Account Title	Number
Preferred Stock	510
Paid-In Capital in Excess of Par–Preferred	511
Stock Subscribed–Preferred	512
Common Stock	520
Paid-In Capital in Excess of Par–Common	521
Paid-In Capital in Excess of Stated Value–Common	522
Stock Subscribed–Common	523
Stock Dividend Distributable	525
Paid-In Capital-Stock Dividend	530
Paid-In Capital–Treasury Stock Transactions	531
Paid-In Capital–Retirement of Stock	532
Minority Interest	540
Retained Earnings	550
Retained Earnings Appropriated	551
Unrealized Gain (Loss) from Available-for-Sale Securities	560
Accumulated Translation Adjustment	562
Treasury Stock	564
Dividends	598
Income Summary	599

REVENUES 收入

Account Title	Number
Revenue	600
Sales	602
Fee Revenue	604
Parking Revenue	606
Repairs Revenue	608
Rent Revenue	610
Cash Sales	612
Credit Sales	614
Interest Revenue	616
Dividends Revenue	618
Miscellaneous Revenue	620
Sales Returns and Allowances	622
Sales Discounts	624
Income from Subsidiary	630

EXPENSES

Account Title	Number
Advertising Expense	700
Bond Issue Expense	701
Cash Over or Short	702
Cleaning Supplies Expense	703
Cost of Goods Sold	704
Depletion Expense	706
Depreciation Expense–Building	708
Depreciation Expense–Delivery Equipment	710
Depreciation Expense–Equipment	712
Depreciation Expense–Equipment Under Capital Lease	713
Depreciation Expense–Land Improvements	714
Depreciation Expense–Office Equipment	716
Employer Payroll Expense	718
Franchise Amortization Expense	720
Fuel Expense	722
Goodwill Amortization Expense	724
Income Tax Expense	726
Insurance Expense	728
Interest Expense	730
Laboratory Expense	732
Licenses Expense	733

Account Title	Number
Maintenance	
Maintenance	
Miscellaneou.	
Office Supplies Expense	740
Organization Costs Amortization Expense	742
Parts Expense	744
Patent Amortization Expense	746
Pension Expense	748
Professional Fees Expense	750
Property Tax Expense	752
Purchases	754
Purchases Discounts	756
Purchases Discounts Lost	758
Purchases Returns and Allowances	760
Rent Expense	762
Research and Development Expense	764
Sales Commissions Expense	766
Sales Expense	768
Sales Supplies Expense	770
Sick Pay Expense	772
Supplies Expense	774
Telephone Expense	775
Transportation-In	776
Uncollectible Accounts Expense	778
Utilities Expense	780
Vacation Pay Expense	782
Wages and Salaries Expense	784

GAINS AND LOSSES
Gains

Account Title	Number
Exchange Gain	800
Gain from Disposal	802
Gain from Retirement of Debt	804
Gain from Sale of Equipment	806
Gain from Sale of Investments	808
Gain from Sale of Property	810
Gain (Loss) from Realization	815
Unrealized Gain (Loss) from Investments	820

Losses

Account Title	Number
Exchange Loss	850
Loss from Damaged Inventory	852
Loss from Decline in Market Value of Merchandise Inventory	853
Loss from Disposal	854
Loss from Inventory Shortage	856
Loss from Sale of Equipment	858
Loss from Sale of Investments	860
Loss from Sale of Mineral Deposits	861
Loss from Sale of Property	862

MANUFACTURING ACCOUNTS

Account Title	Number
Manufacturing Overhead	900
Material Price Variance	905
Material Quantity Variance	910
Labor Efficiency Variance	915
Labor Rate Variance	920
Controllable Overhead Variance	925
Overhead Volume Variance	930

ACCOUNTING

MAY JIAMBALVO McDONALD

ROBERT G. MAY, PhD
KPMG Peat Marwick Centennial Professor of Accounting
Associate Dean, College of Business Administration and
Graduate School of Business
The University of Texas at Austin

JAMES JIAMBALVO, PhD, CPA
Chair, Department of Accounting
University of Washington

CHARLES L. McDONALD, PhD, CPA
Associate Professor and Director,
Center for Accounting Research and Professional Education
University of Florida

SOUTH-WESTERN College Publishing

An International Thomson Publishing Company

DEDICATION
To our families
Robert G. May, James Jiambalvo, and Charles L. McDonald

AB88AA
Copyright © 1995
by South-Western Publishing Co.
Cincinnati, Ohio

I ⓣ P

International Thomson Publishing
South-Western College Publishing is an ITP Company.
The ITP trademark is used under license

Sponsoring Editor: David L. Shaut
Developmental Editor: Minta Berry
Production Editor: Mark Sears
Production House: Berry Publication Services
Cover Design: Bruce Design
Internal Design: Lesiak/Crampton Design
Photographer, Chapter Openers: Kessler Photography
Photo Editor: Jennifer Mayhall
Marketing Manager: Michael O'Brien

Credits:
107, 150   Robert Morris Associates cautions that the Studies be regarded only as a general guidelines and not as an absolute industry norm. This is due to limited samples within categories, the categorization of companies by their primary Standard Industrial Classification (SIC) number only, and different methods of operations by companies within the same industry. For these reasons, Robert Morris Associates recommends that the figures be used only as general guidelines in addition to other methods of financial analysis.
245–283   ClickArt®Images Copyright © 1984–1994® T/Maker Company. All Rights Reserved.
993   David Joel/Tony StoneImages/MacNeal Hospital
1187–1213   Copyright J.C. Penney Company, Inc.–1994.

ISBN: 0-538-83062-X
1 2 3 4 5 6 7 VH 0 9 8 7 6 5 4
Printed in the United States of America

Library of Congress Cataloging-in-Publication Data
May, Robert G.
    Accounting / Robert G. May, James Jiambalvo, Charles L. McDonald.
       p.   cm.
    Includes bibliographical references and index.
    ISBN 0-538-83062-X
    1. Accounting.   I. Jiambalvo, James   . II. McDonald,
Charles L.   . III. Title.
    HF5635.M452   1995
    657—dc20   94-31231
                                                                    CIP

PREFACE

According to the Accounting Education Change Commission (AECC):

> The primary objective of the first course in accounting is for students to learn about accounting as an information development and communication function that supports economic decision-making. The knowledge and skills provided by the first course in accounting should facilitate subsequent learning even if the student takes no additional academic work in accounting or directly related disciplines. For example, the course should help students perform financial analysis; derive information for personal or organization decisions; and understand business, governmental, and other organizational entities.[1]

Accounting directly addresses the AECC's recommendations in the following ways:

1. A decision-making focus is evident in every chapter.
2. Financial analysis is integrated with the presentation of accounting principles and practices.
3. Accounting is discussed in a way that provides insight into how businesses and other organizations function.

This text is suitable for a two-semester or a two- or three-quarter course covering principles of financial and managerial accounting. Material is presented in sufficient depth so that students who aspire to major in accounting will have more than adequate preparation for their intermediate accounting courses. However, the text is aimed primarily at the majority of students who will major in other disciplines. The text stresses basic principles and presents analytical tools in contexts that students will find appealing. Students will appreciate the clear prose, helpful graphics, and emphasis on decision making.

Decision-Making Focus

Each chapter opens with a brief, believable story about a decision maker facing a realistic business decision or dilemma. In the body of the chapter, we introduce accounting information related to the decision maker's problem. By the end of the chapter, we close the loop, describing and illustrating financial ratios and other analyses that specifically address the decision maker's concerns. The scenarios provide a context that aids understanding of the material, and they emphasize the role of accounting information in economic decision making.

Financial Analysis

Throughout the text, we illustrate the tools of financial analysis along with the development of related accounting information. For example, in Chapter 2, which deals with accounting income and accrual concepts, students are introduced to the profit margin as a measure of profitability. Students compare the profit margin of the business in Chapter 2's opening scenario to the profit margin of other ser-

---

[1]Accounting Education Change Commission, *The First Course in Accounting*, Position Statement No. Two, (June 1992).

vice businesses. This comparison helps students understand the usefulness of accounting information. Another example of our approach is in Chapter 4, where students learn about a classified balance sheet. To emphasize the utility of this statement, students are introduced to the current ratio, which uses the classifications of current assets and current liabilities to assess a firm's liquidity.

Insights into Organizations

For many students, principles of accounting is their first business course. Since accounting procedures track business activity, a great opportunity is lost if the principles text and course do not enhance students' understanding of underlying business processes as they learn accounting principles. In the context of our chapter scenarios, we find it natural to implicitly cover important aspects of various business activities as we introduce accounting principles. For example, Chapters 1 through 4 present a continuing scenario of a start-up business, how its financial statements are developed, and how accounting information is used in assessing its relative profitability and liquidity as it goes through its early growth stage. In Chapter 5, we emphasize how merchandising businesses earn profits in contrast to service businesses—by buying and selling goods. We follow the income statement of a merchandising business and introduce the transactions making up net sales and cost of goods sold (and gross profit). Each type of transaction is introduced in the context of running a merchandising business and the importance of managing gross profit is brought home at the end of the chapter where we close the loop on the motivating scenario.

In Chapter 8, we cover accounts and notes receivable. In a progression motivated by the opening scenario, we examine why a business grants credit and how bank card sales and notes receivable represent alternative ways of managing customer credit. The chapter winds up with an analysis of the contribution of credit sales to a business—an analysis, incidentally, that is echoed by a note to J.C. Penney's 1993 financial statements that is the focus of a critical thinking case in the end-of-chapter material.

Similarly in Chapter 12, we cover current liabilities and how they are used to provide short-term funds in a business. The scenario sets up the common business need to manage inventory purchases and collection lags for a peak selling season. In the process of covering accounting for a variety of current liabilities, we cover the features and tradeoffs of different strategies for managing the short-term financing problem.

Far from being distractions, these business activities and the decision contexts that apply are covered subtly and unobtrusively. This is an accounting text, but it enriches and motivates the student's first learning experience in the accounting discipline by presenting accounting in an organizational context that demonstrates a need for accounting information. Throughout the text, we have scattered feature boxes that provide insight into the functioning of businesses and other organizations. They include ethical dilemmas, insights into real-world accounting applications, historical perspectives, and global insights. We use these features judiciously; they season the text without distracting from its main lines of thought.

Analyzing, Thinking, and Communicating

Throughout this text, we emphasize decision making and thinking about problems in a rich business context. The thinking-in-context emphasis is reinforced in the end-of-chapter materials. At the end of each chapter are a set of Critical

Thinking and Communicating cases. They range from thought-provoking ethical situations, to scenarios that promote critical thinking about the limitations of accounting and the motives of managers who choose accounting methods, to cases requiring the analysis and interpretation of financial statements. In most cases, a substantial writing exercise is required or implied. The following icons are used to identify the cases:

Decision Case

Ethical Dilemmas

Financial Analysis Case

Communication Case

Expanded Coverage of Managerial Accounting

As already noted, most students who study accounting principles will go on to become business managers, rather than accountants. As managers, they will need to plan operations, evaluate subordinates, and make a variety of decisions using managerial accounting information and techniques. Consistent with a focus on business majors, rather than accounting majors, as the users of this text, we decided to expand the coverage of managerial accounting compared to other principles texts. *Accounting* has ten chapters covering managerial accounting topics compared to eight or nine for most principle's texts.

While the coverage of managerial accounting is expanded, judicious choices were made as to where expansion was necessary and where cutting was appropriate. For example, recognizing that activity based costing is a critical element of managerial accounting, this topic is covered in both the chapter on job-order costing, Chapter 21, and in the chapter on cost allocation, Chapter 24. Process costing, however, is a somewhat "technical" topic in that the ideas are easily mastered but specific procedures are quite complex. To reduce technical complexity, we present the relatively simple weighted-average approach and ignore the more complex FIFO approach.

Computer Technology, Accounting Systems, and Accounting Controls

Computers are commonplace in the business world, yet, like many instructors, we find that students understand accounting systems and controls more readily in the context of manual systems. What do we do about this? We introduce the topic of computers in accounting right away, in the Introduction, and we comment on their use whenever appropriate in the remainder of the text. In Chapter 6, we set up a decision scenario that requires integration of the sales and purchasing subsystems of a merchandising business to monitor inventory levels and improve purchasing efficiency. We are able to introduce traditional, manual subsystems for sales/cash receipts and purchases/cash disbursements as the existing system in this realistic business scenario. The manual records and procedures are easy to understand and effective in meeting certain accounting control objectives, but they are obviously limited vis a vis the inventory control problem. We then describe a computer system that integrates the subsystems and solves the decision problem while meeting the cost-effectiveness criterion. In subsequent chapters, we assume that computers are used in the accounting systems and describe appropriate controls for a computer environment.

Supplementary Material for the Instructor

Solutions Manual The comprehensive manual contains solutions to questions, exercises, and problems. Suggested solutions and key points of discussion are provided for all cases. All exercises and problems are correlated to the appropriate learning objectives and time estimates are provided for all problems. The manual is also available in electronic media.

Solution Transparencies The solutions to exercises and problems are available on transparency for ease of classroom presentation.

Test Bank A printed test bank includes true/false, multiple choice, and problem materials for all chapters. All items are correlated to the appropriate learning objectives. The level of difficulty for the items is also identified.

MicroExam 4.0 Computerized Test Bank The test bank is available in a MicroExam version. All items that appear in the print test bank are available electronically. Among the features of the electronic version are the ability to customize the test, the ability to prepare multiple versions of the same questions, and the ability to add or edit questions and problems.

Videos *Financial Accounting* explores activities of the firm through interviews with people who use accounting data. *The Role of Management Accounting in the Production Process* features management accounting at work in high-profit companies. *GE Lighting Systems: Continuous Flow Manufacturing* studies employees producing products in both conventional and advanced manufacturing environments.

Supplementary Material for the Student

Working Papers Appropriate forms for students to use in solving end-of-chapter problems are available in two volumes: Chapters 1–19 and Chapters 20–29.

Study Guides Two study guides are available: one for Chapters 1–19 (Financial Accounting) and one for Chapters 20–29 (Managerial Accounting).

Practice Sets and Cases The following practice sets and cases provide additional exposure to the accounting systems of various business entities: *Ice Inc.: An Interactive, Corporate Financial Accounting Practice Case; Cool Company: An Interactive Sole Proprietorship Financial Accounting Practice Case; Mountain Bikes, Inc.*, a merchandising business using perpetual inventory; an *Annual Report Project;* and *Cases in Financial Accounting.*

Solutions Software This general ledger software, prepared by Warren W. Allen and Dale H. Klooster of Educational Technical Systems, may be used to solve selected end-of-chapter problems. The software may be used with DOS or Windows systems.

Acknowledgements

Throughout the text, relevant professional statements of the Financial Accounting Standards Board and other authoritative publications are discussed, quoted, or footnoted. We are indebted to the American Institute of Certified Public Accountants, the Financial Accounting Standards Board, the American Accounting Association, and the Institute of Management Accountants for material from their publications.

During the development of this text, many individuals contributed significant insights and provided guidance to us as we wrote and refined the text. We especially thank Bruce Koch, John Beegle, and David Coffee for their time and effort in assisting with the content development and review of the end of chapter material. We are also grateful for the assistance of Steven Rice in the preparation of the tax appendix.

We sincerely appreciate the efforts of all who have contributed to the final product. The following faculty served as reviewers and class testers during the project:

James Abbott	Broome Community College
Michael Adkins	Lexington Community College
Rainer Albright	The University of Alabama
Herman Andress	Santa Fe Community College
Sue Atkinson	Tarleton State University
Debra Barbeau	Southern Illinois University at Carbondale
Donald J. Barnett	California State University–Dominguez Hills
Homer L. Bates	University of North Florida
Susan Shannon Bates	Boise State University
Anne Connell Baucom	University of North Carolina–Charlotte
Kathleen Bindon	University of Alabama
Dorothy Binger	Tallahassee Community College
Sallie Branscom	Virginia Western Community College
Ronald P. Brooker	Phoenix College
Howard Bryan	Santa Rosa Junior College
James I. Bryant	Catonsville Community College
Carol Buchl	Northern Michigan University
Leon Button	Scottsdale Community College
David Bydalek	Mesa Community College
Eric Carlson	Kean College of New Jersey
Charles F. Chanter	Grand Rapids Junior College
Michael C. Chester	Norfolk State University
C. David Coffee	Western Carolina University
Kenneth L. Coffey	Johnson County Community College
A. Carter Cogle	Southside Virginia Community College
Judith Considine	Rutgers University
Grace M. Conway	Adelphi University
Judith M. Cook	Grossmont College
Tomas Cooper	Parkland College
Fredonna Cox	Eastern Kentucky University
Alan E. Davis	Philadelphia Community College
Paul L. Donohue	Delaware County Community College
Joseph G. Doser	Truckee Meadows Community College
Lola A. Dudley	Eastern Illinois University
Dean Edmiston	Emporia State University
Randy Edwards	Appalachian State University
John A. Elfrink	Southeast Missouri State University
David Fetyko	Kent State University
Carl J. Fisher	Foothill College
R. Leigh Frackelton, Jr.	Mary Washington College
Joseph Gallo	Cuyahoga Community College–Metro Campus
Helen Gernon	University of Oregon
Shirley Glass	Macomb Community College–South
Robert F. Godfrey	Marshall University
Maxwell P. Godwin	Southwest Texas State University
Harold Goedde	North Carolina A & T University
William D. Goodman	Bluefield State College
Donald J. Griffin	Cayuga Community College
Joyce Griffin	Kansas City Kansas Community College
Donald D. Gusarson	Cabrillo College
William T. Hall, Sr.	Fayetteville Technical Community College
Linda Herrington	Community College of Allegheny County
George Holdren	University of Nebraska

Cynthia L. Holloway	Tarrant County Junior College–Northeast
Patty Holmes	Des Moines Area Community College
Anita V. Hope	Tarrant County Junior College–Northeast
George Ihorn	El Paso Community College
Randy Johnston	Penn State University
Brent Joyce	Virginia Highlands Community College
Bruce Koch	University of North Texas
Edward Krohn	Miami-Dade Community College
Michael Layne	Nassau Community College
Marcella Y. Lecky	The University of Southwestern Louisiana
Albert Y. Lew	Wright State University
Norbert Lindskog	Harold Washington College
Johanna D. Lyle	Kansas State University
Thomas Lynch	Hocking Technical College
Rene Manes	The Florida State University
Ken Mark	Kansas City Kansas Community College
Thomas J. McCoy	Middlesex County College
William McFarland	Illinois Central College
Maria Trini U. Melcher	California State University–Fullerton
Phillip Mills	Miami-Dade Community College–South Campus
Thomas P. Moncada	Eastern Illinois University
Paula Morris	Kennesaw State College
C. Lynn Murray	Florida Community College–South Campus
M. Salah Negm	Prince George's Community College
Cletus O'Drobinak	South Suburban College
Leslie Oakes	Rutgers University
Frances Aileen Ormiston	Mesa Community College
John Overton	University of New Hampshire
John Palipchak	Penn State–Beaver Campus
Lynn M. Paluska	Nassau Community College
Joseph S. Patterson	DeKalb Community College–South Campus
Deborah Dianne Payne	Roosevelt University
A. George Petrie	University of Texas–Pan American
Rose Marie Pilcher	Richland College
Sharyll A.B. Plato	Central State University–Oklahoma
Norma C. Powell	Bryant College
Barbara Powers	Wytheville Community College
Robert D. Reid	Germanna Community College
Reg Rezac	Texas Women's University
Carla Lemley Rich	Pensacola Junior College
Juan Rivera	University of Notre Dame
Lawrence A. Roman	Cuyahoga Community College–Eastern
David L. Rozelle	Western Michigan University
Leo Ruggle	Mankato State University
Pearl B. Sandelman	De Anza College
Wallace James Satchell	St. Philip's Community College
John Schryver	Bentley College
Robbie Sheffy	Tarrant County Junior College
Michael T. Stein	Rutgers University
John R. Stewart	University of Northern Colorado
Linda Sugarman	University of Akron
Thomas Sullivan	Quincy College
Lisa Tahlier	North Carolina Wesleyan College
Greg Thom	Parkland College
Ingrid R. Torsay	DeKalb Community College–Central Campus
Charles L. Vawter	Glendale Community College
Vicki S. Vorell	Cuyahoga Community College–Western
DuWayne M. Wacker	University of North Dakota
Lori A. Wahila	Broome Community College
Al Walczak	Linn-Benton Community College
Thomas C. Waller	University of Houston–Clear Lake
Sharon Walters	Morehead State University
Peter R. Wilson	New York University
Frank Zattich	Lincoln Land Community College
Karl M. Zehms	University of Wisconsin–Green Bay

Robert G. May is the KPMG Peat Marwick Centennial Professor of Accounting at The University of Texas at Austin and Associate Dean for Academic Affairs. He has also held appointments at the University of Washington and at Stanford University. He received his Ph.D. from Michigan State University.

Professor May has published articles in scholarly journals and was co-winner of the 1976 AICPA Notable Contribution to the Accounting Literature Award. He has served as Associate Editor of *The Accounting Review*. He has coauthored three textbooks: *A New Introduction to Financial Accounting*, *A Brief Introduction to Managerial and Social Uses of Accounting*, and *Evaluating Business Ventures*. He is the co-developer of SCAD, a Simulated Case for Audit Decisions, under a grant from Price Waterhouse Foundation and developer of Variables Sampling Education Support Software (VSESS) under a grant from Coopers & Lybrand Foundation.

Professor May has taught a variety of graduate and undergraduate courses in accounting. He received teaching awards at the University of Washington and at the University of Texas. He was co-recipient of the American Accounting Association Innovation in Accounting Education Award in 1991 and 1993. Professor May has had public accounting experience and is active in the American Accounting Association.

James Jiambalvo is a Professor of Accounting at the University of Washington. He received undergraduate and masters degrees from the University of Illinois and the Ph.D. degree from The Ohio State University. Professor Jiambalvo has published articles in a number of top accounting journals including *The Accounting Review*, *Contemporary Accounting Research*, the *Journal of Accounting and Economics*, and the *Journal of Accounting Research*. He has also served on the editorial boards of *Auditing: A Journal of Practice and Theory*, *Contemporary Accounting Research*, the *Journal of Management Accounting Research*, and he is a past associate editor of *The Accounting Review*. Professor Jiambalvo is a CPA and he has been recognized at the University of Washington with the Burlington Northern Faculty Achievement Award.

Charles L. McDonald is Associate Professor and Director of the Center for Accounting Research and Professional Education of the Fisher School of Accounting at the University of Florida. He received a Ph.D. in accounting from Michigan State University. Articles by Professor McDonald have appeared in *The Accounting Review*, *Accounting Horizons*, *Corporate Accounting*, and the *Journal of Business Research*. Professor McDonald is a CPA and a member of the American Accounting Association, American Institute of Certified Public Accountants, and the Florida Institute of Certified Public Accountants. He has served on numerous committees of those organizations including the Financial Accounting Standards Committee of the AAA and is currently a member of the Accounting Standards Executive Committee of the AICPA.

CONTENTS

PART 1

FINANCIAL
ACCOUNTING

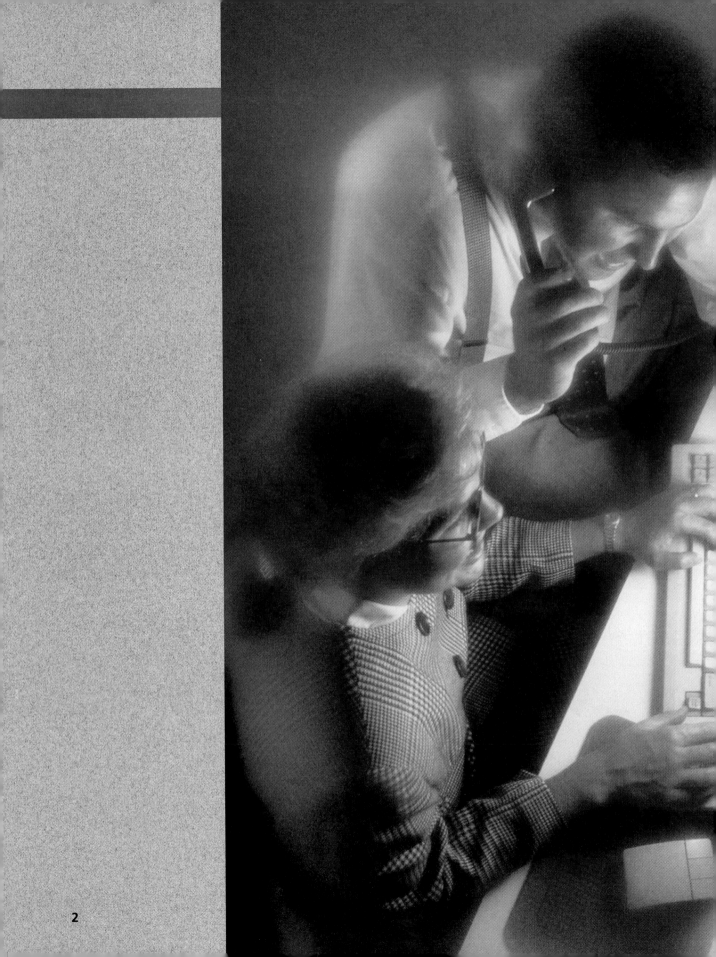

Introduction

Have you ever looked around your home town or city and wondered what makes everything work? When you shop for groceries, why is food on the shelves? Why do the streets (eventually) get repaired? Why do you have power available in your house, apartment, or dorm room? Why is a seat available for you in your accounting class? Why can you buy most things that you need when you need them – without waiting unreasonably long in lines? What holds all these essential goods and services together and makes them work in a coordinated manner? It takes thousands, tens of thousands, millions, or even hundreds of millions of individual economic decisions to make a town or city work. And, to be effective – in order for towns, cities, states, and whole economies to work well – these decisions must be based on sound information about their economic consequences.

Accounting supplies the informational basis for economic decisions. It provides quantitative – usually financial – information about past events and activities that are relevant to current decisions. Whether or not you become an accountant, you will find your knowledge of accounting to be of value in your personal as well as your professional life. Accountants hold many of the most rewarding and best paying jobs, and many top managers of our largest businesses are accountants.

In this Introduction, we describe what accounting information is about and specific ways it is used, by whom it is used, and what kinds of accounting professionals produce it. We also raise the important issue of business ethics and truth in accounting.

1. Define accounting and describe the process of accounting.
2. Identify the users and uses of accounting information.
3. Describe what accountants do in the private sector, in government, and in public accounting practice.
4. Identify the important relationships among ethics, business, and accounting.

LO 1

Define accounting and describe the process of accounting.

ACCOUNTING INFORMATION PROCESSING

Accounting systematically and selectively captures financial data, records these data, summarizes them, and prepares statements that communicate to decision makers relevant information about economic entities, transactions, and events.

The Focus of Accounting Information – Economic Entities

Fundamentally, accounting focuses on economic entities. **Economic entities** carry on economic activities such as buying or selling products or providing or consuming services. Every person, every business, every government organization, every charitable organization, and every educational institution is an economic entity. By systematically processing data, accounting produces information about the transactions economic entities undertake and about the events that happen to them. A **transaction**, a voluntary exchange between economic entities, typically occurs when one entity sells a product or service that the other entity buys.

The transactions of an economic entity make up a large part of its history and constitute most of the raw material in the accounting process. However, the histories of entities are incomplete unless we also take into account the events that affect them involuntarily. These events can be natural such as fires, floods, and storms; political, such as condemnation of land for a freeway right-of-way; or social, such as a boycott of products produced by a company that has been polluting the environment.

The Accounting Process

As Illustration I-1 shows, business documents capture transaction data. For example, the sales slip, a common business document, captures the essential facts about an individual sale. Accountants generally do not record the actual transaction data on documents. Instead, they design procedures and documents so that other employees can gather transaction data accurately. It is much more efficient for employees directly involved in transactions (such as sales clerks) to gather data about transactions. Generally, *everyone who participates in transactions also participates in the accounting process.*

Second, the accounting process selects essential data from the business documents and records these data in chronological records. A cash register tape, a familiar accounting record, contains a listing of all the daily transactions in the order they occurred. In many cases today, employees enter transaction data directly into electronic computer files at the time of the transaction.

Third, accountants (or computers) total the data about individual transactions of each type and then carry these totals forward to record them to various

ILLUSTRATION I-1 The Accounting Process

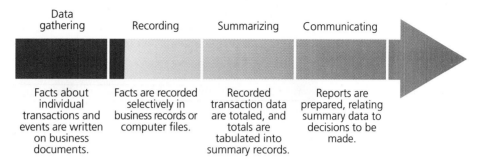

Data gathering	Recording	Summarizing	Communicating
Facts about individual transactions and events are written on business documents.	Facts are recorded selectively in business records or computer files.	Recorded transaction data are totaled, and totals are tabulated into summary records.	Reports are prepared, relating summary data to decisions to be made.

summary records. If computers summarize accounting data, accountants direct the programming of the computers to ensure that the correct accounting result is obtained.

Finally, accountants prepare reports from the summary records for decision makers' use. To be useful to decision makers, accounting reports must convey information relevant to decisions. Thus, an important dimension of accounting – one that we emphasize in this text – is how accounting information can be used to facilitate decision making. *Accountants have a responsibility to construct reports that contain relevant information and to communicate that information to the decision maker.*

Accounting and Computer-Based Information Systems

Until after World War II, bookkeepers, accountants, or other employees performed all accounting functions manually or used bookkeeping machines. Now, computers assist in varying degrees in accounting for all but the smallest organizations – from handling the mechanics of recording accounting data to integrating accounting functions fully with the entity's operations. The more extensively computers are used, the more profoundly they affect the way accounting objectives are accomplished. For example, computers make some types of accounting reports economical or possible for the first time. However, computers have not changed the objectives of the accounting process or the principles and standards governing the preparation of accounting reports.

Accounting information is generally quantitative and predominantly financial in nature. The system many organizations use to accomplish the accounting process also provides managers with a wider range of information than just accounting information. For example, airlines use computers to manage their passenger reservations – clearly one of the most important management functions in an airline. Ultimately, however, when the passengers board a plane and the plane takes off, the data in the passengers' reservation records can be transferred directly to the sales (accounting) record for the day, thus supporting the accounting process as well. In developing such sophisticated systems, organizations should include accountants as part of the team. This way, the systems can fulfill both their accounting and other business objectives.

Accountants and Bookkeepers

Many people often confuse bookkeeping with accounting. **Bookkeeping** includes the mechanical and clerical aspects of the entire accounting process. Bookkeepers work under the supervision of accountants and record accounting data, summarize these data, and prepare routine financial reports. Illustration I-2 contrasts the responsibilities of accountants and bookkeepers.

ILLUSTRATION I-2 Responsibilities of Accountants and Bookkeepers

Accountants	Bookkeepers
• Determine data to be gathered and design business documents and controls to facilitate accurate data gathering.	• Gather data as needed, according to established procedures.
• Design accounting records and advise management about whether data should be recorded manually or by computer.	• Record data and apply control procedures over computer input preparation.
• Establish controls over recorded data to ensure accurate summarization and error detection either by manual procedures or by computer.	• Summarize recorded data and perform control procedures to detect and correct errors.
• Design relevant accounting reports that conform to established standards and design manual or computer procedures for preparing them.	• Prepare draft reports or review computer drafts as needed.
• Perform high-level control procedures to ensure the integrity of the accounting process and the computer-based information system.	• Assist with control procedures as directed.

LO 2

Identify the users and uses of accounting information.

USERS AND USES OF ACCOUNTING INFORMATION

Economic entities are accounting's focus, because they are the subjects of many economic decisions. Accounting supplies valuable information, by recognizing who wants what kinds of information and about what entities.

Information About Individuals

Individuals need information to manage their own financial affairs and frequently ask themselves the following questions:

- How much cash do I have on hand?
- How much cash could I raise if I sold everything I have?
- Will I be able to borrow additional funds to buy a house (or car) and still meet all of my other obligations?

Individuals are not the only ones interested in their financial affairs. In particular, when an individual wants to borrow money to buy a car or a house or take a vacation, a lender of some type enters the picture. The lender wants the answers to such questions as:

- How much income does this individual earn?
- How has the individual performed in paying back previous loans?
- How much of the individual's income is available after personal expenses to pay back a new loan?

- Does the individual own valuable property to pledge as collateral for a loan?

If the individual is an elected public official, then voters feel a need for and have a right to answers to questions such as:

- Does the individual have income from sources other than his or her salary in public office? What sources?
- Do conflicts of interest exist between the other sources of the individual's income and his or her duty to the public?

Information About Businesses

Businesses are private organizations operated to earn profits for their owners. Financial affairs can be much more complex for businesses than they are for most individuals. Hence, the users of information about businesses are numerous, and the questions they ask are more varied. Illustration I-3 summarizes three major classes of users of accounting information managers, owners, and lenders – and gives examples of the questions they ask.

ILLUSTRATION I-3 Users of Accounting Information About Businesses

Managers:
- Will sufficient cash be available to pay bills and retire debts as needed?
- Did expenditures exceed budgets or plans? In which areas?
- Should the business buy or rent new facilities and equipment?
- Should selling prices be increased or decreased?
- Are goods selling as quickly as expected?
- What product lines offer the best prospects for future profitability?

Owners and prospective owners:
- Is the business as profitable as it can be?
- Have sales grown or diminished?
- Is the business performing better or worse than its competition? Why?
- What is the risk that the business will fail financially (not be able to pay its debts)?
- Is it worthwhile making or continuing an investment in this business?

Lenders:
- Is the business profitable?
- Has the business paid its bills and retired its past debts on time?
- Does the business appear to be generating sufficient cash to handle additional debt in the future?
- What is the risk that the business will fail financially?

Besides managers, owners, and lenders, many others use accounting information about businesses. Employees and suppliers naturally want to know whether businesses can generate sufficient cash flows to pay them on time. Customers want to know whether businesses will survive and be steady sources of needed goods and services. The Internal Revenue Service wants to know if businesses (and individuals) have recognized all income, deducted only allowable deductions, and paid the actual amount of taxes owed. Regulators such as public utility commissions want to know if businesses are profiting excessively by charging unfairly high rates to consumers.

Information About Other Entities

Users of accounting information ask many of the same questions about other organizations such as charities and governmental units as they ask about businesses. However, since these entities differ from businesses in certain fundamental ways, some questions applicable to businesses do not apply to them.

For example, **charities** are private organizations that are operated not for profit but for humanitarian purposes. Therefore, questions of profitability do not apply. However, managers, creditors, suppliers, donors, and beneficiaries all want to know whether charities will continue to pay their bills on time and survive. They also want to know what percentages of total donations flow through from donors to beneficiaries and what percentages charities use for operations.

Governments are public organizations formed to supply essential public services to the citizenry and to the state (nation). Generally, financial failure is not an issue with government units – that is, they do not go out of business when they cannot pay their bills. Nevertheless, managers of government units take their ability to pay bills and repay debts very seriously – as do the constituents of the unit, its employees, and suppliers – because vital services and the ability to borrow for capital improvements are affected. Managers and citizens alike want to know whether a government unit spends too much or too little on current services and whether it makes sufficient capital investments to maintain or expand services as needed in the future.

LO 3

Describe what accountants do in the private sector, in government, and in public accounting practice.

PROVIDING ACCOUNTING INFORMATION — ACCOUNTING CAREERS

Accountants pursue two very broad career paths. The vast majority of accountants (close to 85 percent of the approximately one million accountants in the United States) are employed in private or government accounting occupations within economic organizations.[1] **Private accounting** consists of all accounting activities required to meet the information needs of managers of private-sector organizations and of outside users such as prospective owners and lenders. **Government accounting** consists of the same activities as private accounting but is performed in cities, counties, and state and federal agencies. The outside users of information about government organizations are lenders and taxpayers. Other accountants engage in **public accounting**, which consists of providing professional accounting services to individuals, businesses, government units, and other entities for fees – much like the practices of medicine and law.

Accountants and Accounting Within Organizations

Accountants perform the full variety of functions described in Illustration I-2 in all types of economic organizations. Accounting is a "staff function"; that is, it is not a direct part of providing products or services. However, it is a vital and indispensable staff function and usually enjoys a status within the organizational hierarchy that reflects its importance.

Large businesses, charities, education institutions, and government units recognize the persons responsible for the accounting function as high-ranking

[1]Economic organizations consist of all economic entities other than individuals.

members of management. These people generally have the status of vice president and the title of *controller*. In a business, a charity, or an education institution, the controller typically reports to the chief financial officer or CFO (an executive vice president) or to the chief executive officer or CEO (the president). Illustration I-4 shows the relationships among the executive vice president and CFO of J.C. Penney Company, Inc. and the various vice presidents, including the vice president and controller. In a government unit such as a city, the controller reports to an equally high-ranking officer such as the treasurer, city manager, or mayor.

ILLUSTRATION I-4 J.C. Penney Company, Inc., CFO Organization (March 1, 1990)

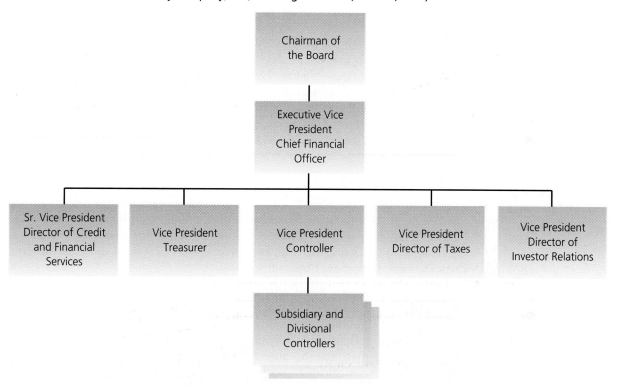

Accounting Specializations Within Organizations

Accountants tend to work in one of four areas within organizations. Financial accountants and managerial accountants prepare information directed at two major classes of users, outsiders and managers, respectively. In addition, accountants work as internal auditors and tax specialists.

Financial Accounting.   The early chapters of this text present the basics of financial accounting. **Financial accounting** consists of the processes and principles used to prepare financial statements. **Financial statements** are standardized reports organizations prepare for use by outsiders such as owners and prospective owners of a business, bankers who have loaned or are considering lending money to a business, and customers and suppliers of a business.

Managerial Accounting.   Managers also find financial statements to be quite relevant in their work; however, they need more detailed information to guide their day-to-day decisions. The later chapters of this text present the basics of managerial accounting. **Managerial accounting** is the process by which information is prepared for use by managers in making decisions about the current and future activities of economic entities. Managerial accounting must accommodate a wide variety of managerial decision making; and, therefore, the reports produced are less standardized than they are in financial accounting. They may be one-of-a-kind reports, tailored to a specific use.

Internal Auditing. Accountants also conduct internal audits within their organizations. An **internal audit** is an investigation intended to determine whether:

1. Employees and departments conform to management (or government) policies.
2. Functions in the organization are performed at reasonable cost.
3. A department or division is fully meeting its goals and objectives.

Internal Tax Management. Larger corporations employ accountants and attorneys in internal tax departments. They plan transactions and structure entities to maximize *profits after taxes* (i.e., they minimize the effect of taxes on profits). While these departments may not be part of the accounting function (for example, they may be part of the treasury function), they employ many accountants who specialize in taxation.

Public Accounting

We estimate that close to 170,000 accountants are public accountants in the United States. Public accountants perform accounting, auditing, tax, and management advisory services for their clients. They practice alone, as sole practitioners, or in firms ranging from two practitioners to several thousand in large multinational accounting firms.

Accounting Services. Small businesses do not always have the resources to hire skilled accountants internally. Until they grow large enough to justify expenditures on accounting salaries, small businesses often hire public accountants to prepare their financial statements and other reports. As businesses become larger, they may be able to hire accountants, but they might not be able to afford sophisticated computer-based accounting information systems. Once again, small businesses may turn to public accountants who operate centralized computer service bureaus to handle their clients' computing needs.

Auditing Services. **Financial auditing** is an *independent* investigative activity through which public accountants lend credibility to the financial statements or other representations of economic entities. Independent auditing services are the most distinguishing feature of public accounting. Because it provides a basis for economic decisions, accounting information is valuable. However, *if information is not trusted, it will neither influence decisions to its full potential nor achieve its full value.*

Managers who prepare financial statements for outsiders realize that it is in their interests to improve the credibility of their organizations' financial statements. They demand the services of independent auditors who test the content of financial statements for conformity with underlying facts and with standards such as Generally Accepted Accounting Principles (defined later in this text). Auditors make an independent report to accompany the financial statements, which contains their opinion about the fairness of presentation of the information contained in the statements. Because fairness in financial reporting is in the public interest, the federal government and many states have passed statutes that require publicly-held corporations to have independent audits of their financial statements. Banks also require audits of their medium- and large-loan customers.

Tax Services. Public accountants offer tax services that consist of assisting clients in filing tax returns, helping them comply with tax laws and regulations, and advising them about ways to maximize their profits after taxes. State and federal tax laws are voluminous and complex and affect both business and individual profitability. Therefore, many businesses and individuals find it beneficial to consult with tax experts. Increasingly, businesses are operating globally and need expert advice on how to balance the tax provisions of several different countries.

Management Advisory Services. Public accountants also provide management advisory services (MAS) to help their clients with many other aspects of running their businesses. As part of every audit, they make suggestions about ways to improve their clients' information systems and their business practices. If clients do not have the expertise to design new information systems or to implement other suggestions themselves, they may hire the MAS division of the public accounting firm that suggested the improvements. Public accountants also perform MAS services for non-audit clients.

Accounting Designations (Certifications)

The public and the managers of organizations rely on the integrity and expertise of accountants. Professional designations or certifications distinguish accountants who meet high standards of qualification and professional conduct.

The CPA Certificate and License to Practice Public Accounting. Because the independent audit function protects a dimension of the public interest, public accounting is the only aspect of accounting practice that requires a license. Each state licenses individuals to practice public accounting as certified public accountants (CPAs).

According to the Department of Labor, there were about 400,000 CPAs in the United States in 1990. Approximately 40 percent of these CPAs practice public accounting, and the other 60 percent are employed in private accounting, government accounting, or other occupations.[2] Although states differ somewhat in their requirements, a candidate for the CPA certificate and license to practice must generally satisfy an education requirement (minimum of a bachelor's degree, with some minimum number of accounting credits), pass the Uniform CPA Examination (administered by the American Institute of Certified Public Accountants), and obtain work experience under a CPA's supervision.[3]

State Boards of Accountancy issue the licenses to practice and the CPA Certificates in most states, and they also enforce codes of conduct and stipulate continuing education requirements for retention of the licenses and certificates. You may wish to contact your State Board of Accountancy to find out the specific requirements and procedures for becoming a CPA in your state.

---

[2]*Occupational Outlook Handbook*, 1992–1993 Edition (U.S. Government Printing Office: U.S. Department of Labor, May, 1992), p. 15.

[3]Increasingly states are requiring more education. For example, as of January 1994, over 30 states were phasing in minimum requirements of 150 semester hours of college credit as well as a bachelor's degree.

Other Professional Accounting Certifications.   Accountants who practice in industry and government have recognized the benefits of setting high professional standards for all accounting practices rather than just for public accounting. They have formed institutes to administer rigorous standardized examinations and to award certificates to individuals who meet their standards. Two such institutes are the Institute of Management Accountants (IMA) and the Institute of Internal Auditors (IIA). They administer examinations to accountants aspiring to be certified management accountants (CMAs) and certified internal auditors (CIAs), respectively.[4]   According to the Department of Labor, in 1990, there were 17,000 CIAs and 10,000 CMAs in the United States.[5]

Professional Accounting Organizations

Most professional accounting organizations have several things in common. They all wish to protect and enhance the reputation of the accounting profession and the productivity of their members. To this end, they set standards of conduct for their members, set technical standards for accounting and auditing practice, represent their members in public forums such as legislative hearings, conduct or support research to improve the discipline of accounting, develop technology for practice, publish books and monographs on professional topics, and publish journals (magazines) to keep their members abreast of current developments. The names, members, and journals of the most influential professional accounting organizations are listed in Illustration I-5.

ILLUSTRATION I-5 Accounting Organizations

Organization Name	Primary Membership	Journal
American Institute of Certified Public Accountants (AICPA)	CPAs	Journal of Accountancy
Institute of Management Accountants (IMA)	Managerial accountants	Management Accounting
Financial Executives Institute (FEI)	Chief financial officers	The Financial Executive
American Accounting Association (AAA)	College and university teachers of accounting	The Accounting Review
The Association of Government Accountants (AGA)	Accountants in all branches of government	The Government Accountants Journal

Opportunities in Accounting

New entrants to the accounting field find both immediate employment and career-long opportunities very favorable. The Bureau of Labor Statistics expects faster than average growth in accounting and auditing jobs through the year

---

[4]Further information may be obtained by writing the following addresses: American Institute of Certified Public Accountants, 1211 Avenue of the Americas, New York, NY 10036; Institute of Internal Auditors, 249 Maitland Avenue, Altamonte Springs, FL 32701-4201; and Institute of Management Accountants, 10 Paragon Drive, Montvale, NJ 07645-1759.

[5]*Op. cit.*

2005 and estimates that approximately 304,000 new accounting and auditing jobs will be created between 1992 and 2005.[6]

The 1991 College Placement Council Survey reported an average *starting* salary of $26,600 for a graduate with a bachelor's degree in accounting and no prior accounting work experience – approximately 40 percent higher than the average personal income in the United States.[7] Of course, actual starting salaries of accountants vary, depending on the region of employment (and its cost of living), the prestige of the school granting the degree, the type of employer, and the performance of the individual earning the degree. Persons with advanced degrees and previous accounting experience generally receive significant premiums. The salaries of top accounting executives and partners in international public accounting firms average as much as ten times the starting salaries. This provides a significant range for upward economic mobility in accounting practice.

<table>
<tr><td>LO 4</td></tr>
</table>

Identify the important relationships among ethics, business, and accounting.

ETHICS IN BUSINESS AND TRUTH IN ACCOUNTING

Many people believe the phrase "business ethics" is a contradiction in terms. Perhaps this cynicism is understandable. In a free-enterprise, market economy, businesses compete vigorously for sales and profits with other businesses; and we know they sometimes bend the rules. In all types of organizations, managers and employees compete with each other for jobs, advancement, bonuses, etc. Hence, we hear expressions such as: "It's a dog-eat-dog world out there." Yet, we are wrong to assume that business and ethics do not mix.

To the contrary, most successful businesspeople know that integrity and ethical behavior are essential ingredients. Why? Because business is actually built on trust. Owners and lenders entrust their money to managers. Employees entrust their safety and future employment to managers. Managers, in turn, entrust employees with valuable resources for which the managers are themselves responsible. Such essential trust relationships cannot work effectively without a high level of confidence that the individuals involved have integrity. As most astute businesspeople know, in the long run, loss of other people's confidence means loss of business, loss of profit, loss of opportunity, etc.

Accountability and Business Ethics

Accountants are acutely aware of the relationship between successful business and integrity. Accounting is the heart of **accountability**, the process by which individuals and groups demonstrate to others that they have properly or effectively discharged their responsibilities. Financial statements, for example, show owners and lenders what management has done with the business's resources. Internal accounting reports show managers where employees are performing well or poorly and may reveal such crucial information as whether stocks of goods are shrinking due to theft or poor handling.

Thus, managers or employees who engage in fraud or other misconduct may attempt to compromise the organization's accountability system by falsify-

---

[6]*Occupational Outlook Quarterly* (U.S. Government Printing Office: U.S. Department of Labor, Fall 1993), p. 15.

[7]*Occupational Outlook Handbook*, 1990–1991 Edition, *ibid.*

ing accounting data or reports.[8] Unethical managers and employees pressure accountants to aid them in the latter. Accountants may also discover managers' or employees' unethical behavior and must decide when and how to "blow the whistle." Thus, accountants – as much or more than other members of society – need to have well-developed senses of ethics and abilities to cope with ethical dilemmas.

Individual and Group Ethics

Webster's defines ethics as "dealing with values relating to human conduct, with respect to the rightness and wrongness of actions."[9] Most of us know what is right and wrong. However, we can be influenced by feelings such as greed, jealousy, ambition, and pride. We know that moral and ethical standards require us to control or overcome our baser feelings. It takes discipline and self-denial to succeed. However, group pressure often works against our best efforts.

For example, during their college careers, most students witness at least one case of scholastic dishonesty such as cheating on examinations. However, these students report only a very few cases. Why? Because they believe their peer group will think less of the person who blows the whistle than of the person who commits the act of dishonesty. As we grow more mature, we should become less sensitive to peer pressure. However, it is also present in the business environment, and you must consider how you will handle it.

Black and White Versus Gray

The "gray zone" is another problem people face in ethical decisions. It is easy to know what one should do if one alternative is clearly right and the other one is clearly wrong. Unfortunately, many situations confront us in which both (all) alternatives have some aspects of right and some of wrong.

Consider an example. Your good friend, through a series of financial misfortunes, has fallen behind on her car payments. Unless she makes a payment immediately, the car will be repossessed. She has tried to borrow money from many sources, including friends, but no one has the money to spare. You are responsible for the office petty cash fund, and she asks you to advance her the money from the fund. Only a few days remain until payday when she says she will repay the money. Your co-workers agree that this is a good solution to her problem. Most people know in their minds that to make a loan from petty cash is wrong. However, in their hearts, they feel it is wrong for their friend to lose something as important as a car because she is late with a payment by just a few days. What would you do?

When you consider gray-zone dilemmas similar to the one above, review alternative ways to look at the situation. That way, you can ultimately do what you know is right and feel right about it. For example, in the case of your friend's car payment, no individual in the office can make a sufficient loan, but what about taking up a collection of smaller loans? Also, consider seeking advice from more experienced individuals who might know more ways to solve the problem. In this case, perhaps a supervisor knows whether your friend can receive an advance against her next paycheck.

---

[8]Clearly, not all unethical behavior within organizations involves accountability and the accounting system. For example, sexual harassment may occur with no compromise of accounting data or reports.

[9]*Webster's College Dictionary* (New York: Random House, Inc.), 1991.

Ethics in This Text

Because ethics in business and accounting are important, and because ethical situations in real life are not black and white and involve peer pressure, we have placed windows entitled "Insights Into Ethics" in many of the chapters of the text. Each contains an ethical decision situation that relates to the contents of the chapter and is printed on a purple background. No right answers are expected or given – reflecting the nature of many ethical choices.

SUMMARY

Define accounting and describe the process of accounting. Accounting is a process of systematically and selectively capturing, recording, and summarizing data and preparing statements that communicate relevant information about economic entities, transactions, and events to decision makers. Accounting focuses on economic entities such as individuals, businesses, and government units and records data about the transactions they enter into. Accountants have a responsibility to construct reports that contain relevant information and to communicate that relevance to decision makers.

Identify the users and uses of accounting information. The users of accounting information include managers, employees, and suppliers of all kinds of organizations and various outside decision makers such as owners and creditors of a business, citizens of a town or city, and donors and beneficiaries of charities. Accounting information about an entity is used to answer questions about its financial condition, its best future alternatives, whether it will be able to pay its bills and debts, and its performance—profitability in the case of a business.

Describe what accountants do in the private sector, in government, and in public accounting practice. Accountants work within organizations to design and operate accounting systems to produce relevant information for managers and outsiders. They also perform internal audits and contribute to tax management. Accountants who practice public accounting perform accounting, auditing, and tax and management advisory services for fees.

Identify the important relationships among ethics, business, and accounting. Successful business is built on many relationships of trust and is impeded when individuals cannot rely on the integrity of others, either within their own organizations or outside. Accounting's central role in accountability puts accountants under pressure to falsify accounting information. Accountants often discover wrongdoing and must decide when and how to blow the whistle on wrongdoers.

KEY TERMS

accountability, *13*
accounting, *4*
bookkeeping, *5*
businesses, *7*
charities, *8*
economic entities, *4*

financial accounting, *9*
financial auditing, *10*
financial statements, *9*
government accounting, *8*
governments, *8*
internal audit, *10*

managerial accounting, *10*
private accounting, *8*
public accounting, *8*
transaction, *4*

QUESTIONS

QI-1   What is the difference between the accountant's role in data gathering and recording?

QI-2   What is the purpose of each of the four steps in the accounting process?

QI-3   What are the differences between the roles of accountants and bookkeepers?

QI-4   What functions do accountants perform within an organization?

QI-5   What type of accounting information might individuals need about their own finances?

QI-6   Name the three major classes of users of accounting information about businesses.

QI-7   What type of accounting information do managers need about their business?

QI-8   What type of accounting information do owners and prospective owners need about a business?

QI-9   What type of accounting information do lenders need about a business?

QI-10   What are the differences between financial and managerial accounting?

QI-11   What services do public accountants typically perform?

QI-12   What major certifications are available to accountants?

QI-13   What are five professional accounting organizations?

QI-14   Why are business ethics important?

QI-15   What is accountability?

CRITICAL THINKING AND COMMUNICATING

CI-1   John Camp works for a high-technology company that is just getting started. The company is working on developing a "wireless" computer network system for colleges and universities. The system will permit schools to provide their students who own their own portable computers full access to the schools' computer network resources such as printers and on-line catalogs without having to use a computer laboratory, a telephone, or a modem. They can connect to the school's computer network anywhere in a given building or within a certain distance of the building. John works in the Accounting Department of his employer. It has come to his attention that the Director of Research and Development has been holding back the paperwork on some research and development expenditures for the wireless system. John has heard that the company is applying for some new loans. Holding back the paperwork on the research and development expenditures prevents them from being included in the reports supplied to the banks, making the company look like a better prospect for loans. Everyone in the company, including John, is aware that the loans are crucial to the survival of the company until the wireless system is ready to sell.

REQUIRED:

a. If John informs the president or other officer of the company of the unrecorded expenditures, what might happen to the company's loan applications?

b. If John informs, do you think the president will welcome the information?

c. If John informs, will his fellow employees applaud his action?

d. What should John do?

CHAPTER 1

Introduction to Financial Accounting

Consider the case of Charlotte Cruz. Over Thanksgiving holiday break from Southwestern State College, she complained to her parents about the lack of parking places on campus. Ever since she moved into an apartment off campus, she had difficulty finding places to park her car and making it to her classes on time. During one long conversation about this problem, Charlotte began forming an idea. Her solution to the problem turned into a proposal to start a business of her own. When she returned to school, she approached the owner of a vacant lot behind the Campus Bookstore. After some negotiations, the owner signed a contract, agreeing to sell the lot to Charlotte for $9,000. Charlotte then withdrew $10,000 from a savings account her grandmother had set up for her, bought the lot, and founded her business, Charlotte's Car Park.

After only one month, the business proved so successful that Charlotte considered opportunities for improving it. However, she faced a difficult decision. She could just continue operating her simple parking lot indefinitely. She could borrow money to add security lighting and operate the parking lot at night as well as in the daytime. Or, she could possibly borrow money to purchase another lot on the opposite side of campus.

What kind of information will Charlotte need to make such a decision? Accounting information – specifically, information about the amounts she can expect to receive and to pay under each of the alternatives. If she has to borrow money from her parents or a bank to pay for lighting or another lot, she will need accounting information to convince them that making the loan is a sound investment. Financial accounting provides information that is relevant to Charlotte and potential lenders in such situations. So, let us look at its basic elements.

1. Define or describe the basic elements of financial accounting.
2. Apply the financial accounting equation and the double-entry technique to processing business transactions.
3. Describe the four basic financial statements.
4. Analyze the profitability of a business from an owner's perspective.
5. Recognize the limitations of accounting information for decision making.

LO 1

Define or describe the basic elements of financial accounting.

[handwritten notes in margin:]
A + L + O where
A = L + O

cash,
land,
buildings,
equipment,
A/C receivable.

debts,
A/C payable

各式各样的

THE FOUNDATION OF FINANCIAL ACCOUNTING

Records similar to those of modern accounting were used in Northern Italy as early as the Middle Ages—at least a century before Columbus discovered America.[1] Began as a means of keeping track of what a merchant owed and what was owed to a merchant, accounting has evolved over several centuries into a more sophisticated way of capturing and transforming data. Its objectives are to report on the financial position and performance of any business and to support the varied management decisions of that business. However, since the business world is ever-changing and increases in complexity each year, authorities, who the government designates directly or indirectly, continuously adapt accounting to the changing environment.

Generally Accepted Accounting Principles

Financial statements that a U.S. business publishes and distributes to outsiders must conform to professional standards called **Generally Accepted Accounting Principles** (GAAP). Before the mid-1930s, GAAP consisted of relatively few foundation elements, including broad assumptions, concepts, and definitions, that had evolved over several centuries. Much judgment was required to apply GAAP to individual businesses and circumstances. In fact, managers of U.S. firms made most judgments regarding what constituted GAAP and how to conform financial statements with them.[2]

The Stock Market Crash of 1929 and the ensuing Great Depression, however, uncovered many abuses of managements' discretion.[3] Although the Crash and Depression were not caused by accounting abuses, such abuses apparently were considered contributing factors. In the mid-1930s, the U. S. government passed the Securities Act of 1933 and the Securities Exchange Act of 1934. Both acts gave the newly formed Securities and Exchange Commission (SEC) the authority to set accounting standards for financial statements filed with the SEC, that is, for financial statements of virtually all large, publicly-owned U.S. corporations.

Interestingly, the SEC has exercised its authority only indirectly. In 1938, the SEC turned to the accounting profession, represented by the American Institute

---

[1]A. C. Littleton, *Essays on Accountancy* (Urbana: University of Illinois Press, 1961), p. 22. Littleton notes the existence of the 500-year-old account books of the Florentine merchant, Francesco di Marco, 1358–1412.

[2]Companies whose securities were listed on the New York Stock Exchange had to conform to some financial reporting requirements imposed by the Exchange in its listing agreement.

[3]A colorful description of some of the pre-Depression abuses of financial reporting in the United States is given in William Z. Ripley, *Main Street and Wall Street* (Lawrence, Kansas: Scholars Book Co., 1972), pp. 162–64. This book was published originally in 1927.

of Certified Public Accountants (AICPA). The AICPA's Committee on Accounting Procedure (CAP) and later its Accounting Principles Board (APB) set standards for financial statements until 1973. In 1973, the Financial Accounting Standards Board (FASB), a new body and independent of the AICPA, was formed to bring representatives of businesses and users of financial statements, as well as CPAs, directly into the standard-setting process. The CAP issued 51 Accounting Research Bulletins, the APB issued 31 Opinions, and the FASB had issued over 100 Statements of Financial Accounting Standards by the early 1990s.[4] As a consequence, Generally Accepted Accounting Principles now include the original foundation elements, those that evolved over centuries, plus an ever-expanding set of authoritative pronouncements on the ways to apply them to specific situations.

Key Financial Accounting Concepts

In spite of all the complexities in the business world – and the related complexities in setting accounting standards – a small and cohesive set of concepts, simple equations, definitions, measurement principles, and assumptions form the foundation of GAAP. These foundation elements guide accountants in recording the activities of businesses and in preparing their financial statements. To understand financial accounting, you must begin with the most fundamental of elements.

Three key concepts of financial accounting are: the accounting entity, the accounting period, and monetary measurement. These concepts give the accounting process its focus.

The Accounting Entity Concept.   The **accounting entity concept** states that the accounting process focuses on specific, separate economic entities. The *focus of financial accounting is on specific business entities, separate from other entities*, including their owners. For example, if Dr. Jessica Brown purchased a new car for her personal use, she would account for the expenditure as a personal expenditure, not as an expenditure of her medical practice.

In the United States, business entities are organized into three basic forms: proprietorships, partnerships, and corporations.

A **proprietorship** is a business owned by an individual. Proprietorships have no legal status apart from their owners; their relationships to other parties (customers, suppliers, employees, etc.) are all interpreted legally as relationships between the owner, as an individual, and the other parties. For example, if the government found a proprietorship had not paid all of its payroll taxes on time, it would bring legal action against the owner, not the business itself. However, for accounting purposes, the proprietor is a separate entity from the business. For example, the proprietor should keep personal funds separate from business funds. This way, the proprietor would know how much cash is available for business expenses and how much is available for personal spending.

Partnerships are businesses conducted by two or more entities acting as co-owners. Like proprietorships, partnerships are not separate, legal entities. The relationships between partnerships and others are interpreted legally as relationships between the partners, individually and collectively, with the other entities. For example, if a customer is injured by a product purchased from a partnership, he or she would sue the partners "jointly and severally" to recover

---

[4]CAP and APB standards are still considered authoritative, unless superceded by FASB Statements.

damages for the injury. Nevertheless, for accounting purposes, partnerships are treated as entities that are separate and distinct from the partners.

Corporations are business entities that are legally separate from their owners. Corporations are nonpersons; they do not exist naturally. A person may not simply begin a business and call it a corporation; a corporation must be chartered under a state's corporation statutes. Corporations can have any number of owners (including one) and still be corporations. Since corporations are separate legal entities, no inconsistency exists between their legal status and their treatment as separate business entities in accounting.

INTERNATIONAL PERSPECTIVES

The world is about to close the books on the 20th century amid a rapid-fire series of historic changes. Europe's markets are uniting. Eastern Bloc countries are embracing capitalist values. The Japanese are aggressively investing abroad. Medium and small companies are scrambling for new international opportunities. And in the midst of all this, issuers, investors, and analysts around the world are grappling with some surprisingly fundamental accounting questions.

For example: If the price/earnings ratio of a Japanese company is dramatically higher than that of an otherwise comparable U.S. company, is it because the cost of funds in Japan is lower? Is it because real prices charged to Japanese customers are higher than those charged to non-Japanese customers in overseas markets, presumably resulting in higher profit margins? Or is it due to an accounting distortion? If so, to what degree? And which of the two markets – U.S., Japan, or both – is distorted?

Granted, the volume of international financial transactions has exploded in recent years and may grow much larger if the United States Securities and Exchange Commission (SEC) eases restrictions on the sale of foreign debts and equity in the U.S. to sophisticated buyers. But what effect has accounting diversity had on the global capital markets so far? And if the purpose of accounting is to portray economic reality, are the economics driving the accounting or vice versa?

Because accountants of the world are not united by a single language like Esperanto or measurement standard like the metric system, cross-border financial participants must translate a bewildering array of financial information with great dispatch and hope nothing important gets lost in the translation. As one executive of a major credit rating agency put it, "Ten years ago, our primary readership was a U.S. audience. Today, it is very much an international market because of the recent explosion in Euro-bond and Euro-commercial paper offerings by companies in the U.S., Europe and Asia. And these international issuers are no longer brand names such as ICI or Siemens. It's a lot of companies that investors don't know, and frankly we're a little worried about this."

Can there be a single standard of comparison? Definite answers are still elusive. The SEC, the U.S.-based Financial Accounting Standards Board (FASB) and many organizations outside the U.S., most significantly the International Accounting Standards Committee, have publicly stated that harmonization of international accounting standards is a priority. But others are more skeptical. As one issuer [of financial statements] stated, "An international set of accounting standards would be a good idea, but we won't see it in our lifetime."

Meanwhile, the world must cope with accounting diversity.

Source: "Valuing Global Securities: Is Accounting Diversity a Mountain or a Molehill?" Arthur Andersen & Co., S.C., and Salomon Brothers, Inc., 1990.

The Accounting Period Concept.   The **accounting period concept** states that financial statements or other reports should be prepared at regular intervals such as every month, quarter, or year. Virtually all businesses prepare annual financial statements. Many also prepare statements at more frequent intervals because users of financial statements, particularly managers, need information more frequently to make decisions. Financial statements are prepared at regular intervals because users of the statements want to analyze performance improvements. For example, they want to know whether a business is doing better this year than last year. Such comparisons require financial statements prepared for two periods of the same length.

The Monetary Measurement Concept.   An almost infinite variety of information could appear in accounting reports – from the business's physical characteristics and appearance to its personnel to the specific ways it provides services or products to customers. Accounting cuts through the infinite set of possibilities and focuses on the business's financial essentials. A business is a pool of financial resources provided by its owners and creditors (lenders). Accounting focuses on the flow of resources through a business and only measures and reports on those business events, resources, and obligations that can be expressed in money terms. This idea is known as the **monetary measurement concept** that underlies GAAP.

Accounting Equations and Definitions[5]

Fundamental equations bind the elements of financial accounting together into a logical whole. The definitions of the elements tell us what aspects of a business are actually recognized and measured by the financial accounting process.

The Accounting Equation. The **accounting equation** states that assets equal liabilities plus owner's equity and governs the relationship between these three elements. It is expressed as follows:

$$\text{Assets} = \text{Liabilities} + \text{Owner's Equity}$$

Assets.   **Assets** are future economic benefits a business owns or controls. In a word, an asset is a resource of the business. Assets include anything that can be used for the business's benefit or any right to receive benefits. Examples of assets are cash, land, buildings, and equipment. **Accounts receivable** are payments due from customers for products or services previously provided on a credit basis. An account receivable is an asset because it represents a right to receive a future payment.

Liabilities.   **Liabilities** are the business's debts and other obligations to transfer cash, other assets, or services to other entities at some time in the future. Debts to lenders are liabilities because they require payment of specific, future amounts to repay and erase the debts. **Accounts payable**, amounts owed to suppliers for goods purchased on credit (charged), are also liabilities.

Owner's equity.   The **owner's equity** of a business is the residual interest owners have in the business's assets after deducting its liabilities. Both creditors and owners supply the funds to buy assets. According to the accounting equation, the total assets of a business are matched by the combined claims of the owners and creditors. However, the claims of creditors come before the claims

---

[5]To avoid unnecessary abstraction, definitions in this section are not direct quotes from *Statement on Financial Accounting Concepts No. 6*, "Elements of Financial Statements of Business Enterprises," (Stamford, Connecticut: FASB, 1985), but are based on the FASB definitions.

of owners. For example, if a business is liquidated (say, in bankruptcy proceedings), the creditors' claims must be paid in full before the owners can receive any of the business's assets. Therefore, owner's equity is a *residual* amount. It equals the net assets of the business, or the difference between the assets and the liabilities.

$$\text{Owner's Equity = Net Assets = Assets − Liabilities}$$

Owner's equity changes when the owners make investments in or receive distributions from the business. When owners contribute cash or other assets to the business, we call the contributions **investments**. Investments increase owner's equity because they increase assets without increasing liabilities. When the business gives cash or other assets to the owners, we call the assets given **distributions**. Distributions of proprietorships and partnerships are also called **withdrawals**, while distributions by corporations are called **dividends**. Distributions decrease owner's equity because they decrease assets without decreasing liabilities. In addition, owner's equity is increased by revenues and decreased by expenses as defined below.

The assets, liabilities, and owner's equity of a business make up its **financial position**. The financial position of a business is communicated in the **balance sheet** (formally known as a **statement of financial position**). The balance sheet takes its name from the accounting equation, which guarantees that assets will be balanced exactly by liabilities and owner's equity. We present a balance sheet later in the chapter as one of the outputs of the financial accounting process.

The Income Equation. **Net income** is defined by a very important equation in accounting:

$$\text{Revenues − Expenses = Net Income}$$

Revenues. **Revenues** are the increases in net assets (owner's equity) that result directly from providing products or services to customers during a specific period. In most cases, the assets received for providing products or services to customers are cash or the rights to receive cash in the future (accounts receivable). Thus, for example, when you buy clothing from a department store, the amount of the sale is revenue to the store, regardless of whether you pay cash or charge your purchase.

Expenses. **Expenses** are decreases in net assets (owner's equity) caused by the revenue-producing activities during a specific period. Examples of expenses are employees' wages, supplies, utilities, and rent. Many expenses represent decreases in cash. However, not all expenses are direct decreases in cash. For example, wages earned by employees during a period but not yet paid as of the end of the period are an obligation to pay. The increase in the liability, called wages payable, is an expense of the period in which the wages are earned.

The revenues, expenses, and net income of a business are communicated in the **income statement**. The income statement follows the income equation – expenses are subtracted from revenues to derive net income. We present an income statement later in the chapter.

Measurement Principles

Several measurement principles have evolved over many years of financial accounting practice. The most pervasive is the cost principle, which guides us in deciding the values to assign to assets, liabilities, revenues, and expenses. We introduce additional measurement principles in later chapters.

According to the **cost principle**, the amounts of assets recorded in the accounting records should be the amounts paid (or promised to be paid) for them when acquired. Also, the amounts of liabilities recorded should be the amounts of assets received when the liabilities are incurred. Suppose, for example, that a convenience store such as 7-Eleven purchases a piece of land for a new store site at a cost of $100,000. For accounting purposes, the value of the land is $100,000, which is also the "fair value" of the land at the date it is acquired. That is, the business presumably paid no more or less than necessary to acquire it. The land may increase in fair value over time, and while its later fair value will be a matter of opinion, its cost remains unchanged and is more objective. Because various users of financial statements such as owners and creditors have different interests in a business, objectivity is an important criterion for accounting information. Thus, the cost principle is often favored over alternatives such as "fair value."

TRANSACTION ANALYSIS USING THE ACCOUNTING EQUATION

LO 2
Apply the financial accounting equation and the double-entry technique to processing business transactions.

The financial accounting process consists of capturing transaction data, recording transactions, summarizing their effects on financial position, and, ultimately, transforming their effects into financial statements. **Transactions** consist of purchases, sales, and other exchanges that change the business's financial position. When a business purchases a piece of equipment, its financial position changes – equipment increases and cash decreases. When a business borrows money, its financial position changes – cash increases and a liability increases.

Maintaining the Equality Condition

Since transactions change the business's financial position, they are subject to the accounting equation, which defines the relationship between the elements of financial position. Therefore, *transactions are recorded according to the equation, and the equation holds both before and after each transaction is recorded.*

Before a business comes into being, its financial position consists of all zeros:

$$\textbf{Assets} = \textbf{Liabilities} + \textbf{Owner's Equity}$$
$$0 = 0 + 0$$

Since the accounting equation is satisfied by the all-zero beginning position, we know that the business's future financial positions will satisfy the equality condition *if, and only if,* all of the changes recognized from this point meet the equality condition. Thus, the rule for recording transactions is: *Each change in an element of the accounting equation must be matched by at least one change that has an equal, but opposite, effect.* Hence, the rule is often called the **double-entry rule**, and financial accounting is often referred to as double-entry accounting.

Suppose, for example, that a house painter buys a paint sprayer for $1,250 on credit. To record the transaction, the asset, equipment, is increased by

$1,250; and the liability, accounts payable, is increased by $1,250. The change in assets equals the change in liabilities with no change in owner's equity – so, the equation is satisfied.

Assets = Liabilities + Owner's Equity

+$1,250 = +$1,250 +   0

Processing Transactions

Now, let us tackle Charlotte Cruz's problem. She needs to prepare financial statements for the month of January 19X1, both for her own information and possibly to convince her parents or a bank to loan her money for expansion of her business. Her business had no assets, no liabilities, and no owner's equity just before she made her initial investment.

Assets = Liabilities + Owner's Equity

1/1/X1   0   =   0   +   0

We now apply the double-entry rule to the transactions and events that took place during January 19X1.

Transaction 1—Owner Investment.   On January 2, 19X1, Charlotte invested $10,000 of her own money in her new business, Charlotte's Car Park. She opened a separate checking account for the business and transferred the funds from her personal savings account. This investment immediately gives life to the business by endowing it with an asset, cash. The corresponding change is an increase in owner's equity.

Transaction	Cash	=	Owner's Equity	
1/1/X1	0	=	0	
(1)	10,000	=	10,000	Investment
New Bal.	10,000	=	10,000	

The equality condition is satisfied by this change in the business's financial position. The new financial position consists of $10,000 cash and $10,000 owner's equity.

Transaction 2—Purchase of Land for a Parking Lot.   On January 2, 19X1, Charlotte completed the purchase of land for the parking lot. This transaction decreased cash by $9,000 and increased the asset, land, by that amount.

Transaction	Cash	+	Land	=	Owner's Equity	
Prev. Bal.	10,000	+		=	10,000	
(2)	(9,000)	+	9,000	=	0	Lot Purchase
New Bal.	1,000	+	9,000	=	10,000	

Notice the result of processing every change so that it satisfies the double-entry rule: The equality condition is met by the new financial position each time. After Transaction 2, assets of cash plus the land total $10,000, and owner's equity is $10,000.

Transaction 3—Revenues Received in Cash.   During the first half of January, Charlotte's Car Park earned $1,200 in cash revenues from customers. These transactions increase cash and increase owner's equity by the amount of revenues earned.

Transaction	Cash	+	Land	=	Owner's Equity	
Prev. Bal.	1,000	+	9,000	=	10,000	
(3)	1,200	+		=	1,200	Revenues
New Bal.	2,200	+	9,000	=	11,200	

Transaction 4—Advertising Expense Incurred.   During January, Charlotte ran the following ad daily in the campus newspaper:

> **NOW OPEN** -- Charlotte's Car Park, 2501 Old College Street. Attended parking 6:00 a.m. to 6:00 p.m. daily. $1.00, first hour; $.50 each additional hour; $5.00 maximum per day. Convenient to bookstores, shops, and all of north campus.

The bill for $200 is due by February 15. This transaction results in a decrease in owner's equity for advertising expense and an increase in the liability, accounts payable.

Transaction	Cash	+	Land	=	Accounts Payable	+	Owner's Equity	
Prev. Bal.	2,200	+	9,000	=			11,200	
(4)		+		=	200	+	(200)	Advert. Exp.
New Bal.	2,200	+	9,000	=	200	+	11,000	

Transaction 5—Wages Expense.   Because of her studies, Charlotte could not be the attendant at the parking lot for more than a few hours each week. She paid a total of $800, which was payment in full for services, to friends to be attendants at the lot in January. This is a decrease in the asset, cash, due to the revenue-producing activities of the business. In other words, it is an expense and is recognized with a decrease to cash and an equal decrease to owner's equity.

Transaction	Cash	+	Land	=	Accounts Payable	+	Owner's Equity	
Prev. Bal.	2,200	+	9,000	=	200	+	11,000	
(5)	(800)	+		=		+	(800)	Wages Exp.
New Bal.	1,400	+	9,000	=	200	+	10,200	

Transaction 6—Uncollected Revenues.   Starting on January 8, Charlotte agreed to reserve five parking spaces for the Campus Bookstore to use as overflow parking on Mondays through Saturdays. The bookstore owed her $4.00 per day for each space, or a total of $400 for the month of January, and agreed to pay by February 15. We record the revenues for January, because the parking fees were earned in January and the right to receive payment in February is an asset as of January 31. To record the revenues earned, we increase a new asset, accounts receivable, and increase owner's equity by $400.

			Accounts				Accounts	Owner's	
Transaction	Cash	+	Receivable	+	Land	=	Payable	+	Equity	
Prev. Bal.	1,400	+			+ 9,000	=	200	+	10,200	
(6)		+	400	+		=		+	400	Revenues
New Bal.	1,400	+	400	+ 9,000	=	200	+	10,600	

Transaction 7—Withdrawal by Owner.   On January 31, 19X1, Charlotte wrote herself a check for $500 to cover her living expenses. This withdrawal reduces cash, but it does not increase any other asset or decrease any liability. Owner withdrawals from a business reduce its net assets and owner's equity. Thus, we reduce cash and owner's equity by $500. However, *because withdrawals are not reductions in owner's equity due to revenue-producing activities, they are not expenses and do not enter into the calculation of income.*

			Accounts				Accounts	Owner's	
Transaction	Cash	+	Receivable	+	Land	=	Payable	+	Equity	
Prev. Bal.	1,400	+	400	+ 9,000	=	200	+	10,600	
(7)	(500)	+		+	=		+	(500)	Withdrawal
New Bal.	900	+	400	+ 9,000	=	200	+	10,100	

Illustration 1-1 summarizes all of the transactions of Charlotte's Car Park for January 19X1. It starts with a hypothetical financial position that satisfies the equality condition with all zeros as of January 1, 19X1. Each transaction of January is processed to satisfy the equality condition (double entry).

ILLUSTRATION 1-1 Accounting History of Charlotte's Car Park—January 19X1

Transaction	Cash	+	ASSETS Accounts Receivable	+	Land	=	LIABILITIES Accounts Payable	+	OWNER'S EQUITY Owner's Equity
1/1/X1	0	+	0	+	0	=	0	+	0
(1) Investment	10,000	+		+		=		+	10,000
(2) Land	(9,000)	+		+	9,000	=		+	
(3) Revenue	1,200	+		+		=		+	1,200
(4) Advertisment		+		+		=	200	+	(200)
(5) wage	(800)	+		+		=		+	(800)
(6) Uncollected Revenue		+	400	+		=		+	400
(7) Withdrawal	(500)	+		+		=		+	(500)
1/31/X1	900	+	400	+	9,000	=	200	+	10,100
			10,300			=		10,300	

After the last transaction of January, we draw a line. Down each column of Charlotte's Car Park's accounting equation, we sum the beginning balance and the effects, if any, of Transactions 1 through 7. The results shown below the line are the balances in the equation elements as of January 31, 19X1. Below the balances note that the sum of the assets ($10,300) does indeed equal the sum of the liability ($200) and owner's equity ($10,100).

LO 3

Describe the four basic financial statements.

BASIC FINANCIAL STATEMENTS

The four basic financial statements – income statement, statement of owner's equity, statement of cash flows, and balance sheet – can be prepared directly from the transaction analysis summary in Illustration 1-1.

Income Statement

The income statement displays the business's revenues, expenses, and net income for a specific time period. Transactions 3-6 represent revenues and expenses of Charlotte's Car Park for January 19X1. They are increases and decreases, respectively, in the Owner's Equity column of Illustration 1-1. To prepare the income statement of Charlotte's Car Park for January 19X1, we format the revenues and expenses from the Owner's Equity column of Illustration 1-1 into the statement shown in Illustration 1-2. The income statement lists revenues first, followed by expenses, which are summed and subtracted from revenues to derive net income.

ILLUSTRATION 1-2 Income Statement

Charlotte's Car Park Income Statement For the Month Ended January 31, 19X1		
Revenues		$1,600
Expenses:		
Advertising expense	$200	
Wages expense	800	
Total expenses		1,000
Net income		$ 600

We label every financial statement with a heading that gives three items of information: the name of the business, the type of statement, and either the date for which it was prepared or the period it covers. Notice that the heading on the income statement in Illustration 1-2 indicates that it covers the month of January 19X1. This label is appropriate because an income statement reports about events that happened *during a period.*

Statement of Owner's Equity

Illustration 1-3 shows the statement of owner's equity. The **statement of owner's equity** reflects the effects of net income, owner's investments, and owner's withdrawals *for a period of time.* We said earlier that the owner's investments and revenues increase owner's equity and the owner's withdrawals and expenses decrease owner's equity. The statement of owner's equity reflects these changes. It can be prepared from the detail of the Owner's Equity column of Illustration 1-1, except that it is customary to offset revenues and expenses and show net income as a single change in owner's equity. Thus, we add net income of $600 to the beginning balance of zero and the owner's initial investment of $10,000 (Transaction 1 in Illustration 1-1). Then, we subtract the owner's withdrawal of $500 (Transaction 7) to determine the ending balance in owner's equity of $10,100 as of January 31, 19X1.

ILLUSTRATION 1-3 Statement of Owner's Equity

Charlotte's Car Park Statement of Owner's Equity For the Month Ended January 31, 19X1	
Beginning balance	$ 0
Add: Owner's investment	10,000
Net income	600
Less: Owner's withdrawal	(500)
Ending balance	$10,100

Statement of Cash Flows

A **statement of cash flows** explains the change in the business's cash balance for the period by presenting the increases and decreases in cash due to the company's operating, investing, and financing activities. The definitions of these activities, the techniques for preparing the statement, and the perceived usefulness of the statement are subjects of a later chapter. However, the statement for Charlotte's Car Park for January 19X1 appears in Illustration 1-4. While you may not know how to format such a statement at this time, you can trace all figures in it to the Cash column of Illustration 1-1.

ILLUSTRATION 1-4 Statement of Cash Flows

Charlotte's Car Park Statement of Cash Flows For the Month Ended January 31, 19X1		
Operations:		
Cash collections for parking	$ 1,200	
Expenditures for wages	(800)	
Cash provided by operations		$ 400
Investing activities:		
Purchase of land		(9,000)
Financing activities:		
Owner's investment	$10,000	
Owner's withdrawal	(500)	
Total cash from financing		9,500
Net increase in cash		$ 900

Balance Sheet

The balance sheet presents a business's financial position *as of a specific date*. A balance sheet is like a snapshot, presenting a picture of the business's financial position at an instant in time. In this case, the point in time is January 31, 19X1.

To prepare the balance sheet in Illustration 1-5, we format the January 31, 19X1, balances at the bottom of the transaction analysis worksheet in Illustration

1-1. The cash balance of $900 from Illustration 1-1 is the cash figure in Illustration 1-5; and the accounts receivable balance from Illustration 1-1 is the accounts receivable balance in Illustration 1-5. Likewise, the land, accounts payable, and owner's equity figures in Illustration 1-5 are all from the bottom line of Illustration 1-1.

ILLUSTRATION 1-5 Balance Sheet

Charlotte's Car Park Balance Sheet January 31, 19X1	
Assets	
Cash	$ 900
Accounts receivable	400
Land	9,000
Total assets	$10,300
Liabilities and Owner's Equity	
Accounts payable	$ 200
Owner's equity	10,100
Total liabilities and owner's equity	$10,300

LO 4
Analyze the profitability
of a business from an
owner's perspective.

INTERPRETATION OF FINANCIAL STATEMENTS

What can be learned from the financial statements that represent Charlotte's business for January? First, the business's cash position improved from a zero balance at the beginning of January to a balance of $900 at the end of January even though Charlotte was able to withdraw $500 for personal expenses. Second, the balance sheet shows that the business's total assets equal $10,300 at the end of January and its owner's equity equals $10,100. Third, seemingly the business was very profitable. It earned $600 in net income in one month with an original investment of $10,000. But just how profitable is this?

Profitability from the Owner's Perspective – Rate of Return

To judge profitability, we like to use a relative measure, one that can be compared to alternative uses of the owner's money. One of the important relative measures of profitability is **rate of return** (ROR) **on owner's equity**:

$$\text{Rate of Return on Owner's Equity} \ = \ \frac{\text{Net Income}}{\text{Average Owners' Equity}}$$

By this measure, Charlotte's Car Park's rate of return for January was:

$$\frac{\$600}{(\$10,000 + \$10,100) \div 2} \ = \ \frac{\$600}{\$10,050} \ = \ 5.97\%$$

The annual equivalent rate of return is 5.97% x 12 (months) = 71.6%, which is very impressive indeed when compared with the likely interest rate on the savings account from which Charlotte withdrew her investment funds.

However, it is important to recognize the nature and limitations of the accounting information used in the calculation. The Car Park's income for the month of January is unique to this first month of business. For example, January required no maintenance of the new parking lot, whereas future months will surely see some expenditures for maintenance. Moreover, Charlotte did some of the actual attending at the parking lot during January, which means the $600 income was partly due to her labor and partly due to her investment.[6]

LO 5

Recognize the limitations of accounting information for decision making.

Limitations of Accounting Information as a *Basis* for Decisions

The lesson is that financial accounting information does not provide answers to decision problems by itself. It merely tracks the history of a business. To make decisions, a user of financial statements must learn to analyze historical accounting information, understand it in the context of the business, and then use it as a basis for projections into the future. It is the projections of past results into the future (with appropriate modifications for expected changes) that are the foundation for actual choices between decision alternatives.

For example, Charlotte may find that, not only will the maintenance costs of the business be substantial in the future, but she may also have to curtail her attendance of the lot to manage the business if she expands it. Thus, the business may face higher wage expenses as well as significant maintenance expenses in the future. Such projected differences from the brief past history of her business should influence:

1. Charlotte's projections about her business in the future.
2. Whether she chooses to expand her business.
3. If she chooses expansion, then Charlotte must decide whether to buy a second lot or to add lighting to the first lot and expand to nighttime hours.

When she compares the rates of return that she projects for the business for these alternatives to the rate on, say, a savings account, Charlotte should consider the risk of her expanded business relative to the safety of a savings account.

SUMMARY

Define or describe the basic elements of financial accounting.   Financial accounting is built on concepts of the accounting entity, the accounting period, and monetary measurement; on definitions of assets, liabilities, owner's equity, revenues, and expenses; on the cost principle; and on two central equations:

$$Assets = Liabilities + Owner's Equity$$
$$Revenues - Expenses = Net Income$$

Apply the financial accounting equation and the double-entry technique to processing business transactions.   Transactions are processed from the business's inception according to the double-entry rule that says for each change in one

---

[6]Although it violates the accounting entity concept, it is a long-standing tradition that the salaries of owners are not considered expenses of proprietorships.

INSIGHTS INTO ETHICS

John Washington started a successful business delivering fast foods for several small restaurants in his college town. Now, about to graduate and move on in his life, John has put his business up for sale. John is negotiating to sell it to James Caldwell, a retired postal worker who has some money he wants to invest. John knows Mr. Caldwell has a limited knowledge of accounting. John also knows that he provided a substantial amount of the actual delivery driving in his business in each of the years he operated. Thus, the wages and salaries expense on his income statements do not reflect his services as proprietor. Mr. Caldwell, however, will not be driving deliveries himself and is relying on John's financial statements to estimate future profits and establish a price he is willing to pay.

What will happen to Mr. Caldwell's estimates of future profitability if he learns of John's role in making deliveries?

What should John do?

element of the accounting equation one or more changes must be made in other elements that equal it in total and have the opposite effect.

Describe the four basic business financial statements.   The four basic financial statements of businesses are the income statement, the statement of owner's equity, the statement of cash flows, and the balance sheet (statement of financial position).

Analyze the profitability of a business from an owner's perspective.   Owners wish to know whether a business is relatively as profitable as other alternatives that they may have for investing funds. The rate of return on owner's equity (net income ÷ average owner's equity) for a period is a relevant measure of profitability for owners.

Recognize the limitations of accounting information for decision making. Accounting information tracks the history of a business. As such, it does not provide answers to business decision problems directly. Rather, accounting information provides a basis for the projections of future consequences of decisions necessary to decide about which courses of action to take.

REVIEW PROBLEM

John Crown, the proprietor of Crown's Dental Clinic, started his practice after graduating from dental school on July 1, 19X1. At that time, the practice had no assets, liabilities, or owner's equity. The transactions for the month of July are given below:

July 1   John Crown invested $28,000 of his own money in Crown's Dental Clinic.
      3   John paid $800 for July's office rent.
      5   John rented used dental equipment for $400 per month.
    31   John billed his patients $5,200 during July. $4,000 of fees were received in cash at the time services were performed, and the remaining $1,200 was still owed by patients as of July 31.
    31   John was billed $1,100 for utilities.
    31   John paid wages of $1,400 owed to the receptionist and hygienist.
    31   John withdrew $1,200 from the business for personal use.

REQUIRED:

a. Determine the effect of each transaction on the accounting equation for Crown's Dental Clinic and total each part of the equation for July.
b. Prepare an income statement for the month of July.
c. Prepare a statement of owner's equity for the month of July.
d. Prepare a balance sheet for July 31.

SOLUTION:

Planning and Organizing Your Work
1. Analyze each transaction.
2. Enter the effect of each transaction in the appropriate columns of the accounting equation following the double-entry rule.
3. Total each column.
4. Verify that the equation is in balance.
5. Select the items to include on the income statement.
6. Prepare the income statement.
7. Select the items to include on the statement of owner's equity.
8. Prepare the statement of owner's equity.
9. Select the items to include on the balance sheet.
10. Prepare the balance sheet.

(a) *Determine the effect of each transaction.*

Transaction	Cash	+	Accounts Receivable	=	Accounts Payable	+	Owner's Equity	
1.	28,000						28,000	Investment
2.	(800)						(800)	Rent expense, office
3.	(400)						(400)	Rent expense, equip.
4.	4,000		1,200				5,200	Revenue
5.					1,100		(1,100)	Utilities expense
6.	(1,400)						(1,400)	Wages expense
7.	(1,200)						(1,200)	Withdrawal
7/31 Total	28,200	+	1,200	=	1,100	+	28,300	

(b) *Prepare an income statement.*

Crown's Dental Clinic
Income Statement
For the Month Ended July 31, 19X1

Fee revenue		$5,200
Expenses:		
Utilities expense	$1,100	
Rent expense, office	800	
Rent expense, equipment	400	
Wages expense	1,400	
Total expenses		3,700
Net income		$1,500

(c) *Prepare a statement of owner's equity.*

Crown's Dental Clinic Statement of Owner's Equity For the Month Ended July 31, 19X1		
Beginning balance	$	0
Add: Owner's investment		28,000
Net income		1,500
Less: Owner's withdrawal		(1,200)
Ending balance		$28,300

(d) *Prepare a balance sheet.*

Crown's Dental Clinic Balance Sheet July 31, 19X1	
Assets	
Cash	$28,200
Accounts receivable	1,200
Total assets	$29,400
Liabilities and Owner's Equity	
Accounts payable	$ 1,100
Owner's equity	28,300
Total liabilities and owner's equity	$29,400

KEY TERMS

accounting entity concept, *21*
accounting equation, *23*
accounting period concept, *23*
accounts payable, *23*
accounts receivable, *23*
assets, *23*
balance sheet, *24*
corporations, *22*
cost principle, *25*
distributions, *24*
dividends, *24*
double-entry rule, *25*

expenses, *24*
financial position, *24*
Generally Accepted Accounting Principles, *20*
income statement, *24*
investments, *24*
liabilities, *23*
monetary measurement concept, *23*
net income, *24*
owner's equity, *23*
partnerships, *21*

proprietorship, *21*
rate of return on owner's equity, *31*
revenues, *24*
statement of cash flows, *30*
statement of financial position, *24*
statement of owner's equity, *29*
transactions, *25*
withdrawals, *24*

SELF-QUIZ

LO 1 1. Which accounting concept requires accountants to separate the owners from their proprietorships?
a. Individual concept
b. Accounting period concept
c. Monetary concept
d. Accounting entity concept

LO 1 2. Which accounting relationship is incorrect?
a. Assets = Liabilities + Owner's Equity
b. Net Income − Expenses = Revenues
c. Net Assets = Assets − Liabilities
d. Owner's Equity = Assets − Liabilities

LO 1 3. Which type of business entities are legally separate from their owners?
a. Corporations
b. Proprietorships
c. Partnerships
d. Both b and c

LO 3 4. Which of the following is not one of the basic financial statements of a business?
a. Income statement
b. Statement of cash flows
c. Liability statement
d. Statement of owner's equity

LO 2 5. What items in the accounting equation (assets, liabilities, or owner's equity) are increased or decreased as a result of an owner investing $15,000 cash in the business?

LO 2 6. What items in the accounting equation are increased or decreased as a result of paying wages of $1,500?

LO 2 7. What items in the accounting equation are increased or decreased as a result of receiving $9,000 cash for services performed?

LO 2 8. What items in the accounting equation are increased or decreased as a result of an owner withdrawing $3,900 cash from a business.

LO 4 9. How is the rate of return on owner's equity calculated?
a. Dividing cash from operations by total assets
b. Dividing net income by 2 and adding owner's equity
c. Dividing net income by average owner's equity
d. Dividing net income by average assets

LO 5 10. True or False? A decision maker can rely solely on accounting information to make a decision.

LO 1 11. Match the definitions with these terms that appear on an income statement:
___ Revenues
___ Net income
___ Expenses
a. Decreases in net assets caused by generating revenues
b. Increases in net assets from providing goods or services to customers
c. Revenues minus expenses

LO 3 12. Match these definitions with the different financial statements:
___ Balance sheet
___ Statement of owner's equity
___ Statement of cash flows
___ Income statement
a. Presents revenues and expenses
b. Presents investments and withdrawals
c. Presents assets, liabilities, and owner's equity
d. Presents operating, investing, and financing cash flows

LO 1 13. Match the definitions with the different types of business entities.
___ Balance sheet
___ Proprietorships
___ Corporations
a. Businesses legally separate from their owners
b. Businesses conducted by more than one owner
c. Businesses conducted by one owner

LO 1 14. The balance sheet is also known as the _____ of _____ _____.

LO 1 15. The _____ _____ prevents an accountant from recording an asset's value greater than the price paid when it was acquired.

LO 3 16. The _____ _____ is the only basic statement prepared as of a specific time instead of for a period of time.

LO 1 17. Distributions of proprietorships are called _____, whereas distributions of corporations are called _____.

LO 2 18. The _____ rule states that at least two elements of the accounting equation must be increased or decreased for each transaction.

SOLUTIONS TO SELF-QUIZ
1. d   2. b   3. a   4. c   5. assets increase; owner's equity increases   6. assets decrease; owner's equity decreases   7. assets increase; owner's equity increases   8. assets decrease; owner's equity decreases   9. c   10. false   11. revenues = b; net income = c; expenses = a   12. balance sheet = c; statement of owner's equity = b; statement of cash flows = d; income statement = a   13. partnerships = b; proprietorships = c; corporations = a   14. statement of financial position   15. cost principle   16. balance sheet   17. withdrawals, dividends   18. double-entry

QUESTIONS

Q1-1 What government body has the right to make accounting rules, even though it has only indirectly exercised this authority?

Q1-2 What do CAP, FASB, and APB have in common?

Q1-3 What are the important differences among a proprietorship, a partnership, and a corporation?

Q1-4 What are the four basic financial statements of businesses?

Q1-5 Why is the accounting period concept necessary?

Q1-6 What are the definitions of the three elements of the accounting equation?

Q1-7 What is the difference between a withdrawal and a dividend?

Q1-8 What is the general rule for recording accounting transactions?

Q1-9 What specific information can you learn about a company from each of its four financial statements?

Q1-10 What feature distinguishes a balance sheet from the other three basic financial statements?

Q1-11 Name a measure that can help an owner judge profitability.

Q1-12 How should a decision maker effectively use financial accounting information?

EXERCISES

LO 1

E1-1 Accounting Relationships Determine owner's equity if total assets re $86,000 and total liabilities are $31,000.

LO 1

E1-2 Accounting Relationships Determine the ending balance of owner's equity if you know the following information:

Investments by owner	$21,600	Beginning owner's equity	$9,800
Withdrawals by owner	9,100	Net income	5,100

LO 1

E1-3 Accounting Relationships Determine revenues if you know the following information:

Total assets (ending)	$13,500	Total liabilities (ending)	$3,600
Expenses	3,100	Beginning owner's equity	600
Investments by owner	4,000	Withdrawals by owner	1,100

LO 2

E1-4 Processing Business Transactions Ann Fernandez started operating U Rent-All on January 1, 19X1. During the month of January, U Rent-All entered into a number of transactions. On a separate sheet of paper, show the effect that each transaction had on assets, liabilities, and owner's equity by using a + for increase; a – for decrease; and an N for no effect. Use the format below for your answer. The first transaction is completed for you.

Transaction	Assets	Liabilities	Owner's Equity
(0)	+	+	N

(0) Borrowed money from the bank.
a. Ann Fernandez invested her own money in U Rent-All.
b. Paid wages.
c. Collected cash from renting equipment.
d. Ann withdrew cash from the business.
e. Paid the utility bill for January.
f. Paid the rent for January.

LO 3   **E1-5**   **Financial Statement Items**   On a separate sheet of paper, place the correct letters next to the following items to show that they belong on the (*B*) balance sheet, (*I*) income statement, or (*O*) statement of owner's equity. It is possible that an item may belong on more than one statement.

Cash	Utility expense
Fee revenue	Investment by owner
Net income	Notes payable
Owner's equity	Withdrawal by owner
	Salaries and wages expense

LO 3   **E1-6**   **Income Statement Preparation**   Using the following data, prepare an income statement for the Clyde Company for the year ended December 31, 19X4.

Rent expense	$17,500	Utilities expense	$3,700
Fee revenue	48,900	Advertising expense	7,700
Salaries and wages expense	23,800	Insurance expense	2,000
Interest revenue	9,600		

LO 3   **E1-7**   **Balance Sheet Preparation**   Using the following data, prepare a balance sheet for the Rolf Company for the year ended December 31, 19X7. Calculate any unknown amounts needed to complete the balance sheet.

Bank loan payable	$35,000
Land	18,000
Cash	16,600
Accounts receivable	13,900

LO 3   **E1-8**   **Statement of Owner's Equity Preparation**   Using the following data, prepare a statement of owner's equity for the Yolanda Company for the year ended December 31, 19X3.

Owner's equity, 1/1/X3	$14,000	Revenues	$27,000
Owner's withdrawal	3,800	Expenses	15,500
Owner's investment	1,200		

LO 4   **E1-9**   **Compute Rate of Return on Owner's Equity**   Using the following data, compute the rate of return on owner's equity for Silverheels Company for the year ended 12/31/X9.

Owner's equity, 1/1/X9	$ 8,000
Assets, 12/31/X9	65,000
Liabilities, 12/31/X9	41,000
Net income, 19X9	4,000

PROBLEM SET A

LO 2   **P1-1A**   **Understanding Business Transactions**   Transactions for Home Decorators for the month ended October 31, 19X5 (the first month of operations), are shown below in equation form.

31/10/9S

	Cash	+	Land	=	Bank Loan	+	Owner's Equity
Beg. Bal.	0		0		0		0
1.	191,000						191,000
2.	134,000				134,000		
3.	(107,300)		107,300				
4.	6,200						6,200
5.	(1,100)						(1,100)
6.	(2,500)				(2,500)		
7.	(2,300)						(2,300)

REQUIRED:

Describe the probable nature of each transaction that occurred during the month of October. For example, Transaction 1 could be described as the proprietor investing $191,000 cash in Home Decorators. Each transaction is different. Assume that Transaction 4 was with customers, Transaction 5 was with employees, and Transaction 7 was with the owner.

LO 2,3

P1-2A   **Process Business Transactions**   Janet Jones, the proprietor of Fix-a-Disk, started her business on May 1, 19X4. At that time, the business had no assets, liabilities, or owner's equity. The transactions for the month of May are given below:

May	1	Janet Jones invested $9,600 of her own money to establish her new business, Fix-a-Disk.
	2	Janet borrowed $5,000 from the bank.
	31	Janet collected $1,900 for repairs in May.
	31	Janet rented a store. She paid $500 for May's rent.
	31	Janet paid her assistant $600 in wages.
	31	Janet repaired a computer hard disk for the Phi Kappa Psi fraternity but will not be paid until next month. The amount charged is $85.
	31	Janet received a utility bill for $160 for the month of May. The bill will be paid in June.
	31	Janet withdrew $1,400 from the business for personal use.

REQUIRED:

a. Determine the effect of each transaction on the accounting equation for Fix-a-Disk and summarize their total effects on each part of the equation for May. The elements of the accounting equation for the store are cash, accounts receivable, accounts payable, bank loan, and owner's equity.

b. Prepare an income statement for the month of May.

c. Prepare a statement of owner's equity for the month of May.

d. Prepare a balance sheet as of May 31.

LO 3

P1-3A   **Financial Statement Preparation**   The following data are presented for Clifton's Auto Repair Shop for 19X1:

Bank loan payable, 12/31/X1	$35,000	Salaries or wages expense	$25,600
Land, 12/31/X1	38,000	Utilities expense	3,500
Cash, 12/31/X1	26,600	Advertising expense	4,200
Accounts receivable, 12/31/X1	24,500	Insurance expense	7,100
Repairs revenue	87,400	Withdrawals by owner	6,800
Rent expense	10,800		

REQUIRED:

Prepare an income statement, statement of owner's equity, and balance sheet for Clifton's Auto Repair Shop for 19X1. Calculate any unknown amounts needed to complete the financial statements.

LO 1,4

P1-4A   **Accounting Relationships and Return on Owner's Equity**   The following information is from Hal's Printing Services for 19X1 and 19X2:

	19X1	19X2
Total assets (ending)	$ 90,000	$?
Total liabilities (ending)	25,000	41,000
Owner's equity (beginning)	31,000	?
Revenues	110,000	130,000
Expenses	?	85,000
Withdrawals by owner	7,000	?
Owner's equity (ending)	?	79,000

REQUIRED:

a. Determine the unknown information for 19X1 and 19X2.
b. Calculate the rate of return on owner's equity for 19X1 and 19X2.

PROBLEM SET B

LO 2

P1-1B   Understanding Business Transactions   Transactions for The Appliance Service Center for the month ended March 31, 19X8 (the first month of operations), are shown below in equation form:

	Cash	+ Equipment	=	Bank Loan	+	Owner's Equity
Beg. Bal.	0	0		0		0
1.	118,500					118,500
2.	(86,900)	86,900				
3.	45,000			45,000		
4.	7,900					7,900
5.	(4,000)			(4,000)		
6.	(2,100)					(2,100)
7.	(3,300)					(3,300)

REQUIRED:

Describe the nature of each transaction during the month of March. For example, Transaction 1 could be described as the owner investing $118,500 cash in The Appliance Service Center. Each Transaction is different. Assume that Transaction 4 was with customers, Transaction 6 was with employees, and Transaction 7 was with the owner.

LO 2,3

P1-2B   Process Business Transactions   Nancy Doubrava, the proprietor of Nancy's Landscape Design Shop, started her business after graduating with a degree in botany on August 1, 19X7. At that time, the business had no assets, liabilities, or owner's equity. The transactions for the month of August are given below:

Aug. 1   Nancy Doubrava invested $11,200 of her own money to establish Nancy's Landscape Design Shop.
     2   Nancy borrowed $7,000 from the bank.
    31   Nancy collected $3,800 for designs prepared for clients in August.
    31   Nancy prepared additional designs in August for $1,800 that will be collected in September.
    31   Nancy paid her two assistants $550 each in wages.
    31   Nancy received a utility bill for $240 for the month of August. Nancy will pay the bill in early September.
    31   Nancy paid August's rent for the shop of $600.
    31   Nancy withdrew $1,100 from the business for personal use.

REQUIRED:

a. Determine the effect of each transaction on the accounting equation for Nancy's Landscape Design Shop and total each part of the equation for August. The elements of the accounting equation for the design shop are cash, accounts receivable, accounts payable, bank loan, and owner's equity.
b. Prepare an income statement for the month of August.
c. Prepare a statement of owner's equity for the month of August.
d. Prepare a balance sheet as of August 31.

LO 3

P1-3B   Financial Statement Preparation   The following data are presented for Dara's Rental Storage for 19X1:

Building, 12/31/X1	$19,000
Accounts receivable, 12/31/X1	12,250
Rent expense	3,700
Salaries and wages expense	2,800
Bank loan payable, 12/31/X1	17,500
Rent revenue	23,700
Withdrawals by owner	3,400
Utilities expense	2,250
Advertising expense	1,600
Cash, 12/31/X1	13,300
Insurance expense	3,550

REQUIRED:

Prepare an income statement, statement of owner's equity, and balance sheet for Dara's Rental Storage for 19X1. Calculate any unknown amounts needed to complete the financial statements.

LO 1,4

P1-4B   Accounting Relationships and Return on Owner's Equity   The following information is from Milano's Computer Training School for 19X8 and 19X9:

	19X8	19X9
Total assets (ending)	$270,000	$360,000
Total liabilities (ending)	105,000	?
Owner's equity (beginning)	163,000	?
Revenues	?	290,000
Expenses	147,000	225,000
Withdrawals	51,000	?
Owner's equity (ending)	?	137,000

REQUIRED:

a. Determine the unknown information for 19X8 and 19X9.
b. Calculate the rate of return on owner's equity for 19X8 and 19X9.

CRITICAL THINKING AND COMMUNICATING

C1-1   John Chang is thinking about investing half of his savings account to purchase an existing motorcycle maintenance business. Before investing, John requested copies of the company's financial statements. John would also like to study additional information about the company before making a decision to invest.

REQUIRED:

a. Determine the information that he should examine from the financial statements.
b. What other information should John examine before making his decision?

C1-2   Carol Higgins was upset after she examined her business's balance sheet. She feels that the total assets shown in the balance sheet are significantly under fair value.

REQUIRED:

Write a memo to Carol explaining why the cost principle may lead to undervaluation of assets relative to their fair values. Include in the memo a discussion of the advantages and disadvantages of the cost principle versus fair value.

CHAPTER 2

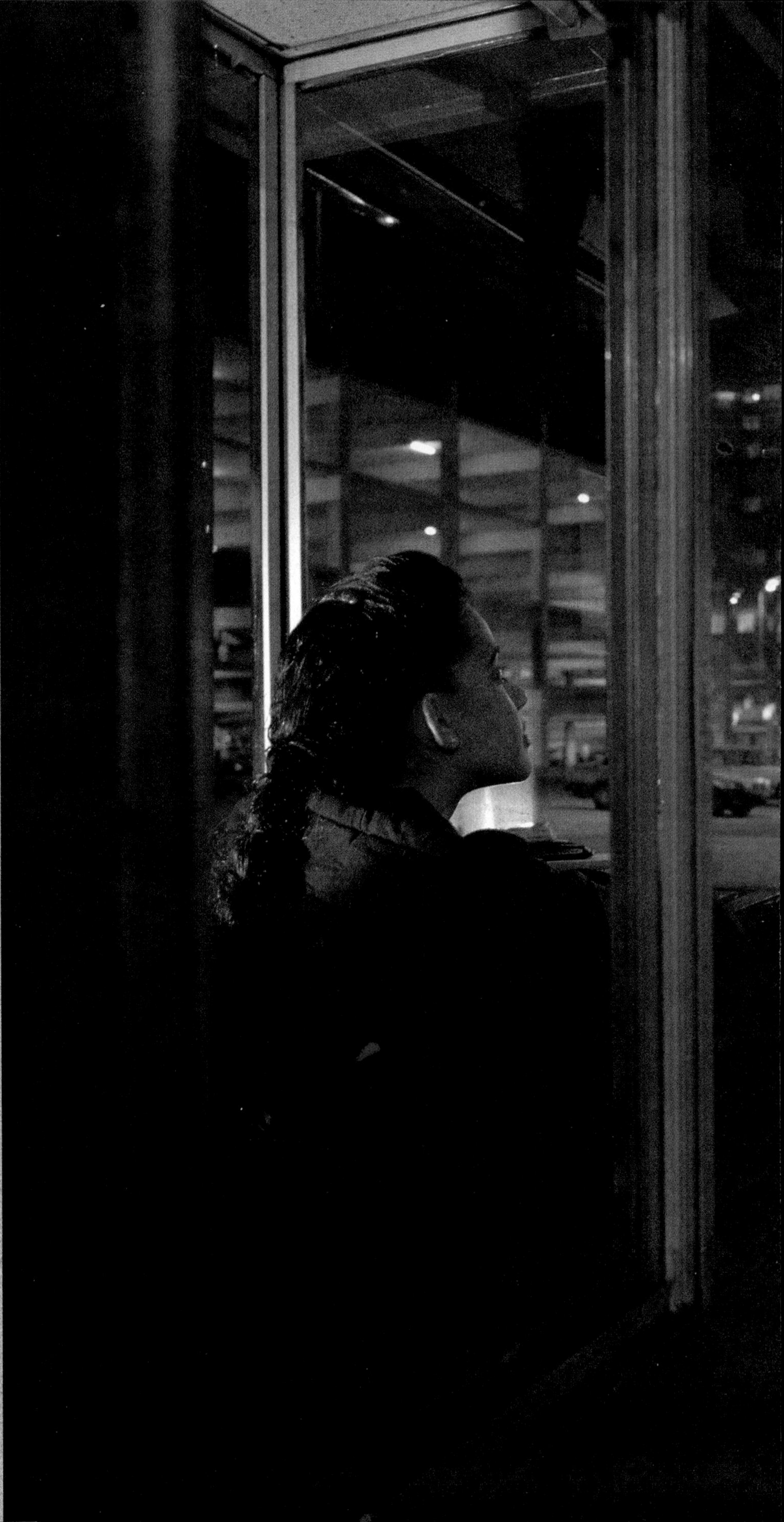

Accounts, Transactions, and Double Entry

Charlotte Cruz decided to provide night parking at Charlotte's Car Park by adding lighting for security. At the beginning of February 19X1, Charlotte received estimates of the cost of the lighting of $3,000. To add the improvements, Charlotte will have to borrow the money. Charlotte decided to take the financial statements for January, which you saw in the previous chapter, to the local banks and to apply for a loan.

Charlotte realizes that her business and the number of transactions it enters into will expand as a result of adding night parking. She recalls how tedious it was during the first month of operations to record just the few transactions directly into the accounting equation. She wonders if there is a more efficient means of recording the transactions. Can you imagine how many transactions a business such as General Motors Corporation enters into each day? She believes there has to be a better system.

This chapter begins a more thorough examination of the financial accounting process to which you were introduced previously. The financial accounting process tracks business events and transactions by recording their effects on the business's financial position. The end product of this process is the financial statements of the business. In this chapter, you are introduced to accounts. Accounts are records used to store and summarize information about business transactions. Through the use of double-entry accounting, we record information about transactions in the accounts. By studying how some common transactions are recorded in the accounts, you are introduced to the mechanics of double entry.

1. Describe accounts and recognize commonly used accounts.
2. Explain the rules of debit and credit and how they relate to the accounting equation.
3. Apply the rules of debit and credit to business transactions.
4. Identify the procedures in the accounting cycle.
5. Apply the procedures to record in the accounting records the effects of business transactions.
6. Explain the relationship between the general journal and the general ledger.
7. Prepare a trial balance.
8. Analyze the various types of errors a trial balance identifies and apply procedures to correct the errors.

LO 1

Describe accounts and recognize commonly used accounts.

ACCOUNTS

Using the accounting equation directly, you previously examined the effects of business transactions on assets, liabilities, and owner's equity. While this procedure may be acceptable for a small number of transactions, most businesses need a more efficient and convenient means of storing and summarizing the effects of a variety of transactions. Many large businesses have thousands of transactions daily; obviously, for them the use of individual accounting equations is impractical.

In actual practice, the device businesses use for storing and summarizing information about the effects of transactions is the account. Using accounts is Charlotte's solution to the inefficiency of recording transactions directly in the accounting equation. An **account**, a subclassification of the accounting equation, is used for storing and summarizing information about transactions that affect a particular element of the business's financial position. Hence, there are asset accounts, liability accounts, and owner's equity accounts. Accounts are a part of the business's formal accounting records and are located in a general ledger, which we discuss later in this chapter.

T-Accounts

In its simplest form, an account resembles the letter T and is referred to as a **T-account**. The basic format of the T-account is illustrated below:

Account Title	
Left side	Right side

The T-account consists of three components:

1. the account title
2. the left side
3. the right side

The account title names an asset, a liability, or an item of owner's equity. We record increases in accounts on one side; decreases, on the other side.

We use the cash account to record the increases and decreases in cash. For example, recall the transactions of Charlotte's Car Park. If those transactions that affected cash are recorded in a T-account, they appear as follows:

Cash			
Investment	10,000	Purchase of parking lot	9,000
Parking revenues earned	1,200	Payment of wages	800
		Withdrawal by owner	500

Account Balance

When we place increases in an account on one side and decreases on the other side, it is easy to sum the increases and the decreases. Then we determine the **account balance** at the end of a period as follows:

Balance at the beginning of the period
Add: Increases during the period
Less: Decreases during the period

Equals: Balance at the end of the period

The balance in the cash account of Charlotte's Car Park is $900, and the account is shown below:

Cash						
Jan.	1	Beginning balance	0	Jan.	1	Purchase of parking lot	9,000
	2	Investment	10,000		31	Payment of wages	800
	15	Parking revenues earned	1,200		31	Withdrawal by owner	500
		Increases	11,200			Decreases	10,300
	31	Ending balance	900				

Notice that the T-account for cash now has the dates of the beginning balance, the cash transactions, and the ending balance. Also, the account balance of $900 is calculated in the T-account. Recall that the amount of cash shown in the January 31, 19X1, balance sheet for Charlotte's Car Park is $900.

Commonly Used Accounts

The types of accounts a business uses depend on the nature of its operations. For example, a service business such as Charlotte's Car Park will have accounts for the assets it uses to provide parking services to its customers. A manufacturing business will have accounts for the assets it uses in its manufacturing operations—factory buildings and equipment. Then, a retail clothing store will have asset accounts different than either those of service and manufacturing businesses. For example, a retail clothing store's assets might include display cases, mannequins, and cash registers. Similarly, liability accounts will vary, depending on the form of the business's borrowing; and owner's equity accounts will vary, depending on how the business is organized—proprietorship, partnership, or corporation. While accounts do vary from business to business, those discussed in the following section are common to most businesses.

Asset Accounts.   Conceivably, a business could have just one account called Assets, one account called Liabilities, and one account called Owner's Equity. However, the result of accounting for the business with only three accounts would not be very informative. For example, neither management nor outside users of financial statements would be able to tell how much of its total assets the business holds in cash and how much it holds in accounts receivable, equipment, buildings, etc. There is no rule that says exactly how many different accounts a business should have. However, it should use as many different asset, liability, and owner's equity accounts as needed to distinguish between the elements of its financial position. These accounts will have different implications for management purposes and for evaluation by outside users of the financial statements. Therefore, a business should have a separate account for each distinctly different category of assets that it uses.

Cash.   We use a cash account to record increases and decreases in the business's cash. The term *cash* includes money or any medium of exchange that a bank will accept at face value for deposit. Common components of cash include coins, currency, checks, and money orders. A cash account includes both cash deposited in a bank and cash on the premises of the business in a cash register or safe.

Accounts receivable.   Many businesses sell goods or provide services to customers for an implied promise to pay in the future. These types of transactions commonly are called *sales on credit* or *sales on account*. The amounts due from customers for sales on credit are called *accounts receivable*, which we record in the accounts receivable account. Sales on credit increase accounts receivable, and collections of amounts due from customers decrease accounts receivable.

Notes receivable.   We use a notes receivable account to record formal written promises of other entities to pay amounts of money on future fixed dates.

Prepaid expenses.   A business often pays for goods and services before using or receiving them. These payments create assets called *prepaid expenses*. Common types of prepaid expenses include insurance and rent. A business may have a separate account for each type of prepaid expense.

Equipment.   Each type of equipment that a business uses in its operations should be recorded in a separate equipment account. The types of equipment used in operations and the types of equipment accounts depend on the nature of the business's operations. A service business has equipment accounts for the equipment needed to provide its services to customers. A manufacturing business uses equipment such as drill presses and lathes and records increases and decreases in this type of equipment in a manufacturing equipment account. Items such as typewriters, photocopying machines, and microcomputers are recorded in an office equipment account. A retail store would record display cases, cash registers, and similar items in a store equipment account. A business that uses trucks and automobiles in its operations would have a transportation equipment account.

Land.   A business often owns land that it uses in operations. For example, a business may own the land on which a factory, retail store, or office building is located. We use a separate land account to record each type of land the business owns.

Land improvements.   A business sometimes adds improvements to the land it owns. We record the cost of the improvements in a land improvements account. Examples of land improvements include driveways, sidewalks, fences, and lighting.

Buildings.   A business also commonly owns buildings that it uses in operations. Types of buildings a business uses include manufacturing plants, office buildings, warehouses, retail stores, and garages. Although a building is physically inseparable from the land on which it is located, we record land in a separate account from the building. The reason for recording land and buildings in separate accounts is that buildings are subject to wear and deterioration and are used up over time, while land is not used up. The using up of a building is called *depreciation* and is discussed in subsequent chapters. A business should have a separate building account for each type of building it owns and uses in its operations.

To illustrate the variety of assets that a business may have, *The Walt Disney Company's* 1992 annual report listed the following assets in its balance sheet:

Cash and cash equivalents
Investments
Receivables
Merchandise inventories
Film and television costs
Theme parks, resorts, and other property

You may not understand all of the asset titles at this point or how they are combined in the balance sheet; but as you continue your study of accounting, the titles will become familiar. For example, the Theme parks, resorts, and other property includes attractions, buildings, projects in progress, and land, all of which were recorded in Disney's actual accounting records. These assets were shown at a total amount of $10.8 billion.

Liability Accounts.   Managers and outside users of financial statements such as bankers are aware that different obligations may have entirely different implications for a business. For example, as a business pays accounts payable, it usually replaces them by new accounts payable through continuous purchases of supplies and services needed for operations. However, a business must pay off a bank loan without assuming any other liability to take its place automatically. Thus, the business must have sufficient cash, that is not required for other purposes, to pay off a bank loan. Once again, there is no clear rule as to how many different liability accounts a business should have. However, because different liabilities have different financial implications, a business should have a separate liability account for each distinctly different type of obligation.

Accounts payable.   Accounts payable are amounts owed to others as a result of an implied promise to pay in the future. Accounts payable generally are the result of purchases of goods and services on credit (on account). When a business purchases goods or services on account, it increases Accounts Payable. When a business pays cash to the vendor, it decreases Accounts Payable by the amount of the payment.

Notes payable.   We record increases and decreases in the amounts owed to others in the form of written promises to pay in Notes Payable.

Other payables.   The types of other liabilities that a business has depend on the nature of its operations. Examples of other liability accounts include Wages and Salaries Payable, Interest Payable, Rent Payable, and Mortgage Payable.

Owner's Equity Accounts.   Owner's equity accounts represent the owner's residual interest in the business's net assets (assets – liabilities). This residual interest is seen in the following version of the accounting equation:

Owner's Equity = Assets – Liabilities

The right side of the equation represents the business's net assets, and the left side represents the owner's interest. To keep the equation in balance, transactions that increase the business's net assets must increase owner's equity; and, conversely, transactions that decrease the business's net assets must decrease owner's equity. We use a separate owner's equity account to record the effects of each type of transaction that affects owner's equity.

Capital.   We use a capital account, in the name of an individual, to record the investment of that person in his or her business. When Charlotte Cruz invested $10,000 to start her business, she established a capital account in her name to record the investment.

Withdrawals.   A primary objective of most businesses is to earn income for the owner. An individual who invests in his or her business expects to use at least part of its earnings for personal living expenses and other personal uses. Although a business does not determine net income until the end of an accounting period, an owner usually withdraws assets (usually cash) periodically for personal use. Withdrawal accounts are owner's equity accounts that proprietorships and partnerships use to accumulate the amounts of withdrawals by owners for a period. Withdrawals represent reductions in the owner's equity and reflect reductions in *net* assets due to the owner's removal of them for personal use. Therefore, *withdrawals are not expenses of the business*.

Revenues.   Revenue accounts are owner's equity accounts used to accumulate the business's revenues for a particular period. For purposes of determining net income (or loss) and preparing income statements, separate accounts for each of the various sources of revenue are maintained. The types of revenue accounts a business uses depend on the nature of its operations. Examples of revenue accounts are Sales, Parking Revenue, Repairs Revenue, Rent Revenue, and Interest Revenue. Generally, the titles of revenue accounts are descriptive of the types of revenue recorded in each account.

The realization principle tells us how much revenue to recognize for a given period. To **recognize** means to record in an account. According to the **realization principle**, we should recognize revenues in a period only if:

1. They are *earned* during the period.
2. They either are collected in cash, or they will be collected from customers in the future.

Generally, we consider revenues as earned if the business has provided products or services to customers.

Expenses.   Expense accounts are owner's equity accounts used to accumulate the business's expenses for a particular period. We use a separate expense account for each type of expense a business incurs; and using this information, we may prepare the income statement. Different types of businesses will have different expense accounts. Examples of expense accounts are Wages and Salaries Expense, Rent Expense, Interest Expense, and Utilities Expense.

The matching principle governs when to recognize expenses. According to the **matching principle**, we should recognize as expenses the costs incurred to produce products and services, which the business sells to its customers, in the same period we recognize the revenues from those products and services.

LO 2

Explain the rules of debit and credit and how they relate to the accounting equation.

DEBIT AND CREDIT

Debit and credit rules determine on which side of an account we record the increases and decreases. In practice, accountants refer to the left side of a T-account as the **debit** side; the right side, as the **credit** side. Debit is abbreviated as *Dr.* and credit is abbreviated as *Cr.* When we record an amount in the left side of an account, we have **debited** the account; and the amount itself is called a debit. Conversely, when we record an amount in the right side of an account, we have **credited** the account; and the amount itself is called a credit. If the sum of the debits exceeds the sum of the credits in an account, the account has a **debit balance**. On the other hand, in an account with a **credit balance**, the sum of the credits exceeds the sum of the debits. Examples of debit-balance and credit-balance accounts follow:

Debit-Balance Account		Credit-Balance Account	
1,250	250	800	1,900
100			1,000
1,100			2,100

Remember: The terms *debit* and *credit* simply refer to the left side and the right side of a T-account. These terms do not mean increases or decreases. Whether a debit or a credit increases or decreases an account depends on the account involved. Illustration 2-1 summarizes the rules for how debits and credits affect the accounts. As shown in Illustration 2-1, assets normally have debit balances. Conversely, liabilities and owner's equity normally have credit balances.

ILLUSTRATION 2-1 Debits and Credits and Changes in Accounts

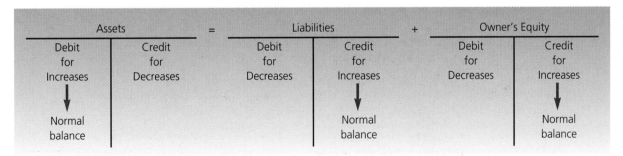

The rules in Illustration 2-1 are generally straightforward. However, experience tells us that you must initially memorize them at this point in your accounting education.

Debits, Credits, and Owner's Equity Accounts

Because some owner's equity accounts accumulate distinctly different types of changes in owner's equity, the debit and credit rules for them need further explanation. Illustration 2-1 indicates that owner's equity is increased by credits and decreased by debits. This translates into the following detailed rules for the different types of owner's equity accounts:

1. The owner's initial investment and any subsequent permanent investments increase owner's equity, and we record them as credits to Capital. We record any permanent decreases in the owner's investment as debits to Capital.
2. The owner's withdrawals of assets for personal use decrease owner's equity, and we record them as debits to Withdrawals.

3. Revenues increase net assets and owner's equity, and we record them as credits to the appropriate revenue accounts.
4. Expenses decrease net assets and owner's equity, and we record them as debits to the appropriate expense accounts.

The T-account representation in Illustration 2-2 of the elements of owner's equity summarizes which accounts are increased by debits (left side) and which accounts are increased by credits (right side). Illustration 2-3 summarizes how the various accounts are affected by debits and credits.

ILLUSTRATION 2-2 Application of Debits and Credits to Owner's Equity Accounts

Owner's Equity			
Withdrawals and Expenses		Capital and Revenues	
Debit for Increases	Credit for Decreases	Debit for Decreases	Credit for Increases
↓			↓
Normal balance			Normal balance

ILLUSTRATION 2-3 Summary of Rules of Debit and Credit

	Assets	Liabilities	Capital	Withdrawals	Revenues	Expenses
Increases	Debit	Credit	Credit	Debit	Credit	Debit
Decreases	Credit	Debit	Debit	Credit	Debit	Credit
Normal balance	Debit	Credit	Credit	Debit	Credit	Debit

Debits, Credits, and the Accounting Equation

The rules for how debits and credits affect the accounts, summarized in Illustration 2-3, are a direct result of applying the accounting equation to transaction analysis. Consider again the accounting equation and the reasoning behind the double-entry rule introduced previously. The accounting equation must hold at all times:

Assets = Liabilities + Owner's Equity

Recall that as we record each transaction, we maintain the accounting equation. If we increase assets by debits (entries to the left side of the account), then it follows that we must increase liabilities and owner's equity by credits (entries to the right side of the account) since they are on the opposite side of the equation. Similarly, if we decrease assets by credits, then we must decrease liabilities and owner's equity by debits. When we apply these rules in recording transactions and events, the result is that *the debits must equal the credits each time we process a transaction or event*. Thus, the accounting equation will always hold.

In the example of Charlotte's Car Park, when Charlotte invested $10,000 in her business, we increased the asset, cash, by $10,000. We also increased the owner's equity account, Charlotte Cruz, Capital, by $10,000. Because we

HISTORICAL PERSPECTIVES

PACIOLI—THE FATHER OF THE BALANCE SHEET

Centuries have elapsed since Fra Pacioli, an Italian Renaissance man, first outlined some of the fundamental principles of accounting. Pacioli, an Italian mathematician who is considered the "Father of the Balance Sheet," lived from about 1445 to 1520 and was a close friend of Renaissance master Leonardo da Vinci. Pacioli is best known for publishing *Summa de Arithmetica, Geometria, Proportione et Proportionalita*, which included a special supplement on double-entry record keeping for merchants. This supplement — a slender tract entitled *De Compatis et Scripturis* — proved to be the most useful and lasting part of the book since it detailed for the first time the system of accounting that had been in wide use in the commercial center of Venice for years.

What sort of man was the monk Luca Pacioli, and how did he acquire such knowledge and background about business? Pacioli was born in Borgo San Sepolcro, a small town in central Italy, and was early apprenticed to a wealthy merchant family. When he was 20, he went to Venice to tutor the sons of a rich merchant named Rompiasi. Later he studied at the great universities of his time. In the 1470s he joined the Franciscans and began to teach both mathematics and theology.

Pacioli was a skilled observer and noticed that Italian merchants kept track of their business affairs by making two entries, a debit and a credit. Each transaction was viewed separately, but the concept of "balance" was then unknown. Also, no attempt was made to find out if a business was operating profitably over a specific period such as a year. Pacioli added an important refinement by recording and classifying transactions and setting forth the necessary elements of a balance sheet.

The system described by Pacioli in his tract was not originated by him but had been employed in Venice as far back as the thirteenth century. But Pacioli was the first to bring many diverse elements together into a coordinated system, which proved to be the foundation of the modern double-entry bookkeeping system.

Source: *Journal of Accountancy* (May 1987), pp. 195–197. Reprinted with permission from the *Journal of Accountancy*, copyright © 1987 by American Institute of Certified Public Accountants, Inc.

increase assets by debits and we increase owner's equity by credits, we record this transaction in the accounts by debiting Cash for $10,000 and crediting Charlotte Cruz, Capital for $10,000. We maintained the equality of debits and credits in recording this transaction.

LO 3
Apply the rules of debit and credit to business transactions.

ANALYZING TRANSACTIONS USING THE RULES OF DEBIT AND CREDIT

Earlier you saw how we use the financial accounting process to track events and transactions by recording their effects on the business's financial position. Analyzing and recording effects of transactions is an essential part of the process by which financial statements are derived. Recording the effects of transactions requires us to analyze each transaction. First, we decide which accounts the transaction affects. Then, we decide by what amounts. Finally, we record these effects in the accounts by applying the rules of debit and credit.

Recording Transactions in T-Accounts

We continue the example of Charlotte's Car Park to illustrate analyzing and recording transactions. We record the transactions in T-accounts, and the entries to the accounts are numbered parenthetically with the same number as the related transaction. Illustration 2-4 shows the beginning balances for February 19X1, recorded in the accounts. The beginning balances are from the financial statements presented in Chapter 1.

ILLUSTRATION 2-4 T-Accounts at the Beginning of February

Cash			Accounts Payable			Charlotte Cruz, Capital	
Jan. 31	900			Jan. 31	200		Jan. 31 10,000

Accounts Receivable						Charlotte Cruz, Withdrawals	
Jan. 31	400					Jan. 31	500

Land						Parking Revenue	
Jan. 31	9,000						Jan. 31 1,600

						Advertising Expense	
						Jan. 31	200

						Wages and Salaries Expense	
						Jan. 31	800

Assets	=	Liabilities	+	Owner's Equity
$10,300		$200		$10,100

Transaction 1—Bank Loan.   Charlotte Cruz received an estimate of $3,000 from Cardinal Construction Co. for adding security lights to her parking lot. Based on the January financial statements that Charlotte presented, North National Bank agreed to lend her $3,000 for the improvements. The interest rate on the loan is 12% per year and is payable on the first of each month beginning March 1, 19X1. The borrowing transaction increased cash and increased the liability, notes payable, $3,000 each. We increase assets by debits, and we increase liabilities by credits. We record the transaction as a debit to Cash for $3,000 and a credit to Notes Payable for $3,000.

Asset   *Liability*

Cash			Notes Payable	
Jan. 31	900		(1)	3,000
(1)	3,000			

Transaction 2—Purchase of Assets.   On February 3, Cardinal Construction Company completed the lights for the parking lot; and Charlotte paid the bill in the amount of $3,000. Charlotte classifies the lights as a land improvement. We record the transaction by debiting Land Improvements for $3,000 and crediting Cash for $3,000.

Asset   *Asset*

Cash				Land Improvements	
Jan. 31	900	(2)	3,000	(2)	3,000
(1)	3,000				

Transaction 3—Prepaid Expense.   Charlotte decided that with the addition of the lights to the parking lot she should acquire some insurance. On February 3, she paid $480 for a 12-month policy. This transaction creates an asset called prepaid insurance. The prepaid insurance will become an expense as the period of time covered by the policy expires. We record the transaction as a debit to Prepaid Insurance and as a credit to Cash for $480 each.

Cash				Prepaid Insurance	
Jan. 31	900	(2)	3,000	(3)	480
(1)	3,000	(3)	480		

(handwritten annotations: "Asset" above Cash area; "Asset" and "OE - Expenses" above Prepaid Insurance)

Transaction 4—Account Receivable Collection.   On February 4, Charlotte collects the $400 account receivable from Campus Bookstore. The account receivable was shown as an asset on the January 31, 19X1, balance sheet. The collection increases cash and decreases accounts receivable. Assets are increased by debits and decreased by credits. We record the transaction as a debit to Cash for $400 and as a credit to Accounts Receivable for $400.

Cash				Accounts Receivable			
Jan. 31	900	(2)	3,000	Jan. 31	400	(4)	400
(1)	3,000	(3)	480				
(4)	400						

(handwritten annotations: "Asset" above Cash; "Asset" above Accounts Receivable)

Transaction 5—Payment of Account Payable.   On February 8, Charlotte pays the campus newspaper for the amount owed for advertising in January. The payment decreases cash and decreases the liability, accounts payable. Liabilities are decreased by debits, and assets are decreased by credits. We record the transaction by debiting Accounts Payable and crediting Cash for $200 each.

Cash				Accounts Payable			
Jan. 31	900	(2)	3,000	(5)	200	Jan. 31	200
(1)	3,000	(3)	480				
(4)	400	(5)	200				

(handwritten annotations: "Asset" above Cash; "Liability" above Accounts Payable)

Transaction 6—Unearned Revenue.   Two of Charlotte's classmates asked if they could reserve spaces on Mondays, Wednesdays, and Fridays to attend their classes. Charlotte agreed to reserve the spaces if the students paid a total of $200 in advance for each month. On February 8, Charlotte received the $200 advance payment from the students for the month of February. The amount received, however, is not revenue to be recognized at the time it is received because it has not been earned. Rather, the amount received creates a liability called unearned revenue. The liability will be satisfied, and revenue will be earned, when the agreed to parking is provided during February. We record the transaction by debiting Cash and crediting Unearned Revenue for $200 each.

Cash				Unearned Revenue	
Jan. 31	900	(2)	3,000	(6)	200
(1)	3,000	(3)	480		
(4)	400	(5)	200		
(6)	200				

(handwritten annotations: "Asset" above Cash; "Liability" above Unearned Revenue)

Transaction 7—Revenues Received in Cash.   During February, Charlotte's Car Park earned $1,800 in cash revenues from parking customers. There transactions increased cash and increased revenues. We increase revenues by credits. We record these transactions by debiting Cash and crediting Parking Revenue by $1,800 each.

Asset   OE : Revenue

Cash			
Jan. 31	900	(2)	3,000
(1)	3,000	(3)	480
(4)	400	(5)	200
(6)	200		
(7)	1,800		

Parking Revenue	
Jan. 31	1,600
(7)	1,800

Transaction 8—Wages Expense. During February, Charlotte had to hire even more help than in January to attend the parking lot. On February 28, she paid attendants a total of $1,200 for their services through February 21. This transaction decreases the asset cash and increases wages and salaries expense. We record the transaction as a credit to Cash and as a debit to Wages and Salaries Expense for $1,200 each.

Asset   OE : Expenses

Cash			
Jan. 31	900	(2)	3,000
(1)	3,000	(3)	480
(4)	400	(5)	200
(6)	200	(8)	1,200
(7)	1,800		

Wages and Salaries Expense			
Jan. 31	800		
(8)	1,200		

Transaction 9—Maintenance Expense. On February 28, Charlotte paid Ed's Lawn Service $60 for mowing the grass around the edge of the parking lot during February. This transaction decreased cash and increased maintenance expense. We record the transaction by crediting Cash for $60 and debiting Maintenance Expense for $60.

Asset   OE : Expenses

Cash			
Jan. 31	900	(2)	3,000
(1)	3,000	(3)	480
(4)	400	(5)	200
(6)	200	(8)	1,200
(7)	1,800	(9)	60

Maintenance Expense			
(9)	60		

Transaction 10—Owner's Withdrawal. Charlotte Cruz withdrew $500 from her business on February 28. The withdrawal decreases cash and decreases owner's equity through the owner's withdrawals account. We record the transaction as a credit to Cash for $500 and as a debit to Charlotte Cruz, Withdrawals for $500.

Asset   OE : Withdrawals

Cash			
Jan. 31	900	(2)	3,000
(1)	3,000	(3)	480
(4)	400	(5)	200
(6)	200	(8)	1,200
(7)	1,800	(9)	60
		(10)	500

Charlotte Cruz, Withdrawals			
Jan. 31	500		
(10)	500		

February Account Balances

At the end of February, Charlotte determined the account balances. Illustration 2-5 shows the balances in the accounts at the end of February. Notice that we have maintained the equality of the accounting equation during the process of recording the transactions for February. Assets of $13,340 equal the sum of liabilities and owner's equity of $13,340 ($3,200 + $10,140).

ILLUSTRATION 2-5 Account Balances at End of February

Cash			
Jan. 31	900	(2)	3,000
(1)	3,000	(3)	480
(4)	400	(5)	200
(6)	200	(8)	1,200
(7)	1,800	(9)	60
		(10)	500
Bal.	860		

Accounts Receivable			
Jan. 31	400	(4)	400
Bal.	0		

Prepaid Insurance	
(3)	480
Bal.	480

Land	
Jan. 31	9,000

Land Improvements	
(2)	3,000
Bal.	3,000

Accounts Payable			
(5)	200	Jan. 31	200
		Bal.	0

Unearned Revenue		
	(6)	200
	Bal.	200

Notes Payable		
	(1)	3,000
	Bal.	3,000

Charlotte Cruz, Capital		
	Jan. 31	10,000

Charlotte Cruz, Withdrawals	
Jan. 31	500
(10)	500
Bal.	1,000

Parking Revenue		
	Jan. 31	1,600
	(7)	1,800
	Bal.	3,400

Advertising Expense	
Jan. 31	200

Wages and Salaries Expense	
Jan. 31	800
(8)	1,200
Bal.	2,000

Maintenance Expense	
(9)	60
Bal.	60

Assets	=	Liabilities	+	Owner's Equity
$13,340		$3,200		$10,140

LO 4

Identify the procedures in the accounting cycle.

THE ACCOUNTING CYCLE

The **accounting cycle** is the sequence of procedures accountants follow to complete the financial accounting process. Illustration 2-6 presents the accounting cycle as a loop, or a continuous process. When one accounting cycle ends —preparing the annual financial statements and closing appropriate accounts— another accounting cycle begins anew with analyzing and recording transactions.

The following procedures are represented in Illustration 2-6.

1. Analyze the transactions.
2. Record the transactions in the general journal.
3. Post the general journal entries to the general ledger accounts.
4. Adjust the general ledger accounts.
5. Prepare the financial statements.
6. Close the revenue, expense, and owner's withdrawals ledger accounts.

ILLUSTRATION 2-6 The Accounting Cycle

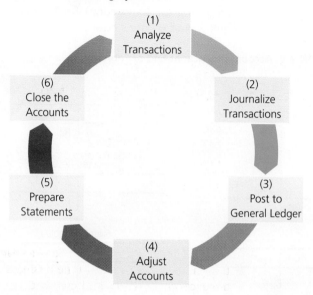

So far in this chapter, we analyzed the transactions for Charlotte's Car Park. Next, we prepare general journal entries for those transactions. The posting of general journal entries to the general ledger accounts is also illustrated in this chapter. Then, in a subsequent chapter, we present the procedures for adjusting the accounts and preparing financial statements. Adjusting accounts is necessary. It brings them into conformity with GAAP so that we may prepare appropriate financial statements. In a following chapter, we examine further the preparation of financial statements and illustrate the final procedure in the accounting cycle—closing the revenue, expense, and owner's withdrawal accounts.

LO 5

Apply the procedures to record in the accounting records the effects of business transactions.

RECORDING TRANSACTIONS

The first step in recording transactions is preparing general journal entries. We then post those entries to the general ledger.

The General Journal

A **general journal** is a chronological listing of transactions. We describe each transaction that affects the business's financial position in an *entry* in the general journal. The entry for Transaction 1 of February for Charlotte's Car Park is shown in Illustration 2-7.

Each general journal entry provides the following information about the transaction or event:

1. The date of the transaction or event.
2. The names of the accounts debited and credited.
3. The amounts debited and credited to each account.
4. An explanation of the transaction.
5. A reference to the posting of the transaction (to be explained later).

ILLUSTRATION 2-7 General Journal Entry

The general journal provides a place to record information about transactions and events that affect the business. As we illustrated earlier, we can record transactions as debits and credits directly in the T-accounts. When we use this method, however, it is difficult to observe all the effects of a transaction. Since each transaction affects at least two accounts (by the double-entry rule), at most, we record only half of the information about a transaction in any one account.

As transactions take place, we first record them in the general journal. Therefore, it is sometimes called the *book of original entry.* We record each transaction as a separate **journal entry** in the general journal, and the process of recording a transaction is **journalizing**.

Illustration 2-8 shows the general journal entries for the February transactions of Charlotte's Car Park. The numbers in parentheses correspond to the transaction numbers listed on pages 52–54.

We can summarize the procedures for recording transactions in the general journal as follows:

1. Record the year at the top of the Date column; record the month in the first column and the day in the second column. You do not need to repeat the year and month for subsequent entries, unless a new year or new month begins or when you begin a new page in the general journal.
2. In the Description column, record the names of all accounts debited and credited and a brief description of the transaction. Record the names of the accounts debited first, aligned with the left margin, followed by the names of the accounts credited, indented about one-half inch. For some transactions, more than one account will be debited and/or more than one account credited. In this case, record first the names of all accounts debited, followed by the names of all accounts credited.
3. In the Debit column, record the amount debited on the same line as the related account name; and in the Credit column, record the amount credited on the same line as the related account name. Do not use dollar signs in the general journal.
4. After each entry, it is common practice to provide a brief explanation and then to skip a line. The explanation reflects the analysis of the transaction or other event.

ILLUSTRATION 2-8 General Journal

GENERAL JOURNAL				PAGE 1	
DATE		DESCRIPTION	POST. REF.	DEBIT	CREDIT
19X1 Feb.	1	Cash		3,000	
		Notes Payable			3,000
		Cash receipts from proceeds of bank loan. (1)			
	3	Land Improvements		3,000	
		Cash			3,000
		Purchase of lights for parking lot. (2)			
	3	Prepaid Insurance		480	
		Cash			480
		Purchase of one-year insurance policy. (3)			
	4	Cash		400	
		Accounts Receivable			400
		Collection of account receivable. (4)			
	8	Accounts Payable		200	
		Cash			200
		Payment of amount owed for ad in campus newspaper. (5)			
	8	Cash		200	
		Unearned Revenue			200
		Receipt of advance payment for reserved parking. (6)			
	28	Cash		1,800	
		Parking Revenue			1,800
		Cash receipts for parking during February. (7)			
	28	Wages and Salaries Expense		1,200	
		Cash			1,200
		Payment of wages for parking lot attendants. (8)			
	28	Maintenance Expense		60	
		Cash			60
		Payment for mowing for February. (9)			
	28	Charlotte Cruz, Withdrawals		500	
		Cash			500
		Withdrawal of cash by owner. (10)			

The General Ledger

Regardless of the number of accounts, they are organized in a **general ledger**, which is the collection of all a business's accounts. For some businesses, the general ledger is a large book with a separate page for each account. However, many businesses maintain their general ledgers in a data storage medium such as a computer disk or tape. We recorded the previous examples of transactions in this chapter in T-accounts. While T-accounts are useful for textbook and classroom presentations, they are not used in practice. Rather, accountants use a ledger account form similar to the one presented in Illustration 2-9.

ILLUSTRATION 2-9 Ledger Account

GENERAL LEDGER ACCOUNT

NAME:				ACCOUNT NO.:	
DATE	DESCRIPTION	POST. REF.	DEBIT	CREDIT	BALANCE

The general ledger account presents the account name, account number, date of the transaction, amount debited or credited, and the account balance. The Post. Ref. column provides a reference to the source of entry in the ledger account. The process of recording transactions in the general ledger accounts is **posting**.

Account Numbers

To locate accounts quickly within the general ledger, businesses have systems of numbering accounts. A three-digit numbering system numbers the accounts as follows:

Asset accounts, 100-299
Liability accounts, 300-499
Owner's equity accounts, 500-599
Revenue accounts, 600-699
Expense accounts, 700-799

In the three-digit numbering system, all asset account numbers begin with the digit 1; all liability account numbers, with the digit 3; and so forth. The second and third digits are used to identify the account further. In the general ledger, accounts are kept in numerical order. Organizing the accounts numerically is more efficient than ordering them alphabetically by account title. Also, using numbers to identify accounts increases the efficiency of data entry for those businesses that use computerized accounting systems. Only the numbers need be used to identify the accounts; the computer keeps a master list with the corresponding account titles in storage.

The numbering system illustrated above is common for a service business. Larger and more complex businesses need an expanded numbering system.

A business maintains a list of account names and their corresponding account numbers with a **chart of accounts**. A chart of accounts for Charlotte's Car Park is shown in Illustration 2-10. When you analyze transactions and work with the accounting records, a chart of accounts is useful for determining the accounts affected. For example, consider Transaction 3 of Charlotte's Car Park. The purchase of an insurance policy for cash indicates that the asset account, Prepaid Insurance, should be debited and the asset account, Cash, should be credited. The chart of accounts shows that Prepaid Insurance can be found in the general ledger as account number 150; Cash, as account number 100. The chart of accounts is usually accompanied by a description of the types of transactions that are recorded in each account. For recording unusual transactions and new employees' reference, this description is particularly useful and significantly improves the efficiency of posting to the general ledger.

Review the chart of accounts shown in Illustration 2-10. In subsequent chapters, you will learn more about these accounts. You do not need to be concerned about them at this point.

ILLUSTRATION 2-10 Chart of Accounts

Charlotte's Car Park Chart of Accounts			
Assets		*Owner's Equity*	
Cash	100	Charlotte Cruz, Capital	500
Accounts Receivable	110	Charlotte Cruz, Withdrawals	502
Prepaid Insurance	150	Income Summary	599
Land	200	*Revenues*	
Land Improvements	210		
Accumulated Depreciation – Land		Parking Revenue	606
Improvements	211	*Expenses*	
Liabilities		Advertising Expense	700
Accounts Payable	302	Depreciation Expense	
Notes Payable	326	–Land Improvements	714
Unearned Revenue	342	Insurance Expense	728
Wages and Salaries Payable	346	Maintenance Expense	734
		Utilities Expense	780
		Wages and Salaries Expense	784

LO 6

Explain the relationship between the general journal and the general ledger.

Relationship Between the General Journal and General Ledger

Both the general journal and the general ledger are important components of the accounting records, and we record the effects of transactions in both of them. Listing transactions chronologically, we record all debit and credit effects of each transaction in the general journal. Then, we post the information about the effects of the entry on individual accounts to the appropriate general ledger accounts.

Illustration 2-11 demonstrates the journalizing *and posting* of Transaction 1 from the set of transactions analyzed earlier in the chapter. The procedures for journalizing and posting transactions can be summarized as follows:

1. Record transactions in the general journal as described on pages 56-58.
2. Periodically, such as at the end of a day or the end of a week, post the journal entries to the ledger accounts. In the ledger, locate the account to be debited. In the Date column, enter the date of the transaction. Next, enter the amount of the debit in the Debit column and adjust the balance to reflect the debit. In the Post. Ref. column, enter the page in the general journal on which the journal entry is located. The page number is preceded by the letters *GJ* to indicate that the source of the posting is the *General Journal.* Do not use dollar signs in either the journal or the ledger. The last step in posting is to record in the general journal's Post. Ref. column the number of the account to which you posted the debit entry. This last step provides a cross-reference between the journal and the ledger. Should your posting process be interrupted, you can then determine which journal entries you have already posted.
3. For the credits, repeat the procedures you followed for the debits.

LO 7

Prepare a trial balance.

THE TRIAL BALANCE

The double-entry requirement of equal debits and credits provides a useful means for finding errors. If the total amounts of those accounts with debit bal-

ILLUSTRATION 2-11 Posting the General Ledger

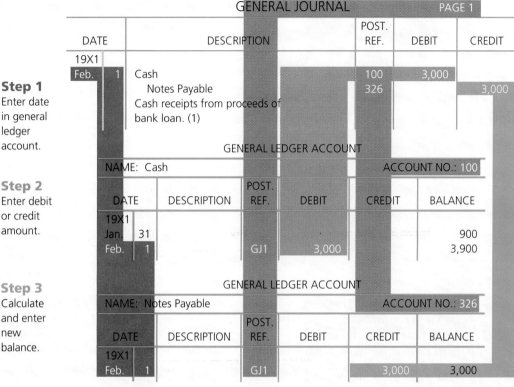

Step 1
Enter date in general ledger account.

Step 2
Enter debit or credit amount.

Step 3
Calculate and enter new balance.

Step 4
Record general journal page number in Post. Ref. column of general ledger. Record account number in Post. Ref. column of general journal.

ances and the total amount of those accounts with credit balances do not equal, then we have made a recording error.

We test the equality of debits and credits periodically by preparing a trial balance such as the one shown in Illustration 2-12. A **trial balance** lists in columns and then totals all the debit balances and all the credit balances in the general ledger accounts. In preparing a trial balance, use the following four procedures:

1. Determine the balance of each account in the ledger.
2. List the ledger account titles in the column at the left side of the trial balance. For debit-balance accounts, enter the balances in the Debits column on the same line as the related account titles. For credit-balance accounts, enter the balances in the Credits column on the same line as the related account titles.
3. Sum the Debits column and the Credits column.
4. Compare the sums of the two columns.

Illustration 2-12 shows a trial balance for Charlotte's Car Park. You can trace each balance back to one of the T-accounts in Illustration 2-5. For example, the balance of Prepaid Insurance in the trial balance is $480 debit, which is the same balance as for the Prepaid Insurance T-account in Illustration 2-5.

LO 8
Analyze the various types of errors a trial balance identifies and apply procedures to correct the errors.

ERROR ANALYZING

In the trial balance in Illustration 2-12, the debits of $16,600 equal the credits of $16,600. The equality provides a check that the debits equal the credits in the

ILLUSTRATION 2-12 Trial Balance

Charlotte's Car Park Trial Balance February 28, 19X1		
	Debits	Credits
Cash	$ 860	
Prepaid Insurance	480	
Land	9,000	
Land Improvements	3,000	
Unearned Revenue		$ 200
Notes Payable		3,000
Charlotte Cruz, Capital		10,000
Charlotte Cruz, Withdrawals	1,000	
Parking Revenue		3,400
Wages and Salaries Expense	2,000	
Maintenance Expense	60	
Advertising Expense	200	
Totals	$16,600	$16,600

general ledger. However, you must take care in interpreting the trial balance. The fact that debits equal credits does *not* ensure that all transactions are recorded, that the analysis of transactions is correct, or that the transactions are recorded in the correct accounts. *If the total debits do not equal total credits, however, we know that one or more of the following errors may have occurred:*

1. Debits and credits of unequal amounts were journalized and/or posted for a transaction.
2. A debit was recorded in an account as a credit, or vice versa.
3. An account balance was determined incorrectly.
4. An error occurred in recording account balances in the trial balance.
5. The Debits and/or Credits columns of the trial balance were summed incorrectly.

You may discover the source of the error by checking the correctness of journalizing, posting, and trial balance preparation procedures. You will find it more efficient to check those procedures in the reverse order that you originally performed them.

A common error is recording a debit-balance amount as a credit in the trial balance, or vice versa. If this type of error occurs, the amount by which the trial balance is "out of balance" is divisible by 2. A second common error is a transposition error. A **transposition error** occurs when two digits are reversed during the process of recording the number. For example, the debit amount of $1,319 is recorded in the trial balance as a debit of $1,391. If you make a transposition error, the amount by which the trial balance is out of balance is evenly divisible by 9. In our example, ($1,391 − $1,319) = $72 ÷ 9 = $8. A third common error is a slide. A **slide** is an error that results from adding or dropping one or more zeros from a number. For example, recording $100 as $1,000 or recording $8,000 as $800. For a slide, the differences between the correct number and the incorrect number is evenly divisible by 9: ($1,000 − $100 = $900 ÷ 9 = $100); or ($8,000 − $800 = $7,200 ÷ 9 = $800).

Correcting Entries

When we discover an error, we must correct it. We do not correct errors in the general journal or general ledger by simply erasing the error because such action may raise questions concerning the integrity of the recording process. The procedures for correcting errors in the general journal and general ledger depend on the nature of the error and at what point in the recording and posting process the error occurs.

Two types of errors may occur in the general journal and general ledger:

1. We recorded an incorrect amount in the general journal, and/or we posted an incorrect amount to a general ledger account.
2. We recorded a transaction as a debit or credit to an incorrect account in the general journal, and/or we posted the transaction to the incorrect account in the general ledger.

To correct the first type of error, the appropriate procedure is to draw a line through the incorrect amount, and then to enter the correct amount directly above the incorrect amount. For the second type of error, you must make a correcting journal entry. For example, assume an enterprise collects an account receivable and makes the following journal entry:

Feb. 12	Cash	75	
	Repairs Revenue		75
	To record the collection of an account receivable.		

The journal entry obviously is in error because the collection of an account receivable requires a credit to Accounts Receivable. If we do not correct the error, both Accounts Receivable and Repairs Revenue will be overstated by $75. The correcting general journal entry for the error is:

Feb. 19	Repairs Revenue	75	
	Accounts Receivable		75
	To correct an error of Feb.12 in which the collection of an account receivable was erroneously recorded as Repairs Revenue.		

Posting the correcting journal entry in the general ledger reduces both Repairs Revenue and Accounts Receivable to their correct balances. The full explanation in the correcting entry provides a complete record of what occurred for anyone who questions the journal entry.

SUMMARY

Describe accounts and recognize commonly used accounts. Businesses store and summarize information about the effects of transactions in accounts. They use separate accounts for each category of assets, liabilities, and owner's equity that are relevant for management purposes or for analysis by outside users of the financial statements.

Explain the rules of debit and credit and how they relate to the accounting equation. The rules of debit and credit dictate how we increase and decrease accounts for the effects of transactions and other events that affect the business's financial position. We increase asset accounts with debits, and we decrease them with credits. We increase liability and owner's equity accounts with credits, and we decrease them with debits. Observing the rule that debits must always equal credits as we record transactions in the business's accounts is equivalent to preserving the accounting equation.

Apply the rules of debit and credit to business transactions.   Recording the effects of transactions requires us to analyze each transaction. First, we decide which accounts are affected. Then, we decide by what dollar amounts. Finally, we record these effects in the accounts, applying the rules of debit and credit.

Identify the procedures in the accounting cycle.   Analyzing, journalizing, and posting transactions and events constitute three of the six stages in the accounting cycle — the process that maintains the accounting records according to GAAP and leads to periodic preparation of financial statements. Later, you are introduced to the next two procedures in the accounting cycle. To prepare financial statements that conform to GAAP, it is necessary to make adjustments to certain accounts at the end of an accounting period. These adjustments are explained, and the preparation of financial statements from the adjusted accounts is illustrated in a subsequent chapter. In another chapter, the last phase of the process, closing temporary accounts, is described, along with a very valuable tool for preparing financial statements, the accountants' worksheet.

Apply the procedures to record in the accounting records the effects of business transactions.   These procedures consist of (1) analyzing the transactions, (2) journalizing an entry in the general journal, and (3) posting the entries in the general journal to the general ledger.

Explain the relationship between the general journal and the general ledger. Businesses store their accounts in General Ledgers. As transactions and events that affect financial position occur, businesses analyze them and record their effects by entries in the general journal. The information in general journal entries consists of the date, accounts affected by the event or transaction, the amounts to be debited and credited to the accounts, and a brief description. The debit and credit amounts are then posted to the individual accounts in the general ledger.

Prepare a trial balance.   The accuracy of the journalizing and posting process can be periodically checked by preparing a trial balance. The trial balance is a listing of all general ledger accounts, with debit balances in one column and credit balances in another. If the sums of the two columns are equal, the double-entry rule has been applied accurately. Otherwise, the accountant is alerted that there has been a recording or posting error.

Analyze the various types of errors a trial balance identifies and apply procedures to correct the errors.   Errors may occur in the process of journalizing and posting transactions, in determining account balances, or in the preparation of the trial balance. When we discover an error, we should correct it, which often involves making a correcting entry.

REVIEW PROBLEM

Eddie's VCR Repair Service began business on January 2, 19X6, and Eddie DeVine has asked you to prepare all the necessary accounting records.

The company uses the following chart of accounts:

ASSETS
100 Cash
110 Accounts Receivable
139 Repair Parts
158 Utility Deposits

LIABILITIES
302 Accounts Payable

OWNER'S EQUITY
500 Eddie DeVine, Capital
502 Eddie DeVine, Withdrawals

REVENUES
608 Repairs Revenue

EXPENSES
728 Insurance Expense
762 Rent Expense
780 Utilities Expense

The following information is available for the month of January:

Jan.   2 Eddie begins business by depositing $2,500 in a new business checking account.
       3 Eddie pays Wimson Insurance Co. a $50 premium for liability insurance for the month.
       3 Eddie pays $250 to Ramon Smith for one month's rent on a small downtown shop.
       3 Eddie makes a $150 deposit with the City Power and Water Company. This utility deposit is refundable.
       3 Electronic repair parts for VCRs are purchased from Smith Co. on credit for $1,000.
       6 Ten VCRs are serviced on credit for the Video Rental Company. Eddie sends Video Rental Company a bill of $600 for the repairs.
       8 Eddie withdraws $225 for personal use.
      11 Eddie cleans and adjusts VCR heads for Marti Gregg and collects a $24 service fee in cash.
      18 Keboe Inc. brought in 7 VCRs for service. It required 6 hours labor to repair the units at $50 per hour. A bill was sent with the units to Keboe Inc.
      21 Eddie receives a $400 check from Video Rental Company for partial payment of the services performed on January 6.
      23 Eddie pays Smith Co. $500 as a partial payment for repair parts purchased on January 3.
      30 Eddie pays $112 to the City Power and Water Company for January utilities.

REQUIRED:

a. Prepare a general journal entry for each transaction as appropriate.
b. Open a general ledger account for each account shown in the chart of accounts.
c. Post each transaction to the proper accounts in the general ledger.
d. Prepare a trial balance for January 31, 19X6.
e. Calculate the totals for the trial balance which would have occurred if the balance of Accounts Payable was incorrectly copied to the trial balance as $50.
f. Calculate the difference between the trial balance totals in *e* above.
g. Explain how the difference determined in *f* indicates a slide error.

SOLUTION:

Planning and Organizing Your Work

1. Analyze each transaction to determine which accounts are increased or decreased and by what amount.
2. Determine whether the effect would be a debit or credit to each of the accounts involved.
3. Prepare general journal entries based on the analysis in 1 and 2.
4. Open a general ledger account for each account in the chart of accounts.
5. Post each transaction in the general journal to the appropriate general ledger accounts.

6. Prepare a trial balance.
7. Analyze the effect of errors in the trial balance.

The first transaction, January 2, would be analyzed as follows:

Eddie's investment in the business increases the asset account, Cash, and the owner's equity account, Eddie DeVine, Capital. Increases in assets are recorded with debits. Increases in owner's equity are recorded with credits.

(a) *Prepare general journal entries.*

		GENERAL JOURNAL		PAGE 1	
DATE		DESCRIPTION	POST. REF.	DEBIT	CREDIT
19X6 Jan.	2	Cash	100	2,500	
		Eddie DeVine, Capital	500		2,500
		Investment by owner.			
	3	Insurance Expense	728	50	
		Cash	100		50
		Payment of liability insurance.			
	3	Rent Expense	762	250	
		Cash	100		250
		Payment of January rent.			
	3	Utilities Deposits	158	150	
		Cash	100		150
		Deposit with utility company.			
	3	Repair Parts	139	1,000	
		Accounts Payable	302		1,000
		Purchased repair parts on credit.			
	6	Accounts Receivable	110	600	
		Repairs Revenue	608		600
		Services performed on credit.			
	8	Eddie DeVine, Withdrawals	502	225	
		Cash	100		225
		Withdrawal for personal use.			
	11	Cash	100	24	
		Repairs Revenue	608		24
		Services performed for cash.			
	18	Accounts Receivable	110	300	
		Repairs Revenue	608		300
		Services performed on credit.			
	21	Cash	100	400	
		Accounts Receivable	110		400
		Collection of account receivable.			
	23	Accounts Payable	302	500	
		Cash	100		500
		Payment of account payable.			
	30	Utilities Expense	780	112	
		Cash	100		112
		Payment of utilities.			

(b), (c) *Open and post general ledger accounts.*

GENERAL LEDGER

NAME: Cash   ACCOUNT NO.: 100

DATE		DESCRIPTION	POST. REF.	DEBIT	CREDIT	BALANCE
19X6						
Jan.	2		GJ1	2,500		2,500
	3		GJ1		50	2,450
	3		GJ1		250	2,200
	3		GJ1		150	2,050
	8		GJ1		225	1,825
	11		GJ1	24		1,849
	21		GJ1	400		2,249
	23		GJ1		500	1,749
	30		GJ1		112	1,637

NAME: Accounts Receivable   ACCOUNT NO.: 110

DATE		DESCRIPTION	POST. REF.	DEBIT	CREDIT	BALANCE
19X6						
Jan.	6		GJ1	600		600
	18		GJ1	300		900
	21		GJ1		400	500

NAME: Repair Parts   ACCOUNT NO.: 139

DATE		DESCRIPTION	POST. REF.	DEBIT	CREDIT	BALANCE
19X6						
Jan.	3		GJ1	1,000		1,000

NAME: Utilities Deposits   ACCOUNT NO.: 158

DATE		DESCRIPTION	POST. REF.	DEBIT	CREDIT	BALANCE
19X6						
Jan.	3		GJ1	150		150

NAME: Accounts Payable   ACCOUNT NO.: 302

DATE		DESCRIPTION	POST. REF.	DEBIT	CREDIT	BALANCE
19X6						
Jan.	3		GJ1		1,000	1,000
	23		GJ1	500		500

NAME: Eddie DeVine, Capital   ACCOUNT NO.: 500

DATE		DESCRIPTION	POST. REF.	DEBIT	CREDIT	BALANCE
19X6						
Jan.	2		GJ1		2,500	2,500

NAME: Eddie DeVine, Withdrawals   ACCOUNT NO.: 502

DATE		DESCRIPTION	POST. REF.	DEBIT	CREDIT	BALANCE
19X6 Jan.	2		GJ1	225		225

NAME: Repairs Revenue   ACCOUNT NO.: 608

DATE		DESCRIPTION	POST. REF.	DEBIT	CREDIT	BALANCE
19X6 Jan.	6		GJ1		600	600
	11		GJ1		24	624
	18		GJ1		300	924

NAME: Insurance Expense   ACCOUNT NO.: 728

DATE		DESCRIPTION	POST. REF.	DEBIT	CREDIT	BALANCE
19X6 Jan.	3		GJ1	50		50

NAME: Rent Expense   ACCOUNT NO.: 762

DATE		DESCRIPTION	POST. REF.	DEBIT	CREDIT	BALANCE
19X6 Jan.	3		GJ1	250		250

NAME: Utilities Expense   ACCOUNT NO.: 780

DATE		DESCRIPTION	POST. REF.	DEBIT	CREDIT	BALANCE
19X6 Jan.	30		GJ1	112		112

(d) *Prepare a trial balance.*

Eddie's VCR Repair Service
Trial Balance
January 31, 19X6

		Debits	Credits
100	Cash	$1,637	
110	Accounts Receivable	500	
139	Repair Parts	1,000	
158	Utilities Deposits	150	
302	Accounts Payable		$ 500
500	Eddie DeVine, Capital		2,500
502	Eddie DeVine, Withdrawal	225	
608	Repairs Revenue		924
728	Insurance Expense	50	
762	Rent Expense	250	
780	Utilities Expense	112	
		$3,924	$3,924

(e) *Explain the effect of errors on trial balances.*

The debit total would remain unaffected at $3,924.
The credit total would be $450 less, or $3,474.

(f) *Calculate the difference in trial balance totals.*

$$
\begin{array}{r}
\$\ 3{,}924 \\
-\ 3{,}474 \\
\hline
\$\quad 450
\end{array}
$$

(g) *Explain how the difference indicates a slide error.*

If the difference in *f* is evenly divisible by 9, a slide or a transposition error has probably occurred (450 ÷ 9 = $50). The actual error was recording a $500 amount as $50. This involves sliding the 5 from the hundreds column to the tens column and would, therefore, be a slide error.

KEY TERMS

account, *44*	**debited,** *49*	**realization principle,** *48*
account balance, *45*	**debit balance,** *49*	**recognize,** *48*
accounting cycle, *55*	**general journal,** *56*	**slide,** *62*
chart of accounts, *59*	**general ledger,** *58*	**T-account,** *44*
credit, *48*	**journal entry,** *57*	**transposition error,** *62*
credited, *49*	**journalizing,** *57*	**trial balance,** *61*
credit balance, *49*	**matching principle,** *48*	
debit, *48*	**posting,** *59*	

SELF QUIZ

LO 1,2   1. Indicate which of the following statements about accounts are true (*T*) and which are false (*F*).
   a. Accounts are used to summarize accounting information.
   b. Accounts are always increased by debits.
   c. Accounts are used to store accounting information.
   d. All accounts appear in the balance sheet.

LO 1   2. Indicate whether the following accounts belong in a balance sheet (*B*) or in an income statement (*I*).
   a. Cash
   b. Utilities Expense
   c. Notes Payable
   d. Land
   e. Interest Revenue
   f. Utilities Deposits

LO 1,2   3. Indicate the normal balances for the following types of accounts. Use *Dr.* for debit or *Cr.* for credit.

   a. Assets
   b. Liabilities
   c. Owner's Equity
   d. Revenues
   e. Expenses

LO 1,2   4. Identify each of the following accounts as to whether it is an asset (*A*), liability (*L*), or owner's equity (*OE*):
   a. Accounts Receivable
   b. Buildings
   c. Wages and Salaries Expense
   d. Prepaid Insurance
   e. Mortgage Payable
   f. Unearned Revenue

LO 1,2   5. Indicate whether each of the following accounts would normally have a debit balance (*Dr.*) or a credit balance (*Cr.*).
   a. Cash
   b. Notes Payable
   c. Fee Revenue
   d. Advertising Expense
   e. I. M. Dove, Capital
   f. I. M. Dove, Withdrawals

LO 2 6. Complete the following statement: Debits will increase _____ accounts, decrease _____ accounts, and decrease _____ accounts.

LO 2 7. Complete the following statement: Credits will increase _____ accounts, increase _____ accounts, and decrease _____ accounts.

LO 2,3 8. A correct statement of the accounting equation would be
a. Assets – Liabilities = Owner's Equity
b. Owner's Equity + Assets = Liabilities
c. Assets = Liabilities + Owner's Equity
d. Both a and c are correct.

LO 2,3,6 9. Match the following accounting terms with the definitions shown below.
a. Account
b. General journal
c. General ledger
d. Credit
e. Debit balance
f. Journalizing
(1) Amount by which the total debits in an account exceed the total credits in that same account
(2) Book of original entry that provides a complete description of a business transaction in one place
(3) Right side of an account
(4) Process of recording business transactions
(5) Collection of all accounts of a business
(6) Subclassification of the accounting equation that is used for storing and summarizing transaction data

LO 3 10. An example of a transaction that increases one asset, decreases another asset, and has no effect on the liabilities or owner's equity is
a. Purchase of equipment on credit
b. Payment of an account payable
c. Recording of revenue
d. Contribution of cash by the owner
e. Purchase of supplies for cash

LO 3 11. An example of a transaction that increases an asset, increases a liability, and has no effect on owner's equity is
a. Purchase of equipment on credit
b. Payment of an account payable
c. Recording of revenue
d. Contribution of cash by the owner
e. Purchase of supplies for cash

LO 3 12. An example of a transaction that decreases an asset, decreases a liability, and has no effect on owner's equity is

a. Purchase of equipment on credit
b. Payment of an account payable
c. Recording of revenue
d. Contribution of cash by the owner
e. Purchase of supplies for cash

LO 4 13. Indicate the proper order of the six steps in the accounting cycle listed below by placing the numbers 1 through 6 in the spaces provided.
___ a. Prepare financial statements.
___ b. Analyze business transactions.
___ c. Post to the general ledger.
___ d. Adjust the accounts.
___ e. Close the accounts.
___ f. Journalize transactions.

LO 4,6,7 14. Match the following accounting terms with the definitions shown below:
a. Matching principle
b. Realization principle
c. General ledger
d. T-account
e. Trial balance
f. Posting
(1) Abbreviation of a general ledger account that is used to simplify problem solutions and to explain how an account is used
(2) Process of transferring transactions data from the book of original entry to the general ledger
(3) Generally Accepted Accounting Principle that mandates that the costs incurred to generate revenues should be recognized in the same accounting period in which the related revenue is recognized
(4) Group of accounts consisting of all of the accounts listed in the chart of accounts.
(5) Generally Accepted Accounting Principle that mandates that revenues should only be recognized during an accounting period if (a) they are earned during the period and (b) cash is collected or expected be collected
(6) Statement that lists in one column the debit balances of general ledger accounts and lists in another column the credit balances

LO 5 15. The Womack Company purchased land for $25,000, paying cash of $10,000 and giving a note payable for the remaining $15,000. Which of the following journal entries would be correct?

a. Notes Payable   15,000
   Cash   10,000
      Land   25,000
   Purchased land.
b. Land   25,000
      Cash   10,000
      Notes Payable   15,000
   Purchased land.
c. Land   10,000
      Cash   10,000
   Purchased land,
   still owe $15,000.
d. Land   25,000
   Cash   10,000
      Notes Payable   15,000
   Purchased land.

LO 6   16. Indicate whether the following statements are true (*T*) or false (*F*).
   a. Transaction data are entered directly into the general ledger.
   b. Transaction data are entered directly into the general journal.
   c. Transaction data are entered into the general ledger from the general journal.

LO 8   17. An example of a transposition error is
   a. A check for $4,512.00 recorded as $451.20
   b. A check for $4,512.00 recorded as $4,215.00
   c. A check for $4,512.00 recorded as $5,512.00
   d. None of the above are transposition errors

LO 8   18. Which of the following recording or posting errors would require a correcting journal entry?

   a. Posting a $300 Cash debit as a debit to Rent Expense
   b. Posting a $500 Cash debit as a $50 debit to Cash
   c. Recording a journal entry for the payment of a $500 Account Payable as a debit to Accounts Receivable and a credit to Cash
   d. Posting a $72 debit to Cash as a $27 debit to Cash in the general ledger

LO 8   19. In preparing a trial balance, the $10,000 Accounts Payable balance is listed in the debit column. Therefore,
   a. The trial balance will be in balance because the $10,000 is included in the trial balance.
   b. The trial balance will be out of balance, with the Debits column $10,000 greater than the Credits column.
   c. The trial balance will be out of balance with the Debits column $20,000 greater than the Credits column.
   d. The trial balance will be out of balance by one-half the amount of the error, $5,000.

LO 8   20. The owner of a business contributes $5,000 cash to start the business. The transaction is recorded with a debit to Cash of $5,000 and a credit to Revenue of $5,000.
   a. The trial balance will be out of balance by $5,000.
   b. The trial balance will be out of balance by $10,000
   c. The trial balance will be in balance.
   d. The trial balance will be out of balance by $2,500.

SOLUTIONS TO SELF-QUIZ
1. a. T b. F c. T d. F   2. a. B b. I c. B d. B e. I f. B   3. a. Dr. b. Cr. c. Cr. d. Cr. e. Dr.   4. a. A b. A c. OE d. A e. L f. L   5. a. Dr. b. Cr. c. Cr. d. Dr. e. Cr. f. Dr.   6. asset, liability, owner's equity   7. liability, owner's equity, asset   8. d   9. a. 6 b. 2 c. 5 d. 3 e. 1 f. 4   10. e   11. a   12. b   13. a. 5 b. 1 c. 3 d. 4 e. 6 f. 2   14. a. 3 b. 5 c. 4 d. 1 e. 6 f. 2   15. b   16. a. F b. T c. T   17. b   18. a and c   19. c   20. c

QUESTIONS

Q2-1   What is the purpose of an account?

Q2-2   What is a ledger?

Q2-3   List five asset accounts and three liability accounts that businesses commonly use.

Q2-4   What is a debit?

Q2-5   Does a debit always increase an account? Explain.

Q2-6   How does a debit affect a liability account?

Q2-7   What is a credit?

Q2-8   What effect would a credit have on an asset account?

Q2-9   Comment on the following statement: "The whole premise of accounting is unnecessarily complex. Why not be consistent with debits and credits. If I designed the system, debits would always increase accounts and credits would always decrease accounts. This would make accounting much simpler."

Q2-10   Accounting transactions are first entered in the general journal and then posted to the general ledger accounts. Some view this as recording the transaction twice. Could time be saved by eliminating the general journal and making entries directly in the general ledger? Discuss.

Q2-11   When you have analyzed a business transaction in preparation for making a journal entry, is it true that one account will always increase and another account will always decrease?

Q2-12   Explain how the balance of a general ledger account is determined.

Q2-13   If all debits and credits recorded in the general journal are posted to the general ledger, is it reasonable to assume that the total of the debit balances in the general ledger will be equal to the total of the credit balances in the general ledger? Discuss.

Q2-14   What is a trial balance and what does it prove?

Q2-15   A credit to Accounts Receivable is inadvertently posted to Cash. What effect will this error have on your trial balance totals?

Q2-16   The trial balance that you prepare does not balance. Where might you look to find your error?

Q2-17   At the end of the accounting period, the trial balance is in balance. Does this ensure that the accounting records are correct? Explain.

Q2-18   A trial balance is taken at the end of the accounting period and is out of balance. The Debits column exceeds the Credits column by $810. Suggest possible errors that might have caused this difference.

Q2-19   Give an example of an error in the accounting records that will not cause the trial balance to be out of balance.

Q2-20   Comment on the following statement: "Taking a trial balance is a waste of time. It doesn't prove that the accounting records are correct; so, why bother?"

EXERCISES

LO 1,2

E2-1   **Recognizing Common Accounts and Their Normal Balances**   The following accounts were selected from the chart of accounts of the Top Shop. Identify each account as an element of assets (*A*), liabilities (*L*), or owner's equity (*OE*) and indicate whether its normal balance is a debit (*Dr.*) or credit (*Cr.*).

a. Peter Drumm, Withdrawals   f.   Wages and Salaries Payable
b. Accounts Receivable   g.   Sales
c. Equipment   h.   Rent Expense
d. Notes Payable   i.   Peter Drumm, Capital
e. Prepaid Insurance   j.   Land

LO 1,2

E2-2   **The Rules of Debit and Credit**   Indicate whether you would debit (*Dr.*) or credit (*Cr.*) each of the following accounts to increase their balances. (First identify the account as an asset, liability, or owner's equity account.)

a. Fee Revenue   f.   Cash
b. Notes Receivable   g.   Accounts Payable
c. Utilities Expense   h.   P. Michaels, Capital
d. Notes Payable   i.   Office Supplies
e. Buildings   j.   P. Michaels, Withdrawals

LO 3,5   **E2-3   The Effect of Business Transactions on Accounts**   The Apex Apple Farm borrowed $25,000 from the N.B.C. Bank at the beginning of the harvesting season to cover labor costs during the picking and packing process. What effect would this transaction have on the company's

a. Assets   d. Expenses
b. Liabilities   e. Owner's capital account
c. Revenues   f. Owner's withdrawals account

LO 3,5   **E2-4   Compound Journal Entry**   A company purchases equipment costing $10,000 by paying $3,000 down and signing a note payable for the balance ($7,000).

REQUIRED:

a. Prepare the necessary journal entry.
b. Explain how you are reasonably sure that you have included all of the elements of the transaction in your entry.

LO 3,5   **E2-5   Applying the Rules of Debit and Credit**   Each of the following unrelated business transactions occurred:

(1) The Too-Sweet Dairy Bar paid salaries for the week in the amount of $575.
(2) Ed McDowell invested an additional $5,000 in his golf equipment shop.
(3) Sue McNerny, M.D., borrowed $15,000 from the bank to expand her medical practice.
(4) On January 2, the accounting firm of Sallho, Texti and Braun paid $7,000 in liability insurance premiums for the first 6 months of the year.
(5) Min Lo collected $2,500 due from customers' accounts receivable.
(6) Raoul Prega purchased a new machine for $6,000, paying $2,000 in cash and signing a note payable for the remaining $4,000.

REQUIRED:

a. Determine the accounts involved
b. Determine if the account is increased or decreased
c. Determine if the account is debited or credited

Use the following format to complete your analysis:

0. The Flaming Arrow Campground received camping fees from patrons totaling $1,500 for the weekend.

	(1)	(2)	(3)
0.	Accounts Involved	Increase/Decrease	Debit/Credit
	Cash	Increase	Debit
	Fee Revenue	Increase	Credit

LO 5,6   **E2-6   The Relationship Between the General Journal and the General Ledger**   The following T-accounts summarize the effect of 5 business transactions on the general ledger accounts of Mountain City Spas:

Cash				Fee Revenue			
(1)	2,500	(4)	1,000			(1)	2,500
(3)	1,750	(5)	250			(2)	3,000

Accounts Receivable				Notes Payable			
(2)	3,000	(3)	1,750			(4)	2,000

Equipment			Rent Expense		
(4)	3,000		(5)	250	

REQUIRED:

a. Review the information contained in the accounts and write descriptions of the 5 transactions that were involved.

b. Prepare general journal entries to match your descriptions of the transactions.

LO 3,5,6

E2-7 Journalizing and Posting Transactions The following business events of the Cullowhee Collection Company occurred in March:

Mar.   1 Tim Trainorh, the owner, invested $500 to start the business.

3 Tim paid $100 to rent desk space in the office of the Paradise Travel Agency for the month of May.

5 Tim paid a $125 refundable deposit for a 3-line telephone from Mountain Phone Company and a 1 month's local service fee of $35. Issued one check.

16 Tim collected a bill for the Climber Tree Company, and received $500 from Ann Climber for this service.

19 Tim collected an old account for the accounting firm of Drew, Grimes, and Brown. He billed them $400 for his services.

29 Tim received payment from Drew, Grimes, and Brown.

REQUIRED:

a. Prepare the journal entry for each transaction.

b. Post the journal entries to the general ledger.

LO 7

E2-8 Preparing a Trial Balance The following list of accounts and related balances is taken from the records of the Optical Shop Co. on June 30, 19X3:

Accounts Payable	$ 12,650
Accounts Receivable	34,630
Advertising Expense	4,800
Buildings	50,000
C. Aldredge, Capital	80,000
C. Aldredge, Withdrawals	16,000
Cash	7,800
Office Supplies	9,700
Laboratory Expense	45,000
Mortgage Payable	65,000
Office Equipment	58,000
Professional Fees Expense	17,500
Wages and Salaries Expense	18,000
Fee Revenue	120,000
Prepaid Insurance	12,000
Utilities Expense	4,220

REQUIRED:

Prepare a trial balance in proper form.

LO 7,8

E2-9 Identifying and Correcting Trial Balance Errors A temporary bookkeeper, who worked while Dandelion's accountant was on vacation, prepared the trial balance shown at the top of the next page.

REQUIRED:

Identify the three errors in this trial balance and prepare a corrected trial balance.

Dandelion Lawn Service Trial Balance August 31, 19X4		
	Debits	Credits
Cash	$ 5,000	
Accounts Receivable	7,200	
Equipment	12,500	
Truck	9,500	
Prepaid Insurance		$ 400
Notes Payable		4,000
Jim Dandelion, Capital		21,300
Jim Dandelion, Withdrawals		1,500
Lawn Service Revenue		18,000
Maintenance Expense	700	
Wages and Salaries Expense	6,500	
	$41,400	$41,400

LO 3,5,8

E2-10 **Correcting Errors** The following unrelated journal entries have been recorded:

(1) On June 4, Jim Smith paid $400 on an account payable.

Accounts Receivable	400	
Cash		400

(2) On June 23, Janet Dyer collected $750 from a customer in full payment of a note.

Cash	750	
Accounts Receivable		750

(3) On July 15, Kerri Middlehopf purchased a computer and printer for $4,000 cash.

Office Equipment	4,000	
Cash		4,000

(4) On August 15, Ajax Scaffold Rental Company paid $350 to a welder who did routine minor repairs to a number of its rental items.

Prepaid Insurance	350	
Cash		350

REQUIRED:

a. Review each transaction narrative and the related entry to determine if an error has been made.
b. Prepare correcting entries for transactions that have been improperly recorded.
c. Indicate the effect the error would have on: total assets, total liabilities, and owner's equity.

Date any required entries the last day of the month in which the error occurred.

PROBLEM SET A

LO 1,2,3 **P2-1A** **Account Recognition and Applying Rules of Debit and Credit**   Joanne Williams runs the Mountain Go-Cart Track Co. She completed the following transactions during the month of June 19X5:

June   7 Joanne received an invoice from State Oil Company for gasoline delivered today, $2,500. The invoice is due June 23, 19X5.
11 Joanne wrote a company check for $1,000 to herself.
14 Joanne borrowed $15,000 from 2nd National Bank of Asheville to finance a second track. A 1-year, 15%, note payable was signed, and the cash was deposited to the company's account.
15 Paid $4,000 wages and salaries for the first half of the month.
16 Track fees received in cash for the first half of June, $2,800.
18 A small, used Spacestar van was purchased to transport riders from area hotels to the track. The purchase price was $11,500. Joanne paid $3,000 in cash and financed the balance through Eastern Finance Company at 6% on a special purchase incentive program.
21 Purchased a 3-acre tract of land next to the current property as a site for the second track, at a cost of $10,000.
23 Issued a check to State Oil Company for the invoice received on June 7.
30 Bills were mailed to local hotels for providing go-cart rides for hotel patrons, $26,840.
30 Joanne paid $4,000 wages and salaries for the second half of June.
30 Paid $2,000 for monthly repairs and maintenance on the go-carts.
30 Track fees received in cash for the second half of June, $2,500.

REQUIRED:

Use the following format to analyze each transaction. The first transaction is completed as an example.

Date	Account Used	Increase/Decrease	Debit/Credit
June 7	Supplies	Increase	Debit
	Accounts Payable	Increase	Credit

LO 1,3,5 **P2-2A** **Analyzing and Journalizing Transactions**   Jackson Meter Company specializes in repairing and adjusting gasoline and other dispensing pumps for service stations and other vendors in the area. The following selected business events are from the company's activities during December 19X6:

Dec.   3 Agreed to adjust 14 gasoline pumps, 2 diesel pumps, and a kerosene dispenser for Super-Five Truck Stop, Inc. This was required because of a violation finding from E.P.A.
6 Performed the work agreed to on Dec. 3 and a bill was mailed to Super-Five Truck Stop, Inc. in the amount of $850.
7 Repair parts costing $540 were purchased from Wend Pump Products Company on credit.
10 Purchased a new cellular phone for a repair truck at a cost of $250 installed. It was paid for at this time.
15 Paid the December 7, Wend Pump Products Company invoice, in the amount of $540.
20 Emory Smith, the owner, withdrew $1,500 for personal expenses.
21 Emory repaired 2 gasoline pumps for Red's Super Serve. He collected $110 from Red for the repairs.
23 Distributed annual bonus checks to the employees totalling $800.
23 Closed the shop down for the holiday weekend. Emory told the employees he would take any emergency calls.

Dec. 25 Emory was called to T. M.'s Self-Serve Gas Company by the fire department to repair a leaking propane dispensing unit. The repair was completed and Emory got home just in time for dinner.

27 Emory mailed a bill to T. M.'s Self-Serve Gas Company for $350 for the emergency repair on December 25.

30 December salary checks were issued for $3,200.

REQUIRED:

a. Analyze each event to determine if a business transaction has occurred.
b. If the event is a business transaction and can be recorded in the accounting records, use the following format to analyze the transactions.

Date	Recordable Transaction	Account Used	Increase/ Decrease	Debit/ Credit
Dec. 3	No	Work performed, amount not given.		
Dec. 6	Yes	Accounts Receivable	Increase	Debit
		Fee Revenue	Increase	Credit

c. Prepare general journal entries for the business transactions.
d. Is this information useful in its present form? How could its usefulness be enhanced?

LO 1,2,3,5 **P2-3A** **Journalizing and Posting Transactions** The following business transactions are from the August 19X7, activities of the Second Life Consignment Shop in Largo. The business accepts used goods from clients and sells them at prices the clients set. The shop is liable to the client for the amount collected from the sale of the goods less a commission, which represents a fee for selling the items in the store. The store owns no merchandise of its own and does not accept responsibility for goods that are stolen.

Aug. 2 Sam Cortez opened a business checking account with a deposit of $2,500.

3 Sam gave a $200 check to Tarpon Springs Realty Management for one month's rent on a small store.

4 Sam placed an advertisement in the *Clearwater Sun* to run during the month and paid $100.

9 Sam received several groups of used items from clients to sell. The clients set the prices. The agreement provides for Sam to receive a commission equal to 25% of the sales price when the item is sold.

10 Two flea market buffs went through all of the goods received yesterday and purchased items totaling $460. Sam recorded his commission as revenue and the amount owed to the client as accounts payable.

14 Sam received several additional groups of used items to be sold. He had sales during the day of $988.

20 Sam had a dental appointment in the afternoon and hired his brother-in-law, Fred, to run the store in the afternoon for $35. The wages are paid when Fred returns to the store.

20 Fred had sales totalling $748 for the afternoon.

31 Sam purchased 6 used display gondolas for $900.

REQUIRED:

a. Prepare general journal entries for the transactions.
b. Open T-accounts as needed and post from the general journal to the T-accounts. Determine the account balances at the end of the month.
c. Discuss how the T-accounts improve the information in terms of usefulness.

LO 3,4,5,6,7 **P2-4A** **Recording Business Transactions, Explaining the Purpose of the Procedures, Preparing a Trial Balance** Dave Morik retired from the Marine Corp after 30 years. He decided to open a Martial Arts Training Center. His intent was to offer classes in a variety of martial arts and related physical fitness training. He began his business in November 19X8.

The Martial Arts Training Center uses the following accounts:

100 Cash	700 Advertising Expense
150 Prepaid Insurance	734 Maintenance Expense
154 Prepaid Advertising	762 Rent Expense
158 Utilities Deposits	
230 Equipment	
302 Accounts Payable	
326 Notes Payable	
500 Dave Morik, Capital	
502 Dave Morik, Withdrawals	
604 Fee Revenue	

The following business activities occurred during November:

Nov.
1 Dave deposited $20,000 in a business checking account at the Valley Bank.

2 Dave prearranged loans with the bank for up to $80,000. (This is known as a line of credit.) Notes would be signed for any funds borrowed. They agreed on an interest rate of 12%.

4 Dave purchased two complete fitness machines at a cost of $26,000 from International Sports Equipment, Inc. The invoice is due November 15.

5 Dave paid $2,400 for 12 large gym mats from Warner Company.

8 Dave completed negotiations for a 5,000-square-foot building at an annual cost of $12 per square foot, per year. He paid the first month's rent.

9 Dave deposited $100 with the local utility company (refundable) to guarantee payment. The utilities were connected.

11 Dave paid a local cleaning company $250 to do general cleanup. He also paid R. M. Greene $400 to paint the walls and ceilings. The cleaning and painting are considered maintenance.

15 Dave drew $20,000 against his line of credit at the bank for deposit in his checking account. He signed a note due in 180 days.

15 Paid the November 4, International Sports Equipment invoice, $26,000.

22 Dave completed installation of the equipment and the mats that were delivered by Warner today.

22 Dave placed a radio spot with KMOC to run four times per day through the end of November, at a cost of $300.

23 Dave took out a liability insurance policy with County Insurance. The $2,400 annual premium was paid. The policy covered the period from December 1, 19X8 through November 30, 19X9.

24 Five persons inquired about Dave's program, and three of them signed up for classes, paying $40 each for the first week.

30 Dave withdrew $400 for personal use.

REQUIRED:

a. Journalize the transactions of Martial Arts Training Center for the month of November.
b. Explain the advantage of first recording the transaction data in a general journal.
c. Set up T-accounts and post the information from the general journal. Determine the balances of the accounts.
d. Prepare a trial balance.
e. Explain how the general ledger makes accounting information easier to use.

LO 5,6,7   **P2-5A**   **The Effect of Business Transactions in the Accounting Records, Posting to the Ledger, and Preparing a Trial Balance**   Ed Martin became bored with retirement after only 6 months and decided to start Chocolate Mountains Trail Rides as a weekend adventure program during the winter months. He located a small base camp facility just a 2-hours' drive from Los Angeles, where he would meet his customers.

You will use the following accounts for Chocolate Mountains Trail Rides:

100 Cash
134 Maintenance Supplies
230 Equipment
245 Livestock
500 Ed Martin, Capital
604 Fee Revenue
700 Advertising Expense
728 Insurance Expense
762 Rent Expense
784 Wages and Salaries Expense

The following business events occurred during Ed's first month of activity, October 19X9:

Oct. 4 Ed Martin rented a base camp facility on the ranch of D. R. Dudley, which was located at the base of the Chocolate Mountains, paying $1,000 for the 6-month season from his personal checking account. He picked the location to capitalize on the legend of the Lost Dutchman's Mine.

7 Ed deposited $30,000 cash in a business checking account.

8 Ed began the process of acquiring the necessary assets. He purchased 20 old but gentle horses from a dude ranch that had closed, for $4,000 delivered to the base camp, where he put them out to pasture.

9 Ed went to a dispersal auction where he managed to acquire a single lot of tack which included 25 saddles, 40 headstalls with bits, 6 pack saddles, and an array of repair leather, straps, etc., for $1,400.

11 Ed placed an advertisement in *The Times* announcing trail rides leaving from the base camp on Saturday mornings and returning Sunday evenings for the fourth and fifth weekends in October. The ad cost $120 for two weeks.

14 Ed spent the last several days repairing the saddles, bridles, and pack saddles in preparation for the first trip. He went to town and purchased cooking utensils, 25 sleeping bags, and arranged for food to be delivered to the base camp on Saturday. The camping gear cost $2,600 and the food cost $460. Food is considered a supply item.

19 A trip liability insurance policy was purchased for the two planned trips for a premium of $150 per trip. He also hired Sara Brown, formerly with the dude ranch, to serve as wrangler and trail guide.

23 Fourteen people had signed in for the ride and paid the $200 fee.

26 Ed sent the wrangler to buy 6 more horses advertised for $250 each. The wrangler returned with 5 sound horses having given the seller a company check for $1,000 for them.

29 The wrangler went to buy the food for tomorrow's trip, taking a company check which she filled out for $410.

30 Sixteen riders registered for the trip, each paying the $200 trail ride fee.

31 Ed wrote the wrangler's paycheck for $300.

REQUIRED:

a. Prepare general journal entries for the business transactions above.
b. Post the general journal entries to T-accounts and determine the balances of the accounts.
c. Prepare a trial balance as of October 31, 19X9.

LO 3,5,6,7   **P2-6A**   **Journalizing and Posting Business Transactions and Preparing a Trial Balance**
Great Plains Charter Service has been operating for 12 months out of Council Bluffs Airpark. They have been flying a leased Cherokee-Six all year. The trial balance for December 31, 19X9 is as follows.

Great Plains Charter Service **Trial Balance** **December 31, 19X9**		
	Debits	*Credits*
Cash	$15,500	
Accounts Receivable	12,800	
Office Supplies	200	
Accounts Payable		$ 700
Harold Whealon, Capital		27,800
	$28,500	$28,500

The following events occurred in January 19X0:

Jan.   4 Harold Whealon found an ad in *Trade-a-Plane* for a Piper Lance Turbo II, which was for sale by Roberta Randall in Omaha. He flew over with a friend to see the plane and negotiated a purchase price of $48,000. He immediately called his bank to arrange a loan.

        5 Harold went to his bank, signed a 5-year, 15% note pledging the plane as collateral. He returned to Omaha with a $42,000 bank check payable to Roberta and a $6,000 company check payable to her. Harold completed the deal and flew the plane home to Council Bluffs.

        5 Harold called Avemco and had the plane covered with insurance. He mailed the first quarter's premium check for $800 that same day.

        6 Harold paid Ted Eure, an aviation mechanic, $600 to service and inspect the plane to certify it for charter service.

        8 Harold topped off the plane's tanks with fuel (billed monthly at the Airpark), and he and Ted took off for a shakedown cruise to Illinois, stopping for lunch at the Air Park Barn Restaurant and topping off the tanks again to check the fuel burn rate. The refueling cost $48 cash. After the return trip, they were both satisfied to place the aircraft in service.

    11 Harold called the leasing company to cancel the lease on the Cherokee-Six. The lessor advised Harold of the penalty clause in his contract, and they agreed to a $1,200 final lease payment in settlement. Harold mailed the check and the leasing company arranged to pick up the aircraft that same day.

    16 Harold got a call at 11:00 p.m. for an air-ambulance run to pick up a patient in Iowa City for transport to the Memphis Burn Center.

    17 Harold returned from Memphis, via Iowa City to drop off the paramedic and the nurse, and arrived back in Council Bluffs at 7:00 a.m. He mailed a bill to Aero-Ambulance Booking Service for $960 for the plane and pilot.

    22 Harold picked up electronic parts at Lambert Field, in St. Louis, for delivery to Mulke Corp. of Janesville, Wisconsin. He billed the Mulke Corp. $600.

    24 Harold flew a group of 5 sightseers out to view the Black Hills from the air, stopping for fuel on the way back. The fuel cost, $96, was paid by check. The group paid $720 for the 6 hours of flying time.

    31 Harold received his fuel bill from Airpark for aviation fuel and oil totalling $620 for the month. He delivered the check to their office.

REQUIRED:

a. Read the event information for an understanding of the company's activities and then develop a chart of accounts. Create a numbering system for the chart of accounts and assign an account number to each account. Enter the account titles, account numbers, and the beginning balances dated January 1, 19X0 in the general ledger accounts.

b. Prepare entries in a general journal to record each of the business transactions that you identify in the above listed events.

c. Post the journal entries to the ledger accounts.

d. Prepare a trial balance dated January 31, 19X0.

PROBLEM SET B

LO 1,2,3   **P2-1B**   **Account Recognition and Applying Rules of Debit and Credit**   Each of the follow-ing events in the activity of the Center City Realty Company occurred during March 19X1:

Mar. 1 Paid March rent of $500.

3 Three homes were listed for sale. The contract provides for Center City to receive a commission equal to 6% of the sales price, provided the home is sold in 6 months.

9 Paid $250 for ads for the 3 homes. The ads will appear in the *Center City News* during March.

11 Purchased office supplies for $300.

15 Salaries of $1,200 were paid for the first half of the month.

18 Sold 1 of the listed homes for $150,000.

25 Arimis Jones, the owner, withdrew $2,500 in cash for personal use.

29 Collected half of the commission from the March 18 sale.

31 Salaries of $1,200 were paid for the second half of the month.

31 Paid $175 for March utilities to the landlord.

REQUIRED:

Use the following format to analyze each transaction. The first transaction is completed as an example.

Date	Account Used	Increase/Decrease	Debit/Credit
Mar. 1	Rent Expense	Increase	Debit
	Cash	Decrease	Credit

LO 1,3,5   **P2-2B**   **Analyzing and Journalizing Transactions**   Patricia Keith has been in the printing business in Hayesville for six years. The following events occurred during the month of February 19X2:

Feb. 1 Patricia Keith received a shipment of ink and assorted papers on credit from Printers' Supply with a bill for $980.

2 Vargo Corporation placed an order with Patricia for 10,000 sheets of imprinted billing paper. Vargo provided the copy with a logo to use in preparing the off-set plate. As this was a two-color layout, Patricia estimated the cost to Vargo at $850.

5 Patricia delivered the Vargo Corporation order with a bill for $850.

8 Patricia received an order from RealeX Realty Co. for 5,000, 7-color, 6-side, tri-fold brochures to be used in selling property in a new recreational develop-ment. She is to do the design and layout. The text was provided by RealeX. Patricia estimated the job at $6,250.

11 Patricia mailed a check for $980 to Printer's Supply in payment of the February 1, shipment.

12 Patricia took the mockups to RealeX for approval. They requested two changes and approved the brochures for production as modified. She collected $2,500 advance payment at this time.

15 Patricia picked up the mail at the post office and it included a check from Vargo Corporation for the balance due from the February 2 order.

18 Patricia completed the RealeX plates, ran the brochures, and stacked them in the dryer.

Feb.   19 Patricia folded the brochures and boxed them for delivery.
       22 Patricia delivered the brochures to RealeX and collected the balance of the $6,250 estimate.
       25 Patricia accepted an order for 10,000 business cards to consist of 1,000 cards for each of Vargo Corporation's 10 salespeople. She estimated the cost to Vargo at $550. She did the setup and ran the cards.
       26 Vargo's sales manager brought in the check for $550 and picked up the business cards.
       26 Patricia wrote herself a check for personal expenses of $2,000.

REQUIRED:

a. Analyze each event to determine if a business transaction has occurred.
b. If the event is a business transaction, determine what accounts would be involved and whether they would increase or decrease.
c. Prepare general journal entries for the business transactions, complete with appropriate explanations.
d. What could be done with this information to make it more useful?

LO 3,5   **P2-3B**   **Journalizing and Posting Transactions**   Jeanne Jackson began her accounting practice as a CPA in January 19X4.

Jeanne uses the following general ledger accounts:

100 Cash
110 Accounts Receivable
136 Office Supplies
152 Prepaid Rent
242 Office Equipment
302 Accounts Payable
326 Notes Payable
500 Jeanne Jackson, Capital
502 Jeanne Jackson, Withdrawals
604 Fee Revenue
780 Utilities Expense

The following business events occurred during the month.

Jan.   4 Jeanne deposited $8,000 of her own cash to open the business checking account.
        5 Jeanne rented a small office for $500 per month, paying the first 6 months' rent.
        7 Jeanne purchased a computer and other office equipment for $10,000, paying $1,000 in cash and signing a note payable for the balance.
       10 Office supplies costing $300 were purchased on account. Payment is due on February 10.
       12 Jeanne set up a set of books for J. R. Reed Oil Company. She received Mr. Reed's check of $3,000 for her services.
       14 Jeanne issued a check for $100 in partial payment for the office supplies purchased earlier in the month.
       17 Jeanne completed the preparation of a financial report for John King and billed him $3,000.
       27 The phone bill of $150 was received and a check was immediately issued and mailed.
       31 A check was received from John King for $1,000, representing one-third of the amount due.
       31 Jeanne withdrew $500 from the business for personal use.

REQUIRED:

a. Prepare general journal entries for the transactions.
b. Open T-accounts and post from the general journal to the T-accounts.
c. Discuss how the T-accounts improve the usefulness of the information.

LO 3,4,5,6,7   **P2-4B**   **Recording Business Transactions, Explaining the Purpose of the Procedures, Preparing a Trial Balance**   Charlene Smider began the DeSoot Chimney Service in September 19X5.

You will use the following accounts for the DeSoot Chimney Service:

100 Cash
230 Equipment
500 Charlene Smider, Capital
600 Revenue
700 Advertising Expense
733 Licenses Expense
784 Wages and Salaries Expense

The following events occurred during the month:

Sept. 1 Charlene Smider deposited $3,000 at Maine State Bank in the name of DeSoot Chimney Service.
1 Charlene purchased a city business license for September at the Rockland City Hall for $10.
1 She placed an ad in the *Rockland Gazette* to run each day in September. The cost was $100.
1 Charlene purchased chimney cleaning equipment from Booklins Hardware at a cost of $1,450.
2 Charlene purchased a used van for $600.
6 Charlene received 5 calls to clean chimneys. She cleaned 3 this date and scheduled the other 2 for the 7th. She collected a total of $180 for the three chimneys.
7 She cleaned the two chimneys scheduled and collected $145.
8 She arranged with her sister, Arline, to work on a part-time basis when needed at $7.50 per hour.
13 Twenty-five calls were received during the day to schedule chimney cleaning services between the 16th and the 30th.
17 Charlene and Arline cleaned 9 chimneys. Charlene received $640.
24 Charlene and Arline cleaned 14 chimneys during the period of September 18 – 24. Cash totaling $940 was received.
30 Charlene cleaned the other 2 scheduled chimneys on Monday and 3 additional chimneys on Wednesday. The total collected was $350.
30 Charlene paid Arline for the 60 hours she worked.

REQUIRED:

a. Journalize the transactions of DeSoot Chimney Service for the month of September.
b. Explain the advantage of first recording the transaction data in a general journal.
c. Set up T-accounts and post the information from the general journal. Determine the balances of the accounts.
d. Prepare a trial balance.
e. Explain how the general ledger makes accounting information more useful.

LO 5,6,7   **P2-5B**   **The Effect of Business Transactions in the Accounting Records, Posting to the Ledger, and Preparing a Trial Balance**   Claude Edwards has opened the Highway 107 Flea Market. He purchased a very large barn on Highway 107 just south of the area known as Tourist Junction. The market will be open only on weekends. The 90 small stalls will rent for $15 per day. The 10 large stalls will be rented to commercial vendors at $250 per month, payable on the first of the month. All collections are considered revenue when received as no refunds are made.

The Highway 107 Flea Market uses the following accounts:

100 Cash
150 Prepaid Insurance

158   Utilities Deposits
220   Buildings
230   Equipment
408   Notes Payable – Noncurrent
500   Claude Edwards, Capital
502   Claude Edwards, Withdrawals
610   Rent Revenue
700   Advertising Expense
734   Maintenance Expense
738   Miscellaneous Expense
780   Utilities Expense

The following events occurred during the month of July 19X6.

July   1   Claude purchased the barn by paying $5,000 in cash from his personal checking account and giving a 5-year note for $25,000.

          1   Claude paid Karen Cleaning $150 from his personal checking to clean up the barn for use. This is maintenance expense.

          2   Claude deposited $8,000 at Mountain Bank to start a business checking account.

          2   Craft Carpenters were hired to repair loose boards and to remove any splinters and stray nails. A check was drawn for $260. Claude treated this cost as maintenance expense.

          3   The building inspector and the fire marshall examined the building for safety considerations. They approved the barn for use as a flea market but required that Claude purchase 12 fire extinguishers and install an outside phone booth. The inspection fee of $350 was paid by check. Treat it as a miscellaneous expense.

          3   Liability insurance was purchased for the balance of the year at a premium of $900.

          5   Mountain Area Fire and Safety installed the fire extinguishers at a cost of $300. This was paid to the installers before they left. The extinguishers are classified as equipment.

          6   Coop Telephone Service installed the phone booth. The required deposit of $250 and the first month service charge of $50 were paid.

          8   A half-page ad was placed to run in the *Sunday Chronicle*, offering to rent the stalls. The $250 cost for the ad was paid.

       12   Eight commercial vendors came by during the day to look over the facilities. Six rented large stalls for $150 for the rest of the month.

       13   During the day, 75 different individuals signed up for booths for Saturday; 50 of these also signed up for Sunday. All monies were collected and deposited in the checking account.

       14   Claude purchased a variety of balloons, small toys, and soft drinks to give away at the grand opening. The cost was $350.

       15   Twenty of the Saturday only renters signed up for booths for Sunday, July 16. The cash was collected and dropped in the night depository at the bank.

       17   Claude paid Karen Cleaning $350 to clean up on July 17, 24, and 31 after the weekend activities. The total was paid and recorded as maintenance expense.

       21   On Friday, 3 more commercial vendors signed up for large stalls at $100 each for the balance of the month and paid in full. All 90 small stalls were rented for Saturday, and 80 were rented for Sunday. All of the cash was collected and deposited.

       28   On Friday, all 90 small stalls were rented for both Saturday and Sunday. The cash was collected and deposited.

       31   Claude withdrew $1,500 for personal expenses.

REQUIRED:

a. Prepare general journal entries to record the above business transactions.
b. Set up T-accounts for each account in the chart of accounts, post the general journal entries, and determine the balances of the accounts.
c. Prepare a trial balance dated July 31, 19X6.

LO 3,5,6,7 **P2-6B** **Journalizing and Posting Business Transactions and Preparing a Trial Balance**
Smelter's Seamless Guttering Co., of Deep Woods, OK, has been hanging gutters and installing aluminum soffit since 19X1. The January 1, 19X7, balances are listed below:

Smelter's Seamless Guttering Co. Trial Balance December 31, 19X6		
	Debits	*Credits*
Cash	$16,000	
Accounts Receivable	6,000	
Equipment	40,000	
Notes Payable — Noncurrent		$ 2,500
Jim Smelter, Capital		59,500
	$62,000	$62,000

The following events occurred during the month of January 19X7.

Jan.　4　Guttering and soffit supplies were purchased from White Metals & Supply on account. The invoice for the supplies totaled $6,500 and was due to be paid in 10 days.

4　Smelter signed a contract with Wallart Construction Co. for the installation of gutters and soffits on a large townhouse development. The job is expected to generate revenues of approximately $45,000. Smelter's crew began the installation.

8　Jim Smelter, the owner, billed the Wallart Construction Co. $8,000 for work done on the townhouses during the week.

13　Received a check from Wallart Construction for the amount billed on January 8.

14　Issued a check to White Metals & Supply for the supplies purchased on January 4.

15　Jim billed Wallart Construction $12,000 for the second week's work.

22　Jim was out sick for 3 days this week, and no bills were sent out.

25　Received an electric and water bill from the City of Deep Woods for $175, which Jim promptly paid.

29　Jim sent a bill to Wallart Construction for two weeks' work in the amount of $19,000.

29　Jim paid $12,500 wages for the month.

29　Jim withdrew $1,800 for personal living expenses.

REQUIRED:

a. Read the event information for an understanding of the company's activities and then develop a chart of accounts. Create a numbering system for the chart of accounts and assign a number to each account. Enter the account titles, account numbers, and the beginning balances dated January 1, 19X7, in the general ledger accounts.
b. Prepare entries in a general journal to record each of the business transactions that are identified in the above events.
c. Post the journal entries to the ledger accounts.
d. Prepare a trial balance.

CRITICAL THINKING AND COMMUNICATING

C2-1 You consider making an offer to purchase a small local business that is currently operated by an elderly couple seeking to retire. They sell locally manufactured crockery dinnerware for a commission. Initially, you were permitted to look through their general journal. The journal contained 74 pages of entries; and although the individual entries were easily followed, you had no luck in getting an overall picture of the business activity. You requested that they prepare a trial balance for your inspection. The couple complied and furnished the following statement:

The Crockery Shop Trial Balance December 31, 19X9		
	Debits	*Credits*
Cash	$ 2,350	
Accounts Receivable	18,000	
Supplies	900	
Prepaid Rent	2,500	
Accounts Payable		$11,450
Notes Payable		1,500
Owner's Capital		5,000
Owner's Withdrawals	24,000	
Sales Commissions Revenue		50,000
Miscellaneous Expense	500	
Rent Expense	15,000	
Sales Supplies Expense	3,500	
Utilities Expense	1,200	
	$67,950	$67,950

REQUIRED:

a. What does the trial balance tell you about the possible profits you might earn should you decide to purchase the business?
b. What kind of a financial statement would provide you with information concerning profitability?
c. What can you tell about the value of the assets listed, and would this information be important in determining the amount of your offer?

C2-2 Sandra Potts, a close friend, has just opened a local carpet cleaning business on September 1, 19X8. She has arranged for a local bookkeeping service to keep her accounting records and to provide her with a monthly trial balance. Sandra asked the bookkeeping service to keep the accounting records as simple as possible because she does not have an accounting background and she also wants to keep the accounting costs as low as possible.

Sandra just received her first trial balance from the bookkeeping service and brings it by for you to inspect, as she knows you are enrolled in a college accounting course. The trial balance is presented on the next page:

Quick Klean		
Trial Balance		
September 30, 19X8		
	Debits	Credits
Cash		$ 1,000
Accounts Receivable	$ 2,000	
Cleaning Supplies	500	
Prepaid Insurance	400	
Equipment	90,000	
Notes Payable — Noncurrent		80,000
Accounts Payable		1,900
Potts, Capital		14,000
Potts, Withdrawals	1,000	
Revenue		6,000
Expenses	8,000	
	$102,900	$102,900

REQUIRED:

Examine the trial balance and make a list of items you should discuss with Sandra.

CHAPTER 3

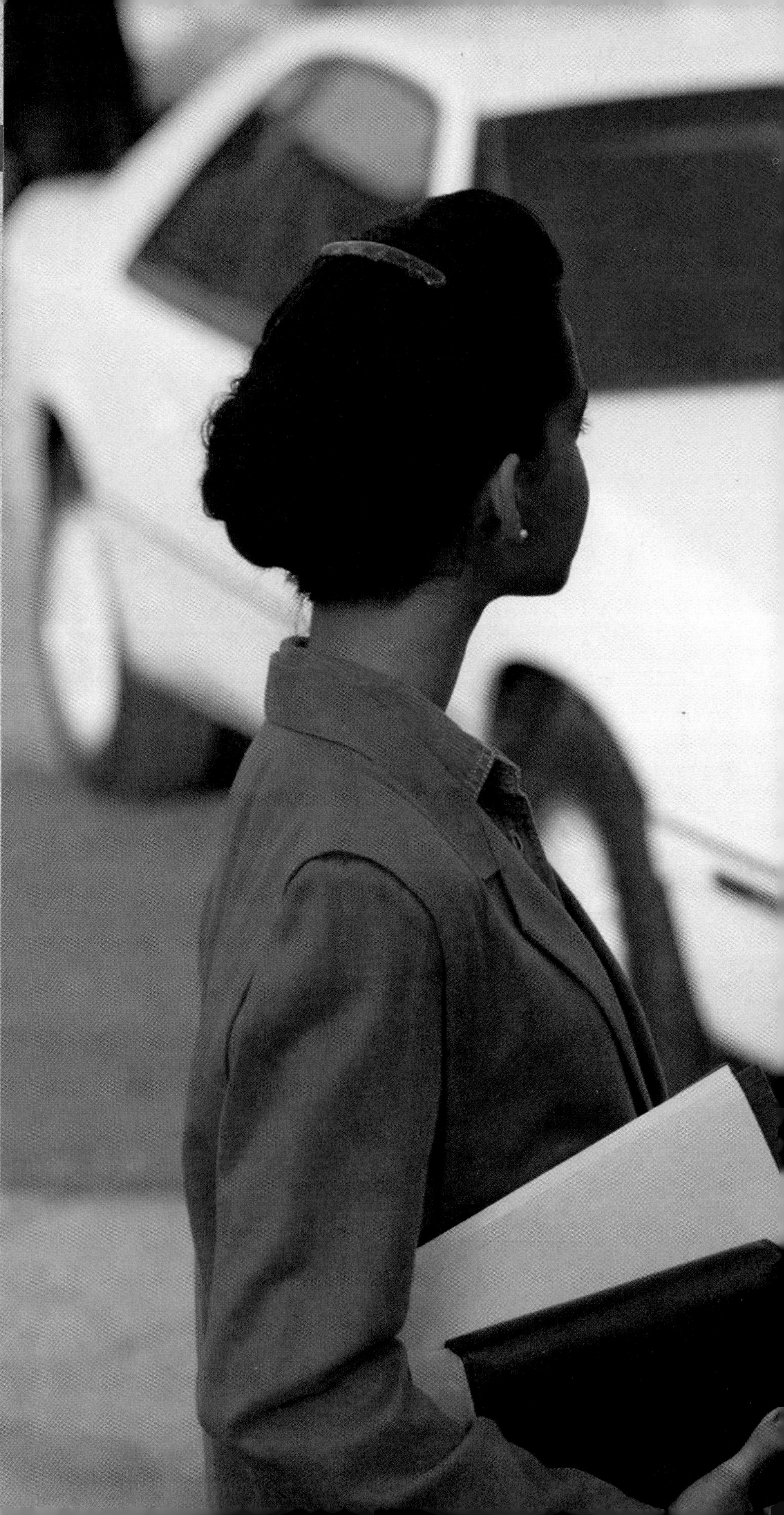

Adjusting Entries, Accounting Income, and Accrual Concepts

Charlotte Cruz considers investing in another parking lot on the opposite side of campus. An important factor is the profitability of her current parking lot. You saw that in January the lot appeared quite profitable. In February, Charlotte added night parking. This addition increased her revenues, but it also increased her expenses. Charlotte is anxious to prepare financial statements at the end of February to assess the profitability of her business for the two-month period.

This chapter begins the discussion of procedures that are necessary to prepare financial statements at the end of an accounting period. (This discussion is completed in the next chapter.) The end-of-period procedures are necessary because many revenue and expense transactions extend beyond one accounting period. As a result, we must adjust the accounts to correct them and to prepare financial statements for the period. Accounting appor-*divide* tions the effects of multiperiod transactions among accounting periods based on the measurement principles introduced previously.

LEARNING OBJECTIVES

1. Define accounting net income.
2. Distinguish between the cash basis and accrual basis of income.
3. Explain the concepts, assumptions, and principles underlying the accrual basis of accounting.
4. Prepare adjusting entries at the end of an accounting period.
5. Prepare financial statements using an adjusted trial balance.
6. Calculate and interpret a business's profit margin.
7. Prepare adjusting entries when certain cash transactions are recorded initially as revenues and expenses (Appendix 3-A).

LO 1

Define accounting net income.

ACCOUNTING NET INCOME

A business enterprise's primary objective is to earn a profit for the owners. Profit, however, means different things to different people—to investors and creditors, economists and accountants. An investor, for example, might consider profit as the increase in the market price of shares of stock that the investor owns. An accountant, on the other hand, considers profit to be the increase in a business enterprise's net assets from operations during a period. Accountants use the concept of net income (rather than profit) to report on the results of a business's operations. **Net income** is the excess of revenues over expenses for a period and may be expressed by the equation:

Net Income = Revenues − Expenses

If expenses exceed revenues for a period, the business has incurred a **net loss**. For 1992, General Motors Corporation reported the largest net loss, $23 billion, in the history of American business. As you saw previously, we report the business's net income (or net loss) in the income statement.

The income statement provides a measure of the business's performance during a period. Net income is important to both the owner and to other users of the financial statements such as creditors. When a business reports net income in its income statement, it means that operations have resulted in an increase in the business's net assets. This information is important to the owner because it signifies the degree of success the business has experienced during the period. The information about net income is important to creditors because it provides a basis for them to assess the business's financial health.

Revenues

Revenues are defined as the increases in assets that result directly from providing products or services to customers during a specific period. In other words, revenues are increases in *net assets* due to the business's operations. For example, Charlotte's Car Park earns revenues by providing parking to customers. IBM earns revenues by selling computers and related products to customers, while McDonald's earns revenues by providing fast-food to customers. Revenues increase assets by increasing cash (through cash sales) or accounts and notes receivable (through credit sales).

However, not all increases in cash or other assets are revenues. For example, borrowing from the bank increases cash, but this cash is not revenue because the transaction does not involve providing products or services to customers. Also, collection of accounts receivable is not revenue because the transaction does not increase net assets. Consider the following example. Cooper's Computer Repair Shop repairs several computers and bills the customers $1,200. Illustration 3-1 shows the effects of this transaction.

The $1,200 is considered revenue because Cooper's has increased its net assets (accounts receivable) by providing repair services to customers. However, when Cooper's collects $300 of the amount owed, the transaction does not result in revenue because net assets have not changed. Notice that in Illustration 3-1 the collection of the account receivable has no effect on owner's equity. The $300 increase in Cash is offset by the $300 decrease in Accounts Receivable so that there is no change in net assets.

ILLUSTRATION 3-1 Revenue Transactions and Net Assets

	Assets			Owner's Equity	
	Cash		Accounts Receivable		Repairs Revenue
Revenue - $1,200 sales on credit			1,200		1,200
Collection of $300 of accounts receivable	300			300	

Expenses

Expenses are defined as decreases in assets and increases in liabilities the business's revenue-producing activities cause during a specific period. In other words, expenses are decreases in *net assets* due to the business's operations. We may view expenses as the sacrifices the business makes to earn the revenues of the period. Examples of expenses include wages and salaries, rent, depreciation, and utilities. When Charlotte Cruz pays the attendants' wages of $1,200, we record the expense as follows:

Feb. 28	Wages and Salaries Expense	1,200	
	Cash		1,200
	Payment of parking lot attendants' wages.		

The payment is an expense because assets (cash) are decreased by revenue-producing activities—providing parking for customers.

Transactions other than expenses can decrease assets or increase liabilities. For example, when Charlotte Cruz makes a withdrawal from her business, we record the following entry:

Feb. 28	Charlotte Cruz, Withdrawals	500	
	Cash		500
	Withdrawal of cash by owner.		

This transaction decreases assets (cash). However, because the withdrawal does not involve the business's revenue-producing activities, it is not an expense.

LO 2
Distinguish between the cash basis and accrual basis of income.

ACCOUNTING BASES

In practice, more than one concept exists for measuring the business's performance during a period. Below we discuss two concepts—the cash basis and the accrual basis of accounting.

Cash Basis

Some small businesses prepare financial statements on the cash basis of accounting. Under the **cash basis of accounting**, *revenues are recorded only in the period that cash payments are received from customers; and expenses are recorded only in the period that cash payments are made.* This method measures the business's performance by the difference between cash receipts and cash disbursements. The primary advantage of the cash basis of accounting is its simplicity.

Accrual Basis

GAAP require the accrual basis of accounting for the preparation of income statements and balance sheets. The **accrual basis of accounting** means that revenues are recorded in the period that they are earned, and expenses are recorded in the period that they are incurred. The period that revenues are earned may be different from the period of the related cash receipts. For example, Charlotte's Car Park provided parking to a customer on credit in one period but did not receive the cash payment until the following period. Under accrual accounting, we record revenue in the period that the business provides the service because that is when the business earns the revenue. Advocates of accrual accounting believe that recording the revenues in the period they are *earned*, rather than in the period that the *cash payments are received*, better measures enterprise performance. The basis for this viewpoint is that providing the product or service to customers is generally the critical event in the earning process. Accountants view the collection of the cash payment as only an incidental (but necessary) part of the earning process.

HISTORICAL PERSPECTIVES

QUEEN ELIZABETH I

BLAME THIS LADY

She's Queen Elizabeth I, who in 1600 chartered the East India Company, one of the world's first "joint stock" companies. The joint stock company had owners who were merely investors and did not participate in the management of the trading ventures of the company. Initially, the company made distributions of all income (if any) to the investors at the end of a trading venture. But in 1661 the company's governor announced that future distributions would be paid periodically out of net income.

All of a sudden, measuring net income was a job for the accountants, who had to start making judgment calls. Assets and net income had to be apportioned among many voyages in different stages of completion. Many subjective judgments were required before calculating each period's net income—the life expectancy of ships, how much capital to retain to keep ships in tip-top shape, when to write off bad debts, etc.

In short, trading companies like East India Company introduced accrual accounting, periodic net income, and most of the accounting problems we face today.

Source: *Forbes* (November 12, 1990), pp. 8, 112. Reprinted by permission of FORBES magazine © Forbes Inc., 1990.

Under accrual accounting and the matching principle, we record expenses in the period that they are incurred, which may be a period different from the one in which the business makes the cash payment for the expense. For example, assume that an employee works for a business in one period but is not paid until the following period. Under accrual accounting, we record wages and salaries expense in the period the employee works for the business, rather than in the following period when the business pays the employee. An employee's salary increases liabilities because the business is obligated to pay the salary. Accrual accounting advocates believe that recording expenses in the period they are incurred—rather than in the period paid—is a superior measure of the sacrifices the business makes in earning the revenues of the period. The important event in the business's earning process is incurring wages and salaries expense for the service the employee provides during the period, not for the payment of the obligation to the employee. Illustration 3-2 summarizes the recording of revenues and expenses under the cash basis and the accrual basis of accounting.

ILLUSTRATION 3-2 Cash Basis and Accrual Basis

	Cash basis	Accrual basis
Revenue recorded	In period cash is received	In period earned (when product or service is provided)
Expense recorded	In period cash is paid	In period expense is incurred

Many businesses keep their records, on a day-to-day basis, using a method similar to the cash basis of accounting. That is, most transactions recorded involve either cash receipts or cash payments. At the end of an accounting period, these businesses must adjust their records to the accrual basis of accounting to prepare financial statements. For example, assume that on January 2, a painter contracts with an apartment complex to paint the interiors of the 20 units that make up the complex. The agreed-upon price for the job is $4,000, to be paid upon completion of all 20 units. In addition, the complex agrees to provide the paint. On the same day, the painter purchases for cash a spray-painting machine at a cost of $900. The painter expects to use the painting machine for 5 years. At the end of January, the painter has completed 15 of the units.

On the cash basis of accounting, the painter has no revenues for January because cash receipts are zero. On the other hand, expenses on a cash basis are $900—the cash payment for the spray-painting machine. In this case, the cash basis of accounting does not accurately reflect the painter's performance for the month. During January, he earned 75 percent of the contract price (15 ÷ 20 units), and he used only 1/60 [1 month ÷ (5 years x 12 months)] of the machine's service potential. To adjust to the accrual basis of accounting for January, the painter should record revenues of $3,000 (75% x $4,000). Expenses should be recorded at only $15 ($900 ÷ 60 months), and the machine should be shown as an asset at the cost of its remaining service potential of $885 ($900 – $15).

Later in this chapter, we provide a full description of the adjustment process that accomplishes accrual basis accounting for such events. Note that even though income statements and balance sheets are prepared on the accrual basis, cash flow information is also important; and the statement of cash flows is a required financial statement. Statements of cash flows are discussed in a subsequent chapter.

LO 3
Explain the concepts,
assumptions, and
principles underlying the
accrual basis of
accounting.

ACCRUAL CONCEPTS, ASSUMPTIONS, AND PRINCIPLES

In previous chapters, we introduced the fundamental elements that compose the foundations of financial accounting. Several of those elements are essential to understanding the role of the accrual basis of accounting and the adjustment of accounts for preparation of financial statements. We review these key elements in this chapter to provide the basis for the discussion of the adjustment process. The elements that we review are: accounting period concept, realization principle, and matching principle. In addition to reviewing these elements, we introduce a new element—the going-concern assumption.

Accounting Period Concept

The previous discussion of accounting net income referred to the business's net income for a period. The period of time for which we determine net income is called the **accounting period**. The accounting period commonly is a year, but we may measure and report income for periods as short as a month. The development of a year as the accounting period may be traced to the requirement for businesses to file income tax returns with federal and state governments on an annual basis. Also, federal and state regulatory agencies require many businesses to file financial statements on an annual basis. In any event, the annual accounting period for businesses is an established practice. When we determine net income for a period of less than a year, the process is usually less formal than that for an annual determination and involves more estimates and assumptions. We present financial information such as net income for a period shorter than a year in reports called **interim financial reports**.

Various Business Fiscal Periods.   A **fiscal year** is the specific twelve-month accounting period a business adopts. Many businesses adopt the calendar year, January 1 to December 31, as their fiscal year. Other businesses, however, use fiscal years different from the calendar year such as July 1 to June 30 or October 1 to September 30. The reason a business often cites for adopting a different fiscal year is to match the end of the fiscal year with a slack season.

The preparation of annual financial statements and annual tax returns requires many procedures and significant effort by the employees. For example, in this chapter, we describe how a business must undertake additional accounting procedures to adjust its accounts to prepare formal financial statements. Other procedures also may be required—namely a physical check for the assets that the accounting records indicate the business owns. Therefore, if the end of the fiscal year comes during the business's slack season, the required additional efforts to prepare its annual financial statements can be accommodated more conveniently.

Income Determination and Multiperiod Transactions.   Determining net income for the accounting period, whether it is the annual period or an interim period, is one of the most difficult problems accountants face. Many transactions extend beyond one accounting period. That is, the transaction begins in one accounting period and concludes in a subsequent accounting period. Some transactions may conclude in the next accounting period; other transactions may span several accounting periods.

To determine net income for a period, the accountant must apportion to the appropriate periods the effects of transactions that extend beyond one period.

INSIGHTS INTO ACCOUNTING

The American Institute of CPAs (AICPA) conducts an annual survey of financial reporting practices of 600 large U.S. businesses. For the years 1988 – 91, the businesses had fiscal years ending in months of the year as follows:

	1991	1990	1989	1988
January	21	22	22	20
February	14	15	15	13
March	12	14	16	15
April	7	7	8	7
May	16	16	15	16
June	62	62	57	54
July	16	16	16	14
August	18	17	16	15
September	31	33	37	38
October	21	21	20	22
November	18	17	17	15
December	364	360	361	371
Total	600	600	600	600

Source: *Accounting Trends and Techniques* (AICPA, 1992), p. 30. Reprinted with permission of the American Institute of Certified Public Accountants, Inc.

For example, Charlotte Cruz purchased lights costing $3,000 in February 19X1, that will benefit the business for several years—the estimated time period that the business can use the lights. Since Charlotte will use the lights to earn revenues over several years, we allocate the cost of the lights to the years that her business benefits from the expenditure.

We accomplish the required apportionment of the cost of the lights by the adjustment process that we illustrate later in this chapter. After the adjustment process, the accounts should reflect the revenues earned and the expenses incurred during the period. To accomplish this objective, however, the adjustment process requires the accountant to make certain critical assumptions.

Going-Concern Assumption

An important assumption accountants make is whether the business is a going-concern. The **going-concern assumption** states that, in the absence of evidence to the contrary, we assume that the enterprise will continue to operate as a viable business. The going-concern assumption is the basis of the adjustment process. To apportion the effects of multiperiod transactions to current and future periods, the accountant assumes that the enterprise is a going-concern, even though thousands of businesses fail each year. Of course, the going-concern assumption is not appropriate if evidence is available that the enterprise is about to go out of business.

Accounting for the lights Charlotte Cruz purchased provides an excellent example of the application of the going-concern assumption. At the date of purchase, we record the lights as an asset. As Charlotte uses the lights, a portion of the asset expires and becomes an expense. If we estimate that the lights can be used for 5 years, we apportion the cost of the lights through the adjustment process to the 5-year period as an expense called *depreciation expense*. For example, we might recognize one-fifth of the total cost as an expense in each of the 5 years. But, the process of spreading the cost of the lights over 5 years is appropriate only if the accountant can reasonably assume that the business will continue and, thereby, utilize the lights to earn revenues in all 5 years.

Realization Principle and Revenue Apportionment

Some revenue transactions extend beyond one accounting period. Earlier we discussed that according to the realization principle, we recognize revenue in the period it is earned. Accountants apportion the effects of multiperiod revenue transactions to current and future periods by recognizing revenues in the period they are earned from delivering goods or providing services.

Matching Principle and Expense Apportionment

Some expense transactions, like some revenue transactions, extend beyond one accounting period. Accountants apportion the effects of multiperiod expense transactions to current and future periods by recognizing expenses in the period they are incurred. An expense is incurred in the period that the business uses up its assets or incurs liabilities from delivering goods or providing services in connection with its normal operations.

According to the matching principle, we should recognize expenses in the same period as the related revenues. Some expenses such as sales commissions are related directly to the revenues of a period. We recognize expenses that are related directly to revenues in the same period we recognize the revenues. Other expenses are only indirectly related to revenues, and their recognition involves much approximation. We allocate these expenses such as rent and insurance *to the periods* in which the business benefits from occupancy and insurance coverage.

ADJUSTING ENTRIES

LO 4
Prepare adjusting entries at the end of an accounting period.

The adjustment process requires the accountant to make adjusting entries at the end of an accounting period. **Adjusting entries** are those necessary to adjust the accounts to their proper balances to conform with GAAP for purposes of preparing appropriate financial statements. The adjustment process involves apportioning multiperiod revenues and expenses to the periods in which they are earned and incurred. The need for adjusting entries does not mean that the account balances are in error. All general journal entries to date may be correct, and all transactions may have been posted correctly to the general ledger accounts. We need adjusting entries because some revenues may have been earned but not yet recorded, and some expenses may have been incurred but not yet recorded. Also, some cash receipts may initially be recorded as revenues, but they are not yet earned; and some cash payments may initially be recorded as expenses, but the expenditures may not be expenses of the current period.

The adjusting entries needed at the end of an accounting period are for the following items:

Expiration of Prepaid Expenses
Recognition of Depreciation Expense
Accrual of Unpaid Expenses
Recognition of Revenues Previously Unearned
Accrual of Revenues Earned

Using Charlotte's Car Park from previous chapters, we discuss and illustrate adjusting entries for these items. Illustration 3-3 reproduces the trial balance at the end of February 19X1. The account balances reflect the transactions analyzed and recorded previously, but they do not reflect the adjusting entries. A trial balance prepared before posting the adjusting entries, is an **unadjusted trial balance**.

ILLUSTRATION 3-3 Unadjusted Trial Balance

Charlotte's Car Park Trial Balance February 28, 19X1		
	Debits	Credits
Cash	$ 860	
Prepaid Insurance	480	
Land	9,000	
Land Improvements	3,000	
Unearned Revenue		$ 200
Notes Payable		3,000
Charlotte Cruz, Capital		10,000
Charlotte Cruz, Withdrawals	1,000	
Parking Revenue		3,400
Advertising Expense	200	
Maintenance Expense	60	
Wages and Salaries Expense	2,000	
Totals	$16,600	$16,600

Expiration of Prepaid Expenses

Prepaid expenses are those that have been paid but not yet incurred. Examples of prepaid expenses include insurance and rent. When prepaid expenses are for periods beyond one accounting period, we need adjusting entries to apportion the expenses to the periods they are incurred.

Insurance policies cover a future period of time and usually require that the premium be paid in advance. The payment of the premium creates an asset—insurance coverage for the period of the policy—and we record the asset in Prepaid Insurance. As time passes, a portion of the asset expires and becomes insurance expense. At the end of an accounting period, we make an adjusting entry to record the expiration of the prepaid insurance. On February 3, 19X1, Charlotte paid for an insurance policy that provides coverage from the beginning of February 19X1, to the end of January 19X2. The transaction created an asset that we record in Prepaid Insurance in the amount of $480. On February 28, 19X1, we need an adjusting entry to recognize the expiration of one month's prepaid insurance. The amount of the expired insurance is $40 ($480 x 1/12). The adjusting entry is:

Feb. 28	Insurance Expense	40	
	Prepaid Insurance		40
	To record the expiration of prepaid insurance.		

Posting the adjusting entry to the general ledger affects the accounts as follows:

Prepaid Insurance				Insurance Expense	
Feb. 3	480	Feb. 28	40	Feb. 28	40
Bal.	440				

The entry reduces (credits) the asset account, Prepaid Insurance, by the amount of the insurance expense ($40) — which we debit to Insurance Expense.

Depreciation

We recognize an expense, called **depreciation expense**, for expiration of portions of the total lifetime usefulness of certain assets such as land improvements, equipment, and buildings. As time passes, a portion of the usefulness of such an asset expires, due to physical wear and such other forces as eventual obsolescence. Generally, it is not possible to observe the diminishing usefulness of assets on a day-to-day basis. However, management knows that a significant amount will expire during the estimated time that the business will use the assets. The matching principle requires that we apportion the cost of the assets to the accounting periods during the assets' useful lives. Apportioning the cost of an asset involves much estimation. Management must estimate both the useful life of the asset and the pattern of the expiration of the asset's usefulness during its useful life.

At the end of an accounting period, we make an adjusting entry to record the portion of the asset's cost that has expired during the period. The entry is a debit to Depreciation Expense. However, the credit is not made directly to the asset account, as you might have expected. Instead, a credit is made to an account called Accumulated Depreciation. **Accumulated Depreciation** represents the cumulative depreciation of the asset since it was acquired. Accumulated depreciation is a **valuation** (or **contra-asset**) **account** that reduces the asset to its correct balance for presentation in the balance sheet. The balance sheet presentation of these accounts is shown in Illustration 3-4.

We credit Accumulated Depreciation for the amount of current depreciation expense so that the asset's original purchase cost will be preserved in the asset account. The balance in the asset account retains the cost of the *total* service potential purchased when the asset was new. The balance of Accumulated Depreciation represents the cost of the estimated service potential *used up* as of the current balance sheet date. The *net* amount, the difference between the asset account balance and Accumulated Depreciation balance, represents the cost of the asset's estimated *remaining* service potential. You should note that the net amount is *not* the current price of similar service potential. Rather, it is the *original cost* of the asset's unused service potential. The net amount is the

ILLUSTRATION 3-4 Undepreciated Cost of an Asset

Asset Account	Original Cost of the Asset
Less: Accumulated Depreciation	Cumulative Depreciation
Carrying Amount	Undepreciated Cost of Asset

asset's undepreciated cost and is called the *carrying amount, carrying value,* or the *net book value.*

Land Improvements.   Charlotte purchased lights on February 3 at a cost of $3,000. Assume Charlotte estimates that she can use the lights in her business for 5 years. The **useful life of an asset** is the period of time the business estimates it can use the asset in its operations. The expense of using the lights for 1 year is one-fifth of $3,000, or $600. The expense of using the lights for 1 month is one-twelfth of $600, or $50. This separate identity is maintained because each asset conceivably depreciates over a different number of periods according to a different pattern. We discuss the varying patterns of depreciation in a subsequent chapter.

Depreciation Expense—Land Improvements.   Charlotte classifies the lights as land improvements of her business. The depreciation expense for land improvements for February as calculated above is $50. At the end of February, Charlotte should record depreciation expense by making the following adjusting entry:

Feb. 28	Depreciation Expense—Land Improvements	50	
	Accumulated Depreciation—Land Improvements		50
	To record February depreciation.		

After we post the adjusting entry to the general ledger, the accounts will appear as follows:

Land Improvements	
Feb. 3 3,000	

Accumulated Depreciation—Land Improvements		Depreciation Expense—Land Improvements	
	Feb. 28 50	Feb. 28 50	

We include Depreciation Expense—Land Improvements in the income statement that we prepare at the end of February. Land Improvements and the contra-asset account, Accumulated Depreciation—Land Improvements, are shown in the February 28 balance sheet as follows:

Land improvements	$3,000	
Less: Accumulated depreciation	50	$2,950

The balance sheet presentation informs the reader that the service potential of the lights when purchased cost $3,000. This amount gives the users of the financial statements some idea of the lights' total service capacity. The cost of the service potential used up is $50, and the cost of the remaining service potential is $2,950. The latter figure gives the users of the financial statements some idea of the lights' remaining capacity to provide service to the business. In subsequent months, the periodic depreciation continues to accumulate in Accumulated Depreciation—Land Improvements at the rate of $50 per month. Therefore, the carrying amount of the asset declines each month by $50.

Accrued Expenses

As previously discussed, the transactions processing methods in most accounting systems are designed to record expenses at the time they are paid. At the end of an accounting period, some expenses may have been incurred but not recorded because they have not been paid. Incurred but unpaid expenses are called **accrued expenses**. Common examples of accrued expenses include wages and salaries, interest, and utilities.

Wages and Salaries Expense.   On February 28, Charlotte paid her parking lot attendants $1,200 for their services through February 21. Assume that for the period February 22 through February 28, the attendants earned an additional $400. Since these wages are unpaid, they are unrecorded. To prepare financial statements at the end of February, however, we must record the attendants' wages that have been incurred since they were last paid. We record the earned but unpaid wages with the following adjusting entry:

Feb. 28	Wages and Salaries Expense	400	
	Wages and Salaries Payable		400
	To record earned but unpaid wages.		

After we post the adjusting entry to the general ledger, the accounts appear as follows:

Wages and Salaries Expense		Wages and Salaries Payable	
Jan. 31 800			Feb. 28 400
Feb. 28 1,200			
Feb. 28 400			
Bal. 2,400			

The effect of the adjusting entry is to increase Wages and Salaries Expense to $2,400, which is the amount of wages and salaries expense Charlotte actually incurred during January and February. Also, we record Wages and Salaries Payable of $400. Charlotte is obligated to pay this amount as of the end of February because the attendants have worked during February after the date they were last paid.

Interest Expense.   On February 1, Charlotte borrowed $3,000 from the bank to purchase the lights. Recall that the interest rate on the loan is 12% per year. As of the end of February, Charlotte has incurred one month's interest. Even though the interest is not due to be paid until March 1, Charlotte incurs the interest expense in February. The amount of interest expense for February is $30 ($3,000 x 12% x 1/12). We record the interest expense for February with the following adjusting entry:

Feb. 28	Interest Expense	30	
	Interest Payable		30
	To record interest expense for February.		

After posting the entry to the general ledger, the accounts appear as follows:

Interest Expense		Interest Payable	
Feb. 28 30			Feb. 28 30

The adjusting entry records the interest expense for February and the liability (interest payable) to pay the interest to the bank.

Utilities Expense.   At the end of February, Charlotte received a $90 bill from City Electric Company for electricity the lights used during February. The cost of the electricity used during the month is an expense of February that Charlotte should record before preparing financial statements. Charlotte records the cost of electricity in Utilities Expense. The following adjusting entry records the expense and the liability to pay City Electric Company:

Feb. 28	Utilities Expense	90	
	Utilities Payable		90
	To record the cost of electricity for February.		

After posting the entry to the general ledger, the accounts appear as follows:

Utilities Expense		Utilities Payable	
Feb. 28 90			Feb. 28 90

Unearned Revenue

When a business receives a cash payment for goods or services before it delivers the goods or performs the services, we record **unearned revenue**. For example, if you subscribe to a magazine at a cost of $36 per year for 12 monthly issues, you pay the subscription price in advance. The magazine company records your payment as unearned revenue. The revenue is unearned until the magazines are delivered to you. Each month, the company earns one-twelfth of the subscription price when it delivers an issue of the magazine to you. Therefore, each month the company decreases unearned revenue and increases revenues by $3 (1/12 of $36).

Charlotte entered into an agreement with two of her classmates to provide reserved parking for $200 per month, payable in advance. We record the receipt of the payment on February 8 as a debit to Cash and a credit to Unearned Revenue. Remember: Unearned Revenue is a liability account because Charlotte is obligated to provide the parking for the month or refund the advance payment to the customers. As of the end of February, however, Charlotte has earned the parking revenue. Therefore, she recognizes the revenue with the following adjusting entry:

Feb. 28	Unearned Revenue	200	
	Parking Revenue		200
	To record parking revenue earned.		

The $200 is classified properly as revenue because net assets have increased (due to a decrease in liabilities) from the business's revenue-producing activities. After we post the adjusting entry to the general ledger, the accounts appear as follows:

Unearned Revenue		Parking Revenue	
Feb. 28 200	Feb. 8 200		Jan. 31 1,600
			Feb. 28 1,800
			Feb. 28 200
			Bal. 3,600

The adjusting entry decreases Unearned Revenue to reflect the satisfaction of the obligation to provide parking and increases Parking Revenue for the revenue earned under the agreement.

Accrued Revenue

A business sometimes earns revenue before receiving payment from the customer. Under the accrual basis of accounting, we record the revenue because it is earned. At the end of the accounting period, we record an adjusting entry for **accrued revenue**—revenue that the business has earned but not yet received. Also, as part of the adjusting entry, we record an account receivable representing the business's right to receive payment from the customer for the services performed. Examples of accrued revenues include interest earned, rent earned, and many types of revenues for services.

In January, Charlotte entered into an agreement with Campus Bookstore to provide overflow parking for its customers. The monthly fee is $400, payable by the 15th of the following month. As of February 28, Charlotte has earned the revenue for the month of February. To record the revenue, we make the following adjusting entry:

Feb. 28	Accounts Receivable	400	
	Parking Revenue		400
	To record parking revenue earned.		

After the adjusting entry is posted to the general ledger, the accounts appear as follows:

Accounts Receivable					Parking Revenue	
Jan. 31	400	Feb. 4	400		Jan. 31	1,600
Feb. 28	400				Feb. 28	1,800
					Feb. 28	200
					Feb. 28	400
					Bal.	4,000

The adjusting entry increases Accounts Receivable and Parking Revenue by the $400 that Charlotte has earned in February under the agreement with the bookstore.

Summary of Adjustments

One way to think of adjusting entries is: Without them, the business's accounts would be misstated. We present a summary of the adjustment process reflecting this view in Illustration 3-5.

ILLUSTRATION 3-5 Summary of Adjustments

Type	Accounts	Account Balances Without Adjustment	Adjusting Entry
1. Expiration of prepaid expenses	Expenses and Assets	Expenses understated Assets overstated	Dr. Expenses Cr. Assets
2. Depreciation expense	Expenses and Assets	Expenses understated Assets overstated	Dr. Expenses Cr. Accumulated Depreciation
3. Accrued expenses	Expenses and Liabilities	Expenses understated Liabilities understated	Dr. Expenses Cr. Liabilities
4. Previously unearned revenue	Liabilities and Revenues	Liabilities overstated Revenues understated	Dr. Liabilities Cr. Revenues
5. Accrued revenue	Assets and Revenues	Assets understated Revenues understated	Dr. Assets Cr. Revenues

THE ADJUSTED TRIAL BALANCE

A trial balance prepared after posting the adjusting entries is an **adjusted trial balance**. Illustration 3-6 shows the adjusted trial balance for Charlotte's Car Park. If we have correctly posted the adjusting entries, the debits and credits will be equal in the trial balance. Illustration 3-6 shows they are equal.

ILLUSTRATION 3-6 Adjusted Trial Balance

Charlotte's Car Park Trial Balance February 28, 19X1		
	Debits	Credits
Cash	$ 860	
Accounts Receivable	400	
Prepaid Insurance	440	
Land	9,000	
Land Improvements	3,000	
Accumulated Depreciation—Land Improvements		$ 50
Interest Payable		30
Notes Payable		3,000
Utilities Payable		90
Wages and Salaries Payable		400
Charlotte Cruz, Capital		10,000
Charlotte Cruz, Withdrawals	1,000	
Parking Revenue		4,000
Advertising Expense	200	
Depreciation Expense—Land Improvements	50	
Insurance Expense	40	
Interest Expense	30	
Maintenance Expense	60	
Utilities Expense	90	
Wages and Salaries Expense	2,400	
Totals	$17,570	$17,570

LO 5
Prepare financial statements using an adjusted trial balance.

Preparing Financial Statements From the Adjusted Trial Balance

The account balances in the adjusted trial balance conform with GAAP and, therefore, are appropriate for the preparation of financial statements. We can prepare the income statement as shown in Illustration 3-7, by extracting the revenue and expense accounts from the adjusted trial balance. We prepare the statement of owner's equity as shown in Illustration 3-8, by using the owner's capital and withdrawals accounts from the adjusted trial balance and the net income figure from the income statement. Finally, we prepare the balance sheet, as shown in Illustration 3-9, by extracting the balance sheet accounts from the adjusted trial balance and the ending balance for owner's equity from the statement of owner's equity.

A Note About Preparing Financial Statements

As demonstrated in this chapter, accountants may prepare financial statements for relatively simple businesses such as Charlotte's Car Park directly from the

ILLUSTRATION 3-7 Preparation of the Income Statement

Charlotte's Car Park
Trial Balance
February 28, 19X1

	Debits	Credits
Cash	$ 860	
Accounts Receivable	400	
Prepaid Insurance	440	
Land	9,000	
Land Improvements	3,000	
Accumulated Depreciation—Land Improvements		$ 50
Interest Payable		30
Notes Payable		3,000
Utilities Payable		90
Wages and Salaries Payable		400
Charlotte Cruz, Capital		10,000
Charlotte Cruz, Withdrawals	1,000	
Parking Revenue		4,000
Advertising Expense	200	
Depreciation Expense—Land Improvements	50	
Insurance Expense	40	
Interest Expense	30	
Maintenance Expense	60	
Utilities Expense	90	
Wages and Salaries Expense	2,400	
Totals	$17,570	$17,570

Charlotte's Car Park
Income Statement
For the Two Months Ended February 28, 19X1

Parking revenue		$ 4,000
Expenses:		
Advertising expense	$ 200	
Depreciation expense—land improvements	50	
Insurance expense	40	
Interest expense	30	
Maintenance expense	60	
Utilities expense	90	
Wages and salaries expense	2,400	
Total expenses		2,870
Net income		$ 1,130

adjusted trial balance. The preparation of financial statements from the adjusted trial balance requires knowledge of:

1. Which accounts are listed in each financial statement.
2. The format of financial statements.

For more complex businesses, accountants use a worksheet, which we demonstrate in a subsequent chapter.

ILLUSTRATION 3-8 Preparation of the Statement of Owner's Equity

Charlotte's Car Park
Trial Balance
February 28, 19X1

	Debits	Credits
Cash	$ 860	
Accounts Receivable	400	
Prepaid Insurance	440	
Land	9,000	
Land Improvements	3,000	
Accumulated Depreciation—Land Improvements		$ 50
Interest Payable		30
Notes Payable		3,000
Utilities Payable		90
Wages and Salaries Payable		400
Charlotte Cruz, Capital		10,000
Charlotte Cruz, Withdrawals	1,000	
Parking Revenue		4,000
Advertising Expense	200	
Depreciation Expense—Land Improvements	50	
Insurance Expense	40	
Interest Expense	30	
Maintenance Expense	60	
Utilities Expense	90	
Wages and Salaries Expense	2,400	
Totals	$17,570	$17,570

Charlotte's Car Park
Statement of Owner's Equity
For the Two Months Ended February 28, 19X1

Beginning balance	$ 0
Add: Owner's investment	10,000
Net income	1,130
Less: Owner's withdrawals	(1,000)
Ending balance	$10,130

LO 6
Calculate and interpret a
business's profit margin.

PROFITABILITY OF CHARLOTTE'S CAR PARK

Now that Charlotte has prepared her financial statements, just how profitable
was her business during January and February? Her income statement for the
two months shows net income of $1,130. But how does this amount compare to
the profitability of other service businesses? One measure of profitability is the
profit margin. **Profit margin** is the amount of net income as a percent of revenues, or:

Profit Margin = Net Income ÷ Revenues

The profit margin is an indication of the business's ability to generate revenues
that are profitable. For the two-month period, Charlotte's profit margin is 28%

ILLUSTRATION 3-9 Preparation of the Balance Sheet

Charlotte's Car Park
Trial Balance
February 28, 19X1

	Debits	Credits
Cash	$ 860	
Accounts Receivable	400	
Prepaid Insurance	440	
Land	9,000	
Land Improvements	3,000	
Accumulated Depreciation—Land Improvements		$ 50
Interest Payable		30
Notes Payable		3,000
Utilities Payable		90
Wages and Salaries Payable		400
Charlotte Cruz, Capital		10,000
Charlotte Cruz, Withdrawals	1,000	
Parking Revenue		4,000
Advertising Expense	200	
Depreciation Expense—Land Improvements	50	
Insurance Expense	40	
Interest Expense	30	
Maintenance Expense	60	
Utilities Expense	90	
Wages and Salaries Expense	2,400	
Totals	$17,570	$17,570

Charlotte's Car Park
Balance Sheet
February 28, 19X1

Assets		
Cash		$ 860
Accounts receivable		400
Prepaid insurance		440
Land		9,000
Land improvements	$3,000	
Accumulated depreciation	(50)	2,950
Total assets		$13,650
Liabilities and Owner's Equity		
Interest payable		$ 30
Notes payable		3,000
Utilities payable		90
Wages and salaries payable		400
Total liabilities		$ 3,520
Owner's equity		10,130
Total liabilities and owner's equity		$13,650

($1,130 ÷ $4,000). How does a 28% profit margin compare to those of other service businesses? The following data represent the average profit margins of certain service industries for 1992.

Industry	Profit Margin
Advertising agencies	1.9%
Car washes	3.5%
Auto repair	3.7%
Legal services	12.8%
Accounting services	15.4%

Reprinted with permission, copyright Robert Morris Associates 1992.

Compared to other service businesses, Charlotte's Car Park appears to be very profitable. However, one must be careful in interpreting these data. For example, is January—February a typical period? Will the same level of business continue throughout the year? Also, other investors may open parking lots in the area and take away some of Charlotte's business.

SUMMARY

Define accounting net income.   Net income is the excess of revenues over expenses for a period. Net income provides a measure of the business's performance for a period. When a business reports net income in its income statement, it means that the operations have increased the business's net assets.

Distinguish between the cash basis and accrual basis of accounting.   Businesses that use the cash basis of accounting recognize revenues when they receive cash and recognize expenses when they make cash payments. Businesses that use the accrual basis of accounting recognize revenues when they are earned and recognize expenses in the period they are incurred. GAAP requires the use of the accrual basis of accounting for the preparation of financial statements.

Explain the concepts, assumptions, and principles underlying the accrual basis of accounting.   The accrual basis of accounting relies on the principles of revenue realization and expense recognition. Costs that are associated directly with revenues are recognized as expenses in the period that the related revenues are recognized. Costs that are not directly associated with revenues are recognized as expenses in the period that the business benefits from the costs. The accountant relies on the going-concern assumption as well as on assumptions about the useful lives of specific assets in apportioning the effects of multiperiod transactions.

Prepare adjusting entries at the end of the accounting period.   Accountants use adjusting entries to prepare financial statements. Adjusting entries apportion the effects of multiperiod transactions to the proper periods.

Prepare financial statements using an adjusted trial balance.   An adjusted trial balance reflects the debit and credit effects of the adjusting entries; and the resulting adjusted account balances are appropriate for preparing the financial statements. Financial statements may be prepared directly from the adjusted trial balance. The income statement is prepared by using the adjusted revenue and expense accounts. The statement of owner's equity is prepared by using the owner's equity accounts from the adjusted trial balance and net income from the income statement. The balance sheet uses adjusted asset and liability accounts from the adjusted trial balance and owner's equity from the statement of owner's equity.

Calculate and interpret a business's profit margin.   A business's profit margin is the ratio of net income to revenues. The profit margin is an indication of the business's ability to generate revenues that are profitable.

LO 7
Prepare adjusting entries when certain cash transactions are recorded initially as revenues and expenses.

APPENDIX 3-A: UNEARNED REVENUE AND PREPAID EXPENSES INITIALLY RECORDED AS REVENUES AND EXPENSES

The discussion of payments for services received before rendering them showed that a business initially records such payments as liabilities—Unearned Revenue. Similarly, when a business makes payments for expenses before incurring them, it initially records the payments as assets—Prepaid Expenses. When revenues are earned and expenses are incurred, a business records adjusting entries to recognize them. However, some businesses find it more convenient to reverse the order of recording because most revenues are earned and most expenses are incurred by the end of the accounting period. Therefore, they first record all such cash transactions as revenues or expenses. Then, they make adjustments at the end of the period to recognize the remaining liability and asset amounts as of that time.

UNEARNED REVENUE

Consider the case of Southeastern Computing Services. Assume that on January 24, 19X1, Southeastern received $2,400 in advance for one month's computing services. Under the method used in the chapter, Southeastern would initially record the payment in a liability account as follows:

Jan. 24	Cash	2,400	
	Unearned Revenue		2,400
	Receipt of advance payment for computing agreement.		

On January 31, we record the following adjusting entry to recognize that one-fourth of the services have been performed:

Jan. 31	Unearned Revenue	600	
	Revenue		600
	To record computing revenue earned.		

Assume instead that Southeastern initially records the receipt as revenue with the following entry:

Jan. 24	Cash	2,400	
	Revenue		2,400
	To record receipt of cash for computing services.		

At the end of the January accounting period, the following relationships indicate the need for adjustment:

1. Revenues are overstated by $1,800 ($2,400 – $600).
2. Liabilities are understated by $1,800.

Therefore, on January 31, we record the following adjusting entry:

Jan. 31	Revenue	1,800	
	Unearned Revenue		1,800
	To adjust Revenue for unearned revenue.		

The ultimate effects of the two alternative treatments are identical, as illustrated with T-accounts below. These T-accounts reflect the effects of only the one transaction.

Initial recording as a liability:

Revenue		Unearned Revenue	
Jan. 31 600 ◄───		Jan. 31 600	Jan. 24 2,400
			Bal. 1,800

Initial recording as a revenue:

Revenue		Unearned Revenue	
Jan. 31 1,800	Jan. 24 2,400		Jan. 31 1,800
	Bal. 600		

Notice that in both cases, after adjustment, the balance of Revenue is $600 and the balance of Unearned Revenue is $1,800.

PREPAID EXPENSES

On January 2, 19X1, Southeastern paid $12,000 in advance for rent for 19X1. Under the method used in the chapter, Southeastern would record the following entry:

Jan. 2	Prepaid Rent	12,000	
	Cash		12,000
	Payment in advance for 19X1 rent.		

On January 31, $1,000 ($12,000 ÷ 12) of the prepaid rent has expired; and we record the following entry to recognize the partial expiration of the asset prepaid rent:

Jan. 31	Rent Expense	1,000	
	Prepaid Rent		1,000
	To record rent for January.		

Assume instead that Southeastern initially records the prepaid rent as an expense with the following entry:

Jan. 2	Rent Expense	12,000	
	Cash		12,000
	To record rent expense.		

At the end of the January accounting period, the following relationships indicate the need for adjustment:

1. Expenses are overstated by $11,000 ($12,000 – $1,000).
2. Assets are understated by $11,000.

Therefore, on January 31, the following adjusting entry is required:

Jan. 31	Prepaid Rent	11,000	
	Rent Expense		11,000
	To record unexpired rent.		

The ultimate effects of the two alternative treatments are identical, illustrated with T-accounts. Notice that in both cases, after adjustment, the balance of Prepaid Rent is $11,000 and the balance of Rent Expense is $1,000.

Initial recording as an asset:

Prepaid Rent		Rent Expense	
Jan. 2 12,000	Jan. 31 1,000 ⟶	Jan. 31 1,000	
Bal. 11,000			

Initial recording as an expense:

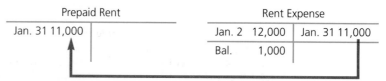

Prepaid Rent		Rent Expense	
Jan. 31 11,000		Jan. 2 12,000	Jan. 31 11,000
		Bal. 1,000	

REVIEW PROBLEM

Jack Ford organized Wildwater Expeditions several years ago to provide raft trips down the Big South Fork of the Cumberland River. Wildwater has an annual accounting period based on the calendar year. Jack Ford provides the unadjusted trial balance and additional information shown on the next page.

Additional Information:

1. The balance in Prepaid Insurance is the result of a comprehensive river liability policy that was purchased on April 1, 19X3. The policy cost $2,400 and covers the period of April 1, 19X3, through March 31, 19X4.
2. The equipment, purchased on January 1, 19X1, consists of 25 Northwest River Supply Scout Rafts at a cost of $2,000 each. These rafts have an estimated life of 5 years and are estimated to be worthless at the end of the 5-year period.
3. Wildwater records walk-in trip ticket sales (which result from customers purchasing trip tickets on the days of the trip) by crediting Fee Revenue. Most of its business, however, consists of trips booked and paid for in advance. Advance bookings are recorded with a credit to Unearned Fees. Unearned Fees is adjusted at the end of the accounting year based on the amount of advance booking customers that have

Wildwater Expeditions **Trial Balance** **December 31, 19X3**		
	Debits	*Credits*
Cash	$ 6,500	
Accounts Receivable	4,500	
Prepaid Insurance	2,400	
Office Supplies	500	
Equipment	50,000	
Accumulated Depreciation–Equipment		$ 20,000
Accounts Payable		3,000
Unearned Fees		80,000
Ford, Capital		14,400
Ford, Withdrawals	25,000	
Fee Revenue		32,000
Miscellaneous Expense	4,000	
Rent Expense	15,000	
Utilities Expense	1,500	
Wages and Salaries Expense	40,000	
	$149,400	$149,400

completed the raft trip. On December 31, $65,000 of the $80,000 advance booking revenue is earned.

4. Wildwater rents paddles, helmets, and wetsuits from Whitewater Sales and Service. The bill for December rentals is $1,500 and is due January 31, 19X4.

5. Office supplies on hand on December 31 total $200.

REQUIRED:

a. Prepare the necessary adjusting entries.
b. Prepare an adjusted trial balance.
c. Prepare an income statement, a statement of owner's equity, and a balance sheet for Wildwater as of December 31, 19X3.
d. Calculate the profit margin for the 19X3 operations and comment on what it tells us about Wildwater.

SOLUTION:

Planning and Organizing Your Work

1. Analyze the information in the problem to determine which accounts require adjustment.
2. Journalize the adjusting entries.
3. Prepare an adjusted trial balance. Make sure the debits equal the credits.
4. Prepare the financial statements.
5. Use the appropriate figures to determine the profit margin from 19X3 operations.

(a) *Prepare adjusting entries.*

Dec. 31	Insurance Expense	1,800	
	Prepaid Insurance		1,800
	To record expired insurance.		
	($2,400 x 9/12 = $1,800)		
31	Depreciation Expense—Equipment	10,000	
	Accumulated Depreciation–Equipment		10,000
	To record 19X3 depreciation.		
	((25 x $2,000)/5 = $10,000)		

Dec. 31	Unearned Fees	65,000	
	Fee Revenue		65,000
	To record advance booking revenues		
	that have been earned.		
31	Rent Expense	1,500	
	Accounts Payable		1,500
	To accrue rental expense.		
31	Office Supplies Expense	300	
	Office Supplies		300
	To record office supplies used.		

(b) *Prepare an adjusted trial balance.*

Note: A worksheet, presented in a subsequent chapter, will simplify the preparation of an adjusted trial balance. Without the worksheet, two approaches are possible: (1) Use T-accounts and place the balance from the trial balance in the accounts and then "post" the adjusting entries to the accounts and prepare an adjusted trial balance from the resulting account balances. (2) Use an "eyeball" approach, increasing and decreasing the account balances in the trial balance as required by the adjustments and adding account balances as required. The T-account approach is illustrated.

TB = Trial balance
Bal. = Balance
( ) = Adjustment; keyed to "Additional Information"

Cash

| TB | 6,500 | |
| Bal. | 6,500 | |

Accounts Receivable

| TB | 4,500 | |
| Bal. | 4,500 | |

Prepaid Insurance

| TB | 2,400 | (1) | 1,800 |
| Bal. | 600 | | |

Office Supplies

| TB | 500 | (5) | 300 |
| Bal. | 200 | | |

Equipment

| TB | 50,000 | |
| Bal. | 50,000 | |

Accumulated Depreciation— Equipment

		TB	20,000
		(2)	10,000
		Bal.	30,000

Accounts Payable

		TB	3,000
		(4)	1,500
		Bal.	4,500

Unearned Fees

| (3) | 65,000 | TB | 80,000 |
| | | Bal. | 15,000 |

Ford, Capital

| | | TB | 14,400 |
| | | Bal. | 14,400 |

Ford, Withdrawals

| TB | 25,000 | |
| Bal. | 25,000 | |

Fee Revenue

		TB	32,000
		(3)	65,000
		Bal.	97,000

Wages and Salaries Expense

| TB | 40,000 | |
| Bal. | 40,000 | |

Utilities Expense

| TB | 1,500 | |
| Bal. | 1,500 | |

Rent Expense

TB	15,000	
(4)	1,500	
Bal.	16,500	

	Miscellaneous Expense			Insurance Expense
TB	4,000		(1)	1,800
Bal.	4,000		Bal.	1,800

	Depreciation Expense–Equipment			Supplies Expense
(2)	10,000		(5)	300
Bal.	10,000		Bal.	300

Wildwater Expeditions
Adjusted Trial Balance
December 31, 19X3

	Debits	Credits
Cash	$ 6,500	
Accounts Receivable	4,500	
Prepaid Insurance	600	
Office Supplies	200	
Equipment	50,000	
Accumulated Depreciation—Equipment		$ 30,000
Accounts Payable		4,500
Unearned Fees		15,000
Ford, Capital		14,400
Ford, Withdrawals	25,000	
Fee Revenue		97,000
Depreciation Expense—Equipment	10,000	
Insurance Expense	1,800	
Miscellaneous Expense	4,000	
Rent Expense	16,500	
Supplies Expense	300	
Utilities Expense	1,500	
Wages and Salaries Expense	40,000	
Totals	$160,900	$160,900

(c) *Prepare financial statements.*

Wildwater Expeditions
Income Statement
For the Year Ended December 31, 19X3

Fee revenue		$97,000
Expenses:		
Wages and salaries	$40,000	
Rent	16,500	
Depreciation—equipment	10,000	
Insurance	1,800	
Utilities	1,500	
Supplies	300	
Miscellaneous	4,000	
Total expenses		74,100
Net income		$22,900

Wildwater Expeditions Statement of Owner's Equity For the Year Ended December 31, 19X3	
Beginning balance, 1-1-X3	$14,400
Add: Net income	22,900
Less: Owner's withdrawals	(25,000)
Ending balance, 12-31-X3	$12,300

Wildwater Expeditions Balance Sheet December 31, 19X3		
Assets		
Cash		$ 6,500
Accounts receivable		4,500
Prepaid insurance		600
Office supplies		200
Equipment	$50,000	
Accumulated depreciation—equipment	(30,000)	20,000
Total assets		$31,800
Liabilities and Owner's Equity		
Liabilities:		
Accounts payable		$ 4,500
Unearned fees		15,000
Total liabilities		$19,500
Owner's equity		12,300
Total liabilities and owner's equity		$31,800

(d) *Calculate profit margin.*

Profit Margin =   Net Income ÷ Revenues

Profit Margin =   22,900 ÷ 97,000

Profit Margin =   23.61%

Comments: The profit margin indicates that nearly 24 cents of each dollar of revenue is profit. Conversely, we can conclude that 76 cents ($1 – 24 cents) of each dollar of revenue go to cover the expenses of the business. This seems to indicate good profit potential for Wildwater. Better information about the business's operating performance could be obtained by: (1) comparing the margin with past years to identify any trends that may appear and (2) obtaining industry profit margin data from a source such as Robert Morris to learn how Wildwater compares with other businesses providing guided outdoor activities.

KEY TERMS

accounting period, *94*

accrual basis of accounting, *92*

accrued expenses, *100*

accrued revenue, *102*

Accumulated Depreciation, *98*

adjusted trial balance, *103*

adjusting entries, *96*

cash basis of accounting, *92*

depreciation expense, *98*

fiscal year, *94*

going-concern assumption, *95*

interim financial reports, *94*

net income, *90*

net loss, *90*

profit margin, *105*

unadjusted trial balance, *97*

unearned revenue, *101*

useful life of an asset, *99*

valuation account (contra-asset account), *98*

SELF-QUIZ

LO 1 1. The best representation of net income is
  a. An increase in the market value of shares of stock
  b. An increase in the cash balance during the accounting period
  c. Assets minus liabilities
  d. Revenues minus expenses

LO 1 2. The best representation of a net loss is
  a. An excess of liabilities over assets
  b. An excess of expenses over revenues
  c. The total of liabilities at the end of the accounting period
  d. An excess of cash payments over cash receipts

LO 2 3. The best representation of revenue is
  a. The cash collected during an accounting period
  b. The total assets at the end of the accounting period
  c. The excess of cash receipts over cash disbursements during the accounting period
  d. An increase in assets resulting from providing products or services during the accounting period

LO 2 4. Each of the following transactions increases cash, but only one increases revenue. Identify the transaction that increases revenue.
  a. $10,000 is borrowed from the bank.
  b. A $1,000 account receivable is collected.
  c. The owner invests $1,000 in the business.
  d. A service is provided to a customer, and $400 cash is received in payment.

LO 2 5. The best representation of an expense is
  a. A decrease in an asset or increase in a liability caused by the revenue-producing activity of the business
  b. A cash payment made during the accounting period
  c. The payment of liabilities
  d. A withdrawal of cash by the owner of the business

LO 2 6. The accrual basis of accounting
  a. Is considered better than the cash basis of accounting because it is simpler
  b. Recognizes revenue when cash is collected
  c. Is not considered a Generally Accepted Accounting Principle
  d. Recognizes revenue in the accounting period it is earned

LO 2 7. The cash basis of accounting
  a. Is a better accounting method than the accrual basis of accounting because it provides better information about cash
  b. Is not considered a Generally Accepted Accounting Principle
  c. Is a more complex method of accounting than accrual accounting
  d. Usually requires more end-of-period adjustments than accrual accounting

LO 2 8. An employee works in March but is not paid until April. Under the accrual accounting method
  a. We recognize the wage expense in March.
  b. We recognize the wage expense in April.
  c. The wage expense may be recognized in March or April.
  d. We recognize half the wage expense in the month worked (March) and the other half in the month paid (April).

LO 3 9. According to the _____ principle, we should recognize expenses in the same period as the related revenues.

LO 3 10. The _____ assumption states that, in the absence of evidence to the contrary, we assume that the enterprise will continue to operate as a viable business.

LO 3 11. Key terms related to accounting periods and their definitions are presented below. Match the terms with the definitions.
  ___ a. Accounting period
  ___ b. Fiscal year
  ___ c. Calendar year
  ___ d. Interim financial reports

(1) The specific 12-month accounting period a business adopts

(2) The most popular accounting period

(3) Financial statements provided for periods shorter than a year

(4) The period of time for which we determine net income

LO 4   12. Adjusting entries

   a. Indicate the account balances are in error and corrections must be made

   b. Are often made because some revenues earned have not been recorded and some expenses incurred have not been recorded

   c. Are needed only if the trial balance is out of balance

   d. Are normally made at the beginning of the accounting period

LO 4   13. Key terms and their definitions are listed below. Match the definitions with the key terms.

   ___ a. Depreciation expense

   ___ b. Accumulated depreciation

   ___ c. Prepaid expense

   ___ d. Adjusting entries

   ___ e. Accrued expenses

   ___ f. Unearned revenue

   ___ g. Accrued revenue

   ___ h. Adjusted trial balance

   ___ i. Unadjusted trial balance

(1) Entries made at the end of the accounting period to record unrecorded expenses and revenues

(2) An expense that has been paid but not yet incurred

(3) Expenses recognized for the expiration of portions of the total lifetime usefulness of long-term assets

(4) Expenses that are incurred but unpaid

(5) Trial balance taken at the end of the accounting period prior to recording adjusting entries

(6) Revenue that the business has earned but not yet received

(7) Trial balance used to prepare the financial statements

(8) Account credited when a business receives cash payment for goods or services before it delivers or performs them

(9) Account representing the asset's cumulative depreciation since it was acquired

LO 4   14. Five types of adjusting entries are described below. Match the adjusting entry with the description.

   ___ a. Expiration of prepaid expenses

   ___ b. Recognition of depreciation expense

   ___ c. Accrual of unpaid expenses

   ___ d. Recognition of revenue previously unearned

   ___ e. Accrual of revenues earned

(1) Insurance Expense   XX

      Prepaid Insurance   XX

(2) Accounts Receivable   XX

      Revenue   XX

(3) Utilities Expense   XX

      Accounts Payable   XX

(4) Unearned Revenue   XX

      Revenue   XX

(5) Depr. Exp.—Equip.   XX

      Accum. Depr.—Equip.   XX

LO 6   15. _____ is calculated by dividing net income by revenues.

LO 5   16. Financial statements are prepared from an adjusted trial balance. Each account in the adjusted trial balance will appear on the income statement or on the balance sheet.

   a. Identify the types of accounts that appear on the income statement. _____ _____

   b. Identify the types of accounts that appear on the balance sheet. _____, _____ , and _____

LO 4   17. The accounting year begins with a $375 balance in Office Supplies. During the year, we purchase supplies costing $600, debiting the supplies account. At the end of the year, an inventory is taken, and supplies costing $100 are on hand. Prepare the adjusting entry at the end of the year to record the supplies used.

LO 4   18. On December 1, 19X3, we rent an empty warehouse to another company for the 6-month period beginning December 1 and ending May 31. We receive the entire $200 per month rent in advance and record the transaction by debiting Cash and crediting Unearned Rent Revenue for $1,200. Prepare the necessary adjusting entry on December 31, 19X3, the end of our accounting year.

LO 7   19. (Appendix 3-A) On December 1, 19X3, we rent an empty warehouse to another company for the 6-month period beginning December 1 and ending May 31. We receive the entire $200 per month rent in advance and record the transaction by debiting Cash and crediting Rent Revenue for $1,200. Prepare the necessary adjusting entry on December 31, 19X3, the end of our accounting year.

LO 7   20. (Appendix 3-A) During our first year of operations, we purchase $600 of supplies, debiting Supplies Expense. At the end of the year, an inventory count determines that $100 of supplies are on hand. Prepare the adjusting entry at the end of the year to record the supplies used.

SOLUTIONS TO SELF-QUIZ
1. d   2. b   3. d   4. d   5. a   6. d   7. b   8. a   9. matching   10. going-concern   11. a. 4 b. 1
c. 2 d. 3   12. b   13. c i b a d h f g e   14. a e c d b   15. Profit margin   16. a. expenses and revenues
b. assets, liabilities, and owner's equity

17. Office Supplies Expense	875	
Office Supplies		875
18. Unearned Revenue	200	
Rent Revenue		200
19. Rent Revenue	1,000	
Unearned Revenue		1,000
20. Office Supplies	100	
Office Supplies Expense		100

QUESTIONS

Q3-1   Revenues are defined as the increase in net assets that result from providing products or services to customers. Does this mean that Revenue is an asset account? Explain.

Q3-2   A transaction that results in recording revenue affects the income statement. Does this transaction also affect the balance sheet? Explain.

Q3-3   A transaction that results in recording an expense affects the income statement. Does this transaction also affect the balance sheet? Explain.

Q3-4   Revenues increase net assets; expenses decrease net assets. Distinguish between net assets and total assets and restate the accounting equation to emphasize the concept of net assets better.

Q3-5   Comment on the following statement made by a business owner: "Revenues are down this accounting period, and I am worried about the income statement....Guess I'll have to contribute some cash to keep net income from falling below last year's level."

Q3-6   Describe an accounting entry that recognizes an expense without decreasing an asset.

Q3-7   Describe an accounting entry that recognizes revenue without increasing assets.

Q3-8   Describe an accounting entry that involves receipt of cash from a customer for services performed but does not involve the recognition of revenue.

Q3-9   Comment on the following statement made by a loan officer at Citizens Trust Bank: "Sure, their financial statements look OK; but they are on the cash basis, and this worries me....If they want money from us, they will have to produce accrual basis statements."

Q3-10 Comment on the following statement made by a business owner: "Look, these accrual accounting numbers are OK if you want something to play around with; but for my money, accrual basis accounting is just so much mumbo jumbo....Cash is what is important, and I want my income statements prepared on a cash basis."

Q3-11 Explain the basic difference in revenue recognition under the cash and accrual bases of accounting. Which method provides the best indication of a company's economic performance during a specific time period?

Q3-12 Explain the basic difference in expense recognition under the cash and accrual bases of accounting. Which method provides the best indication of a company's economic performance during a specific time period?

Q3-13 A company fails to make an adjusting entry to accrue revenue as of the end of the accounting period. Explain the effect this omission will have on the income statement, the statement of owner's equity, and the balance sheet.

Q3-14 Why might a company choose to have its accounting year different from the calendar year?

Q3-15 Comment on the following statement made by a business owner: "The accountants complain about all the work involved in adjusting entries at the end of the monthly accounting period, and I'm tired of hearing it....I say if they keep the books up-to-date during the month like they are supposed to, they wouldn't have all this adjustment stuff to do at the end of the month."

Q3-16   (Appendix 3-A) Company A records the purchase of supplies by debiting the asset Supplies. Company B records the same transaction by debiting Supplies Expense. Which company is correct? Explain.

EXERCISES

LO 1

E3-1   Accounting Net Income   Determine net income from the following information:

Revenues	$100,000
Owner withdrawals	30,000
Cash borrowed from bank	10,000
Owner contributions	50,000
Payment of liabilities	5,000
Expenses	80,000

LO 1,2,3

E3-2   Revenue Recognition   Assuming the accrual basis of accounting, indicate the amount of revenue earned in each of the following transactions during the month of March for the Quick Computer Repair Shop:

a. March 1 — Quick Computer signs a contract with Fast Tax Incorporated to provide on-call service for Fast's computers during the month of April. The fee is $2,500, and Quick collects $500 in advance on March 1.

b. March 7 — Quick replaces the defective hard drive in George Smith's computer and bills Smith $418. The account is due April 7.

c. March 10 — Quick collects a $750 account from Hardwood University for services performed in February.

d. March 25 — Allen Enterprises brings in a PC and leaves it with Quick to be repaired.

e. March 31 — Quick bills the City School System $500 for the month of March, as provided in their monthly service contract, which requires Quick to be on-call for service. There were no service calls in March.

LO 2

E3-3   Revenue Recognition   Referring to Quick's transactions in E3-2 above, indicate the revenue that Quick would recognize for each transaction during the month of March, assuming the cash basis of accounting.

LO 1,2,3

E3-4   Expense Recognition   Applying the accrual basis of accounting, indicate for each transaction the amount of expense that would be recognized on the date the transaction occurs for Slow Joe's Shoe Repair Shop.

a. May 1 — Slow purchases a heavy-duty sewing machine for $3,000 cash.

b. May 10 — Slow purchases $900 of repair supplies on account. The supplies are expected to be used over the next few months.

c. May 15 — Slow pays the utilities bill for the month of April, $190.

d. May 25 — Slow places an advertisement in the *City News*. The ad will appear twice in May and 3 times in June. Slow pays the $250 fee in cash.

e. May 31 — Slow receives a utility bill for the month of May for $175. The bill is due June 30.

LO 2

E3-5   Expense Recognition   Referring to Slow's transactions in E3-4 above, indicate the expenses that Slow would recognize on the date each transaction occurs, assuming the cash basis of accounting.

LO 4 **E3-6** **Adjusting Entries**   The balance of Cleaning Supplies at the end of the accounting period is $815. An inventory count indicates cleaning supplies costing $276 are on hand at the end of the accounting period.

REQUIRED:

Prepare the necessary adjusting entry.

LO 4 **E3-7** **Adjusting Entries**   Northern Airlines has a balance in Unearned Revenue of $385,000 at the end of the accounting period. Cancelled ticket information indicates that $175,000 of this $385,000 has been earned.

REQUIRED:

Prepare the necessary adjusting entry.

LO 4 **E3-8** **Adjusting Entries**   The only employee of White Company, Helen Gibson, earns $100 per day and works a 5-day week, Monday through Friday. Helen is paid every Friday for the work of that week. The last payday of the accounting period ending December 31, 19X3, is on Friday, December 27. Helen works Monday, December 30, and Tuesday, December 31.

REQUIRED:

a. Prepare the adjusting entry necessary on December 31.
b. Prepare the journal entry on Friday, January 3, 19X4, to record the payment to Helen.

LO 4 **E3-9** **Adjusting Entries**   On September 1, 19X4, Black Company signs a contract with James Farmer requiring Black to manage Farmer's rental cabins for the period from September 1, 19X4, through May 31, 19X5. Black is required to maintain the property in good condition and to provide weekly security inspections. The $450 fee for this service ($50 per month) is collected in advance. Black credits Unearned Fees.

REQUIRED:

Prepare the adjusting entry necessary on December 31, 19X4, Black's year-end.

LO 4 **E3-10** **Adjusting Entries**   On October 1, 19X1, Green River Supply Company purchases a 12-month insurance policy, which provides fire and other protection for the period October 1, 19X1, through September 30, 19X2. The cost of the policy, $1,800, is paid in advance. Green records the transaction by debiting Prepaid Insurance.

REQUIRED:

Prepare the necessary adjusting entry on December 31, 19X1, the end of Green's accounting period.

LO 7 **E3-11** **Adjusting Entries (Appendix 3-A)**   Prepare the adjusting entry for Green River in E3-10, assuming it recorded the purchase of the policy by debiting Insurance Expense.

LO 5,6 **E3-12** **Financial Statements**   The adjusted trial balance for Brown Bag Consulting Company is shown on the next page. Brown Bag prepares financial statements on December 31; the owner made no capital contributions during the year.

Brown Bag Consulting Company
Adjusted Trial Balance
December 31, 19X6

	Debits	Credits
Cash	$ 1,500	
Accounts Receivable	8,000	
Prepaid Insurance	600	
Office Supplies	400	
Equipment	75,000	
Accumulated Depreciation—Equipment		$ 15,000
Accounts Payable		3,000
Notes Payable		25,000
Wages and Salaries Payable		1,000
Unearned Fees		2,000
Robert Brown, Capital		32,400
Robert Brown, Withdrawals	24,000	
Fee Revenue		55,000
Depreciation Expense—Equipment	5,000	
Insurance Expense	1,200	
Miscellaneous Expense	1,200	
Office Supplies Expense	500	
Wages and Salaries Expense	16,000	
Totals	$133,400	$133,400

REQUIRED:

a. Prepare an income statement.
b. Prepare a statement of owner's equity.
c. Prepare a balance sheet.
d. Calculate the profit margin.

PROBLEM SET A

LO 1,2,3,4,5   **P3-1A   Recording and Posting Basic Transactions Including Revenues and Expenses, Adjusting Entries, Preparing Financial Statements, Distinguishing Between Cash and Accrual Basis Income**   Greg Lighthead starts a business on March 1, 19X3. Greg will provide sailboard lessons for a fee. The following events occurred during March:

Mar. 1 Greg deposits $500 cash in a newly opened account, Lighthead Aqua Dimensions.

2 Greg purchases 4 sailboards at $900 each on account. The boards are estimated to have a useful life of 36 months. Greg will depreciate the boards.

2 Greg signs a contract with Island Breeze Resorts to provide instruction to registered Breeze guests for March, April, and May. Greg receives $1,500 per month for the service and collects $4,500 for the 3 months as payment in advance.

3 Greg purchases liability insurance for the 3-month period of March, April, and May. The cost of the policy is $600 and is paid in cash.

15 Greg provides instruction to Joe Green (not a Breeze guest) and bills Joe $75. Payment is due April 15.

25 Greg withdraws $1,000 from the business as a payment to himself for providing instruction for March.

27 Greg places an ad in the *Beach Bulletin* to be run in April and May. The cost is $100 per month, and the amount for the 2 months is paid in full.

Use the following accounts:

	Acct. No.
Cash	100
Accounts Receivable	110
Prepaid Insurance	150
Prepaid Advertising	154
Equipment	230
Accumulated Depreciation–Equipment	231
Accounts Payable	302
Unearned Fees	340
Lighthead, Capital	500
Lighthead, Withdrawals	502
Fee Revenue	604
Depreciation Expense-Equipment	712
Insurance Expense	728

REQUIRED:

a. Prepare journal entries to record the transactions, using accrual basis accounting.
b. Post the transactions to the general ledger. Use T-accounts.
c. Prepare the necessary adjusting entries required at the end of March. Greg has a monthly accounting period.
d. Post the adjusting entries to the T-accounts in the general ledger.
e. Prepare an adjusted trial balance.
f. Prepare an income statement for March.
g. Prepare a statement of owner's equity for March.
h. Prepare a balance sheet as of March 31.
i. Review the transactions and prepare an income statement, using cash basis accounting. Compare the cash basis and accrual basis income statements and explain which one provides a better picture of Lighthead's operating performance for March.

LO 4   **P3-2A   Adjusting Entries**   Following is a transaction requiring an adjusting entry:

On July 1, 19X7, the Tellico Development Company rented the 29th and 30th floors of the Cumberland Building for the 12-month period July 1, 19X7, through June 30, 19X8. The fee of $192,000 ($16,000 per month) is paid in advance.

REQUIRED:

a. Prepare the necessary adjusting entry on the books of Tellico, assuming: (1) it recorded the transaction with a debit to Prepaid Rent, and (2) Tellico's accounting period ends on September 30, 19X7.
b. Prepare the necessary adjusting entry on the books of Cumberland, assuming   it recorded the transaction with a credit to Unearned Revenue, and Cumberland's accounting period ends December 31, 19X7.

LO 1,2,3,4,5   **P3-3A   Recording and Posting Basic Transactions Including Revenues and Expenses, Adjusting Entries, Preparing Financial Statements, Distinguishing Between Cash and Accrual Basis Income**   In 19X3, Ralph Carson resigned from the FBI to establish a business offering security and intelligence gathering services to the corporate community. The following events occurred during the first month of operations:

May 1   Ralph deposits $35,000 in a checking account opened in the name of the business, North American Security and Intelligence (NASI).

     1   Ralph purchases electronic surveillance and monitoring equipment for $270,000. A cash down payment of $25,000 is made and a $245,000 note payable due in 3 years is given to the vendor. Interest of 12% is payable at the end of each year. The equipment has an expected useful life of 4 years,

after which time Ralph expects it to be obsolete. Ralph will depreciate the equipment over its 4-year life.

May 3 Ralph leases a Mini-Storage warehouse to store the equipment. The warehouse is leased for 6 months at a cost of $50 per month. The first month's rent (pro-rated to $46 for May) and the last month's rent are paid in advance. Record the payment by debiting Prepaid Rent.

4 Ralph arranges to lease a van on a monthly basis, at a cost of $400 per month. Rent for May 4 through May 31 ($348) is paid.

5 Ralph leases an office from TurnKey Business Services, which includes telephone service and other office support services at a cost of $750 per month. Ralph pays the first 3 months in advance, including a full month's rent for May.

14 Ralph signs a contract with Global Defense Systems to compile intelligence information on individuals who are assigned to Global's classified Lone Wolf project. For this service, Ralph is to receive $1,000 per day. The contract starts May 15 and terminates on December 15. Global has the option to renew the contract for up to an additional 7 months. Contractual arrangements call for Global to pay each month's fees on the 15th day of the following month. For example, the fee for May (17 days at $1,000 per day) is payable on June 15.

15 Ralph hires 3 employees, all with extensive security and intelligence backgrounds, to work with him in the Global contract.

Use the following accounts:

	Acct. No.
Cash	100
Accounts Receivable	110
Prepaid Rent	152
Equipment	230
Accumulated Depreciation—Equipment	231
Interest Payable	318
Wages and Salaries Payable	346
Notes Payable—Noncurrent	408
Carson, Capital	500
Fee Revenue	604
Depreciation Expense—Equipment	710
Interest Expense	730
Rent Expense	762
Wages and Salaries Expense	784

REQUIRED:

a. Prepare journal entries to record the transactions, using accrual basis accounting.
b. Post the transactions to the general ledger. Use T-accounts.
c. Prepare the necessary adjusting entries required at the end of the month. Ralph has a monthly accounting period. Salaries earned but unpaid for the 3 employees for May total $4,000.
d. Post the adjusting entries to the T-accounts in the general ledger.
e. Prepare an adjusted trial balance.
f. Prepare an income statement for May.
g. Prepare a statement of owner's equity for May.
h. Prepare a balance sheet as of May 31.
i. Review the transactions and prepare an income statement, using cash basis accounting. Compare the cash basis and accrual basis income statements and explain which one provides a better picture of NASI's operating performance for May.

LO 4,5,6   **P3-4A**   **Preparing Adjusting Entries, Preparing Financial Statements Using an Adjusted Trial Balance**   Presented on the next page is a trial balance for Lynn's Window Cleaning Service for June 30, 19X8. Lynn prepares financial statements each month.

Lynn's Window Cleaning Service Unadjusted Trial Balance June 30, 19X8		
	Debits	*Credits*
Cash	$ 14,000	
Accounts Receivable	40,000	
Cleaning Supplies	6,000	
Prepaid Insurance	3,000	
Prepaid Rent	2,000	
Equipment	90,000	
Accumulated Depreciation–Equipment		$ 18,000
Office Equipment	24,000	
Accumulated Depreciation–Office Equipment		6,000
Unearned Revenue		5,000
Accounts Payable		41,000
Lynn Lance, Capital		94,000
Lynn Lance, Withdrawals	3,000	
Revenue		60,000
Advertising Expense	400	
Professional Fees Expense	1,000	
Telephone Expense	350	
Utilities Expense	250	
Wages and Salaries Expense	40,000	
Totals	$224,000	$224,000

Information for adjusting entries as of June 30, 19X8 follows:

(1) Windows cleaned in June but not billed, $4,000.
(2) The $5,000 balance in Unearned Revenue represents an advance payment by Capital Enterprises received on June 1, 19X8, for the cleaning of 500 windows facing Broadway on the north side of Capital's office building. Lynn's foreman tells her "about 300" of these windows have been cleaned.
(3) Lynn charges the asset account, Cleaning Supplies, for purchases of the various solvents used in cleaning. An inventory was taken by Lynn's foreman who estimated that there were $2,000 of cleaning supplies on hand at June 30.
(4) On June 1, a $3,000 premium was paid on a comprehensive insurance policy covering the period June 1, 19X8, through November 30, 19X8.
(5) On January 1, 19X8, 9 months' rent, at $500 per month, was paid in advance. The balance in Prepaid Rent represents the prepaid rent remaining at the beginning of the June accounting period.
(6) The equipment is depreciated over its estimated 5-year life.
(7) Office equipment is depreciated over its estimated 10-year life.
(8) Lynn's accounting firm charges $1,000 per month for monthly accounting services, payable at the beginning of the month. In addition to the monthly fee, paid on June 5 for the month of June, the firm advises Lynn that it has accumulated 50 billable hours of work during June on a Tax Court Case involving Lynn's 19X6 business tax returns. The firm's rate is $75 per hour.
(9) Wages owed to employees at June 30, $1,000.

Lynn uses the following accounts:

	Acct. No.
Cash	100
Accounts Receivable	110
Cleaning Supplies	132
Prepaid Insurance	150
Prepaid Rent	152
Equipment	230
Accumulated Depreciation–Equipment	231
Office Equipment	242
Accumulated Depreciation—Office Equipment	243
Accounts Payable	302
Unearned Revenue	342
Wages and Salaries Payable	346
Lynn Lance, Capital	500
Lynn Lance, Withdrawals	502
Revenue	600
Advertising Expense	700
Cleaning Supplies Expense	703
Depreciation Expense–Equipment	712
Depreciation Expense–Office Equipment	716
Insurance Expense	728
Professional Fees Expense	750
Rent Expense	762
Telephone Expense	775
Utilities Expense	780
Wages and Salaries Expense	784

REQUIRED:

a. Create a general ledger by opening T-accounts and entering the June 30 unadjusted balances in the accounts.
b. Prepare adjusting entries. To save time, instead of entering the adjustments in the general journal, which is the proper procedure, enter them directly in the T-accounts. Code each adjustment with the number corresponding to the adjustment information. Add T-accounts as necessary.
c. Prepare an adjusted trial balance as of June 30, 19X8.
d. Prepare an income statement for the month of June.
e. Prepare a statement of owner's equity for the month of June. Assume Lynn made no capital contributions in June.
f. Prepare a balance sheet as of June 30, 19X8.
g. Calculate Lynn's profit margin for June and evaluate the operating performance for June. Discuss what information (that is not given in this problem) you might need to perform the evaluation.

LO 5   **P3-5A**   **Prepare Financial Statements Using an Adjusted Trial Balance**   An adjusted trial balance for the Atlanta Lawn Service is presented on the next page. Atlanta's fiscal year ends December 31.

REQUIRED:

a. Prepare an income statement for the year ended December 31, 19X4.
b. Prepare a statement of owner's equity for the year ended December 31, 19X4. Assume the Capital balance includes a $25,000 investment by Perez during 19X4.
c. Prepare a balance sheet as of December 31, 19X4.

Atlanta Lawn Service
Adjusted Trial Balance
December 31, 19X4

	Debits	Credits
Cash	$ 35,000	
Accounts Receivable	175,000	
Prepaid Insurance	5,000	
Maintenance Supplies	20,000	
Land	30,000	
Buildings	250,000	
Accumulated Depreciation—Buildings		$ 100,000
Equipment	80,000	
Accumulated Depreciation—Equipment		50,000
Delivery Equipment	100,000	
Accumulated Depreciation—Delivery Equipment		60,000
Accounts Payable		30,000
Interest Payable		2,000
Notes Payable		200,000
Unearned Revenue		25,000
Wages and Salaries Payable		4,000
Ramon Perez, Capital		89,000
Ramon Perez, Withdrawals	50,000	
Revenue		900,000
Professional Fees Expense	24,000	
Advertising Expense	30,000	
Depreciation Expense—Buildings	10,000	
Depreciation Expense—Equipment	8,000	
Depreciation Expense—Delivery Equipment	20,000	
Insurance Expense	3,000	
Supplies Expense	200,000	
Miscellaneous Expense	10,000	
Telephone Expense	6,000	
Utilities Expense	4,000	
Wages and Salaries Expense	400,000	
Totals	$1,460,000	$1,460,000

d. Explain why the income statement and statement of owner's equity are dated for a designated period of time (the year) ending on December 31, while the balance sheet is dated for a point in time (December 31).

e. You were asked to prepare the statements in this order: income statement, statement of owner's equity, and balance sheet. Is this order necessary, or could you prepare the balance sheet or statement of owner's equity first? Explain.

LO 7   **P3-6A   Adjusting Entries (Appendix 3-A)**   Four account balances from the December 31, 19X6, general ledger of Executive Miniature Golf are presented on the next page. These accounts have not been adjusted.

	Debits	*Credits*
Maintenance Supplies	– 0 –	
Maintenance Supplies Expense	$17,500	
Unearned Fees		– 0 –
Fee Revenue		$258,000

Dae Sung Lee, the putting pro and owner of Executive, knows you are taking a college accounting course and asks you to help him make adjusting entries for the supplies and revenue accounts. His bookkeeper is out sick, and these accounts are the only ones that have not been adjusted. You make some inquiries and learn that: (1) the supplies inventory on December 31 is "about $5,000" and that (2) $18,000 of the green fees tickets sold have not been presented for play. Dae Sung states that these tickets are typically purchased as gifts and most of them will be used in the spring.

REQUIRED:

a. Prepare the necessary adjusting entry for the supplies.
b. Suppose that Executive charged (debited) Maintenance Supplies when purchasing supplies, instead of its current procedure of charging Maintenance Supplies Expense. Prepare the appropriate adjusting entry on December 31.
c. Prepare the necessary adjusting entry for revenue.
d. Suppose that Executive credits Unearned Fees when collecting cash for green fees tickets. Prepare the appropriate adjusting entry on December 31.
e. Which account would you recommend be debited for the purchase of supplies? Explain. Which account would you recommend be credited for the collection of green fees tickets? Explain.

PROBLEM SET B

LO 1,2,3,4,5   **P3-1B**   **Recording and Posting Basic Transactions Including Revenues and Expenses, Adjusting Entries, Preparing Financial Statements, Distinguishing Between Cash and Accrual Basis Income**   Janet Lopez starts a business on September 1, 19X7. Janet's business will provide automobile driver training. The following events occurred during September:

Sept. 1   Janet opens a checking account in the name of the business, Safeway Driver Training, and deposits $15,000 cash in the account.

1   Janet leases 2 automobiles specially equipped for driver instruction. The cars are leased on a monthly basis, and the rent for each car is $450 per month. Janet pays the first 3 months' rent in advance. Record the transaction with a debit to Prepaid Rent.

1   Janet purchases comprehensive liability insurance for the period September 1, 19X7, through August 31, 19X8. The annual premium, $3,000, is paid on September 1.

2   Janet obtains a probationary license and certification to provide driver training from the state for the period September 1, 19X7, through August 31, 19X8. The annual fee is $600 and is paid in advance on September 2.

3   Janet signs a contract with a local private high school to provide driving instruction for the school's students. There are 50 students involved, and the instruction will be started in September and completed by December. The contract calls for each student to receive 4 hours of hands-on driver training and 2 hours of classroom training. The fee for providing the instruction is $15,000, paid in advance on September 3. (50 students, 6 hrs. each, $50 per hr.)

4   Janet hires 2 driving instructors. Each instructor will be paid a flat rate of $12 per instructional hour.

Sept. 30   Instructors are paid for 100 instructional hours provided during September. (Note: This information is also used to prepare the entry to adjust Unearned Fees in Requirement *c*.)

30   Janet withdraws $2,000 from the business.

Use the following accounts:

	Acct. No.
Cash	100
Prepaid Insurance	150
Prepaid License	151
Prepaid Rent	152
Unearned Fees	340
Lopez, Capital	500
Lopez, Withdrawals	502
Fee Revenue	604
Insurance Expense	728
License Expense	733
Rent Expense	762
Wages and Salaries Expense	784

REQUIRED:

a. Prepare journal entries to record the transactions, using accrual basis accounting.
b. Post the transactions to the general ledger. Use T-accounts.
c. Prepare the necessary adjusting entries required at the end of September.
d. Post the adjusting entries to the T-accounts in the general ledger.
e. Prepare an adjusted trial balance.
f. Prepare an income statement for September.
g. Prepare a statement of owner's equity for September.
h. Prepare a balance sheet as of September 30.
i. Review the transactions and prepare an income statement, using cash basis accounting. Compare the cash basis and accrual basis income statements and explain which one provides a better picture of Safeway Driver Training's operating performance for September.

LO 4   **P3-2B   Adjusting Entries**   Below is a transaction requiring an adjusting entry:

On November 1, 19X2, Ocoee Rafting Adventures (ORA) entered into a contract with Ducktown Protection Services. ORA paid Ducktown $24,000 to provide weekend parking and traffic management on the Ocoee River. The period of the contract is November 1, 19X2, through October 31, 19X3. ORA classifies the parking and traffic management as a general and administrative expense.

REQUIRED:

a. Prepare the necessary adjusting entry on the books of ORA, assuming: (1) it recorded the transaction with a debit to Prepaid Professional Fees and (2) ORA's accounting period ends on December 31, 19X2.
b. Prepare the necessary adjusting entry on the books of Ducktown Protection Services, assuming: (1) it recorded the transaction with a credit to Unearned Fees and (2) Ducktown's accounting period ends on March 31, 19X3.

LO 1,2,3,4,5   **P3-3B   Recording and Posting Basic Transactions Including Revenues and Expenses, Adjusting Entries, Preparing Financial Statements, Distinguishing Between Cash and Accrual Basis of Income**   David Harris establishes a carpet installation and cleaning business. The following events occur during April 19X3, the first month of operations:

Apr. 1 David deposits $6,000 in a newly opened checking account in the name of the business, Reliable Carpet Services.

1 David purchases 2 carpet shampoo machines at a cost of $1,800 each. The machines have an estimated useful life of 3 years. A cash down payment of $100 is made, and the balance is due in 30 days.

1 David leases a van at a rate of $400 per month and pays the first 3 months in advance.

2 David purchases carpet installation tools. The tools cost $2,700 and have an estimated useful life of 3 years. A cash down payment of $800 is paid, and the balance is due in 90 days.

3 David purchases cleaning solvents and supplies on account. The cost is $500, and payment is due in 30 days.

15 During the first 15 days of April, David installed carpet in 2 houses for Executive Home Builders. The $2,500 fee is billed to Executive.

25 David cleaned the carpet of Lynn Bowman and collected the fee in cash, $100.

29 David received $1,500 from Executive Home Builders as a partial payment of the amount owed for the April 1-15 work.

30 David withdrew $1,000 from the business for personal living expenses.

30 David paid the $3,500 balance due on the April 1 purchase of the shampoo machines.

Use the following accounts:

	Acct. No.
Cash	100
Accounts Receivable	110
Cleaning Supplies	132
Prepaid Rent	152
Equipment	230
Accumulated Depreciation—Equipment	231
Accounts Payable	302
Harris, Capital	500
Harris, Withdrawals	502
Revenue	600
Cleaning Supplies Expense	703
Depreciation Expense—Equipment	712
Rent Expense	762

REQUIRED:

a. Prepare journal entries to record the transactions, using accrual basis accounting.
b. Post the transactions to the general ledger. Use T-accounts.
c. Prepare the necessary adjusting entries required at the end of the month. Supplies on hand on April 30 total $100.
d. Post the adjusting entries to the T-accounts in the general ledger.
e. Prepare an adjusted trial balance.
f. Prepare an income statement for the month of April.
g. Prepare a statement of owner's equity for April.
h. Prepare a balance sheet as of April 30, 19X3.
i. Review the transactions and prepare an income statement, using cash basis accounting. Compare the cash basis and accrual basis income statements and explain which one provides a better picture of Reliable's operating performance for April.

LO 4,5   P3-4B   **Preparing Adjusting Entries, Preparing Financial Statements Using an Adjusted Trial Balance**   Presented on the next page is a trial balance for Longview Bicycle Repair for March 31, 19X5. Longview prepares financial statements each month.

Longview Bicycle Repair Unadjusted Trial Balance March 31, 19X5		
	Debits	*Credits*
Cash	$ 1,500	
Accounts Receivable	4,000	
Maintenance Supplies	9,000	
Prepaid Insurance	600	
Prepaid Rent	900	
Equipment	18,000	
Accumulated Depreciation-Equipment		$ 3,000
Unearned Revenue		2,000
Accounts Payable		1,000
Ronnie Dibbs, Capital		25,000
Ronnie Dibbs, Withdrawals	900	
Repairs Revenue		6,000
Miscellaneous Expense	500	
Professional Fees Expense	200	
Telephone Expense	100	
Utilities Expense	300	
Wages and Salaries Expense	1,000	
Totals	$37,000	$37,000

Information for adjusting entries for March 31, 19X5, follows:

(1) Repair work performed in March but not billed, $1,000.
(2) The $2,000 balance in Unearned Revenue represents an advance payment by Smoky Mountain Bike Rentals. The payment was made March 1 and requires Longview to perform routine periodic maintenance on Smoky's rental fleet of mountain bikes for the 10-month period March 1 through December 31. Unearned Revenue, Repairs Revenue
(3) Maintenance supplies inventory on March 31 is $7,000.
(4) On March 1, the premium was paid on a 6-month comprehensive insurance policy covering the period March 1 through August 31.
(5) On March 1, 3 months' rent at $300 per month was paid in advance.
(6) Equipment has an estimated life of 6 years.
(7) Wages owed to employees at March 31, $1,500.

REQUIRED:

a. Create a general ledger by opening T-accounts and entering the March 31 unadjusted balances in the accounts. Add any accounts needed to complete the adjusting entries.
b. Prepare adjusting entries. To save time, instead of entering the adjustments in the general journal, which is the proper procedure, enter them directly in the T-accounts. Code each adjustment with the number corresponding to the adjustment information. Add T-accounts as necessary.
c. Prepare an adjusted trial balance as of March 31, 19X5.
d. Prepare an income statement for the month of March.
e. Prepare a statement of owner's equity for the month of March. Dibbs did not make a capital contribution during March.
f. Prepare a balance sheet as of March 31, 19X5.
g. Calculate Longview's profit margin for March and evaluate Longview's operating performance. Discuss what information (that is not given in this problem) you might need to perform the evaluation.

LO 5

P3-5B   Prepare Financial Statements Using an Adjusted Trial Balance   An adjusted trial balance for Bluegrass Charter Flights is presented below. Bluegrass' fiscal year ends December 31.

Bluegrass Charter Flights Adjusted Trial Balance December 31, 19X9		
	Debits	Credits
Cash	$ 12,000	
Accounts Receivable	18,000	
Office Supplies	1,000	
Prepaid Insurance	10,000	
Equipment	500,000	
Accumulated Depreciation–Equipment		$ 200,000
Office Equipment	25,000	
Accumulated Depreciation–Office Equipment		10,000
Accounts Payable		20,000
Interest Payable		30,000
Notes Payable		100,000
Unearned Fees		20,000
Wages and Salaries Payable		5,000
Sally Porter, Capital		147,000
Sally Porter, Withdrawals	50,000	
Fee Revenue		500,000
Depreciation Expense–Equipment	50,000	
Depreciation Expense–Office Equipment	5,000	
Fuel Expense	100,000	
Insurance Expense	30,000	
Maintenance Expense	50,000	
Miscellaneous Expense	3,000	
Professional Fees Expense	15,000	
Rent Expense	10,000	
Telephone Expense	2,000	
Utilities Expense	1,000	
Wages and Salaries Expense	150,000	
	$1,032,000	$1,032,000

REQUIRED:

a. Prepare an income statement for the year ended December 31, 19X9.
b. Prepare a statement of owner's equity for the year ended December 31, 19X9. There were no owner investments during the year.
c. Prepare a balance sheet as of December 31, 19X9.
d. Explain why the income statement and statement of owner's equity are dated for a designated period of time (the year) ending December 31, while the balance sheet is for a point in time (December 31).
e. You were asked to prepare the statements in this order: income statement, statement of owner's equity, and balance sheet. Is this order necessary, or could you prepare the balance sheet or statement of owner's equity first? Explain.

LO 7

P3-6B   Adjusting Entries (Appendix 3-A)   Four account balances from the December 31, 19X2, general ledger of Glendale Salvage and Demolition are presented on the next page. These accounts have not been adjusted.

	Debits	*Credits*
Prepaid Insurance	– 0 –	
Insurance Expense	$24,000	
Unearned Fees		– 0 –
Fee Revenue		$600,000

Mike Steel, the owner, asks you to help him adjust the insurance and fees accounts. You learn that the balance in Insurance Expense is from the payment of the premium for a 2-year liability policy covering the period October 1, 19X2, through September 30, 19X4. Included in the balance of Fee Revenue is an entry for recording the advance payment of $100,000 to demolish a warehouse the state condemned because of asbestos standards. Mike expects the demolition to take place in March 19X4. All other demolition fees have been earned.

REQUIRED:

a. Prepare the necessary adjusting entry for the insurance.
b. Suppose that Glendale charged (debited) Prepaid Insurance when recording the premium payment, instead of its current practice of debiting Insurance Expense. Prepare the appropriate adjusting entry on December 31.
c. Prepare the necessary adjusting entry for the fee accounts.
d. Suppose that Glendale credits Unearned Fees when collecting demolition fees. Prepare the appropriate adjusting entry for December 31.

CRITICAL THINKING AND COMMUNICATING

C3-1   Using Generally Accepted Accounting Principles, which requires accrual accounting, Feldon Company reported a quarterly loss in excess of $1 million for the first quarter of 19X5.

REQUIRED:

a. Does this indicate that Feldon's cash disbursements exceeded cash receipts by $1 million during the first quarter? Discuss.
b. Assuming Feldon had no contributions from the owner during the first quarter and there were no withdrawals during this period, what impact will this loss have on Feldon's capital? Discuss.
c. Does this loss indicate that Feldon was unable to pay its bills during the first quarter? Would a creditor be willing to loan Feldon money, after the reporting of the loss? Discuss.
d. How will this loss impact Feldon's balance sheet? Discuss.
e. Is it possible that Feldon could have shown a net income under cash basis accounting for the first quarter? Discuss.

C3-2   You have been employed as the chief accountant of the Dellwood Property Management Company for about 1 year. Sandra Dellwood owns and manages the company. You have a good professional relationship with Sandra, a liberal arts major in college who has not had a course in accounting; and she has come to trust your judgment in financial matters related to the company's operations.

A month ago, Sandra signed a $30,000 contract with the Bridgetown Apartments to manage a 250-unit complex. The contract is for 6 months, starting on December 1 and concluding on May 31, calling for a $5,000 per month management fee for the 6-month period. Dellwood's responsibility is to collect monthly rents, arrange for vacant apartments to be cleaned, and rent vacant apartments. The $30,000 was paid to Dellwood in advance on December 1. You recorded the receipt by debiting Cash and crediting Unearned Fees. You are now in the process of preparing financial statements for the year ended December 31 and have submitted your proposed adjusting entries to Sandra for her review. Included in your adjusting entries is an entry debiting Unearned Fees and crediting Fee Revenue for $5,000.

Sandra returns your adjustments with a note requesting you to recognize the entire $30,000 as earned. You meet with her to discuss the request, and she says: "We have the money; we won't have to refund it; so, we may as well recognize it as income. It will improve our income statement and balance sheet, and I'm applying for a loan at the bank. The loan officer, William O'Day, is an old friend and has already approved the loan. However, he suggested that we go ahead and classify the contract as income because we have the cash, and he is confident that we won't have to give it back. The improved financial statements will ensure that the senior vice-president on the bank's loan board won't question the loan."

REQUIRED:

a. Explain the effect that Sandra's reclassification suggestion would have on the income statement, the statement of owner's equity, and the balance sheet.
b. How would you, as the chief accountant, respond to Sandra's suggestion?

CHAPTER 4

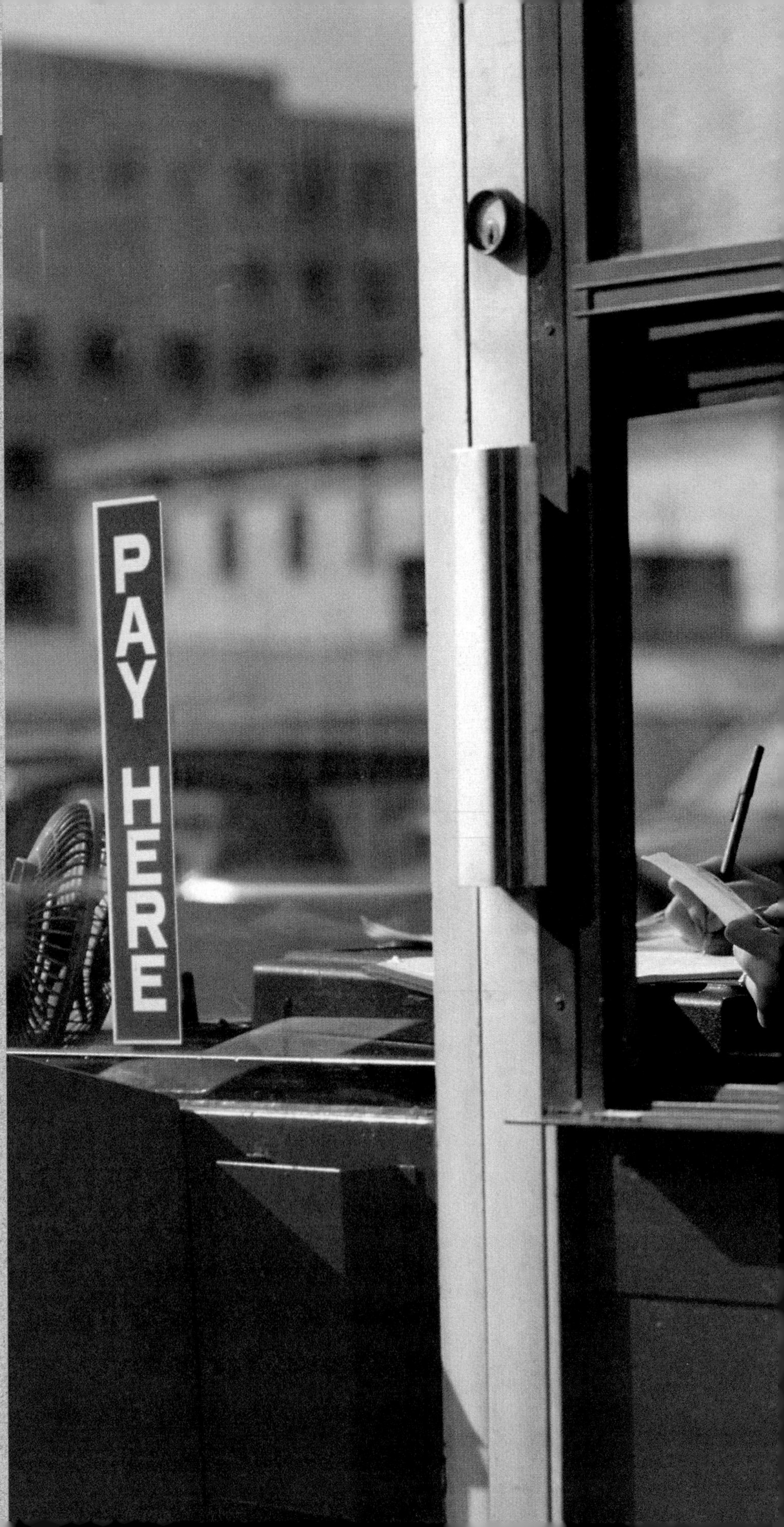

Worksheets, Closing Entries, and Preparing Financial Statements

Charlotte Cruz is so pleased with the profitability of her Car Park that she still considers investing in another parking lot on the opposite side of campus. If she acquires the second lot, she knows she will have to finance the purchase with a loan. To get a loan, she will have to apply for one at a bank. To analyze her ability to pay interest and to repay the loan on the scheduled payment dates, the bank will require her to submit financial statements. Charlotte wonders how the bank uses the financial statements to assess her ability to make the required payments on time.

This chapter continues the discussion of the accountant's procedures at the end of an accounting period. The adjustment process, discussed previously, involves adjusting the accounts to their correct balances at the end of the period to prepare financial statements. You will see how accountants use a worksheet in the adjustment process and in preparing financial statements. Also, we discuss in this chapter the additional end-of-period procedures that are necessary to complete the accounting cycle. These procedures involve closing the owner's withdrawals, revenue, and expense accounts to begin the accounting cycle for the next accounting period. Finally, we discuss how creditors such as banks assess the borrower's debt-paying ability by using the current ratio.

1. Complete the accountant's worksheet and prepare financial statements using the worksheet.
2. Journalize and post the adjusting entries from the information in the completed worksheet.
3. Explain the closing process and prepare closing entries.
4. Prepare a post-closing trial balance.
5. Describe the timing of the various steps in the accounting cycle.
6. Describe the significant groupings of a classified balance sheet.
7. Calculate and interpret the current ratio.
8. Explain how reversing entries are used for certain adjusting entries (Appendix 4-A).

LO 1

Complete the accountant's worksheet and prepare financial statements using the worksheet.

THE ACCOUNTANT'S WORKSHEET

A worksheet, as shown in Illustration 4-1, is a tool accountants use at the end of an accounting period to prepare financial statements; it is *not* a formal part of the accounting records. The worksheet begins with the unadjusted trial balance, then adjusting entries, and then extensions of the amounts to an adjusted trial balance. Finally, the worksheet includes Income Statement and Balance Sheet columns. Using these columns, accountants can prepare these two financial statements. Using the worksheet to prepare financial statements is not only more convenient than preparing them from an adjusted trial balance, but it also minimizes the chances of errors in the end-of-period procedures. In fact, accountants generally prepare adjusting entries on the worksheet *and then journalize and post the entries* to the general journal and general ledger after completing the worksheet.

Procedures for Preparing the Worksheet

The worksheet format presented in Illustration 4-1 has 11 columns. The first column, starting from the left, is for listing account titles. The next five pairs of columns are for entering monetary amounts. Each pair of columns has a left column Dr. (debits) and a right column Cr. (credits). The sequence of procedures below for preparing the worksheet are demonstrated in the overlay Illustrations 4-2 through 4-5.

1. Prepare the unadjusted trial balance in Illustration 4-2 by entering all general ledger account titles in the first column. Then, enter the unadjusted account balances in the first pair of monetary columns, Trial Balance. The trial balance is the same as the one you saw previously for Charlotte's Car Park, except that accounts with zero balances are also listed here. After entering all account balances, check the equality of debits and credits to make sure the account balances have equal debits and credits and that the balances are entered correctly in the worksheet.
2. Next, prepare adjusting entries as in overlay Illustration 4-3 by entering the adjustments (same as you saw previously) in the second pair of monetary columns, Adjustments. In the column with each part of an adjusting entry is a letter reference enclosed in parentheses. These references allow you to match the debit and credit parts of each adjusting

ILLUSTRATION 4-1 Format of a Worksheet for the Financial Statements

(WORKSHEET HEADING)

ACCOUNTS	TRIAL BALANCE		ADJUSTMENTS		ADJUSTED TRIAL BALANCE		INCOME STATEMENT		BALANCE SHEET	
	Dr.	Cr.	Dr.	Cr.	Dr.	Cr.	Dr.	Cr.	Dr.	Cr.
(Account titles)	(Account balances)		(Amounts of adjustments)		(Account balances for the adjusted trial balance)		(Income statement account from the adjusted trial balance)		(Balance sheet accounts from the adjusted trial balance)	

entry so that the entire entry can be assessed. After entering all adjusting entries, check the equality of debits and credits in the Adjustments columns. By checking for equality, you can quickly discover and easily correct adjusting entries with unequal debits and credits.

3. Prepare the Adjusted Trial Balance as in overlay Illustration 4-3 by summing each account across the Trial Balance and Adjustments columns. This process involves taking the trial balance amount of each account, adding and subtracting the adjustments to that account, and then entering the adjusted balance in the appropriate column of the Adjusted Trial Balance. For accounts with zero balances in the Trial Balance columns, the amount entered in the Adjusted Trial Balance columns is composed solely of the amounts entered in the account in the Adjustments columns. After entering all adjusted account balances, check the equality of debits and credits in the Adjusted Trial Balance columns.

4. Complete the Income Statement columns as in overlay Illustration 4-4 by transferring adjusted revenue and expense account balances to the Income Statement pair of columns. The revenue accounts have credit balances, so enter them in the Cr. column. Similarly, expense accounts have debit balances, so enter them in the Dr. column.

   Compute net income as in overlay Illustration 4-4 by summing the Dr. and Cr. columns and finding the difference in the balances. The amount by which the balance of the Cr. (revenues) column exceeds the balance of the Dr. (expenses) column is the amount of net income. If the business incurred a net loss, the balance of the Dr. (expenses) column would exceed the balance of the Cr. (revenues) column.

   When the Dr. and Cr. columns of the Income Statement in Illustration 4-4 are summed, the credits exceed the debits by $1,130 ($4,000 − $2,870). The $1,130 is net income. Enter the title "Net income" in the Accounts column at the left, and enter $1,130 in the Dr. column of the Income Statement *and* in the Cr. column of the Balance Sheet (shown in Illustration 4-5). Entering the amount of net income in the Dr. column of the Income Statement balances the sums of the Dr. and Cr. columns. Net income represents an increase in owner's equity due to the business's operations, and it has not yet been added to the owner's capital account. Also, this balances the sums of the Dr. and Cr. Balance Sheet columns.

5. Complete the Balance Sheet columns as in overlay Illustration 4-5 by transferring the adjusted asset, liability, and owner's equity account balances to the Balance Sheet columns. Assets have debit balances, so enter them in the Dr. column. Liability accounts have credit balances, so enter them in the Cr. column. Take special care to enter accumulated depreciation account balances in the Balance Sheet Cr. column, even though accumulated depreciation is related to assets.

   Owner's equity accounts have both debit and credit balances. The owner's capital account has a credit balance, so enter it in the Cr. column of the Balance Sheet. However, the owner's capital account from the adjusted trial balance is not the correct account balance for the end-of-period balance sheet. It does not reflect the income for the period or the owner's withdrawals. These amounts have been accumulated in Withdrawals and in the revenue and expense accounts, and ultimately you must transfer those amounts to the owner's capital account. The transfer takes place through the closing entries (described later), after you complete the worksheet, In the worksheet, you accomplish the same effect on owner's capital by taking the debit balance of Withdrawals to the Dr. column of the Balance Sheet. The amount of net income has already been included in the Cr. column by the procedures described in No. 4 above. The ending owner's capital balance does not appear directly in the Balance Sheet columns. The beginning balance in the capital account appears in the Balance Sheet columns. The ending balance in the capital account that will appear in the balance sheet is composed of three items that do appear in the worksheet: (a) the balance in the owner's capital account, (b) *minus* the balance in Withdrawals, (c) *plus* net income (or *minus* net loss) for the period.

Next, sum the Balance Sheet columns. If you have made no errors in completing the worksheet, the sum of the Dr. column should equal the sum of the Cr. column. Notice the equality of debits and credits for each pair of the financial statement columns in Illustration 4-5.

Preparing Financial Statements Using a Worksheet

The completed worksheet contains all the information necessary to prepare the formal financial statements for Charlotte's Car Park. We prepare the income statement from the information in the Income Statement columns, and we prepare the statement of owner's equity and balance sheet from the information in the Balance Sheet columns. While all the information necessary for the financial statements is in the worksheet, the financial statement columns are *not* in financial statement format *per se*. That is, the columns do not show the proper headings, and they list many of the accounts out of order. Therefore, we prepare the financial statements by first extracting the information from the completed worksheet and then arranging the information in the proper financial statement format. The financial statements prepared from the worksheet are presented in Illustration 4-6.

LO 2

Journalize and post the adjusting entries from the information in the completed worksheet.

JOURNALIZING AND POSTING ADJUSTING ENTRIES

To complete the adjustment process after preparing financial statements, we must record the adjusting entries entered on the worksheet in the general journal and post them to the general ledger accounts. When accountants use a worksheet, they usually do not journalize and post adjusting entries until after they complete the worksheet. The adjusting entries as they would appear in the general journal for Charlotte's Car Park are shown in Illustration 4-7. For each adjusting entry in Illustration 4-7, the letter in parentheses at the end of the explanation corresponds to the letter reference on the worksheet in Illustration 4-5. We include the letter references in the explanation to aid your understanding of the worksheet. In practice, the adjusting entries recorded in the general journal generally do not include references to worksheets. The owner's equity, revenue, and expense accounts of Charlotte's Car Park are shown in Illustration 4-8. These accounts show the balances after we have posted the adjusting entries.

ILLUSTRATION 4-2 Worksheet for Charlotte's Car Park (Accounts and Trial Balance Columns)

Charlotte's Car Park
Worksheet for Financial Statements
February 28, 19X1

ACCOUNTS	TRIAL BALANCE Dr.	TRIAL BALANCE Cr.	ADJUSTMENTS Dr.	ADJUSTMENTS Cr.	ADJUSTED TRIAL BALANCE Dr.	ADJUSTED TRIAL BALANCE Cr.	INCOME STATEMENT Dr.	INCOME STATEMENT Cr.	BALANCE SHEET Dr.	BALANCE SHEET Cr.
Cash	860									
Accounts Receivable										
Prepaid Insurance	480									
Land	9,000									
Land Improvements	3,000									
Accum. Depr.—Land Improv.										
Interest Payable		3,000								
Notes Payable		200								
Unearned Revenue										
Utilities Payable										
Wages and Salaries Payable		10,000								
Charlotte Cruz, Capital	1,000									
Charlotte Cruz, Withdrawals		3,400								
Parking Revenue										
Advertising Expense	200									
Depr. Exp.—Land Improv.										
Insurance Expense										
Interest Expense	60									
Maintenance Expense										
Utilities Expense										
Wages and Salaries Expense	2,000									
Totals	16,600	16,600								

ILLUSTRATION 4-6 Financial Statements for Charlotte's Car Park

Charlotte's Car Park
Income Statement
For the Two Months Ended February 28, 19X1

Parking revenue		$4,000
Expenses:		
Advertising expense	$ 200	
Depreciation expense	50	
Insurance expense	40	
Interest expense	30	
Maintenance expense	60	
Utilities expense	90	
Wages and salaries expense	2,400	
Total expenses		2,870
Net income		$1,130

Charlotte's Car Park
Statement of Owner's Equity
For the Two Months Ended February 28, 19X1

Beginning balance	$ 0
Add: Owner's investment	10,000
Net income	1,130
Less: Owner's withdrawals	(1,000)
Ending balance	$10,130

Charlotte's Car Park
Balance Sheet
February 28, 19X1

Assets

Cash		$ 860
Accounts receivable		400
Prepaid insurance		440
Land		9,000
Land improvements	$3,000	
Less: Accumulated depreciation	50	2,950
Total assets		$13,650

Liabilities and Owner's Equity

Interest payable	$ 30	
Notes payable	3,000	
Utilities payable	90	
Wages and salaries payable	400	
Total liabilities		$ 3,520
Owner's equity		10,130
Total liabilities and owner's equity		$13,650

ILLUSTRATION 4-7 Adjusting Entries

GENERAL JOURNAL   PAGE 3

DATE		DESCRIPTION	POST. REF.	DEBIT	CREDIT
19X1 Feb.	28	Insurance Expense Prepaid Expense To record the expiration of prepaid insurance. (a)		40	40
	28	Depreciation Expense–Land Improvements Accumulated Depreciation–Land Improvements To record February depreciation. (b)		50	50
	28	Wages and Salaries Expense Wages and Salaries Payable To record earned but unpaid wages. (c)		400	400
	28	Interest Expense Interest Payable To record interest expense for February. (d)		30	30
	28	Utilities Expense Utilities Payable To record the cost of electricity for February. (e)		90	90
	28	Unearned Revenue Parking Revenue To record parking revenue earned. (f)		200	200
	28	Accounts Receivable Parking Revenue To record parking revenue earned. (g)		400	400

ILLUSTRATION 4-8 General Ledger Accounts After Adjustments

GENERAL LEDGER

NAME: Charlotte Cruz, Capital   ACCOUNT NO.: 500

DATE		DESCRIPTION	POST. REF.	DEBIT	CREDIT	BALANCE
19X1 Jan.	2		GJ1		10,000	10,000

NAME: Charlotte Cruz, Withdrawals   ACCOUNT NO.: 502

DATE		DESCRIPTION	POST. REF.	DEBIT	CREDIT	BALANCE
Jan.	31		GJ1	500		500
Feb.	28		GJ2	500		1,000

(Continues)

ILLUSTRATION 4-8 (Concluded) General Ledger Accounts After Adjustments

NAME: Parking Revenue   ACCOUNT NO.: 606

DATE		DESCRIPTION	POST. REF.	DEBIT	CREDIT	BALANCE
19X1						
Jan.	31		GJ1		1,200	1,200
	31		GJ1		400	1,600
Feb.	28		GJ1		1,800	3,400
	28	Adjusting (f)	GJ3		200	3,600
	28	Adjusting (g)	GJ3		400	4,000

NAME: Advertising Expense   ACCOUNT NO.: 700

DATE		DESCRIPTION	POST. REF.	DEBIT	CREDIT	BALANCE
Jan.	31		GJ1	200		200

NAME: Deprec. Expense–Land Impr.   ACCOUNT NO.: 714

DATE		DESCRIPTION	POST. REF.	DEBIT	CREDIT	BALANCE
Feb.	28	Adjusting (b)	GJ3	50		50

NAME: Insurance Expense   ACCOUNT NO.: 728

DATE		DESCRIPTION	POST. REF.	DEBIT	CREDIT	BALANCE
Feb.	28	Adjusting (a)	GJ3	40		40

NAME: Interest Expense   ACCOUNT NO.: 730

DATE		DESCRIPTION	POST. REF.	DEBIT	CREDIT	BALANCE
Feb.	28	Adjusting (d)	GJ3	30		30

NAME: Maintenance Expense   ACCOUNT NO.: 734

DATE		DESCRIPTION	POST. REF.	DEBIT	CREDIT	BALANCE
Feb.	28		GJ2	60		60

NAME: Utilities Expense   ACCOUNT NO.: 780

DATE		DESCRIPTION	POST. REF.	DEBIT	CREDIT	BALANCE
Feb.	28	Adjusting (e)	GJ3	90		90

NAME: Wages and Salaries Expense   ACCOUNT NO.: 784

DATE		DESCRIPTION	POST. REF.	DEBIT	CREDIT	BALANCE
Jan.	31		GJ1	800		800
Feb.	28		GJ1	1,200		2,000
	28	Adjusting (c)	GJ3	400		2,400

Explain the closing process
and prepare closing
entries.

CLOSING THE TEMPORARY ACCOUNTS

After we have prepared the financial statements and have journalized and posted the adjusting entries, the final step in the accounting cycle is to close the
revenue, expense, and withdrawals accounts. This section discusses the need
for closing entries, describes the closing process, and shows the closing entries
for Charlotte's Car Park.

The Need for Closing Entries

Revenues, expenses, and withdrawals could be recorded directly as increases
and decreases in owner's equity. In practice, however, the detailed amounts
and types of the business's individual revenues and expenses must be conveniently available to the accountant to facilitate calculating and presenting net
income. To satisfy this requirement, we use a separate account for each type of
revenue and expense. Similarly, accumulating withdrawals in a separate account
facilitates the preparation of the statement of owner's equity.

The revenue, expense, and withdrawals accounts are **temporary
accounts**. During an accounting period, we record revenues, expenses, and
withdrawals in the appropriate accounts, which always begin the period with
zero balances. The net income measured in the revenue and expense accounts
is for that period only, as are the withdrawal amounts accumulated in
Withdrawals. At the end of the period, we transfer the temporary account balances to owner's capital to state correctly the business's financial position as of
the end of the period. Therefore, at both the beginning and the end of an
accounting period, temporary accounts have zero balances. We simply use temporary accounts in the interim to accumulate information in convenient form for
the preparation of the financial statements. We call the process of transferring
temporary account balances to owner's capital **closing temporary accounts**,
or simply **closing the accounts**.

The Closing Process

The closing process for a proprietorship involves transferring net income and
the owner's withdrawals to the owner's capital account. The revenue and
expense accounts contain the information about net income. We could close
(transfer) the revenue and expense accounts directly to the owner's capital
account, but this would result in too much detailed information in the owner's
permanent capital account. For this reason, we close the revenue and expense
accounts first to an account called **Income Summary**. After we close the revenue and expense account balances to Income Summary, the balance of
Income Summary is equal to the net income or net loss for the period.

The closing process for a proprietorship is shown in Illustration 4-9. The
process consists of four entries that we journalize in the general journal and
post to the general ledger. The four entries are:

1. Close the revenue accounts by debiting each revenue account with the
   amount of its credit balance and crediting Income Summary with an
   amount equal to the sum of the debits. After posting this entry, the revenue accounts have zero balances.
2. Close the expense accounts by crediting each expense account with the
   amount of its debit balance and debiting Income Summary with an
   amount equal to the sum of the credits. After posting this entry, the

expense accounts have zero balances. After the first two entries, the balance of Income Summary is equal to the net income (credit balance) or net loss (debit balance) for the period.

3. Close Income Summary to the owner's capital account. For net income (assumed in Illustration 4-9), the entry is a debit to Income Summary in an amount equal to its credit balance and a credit to the owner's capital account for the same amount. For a net loss, the entry is a credit to Income Summary and a debit to owner's capital in the amount of the debit balance in Income Summary. After this closing entry, Income Summary has a zero balance, and the net income (loss) has been added to (subtracted from) the owner's capital account.

4. Close the owner's withdrawals account to the capital account. The entry is a credit to the withdrawals account and a debit to the capital account in an amount equal to the debit balance in the withdrawals account. After this entry, the withdrawals account has a zero balance.

ILLUSTRATION 4-9 Closing Process

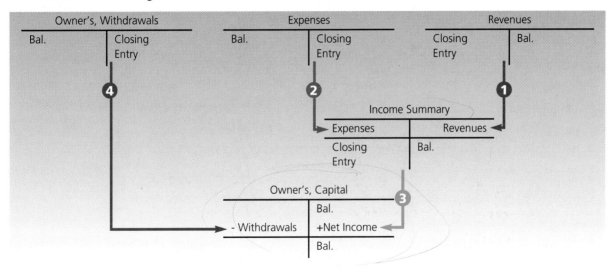

Closing Entries for Charlotte's Car Park

You may find the information necessary to prepare closing entries in the general ledger or in the Adjusted Trial Balance, Income Statement, and Balance Sheet columns of the worksheet. We base the closing entries for Charlotte's Car Park on the information in the worksheet in Illustration 4-5.

Closing the Revenue Account.   Charlotte's Car Park only has one revenue account, Parking Revenue, and the closing entry is:

Feb. 28	Parking Revenue	4,000	
	Income Summary		4,000
	To close revenue account to Income Summary.		

The effect of the closing entry for revenue is shown below:

Closing the Expense Accounts.   The closing entry for Charlotte's Car Park expense accounts is:

Feb. 28	Income Summary	2,870	
	Advertising Expense		200
	Depreciation Expense – Land Improvements		50
	Insurance Expense		40
	Interest Expense		30
	Maintenance Expense		60
	Utilities Expense		90
	Wages and Salaries Expense		2,400
	To close expense accounts to Income Summary.		

The effects of the closing entry for expenses may be illustrated as follows:

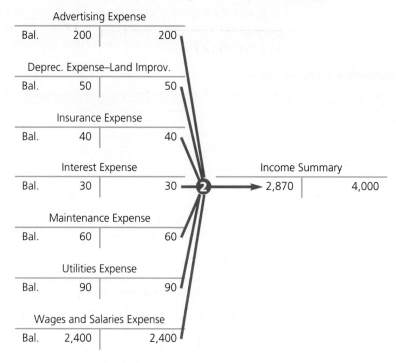

Closing the Income Summary Account.   After the first two closing entries above, the balance of $1,130 in Income Summary is equal to the net income for the period. The closing entry for Income Summary is:

Feb. 28	Income Summary	1,130	
	Charlotte Cruz, Capital		1,130
	To close Income Summary.		

The effect of closing Income Summary may be illustrated as follows:

Charlotte Cruz, Capital				Income Summary			
		Bal.	10,000	2,870		4,000	
			1,130	1,130	Bal.	1,130	

Closing the Withdrawals Account.   The final closing entry is to close the owner's withdrawals account to the owner's capital account:

Feb. 28	Charlotte Cruz, Capital	1,000	
	Charlotte Cruz, Withdrawals		1,000
	To close Withdrawals.		

The effect of this closing entry may be illustrated as follows:

Charlotte Cruz, Withdrawals			Charlotte Cruz, Capital	
Bal.	1,000	1,000 ④ →	Bal.	10,000
		1,000		1,130
			Bal.	10,130

The General Ledger Accounts After Closing

Illustration 4-10 presents the owner's equity, revenue, and expense general ledger accounts for Charlotte's Car Park after we post the closing entries.

Notice that the temporary accounts—the withdrawals, revenue, and expense accounts—have zero balances after we post the closing entries. The permanent accounts—the asset, liability, and owner's capital accounts—have non-zero balances.

ILLUSTRATION 4-10 General Ledger Accounts After Closing

GENERAL LEDGER

NAME: Charlotte Cruz, Capital   ACCOUNT NO.: 500

DATE		DESCRIPTION	POST. REF.	DEBIT	CREDIT	BALANCE
19X1						
Jan.	2		GJ1		10,000	10,000
Feb.	28	Closing	GJ4		1,130	11,130
	28	Closing	GJ4	1,000		10,130

NAME: Charlotte Cruz, Withdrawals   ACCOUNT NO.: 502

DATE		DESCRIPTION	POST. REF.	DEBIT	CREDIT	BALANCE
Jan.	31		GJ1	500		500
Feb.	28		GJ2	500		1,000
	28	Closing	GJ4		1,000	0

NAME: Parking Revenue   ACCOUNT NO.: 606

DATE		DESCRIPTION	POST. REF.	DEBIT	CREDIT	BALANCE
Jan.	31		GJ1		1,200	1,200
	31		GJ1		400	1,600
Feb.	28		GJ1		1,800	3,400
	28	Adjusting (f)	GJ3		200	3,600
	28	Adjusting (g)	GJ3		400	4,000
	28	Closing	GJ4	4,000		0

NAME: Advertising Expense   ACCOUNT NO.: 700

DATE		DESCRIPTION	POST. REF.	DEBIT	CREDIT	BALANCE
Jan.	31		GJ1	200		200
Feb.	28	Closing	GJ4		200	0

(Continues)

ILLUSTRATION 4-10 (Concluded) General Ledger Accounts After Closing

NAME: Deprec. Expense–Land Impr. ACCOUNT NO.: 714

DATE		DESCRIPTION	POST. REF.	DEBIT	CREDIT	BALANCE
19X1						
Feb.	28	Adjusting (b)	GJ3	50		50
	28	Closing	GJ4		50	0

NAME: Insurance Expense ACCOUNT NO.: 728

DATE		DESCRIPTION	POST. REF.	DEBIT	CREDIT	BALANCE
Feb.	28	Adjusting (a)	GJ3	40		40
	28	Closing	GJ4		40	0

NAME: Interest Expense ACCOUNT NO.: 730

DATE		DESCRIPTION	POST. REF.	DEBIT	CREDIT	BALANCE
Feb.	28	Adjusting (d)	GJ3	30		30
	28	Closing	GJ4		30	0

NAME: Maintenance Expense ACCOUNT NO.: 734

DATE		DESCRIPTION	POST. REF.	DEBIT	CREDIT	BALANCE
Feb.	28		GJ2	60		60
	28	Closing	GJ4		60	0

NAME: Utilities Expense ACCOUNT NO.: 780

DATE		DESCRIPTION	POST. REF.	DEBIT	CREDIT	BALANCE
Feb.	28	Adjusting (e)	GJ3	90		90
	28	Closing	GJ4		90	0

NAME: Wages and Salaries Expense ACCOUNT NO.: 784

DATE		DESCRIPTION	POST. REF.	DEBIT	CREDIT	BALANCE
Jan.	31		GJ1	800		800
Feb.	28		GJ1	1,200		2,000
	28	Adjusting (c)	GJ3	400		2,400
	28	Closing	GJ4		2,400	0

LO 4

Prepare a post-closing trial balance.

The Post-Closing Trial Balance

A **post-closing trial balance** is prepared after we have posted the closing entries to the general ledger. A post-closing trial balance for Charlotte's Car Park is presented in Illustration 4-11. Since revenue and expense accounts have zero balances after closing, the post-closing trial balance lists only the balance sheet accounts — asset, liability, and owner's capital. The post-closing trial balance serves as a check that no errors occurred in preparing and posting the closing entries.

ILLUSTRATION 4-11 Post-Closing Trial Balance

Charlotte's Car Park Post-Closing Trial Balance February 28, 19X1		
	Debits	*Credits*
Cash	$ 860	
Accounts Receivable	400	
Prepaid Insurance	440	
Land	9,000	
Land Improvements	3,000	
Accumulated Depreciation – Land Improvements		$ 50
Interest Payable		30
Notes Payable		3,000
Utilities Payable		90
Wages and Salaries Payable		400
Charlotte Cruz, Capital		10,130
Totals	$13,700	$13,700

LO 5

Describe the timing of the various steps in the accounting cycle.

THE ACCOUNTING CYCLE

You have seen the six steps in the accounting cycle. These steps are summarized in Illustration 4-12. Not all of the steps are performed at equal time intervals. On a daily basis, we perform the first three steps. That is, we analyze transactions, enter them in the general journal, and post them to the general ledger. We adjust the accounts whenever the business prepares financial state-

ILLUSTRATION 4-12 The Accounting Cycle

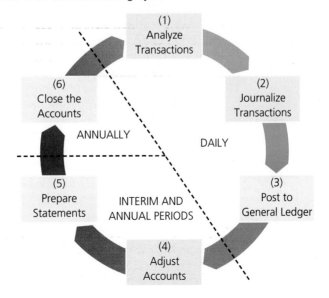

ments. Most businesses prepare statements for interim periods such as monthly or quarterly; and we adjust the accounts to prepare the financial statements for those time intervals. We close the temporary accounts annually, so that the accumulation of revenue and expense information is for the annual accounting period. In this chapter, we closed the temporary accounts at the end of the second month of operations for discussion purposes only.

THE CLASSIFIED BALANCE SHEET

LO 6

Describe the significant groupings of a classified balance sheet.

The balance sheet for Charlotte's Car Park, presented in Illustration 4-6, is an *unclassified* balance sheet. It lists the business's asset, liability, and owner's capital accounts. Many businesses, however, prepare classified balance sheets. A **classified balance sheet** presents the assets and liabilities arranged in certain customary groupings. No specifically required format exists under GAAP for classifying balance sheet elements. However, the customary classification format presents assets according to the following groupings:

1. Current assets
2. Long-term investments
3. Property, plant, and equipment
4. Intangible assets

Liabilities generally are classified into only two groupings:

1. Current liabilities
2. Noncurrent (or long-term) liabilities

The classified balance sheet for Charlotte's Car Park at the end of February is shown in Illustration 4-13. Because Charlotte's Car Park is small and not complex, its balance sheet only contains two groupings of assets—current assets and property, plant, and equipment. However, it does have both current and noncurrent liabilities.

Two significant asset and liability classifications are current assets and current liabilities. In relation to assets, the term *current* deals with the length of time before the assets are realized—meaning converted into cash or used. In relation to liabilities, the term *current* refers to how soon the liabilities are due. Current assets and liabilities are assets that will be realized and liabilities that are due within one year or within one operating cycle, whichever is longer.

The **operating cycle** is the average period of time between committing resources to providing goods or services and collecting cash from customers. The operating cycle of a service business, such as Charlotte's Car Park, is the period of time between rendering the service and collecting cash from the customer. The operating cycle of a merchandising business, which buys merchandise from wholesalers and resells it to retail customers, is the average period of time between the acquisition of merchandise and receipt of cash from the sale of the merchandise. For a manufacturing business, which manufactures a product and sells it to customers, the operating cycle is the average period of time between the acquisition of raw materials and the receipt of cash from the sale of the product.

Because they have operating cycles of one year or shorter, most businesses use one year to classify assets and liabilities as current and noncurrent. Some businesses, however, have operating cycles longer than one year. For example, construction businesses enter into long-term contracts to build bridges, high-

ILLUSTRATION 4-13 Classified Balance Sheet

Charlotte's Car Park Balance Sheet February 28, 19X1			
Assets			
Current assets:			
Cash		$ 860	
Accounts receivable		400	
Prepaid insurance		440	
Total current assets			$ 1,700
Property, plant, and equipment:			
Land		$9,000	
Land improvements	$3,000		
Less: Accumulated depreciation	50	2,950	
Total property, plant, and equipment			11,950
Total assets			$13,650
Liabilities and Owner's Equity			
Current liabilities:			
Interest payable		$ 30	
Wages and salaries payable		400	
Utilities payable		90	
Total current liabilities			$ 520
Noncurrent liabilities:			
Notes payable			3,000
Total liabilities			$ 3,520
Owner's equity			10,130
Total liabilities and owner's equity			$13,650

ways, buildings, etc. and take several years to complete the projects. These businesses use a period longer than one year to classify assets and liabilities as current and noncurrent. Since they neither sell nor manufacture a product, service businesses—such as Charlotte's Car Park—use one year for classification of current assets and liabilities.

In reviewing a classified balance sheet, the reader can assess the business's ability to pay its liabilities when they come due. Also, the reader can assess the extent of investment in various types of assets. A business that has current assets in excess of current liabilities should be able to pay its current liabilities because the current assets will be realized within the same time period that the current liabilities come due. On the other hand, a business with current liabilities greater than its current assets may have to borrow money to pay the liabilities. The noncurrent asset classifications show the amounts and types of assets that the business uses in its long-term operations. The noncurrent liability and owner's equity classifications show the business's sources—borrowing and investing by the owner—of long-term financing.

Asset Classifications

Some businesses' classified balance sheets contain all of the asset classifications listed previously. Other businesses, however, only list some of the classifications in their classified balance sheets, depending on the nature of their operations.

Current Assets.   **Current assets** consist of cash and assets that the business reasonably expects to sell, consume, or convert into cash within one year or within one operating cycle, whichever is longer. Current assets generally include cash, short-term investments, notes and accounts receivable, inventories, prepaid expenses, and unused supplies. Accounts receivable are expected to be converted into cash within a short period, typically 30 to 90 days. Short-term investments (often called *trading securities*) are temporary investments of cash that the business does not currently need. Investments are classified as short-term if management expects to sell them within a year or within an operating cycle. Inventories are goods that the business expects to sell to customers either for cash or for notes or accounts receivable, which are ultimately converted into cash. Charlotte's Car Park does not have inventories on its balance sheet because it provides services, rather than goods, to its customers. A business will use or consume prepaid expenses and unused supplies in the short run, usually within a year.

IBM's 1992 balance sheet reported the following current assets (rounded to the nearest $1 million):

Cash and cash equivalents	$ 4,446,000,000
Marketable securities	1,203,000,000
Receivables	21,604,000,000
Inventories	8,385,000,000
Prepaid expenses and other current assets	4,054,000,000
Total	$39,692,000,000

A classified balance sheet presents current assets in order of the assets' liquidity. In this context, the term **liquidity** refers to the expected length of time needed to convert an asset into cash. Cash, obviously, is the most liquid asset and is generally listed first in the current assets section. Following cash, and in the order of their liquidity, are: short-term investments, accounts receivable, notes receivable, and inventories. Prepaid expenses and unused supplies are not generally realized in cash and, by convention, are commonly listed last in the current asset section.

Long-Term Investments.   **Long-term investments** include stocks, bonds, and promissory notes that the business does not expect to sell or collect within one year or within the operating cycle, whichever is longer. A **promissory note** is a formal written promise to pay a certain amount of money on a fixed date in the future.

Property, Plant, and Equipment.   **Property, plant, and equipment** includes the long-lived assets that the business uses to sell and/or manufacture a product or to provide a service. Assets commonly classified as property, plant, and equipment are the land and buildings in which the business is housed and the equipment the business uses. For a business such as Charlotte's Car Park, which provides a service, this classification might include land and buildings, office equipment, and equipment used in providing parking services.

To classify as property, plant, and equipment, assets must have relatively long useful lives and must be used in selling or manufacturing a product or in providing a service. Assets such as land and buildings that the business does not currently use but holds for future expansion or sale should be classified as long-term investments. Property, plant, and equipment assets are sometimes called *plant assets, operating assets, fixed assets, tangible assets,* or *long-lived assets.*

Intangible Assets.   **Intangible assets** include those that have no physical substance. Examples of intangible assets are patents, copyrights, franchises, and trademarks. The value of these assets results from the rights or privileges granted to the owner of the assets.

Liability Classifications

Liabilities are classified as either current or noncurrent. Most businesses have both of these classifications on their balance sheets.

Current Liabilities.   **Current liabilities** are those obligations due within one year or within one operating cycle, whichever is longer. Businesses pay current liabilities with current assets or by incurring new current liabilities. Examples of current liabilities, some of which are shown in Charlotte's Car Park's balance sheet, are notes payable and accounts payable, wages and salaries payable, interest payable, taxes payable, and unearned revenue. Current liabilities are discussed in greater detail in subsequent chapters.

IBM's current liabilities for 1992 are as follows (rounded to the nearest $1 million):

Taxes	$ 979,000,000
Short-term debt	16,467,000,000
Accounts payable	3,147,000,000
Compensation and benefits	3,476,000,000
Deferred income	3,316,000,000
Other accrued expenses and liabilities	9,352,000,000
Total	$36,737,000,000

Noncurrent Liabilities.   **Noncurrent liabilities** are those obligations due in more than one year or more than one operating cycle, whichever is longer, from the balance sheet date. Examples of noncurrent liabilities are notes and bonds payable and mortgages payable. When the due date for noncurrent liabilities approaches to within one year or within one operating cycle, businesses reclassify the liabilities as current liabilities. At that point, they meet the definition of a current liability. Noncurrent liabilities are also called *long-term liabilities* and are discussed further in a subsequent chapter.

Owner's Equity Classifications

The owner's equity section of a proprietorship's balance sheet shows the amount of owner's capital at the balance sheet date. The statement of owner's equity presents detailed information about the changes in the amount of owner's capital that occurred during the accounting period, ending at the balance sheet date. Different forms of business organizations (partnerships and corporations) have different owners' equity sections in their balance sheets. The owners' equity accounts of these forms of business organizations are discussed in subsequent chapters.

A Note About Classified Financial Statements

Many businesses prepare classified income statements, in addition to classified balance sheets. Why doesn't Charlotte Cruz need a classified income statement? Such an income statement is not meaningful for Charlotte's Car Park since she uses only one revenue and a few expense accounts. However, in a later chapter, you will see a classified income statement illustrated. It is an appropriate statement for the merchandising business discussed in that chapter.

LO 7
Calculate and interpret the current ratio.

Using Classified Balance Sheets to Assess Liquidity

Financial statements readers can use classified balance sheets to assess the business's liquidity. Of particular interest to creditors—and to potential creditors—is the relationship between current assets and current liabilities. This relationship gives an indication of the business's ability to pay current liabilities with current assets. This relationship may be observed with a classified balance sheet since current assets and current liabilities are two of the classifications.

A financial ratio commonly used to assess the relative liquidity and debt-paying ability is the current ratio. The **current ratio** compares current assets to current liabilities as of the balance sheet date as follows:

$$\text{Current Ratio} = \frac{\text{Current Assets}}{\text{Current Liabilities}}$$

Based on the information about current assets and current liabilities presented earlier, IBM's current ratio is calculated as follows:

$$1.08 = \frac{\$39,692,000,000}{\$36,737,000,000}$$

The average current ratios for several service businesses are shown in Illustration 4-14.

ILLUSTRATION 4-14 Current Ratios of Certain Service Businesses

Industry	Current ratio
Car washes	.5
Radio stations	1.2
Auto repairs	1.3
Advertising agencies	1.3
Employment agencies	1.7

Reprinted with permission, copyright Robert Morris Associates 1992.

The Current Ratio for Charlotte's Car Park

Using the information from the classified balance sheet in Illustration 4-13, the current ratio for Charlotte's Car Park as of February 28, 19X1 is computed as follows:

$$\text{Current Ratio} = \frac{\text{Current Assets}}{\text{Current Liabilities}}$$

$$3.27 = \frac{\$1,700}{\$520}$$

Compared with other service businesses, Charlotte's Car Park appears to have a strong current ratio. The bank would probably conclude that the business appears to have no problem in paying its debts as they come due. Care must be exercised, however, in relying too heavily on the current ratio. The ratio represents the business's relative liquidity *as of the balance sheet date.* Debt-paying ability depends very much on *future* cash inflows. So while the current ratio is helpful for assessing debt-paying ability, it is not a perfect gauge. The bank would want to analyze other financial information in making a final lending decision.

SUMMARY

Complete the accountant's worksheet and prepare financial statements using the worksheet.   In this chapter, you saw the completion of the accounting cycle. At the end of an accounting period, an accountant may use the worksheet to prepare financial statements. The worksheet is helpful, especially in the preparation of financial statements for businesses that have numerous accounts.

Journalize and post the adjusting entries from the information in the completed worksheet.   After the worksheet is completed, the adjusting entries that we enter on the worksheet should be journalized and posted.

Explain the closing process and prepare closing entries.   The final step in the accounting cycle is to close the temporary accounts to the owner's capital account. The temporary accounts are the income statement accounts—revenue and expense accounts—and the owner's withdrawals account. The temporary accounts begin each annual accounting period with zero balances and are used to accumulate information about net income and withdrawals for the year. At the end of the year, the temporary accounts are returned to zero balances by transferring (closing) their balances to the owner's capital account. After closing, the temporary accounts are ready to accumulate the applicable information for the next year.

Prepare a post-closing trial balance.   An optional procedure after closing is to check the equality of the permanent (balance sheet) accounts by preparing a post-closing trial balance.

Describe the timing of the various steps in the accounting cycle.   We perform the steps in the accounting cycle at varying time intervals. We daily analyze transactions, enter them in the general journal, and post them to the general ledger. We adjust the accounts whenever the business prepares financial statements. We close the accounts annually so that the accumulation of net income information is for the annual accounting period.

Describe the significant groupings of a classified balance sheet.   Most businesses prepare classified balance sheets, which present assets and liabilities arranged in certain customary groupings. The customary groupings for asset accounts are: current assets; long-term investments; property, plant and equipment; and intangible assets. The customary groupings for liabilities are current and noncurrent.

Calculate and interpret the current ratio.   We calculate the current ratio by dividing current assets by current liabilities. The current ratio gives an indication of the business's debt-paying ability as of the balance sheet date.

LO 8
Explain how reversing
entries are used for
certain adjusting entries.

APPENDIX 4-A: REVERSING ENTRIES

When making adjusting entries at the end of an accounting period, we should
take precautions to ensure that, in the subsequent period, we record properly
the settlements of the transactions related to the adjusting entries. In particular,
the settlement of accrued revenue and accrued expenses that arise from adjusting entries require consideration. For example, the adjusting entry for accrued
revenues results in a debit to Accounts Receivable and a credit to Parking
Revenue. When a cash payment is received, it is in settlement of the accounts
receivable for revenue earned the preceding accounting period. In recording
the cash receipt, we must take care to decrease accounts receivable, not to
record additional revenue.

Some businesses avoid the problem of allocating subsequent cash transactions related to accrued revenue and accrued expenses by making reversing
entries immediately at the beginning of a new accounting period. A **reversing
entry** is one that is exactly the opposite of an adjusting entry made at the end
of the preceding accounting period. Reversing entries allow the subsequent
cash settlement of the accrued revenue and accrued expense transactions to be
recorded without giving consideration to the previous adjusting entries. This is
especially beneficial when clerks, who may be unsophisticated in accounting
matters, are recording the cash transactions. Also, if we make reversing entries,
computerized accounting systems can be more simply programmed to handle
the subsequent cash transactions.

ACCRUED REVENUE

To show the effects of reversing entries, consider the agreement between
Charlotte's Car Park and the Campus Bookstore. For simplicity, *we consider the
effects of just this one transaction.* In January 19X1, Charlotte entered into an
agreement to provide overflow parking for $400 per month. Charlotte is to
receive the monthly payment by the 15th of the following month. On February
28, 19X1, at the end of the two-month accounting period, we made the following adjusting entry to recognize that Charlotte's Car Park earned $400 of rev-
enue for which she will receive payment in March:

Feb. 28	Accounts Receivable	400	
	Parking Revenue		400
	To record parking revenue earned.		

The closing entry for Parking Revenue has the following effect:

Feb. 28	Parking Revenue	400	
	Income Summary		400
	To close revenue.		

The closing entry leaves a zero balance in Parking Revenue as of March 1, 19X1.
Whether or not a reversing entry is made on March 1 determines the type of
entry that must be made to record the $400 cash payment received on March 15:

Subsequent cash receipt without reversing entries:

Feb. 16	Cash	400	
	Accounts Receivable		400
	To record the receipt of cash for parking.		

Reversing entry:

Mar. 1	Parking Revenue	400	
	Accounts Receivable		400
	To reverse adjusting entry for accrued revenue.		

Subsequent cash receipt with reversing entry:

Mar. 15	Cash	400	
	Parking Revenue		400
	To record the receipt of cash for parking.		

Because the February 28 balance in Parking Revenue is zero after the closing entry for February, the reversing entry results in a debit balance in Parking Revenue on March 1. A debit balance is the opposite of the normal balance of a revenue account. This situation is temporary, however, since the cash receipt offsets the debit balance. The effects of the two alternative methods in T-account form is shown below:

Without reversing entry:

Accounts Receivable		Parking Revenue	
Feb. 28 (A) 400	Mar. 15 400	Feb. 28 (C) 400	Feb. 28 (A) 400

With reversing entry:

Accounts Receivable		Parking Revenue	
Feb. 28 (A) 400	Feb. 28 (R) 400	Feb. 28 (C) 400	Feb. 28 (A) 400
		Mar. 1 (R) 400	Mar. 15 400

> A = Adjusting
> C = Closing
> R = Reversing

Under both methods, the amount of revenue recognized in February is $400, which we close to Income Summary as of February 28, and the amount of revenue recognized in March related to the receipt of payment is zero.

ACCRUED EXPENSES

To illustrate reversing entries for accrued expenses, consider Charlotte's payment of the attendants' salaries in Transaction 8. On February 28, Charlotte paid the attendants $1,200 for services through February 21. On February 28, the following adjusting entry was recorded to recognize that the attendants had worked in February after the 21st (the last date for which they had been paid):

Feb. 28	Wages and Salaries Expense	400	
	Wages and Salaries Payable		400
	To record earned but unpaid salary.		

On February 28, the closing entry for Wages and Salaries Expense is:

Jan. 31	Income Summary	2,400	
	Wages and Salaries Expense		2,400
	To close salaries expense.		

When Charlotte pays the attendants on March 5 for their services through February 28th, the entries under the two alternative methods are:

Subsequent payment without reversing entry:

Mar. 5	Wages and Salaries Payable	400	
	Cash		400
	To record payment of attendants' salaries.		

Reversing entry:

Mar. 1	Wages and Salaries Payable	400	
	Wages and Salaries Expense		400
	To reverse adjusting entry for accrued salaries expense.		

Subsequent payment with reversing entry:

Mar. 5	Wages and Salaries Expense	400	
	Cash		400
	To record payment of attendants' salaries.		

The effects of the two alternative methods in T-account form are:

Without reversing entry:

Wages and Salaries Expense			Wages and Salaries Payable		
Jan. 31	800		Mar. 5	400	Feb. 28 (A) 400
Feb. 21	1,200				Bal. 0
Feb. 28 (A) 400		Feb. 28 (C) 2,400			
Bal.	0				

With reversing entry:

Wages and Salaries Expense			Wages and Salaries Payable		
Jan. 31	800		Mar. 1 (R) 400		Feb. 28 (A) 400
Feb. 21	1,200				Bal. 0
Feb. 28 (A) 400		Feb. 28 (C) 2,400			
Mar. 5	400	Mar. 1 (R) 400			
Bal.	0				

> A = Adjusting
> C = Closing
> R = Reversing

The amount of wages and salaries expense recognized through February 28 under both methods is $2,400, and the amount of expense recognized as a result of the payment of $400 in March is zero.

REVIEW PROBLEM

The unadjusted trial balance for Mike's Advertising Agency is given below:

Mike's Advertising Agency Trial Balance January 31, 19X1		
	Debits	*Credits*
Cash	$ 9,700	
Accounts Receivable	1,100	
Office Supplies	1,700	
Prepaid Insurance	2,400	
Prepaid Rent	6,000	
Equipment	12,000	
Accumulated Depreciation – Equipment		$ 1,200
Accounts Payable		3,700
Unearned Revenue		4,100
Notes Payable – Noncurrent		8,000
Mike Doyle, Capital		15,200
Mike Doyle, Withdrawals	1,200	
Fee Revenue		4,800
Utilities Expense	700	
Wages and Salaries Expense	2,200	
Totals	$37,000	$37,000

Additional Information:

(a) A count of supplies revealed that $1,300 remained on hand as of January 31.

(b) Mike purchased a 1-year insurance policy for $2,400 on January 1, 19X1.

(c) Mike paid 1 year's rent of $6,000 in advance on January 1, 19X1.

(d) Purchased equipment on January 1, 19X0. Its expected useful life is 10 years.

(e) Palmer Company paid $4,100 on January 3 for advertising services to be performed in January and February. On January 31, $3,200 of these services have been performed.

(f) Assume that the balance in Mike Doyle, Capital represents the January 1 balance in the accounts.

REQUIRED:

a. Prepare a worksheet for the month ended January 31, 19X1.

b. Prepare financial statements.

c. Journalize and post adjusting entries.

d. Journalize and post closing entries.

e. Prepare a post-closing trial balance.

f. Calculate the current ratio for Mike's Advertising Agency.

SOLUTION:

Planning and Organizing Your Work

1. Transfer the information from the unadjusted trial balance to the first two columns of the worksheet and sum these worksheet columns.

2. Using the additional information, record adjusting entries in the Adjustments columns of the worksheet, and sum these worksheet columns.

3. Prepare the adjusted trial balance by summing across the Trial Balance columns and the Adjustments columns and sum the Adjusted Trial Balance columns.
4. Complete the Income Statement columns by transferring adjusted revenue and expense account balances to the Income Statement columns. Sum each column and place the difference in the Net Income row in the Dr. column such that the two columns are equal.
5. Complete the Balance Sheet columns by transferring the adjusted asset, liability, and owner's equity account balances to the Balance Sheet columns. Transfer the Net Income amount from Step 4 to the Balance Sheet Cr. column. Sum the Balance Sheet columns.
6. Prepare the income statement from the Income Statement columns of the worksheet.
7. Prepare the statement of owner's equity.
8. Prepare a classified balance sheet from the Balance Sheet columns of the worksheet.
9. Journalize and post the adjusting entries from the Adjustments columns of the worksheet.
10. Journalize and post closing entries for revenue, expense, and withdrawal accounts.
11. Prepare the post-closing trial balance.

(a) *Prepare a worksheet.*

Mike's Advertising Agency
Worksheet
For the Month Ended January 31, 19X1

ACCOUNTS	TRIAL BALANCE Dr.	TRIAL BALANCE Cr.	ADJUSTMENTS Dr.	ADJUSTMENTS Cr.	ADJUSTED TRIAL BALANCE Dr.	ADJUSTED TRIAL BALANCE Cr.	INCOME STATEMENT Dr.	INCOME STATEMENT Cr.	BALANCE SHEET Dr.	BALANCE SHEET Cr.
Cash	9,700				9,700				9,700	
Accounts Receivable	1,100				1,100				1,100	
Office Supplies	1,700			(a) 400	1,300				1,300	
Prepaid Insurance	2,400			(b) 200	2,200				2,200	
Prepaid Rent	6,000			(c) 500	5,500				5,500	
Equipment	12,000				12,000				12,000	
Accum. Deprec.–Equip.		1,200		(d) 100		1,300				1,300
Accounts Payable		3,700				3,700				3,700
Unearned Revenue		4,100	(e) 3,200			900				900
Notes Pay.–Noncurrent		8,000				8,000				8,000
Mike Doyle, Capital		15,200				15,200				15,200
Mike Doyle, Withdrawals	1,200				1,200				1,200	
Fee Revenue		4,800		(e) 3,200		8,000		8,000		
Deprec. Expense–Equip.			(d) 100		100		100			
Insurance Expense			(b) 200		200		200			
Rent Expense			(c) 500		500		500			
Supplies Expense			(a) 400		400		400			
Utilities Expense	700				700		700			
Wages and Salaries Exp.	2,200				2,200		2,200			
	37,000	37,000	4,400	4,400	37,100	37,100	4,100	8,000	33,000	29,100
Net Income							3,900			3,900
							8,000	8,000	33,000	33,000

(b) *Prepare financial statements.*

Mike's Advertising Agency
Income Statement
For the Month Ended January 31, 19X1

Fee revenue		$8,000
Expenses:		
Depreciation expense–equip.	$ 100	
Insurance expense	200	
Rent expense	500	
Supplies expense	400	
Utilities expense	700	
Wages and salaries expense	2,200	
Total expenses		4,100
Net income		$3,900

Mike's Advertising Agency
Statement of Owner's Equity
For the Month Ended January 31, 19X1

Beginning balance	$15,200
Add: Net income	3,900
Less: Owner's withdrawal	(1,200)
Ending balance	$17,900

Mike's Advertising Agency
Balance Sheet
January 31, 19X1

Assets

Current assets:		
Cash		$ 9,700
Accounts receivable		1,100
Office supplies		1,300
Prepaid rent		5,500
Prepaid insurance		2,200
Total current assets		$19,800
Property, plant, and equipment:		
Equipment	$12,000	
Less: Accumulated depreciation	1,300	
Total property, plant, and equipment		10,700
Total assets		$30,500

Liabilities and Owner's Equity

Current liabilities:	
Accounts payable	$ 3,700
Unearned revenue	900
Total current liabilities	$ 4,600
Noncurrent liabilities:	
Notes payable–noncurrent	8,000
Total liabilities	$12,600
Owner's equity	17,900
Total liabilities and owner's equity	$30,500

(c) *Journalize and post adjusting entries.*

Jan. 31	Supplies Expense	400	
	Office Supplies		400
	To record the use of $400 ($1,700 – $1,300) of supplies.		
31	Insurance Expense	200	
	Prepaid Insurance		200
	To record insurance expense of $200 ($2,400 ÷ 12 mo.).		
31	Rent Expense	500	
	Prepaid Rent		500
	To record rent expense of $500 ($6,000 ÷ 12 mos.).		
31	Depreciation Expense	100	
	Accumulated Depreciation – Equipment		100
	To record depreciation expense of $100 ($12,000 ÷ 120 mos.).		
31	Unearned Revenue	3,200	
	Fee Revenue		3,200
	To record earned revenue.		

See pages 159–160 for the postings to the general ledger.

(d) *Journalize and post closing entries.*

Refer to the Adjusted Trial Balance columns on the worksheet in section (a) of this solution to determine the correct amounts to close the books.

Jan. 31	Fee Revenue	8,000	
	Income Summary		8,000
	To close Fee Revenue.		
31	Income Summary	4,100	
	Depreciation Expense—Equipment		100
	Insurance Expense		200
	Rent Expense		500
	Supplies Expense		400
	Utilities Expense		700
	Wages and Salaries Expense		2,200
	To close expense accounts.		
31	Income Summary	3,900	
	Mike Doyle, Capital		3,900
	To close Income Summary.		
31	Mike Doyle, Capital	1,200	
	Mike Doyle, Withdrawals		1,200
	To close Withdrawals.		

GENERAL LEDGER

NAME: Office Supplies   **ACCOUNT NO.: 136**

DATE		DESCRIPTION	POST. REF.	DEBIT	CREDIT	BALANCE
Jan.	31	Balance				1,700
	31	Adjusting (a)			400	1,300

NAME: Prepaid Insurance   **ACCOUNT NO.: 150**

DATE		DESCRIPTION	POST. REF.	DEBIT	CREDIT	BALANCE
Jan.	31	Balance				2,400
	31	Adjusting (b)			200	2,200

NAME: Prepaid Rent   **ACCOUNT NO.: 152**

DATE		DESCRIPTION	POST. REF.	DEBIT	CREDIT	BALANCE
Jan.	31	Balance				6,000
	31	Adjusting (c)			500	5,500

NAME: Accumulated Deprec.–Equip.   **ACCOUNT NO.: 231**

DATE		DESCRIPTION	POST. REF.	DEBIT	CREDIT	BALANCE
Jan.	31	Balance				1,200
	31	Adjusting (d)			100	1,300

NAME: Unearned Revenue   **ACCOUNT NO.: 342**

DATE		DESCRIPTION	POST. REF.	DEBIT	CREDIT	BALANCE
Jan.	31	Balance				4,100
	31	Adjusting (e)		3,200		900

NAME: Mike Doyle, Capital   **ACCOUNT NO.: 500**

DATE		DESCRIPTION	POST. REF.	DEBIT	CREDIT	BALANCE
Jan.	31	Balance				15,200
	31	Closing			3,900	19,100
	31	Closing		1,200		17,900

NAME: Mike Doyle, Withdrawals   **ACCOUNT NO.: 502**

DATE		DESCRIPTION	POST. REF.	DEBIT	CREDIT	BALANCE
Jan.	31	Balance				1,200
	31	Closing			1,200	0

NAME: Income Summary   ACCOUNT NO.: 599

DATE		DESCRIPTION	POST. REF.	DEBIT	CREDIT	BALANCE
Jan.	31	Closing			8,000	8,000
	31	Closing		4,100		3,900
	31	Closing		3,900		0

NAME: Fee Revenue   ACCOUNT NO.: 604

DATE		DESCRIPTION	POST. REF.	DEBIT	CREDIT	BALANCE
Jan.	31	Balance				4,800
	31	Adjusting (e)			3,200	8,000
	31	Closing		8,000		0

NAME: Depreciation Expense–Equip.   ACCOUNT NO.: 712

DATE		DESCRIPTION	POST. REF.	DEBIT	CREDIT	BALANCE
Jan.	31	Adjusting (d)		100		100
	31	Closing			100	0

NAME: Insurance Expense   ACCOUNT NO.: 728

DATE		DESCRIPTION	POST. REF.	DEBIT	CREDIT	BALANCE
Jan.	31	Adjusting (b)		200		200
	31	Closing			200	0

NAME: Rent Expense   ACCOUNT NO.: 762

DATE		DESCRIPTION	POST. REF.	DEBIT	CREDIT	BALANCE
Jan.	31	Adjusting (c)		500		500
	31	Closing			500	0

NAME: Supplies Expense   ACCOUNT NO.: 774

DATE		DESCRIPTION	POST. REF.	DEBIT	CREDIT	BALANCE
Jan.	31	Adjusting (a)		400		400
	31	Closing			400	0

NAME: Utilities Expense   ACCOUNT NO.: 780

DATE		DESCRIPTION	POST. REF.	DEBIT	CREDIT	BALANCE
Jan.	31	Balance				700
	31	Closing			700	0

NAME: Wages and Salaries Expense   ACCOUNT NO.: 784

DATE		DESCRIPTION	POST. REF.	DEBIT	CREDIT	BALANCE
Jan.	31	Balance				2,200
	31	Closing			2,200	0

(e) *Prepare a post-closing trial balance.*

Mike's Advertising Agency Post-Closing Trial Balance January 31, 19X1		
	Debits	*Credits*
Cash	$ 9,700	
Accounts Receivable	1,100	
Office Supplies	1,300	
Prepaid Insurance	2,200	
Prepaid Rent	5,500	
Equipment	12,000	
Accumulated Depreciation – Equipment		$ 1,300
Accounts Payable		3,700
Unearned Revenue		900
Notes Payable – Noncurrent		8,000
Mike Doyle, Capital		17,900
Totals	$31,800	$31,800

(f) *Calculate the current ratio.*

$19,900 ÷ $4,600 = 4.33

KEY TERMS

classified balance sheet, *146*
closing temporary accounts, *140*
current assets, *148*
current liabilities, *149*
current ratio, *150*

Income Summary, *140*
intangible assets, *149*
liquidity, *148*
long-term investments, *148*
noncurrent liabilities, *149*
operating cycle, *146*

post-closing trial balance, *144*
promissory note, *148*
property, plant, and
  equipment, *148*
reversing entry, *152*
temporary accounts, *140*

SELF-QUIZ

LO 1   1. True or False? All columns on an accountant's worksheet should sum to the same total.

LO 1   2. Which of the following is *not* a purpose of preparing a worksheet?
   a. Assist in the adjustment process
   b. Help calculate net income
   c. Determine if journal entries are posted to the correct account
   d. Help prepare financial statements

LO 2   3. After accountants prepare adjusting entries, they journalize them in the _____ _____ _____ and post the entries to the _____ _____.

LO 3   4. Name the three types of temporary accounts.

LO 3   5. Which of the alternatives describe the balances in the temporary accounts after the closing process is complete?

   a. All of these accounts will have a debit balance.
   b. All of theses accounts will have a credit balance.
   c. Some of these accounts will have debit balances, and others will have credit balances.
   d. All of these accounts will have a zero balance at the beginning and at the end of each accounting period.

LO 3   6. For the following accounts, which of the indicated balances is an *incorrect* normal balance?
   a. Capital has a credit balance.
   b. Withdrawals has a debit balance.
   c. Revenue accounts have a debit balance.
   d. Expense accounts have a debit balance.

LO 3 7. Revenue and expense accounts are first closed to _____ _____.

LO 3 8. After we close the revenue and expense accounts, we should close Owner's Withdrawals to Owner's _____.

LO 5 9. Name the three steps in the accounting cycle that are performed on a daily basis.

LO 5 10. Name the two steps in the accounting cycle performed at the end of both interim and annual periods.

LO 5 11. Name the step of the accounting cycle that is performed only annually.

LO 5 12. Which partial list of steps in the accounting cycle is in the right order.
   a. Journalize, prepare statements, adjust, close temporary accounts
   b. Journalize, post to general ledger, close temporary accounts, adjust accounts
   c. Post to general ledger, close temporary accounts, journalize, prepare statements
   d. Adjust, close temporary accounts, analyze transactions, prepare statements

LO 6 13. Which list of asset classifications is found in the classified balance sheet?
   a. Current assets; long-term investments; property, plant, and equipment; intangible assets
   b. Revenues, expenses, gains, losses
   c. Cash, accounts receivable, inventories, prepaid expenses
   d. Land, equipment, accumulated depreciation

LO 6 14. Match these definitions with the asset classifications that appear in a classified balance sheet.
   a. Current assets
   b. Long-term investments
   c. Property, plant, and equipment
   d. Intangible assets

   (1) Assets that typically include land, equipment, and buildings
   (2) Assets that include patents and trademarks
   (3) Assets that include stocks and bonds that are not expected to be sold in the foreseeable future
   (4) Assets that are short-term and are arranged in order of liquidity

LO 6 15. The two classifications of liabilities on the balance sheet are _____ liabilities and _____ liabilities.

LO 7 16. True or False? Liquidity is a measure of how fast a business spends cash.

LO 7 17. True or False? The current ratio is useful to assess the business's debt-paying ability.

LO 7 18. Compute the current ratio if total current assets equal $2,500 and total current liabilities equal $500.

SOLUTIONS TO SELF-QUIZ
1. False   2. c   3. general journal, general ledger   4. Revenues, expenses, and withdrawals   5. d   6. c
7. Income Summary   8. Capital   9. Analyze transactions, journalize transactions, post to general ledger   10. Adjust accounts and prepare statements   11. Close temporary accounts   12. a   13. a   14. a. 4 b. 3 c. 1 d. 2
15. Current, noncurrent   16. False   17. True   18. $2,500 ÷ $500 = 5:1

QUESTIONS

Q4-1 Explain to a new business associate why it is necessary to prepare a worksheet.
Q4-2 How does a worksheet assist the accountant in preparing financial statements?
Q4-3 Why is it necessary to close the temporary accounts?
Q4-4 What are the necessary steps to close temporary accounts?
Q4-5 What is the purpose of Income Summary?
Q4-6 What are the steps in the accounting cycle?
Q4-7 What is the purpose of a post-closing trial balance?
Q4-8 What are the typical classifications of a classified balance sheet?
Q4-9 What is the purpose of preparing a classified balance sheet?
Q4-10 How is the concept of liquidity applied to the preparation of the balance sheet?
Q4-11 Explain why a high current ratio is not always better than a low current ratio.

EXERCISES

LO 1

E4-1 **Worksheet Preparation** Determine whether the following items from the Adjusted Trial Balance columns in a worksheet should be extended to: (*a*) the Income Statement Dr. column, (*b*) the Income Statement Cr. column, (*c*) the Balance Sheet Dr. column, or (*d*) the Balance Sheet Cr. column.

____ Notes Payable	____ Repair Revenue
____ Owner's, Withdrawals	____ Wages and Salaries Payable
____ Depreciation Expense—Equipment	____ Owner's, Capital
____ Unearned Revenue	____ Utilities Expense
____ Accumulated Depreciation—Equipment	____ Accounts Payable
____ Equipment	____ Prepaid Rent
____ Accounts Receivable	____ Rent Expense

LO 5

E4-2 **The Accounting Cycle** Indicate the appropriate order of the following steps in the accounting cycle. Use numbers 1 through 6.

____ Close temporary accounts	____ Journalize transactions
____ Post to general ledger	____ Prepare statements
____ Adjust accounts	____ Analyze transactions

LO 6

E4-3 **Asset Classification** Place the correct letter next to each item below after determining if the item is classified as a current asset (*C*); a long-term investment (*L*); property, plant, and equipment (*P*); an intangible asset (*I*); or not an asset (*N*).

____ Cash	____ Land held for investment
____ Factory building	____ Accounts receivable
____ Accumulated depreciation	____ Patents
____ Unearned revenue	____ Prepaid expenses
____ Supplies	____ Withdrawals

LO 6

E4-4 **Balance Sheet Classification** Place the correct letter next to each item below after determining if the item appears on a balance sheet as a current asset (*C*); a long-term investment (*L*); property, plant, and equipment (*P*); an intangible asset (*I*); a current liability (*CL*); a noncurrent liability (*NL*); owner's equity (*O*); or not on the balance sheet (*N*).

____ Notes payable	____ Owner's capital
____ Trademarks	____ Accounts payable
____ Unearned revenue	____ Utilities expense
____ Owner's, withdrawals	____ Accounts receivable
____ Land	____ Accumulated depreciation—equipment
____ Bonds payable	____ Interest payable
____ Sales revenue	____ Securities held for more than a year

LO 3

E4-5 **Closing Entries** Prepare closing entries from the following list of account balances:

Accounts Receivable	$43,500	Utilities Expense	$13,900
Accumulated Deprec.—Equip.	21,000	Interest Payable	7,600
Wages and Salaries Expense	13,200	Rent Expense	3,600
Repairs Revenue	68,500	Insurance Expense	8,100
Owner's, Withdrawals	12,200	Deprec. Expense—Equip.	12,900
Owner's, Capital	49,900	Notes Payable	46,600

LO 3,4

E4-6 **Prepare a Post-Closing Trial Balance** Prepare the closing entries and a post-closing trial balance for Reither's Travel Service from the adjusted trial balance given on the next page:

Reither's Travel Service Adjusted Trial Balance December 31, 19X4		
	Debits	Credits
Cash	$14,550	
Accounts Receivable	1,650	
Office Supplies	2,550	
Prepaid Insurance	3,600	
Prepaid Rent	9,000	
Equipment	18,000	
Accumulated Depreciation – Equipment		$ 1,800
Accounts Payable		5,550
Unearned Revenue		6,150
Notes Payable – Noncurrent		12,000
Walter Reither, Capital		22,800
Walter Reither, Withdrawals	1,800	
Fee Revenue		7,700
Supplies Expense	650	
Utilities Expense	900	
Wages and Salaries Expense	3,300	
Totals	$56,000	$56,000

LO 6

E4-7   Classified Balance Sheet Preparation   Using the following data, prepare a classified balance sheet for the Gunther Company as of December 31, 19X2.

Building	$100,000
Accumulated deprec.—bldg.	12,500
Cash	6,000
Accounts payable	30,000
Equipment	30,000
Supplies	37,500
Long-term investment	5,000
Wages and salaries payable	14,000
Notes payable—noncurrent	53,000
Land	50,000
Accumulated deprec.—equip.	5,000
Notes payable—current	20,000
Trademarks	2,500
Accounts receivable	25,000
Unearned revenue	13,000
Amelia Gunther, capital	?

LO 2

E4-8   Preparing Adjusting Entries from a Worksheet   From the partial worksheet for Eagle for the year ended December 31, 19X2, prepare the adjusting entries that apparently were made to proceed from the unadjusted to the adjusted trial balance and explain each entry.

Eagle
Partial Worksheet for Financial Statements
December 31, 19X2

ACCOUNTS	TRIAL BALANCE Dr.	TRIAL BALANCE Cr.	ADJUSTED TRIAL BALANCE Dr.	ADJUSTED TRIAL BALANCE Cr.
Cash	9,700		9,700	
Accounts Receivable	1,100		1,100	
Office Supplies	1,700		1,100	
Prepaid Insurance	2,400		2,200	
Prepaid Rent	6,000		5,500	
Equipment	12,000		12,000	
Accumulated Deprec.–Equip.		1,200		1,800
Accounts Payable		3,700		3,700
Unearned Revenue		4,100		900
Notes Payable–Noncurrent		8,000		8,000
T. Eagle, Capital		15,200		15,200
T. Eagle, Withdrawals	1,200		1,200	
Revenue		4,800		8,000
Depreciation Expense–Equipment			600	
Insurance Expense			200	
Rent Expense			500	
Supplies Expense			600	
Utilities Expense	700		700	
Wages and Salaries Expense	2,200		2,200	
	37,000	37,000	37,600	37,600

LO 3

E4-9   Prepare Closing Entries   Prepare closing entries from the worksheet for Eagle presented in E4-8.

LO 1

E4-10   Completing a Worksheet   Complete the worksheet for Tribeca, shown on the next page, and prepare an income statement and a balance sheet.

LO 6

E4-11   Calculating the Current Ratio   Calculate the current ratio for Tribeca from the adjusted trial balance presented in the partial worksheet in E4-10.

LO 8

E4-12   Reversing Entries (Appendix 4-A)   Prepare adjusting entries, reversing entries, and subsequent cash transaction entries for events (a) and (b) for the Ultra Cleaning Company in 19X8.
   a. On December 1, 19X7, the Ultra Cleaning Company entered into an agreement to clean floors for the White Company for $2,000 per month. The cleaning services started immediately. Ultra collects $2,000 of cash from White on January 15, 19X8.
   b. Jim Broom, an employee of Ultra, receives $250 every Friday for five days of work. Jim worked 3 days at the end of 19X7 and 2 days to complete the first week ending in 19X8. Payment was made to Jim on Friday, January 2, 19X8.

Tribeca
Partial Worksheet for Financial Statements
December 31, 19X2

ACCOUNTS	ADJUSTED TRIAL BALANCE		INCOME STATEMENT		BALANCE SHEET	
	Dr.	Cr.	Dr.	Cr.	Dr.	Cr.
Cash	4,850					
Accounts Receivable	550					
Office Supplies	550					
Prepaid Insurance	1,100					
Prepaid Rent	4,750					
Equipment	16,000					
Accumulated Deprec.—Equip.		1,200				
Accounts Payable		1,500				
Unearned Revenue		1,900				
Notes Payable—Noncurrent		10,000				
D. Tribeca, Capital		12,225				
D. Tribeca, Withdrawals	600					
Revenue		3,975				
Depreciation Expense—Equip.	300					
Insurance Expense	100					
Rent Expense	250					
Supplies Expense	300					
Utilities Expense	350					
Wages and Salaries Expense	1,100					
	30,800	30,800				
Net Income						

PROBLEM SET A

LO 1,2,3,6 **P4-1A** **Preparing a Worksheet** The trial balance for Dara's Services International at December 31, 19X5, is presented on the next page:

Additional Information:

(1) A count of supplies revealed that $3,900 remained on hand as of December 31.
(2) Dara purchased a 2-year insurance policy for $1,200 on January 1, 19X5.
(3) Paid 2 year's rent of $18,000 in advance on January 1, 19X5.
(4) The equipment was purchased on January 1, 19X4. The expected life of the equipment was 10 years at the time of purchase.
(5) Dara's Services International was paid $12,300 on December 5 for services to be performed in December and January. On December 31, $9,600 of these services have been performed.

REQUIRED:

a. Prepare a worksheet similar to Illustration 4-5.
b. Prepare an income statement for the year ended December 31, 19X5.
c. Prepare a classified balance sheet as of December 31, 19X5.
d. Journalize adjusting entries for 19X5.
e. Journalize closing entries for 19X5.
f. Prepare a post-closing trial balance.
g. Calculate the current ratio as of December 31, 19X5.

Dara's Services International
Trial Balance
December 31, 19X5

	Debits	Credits
Cash	$ 29,100	
Accounts Receivable	3,300	
Office Supplies	5,100	
Prepaid Insurance	1,200	
Prepaid Rent	18,000	
Equipment	36,000	
Accumulated Depreciation—Equipment		$ 3,600
Accounts Payable		11,100
Unearned Revenue		12,300
Notes Payable—Noncurrent		24,000
Evan Dara, Capital		39,600
Evan Dara, Withdrawals	3,600	
Fee Revenue		14,400
Wages and Salaries Expense	6,600	
Utilities Expense	2,100	
Totals	$105,000	$105,000

LO 1,2,3,4,6   **P4-2A**   **Preparing a Worksheet**   The trial balance for Carol's Consulting Company at January 31, 19X3, and additional information are presented below.

Carol's Consulting Company
Trial Balance
January 31, 19X3

	Debits	Credits
Cash	$ 67,720	
Accounts Receivable	55,900	
Office Supplies	9,010	
Prepaid Rent	12,000	
Prepaid Insurance	28,000	
Office Equipment	84,000	
Accumulated Depreciation—Office Equipment		$ 31,500
Accounts Payable		14,600
Unearned Fees		12,000
Notes Payable—Noncurrent		100,000
June Carol, Capital		45,330
Fee Revenue		130,000
Miscellaneous Expense	11,400	
Rent Expense	4,800	
Utilities Expense	6,600	
Wages and Salaries Expense	54,000	
Totals	$333,430	$333,430

Additional Information:
(1) A count of remaining supplies revealed that $7,580 remained on hand as of January 31.
(2) Prepaid rent of $4,800 expired during the month.

(3) The January 31 balance of Prepaid Insurance should be $21,000.
(4) Depreciation for one month on the office furniture is $875.
(5) One-third of the balance of the unearned fees account was not earned during the month.
(6) Salary expense of $1,800 should be accrued at the end of January.

REQUIRED:

a. Prepare a worksheet similar to the one in the text.
b. Prepare an income statement for the month ended January 31, 19X3.
c. Prepare a classified balance sheet as of January 31, 19X3.
d. Journalize adjusting entries for January.
e. Journalize closing entries for January.
f. Prepare a post-closing trial balance.

LO 3   **P4-3A   Closing Entries**   A listing of account balances is given below:

Accounts Receivable	$27,900	Wage and Salaries Expense	$29,900
Accumulated Deprec.—Bldgs.	11,000	Sales Taxes Payable	6,700
Insurance Expense	10,200	Rent Expense	5,600
Revenue	98,600	Sales Tax Expense	18,700
Owner's, Withdrawals	9,200	Deprec. Expense—Bldgs.	12,900
Owner's, Capital	78,100	Wages and Salaries Payable	6,600
Miscellaneous Revenue	7,900	Utilities Expense	5,300
Unearned Revenue	44,440	Supplies Expense	13,900

REQUIRED:

Prepare closing entries from the list of account balances.

LO 1   **P4-4A   Income Statement Errors**   The income statement for CHK Company contains several errors.

Income Statement
CHK Company
February 30, 19X9

Revenue:		
Repair Revenue		$ 8,000
Unearned Revenue		2,200
Total Revenue		$12,200
Utilities Expense	$ 700	
Supplies Expense	400	
Accumulated Depreciation	1,300	
Insurance Expense	100	
Rent Expense	500	
Prepaid Insurance	600	
Depreciation Expense	200	
Subtract		6,100
Profit		$ 4,900

REQUIRED:

a. Identify each error.
b. Prepare a corrected income statement for CHK Company.

LO 6   **P4-5A   Balance Sheet Errors**   The balance sheet for Copeland Accounting Services contains several errors.

Balance Sheet For the year ended March 31, 19X4		
Assets		
Property, Plant and Equipment		
Equipment	$12,000	
Supplies	1,300	
Total Property, Plant & Equipment		13,300
Current Assets:		
Prepaid Insurance	3,300	
Cash	9,700	
Accounts Receivable	1,100	
Prepaid Rent	8,400	
Total Current Assets		$19,900
Total Assets		$40,500
Liabilities		
Current Liabilities:		
Accounts Payable	$6,600	
Less Accumulated Depreciation—Equipment	1,400	
Unearned Revenue	900	
Total Current Liabilities		$ 6,000
Wages and Salaries Payable		13,600
Notes Payable—Noncurrent		$ 8,000
Total Liabilities		$25,300
Owner's Equity:		
Amanda Copeland, Capital, March 1		$?
Less: March Net Income	$ 3,900	
Plus Withdrawals	1,200	
Excess of Income Over Withdrawals	(2,700)	
Amanda Copeland, Capital, January 31		$21,600
Total Liabilities and Owner's Equity		$46,900

REQUIRED:

a. Identify each error.
b. Prepare a corrected classified balance sheet for Copeland Accounting Services.

PROBLEM SET B

LO 1,2,3,6   **P4-1B   Preparing a Worksheet**   The trial balance for Travel Time at December 31, 19X6, is presented on the next page.

Additional Information:
(1) Used $1,600 of supplies during 19X6.
(2) Travel Time purchased an 18-month insurance policy on January 1, 19X6, for $3,600.
(3) Paid 2 year's rent in advance on January 1, 19X6.
(4) The equipment was purchased on January 1, 19X5. The expected useful life was 10 years at the time of purchase.
(5) Collected $2,100 of travel deposits in 19X6 for trips to be taken in 19X7. The deposits were credited to the revenue account.

Travel Time Trial Balance December 31, 19X6		
	Debits	Credits
Cash	$ 9,100	
Accounts Receivable	13,800	
Office Supplies	4,800	
Prepaid Insurance	3,600	
Prepaid Rent	24,000	
Equipment	36,500	
Accumulated Depreciation—Equipment		$ 3,650
Accounts Payable		11,300
Notes Payable—Noncurrent		30,600
Indigo Collins, Capital		22,150
Indigo Collins, Withdrawals	2,800	
Revenue		36,800
Utilities Expense	1,600	
Wages and Salaries Expense	8,300	
Totals	$104,500	$104,500

REQUIRED:

a. Prepare a worksheet similar to the one in the Illustration 4-5.
b. Prepare an income statement for the year ended December 31, 19X6.
c. Prepare a classified balance sheet as of December 31, 19X6.
d. Journalize adjusting entries for 19X6.
e. Journalize closing entries for 19X6.
f. Prepare a post-closing trial balance.
g. Calculate the current ratio as of December 31, 19X6.

LO 1,2,3,4,6   **P4-2B**   **Preparing a Worksheet**   The trial balance for Koch Services at January 31, 19X7, is presented on the next page.

Additional Information:

(1) A count of office supplies revealed that $12,300 remained on hand as of January 31.
(2) One-third of the prepaid rent expired during the month.
(3) The amount of $15,100 of prepaid insurance remained as of January 31.
(4) Depreciation for the month on the office equipment is $825.
(5) One-half of the balance of the Unearned Fees account was earned during the month.
(6) Salary expense of $4,100 should be accrued at the end of January.

REQUIRED:

a. Prepare a worksheet similar to the one in Illustration 4-5.
b. Prepare an income statement for the month ended January 31, 19X7.
c. Prepare a classified balance sheet as of January 31, 19X7.
d. Journalize and post adjusting entries for January.
e. Journalize and post closing entries for January.
f. Prepare a post-closing trial balance.

Koch Services Trial Balance January 31, 19X7		
	Debits	Credits
Cash	$ 56,350	
Accounts Receivable	41,600	
Office Supplies	17,900	
Prepaid Rent	6,600	
Prepaid Insurance	18,600	
Office Equipment	99,000	
Accum. Depr. – Office Equipment		$ 9,900
Accounts Payable		17,600
Unearned Fees		21,960
Notes Payable – Noncurrent		100,000
Wages and Salaries Payable		3,000
Thomas Koch, Capital		51,990
Fee Revenue		108,300
Miscellaneous Expense	10,700	
Rent Expense	11,600	
Utilities Expense	4,900	
Wages and Salaries Expense	45,500	
Totals	$312,750	$312,750

LO 3

P4-3B   Closing Entries   A listing of account balances is given below:

Equipment	$ 45,700
Accumulated Deprec.—Equip.	16,000
Wages and Salaries Payable	1,100
Unearned Fees	88,600
Owner's, Withdrawals	19,800
Owner's, Capital	66,200
Miscellaneous Revenue	9,700
Fee Revenue	114,440
Wages and Salaries Expense	32,400
Rent Payable	7,600
Insurance Expense	5,500
Insurance Premium Payable	16,700
Deprec. Expense—Equip.	10,900
Prepaid Rent	16,600
Utilities Expense	9,700
Supplies Expense	18,800

REQUIRED:

Prepare closing entries from the list of account balances.

LO 1

P4-4B   Income Statement Errors   The income statement for BSK Company shown on the next page contains several errors.

REQUIRED:

a. Identify each error.

b. Prepare a corrected income statement for BSK Company.

Profit Statement BSK On April 31, 19X4		
Expenses:		
Supplies Expense	700	
Repair Revenue		$18,000
Total Revenue		11,200
Utilities Expense	600	
Accumulated Depreciation—Equipment	31,300	
Unearned Revenue		2,200
Wages and Salaries Expense	800	
Withdrawals	9,900	
Prepaid Rent	1,200	
Depreciation Expense—Equipment	900	
Subtract		86,100
Profit		$ 4,900

LO 6   **P4-5B**   **Balance Sheet Errors**   The balance sheet for Carlson Repairs contains several errors.

Balance Sheet For the year ended June 31, 19X2		
Assets		
Property, Plant and Equipment		
Accumulated Deprec.,Equip.	$12,000	
Supplies	1,300	
Total Property, Plant & Equipment		13,300
Current Assets:		
Prepaid Insurance	13,300	
Cash	6,200	
Accounts Receivable	1,900	
Rent Expense	18,400	
Total Current Assets		17,400
Total Assets		$49,100
Liabilities		
Current Liabilities:		
Accounts Payable	$8,700	
Less Depreciation Expense—Equipment		1,400
Total Current Liabilities		$6,000
Equipment		61,000
Wages and Salaries Payable		31,600
Notes Payable—Noncurrent		$18,000
Total Liabilities		$28,920
Owner's Equity:		
Coda, Capital, March 1		$?
Less: March Net Income	$7,900	
Plus Withdrawals	2,100	
Excess of Income Over Withdrawals	(3,300)	
Coda, Capital, January, 31		$24,300
Total Liabilities and Owner's Equity		$66,900

REQUIRED:

a. Identify each error.
b. Prepare a corrected classified balance sheet for Carlson Repairs.

CRITICAL THINKING AND COMMUNICATING

C4-1 Jill Smith decided to expand her small restaurant, which has been overcrowded for the last several years. Unfortunately, Smith did not have sufficient cash to pay for the expansion; so, she decided to see her banker and to apply for a loan. Smith had anticipated that the banker would want to analyze her financial condition; so she brought along her restaurant's financial statements. In examining Smith's financial statements, the banker said he was pleased that she had prepared a classified balance sheet because it made his analysis of the restaurant's financial condition easier.

REQUIRED:

a. Explain why the banker prefers to use a classified balance sheet.
b. Consider the account balances that are used in assessing the liquidity of a business. Discuss how some of the accounts could lead to the understatement or overstatement of a business's liquidity.

C4-2 You are a consultant to the owner of an auto repair shop that is growing rapidly. The business received a $20,000 business loan with the First National Bank of San Jose on January 3, 19X3. The loan is due on December 31, 19X7. The terms of the loan specify that the business must maintain a current ratio of at least 2:1 or the bank will demand immediate payment of the entire loan balance. The accountant has just informed the owner that this ratio will fall to 1.75:1 on the December 31, 19X5, balance sheet. The business has a good credit history and always pays its loans on a timely basis.

REQUIRED:

Write a memo to the owner of the auto repair shop, Debbie Schwartz, suggesting possible actions that she could take that would remedy the too-low current ratio.

CHAPTER 5

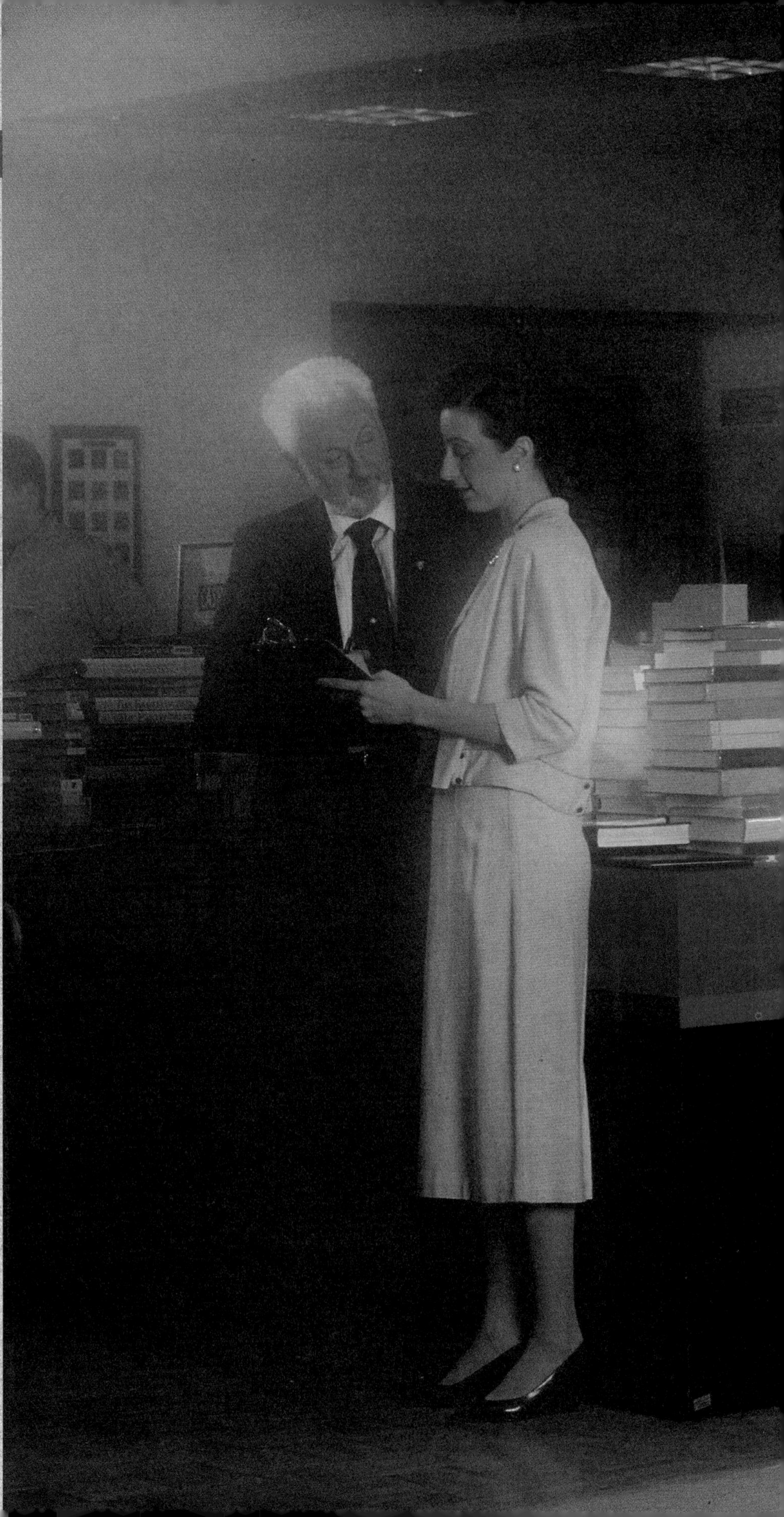

Accounting for Merchandising Businesses

Robert Good plans to retire at the end of the current business year on December 31, 19X2. He has owned and operated Good's Campus Books for 30 years but has arranged to sell it to his manager, Sheila Pell. Sheila has agreed to pay a price equal to 12 times the business's average net income for the last 5 years. Robert believes this is a fair arrangement, but he is worried because the income for the year just ended was disappointing. He wants to know what went wrong and how to turn things around for his last year. His retirement income depends on receiving a favorable price for his business. How can Robert diagnose the problem and focus his attention on the most important ways to improve his business's profitability?

In this chapter, we introduce the components of income of a merchandising business, the concept of gross profit, and a specially formatted income statement designed to reflect the way merchandising businesses earn income. After we cover the components of income and the preparation of financial statements of merchandising businesses, you will see how Robert can use financial statement information in planning to maximize the bookstore's income in his last year before retirement.

1. Describe a multistep income statement and explain why a merchandising business uses it.
2. Record gross sales, sales returns and allowances, and sales discounts and calculate net sales for a merchandising business.
3. Record gross purchases, purchases returns and allowances, purchases discounts, and transportation costs for purchased goods and calculate cost of goods purchased.
4. Describe the periodic method of inventory valuation, contrast it with the perpetual method, and calculate cost of goods sold under the periodic inventory method.
5. Describe the operating expenses of a merchandising business and distinguish between selling expenses and general and administrative expenses.
6. Use a worksheet to prepare the adjusting and closing entries for a merchandising business using the periodic inventory method.
7. Prepare the financial statements of a merchandising business, using the worksheet.
8. Calculate the cost of goods sold and gross profit ratios and use them to assess profitability.
9. Distinguish between the gross and net methods of recording purchases (Appendix 5-A).
10. Prepare a worksheet based on the closing entry method (Appendix 5-B).

MERCHANDISING OPERATIONS AND INCOME STATEMENTS

Service businesses earn their income by providing services to their customers for fees or commissions. The income statement of any business should reflect the nature of its operations—how it earns income. Service businesses have very straightforward income statements containing only three principal parts: revenues, expenses, and net income. In contrast, merchandising businesses earn their income by buying products from suppliers and then selling those products to their customers.

LO 1

Describe a multistep income statement and explain why a merchandising business uses it.

Merchandising Operations

Some merchandising businesses engage in retail trade, selling products directly to consumers. Grocery stores, drugstores, bookstores, record stores, and consumer electronics stores are examples. Another type of merchandising business sells products only on a wholesale basis to other businesses. For example, industrial electronics dealers buy and sell the basic components used to manufacture radios, televisions, stereos, and other appliances. Still another type of merchandising business sells both to other businesses and to consumers. Lumber yards and auto parts dealers are good examples in this category.

Merchandising Income Statements

Since merchandising businesses earn revenues primarily by selling products to customers, they report their expenses in two main categories: the cost of the

goods sold and operating expenses. The condensed, multistep income statement of Good's Campus Books in Illustration 5-1 reflects this format.

ILLUSTRATION 5-1 Income Statement of Good's Campus Books

Good's Campus Books Income Statement For the Year Ended December 31, 19X1	
Net sales	$697,910
Less: Cost of goods sold	447,532
Gross profit	$250,378
Less: Operating expenses	165,928
Net income	$ 84,450

In the first step of the multistep income statement, we display the net sales
(revenue) and the cost of the goods sold and calculate gross profit. **Net sales**
consists of the total amounts a business receives or expects to be collected for
the period's sales of merchandise to customers. The components and calculation of net sales are covered in later sections of this chapter. **Cost of goods
sold** represents the total purchase costs of the goods the business provides to
customers for the period. It includes the purchase costs and any costs incidental
to the purchase of the goods from suppliers—e.g., the cost of shipping from the
supplier's location. **Gross profit** is the difference between net sales and the
cost of goods sold. Good's Campus Books earned a gross profit for 19X1 of
$250,378, the difference between net sales (revenue) of $697,910 and cost of
goods sold of $447,532. *Gross profit may be interpreted as the portion of net
sales that is available to cover operating expenses and to produce a profit or net
income.*

In the second step of the multistep income statement, we subtract operating
expenses from gross profit to derive net income. **Operating expenses** consist
of all the expenses of running the business for a period, *other than the cost of
goods sold.* Operating expenses include salaries, wages, depreciation, rent, and
utilities expenses. Good's Campus Books earned net income of $84,450,
because it generated a gross profit of $250,378 in 19X1 and incurred operating
expenses of $165,928.[1] Illustration 5-2 graphically shows the logical flow of the
multistep income statement.

Illustrations 5-1 and 5-2 give you a simple, straightforward picture of the
merchandising business's income components. Actually, several important types
of transactions make up both net sales and cost of goods sold. In addition, you
will find that calculating cost of goods sold is a challenge when the business
uses the periodic inventory method (defined later in the chapter). In the following sections, we acquaint you with the major types of merchandising transactions *in the order they appear in the income statement*—first, net sales; then,
cost of goods sold. By learning to account for these transactions and learning to
calculate net sales and cost of goods sold, you will better understand merchan-

---

[1]A single-step presentation of the same income statement would appear as follows:

Net sales	$697,910
Less: Expenses	613,460
Net income	$ 84,450

ILLUSTRATION 5-2 Multistep Income Statement

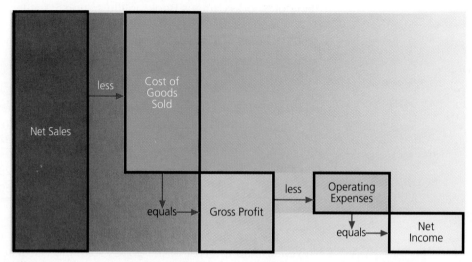

dising operations and be prepared to analyze the accounting information of merchandising businesses.

NET SALES

The term *net* in *net sales* implies that offsetting components make up the overall figure. This is the case. Several transaction components make up the net sales figure, as shown in Illustration 5-3.

ILLUSTRATION 5-3 Calculation of Net Sales

Good's Campus Books Income Statement (Partial)		
Gross sales		$736,400
Less: Sales returns and allowances	$27,444	
Sales discounts	11,046	38,490
Net sales		$697,910

Notice that the bottom figure in Illustration 5-3, net sales, is the same number as the net sales figure of Illustration 5-1. Illustration 5-3 shows the detail of how we derive a net sales figure. **Gross sales** equals the sum of the prices of all goods a business sells in a period. **Net sales** equals gross sales less sales returns and allowances and sales discounts. Net sales represents the revenue Good's Campus Books actually earned.

The merchandising business does not earn the full sales price for every sales transaction. Sometimes the merchandise sold does not satisfy the customer or is found defective, resulting in sales returns. In a **sales return** transaction, the customer returns goods previously purchased, and the seller gives a refund of the price paid. When a business gives a refund to a customer, it does not earn the revenue originally recorded.

In other cases, the goods sold are *basically* acceptable, but the customer discovers minor flaws in them. The customer often agrees to keep the goods if the business concedes to a reduction in price. A reduction in price given because merchandise is partially flawed is called a **sales allowance**. Sales allowances reduce the amount of the original price actually earned.

Additionally, in the case of credit sales, a merchant frequently offers reductions in payments on purchases to its customers to induce them to pay early. Reductions in payments to induce early payments are called **sales discounts**.

A merchandising business records sales, sales returns and allowances, and sales discounts in separate accounts as transactions occur. Net sales is not recorded directly, but is calculated in the income statement from the other components (as we demonstrate in Illustration 5-3).

Gross Sales

Gross sales is the total amount of revenue a merchandising business would earn if it always collects the full sales prices on all sales transactions—that is, if it gives no discounts, accepts no sales returns, and grants no allowances. A business uses the sales account to record gross sales. Two types of sales transactions combine to make up gross sales: cash sales and credit sales.

In a cash sale, the merchant's employees enter the prices of the merchandise sold or scan the prices marked in bar codes on the merchandise with an optical scanner connected to the cash register. The store manager, other senior employee, or a computer totals the daily sales from all the store's cash registers and records the daily total. Good's Campus Books made a total of $2,310 in cash sales for January 27, 19X1, and recorded the sales with the following general journal entry:

Jan. 27	Cash	2,310	
	Sales		2,310
	To record daily cash sales.		

In a credit sale, an employee or a computer (or, in some cases, a sophisticated cash register) lists the customer's purchases on a sales invoice. The prices and quantities of individual products are multiplied, and the product subtotals are added; the terms of payment are noted; and the customer receives a copy of the invoice (or it is mailed, if the goods are shipped to the customer). On January 27, 19X1, Good's Campus Books made a sale of used books to College Book Brokers. The details of the sale are shown on the invoice in Illustration 5-4. The entry to record the sale is:

Jan. 27	Accounts Receivable	1,500	
	Sales		1,500
	To record credit sale to College Book Brokers.		

Sales Returns and Allowances

Many businesses accept returned merchandise within a short time after the sale, *whether or not the merchandise is defective.* For example, Nordstrom's, a department store chain based in Seattle, Washington, built a remarkably loyal customer base around its policy that all returns are accepted for full refunds with no questions asked. While not all merchandising businesses have such generous policies, most accept the return of merchandise that is defective and grant

ILLUSTRATION 5-4 A Sales Invoice

<table>
<tr><td colspan="4" align="center">

Good's Campus Books
4500 Broad Street
College Place, TX 01122–3456

SALES INVOICE   568234
</td></tr>
<tr><td colspan="2">**Date:** 1/27/x1</td><td colspan="2">**Invoice Number: 568234**</td></tr>
<tr>
<td colspan="2">

Sold to
College Book Brokers
7629 Foundation Dr.
Solstice, CA 93989-4524
</td>
<td colspan="2">

Shipped to
Buyer
</td>
</tr>
<tr>
<td>**Shipping Adv.** 61204</td>
<td colspan="2">**Sales Order** 44332211</td>
<td>**Your P.O.** 24677</td>
</tr>
<tr>
<td>**Qty.**</td>
<td colspan="2">**Description**</td>
<td>**Unit Price**</td>
<td>**Amount**</td>
</tr>
<tr>
<td>200</td>
<td colspan="2">Introductory Economics
(Western College Press)</td>
<td>7.50</td>
<td>1,500.00</td>
</tr>
<tr>
<td colspan="3">

Terms: 2/10, n/30
Freight: F.O.B. shipping point
</td>
<td colspan="2">**Page total:** $ 1,500.00</td>
</tr>
<tr>
<td colspan="3">**Prepared By:** *RGM*</td>
<td colspan="2">**Verified by:** *JDG*</td>
</tr>
</table>

allowances to induce customers to keep merchandise that has only minor defects.

Sales returns and allowances are gross sales dollars that ultimately are not earned. Therefore, when sales returns and allowances occur, they could be debited directly to Sales. That is, the balance of sales for the period could be reduced directly. Would this be good business practice? No, because most merchandising managers need to keep track of sales returns and allowances separately for management reasons.

Every merchandising business can expect a certain percentage of merchandise sold to be returned. Likewise, it can expect to grant allowances up to a certain percentage of gross sales. However, unexpectedly high sales returns and allowances signal that something is wrong. For example, the merchandise it has purchased may be of poor quality, or employees may be mishandling it and causing damage. The manager will want this "signal" so that the manager can take steps to investigate the cause and to correct the situation. Debiting sales returns and allowances directly to Sales buries the returns in the balance of that account, and the manager would have no convenient way to keep track of them. *Thus, a merchandising business records its sales returns and allowances in a separate contra-account to Sales, entitled Sales Returns and Allowances.*

To record sales returns and allowances, the business credits the account that was originally debited to record the sale, either Cash or Accounts Receivable, and debits Sales Returns and Allowances. So, for example, if Good's Campus Books gave $50 of cash allowances and allowed $350 in returns of previous credit sales on February 5, 19X1, it would record returns and allowances for the day as follows:

Feb. 5	Sales Returns and Allowances	400	
	Accounts Receivable		350
	Cash		50
	To record the day's sales returns and allowances on cash and credit sales.		

Sales Discounts

Merchants commonly offer sales discounts of 1/2% to 2% to credit-sales customers to encourage them to pay their accounts earlier than the due dates. The specific amount of discount varies, depending on the level of interest rates and the amount of competition. If interest rates are low, businesses tend to offer small discounts; if interest rates are high, they tend to offer high discounts. However, if a particular business offers large sales discounts to attract credit customers, its competitors may have to do the same, regardless of the general level of interest rates.

Typically, merchants offer sales discounts for payment within 10 days. For example, a wholesale business commonly requires payment in full on all invoices within 30 days and offers a 1% discount for payment within 10 days. Such terms are usually abbreviated on invoices. For example, we abbreviate the above terms as 1/10, n/30. The *1* is the discount percent; *10* the discount period in days; *n* means *net*, referring to the full invoice total; and *30*, the period when the full amount is due (in days) if the discount is not taken. You would quote these terms to a customer as "one ten, net thirty."

Because *customers decide after the sale* whether or not to take sales discounts, we initially record credit sales at the full amounts. When customers take advantage of discounts and pay the lesser amounts, we debit the difference to an account entitled Sales Discounts. Notice the terms (2/10, n/30) of Good's Campus Books' sale of used books to College Book Brokers in Illustration 5-4 (lower left area of the invoice). Now assume that College Book Brokers pays for the used books on February 5—within the discount period of 10 days. College Book Brokers pays $1,470, and Good's records the transaction as follows:

Feb. 5	Cash	1,470	
	Sales Discounts	30	
	Accounts Receivable		1,500
	To record cash received for credit sale and discount taken.		

Sales Discounts is a contra-revenue account. It represents revenue the merchant sacrifices to secure cash from customers at an earlier date to have more cash available for business use. Assuming a business has both sales returns and allowances and sales discounts, the revenue section of its income statement would resemble Illustration 5-3 on page 178.

LO 3

Record gross purchases, purchases returns and allowances, purchases discounts, and transportation costs for purchased goods and calculate cost of goods purchased.

PURCHASE TRANSACTIONS

The cost of goods sold figure in a merchandising business's income statement is actually the net amount of several components. Purchase transactions account for several of these components. The aggregate of the costs suppliers bill to a business is the most significant component. However, this total is subject to discounts and returns and allowances; and a business also incurs additional costs such as those for transportation to put goods in place for sale.

Gross Purchases

Typically, we record purchases at the full or gross amounts the sellers charge. For example, on March 15, 19X1, Good's Campus Books purchased textbooks costing $2,000 on terms of 2/10, n/30, from Foster Publishing Company. The purchase entry is:

Mar. 15	Purchases	2,000	
	Accounts Payable		2,000
	To record the purchase of textbooks on credit.		

Purchases Returns and Allowances

Just as a merchant's customers may be dissatisfied with goods they buy, the merchant may also find purchased goods unacceptable in quality or condition. A merchant records **purchase returns** when the goods are sent back to the supplier because they are unacceptable. The supplier records them as sales returns. A merchant records **purchase allowances** when the goods are deficient in only minor ways and the supplier concedes an acceptable reduction in the amount owed for the goods.

Suppose on March 20, Good's Campus Books returned one-fourth of the textbooks it purchased from Foster Publishing on March 15. Good's entry to record the return is:

Mar. 20	Accounts Payable	500	
	Purchases Returns and Allowances		500
	To record return of textbooks purchased.		

Purchases Returns and Allowances is a *contra-account* whose balance is subtracted from gross purchases to calculate net purchases. (See Illustration 5-5.)

Purchases Discounts

Vendors (suppliers) frequently offer **purchase discounts** for early payment on credit purchases. Tradition dictates that we account for these discounts in a way that mirrors the treatment of sales discounts. An alternative treatment, which some accountants consider theoretically superior, is discussed in Appendix 5-A. According to tradition, we record credit purchases initially at the full prices suppliers charged for the goods purchased. Then, if the business takes a purchase discount, we debit Accounts Payable for the *full amount owed*, credit Cash for the *amount actually paid*, and credit a *contra-account*, Purchases Discounts, for the *amount of the discount taken*. Assume, for example, that on March 24 Good's Campus Books paid for the remaining $1,500 in textbooks purchased from Foster Publishing on March 15. We record the payment, which is within the 10-day discount period, as follows:

Mar. 24	Accounts Payable	1,500	
	Cash		1,470
	Purchases Discounts		30
	To record payment for purchase and 2% discount taken.		

Calculating Net Purchases

When a business returns defective goods, receives allowances for goods with minor flaws, or receives discounts from suppliers for paying its accounts early, the correct cost of the purchased goods is net purchases. **Net purchases** equals purchases less purchases returns and allowances and purchases discounts. The net purchases calculation of Good's Campus Books for 19X1 is shown in Illustration 5-5.

ILLUSTRATION 5-5 Calculation of Net Purchases

Good's Campus Books Income Statement (Partial)	
Purchases	$460,000
Less: Purchases returns and allowances	(5,676)
Purchases discounts	(8,924)
Net purchases	$445,400

Transportation-In

According to GAAP, an asset's cost is its net purchase price plus any costs incidental to placing the asset in the appropriate location for its intended use. Transportation costs, those incurred in moving goods from the seller's to the purchaser's location, are the most common incidental costs. Practice varies widely as to whether the purchaser or the seller pays for transportation costs. As a consequence, purchasers and suppliers make sure that shipping charges are mentioned explicitly in the terms of the purchase transaction.

Businesses traditionally use certain abbreviations, such as *F.O.B. shipping point* and *F.O.B. destination*, to describe the seller's terms for handling shipping charges. The letters *F.O.B.* stand for "free on board," meaning the goods are the property of the buyer at the location referred to. Thus, F.O.B. shipping point means the buyer owns the goods at the point of shipment. The buyer bears the risk that the goods will be lost or damaged in transit, and the buyer pays for any transportation. On the other hand, F.O.B. destination means the seller owns the goods at the point of shipment, and ownership transfers to the buyer when they are delivered. The seller pays the freight and insurance and assumes responsibility for loss or damage to the goods.

We accumulate transportation charges for purchases in a separate account called Transportation-In. If the carrier (railroad, trucking company, airline, etc.)

charges separately for freight, we make separate entries for the purchase and the transportation charges. If Good's Campus Books purchased $3,000 of T-shirts on April 1, 19X1, with terms of F.O.B. shipping point and $100 freight to be charged directly by the trucking company, the entries are:

Apr. 1	Purchases	3,000	
	Accounts Payable		3,000
	To record credit purchase of goods shipped F.O.B. shipping point.		
5	Transportation-In	100	
	Accounts Payable		100
	To record shipping charges for goods purchased on April 1.		

Frequently, sellers prepay the freight charges on goods purchased F.O.B. shipping point as a service to their customers. When this happens, the seller usually shows the shipping charges as well as the cost of the goods on the seller's invoice. Then, the buyer records the purchase and transportation-in in one entry.

Apr. 1	Purchases	3,000	
	Transportation-In	100	
	Accounts Payable		3,100
	To record purchases and shipping charges prepaid by supplier.		

When suppliers prepay transportation charges and add the charges to their invoices, any cash discounts offered do not apply to the transportation charges.

Cost of Goods Purchased

Since transportation charges are considered part of the total cost of purchased goods, the **cost of goods purchased** equals net purchases plus transportation-in as demonstrated in Illustration 5-6.

ILLUSTRATION 5-6 Calculation of Cost of Goods Purchased

Good's Campus Books Income Statement (Partial)	
Purchases	$460,000
Less: Purchases returns and allowances	(5,676)
Purchases discounts	(8,924)
Net purchases	$445,400
Add: Transportation-in	10,123
Cost of goods purchased	$455,523

ACCOUNTING FOR MERCHANDISE INVENTORIES

LO 4
Describe the periodic method of inventory valuation, contrast it with the perpetual method, and calculate cost of goods sold under the periodic inventory method.

The calculation of the cost of goods purchased is only a step in calculating cost of goods sold. When a business purchases goods for resale to its customers, it adds the goods to its merchandise inventory upon delivery. **Merchandise inventory** is a merchandising business's stock of goods available for sale as of a particular point in time. When goods are sold during a period, they flow out of the business's merchandise inventory into the customers' possession. Therefore, for any period, the relationship in Illustration 5-7 holds. That is, the beginning merchandise inventory plus the goods purchased represent the goods available for sale. The goods available for sale less the goods sold equals the goods remaining in the ending merchandise inventory.

ILLUSTRATION 5-7 Inventory and Cost Relationships for a Period

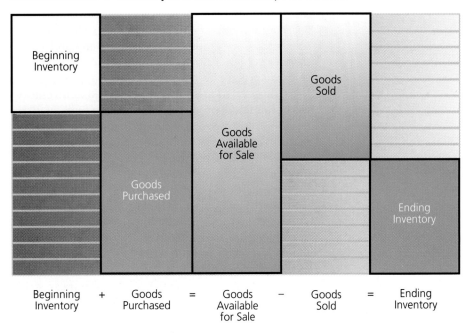

| Beginning Inventory | + | Goods Purchased | = | Goods Available for Sale | − | Goods Sold | = | Ending Inventory |

Consistent with the physical relationship above is a basic cost relationship:

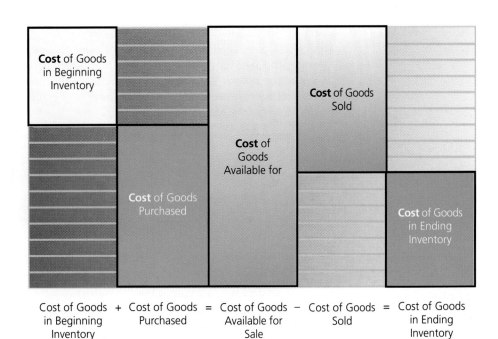

| Cost of Goods in Beginning Inventory | + | Cost of Goods Purchased | = | Cost of Goods Available for Sale | − | Cost of Goods Sold | = | Cost of Goods in Ending Inventory |

The fundamental equation shown at the bottom of Illustration 5-7 governs accounting for inventories and cost of goods sold. However, we have two distinctly different ways to apply this relationship in practice, which lead to two different ways to calculate cost of goods sold. One is the perpetual method of inventory accounting; the other, the periodic method.

The Perpetual Inventory Method

Under the **perpetual inventory method**, we record the costs of purchases and the cost of goods sold on a daily or even a continuous basis. As a business purchases goods, we debit their costs to Merchandise Inventory; as the business sells goods, we credit their costs to Merchandise Inventory and *debit their costs directly to Cost of Goods Sold.* Thus, the inventory balance and the cost of goods sold balance are kept up-to-date *perpetually.*

However, to implement the perpetual inventory method, as a business purchases and sells products, it must keep track of all individual products. Also, the business must keep a separate inventory record for each product it handles to record the physical quantities purchased and sold and their per-unit costs. When a business purchases goods, we add the physical units to the individual inventory record and note the cost per unit. When a business sells goods, we subtract the physical units from the number available and multiply the quantity sold by their unit costs to determine the amount to debit to Cost of Goods Sold. The perpetual inventory method, therefore, can be very intricate and costly to implement. However, availability of relatively inexpensive and powerful computers has made it more feasible to apply the perpetual method to almost any merchandising situation.

The perpetual inventory method contrasts sharply with the periodic inventory method described below. The periodic method is the basis for the discussion in the rest of this chapter. The perpetual method is described in more detail in a later chapter.

The Periodic Inventory Method

Under the **periodic inventory method**, we update the Merchandise Inventory balance and calculate the cost of goods sold *at the end of an accounting period,* based on physical inventory counts. Under the periodic method, we do not change the beginning balance in Merchandise Inventory until the end of an accounting period. We accumulate purchases for the period in Purchases, not in Merchandise Inventory. *We calculate the cost of goods sold as a by-product of the calculation of the ending inventory:*

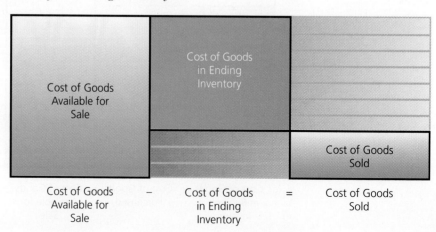

| Cost of Goods Available for Sale | − | Cost of Goods in Ending Inventory | = | Cost of Goods Sold |

Determining the Cost of Ending Inventory. At the end of each period, the business conducts a physical inventory to derive the ending inventory balance independent of purchases and sales of the period. A **physical inventory** is a process of physically counting all goods of each kind in the merchandise inventory as of a particular date. As they count the physical goods on hand, employees also inspect them, set aside spoiled, obsolete, and damaged goods, and count them in separate categories. Employees record the descriptions and tabulate the physical counts of goods on hand. Accounting clerks determine the cost of each inventory item from records of purchases and enter them in the tabulation. They also multiply the costs and quantities and add the individual results to arrive at a total cost of ending inventory, as shown in Illustration 5-8.

ILLUSTRATION 5-8 Periodic Inventory Tabulation

Inventory item number	Quantity counted	x	Unit cost	=	Item amount
1001	25		$ 49.95		$ 1,248.75
1002	56		45.23		2,532.88
1003	3,700		5.01		18,537.00
1004	158		25.00		3,950.00
1005	10		250.00		2,500.00
Total					$28,768.63

Conducting Physical Inventories with Computers. Computers make the process of conducting physical inventories and tabulating the results easier, faster, and more accurate. As they count goods of particular descriptions, employees enter the counts directly in hand-held computers linked to the computer that maintains the inventory records. From its stored records of purchases, the latter computer determines the unit cost of each item. Finally, the computer completes all the arithmetic operations of the inventory tabulation with great speed and accuracy.

COST OF GOODS SOLD

Illustration 5-9 summarizes the calculation of cost of goods sold under the periodic inventory method. The general ledger account balances supply beginning inventory and purchases amounts for the period. Together, they sum to the cost of goods available for sale. The goods available during the period must either

ILLUSTRATION 5-9 Calculation of Cost of Goods Sold

Good's Campus Books Income Statement (Partial)	
Inventory, January 1, 19X1	$127,686
Add: Cost of goods purchased	455,523
Cost of goods available for sale	$583,209
Less: Inventory, December 31, 19X1	135,677
Cost of goods sold	$447,532

have been sold during the period or must still be in inventory at the end of the period. Therefore, when the independently derived ending inventory figure is subtracted from the cost of goods available for sale, the result is the correct cost of goods sold for the period.

The detailed calculation of cost of goods sold, including the calculation of net purchases and the cost of goods purchased, can now be examined in Illustration 5-10.

ILLUSTRATION 5-10 Detailed Calculation of Cost of Goods Sold

Good's Campus Books Income Statement (Partial)		
Inventory, January 1, 19X1		**$127,686**
Add: Cost of goods purchased:		
Purchases	$460,000	
Less: Purchases returns and allowances	(5,676)	
Purchases discounts	(8,924)	
Net purchases	$445,400	
Add: Transportation-in	10,123	
Cost of goods purchased		455,523
Cost of goods available for sale		**$583,209**
Less: Inventory, December 31, 19X1		135,677
Cost of goods sold		**$447,532**

LO 5
Describe the operating expenses of a merchandising business and distinguish between selling expenses and general and administrative expenses.

OPERATING EXPENSES

Merchandising businesses incur the same types of operating expenses as service businesses. They consist of the costs of wages, salaries, supplies, rent, utilities, depreciation, etc. However, managers of merchandising businesses find it useful to see expenses divided into two categories: selling expenses and general and administrative expenses. **Selling expenses** are directly related to storing, handling, displaying, selling, and shipping or delivering products to customers. For example, the wages and salaries of sales, warehouse, and delivery personnel are selling expenses. On the other hand, expenses that do not relate directly to the selling function such as the wages and salaries of the general managers, accountants, bookkeepers, and office clerks are considered **general and administrative expenses**.

Technically, certain common expenses such as depreciation and utilities expenses—say of a building that houses both a store and administrative offices—can be allocated between the selling category and the administrative and general category. However, managers, in consultation with accountants, may decide to forego the extra detail in the accounts and income statement, unless they actually can manage the expenses separately for the two business functions. The 19X1 operating expenses of Good's Campus Books are presented in the partial income statement in Illustration 5-11. Notice that the only costs actually divided between the two functions in this case are wages and salaries expenses. Advertising expense only applies to the selling function. Robert Good apparently has chosen to regard all other expenses exclusively as general and administrative expenses.

ILLUSTRATION 5-11 Operating Expenses

Good's Campus Books Income Statement (Partial)		
Selling expenses:		
Advertising expense	$23,555	
Wages and salaries expense	67,500	
		$ 91,055
General and administrative expenses:		
Depreciation expense	$ 8,500	
Insurance expense	2,666	
Supplies expense	8,162	
Utilities expense	15,545	
Wages and salaries expense	40,000	
		74,873
Total operating expenses		$165,928

LO 6

Use a worksheet to prepare the adjusting and closing entries for a merchandising business using the periodic inventory method.

WORKSHEET OF A MERCHANDISING BUSINESS

Like service businesses, merchandising businesses find worksheets helpful for preparing their financial statements. Worksheets organize their adjusting and closing entries and facilitate preparation of their financial statements. The format of Good's Campus Books' worksheet is shown in Illustration 5-12. Its adjustments columns contain the following adjustments:

- a. Accrual of additional supplies used during December 19X1.
- b. Recognition of expiration of one year's insurance coverage under a prepaid policy.
- c. Accrual of wages payable for the last two-week payroll period of December, 19X1.
- d. Depreciation expense on equipment.

All of these adjustments and the ways they are handled in the worksheet are similar to those you have experienced before.

Worksheet Treatment of Merchandise Inventory — Adjusting Entry Method

Now focus on adjustments e and f to Merchandise Inventory. These adjustments are something new. Their purposes are to change the inventory figure in the balance sheet from the beginning balance to the ending balance, according to the periodic inventory method, and to provide beginning and ending inventory figures in the income statement to calculate cost of goods sold. We achieve the first purpose in Illustration 5-12 by two adjustments. Adjustment (e) credits Merchandise Inventory for $127,686, which offsets the beginning balance and, therefore, removes it from the account. Adjustment (f) debits Merchandise Inventory, establishing its new balance of $135,677. The offsetting entries debit Income Summary with $127,686 in entry (e) and credit it with $135,677 in entry (f).

When the inventory adjustments to Income Summary are carried through the Adjusted Trial Balance to the Income Statement columns, the second purpose of the adjustments is achieved. Recall that in calculating cost of goods sold

ILLUSTRATION 5-12 Worksheet of a Merchandising Business

Good's Campus Books
Worksheet
For the Year Ended December 31, 19X1

ACCOUNTS	TRIAL BALANCE Dr.	TRIAL BALANCE Cr.	ADJUSTMENTS Dr.	ADJUSTMENTS Cr.	ADJUSTED TRIAL BALANCE Dr.	ADJUSTED TRIAL BALANCE Cr.	INCOME STATEMENT Dr.	INCOME STATEMENT Cr.	BALANCE SHEET Dr.	BALANCE SHEET Cr.
Cash	20,000				20,000				20,000	
Accounts Receivable	85,126				85,126				85,126	
Merchandise Inventory	127,686		(f) 135,677	(e) 127,686	135,677			135,677	135,677	
Office Supplies	3,241			(a) 577	2,664				2,664	
Prepaid Insurance	5,666			(b) 2,666	3,000				3,000	
Land	50,600				50,600				50,600	
Equipment	85,000				85,000				85,000	
Accum. Deprec.–Equipment		25,000		(d) 8,500		33,500				33,500
Accounts Payable		26,795				26,795				26,795
Wages and Salaries Payable				(c) 2,500		2,500				2,500
Robert Good, Capital		234,822				234,822				234,822
Income Summary			(e) 127,686	(f) 135,677	127,686	135,677	127,686	135,677		
Sales		736,400				736,400		736,400		
Sales Discounts	11,046				11,046		11,046			
Sales Ret. and Allow.	27,444				27,444		27,444			
Purchases	460,000				460,000		460,000			
Transportation-In	10,123				10,123		10,123			
Purch. Ret. and Allow.		5,676				5,676		5,676		
Purchases Discounts		8,924				8,924		8,924		
Advertising Expense	23,555				23,555		23,555			
Depreciation Expense–Equip.			(d) 8,500		8,500		8,500			
Insurance Expense			(b) 2,666		2,666		2,666			
Supplies Expense	7,585		(a) 577		8,162		8,162			
Utilities Expense	15,545				15,545		15,545			
Wages and Sal. Exp.–Office	40,000				40,000		40,000			
Wages and Sal. Exp.–Sales	65,000		(c) 2,500		67,500		67,500			
	1,037,617	1,037,617	277,606	277,606	1,184,294	1,184,294	802,227	886,677	382,067	297,617
Net Income							84,450			84,450
							886,677	886,677	382,067	382,067

(see Illustration 5-10), we add the beginning inventory balance of $127,686 to the cost of goods purchased of $455,523 to derive cost of goods available for sale of $583,209. From this figure, we deduct ending inventory of $135,677 to determine the cost of goods sold of $447,532. The cost of goods sold, which is an expense, should be a net debit in calculating net income. By debiting Income Summary for the beginning inventory balance, in effect, we add the balance to the cost of goods sold calculation. By crediting Income Summary for the ending inventory balance, in effect, we subtract the balance from the cost of goods sold calculation. When we carry the adjustments over to the Income Statement, they provide the correct data in the appropriate columns (debit for the beginning inventory figure, credit for the ending inventory figure) to calculate cost of goods sold in the income statement.

We journalize adjustments (e) and (f) as follows:

Dec. 31	Income Summary	127,686	
	Merchandise Inventory		127,686
	To remove the beginning inventory balance and carry it to Income Summary.		
31	Merchandise Inventory	135,677	
	Income Summary		135,677
	To enter the ending inventory balance and carry it to Income Summary.		

After posting these two entries to Income Summary, the account would look like this:

Income Summary	
Dec. 31 127,686	Dec. 31 135,677

In Appendix 5-B, we present an alternative to the adjusting entry method of handling inventory in the worksheet. The alternative is the closing entry method.

Worksheet Treatment of Cost of Goods Sold

Note that no cost of goods sold account *per se* appears on the worksheet in Exhibit 5-12. Instead, all the components of the cost of goods sold calculation, including the inventory components, appear highlighted in the Income Statement columns. If you trace each of the highlighted numbers to Illustration 5-10, you will see that they agree with the components of the cost of goods sold calculation for Good's Campus Books for 19X1.

Closing Entries Based on the Worksheet

Closing entries prepared from the worksheet are shown in Illustration 5-13. All account balances in the Income Statement columns, *except* Income Summary, are closed together in just two, basic closing entries. First, all of the debit-balance accounts are credited and their total of $674,541 is debited to Income Summary. Next, all of the credit-balance accounts are debited and their total of $751,000 is credited to Income Summary. When Income Summary is summarized, as in Illustration 5-14, we find it has a balance equal to the net income amount of $84,450. This income amount is closed to Robert Good, Capital in the final entry of Illustration 5-13.

ILLUSTRATION 5-13 Closing Entries Prepared from the Worksheet

Dec. 31	Income Summary	674,541	
	Sales Returns and Allowances		27,444
	Sales Discounts		11,046
	Advertising Expense		23,555
	Depreciation Expense—Equipment		8,500
	Insurance Expense		2,666
	Purchases		460,000
	Supplies Expense		8,162
	Transportation-In		10,123
	Utilities Expense		15,545
	Wages and Salaries Expense—Sales		67,500
	Wages and Salaries Expense—Office		40,000
	To close the expenses and contra-revenues to Income Summary.		
31	Sales	736,400	
	Purchases Discounts	8,924	
	Purchases Returns and Allowances	5,676	
	Income Summary		751,000
	To close revenues and contra-purchases to Income Summary.		
31	Income Summary	84,450	
	Robert Good, Capital		84,450
	To close Income Summary to Robert Good, capital.		

ILLUSTRATION 5-14 Income Summary Account

Income Summary

Dec. 31	127,686	Dec. 31	135,677
Dec. 31	674,541	Dec. 31	751,000
Dec. 31	84,450	Bal.	84,450
		Bal.	0

The net income figure of $84,450 is also the difference between the preliminary debit and credit totals of the Income Statement *and* Balance Sheet columns in Illustration 5-12. When this amount is entered below the preliminary Income Statement Dr. column total and also below the preliminary Balance Sheet Cr. column total of Illustration 5-12, it balances both the Income Statement and Balance Sheet columns.

LO 7
Prepare the financial statements of a merchandising business, using the worksheet.

FINANCIAL STATEMENTS OF A MERCHANDISING BUSINESS

Illustrations 5-15 through 5-17 show the financial statements that we can prepare from the worksheet in Illustration 5-12. They are the income statement, the statement of owner's equity, and the balance sheet. Discussion of the statement of cash flows is deferred to a later chapter.

Classified Income Statement

You prepare an income statement, such as the one in Illustration 5-15, from the Income Statement columns of the worksheet in Illustration 5-12. All of the data for preparing the income statement come from the worksheet, but this income statement organizes the data into several major categories. The major categories correspond to the individual figures in the very simple income statement in Illustration 5-1.

First, Illustration 5-15 begins with a revenue section that corresponds to the calculation presented in Illustration 5-3. Next, the statement displays all of the items making up the cost of goods sold, as shown in Illustration 5-10. We subtract cost of goods sold from net sales revenue to calculate gross profit and deduct operating expenses from gross profit to derive net income from operations. Obviously, Illustration 5-15 is a more detailed presentation of Good's

ILLUSTRATION 5-15 Complete Income Statement of Good's Campus Books

Good's Campus Books Income Statement For the Year Ended December 31, 19X1			
Revenue:			
Gross sales			$736,400
Less: Sales returns and allowances		$ 27,444	
Sales discounts		11,046	38,490
Net sales			$697,910
Cost of goods sold:			
Inventory, January 1, 19X1		$127,686	
Add: Cost of goods purchased:			
Purchases	$460,000		
Less: Purchases returns and allowances	(5,676)		
Purchases discounts	(8,924)		
Net purchases	$445,400		
Add: Transportation-in	10,123		
Cost of goods purchased		455,523	
Cost of goods available for sale		$583,209	
Less: Inventory, December 31, 19X1		135,677	
Cost of goods sold			447,532
Gross profit			$250,378
Selling expenses:			
Advertising expense	$ 23,555		
Wages and salaries expense	67,500		
		$91,055	
General and administrative expenses:			
Depreciation expense–equipment	$ 8,500		
Insurance expense	2,666		
Supplies expense	8,162		
Utilities expense	15,545		
Wages and salaries expense	40,000		
		74,873	
Total operating expenses			165,928
Net income			$ 84,450

Campus Books' 19X1 operations than is Illustration 5-1. Illustration 5-15 contains the type of detail that an owner or manager like Robert Good would want. To communicate summary information to outsiders, Robert would most likely use a condensed income statement, such as Illustration 5-1.

Statement of Owner's Equity

The statement of owner's equity is generally the simplest of the four major financial statements. This is very evident in Illustration 5-16, which presents the statement of owner's equity for Good's Campus Books. The statement of owner's equity begins with the beginning balance in the owner's capital account. To this we add the net income of the period and subtract withdrawals (not applicable in this case). In other cases, additional capital contributions as with net income, would be added to the beginning balance in the owner's capital account, and withdrawals would be subtracted.

ILLUSTRATION 5-16 Statement of Owner's Equity

Good's Campus Books Statement of Owner's Equity For the Year Ended December 31, 19X1	
Robert Good, capital, January 1, 19X1	$234,822
Net income for the year ended December 31, 19X1	84,450
Robert Good, capital, December 31, 19X1	$319,272

Classified Balance Sheet

The classified balance sheet of Good's Campus Books is shown in Illustration 5-17. The only component of a merchandising business's balance sheet not found in a service business's balance sheet is Merchandise Inventory, which the merchandising business includes among its current assets. The typical time period it takes to buy merchandise, resell it, and collect cash defines the merchandising business's operating cycle. Current assets are those that convert to cash within one year or within one operating cycle, whichever is longer. Thus, merchandise inventories are always classified as current assets.

The balance in Robert Good, Capital from the worksheet of $234,822 is a "pre-income" balance. In the statement of owner's equity in Illustration 5-16, we combine it with the income figure of $84,450 to determine the appropriate balance in Capital of $319,272 as of December 31, 19X1.

LO 8

Calculate the cost of goods sold and gross profit ratios and use them to assess profitability.

USING THE MULTISTEP INCOME STATEMENT

The multistep income statement of merchandising businesses is no accident. All expenses are basically alike in that they must be covered by revenues before a business generates a profit. Nevertheless, for a merchandising business, the relationship between revenue and cost of goods sold and the resulting gross profit

ILLUSTRATION 5-17 Balance Sheet of Good's Campus Books

Good's Campus Books Balance Sheet December 31, 19X1			
Assets			
Current assets:			
Cash		$ 20,000	
Accounts receivable		85,126	
Merchandise inventory		135,677	
Supplies		2,664	
Prepaid insurance		3,000	
Total current assets			$246,467
Property, plant, and equipment:			
Land		$ 50,600	
Equipment	$85,000		
Less: Accumulated depreciation	33,500	51,500	
Total property, plant, and equipment			102,100
Total assets			$348,567
Liabilities and Owner's Equity			
Current liabilities:			
Accounts payable			$ 26,795
Wages and salaries payable			2,500
Total current liabilities			$ 29,295
Owner's equity:			
Robert Good, capital			319,272
Total liabilities and owner's equity			$348,567

is especially important. If a business cannot sell merchandise for more than its cost, then its gross profit will be negative; and with additional expenses to deduct, "it's all downhill from there." Therefore, owners and managers of merchandising businesses give a great deal of attention to trying to manage gross profit.

Gross Profit and Cost of Goods Sold Ratios

Let us now return to the case of Robert Good, who is worried about a drop in the profitability of Good's Campus Books in 19X1. Consider the store's income statement for 19X1 compared to its income statement for 19X0 in Illustration 5-18. The side-by-side statements tell us a few things without any additional diagnostic tools. Most importantly, we observe that net sales grew from 19X0 to 19X1, but net income fell—so Mr. Good has reason to be concerned.

In diagnosing what caused this adverse pattern, Robert will want to review the comparative gross profit ratios. The **gross profit ratio** is the ratio of gross profit to the net sales of a given year:

$$\text{Gross Profit Ratio} = \frac{\text{Gross Profit}}{\text{Net Sales}}$$

ILLUSTRATION 5-18 Comparative Income Statements

Good's Campus Books Comparative Income Statement For the Years Ended December 31, 19X0 and 19X1		
	19X0	*19X1*
Net sales	$606,878	$697,910
Less: Cost of goods sold	370,196	447,532
Gross profit	$236,682	$250,378
Less: Operating expenses	144,285	165,928
Net income	$ 92,397	$ 84,450

Since cost of goods sold is subtracted from net sales to calculate gross profit, the **cost of goods sold ratio** is the complement of the gross profit ratio:

$$\text{Cost of Goods Sold Ratio} = \frac{\text{Cost of Goods Sold}}{\text{Net Sales}}$$

The two ratios for Good's Campus Books for 19X0 and 19X1 reveal a considerable amount about Robert's profitability problem:

	19X0		*19X1*	
Cost of goods sold ratio:	$\dfrac{\$370,196}{\$606,878}$	= .610	$\dfrac{\$447,532}{\$697,910}$	= .641
Gross profit ratio:	$\dfrac{\$236,682}{\$606,878}$	= .390	$\dfrac{\$250,378}{\$697,910}$	= .359
		1.000		1.000

Using the Cost of Goods Sold and Gross Profit Ratios

The gross profit and cost of goods sold ratios of Good's Campus Books tell us that in 19X1, .031 (.641 − .610) more of every net sales dollar went for the cost of goods sold and, therefore, .031 less flowed through to gross profit. That is, of every net sales dollar earned, only .359 became gross profit—to cover operating expenses and generate net income—in 19X1, as opposed to .390 per net sales dollar earned in 19X0. To see the significance of this difference in the cost of goods sold/gross profit split, we multiply the decline in gross profit ratio in 19X1 (.390 − .359) by 19X1 net sales:

$$.031 \times \$697,910 = \$21,635$$

Now we know that, if the gross profit (and cost of goods sold) ratio had been the same in 19X1 as it was in 19X0, Good's Campus Books would have had over $20,000 of additional net income than it actually earned in 19X1. This is certainly a significant amount. It shows how small changes in a merchandising business's cost of goods sold/gross profit ratio can have a significant impact on its profitability. It also tells Robert that it would be very worthwhile to investigate the components of cost of goods sold to find out why it was a higher percentage of net sales in 19X1 than it was in 19X0.

INSIGHTS INTO ETHICS

It is now January 10, 19X3. Amy Parks, the accounting clerk at Good's Campus Books, overheard Frank Diaz, manager of used books, say that the December 31, 19X2, physical inventory included several hundred introductory psychology books that Good's had bought back from students at $15 each. At the end of fall term, Frank assumed the used textbooks would be sold to other students for $30 each at the beginning of spring term. Unfortunately, in December the Psychology Department unexpectedly changed books for spring term; and now the used books must be sold to a broker for only $5 each. Amy realizes immediately that the ending inventory tabulation for 19X1 was overstated, cost of goods sold was thereby understated, and net income was overstated. Amy has always admired Robert Good but has not been particularly fond of Sheila Pell who will soon replace him as the owner. She knows that the price Sheila will pay Robert for the business depends on net income, and she also noticed during 19X2 that Sheila authorized early maintenance and other expenditures to inflate expenses during 19X2. To revise the inventory tabulation, financial statement worksheet, and financial statements themselves will be a lot of work. What should Amy do?

To see just how important managing cost of goods sold and gross profit are in the real world, consider the following ratios of Crown Books Corporation, which operates retail specialty bookstores.

	1990	1991	1992
Cost of goods sold ratio	.783	.781	.785
Gross profit ratio	.217	.219	.215

Notice that the fluctuations from year to year are less than .005 of sales, indicating relatively tight control of costs of goods sold in relationship to sales.

SUMMARY

Describe a multistep income statement and why a merchandising business uses it. The multistep income statements of merchandising businesses consist of two stages. First, we subtract cost of goods sold from net sales to arrive at gross profit. Second, we subtract operating expenses from gross profit to derive net income. Since merchandising businesses earn revenues primarily by selling products to customers, managers and other users of their financial statements find it useful to see expenses split into two main categories: the cost of the goods sold and operating expenses.

	Net Sales
Less:	**Cost of Goods Sold**
Equals:	**Gross Profit**
Less:	**Operating Expenses**
Equals:	**Net Income**

Record gross sales, sales returns and allowances, and sales discounts and calculate net sales for a merchandising business.   The prices customers pay or agree to pay for merchandise at the time of sale are the gross sales of the business recorded in Sales. We record sales returns and allowances and sales discounts in *contra-revenue* accounts and subtract their balances from gross sales to derive net sales in the income statement.

	Gross Sales
Less:	**Sales Returns and Allowances**
Less:	**Sales Discounts**
Equals:	**Net Sales**

Record gross purchases, purchases returns and allowances, purchases discounts, and transportation costs for purchased goods and calculate cost of goods purchased.   Under the gross method, we record purchases at the full prices suppliers charge. We record purchases returns and allowances and purchases (cash) discounts in contra-accounts and subtract them from gross purchases to calculate net purchases. Further, we record transportation costs of purchases in Transportation-In and add its balance to net purchases to derive the cost of goods purchased.

	Gross Purchases
Less:	**Purchases Returns and Allowances**
Less:	**Purchases Discounts**
Equals:	**Net Purchases**
Add:	**Transportation-In**
Equals:	**Cost of Goods Purchased**

Describe the periodic method of inventory valuation, contrast it with the perpetual method, and calculate cost of goods sold under the periodic inventory method. Under the periodic inventory method, we update the Merchandise Inventory balance and calculate the cost of goods sold *only at the ends of accounting periods*, based on physical inventory counts. We do not change the beginning balance in Merchandise Inventory until the end of an accounting period. We accumulate the components of the cost of goods purchased in separate accounts, not in Merchandise Inventory. At the end of the period, we calculate cost of goods available for sale by adding the cost of goods purchased to the beginning inventory balance. The ending inventory balance from the physical inventory is subtracted to derive cost of goods sold.

	Beginning Inventory
Add:	**Cost of Goods Purchased**
Equals:	**Cost of Goods Available for Sale**
Less:	**Ending Inventory**
Equals:	**Cost of Goods Sold**

Describe the operating expenses of a merchandising business and distinguish between selling expenses and general and administrative expenses.   Selling expenses are directly related to storing, handling, displaying, selling, and shipping or delivering products to customers. For example, the wages and salaries of sales, warehouse, and delivery personnel are selling expenses. On the other hand, the wages and salaries of general managers, accountants, bookkeepers, and office clerks are considered general and administrative expenses.

Use a worksheet to prepare the adjusting and closing entries for a merchandising business using the periodic inventory method.   The worksheet of a merchandising business is fundamentally the same as the worksheet of a service business, and it serves exactly the same functions. However, some modifications are required to handle merchandise inventories and cost of goods sold under the periodic inventory method. The cost of goods sold never appears in the worksheet directly. After appropriate adjustments are made, all the components are carried to the Income Statement columns of the worksheet. We handle the transition from the beginning to ending inventory in two adjustments, crediting Merchandise Inventory with the beginning balance and debiting it with the ending balance. The offsetting entries are made to Income Summary, and both balances are carried to the Income Statement columns to be included in the cost of goods sold calculation. All debit and credit balances in the Income Statement columns, *except* Income Summary, are closed in two entries.

Prepare the financial statements of a merchandising business using the worksheet.   All the account balances needed for preparing the income statement, balance sheet, and statement of owner's equity are displayed in the respective columns of the worksheet and need only be formatted into suitable statements.

Calculate the cost of goods sold and gross profit ratios and use them to assess profitability.   We calculate the cost of goods sold and gross profit ratios by dividing their respective amounts by net sales. Because the cost of goods sold is a significant expense to most merchandising businesses, small fluctuations in the cost of goods sold and gross profit ratios usually imply significant effects on net income. The ratios are very useful in assessing the profitability of merchandising businesses.

LO 9
Distinguish between the gross and net methods of recording purchases.

APPENDIX 5-A: RECORDING PURCHASES NET OF DISCOUNTS

Some accountants and managers criticize the traditional method of handling cash discounts on purchases—that is, deducting purchases discounts from gross purchases to derive net purchases. First, purchases discounts are related to the business's cash management, not to its purchasing function. Generally speaking, if the business has adequate cash on hand, it should take all cash discounts on purchases. (In a later chapter, we justify this rule of thumb.) If a business does not take the discounts, the discounts lost are costs of financing purchases using supplier credit, not costs of the goods purchased. From the cash-management perspective, a manager should want the discounts lost categorized as a separate controllable expense, rather than as a component of the net purchases calculation. Thus, many managers and accountants prefer an alternative to the traditional way of accounting for cash discounts on purchases.

Under the alternative method, when a supplier offers a business a cash discount on purchases, we record the purchases at the discounted purchase price. For example, we record the purchase of $4,000 worth of goods under terms of 1/10, n/30 as:

(Date)	Purchases	3,960	
	Accounts Payable		3,960
	To record purchases net of available cash discounts.		

Only the costs necessary to acquire the goods are regarded as part of the purchase cost. When discounts are not taken, in effect, the merchant borrows money from the supplier. In the case above, the period of the loan is 20 days, the difference between the 10-day discount period and the 30 days allowed for full payment. If the merchant does not take the discount offered in the case above, we debit the amount of the discount lost to an expense account entitled Purchases Discounts Lost.

(Date)	Accounts Payable	3,960	
	Purchases Discounts Lost	40	
	Cash		4,000
	To record payments on accounts payable after the discount period.		

Otherwise, if the merchant pays the invoice within 10 days, the payment on the purchase is the discounted amount and we record it as:

(Date)	Accounts Payable	3,960	
	Cash		3,960
	To record payments on accounts payable within the discount periods.		

Under this method, cash discounts on purchases do not enter into calculating net purchases. *Purchases are already recorded net of discounts.* We continue to subtract purchases returns and allowances from purchases to calculate net purchases. Since Purchases Discounts Lost is akin to (and sometimes is combined with) interest expense, we typically report it on the income statement in an other income and expense category or after operating expenses.

LO 10
Prepare a worksheet based on the closing entry method.

APPENDIX 5-B: WORKSHEET TREATMENT OF MERCHANDISING INVENTORY—CLOSING ENTRY METHOD

Illustration 5-19 is a worksheet that accomplishes the same objectives as the worksheet in Illustration 5-12. However, it uses a slightly different method for handling Merchandise Inventory. In this worksheet, no adjustments to inventory are made in the Adjustments columns. Good's Campus Books' *beginning* inventory balance as of January 1, 19X1, of $127,686 is taken to the Dr. column of the Adjusted Trial Balance and is then carried over to the Dr. column of the Income Statement. Good's Campus Books' *ending* inventory figure of $135,677 as of December 31, 19X1, is "plugged" into the worksheet in the Cr. column of the Income Statement and the Dr. column of the Balance Sheet. (Debits still equal credits for the worksheet as a whole.)

These two inventory entries accomplish two objectives. First, they record the ending balance in Merchandise Inventory (the entry in the Dr. column of the Balance Sheet). Second, they ensure the proper calculation of cost of goods sold under the periodic method. That is, beginning inventory is in the Dr. column of the Income Statement, which is equivalent to adding it to purchases to derive cost of goods available for sale. Ending inventory is in the Cr. column of the Income Statement, which is equivalent to deducting it from cost of goods available for sale to derive cost of goods sold. Since we do not record *adjustments* to Merchandise Inventory in Income Summary under this method, we

ILLUSTRATION 5-19 Worksheet of a Merchandising Business—Closing Entry Method

Good's Campus Books
Worksheet
For the Year Ended December 31, 19X1

ACCOUNTS	TRIAL BALANCE Dr.	TRIAL BALANCE Cr.	ADJUSTMENTS Dr.	ADJUSTMENTS Cr.	ADJUSTED TRIAL BALANCE Dr.	ADJUSTED TRIAL BALANCE Cr.	INCOME STATEMENT Dr.	INCOME STATEMENT Cr.	BALANCE SHEET Dr.	BALANCE SHEET Cr.
Cash	20,000				20,000				20,000	
Accounts Receivable	85,126				85,126				85,126	
Merchandise Inventory	127,686				127,686		127,686	135,677	135,677	
Office Supplies	3,241			(a) 577	2,664				2,664	
Prepaid Insurance	5,666			(b) 2,666	3,000				3,000	
Land	50,600				50,600				50,600	
Equipment	85,000				85,000				85,000	
Accum. Deprec.-Equipment		25,000		(d) 8,500		33,500				33,500
Accounts Payable		26,795				26,795				26,795
Wages and Salaries Payable				(c) 2,500		2,500				2,500
Robert Good, Capital		234,822				234,822				234,822
Sales		736,400				736,400		736,400		
Sales Discounts	11,046				11,046		11,046			
Sales Ret. and Allow.	27,444				27,444		27,444			
Purchases	460,000				460,000		460,000			
Transportation-In	10,123				10,123		10,123			
Purch. Ret. and Allow.		5,676				5,676		5,676		
Purchases Discounts		8,924				8,924		8,924		
Advertising Expense	23,555				23,555		23,555			
Depreciation Expense-Equip.			(d) 8,500		8,500		8,500			
Insurance Expense			(b) 2,666		2,666		2,666			
Supplies Expense	7,585		(a) 577		8,162		8,162			
Utilities Expense	15,545				15,545		15,545			
Wages and Sal. Exp.-Office	40,000				40,000		40,000			
Wages and Sal. Exp.-Sales	65,000		(c) 2,500		67,500		67,500			
	1,037,617	1,037,617	14,243	14,243	1,048,617	1,048,617	802,227	886,677	382,067	297,617
Net Income							84,450			84,450
							886,677	886,677	382,067	382,067

merely include the beginning and ending inventory balances in the closing entries that are based on the Income Statement columns of the worksheet. For example, the closing entry for all balances in the Income Statement Dr. columns now includes the beginning inventory balance as:

Dec. 31	Income Summary	802,227	
	Merchandise Inventory, 1/1/X1		127,686
	Sales Returns and Allowances		27,444
	Sales Discounts		11,046
	Advertising Expense		23,555
	Depreciation Expense—Equipment		8,500
	Insurance Expense		2,666
	Purchases		460,000
	Supplies Expense		8,162
	Transportation-In		10,123
	Utilities Expense		15,545
	Wages and Salaries Expense—Sales		67,500
	Wages and Salaries Expense—Office		40,000
	To close the expenses, contra-revenues, and beginning inventory to Income Summary.		

The worksheet based on the closing entry method (Illustration 5-19) results in exactly the same financial statements as the worksheet based on the adjusting entries for inventory and closing entries for the other balances in the Income Statement columns (Illustration 5-12). Because they believe it is simpler, some accountants prefer the closing entry method.

REVIEW PROBLEM

The partial worksheet for the Small-Fry Toy Company appears on the next page. Small-Fry uses the adjusting entry method to account for Merchandise Inventory on the worksheet.

REQUIRED:

a. Complete the worksheet.
b. Calculate net sales.
c. Prepare a detailed calculation of cost of goods sold.
d. Prepare a multistep income statement for 19X1.
e. Prepare a balance sheet as of December 31, 19X1.
f. Prepare closing entries for temporary accounts.

SOLUTION:

Planning and Organizing Your Work

1. Extend the balances in the Adjusted Trial Balance columns to the appropriate Income Statement or Balance Sheet columns.
2. Total all Balance Sheet and Income Statement columns.
3. Select appropriate sales-related accounts from the Income Statement columns to calculate net sales.
4. Select appropriate accounts from the Income Statement columns to calculate cost of goods sold.

Small-Fry Toy Company
Partial Worksheet
For the Year Ended December 31, 19X1

ACCOUNTS	ADJUSTED TRIAL BALANCE Dr.	Cr.	INCOME STATEMENT Dr.	Cr.	BALANCE SHEET Dr.	Cr.
Cash	19,500					
Accounts Receivable	8,100					
Merchandise Inventory	16,100					
Supplies	2,700					
Prepaid Insurance	1,400					
Land	8,000					
Building	42,000					
Accumulated Deprec.—Equip.		11,200				
Accounts Payable		5,700				
Wages and Salaries Payable		4,700				
Notes Payable—Noncurrent		8,500				
J. Smith, Capital		37,400				
J. Smith, Withdrawals	7,200					
Income Summary	9,800	16,100				
Sales		157,600				
Sales Returns and Allowances	3,900					
Sales Discounts	1,800					
Purchases	62,600					
Transportation-In	3,100					
Purchases Returns and Allow.		2,300				
Purchases Discounts		2,700				
Deprec. Expense—Off. Equip.	1,600					
Depreciation Expense—Sales	1,200					
Insurance Expense	2,700					
Supplies Expense—Office	2,100					
Supplies Expense—Sales	1,500					
Utilities Expense—Office	700					
Utilities Expense—Sales	900					
Wages and Sal. Exp.—Off.	22,200					
Wages and Sal. Exp.—Sales	27,100					
	246,200	246,200				

5. Prepare a multistep income statement using the Income Statement columns from the partial worksheet.
6. Prepare a balance sheet using the Balance Sheet columns from the partial worksheet. Calculate the ending J. Smith, Capital balance and use this amount in the owner's equity portion of the balance sheet.
7. Select income-statement related temporary accounts from the Income Statement columns and close these accounts to Income Summary. Note: Income Summary already contains the adjustments to Merchandise Inventory.
8. Close Income Summary to J. Smith, Capital.
9. Close J. Smith, Withdrawals to J. Smith, Capital.

(a) *Complete the worksheet.*

Small-Fry Toy Company
Partial Worksheet
For the Year Ended December 31, 19X1

ACCOUNTS	ADJUSTED TRIAL BALANCE Dr.	ADJUSTED TRIAL BALANCE Cr.	INCOME STATEMENT Dr.	INCOME STATEMENT Cr.	BALANCE SHEET Dr.	BALANCE SHEET Cr.
Cash	19,500				19,500	
Accounts Receivable	8,100				8,100	
Merchandise Inventory	16,100				16,100	
Supplies	2,700				2,700	
Prepaid Insurance	1,400				1,400	
Land	8,000				8,000	
Building	42,000				42,000	
Accumulated Deprec.—Equip.		11,200				11,200
Accounts Payable		5,700				5,700
Wages and Salaries Payable		4,700				4,700
Notes Payable—Noncurrent		8,500				8,500
J. Smith, Capital		37,400				37,400
J. Smith, Withdrawals	7,200				7,200	
Income Summary	9,800	16,100	9,800	16,100		
Sales		157,600		157,600		
Sales Returns and Allowances	3,900		3,900			
Sales Discounts	1,800		1,800			
Purchases	62,600		62,600			
Transportation-In	3,100		3,100			
Purchases Returns and Allow.		2,300		2,300		
Purchases Discounts		2,700		2,700		
Deprec. Expense—Off. Equip.	1,600		1,600			
Depreciation Expense—Sales	1,200		1,200			
Insurance Expense	2,700		2,700			
Supplies Expense—Office	2,100		2,100			
Supplies Expense—Sales	1,500		1,500			
Utilities Expense—Office	700		700			
Utilities Expense—Sales	900		900			
Wages and Sal. Exp.—Off.	22,200		22,200			
Wages and Sal. Exp.—Sales	27,100		27,100			
	246,200	246,200	141,200	178,700	105,000	67,500
Net Income			37,500			37,500
			178,700	178,700	105,000	105,000

(b) *Calculate net sales.*

Gross sales		$157,600
Less: Sales returns and allowances	$ 3,900	
Sales discounts	1,800	5,700
Net sales		$151,900

(c) *Calculate cost of goods sold.*

Merchandise inventory, January 1, 19X1		$ 9,800
Add: Cost of goods purchased:		
Purchases	$62,600	
Less: Purchases returns and allowances	2,300	
Purchases discounts	2,700	
Net purchases	$57,600	
Add: Transportation-in	3,100	
Cost of goods purchased		60,700
Cost of goods available for sale		$70,500
Less: Merchandise inventory, December 31, 19X1		16,100
Cost of goods sold		$54,400

(d) *Prepare a multistep income statement.*

Small-Fry Toy Company
Income Statement
For the Year Ended December 31, 19X1

Revenue:			
Gross sales			$157,600
Less: Sales returns and allowances		$ 3,900	
Sales discounts		1,800	5,700
Net sales			$151,900
Cost of goods sold:			
Merchandise inventory, January 1, 19X1		$ 9,800	
Add: Cost of goods purchased:			
Purchases	$62,600		
Less: Purchases returns and allowances	(2,300)		
Purchases discounts	(2,700)		
Net purchases	$57,600		
Add: Transportation-In	3,100		
Cost of goods purchased		60,700	
Cost of goods available for sale		$70,500	
Less: Merchandise inventory, December 31, 19X1		16,100	
Cost of goods sold			54,400
Gross profit			$ 97,500
Selling expenses:			
Depreciation expense–sales	$ 1,200		
Supplies expense	1,500		
Utilities expense	900		
Wages and salaries expense	27,100	$30,700	
General and administrative expenses:			
Depreciation expense–office equip.	$ 1,600		
Insurance expense	2,700		
Supplies expense	2,100		
Utilities expense	700		
Wages and salaries expense	22,200	29,300	
Total operating expenses			60,000
Net income			$ 37,500

(e) *Prepare a balance sheet.*

Small-Fry Toy Company
Balance Sheet
December 31, 19X1

Assets

Current assets:			
Cash		$19,500	
Accounts receivable		8,100	
Merchandise inventory		16,100	
Supplies		2,700	
Prepaid insurance		1,400	
Total current assets			$47,800
Property, plant, and equipment:			
Land		$ 8,000	
Building	$42,000		
Less: Accumulated depreciation	11,200	30,800	
Total property, plant, and equipment			38,800
Total assets			$86,600

Liabilities and Owner's Equity

Current liabilities:	
Accounts payable	$ 5,700
Wages and salaries payable	4,700
Total current liabilities	$10,400
Long-term liabilities:	
Notes payable–noncurrent	8,500
Owner's equity:	
J. Smith, capital	67,700
Total liabilities and owner's equity	$86,600

(f) *Prepare closing entries.*

Dec. 31	Income Summary	131,400	
	Sales Returns and Allowances		3,900
	Sales Discounts		1,800
	Depreciation Expense–Office Equipment		1,600
	Depreciation Expense–Sales		1,200
	Insurance Expense		2,700
	Purchases		62,600
	Supplies Expense–Office		2,100
	Supplies Expense–Sales		1,500
	Transportation-In		3,100
	Utilities Expense–Office		700
	Utilities Expense–Sales		900
	Wages and Salaries Expense–Office		22,200
	Wages and Salaries Expense–Sales		27,100
	To close the expenses, contra-revenues, and beginning inventory to Income Summary.		

Dec. 31	Sales	173,700	
	Purchases Discounts	2,700	
	Purchases Returns and Allowances	2,300	
	Income Summary		178,700
	To close revenues and contra-purchases to the		
	Income Summary account and to recognize		
	ending inventory.		
31	Income Summary	37,500	
	J. Smith, Capital		37,500
	To close Income Summary to J. Smith, Capital.		
31	J. Smith, Capital	7,200	
	J. Smith, Withdrawals		7,200
	To close J. Smith, Withdrawals to J. Smith, Capital.		

KEY TERMS

cost of goods purchased, *184*
cost of goods sold, *177*
cost of goods sold ratio, *196*
general and administrative
    expenses, *188*
gross profit, *177*
gross profit ratio, *195*
gross sales, *178*

merchandise inventory, *184*
net purchases, *183*
net sales, *177*
operating expenses, *177*
periodic inventory method,
    186
perpetual inventory method,
    186

physical inventory, *187*
purchase allowances, *182*
purchase discounts, *182*
purchase returns, *182*
sales allowance, *179*
sales discounts, *179*
sales return, *178*
selling expenses, *188*

SELF-QUIZ

LO 1 1. Which of the following is *not* a principal part of a merchandising firm's income statement?
    a. Operating expenses
    b. Net profit
    c. Gross profit
    d. Cost of goods sold

LO 2 2. Net sales equals gross sales minus _____ _____ _____ _____ and _____ _____ .

LO 2 3. Sales discounts is classified as a _____ account.

LO 2 4. Which of the following is the correct meaning of the term *2/10, n/30?*
    a. Payment is due between February 10 and November 30.
    b. A discount of between 2% and 10% will be given if payment is received within 30 days.
    c. A 2% discount will be given if payment is received between 10 to 30 days.
    d. A 2% discount will be given if payment is received within 10 days, or the full amount is due within 30 days of purchase.

LO 3 5. Net purchases equals purchases less _____ _____ _____ _____ and _____ _____.

LO 3 6. Which of the following is *not* correct about the term *F.O.B shipping point?*

    a. F.O.B. stands for "free on board."
    b. The buyer is responsible for the cost of the shipping.
    c. The buyer owns the goods when they are shipped.
    d. The seller is responsible for purchasing insurance for the shipment.

LO 3 7. True or False? If a good is shipped F.O.B. shipping point, the purchaser is responsible for paying the freight.

LO 3 8. Net purchases plus transportation-in is equal to _____ __ _____ _____ .

LO 4 9. Which of the following is not correct about the perpetual inventory method?
    a. Purchased goods are debited directly to Merchandise Inventory.
    b. Cost of Goods Sold is debited and Merchandise Inventory is credited with each sale.
    c. The perpetual inventory system is usually easy and inexpensive to implement.
    d. This method is only associated with businesses containing few individual inventory items.

LO 4 10. Which of the following is a correct computation of cost of goods sold?
   a. Beginning Inventory + Net Purchases + Transportation-In – Ending Inventory
   b. Ending Inventory + Net Purchases + Transportation-In – Beginning Inventory
   c. Goods Available for Sale – Beginning Inventory
   d. Beginning Inventory + Net Purchases – Transportation-In – Ending Inventory

LO 4 11. True or False? It is generally not necessary to count inventory to determine cost of goods sold under the periodic inventory system.

LO 4 12. Which of the following is *not* correct about the periodic inventory method?
   a. Purchased goods are debited directly to Merchandise Inventory.
   b. Cost of goods sold is not calculated until the end of the period.
   c. The Merchandise Inventory balance is updated only at the end of the accounting period based on physical inventory counts.
   d. The periodic method is often easier and less expensive to implement than the perpetual inventory method.

LO 4 13. What are the two purposes of adjusting Merchandise Inventory under the periodic inventory system?

LO 6 14. True or False? Cost of Goods Sold is an account on a merchandising business's worksheet?

LO 6 15. Indicate whether the following accounts are debited or credited when they are closed.
   a. Sales Discounts
   b. Sales
   c. Purchases Discounts
   d. Transportation-In

LO 7 16. What is the label of the amount that represents net sales minus cost of goods sold on a classified income statement?

LO 7 17. What is the only different account on a merchandising company's classified balance sheet compared with that of a service company?

LO 8 18. What is the gross profit ratio if net sales are $50,000 and cost of goods sold is $30,000?

LO 8 19. True or False? The gross profit ratio subtracted from one is equal to the cost of goods sold ratio.

LO 8 20. What does it mean if the gross profit ratio decreases and net sales do not decline?

SOLUTIONS TO SELF-QUIZ

1. b   2. sales returns and allowances, sales discounts   3. contra-revenue   4. d   5. purchases returns and allowances, purchases discounts   6. d   7. True   8. cost of goods purchased   9. c   10. a   11. False   12. a
13. (1) To change inventory on the balance sheet from the beginning balance to the ending balance according to the inventory count   (2) To provide the beginning and ending inventory amounts in the income statement to calculate cost of goods sold
14. False   15. a credited b. debited c. debited d. credited   16. Gross profit   17. Merchandise inventory
18. ($50,000 – $30,000) ÷ $50,000 = 40%   19. True   20. Cost of goods sold is higher than before.

QUESTIONS

Q5-1   What are the major differences between how a service business and a merchandising business earns profits?

Q5-2   What are the differences between a service business's and a merchandising business's income statements?

Q5-3   What is the difference between a sales allowance and a sales discount?

Q5-4   How do you compute net sales?

Q5-5   Why do businesses accept returned merchandise even if it is not defective?

Q5-6   Why is Sales Discounts classified as a contra-revenue account?

Q5-7   What is the definition of F.O.B.? Why is it important for an accountant to know the F.O.B. terms of a purchase?

Q5-8   What are the advantages and disadvantages of using the perpetual inventory method compared with using the periodic inventory method?

Q5-9   Why is it necessary to count inventory under the periodic inventory system?

Q5-10 What type of operating expenses does your local drug store incur?

Q5-11 How are worksheets helpful to merchandising businesses?

Q5-12 What is the purpose of computing a cost of goods sold ratio?

EXERCISES

LO 1   **E5-1**   **Determining Gross Profit**   Determine gross profit if sales are $500,000 and cost of goods sold is 60% of sales.

LO 2   **E5-2**   **Recording Basic Sales Transactions**   Prepare journal entries for the following list of events:

Jan. 2 Sold merchandise in exchange for $1,300 cash.
      5 Sold merchandise on credit for $2,100.
     12 One-half of the goods sold on January 5 were defective and were returned.
     21 Sold merchandise for $2,200, of which one-half was paid in cash and the remainder was sold on credit.

LO 2   **E5-3**   **Recording Sales Transactions**   Prepare journal entries for the Home Builders Supply Company for the following list of events:

Mar. 2 Sold building supplies to Charles Smith for $13,500 on account, terms 2/10, n/30.
      7 Sold plumbing fixtures to Fantasy Builders on account for $30,000. No discount was given.
     13 Sold lumber to Abbey Street Stores on account for $8,000, terms 2/10, n/30.
     15 Charles Smith returned $2,000 of building supplies from the March 2 sale.
     21 Payment was received from Abbey Street Stores.
     28 Payment was received from Charles Smith.
     31 Payment was received from Fantasy Builders.

LO 2   **E5-4**   **Calculate Sales Discounts**   Maria's Art Supply House had net sales of $184,000, gross sales of $207,000, and sales returns and allowances of $19,175 for 19X4.

REQUIRED:

Calculate the amount of sales discounts given by Maria's Art Supply House for 19X4.

LO 3   **E5-5**   **Recording Basic Purchases Transactions**   Prepare journal entries for the following list of events. The company uses the periodic inventory method and records purchases at the gross amount.

May 3 Purchased $1,900 of merchandise in exchange for cash.
     5 Purchased $4,300 of merchandise on credit.
    16 One-half of the goods purchased on May 5 were defective and were returned.
    24 Purchased $3,700 of merchandise, of which one-half was paid in cash and the remainder was purchased on credit.

LO 3   **E5-6**   **Purchases Discount Transactions**   Prepare journal entries for Middaugh's Hobby Shop for the following list of events. The company uses the periodic inventory method and records purchases at the gross amount.

July 1 Purchased $5,000 of toy model kits with terms of 1/10, n/30, F.O.B. shipping point.
      9 Ordered $3,500 of remote-controlled racing cars on terms of 2/10, n/30, F.O.B. destination.
     11 Received the remote-controlled cars ordered on July 9. The attached invoice listed the freight charge at $95.
     12 Received a freight bill for $135 due on August 1 for the July 1 purchase.
     13 Returned $600 of the toy model kits purchased on July 1 because they were defective.

July 18 Paid the balance owed for the remote-controlled racing cars received on July 11.
     28 Paid the balance owed for the toy model kits.

LO 9

E5-7   Recording Purchases Net of Discounts (Appendix 5-A)   Prepare journal entries for the events described in E5-6, assuming Middaugh's Hobby Shop uses the net of discount method for recording purchases.

LO 4

E5-8   Basic Inventory Relationships   Determine the missing amounts for the following information:

	January	February	March
Beginning merchandise inventory	$1,400	?	$1,800
Goods purchased	?	?	$2,000
Goods available for sale	$3,100	$5,600	?
Cost of goods sold	$1,100	?	?
Ending merchandise inventory	?	?	$1,100

LO 5

E5-9   Calculate Operating Expense   Determine the total selling expenses and the total general and administrative expenses from the total operating expenses listed below. The sales department and the administrative offices are located in the same building. Each function occupies one-half of the total space. Allocate as many of the total operating expenses as you can to the separate categories of selling expenses and general and administrative expenses.

Sales commissions	$13,150
Insurance expense	12,980
Wages and salaries expense—administrative	89,500
Wages and salaries expense—sales	76,890
Advertising expense	31,160
Depreciation expense—building	19,800
Utilities expense	2,985

LO 6

E5-10   Adjusting and Closing Entries for Cost of Goods Sold   Prepare adjusting and closing entries for cost of goods sold using the adjusting entry method from the following list of accounts. (Ignore the absence of other revenue, contra-revenue, and expense accounts that ordinarily would be closed as well.)

Merchandise Inventory, 1/1/X7	$33,500
Merchandise Inventory, 12/31/X7	21,000
Transportation-In	3,200
Purchases	42,000
Purchases Returns and Allowances	4,600
Purchases Discounts	1,100

LO 10

E5-11   Closing Entries for Cost of Goods Sold (Appendix 5-B)   Prepare closing entries for the merchandise inventory accounts given in E5-10, using the closing entry method.

LO 4,6

E5-12   Completing the Worksheet and Calculating Cost of Goods Sold   Complete the following worksheet for the Discount Furniture Company and calculate cost of goods sold.

Discount Furniture Company
Partial Worksheet
For the Year Ended December 31, 19X9

ACCOUNTS	TRIAL BALANCE Dr.	TRIAL BALANCE Cr.	ADJUSTMENTS Dr.	ADJUSTMENTS Cr.	ADJUSTED TRIAL BALANCE Dr.	ADJUSTED TRIAL BALANCE Cr.
Cash	29,400				29,400	
Accounts Receivable	12,200				12,200	
Merchandise Inventory	36,900		(f) 44,200	(e) 36,900	44,200	
Sales Supplies	3,400			(a) 1,200	2,200	
Prepaid Insurance	4,800			(b) 400	4,400	
Prepaid Rent	12,000			(c) 1,000	11,000	
Equipment	24,000				24,000	
Accum. Deprec.—Equip.		2,400		(d) 1,200		3,600
Accounts Payable		7,400				7,400
Notes Payable		16,000				16,000
F. Fernandez, Capital		77,700				77,700
F. Fernandez, Withdrawals	2,400				2,400	
Income Summary			(e) 36,900	(f) 44,200	36,900	44,200
Sales		147,000				147,000
Sales Returns and Allow.	3,500				3,500	
Sales Discounts	8,400				8,400	
Purchases	112,300				112,300	
Transportation-In	3,600				3,600	
Purchases Returns and Allow.		7,100				7,100
Purchases Discounts		1,100				1,100
Deprec. Expense—Equip.			(d) 1,200		1,200	
Insurance Expense			(b) 400		400	
Rent Expense			(c) 1,000		1,000	
Supplies Expense			(a) 1,200		1,200	
Utilities Expense	1,400				1,400	
Wages and Sal. Expense	4,400				4,400	
	258,700	258,700	84,900	84,900	304,100	304,100
Net Income						

LO 7   **E5-13**   **Preparing an Income Statement from a Worksheet**   Prepare a multistep income statement for Carmen's Beauty Supply from the following worksheet (shown on the next page). Assume all operating expenses are categorized as general and administrative expenses.

LO 7   **E5-14**   **Preparing a Balance Sheet from a Worksheet**   Prepare a classified balance sheet for Carmen's Beauty Supply from the worksheet given on the next page.

LO 8   **E5-15**   **Calculate Cost of Goods Sold and Gross Profit Ratios**   During 19X1, Kumar's Computer Store had net income of $158,000, operating expenses of $59,600, and cost of goods sold of $679,200.

REQUIRED:

Determine the gross profit and the cost of goods sold ratios for 19X1.

Carmen's Beauty Supply
Worksheet
For the Year Ended December 31, 19X4

ACCOUNTS	TRIAL BALANCE Dr.	TRIAL BALANCE Cr.	ADJUSTMENTS Dr.	ADJUSTMENTS Cr.	ADJUSTED TRIAL BALANCE Dr.	ADJUSTED TRIAL BALANCE Cr.	INCOME STATEMENT Dr.	INCOME STATEMENT Cr.	BALANCE SHEET Dr.	BALANCE SHEET Cr.
Cash	73,500				73,500				73,500	
Accounts Receivable	30,500				30,500				30,500	
Merchandise Inventory	92,250		(f) 110,500	(e) 92,250	110,500				110,500	
Office Supplies	8,500			(a) 3,000	5,500				5,500	
Prepaid Insurance	12,000			(b) 1,000	11,000				11,000	
Prepaid Rent	30,000			(c) 2,500	27,500				27,500	
Equipment	60,000				60,000				60,000	
Accumulated Deprec.—Equip.		6,000		(d) 3,000		9,000				9,000
Accounts Payable		18,500				18,500				18,500
Notes Payable		40,000				40,000				40,000
C. Smith, Capital		194,250				194,250				194,250
C. Smith, Withdrawals	6,000				6,000				6,000	
Income Summary			(e) 92,250	(f) 110,500	92,250	110,500	92,250	110,500		
Sales		367,500				367,500		367,500		
Sales Returns and Allow.	8,750				8,750		8,750			
Sales Discounts	21,000				21,000		21,000			
Purchases	280,750				280,750		280,750			
Transportation-In	9,000				9,000		9,000			
Purchases Returns and Allow.		17,750				17,750		17,750		
Purchases Discounts		2,750				2,750		2,750		
Depreciation Expense			(d) 3,000		3,000		3,000			
Insurance Expense			(b) 1,000		1,000		1,000			
Rent Expense			(c) 2,500		2,500		2,500			
Supplies Expense			(a) 3,000		3,000		3,000			
Utilities Expense	3,500				3,500		3,500			
Wages and Salaries Expense	11,000				11,000		11,000			
	646,750	646,750	212,250	212,250	760,250	760,250	435,750	498,500	324,500	261,750
Net Income							62,750			62,750
							498,500	498,500	324,500	324,500

PROBLEM SET A

LO 2,3   **P5-1A   Sale and Purchase Transactions**   Merino's Sweater Store uses the periodic inventory method and the gross method of recording purchases. A list of events for Merino's Sweater Store during the month of October is given below:

Oct. 1 Purchased $3,500 of cashmere sweaters from Liz's Sweater Supply on account with terms of 2/10, n/30. The sweaters were picked up by a Merino's employee.
   3 Sold sweaters for $830 cash.
   5 Sold sweaters for $760 on credit with terms of 1/10, n/30.
   6 Returned $300 of the cashmere sweaters to Liz's Sweater Supply because they were defective.
   7 Purchased $1,300 of sweaters, F.O.B. shipping point, from Wool-Enz Company on account with terms of 2/10, n/30. Freight, prepaid by the seller, was $50.
   9 Sold sweaters for $660 cash.
   12 Sweaters that sold for $200 on October 5 were returned due to defects.
   14 Paid for the sweaters purchased on October 7, including the freight prepaid by the seller of $50.
   17 Collected cash for the sweaters sold on October 5.
   19 Sold sweaters on credit for $4,300 with terms of 1/10, n/30. The customer picked up the sweaters at the store.
   26 Paid the balance due on the October 1 purchase.
   28 Collected cash for the sweaters sold on October 19.
   30 Sold sweaters for $900. One-half was paid in cash and the remainder was on account. The customer took possession of the sweaters at the time of sale.

REQUIRED:

a. Record journal entries for each of the events.
b. Calculate net sales.
c. Calculate cost of goods purchased.

LO 3,4   **P5-2A   Accounting for Purchases**   Wilner's Hardware uses the periodic inventory method and the gross method of recording purchases. A list of events for Wilner's Hardware during the month of June is given below:

June 1 Purchased $600 of hammers from Armand Company on account with terms of 2/10, n/30, F.O.B. destination. Freight charges of $30 were paid by Armand Company. The hammers were received on June 2.
   5 Purchased $4,200 of power drills from Tools International on account with terms of 1/10, n/30, F.O.B. shipping point. Freight charges of $120 were paid by Tools International.
   10 Paid the balance due to Tools International for the June 5 purchase.
   12 Purchased $2,600 of lawn trimmers from Grass Eater Company on account with terms of 1/10, n/30, F.O.B. shipping point. Freight charges of $190 were paid by Wilner at the time of delivery on June 15.
   18 Returned $200 of hammers to Armand Company.
   28 Paid the balance due to Armand Company for the June 2 purchase.
   30 Paid the balance due to the Grass Eater Company for the June 12 purchase.

REQUIRED:

a. Record journal entries for each of the events.
b. Calculate cost of goods purchased.
c. Calculate cost of goods sold, assuming the beginning and ending balances of Merchandise Inventory are $32,600 and $29,700, respectively.

LO 3,4,6

P5-3A   **Cost of Goods Sold Relationships**   Selected information for Bayer Company for the years ended 19X5 and 19X6 is presented below:

	19X5	19X6
Purchases returns and allowances	2,100	?
Cost of goods sold	10,500	?
Cost of goods purchased	?	?
Net purchases	?	21,500
Transportation-in	1,100	1,500
Ending merchandise inventory	?	4,200
Goods available for sale	20,000	?
Purchases discounts	700	400
Beginning merchandise inventory	3,500	?
Gross purchases	?	24,100

REQUIRED:

a. Fill in the missing information for 19X5 and 19X6.

b. Prepare all appropriate adjusting and closing entries for the accounts shown for 19X6.

LO 1,2,3,4,8

P5-4A   **Merchandising Income Statement Relationships**   Selected information for Ralph's Plumbing Supply for the years ended 19X2 and 19X3 is presented below:

	19X2	19X3
Purchases returns and allowances	?	6,000
Net income	37,200	41,100
Gross sales	223,500	?
Cost of goods purchased	?	?
Beginning merchandise inventory	?	?
Sales expense	?	18,100
Cost of goods available for sale	176,100	?
Purchases discounts	2,400	9,200
Gross profit	81,700	?
Sales discounts	?	4,700
Ending merchandise inventory	?	41,900
Net sales	?	221,000
Transportation-in	8,700	4,300
Cost of goods sold	120,100	?
General and administrative expense	27,100	27,300
Purchases	152,600	?
Sales returns and allowances	11,600	9,100
Net purchases	144,500	?

REQUIRED:

a. Fill in the missing information for 19X2 and 19X3.

b. Prepare a classified income statement for Ralph's Plumbing Supply for 19X3.

c. Calculate the gross profit ratios for 19X2 and 19X3.

d. Calculate the cost of goods sold ratios for 19X2 and 19X3.

LO 6,7

P5-5A   **Preparing a Worksheet for a Merchandising Business**   The partial worksheet for the year ended 12/31/X8 for A. Leathers Company is shown on the next page.

REQUIRED:

a. Complete the worksheet in good form.

b. Explain what the adjustments to Merchandise Inventory accomplish.

c. Prepare an income statement for the year ended 19X8. Classify all operating expenses not identified to be sales-related as general and administrative.

A. Leathers Company
Partial Worksheet
For the Year Ended December 31, 19X8

ACCOUNTS	TRIAL BALANCE Dr.	TRIAL BALANCE Cr.	ADJUSTMENTS Dr.	ADJUSTMENTS Cr.	ADJUSTED TRIAL BALANCE Dr.	ADJUSTED TRIAL BALANCE Cr.
Cash	23,800				23,800	
Accounts Receivable	14,350				14,350	
Merchandise Inventory	64,180		(e) 99,640	(d) 64,180	99,640	
Office Supplies	16,600			(a) 12,200	4,400	
Prepaid Insurance	8,400			(b) 4,800	3,600	
Equipment	204,000				204,000	
Accum. Deprec.—Equip.		39,600		(c) 10,200		49,800
Accounts Payable		11,450				11,450
Notes Payable		118,000				118,000
A. Leathers, Capital		128,670				128,670
A. Leathers, Withdrawals	8,400				8,400	
Income Summary			(d) 64,180	(e) 99,640	64,180	99,640
Sales		313,560				313,560
Sales Returns and Allow.	6,200				6,200	
Sales Discounts	4,180				4,180	
Purchases	218,650				218,650	
Transportation-In	11,100				11,100	
Purchases Returns and Allow.		8,240				8,240
Purchases Discounts		4,160				4,160
Deprec. Exp.—Equip. (G&A)			(c) 1,200		1,200	
Deprec. Exp.—Equip. (Sales)			(c) 9,000		9,000	
Insurance Expense			(b) 4,800		4,800	
Supplies Expense			(a) 12,200		12,200	
Utilities Expense	9,620				9,620	
Wages and Sal. Exp. (G&A)	24,400				24,400	
Wages and Sal. Exp. (Sales)	9,800				9,800	
	623,680	623,680	191,020	191,020	733,520	733,520
Net Income						

d. Prepare a balance sheet as of December 31, 19X8.
e. Journalize the necessary closing entries for 19X8.

LO 6,7   **P5-6A**   **Preparing a Worksheet for a Merchandising Business**   The trial balance as of December 31, 19X6 for Frank Higgins Company is shown on the next page.

Additional Information:
(1) A count of remaining supplies revealed that $400 remained on December 31, 19X6.
(2) A 2-year insurance policy was purchased for $2,800 on January 1, 19X6.
(3) Total depreciation of the building for the year was $10,500.
(4) Total depreciation of the equipment for the year was $6,000.
(5) Frank Higgins chooses to classify all depreciation expense, supplies expense, and insurance expense as general and administrative expense.
(6) The December 31, 19X6 amount of merchandise inventory is $43,700.
(7) All advertising expense is categorized as selling.
(8) Wages and salaries owed to employees, but unpaid at December 31, 19X6 were $5,000 for sales personnel and $4,400 for other employees.

Frank Higgins Company
Trial Balance
December 31, 19X6

	Debits	Credits
Cash	$39,000	
Accounts Receivable	16,200	
Merchandise Inventory, January 1, 19X6	19,600	
Office Supplies	5,400	
Prepaid Insurance	2,800	
Land	16,000	
Building	84,000	
Accumulated Depreciation - Building		$ 21,000
Equipment	60,000	
Accumulated Depreciation - Equipment		6,000
Accounts Payable		11,400
Notes Payable		8,500
F. Higgins, Capital		119,100
F. Higgins, Withdrawals	14,400	
Sales		315,200
Sales Returns and Allowances	7,800	
Sales Discounts	3,600	
Purchases	125,200	
Transportation-In	6,200	
Purchases Returns and Allowances		5,600
Purchases Discounts		5,400
Advertising Expense	2,800	
Wage and Salaries Expense–Office	40,000	
Wage and Salaries Expense–Sales	49,200	
Totals	$492,200	$492,200

REQUIRED:

a. Prepare a worksheet in good form.
b. Prepare an income statement for the year ended 19X6.
c. Prepare a statement of owner's equity for the year ended 19X6.
d. Prepare a balance sheet as of December 31, 19X6.
e. Journalize the necessary closing entries for 19X6.

PROBLEM SET B

LO 2,5

P5-1B   Sale and Purchase Transactions   Jean's Lighting Store uses the periodic inventory method and the gross method of recording purchases. A list of events for Jean's Lighting Store during the month of September is given below:

Sept. 2 Purchased $4,500 of lighting fixtures from Eastern Electric on account with terms of 2/10, n/30. The fixtures were picked up by one of Jean's employees.
3 Sold light fixtures for $2,130 cash.
5 Sold chandeliers for $3,260 on credit with terms of 1/10, n/30. The chandeliers were delivered to the customer at the store.
7 Returned $900 of the lighting fixtures to Eastern Electric because they were defective.

Sept. 8 Purchased $4,300 of bathroom lighting fixtures F.O.B. shipping point from A-One Wholesale Electronics on account with terms of 2/10, n/30. Freight of $250 was paid by A-One.

10 Sold lighting fixtures for $4,660 cash. The fixtures were delivered to the customer at the store.

12 Chandeliers that were sold for $1,700 on September 5 were returned due to defects.

14 Paid for the bathroom lighting fixtures purchased on September 8, including the prepaid freight of $250.

17 Collected cash for the chandeliers sold on September 5.

19 Sold lighting fixtures for $8,300 on credit with terms of 1/10, n/30. The customer took possession of the fixtures at the store.

26 Paid the balance due on the September 2 purchase.

28 Collected cash for the fixtures sold on September 19.

30 Sold bathroom lighting fixtures for $1,800. One-half was paid in cash and the remainder was on account. The customer picked up the fixtures.

REQUIRED:

a. Record journal entries for each of the events.
b. Calculate net sales.
c. Calculate net cost of goods purchased.

LO 3,4   **P5-2B**   **Accounting for Purchases**   The Appliance Den uses the periodic inventory method. A list of events for The Appliance Den during the month of March is given below:

Mar. 2 Received $900 of blenders purchased from Shaker Company on account with terms of 2/10, n/30, F.O.B. destination. Freight charges of $30 were paid by Shaker Company.

5 Purchased $6,300 of vacuum cleaners from Kauffman Distributors on account with terms of 1/10, n/30, F.O.B. shipping point. Freight charges of $120 were paid by Kauffman Distributors.

10 Paid the balance due to Kauffman Distributors for the March 5 purchase.

12 Purchased $3,900 of toaster ovens from Westend Company on account with terms of 1/10, n/30, F.O.B. shipping point. Freight charges of $190 were paid in cash on delivery by The Appliance Den on March 15.

18 Returned $300 of blenders to Shaker Company.

28 Paid the balance due to Shaker Company for the March 2 purchase.

30 Paid the balance due to Westend Company for the March 12 purchase.

REQUIRED:

a. Record journal entries for each of the events.
b. Calculate cost of goods purchased.
c. Calculate cost of goods sold, assuming the beginning and ending balances of Merchandise Inventory are $48,900 and $44,550, respectively.

LO 3,4   **P5-3B**   **Cost of Goods Sold Relationships**

Selected information for Butler Company for the years ended 19X1 and 19X2 is presented below:

	19X1	*19X2*
Purchases returns and allowances	5,250	5,500
Cost of goods sold	26,250	?
Net cost of goods purchased	?	?
Net purchases	?	53,750
Transportation-in	2,750	3,750
Ending merchandise inventory	?	10,500

	19X1	19X2
Goods available for sale	50,000	?
Purchase discounts	1,750	?
Beginning merchandise inventory	8,750	?
Gross purchases	?	60,250

REQUIRED:

a. Fill in the missing information for 19X1 and 19X2.

b. Prepare all appropriate adjusting and closing entries for the accounts shown for 19X2.

LO 1,2,3 4,8   **P5-4B**   **Merchandising Income Statement Relationships**   Selected information for Ace Auto Parts for the years ended 19X8 and 19X9 is presented below:

	19X8	19X9
Purchases returns and allowances	?	3,000
Net income	18,600	20,550
Gross sales	111,750	?
Cost of goods purchased	?	?
Beginning merchandise inventory	?	?
Sales expense	?	9,050
Cost of goods available for sale	88,050	?
Purchases discounts	1,200	4,600
Gross profit	40,850	?
Sales discounts	?	2,350
Ending merchandise inventory	?	20,950
Net sales	?	110,500
Transportation-in	4,350	2,150
Cost of goods sold	60,050	?
General and administrative expense	13,550	13,650
Purchases	76,300	?
Sales returns and allowances	5,800	4,550
Net purchases	72,250	?

REQUIRED:

a. Fill in the missing information for 19X8 and 19X9.

b. Prepare a classified income statement for Ace Auto Parts for 19X9.

c. Calculate the gross profit ratios for 19X8 and 19X9.

d. Calculate the cost of goods sold ratios for 19X8 and 19X9.

LO 6,7   **P5-5B**   **Preparing a Worksheet for a Merchandising Business**   The partial worksheet for the year ended December 31, 19X4 for N. Suhm Company is shown on the next page:

REQUIRED:

a. Complete the worksheet in good form.

b. Explain what the adjustments to Merchandise Inventory accomplish.

c. Prepare an income statement for the year ended 19X4. Advertising expense is classified as a sales expense. All other expenses may be split, 40% selling and 60% general and administrative.

d. Prepare a balance sheet as of December 31, 19X4.

e. Journalize the closing entries for 19X4.

N. Suhm Company
Partial Worksheet
For the Year Ended December 31, 19X4

ACCOUNTS	TRIAL BALANCE Dr.	TRIAL BALANCE Cr.	ADJUSTMENTS Dr.	ADJUSTMENTS Cr.	ADJUSTED TRIAL BALANCE Dr.	ADJUSTED TRIAL BALANCE Cr.
Cash	35,700				35,700	
Accounts Receivable	21,525				21,525	
Merchandise Inventory	96,270		(e) 149,460	(d) 96,270	149,460	
Office Supplies	24,900			(a) 18,300	6,600	
Prepaid Insurance	12,600			(b) 7,200	5,400	
Equipment	306,000				306,000	
Accum. Deprec.—Equip.		59,400		(c) 15,300		74,700
Accounts Payable		17,175				17,175
Notes Payable		177,000				177,000
N. Suhm, Capital		193,005				193,005
N. Suhm, Withdrawals	12,600				12,600	
Income Summary			(d) 96,270	(e) 149,460	96,270	149,460
Sales		470,340				470,340
Sales Returns and Allow.	9,300				9,300	
Sales Discounts	6,270				6,270	
Purchases	327,975				327,975	
Transportation-In	16,650				16,650	
Purchases Returns and Allow.		12,360				12,360
Purchases Discounts		6,240				6,240
Advertising Expense	14,700				14,700	
Depreciation Expense			(c) 15,300		15,300	
Insurance Expense			(b) 7,200		7,200	
Supplies Expense			(a) 18,300		18,300	
Utilities Expense	14,430				14,430	
Wages and Sal. Expense	36,600				36,600	
	935,520	935,520	286,530	286,530	1,100,280	1,100,280
Net Income						

LO 6,7   **P5-6B   Preparing a Worksheet for a Merchandising Business**   The trial balance on December 31, 19X5 for The Silverman Company is shown on the next page:

Additional Information:
(1) A count of remaining supplies revealed that $600 remained on December 31, 19X5.
(2) A 2-year insurance policy was purchased for $3,700 on January 1, 19X5.
(3) Depreciation on the equipment for the year was $15,500.
(4) Depreciation for the year on the building was $9,000.
(5) Wages and salaries owed but unpaid at December 31, 19X5 were $6,600 for office personnel and $7,500 for sales employees.
(6) The December 31, 19X5 amount of merchandise inventory is $65,550.
(7) Silverman chooses to view all depreciation expense, supplies expense, and insurance expense as general and administrative expense.
(8) All advertising expense is selling.

The Silverman Company Trial Balance December 31, 19X5		
	Debits	Credits
Cash	$58,500	
Accounts Receivable	24,300	
Merchandise Inventory	29,400	
Office Supplies	8,100	
Prepaid Insurance	3,700	
Land	24,000	
Equipment	126,000	
Accumulated Depreciation—Equipment		$ 31,500
Building	90,000	
Accumulated Depreciation—Building		9,000
Accounts Payable		17,100
Notes Payable		12,750
L. Silverman, Capital		178,650
L. Silverman, Withdrawals	21,600	
Sales		472,800
Sales Discounts	11,700	
Sales Returns and Allowances	5,400	
Purchases	187,800	
Transportation-In	9,800	
Purchases Returns and Allowances		8,400
Purchases Discounts		8,100
Advertising Expense	4,200	
Wages and Salaries Expense–Office	60,000	
Wages and Salaries Expense–Sales	73,800	
Totals	$738,300	$738,300

REQUIRED:

a. Prepare a worksheet in good form.
b. Prepare an income statement for the year ended 19X5.
c. Prepare a statement of owner's equity for the year ended 19X5.
d. Prepare a balance sheet as of December 31, 19X5.
e. Journalize the closing entries for 19X5.

CRITICAL THINKING AND COMMUNICATING

C5-1   Fred Wang owns and operates a regional chain of pet supply stores. Many of Mr. Wang's suppliers offer purchase discounts with the terms of 2/10, n/30. Mr. Wang suspects some of his store managers, hired in the last year, are not paying the suppliers in time to receive the discounts. Mr. Wang's stores record purchases at gross prices and deduct discounts received to derive net purchases. Mr. Wang prefers not to change his accounting method to the "net" method (see Appendix 5-A). Mr. Wang discusses the problem with his accountant, Mrs. Greenleaf, and asks her how to analyze it.

REQUIRED:

a. Explain why Mr. Wang is concerned about his managers' not receiving purchases discounts.

b. Describe the analysis that Mrs. Greenleaf should recommend to Mr. Wang and explain how it will help him determine the extent of the problem.

c. Explain to Mr. Wang what the impact of not taking purchases discounts would have on the gross profit ratio.

C5-2 Yvette Bescos owns and operates a women's boutique. She has been replacing the lines of clothing she carries with well-known designer labels. Yvette believes her net income has been increasing as a result of carrying these labels, but she is concerned about the decline in sales last year. A comparative income statement for her store is given below:

Yvette's Boutique Comparative Income Statement For the Years Ended December 31, 19X7 and 19X8		
	19X7	*19X8*
Net sales	$198,000	$195,000
Less: Cost of goods sold	110,000	93,000
Gross profit	$ 88,000	$102,000
Less: Operating expenses	38,000	39,000
Net income	$ 50,000	$ 63,000

REQUIRED:

a. Calculate the gross profit ratios for 19X7 and 19X8.

b. Explain why sales are declining.

c. Advise Yvette whether or not to continue her current strategy.

C5-3 The financial statements of J.C. Penney Company, Inc. a major retail merchandising company, are reprinted in Appendix B at the end of the text. Examine J. C. Penney's income statement carefully. Note two things. The company does not calculate gross profit in the income statement and it includes "occupancy, buying, and warehousing costs" with cost of goods sold.

REQUIRED:

1. Ignore the additional costs included with cost of goods sold and calculate J.C. Penney's gross profit, gross profit percentage, and cost of goods sold percentage for 1991, 1992, and 1993. Use retail sales rather than total revenue in your calculations.

2. Comment on the degree of fluctuation in J.C. Penney's gross profit percentage over the three years.

3. Calculate the effect an increase in cost of goods sold equal to 1% of retail sales would have had on J.C. Penney's net income for 1993.

4. Considering that J.C. Penney operates stores in many different locations, comment on why you think that management lumps "occupancy, buying, and warehousing costs" with cost of goods sold in the income statement.

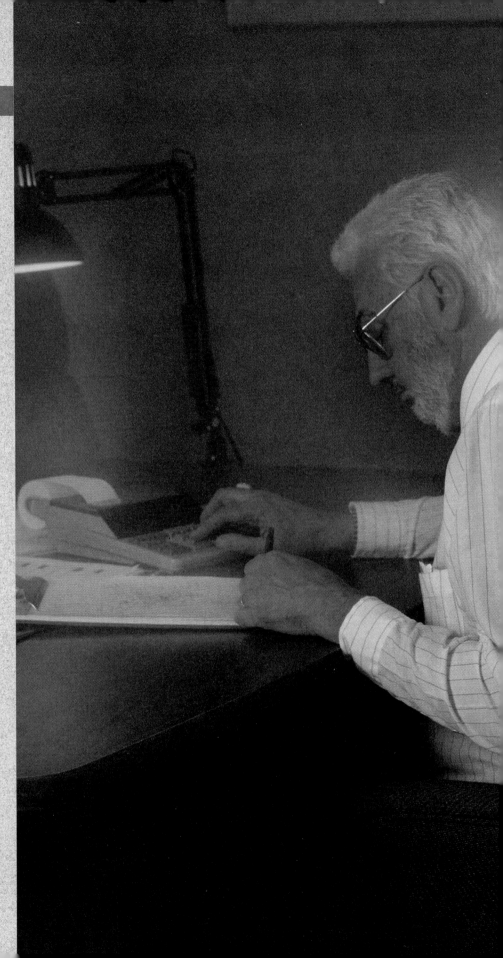

CHAPTER 6

Accounting Systems

Robert Good analyzed comparative income statements for 19X0 and 19X1 to find out why the profitability of Good's Campus Books had declined in 19X1. The bookstore's gross profit ratio was lower in 19X1, and its cost of goods sold ratio was higher than in 19X0. Upon further analysis, Robert found that the store paid too much for purchases. Too often the store ran out of books and other stock before placing re-orders. The bookstore also paid more for rush orders because employees had less time to shop for the best prices, and transportation charges on rush orders were much higher than on normal purchases. Now Robert knows the problem, but he is not sure what to do about it. Apparently, the bookstore's accounting system does not support timely purchasing. Robert talked about the problem with his friend, Jonathan Fine, owner of Fine Appliances. Jonathon confessed that he was also experiencing the same problem in his business and was comparing various computer systems that might improve purchasing and other operations as well as perform accounting functions more efficiently.

In this chapter, you will learn about accounting systems. We introduce you to accounting control objectives and how they are achieved. Computers can not only speed accounting processing, but they can also enhance achievement of control objectives and improve a business's efficiency and effectiveness. You will see how computer systems can solve problems similar to those Robert and Jonathon have encountered.

LO 1

Describe the broad objectives of accounting systems.

ACCOUNTING SYSTEMS DESIGN AND OPERATION

To ensure that their accounting reports are reliable, businesses implement accounting systems. An **accounting system** is an organization of physical facilities, personnel, equipment, documents, records, and procedures designed to provide relevant information and to accomplish accounting control objectives. Although specific component configurations vary, depending on the size and nature of the business and on the types of transactions processed, certain broad objectives are common to all accounting systems.

Objectives of Accounting Systems

To be effective, any accounting system must implement the accounting process and support management decisions. In addition, the system must ensure the reliability of information produced. Finally, systems must be economical so that they are worth their cost to the business.

Implementing the Accounting Process.   Accounting systems must provide the accounting numbers that are ultimately summarized in financial statements that conform to GAAP. A system is unlikely to achieve this broad systems objective unless it achieves the six specific accounting control objectives described later.

Supporting Management Decisions.   Management's responsibilities include making a wide variety of business decisions. The accounting system must be designed to provide reports and other information useful in making these decisions. While formal financial statements provide useful information, managers usually need a variety of additional information.

To meet management's decision needs, accounting systems must achieve two corollary objectives: timeliness and flexibility. **Timeliness** requires that information be supplied with sufficient lead time to permit management to assimilate and use it in the decision at hand. Information has value because it improves the expected outcomes of decisions. However, if managers make decisions before relevant information is available, that information cannot influence the outcomes of decisions and, therefore, is useless. Both Robert and

Jonathon are experiencing precisely this problem. Purchase orders are delayed because the information indicating that stocks are running low is not available until after stock-outs occur.

An accounting system has **flexibility** if it can provide information to support new decisions without needing major modifications. Not only does management require support for a variety of decisions, but the specific types of decisions and information they need also change—often frequently and rapidly. If an information system is *not flexible* (cannot provide new types of information without major modification), *it cannot be timely in providing information as needs change.*

Control.   If information is unreliable, it may not improve the outcomes of decisions and will lose some or all of its potential value. If the information the system generates is to be reliable, then the system must satisfy the six specific control objectives described below.

Cost-Effectiveness.   The more effective an information system is in achieving the above systems objectives, the more it will improve the expected outcomes of business decisions. However, information systems add to administrative costs as well. Therefore, entire information systems, as well as individual controls, must be **cost-effective**. In other words, benefits must outweigh costs.

LO2

List the specific accounting control objectives.

Control Objectives in Accounting Systems

A business cannot earn a competitive profit by being sloppy or inefficient, especially when it must compete with other businesses. It must be effective in achieving its sales, production, and other goals; and it must be efficient in utilizing its assets and personnel to achieve those goals at the least cost. In other words, it must be disciplined and operate under management's control.

Control consists of all the steps management takes to ensure that:

1. Goals are achieved (effectiveness).
2. Only necessary costs are incurred in achieving goals (efficiency).
3. Activities are conducted only in accordance with management's policies, and all transactions are preauthorized.
4. The assets of the business are safeguarded.
5. The financial reports used by management and prepared for outside users are reliable.

Similar to all other business functions, the accounting function requires discipline or control. If the accounting process is not controlled carefully, the objective of ensuring reliable financial reports cannot be achieved. Accounting also contributes significantly to the overall control of the business. For example, the efficiency of the sales department cannot be judged without reliable accounting information about the expenses incurred to support the sales effort.

Control is achieved in an organization through accounting and administrative controls. **Accounting controls** are those management implements to ensure that accounting reports are reliable. All other controls are called **administrative controls**.

Accounting Control Objectives

To produce reliable financial reports for management and outside users, an accounting system must satisfy certain specific control objectives. Any accounting system for processing transactions should meet these objectives: authorization, validity, valuation, classification, completeness, and accuracy.

Proper Authorization.   Employees with appropriate authority should evaluate each transaction for compliance with management policy and approve the transaction before it takes place. For example, Jonathon requires Judy Cohen, credit manager/office manager, to check all credit sales orders and to approve or deny the sale. With this requirement, Jonathon knows that appliances will be sold only to creditworthy customers. Since Judy does not sell appliances and receives no commissions on sales, she has no incentive to approve a sale to a customer who is unlikely to pay.

Validity.   The accounting system should record only real transactions and reject fake or fraudulent ones. For example, Jonathon has instructed his accountant not to record any purchase unless concrete evidence exists that goods have actually been received (e.g., a receiving report is received from the warehouse personnel). Jonathon also reviews all cash disbursements himself before they are paid. He will not authorize payment for recorded purchases unless the receiving report is included in the documentation he reviews.

Proper Valuation.   Employees must enter correct quantities and prices on the documents that represent transactions, and all arithmetic must be accurate. In preparing credit sales invoices, James Meyers, an accounting assistant at Fine Appliances, compares quantities and prices from customer orders to quantities recorded on delivery documents and approved price lists, respectively; if everything agrees, he enters the correct quantities and prices on sales invoices and calculates the amount of sale.

Proper Classification.   Accounting personnel must correctly analyze transactions for posting to the proper accounts, and they must record all transactions as of the correct dates. In Jonathon's business, sales on F.O.B. shipping point terms are recorded properly as of the date of shipment; and sales on F.O.B. destination terms are properly recorded as of the date of delivery.

Completeness of Recording.   A business should record a journal entry for every transaction that actually takes place. At Fine Appliances, accounting assistants record every individual transaction with an individual journal entry, except cash sales transactions. Cash sales are summarized for a day, and an accounting assistant makes one entry for the daily total. As long as every cash sale is included in the daily total, every cash sale is thus recorded with a daily journal entry. (A subsequent chapter describes specific controls to ensure that all cash sales are recorded.)

Recording Accuracy.   Once recorded with journal entries, transactions must be accurately posted to *all* appropriate accounting records management uses, including the appropriate general ledger accounts. In addition, the general ledger accounts must be correctly adjusted and transformed into financial reports. The next section of this chapter illustrates the use of subsidiary ledgers and special journals and related procedures to achieve recording accuracy.

LO 3

Describe the accounting system life cycle.

System Life Cycle

Accounting systems must meet multiple objectives, including multiple control objectives. Although good systems are flexible, every accounting system inevitably becomes obsolete. All information systems, including accounting systems, generally pass through a distinct life cycle. The typical life cycle of an accounting information system is depicted in Illustration 6-1.

ILLUSTRATION 6-1 Accounting System Life Cycle

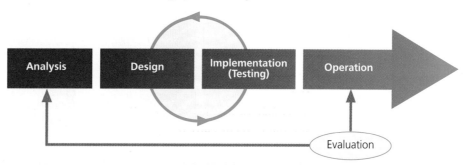

Analysis.   When a business believes it needs a new or improved accounting information system, it must analyze the need. An important part of this analysis is to determine what kinds of information and reports are needed. This process involves questioning managers about what they need. From the analysis comes a detailed set of system objectives.

Design.   Designing a system involves specifying all the personnel, organizational units, documents, records, procedures, and other controls needed and reviewing the relationships among them to meet the detailed system objectives. To put together a complex system composed of many of the above components and to coordinate their interactions, system designers usually prepare system flowcharts. **System flowcharts** are symbolic representations of systems. The advantage of flowcharts is that we can represent people, departments, objects, documents, procedures, and communications in relatively little space. Illustration 6-2 is a segment of a flowchart of the cash sales system of Fine Appliances. Notice that different symbols represent documents, actions, files, transfers of money, and transfers of documents to and from customers and internal personnel. Vertical columns with headings represent employees and departments and emphasize separation of incompatible duties. The documents and actions flow downward and to the right, the way we read text. These features are standard flowcharting techniques that permit others less familiar with the business, such as new employees, to examine and understand its system or procedures.

Implementation.   Implementation of the system involves installing the new system and then testing it for proper functioning. Experienced systems and accounting personnel always run the new system *parallel* to the old system. They compare the reports and other information the two systems produce from the same raw data to check the new system's effectiveness. Also, the old system temporarily serves as a backup system in case the new system fails. If the new system proves deficient in some way, the process cycles back for further design work as shown by the circular arrows in Illustration 6-1.

Operation.   Once the business implements and thoroughly tests the new system, it can phase out the old system and allow the new system to operate in its place.

Evaluation.   During the operational phase, the business should monitor the new system for malfunctions and evaluate its performance periodically. If well-

ILLUSTRATION 6-2 Anatomy of a Flowchart

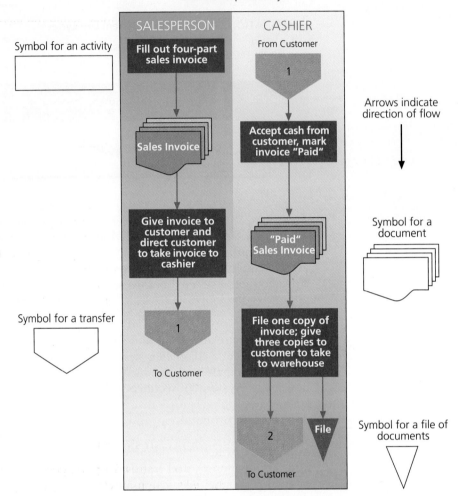

designed, the system will serve the needs of the business for a long enough period to justify all its development costs. Eventually, however, the system will cease to meet the business's needs adequately, and the cycle will start over.

ACCOUNTING SYSTEMS FOR RECORDING TRANSACTIONS

LO 4
Describe the need for and functions of subsidiary ledgers and special journals.

In earlier chapters, we showed you how to use the general journal and general ledger to record and summarize data about transactions and other events and to prepare financial statements. However, the general journal and general ledger have limitations. They can handle the transaction processing and management and control needs of only the smallest businesses. If the general journal and general ledger were the only accounting records other businesses used, these basic records would become choked with detail and would cease to be useful to management for any purpose other than preparation of financial statements. Thus, most businesses supplement the general ledger with subsidiary ledgers and supplement the general journal with various special journals.

Subsidiary ledgers are sets of ledger accounts that contain the details of balances in individual general ledger asset, liability, and owner's equity accounts. Examples of subsidiary ledgers are the accounts receivable subsidiary ledger, accounts payable subsidiary ledger, and inventory subsidiary ledger. The first two are illustrated in this chapter, while the inventory subsidiary ledger is illustrated in a subsequent chapter.

Special journals are substitutes for the general journal used to record particular classes of transactions. Examples of special journals are the sales journal, cash receipts journal, purchases journal, and cash disbursements journal—all of which are illustrated in this chapter.

Advantages of Subsidiary Ledgers

Subsidiary ledgers give managers information at the level and in the detail required to manage individual assets and liabilities. As you can imagine, a business would have significant difficulty managing its accounts receivable if its only record of the amounts customers owe is the total debit balance in Accounts Receivable in the general ledger. This is all that Jonathon had when he started his business, and he learned the hard way. If a particular customer had not paid for a sale by the due date, he had no way of knowing. If the customer ordered additional merchandise before paying the overdue amount, Jonathon had no way of knowing that he should withhold credit for the additional sale. Having no specific record of what that particular customer owed, Jonathon had to sort through all postings to Accounts Receivable in the general ledger and trace them to the related journal entries to determine which customers owed what amounts. He soon realized he needed a way to manage the details of accounts receivable on a customer-by-customer basis. As soon as he could afford it, he hired a public accountant to set up subsidiary ledgers for him.

Accounts Receivable Subsidiary Ledger

The **accounts receivable subsidiary ledger** consists of an individual ledger account for each credit customer. We post a particular customer's sales (debits), sales returns (credits), cash payments (credits), and write-offs of bad debts (credits) to that customer's individual account. (Write-offs are discussed in a subsequent chapter.)

Fine Appliances' accounts receivable subsidiary ledger is shown in Illustration 6-3.[1] Notice that the sum of the balances in the individual customer accounts equals the balance in Accounts Receivable in the general ledger. Because of this relationship, Accounts Receivable in the general ledger is called a control account. **A control account** is the general ledger account that relates in total to the details contained in a particular subsidiary ledger.

---

[1]Although the advantages of subsidiary journals and ledgers are greatest when there are many transactions with many customers and suppliers, we intentionally choose to illustrate only a representative few of each in this and other illustrations of subsidiary ledgers and journals. Our purpose is to give you a clear picture of the procedures used to implement subsidiary ledgers and special journals and the relationships among them and the general ledger. Representative numbers of items would interfere with this purpose.

ILLUSTRATION 6-3 Accounts Receivable Subsidiary Ledger and Control Account

ACCOUNTS RECEIVABLE SUBSIDIARY LEDGER

NAME: ABC Homes   ACCOUNT NO.: 1041

DATE	DESCRIPTION	POST. REF.	DEBIT	CREDIT	BALANCE
19X0 Dec. 5		SJ1	2,300		2,300
26		CR1		2,300	0

NAME: Brown Construction   ACCOUNT NO.: 1052

DATE	DESCRIPTION	POST. REF.	DEBIT	CREDIT	BALANCE
19X0 Dec. 28		SJ1	7,750		7,750

NAME: Colby Custom Homes   ACCOUNT NO.: 1075

DATE	DESCRIPTION	POST. REF.	DEBIT	CREDIT	BALANCE
19X0 Dec. 11		SJ1	3,100		3,100

GENERAL LEDGER

NAME: Accounts Receivable   ACCOUNT NO.: 110

DATE	DESCRIPTION	POST. REF.	DEBIT	CREDIT	BALANCE
19X0 Dec. 31		SJ1	13,150		13,150
31		CR1		2,300	10,850

Advantages of Special Journals

Special journals remove excessive detail from the general journal and general ledger accounts, group like transactions together for easier reference, and contribute to efficiency in posting to general ledger accounts. In merchandising businesses, sales generally account for the largest percentage of all transactions. Most merchandising businesses have at least several hundred sales transactions per year; and the number increases to the hundreds of millions per year among large retail chains such as Kmart. For its fiscal year ended January 31, 1993, Kmart reported sales of $37.7 billion. If we assume that the average sale by Kmart is $100 or less, Kmart must have made at least 377 million individual sales transactions. If all transactions are recorded individually in the general journal, searching to find information about any individual transaction would be very difficult or impossible. Moreover, since transactions of all different varieties would be intermingled, management would have difficulty tracking key flows in the business such as weekly or monthly sales volume. Finally, since every transaction recorded in the general journal must be individually posted to a general ledger account, the general ledger accounts would also be congested with detail.

In contrast, special journals are set up to handle each type of frequent business transaction, keeping details of those entries out of the general journal. Entries in special journals are not all posted to the general ledger accounts as they take place. Instead, many are summarized periodically such as monthly. The periodic totals, rather than the detailed transactions, are then posted to the general ledger accounts. The public accounting firm Jonathon hired to set up subsidiary ledgers for Fine Appliances strongly recommended the use of special journals—a recommendation Jonathon wisely accepted.

Sales Journal

The **sales journal** is the special journal for recording credit sales transactions. Illustration 6-4 shows the sales journal of Fine Appliances for January 19X1. The transactions journalized in the sales journal are:

Date of sale	Customer	Description	Amount
1/3	ABC Homes	One deluxe refrigerator	$ 2,300
1/7	Brown Construction	Two refrigerators; two cooktop stoves	7,750
1/13	Colby Custom Homes	Cooktop, microwave, and oven	3,100
1/20	Manor Contracting	Refrigerator, cooktop, microwave, and oven	4,700
1/23	ABC Homes	Refrigerator; three ovens	5,600
1/28	Brown Construction	Cooktop and oven	1,850
1/31	Good Construction	Five refrigerators	10,500

ILLUSTRATION 6-4 Sales Journal of Fine Appliances

SALES JOURNAL

Page 1

DATE		ACCOUNT DEBITED	INVOICE NO.	POST. REF.	DR./CR. AMOUNT
19X1					
Jan.	3	ABC Homes	1011	✓	2,300
	7	Brown Construction	1012	✓	7,750
	13	Colby Custom Homes	1013	✓	3,100
	20	Manor Contracting	1014	✓	4,700
	23	ABC Homes	1015	✓	5,600
	28	Brown Construction	1016	✓	1,850
	31	Good Construction	1017	✓	10,500
					35,800

In organizing all special journals, certain customary methods are used. Special journals have the following columns for recording and describing each transaction:

1. The Date column on each page is used just like its counterpart in the general journal.
2. A column used to identify the other party to the transaction—the customer in the case of the sales journal—is labeled Account Debited. This refers to the individual customer's accounts receivable subsidiary ledger account.
3. At least one column is provided to record the number of a source document or business paper that backs up the entry to the journal. In the sales journal, we enter the number of the sales invoice used to summarize the sale and to bill the customer in the Invoice No. column.
4. The Post. Ref. column in a special journal serves the same purpose as the Post. Ref. column of the general journal—to note when posting an entry to the appropriate account(s) is complete.
5. One or more Amount columns are used to represent general ledger accounts to which summary totals are to be posted. These account columns give the special journals an advantage over the general journal. Each transaction is recorded in a special journal on only one line. The sales journal in Illustration 6-4 has an additional advantage of only requiring one amount column, because each sale in the example results in a debit to Accounts Receivable *and an equal credit* to Sales.

RECORDING TRANSACTIONS—
SALES AND CASH RECEIPTS CYCLE

We typically organize accounting records and systems around the business's major transaction cycles. In an earlier chapter, we described the fundamental way that a merchandising business earns income—purchasing and selling goods. Each of these two fundamental business functions is part of a larger transaction cycle. For example, sales is one-half of the sales and cash receipts cycle, and purchases is one-half of the purchases and cash disbursements cycle. We cover the accounting records and procedures used in these two cycles in this chapter. There are other cycles in most businesses such as an inventory cycle and a payroll cycle, which we cover in subsequent chapters. Each cycle requires its own combination of special journals and subsidiary ledgers. We use a sales journal, cash receipts journal, and an accounts receivable subsidiary ledger to record sales and cash receipts transactions.

Journalizing and Posting Credit Sales Transactions

Illustration 6-5 shows the relationships among the sales journal, accounts receivable subsidiary ledger, and relevant general ledger accounts for journalizing and posting the credit sales transactions listed earlier. The procedure for journalizing and posting credit sales transactions consists of these three steps:

1. Record each sales transaction on one line of the sales journal, filling in all columns except the Post. Ref. column.
2. Post individual sales daily to the accounts receivable subsidiary ledger as shown in Illustration 6-5.
   a. Enter the same date of the transaction as in the sales journal.
   b. In the Post. Ref. column of the individual customer account, enter the letters SJ, indicating sales journal, followed by the page number on which the transaction is entered in the journal.
   c. After each posting to the appropriate individual customer account, place a check mark (✓) in the Post. Ref. column of the sales journal.
3. Sum the columns monthly and post the total of the credit sales for the month to Accounts Receivable (debit) and Sales (credit) in the general ledger.
   a. Date these postings as of the end of the month and reference them to the sales journal page in the Post. Ref. column of the account.
   b. When the posting is complete, write the account numbers of the general ledger accounts below the Amount Dr./Cr. column total of the sales journal.

We post individual transactions to the accounts receivable subsidiary ledger accounts on a daily basis because management wants up-to-date information for managing collections and granting credit. However, we make summary postings to the general ledger accounts at monthly intervals because summarizing greatly reduces the volume of postings in the general ledger, saves space, and saves posting effort. The sales journal itself is available if management wishes to follow the details of sales as a month progresses. Also, if management needs details of a past month's sales, those details can be accessed by tracing the posting to the sales journal page noted in the Post. Ref. column of the general ledger sales account.

ILLUSTRATION 6-5 Recording Sales Transactions

SALES JOURNAL

Page 1

	DATE	ACCOUNT DEBITED	INVOICE NO.	POST. REF	DR./CR. AMOUNT
	19X1 Jan. 3	ABC Homes	1011	✓	2,300
	7	Brown Construction	1012	✓	7,750
	13	Colby Custom Homes	1013	✓	3,100
	20	Manor Contracting	1014	✓	4,700
	23	ABC Homes	1015	✓	5,600
	28	Brown Construction	1016	✓	1,850
	31	Good Construction	1017	✓	10,500
					35,800
					(110/602)

Step 1: DAILY journalize individual transactions.

Step 2: DAILY post individual sales to individual customer accounts receivable.

Step 3: MONTHLY post column total to general ledger accounts.

ACCOUNTS RECEIVABLE SUBSIDIARY LEDGER

NAME: ABC Homes   ACCOUNT NO.: 1041

DATE	DESCRIPTION	POST. REF.	DEBIT	CREDIT	BALANCE
19X1 Jan. 3		SJ1	2,300		2,300
23		SJ1	5,600		7,900

NAME: Brown Construction   ACCOUNT NO.: 1052

DATE	DESCRIPTION	POST. REF.	DEBIT	CREDIT	BALANCE
19X1 Jan. 7		SJ1	7,750		7,750
28		SJ1	1,850		9,600

NAME: Colby Custom Homes   ACCOUNT NO.: 1075

DATE	DESCRIPTION	POST. REF.	DEBIT	CREDIT	BALANCE
19X1 Jan. 13		SJ1	3,100		3,100

NAME: Good Construction   ACCOUNT NO.: 1378

DATE	DESCRIPTION	POST. REF.	DEBIT	CREDIT	BALANCE
19X1 Jan. 31		SJ1	10,500		10,500

NAME: Manor Contracting   ACCOUNT NO.: 1561

DATE	DESCRIPTION	POST. REF.	DEBIT	CREDIT	BALANCE
19X1 Jan. 20		SJ1	4,700		4,700

GENERAL LEDGER

NAME: Accounts Receivable   ACCOUNT NO.: 110

DATE	DESCRIPTION	POST. REF.	DEBIT	CREDIT	BALANCE
19X1 Jan. 31		SJ1	35,800		35,800

NAME: Sales   ACCOUNT NO.: 602

DATE	DESCRIPTION	POST. REF.	DEBIT	CREDIT	BALANCE
19X1 Jan. 31		SJ1		35,800	35,800

Journalizing and Posting Cash Receipts Transactions

Journalizing and posting all other types of transactions, including cash receipts transactions, follow the same three steps as journalizing and posting sales transactions. The only real difference is the organization of the special journal involved in the particular type of transaction. Consider the following cash receipts transactions of Fine Appliances for January 19X1, that are journalized and posted in Illustration 6-6 using the three-step method:

Jan.   2 J. Fine, proprietor of Fine Appliances, invests $40,000.
       8 A cash sale is made for $4,500.
      13 A cash sale is made for $7,900.
      15 $20,000 in proceeds of a bank loan are received.
      17 Brown Construction pays, within the 2% discount period, the amount owed on Invoice 1012 (credit sale of Jan. 7).
      20 A cash sale is made for $6,600.
      23 Colby Custom Homes pays, within the 2% discount period, the amount owed on Invoice 1013 (credit sale of Jan. 13).
      24 A cash sale is made for $9,700.
      29 Manor Contracting pays, within the 2% discount period, the amount owed on Invoice 1014 (credit sale of Jan. 20).
      31 ABC Homes pays in full for Invoice No. 1011.

The above list implies that Fine Appliances needs a special journal to record cash received from customers and other cash inflows, a **cash receipts journal**, that is more sophisticated than the sales journal illustrated previously. First, the variety of cash receipts transactions contrasts with the single credit sales transaction. Second, entries, therefore, will not necessarily have equal amounts debited and credited to just two general ledger accounts. All entries involve debits to Cash, but the credits may be to Accounts Receivable, Cash Sales, or other accounts such as Notes Payable. Moreover, when cash is received from customers paying within the discount period on credit sales, a debit is made to Sales Discounts. These additional requirements are handled by adding columns, as shown in the cash receipts journal at the top of Illustration 6-6.

Following the Date column is an Explanation column where a very brief description of each transaction is entered. Thus, a variety of transactions can be handled without confusion. Following the Explanation column, the Account Credited column is for two types of entries: names of credit sales customers whose payments should be posted to their individual accounts receivable and the names of general ledger accounts other than those named in specific column headings. Next are columns for each general ledger account that is frequently debited or credited in cash receipts transactions. The final column, Other Accounts, is for recording credits to *other* general ledger accounts that are infrequently involved in cash receipts transactions. These multiple columns make it feasible to enter the amounts debited and credited for cash receipts transactions on one line, even though the transaction may involve three or more accounts. Because of the multiple columns, however, inaccuracies may arise. Thus, whoever is in charge of recording or posting transactions in the journal should make sure that the monthly totals of the debit columns equal the monthly totals of the credit columns.

Sales Tax and a Multicolumn Sales Journal

The contrast between the sales journal and cash receipts journal in Illustrations 6-5 and 6-6 makes it clear that the sales journal, with its single amount column, is a very simple special journal. In this respect, all sales journals are not alike. Suppose, for example, that Fine Appliances operates in a state that charges sales tax on its sales transactions. In such states, businesses collect the sales tax from customers and pay it to the state. Collection of the tax from customers gives rise to a liability. Fine Appliances would switch to a more sophisticated sales journal with three amount columns as shown in Illustration 6-7.

ILLUSTRATION 6-6 Recording Cash Receipts Transactions

CASH RECEIPTS JOURNAL

Page 1

DATE	EXPLANATION	ACCOUNT CREDITED	POST. REF.	CASH DR.	SALES DISCOUNTS DR.	ACCOUNTS RECEIVABLE CR.	SALES CR.	OTHER ACCOUNTS CR.
19X1								
Jan. 2	Investment	J. Fine, Capital	500	40,000				40,000
8	Cash sale			4,500			4,500	
13	Cash sale			7,900			7,900	
15	Bank loan	Notes Payable	326	20,000				20,000
17	Collection in full	Brown Construction	✓	7,595	155	7,750		
20	Cash sale			6,600			6,600	
23	Collection in full	Colby Custom Homes	✓	3,038	62	3,100		
24	Cash sale			9,700			9,700	
29	Collection in full	Manor Contracting	✓	4,606	94	4,700		
31	Collection in full	ABC Homes	✓	2,300		2,300		
				106,239	311	17,850	28,700	60,000
				(100)	(624)	(110)	(602)	(N/A)

Step 1: DAILY journalize individual transactions.

Step 2: DAILY post individual receipts to individual customer accounts receivable.

Step 3: MONTHLY post column totals and individual amounts to general ledger accounts.

ACCOUNTS RECEIVABLE SUBSIDIARY LEDGER

NAME: ABC Homes ACCOUNT NO.: 1041

DATE	DESCRIPTION	POST. REF.	DEBIT	CREDIT	BALANCE
19X1					
Jan. 3		SJ1	2,300		2,300
23		SJ1	5,600		7,900
31		CR1		2,300	5,600

NAME: Brown Construction ACCOUNT NO.: 1052

DATE	DESCRIPTION	POST. REF.	DEBIT	CREDIT	BALANCE
19X1					
Jan. 7		SJ1	7,750		7,750
17		CR1		7,750	0
28		SJ1	1,850		1,850

NAME: Colby Custom Homes ACCOUNT NO.: 1075

DATE	DESCRIPTION	POST. REF.	DEBIT	CREDIT	BALANCE
19X1					
Jan. 13		SJ1	3,100		3,100
23		CR1		3,100	0

NAME: Good Construction ACCOUNT NO.: 1378

DATE	DESCRIPTION	POST. REF.	DEBIT	CREDIT	BALANCE
19X1					
Jan. 31		SJ1	10,500		10,500

NAME: Manor Contracting ACCOUNT NO.: 1561

DATE	DESCRIPTION	POST. REF.	DEBIT	CREDIT	BALANCE
19X1					
Jan. 20		SJ1	4,700		4,700
29		CR1		4,700	0

GENERAL LEDGER

NAME: Cash ACCOUNT NO.: 100

DATE	DESCRIPTION	POST. REF.	DEBIT	CREDIT	BALANCE
19X1					
Jan. 31		CR1	106,239		106,239

NAME: Accounts Receivable ACCOUNT NO.: 110

DATE	DESCRIPTION	POST. REF.	DEBIT	CREDIT	BALANCE
19X1					
Jan. 31		SJ1	35,800		35,800
31		CR1		17,850	17,950

NAME: Notes Payable ACCOUNT NO.: 326

DATE	DESCRIPTION	POST. REF.	DEBIT	CREDIT	BALANCE
19X1					
Jan. 15		CR1		20,000	20,000

NAME: J. Fine, Capital ACCOUNT NO.: 500

DATE	DESCRIPTION	POST. REF.	DEBIT	CREDIT	BALANCE
19X1					
Jan. 2		CR1		40,000	40,000

NAME: Sales ACCOUNT NO.: 602

DATE	DESCRIPTION	POST. REF.	DEBIT	CREDIT	BALANCE
19X1					
Jan. 31		SJ1		35,800	35,800
31		CR1		28,700	64,500

NAME: Sales Discounts ACCOUNT NO.: 624

DATE	DESCRIPTION	POST. REF.	DEBIT	CREDIT	BALANCE
19X1					
Jan. 31		CR1	311		311

ILLUSTRATION 6-7 Multicolumn Sales Journal

SALES JOURNAL

Page 1

DATE		ACCOUNT DEBITED	INVOICE NO.	POST. REF.	ACCOUNTS RECEIVABLE DR.	SALES TAX PAYABLE CR.	CREDIT SALES CR.
19X1							
Feb.	3	ABC Homes	1011	✓	2,300	110	2,190
	7	Brown Construction	1012	✓	7,750	369	7,381
	11	Colby Custom Homes	1013	✓	3,100	148	2,952
	20	Manor Contracting	1014	✓	4,700	224	4,476
	23	ABC Homes	1015	✓	5,600	267	5,333
	28	Brown Construction	1016	✓	1,850	88	1,762
	31	Good Construction	1017	✓	10,500	500	10,000
					35,800	1,706	34,094
					(110)	(332)	(602)

LO 6

Journalize and post credit purchases and cash disbursements transactions using a purchases journal, a cash disbursements journal, accounts payable subsidiary ledger accounts, and general ledger accounts.

RECORDING PURCHASES AND CASH DISBURSEMENTS

The series of steps that must be linked together from the purchase of goods to the payment of suppliers is called the purchases and cash disbursements cycle. This cycle typically involves more general ledger accounts than any other business transaction cycle because businesses make disbursements for a variety of goods and services.

Journalizing and Posting Purchases Transactions

The following purchases made by Fine Appliances during January 19X1, are recorded in Illustration 6-8 using the three-step method:

Date received	Nature of purchase	Supplier	Invoice date	Terms	Amount
Jan. 3	Merchandise	Ace Appliance Mfrs.	Jan. 3	2/10, n/30	$15,000
6	Merchandise	Red Dot Stoves	3	2/10, n/30	10,000
10	Office supplies	XYZ Office Supply	10	1/10, n/30	500
15	Showroom supplies	Sales Products	15	1/10, n/30	1,500
20	Merchandise	Kitchen Products	17	2/10, n/30	8,000
24	Merchandise	Red Dot Stoves	23	2/10, n/30	5,000
27	Merchandise	Ace Appliance Mfrs.	27	2/10, n/30	18,000
29	Office supplies	XYZ Office Supply	29	1/10, n/30	100

The special journal used to record purchases of merchandise and supplies, the **purchases journal**, is basically organized the same as the cash receipts journal. There are four columns for dollar entries. The credit to Accounts Payable is entered first, followed by a debit to at least one of the three debit columns, Purchases, Sales Supplies, and Office Supplies. The unique features of the purchases journal are the column for the date of the supplier's invoice and the column for the terms of credit. The dates of the suppliers' invoices are

ILLUSTRATION 6-8 Recording Purchases Transactions

PURCHASES JOURNAL

Page 1

	DATE		ACCOUNT CREDITED	DATE OF INVOICE	TERMS	POST. REF.	ACCOUNTS PAYABLE CR.	PURCHASES DR.	SALES SUPPLIES DR.	OFFICE SUPPLIES DR.
Step 1: DAILY journalize individual transactions.	19X1 Jan.	3	Ace Appliance Mfrs.	1/3/X1	2/10,n/30	✓	15,000	15,000		
		6	Red Dot Stoves	1/3/X1	2/10,n/30	✓	10,000	10,000		
		10	XYZ Office Supply	1/10/X1	1/10,n/30	✓	500			500
		15	Sales Products	1/15/X1	1/10,n/30	✓	1,500		1,500	
		20	Kitchen Products	1/17/X1	2/10,n/30	✓	8,000	8,000		
		24	Red Dot Stoves	1/23/X1	2/10,n/30	✓	5,000	5,000		
		27	Ace Appliance Mfrs.	1/27/X1	2/10,n/30	✓	18,000	18,000		
		29	XYZ Office Supply	1/29/X1	1/10,n/30	✓	100			100
							58,100	56,000	1,500	600
							(302)	(754)	(138)	(136)

Step 2: DAILY post individual purchases to individual supplier accounts payable.

Step 3: MONTHLY post column totals to general ledger accounts.

ACCOUNTS PAYABLE SUBSIDIARY LEDGER

NAME: Ace Appliance Mfrs.   ACCOUNT NO.: 3045

DATE	DESCRIPTION	POST. REF.	DEBIT	CREDIT	BALANCE
19X1 Jan. 3		PJ1		15,000	15,000
27		PJ1		18,000	33,000

NAME: Kitchen Products   ACCOUNT NO.: 3413

DATE	DESCRIPTION	POST. REF.	DEBIT	CREDIT	BALANCE
19X1 Jan. 20		PJ1		8,000	8,000

NAME: Red Dot Stoves   ACCOUNT NO.: 3721

DATE	DESCRIPTION	POST. REF.	DEBIT	CREDIT	BALANCE
19X1 Jan. 6		PJ1		10,000	10,000
24		PJ1		5,000	15,000

NAME: Sales Products   ACCOUNT NO.: 3838

DATE	DESCRIPTION	POST. REF.	DEBIT	CREDIT	BALANCE
19X1 Jan. 15		PJ1		1,500	1,500

NAME: XYZ Office Supply   ACCOUNT NO.: 3900

DATE	DESCRIPTION	POST. REF.	DEBIT	CREDIT	BALANCE
19X1 Jan. 10		PJ1		500	500
29		PJ1		100	600

GENERAL LEDGER

NAME: Office Supplies   ACCOUNT NO.: 136

DATE	DESCRIPTION	POST. REF.	DEBIT	CREDIT	BALANCE
19X1 Jan. 31		PJ1	600		600

NAME: Sales Supplies   ACCOUNT NO.: 138

DATE	DESCRIPTION	POST. REF.	DEBIT	CREDIT	BALANCE
19X1 Jan. 31		PJ1	1,500		1,500

NAME: Accounts Payable   ACCOUNT NO.: 302

DATE	DESCRIPTION	POST. REF.	DEBIT	CREDIT	BALANCE
19X1 Jan. 31		PJ1		58,100	58,100

NAME: Purchases   ACCOUNT NO.: 754

DATE	DESCRIPTION	POST. REF.	DEBIT	CREDIT	BALANCE
19X1 Jan. 31		PJ1	56,000		56,000

entered as references because the suppliers' invoices are backup documents for entries in the journal. They should be kept in files by supplier, in date order, for easy reference. The terms of credit are entered for ease of reference when paying bills.

The accounts payable subsidiary ledger serves the same purpose for amounts owed to suppliers as the accounts receivable subsidiary ledger serves for amounts credit customers owe to the business.

Journalizing and Posting Cash Disbursements Transactions

The following January 19X1, cash disbursements of Fine Appliances are recorded and posted in Illustration 6-9 using the three-step method:

Date	Payee	Explanation	Amount
Jan. 3	Casualty Insurance	Eighteen-month policy premium	$ 1,800
6	Justice Buildings	Monthly rent	900
7	COD Supply	Display supplies (showroom)	200
13	Ace Appliance Mfrs.	Payment on account within discount period	14,700
16	Red Dot Stoves	Payment on account within discount period	9,800
17	XYZ Office Supply	Payment on account within discount period	495
24	Sales Products	Payment on account within discount period	1,485
30	Kitchen Products	Payment on account within discount period	7,840
31	J. Fine	Monthly withdrawal	2,500

The special journal used to record payments to suppliers and service
providers, the **cash disbursements journal**, is organized similar to the other
special journals. However, the cash disbursements journal in Illustration
6-9 doubles as a check register. You will notice that after the Date column is a
column to enter the number of the check issued to pay each item. Next is a column to enter the payee of the check, followed by a column to enter the name
of the account to be debited. The account to be debited will either be the
account of a supplier (payee), if the check is issued to pay for a previous purchase, or it will be the name of a general ledger account. Each disbursement
involves a credit entry to Cash and possibly a credit to Purchases Discounts.
The Accounts Payable column is used to record payments to suppliers.
Disbursements for other purposes result in debits in the Other Accounts column. The general ledger account affected is named in the Account Debited column of the journal.

LO 7
Use a trial balance and
reconciliations of
subsidiary ledger accounts
with control accounts to
control accuracy in
journalizing and posting.

CONTROLS OVER JOURNALIZING AND POSTING ACCURACY

Earlier in the chapter, we discussed specific control procedures as one of the
principal components of accounting systems. Reconciliation is one of the most
powerful of these procedures. Three reconciliations apply to the journalizing
and posting we have described to this point. You are familiar with one—the
trial balance; the others are new. The individual accounts receivable subsidiary
ledger balances should reconcile to the Accounts Receivable control account
balance, and the individual accounts payable subsidiary ledger balances should
reconcile to the Accounts Payable control account balance.

Proving the Accounts after Journalizing and Posting Transactions

As we point out in in an earlier chapter, if the journalizing and posting to the
general ledger accounts have been completed with accuracy, the total debit balances should equal the total credit balances in the general ledger accounts. This
equality condition should hold when only a general journal is used, as you
have seen before, *and* when special journals are used, as in this chapter. The

ILLUSTRATION 6-9 Recording Cash Disbursements Transactions

CASH DISBURSEMENTS JOURNAL

Page 1

	DATE	CHECK NO.	PAYEE	ACCOUNT DEBITED	POST. REF.	OTHER ACCOUNTS DR.	ACCOUNTS PAYABLE DR.	PURCHASES DISCOUNTS CR.	CASH CR.
Step 1: DAILY journalize individual transactions.	19X1 Jan. 3	101	Casualty Insurance	Prepaid Insurance	150	1,800			1,800
	6	102	Justice Buildings	Rent Expense	762	900			900
	7	103	COD Supply	Sales Supplies	138	200			200
	13	104	Ace Appliance Mfrs.	Ace Appliance Mfrs.	✓		15,000	300	14,700
	16	105	Red Dot Stoves	Red Dot Stoves	✓		10,000	200	9,800
	17	106	XYZ Office Supply	XYZ Office Supply	✓		500	5	495
	24	107	Sales Products	Sales Products	✓		1,500	15	1,485
	30	108	Kitchen Products	Kitchen Products	✓		8,000	160	7,840
	31	109	J. Fine	J. Fine, Withdrawals	502	2,500			2,500
						5,400	35,000	680	39,720
						(N/A)	(302)	(756)	(100)

Step 2: DAILY post individual payments to individual supplier accounts payable.

Step 3: MONTHLY post column totals and individual amounts to general ledger accounts.

ACCOUNTS PAYABLE SUBSIDIARY LEDGER

NAME: Ace Appliance Mfrs.   ACCOUNT NO.: 3045

DATE	DESCRIPTION	POST. REF.	DEBIT	CREDIT	BALANCE
19X1 Jan. 3		PJ1		15,000	15,000
13		CD1	15,000		0
27		PJ1		18,000	18,000

NAME: Kitchen Products   ACCOUNT NO.: 3413

DATE	DESCRIPTION	POST. REF.	DEBIT	CREDIT	BALANCE
19X1 Jan. 20		PJ1		8,000	8,000
30		CD1	8,000		0

NAME: Red Dot Stoves   ACCOUNT NO.: 3721

DATE	DESCRIPTION	POST. REF.	DEBIT	CREDIT	BALANCE
19X1 Jan. 6		PJ1		10,000	10,000
16		CD1	10,000		0
24		PJ1		5,000	5,000

NAME: Sales Products   ACCOUNT NO.: 3838

DATE	DESCRIPTION	POST. REF.	DEBIT	CREDIT	BALANCE
19X1 Jan. 15		PJ1		1,500	1,500
24		CD1	1,500		0

NAME: XYZ Office Supply   ACCOUNT NO.: 3900

DATE	DESCRIPTION	POST. REF.	DEBIT	CREDIT	BALANCE
19X1 Jan. 10		PJ1		500	500
17		CD1	500		0
29		PJ1		100	100

GENERAL LEDGER

NAME: Cash   ACCOUNT NO.: 100

DATE	DESCRIPTION	POST. REF.	DEBIT	CREDIT	BALANCE
19X1 Jan. 31		CR1	106,239		106,239
31		CD1		39,720	66,519

NAME: Sales Supplies   ACCOUNT NO.: 138

DATE	DESCRIPTION	POST. REF.	DEBIT	CREDIT	BALANCE
19X1 Jan. 31		PJ1	1,500		1,500
7		CD1	200		1,700

NAME: Prepaid Insurance   ACCOUNT NO.: 150

DATE	DESCRIPTION	POST. REF.	DEBIT	CREDIT	BALANCE
19X1 Jan. 3		CD1	1,800		1,800

NAME: Accounts Payable   ACCOUNT NO.: 302

DATE	DESCRIPTION	POST. REF.	DEBIT	CREDIT	BALANCE
19X1 Jan. 31		PJ1		58,100	58,100
31		CD1	35,000		23,100

NAME: J. Fine, Withdrawals   ACCOUNT NO.: 502

DATE	DESCRIPTION	POST. REF.	DEBIT	CREDIT	BALANCE
19X1 Jan. 31		CD1	2,500		2,500

NAME: Purchases Discounts   ACCOUNT NO.: 756

DATE	DESCRIPTION	POST. REF.	DEBIT	CREDIT	BALANCE
19X1 Jan. 31		CD1		680	680

NAME: Rent Expense   ACCOUNT NO.: 762

DATE	DESCRIPTION	POST. REF.	DEBIT	CREDIT	BALANCE
19X1 Jan. 6		CD1	900		900

equality of the debits and credits posted above to the accounts of Fine Appliances in the sales-collections cycle *and* the purchases-disbursements cycle is proved by the trial balance in Illustration 6-10. Account balances in Illustration 6-10 are based only on the transactions journalized and posted in this chapter and come from the general ledger accounts as they would appear after posting all transactions in Illustrations 6-5, 6-6, 6-8, and 6-9.

ILLUSTRATION 6-10 General Ledger Trial Balance

Fine Appliances Trial Balance January 31, 19X1		
	Debits	*Credits*
Cash	$ 66,519	
Accounts Receivable	17,950	
Office Supplies	600	
Sales Supplies	1,700	
Prepaid Insurance	1,800	
Accounts Payable		$ 23,100
Notes Payable		20,000
J. Fine, Capital		40,000
J. Fine, Withdrawals	2,500	
Cash Sales		28,700
Credit Sales		35,800
Sales Discounts	311	
Purchases	56,000	
Purchases Discounts		680
Rent Expense	900	
Totals	$148,280	$148,280

Reconciling Accounts Receivable to the Control Account

If the three-step procedure for journalizing and posting is executed accurately, the debits and credits posted to the accounts receivable subsidiary ledger accounts should equal the debits and credits posted to the Accounts Receivable control account. This equality is proved by comparing the total of the balances in the individual accounts receivable to the balance in the control account as we demonstrate in Illustration 6-11. The balances in Illustration 6-11 come from the accounts as they appeared in Illustration 6-6, after all sales and cash receipts transactions had been journalized and posted.

Reconciling Accounts Payable to the Control Account

Likewise, the balances in the individual accounts payable subsidiary ledger accounts should equal the balance in the Accounts Payable control account as shown in Illustration 6-12. The balances in Illustration 6-12 come from the accounts as they appear in Illustration 6-9 after all purchases and cash disbursements had been journalized and posted.

ILLUSTRATION 6-11 Reconciliation of Accounts Receivable

Fine Appliances Schedule of Accounts Receivable January 31, 19X1		
Account Number	*Account*	*Balance*
1041	ABC Homes	$ 5,600
1052	Brown Construction	1,850
1075	Colby Custom Homes	0
1561	Manor Contracting	0
1378	Good Construction	10,500
	Total	$17,950
	Balance in control account	$17,950

ILLUSTRATION 6-12 Reconciliation of Accounts Payable

Fine Appliances Schedule of Accounts Payable January 31, 19X1		
Account Number	*Account*	*Balance*
3045	Ace Appliance Mfrs.	$18,000
3413	Kitchen Products	0
3721	Red Dot Stoves	5,000
3838	Sales Products	0
3900	XYZ Office Supply	100
	Total	$23,100
	Balance in control account	$23,100

LO 8
Describe what computers can do, what they can do for accounting systems, and how they affect the control environment.

COMPUTER-BASED ACCOUNTING SYSTEMS

In the accounting systems described in previous chapters and in the previous sections of this chapter, it is assumed that all functions are performed manually. Manual systems are still prevalent in accounting for very small businesses, and they are the easiest systems for beginners to understand. Hence, they are very suitable for introduction in texts such as this one. However, accounting for all but the smallest businesses is usually done with some degree of computer assistance. Computers are used in accounting to varying degrees, from handling only the mechanics of doing arithmetic and recording transactions to integrating accounting functions fully with the business's operations. The greater the degree of computer utilization in accounting, the more profoundly the computer affects the ways control objectives and other information systems objectives are met.

What Computers Can Do

Now that computers are so widespread, most everyone knows, at least intuitively, some of the things computers can do and how they work. So, we will give you only a brief, nontechnical review here. Computers themselves do not do anything except consume electric power if you turn them on. *Computer systems*, however, do everything that we attribute to computers and consist of both hardware and software.

Computer hardware includes all of the system's mechanical and electronic components. For a basic PC, the hardware configuration consists of a system unit (the computer itself) with one or more built-in floppy disk and hard disk drives, a keyboard, a video monitor, a printer, and perhaps a compact disc (CD) drive. The hardware provides physical capabilities such as basic computing, sending and receiving electronic signals, displaying images, printing output, and storing files of data.

Computer software consists of sets of instructions that control the hardware's operations and direct it to perform computational and other logical tasks. Basically, two kinds of software work together to make the computer perform useful functions: operating systems and application programs.

Operating systems are very fundamental programs that tell the computer how to coordinate the parts of the system—that is, what steps to follow to receive input, provide output, communicate with storage devices, etc. While the hardware of different computer manufacturers does not differ fundamentally, the operating systems used can make the hardware perform its basic functions very differently. Windows™ is an operating system used with many PCs; the System and Finder perform the operating system functions on Macintosh® equipment—but with a style similar to Windows. Together, computer hardware and operating systems perform the following basic functions:

1. Receive data and instructions from various sources through input devices. Computers receive data and instructions from users directly through keyboards, mice, light pens, and bar-code readers and from various other input devices such as electronic disk drives, electronic tape drives, and CDs.
2. Interpret and process instructions and data. The processor chips or circuitry of the computer performs these functions.
3. Output and store data and instructions. Output may be sent without storing it to such devices as printers and video displays. Output may also be stored on media such as electronic tapes and disks.
4. Communicate with and transfer information to and from other computers. To communicate with each other, computers must be linked, either directly with cables connected to their communication ports or indirectly through modems and telecommunication channels.

Application programs are sets of computer instructions to accomplish specific tasks. Word processing programs such as Microsoft® Word and spreadsheet programs such as Lotus 1-2-3® are application programs. Specific combinations of hardware and operating systems create different "environments" in which various applications can be developed and used. Thus, an application program must be tailored to the system's hardware and an operating system, as well as to its own specific purpose.

Application programs manipulate the basic functions listed above to perform the task a computer user wishes to accomplish. For example, a word processing program causes the computer to receive the words you key on the keyboard (input) and displays them on the screen (output). It also causes the computer to recognize and act on commands you enter on the keyboard or select by using a mouse to delete, insert, or copy words or to otherwise alter your manuscript. When you enter or select a *Save* command, your words, as edited, become output that the word processing program instructs the computer to write on a storage medium such as a floppy disk or a fixed disk (hard disk). When you select the *Print* command, the word processor instructs the computer to send your words as output to a printer.

What Computers Can Do for Accounting Systems

Now that we have reviewed briefly what computers can do in general, let us look at what they can do to solve accounting problems. Consider again the problem Jonathon has discovered. A schematic of his manual accounting system is presented in Illustration 6-13. It shows how the system handles the transac-

ILLUSTRATION 6-13 Fine Appliances' Accounting System Schematic

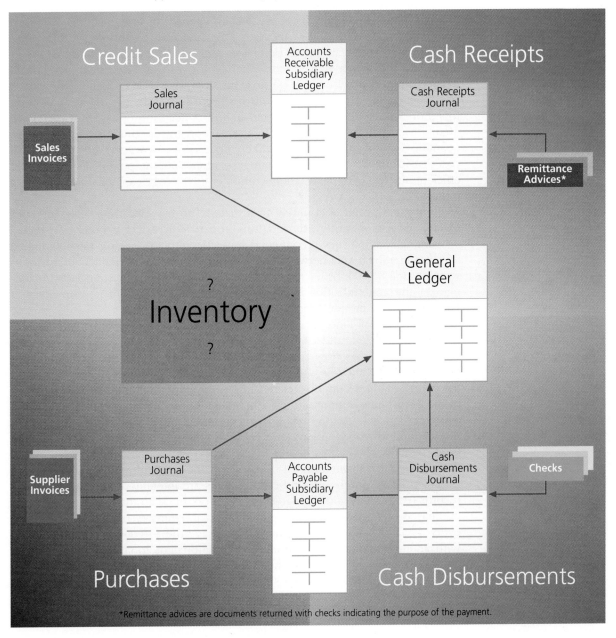

*Remittance advices are documents returned with checks indicating the purpose of the payment.

tions of the sales-cash receipts cycle (top) and the purchases-cash disbursements cycle (bottom)—the two cycles that affect the quantities of inventory on hand. It also shows that the transaction data from the two key cycles are not used to maintain up-to-date inventory records.

Some years ago, when his special journals and subsidiary ledgers were being set up, Jonathon opted for the periodic inventory method. At the end of each month, he and his accounting staff count and price the inventory on hand to determine the cost of goods sold. However, while a once-a-month update of inventory quantities on hand may be timely for financial statement purposes, it is far too infrequent to help with day-to-day purchases. When his business was small, Jonathon could walk through the warehouse each morning and see which items of stock were getting low, and he could scan the sales invoices at the end of each day and see which items were selling quickly. This was all he needed to make timely purchase orders. Now that his business is larger, the variety of appliances it sells is greater; and Jonathon is much too busy with overall management to follow the daily sales breakdowns and physical inventory stocks. After analyzing both purchases and sales, he estimates that he is losing at least $10,000 a year in extra charges for rush orders or lost gross profit when customers go elsewhere because his store is out of a particular appliance.

To maintain up-to-date inventory records within the manual system, Jonathon would need an additional half-time accounting assistant to record quantities purchased of each item from receiving documents and to record quantities sold from invoices or delivery documents. However, the assistant will cost $18,500 in salary and fringe benefits—more than the potential savings from efficient purchasing! This is where computer technology can come to Jonathon's rescue.

The same public accounting firm that set up his special journals and subsidiary ledgers recently advised Jonathon to convert to a computer-based accounting system. They recommend several computers costing $15,000, linked together in a local area network (LAN) costing $3,000, running accounting software costing $2,000, or a total of $20,000 for the system. Illustration 6-14 summarizes the general differences between the manual system now in place at Fine Appliances and the proposed computer-based system.

Three types of Fine Appliances' transactions affect its inventory levels: credit sales, purchases, and cash receipts (through cash sales). Illustration 6-15 schematically shows how these transactions will be processed using the proposed system. Notice how the proposed computer system will greatly reduce the effort Jonathon's employees must put into the accounting process. For each of the three types of transactions, employees key in a few basic data items; the computer system does the rest. Jonathon estimates that he can actually reduce his accounting work force by one position and save $20,000 a year, including fringe benefits.

Additionally, Illustration 6-15 shows how the transaction processing systems for credit sales, purchases, and cash receipts are integrated with the inventory records (each application updates the inventory file with the quantities of items purchased or sold). Together, they maintain an inventory file that is up-to-date every day and will permit the business to save the $10,000 a year it is losing with its current, inefficient purchasing function. For Jonathon, there was no question that he should make the switch to a computer-based accounting system. At a cost of $20,000 and a savings potential of $30,000 per year, the computer may be the most productive asset on Fine Appliances' balance sheet.

ILLUSTRATION 6-14 Manual Versus Computer-Based Accounting System

Function	Manual Accounting System	Computer-Based System
Document Preparation	Personnel prepare all documents by hand, entering names, addresses, quantities, product descriptions, etc.	Personnel enter identifications such as customer ID numbers, product numbers, and quantities; the computer retrieves names, addresses, product descriptions, etc., from master files; the computer prepares and prints all documents and stores transaction data in transaction files.
Arithmetic	Personnel perform all arithmetic manually, with the aid of electronic calculators.	The computer performs all arithmetic.
Journalizing and Posting	Personnel do all recording and posting manually.	The computer performs all recording and posting, using data from transaction (document) files and minimal input from personnel.
Verifications	Personnel with separate responsibilities verify all input data, arithmetic, recording, and posting.	Only input data need be verified; the computer performs accurately all arithmetic, recording, and posting.
Financial Statement Preparation	Personnel prepare worksheets, journalize and post adjustments, transcribe data to financial statements, and journalize and	Personnel enter data for adjusting entries; the computer prepares financial statements and performs all necessary

ILLUSTRATION 6-15 Computer-Based Processing

Credit Sales Processing

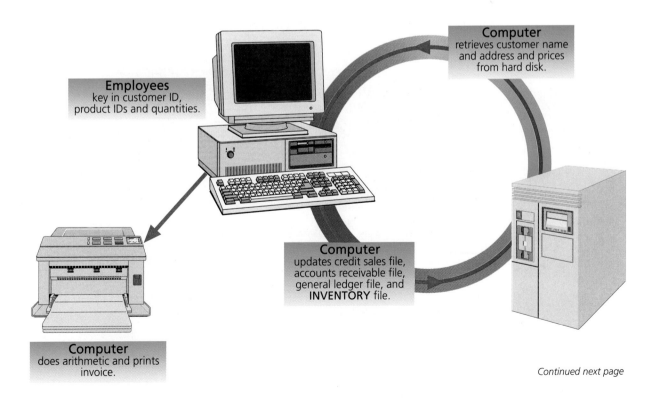

Employees key in customer ID, product IDs and quantities.

Computer retrieves customer name and address and prices from hard disk.

Computer updates credit sales file, accounts receivable file, general ledger file, and **INVENTORY** file.

Computer does arithmetic and prints invoice.

Continued next page

ILLUSTRATION 6-15 (Continued) Computer-Based Processing

Purchases Processing

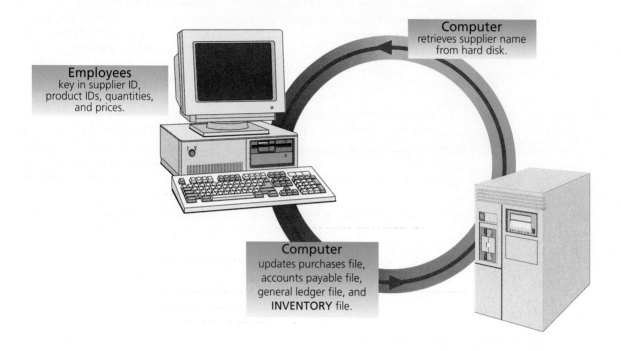

Employees key in supplier ID, product IDs, quantities, and prices.

Computer retrieves supplier name from hard disk.

Computer updates purchases file, accounts payable file, general ledger file, and **INVENTORY** file.

Cash Receipts Processing

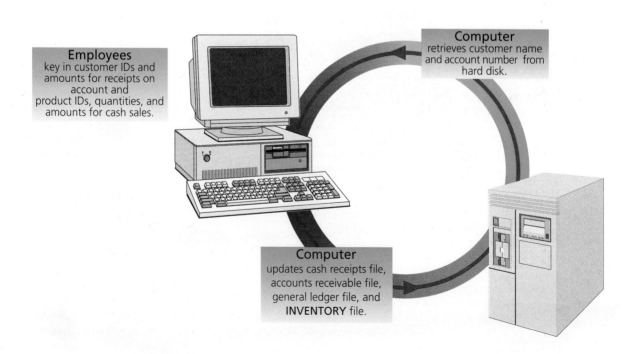

Employees key in customer IDs and amounts for receipts on account and product IDs, quantities, and amounts for cash sales.

Computer retrieves customer name and account number from hard disk.

Computer updates cash receipts file, accounts receivable file, general ledger file, and **INVENTORY** file.

Accounting Controls in a Computer Environment

Computer systems can do much to reduce labor and to enhance the value of the information an accounting system generates. However, by changing the way both operations and accounting objectives are accomplished, computers change the control environment and the way control objectives can be accomplished. For example, since computers are more accurate and faster at arithmetic than humans, most calculations should be incorporated into application programs. This eliminates the need for employees to verify each others' calculations. However, accounting application programs can be improperly programmed or improperly run, and input data can be erroneous. In such cases, computers make mistakes and can facilitate fraud at the same incredible speed at which they perform useful tasks. To prevent these things from happening, many businesses apply controls over computer-based accounting systems that fall into two broad categories: general controls and application controls.

General controls are oriented toward organizing the data processing function and protecting computer equipment and related documents, files, etc. For example, if employees enter data directly into the computer system, passwords should be issued to authorized employees only. Passwords should give employees access only to those application programs and files they need to do their work. **Application controls** are controls over the inputs, outputs, and processing logic of a particular accounting application. These controls should be designed to ensure that data are entered accurately, new data and existing files are processed correctly, new files are created accurately, and reports correctly reflect the contents of the underlying files. The program should test input data for conformity with expectations. For instance, transaction data should not include negative numbers—that is, we do not expect to have sold a –200 units of a product in a sales transaction. The computer test would detect and reject the negative sales and prevent the improper data from being recorded.

SUMMARY

Describe the broad objectives of accounting systems. Accounting systems must provide the accounting numbers that are ultimately summarized in financial statements that conform to Generally Accepted Accounting Principles. The accounting system must be designed to provide reports and other information useful in making management decisions. To meet management's decision needs, accounting systems must achieve two corollary objectives: timeliness and flexibility. For the information the system generates to be reliable, the system must satisfy six specific control objectives. The entire accounting information system, as well as individual controls, must be cost-effective.

List the specific accounting control objectives. To produce reliable financial reports for management and outside users, an accounting system must satisfy these specific control objectives:

1. Employees with appropriate authority should evaluate each transaction for compliance with management policy and preapprove the transaction.
2. The accounting system should record only *real* transactions and reject fake or fraudulent transactions.
3. Accounting personnel must enter correct quantities and prices on the documents that represent transactions, and all arithmetic must be accurate.

4. Accounting personnel must correctly analyze transactions for posting to the proper accounts, and they must record all transactions as of the correct dates.
5. A business should record a journal entry for every transaction that actually takes place.
6. Once journalized, transactions must be accurately posted to *all* appropriate subsidiary ledgers and to the appropriate general ledger accounts.

Describe the accounting system life cycle. All information systems, including accounting systems, generally pass through a distinct life cycle. The cycle begins with analysis of management's information needs and continues with the design, implementation, and, finally, operation of the new system. During its operation, the system is evaluated; and, as new, significant needs or limitations in the existing system warrant a change, the cycle begins anew.

Describe the need for and functions of subsidiary ledgers and special journals. Subsidiary ledgers are sets of ledger accounts that contain the details of balances in individual general ledger asset, liability, and owner's equity accounts. Subsidiary ledgers give managers information at the level and in the detail required to manage individual assets and liabilities. A control account is the general ledger account that relates in total to the details contained in a particular subsidiary ledger. Good control procedure dictates that the details of the subsidiary ledger should be reconciled periodically to the balance of the related control account.

Special journals are substitutes for the general journal, used to record particular classes of transactions. Special journals remove excessive detail from the general journal and general ledger accounts, group like transactions together for easier reference, and contribute to efficiency by permitting periodic totals, rather than individual transaction amounts, to be posted to general ledger accounts.

Journalize and post credit sales and cash receipts transactions using a sales journal, a cash receipts journal, accounts receivable subsidiary ledger accounts, and general ledger accounts. The procedures for journalizing and posting transactions in special journals and subsidiary ledgers are:

1. Record each sale transaction on one line of the special journal, filling in all columns except the Post. Ref. column.
2. Post individual transactions daily to the subsidiary ledger accounts.
3. Post the total of the transactions monthly to the appropriate general ledger accounts.

Journalize and post credit purchases and cash disbursements transactions using a purchases journal, a cash disbursements journal, accounts payable subsidiary ledger accounts, and general ledger accounts. In the purchases and cash disbursements cycle, the same three-step journalizing and posting procedure is used as in the sales and cash receipts cycle. The special journals and subsidiary ledger of this cycle differ from the records used in other cycles only in their layouts—for example, numbers of columns. However, their roles in the accounting system are the same.

Use a trial balance and reconciliations of subsidiary ledger accounts with control accounts to control accuracy in journalizing and posting. As we point out in an earlier chapter, if the journalizing and posting to the general ledger accounts have been completed with accuracy, the total debit balances should equal the total credit balances in the general ledger accounts. This equality condition should hold when only a general journal is used, as you have seen before, *and* when special journals are used, as in this chapter. To test the equality condition, we typically prepare a trial balance.

If the three-step procedure for journalizing and posting is executed accurately, the debits and credits posted to the accounts receivable subsidiary ledger accounts should equal the debits and credits posted to Accounts Receivable (control account), and the debits and credits posted to the accounts payable subsidiary ledger accounts should equal the debits and credits posted to Accounts Payable (control account). These equalities are proved by comparing the totals of the balances in the individual subsidiary ledger accounts to the balances in the respective control accounts.

Describe what computers can do, what they can do for accounting systems, and how they affect the control environment.   Computer systems do everything that we attribute to computers and consist of both hardware and software. Computer hardware includes all of the system's mechanical and electronic components. Computer software consists of sets of instructions that control the hardware's operations and direct it to perform computational and other logical tasks. Operating systems are very fundamental programs that tell the computer how to coordinate the parts of the system—that is, what steps to follow to receive input, provide output, communicate with storage devices, etc. Application programs are sets of computer instructions that utilize these basic functions to accomplish specific tasks such as accounting for a business's transactions.

In accounting systems, computers reduce labor by performing arithmetic, preparing documents, creating transaction files, and recording and posting transactions, while employees input only the minimum data to process each transaction. The computational efficiency of computers makes it possible to integrate accounting records cost-effectively—say, from the sales and cash receipts cycle and the purchases and cash disbursements cycle—and provides management with greater access to useful information on a timely basis.

When computers are used in place of manual procedures, the control emphasis shifts away from separating employee duties and performing many verifications of manual accuracy. The emphasis is instead placed on ensuring the proper functioning of application programs, using security procedures to limit access to the computer system, application programs, and files to authorized employees, verifying the accuracy of input, and reconciling outputs to inputs.

▍REVIEW PROBLEM

Good Morning Distribution Company is a wholesale distributor of several brands of coffee. They have a manual accounting system which uses special journals and ledgers for Accounts Receivable and Accounts Payable. Selected information from the accounting system and the transactions for January 19X3, are presented below.

The Accounts Receivable subsidiary ledger at December 31, 19X2 is shown on the next page. (The page numbers of the posting references arbitrarily assume page 9 for all journals.)

ACCOUNTS RECEIVABLE SUBSIDIARY LEDGER

NAME: Economy Supermarket   ACCOUNT NO.: 101

DATE		DESCRIPTION	POST. REF.	DEBIT	CREDIT	BALANCE
19X2						
Dec.	2		SJ9	3,000		3,000
	12		CR9		3,000	0
	26		SJ9	2,000		2,000

NAME: Dan's Market   ACCOUNT NO.: 105

DATE		DESCRIPTION	POST. REF.	DEBIT	CREDIT	BALANCE
Dec.	15		SJ9	5,000		5,000
	23		CR9		5,000	0
	28		SJ9	6,000		6,000

NAME: Yankee's Superstore   ACCOUNT NO.: 110

DATE		DESCRIPTION	POST. REF.	DEBIT	CREDIT	BALANCE
Dec.	5		SJ9	10,000		10,000
	15		CR9		10,000	0
	29		SJ9	15,000		15,000

The Accounts Payable subsidiary ledger on December 31, 19X2 is shown below:

ACCOUNTS PAYABLE SUBSIDIARY LEDGER

NAME: Old Cabin Coffee Company   ACCOUNT NO.: 210

DATE		DESCRIPTION	POST. REF.	DEBIT	CREDIT	BALANCE
19X2						
Dec.	12		PJ9		4,000	4,000
	17		PJ9		3,500	7,500
	22		CD9	4,000		3,500

NAME: American Foods   ACCOUNT NO.: 215

DATE		DESCRIPTION	POST. REF.	DEBIT	CREDIT	BALANCE
Dec.	1		PJ9		1,000	1,000
	11		CD9	1,000		0
	28		PJ9		4,500	4,500

NAME: Campfire Coffee Company   ACCOUNT NO.: 220

DATE		DESCRIPTION	POST. REF.	DEBIT	CREDIT	BALANCE
Dec.	14		PJ9		9,000	9,000
	23		CD9	9,000		0
	30		PJ9		8,000	8,000

NAME: Redbird Office Supply   ACCOUNT NO.: 225

DATE	DESCRIPTION	POST. REF.	DEBIT	CREDIT	BALANCE
					0

Selected general ledger account balances as of December 31, 19X2 are shown below.

GENERAL LEDGER

NAME: Cash   ACCOUNT NO.: 100

DATE		DESCRIPTION	POST. REF.	DEBIT	CREDIT	BALANCE
19X2 Dec.	31	Balance				25,000

NAME: Accounts Receivable   ACCOUNT NO.: 110

DATE		DESCRIPTION	POST. REF.	DEBIT	CREDIT	BALANCE
19X2 Dec.	31		SJ9	41,000		41,000
	31		CR9		18,000	23,000

NAME: Office Supplies   ACCOUNT NO.: 127

DATE		DESCRIPTION	POST. REF.	DEBIT	CREDIT	BALANCE
19X2 Dec.	31	Balance				2,000

NAME: Sales Supplies   ACCOUNT NO.: 138

DATE		DESCRIPTION	POST. REF.	DEBIT	CREDIT	BALANCE
19X2 Dec.	31	Balance				1,000

NAME: Accounts Payable   ACCOUNT NO.: 302

DATE		DESCRIPTION	POST. REF.	DEBIT	CREDIT	BALANCE
19X2 Dec.	31		PJ9		30,000	30,000
	31		CD9	14,000		16,000

Good Morning uses the following special journals:

(1) a one-column sales journal
(2) a multicolumn cash receipts journal
(3) a multicolumn purchases journal
(4) a multicolumn cash disbursements journal

The special journals are similar in format to the ones found in Illustrations 6-5, 6-6, 6-8, and 6-9.

Good Morning's January 19X3, transactions are as follows:

Jan.   2 Issued Check Number 200 to Old Cabin Coffee Company for payment of invoice of December 17, 19X2, for $3,500. Terms are 2/10, n/30. Good Morning is not entitled to the 2% discount.

5 Received payment less the 2% discount from Economy Supermarket for invoice of December 26, 19X2, for $2,000. Terms are 2/10, n/30.

7 Received payment less the 2% discount from Dan's Market for invoice dated December 28, 19X2, for $6,000. Terms are 2/10, n/30.

7 Paid American Foods invoice dated December 29, 19X2, for $4,500, issuing Check Number 201. The 2% discount was taken. The terms are 2/10, n/30.

8 Received payment from Yankee's Superstore for the December 29, 19X2, invoice of $15,000 less the 2% discount. Terms are 2/10, n/30.

9 Paid Campfire Coffee Company one-half of the December 30, 19X2, invoice for $8,000, less a 2% discount, issuing Check Number 202.

10 Purchased $500 of sales supplies from Redbird Office supply on credit, terms 1/15, n/60.

15 Purchased $25 of office supplies from Redbird Office Supply Company, issuing Check Number 203 for full payment.

20 Shipped coffee to Economy Supermarket, Invoice Number 251, $2,500, terms 2/10, n/30.

21 Shipped coffee to Dan's Market, Invoice Number 252, $6,000, terms 2/10, n/30.

21 Received shipment of coffee from Old Cabin, invoice for $5,000 dated January 21, 19X3, terms 2/10, n/30.

29 Paid the remaining one-half of the December 30, 19X2, Campfire invoice, issuing Check Number 204.

30 Paid wages and salaries of $5,000, issuing Check Number 205. The check is made payable to Payroll.

31 Shipped coffee to Yankee's, Invoice Number 253, $20,000, terms 2/10, n/30.

31 Recorded cash sales for the month, $2,000.

31 Borrowed $10,000 from the American Bank and signed a note payable due in 90 days.

REQUIRED:

a. Enter the January 19X3 transactions in the appropriate journals. Post to subsidiary ledgers at the time the entries are recorded in the journals. Provide appropriate posting references in both the journals and subsidiary ledgers. For posting reference purposes, assume page 10 for all journals.

b. Total the special journal columns and post the totals to the appropriate general ledger accounts. Provide appropriate posting references in both the journals and ledger accounts.

c. Prepare a schedule of accounts receivable and a schedule of accounts payable and reconcile the totals to the control accounts.

SOLUTION:

Planning and Organizing Your Work

1. Analyze each transaction and determine which journal to use.
2. Journalize each transaction.
3. Post as needed to subsidiary ledgers.
4. Total the columns in the special journals.
5. Post the column totals to the general ledger.
6. Prepare a schedule of accounts receivable and a schedule of accounts payable.
7. Reconcile the totals on the schedules with the control accounts.

(a), (b) *Enter and post transactions.*

SALES JOURNAL

Page 10

DATE		ACCOUNT DEBITED	INVOICE NO.	POST. REF.	DR./CR. AMOUNT
19X3					
Jan.	20	Economy Super Market	251	✓	2,500
	21	Dan's Market	252	✓	6,000
	31	Yankee's Super Store	253	✓	20,000
					28,500
					(110/612)

CASH RECEIPTS JOURNAL

Page 10

DATE		EXPLANATION	ACCOUNT CREDITED	POST. REF.	CASH DR.	SALES DISCOUNTS DR.	ACCOUNTS RECEIVABLE CR.	SALES CR.	OTHER ACCOUNTS CR.
19X3									
Jan.	5	Collection	Economy	✓	1,960	40	2,000		
	7	Collection	Dan's	✓	5,880	120	6,000		
	8	Collection	Yankee's	✓	14,700	300	15,000		
	31	Cash Sales	Sales		2,000			2,000	
	31	Bank loan	Notes Payable	326	10,000				10,000
					34,540	460	23,000	2,000	10,000
					(100)	(624)	(110)	(612)	(N/A)

PURCHASES JOURNAL

Page 10

DATE		ACCOUNT CREDITED	DATE OF INVOICE	TERMS	POST. REF.	ACCOUNTS PAYABLE CR.	PURCHASES DR.	SALES SUPPLIES DR.	OFFICE SUPPLIES DR.
19X3									
Jan.	10	Redbird	1/10/X3	1/15, n/60	✓	500		500	
	21	Old Cabin	1/21/X3	2/10, n/30	✓	5,000	5,000		
						5,500	5,000	500	
						(302)	(754)	(138)	

CASH DISBURSEMENTS JOURNAL

Page 10

DATE		CHECK NO.	PAYEE	ACCOUNT DEBITED	POST. REF.	OTHER ACCOUNTS DR.	ACCOUNTS PAYABLE DR.	PURCHASES DISCOUNTS CR.	CASH CR.
19X3									
Jan.	2	200	Old Cabin	Old Cabin	✓		3,500		3,500
	7	201	American Foods	American Foods	✓		4,500	90	4,410
	9	202	Campfire	Campfire	✓		4,000	80	3,920
	15	203	Redbird	Office Supplies	136	25			25
	29	204	Campfire	Campfire	✓		4,000		4,000
	30	205	Payroll	Wages and Salaries	784	5,000			5,000
						5,025	16,000	170	20,855
						(N/A)	(302)	(756)	(100)

ACCOUNTS RECEIVABLE SUBSIDIARY LEDGER

NAME: Economy Supermarket   ACCOUNT NO.: 101

DATE		DESCRIPTION	POST. REF.	DEBIT	CREDIT	BALANCE
19X2						
Dec.	2		SJ9	3,000		3,000
	12		CR9		3,000	0
	26		SJ9	2,000		2,000
19X3						
Jan.	5		CR10		2,000	0
	20		SJ10	2,500		2,500

NAME: Dan's Market   ACCOUNT NO.: 105

DATE		DESCRIPTION	POST. REF.	DEBIT	CREDIT	BALANCE
19X2						
Dec.	15		SJ9	5,000		5,000
	23		CR9		5,000	0
	28		SJ9	6,000		6,000
19X3						
Jan.	7		CR10		6,000	0
	21		SJ10	6,000		6,000

NAME: Yankee's Superstore   ACCOUNT NO.: 110

DATE		DESCRIPTION	POST. REF.	DEBIT	CREDIT	BALANCE
19X2						
Dec.	5		SJ9	10,000		10,000
	15		CR9		10,000	0
	29		SJ9	15,000		15,000
19X3						
Jan.	8		CR10		15,000	0
	31		SJ10	20,000		20,000

ACCOUNTS PAYABLE SUBSIDIARY LEDGER

NAME: Old Cabin Coffee Company   ACCOUNT NO.: 210

DATE		DESCRIPTION	POST. REF.	DEBIT	CREDIT	BALANCE
19X2						
Dec.	12		PJ9		4,000	4,000
	17		PJ9		3,500	7,500
	22		CD9	4,000		3,500
19X3						
Jan.	2		CD10	3,500		0
	21		PJ10		5,000	5,000

NAME: American Foods ACCOUNT NO.: 215

DATE		DESCRIPTION	POST. REF.	DEBIT	CREDIT	BALANCE
19X2						
Dec.	1		PJ9		1,000	1,000
	11		CD9	1,000		0
	28		PJ9		4,500	4,500
19X3						
Jan.	7		CD10	4,500		0

NAME: Campfire Coffee Company ACCOUNT NO.: 220

DATE		DESCRIPTION	POST. REF.	DEBIT	CREDIT	BALANCE
19X2						
Dec.	14		PJ9		9,000	9,000
	23		CD9	9,000		0
	30		PJ9		8,000	8,000
19X3						
Jan.	9		CD10	4,000		4,000
	29		CD10	4,000		0

NAME: Redbird Office Supply ACCOUNT NO.: 225

DATE		DESCRIPTION	POST. REF.	DEBIT	CREDIT	BALANCE
19X3						
Jan.	10		PJ10		500	500

GENERAL LEDGER

NAME: Cash ACCOUNT NO.: 100

DATE		DESCRIPTION	POST. REF.	DEBIT	CREDIT	BALANCE
19X2						
Dec.	31	Balance				25,000
19X3						
Jan.	31		CR10	34,540		59,540
	31		CD10		20,855	38,685

NAME: Accounts Receivable ACCOUNT NO.: 110

DATE		DESCRIPTION	POST. REF.	DEBIT	CREDIT	BALANCE
19X2						
Dec.	31		SJ9	41,000		41,000
	31		CR9		18,000	23,000
19X3						
Jan.	31		SJ10	28,500		51,500
	31		CR10		23,000	28,500

NAME: Office Supplies   ACCOUNT NO.: 136

DATE		DESCRIPTION	POST. REF.	DEBIT	CREDIT	BALANCE
19X2 Dec.	31	Balance				2,000
19X3 Jan.	15		CD10	25		2,025

NAME: Sales Supplies   ACCOUNT NO.: 138

DATE		DESCRIPTION	POST. REF.	DEBIT	CREDIT	BALANCE
19X2 Dec.	31	Balance				1,000
19X3 Jan.	31		PJ10	500		1,500

NAME: Accounts Payable   ACCOUNT NO.: 302

DATE		DESCRIPTION	POST. REF.	DEBIT	CREDIT	BALANCE
19X2 Dec.	31		PJ9		30,000	30,000
	31		CD9	14,000		16,000
19X3 Jan.	31		PJ10		5,500	21,500
	31		CD10	16,000		5,500

NAME: Notes Payable   ACCOUNT NO.: 326

DATE		DESCRIPTION	POST. REF.	DEBIT	CREDIT	BALANCE
19X3 Jan.	31		CR10		10,000	10,000

NAME: Sales   ACCOUNT NO.: 612

DATE		DESCRIPTION	POST. REF.	DEBIT	CREDIT	BALANCE
19X3 Jan.	31		SJ10		28,500	28,500
	31		CR10		2,000	30,500

NAME: Sales Discounts   ACCOUNT NO.: 624

DATE		DESCRIPTION	POST. REF.	DEBIT	CREDIT	BALANCE
19X3 Jan.	31		CR10	460		460

NAME: Purchases   ACCOUNT NO.: 754

DATE		DESCRIPTION	POST. REF.	DEBIT	CREDIT	BALANCE
19X3 Jan.	31		PJ10	5,000		5,000

NAME: Purchases Discounts   ACCOUNT NO.: 756

DATE		DESCRIPTION	POST. REF.	DEBIT	CREDIT	BALANCE
19X3 Jan.	31		CD10		170	170

NAME: Wages and Salaries Expense   ACCOUNT NO.: 784

DATE		DESCRIPTION	POST. REF.	DEBIT	CREDIT	BALANCE
19X3 Jan.	31		CD10	5,000		5,000

(c) *Prepare schedules.*

**Good Morning Distribution Company
Schedule of Accounts Receivable
January 31, 19X3**

Account Number	Account	Balance
101	Economy Supermarket	$ 2,500
105	Dan's Market	6,000
110	Yankee's Superstore	20,000
	Total	$28,500
	Balance in control account	$28,500

**Good Morning Distribution Company
Schedule of Accounts Payable
January 31, 19X3**

Account Number	Account	Balance
210	Old Cabin Coffee Company	$5,000
225	Redbird Office Supply	500
	Total	$5,500
	Balance in control account	$5,500

KEY TERMS

accounting controls, *225*
accounting system, *224*
accounts receivable subsidiary
   ledger, *229*
administrative controls, *225*
application controls, *247*
application programs, *242*
cash disbursements journal,
   238

cash receipts journal, *234*
computer hardware, *242*
computer software, *242*
control, *225*
control account, *229*
cost-effective, *225*
flexibility, *225*
general controls, *247*
operating systems, *242*

purchases journal, *236*
sales journal, *230*
special journals, *229*
subsidiary ledgers, *229*
system flowcharts, *227*
timeliness, *224*

SELF-QUIZ

LO 1
LO 2
LO 8

1. Key terms and their definitions are listed below. Match the definitions with the key terms.

_____ a. Accounting controls
_____ b. Accounting system
_____ c. Administrative controls
_____ d. Control
_____ e. Application controls
_____ f. General controls
_____ g. Timeliness
_____ h. Flexibility

   (1) All the steps that management takes to ensure that: (1) goals are achieved; (2) only necessary costs are incurred; (3) activities are conducted in accordance with management's authorization; (4) assets are safeguarded; and (5) financial reports are reliable
   (2) Controls in an organization other than accounting controls
   (3) Organization of physical facilities, personnel, documents, records, and procedures designed to accomplish specific accounting control objectives
   (4) Controls over the inputs, outputs, and processing logic of a particular accounting application
   (5) Controls management implements to ensure that accounting reports are reliable
   (6) Characteristic of an accounting system that can provide information to support new decisions without major modification of the system
   (7) Controls oriented toward the organization of the data processing function and the protection of computer-related assets
   (8) Information supplied with sufficient lead time to be useful to management

LO 8 2. Key terms and their definitions are listed below. Match the definitions with the key terms.

_____ a. System flowcharts
_____ b. Application programs
_____ c. Computer hardware
_____ d. Operating systems
_____ e. Cost-effective
_____ f. Computer software

   (1) Benefits of a policy, procedure, or action outweigh its cost
   (2) Symbolic representations of systems
   (3) Mechanical and electronic components of a computer system
   (4) Set of instructions that control the operations of computer hardware and direct it

to perform computational and other logical tasks
   (5) Fundamental programs that direct the computer to coordinate the parts of the computer system
   (6) Sets of computer instructions to accomplish specific tasks (Examples: Microsoft® Word and Lotus 1-2-3®)

LO 4
LO 5
LO 6

3. Key terms and their definitions are listed below. Match the definitions with the key terms.

_____ a. Accounts receivable subsidiary ledger
_____ b. Cash disbursements journal
_____ c. Cash receipts journal
_____ d. Purchases journal
_____ e. Sales journal
_____ f. Special journals
_____ g. Subsidiary ledgers

   (1) Sets of ledger accounts that contain the details of balances in individual general ledger accounts
   (2) Typically contains one column, whose total is posted to Accounts Receivable and Sales in the general ledger
   (3) Substitutes for the general journal used to record particular classes of transactions
   (4) Consists of an individual ledger account for each credit customer
   (5) Typically has a Cash Dr. column, Sales Discounts Dr. column, Accounts Receivable Cr. column, Sales Cr. column, and Other Accounts Cr. column
   (6) Typically has an Accounts Payable Cr. column, Purchases Dr. column, and sometimes Dr. columns for various other accounts
   (7) All transactions entered in this journal require an amount entered in the Cash Cr. column

LO 2 4. To produce reliable financial reports, an accounting system must satisfy six accounting control objectives:

   (1) _____   (4) _____
   (2) _____   (5) _____
   (3) _____   (6) _____

LO 1 5. When the benefits of any policy, procedure, or action outweigh its cost:
   a. The company is operating at a profit.
   b. The policy, procedure, or action is said to be cost-effective.
   c. The policy, procedure, or action is said to have validity.
   d. All of the above

LO 1   6. Four objectives of the accounting system are:
(1)_____
(2)_____
(3)_____
(4)_____

LO 1   7. To meet management's decision needs, accounting systems must achieve two corollary objectives:
(1)_____
(2)_____

LO 3   8. Although good accounting systems are flexible, every accounting system inevitably becomes obsolete. All information systems, including accounting systems, pass through a distinct life cycle. The five stages in the typical life cycle of an accounting information system are:
(1)_____
(2)_____
(3)_____
(4)_____
(5)_____

LO 5   9. The total of the one-column sales journal is posted
a. To Sales as a credit
b. Accounts Receivable (control account) as a debit
c. To the accounts receivable subsidiary accounts receivable ledger as a credit
d. Both a and b
e. To Sales as a debit

LO 6   10. The total of the Cash column in the cash disbursements journal is
a. Not posted because the individual entries in the Cash column are posted to Cash at the time the entry is recorded
b. Posted to Cash as a debit
c. Posted to Cash as a credit
d. Posted to the accounts payable subsidiary ledger as a credit

LO 4   11. True or False? The use of a cash receipts journal
LO 5   increases the number of postings to Cash.

LO 7   12. A company uses special journals and a subsidiary accounts receivable ledger. It incorrectly totals the Accounts Receivable Cr. column in the cash receipts journal. An error in the system will be discovered when

a. The debit column totals of the cash receipts journal are added, the credit column total of the cash receipts journal are added, and the totals of the debit and credit columns are compared for equality
b. The total of the accounts receivable subsidiary accounts is compared to the total in Accounts Receivable (control account)
c. A trial balance is prepared
d. All of the above
e. None of the above

LO 7   13. A company uses special journals and an accounts receivable subsidiary ledger. It incorrectly records a $1,000 sales invoice as $10,000 in the sales journal. An error in the accounting system will probably be detected when
a. The accounts receivable subsidiary ledger totals are compared with Accounts Receivable (control account)
b. The equality of debit column totals and credit column totals in the sales journal is compared
c. A trial balance is taken
d. The customer pays the correct amount of cash according to the invoice
e. None of these procedures will detect the existence of an error

LO 8   14. Lotus 1-2-3® is an example of
a. Computer hardware
b. Computer software
c. An operating system
d. An application program
e. Both b and d

LO 8   15. Accounting controls in a computer environment are classified as _____ controls and _____ controls.

LO 8   16. Errors in a computerized accounting system are most likely to occur
a. During the process of posting transactions to the general ledger
b. During the computation of account balances
c. During the inputting of transactions into the system
d. During the process of preparing financial statements from the adjusted trial balance

---

SOLUTIONS TO SELF-QUIZ
1. a. 5 b. 3 c. 2 d. 1 e. 4 f. 7 g. 8 h. 6   2. a. 2 b. 6 c. 3 d. 5 e. 1 f. 4   3. a. 4 b. 7 c. 5 d. 6 e. 2
f. 3 g. 1   4. authorization, validity, valuation, classification, completeness, accuracy   5. b   6. Implement the accounting
process, support management decisions, provide reliable information, be cost-effective   7. timeliness, flexibility   8. analysis,
design, implementation, operation, evaluation   9. d   10. c   11. False   12. d   13. d   14. e   15. general, application   16. c

QUESTIONS

Q6-1   Accounting controls are the controls management implements to ensure that accounting reports are reliable. All other controls are called administrative controls. Discuss how accounting controls assist management in establishing effective administrative controls.

Q6-2   One accounting control objective is that of completeness—i.e., ensuring that all transactions are recorded. Listed below are two kinds of transactions. Discuss which type of transaction would probably have the greater risk of not being recorded in the accounting system.

a. Cash sales
b. Purchases on credit

Q6-3   Should a business implement all of the accounting controls illustrated in this chapter? Discuss.

Q6-4   Assume the accounting records are accurate. During the middle of the month, the total of the accounts payable accounts in the subsidiary ledger is compared with the balance in the accounts payable control account in the general ledger and the numbers do not agree. Explain why they do not agree.

Q6-5   To meet management's decision needs, accounting systems must achieve two corollary objectives—timeliness and flexibility. Discuss how the movement from a manual accounting system to a computerized accounting system might impact these two objectives.

Q6-6   Although good accounting systems are flexible, every accounting system inevitably becomes obsolete. Discuss some changes in business conditions that might make even a flexible accounting system become obsolete.

Q6-7   If a company uses special journals similar to those illustrated in the chapter, explain why there is still a need for a general journal.

Q6-8   Explain how special journals contribute to a more efficient accounting system.

Q6-9   Explain how control accounts and subsidiary ledgers contribute to a more efficient accounting system.

Q6-10 Hardware and software are both part of a computerized accounting system. Distinguish between hardware and software. Is one more important than the other? Discuss.

Q6-11 A dishonest employee creates a dummy company posing as a supplier. After regular hours, the employee uses the cash disbursements program, which is a part of the company's integrated computerized general ledger program, to record cash disbursements and write checks to the dummy company. The company treasurer signs and mails the checks to the dummy company, where the dishonest employee picks them up from a post office box and deposits them in the dummy company's checking account. Identify control procedures that could detect this fraud.

EXERCISES

LO 4,5,6

E6-1   **Special Journals**   A company uses a sales journal (*S*), cash receipts journal (*CR*), purchases journal (*P*), cash disbursements journal (*CD*), and general journal (*G*). Identify in which journal each of the following transactions would be entered:

___ a. Cash sale
___ b. Purchase of office equipment on account
___ c. Cash withdrawal by owner
___ d. Purchase of merchandise for cash
___ e. Sale of merchandise on credit
___ f. Purchase of office supplies on credit
___ g. Adjusting entry to record depreciation

___ h. Check issued for payment of merchandise purchased on credit
___ i. Check received in payment of a customer's account
___ j. Cash received from insurance company in payment of insurance claim
___ k. Closing entries
___ l. Purchase of a building needed for additional space, paying 10% down and signing a note for the balance

LO 5,7

E6-2   Special Journals, Control Accounts, Subsidiary Ledgers   Below is the accounts receivable control account. Assume the company uses special journals like those illustrated in the chapter.

Accounts Receivable			
Beg. Bal.	65,335	Jan. 31	70,859
Jan. 31	91,722		

REQUIRED:

a. Identify the journal that is the source of the $91,722 posting.
b. Identify the journal that is the source of the $70,859 posting.
c. If we prepare a list of accounts receivable accounts from the subsidiary ledger, we would expect the total of the subsidiary accounts to be $_____.

LO 6,7

E6-3   Special Journals, Control Accounts, Subsidiary Ledgers   Below is the accounts payable control account. Assume the company uses special journals like those illustrated in the chapter.

Accounts Payable			
Jan. 31	47,600	Beg. Bal.	38,950
		Jan. 31	41,445

REQUIRED:

a. Identify the journal that is the source of the $47,600 posting.
b. Identify the journal that is the source of the $41,445 posting.
c. If we prepare a list of accounts payable accounts from the subsidiary ledger, we would expect the total of the subsidiary accounts to be $_____.

LO 4,7

E6-4   Accounts Receivable Subsidiary Ledgers and General Ledger Control Accounts   A company using special journals, like those illustrated in the chapter, correctly enters a sale on account of $900 in the sales journal. When posting to the accounts receivable subsidiary ledger, it incorrectly posts $90 to the subsidiary account.

REQUIRED:

a. Identify the accounting control procedure that will detect the existence of an error in the system.
b. Calculate the difference in the balance in the accounts receivable control account and the total of the accounts in the subsidiary ledger.

LO 5,7

E6-5   Journalizing and Posting Credit Sales and Cash Receipts Transactions, Reconciling Subsidiary Ledger and Control Account   Following are January transactions for a new company that started business on January 1:

Jan. 7 Sold merchandise on credit to Green Company, terms 2/10, n/30. Invoice No. 1, $10,000.
     17 Sold merchandise on credit to Red Company, terms 2/10, n/30. Invoice No. 2, $20,000.
     25 Received full payment from Red Company, less the 2% discount.

REQUIRED:

a. Set up whatever journals and ledger accounts you need. Assume zero beginning balances for January. Enter the three transactions in the journals, post individual transactions to the subsidiary ledger accounts, and post journal column totals to the general ledger accounts. Include all appropriate posting references in the journals and ledger accounts.

b. Prepare a list of accounts receivable subsidiary ledger accounts and compare the total with the total in the accounts receivable control account.

LO 6,7

E6-6 **Journalizing and Posting Credit Purchases and Cash Disbursements Transactions, Reconciling Subsidiary Ledger and Control Account**   Following are January transactions for a new company that started business on January 1:

Jan. 7 Purchased merchandise on credit from Blue Company, terms 2/10, n/30, $6,000.
   17 Purchased merchandise on credit from White Company, terms 2/10, n/30, $12,000.
   25 Paid White Company in full, less the 2% discount, issuing Check No. 1

REQUIRED:

a. Set up whatever journals and ledger accounts you need. Enter a beginning balance of $15,000 in Cash. Assume zero beginning balances for all other accounts.

b. Enter the three transactions in the journals, post individual transactions to the subsidiary ledger accounts, and post journal column totals to the general ledger accounts. Include all appropriate posting references in the journals and ledger accounts.

c. Prepare a list of accounts payable subsidiary ledger accounts and compare the total with the total in the accounts payable control account.

LO 5

E6-7 **Journalizing Credit Sales with Sales Tax**   Surplus Supply operates in a state that has a 6% sales tax. Following are Surplus' January transactions:

Jan. 5 Sold merchandise on credit to C. Williams, $5,000 plus tax, Invoice No. 101, terms 2/10, n/30.
   15 Sold merchandise on credit to P. Carter, $10,000 plus tax, Invoice No. 102, terms 2/10, n/30.
   25 Sold merchandise to C. Williams, $400 plus tax, Invoice No. 103, terms 2/10, n/30.

REQUIRED:

In a sales journal like the one in Illustration 6-7, enter the three transactions.

LO 5,6

E6-8 **Special Journals and Subsidiary Ledgers**   Identify the journal (sales–*S*, cash receipts–*CR*, purchases–*P*, cash disbursements–*CD*, general–*G*) that is the most likely source of each posting indicated below:

___ a. Debit posting to the accounts receivable control account in the general ledger
___ b. Debit posting to an accounts receivable subsidiary ledger account
___ c. Debit posting to Depreciation Expense in the general ledger
___ d. Credit posting to Cash in the general ledger
___ e. Debit posting to Cash in the general ledger
___ f. Debit posting to Purchases in the general ledger
___ g. Debit posting to Sales Discounts in the general ledger
___ h. Credit posting to Purchases Discounts in the general ledger
___ i. Credit posting to an accounts payable subsidiary ledger account
___ j. Credit posting to an accounts receivable subsidiary ledger account
___ k. Debit posting to an accounts payable subsidiary ledger account

___ l. Debit posting to Sales Returns and Allowances in the general ledger
___ m. Debit posting to Office Equipment in the general ledger
___ n. Debit posting to Income Summary in the general ledger

LO 8   **E6-9**   **General and Application Controls in Computer-Based Systems**   Greune Company has just installed a new computer-based system, and enters all sales in the computer at the point of sale. Entries are made from four different terminals, and an average of 300 sales transactions occur each day. Management is worried about the reliability of the new system.

REQUIRED:

Identify some general and application controls that Greune can implement to help ensure the reliability and accuracy of the system.

PROBLEM SET A

LO 1,2,3   **P6-1A**   **Accounting Systems Design and Operation**   The Western Warehouse Company is a discount mail-order supplier of parts for luxury touring motorcycles. It stocks a large inventory of parts and accessories. In recent years, the supply business has become very competitive; and Western considers implementing a new promotion program that will guarantee shipment within 12 hours of order placement. Currently, Western has a manual accounting system that uses special journals, subsidiary ledgers for receivables and payables, and a periodic inventory system.

REQUIRED:

a. Briefly explain the concepts of timeliness and flexibility as they relate to accounting systems in general.
b. Based on the brief description of Western, evaluate its accounting system in terms of timeliness and flexibility.
c. Briefly describe the steps that would be involved in designing a new accounting system for Western.
d. In implementing the first step, analysis, identify the accounting information and reports that the new promotion program will require.

LO 4,5,6,7   **P6-2A**   **Special Journals, Subsidiary Ledgers, Accounting Controls**   The Great Western Boot Distribution Company is a wholesale distributor of several brands of western-style boots and leather apparel. It began operations following the owner's initial investment on January 1, 19X7, and established a manual accounting system that utilizes special journals and subsidiary accounts receivable and payable ledgers similar to the ones illustrated in this chapter. *Selected* transactions for January 19X7 follow:

Jan. 1 The owner, Kenneth Ray, started the business with an investment of $100,000 cash.
      4 Purchased merchandise from Texas Boot Company for $10,000, terms 2/10, n/30.
      4 Purchased merchandise from Great Plains Boots for $20,000, terms 1/5, n/30.
      6 Sold merchandise to the Louisville Leather Shop for $3,000, Invoice No. 1, terms 2/10, n/30.
      7 Sold merchandise to the Dodge City Mail Order Company for $35,000, Invoice No. 2, terms 2/10, n/30.
     11 Received full payment on Invoice No. 2, less the cash discount.
     12 Issued Check No. 601 to the Texas Boot Company in payment of the January 4, 19X7 purchase, less the cash discount.
     15 Received full payment on Invoice No. 1, less the cash discount.

Jan. 18 Paid Great Plains Boots the full amount for the January 4, 19X7 purchase, issuing Check No. 602.

   25 Issued Check No. 603 to Kenneth Ray, the owner, for a $1,000 withdrawal from the business.

   27 Purchased a 3-year insurance policy from Mayflower, issuing Check No. 604 for $3,000.

   28 Purchased merchandise on credit from Desert Apparel, $15,000, terms 2/10, n/30.

   29 Sold merchandise to Quest Exports, $20,000, Invoice No. 3, terms 2/10, n/30.

   30 Sold merchandise to Louisville Leather Shop for $6,000, Invoice No. 4, terms 2/10, n/30.

   30 Agreed to take back $1,000 of the merchandise purchased by Quest on January 29, 19X7. (Record in the general journal.)

   31 Purchased merchandise from Great Plains Boots for $4,000, terms 1/5, n/30.

   31 Sold merchandise to New World Exports for $7,000 cash.

   31 Recorded depreciation expense on equipment for the month, $2,500.

   31 Paid Wages and Salaries for the month, $5,000, issuing Check No. 605.

REQUIRED:

a. Open the following general ledger accounts:

Cash	100
Accounts Receivable	110
Prepaid Insurance	150
Accumulated Depreciation–Equipment	231
Accounts Payable	302
Kenneth Ray, Withdrawals	502
Sales	602
Sales Returns and Allowances	622
Sales Discounts	624
Depreciation Expense–Equipment	712
Purchases	754
Purchases Discounts	756
Wages and Salaries Expense	784

b. Open the following subsidiary ledger accounts:

Accounts Receivable:

Louisville Leather Shop	101
Dodge City Mail Order Company	102
Quest Exports	103

Accounts Payable:

Texas Boot Company	201
Great Plains Boots	202
Desert Apparel	203

c. Record the January transactions in the appropriate journal. Post all transactions affecting the subsidiary ledgers to the subsidiary ledger accounts at the time the entry is recorded in the journals. Include appropriate posting references in the journals and ledgers.

d. Post the totals of the special journals at the end of the month. Include appropriate posting references in the journals and ledgers.

e. Prepare schedules of the accounts in the subsidiary ledgers and compare the totals to the balances in the control accounts.

f. Explain how Step *e* serves as a good accounting control procedure.

LO 4,5   **P6-3A   Subsidiary Ledgers and Special Journals, Credit Sales and Cash Receipts Transactions**   The accounts receivable subsidiary ledger of the Maryville Heating Oil Company is presented on the following page:

ACCOUNTS RECEIVABLE SUBSIDIARY LEDGER

NAME: Maryville High School   ACCOUNT NO.: 101

DATE		DESCRIPTION	POST. REF.	DEBIT	CREDIT	BALANCE
19X6						
Apr.	1	Balance				7,500
	5		CR12		7,500	0
	13		SJ8	2,500		2,500

NAME: Maryville Hospital   ACCOUNT NO.: 102

DATE		DESCRIPTION	POST. REF.	DEBIT	CREDIT	BALANCE
19X6						
Apr.	1	Balance				25,000
	6		SJ8	10,000		35,000
	14		CR12		25,000	10,000

NAME: Maryville Community College   ACCOUNT NO.: 103

DATE		DESCRIPTION	POST. REF.	DEBIT	CREDIT	BALANCE
19X6						
Apr.	1	Balance				8,000
	10		SJ8	5,000		13,000
	15		CR12		8,000	5,000
	29		SJ8	6,000		11,000

NAME: Maryville Retirement Village   ACCOUNT NO.: 104

DATE		DESCRIPTION	POST. REF.	DEBIT	CREDIT	BALANCE
19X6						
Apr.	1	Balance				6,000
	18		CR12		3,000	3,000
	20		SJ8	9,000		12,000

NAME: Maryville Amusement Park   ACCOUNT NO.: 105

DATE		DESCRIPTION	POST. REF.	DEBIT	CREDIT	BALANCE
19X6						
Apr.	1	Balance				9,000
	5		GJ5		1,000	8,000
	6		CR12		8,000	0

NAME: Maryville Technical Institute   ACCOUNT NO.: 106

DATE		DESCRIPTION	POST. REF.	DEBIT	CREDIT	BALANCE
19X6						
Apr.	1	Balance				2,000

REQUIRED:

a. From the information in the subsidiary ledger accounts, recreate the Accounts Receivable control account in the general ledger. Include in your control account the beginning balance for April 1,19X6, all postings for April, the appropriate posting references, and the ending balance as of April 30, 19X6.

b. What transaction might have caused the $1,000 credit to the Maryville Amusement Park account?

LO 2,4   **P6-4A   Accounting Controls, Subsidiary Ledgers, Special Journals**   In each independent situation presented, identify the control procedure or event, if any, that would discover the existence of an error or irregularity in the accounting system.

a. Merchandise that was never received is being paid for.

b. Underbilling for merchandise because of a mathematical error in preparing the sales invoice: 12 items @ $100 = $120.

c. The following journal entry for depreciation expense was made at the end of the month:

Depreciation Expense–Office Equipment	2,600	
Depreciation Expense–Sales Equipment	2,300	
Accumulated Depreciation–Office Equipment		2,600
Accumulated Depreciation–Sales Equipment		3,200

d. A $5,000 sale of merchandise to Mullins Company on credit was posted to Miller Company in the accounts receivable subsidiary ledger.

e. A $1,000 sale of merchandise to Higgons Inc. was posted to the Higgons account in the subsidiary ledger as a credit.

f. The Amount column in the sales journal actually added to $100,000 for the month but was incorrectly added to arrive at a total of $110,000.

g. A math error was made in calculating the balance in Cash in the general ledger.

h. A math error was made in adding the Cash Dr. column in the cash receipts journal.

LO 1,4   **P6-5A   Accounting Systems, Subsidiary Ledgers, and Special Journals**   The Mountain Crafts Quilt Company sells handmade quilts to retail outlets across the country and to several importers from overseas. Mountain Crafts started as a small, part-time operation 10 years ago and has grown steadily over the years. During the past 2 years, handcrafted quilts have become popular, with a particularly strong export market.

Mountain Crafts utilizes the same accounting system designed for the company when it began operations—a manual bookkeeping system with a general journal and a general ledger.

Currently, the company has a separate accounts receivable account for each customer (approximately 100) and a separate accounts payable account for each supplier (approximately 20). It has an average of 200 credit sales each month and an average of 10 credit purchase transactions each month.

Mountain Crafts considers upgrading their accounting system to incorporate special journals and subsidiary ledgers.

REQUIRED:

a. How would the adoption of subsidiary ledgers impact the size of its general ledger? Calculate the approximate reduction in accounts.

b. How would the adoption of special journals impact the number of postings to Sales each month? Calculate the approximate reduction in the number of postings.

c. How would the adoption of special journals impact the number of debit and credit postings to Cash?

d. What additional accounting controls result from control accounts and subsidiary ledgers?

LO 1,8   **P6-6A   Accounting Systems, Computer-Based Systems**   The Iron Forge Hardware Store has been in business for 3 generations. It uses a manual accounting system with special journals and a subsidiary ledger for accounts payable and a periodic inventory system. It does not use a subsidiary accounts receivable ledger, as nearly all its sales are cash or credit card.

Iron Forge considers adopting a computer-based accounting system. However, the owner, Sharon Givens, is concerned about adopting a new system. "Our manual book-keeping may take a little more time, but at least I trust the numbers. We understand where the numbers come from, and we know they are accurate. Any math errors we make are always detected by the trial balance, and all our invoices are independently verified as to mathematical accuracy."

REQUIRED:

a. Explain how a computer-based system might be able to provide accounting information that would improve Iron Forge's management decision making.
b. Identify some general controls that Iron Forge can establish to help ensure an accurate and reliable computer-based accounting system.
c. Identify some application controls that Iron Forge can establish to help ensure an accurate and reliable accounting system.

PROBLEM SET B

LO 2

P6-1B   Accounting Controls   Accounting controls are the controls management implements to ensure that accounting reports are reliable.

REQUIRED:

a. Discuss how double-entry accounting helps ensure that mathematical errors are not included in accounting reports.
b. Are the control features incorporated in double-entry accounting more useful in a manual accounting system or a computer-based accounting system? Discuss.

LO 4,5,6,7

P6-2B   Special Journals, Subsidiary Ledgers, Accounting Controls   The Technical Synthetic Supply Company is a wholesale distributor of several types of high-tech materials that manufacturers of brakes and clutches use. It began operations following the owner's initial investment on July 1, 19X9, and has established a manual accounting system that utilizes special journals and subsidiary accounts receivable and payable ledgers similar to the ones illustrated in this chapter. *Selected* transactions for July 19X9 are listed below:

July 1 The owner, Juanita Cortez, started the business with an initial investment of $150,000.
   3 Purchased merchandise from Universal Corporation for $50,000, terms 1/15, n/45.
   5 Purchased merchandise from Western Chemical for $75,000, terms 1/10, n/30.
   6 Sold merchandise to the Southern Brake Company for $60,000, Invoice No. 1, terms 2/10, n/30.
   7 Sold merchandise to the Charlotte Clutch Company for $75,000, Invoice No. 2, terms 2/10, n/30.
   11 Received full payment on Invoice No. 2, less the cash discount.
   12 Paid Universal Corporation for the July 3, 19X9, purchase, less the cash discount (Check No. 100).
   15 Received full payment on Invoice No. 1, less the cash discount.
   18 Paid Western Chemical the full amount for the July 5, 19X9, purchase (Check No. 101).
   25 Juanita Cortez, the owner, made an additional $10,000 capital contribution to the business.
   26 Purchased a 3-year insurance policy from Eastern Security, paying $3,600 cash (Check No. 102).
   28 Purchased merchandise on credit from Western, $80,000, terms 2/10, n/30.
   29 Sold merchandise to Southern Brake Company, $90,000, Invoice No. 3, terms 2/10, n/30.

July 30 Sold Merchandise to Charlotte Clutch Company for $40,000, Invoice No. 4, terms 2/10, n/30.

   30 Agreed to take back $10,000 of the merchandise purchased by Southern Brake Company on July 29, 19X9. (Record in the general journal.)

   31 Purchased merchandise from Universal Corporation for $45,000, terms 1/15, n/30,

   31 Sold merchandise to Bradley Technology for $20,000 cash.

   31 Recorded depreciation expense for equipment for the month, $5,000.

   31 Paid wages and salaries for the month, $6,000 (Check No. 103).

REQUIRED:

a. Open the following general ledger accounts:

Cash	100
Accounts Receivable	110
Prepaid Insurance	150
Accumulated Depreciation–Equipment	231
Accounts Payable	302
Juanita Cortez, Capital	500
Sales	602
Sales Returns and Allowances	622
Sales Discounts	624
Depreciation Expense–Equipment	712
Purchases	754
Purchases Discounts	756
Wages and Salaries Expense	784

b. Open the following subsidiary ledger accounts:

Accounts Receivable:

Southern Brake Company	101
Charlotte Clutch Company	102
Bradley Technology	103

Accounts Payable:

Universal Corporation	201
Western Chemical	202

c. Record the July transactions in the appropriate journals. Post all transactions affecting the subsidiary ledgers to the subsidiary ledger accounts at the time the entry is recorded in the journals. Include appropriate posting references in the journals and ledgers.

d. Post the totals of the special journals at the end of the month. Include appropriate posting references in the journals and ledgers.

e. Prepare schedules of the accounts in the subsidiary ledgers and compare the totals to the balances in the control accounts.

f. Explain how Step *e* serves as a good accounting control procedure.

LO 4,5   **P6-3B** **Subsidiary Ledgers and Special Journals, Credit Sales and Cash Receipts Transactions** The accounts payable subsidiary ledger of the Sunset Tile Company is presented below:

ACCOUNTS PAYABLE SUBSIDIARY LEDGER

NAME: Southern Tile Manufacturing				ACCOUNT NO.: 101	
DATE	DESCRIPTION	POST. REF.	DEBIT	CREDIT	BALANCE
19X5					
Feb. 1	Balance				10,000
5		CD12	10,000		0
13		PJ8		8,000	8,000

NAME: Boston Tile Company   ACCOUNT NO.: 102

DATE		DESCRIPTION	POST. REF.	DEBIT	CREDIT	BALANCE
19X5						
Feb.	1	Balance				5,000
	6		PJ8		4,000	9,000
	14		CD12	5,000		4,000

NAME: Tidewater Tile   ACCOUNT NO.: 103

DATE		DESCRIPTION	POST. REF.	DEBIT	CREDIT	BALANCE
19X5						
Feb.	1	Balance				20,000
	10		PJ8		5,000	25,000
	15		CD12	20,000		5,000
	29		PJ8		18,000	23,000

NAME: Red Sky Tile Company   ACCOUNT NO.: 104

DATE		DESCRIPTION	POST. REF.	DEBIT	CREDIT	BALANCE
19X5						
Feb.	1	Balance				7,000
	18		CD12	7,000		0
	20		PJ8		9,000	9,000

NAME: Kustom Tile Kiln   ACCOUNT NO.: 105

DATE		DESCRIPTION	POST. REF.	DEBIT	CREDIT	BALANCE
19X5						
Feb.	1	Balance				13,000
	5		GJ5	3,000		10,000
	6		CD12	10,000		0

NAME: Koole Fire Productions   ACCOUNT NO.: 106

DATE		DESCRIPTION	POST. REF.	DEBIT	CREDIT	BALANCE
19X5						
Feb.	1	Balance				12,000

REQUIRED:

a. From the information in the subsidiary ledger accounts, recreate the Accounts Payable control account in the general ledger. Include in your control account the beginning balance for February 1, 19X5, all postings for February, the appropriate posting references, and the ending balance as of February 28, 19X5.

b. What transaction might have caused the $3,000 debit to the Kustom Tile Kiln account?

LO 2,4   **P6-4B   Accounting Controls, Subsidiary Ledgers, Special Journals**   In each independent situation presented, identify the control procedure or event, if any, that would discover the existence of an error, weakness, or irregularity in the accounting system.

a. Merchandise that was never received is being paid for.

b. A math error was made in adding the Amount column in a single-column sales journal.

c. A $987 sale on credit was entered correctly in the sales journal but posted to the customer account as $897.

d. The company has had increasing difficulty collecting accounts receivable because of sales to poor credit risks.

e. A math error is made in computing the balance of a customer account in the accounts receivable subsidiary ledger.

f. Journal entries made in a general ledger computer-based accounting system frequently have unequal debits and credits.

g. A $2,000 credit sale to Schmidt was posted erroneously to the accounts receivable subsidiary ledger account of Schwandt.

LO 1,4 **P6-5B** **Accounting Systems, Subsidiary Ledgers, and Special Journals**   The Mountain Chair Company sells handmade rocking chairs to retail outlets across the country and to several importers from overseas. Mountain Chair started as a small, part-time operation 10 years ago and has grown steadily over the years. During the past 2 years, rocking chairs have become popular, with a particularly strong export market.

Mountain Chair utilizes the same accounting system designed for the company when it began operations—a manual bookkeeping system with a general journal and a general ledger.

Currently, the company has a separate accounts receivable account for each customer (approximately 100) and a separate accounts payable account for each supplier (approximately 20). It has an average of 200 credit sales each month and an average of 10 credit purchase transactions each month.

Mountain Chair considers upgrading their accounting system to incorporate special journals and subsidiary ledgers.

REQUIRED:

a. How would the adoption of subsidiary ledgers impact the size of its general ledger? Calculate the approximate reduction in accounts.

b. How would the adoption of special journals impact the number of postings to Sales each month? Calculate the approximate reduction in the number of postings.

c. How would the adoption of special journals impact the number of debit and credit postings to Cash?

d. What additional accounting controls result from control accounts and subsidiary ledgers?

LO 8 **P6-6B** **Accounting Controls in a Computer Environment**   Any accounting system for processing transactions should meet these objectives: authorization, validity, valuation, classification, completeness, and accuracy.

REQUIRED:

Discuss how a computer-based accounting system might impact the way each control objective is accomplished.

CRITICAL THINKING AND COMMUNICATING

C6-1   The use of the computer as a tool in accounting information systems has expanded exponentially over the past 3 decades. The computer is ideally suited to processing accounting information through an accounting information system. After the initial entry of data, the system processes it through the posting process, the trial balance, and the financial statements in a structured sequence. Processing procedures can be clearly and precisely programed in advance, employing the logic of the double-entry bookkeeping system. Processing accounting information is a task for which the computer is very well-suited.

The capability of computer hardware and software advances almost daily, and the cost reductions in recent years are staggering. A company can purchase accounting hardware and software at a very small fraction of the cost of state-of-the-art 1960s equipment, and the current equipment is much more sophisticated. Indeed a computerized system costing hundreds of thousands of dollars in the 60s can be purchased for less than the price of a small compact car. There no longer seems to be any real reason for not having a computer-based accounting system.

Given the current widespread use of computer-based accounting systems, one first-year accounting student was heard to say: "Studying manual accounting systems with general journals, special journals, subsidiary ledgers is a waste of time. No one uses a manual system anymore. We should be using general ledger software to learn how accounting systems work."

REQUIRED:

Do you agree or disagree with the student's comment? Discuss.

C6-2 Sung Lee Kim owns and operates a greeting card shop, Special Moments, which carries a comprehensive line of cards from several major suppliers. Over the past 5 years, the business has grown steadily; and Sung Lee has expanded the operations into the mail-order market, producing a catalog that will be mailed to about 2,000 prospective customers during the upcoming year. Sung Lee uses a manual accounting system with special journals and accounts receivable and payable subsidiary ledgers. The business uses a periodic inventory system for financial accounting purposes but keeps an up-to-date inventory record of the quantities of the 100 or so best-selling cards. The inventory record is primarily used for ordering purposes. Two long-time employees perform the accounting work on a full-time basis.

In a discussion over lunch, Sung Lee asks your advice. Sung realizes that the business has grown to the point that a computer-based accounting system seems logical but is reluctant to abandon the manual system. "I could let one of my accountants go; and with the money I would save, I could install a computer-based system and still have money left over. But there is a loyalty issue here, and I just don't think I would be doing the right thing. The system we have is working and the business is growing. I would rather spend my money preserving a job for a person who has been a part of the success of my business, than to spend the money on some machine." Sung Lee then turns to you and asks, "Am I doing the right thing?"

REQUIRED:

Provide your response to Sung Lee Kim.

C6-3 Refer to the financial statements of J.C. Penney Company, Inc. in Appendix B at the end of the text. Find the company statement on financial information that follows the independent auditors' report and precedes the income statement.

REQUIRED:

You may assume that the statement is written primarily for the benefit of the owners of the company (its shareholders). Consider each of the paragraphs contained in the statement and the statement as a whole. Write a brief essay analyzing the message(s) contained in the statement from a concerned shareholder's point of view. Indicate why you think the Chairman of the Board and Executive Vice President would want to include such a statement with the financial statements of the company. Also, indicate why an authority such as the Securities and Exchange Commission might want to require top management to make such a statement in the case of a large company owned by many members of society.

CHAPTER 7

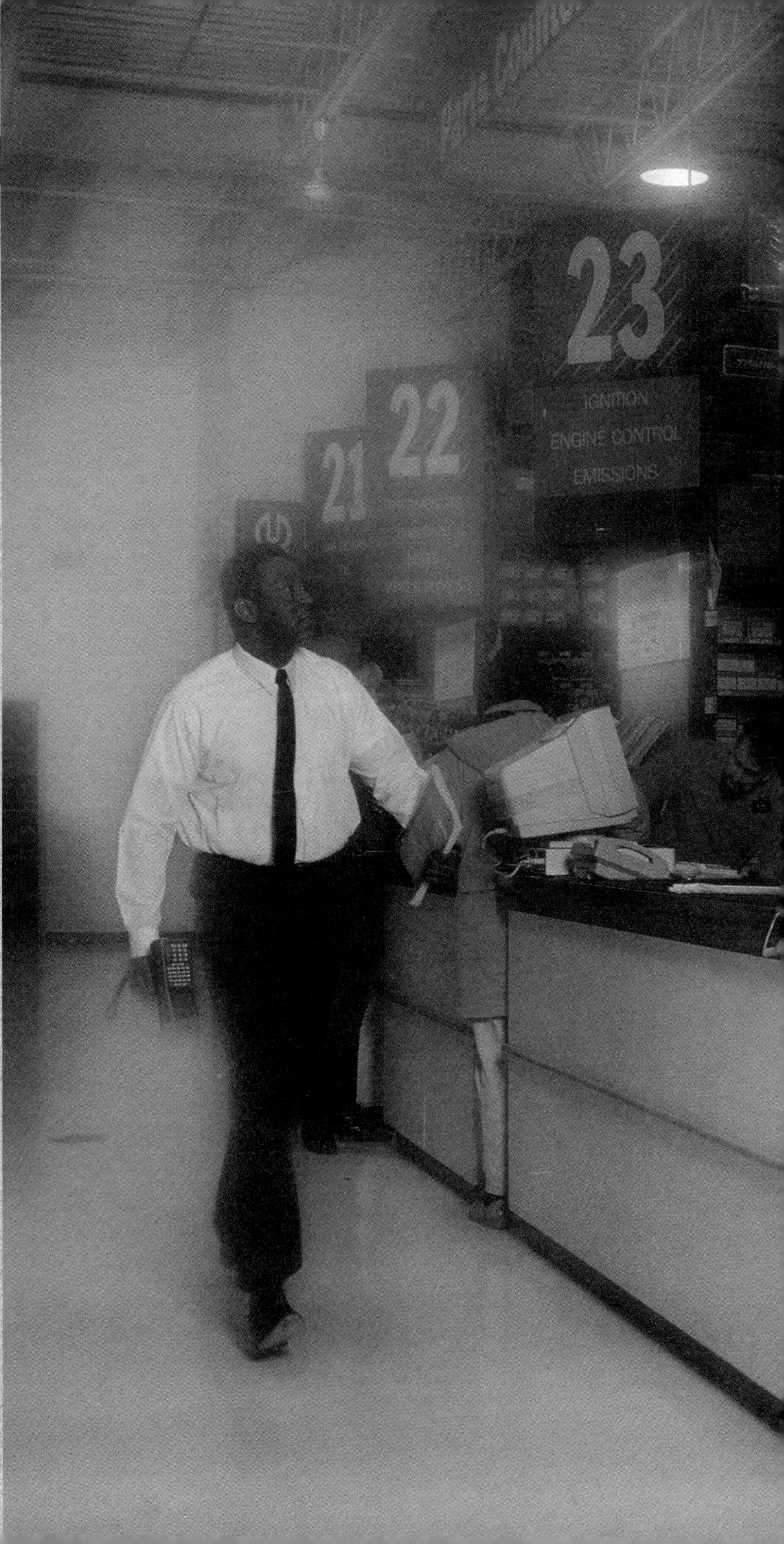

Internal Control and Cash

Frank Brown, owner of Ready Auto Parts, believed he really was in touch with the successful business he founded a few years ago—that is, until today. Having just finished a meeting with some officers of his bank, Frank now feels confused. Wanting to establish a line of credit—a pre-arranged loan—that he could draw on as needed to help him finance further business growth, Frank had arranged the meeting. The bankers had analyzed his financial statements and had asked many specific questions Frank could easily answer. Then, when they had asked specifically about how his business controlled its cash and about its liquidity position, Frank felt less prepared. He knows he has done a good job of organizing his business, and he has implemented most of the internal control suggestions made by the CPAs who help his accounting personnel prepare the financial statements each year. However, Frank is no longer familiar with many of the details, and he has never learned about the financial ratios that best measure a business's liquidity. Before his meeting with the bankers ended, Frank asked for a second meeting in a week to prepare answers to their questions.

= ability to pay debt

This chapter covers the methods businesses commonly use to control cash. A well-designed system controls cash receipts, cash disbursements, and any cash the business holds. Cash control systems must be "tight" because cash is the asset that employees most easily convert to personal use and it is the business's life-blood—the means by which it pays its bills and survives. The liquidity of a business is its ability to pay its bills in the short run. At the end of the chapter, we introduce you to the colorfully named acid-test ratio, the toughest of the widely used tests of a business's liquidity position.

LEARNING OBJECTIVES

1. Describe control procedures for cash received from credit sales.
2. Describe control procedures for cash received in cash sales transactions.
3. Describe control procedures for cash disbursements, including the voucher system and voucher documents.
4. Describe the operation of a petty cash fund and record petty cash expenditures in the accounting records.
5. Identify the reconciling items that make the business's cash balance differ from the balance on its bank statement.
6. Follow the steps required to prepare a bank reconciliation and record any needed adjustments in the accounting records.
7. Describe two major categories of electronic funds transfers businesses use.
8. Define and interpret the acid-test ratio.

CONTROL OBJECTIVES AND SYSTEMS FOR CASH

Earlier we described the broad control objectives of accounting systems:

1. Goals are achieved (effectiveness).
2. Only necessary costs are incurred in achieving goals (efficiency).
3. Activities are conducted only in accordance with management's policies, and all transactions are preauthorized.
4. The assets of the business are safeguarded.
5. The financial reports used by management and prepared for outside users are reliable.

Different areas of an overall control system will emphasize these broad objectives to different degrees. Because employees and others can readily convert cash to personal use, cash control systems predominantly focus on *safeguarding cash* (objective 4). However, a business cannot safeguard its cash unless employees *conform strictly to company policies (objective 3) and maintain reliable records* (objective 5). So, good cash control systems must meet three of the five major control objectives.

Illustration 7-1 gives you an overview of the major components of a cash control system. An overall **cash control system** includes both strong cash receipts and strong cash disbursements controls. Using a bank checking account physically protects cash reserves and disbursements. A checking account is so crucial to cash control that we do not consider cases where this essential control is absent. When a business uses a checking account, the only significant amounts of cash employees actually handle are cash receipts, which should be deposited promptly in the bank. All significant payments should be made by check, and minor expenditures should be made with a petty cash fund. The monthly bank statement is the bank's independent record of the cash transactions and the cash balance. A business should use the bank statement monthly to verify its recorded cash balance by preparing a schedule known as a bank reconciliation.

ILLUSTRATION 7-1 Overview of a Cash Control System

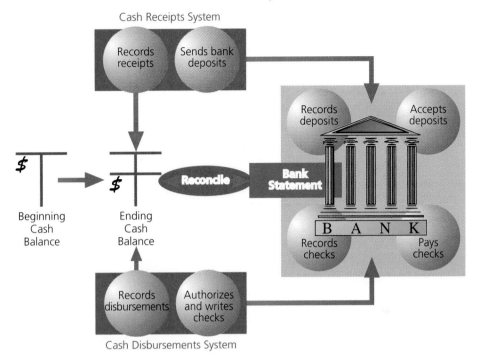

CONTROL OF CASH RECEIPTS

Processing cash receipts consists of:

1. Receiving and recording cash at the point of receipt
2. Preparing deposit slips and depositing cash in the bank
3. Recording cash receipts in the cash receipts journal

Whenever possible (cost-effective), no employee should be allowed to perform more than one of these basic functions. By separating these responsibilities, no individual employee can commit theft of cash and avoid detection by covering up the theft in the accounting records. Employees who work independently of each other should perform verifications and reconciliations as we describe below.

Control of Cash Receipts from Credit Sales

LO 1

Describe control procedures for cash received from credit sales.

Ready Auto Parts' system for processing cash receipts on credit sales is shown in Illustration 7-2.

Receiving Cash. Generally, businesses receive cash receipts from credit sales through the mail. Businesses should discourage their customers from remitting currency or coins when paying their accounts. At Ready Auto Parts, Frank Brown's secretary, Leticia Jackson, opens the mail, separates the checks from the rest of the mail, and restrictively endorses each check immediately. A restrictive endorsement, as shown in Illustration 7-3, says that the check may only be deposited to the account of the payee business. After restrictively

ILLUSTRATION 7-2 Processing Cash Receipts from Credit Sales

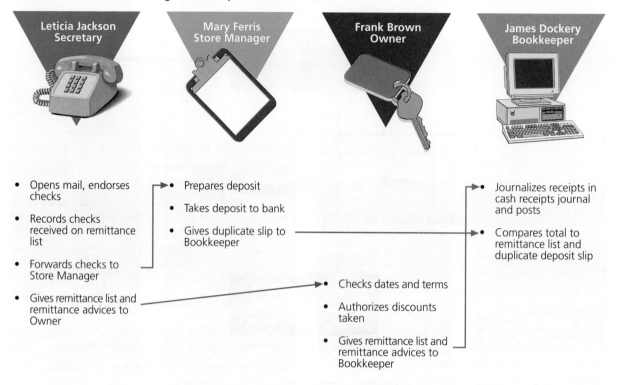

- Opens mail, endorses checks
- Records checks received on remittance list
- Forwards checks to Store Manager
- Gives remittance list and remittance advices to Owner

- Prepares deposit
- Takes deposit to bank
- Gives duplicate slip to Bookkeeper

- Checks dates and terms
- Authorizes discounts taken
- Gives remittance list and remittance advices to Bookkeeper

- Journalizes receipts in cash receipts journal and posts
- Compares total to remittance list and duplicate deposit slip

ILLUSTRATION 7-3 Restrictive Endorsement

Back of Check

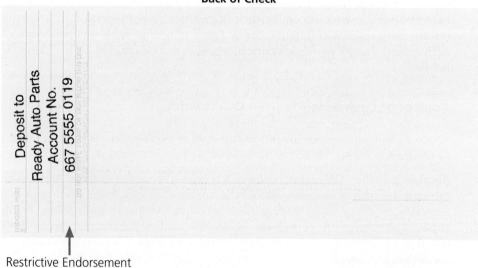

Restrictive Endorsement

endorsing the checks, Leticia enters them on a remittance list that includes the names of the companies or individuals making the payments and the amounts of the checks. After entering and double-checking all the checks, Leticia signs the remittance list, thus taking personal responsibility for its accuracy.

Depositing Cash.   Leticia immediately gives the checks to the Store Manager, Mary Ferris, who makes the bank deposits. Mary fills out deposit slips such as the one shown in Illustration 7-4. Notice that the deposit slip includes currency and coins from cash sales (discussed below) as well as checks from credit sales customers. Either Mary or Frank personally delivers the daily deposit to the bank, and Mary then gives a copy of the deposit slip to James Dockery, the bookkeeper.

Authorizing Discounts.   Leticia gives the remittance advices to Frank to review and to approve the discounts customers take. Customers should return the Ready Auto Parts' remittance advices (second copies of the original invoices sent to them) when they make payments on their accounts. When customers forget to return remittance advices with their checks, Leticia makes photocopies of the original invoices. The important point is that a document other than the check is ultimately used to record each cash receipt. This procedure separates the incompatible duties of handling the checks for deposit purposes and recording cash receipts.

Before the recording takes place, Frank compares the date of receipt of payment with the due dates for discounts, according to the terms of the original sales transaction. He approves discounts taken by initialing the discount on the remittance advice. When Frank denies a discount, he indicates so on the remittance advice, and James subsequently records only the amount of the payment in the cash receipts journal and the customer's account. The improper discount is not recognized and remains receivable from the customer.

Recording Cash Receipts.   Frank gives the remittance advices to James to enter the data using the computer program that prepares the cash receipts journal and posts cash receipts to the individual accounts receivable ledger accounts. James uses the program to print a list of the day's entries and to reconcile the list total with the deposit slips and the remittance listing forwarded to him by Mary and Frank, respectively. He corrects any entry errors he has made and reports other discrepancies to Frank immediately.

How Controls Protect Cash Received.   Even in a small business like Ready Auto Parts, control over cash receipts is built not just on the trustworthiness of key employees, but also on basic controls. In Illustration 7-2 and the discussion above, Mary handles checks received only after they are restrictively endorsed, and she does not record cash receipts transactions. James, on the other hand, enters the cash receipts into the computer, but he does not handle any cash. Neither of these employees can take cash from the business and cover up the theft without the cooperation of another employee. The **separation of incompatible duties** works on a common-sense principle of accounting control: The likelihood that two or more employees will be dishonest is less than the likelihood that one employee will be dishonest. The separation of incompatible duties denies the single dishonest employee an easy opportunity to harm the business.

So, you might ask: "What about Leticia, who opens the mail and handles *both* the checks and the remittance advices?" Frank has employed her for many years and is absolutely sure of her honesty and integrity. However, even if his

ILLUSTRATION 7-4 Business Deposit Slip

| CASH | CURRENCY | 1,550 | 00 |
| | COIN | 45 | 50 |

DEPOSIT SLIP
Ready Auto Parts
105 S. Main
Twin City, MO 11223-4578

Date: June 10, 19X1

North National Bank
232 North Elm Street, Twin City, MO 11223

":055500010 ":40566755550119" '4564

00-001 / 555

		Amount	
CASH	CURRENCY	1,550	00
	COIN	45	50
CHECKS	Attach list		
		3,110	00
TOTAL DEPOSIT		4,705	50

Ready Auto Parts
Remittance List

Date: 06/10/X1	Page 1	
Maker	**Amount**	
Windler Garage	530	00
Ace Repair	1,060	00
Don's Auto Repair	125	00
Vern's Body Shop	545	00
Bob's Top Shop	850	00
Total	3,110	00

judgment is wrong, according to the schematic in Illustration 7-2, there are implicit controls over her role in handling cash. As long as Leticia has no access to accounting records, if she takes checks and converts them to her own use (and destroys the remittance advices), the customers' accounts will not be credited with their payments. Eventually, Frank will try to collect what appear to be past-due accounts, and an investigation will follow. Thus, the virtual certainty of ultimate detection acts as a deterrent, albeit not a perfect one, to the person in Leticia's position in the control system.

Controlling Cash Sales

LO 2

Describe control procedures for cash received in cash sales transactions.

While cash receipts on credit sales generally involve only receipt of checks, cash sales involve the receipt of checks, currency, and coins, as well as giving change to customers. Since receipts on cash sales give rise to greater risks of employee errors and dishonesty, the procedures for controlling cash received from cash sales differ slightly from those involving credit sales. Effective control for cash sales involves the use of cash registers and separation of duties of receiving cash, depositing cash, and recording and reconciling cash received to the cash register record of cash sales. A schematic for processing cash sales is shown in Illustration 7-5.

ILLUSTRATION 7-5 Cash Sales Processing

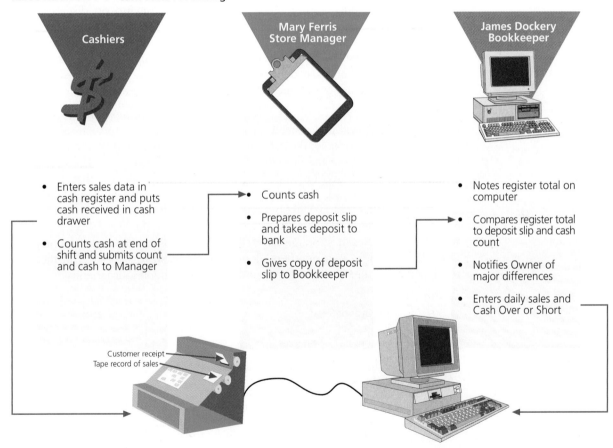

Receipt of Cash Using Cash Registers. Cashiers at Ready Auto Parts enter each cash sale into electronic cash registers at the time of sale. As cashiers enter the amounts, customers can see them on a display. As a cash register receives the information entered, it prints this information and the total of each sale on two tapes. One tape provides sales receipts to customers. Because customers generally will pay only for the amount on the receipts, the register cashier is not able to collect more cash than is recorded and keep the difference. The other tape is locked in (inaccessible to the cashier) and keeps a paper record of the sales made with the register. The cash register totals the sales keyed in for a particular shift or for the day and prints the total to the locked-in tape. The cash register is also connected to Ready Auto Parts' computer network, and it transmits its totals to a computer as well. At the end of the shift or end of the day, each cashier is required to count the cash in his or her cash drawer and turn it over to the Store Manager, Mary Ferris.

Depositing Cash. Mary Ferris recounts the cash to check on the accuracy of the cashiers' counts and includes the coins, currency, and checks collected in the daily deposit. As shown in Illustration 7-5, she gives a copy of the deposit slip to the Bookkeeper, James Dockery.

Reconciling Cash Sales to Deposits. James has access to the cash register totals through his computer. He compares the register totals to the cash count on the deposit slip and calls any significant discrepancies to Frank's attention immediately.

Recording Cash Sales. After reconciling and following up on discrepancies, James enters the (corrected) cash count from the deposit slip into the computer, which then records it in the cash receipts journal file. Typically, cash sales are recorded in the cash receipts journal file as a single sum for each day. Minor discrepancies between cash deposited and the cash sales per the cash register tapes are recorded as "cash over or short."

Recording Cash Over or Short. Regardless of how honest and careful the cashiers are, they will make small errors in handling cash from cash sales. Thus, at the end of the workday, the amount of cash sales indicated by the cash register total will differ from the amount of cash on hand for deposit. The discrepancy is recorded in an account called Cash Over or Short. Assume that at the end of business on June 10, 19X1, the cash register total of Ready Auto Parts indicates cash sales of $1,597.75, but the cash listed on the deposit slip is only $1,595.50, meaning that there is a cash shortage for the day of $2.25. James would enter the cash shortage as well as the deposit total, and the computer would record these two numbers along with the cash register total in the cash receipts journal file. The effect is the same as this general journal entry:

June 10	Cash	1,595.50	
	Cash Over or Short	2.25	
	Cash Sales		1,597.75
	To record day's cash sales.		

On the other hand, if cash sales had been $1,593.25, the amounts recorded effectively would be:

June 10	Cash	1,595.50	
	Cash Over or Short		2.25
	Cash Sales		1,593.25
	To record day's cash sales.		

Over time, the cash shortages and the cash overages should be about equal. Of course, any individually large daily shortages or overages should be investigated—as should any large *cumulative* debit or credit balances in Cash Over or Short. At the end of an accounting period, the balance of Cash Over or Short is closed to Income Summary. In the income statement, a debit balance in

Cash Over or Short is shown as part of selling expense or miscellaneous expense. A credit balance is shown as a part of miscellaneous revenue.

Separation of Incompatible Duties.   While Ready Auto Parts' accounting system is not foolproof, the separation of incompatible duties for cash sales should be reasonably effective. James, who has access to the cash register totals, does not have access to the cash. On the other hand, the cashiers and Mary, who physically handle the cash, do not have access to the cash register totals.

If employees with access misappropriate cash, their actions would be detected almost immediately. James would notice a significant discrepancy between the amount of the cash register total and the cash count per the deposit slip—more than would be explained by ordinary cash over or short. He would immediately take his findings to Frank, the owner. The internal cash register tapes serve as a backup in case of an electronic problem with a cash register or the computer network. They are saved for a few months, and Frank occasionally compares a day's tape total to the daily entry in the cash receipts file. This is a reasonable overall check on all the personnel involved in handling and recording cash sales.

CONTROLLING CASH DISBURSEMENTS

LO 3

Describe control procedures for cash disbursements, including the voucher system and voucher documents.

Controlling cash disbursements requires some fairly sophisticated accounting controls. They focus not only on the direct expenditure of funds, but also on the acquisition of goods and services. It makes little difference to a business whether an employee steals cash directly from a cash register or indirectly. For example, an employee might submit fake purchase documents, and the business would issue a check to the employee or to the employee's business without receiving any goods or services in exchange.

Voucher System

To integrate controls over acquisitions and expenditures, many businesses use the voucher system. The **voucher system** takes its name from the word *vouch*, which means to support (with evidence or testimony). The **voucher** is the document on which relevant data about an obligation to pay are summarized for approval, recording, and payment. Illustration 7-6 is the voucher for the June 2, 19X1, receipt by Ready Auto Parts of a shipment of mufflers purchased from Quiet Mufflers, Inc. Some small businesses use the voucher system without having a separate voucher document. They merely use a stamp that makes an impression on the supplier's invoice. The impression is a condensed voucher form that employees fill out right on the face of the invoice. This is a simple, cost-saving alternative to the full voucher documentation.

Processing Purchases

Vouchers represent purchase transactions and cash disbursements for both goods and services. They are supported by purchase requisitions, purchase orders, receiving reports, and supplier invoices. The individual responsible for maintaining stocks on hand submits a **purchase requisition**, a request to purchase needed goods. For example, John Thomas, inventory manager, requisi-

ILLUSTRATION 7-6 Voucher

(Front of Voucher)

Ready Auto Parts
Voucher

Payee:	Quiet Mufflers, Inc.	Voucher No:	**10001**
Address:	666 S. Second Avenue		
	Rockport, ME 11223	Date:	06/02/X1
		Date Due:	06/12/X1
Terms:	2/10, n/30	Check No.	221

Date	Invoice Number	Description	Amount
06/02/X1	INV606076	250 Universal Mufflers	5,000

Attach Supporting Document

Supporting Documents Attached____*CLM*____
Amount and Terms Correct____*CLM*____   Approved____*MF*____

(Back of Voucher)

Debit to Account	Amount
754 Purchases	5,000
776 Transportation-In	
Other Accounts:	
Number Name	
Credit to 212 Vouchers Payable	5,000
Distribution Reviewed and Approved *MF*	

Date Due:	06/12/X1
Amount:	5,000
Discount:	100
Check Amount:	4,900
Payment Approved:	*FB*
Check Number:	221

tioned the mufflers Ready purchased. John reviews the existing stocks of goods in the store and reorders them when necessary. A **purchase order**, a formal offer to buy goods, is sent to the supplier after a person with authority approves the transaction. A clerk prepares purchase orders at Ready Auto Parts and Mary Ferris, store manager, approves them. A **receiving report**, a document completed by the employees who physically receive goods on the business's behalf, contains evidence of the quantities and condition of goods actually received from suppliers. John Thomas signs receiving reports when goods are received. The **supplier's invoice**, the supplier's billing document, contains the descriptions, quantities shipped and prices of goods, the total amount owed, and the terms of credit.

Preparing Vouchers.   Illustration 7-7 presents a schematic of a system for preparing vouchers and controlling cash disbursements, once purchased goods are received. At Ready Auto Parts, office assistants working for Mary Ferris prepare vouchers from the basic information on the supplier's invoice. They compare the invoice to the requisition, purchase order, and the receiving report so the business recognizes liabilities and pays suppliers only for goods and services actually ordered and received. Only originals or carbon copies of supporting documents are accepted (no photocopies) to reduce the chance of duplicate payments. The assistants also enter on the back of the voucher the "account distribution" of the transaction—the appropriate accounts and amounts to be debited in recording the purchase. (See Illustration 7-6.)

ILLUSTRATION 7-7 Voucher Processing Schematic

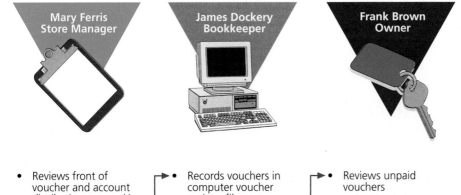

Mary Ferris Store Manager	James Dockery Bookkeeper	Frank Brown Owner	Leticia Jackson Secretary
• Reviews front of voucher and account distribution prepared by her assistant • Approves vouchers for recording • Runs tape of approved vouchers • Forwards vouchers with supporting documents attached and tape to Bookkeeper	• Records vouchers in computer voucher register file • Places vouchers in Unpaid Vouchers File in Frank's office • Reconciles list of daily entries of vouchers to tape	• Reviews unpaid vouchers • Approves payment and payment date • Gives vouchers to Leticia for check preparation • Signs checks after preparation by Leticia • Reconciles Unpaid Vouchers File to Vouchers Payable monthly	• Prepares checks for vouchers using a computer program that records checks in disbursements file and prints check register • Marks vouchers "paid" • Files vouchers • Forwards checks to Frank for signing

Approving Vouchers for Recording.   Mary Ferris examines the underlying documentation attached to each voucher and checks the voucher and the account distribution on the back for accuracy. If satisfied, she initials both sides of the voucher, indicating that it is approved for recording. She also runs a tape of the totals of all vouchers approved for recording each day and passes the tape along to James Dockery with the vouchers.

Recording Vouchers.   James Dockery enters the information on the vouchers into his computer using a program that maintains a voucher file and prepares and prints the voucher register (journal). The printed voucher register is shown in Illustration 7-8.

ILLUSTRATION 7-8 Voucher Register

VOUCHER REGISTER

Page 1

DATE		VOUCHER NUMBER	PAYEE	CHECK NO.	DATE	VOUCHERS PAYABLE CR.	PURCHASES DR.	TRANSPOR-TATION-IN DR.	OTHER ACCOUNT DR.		
									NAME	NO.	AMOUNT
19X1											
June	2	10001	Quiet Mufflers, Inc.	221	06/12/X1	5,000	5,000				
	4	10002	Carter Trucking	219	06/05/X1	125		125			
	10	10003	Western Utility District	220	06/11/X1	1,000	1,000				
	12	10004	Spencer Supplies	222	06/15/X1	250			Office Supplies	136	250
	15	10005	Clear Auto Glass	223	06/25/X1	6,500	6,500				
	17	10006	Roller-Ball Bearings	225	06/26/X1	3,500	3,500				
	19	10007	Swift Transit	224	06/22/X1	90		90			
	23	10008	Flexible Rubber Products			560	560				
	30	10009	United Parcel Service	226	06/30/X1	25		25			
	30	10010	Daily Alarmist	227	06/30/X1	200			Advertising Exp.	700	200
	30	10011	U.S. Postmaster			350			Miscellaneous Exp.	738	350
	30	10012	Wireless Phone Co.			1,050			Telephone Exp.	775	1,050
						18,650	16,560	240			1,850

Unlike the purchases journal illustrated in an earlier chapter, the voucher register records obligations for all kinds of goods and services. Every acquisition of goods or required payment for services is recorded at the first opportunity, whether it is due the day it is recorded or at some time in the future. Every item results in an entry in the Vouchers Payable Cr. column. Purchases of merchandise and Transportation-In have separate debit columns and all other debits, including supplies and expenses, are recorded in the Other Account Dr. column.

At the end of the month, the computer program summarizes the entries in the voucher register and updates the general ledger file (which, in Ready's computer system, is equivalent to posting to the general ledger accounts). However, Ready Auto Parts does not use an accounts payable subsidiary ledger. Instead, James Dockery places recorded vouchers in order of the date payment is due in the Unpaid Vouchers File in Frank's office; and the computer provides Frank with an Unpaid Vouchers List organized in the same order.

The Unpaid Voucher File serves two purposes. First, its due-date order ensures timely payment of obligations and taking as many discounts as possible. Second, it also represents the details supporting the balance in the general ledger Vouchers Payable at any time. When the computer completes all posting at the end of a month, Frank compares the sum of the unpaid vouchers to the balance of the general ledger Vouchers Payable and investigates discrepancies.

Approving Vouchers for Payment.   Reviewing vouchers on the day they are due, Frank focuses primarily on the validity of the attached documents. He indicates his approval by writing his initials in the appropriate place on the back of the vouchers and then passes them along to Leticia for check preparation. After Leticia prepares the checks, she presents them to Frank for signature.

Paying Vouchers.   Leticia Jackson prepares checks like the one in Illustration 7-9 for all approved vouchers. Notice that an extension document, called a remittance advice, is attached to the bottom of the check. The **remittance advice** notifies the payee of the purpose of the payment so that Ready Auto Parts' account with the payee will be credited properly. Leticia uses a computer program that permits her to select the vouchers to be paid from the Unpaid Voucher List. The computer prints the checks and enters the data on payment

ILLUSTRATION 7-9 Business Check with Attached Remittance Advice

Ready Auto Parts
105 S. Main
Twin City, MO 11223-4578

221

00-001
555

June 12   19 X1

PAY TO THE
ORDER OF Quiet Mufflers, Inc. $ 4,900.00

Four thousand nine hundred and 00/100————————————DOLLARS

North National
232 North Elm Street, Twin City, MO
11223

Frank Brown

MEMO

":055500010 ":40566755550119" '0221

REMITTANCE ADVICE			Ready Auto Parts	
Date	P.O. No.	Description		Amount
06/12/X1	PO67561	250 Universal Mufflers (Terms: 2/10, n/30) Your Invoice No. INV606076		$5,000.00
		Less applicable discount		100.00
		Net		$4,900.00

into a simplified cash disbursements file from which the **check register**, shown in Illustration 7-10, is printed. Recall that all expenditures are first recorded as liabilities and the related asset or expense accounts are updated (debited) by the program that prepares the voucher register. Thus, actual expenditures involve only debits to Vouchers Payable and credits to Cash and Purchases Discounts (where applicable).

After the computer prepares and records the checks, Leticia marks the voucher and all the attached documents "Paid" to prohibit their use another time to support duplicate payments. She presents the checks (with the vouchers) to Frank for signature and then mails them to the payees. Finally, she files the paid vouchers by payee.

LO 4
Describe the operation of a petty cash fund and record petty cash expenditures in the accounting proceeds.

PETTY CASH FUND

Although businesses should make most of their cash payments by check, some expenditures are too small to justify the expense and time of preparing a voucher, securing the necessary approvals, and writing a check. Thus, many businesses use a **petty cash fund** from which to make small cash payments.

ILLUSTRATION 7-10 Check Register

CHECK REGISTER

Page 1

DATE		CHECK NO.	CHECK CLEARED[1]	PAYEE	VOUCHER NUMBER	VOUCHERS PAYABLE DR.	PURCHASES DISCOUNTS CR.	CASH CR.
19X1								
June	3	218	✔	Reliable Brake Pads	10000	7,500	150	7,350
	5	219	✔	Carter Trucking	10002	125		125
	11	220	✔	Western Utility District	10003	1,000		1,000
	12	221	✔	Quiet Mufflers, Inc.	10001	5,000	100	4,900
	15	222	✔	Spencer Supplies	10004	250		250
	25	224	✔	Clear Auto Glass	10005	6,500	130	6,370
	22	223		Swift Transit	10007	90		90
	26	225	✔	Roller-Ball Bearings	10006	3,500	70	3,430
	30	226		United Parcel Service	10009	25		25
	30	227		Daily Alarmist	10010	200		200
				Totals		24,190	450	23,740

Setting Up the Petty Cash Fund

Frank Brown decided to establish a petty cash fund on July 1, 19X1. He estimated that $75 should be sufficient for one month's operation of the fund. He gave Leticia Jackson an approved voucher debiting Petty Cash and asked her to prepare a check for his signature payable to "Cash" in the amount of $75. He also asked her to cash the check and to set up and run the petty cash fund. She keeps the petty cash fund in a small metal cash box locked in her desk. Leticia entered the check in the check register, but its effect together with the entry in the voucher register can best be illustrated with a single equivalent general journal entry:

July 1	Petty Cash	75.00	
	Cash		75.00
	To establish a petty cash fund to be managed by Leticia Jackson.		

The effect of the entry is to transfer $75 from Cash to Petty Cash. Once the petty cash fund is established and recorded, Petty Cash is not debited or credited until the amount of the fund is changed. The amount of the fund is changed when experience indicates that the original amount of the fund is either too small or too large.

Expenditures from Petty Cash

When she makes a payment out of the petty cash fund, Leticia requires the person receiving the cash to sign a **petty cash receipt**. On the petty cash receipt, Leticia records the date, the amount of the expenditure, what the expenditure is for, and the account to which the expenditure should ultimately be posted. As

---

[1]The Check Cleared column in the check register is used to note which checks have cleared (have been paid by) the bank as part of the bank reconciliation explained later in the chapter.

shown in Illustration 7-11, the petty cash receipt also has a space for Leticia's signature as the person with the authority to approve petty cash expenditures.

ILLUSTRATION 7-11 Petty Cash Receipt

Petty Cash Receipt

Date: _____7/20/X1_____   Receipt No.: _____5_____

Amount: _____$3.14_____

For: _____Typewriter ribbon_____   _____Judy Gold_____
                                                              Received by

Charge to: _____Office Supplies_____   _____Leticia Jackson_____
                                                              Approved by

Leticia places the petty cash receipts in the cash box with the remaining cash. Therefore, *the sum of the petty cash receipts and the remaining cash should always equal the amount of the petty cash fund.* This feature provides an element of control over the use of the petty cash fund. When Leticia performs a count, the amount of cash in the fund should equal the amount at which the fund is established less the amount of the petty cash receipts.

Replenishment of Petty Cash

At the end of July, Leticia lists the petty cash receipts:

Receipt no.	Purpose	Amount	Debit account
1	Postage stamps	$22.00	Office Supplies
2	Freight on purchase	7.50	Transportation-In
3	Flowers for office party	15.75	Miscellaneous Expense
4	Coffee service	12.60	Miscellaneous Expense
5	Typewriter ribbon	3.14	Office Supplies
6	Freight on purchase	9.89	Transportation-In
	Total	$70.88	

Only $4.12 remains in the petty cash fund, a balance which probably is insufficient to make another payment. To replenish the fund, Leticia gives the petty cash receipts to Mary Ferris, who prepares a voucher. Frank approves the voucher after reviewing the petty cash expenditures and has Leticia prepare another check payable to "Cash" for $70.88. She cashes the check and puts the $70.88 in the petty cash box, restoring the fund to its original amount of $75. James Dockery would enter the voucher into the voucher register, but the effect on the accounts of replenishing the fund can best be seen in general journal form as follows:

July 31	Office Supplies	25.14	
	Transportation-In	17.39	
	Miscellaneous Expense	28.35	
	Cash		70.88
	To record the replenishment of the petty cash fund.		

The entry debits the asset and expense accounts that are affected by the cash payments and reduces Cash. Occasionally, the petty cash receipts and remaining balance do not sum to the proper amount—the amount of the petty cash fund. Small discrepancies are debited or credited to Cash Over and Short when the fund is replenished.

Because the entry to replenish petty cash is necessary to record the effects of petty cash payments, it is preferable to replenish the petty cash fund at the end of every accounting period, whether or not the fund is exhausted. Technically, failure to do so results in overstating the amount of Cash and understating the assets and expenses resulting from the petty cash payments in the financial statements. However, the amounts usually are too small to make a material difference, and it may be cost-effective to replenish the fund only as needed. In the balance sheet, petty cash generally is combined with the other cash accounts and the total is shown as the Cash balance.

THE BANK STATEMENT

Once each month, banks mail statements to their depositors. A **bank statement** lists the activity in the depositor's bank account for a month. The bank statement reports the items listed at the top of the next page.

INSIGHTS INTO ACCOUNTING

Separation of Incompatible Duties

Below are the first two paragraphs from an actual memo dated February 18, 1994, to all administrators from the Vice President of Business Affairs of a major state university.

Embezzlement. As a result of a major cash loss which recently led to criminal charges against a University employee, a special committee of accountants and auditors has been formed to review and improve University fiscal controls (internal controls). Without delay, however, I want to ask all individuals who have responsibility for University accounts to be aware of several specific fiscal practices which should be followed.

[Payments for] Goods and Services. There should be a clear separation of assigned duties between individuals who are involved in ordering, receiving, and processing payments for goods and services. That is, the same person should not be authorized to (1) place orders for goods/services, (2) certify that goods/services have been received, and (3) approve payment vouchers. It is best to have a different person perform each of these functions, but, as a minimum, the person who certifies that goods and services have been received should not also be authorized to sign and process payment vouchers. Obviously, if a person is in a position to process a payment for goods/services which have not actually been received, internal controls are not adequate to avoid embezzlement.

1. The account balance at the beginning of the month
2. Deposits for the month
3. Checks the bank paid during the month
4. Monthly bank service charges and fees for certain transactions
5. The account balance at the end of the month

The information reported in the bank statement is based on the bank's records. Since the customer's account is a liability of the bank, increases such as deposits are called credits and decreases such as paid checks are called debits (or charges). A bank statement is shown in Illustration 7-12.

The bank includes several documents when it mails the statement to the depositor. The depositor's paid checks and copies of any debit or credit memoranda applied to the depositor's account are sent with the statement. The checks returned with the statement are the depositor's checks that the bank paid during the month. The paid checks returned with the statement are commonly called **canceled checks** because at the time of payment the bank either stamps or perforates the checks to indicate that they have been paid. The debit and credit memoranda are the bank's notifications that the depositor's account has been decreased or increased for certain transactions the bank has handled. A **debit memorandum** reports a decrease in the account for such things as previous bank credit errors or service charges and fees. A **credit memorandum** reports an increase in the depositor's account for such things as previous bank debit errors and notes receivable the bank has collected for the depositor.

When a business deposits all cash receipts in the bank and makes cash disbursements with checks, it may use the bank statement to verify the balance in Cash and recorded cash receipts and cash disbursements. However, only rarely will the ending balance shown on the bank statement agree with the balance of Cash. There are two principal reasons why the two amounts may not be equal:

1. The bank often records checks, deposits, and other increases and decreases in cash on dates different than the ones the business records.
2. Either the bank or the business may have made errors.

Therefore, verifying Cash involves **reconciling** it to the bank balance. At Ready Auto Parts, Frank Brown reconciles the bank account to Cash each month. The bank reconciliation process permits Frank to discover errors or omissions that got by his cash controls. Large discrepancies will alert him to possible employee theft or fraud.

THE BANK RECONCILIATION

A **bank reconciliation** is a schedule that adjusts the company's cash balance and the balance on the bank statement until they each equal the correct amount of cash as of a given date. The bank reconciliation for Ready Auto Parts is shown in Illustration 7-13.

The reconciliation starts with the balance in Cash on June 30, 19X1, $19,958.58. This figure is corrected for unrecorded items and for any errors Ready committed in accounting for its cash. After the adjustments, the correct balance is $19,543.58. In the lower half of the bank reconciliation, the same procedure is followed, starting with the balance from the bank statement in Illustration 7-12 of $17,343.91 and ending with the correct figure of $19,543.58.

ILLUSTRATION 7-12 Bank Statement

Closing Date:	June 30, 19X1
Statement Date:	July 6, 19X1
Account No.:	66755550119

STATEMENT OF ACCOUNT

Ready Auto Parts
105 S. Main
Twin City, MO 11223

	No.	Total
Previous Balance:		9,865.71
Credits:	15	36,145.20
Debits:	14	28,667.00
New Balance:		17,343.91

Checks				Deposits	Date	Balance
					05/31/X1	9,865.71
213	2,525.00	214	637.00	3,531.25	06/02/X1	10,234.96
216	50.00			1,567.83	06/03/X1	11,752.79
NSF	500.00	215	325.00	2,547.12	06/05/X1	13,474.91
218	7,650.00	219	125.00	1,715.15	06/08/X1	7,415.06
				4,705.50	06/10/X1	12,120.56
				2,424.56	06/11/X1	14,545.12
220	1,000.00	221	4,900.00	1,935.80	06/15/X1	10,580.92
				3,598.99	06/17/X1	14,179.91
222	250.00			2,654.33	06/18/X1	16,584.24
				3,636.96	06/23/X1	20,221.20
217	900.00			2,161.89	06/25/X1	21,483.09
				4,286.37	06/26/X1	25,769.46
224	6,370.00	225	3,430.00	1,316.45	06/29/X1	17,285.91
DM	5.00			CM 63.00	06/30/X1	17,343.91

Please refer any discrepancies within ten days for correction.

DM   Debit Memo
CM   Credit Memo
NSF Not Sufficient Funds

LO 5

Identify the reconciling items that make the business's cash balance differ from the balance on its bank statement.

Finding the Reconciling Items for a Bank Reconciliation

To prepare a bank reconciliation, you must first find the reconciling items and their amounts. If a business's cash balance does not agree with the balance on its bank statement, the difference implies that cash receipts disagree with the credits recorded on the bank statement and/or cash disbursements (checks

ILLUSTRATION 7-13 Bank Reconciliation

Ready Auto Parts Bank Reconciliation June 30, 19X1		
Balance per books, June 30, 19X1		$19,958.58
Add: Bank credit for previous excess charges	$ 63.00	
Error in recording Check No. 219	27.00	90.00
		$20,048.58
Less: NSF check of Sterling Auto Body	$ 500.00	
Service charge for NSF check	5.00	505.00
Correct cash balance		$19,543.58
Balance per bank, June 30, 19X1		$17,343.91
Add: Deposit-in-transit at June 30, 19X1	$2,214.67	
Bank error in recording Check No. 218	300.00	2,514.67
		$19,858.58
Less: Outstanding checks:		
No. 223	$ 90.00	
No. 226	25.00	
No. 227	200.00	315.00
Correct cash balance		$19,543.58

issued) disagree with the charges on the bank statement. You will find the reconciling items and their amounts by organizing your search into two phases.

Compare Bank Debits to Checks Issued. When he receives the monthly bank statement, Frank Brown makes a detailed comparison between the debits in the bank statement and the checks issued during the month or on the outstanding check list of the previous month. He traces each check appearing on a bank statement to the check register to be sure the bank has charged the correct amount. When Frank performs this procedure, he places a check mark (✔) in the "Check Cleared" column of that check's entry in the check register. The comparison of bank charges to checks issued will turn up three types of possible discrepancies:

1. Outstanding checks. **Outstanding checks** are those the business has issued and recorded but which have not been presented to the bank for payment. These checks have not appeared as charges on a bank statement and are easily identified as the checks that have not been ✔-marked in the Checks Cleared column of the check register.
   Example. Ready Auto Parts had issued the following checks during June 19X1, that the bank had not paid as of June 30:

Check No. 223, issued 06/22	$ 90.00
Check No. 226, issued 06/30	25.00
Check No. 227, issued 06/30	200.00

2. Bank charges. **Bank charges** may be made for check printing charges, other service charges, fees, and for previously deposited checks that have been refused for lack of funds by the banks that they are drawn on. The latter are called **NSF** (nonsufficient funds) **checks**. The former are represented by debit memorandums (DMs) the bank returns with the

statement. DMs should be reviewed carefully to make certain that the charges are proper and that the amounts are reasonable. *Example.* Ready deposited a check for $500 from one of its customers on June 2. When the bank tried to collect from that customer's bank, it was refused due to nonsufficient funds. The bank charged (debited) this item back to Ready's account on June 5 and charged a $5 fee at the end of the month for handling it.

3. Errors. Either the company or the bank may have made errors in recording checks, fees, or charges. *Example.* Ready erroneously recorded Check No. 219 at $152, instead of the correct amount, $125. The bank recorded the check correctly on June 8. The bank erroneously recorded Check No. 218 at $7,650 on June 8. Ready correctly recorded it at $7,350.

Compare Bank Credits to Deposits.   Frank also compares deposits per the company's books and deposits-in-transit from last month's reconciliation to deposits per the bank statement. This examination will also turn up three types of possible discrepancies.

1. Deposits-in-transit. **Deposits-in-transit** are amounts the company deposits in the bank but which the bank does not record until the next period. They usually occur on the last day of business of a period. The company closes for the day, prepares its deposit, and takes it to the bank. The bank has an after-hours deposit box that receives deposits after closing time. The bank records the deposit as of the next day, the first day of a new period. *Example.* Ready dropped a deposit of $2,214.67 in the bank's night deposit box on June 30. The bank did not record the deposit until July 1.

2. Bank credits. Bank credits are credits the bank makes to the customer's account, of which the customer was unaware. Banks often collect notes receivable and deposit them directly for their customers. Another such credit is a correction of a past debit error by the bank. The bank sends credit memorandums (CMs) with the bank statements describing such items. *Example.* On June 30 the bank credited Ready's account with a refund of $63.00 of previous excessive service charges that Ready had previously recorded as bank charges.

3. Errors. Either the bank or the company may have made errors in recording deposits or other credits. *Example.* In the case at hand, neither Ready nor the bank made errors of this type.

LO6

Follow the steps required to prepare a bank reconciliation and record any needed adjustments in the accounting records.

Preparing a Bank Reconciliation

As noted earlier, a bank reconciliation is composed of two parts. The first part is prepared by reconciling the business's cash balance to the correct amount; the second part is prepared by reconciling the bank balance to the correct amount. Thus, at the end of the reconciliation process, the correct balance per the company's books should equal the correct balance per the bank. If not, an error has been made and the process should be reviewed.

Part 1. *Start with the cash balance per the company's books.*   That is, the debit balance of the general ledger Cash account as of the date of the reconciliation, after the cash receipts and cash disbursements journals have been summarized and the totals for the period have been posted to Cash. This is illustrated in the top half of Illustration 7-13. *Example.* Ready's Cash balance in its general ledger account on June 30 was $19,958.58.

Add:
1. Credits from the bank statement that have not yet been recorded as debits to Cash. *Example.* The bank credited Ready with $63 for past excessive charges.
2. Errors discovered *in the company's records* that tended to understate the cash balance—for example, understated deposits or overstated checks. *Example.* Ready overstated Check No. 219 by $27 (thus, understating its cash balance).

Subtract:
1. Debits from the bank statement that have not yet been recorded as credits to Cash. *Example.* The bank charged Ready for an NSF check of $500 and a handling fee of $5.
2. Errors discovered *in the company's records* that tended to overstate the cash balance—for example, overstated deposits or understated checks. *Example.* None in this case.

Calculate the correct cash balance. *Example.* The correct cash balance for Ready as of June 30 is $19,543.58. See the last figure in the top half of Illustration 7-13.

Part 2. *Start with the cash balance per the bank statement.* This stage is illustrated in the bottom half of Illustration 7-13. *Example.* The bank balance from the statement in Illustration 7-12 is $17,343.91.

Add:
1. Deposits-in-transit. *Example.* There was a deposit-in-transit of $2,214.67 that the bank recorded after June 30.
2. Errors discovered *in the bank statement* that tended to understate the bank balance—for example, understated deposits or overstated checks. *Example.* The bank recorded Check No. 218 at $300 in excess of the correct amount.

Subtract:
1. Outstanding checks. *Example.* There were three outstanding checks (223, 226, and 227) totaling $315 at June 30.
2. Errors discovered *in the bank statement* that tended to overstate the cash balance—for example overstated deposits or understated checks. *Example.* None in this case.

Calculate the correct cash balance. *Example.* The correct cash balance for Ready as of June 30 is $19,543.58.

Adjusting Cash for Errors and Omissions

After completing the bank reconciliation, the company should adjust Cash to the correct balance. For Ready Auto Parts, the bank reconciliation shows a correct cash balance of $19,543.58. However, Cash shows a balance of $19,958.58. To establish the correct balance in Cash, Ready needs to make adjustments for unrecorded items and errors in its *accounting records*. These are the amounts added to and deducted from the "Balance per books" in upper half of the bank reconciliation. Adjustments are *not* made to the accounting records for items added to and deducted from the "Balance per bank," because the bank will ultimately record these items. For example, the bank has already recorded the June 30 deposit on July 1; and it will record the outstanding checks when they are presented for payment. The adjustments for Ready are as follows:

June 30	Accounts Receivable – Sterling Auto Body	505.00	
	Cash		505.00
	To record NSF check returned by bank and related service charge ($5).		
30	Cash	27.00	
	Vouchers Payable		27.00
	To correct error in recording Check No. 219.		
30	Cash	63.00	
	Miscellaneous Expense		63.00
	To record refund of previously recorded excess service charges by the bank.		

LO 7

Describe two major categories of electronic funds transfers businesses use.

COMPUTER-ASSISTED CASH RECEIPTS AND DISBURSEMENTS

Electronic funds transfers, an innovation in cash receipts and disbursements systems, are cash payments made by computer rather than by coins, currency, or checks. Not only do electronic funds transfers dramatically increase the speed at which payments and receipts occur, but they also cost much less to process than does processing checks. In this section, we discuss two types of electronic funds transfer systems that certain businesses use.

Types of Electronic Funds Transfer Systems

Businesses use two types of electronic funds transfer systems: point-of-sale systems and automated clearing houses.

Point-of-Sale Systems. **Point-of-sale systems** are computer-based cash receipts systems that allow customers to transfer funds immediately from their bank accounts to the merchant's bank account at the time of a sale. On-line terminals that have immediate access to a bank's computer are located at checkout counters or at other locations where sales occur. Inserting a plastic bank account card into the terminal that reads the information encoded on the card, the customer keys in a personal identification number (PIN). Using a cash register or a bar-code reader connected to the terminal, the salesperson enters other information about the transaction.

If the customer and the merchant have accounts at the same bank, the bank's computer transfers the appropriate amount of funds from the customer's account to the merchant's account. If the customer's and merchant's banks are different, a switching and processing center connects the computers of the two banks. The computer at the customer's bank verifies the validity of the card, the encoded information, and whether the customer has sufficient funds in his/her account to cover the amount of the purchase. The customer's account is then reduced by the amount of the purchase, and the merchant's account is increased by the same amount. Both parties to the transaction receive a printed statement (receipt) at the time of the transaction.

Automated Clearing Houses. An **automated clearing house** is a system for the transfer of funds between banks. A traditional bank clearing house processes checks and clears the transfer of funds between banks according to the writer of each check and the payee. In an automated clearing house, the payments must enter the system in the form of electronic data, usually computer-generated magnetic tapes or disks.

For example, consider how a business could pay its suppliers through an automated clearing house. At the end of the month, the company prepares a computer tape or disk that contains information about the names of the payees, bank and customer account identification numbers for each payee, and the amount of each payment. The business then delivers the computer tape to its bank or directly to the automated clearing house. The transfers of funds between banks and adjustment of the various bank accounts take place the same as with paper checks. Because they eliminate the need for the business to write checks and for the payees to receive, endorse, deposit, and send checks, automated clearing houses are efficient.

Control Considerations

Point-of-sale systems essentially are cash receipts systems. In fact, point-of-sale systems enhance control over cash receipts from sales because employees do not physically handle cash or checks. The primary control procedure for these transactions is reconciliation. At the end of each day, a designated employee will retrieve the cash register total on the business's computer and reconcile it to actual cash receipts and the amount credited to the business's bank account directly.

Automated clearing houses, used as described above, essentially are cash disbursement systems. The control procedures for these systems are the same as those for cash disbursements systems that use checks—as discussed in this chapter. The difference is that a computer entry is made on the expenditure tape or disk file for each authorized expenditure, instead of printing a check.

LO 8
Define and interpret the acid-test ratio.

USING INFORMATION ABOUT CONTROLS AND LIQUID ASSETS

Remember Frank Brown's problem from the beginning of the chapter? While satisfied with Frank's expansion plans and the profitability of his present business, the bankers wanted a description of the controls Frank had established for his cash system, and they also wanted to discuss Ready Auto Parts' liquidity position. At their second meeting with Frank, the bankers explained that many small profitable businesses have failed because employees embezzle cash at crucial times and render the businesses unable to pay their bills. However, the bankers are satisfied—even impressed—that a small business such as Ready Auto Parts would have the kind of controls Frank had just summarized for them. So, the discussion advanced to the acid-test ratio, the final criterion the bankers wished to apply before approving Frank's loan.

Calculating the Acid-Test Ratio

The **acid-test ratio** (or **quick ratio**) compares liquid current assets to current liabilities:

$$\text{Acid-Test Ratio} = \frac{\text{Liquid Current Assets}}{\text{Current Liabilities}}$$

Liquid current assets typically consist of cash, liquid investments (certificates of deposit at banks and readily marketable securities), and net accounts receivable. The acid-test ratio is a more stringent test of a business's **liquidity** than the current ratio because it focuses only on the current assets that can be most readily converted into cash to satisfy current liabilities. In the acid-test ratio, inventories and prepaid expenses are excluded from the numerator because the ability to convert them into cash in the very short run is often doubtful.

Interpreting the Acid-Test Ratio

The acid-test ratio compares the business's liquid assets to the amount of liabilities that it will have to pay in the short run. Hence, the ratio is a measure of the business's ability to pay short-term obligations. From this perspective, the larger the ratio, the better. After reviewing all the other information Frank supplied, the bankers decided that they could accept an acid-test ratio of 1.25 or greater. At June 30, 19X1, Ready Auto Parts had a cash balance of $19,544, no liquid investments, and net accounts receivable of $40,000. Its current liabilities consisted of accounts payable of $25,600 and wages and salaries payable of $3,450. Therefore, since its acid-test ratio was more than adequate, the bankers approved the loan:

$$\text{Acid-Test Ratio} = \frac{\$59,544}{\$29,050} = 2.05$$

Limitations of the Acid-Test Ratio

While the acid-test ratio provides a measure of a business's ability to pay its short-term obligations, users of financial statement information should interpret it with care. Most importantly, the numerator of the ratio contains accounts receivable that may or may not be collectible. Those amounts not collected will not be available to pay obligations. If the business's financial statements are not audited, users of the financial statements may want to assure themselves that sound valuation principles have been applied to accounts receivable and that the amount shown in the balance sheet can reasonably be expected to be collected. A subsequent chapter covers the problems of collectibility and proper valuation of receivables.

SUMMARY

Describe control procedures for cash received from credit sales. To control cash received from credit sales, one employee should open the mail, separate all checks, restrictively endorse the checks, and prepare a remittance list of the checks. This employee should then give the checks to a second employee for deposit. Then, an employee with authority to approve discounts taken by customers should receive the remittance lists and remittance advices. The remittance advices, remittance list, and a copy of the deposit slip should be given to a fourth employee who records the remittances and reconciles the total recorded to the remittance list and the deposit slip.

Describe control procedures for cash received in cash sales transactions. Businesses should use cash registers with locked-in tapes, preferably connected directly to the computer(s) used in their accounting systems, to record cash sales. Cashiers should count their cash drawers at the end of a shift and turn their cash over to the employee who prepares the bank deposit. The employee who prepares the bank deposit should give a copy of the deposit slip to the employee who records cash receipts. The person who records cash receipts should record sales for the day equal to the amount of the cash register totals, the increase in cash in the amount of the total on the deposit slip, and the difference as cash over or short. Large daily or cumulative amounts of cash over or short should be investigated.

Describe control procedures for cash disbursements, including the voucher system and voucher documents. Businesses can achieve control of cash disbursements through use of a voucher system. Original or carbon copies (no photocopies) of requisitions, purchase orders, receiving reports, and supplier invoices should be attached to vouchers. Before being approved for recording, the vouchers should be checked carefully for agreement with the descriptions, quantities, prices, and total charges for goods and services on these underlying support documents. A separate employee should be responsible for recording the vouchers. An employee with authority should monitor vouchers in the Unpaid Voucher File to ensure timely payment and to review and approve the underlying documents before checks are prepared.

Describe the operation of a petty cash fund and record petty cash expenditures in the accounting records. Many businesses use a petty cash fund to make cash payments that are too small to be made efficiently by individual checks. The procedures employed for the operation of a petty cash fund are designed to deter employee misconduct in handling the petty cash fund and to provide documentation for recording petty cash transactions in the accounting records. Because the petty cash fund is periodically reimbursed by check, the controls of the voucher system and bank reconciliation are maintained over petty cash as well as cash in the bank.

Identify the reconciling items that make the business's cash balance differ from the balance on its bank statement. Any differences between a business's cash balance and its bank statement balance will be due to differences between its recorded receipts and the credits on its bank statement and/or differences between its recorded expenditures and the charges on its bank statement. To find the items to be used in the bank reconciliation, you should systematically compare receipts to bank credits and expenditures to bank charges. You may find credits such as bank collections of notes receivable not recorded among the receipts, charges such as those for check printing that are not recorded as expenditures, and errors in the business's cash balance. You may also find deposits-in-transit not recorded, outstanding checks that have not cleared, and errors on the bank statement.

Follow the steps required to prepare a bank reconciliation and record any needed adjustments in the accounting records. When a business uses a bank account for all cash receipts and cash disbursements, a bank reconciliation becomes an important procedure for ensuring the accuracy of the accounting records. In a bank reconciliation, the cash balance in the business's records and the bank statement balance are each reconciled to the correct cash balance. In the process, errors the business made and previously unrecorded cash receipts and disbursements are discovered, leading to adjusting entries to Cash. These adjustments never include bank errors or deposits or checks the bank has not yet recorded.

Describe two major categories of electronic funds transfers businesses use. Cash transactions can be facilitated significantly by electronic funds transfers. Point-of-sale transfers involve on-line terminals at sales check-out counters. Information about the customer and the sale are entered, and computers transfer funds directly from the customer's bank account to the seller's bank account. No currency or checks change hands. However, it is still important to reconcile total funds transferred to cash register totals. Similarly, businesses that wish to pay their bills electronically can send machine-readable files of expenditure information to automated clearing houses. There, computers read the files, and the funds to pay each bill are transferred from the payer's bank account to the payee's bank account. Once again, no cash or checks change hands. However, expenditures should still be properly documented and authorized before they are entered on the file sent to the clearing house.

Define and interpret the acid-test ratio. The acid-test ratio compares liquid current assets to current liabilities:

$$\text{Acid-Test Ratio} = \frac{\text{Liquid Current Assets}}{\text{Current Liabilities}}$$

Liquid current assets typically consist of cash, liquid investments (certificates of deposit at banks and readily marketable securities), and accounts receivable. The ratio is generally thought to be a stringent measure of the business's ability to pay short-term obligations. However, it should be interpreted with care because its numerator may contain receivables of questionable collectibility.

REVIEW PROBLEM 1: PETTY CASH

The Action Sales Company is establishing a petty cash fund to facilitate the cash payment of small amounts for which immediate cash is necessary. The petty cash fund is established on September 1, 19X3, in the amount of $150.00. The following payments were made during the month of September.

Petty Cash Voucher	Amount	Purpose
No. 1	$15.00	Transportation-In
No. 2	26.00	Computer Ribbons
No. 3	10.50	Transportation-In
No. 4	7.50	Transportation-In
No. 5	22.60	Flowers
No. 6	18.74	Stationery

The cash count of the petty cash box at the end of the month was $48.56.

REQUIRED:

a. Prepare the journal entry to establish the petty cash fund on September 1, 19X3.
b. Prepare the journal entry to reimburse the petty cash fund at the end of the business day on September 30, 19X3.

SOLUTION:

Planning and Organizing Your Work
1. To establish a petty cash fund, consider the accounts that should be debited and credited and write the necessary journal entry.
2. Sum the amounts of the petty cash receipts and the petty cash fund balance to determine if there is cash over or short.

3. Sum the receipts that apply to individual accounts. Any petty cash expenditure that cannot be identified with a specific account may be considered a miscellaneous expense.
4. Write the journal entry to replenish the petty cash fund, debiting the various asset, expense, and other accounts and crediting Cash.

(a) *Prepare the journal entry to establish fund.*

Sept. 1	Petty Cash	150.00	
	Cash		150.00
	To establish a petty cash fund.		

(b) *Prepare the journal entry to reimburse fund.*

Sept. 30	Miscellaneous Expense	22.60	
	Transportation-In	33.00	
	Office Supplies	44.74	
	Cash Over or Short	1.10	
	Cash		101.44
	To reimburse petty cash fund and record expenses paid and cash shortage.		

REVIEW PROBLEM 2: BANK RECONCILIATION

DuMont Deli began business April 1, 19X4, and opened a checking account at the Central Plaza Bank on April 2 with a deposit of $10,000. During the month, deposits of sales receipts were made totaling $15,000 and checks were written totaling $18,500. Thus, the Deli's Cash balance on April 30 was $6,500. The bank statement was received on May 4, indicating a closing date of April 30 and a closing balance of $8,860. The owner compares the canceled checks with the cash disbursements journal and finds three checks still outstanding: Number 14 to Wheaton Deli Supply for $2,986.00; Number 16 to Bost Bakeries for $48.50; and Number 17 to Central Power Corporation for $199.00.

She also discovered that Check No. 7 had been correctly written for $209.00 in payment of an account payable but had been recorded in the books at $290.00. A comparison of the cash receipts journal with the bank statement and the deposit slips identified a check deposited on April 8 in the amount of $210.00 omitted from the Deli's books and a deposit on April 30 of $1,089 that the bank had not yet recorded. The check for $210.00 was from a customer in payment of an account receivable balance. There were two debit memoranda included with the bank statement, indicating an NSF check in the amount of $35.00 from R. A. Brown and a charge for printing checks of $55.00. A credit memo indicated the interest earned for the month was $14.50.

REQUIRED:

a. Prepare a bank reconciliation for DuMont Deli as of April 30, 19X4.
b. Prepare general journal entries required to adjust Cash to the correct cash balance.

SOLUTION:

Planning and Organizing Your Work
1. Compare the charges on the bank statement with the check register and the credits on the bank statement with the cash receipts journal.
2. Identify each item in the bank reconciliation as one of the following:
   Adjustments to balance per books:
   An unrecorded bank charge to be subtracted from the balance per books.
   An unrecorded bank credit to be added to the balance per books.

An error overstating Cash to be subtracted from the balance per books.
An error understating Cash to be added to the balance per books.
Adjustments to balance per bank:
An outstanding check to be subtracted from the balance per bank.
A deposit in transit to be added to the balance per bank.
An error overstating the bank balance to be subtracted from the balance per bank.
An error understating the bank balance to be added to the balance per bank.

3. Prepare the bank reconciliation by beginning with the balance per books and adjusting it to the correct balance. Then, begin again with the balance per bank and adjust it to the correct balance. When the two "correct" balances are equal, the reconciliation is complete.
4. Write journal entries to record the adjustments to the balance per books.

(a) *Prepare a bank reconciliation.*

DuMont Deli Bank Reconciliation April 30, 19X4		
Balance per books, April 30, 19X4		$6,500.00
Add: Error in recording Check No. 7		
($209.00 recorded as $290.00)	$ 81.00	
Interest earned	14.50	
Deposit not recorded for April 8	210.00	305.50
		$6,805.50
Less: Bank charge, Check Printing	$55.00	
NSF check	35.00	90.00
Correct cash balance		$6,715.50
Balance per bank, April 30, 19X4		$8,860.00
Add: Deposit-in-transit at April 30, 19X4		1,089.00
		$9,949.00
Less: Outstanding checks:		
No. 14	$2,986.00	
No. 16	48.50	
No. 17	199.00	3,233.50
Correct cash balance		$6,715.50

(b) *Prepare journal entries.*

Apr. 30	Cash	290.00	
	Accounts Payable		290.00
	To reverse effects of Check No. 7 recorded at incorrect amount.		
30	Accounts Payable	209.00	
	Cash		209.00
	To record Check No. 7 at the correct amount.		
30	Cash	14.50	
	Interest Revenue		14.50
	To record interest revenue credited by the bank.		
30	Cash	210.00	
	Accounts Receivable		210.00
	To record a check deposited on April 8 but not recorded in cash receipts.		

30	Miscellaneous Expense	55.00	
	Cash		55.00
	To record bank charge for check printing.		
30	Accounts Receivable	35.00	
	Cash		35.00
	To record a check returned by the bank due to NSF.		

REVIEW PROBLEM 3: ACID-TEST RATIO

The balance sheet of Arapaho Products Co. included the following current assets and current liabilities:

Current assets:		Current liabilities:	
Cash	$ 3,250	Notes payable	$ 2,500
Current investments	11,200	Accounts payable	12,500
Accounts receivable (net)	14,200	Sales tax payable	1,800
Merchandise inventory	25,600	Total current liabilities	$16,800
Prepaid insurance	1,800		
Prepaid rent	6,000		
Total current assets	$62,050		

REQUIRED:

Calculate the acid-test ratio and discuss what it means to creditors.

SOLUTION:

Planning and Organizing Your Work

1. Determine which current assets meet the test of being "liquid" current assets and sum them for the numerator of the ratio.
2. Calculate the ratio.
3. Express what the specific value of the ratio means.

Acid-test ratio:

$$\frac{\$3,250 + \$11,200 + \$14,200}{\$16,800} = \frac{\$28,650}{\$16,800} = 1.7054$$

What it means:
Arapaho Products Co. has $1.71 in liquid current assets for each dollar in current liabilities. This suggests that the company is able to pay its short-term debts on time if the accounts receivables and current investments are properly valued.

KEY TERMS

acid-test ratio, *295*
automated clearing house, *294*
bank charges, *291*
bank reconciliation, *289*
bank statement, *288*
canceled checks, *289*
cash control systems, *274*
check register, *285*
credit memorandum (CM), *289*
debit memorandum (DM), *289*

deposits-in-transit, *292*
electronic funds transfers, *294*
liquidity, *296*
NSF checks, *291*
outstanding checks, *291*
petty cash fund, *285*
petty cash receipt, *286*
point-of-sale systems, *294*
purchase order, *282*
purchase requisition, *281*

quick ratio, *295*
receiving report, *282*
reconciling, *289*
remittance advice, *284*
**separation of incompatible
    duties,** *277*
supplier's invoice, *282*
voucher, *281*
voucher system, *281*

SELF-QUIZ

LO 1 1. Indicate which of the following broad control objectives of accounting systems are required in a good cash control system. (*Yes, No*)
    __a. Effectiveness in achieving goals
    __b. Efficiency in incurring costs
    __c. Activities in accordance with management's policy
    __d. Assets safeguarded
    __e. Reliable financial reports

LO 1 2. Checks received from customers should be immediately _____ _____ to protect them from risk of misappropriation.

LO 2 3. Differences between the actual cash count and the cash receipts recorded on the cash register are called ____ ____ ____ _____.

LO 2 4. Which of the following is *not* a normal element of control over cash received from cash sales transactions?
    a. Recording cash sales with a cash register
    b. Preparation of a daily cash report and cash count by the cashier
    c. Cash recount and preparation of duplicate deposit slips by someone other than the cashier
    d. Deposit of daily cash receipts by the cashier
    e. Reconciliation of cash sales to deposits

LO 3 5. Which of the following items is *not* used to ensure that a payment should be authorized?
    a. Vendor's invoice   c. Shipping report
    b. Receiving report   d. Purchase order

LO 3 6. A control against duplicate payments based on a particular voucher and its supporting documentation would be to....

LO 4 7. The contents of a petty cash box should be:
    a. Petty cash receipts
    b. Currency and coins
    c. Petty cash receipts, currency, and coins, which should total to the amount of the petty cash fund
    d. None of the above are correct.

LO 5 8. Canceled checks are checks that
    a. The company has voided before mailing due to errors made in writing the checks
    b. Have cleared the bank and that the bank has canceled because they have been paid
    c. The company has written but which the bank has returned due to a lack of sufficient funds
    d. None of the above

LO 5 9. Debit memoranda are received
    a. From the bank to indicate that a debit has been made on the bank's records to reflect a reduction in our account because of errors or fees the bank charged
    b. From the bank to indicate that it has credited our cash account at the bank and that we should debit Cash in the company books
    c. From the bank to indicate that it has increased our account at the bank
    d. None of the above

LO 5 10. Credit memoranda are received
    a. From the bank to indicate that it has debited our cash account at the bank and that we should credit Cash in the company books
    b. From the bank to indicate that a credit has been made on the bank's records to reflect an increase in our account because of errors or transactions the bank made on our behalf.
    c. From the bank to indicate that it has decreased our account at the bank.
    d. None of the above

LO 5 11. Indicate which one of the following items would be added to the "Balance per books" on a bank reconciliation.
    a. Nonsufficient funds check the bank returned
    b. Interest earned on the checking account
    c. Outstanding checks at the end of the month
    d. Deposits-in-transit

LO 6 12. Journal entries required as the result of the preparation of a bank reconciliation are taken from the reconciling items that adjust the _____ _____ _____ to the corrected cash balance.

LO 7 13. By numbering them 1 and 2, indicate which of the following are the two major categories of electronic funds transfers businesses use.
    __a. Bank clearing houses
    __b. Point-of-sale systems
    __c. Wire fund transfer systems
    __d. Federal reserve clearing houses
    __e. Automated clearing houses

LO 8 14. The acid-test ratio (quick ratio) measures:
    a. Solvency
    b. Liquidity
    c. Excess cash reserves
    d. Current assets to current liabilities

SOLUTIONS TO SELF-QUIZ

1. a. No b. No c. Yes d. Yes e. Yes   2. restrictively endorsed   3. Cash Over or Short   4. d   5. c
6. mark the voucher and supporting documentation "paid"   7. c   8. b   9. a   10. b   11. b   12. "Balance per books"   13. b is 1; e is 2.   14. b

QUESTIONS

Q7-1   Briefly explain why the control of cash is critical to the successful operation of a business.

Q7-2   Discuss what is meant by the "separation of incompatible duties" when applied to cash.

Q7-3   Explain how the separation of incompatible duties contributes to the overall control of cash.

Q7-4   Which of the following provides the appropriate steps for processing cash receipts from credit sales received through the mail?
  a. Open the mail, separate the envelopes with checks and turn them over to the office manager who removes the checks, prepares a deposit slip, and deposits them in the bank.
  b. Open the mail, separate the checks, prepare a remittance list, and turn over the checks and the remittance list to the bookkeeper for recording purposes. The book-keeper then turns the checks over to the office manager who prepares a deposit slip and makes the deposit.
  c. Open the mail and separate the checks from the rest of the mail. With each check being restrictively endorsed, record the amounts and names of the payers on a remit-tance list, total the remittance list, sign and send a copy of the list to the bookkeeper. The checks are turned over to another employee not associated with bookkeeping to prepare a deposit slip and deposit in the bank.
  d. None of the above are adequate to control cash receipts through the mail.

Q7-5   What can be done to ensure that only the discounts actually earned by customers are granted?

Q7-6   The entries in a cash receipts journal, for cash received from credit customers, are made from
  a. The individual checks since they show both the amount paid and the payer's name and address
  b. The remittance list since the checks are deposited shortly after being received
  c. The remittance advices or from photocopies of the remittance advices when cus-tomers fail to return them with their checks
  d. Copies of the customer's purchase orders

Q7-7   Cash received in the course of business should be recorded in the accounting records by
  a. The cashier
  b. The individual who prepares the bank deposit slips and makes the bank deposits
  c. Either a or b above as the cited controls are adequate
  d. Neither a nor b since they both handle cash

Q7-8   Indicate which of the following is a part of a voucher system used to control cash disbursements.
  a. A properly authorized voucher to support each check written
  b. A properly authorized voucher supported by the purchase requisition, purchase order, receiving report, and supplier's invoice
  c. Payments of vouchers payable recorded in a check register
  d. A voucher register
  e. All of the above are part of a voucher system.

Q7-9   Indicate which of the following statements is incorrect concerning a check register.
  a. In the voucher system, the check register replaces the cash disbursements journal as the special journal for cash payments.
  b. The Check Cleared column in the check register is used to note which checks have cleared the bank.
  c. The check register shows both the payee and the number of the voucher being paid as well as the number of the check being issued.
  d. The check register is used in conjunction with a cash disbursements journal.

Q7-10   Explain why Cash Over or Short would be debited if the cash received is less than that indicated by the cash register totals and why it would be credited if the cash received is greater than that of the cash register totals.

Q7-11 The petty cash fund is reimbursed at the end of the accounting period so that
   a. The amount in the fund will be sufficient to carry the firm through the first month of the new year
   b. The financial statements will not be materially misstated by omitting some of the expenses
   c. The expenses of the current year paid from the petty cash fund will be included in the current year's income statement and Petty Cash will not be overstated in the balance sheet
   d. None of the above

Q7-12 Petty Cash is
   a. Debited to record its creation
   b. Credited for expenditures made from the account
   c. Debited when it is reimbursed
   d. Credited when it is reimbursed

Q7-13 A properly completed petty cash receipt includes all of the following except
   a. Date of the payment and the amount paid
   b. Purpose of expenditure and the account to be charged
   c. The signature of the bookkeeper to validate it
   d. The signature of the person receiving the payment
   e. The signature of the petty cashier

Q7-14 Indicate which one of the following items is added to the "Balance per books" in preparing a bank reconciliation.
   a. A bank deposit representing an amount collected from a customer that was omitted from recorded cash receipts
   b. An NSF check of a customer returned by the bank
   c. A deposit-in-transit
   d. The total of the outstanding checks at month-end

Q7-15 Indicate which one of the following items is added to the "Balance per bank" in preparing a bank reconciliation.
   a. A bank deposit representing an amount collected from a customer that was omitted from recorded cash receipts
   b. An NSF check of a customer returned by the bank
   c. A deposit-in-transit
   d. The total of outstanding checks at month-end

Q7-16 Indicate which one of the following items is deducted from the "Balance per books" in preparing a bank reconciliation.
   a. A bank deposit representing an amount collected from a customer that was omitted from recorded cash receipts
   b. An NSF check of a customer returned by the bank
   c. A deposit-in-transit
   d. The total of outstanding checks at month-end

Q7-17 Indicate which one of the following items is deducted from the "Balance per bank" in preparing a bank reconciliation.
   a. A bank deposit representing an amount collected from a customer that was omitted from recorded cash receipts
   b. An NSF check of a customer returned by the bank
   c. A deposit-in-transit
   d. The total of outstanding checks at month-end

Q7-18 The correct cash balance on the bank reconciliation represents
   a. A check figure used to find errors in the books or on the bank records
   b. A total, like the total of the trial balance, which proves equality of debits and credits but does not appear elsewhere
   c. The account balance that will appear on the next month's bank statement
   d. The balance of Cash on the books after the adjustments required by the reconciliation have been journalized and posted

Q7-19 Point-of-sale systems and automated clearing houses are two types of electronic funds transfer systems some businesses use. Which two of the following statements regarding these systems are incorrect?

a. A point-of-sale system transfers funds from one business to another in settlement of accounts with the use of checks.

b. An automated clearing house transfers funds from one business to another in settlement of accounts without the use of checks by using electronic input.

c. A point-of-sale system transfers funds immediately from a customer's account to the business's account when the transaction is input using the customer's plastic bank account card at the check-out counter.

d. An automated clearing house transfers funds immediately from a customer's account to the business's account when the transaction is input using the customer's plastic bank account card at the check-out counter.

Q7-20 Indicate which of the following statements about the acid-test ratio is incorrect.

a. The numerator of the equation includes cash, liquid investments, and accounts receivable (net).

b. The acid-test ratio is a measure of a firm's "liquidity," or its ability to pay its current debt.

c. The acid-test ratio is very reliable because the items included are not subject to any valuation problems.

d. The denominator of the equation includes all of the current liabilities.

EXERCISES

LO 1   **E7-1**   **Identifying Control Procedures for Cash Received from Credit Sales**   Indicate which of the following are major components of a cash control system. (*Yes, No*)

___a.   Use of a bank checking account

___b.   Recording receipts from remittance advices

___c.   Prompt deposit of cash receipts (daily)

___d.   Making all disbursements in cash

___e.   Use of a petty cash fund

___f.   Timely recording of cash receipts

___g.   Separation of incompatible duties

___h.   Use of a remittance list

___i.   Authorization required for discounts taken

___j.   Timely preparation of bank reconciliations

LO 2   **E7-2**   **Identifying Control Procedures for Cash Received from Cash Sales**   Employee duties related to cash received from cash sales include the following:

(1) Recording the cash in the accounting records

(2) Recording the cash received in a cash register

(3) Physical receipt of the payment from the customer

(4) Making the bank deposits

(5) Preparing the bank deposit slips

Complete the following by inserting the numbers of the above statements in the proper blanks.

a. ___ is not compatible with any of the other four.

b. ___ is compatible with 2.

c. ___ is compatible with 5.

d. ___ and 3 are not compatible with 4 and _____.

LO 2   **E7-3**   **Cash Receipts from Cash Sales**   Which of the following carries the greatest risk of employee error and dishonesty? Explain why the item you select involves a significant risk. Assume that cash registers with locked-in tapes are used for cash sales.

a. An employee who does not open the mail completing deposit slips and depositing cash received from credit customers

b. An employee who does not handle cash making entries in both the cash receipts journal and the general journal

c. An employee receiving cash from customers in cash sales

d. An employee completing a daily cash report

LO 3   **E7-4   Cash Disbursements and the Voucher System**   Wheels Unlimited uses a voucher system for control of its cash disbursements. Selected transactions for September are:

Sept. 2 Issued Check No. 2021 to Winson Corp. in payment of Voucher 2117 for $2,150.00, less a 2% purchase discount.

4 Check No. 2022 was issued to Postmaster for $116.00 in payment of Voucher 2175.

7 Check No. 2023 was incorrectly completed and voided by the payments clerk.

7 Check No. 2024 was issued to Metzo Metal for $4,000.00, less a 3% purchase discount in payment of Voucher 2121.

11 Issued Check No. 2025 to Marvin Company for $600.00 in payment of Voucher 2124.

13 Check No. 2026 was issued in payment of Voucher 2176 payable to Melanie McNeal, Petty Cashier, for $474.10.

15 Issued Check No. 2027 to the IRS for $3,400.50 in payment of Voucher 2177.

18 Check No. 2028 was issued to Wilco Oil for $426.75 in settlement of Voucher 2118.

22 Check No. 2029 issued to Wilburn Parts for $2,650.00, less 5% discount in payment of Voucher 2122.

30 Issued Check No. 2030 to the Payroll Bank Account in the amount of $4,250.00 in payment of Voucher 2178.

REQUIRED:

a. Record the above transactions in a check register similar to the one in Illustration 7-10.

b. Prove the equality of the debits and credits in your check register.

LO 3,4,5   **E7-5   Cash Control Systems**   Indicate whether the following statements regarding cash control systems are True (*T*) or False (*F*).

___a.   Small cash shortages do not necessarily indicate dishonesty on the cashier's part.

___b.   A voucher register is used in conjunction with a check register.

___c.   Vouchers Payable is not a substitute for Accounts Payable when a voucher system is used.

___d.   Petty Cash is debited when the amount of the fund is to be increased.

___e.   Items added to the "Balance per books" in a bank reconciliation require an adjusting entry at the end of the month.

LO 4   **E7-6   Reimbursement of Petty Cash**   The petty cash box of Horvath, Cochran, and Co. has a cash count totalling $34.68 and petty cash receipts as follows:

Voucher	Amount	Expense Category
No. 154	$24.12	Transportation-In
No. 155	29.00	Office Supplies Expense
No. 156	5.00	Miscellaneous Expense
No. 157	24.50	Maintenance Expense
No. 158	45.20	Parts Expense
No. 159	38.42	Maintenance Expense
No. 160	39.20	Office Supplies Expense
No. 161	7.11	Miscellaneous Expense

The debit balance of Petty Cash in the general ledger is $250.00.

REQUIRED:

Prepare the journal entry to reimburse the fund on August 31, 19X3, in general journal format.

LO 5   E7-7   **Identifying Reconciling Items**   Indicate which of the following statements related to bank reconciliations is *not* correct. State why the item that you select is incorrect.

a. Credits shown on the bank statement that have not yet been recorded as debits to the company's Cash should be added to the "Balance per books."

b. Debits from the bank statement that have not yet been recorded as credits to the company's Cash should be deducted from the "Balance per books."

c. Debits to Cash that have not yet been recorded on the bank statement should be deducted from the "Balance per bank."

d. Credits to Cash that have not yet been recorded as debits on the bank statement should be deducted from the "Balance per bank."

LO 5   E7-8   **Identifying the Additions and Deductions to be Made in a Bank Reconciliation**
Indicate whether the items listed below are:

(1) Added to the "Balance per books."
(2) Deducted from the "Balance per books."
(3) Added to the "Balance per bank."
(4) Deducted from the "Balance per bank."

___a.   Outstanding checks
___b.   Funds collected by the bank for us and added to the bank account
___c.   NSF checks returned to us
___d.   Deposits-in-transit
___e.   Bank charge for printing checks
___f.   Interest earned on the checking account for the month
___g.   Bank error in omitting one of our deposits
___h.   Error in recording checks that overstated the credit to cash in the cash disbursements book

LO 6   E7-9   **Recording Adjustments from Bank Reconciliations**   Following are possible treatments of a reconciling item in a bank reconciliation:

(1) Added to the "Balance per books."
(2) Deducted from the "Balance per bank."
(3) Added to the "Balance per books."
(4) Deducted from the "Balance per bank."

REQUIRED:

a. Journal entries are required for which of the above items:

(a) 1 and 2 only   (d) 2 and 4 only
(b) 3 and 4 only   (e) All of the above
(c) 1 and 3 only

b. Explain why the items selected require journal entries.

LO 5   E7-10   **Reconciling Items**   An entry is made in the cash disbursements journal for Check No. 3110, an owner withdrawal. The check was correctly written for $615.00 and recorded in the journal for $165.00.

REQUIRED:

a. Explain how the item would be treated in a bank reconciliation.

b. Prepare the adjusting entry for the item, if necessary.

LO 5,6   **E7-11**   **Bank Reconciliation**   Use the following information to prepare a bank reconciliation at month-end:

(1) The balance per Cash in the general ledger is $4,350.00 at month-end.
(2) The list of outstanding checks totals $1,780.00.
(3) Bank service charges for the month total $85.00.
(4) Deposits-in-transit total $840.00.
(5) The bank collected $2,500 on a noninterest-bearing note receivable as our agent.
(6) The bank returned an NSF check of Bulloch Concrete Co., our customer, in the amount of $750.00.
(7) The balance per bank statement at month-end is $6,955.00.

LO 5,6   **E7-12**   **Bank Reconciliation and Adjusting Entries**   Use the following information to prepare a bank reconciliation at month-end and prepare any necessary journal entries.

(1) The closing balance per bank statement is $6,000.00.
(2) The list of outstanding checks totals $2,400.00.
(3) Bank service charges for the month total $150.00.
(4) Deposits-in-transit total $1,000.00.
(5) The bank collected $4,000 on a noninterest-bearing note for us.
(6) The bank returned an NSF check of Cullowhee Corp., our customer, in the amount of $500.00.
(7) The balance per Cash in the general ledger is $1,250.00 at month-end.

PROBLEM SET A

LO 1,2   **P7-1A**   **Controlling Cash Receipts from Credit Sales**   Ramond Barr Wholesale Appliances has two office employees, Walter and Hazel, and an accountant, Alfred. The owner, Ramond, works full-time in the business. All sales are made on credit with payment due within 10 days of the invoice date. All mail is delivered to the company office during working hours.

REQUIRED:

a. Describe the critical elements in controlling checks received through the mail.
b. Develop a set of accounting controls for Ramond Barr to handle the receipt of payments from customers through the mail that will provide for adequate separation of incompatible duties. Identify the employee performing each function in your system.

LO 3,4   **P7-2A**   **Cash Disbursements, Petty Cash, and the Voucher System**   The Vendall Company makes all disbursements by check, excluding small amounts paid out of the petty cash fund. It uses a voucher system to record the disbursements. The system requires an approved voucher accompanied by supporting documentation for each check written. All payments to be made by check are first recorded in a voucher register similar to the one shown in Illustration 7-8. The checks are recorded in a check register similar to that shown in Illustration 7-10.

The following selected transactions related to payables and disbursements are presented for Vendall for August:

Aug. 1 Purchased merchandise on account, $490.00, terms 2/10, n/30, and recorded Voucher No. 156 in the voucher register.

4 Purchased office supplies on account, $130.00, terms 1/10, n/30, and recorded Voucher No. 157 in the voucher register.

8 Purchased a 1-year insurance policy for comprehensive protection and paid the premium in advance, $300.00, recording Voucher No. 158 in the voucher register and recording Check No. 145 in the check register.

11 Recorded Check No. 146 in the check register to pay Voucher No. 156, taking the discount.

12 Established a petty cash fund for $100.00, recording Voucher No. 159 (debit to Petty Cash) in the voucher register and recording Check No. 147 in the check register.

20 Received a statement from the city for property taxes due, $867.55. Recorded Voucher No. 160 in the voucher register.

25 Paid Voucher No. 157 with Check No. 148.

31 Reimbursed the petty cash fund. The fund contained petty cash vouchers totaling $94 for miscellaneous expenses and $6 cash. Recorded Voucher No. 161 in the voucher register and recorded Check No. 149 in the check register.

REQUIRED:

Illustrate the entries in the voucher register and check register in general journal entry form. For each entry, indicate the register in which it is recorded. The August 1 transaction is shown as an example.

Example:

Aug. 1	*Voucher Register*		
	Purchases	490.00	
	Vouchers Payable (No. 156)		490.00

LO 4

P7-3A Petty Cash Funds, Operation, Reimbursement, and Journal Entries Zebra Petting Zoo frequently has to write small checks for supplies acquired. Management has decided that a petty cash fund would be appropriate to handle purchases of leftover vegetables from grocery outlets, which are fed to the animals, and for other small disbursements that arise for which immediate cash payment is necessary or desirable.

Petty cash activities for October 19X6 are presented below:

Oct. 4 The fund is started with $250.00.

9 $25.00 is disbursed to Ingles Produce Market for a pickup truck load of wilted lettuce (Petty Cash Receipt No. 001).

15 $32.00 is disbursed for 800 pounds of soft cantaloupe, Fruit Delivery Service (Receipt No. 002).

21 Postage due was disbursed to a postal worker in the amount $2.10 for a package delivered (Receipt No. 003).

26 $37.50 is disbursed for 40, fifty-pound bags of dog food in torn bags (Receipt No. 004).

30 Receipt No. 005 was completed for $2.90 to reimburse Jane Wilsong for postage to mail a package.

31 The petty cash fund contained $150.25 and Receipts 001–005 above. The fund was replenished.

REQUIRED:

a. Discuss the types of controls that Zebra might establish for the petty cash system.

b. Prepare general journal entries to record the activities related to the petty cash fund for October.

c. Assume the October 31 replenishment of the fund included a reduction in the size of the fund to $200. Prepare the October 31 journal entry.

d. If Zebra failed to replenish the fund on October 31, identify the errors that would be present in the October 31 balance sheet and income statement for the month.

LO 6

P7-4A Bank Reconciliations, Determining the Cash Balance per Books, Journal Entries
The following information relates to Topico Fruit Company's June 30, 19X8, bank reconciliation.

(1) The balance per the bank statement at June 30, 19X8, is $3,600.00.

(2) The outstanding checks at June 30, 19X8, total $1,150.00.

(3) Bank service charges total $38.00 for the month of June.

(4) Interest earned on the checking account for the month of June is $4.50.

(5) A deposit of $250.00 was in transit as of the cutoff date, June 30, 19X8. There are no other items affecting the bank reconciliation except the "Balance per books."

REQUIRED:

a. Prepare the part of a bank reconciliation that reconciles the "Balance per bank" to the correct cash balance.

b. Compute the apparent balance in Cash on the books of Topico as of June 30, 19X8.

c. Complete the part of the bank reconciliation that reconciles the "Balance per books" to the correct cash balance.

d. Prepare the journal entries required by the reconciliation.

LO 6   **P7-5A**   **Preparation of a Bank Reconciliation, Journal Entries**   Comet Construction Co., in preparing the July 31, 19X7, bank reconciliation, identified four checks outstanding at the end of the month: No. 714 for $231.20, No. 716 for $450.50, No. 720 for $711.13, and No. 721 for $196.96. A check for $200.00 from Welbilt Co. was returned as NSF, and a debit memorandum was included in the amount of $25.50 as a collection fee the bank charged for collecting a 60-day, noninterest-bearing note receivable of $5,000.00. The bank statement reported interest earned on the checking account of $18.00. The comparison of the deposits on the bank statement with the daily receipts deposited per the cash receipts journal found a deposit-in-transit as of July 31 in the amount of $2,310.00 and a deposit on July 17 of $330 the bank recorded in error as $300. The balance per books on July 31 was $742.51, and the balance per bank on July 31 was $4,784.80.

REQUIRED:

a. Prepare a bank reconciliation as of July 31, 19X7, for Comet Construction Co.

b. Explain how Comet probably identified the outstanding checks.

c. What action should Comet take when it discovers the error in the July 17 deposit?

d. Prepare the journal entries required by the reconciliation.

LO 5   **P7-6A**   **Preparation of a Bank Reconciliation and Related Journal Entries**   Aardvark Pest Control Company received its bank statement on August 8 for the month ending July 31, 19X7. The bank statement and excerpts from the cash receipts journal for July and the check registers for June and July are provided on the following pages. Additional information is as follows:

(1) The NSF check had been received from Family Restaurant in payment of May services.

(2) The debit memorandum was for bank service charges.

(3) The balance in Cash on June 30 was $3,410.00.

(4) All checks cleared the bank for the correct amounts.

REQUIRED:

a. Determine the outstanding checks as of July 31.

b. Determine the deposits-in-transit as of July 31.

c. Identify the error on Aardvark's books.

d. Compute the cash balance per books on July 31.

e. Prepare a bank reconciliation as of July 31.

f. Prepare the journal entries required by the reconciliation.

3rd National Bank of Inverness
P.O. Box 151852
Inverness, FL 31321

STATEMENT OF ACCOUNT: Aardvark Pest Control   CLOSING DATE: Jul. 31, 19X7
5541 S. Thrush Pt.   STATEMENT DATE: Aug. 6, 19X7
Inverness, FL 31323   ACCOUNT NO.: 421-11552-01

PREVIOUS BALANCE	CREDITS		DEBITS		NEW BALANCE
	NUMBER	TOTAL	NUMBER	TOTAL	
$3,710.00	7	$12,850.00	12	$5,870.00	$10,690.00

DATE	CHECKS				DEPOSITS	BALANCE
07/01/X7						$ 3,710.00
07/02/X7	830	$125.00				3,585.00
07/03/X7	828	199.00	829	$ 101.00		3,285.00
07/07/X7	831	350.00			$2,400.00	5,335.00
07/11/X7	832	80.00			1,200.00	6,455.00
07/17/X7	833	25.00	834	2,150.00	1,500.00	5,780.00
07/20/X7					2,200.00	7,980.00
07/25/X7	835	870.00			2,650.00	9,760.00
07/30/X7	836	420.00	837	1,210.00	1,900.00	10,030.00
07/31/X7	NSF	300.00	DM	40.00	1,000.00	10,690.00

CHECK REGISTER

DATE	CHECK NO.	CHECK CLEARED	AMOUNT
19X7			
Jun. 26	826	✔	418.00
28	827	✔	315.75
30	828		199.00
30	829		101.00
Totals			6,950.75 (100)

===== Indicates columns omitted

----- Indicates lines omitted

CHECK REGISTER

DATE	CHECK NO.	CHECK CLEARED	AMOUNT
19X7			
Jul. 1	830		125.00
5	831		350.00
9	832		80.00
15	833		52.00
15	834		2,150.00
22	835		870.00
26	836		420.00
29	837		1,210.00
30	838		660.00
31	839		148.00
Totals			6,065.00 (100)

CASH RECEIPTS JOURNAL

DATE	EXPLANATION	ACCOUNT CR.	POST. REF.	CASH DR.	OTHER ACCOUNTS CR.
19X7					
Jul. 5				2,400.00	
11				1,200.00	
16				1,500.00	
19	COLUMN DATA OMITTED			2,200.00	
24				2,650.00	
29				1,900.00	
30				1,000.00	
31				350.00	
	Totals			13,200.00	
				(100)	

LO 8

P7-7A **Calculating and Interpreting the Acid-Test Ratio** Below are the current assets and current liabilities excerpted from Wal-Mart's 1993 annual report.

(Amounts in thousands)

	January 31, 1993	1992
Current assets:		
Cash and cash equivalents	$ 12,363	$ 30,649
Receivables	524,555	418,867
Recoverable costs from sale/leaseback	312,016	681,387
Inventories	9,268,309	7,384,299
Prepaid expenses	80,347	60,221
Total current assets	$10,197,590	$8,575,423
Current liabilities:		
Commercial paper	$ 1,588,825	$ 453,964
Accounts payable	3,873,331	3,453,529
Accrued liabilities	1,042,108	829,381
Accrued federal and state income taxes	190,620	226,828
Long-term debt due within one year	13,849	5,156
Obligations under capital leases due within one year	45,553	34,917
Total current liabilities	$ 6,754,286	$5,003,775

REQUIRED:

a. Calculate Wal-Mart's acid-test ratio for January 31, 1992 and 1993.
b. Explain whether you think the change is significant or not.

PROBLEM SET B

LO 3

P7-1B **Control Procedures for Cash Disbursements, Voucher Systems** The following *elements* are all used in a cash disbursements control system that includes a voucher system:

1. Purchase requisition
2. Purchase order
3. Receiving report
4. Supplier's invoice
5. Vouchers
6. Voucher register
7. Check register
8. Checkbook
9. Unpaid Vouchers file
10. Paid Vouchers file
11. Bank reconciliation
12. "PAID" stamp

The following *activities* are used in controlling the payments under a voucher system:

A. Prepare vouchers and accounting distribution
B. Record vouchers
C. File unpaid vouchers
D. File paid vouchers
E. Prepare checks
F. Record checks
G. Sign checks
H. Approve vouchers for recording
I. Approve vouchers for payment
J. Attach documentation
K. Prepare bank reconciliation
L. Recording reconciliation adjustments
M. Review Unpaid Vouchers file
N. Forward vouchers to bookkeeper
O. Run tape of approved vouchers
P. Record check numbers on vouchers
Q. Stamp documents and vouchers paid
R. Post check register; post voucher register

REQUIRED:

Divide the *activities* among three employees—receptionist/clerk, accountant, and office manager—and the owner of a business in a manner that will provide a separation of incompatible duties and enhance internal control over disbursements. Relate each of the *elements* to the activities assigned.

LO 3,4   **P7-2B**   **Cash Disbursements, Petty Cash, and the Voucher System**   The Kendall Company makes all disbursements by check, excluding small amounts paid out of the petty cash fund. It uses a voucher system to record the disbursements. The system requires an approved voucher accompanied by supporting documentation for each check written. All payments to be made by check are first recorded in a voucher register similar to the one in Illustration 7-8. The checks are recorded in a check register similar to the one in Illustration 7-10.

The following selected transactions related to payables and disbursements are presented for Kendall for August:

Aug. 1 Purchased merchandise on account, $600.00, terms 1/10,n/30, and recorded Voucher No. 201 in the voucher register.
   4 Purchased office equipment on account, $900.00, and recorded Voucher No. 202 in the voucher register.
   8 Signed a 1-year rental agreement to rent a warehouse and paid the rent in advance, $3,600.00, recording Voucher No. 203 in the voucher register and recording Check No. 120 in the check register.
   11 Recorded Check No. 121 in the check register to pay Voucher No. 201, taking the discount.
   12 Established a petty cash fund for $200.00, recording Voucher No. 204 (debiting Petty Cash) in the Voucher Register and recording Check No. 122 in the check register.
   20 Received a statement from the city for property taxes due, $945.50. Recorded Voucher No. 205 in the voucher register.
   25 Paid Voucher No. 202 with Check No. 123.
   31 Reimbursed the petty cash fund. The fund contained petty cash vouchers totaling $164 for miscellaneous expenses and $36 cash. Recorded Voucher No. 206 in the voucher register and recorded Check No. 124 in the check register.

REQUIRED:

Illustrate the entries in the voucher register and check register in general journal entry form. For each entry, indicate the register in which it is recorded. The August 1 transaction is shown as an example.

Example:

Aug. 1	Voucher Register		
	Purchases	600.00	
	Vouchers Payable (No. 201)		600.00

LO 4

P7-3B **Petty Cash Funds, Operation, Reimbursement, and Journal Entries** Wilkes Mailing Service receives and forwards mail for individuals whose work requires them to relocate frequently. Marvin Wilkes takes advantage of special rates for packages with various parcel services and the post office. The result is a large number of small payments each month, which Marvin classifies as Office Expense. Writing checks for these payments is awkward and time-consuming, and Marvin has decided to try a petty cash fund to handle these payments and simplify the process.

The following petty cash transactions occurred during April 19X8:

Apr. 1 The petty cash fund is established for $250.00

Vouchers issued:

	No.	Amount	Payee
Apr. 2	001	$ 2.90	USPS
3	002	3.85	UPS
5	003	2.90	USPS
6	004	4.52	RPS
7	005	7.40	RRE
7	006	5.90	UPS
8	007	18.92	FX
9	008	7.52	EAF
10	009	5.20	RPS
12	010	2.90	USPS
13	011	24.17	FX
13	012	13.82	UPS
15	013	5.45	USPS
15	014	31.12	EAF
16	015	14.85	RPS
17	016	4.54	UPS
19	017	2.90	USPS
20	018	17.82	FX
22	019	5.80	RPS
23	020	6.80	FX
26	022	5.80	USPS
27	023	6.15	RRE
27	024	6.60	RRE
28	025	5.80	USPS
29	026	2.90	USPS
30	027	7.40	EAF

30 Marvin reimbursed the fund on April 30, the end of the fiscal year. The cash in the petty cash box was $12.64.

REQUIRED:

a. Write a brief explanation as to how the petty cash fund would work.
b. Prepare the journal entries required to record all of the activities related to the petty cash fund during April 19X8.

c. After replenishing on April 30, Marvin decided the fund may not be large enough for every month's activity. Prepare the journal entry to increase the fund to $300.00.

d. If Marvin failed to replenish the fund on April 30, identify the errors in the April 30 balance sheet and the April income statement.

LO 6   **P7-4B**   **Bank Reconciliations, Determining the Cash Balance per Books, Journal Entries**   The following information relates to the Truck Cap Company's August 31, 19X3, bank reconciliation.

(1) The balance per the bank statement at August 31, 19X3, is $5,120.00.
(2) Outstanding checks at August 31, 19X3, total $785.00.
(3) Bank service charges total $22.00 for the month of August.
(4) Interest earned on the checking account for the month of August is $128.60.
(5) A deposit of $400.00 was in-transit at August 31, 19X3. There are no other items affecting the bank reconciliation except the "Balance per books."

REQUIRED:

a. Prepare the part of a bank reconciliation that reconciles the "Balance per bank" to the correct cash balance.

b. Compute the apparent balance in Cash on the books of Truck Cap Company at August 31, 19X3.

c. Complete the part of the bank reconciliation that reconciles the "Balance per books" to the correct cash balance.

d. Prepare the journal entries required by the reconciliation.

LO 6   **P7-5B**   **Preparation of a Bank Reconciliation**   Alabama Record Co., in preparing the December 31, 19X5, bank reconciliation, identified four checks outstanding at the end of the month: No. 326 for $721.00, No. 328 for $150.00, No. 330 for $425.50, and No. 331 for $290.40. A check for $150.00 from Marvin Co. was returned as NSF, and a debit memorandum was included in the amount of $65.00 as a fee the bank charged for check printing. The bank statement reported interest earned on the checking account of $32.10. The comparison of the deposits on the bank statement with the daily receipts deposited per the cash receipts journal found a deposit-in-transit as of December 31, in the amount of $2,200.00, and a deposit on December 17 of $340 was recorded in error by the bank as $430. The balance per books at December 31, 19X5, was $8,972.71. The bank's balance at December 31, 19X5, was $8,266.71.

REQUIRED:

a. Prepare a bank reconciliation as of December 31, 19X5, for Alabama Record.

b. Explain how Alabama probably identified the outstanding checks.

c. What action should Alabama take when it discovers the error in the December 17 deposit.

d. Prepare the journal entries required by the reconciliation.

LO 5   **P7-6B**   **Preparation of a Bank Reconciliation and Related Journal Entries**   Alexia Movorik Co. received its bank statement on April 7 for the month ending March 31, 19X2. The bank statement and excerpts from the cash receipts journal for March and the check registers for February and March are shown on the following pages. Additional information is as follows:

(1) The debit memorandum was $45.00 for check printing.
(2) Cash was $2,015.00 on February 28, 19X2, after adjustments.
(3) There was a $500.00 deposit in transit as of February 28, 19X2.
(4) The NSF check had been received from B. B. Ballik, a customer, for payment on account.
(5) All checks cleared the bank at the correct amounts.

Bank of Gerald
2 South Spring Street
Gerald, MO 63121

STATEMENT OF ACCOUNT: Alexia Movorik Co.   CLOSING DATE: Mar. 31, 19X2
41 N. Oak Street   STATEMENT DATE: Apr. 5, 19X2
Lone Spring, MO 63142   ACCOUNT NO.: 16-0115

| PREVIOUS BALANCE | CREDITS | | DEBITS | | NEW BALANCE |
	NUMBER	TOTAL	NUMBER	TOTAL	
$2,340.50	8	$5,270.00	11	$4,274.50	$3,336.00

DATE	CHECKS				DEPOSITS	BALANCE
03/01/X2						$ 2,340.50
03/01/X2	216	$ 315.50			$ 500.00	2,525.00
03/07/X2	218	145.00	217	$275.00	800.00	2,905.00
03/10/X2	219	190.00			1,300.00	4,015.00
03/22/X2	222	670.00			350.00	3,695.00
03/24/X2	220	25.00			750.00	4,420.00
03/25/X2	221	1,140.00			410.00	3,690.00
03/26/X2	215	84.00			850.00	4,456.00
03/30/X2	224	1,320.00			310.00	3,446.00
03/31/X2	NSF	65.00	DM	45.00		3,336.00

CHECK REGISTER

DATE	CHECK NO.	CHECK CLEARED	AMOUNT
19X7			
Feb. 26	211	✔	246.00
27	212	✔	110.00
27	213	✔	125.00
28	214		426.00
28	215		84.00
28	216		315.50
Totals			6,306.50
			(100)

CHECK REGISTER

DATE	CHECK NO.	CHECK CLEARED	AMOUNT
19X2			
Mar. 1	217		275.00
5	218		415.00
9	219		190.00
15	220		25.00
15	221		1,140.00
22	222		670.00
26	223		310.00
29	224		1,320.00
30	225		460.00
31	226		1,435.00
Totals			6,240.00
			(100)

===== Indicates columns omitted

----- Indicates lines omitted

CASH RECEIPTS JOURNAL

DATE	EXPLANATION	ACCOUNT CR.	POST. REF.	CASH DR.	OTHER ACCOUNTS CR.
19X2					
Mar. 6				800.00	
9				1,300.00	
21				350.00	
23	COLUMN DATA OMITTED			750.00	
24				410.00	
25				850.00	
29				310.00	
30				160.00	
31				1,250.00	
	Totals			6,180.00	
				(100)	

REQUIRED:

a. Determine the outstanding checks as of March 31.
b. Determine the deposits-in-transit as of March 31.
c. Identify the error on Movorik's books.
d. Compute the cash balance per books on March 31.
e. Prepare a bank reconciliation as of March 31.
f. Prepare the journal entries required by the reconciliation.

LO 8   **P7-7B**   **Calculating and Interpreting the Acid-Test Ratio**   Below are the current assets and current liabilities excerpted from Kmart's 1993 annual report.

(Amounts in millions)	End of January 1993	1992
Current assets:		
Cash (including temporary investments of $260 and $309, respectively)	$ 611	$ 565
Merchandise inventories	8,752	7,546
Accounts receivable and other current assets	1,146	879
Total current assets	$10,509	$8,990
Current liabilities:		
Long-term debt due within one year	$ 117	$ 39
Notes payable	590	0
Accounts payable—trade	2,959	2,722
Accrued payrolls and other liabilities	1,215	1,014
Taxes other than income taxes	368	322
Income taxes	246	211
Total current liabilities	$ 5,495	$4,308

REQUIRED:

a. Calculate Kmart's acid-test ratio for January 29, 1992, and January 27, 1993. (Some companies such as Kmart choose an accounting period of 52 weeks instead of a calendar year. Hence, the exact day of their fiscal year-ends generally fluctuate one or two days each year.)
b. Explain whether you think the change is significant or not.

CRITICAL THINKING AND COMMUNICATING

C7-1 Jim Gordon has worked for the Robbins Company for many years and is a trusted employee. Unknown to his employer and friends, Jim is experiencing severe financial and personal problems.

One of the duties that Jim performs is the monthly reconciliation of the bank statement and Cash. Jim does not perform any other duties related to cash. Robbins Company manages estates and trusts and has receipts and disbursements of several million dollars each month.

Jim Gordon's friend, Roger Simmons, is a systems analyst at the local bank where Robbins maintains its general checking account. Roger has convinced Jim that he has a tip on an investment that can make them both a lot of money. The investment would require $25,000 and would have to be held about 6 months before it could be sold at an expected significant gain.

Roger suggests to Jim that he can transfer $25,000 from Robbins' account to a Swiss account that the two men would have access to. The only problem, states Roger, is that "You will have to figure out a way to conceal the cash shortage until we can sell the investment and put the money back in Robbins' account."

REQUIRED:

a. How might Jim conceal the shortage?
b. What control procedures would identify the concealment?
c. Do you think a scenario such as this happens often in business? Discuss.
d. If the scheme works and the $25,000 is restored to the account, is there anything wrong with what Jim and Roger have done?

C7-2 You have worked for the Watson Sales Company since you started college. You spend 2 hours each afternoon and a full day on Saturdays helping with a variety of office tasks, including calling delinquent customers to urge payment, taking bank deposits to the bank, picking up the mail at the post office, filing paid and unpaid invoices, and other office work. You are well-liked by everyone in the office, and your boss has always allowed you an afternoon off to prepare for tests in your classes. It has been a really good experience for you, especially since you are a business major.

One Saturday, while filing invoices, you notice one of the full-time salespersons going through the company's journals and ledgers and occasionally copying down information. You had never seen anyone other than the owner work on the accounting records. You pretend to concentrate on your filing. About a month later, you see the same person again going through the financial records and making notes. You become concerned. It seems to you that the owner has always been careful to lock the accounting records in the safe when he finishes with them.

You like your employer and all of the staff and don't want to "get involved" but wonder if you have some obligation to relate what you have seen to your employer. You also worry that if the salesperson is supposed to be in the records and you report him it will become some sort of office joke at your expense.

REQUIRED:

a. Discuss what kinds of information the salesperson could be getting from the financial records that could be of financial benefit or could provide an advantageous edge to a competitor of the company.
b. Discuss what controls would have prevented this problem from occurring.
c. Discuss your ethical obligation to your employer and to the company with respect to what you have seen.
d. Discuss how you might deal with the problem and meet your obligation.

C7-3   The financial statements of J.C. Penney Company, Inc. are reprinted in Appendix B at

the end of the text. Find J.C. Penney's balance sheets.

REQUIRED:

a. Which of J.C. Penney's current assets should be included in the numerator of the acid-test ratio? Explain.
b. Calculate J.C. Penney's acid-test ratios for 1991, 1992, and 1993.
c. Write an appropriate general interpretation of the acid-test ratio.
d. Comment on any trend you see in J.C. Penney's acid-test ratios.

CHAPTER 8

Accounts Receivable and Notes Receivable

Jane Trevor decided several years ago that her business, Trevor's Wholesale Warehouse, should extend credit to its customers. Since that time, cash sales have stayed about the same each year, but credit sales have grown dramatically. However, the profitability of her business is now down, and Jane wonders if she has carried credit sales growth too far. She would like to have some diagnostic tools to help her determine whether her credit sales are actually hurting, instead of helping, the business.

In this chapter, we introduce you to the costs and benefits of credit sales. One of the costs of credit sales is uncollectible accounts, which present some interesting challenges in accounting for accounts receivable. We show you how to handle these challenges, and you will see how you can use some simple diagnostic tools to keep track of the effect on a business of credit sales and accounts receivable. In addition to learning about credit sales and more about accounts receivable, you will learn about bank card sales such as VISA and MasterCard sales. We will also introduce you to notes receivable and why businesses accept notes receivable, as well as accounts receivable, from customers.

LEARNING OBJECTIVES

1. Explain why businesses grant credit to their customers, why they should expect to experience uncollectible accounts, and how they can control uncollectible accounts expense.
2. Account for estimated uncollectible accounts, uncollectible accounts expense, and subsequent write-offs of uncollectible accounts according to the allowance method.
3. Account for third-party credit card sales and explain how they can reduce problems of collecting on credit sales.
4. Describe a promissory note receivable and distinguish between negotiable and nonnegotiable notes.
5. Calculate explicit and implicit interest on notes receivable.
6. Account for receipt of notes receivable, accrual of interest on notes receivable, and receipt of payment on notes receivable.
7. Account for the discounting of notes receivable.
8. Calculate the number of days-sales-in-receivables and uncollectible-accounts-expense-as-a-percent-of-credit sales and use these tools to diagnose problems.

LO 1

Explain why businesses grant credit to their customers, why they should expect to experience uncollectible accounts, and how they can control uncollectible accounts expense.

CREDIT SALES AND UNCOLLECTIBLE ACCOUNTS

Businesses extend credit to their customers to increase sales. However, inevitably some customers do not pay. The decision to grant credit to customers should satisfy the following criterion: Will granting credit add to profitability? Granting credit involves adding to the firm's assets (accounts receivable), and the business must earn competitive profits on this additional investment. The benefit of granting credit to customers is measured as follows:

$$\text{Additional Earnings} = \text{Additional Sales Revenue} -$$
$$\text{Cost of Additional Goods Sold} -$$
$$\text{Additional Expenses Incurred}$$

The expense of uncollectible accounts receivable is one of the additional expenses that results from granting credit.

Uncollectible accounts expense is the estimated portion of a period's credit sales that a business ultimately will not collect from customers. Uncollectible accounts expense can make credit sales unprofitable or, at least, not sufficiently profitable to justify the necessary investment in accounts receivable.

Controlling Uncollectible Accounts Expense

The best protection for any individual business against excessive uncollectible accounts expense is a sound credit policy. A business should establish criteria for screening credit customers and impose control over authorizing credit sales transactions.

Screening Credit Customers.   The first rule of a sound credit policy is obvious: "Do not sell goods on credit to those who cannot or will not pay." Though obvious, this rule is not easy to apply. At the time of sale, it is impossible to recognize every customer who ultimately will not pay. As a result, the business must establish criteria to distinguish between customers who are likely to pay and those who are *unlikely* to pay. Thus, the business must set up procedures to screen potential credit customers in advance of any sales transactions. Personnel other than salespeople should conduct credit screening. This way, conflicts of interest can be avoided, especially if sales personnel are paid commissions on the sales they complete.

Credit Applications. The first-time credit sale customer usually has to apply for credit. A credit application may involve no more than a telephone interview, or it may require detailed financial information provided on elaborate forms. Illustration 8-1 is an application for a Sears charge account. The business granting credit uses such an application to collect certain facts about the applicant's financial condition and history to serve as a basis for credit evaluation. Notice that the Sears application asks the customer for personal information and history under the caption TELL US ABOUT YOURSELF, information about income

ILLUSTRATION 8-1 Sears Credit Application

SEARSCHARGE INDIVIDUAL CREDIT ACCOUNT APPLICATION ID 63

IMPORTANT: COMPLETE ALL SPACES AND SIGN BELOW

1 TELL US ABOUT YOURSELF:

FIRST NAME | MIDDLE INITIAL | LAST NAME

RESIDENCE ADDRESS | APT. # | CITY | STATE | ZIP CODE

HOME TELEPHONE ( ) | BUSINESS TELEPHONE ( ) | SOCIAL SECURITY NUMBER | AGE | NO. OF DEPENDENTS (EXCLUDE YOURSELF)

ARE YOU A U.S. CITIZEN? ☐ YES ☐ NO (IF NO, EXPLAIN IMMIGRATION STATUS) | ARE YOU A PERMANENT RESIDENT? ☐ YES ☐ NO | HOW LONG AT PRESENT ADDRESS? ______ YRS. ______ MOS.

TYPE OF RESIDENCE ☐ OWN ☐ LIVE WITH PARENTS ☐ RENT ☐ BOARD ☐ OTHER ______ | MONTHLY RENT OR MORTGAGE $

PREVIOUS ADDRESS (If less than 2 years at present address) | APT. # | CITY | STATE | ZIP CODE

2 ABOUT YOUR EMPLOYER:

EMPLOYER (RETIRED/STUDENT) | CITY | STATE | HOW LONG? ☐ MOS. ☐ YRS. | OCCUPATION

NET INCOME (TAKE HOME PAY) $ ☐ PER MONTH ☐ PER WEEK | ADDITIONAL* INCOME $ ☐ PER MONTH ☐ PER WEEK | SOURCES:

3 ABOUT YOUR CREDIT REFERENCES:

CHECK MAJOR CREDIT CARDS YOU HAVE: ☐ DISCOVER CARD ☐ J C PENNEY ☐ AMERICAN EXPRESS ☐ MASTERCARD ☐ WARDS ☐ VISA ☐ OTHER (LIST)

DO YOU HAVE A (MARK ALL THAT APPLY) ☐ NOW ACCOUNT ☐ CD ☐ CHECKING ACCOUNT ☐ SAVINGS ACCOUNT ☐ MONEY MARKET ☐ NONE

NAME OF YOUR FINANCIAL INSTITUTIONS ______

4 ABOUT YOUR SPOUSE:

Complete this section if: (1) your spouse is an authorized buyer, (2) you reside in a community property state (AZ, CA, ID, LA, NV, NM, TX, WA, WI), or (3) you are relying on the income or assets of a spouse as a source for payment.

SPOUSE, FIRST NAME | MIDDLE INITIAL | LAST NAME | SOCIAL SECURITY NUMBER

EMPLOYER | NET INCOME (TAKE HOME PAY) $ ☐ PER MONTH ☐ PER WEEK

I agree to pay Sears in accordance with the credit terms disclosed to me and to comply with all terms of the SearsCharge Agreement. A copy of the SearsCharge Agreement will be given to me to keep when my application is approved. Sears will retain a security interest where permitted by law under the Uniform Commercial Code on all merchandise charged to the account. Sears is authorized to investigate my credit, employment, and income references and to report to proper persons and credit bureaus my performance of the account. Finance charges not in excess of those permitted by law will be charged on the outstanding balance from month to month.

SEE OTHER SIDE FOR IMPORTANT CREDIT TERMS.

X ______ APPLICANT'S SIGNATURE ______ DATE

SearsCharge Credit Protection Plan **200G3NGT**

☐ **YES!** I accept this optional insurance from Allstate to protect my account. I authorize Sears to add the insurance charges to my account each month (subject to approval). I have read and agree to the terms to the right of this application.

☐ **NO!** I waive my right to enroll for credit insurance at this time.

______ YOUR BIRTHDATE

X ______ APPLICANT'S SIGNATURE ______ DATE

© 1993 Sears, Roebuck and Co. Rev. 4/93

*NOTE: Alimony, child support or separate maintenance income need not be disclosed if you do not wish to have it considered as a basis for paying this obligation.

(ability to pay) under ABOUT YOUR EMPLOYER, and information about credit cards and banking relationships under the caption ABOUT YOUR CREDIT REFERENCES.

If the applicant is a business, the company granting credit often requests financial statements (and income tax returns) to evaluate and to judge the applicant's ability to pay. In addition, the company may consult various credit bureaus or credit rating services such as Dun & Bradstreet, Inc. to obtain a summary of the applicant's credit history. Illustration 8-2 displays an excerpt from a Dun & Bradstreet report showing the most recent payment history of a particular business as reported by its suppliers to Dun & Bradstreet. Notice that this particular business is slow in paying some of its recent bills and is past due with certain amounts—which might make other businesses reluctant to grant it credit.

If the overall credit evaluation of an individual or a business indicates that the applicant is creditworthy, then the company sets up an account in the accounts receivable subsidiary ledger and sets an initial credit limit.

ILLUSTRATION 8-2 Excerpt from a Dun & Bradstreet Report[1]

PAYMENTS REPORTED	PAYING RECORD	HIGH CREDIT	NOW OWES	PAST DUE	SELLING TERMS	LAST SALE WITHIN
	(Amounts may be rounded to nearest figure in prescribed ranges)					
02/X5	Ppt-Slow 30	250	50	50		1 Mo
01/X5	Ppt	500				1 Mo
	Lease agreement					
	Ppt-Slow 30	2500	750	100	N15	1 Mo
10/X4	Ppt	5000			N30	
	Ppt	2500		-0-	N30	

* Payment experiences reflect how bills are met in relation to the terms granted. In some instances payment beyond terms can be the result of disputes over merchandise, skipped invoices etc.

* Each experience shown represents a separate account reported by a supplier. Updated trade experiences replace those previously reported.

Authorizing Credit Sales

Personnel should check the customer's credit status before a credit sale is made.

Retail Credit Sales. In a retail setting, a business often issues its customers plastic credit cards with the customers' account numbers embossed on them. Salesclerks either check the numbers manually against lists of unauthorized accounts, key the numbers into cash registers that are linked to computers, or pass them through devices linked to computers that read the numbers off magnetic strips on the back of the cards. In any case, the sale is rejected if the customer's account is either over the limit or past due or if the customer is otherwise considered unworthy of credit at the time.

Wholesale Credit Sales. In a wholesale or industrial setting, the customer typically sends the seller a written purchase order (which may be preceded by a

---

[1]The report shown is reproduced from an actual computer-printed report from Dun & Bradstreet. However, dates have been changed and the company's name has been omitted. Individual company's credit records change over time; and it would be unfair to print a company's slow-payment record as of a past point in time, when the company may have since improved its record.

Linda Bonaventure is concerned about her own and a co-worker's welfare. Her co-worker, Larry Farnsworth, and she are salespersons for Sleep Tight Waterbeds. Sleep Tight pays its salespersons basic salaries, 15% commissions on all sales they make, and annual bonuses for high sales performers. Larry has confided in her that he is under financial stress. He and his wife recently bought a home that has needed unexpected emergency repairs. He has had to pay for the repairs, but he hopes to be repaid eventually by his homeowner's insurance company.

Linda has noticed that Larry recently has been very aggressive in his sales tactics and, in at least one case, approved a couple for credit on a very expensive bedroom set after Linda had to turn them down for credit just one week earlier. Management has emphasized time and again that salespersons must be careful to approve credit only for customers with ability to pay.

However, Linda is reluctant to say anything to Larry or to management about the credit approval. Linda and Larry and his wife are good friends and she and Larry are "friendly rivals" on the sales floor. Each year they end up number 1 and 2 in sales for the company. The number 1 salesperson always receives a significantly larger bonus than the others. Until just recently, Linda was ahead of Larry in year-to-date sales. She worries that if she talks to management about the bad credit approval Larry will lose his job because of temporary financial pressure beyond his control and her co-workers will think she told on him to win the top annual bonus. If she talks to Larry, she is apt to lose a good friend because he resents her making judgments about his behavior. However, she is also concerned that given Larry's increased sales volume, if he approves too many uncreditworthy customers, he may do serious damage to the business and jeopardize all of their jobs.

What should Linda do about Larry's behavior?

Can she offer management any advice about how to avoid this type of problem?

telephone order). The sales department transforms the information on the customer's order into an internal sales order, which the credit department reviews. The credit department authorizes the sale only if the customer's current balance is not past due and if the customer's current balance and the proposed sale do not exceed the customer's credit limit. The shipping department should never ship goods to a customer unless credit approval is indicated on the sales order.

LO 2

Account for estimated uncollectible accounts, uncollectible accounts expense, and subsequent write-offs of uncollectible accounts according to the allowance method.

ACCOUNTING FOR UNCOLLECTIBLE ACCOUNTS EXPENSE—THE ALLOWANCE METHOD

A sound credit policy does not mean that customers will always pay their accounts. It means only that the amounts of noncollections—called *uncollectible accounts*—will be kept within acceptable limits. According to the matching principle, a business should recognize the amount of uncollectible accounts as an expense in the same period it recognizes related gross revenues. However, accounts receivable are frequently not determined to be uncollectible until some later period. Under the **allowance method** of accounting for receivables, a business anticipates and estimates uncollectible accounts to be recognized as uncollectible accounts expense in the period of sale. The business then records the estimated amount of uncollectible accounts expense in an entry that is independent of any actual write-offs of specific accounts deemed to be uncollectible.

A business can use two approaches for estimating uncollectible accounts expense: the income statement (percentage of sales) approach and the balance sheet (percentage of accounts receivable) approach. We first illustrate the accrual of uncollectible accounts expense under the income statement approach.

Income Statement (Percentage of Sales) Approach

Under the **income statement approach**, a business accrues estimated uncollectible accounts expense based on its past experience with average collections per dollar of credit sales—with appropriate consideration given to changes in economic conditions or credit policy. For example, Trevor's Wholesale Warehouse (TWW) made its decision to offer credit to its customers five years ago. Its experience with uncollectible accounts for the five years preceding the current year (19X5) is summarized in Illustration 8-3.

ILLUSTRATION 8-3 Uncollectible Accounts as Percentages of Credit Sales

Year	Credit sales	Uncollectible accounts	Percent of sales uncollectible
19X0	$ 204,000	$ 4,039	1.98%
19X1	214,200	4,984	2.33%
19X2	235,620	4,948	2.10%
19X3	240,332	5,440	2.26%
19X4	252,349	5,252	2.08%
Total	$1,146,501	$24,663	2.15%

Although it has experienced year-to-year fluctuations, TWW has had an average of 2.15% uncollectible credit sales over the last five years. Assume that TWW has maintained a stable credit policy for the past five years, that general economic conditions have been stable, and that conditions in the industry have been relatively unchanged. Under these assumed conditions, TWW may reasonably project its overall average experienced rate of 2.15% uncollectible sales to its credit sales in 19X5. Therefore, as it recognizes credit sales revenues in 19X5, TWW can appropriately accrue uncollectible accounts expense at 2.15% of the new credit sales.

Now, assuming credit sales for January, February, and March totaled $69,767, TWW's entry to accrue the uncollectible accounts expense for the first quarter would be:

Mar. 31	Uncollectible Accounts Expense	1,500	
	Allowance for Uncollectible Accounts		1,500
	To accrue estimated uncollectible accounts expense for the quarter ended March 31. ($69,767 x .0215 = $1,500)		

If the company changes its credit policy or if changes take place in the economy or industry that suggest changes in collectibility of accounts, TWW should adjust its historical percentage for the new conditions before accruing its uncollectible accounts expense.

Allowance for Uncollectible Accounts.   As you would expect, the debit entry increases uncollectible accounts expense by $1,500. However, we do not credit Accounts Receivable directly, as you might have expected. Instead, we credit a new account, Allowance for Uncollectible Accounts. The **Allowance for Uncollectible Accounts** is a valuation, or contra-account, representing the cumulative amount of past sales that a business estimates to be uncollectible but has not written off. The Allowance for Uncollectible Accounts typically has a credit balance that offsets the debit balance of Accounts Receivable.

Allowance for Uncollectible Accounts in the Financial Statements.   In its balance sheet, a business can combine the balance of Allowance for Uncollectible Accounts with the balance in Accounts Receivable in different ways to disclose net receivables. Two acceptable methods are shown in Illustration 8-4. The $49,570 figure for accounts receivable equals the balance in the general ledger Accounts Receivable control account and the amount individual customers actually owe for past sales. The valuation account (Allowance for Uncollectible Accounts) balance of $3,570 is the amount that TWW does not expect to collect.

ILLUSTRATION 8-4 Allowance for Uncollectible Accounts in the Balance Sheet

Direct Disclosure			Indirect (Net) Disclosure		
TWW Balance Sheet (Partial) March 31, 19X5			**TWW Balance Sheet (Partial) March 31, 19X5**		
Current assets:			Current assets:		
Cash		$20,000	Cash		$20,000
Accounts receivable	$49,570		Accounts receivable,		
Less: Allowance for			net of allowance of		
uncollectible			$3,570		46,000
accounts	3,570	46,000			

Either of the two methods shown in Illustration 8-4 is acceptable, but most large public companies use the **indirect (net) method**. They also frequently use the terms "bad debts" or "doubtful accounts" in place of "uncollectible accounts."

As seen in the following excerpt from its March 31, 1993, annual report, Communications Group, Inc. uses the net method for balance sheet disclosure and uses the term "doubtful accounts" in place of "uncollectible accounts."

	March 31	
	1993	1992
Receivables:		
Trade, less allowance for doubtful accounts of $175,000 and $200,000 at March 31, 1993 and 1992	$584,960	$925,650

As an alternative to showing the allowance in the balance sheet, some large companies such as L.A.Gear, Inc. merely report accounts receivable and indicate that they are reported "net." Other companies such as General Electric report accounts receivable "net" in the balance sheet, but they refer the reader to a note following the financial statements that offsets the allowance against gross receivables and derives the net figure disclosed in the balance sheet.

Uncollectible Accounts Expense.   In practice, businesses disclose their uncollectible accounts expenses according to two different methods in income statements, depending on the point of view taken regarding the nature of uncollectible accounts. The revenue-reduction or contra-revenue view calls for inclusion of uncollectible accounts expense in the calculation of net revenue. Suppose TWW had sales returns and allowances of $1,575 but had no sales discounts in the quarter ended March 31, 19X5. The net revenue section of its income statement for the the quarter ending on March 31 would appear as in Illustration 8-5.

ILLUSTRATION 8-5 Uncollectible Accounts Expense in the Income Statement

TWW Income Statement (Partial) Quarter Ended March 31, 19X5	
Revenue from sales	$69,767
Less: Sales returns and allowances	(1,575)
Uncollectible accounts expense	(1,500)
Net revenue from sales	$66,692

Many large companies such as Reebok International, Inc. only report "net sales" in their income statements, giving no details about the deductions used to derive net sales from total sales revenues.

The selling-expense view implies that uncollectible accounts expense will be included in selling expenses and may not be distinguished from other selling expenses. However, some companies such as Communications Group, Inc. show uncollectible accounts expense (bad debt expense) as a separate expense of the business on a specific line in the income statement as you can see from the following excerpt from its March 1993 annual report.

	1993	1992
Net sales	$4,833,570	$4,252,240
Costs and expenses:		
Cost of sales (exclusive of depreciation and amortization	1,770,060	1,727,710
Selling, general and administrative expenses	1,814,380	2,092,430
Bad debt expense	89,630	260,240
Depreciation and amortization	486,100	425,750

Writing Off Uncollectible Accounts

Suppose TWW sold $300 worth of merchandise to Freida Smith on credit on January 15, 19X5. Assuming that Freida's account was paid-up prior to this sale, her account would have the following balance on January 15:

Freida Smith	
Jan. 15 300	

Now, suppose Freida did not pay her account and TWW concluded it was uncollectible on October 31, 19X5. Under the allowance method, TWW would make the following general journal entry on October 31:

Oct. 31	Allowance for Uncollectible Accounts	300	
	Accounts Receivable—Freida Smith		300
	To write off an uncollectible account.		

TWW posts this entry to Accounts Receivable and Allowance for Uncollectible Accounts general ledger accounts and to Freida Smith's individual account in the accounts receivable subsidiary ledger. After the entry is posted, Freida Smith's account (shown below) has a zero balance. That is, her $300 balance would have been *written off* TWW's accounts. However, the write-off leaves uncollectible accounts expense unaffected. TWW previously recognized the uncollectible accounts expense with the adjusting entry (accrual) of $1,500 of *estimated* expense it recognized on March 31 to match sales revenues of January, February, and March, 19X5. At the time of the accrual, TWW credited Allowance for Uncollectible Accounts but did not know which specific sales of January, February, or March ultimately would not be collected. Now, Freida Smith's account has been specifically identified as uncollectible. Hence, TWW reduces both Accounts Receivable and the allowance account, and it also credits the reduction to Freida's individual account.

	Freida Smith		
Jan. 15	300		
		Oct. 31	300

Illustration 8-6 summarizes the allowance method for handling estimated uncollectible accounts expense and actual write-offs of uncollectible accounts. Notice that the accrual of uncollectible accounts expense does not affect Accounts Receivable or the individual customer account. Also, notice that the subsequent write-off of a specific customer's account does not affect Uncollectible Accounts Expense.

ILLUSTRATION 8-6 Allowance Method for Uncollectible Accounts

		General Ledger				Accounts Receivable Subsidiary Ledger
		Sales	Accounts Receivable	Allowance for Uncollectible Accounts	Uncollectible Accounts Expense	Freida Smith
Jan. 15	Sale	300	300			300
Mar. 31	Accrual			1,500	1,500	
Oct. 31	Write-off		300	300		300

Subsequent Collection of Accounts Previously Written Off.   Although it may be unusual, some former customers pay their accounts after the accounts have been written off. Upon subsequent collection, we debit Accounts Receivable and credit Allowance for Uncollectible Accounts for the amount of the payment. The amount of the payment is posted to the general ledger accounts and to the individual customer's account. Thus, we restore the customer's balance to the customer's individual account in the accounts receivable subsidiary ledger. After the restoration entry, we record the cash receipt in the usual way:

Dec. 15	Accounts Receivable—Freida Smith	300	
	Allowance for Uncollectible Accounts		300
	To restore balance previously written off.		

Dec. 15	Cash	300	
	Accounts Receivable—Freida Smith		300
	To record collection of account previously written off.		

Balance Sheet Approach for Estimating Uncollectible Accounts Expense

An alternative to the income statement (percentage of sales) approach for estimating uncollectible accounts expense is the **balance sheet** (percentage of accounts receivable) **approach**. According to GAAP, both the income statement relationship (match uncollectible amounts with the related sales) and the balance sheet relationship (net receivables should be valued at the amount expected to be collected) must be maintained. A business can use the latter as well as the former relationship as a basis for accruing uncollectible accounts expense.

Aged Schedule of Accounts Receivable.   To apply the balance sheet approach, a business uses an *aged schedule of accounts receivable* to evaluate the makeup of the accounts receivable balance at the end of a period.

ILLUSTRATION 8-7 Aged Schedule of Accounts Receivable

TWW
Aged Schedule of Accounts Receivable
March 31, 19X5

CUSTOMER NUMBER	AMOUNT WITHIN DISCOUNT	AMOUNT WITHIN 30 DAYS	AMOUNT 1–30 DAYS PAST DUE	AMOUNT 31–60 DAYS PAST DUE	AMOUNT 61–90 DAYS PAST DUE	AMOUNT 91–120 DAYS PAST DUE	OVER 120 DAYS PAST DUE	CUSTOMER TOTAL
1101						650		650
1102						390	567	957
1103		401						401
1104		445						445
1105		368						368
1106	456							456
1107		679						679
1108			230	120				350
1109				150	400			550
1110	540							540
Page Total	996	1,893	230	270	400	1,040	567	5,396
Total	9,900	17,037	2,070	2,430	3,600	9,360	5,103	49,500
Allowance %	0.80%	1.20%	2.50%	5.50%	9.10%	15.50%	25.90%	
Allowance	79	204	52	134	328	1,451	1,322	3,570

Illustration 8-7 shows the last page of TWW's aged schedule of accounts receivable as of March 31, 19X5. At the bottom of the page is a summary of the entire schedule. The schedule identifies the customers by account numbers in the first column and lists all of the individual customers' accounts receivable balances in the last column. The columns in between show the breakdown of each customer's balance according to when the amounts making up the balance are (were) due. For example, the amounts in the second column are "within discount." They represent credit sales to customers within the 10 days prior to March 31. In the next column are sales made 11 to 30 days prior to March 31. These amounts are not yet past due. Then, there are five columns representing sales to customers more than 30 days prior to March 31. These amounts are categorized in the columns according to how many days they are past due. For example, Customer 1108's balance of $350 is composed of $230 that is 1 to 30 days past due and $120 that is 31 to 60 days past due.

Estimating the Appropriate Balance for the Allowance for Uncollectible Accounts.

The credit manager should review the amounts in each age category to determine if it is appropriate to apply past experience with collections from each of the age categories. For example, suppose TWW has a history of ultimately collecting 97.5% of accounts once they become past due by 1-30 days. In a "normal" period, TWW should establish a 2.5% allowance for uncollectible accounts in this category of total accounts receivable as shown at the bottom of Illustration 8-7. However, the credit manager may conclude that conditions have changed or that the customers whose accounts are in the particular age category are more or less likely to pay than past experience dictates. In either case, the credit manager should adjust the percentage for that category.

In the above manner, the credit manager or other responsible employee sets appropriate uncollectible percentages for all the age layers. Notice that the percentages increase with the age of the accounts because generally the longer a customer takes to pay, the higher the probability of nonpayment. The appropriate percentages are then multiplied by the total balance in each age category as shown at the bottom of Illustration 8-7, and the allowance amounts are summed across to determine the total allowance estimate. The total allowance estimate of $3,570 in Illustration 8-7 is the estimated amount that will not be collected from the total accounts receivable balance of $49,500 as of March 31, 19X5.

The credit manager compares this total allowance to the *unadjusted balance* in Allowance for Uncollectible Accounts to determine the appropriate expense accrual. Assuming that the *unadjusted* balance in the account is $2,050 at March 31, 19X5, the manager determines the accrual as:

Estimated allowance for uncollectible accounts, March 31, 19X5:	$3,570
Less: Balance in Allowance for Uncollectible Accounts, March 31, 19X5	2,050
Estimated uncollectible accounts expense, January-March, 19X5	$1,520

The journal entry to record the accrual adjustment is:

Mar. 31	Uncollectible Accounts Expense	1,520	
	Allowance for Uncollectible Accounts		1,520
	To adjust the allowance account and to estimate and accrue uncollectible accounts expense for the quarter ended March 31 ($3,570 - $2,050 = $1,520).		

Income Statement and Balance Sheet Approaches Compared

Illustration 8-8 compares the sequence of entries affecting Allowance for Uncollectible Accounts under the balance sheet and income statement approaches. Notice that the only event that differs is the accrual adjustment. Theoretically, the amounts of the accruals and the balances in the account should be the same under both approaches. However, both approaches involve estimations, and different approaches frequently produce different estimates (as we illustrated in the TWW examples above).

The income statement approach is simpler and less costly to apply, and some businesses use it especially for monthly or quarterly accruals. The balance sheet approach, as we have illustrated it, is more detailed and complicated and involves greater cost to implement; but it generally produces more accurate estimates. In addition, because it focuses attention on accounts that are past due and in need of extra collection effort, the review of an aged schedule of accounts receivable is an important part of the management of the collection process. With the widespread proliferation of computers—even in small businesses—preparing an aged schedule of accounts receivable is not the time-consuming task it used to be. Thus, more and more businesses are using the balance sheet approach of estimating the allowance for and accrual of uncollectible accounts expense.

ILLUSTRATION 8-8 Comparing the Income Statement and Balance Sheet Approaches

Income Statement Approach	Balance Sheet Approach
1. Beginning balance, Allowance for Uncollectible Accounts	1. Beginning balance, Allowance for Uncollectible Accounts
2. Deduct write-offs as accounts are deemed uncollectible.	2. Deduct write-offs as accounts are deemed uncollectible.
3. **Estimate and accrue uncollectible accounts expense as a percent of credit sales for the period.**	3. **Estimate appropriate balance in the allowance account from aged schedule of individual accounts and accrue uncollectible accounts expense to achieve the target balance.**
4. Ending balance, Allowance for Uncollectible Accounts	4. Ending balance, Allowance for Uncollectible Accounts

Accounting for Uncollectible Accounts—Direct Write-Off Method

Some businesses use the direct write-off method of accounting for uncollectible accounts receivable—even though it is not acceptable under GAAP. Under the **direct write-off method**, customers' accounts are credited and Uncollectible Accounts Expense is debited when amounts owed are deemed uncollectible. Recall the example of Freida Smith who purchased $300 worth of merchandise on credit from TWW on January 15, 19X5. Under the direct write-off method, TWW would not have accrued any uncollectible accounts expense on March 31 to match against January, February, and March sales as it did under the allowance method. Instead, when TWW deemed Freida's account uncollectible on October 31, it would make the following entry:

Oct. 31	Uncollectible Accounts Expense	300	
	Accounts Receivable—Freida Smith		300
	To write off uncollectible account and		
	to recognize uncollectible accounts expense.		

TWW would post the entry to the general ledger accounts, resulting in a reduction in Accounts Receivable and a recognition of Uncollectible Accounts Expense. When posted to Freida Smith's account, the entry has the same effect as a write-off under the allowance method:

Freida Smith			
Jan. 15	300		
		Oct. 31	300

Direct Write-Off Versus Allowance Method — a Matter of Materiality

Many businesses prefer the direct-write-off method because of its simplicity. In addition, the Internal Revenue Code allows taxpayers to use the direct write-off method for recognizing uncollectible accounts expense, but it does not permit the allowance method. Thus, businesses that cannot afford to keep separate records for financial accounting and tax purposes (including many small businesses) use the direct write-off method. However, direct write-off method violates accrual accounting concepts (GAAP). From a GAAP perspective, a business should recognize and match uncollectible accounts expense against the related revenues in the period it recognizes revenues. The direct write-off method recognizes the expense when accounts are written off. This may or may not be the same accounting period in which the sales were made. When it is not the same period, uncollectible accounts expense will be misstated from an accrual perspective. In addition, according to GAAP, a business should not value the accounts receivable above the amounts actually expected to be collected. Under the direct write-off method, however, no allowance for uncollectible accounts is created to offset gross accounts receivable. Thus, the direct write-off method is not acceptable under GAAP.

However, the principle of materiality makes it possible for some businesses to use the direct write-off method and *still not violate GAAP*. **Materiality** is the amount of error or incorrectness in a set of financial statements that could change a decision of a knowledgeable user of the financial statements. By this definition, immaterial amounts of error or incorrectness in financial statements do not matter to users of the statements. Thus, a business may use a simpler, less expensive non-GAAP method of accounting, provided the differences in its financial statements compared to using the GAAP method are *immaterial*.

THIRD-PARTY CREDIT CARDS

LO 3
Account for third-party credit card sales and explain how they can reduce problems of collecting on credit sales.

A business can avoid collection problems and uncollectible accounts expense by accepting third-party credit cards. These credit cards are of two basic types: bank cards and all other credit cards.

Bank Cards

Bank cards such as MasterCard and VISA permit a customer to purchase goods on credit, while the merchant receives immediate cash payment. These cards are called bank cards because the merchant and the customer each have a bank or other financial service business involved in the transaction.

The customer deals with an "issuing bank." The issuing bank takes applications for bank cards from consumers, reviews their credit records, and either issues or denies them bank cards. Once the cards are issued, the issuing banks guarantee payment on all *properly authorized* transactions charged to the card.

The merchant deals with a "service bank." The service bank typically solicits business from merchants by encouraging them to accept bank cards. The service bank evaluates the merchant's actual or likely volume of bank card sales and other cost factors and quotes the merchant a discount rate. Upon depositing the credit card sales slips, the merchant receives an immediate credit to (increase in) his or her bank account for the amount of the sales minus the discount.

Bank cards create a hybrid situation. By accepting bank cards, the merchant gives customers the benefit of credit sales and enjoys a higher sales volume as a result. Compared to regular credit sales, the merchant receives three benefits from the bank card sales arrangement:

1. The merchant receives cash immediately.
2. The merchant avoids any uncollectible account losses from customers.
3. The merchant avoids the costs of credit reviews, collection efforts, and maintenance of customer accounts.

However, the typical discount of $3^1/2$ to 5% offsets these benefits. The amount of the discount depends on a number of factors, including volume of sales and whether authorization is secured by voice (which requires a live operator at the bank to respond) or electronically. The discount is the lowest if the merchant invests in devices that can read the customers' card numbers off the magnetic strips on the backs of the cards and electronically check the status of the cards with a bank card computer system.

Bank card sales revenues and bank card discounts are recorded as of the date of sale. On March 1, 19X5, TWW had bank card sales of $500, and its discount rate is 4%. TWW's entry to record the bank card sales is:

Mar. 1	Cash	480	
	Sales Discounts	20	
	Sales		500
	To record daily bank card sales.		

Other Third-Party Credit Cards

Other third-party credit cards such as American Express cards work in one of two ways. Similar to bank cards, they offer instantaneous payment by working through a bank. Or, if the seller is willing to wait for payment—say six weeks—third-party credit cards offer a lower discount (called a service fee). The seller has the choice of having a higher discount taken out of sales revenues and avoiding uncollectible accounts *and* avoiding waiting for payment or avoiding only the uncollectible accounts problem and enjoying a lower discount. In either case, sales should be stimulated by the seller's willingness to accept the buyer's credit card.

If the seller chooses the full service, the entries for other third-party credit cards are the same as for bank cards. However, if the seller chooses the second alternative, the entries are similar to ordinary credit sales. For example, suppose TWW had $500 of American Express card sales on March 10. The arrangement between TWW and American Express is for TWW to bill American Express for sales and enclose the credit card slips. American Express pays the amounts billed, less a service fee of 2%, in 30 days. TWW's entries to record the sales and subsequent remittance are:

Mar. 10	Accounts Receivable—American Express		490	
	Sales Discounts		10	
	Sales			500
	To record daily American Express card sales.			
Apr. 11	Cash		490	
	Accounts Receivable—American Express			490
	To record collection on American Express card sales.			

LO 4

Describe a promissory note receivable and distinguish between negotiable and nonnegotiable notes.

NOTES RECEIVABLE

Accounts receivable are not the only types of receivables a business may accept from customers or others in exchange for assets. It may also accept promissory notes receivable. A **promissory note** is a written promise by one party (the **maker** of the note) to pay a specified amount of money, usually with interest, to another party (the **payee**) on a specified date at a specified place. Illustration 8-9 is an example of a promissory note.

ILLUSTRATION 8-9 Promissory Note

$____ *1,000* (a)	(b) *January 15*____, 19X1
____*Ace Cleaning Supply* (c)____	____promises to pay to the order of
____*Superior Cleanser Company* (d)____	
One thousand and 00/100————————(e)————————————————Dollars	
At____*First National Bank* (f)____	
Value received with interest at__*12*__percent. (g)	
__*120*__ days after date. (h)	
____*Unsecured* (i)____	
No.____*101* (j)	(k) Signed____*Bruce E. Hobbitt, President*____

Corresponding to the labels in Illustration 8-9, the components of the promissory note are:

(a) The **face amount** of the note in numbers; for example, *$1,000*.

(b) The date the note becomes effective—from which interest and the due date are calculated.

(c) The name of the maker of the note—the person or entity who (which) is promising the payment.

(d) The payee of the note to whom (to which) the amount is owed.

(e) The face amount in words; for example, *One thousand and 00/100*.

(f) The location at which it is agreed the payment will be made when due.

(g) The annual **interest rate** that applies to the face amount of the note.

(h) The **period**, **term**, or **duration** of the note in days (or months or years); for example, *one hundred twenty* or *120* days.

(i) Any supplemental information or conditions; for example, the word *unsecured* indicates that there is no particular property of the maker

that provides a "collateral" way of settling the note if the maker fails to pay cash.
(j) The number of the note if it is in a series of notes the maker writes.
(k) The signature of the maker or its authorized representative.

A business may accept promissory notes in exchange for almost any consideration (asset or service). For example, a business sometimes accepts notes as payment for sales or services rendered. It sometimes accepts notes in exchange for accounts receivable that have or will become past due. In such cases, the customer cannot pay on time but plans to pay in the future. The seller wants a written promise to pay by a particular date and requires an interest rate that adequately compensates the seller for waiting for payment. In other cases, a business accepts promissory notes in exchange for cash loans—as in many bank lending arrangements.

Negotiable Promissory Notes Receivable

A **negotiable promissory note** is an instrument of debt that the original payee can sell readily to collect cash earlier than the due date of the note. A negotiable promissory note actually can confer equal or greater rights to the buyer (called a **holder in due course**) than to the original payee. However, not all notes are negotiable, and not all buyers are holders in due course. To gain the full benefits of negotiability, the note and the buyer (holder) must satisfy certain conditions specified in the U.S. Uniform Commercial Code (UCC). The UCC is the model statutory law governing commercial transactions and relationships. Most states have adopted the UCC in its entirety. All 50 states and the District of Columbia have adopted Article 3 governing negotiable instruments. It is beyond the scope of this text to go into greater detail about the conditions the UCC sets forth. We assume that all of the notes illustrated in this chapter are negotiable.

A holder in due course of a negotiable note is entitled to collect the note, regardless of any offsetting claims or defenses that the maker might have against the original payee. For example, suppose that Ace Cleaning Supply, the maker of the note in Illustration 8-9, buys cleaning products from Superior Cleanser Company for $1,000 and gives the negotiable note in exchange. If the goods turn out to be defective, Ace can claim an offset against the note (or that it should not be paid at all), *if Superior tries to collect.* However, suppose Superior sells the note to First National Bank in exchange for cash and First National becomes a holder in due course. Ace will have to pay First National in full when the note becomes due and will have no defense due to the defects in the goods. However, do not conclude that negotiable notes are a means for sellers to evade responsibility for defects in goods sold. To the contrary, in the above example, Superior has a responsibility for the defects, whether or not the note is sold—but a holder in due course of a negotiable note does not.

Non-Negotiable Promissory Notes

A **non-negotiable promissory note** is a note that does not satisfy the legal conditions for negotiability. A holder of a non-negotiable promissory note does not have an unconditional right to collect the note. Therefore, the payee of a non-negotiable note will not be able to sell it as readily as a negotiable note and will be less likely to accept such a note from the maker.

ACCOUNTING FOR NOTES RECEIVABLE

You must master a few mechanics to account for notes receivable. Notes have fixed terms to maturity and provide the payee with interest. To allocate interest revenue properly between accounting periods, you will have to determine the due dates and numbers of days in the duration of notes accurately, and you will need to calculate both explicit and implicit interest.

Determining the Due Dates of Notes

Several ways are used to express the duration or due date of a note. Some notes begin the promise to pay section with the words "On demand, I (we) promise to pay...." Such notes are demand notes. **Demand notes** are promissory notes that are due at any time the payee or holder in due course presents them for payment. Other notes are of fixed durations. That is, their due dates are fixed by either a stated period such as 90 days from the date made or by a specified due date. The note in Illustration 8-9 is due 120 days from January 15, 19X1. Therefore, it is due on May 15, 19X1:

January 16–31	16 days
February	28 days
March	31 days
April	30 days
May 1–15	15 days
Total	120 days

LO 5

Calculate explicit and implicit interest on notes receivable.

Interest on Notes

To understand how to account for promissory notes, you must understand interest calculations. **Interest** is the expense a borrower incurs for the use of money owed in fixed-amount agreements such as promissory notes; and it is the revenue the creditor earns for lending the money. An **interest-bearing note** explicitly mentions an interest rate to be applied to the face amount of the note. If an interest rate is not mentioned, the note is said to be **noninterest-bearing**. For example, suppose a purchaser of goods worth $950 gives the seller a note that makes no mention of interest but has a face value of $1,000. The note carries $50 of interest cost to the maker even though no interest rate is mentioned.

We customarily state interest rates in annual terms. For example, if a note such as the one in Illustrated 8-9 quotes an interest rate of 12%, it means that the borrower must repay the amount borrowed plus interest of 12% of the amount borrowed for use of the money for one full year. However, the term of a note (the period from the date it is made until its due date) may be for more or less than one year. Thus, you must be able to calculate interest amounts for both fractions and multiples of years. In this chapter, discussion is restricted to periods of less than one year, which usually are expressed in days. For example, notes due in 30, 60, 90, and 120 days are common. Interest for multiple periods and multiple years is covered in a subsequent chapter.

Calculating Explicit Interest.   The general formula for calculating explicit interest for a fraction of a year is:

Interest = Principal x Rate x Time

or

I = PRT

Principal is the face amount of the note; rate, the stated annual interest rate; and time, the fraction of a year for which interest is being calculated. To illustrate, suppose that a 90-day note was made for a face value of $2,000 (the amount mentioned on the face of the note), with explicit interest at 11%. The interest for 90 days on the note is:

$$\$54.25 = \$2,000 \times 11\% \times \frac{90 \text{ days}}{365 \text{ days}}$$

The calculation means that the amount to be paid when the note is due is $2,054.25, the face amount of $2,000, plus $54.25 interest for 90 days. The amount to be paid when the note is due is called the **maturity value** of the note.

You may use the above formula to calculate interest for any subperiod in the term of a note as well as to calculate the full interest over the term (as illustrated). For example, the interest for the first 30 days of the note of the previous example is:

$$\$18.08 = \$2,000 \times 11\% \times \frac{30 \text{ days}}{365 \text{ days}}$$

Calculating Implicit Interest.   Notes that carry implicit interest do not state interest rates on them. They only mention the promised amount and when it is due. Thus, the face amount of such a note is also its maturity value. However, such notes typically are accepted in exchange for amounts of goods or services worth less than the face amounts. For example, as an alternative to the previous example, a $2,000 noninterest-bearing, 90-day note might be accepted in exchange for goods worth $1,945.75. In this way, the seller of the goods would earn the same $54.25 for waiting 90 days as the payee in the previous example who accepts a note bearing 11% explicit interest.

Use the following formula to calculate implicit interest for fractions of the duration of a note carrying implicit interest:

$$\text{Interest} = \text{Total Interest} \times \frac{\textbf{Days}}{\textbf{Term}}$$

Total interest is the difference between the face value of the note and the value exchanged for it (in this example $54.25); days, the number of days for which you wish to calculate interest; and term, the full term of the note in days. To find the amount of interest applicable to 60 days of the note in the preceding example, perform the following calculation:

$$\$36.17 = \$54.25 \times \frac{60 \text{ days}}{90 \text{ days}}$$

LO 6

Account for receipt of notes receivable, accrual of interest on notes receivable, and receipt of payment on notes receivable.

Recording Receipt of Notes Receivable

As mentioned above, a business may accept a note receivable in almost any type of exchange transaction with another entity. A common example is a sales transaction. When Ace Cleaning Supply purchased $1,000 worth of cleaning products from Superior Cleanser on January 15, 19X1, with the note in

Illustration 8-9, Superior would have recorded the exchange with an entry such as this:

Jan. 15	Notes Receivable—Ace Cleaning Supply	1,000	
	Sales		1,000
	To record sale and note receivable.		

When a business accepts a note in transactions other than the sale of goods, it is usually in exchange for assets other than merchandise or to convert a previous account receivable into a note receivable. Assume Ace Cleaning Supply gave the note to Superior Cleanser to pay an account receivable before it became past due. Superior's entry to record the note would have been:

Jan. 15	Notes Receivable—Ace Cleaning Supply	1,000	
	Accounts Receivable—Ace Cleaning Supply		1,000
	To record acceptance of a note receivable in payment of an account receivable.		

Interest Revenue From Notes Receivable

The interest the maker of a note promises is revenue to the payee (or holder). If the note runs full-term during a single accounting period, the payee can simply postpone recording the revenue until the note is collected.

Recording Interest Upon Receipt of Payment.   Ace's $1,000 note made in favor of Superior is due on May 15, 19X1, with 12% interest. The total interest revenue from the note will be $39.45:

$$\$39.45 = \$1,000 \times 12\% \times \frac{120 \text{ days}}{365 \text{ days}}$$

Assuming Superior does not end an accounting period between January 15 and May 15, it can record the revenue from the note upon receipt of the payment.

May 15	Cash	1,039.45	
	Notes Receivable—Ace Cleaning Supply		1,000.00
	Interest Revenue		39.45
	To record receipt of payment of a note receivable.		

Accruing Interest on Notes Before Receipt of Payment.   However, if the payee ends an accounting period during the term of a note, it *accrues* interest revenue as of the end of the period in proportion to the amount of the term of the note that has passed during the period that is ending. Suppose that, in the previous example, Superior wants to prepare financial statements as of March 31, 19X1. The term of the note is split between quarters, 75 days in the fiscal quarter ended March 31, 19X1 (from January 16 through March 31) and 45 days in the fiscal quarter ended June 30, 19X1 (from April 1 to May 15). Superior should recognize the following amounts of interest earned in the two quarters:

$$\text{Quarter ended March 31:} \quad \$24.66 = \$1,000 \times 12\% \times \frac{75 \text{ days}}{365 \text{ days}}$$

$$\text{Quarter ended June 30:} \quad \$14.79 = \$1,000 \times 12\% \times \frac{45 \text{ days}}{365 \text{ days}}$$

Total interest earned: $39.45

To recognize the splitting of revenue between fiscal periods (in this case, quarters), requires an accrual as of March 31, 19X1, of 75 days' revenue recognized with an adjusting entry:

Mar. 31	Interest Receivable—Note	24.66	
	Interest Revenue		24.66
	To accrue interest on note receivable.		

After the above entry, the balance in Notes Receivable (with respect to this note) will be $1,000 and the balance in Interest Receivable—Note will be $24.66. Superior would recognize the remaining interest revenue in the quarter ended June 30 ($14.79) upon receipt of the payment of the note on May 15, with the entry:

May 15	Cash	1,039.45	
	Notes Receivable		1,000.00
	Interest Receivable—Note		24.66
	Interest Revenue		14.79
	To record receipt of payment and interest on note receivable.		

Recording Dishonored Notes Receivable

When the maker of a note declines to pay on the date it is due, the maker is said to have *dishonored* the note. If the maker dishonors a note, then the payee must make certain entries. While the note's terms cover its original time period and indicate that it is due now, they do not apply to the period subsequent to the due date. However, the maker of the note still owes the payee the full debt. To recognize this may require two entries. First, any accrued interest not previously recognized is recorded with an adjusting entry. Referring to the previous example, suppose Ace Cleaning Supply dishonors the $1,000 note on May 15. Further, suppose Superior Cleanser had recorded the accrued interest revenue on the note of $24.66 through March 31. As of May 15, the carrying value of the note (including interest receivable) is $1,024.66. When Ace dishonored the note on May 15, Superior should recognize the remaining interest due on the note of $14.79 with an entry like this:

May 15	Interest Receivable—Note	14.79	
	Interest Revenue		14.79
	To accrue interest on note receivable dishonored.		

At this point, the Notes Receivable balance is $1,000 and the Interest Receivable—Note balance is $39.45—for a total of $1,039.45, the full amount due from Ace. The next entry converts the full amount of the note receivable into an account receivable:

May 15	Accounts Receivable—Ace Cleaning Supply	1,039.45	
	Notes Receivable—Ace Cleaning Supply		1,000.00
	Interest Receivable—Note		39.45
	To record account receivable for note plus accrued interest dishonored by Ace Cleaning Supply.		

After May 15, Superior will treat Ace's obligation like any other account receivable except that Ace probably is entitled to accrue interest. Of course, since the note was not paid on time, the collectibility of the account receivable and any interest may be in doubt. Thus, the collectibility of this new account receivable should enter into Superior's evaluation of the adequacy of its Allowance for Uncollectible Accounts balance as described earlier in the chapter.

Allowance Method for Notes Receivable

The GAAP considerations that apply to uncollectible accounts receivable apply equally to notes receivable. Thus, if any risk that notes receivable will not be collected exists, then the business should accrue uncollectible notes expense and set up an allowance for uncollectible notes. A business may ignore this requirement only if it would lead to immaterial effects on its financial statements—as would be the case if a business only accepted an occasional note receivable in the normal course of its business.

LO 7

Account for the discounting of notes receivable.

Discounting Notes Receivable

The payee of a negotiable note has a choice of holding it until it is due or discounting it (selling it) to a third party. The third party may be anyone other than the maker or the payee. Frequently, the third party is a bank. When a payee sells a note to a third party, the third party does the waiting until the note is due. Hence, the third party requires some compensation or interest in return for waiting for the receipt of cash. This is usually handled by setting a selling price that is less than the note's maturity value. This difference is called a **discount**, and the process of selling or assigning a note is called **discounting a note**.

To illustrate, consider a $2,000, 10% note Credit Corporation holds. Credit Corporation received the note on September 15, 19X1, from DBT Company in exchange for services provided. The term of the note is 90 days, so it is due on December 14, 19X1. The note's maturity value (face value plus interest) is:

Face value	$2,000.00
Interest	$49.32 = \$2,000 \times 10\% \times \dfrac{90 \text{ days}}{365 \text{ days}}$
Maturity value	$2,049.32

Now, suppose Credit Corporation discounts the note with Federal Bank on September 30. The Bank requires an interest rate of 14% on the note's maturity value. The Bank's interest requirement (discount) is calculated using an interest rate of 14% for 75 days (instead of 90 days because Credit Corporation has held the note for 15 days) and a principal amount equal to maturity value:

$$\$58.95 = \$2,049.32 \times 14\% \times \frac{75 \text{ days}}{365 \text{ days}}$$

The Bank is willing to buy the note for $2,049.32 - $58.95 = $1,990.37. If the Bank then holds the note to maturity, it will receive $2,049.32 and earn $58.95 in interest.

The first thing Credit Corporation must do in recording the discounting transaction is to make sure the note is properly valued in its accounts. If Credit Corporation does not automatically accrue interest monthly, it must now accrue the interest through September 30:

$$\$8.22 = \$2,000 \times 10\% \times \frac{15 \text{ days}}{365 \text{ days}}$$

Sept. 30	Interest Receivable—Note	8.22	
	Interest Revenue		8.22
	To accrue interest on note receivable from DBT Company through September 30.		

After the interest is accrued with the above entry, the carrying value of the note is $2,008.22, a combination of the balance in Notes Receivable ($2,000) and Interest Receivable – Note ($8.22). Now, when Credit Corporation discounts the note to the Bank, Credit's cost of receiving cash for the note 75 days before maturity is easily calculated. It is the difference between the carrying value of the note ($2,008.22) and the amount received from the Bank ($1,990.37) or $17.85. Credit Corporation should classify this cost as interest expense, since it is a cost of having cash for a period of time. Credit Corporation would record the discounting of the note to the Bank as follows:

Sept. 30	Cash	1,990.37	
	Interest Expense	17.85	
	Notes Receivable		2,000.00
	Interest Receivable—Note		8.22
	To record discounting of note receivable from DBT Company with Federal Bank.		

Discounted Notes Receivable Dishonored

When the original payee of a negotiable note discounts it to a third party (holder), the payee endorses the note. To endorse a note, the payee signs the back of the note, just as one endorses a check. By endorsing the note with an appropriate *qualification*, the endorser of a note can avoid any liability for payment, should the maker dishonor the note. With qualified endorsement, the payee specifically states that he/she does not assume obligation to pay a discounted note if the maker dishonors it. To make qualified endorsement, the endorser writes "Without recourse" above his/her signature. If the holder accepts the endorsed note, the holder accepts the restriction.

Unless the endorsement is qualified, the original payee is obligated to pay the maturity value (plus a small penalty called a *protest fee*) to the holder in the event that the maker dishonors the note. While the note is outstanding, the original payee of a discounted note (with an unqualified endorsement) is said to have a contingent liability. A **contingent liability** is an obligation that depends on the outcome of future events – in this case, the liability of the original payee depends on whether the maker dishonors the note. If the maker fails to pay the note at the maturity date, the holder is obligated to make a reasonable effort to collect. Failing in this effort, the holder sends a *notice of protest*, usually witnessed by a notary public, to any *unqualified* endorser(s) of the note.

Upon receipt of the notice of protest, the unqualified endorser of the note must pay the holder in full, including any protest fee. The note again becomes the endorser's property and is transferred back by the purchaser in exchange for the endorser's payment in full. At this point, the note is treated just like a dishonored note that the endorser held to maturity—by recording it as an account receivable. Assume, for example, that on December 14, DBT Company dishonored the $2,000 note originally made in favor of Credit Corporation, which Credit Corporation discounted to Federal Bank. After making a reasonable effort to collect the note from DBT Company, the bank sends a notice of protest to Credit Corporation on December 20. The notice demands payment of the note's maturity value, $2,049.32, plus a protest fee equal to 1% of the matu-

343

rity value, or a total of $2,049.32 + 20.49 = $2,069.81. The entry to record Credit Corporation's payment of the note and fee is:

Dec. 20	Accounts Receivable—DBT Company	2,069.81	
	Cash		2,069.81
	To record payment of discounted note dishonored by DBT Company.		

Upon paying the bank, Credit Corporation now has the right, once again, to collect from DBT Company. Moreover, it has the right to collect interest on the account balance of $2,069.80 for the period until the full amount is paid. Credit should expend all reasonable efforts within legal limits to collect the account, subject to the cost-effectiveness standard. However, a dishonored note is evidence of the maker's unwillingness or inability to pay and, therefore, the collectibility of such an account is generally doubtful. Therefore, Credit may have to write off the account eventually. In the meantime, Credit should not accrue further interest. Although the interest is *earned*, it may not be *collectible*.

USING INFORMATION ABOUT RECEIVABLES

LO 8
Calculate the number of days-sales-in-receivables and uncollectible-accounts-expense-as-a-percent-of-credit sales and use these tools to diagnose problems.

Now, let us return to the problem Jane Trevor faced. She has used credit sales to stimulate sales growth for several years. But, after reviewing her results for 19X5, she is dissatisfied with profits and has asked her accountant to produce the comparative information in Illustration 8-10. Jane has already noted that profits declined from 19X4 to 19X5, while gross sales increased. Although she suspects problems with credit sales, she is not sure. She needs some analytical tools to aid her inquiry.

ILLUSTRATION 8-10 Comparative Financial Data

Trevor's Wholesale Warehouse Comparative Financial Data For the Years Ended December 31, 19X4 and 19X5		
	19X4	*19X5*
Income statement data:		
Cash sales	$102,550	$104,675
Credit sales	252,349	275,565
Gross sales	$354,899	$380,240
Less: Sales returns and allowances	(6,536)	(7,558)
Uncollectible accounts expense	(5,359)	(10,595)
Net sales	$343,004	$362,087
Less: Cost of goods sold	212,939	228,144
Gross profit	$130,065	$133,943
Less: Operating expenses	88,725	95,060
Net income	$ 41,340	$ 38,883
Selected balance sheet data:		
Gross accounts receivable (December 31)	$ 45,560	$ 65,240
Less: Allowance for uncollectible accounts	3,450	6,524
Net receivables	$ 42,110	$ 58,716

Days-Sales-in-Receivables

One common financial ratio Jane can use to analyze her accounts receivable is **days-sales-in-receivables**, defined as follows:

$$\text{Days-Sales-in-Receivables} = \frac{\text{Receivables Balance}}{\text{Credit Sales}} \times \text{Days in Period}$$

The receivables balance is the amount of gross receivables as of any balance sheet date (or the average for a period);[2] credit sales, for the period ended on the balance sheet date (a month, a quarter, or a year); and days in the period, the number of days in the period used to measure credit sales. Jane's ratios, using the data in Illustration 8-10 (the period is a year), are:

	19X4		*19X5*

$$\frac{\$45{,}560}{\$252{,}349} \times 365 \text{ days} = 66 \text{ days} \qquad\qquad \frac{\$65{,}240}{\$275{,}565} \times 365 \text{ days} = 86 \text{ days}$$

These comparative ratios tell Jane that on average the receivables her customers owed are 86 days old as of December 31, 19X5; the average receivable was 66 days old as of December 31, 19X4. What can Jane infer from this change?

1. The investment in accounts receivable has grown more than in proportion to credit sales; credit sales grew 9.2%, while receivables grew 43.2%.[3]
2. Her credit sales customers are paying slower at the end of 19X5 than they were at the end of 19X4. This may be due either to a change in customers' abilities to pay or to poor application of credit and collection policies in her business. If employees authorize credit for less credit worthy customers, the new customers will take longer to pay and a higher percentage will fail to pay. If employees do not pursue collections vigorously, customers will take longer to pay.
3. There is a higher risk of customers not paying at all. That is, as a general rule, when customers take longer to pay, more of them fail to pay.
4. Because accounts receivable grew much faster than credit sales, collections have slowed, and the risk of uncollectibility is higher, the allowance for uncollectible accounts should have expanded considerably—and it did, by 89.1%. Such an expansion generally means that uncollectible accounts expense also grew substantially, reducing the profitability of credit sales.

Uncollectible-Accounts-Expense-as-a-Percent-of-Credit Sales

Uncollectible-accounts-expense-as-a-percent-of-credit sales can add further to Jane's diagnosis of her profitability problem. Assume the credit manager of Trevor's Wholesale Warehouse wrote off all accounts that should have been written off in 19X5, accurately estimated the required ending allowance for uncollectible accounts, and caused the appropriate adjusting entry to be made

---

[2]The average gross receivables for a period is often approximated by adding the beginning and ending balances and dividing by 2.

[3]Growth rates are calculated as follows:

$$\text{Growth Rate} = 100\% \times \left(\frac{\text{New Amount}}{\text{Previous Amount}} - 1\right)$$

for the final year-end accrual of uncollectible accounts expense. Under these circumstances, the uncollectible accounts expense is an accurate estimate of the portion of credit sales for the year that will not be collected. Jane can use the uncollectible-accounts-expense-as-a-percent-of-credit sales as an indicator of the profitability effects of credit sales. The percent is calculated as follows:

$$\text{Percent} = 100 \times \frac{\text{Uncollectible Accounts Expense}}{\text{Credit Sales}}$$

The percents for 19X4 and 19X5 are as follows:

19X4	*19X5*
$100 \times \left(\dfrac{\$5,349}{\$252,349}\right) = 2.12\%$	$100 \times \left(\dfrac{\$10,595}{\$275,565}\right) = 3.84\%$

These comparative ratios show a significant change in uncollectible accounts expense. If uncollectible accounts expense had remained the same percent of credit sales in 19X5 as in 19X4 (2.12%), TWW would have saved $4,740 [(3.84% - 2.12%) x $275,565 = $4,740]. The net income of $38,883 would have been higher by $4,740, or by more than 11%.

In summary, the days-sales-in-receivables and uncollectible-accounts-expense-as-a-percent-of-credit sales ratios tell Jane that her customers are paying slower, more are failing or will fail to pay, her investment in receivables has escalated out of proportion to credit sales, and the profitability of credit sales has clearly declined. She definitely will want to investigate her employees' application of TWW's credit and collections policies.

SUMMARY

Explain why businesses grant credit to their customers, why they should expect to experience uncollectible accounts, and how they can control uncollectible accounts expense.   Businesses grant credit to customers to increase sales and net income. However, some customers ultimately do not pay their accounts. The best ways to control uncollectible accounts expense are a sound credit policy and a system of authorizing sales only to creditworthy customers.

Account for estimated uncollectible accounts, uncollectible accounts expense, and subsequent write-offs of uncollectible accounts according to the allowance method.   A business should recognize uncollectible accounts expense in the same period it records the related credit sales. However, the business does not always know the exact credit sales that will not be collected in the same period as the sales were made. Therefore, as it recognizes uncollectible accounts expense (debited), it increases the contra-receivables account Allowance for Uncollectible Accounts, (credited). When individual accounts are deemed uncollectible, the business writes off accounts in both Accounts Receivable (credit) and Allowance for Uncollectible Accounts (debit) and credits the individual customer accounts. The business may accrue uncollectible accounts expense according to the income statement (percent of credit sales) method or the balance sheet (percent of receivables) method.

Account for third-party credit card sales and explain how they can reduce problems of collecting on credit sales.   Third-party credit cards have the advantage of providing credit to customers and immediate cash to merchants. However, credit card companies charge a discount on credit card sales—that is, the cash received is less than the amount of the sale. Merchants may willingly sacrifice the discount to have cash immediately and to avoid uncollectible accounts.

Describe a promissory note receivable and distinguish between negotiable and nonnegotiable notes.   A note receivable is an explicit, written promise by the maker to pay a specific sum on a specific date (or on demand) at a specific location. A negotiable note is one that meets certain criteria so that a holder in due course to whom the payee has sold the note may collect it, regardless of any dispute the maker may have with the original payee. The advantage of a negotiable note is that it can be sold readily. All other notes are nonnegotiable and cannot be sold as readily as negotiable notes.

Calculate explicit and implicit interest on notes receivable.   Whether stated explicitly or not, most notes receivable pay interest to the payee or holder. The following formula is used to calculate interest on short-term notes carrying explicit interest:

$$\text{Interest} = \text{Principal} \times \text{Rate} \times \text{Time}$$

Principal is the face amount of the note; rate, the stated annual interest rate; and *time, the fraction of a year* for which interest is being calculated.

If a short-term note carries no explicit interest rate, interest revenue for a period is calculated according to this formula:

$$\text{Interest} = \text{Total Interest} \times \frac{\text{Days}}{\text{Term}}$$

Total interest is the difference between the note's face value and the value exchanged for it; days, the number of days for which you wish to calculate interest; and term, the full term of the note in days.

Account for receipt of notes receivable, accrual of interest on notes receivable, and receipt of payment on notes receivable.   When a note is issued—usually in exchange for cash or merchandise—we record the note at the value given in exchange for it. Interest revenue on notes receivable is recorded in each accounting period in proportion to the amount of the term of the note that has expired. When payment is received, any remaining interest is recognized as the difference between the carrying value of the note (original value plus accrued interest) and the cash received.

Account for the discounting of notes receivable.   When a payee sells the note to a holder, we say it is discounted. The holder pays less (by the amount of a discount) than maturity value to the original payee or other seller of the note. The seller then recognizes the difference between the discounted maturity value and the seller's carrying value of the note as interest income or expense (depending on the amount of the discount).

Calculate the number of days-sales-in-receivables and uncollectible-accounts-expense-as-a-percent-of-credit sales and use these tools to diagnose problems. Days-sales-in-receivables is calculated according to the following formula:

$$\text{Days-Sales-in-Receivables} = \frac{\text{Receivables Balance}}{\text{Credit Sales}} \times \text{Days in Period}$$

The receivables balance is the amount of gross receivables as of any balance sheet date (or the average for a period); credit sales, the sales for the period ended on the balance sheet date (a month, a quarter, or a year); and days in the period, the number of days in the period used to measure credit sales.

Uncollectible-accounts-expense-as-a-percent-of-credit sales is calculated as follows:

$$\text{Percent} = 100 \times \frac{\text{Uncollectible Accounts Expense}}{\text{Credit Sales}}$$

Managers can use these two ratios to diagnose problems with credit granting, sales authorization, collection efforts, and profitability of credit sales.

REVIEW PROBLEM 1: ACCOUNTS RECEIVABLE

The Smith Company uses the allowance method of accounting for uncollectible accounts receivable. Accounts receivable information for Smith Company for the year ended 19X1 is presented below:

Cash sales	$ 23,600
Credit sales	170,000
Accounts to be written off, 12-31-X1	2,700
Allowance for uncollectible accounts, 1-1-X1	3,100
Accounts receivable, 12-31-X1, before write offs	48,720

Smith Company
Aged Schedule of Accounts Receivable
December 31, 19X1

CUSTOMER NUMBER	AMOUNT WITHIN DISCOUNT	AMOUNT WITHIN 30 DAYS	AMOUNT 1–30 DAYS PAST DUE	AMOUNT 31–60 DAYS PAST DUE	AMOUNT 61–90 DAYS PAST DUE	AMOUNT 91–120 DAYS PAST DUE	AMOUNT 120 DAYS PAST DUE	CUSTOMER TOTAL
101	3,720		2,190					5,910
102	3,360							3,360
103		4,890	4,810		860	1,020		11,580
104				2,540	920			3,460
105				1,760				1,760
106	2,220							2,220
107					2,220	3,120		5,340
108							960	960
109				1,310				1,310
110		8,930		1,190				10,120
Total	9,300	13,820	7,000	6,800	4,000	4,140	960	46,020
Allowance %	1.5%	3.0%	4.0%	5.0%	7.0%	12.0%	18.0%	
Allowance								

REQUIRED:

a. Prepare all necessary journal entries, assuming that 2.0% of all credit sales will be uncollectible (income statement method).
b. Prepare the balance sheet (direct disclosure method) and income statement (contra-revenue) presentation of accounts receivable, assuming that 2.0% of all credit sales will be uncollectible.
c. Complete the aged schedule of accounts receivable.
d. Calculate uncollectible accounts expense for 19X1 from the information determined in c above (balance sheet method).

SOLUTION:

Planning and Organizing Your Work

1. Calculate uncollectible accounts expense by multiplying the estimated uncollectible percentage times credit sales.
2. Record the uncollectible accounts expense calculated in Step 1.
3. Record the write-off of uncollectible accounts.
4. Determine the balances in Accounts Receivable and Allowance for Uncollectible Accounts.
5. Prepare the income statement and balance sheet presentations.
6. Complete the aged schedule of accounts receivable by multiplying the total in each category times the allowance percentage.
7. Determine the ending balance in the Allowance for Uncollectible Accounts by summing the amounts calculated in Step 6.
8. Determine the uncollectible accounts expense for 19X1 by calculating the amount of increase necessary to bring the Allowance for Uncollectible Accounts to the correct balance calculated in Step 7. (Note: Ignore any previous accrual of uncollectible accounts expense under the income statement method.)

(a) *Prepare all journal entries.*

Dec. 31	Allowance for Uncollectible Accounts	2,700	
	Accounts Receivable		2,700
	To write off uncollectible accounts.		
31	Uncollectible Accounts Expense	3,400	
	Allowance for Uncollectible Accounts		3,400
	To accrue estimated uncollectible accounts expense for the year ended December 31. ($170,000 x 2%)		

(b) *Prepare the balance sheet and income statement presentation.*
The T-accounts for Accounts Receivable and Allowance for Uncollectible Accounts are presented below:

Accounts Receivable

End. Bal. 48,720	
	Write-offs 2,700
Adj. Bal. 46,020	

Allowance for Uncollectible Accounts

	Beg. Bal. 3,100
	Accrual 3,400
Write-offs 2,700	
	End. Bal. 3,800

Therefore, the partial balance sheet would appear as follows:

Smith Company
Balance Sheet (Partial)
December 31, 19X1

Current assets:
Accounts receivable $48,720
Less: Allowance for uncollectible accounts 3,800 $44,920

Smith Company
Income Statement (Partial)
For the Year Ended December 31, 19X1

Revenue from sales $193,600
Less: Uncollectible accounts expense 3,400

(c) *Complete the Aged Schedule of Accounts Receivable.*

Smith Company
Aged Schedule of Accounts Receivable
December 31, 19X1

CUSTOMER NUMBER	AMOUNT WITHIN DISCOUNT	AMOUNT WITHIN 30 DAYS	AMOUNT 1–30 DAYS PAST DUE	AMOUNT 31–60 DAYS PAST DUE	AMOUNT 61–90 DAYS PAST DUE	AMOUNT 91–120 DAYS PAST DUE	OVER 120 DAYS PAST DUE	CUSTOMER TOTAL
101	3,720		2,190					5,910
102	3,360							3,360
103		4,890	4,810		860	1,020		11,580
104				2,540	920			3,460
105				1,760				1,760
106	2,220							2,220
107					2,220	3,120		5,340
108							960	960
109				1,310				1,310
110		8,930		1,190				10,120
Total	9,300	13,820	7,000	6,800	4,000	4,140	960	46,020
Allowance %	1.5%	3.0%	4.0%	5.0%	7.0%	12.0%	18.0%	
Allowance	140	415	280	340	280	497	173	2,125

(d) *Calculate uncollectible accounts expense for 19X1.*
The calculation of uncollectible accounts expense is shown below:

Estimated allowance for uncollectible accounts, December 31, 19X1	$2,125
Less: Balance in Allowance for Uncollectible Accounts after	
write-offs on December 31, 19X1 ($3,100 - $2,700)	400
Estimated uncollectible accounts expense for 19X1	$1,725

REVIEW PROBLEM 2: NOTES RECEIVABLE

Olympic Company received a $15,000, 90-day, 10% note from Mountain, Inc. on December 31, 19X1, in exchange for services performed.

REQUIRED:

a. Prepare the journal entry for Olympic Company to record the issuance of the note.
b. Prepare the journal entry for Olympic Company to record the recognition of interest and collection of the note.
c. Calculate the proceeds for Olympic if it discounted the note with First National Bank at 12%, 60 days after the note was received.
d. Prepare the journal entries for Olympic if it discounted the note at 12%, 60 days after the note was received.
e. Prepare the journal entry assuming Mountain does not honor the discounted note. Assume a protest fee of $150.

SOLUTION:

Planning and Organizing Your Work
1. Analyze the transaction in which the note is received and record the journal entry.
2. Calculate interest for 90 days on the note. Prepare a journal entry to accrue interest revenue for 90 days and the collection of cash.
3. Calculate the interest First National Bank must receive at maturity of the note (the discount).

4. Deduct the discount from the maturity value of the note—face value plus interest for 90 days—to determine the discounted value (proceeds of discounting).
5. Calculate the carrying value of the note after 60 days—face value plus accrued interest.
6. Compare the discounted value (proceeds) to carrying value to determine the interest expense or revenue associated with the discounting.
7. Write the journal entry to accrue interest on the note for 60 days.
8. Write a journal entry to record discounting the note. Debit (credit) Interest Expense (Revenue) with the difference between carrying value and the proceeds of discounting.
9. Prepare a journal entry for the cash payment to First National Bank for the dishonored note at maturity value plus the $150 protest fee.

(a) *Record the issuance of the note.*

19X1			
Dec. 31	Notes Receivable—Mountain, Inc.	15,000.00	
	Revenue		15,000.00
	To record the receipt of the note in exchange for services performed.		

(b) *Record the recognition of interest and collection of the note.*

19X2			
Mar. 31	Cash	15,369.86	
	Notes Receivable—Mountain, Inc.		15,000.00
	Interest Revenue—Mountain, Inc.		369.86
	To recognize collection of the note plus interest. ($15,000 x 10% x 90/365 = $369.86)		

(c) *Calculate the proceeds if the note is discounted.*

1. Calculate maturity value: ($15,000 x 10% x 90/365) + $15,000 = $15,369.86
2. Calculate discount: ($15,369.86 x 12% x 30/365)   =   151.59
3. Calculate proceeds: $15,369.86 - $151.59   = $15,218.27

(d) *Record the discounting of the note.*

19X2			
Mar. 1	Interest Receivable—Note	246.58	
	Interest Revenue—Note		246.58
	To accrue interest of $246.58 on note receivable from Mountain. ($15,000 x 10% x 60/365 before discounting).		
1	Cash	15,218.27	
	Interest Expense	28.31	
	Notes Receivable—Mountain, Inc.		15,000.00
	Interest Receivable—Note		246.58
	To record discounting of note receivable from Mountain.		

The cash received is calculated above. The carrying value of the note receivable equals the original amount ($15,000) plus the interest that would have been recognized after 60 days. The interest expense is the difference between the carrying value and the cash received.

(e) *Prepare the journal entry assuming Mountain does not honor the note.*

19X2			
Mar. 31	Accounts Receivable—Mountain, Inc.	15,519.86	
	Cash		15,519.86
	To record payment of discounted note dishonored by Mountain. ($15,369.86 + $150 protest fee)		

KEY TERMS

allowance for uncollectible
    accounts, *327*
allowance method, *325*
balance sheet approach, *330*
bank card, *333*
contingent liability, *342*
days-sales-in-receivables, *344*
demand notes, *337*
direct write-off method, *332*
discount, *341*
discounting a note, *341*
face amount, *335*

holder in due course, *336*
income statement approach,
    326
indirect (net) method, *327*
interest, *337*
interest-bearing, *337*
interest rate, *335*
maker, *335*
materiality, *333*
maturity value, *338*
negotiable promissory note,
    336

noninterest-bearing, *337*
non-negotiable promissory
    note, *336*
payee, *335*
period (term, duration), *335*
promissory note, *335*
uncollectible accounts expense,
    332
uncollectible-accounts-
    expense-as-a-percent-of-
    credit sales, *344*

SELF-QUIZ

LO 1   1. How do you calculate the additional profits from granting credit?
    a. Additional Cost of Goods Sold - Additional Sales Revenues
    b. Additional Sales Revenue - Additional Cost of Goods Sold
    c. Additional Sales Revenue - Additional Cost of Goods Sold - Additional Expenses, including Uncollectible Accounts Expense
    d. Additional Sales Revenue - Additional Uncollectible Accounts Expense

LO 1   2. True or False? Sales personnel on commission should conduct credit screenings since they know the most about customers.

LO 1   3. According to the _____ principle, a business should recognize the estimated amount of uncollectible accounts from a period's sales revenues as an expense in the same period it recognizes the revenues.

LO 2   4. Which of the following is *not* true about the allowance method?
    a. The accrual of uncollectible accounts expense is independent of any actual write-offs.
    b. This method uses a contra-asset account called Allowance for Uncollectible Accounts.
    c. It is consistent with the matching concept.
    d. Uncollectible Accounts Expense is debited when amounts owed are deemed uncollectible.

LO 2   5. True or False? Under the income statement approach, businesses accrue estimated uncollectible accounts expense based on the average collections per dollar of credit sales.

LO 2   6. Which of the following statements is *not* true under the allowance method?
    a. Recognition of uncollectible accounts expense reduces Accounts Receivable.

    b. The write-off of a customer's account receivable does not affect Uncollectible Accounts Expense.
    c. Uncollectible accounts expense can be presented in the income statement as a reduction of revenue.
    d. Uncollectible accounts expense can be presented in the income statement in the category "Other income and expense."

LO 2   7. To apply the _____ _____ approach, an aged trial balance is used to evaluate the makeup of the Accounts Receivable balance at the end of a period.

LO 2   8. Which of the following is *not* true about the direct write-off method?
    a. It is the simplest method of handling uncollectible accounts.
    b. Uncollectible Accounts Expense is debited when amounts owed are deemed uncollectible.
    c. It is consistent with the matching concept.
    d. Subsequent collections are accounted for by a credit to Uncollectible Accounts Expense.

LO 3   9. With respect to bank cards, the customer deals with an _____ bank and the merchant deals with a _____ bank.

LO 4 10. A promissory note is a written promise by the _____ of the note to pay a specified amount of money to the _____ on a specified date at a specified place.

LO 4 11. Which of the following is *not* a component of a promissory note?
    a. The signature of the payee
    b. The interest rate
    c. The period, term, or duration
    d. The name of the maker

LO 4 12. True or False? Demand notes are promissory notes that are due on a specified date.

LO 5 13. What is the formula for calculating explicit interest?

LO 6 14. It is necessary to accrue _____ _____ on a note receivable if the payee ends an accounting period during the term of the note.

LO 6 15. True or False? When the payee of a note declines to pay on the date it is due, the payee is said to have dishonored the note.

LO 7 16. The process of selling a negotiable note receivable to a third party is called _____ a note.

LO 7 17. Which of the following is *not* true about discounting a note receivable?
   a. The original payee will receive cash before the note is due.
   b. The selling price of the note is usually equal to its maturity value.
   c. The original payee has a contingent liability for the note's maturity value if it is endorsed without qualification.
   d. When a note is dishonored, the holder of the note may collect a protest fee.

LO 8 18. How much is Trevino Company's days sales in receivables if Trevino's ending receivable balance and credit sales for the year are $40,000 and $200,000, respectively?

LO 8 19. True or False? The lower the days-sales-in-receivables, the higher the risk that credit customers will not pay.

LO 8 20. True or False? To be useful in analyzing a company's credit policy, a reasonably accurate estimate of uncollectible accounts expense for uncollectible-accounts-expense-as-a-percent-of-credit sales is necessary.

SOLUTIONS TO SELF-QUIZ
1. c   2. False   3. Matching   4. d   5. True   6. a   7. Balance sheet   8. c   9. issuing, service
10. maker, payee   11. a   12. False   13. Interest = Principal x Rate x Time   14. interest revenue   15. False
16. discounting   17. b   18. ($40,000/$240,000) x 365 = 61days   19. False   20. True

QUESTIONS

Q8-1 Why do businesses grant credit to their customers even though they sometimes cannot collect all of the amounts due?

Q8-2 How can uncollectible accounts expense be controlled?

Q8-3 What are the differences between the income statement approach and the balance sheet approach to estimating uncollectible accounts expense?

Q8-4 What are the advantages and disadvantages of using an aged schedule of accounts receivable?

Q8-5 What are the two different formats for disclosing the allowance for uncollectible accounts on the balance sheet?

Q8-6 What are the differences between the direct write-off method and the allowance method of accounting for receivables?

Q8-7 Why do businesses accept third-party credit cards?

Q8-8 What are the differences between bank cards and other third-party credit cards?

Q8-9 What are the two types of promissory notes and how do they differ?

Q8-10 What is a holder in due course?

Q8-11 What is the difference between explicit interest and implicit interest?

Q8-12 Under what circumstances should the allowance method be applied to notes receivable?

Q8-13 What is the difference between a discount on a note and discounting a note?

Q8-14 What are the advantages and disadvantages of a very low number of days-sales-in-receivables?

EXERCISES

LO 2   **E8-1**   **Allowance Method for Uncollectible Accounts**   Using the allowance method, record journal entries for the Caster Company for the following transactions:

19X0

Mar. 31 Caster estimated that $7,300 of March credit sales will be uncollectible.

Apr. 3 Sold $2,900 of goods on credit to R. Ricketts.

Nov. 28 R. Ricketts' account was deemed to be uncollectible.

19X1

Feb. 3 R. Ricketts paid the $2,900 owed to Caster.

LO 2   **E8-2** **Income Statement Method**   Gadgets Unlimited decided to grant credit 4 years ago, and it uses the percentage of sales method. Since it has a relatively stable credit experience, Gadgets bases the calculation of uncollectible accounts expense on the average uncollectible percentage over the past 4 years. During 19X1, the company had $420,000 of credit sales.

Years past	Credit sales	Uncollectible accounts
4 years	$325,000	$ 7,800
3 years	380,000	8,360
2 years	360,000	8,280
1 year	435,000	10,614

REQUIRED:

Calculate the 19X1 uncollectible accounts expense given the above information.

LO 2   **E8-3** **Financial Statement Presentation Using the Allowance Method**   Given the following information, show the income statement (contra-revenue) and balance sheet (direct disclosure) presentation for the Krish Company:

Item	Amount
Allowance for uncollectible accounts (1/1/X2)	$ 5,100
Write-offs for 19X2	23,500
Estimated uncollectible accounts expense for 19X2	29,200
Accounts receivable (12/31/X2)	188,300
Sales revenue	356,000
Sales returns and allowances	21,600

LO 2   **E8-4** **Balance Sheet Method**   Bright Lights uses an aged schedule of accounts receivable to estimate uncollectible accounts expense. The balance of Allowance for Uncollectible Accounts is $2,900 (credit) after write-offs have been recorded but before uncollectible accounts expense has been estimated. The following summary information is from an aged schedule of accounts receivable:

Age	Accounts receivable balance	Percent uncollectible
Current	$138,000	2%
31–60 days	152,000	4
61–90 days	110,000	6
Over 90 days	85,000	10

REQUIRED:

Write the necessary journal entry to record Uncollectible Accounts Expense for Bright Lights.

LO 3   **E8-5** **Accepting Bank Cards**   To have the benefit of accepting credit sales without having to initiate its own credit system, Premier Jewelry accepts only bank cards and cash. The service bank charges a discount rate of 4% on all bank card sales. During January, Premier customers bought $47,600 of jewelry, of which $13,600 was for cash and the remainder was charged to bank cards.

REQUIRED:

Record the necessary journal entries for January sales.

LO 5   **E8-6**   **Calculating Explicit Interest**   Boone Company received a $1,000, 120-day, 13% note from J. Lewis.

REQUIRED:

Determine the explicit interest and the maturity value of the note.

LO 5   **E8-7**   **Calculating Implicit Interest**   New Ohio Company received an $8,000, noninterest-bearing, 90-day note in exchange for goods worth $7,783.

REQUIRED:

Calculate the amount of interest that New Ohio Company would accrue at the end of the fiscal year, 60 days after the note is dated.

LO 6   **E8-8**   **Accounting for Notes Receivable**   Faultless Laundry purchased $5,000 of cleaning chemicals on credit from Rodger's Chemical Supplies on August 12, 19X3. On December 1, Rodger's Chemical Supplies agreed to accept a 90-day, 10% note receivable from Faultless Laundry to pay for the account receivable from the purchase on August 12.

REQUIRED:

Record the necessary journal entries for the receipt of the note, the accrual of interest on December 31, and the collection of the note for Rodger's Chemical Supplies.

LO 6   **E8-9**   **Recording Dishonored Notes Receivable**   Assuming Faultless Laundry dishonors the note on the due date, record the journal entry for the note receivable for Rodger's Chemical Supplies described in E8-8 above.

LO 7   **E8-10**   **Calculating the Proceeds for a Discounted Note Receivable**   The Sun Company discounted at a rate of 15%, a $10,000 face value, 90-day, 12% note receivable 60 days after the note was issued.

REQUIRED:

Calculate the proceeds to Sun Company.

LO 7   **E8-11**   **Discounting of Notes Receivable**   Record journal entries for the Pei Company for the following transactions:

Apr.   1   Sold $8,000 of merchandise to Discount Stores in exchange for a 60-day, 10% note receivable.
      16   Discounted the note receivable at Last National Bank at 14%.
May 31   Discount Stores paid the amount due to Last National Bank.

LO 7   **E8-12**   **Discounted Notes Receivable Dishonored**   Junipers discounted a $5,000 note from Trillo Company to the Second National Bank. The note has a maturity value of $5,460. Second National Bank charges a protest fee of 2% of the maturity value for all dishonored notes.

REQUIRED:

Assuming Trillo dishonors the note, record the journal entry for Junipers.

LO 8   **E8-13**   **Calculating Days-Sales-in-Receivables and Uncollectible-Accounts-Expense-as-a-Percent-of-Credit Sales**   Calculate the days-sales-in-receivables and the uncollectible-accounts-expense-as-a-percent-of-credit sales for Wetscapes given the following information:

Credit sales	$271,890
Accounts receivable	61,289
Uncollectible accounts expense	3,245

▍PROBLEM SET A

LO 2   **P8-1A**   **Income Statement Method**   The Kumar Company uses the allowance method of accounting for accounts receivable. Kumar estimates uncollectible accounts expense to be 3.5% of net credit sales. During 19X5, Kumar had sales on account of $846,300. Sales returns and allowances on credit sales were $11,200, and sales discounts amounted to $4,800. In addition, Kumar deemed $24,200 of accounts receivable to be uncollectible during the year, and it collected $1,300 of accounts receivable written off in prior years. The balance in Allowance for Uncollectible Accounts as of January 1, 19X5, was $21,600. The December 31, 19X5, balance in Accounts Receivable was $207,200.

REQUIRED:

a. Calculate the estimated uncollectible accounts expense for 19X5.
b. Record the journal entries for the 19X5 events given above.
c. Show how Kumar would disclose the estimated uncollectible accounts expense on the 19X5 income statement (contra-revenue method).
d. Show how Kumar would disclose the allowance for uncollectible accounts on the December 31, 19X5, balance sheet using both disclosure formats.

LO 2   **P8-2A**   **Using an Aged Schedule of Accounts Receivable**   The Jones Company uses the allowance method of accounting for uncollectible accounts receivable. Accounts receivable information for Jones Company for the year ended 19X7 is presented below:

Cash sales	$ 354,000
Credit sales	1,275,000
Accounts written off	40,500
Allowance for uncollectible accounts, 1-1-X7	46,500
Accounts receivable, 1-1-X7	453,000
Estimated percent uncollectible:	

Age of receivable	Percent uncollectible
0 – 30 Days	1.5%
31 – 60 Days	3.0
61 – 90 Days	5.0
91 – 120 Days	6.0
Over 120 Days	10.0

Accounts receivable for Jones by customer (after writeoffs) is presented below:

Customer number	Amount	Time outstanding
101	$ 37,500	20 days
101	19,100	47 days
213	38,000	130 days
284	13,300	15 days
312	27,000	112 days
330	18,600	40 days
401	46,900	32 days
402	11,100	5 days

Customer number	Amount	Time outstanding
569	102,200	12 days
612	24,000	88 days
671	72,300	53 days
691	69,900	27 days

REQUIRED:

a. Prepare an aged schedule of accounts receivable similar to the one in Illustration 8-7. Jones does not offer sales discounts, but sells on terms of net 30 days.
b. Prepare the journal entry for the accounts written off.
c. Determine uncollectible accounts expense and prepare the journal entry to record it.
d. Show how The Jones Company would disclose the estimated uncollectible accounts expense (contra-revenue) and the allowance for uncollectible accounts on the 19X7 financial statements. Use the direct disclosure method for the balance sheet.

LO 2

P8-3A   **Determining Missing Information for Accounts Receivable**   Tom's Electronics Distributors estimates that 2% of all credit sales are uncollectible. Selected information for Tom's Electronics Distributors for the years ended 19X8 and 19X9 is presented below:

	19X8	19X9
Accounts receivable, 1/1	$130,000	$140,000
Accounts receivable, 12/31	?	?
Allowance for uncollectible accounts, 1/1	8,400	?
Allowance for uncollectible accounts, 12/31	?	13,600
Credit sales	540,000	?
Collections	?	620,000
Write-offs	6,200	?
Uncollectible accounts expense	?	14,100

REQUIRED:

a. Fill in the missing information for 19X8 and 19X9.
b. Using the direct disclosure method, show how Tom's will disclose accounts receivable and allowance for uncollectible accounts on the 19X8 and 19X9 balance sheet.

LO 6

P8-4A   **Accounting for Notes Receivable**   The Rojo Company had the following transactions during 19X3:

Apr.   1   The Grunstadt Company purchased goods at a price of $20,000 from Rojo. Because Grunstadt is a marginal credit risk, Rojo insisted that Grunstadt pay by issuing a 14%, $20,000, 120-day note in exchange for the goods purchased.

July   1   Rojo Company loaned $25,000 to one of its best customers, Bill Schwartz, in exchange for a note. The note is due in 1 year and has an interest rate of 12%.

       30   Grunstadt Company dishonored the note issued on April 1.

Sept.   1   Blanco Company, which purchased goods for $10,000 on credit, was unable to pay the amount owed. Rojo accepted a 15%, $10,000, 90-day note in exchange.

Nov.   1   Rojo Company loaned $5,000 to a trusted employee in exchange for a note. The note is due in 120 days and has an interest rate of 10%.

       30   Blanco paid Rojo Company in full.

REQUIRED:

a. Prepare journal entries for the above transactions.
b. Prepare appropriate adjusting entries at December 31, 19X3.

LO 7

P8-5A   **Notes Receivable Discounted**   The Travis Company had the following transactions during 19X6:

Mar. 31 The McGee Company purchased goods for $20,000 from Travis. Because the purchase was large and would take several months for McGee to sell, Travis allowed McGee to pay by issuing a 14%, $20,000, 120-day note in exchange for the goods purchased.

Apr. 30 Travis Company discounted the note from McGee to the Everglades National Bank at a discount rate of 16%. Travis endorsed the note with no qualifications.

July 29 McGee dishonored the note. Travis made the necessary payment to Everglades National Bank, including a protest fee of $40.

Oct. 1 Abernathy Company, which previously purchased goods for $10,000 on credit, was unable to pay the amount owed. Travis accepted a 15%, $10,000, 90-day note in exchange.

Nov. 30 Travis Company discounted the note from Abernathy to the Gator National Bank at a discount rate of 17%. Travis endorsed the note with no qualifications.

Dec. 30 Abernathy paid the Gator National Bank in full.

REQUIRED:

Prepare journal entries for the above transactions.

LO 8 **P8-6A** **Calculate the Number-of-Days-Sales-in-Receivables and Uncollectible-Accounts-Expense-as-a-Percent-of-Credit Sales and Use these Tools to Diagnose Problems** Trudy's Shoe Barn has experienced a 40% increase in gross sales in 19X1 compared to 19X0—mostly due to increased credit sales. However, net income increased by only 25%. Trudy is worried that credit sales may be reducing her company's profitability. She asks her accountant to prepare a schedule of the relevant financial data.

Trudy's Shoe Barn Comparative Financial Data For the Years Ended December 31, 19X0 and 19X1		
	19X0	*19X1*
Income statement data:		
Cash sales	$ 90,000	$100,000
Credit sales	160,000	250,000
Gross sales	$250,000	$350,000
Less: Sales returns and allowances	(5,000)	(7,000)
Uncollectible accounts expense	(5,000)	(17,500)
Net sales	$240,000	$325,500
Less: Cost of goods sold	155,000	217,000
Gross profit	$ 85,000	$108,500
Less: Operating expenses	65,000	83,500
Net income	$ 20,000	$ 25,000
Selected balance sheet data:		
Gross accounts receivable (December 31)	$ 32,000	$ 60,000
Less: Allowance for uncollectible accounts	3,200	10,000
Net receivables	$ 28,800	$ 50,000

REQUIRED:

Analyze the data using the number-of-days-sales-in-receivables and uncollectible-accounts-expense-as-a-percent-of-credit sales. Comment on whether Trudy's concerns about credit sales are well founded.

PROBLEM SET B

LO 2   **P8-1B**   **Income Statement Method**   The Reinbold Company uses the allowance method of
accounting for accounts receivable. Reinbold estimates uncollectible accounts expense to
be 4% of net credit sales. Reinbold deemed $35,100 of accounts receivable to be uncol-
lectible during the year, and it collected $3,200 of accounts receivable written off in prior
years. The Allowance for Uncollectible Accounts had a January 1, 19X9, balance of
$33,100. The December 31, 19X9, balance in Accounts Receivable was $231,800. Sales
information for Reinbold during 19X9 is presented below:

Sales on account	$958,200
Sales returns and allowances on credit sales	16,200
Sales discounts	5,500

REQUIRED:

a. Calculate the estimated uncollectible accounts expense for 19X9.
b. Record the journal entries for the 19X9 events given above.
c. Show how Reinbold would list the estimated uncollectible accounts expense (contra-
revenue) on the 19X9 income statement.
d. Show how Reinbold would disclose the allowance for uncollectible accounts on the
December 31, 19X9, balance sheet using both disclosure formats.

LO 3   **P8-2B**   **Using an Aged Schedule of Accounts Receivable**   The Schwartz Company uses the
allowance method of accounting for uncollectible accounts receivable. Accounts receivable information for Schwartz Company for the year ended 19X2 is presented below:

Cash sales	$ 427,000
Credit sales	1,476,000
Accounts written off	52,300
Allowance for uncollectible accounts, 1-1-X2	49,100
Accounts receivable, 1-1-X2	432,600
Estimated percent uncollectible:	

Age of receivable	Percent uncollectible
0 – 30 Days	2.0%
31 – 60 Days	3.5
61 – 90 Days	4.5
91 – 120 Days	7.0
Over 120 Days	9.0

Accounts receivable information for Schwartz by customer (after writeoffs) is presented
below:

Customer number	Amount	Time outstanding
1010	$ 87,500	23 days
1017	27,900	47 days
1213	41,100	130 days
1284	23,300	5 days
3112	42,200	102 days
3430	14,700	33 days
4501	46,200	42 days
4829	60,300	72 days
4902	111,100	19 days
5669	49,400	8 days
6120	6,300	113 days
6671	15,200	58 days
6991	69,900	27 days
7824	33,300	88 days

REQUIRED:

a. Prepare an aged schedule of accounts receivable similar to the one in Illustration 8-7. Schwartz does not offer sales discounts, and sells only on terms of net 30 days.
b. Prepare the journal entry for the accounts written off.
c. Determine uncollectible accounts expense and prepare the journal entry to record it.
d. Show how Schwartz would disclose the estimated uncollectible accounts expense (contra-revenue) and the allowance for uncollectible accounts on the 19X2 financial statements. Use the direct disclosure method for the balance sheet.

LO 2

P8-3B **Determining Missing Information for Accounts Receivable** Semiconductors Unlimited estimates that 3% of all credit sales are uncollectible. Selected information for Semiconductors Unlimited for the years ended 19X6 and 19X7 is presented below:

	19X6	*19X7*
Accounts receivable, 1/1	$210,000	?
Accounts receivable, 12/31	195,000	?
Allowance for uncollectible accounts, 1/1	10,300	?
Allowance for uncollectible accounts, 12/31	?	$ 25,450
Credit sales	?	?
Collections	817,200	890,900
Write-offs	?	19,100
Uncollectible accounts expense	24,600	?

REQUIRED:

a. Fill in the missing information for 19X6 and 19X7.
b. Using the direct disclosure method, show how Semiconductors will disclose accounts receivable and allowance for uncollectible accounts on the 19X6 and 19X7 balance sheets.

LO 6

P8-4B **Accounting for Notes Receivable** The Trail Company had the following transactions during 19X8:

Apr. 1 The Vert Company purchased goods at a price of $30,000 from Trail. Because Vert is a marginal credit risk, Trail insisted that Vert pay by issuing a 13%, $30,000, 120-day note in exchange for the goods purchased.
July 1 Trail Company loaned $20,000 to one of its best customers, Bill Black, in exchange for a note. The note is due in 1 year and has an interest rate of 14%.
30 Vert Company dishonored the note issued on April 1.
Sept. 1 Blanche Company, which purchased goods for $15,000 on credit, was unable to pay the amount owed. Trail accepted a 16%, $15,000, 90-day note in exchange.
Nov. 1 Trail Company loaned $10,000 to a trusted employee in exchange for a note. The note is due in 120 days and has an interest rate of 12%.
30 Blanche paid Trail Company in full.

REQUIRED:

a. Prepare journal entries for the above transactions.
b. Prepare appropriate adjusting entries at December 31, 19X8.

LO 7

P8-5B **Notes Receivable Discounted** The Bond Company had the following transactions during 19X4:

Mar. 31 The Lane Company purchased goods for $15,000 from Bond. Because this is a large purchase for Lane and it will take Lane several months to sell the goods, Bond allowed Lane to pay by issuing a 13%, $15,000, 120-day note in exchange for the goods purchased.

Apr. 30 Bond Company discounted the note from Lane to the Washington National Bank at a discount rate of 15%. Bond endorsed the note with no qualifications.

July 29 Lane dishonored the note. Bond made the necessary payment to Washington National Bank, including a protest fee of $25.

Oct. 1 Cain Company, which previously purchased goods for $25,000 on credit, was unable to pay the amount owed. Bond accepted a 15%, $25,000, 90-day note in exchange.

Nov. 30 Bond Company discounted the note from Cain to the Second National Bank at a discount rate of 16%. Bond endorsed the note with no qualifications.

Dec. 30 Cain paid the Second National Bank in full.

REQUIRED:

Prepare journal entries for the above transactions.

LO 8

P8-6B **Calculate the Number-of-Days-Sales-in-Receivables and Uncollectible-accounts-Expense-as-a-Percent-of-Credit Sales and Use these Tools to Diagnose Problems**
Roy's Boot Warehouse has experienced stagnant gross sales (no growth) for several years. Roy believes he can increase credit sales by as much as 50% and total sales by at least 35% by relaxing his credit policy. He asks his accountant to prepare a schedule of the relevant financial data for 19X0 (the year just ended) and projections for 19X1.

Roy's Boot Warehouse
Comparative Financial Data
For the Years Ended December 31, 19X0 and 19X1

	Actual 19X0	Projected 19X1
Income statement data:		
Cash sales	$ 80,000	$ 90,000
Credit sales	140,000	210,000
Gross sales	$220,000	$300,000
Less: Sales returns and allowances	(7,000)	(10,000)
Uncollectible accounts expense	(3,000)	(15,000)
Net sales	$210,000	$275,000
Less: Cost of goods sold	130,000	175,000
Gross profit	$ 80,000	$100,000
Less: Operating expenses	45,000	60,000
Net income	$ 35,000	$ 40,000
Selected balance sheet data:		
Gross accounts receivable (December 31)	$ 28,000	$ 60,000
Less: Allowance for uncollectible accounts	2,800	10,000
Net receivables	$ 25,200	$ 50,000

REQUIRED:

Analyze the data using the number-of-days-sales-in-receivables and uncollectible-accounts-expense-as-a-percent-of-credit sales. Comment on whether Roy should pursue his plans to relax his credit policy, assuming the accountant's projections are accurate.

CRITICAL THINKING AND COMMUNICATING

C8-1 Odd Job Trading Company purchases excess goods from manufacturers at reduced rates and sells them for highly discounted prices in stores throughout the greater Dallas-Ft. Worth metropolitan area. Because of its low prices, Odd Job Trading Company has always operated on a cash only basis. Mr. Dawson, the owner of the company, recently attended a meeting of retailers where the speaker discussed the advantages of granting credit. Mr. Dawson always avoided granting credit because he knew that some of his customers would not pay their bills. However, until the meeting, Mr. Dawson did not realize the impact that granting credit would have on his business.

To determine whether or not to grant credit, Mr. Dawson hired Ms. Bosh, a credit consultant. Mr. Dawson asked Ms. Bosh for her recommendations. Mr. Dawson was particularly interested in two issues. First, should he have his own credit operation, accept bank cards, or both? Second, if he initiates his own credit operation, how should he implement it?

REQUIRED:

Summarize the information Ms. Bosh would need to collect to answer Mr. Dawson's questions and how she should analyze the information.

C8-2 Guillermo Lopez works in the accounts receivable department for Bicycles Unlimited, a large chain of retailers in the Los Angeles area. One of Guillermo's duties is reviewing credit applications. While reviewing these applications, Guillermo ran across a friend's credit application for an $800 bicycle. On this application, his friend lied by stating he was employed; Guillermo knew that his friend had quit his job several weeks ago. Guillermo's friend met all other conditions for obtaining credit. Bicycles Unlimited typically does not verify employment on credit applications under $1,000. Guillermo's friend knows that he reviews credit applications and will be very upset if his credit application is denied. Guillermo also knows that his friend has already interviewed for several jobs, and his chances of having a new job in the near future are good. Guillermo believes it is a virtual certainty that his friend will repay the debt.

REQUIRED:

Should Guillermo allow his friend to obtain credit from Bicycles Unlimited? Justify your answer and explain how you think Guillermo should handle the situation.

C8-3 Refer to the financial statements of J.C. Penney in Appendix B at the end of the text. Find the note section entitled Receivables in the *Summary of Accounting Policies* and the section entitled Credit Operations under *Supplemental Information*. In the section entitled Receivables, you will find a table in which the top figures for 1991–3 are labeled Customer receivables serviced. Make a note of these three figures. In the section entitled Credit Operations find the table labeled Credit sales. The first line of this table discloses JCPenney credit card sales for the three years. Make a note of these three figures.

REQUIRED:

a. From the figures you have noted, calculate J.C. Penney's days sales in receivables.
b. How do you interpret the number of days sales in J.C. Penney's receivables? Is there any hint in the section on Receivables as to why J.C. Penney carries so many days sales in receivables?
c. In the section on Credit Operations is a table and paragraph on Pre-tax cost of the JCPenney credit card. Compare the J.C. Penney analysis to the one illustrated in the chapter. Do you see any similarities? Differences? Comment on the apparent cost of credit card sales to J.C. Penney. Does the cost mean credit card sales are not worthwhile?

CHAPTER 9

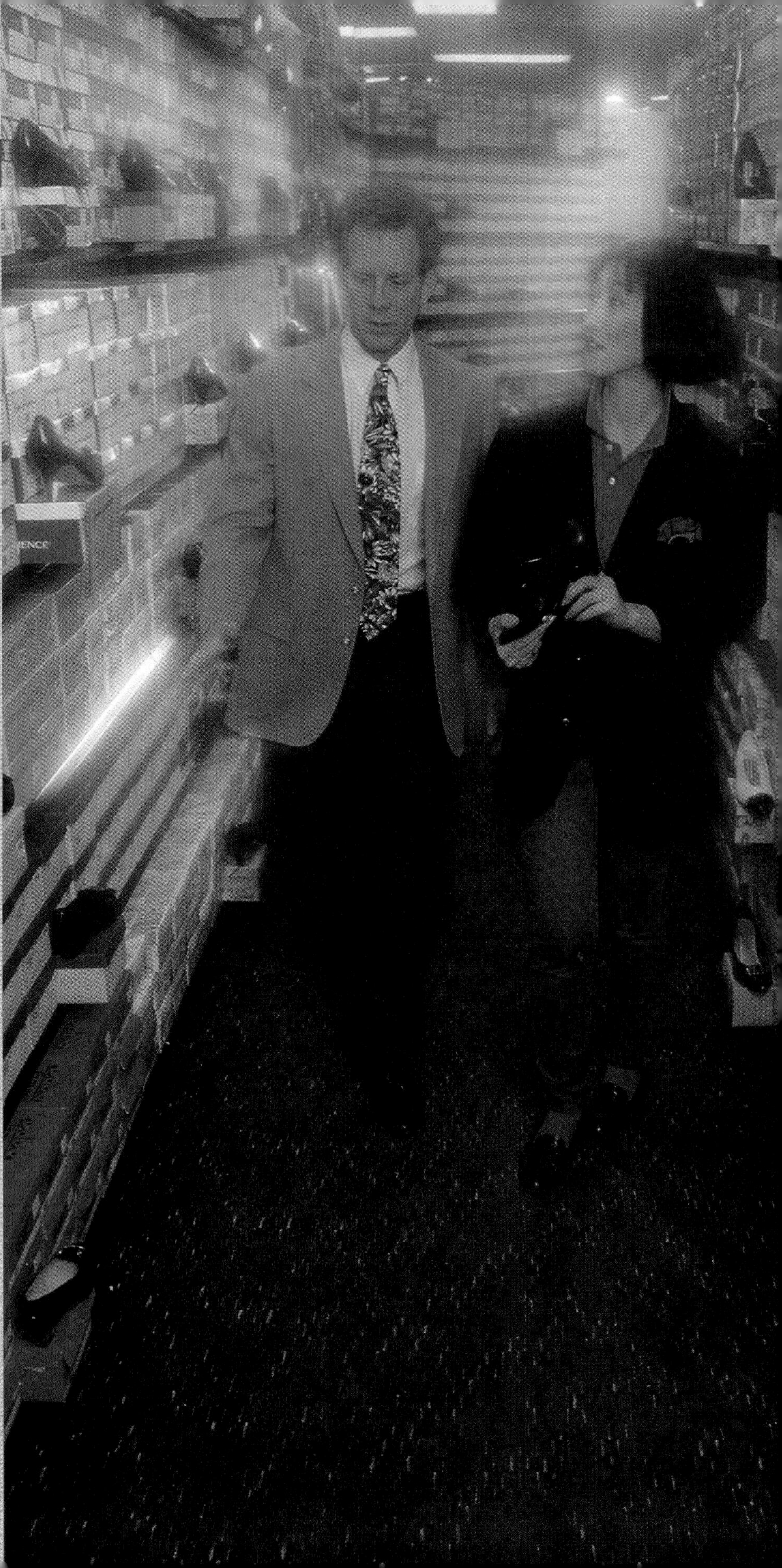

Inventories

"Why don't you ever have my size in stock?" asked Marie. Once again, Marie was frustrated at Bob's Discount Shoe Mart for not having her size of an attractive style of shoe. Marie wanted to wear the shoes to the spring graduation ceremony at Gulfside College. Although she knew she could probably buy the shoes at European Shoe Boutique, which always carried a complete selection of all sizes in a wide variety of styles, Marie also knew the mall stores charge nearly twice as much for similar shoes. Marie, being a college student, had a limited budget; and she preferred to buy the shoes at Bob's to save money. Marie wondered why a business such as Bob's Discount Shoe Mart sold a large volume of shoes but was often out of a particular size or style of shoe. On the other hand, a business such as European Shoe Boutique sold a much smaller volume of shoes but always had a complete selection of sizes and styles. In her accounting class, Marie was beginning to study accounting for merchandise inventories. She wondered if accounting information about inventories could help her understand the different ways the two shoe stores operated.

This chapter discusses accounting for merchandise inventories. You were introduced to this topic in a previous chapter, but many of the issues were deferred to this chapter. Since inventory items are purchased and sold continuously, activities concerning merchandise inventory are a major portion of a merchandising business's operations. Typically, inventory is a merchandising business's largest current asset, and cost of goods sold is usually the largest expense in its income statement. In its 1992 financial statements, General Mills, Inc. reported inventories of $487 million, compared to total current assets of $1.03 billion. Cost of goods sold for General Mills was $4.1 billion, compared to sales of $7.8 billion. For Kmart, the impact of inventories is even more dramatic. For 1991, Kmart reported inventories of $7.5 billion, compared to total assets of $16 billion. Cost of goods sold was $25.9 billion, compared to sales of $34.6 billion.

LEARNING OBJECTIVES

1. Describe the process for determining inventory quantities at the end of an accounting period.
2. Calculate cost of goods available for sale and allocate it to units in ending inventory and to the units sold during the period.
3. Describe the importance of inventory errors.
4. Apply the alternative methods of assigning costs to ending inventory.
5. Discuss the factors management should consider in selecting an inventory method.
6. Discuss when inventories should be valued at less than cost and calculate the relevant values.
7. Describe perpetual inventory systems and prepare the necessary entries.
8. Apply the two methods of estimating inventories.
9. Calculate and interpret the inventory turnover ratio.

LO 1

Describe the process for determining inventory quantities at the end of an accounting period.

ACCOUNTING FOR MERCHANDISE INVENTORIES AT THE END OF A PERIOD

At the end of an accounting period, a business adjusts Merchandise Inventory to reflect the ending inventory and to calculate the cost of goods sold. These procedures are shown in Illustration 9-1. The first procedure is to determine the number of units of merchandise that are on hand at the end of the period. The second procedure is to assign costs to the ending inventory. The final procedure is to determine cost of goods sold. As you saw in an earlier chapter, the number of units sold is the number of units available for sale less the number of units in ending inventory.

ILLUSTRATION 9-1 End-of-Period Procedures for Merchandise Inventories

Determine units in ending inventory	Assign costs to ending inventory	Determine cost of goods sold

Determining Inventory Quantities

Determining the number of units of merchandise that make up the ending inventory involves taking a physical inventory and analyzing goods in transit at the end of the accounting period.

Taking a Physical Inventory.   Employees commonly take the physical inventory. As an alternative, some businesses take physical inventories for other businesses for a fee. The end result of a physical inventory is the determination of the total cost of the ending inventory. Computers have made the process of conducting physical inventories and tabulating the results easier, faster, and more accurate. Physical inventory procedures were discussed in an earlier chapter where you were introduced to merchandising businesses.

Analyzing Goods In Transit. **Goods in transit** are items of merchandise in the possession of a carrier, such as a trucking, railroad, shipping, or airline company. Since the goods are in the process of being transported, those taking inventory cannot possibly include them in the physical inventory. Therefore, in determining the quantity of the merchandise inventory, a business should analyze the goods in transit at the end of the accounting period for possible inclusion in the ending inventory. The ending inventory should include goods in transit that the business owns at the end of the period.

Remember: Businesses determine the ownership of the merchandise in transit by the terms of the transaction. Goods may be shipped F.O.B. shipping point or F.O.B. destination. For a business, goods in transit may include both items of merchandise it has sold to customers and items of merchandise it has purchased from suppliers.

At the end of 19X1, Donald's TV Store had the following goods in transit:

Merchandise Purchases		Merchandise Sales	
Item	Terms	Item	Terms
5 – 19" televisions	F.O.B. shipping point	2 – 25" televisions	F.O.B. shipping point
10 – TV stands	F.O.B. destination		

Among the purchases in transit, the 19" televisions should be included in the ending inventory because Donald's became the owner of them when they were shipped. However, since the company does not become the owner of the TV stands until the carrier delivers them, Donald's should not include them in ending inventory. Ownership of the sold televisions transferred to the customers when Donald's delivered them to the carrier. Therefore, Donald's should not include the sold televisions in the ending inventory. If the televisions had been sold with F.O.B. destination terms, then Donald's would have included them in the ending inventory because the company would have continued to have ownership at the end of the period.

Assigning Inventory Costs

LO 2
Calculate cost of goods available for sale and allocate it to units in ending inventory and to the units sold during the period.

The **cost of goods available for sale** consists of the cost of the beginning inventory plus the cost of purchases during the year. The cost of merchandise inventory purchases should include all costs incurred to get the merchandise to a marketable condition, including acquisition and transportation costs. These costs include:

Purchase Price – Purchases Discounts and Cash Discounts + Transportation-In and Insurance-In-Transit

Conceptually, a business should include such incidental costs as purchasing, handling, and storing in the cost of merchandise inventory. In practice, however, these costs are often difficult to trace directly to individual items of inventory. Typically, a business simply charges these costs to operating expenses for the period. (See a previous chapter for a discussion of the accounting procedures for recording the cost of merchandise inventory purchases.)

At the end of the year, a business allocates the cost of goods available for sale to the units in the ending inventory and to the units sold during the period. The allocation procedures are:

Allocation 1: Assign costs to the units in ending inventory.
Allocation 2: Calculate the cost of goods sold by subtracting the cost of the
ending inventory from the cost of goods available for sale.

To illustrate the allocation of the cost of goods available for sale, assume
Brown's Garden Supplies determines that its cost of goods available for sale is
$75,000. This amount consists of beginning inventory of $25,000 and the cost of
purchases of $50,000. The physical inventory indicates that 4,000 units are on
hand at the end of the year. The per-unit cost of the ending inventory is $5. The
allocation of the cost of goods available for sale is shown in Illustration 9-2.

ILLUSTRATION 9-2 Allocation of Cost of Goods Available for Sale

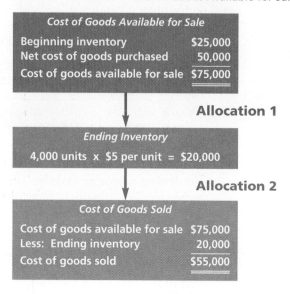

As shown above, the $75,000 cost of goods available for sale is allocated
$20,000 to the ending inventory and $55,000 to the cost of goods sold.

THE IMPORTANCE OF INVENTORY ERRORS

LO 3
Describe the importance
of inventory errors.

Errors may occur in the process of determining the cost of ending inventory.
Such errors include those made in counting the number of items in the inventory or those made in assigning costs to inventory items. When an error occurs in
determining the cost of the ending inventory, cost of goods sold, net income,
owner's equity, and current assets are all misstated in the financial statements.
Therefore, for accurate financial reporting, it is important that businesses determine correctly the inventory quantities and assign the correct costs to the units
in inventory.

To illustrate the effects of errors in the ending inventory for the current
year, consider the three examples shown in Illustration 9-3. In the first example,
the ending inventory is stated correctly at $20,000. In the second example, the
ending inventory is overstated by $5,000; and in the third example, the ending
inventory is understated by $5,000. The errors in ending inventory and the
errors in other income statement items that result are highlighted in Illustration
9-3.

ILLUSTRATION 9-3 Effects of Inventory Errors

	Correct Inventory	Ending Inventory Overstated	Ending Inventory Understated
Beginning inventory	$20,000	$20,000	$20,000
Add: Purchases	45,000	45,000	45,000
Cost of goods available for sale	$65,000	$65,000	$65,000
Less: Ending inventory	20,000	**25,000**	**15,000**
Cost of goods sold	$45,000	**$40,000**	**$50,000**
Sales	$80,000	$80,000	$80,000
Cost of goods sold (above)	45,000	**40,000**	**50,000**
Gross profit	$35,000	**$40,000**	**$30,000**

When the ending inventory is overstated, cost of goods sold is understated and gross profit is overstated. Conversely, when ending inventory is understated, cost of goods sold is overstated and gross profit is understated.

Because the ending inventory of one year is the beginning inventory of the next year, an inventory error affects not only the current year's income statement, but it also affects the subsequent year's financial statements. To illustrate this point, consider the example in Illustration 9-4. In 19X1, the ending inventory is overstated by $5,000; and this results in the 19X2 beginning inventory also being overstated by $5,000. The ending inventory for 19X2 is stated correctly, as is the 19X3 beginning inventory.

ILLUSTRATION 9-4 Inventory Errors in Subsequent Periods

	19X1	19X2	19X3
Sales	$80,000	$80,000	$80,000
Cost of goods sold:			
Beginning inventory	$20,000	$25,000	$20,000
Net purchases	45,000	45,000	45,000
Cost of goods available	$65,000	$70,000	$65,000
Ending inventory	25,000	20,000	20,000
Cost of goods sold	$40,000	$50,000	$45,000
Gross profit	$40,000	$30,000	$35,000

The 19X1 overstatement of ending inventory causes the 19X1 cost of goods sold to be understated by $5,000 and gross profit to be overstated by $5,000. Cost of goods sold should be $45,000 ($65,000 − $20,000), and gross profit should be $35,000 ($80,000 − $45,000). The effects on 19X2 are just the opposite. The overstatement of beginning inventory causes the cost of goods sold to be overstated by $5,000 and gross profit to be understated by $5,000. Cost of goods sold should be $45,000 ($20,000 + $45,000 − $20,000), and gross profit should be $35,000 ($80,000 − $45,000). For the two-year period, 19X1 and 19X2, the effects of the error in 19X1 cancel out. This is because the effects of the error in 19X2 are equal in amount, but in the opposite direction, of the effects of the error in 19X1. The correct gross profit for the two-year period is $70,000.

Even though the effects of inventory errors cancel out over a two-year period, such errors should be avoided. Although the total gross profit for the two-year period is correct, the individual financial statements for each year are incorrect. Because financial statement users make decisions based on the financial statements of each period, the accountant has an obligation to make sure that each period's financial statements are correct.

The effects of inventory errors on the elements of financial statements may be summarized as follows:

ILLUSTRATION 9-5 Summary of Effects of Inventory Errors

	Cost of Goods Sold	Gross Profit	Net Income	Ending Owner's Equity	Ending Current Assets
If ending inventory:					
Overstated	U	O	O	O	O
Understated	O	U	U	U	U
If beginning inventory:					
Overstated	O	U	U	U	no error
Understated	U	O	O	O	no error

U=understated
O=overstated

LO 4

Apply the alternative methods of assigning costs to ending inventory.

METHODS USED TO ASSIGN COSTS TO INVENTORIES

The allocation of the cost of goods available for sale to the ending inventory and to cost of goods sold is made more difficult when the business incurs different costs for purchases of an item at different times during a year. For example, the cost of an item that is purchased for inventory may increase during the year. On the other hand, costs may also decrease or fluctuate. In any event, when the cost of inventory items changes during a year, the accountant must decide which costs to assign to the units in the ending inventory. Accountants follow two general approaches to assigning costs to inventory: actual physical flow and assumed cost flow. Under these approaches, the accountant can use these methods:

Approaches	Methods
Actual physical flow	Specific identification
Assumed cost flow	Weighted-average cost First-in, first-out (FIFO) Last-in, first-out (LIFO)

Actual Physical Flow Approach

One method a merchant uses to assign costs to the ending inventory is specific identification. The **specific identification method** keeps track of the actual physical flow of units during the period. That is, using serial numbers or tags and other coding devices, the merchant specifically identifies the actual units remaining in the ending inventory and the actual units sold during the period. The merchant keeps a record of each inventory item's actual cost. When an item is sold, the merchant adds its invoice cost to cost of goods sold and measures the ending inventory at the invoice cost of the unsold inventory items.

For example, assume that during 19X1, Anna's Antiques purchased three antique desks for $2,500, $2,650, and $2,700, respectively. At the end of the year, the desk that cost $2,650 remains unsold. Using the specific identification method, the cost of goods sold is $5,200 ($2,500 + $2,700); and the ending inventory is the cost of the unsold desk, or $2,650. Illustration 9-6 demonstrates the specific identification method for these transactions of Anna's Antiques.

ILLUSTRATION 9-6 Specific Identification Method

While the specific identification method is simple and logical, its use in practice is generally restricted to unique items of high value such as fine jewelry, automobiles, and antique furniture. A criticism of the specific identification method is that when the inventory is composed of identical items, management can choose to sell either lower-cost or higher-cost items, thereby manipulating the income the business reports. For example, if management desires to report higher net income, it can choose to sell the lower-cost units. Conversely, management can report lower net income by selling the higher-cost units. Also, when the inventory consists of a high volume of identical items such as 8.2 oz. tubes of Crest toothpaste or 32 oz. jars of Crisco vegetable oil, the specific identification method is inefficient and other methods are used.

Assumed Cost Flow Approach

To avoid the limitations of the specific identification method, under GAAP businesses may assign costs to the ending inventory by *assuming* some pattern of cost flows related to units of merchandise. Three assumed cost flow methods are:

1. Weighted-average cost
2. First-in, first-out (FIFO)
3. Last-in, first-out (LIFO)

Illustration 9-7 shows what percentages of businesses use the various inventory cost methods.

When a business uses an assumed cost flow method, the assumed cost flow is not required to conform with the actual physical flow of goods. Management must decide what is the appropriate cost flow method for the business. However, once management adopts a particular method, the *consistency principle* requires that the business use the method consistently from year to year.

ILLUSTRATION 9-7 Relative Use of Inventory Methods

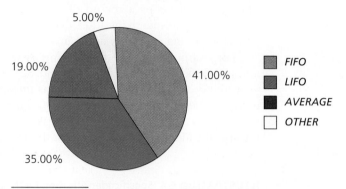

Source: *Accounting Trends and Techniques*, AICPA, 1992.

The consistent use of an inventory costing method allows financial statement users to assess the business's financial position and results of operations consistently across time. Changes in accounting methods disrupt the relationship between financial statements and actual activities of the business.

The three assumed cost flow methods will be illustrated with the following example of Exotic Electronics and its experience with Model 89X Transformers during 19X1. Illustration 9-8 provides information about the beginning inventory, purchases, sales, and ending inventory of Model 89X during the year.

Exotic Electronics uses the periodic inventory method. Recall that under the periodic inventory method, we update the Merchandise Inventory balance and Cost of Goods Sold only at the ends of accounting periods, based on physical inventory counts. The information in Illustration 9-8 about the beginning inventory comes from the prior year's ending inventory. The information about the purchases is found in the purchases journal. The sales journal provides the information about sales. The ending inventory is the result of the physical inventory taken at the end of 19X1.

ILLUSTRATION 9-8 Model 89X Transformers Inventory Data

Exotic Electronics Model 89X Transformers				
19X1		*Units*	*Unit Cost*	*Total Cost*
Jan. 1	Beginning inventory	10	$60	$ 600
Mar. 28	Purchase	20	66	1,320
Aug. 22	Purchase	20	70	1,400
Oct. 14	Purchase	25	76	1,900
Cost of goods available for sale		75		$5,220

Ending inventory = 30 units
Sales   = 45 units
Units available = 75 units

Weighted-Average Cost Method.   Under the **weighted-average cost method**, the costs assigned to the ending inventory and to cost of goods sold are based on the average cost per unit, which consists of the combined cost of the beginning inventory and the purchases made during the year. Exotic Electronics calculates the average cost per unit by the following formula, using the data from Illustration 9-8:

$$\textbf{Average Cost Per Unit} = \frac{\textbf{Cost of Goods Available for Sale}}{\textbf{Number of Units Available for Sale}}$$

$$\$69.60 = \frac{\$5,220}{75}$$

The weighted-average cost method is based on the assumption that all the units available for sale during the year are identical and, therefore, each unit should have the same cost.

Illustration 9-9 shows the application of the weighted-average cost method. First, the average cost per unit is calculated. Then, the resulting weighted-average cost is assigned to the units in ending inventory. Finally, the accountant calculates the cost of goods sold by subtracting the cost of ending inventory from the cost of goods available for sale. To verify the cost of goods sold figure, the number of units sold is multiplied by the average cost per unit (45 x $69.60 = $3,132).

ILLUSTRATION 9-9 Weighted-Average Cost Method

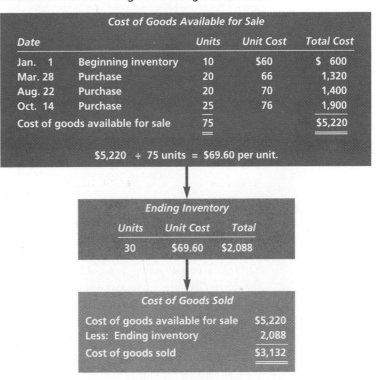

First-In, First-Out Method.   The **first-in, first-out (FIFO)** method *assumes* that the cost of the ending inventory consists of the costs of the most recent purchases, as shown in Illustration 9-10. Illustration 9-10 is based on the same purchases and sales data as those of Illustration 9-8. For Exotic Electronics, the FIFO method *assumes* that the ending inventory of 30 units consists of the 25 units purchased on October 14, plus 5 of the 20 units purchased on August 22. The FIFO method *assumes* that the cost of goods sold consists of the cost of units in beginning inventory and the costs of the earliest purchases during the year. Under FIFO, the 45 units Exotic Electronics sold are *assumed* to consist of the 10 units that are in the beginning inventory, the 20 units purchased on March 28, and 15 of the units purchased on August 22. Illustration 9-11 shows the allocation of the cost of goods available for sale to the ending inventory and cost of goods sold for the Model 89X Transformers under the FIFO method.

ILLUSTRATION 9-10 FIFO Time Line

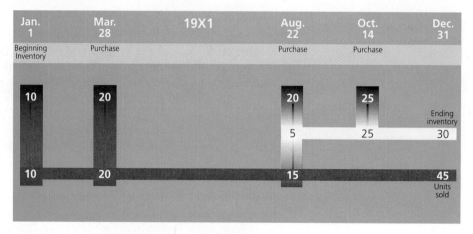

The cost of goods sold of $2,970 that is calculated in Illustration 9-11 may be verified by assigning the appropriate costs to the 45 units assumed to be sold, as follows:

Beginning inventory	10 units	x	$60	=	$ 600
Mar. 28 purchase	20 units	x	66	=	1,320
Aug. 22 purchase	15 units	x	70	=	1,050
Cost of goods sold	45 units				$2,970

The FIFO assumption that the first units purchased are the first units sold is consistent with the actual physical flow of goods of many businesses. When merchants purchase goods and place them on shelves in their stores, they typically place the newly purchased units behind the units already on the shelves. This minimizes the chances of merchants accumulating old units of merchandise that may spoil or become obsolete. However, to use the FIFO method, the business's actual physical flow of goods is irrelevant. Accountants view FIFO as a cost assumption, not a description of actual flows.

Last-In, First-Out Method.   The **last-in, first-out (LIFO) method** *assumes* that the cost of the ending inventory consists of the costs of the units in beginning inventory and the costs of the earliest purchases made during the period. On the other hand, LIFO *assumes* that the cost of goods sold consists of the costs of the most recent purchases. In other words, the LIFO method *assumes* that the last goods purchased are the first goods sold, hence, the name "last-in, first-out." Illustration 9-12 shows a time line for the LIFO method when applied to the Model 89X Transformers.

ILLUSTRATION 9-11 FIFO Method

Cost of Goods Available for Sale			
Date	Units	Unit Cost	Total Cost
Jan. 1 Beginning inventory	10	$60	$ 600
Mar. 28 Purchase	20	66	1,320
Aug. 22 Purchase	20	70	1,400
Oct. 14 Purchase	25	76	1,900
Cost of goods available for sale	75		$5,220

Ending Inventory			
Date	Units	Unit Cost	Total
Oct. 14	25	$76	$1,900
Aug. 22	5	70	350
Total	30		$2,250

Cost of Goods Sold	
Cost of goods available for sale	$5,220
Less: Ending inventory	2,250
Cost of goods sold	$2,970

ILLUSTRATION 9-12 LIFO Time Line

LIFO *assumes* the ending inventory of 30 units consists of the 10 units in the beginning inventory plus the 20 units purchased on March 28. The 45 units sold are *assumed* to consist of the 25 units purchased on October 14, plus the 20 units purchased on August 22. Illustration 9-13 shows the allocation of the cost of goods available for sale to the ending inventory and to cost of goods sold.

ILLUSTRATION 9-13 LIFO Method

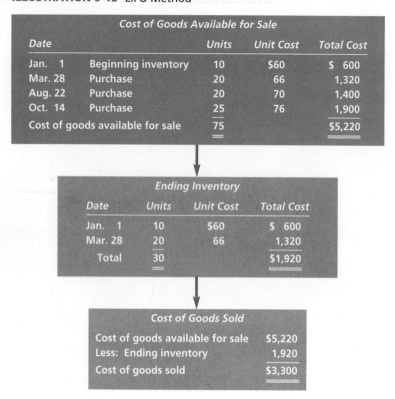

Cost of Goods Available for Sale				
Date		Units	Unit Cost	Total Cost
Jan. 1	Beginning inventory	10	$60	$ 600
Mar. 28	Purchase	20	66	1,320
Aug. 22	Purchase	20	70	1,400
Oct. 14	Purchase	25	76	1,900
Cost of goods available for sale		75		$5,220

Ending Inventory			
Date	Units	Unit Cost	Total Cost
Jan. 1	10	$60	$ 600
Mar. 28	20	66	1,320
Total	30		$1,920

Cost of Goods Sold	
Cost of goods available for sale	$5,220
Less: Ending inventory	1,920
Cost of goods sold	$3,300

The cost of goods sold of $3,300 in Illustration 9-13 may be verified by assigning the appropriate cost to the 45 units assumed to be sold, as follows:

Oct. 14 purchase	25 units x $76 =	$1,900
Aug. 22 purchase	20 units x 70 =	1,400
Cost of goods sold	45 units	$3,300

Under the LIFO method, the assumed flow of costs is not consistent with the actual physical flow of goods for most merchandising businesses.

INTERNATIONAL PERSPECTIVES

Other countries have accounting principles for merchandise inventories that differ from GAAP in the United States. These different principles have developed for various reasons, such as different degrees of self-regulation by the accounting profession, business customs, legal traditions, and rates of inflation. In most countries, the LIFO method is not an acceptable method. LIFO is acceptable, however, in Germany, Italy, the Netherlands, and South Africa, provided that the market value of the inventory is disclosed in the notes to the financial statements.

Comparison of Alternative Inventory Methods

During periods when the costs of merchandise change, the three alternative cost flow assumptions result in different amounts for cost of goods sold and for ending inventory. The previous example for Model 89X Transformers for 19X1 illustrates what happens in a period of increasing costs. Illustration 9-14 presents a comparison of the effects of applying the three inventory methods, assuming net revenues in each case of $4,000.

ILLUSTRATION 9-14 Comparison of Alternative Inventory Methods

	Weighted-Average Cost	FIFO	LIFO
Net revenue	$4,000	$4,000	$4,000
Cost of goods sold:			
Beginning inventory	$ 600	$ 600	$ 600
Purchases	4,620	4,620	4,620
Cost of goods available for sale	$5,220	$5,220	$5,220
Less: Ending inventory	2,088	2,250	1,920
Cost of goods sold	$3,132	$2,970	$3,300
Gross profit	$ 868	$1,030	$ 700

Income Statement Effects

During periods of increasing purchase costs, LIFO results in the highest cost of goods sold and the lowest gross profit, while the FIFO method produces the lowest cost of goods sold and the highest gross profit. The weighted-average cost method smooths out the effects of changing prices and produces measurements of cost of goods sold and gross profit that are between the LIFO and FIFO amounts.

Balance Sheet Effects

The effects of the methods on the cost of inventory reported in the balance sheet are just the opposite of their effects on cost of goods sold. The following presents a comparison of the balance sheet effects of the alternative methods:

	Weighted-Average Cost	FIFO	LIFO
Ending inventory	$2,088	$2,250	$1,920

During periods of increasing costs, the LIFO method produces the lowest amount for ending inventory since it assumes that the inventory consists of the oldest, and lowest, costs. On the other hand, the FIFO method produces the highest amount for ending inventory since it assumes that the inventory consists of the most recent, and highest, costs. The weighted-average cost method produces an amount for ending inventory that is between the amounts produced by the LIFO and FIFO methods.

LO 5

Discuss the factors management should consider in selecting an inventory method.

Factors In Selection of Inventory Methods

Because inventory is such a significant financial statement component for many businesses, management's selection of an inventory method is important. Management should give careful thought to the selection because once a business adopts a method, the *consistency principle* requires that the business use the method in subsequent periods. The following discussion presents some of the factors that management may consider in selecting an inventory method.

Those who support the LIFO method argue that it is the superior method for measuring net income. Since the LIFO method measures cost of goods sold at the most recent costs, they argue that it results in a better matching of current costs (the most relevant costs) and revenues. A going-concern must maintain some minimum level of inventory; and when it sells an item, the business must replace it. Therefore, the appropriate cost to match against revenues is the cost of replacing the item sold. Also, during periods of increasing costs, the LIFO method produces the lowest measurement of net income, which minimizes the amount of income taxes paid. (See Appendix A to this text for an explanation of income taxes.)

During periods of steadily increasing costs of inventory purchases, the LIFO method assigns the higher, recent costs to the cost of goods sold, which produces the lowest net income. On the other hand, the LIFO method assigns the lowest costs to the ending inventory. Critics argue that under the LIFO method, the ending inventory a business reports in its balance sheet does not reflect the value (cost) of its inventory. During periods of steadily decreasing costs of inventory purchases, the effects of LIFO are just the opposite—reporting low cost of goods sold, high net income, high income taxes, and high ending inventory cost.

Supporters of the FIFO method argue that it produces the most realistic measurement of the ending inventory reported in the balance sheet. Under the FIFO method, ending inventory is measured at the most recent costs, which generally approximates the current cost of the inventory. Also, supporters of the FIFO method argue that first-in, first-out more closely approximates the physical flow of goods for most merchandising businesses.

Both the FIFO and LIFO methods have strong points and weak points. Both are acceptable under GAAP. The weighted-average cost method is simply a compromise and is acceptable because it is easy to apply. Management's decision about which inventory costing method to use depends on its expectation about future costs of inventory items and the relative amount of net income and taxable income it desires to report. For example, if management expects inventory costs to increase in the future and wants to report the highest relative amount of income, then it should choose the FIFO method to produce the desired results. On the other hand, if management wishes to minimize the amount of income taxes paid currently, it should choose the LIFO method.

The comparisons of the alternative inventory methods discussed above are valid for periods of increasing costs. During periods of decreasing costs, the comparisons of the methods are just the opposite in their relationships. Because of the effects the selection of an inventory method can have on the income statement and the balance sheet, GAAP require a business to disclose in the financial statements the inventory method that it uses. Financial statement users need to know the inventory costing methods underlying the statements to compare accurately the income and financial position of one business to another. For example, Air Products and Chemicals, Inc. had the following accounting policy disclosure in the notes to the financial statements:

Inventories—To determine the cost of chemical inventories and some gas and equipment inventories in the United States, the company uses the last-in, first-out (LIFO) method. This method assumes the most recent cost is closer to the cost of replacing an item that has been sold. During periods of rising prices, LIFO maximizes the cost of goods sold and minimizes the profit reported on the company's income statement.

LO 6

Discuss when inventories should be valued at less than cost and calculate the relevant values.

INVENTORIES AND THE PRINCIPLE OF CONSERVATISM

Merchandise a business holds for resale to customers may decrease below its assigned cost. The decrease in value may be the result of damage or obsolescence that occurs while the inventory is held. For example, the value of personal computers held in inventory may decrease below cost because of technological advances that make the computers obsolete. Items of inventory may be damaged while being handled or while serving as floor samples for customers' inspection. In addition to damage and obsolescence, the value of goods in inventory also may decrease because of a decline in consumer demand for the particular good. In this case, the merchant may have to decrease the selling price below cost to sell the goods. A business should not report inventories in the balance sheet at more than **estimated net realizable value**, which is the estimated selling price less the estimated costs of disposing of the merchandise.

INSIGHTS INTO ETHICS

Amy Brown is the Assistant Controller of Telmax Company. The employees just completed the physical inventory for the current year and she is comparing the inventory costs with the costs of the previous year. She realizes that for most of the inventory items the costs have actually declined since last year. This realization disturbs Amy because just last year she proposed to management that the business change from the FIFO inventory method to the LIFO method. Her proposal claimed that the LIFO method would save income taxes for the business even though it would result in lower net income. Her proposal had been vigorously opposed by Roy Stein, a new employee in the accounting department, who was very vocal about his ambitions to rise to the management ranks of the business. After a meeting with top management, attended by both Amy and Roy in which Roy had argued strongly against Amy's proposal, management accepted the proposal and switched to the LIFO method.

Amy is considering whether to report the information about the declining inventory costs to management. With the benefit of hindsight, she will be admitting that her proposal was wrong and she will have to listen to Roy say, "I told you so." Management probably will discuss switching back to the FIFO method in order to reduce income taxes. Amy knows that switching inventory methods requires Internal Revenue Service approval. Receiving approval for changing inventory methods for two consecutive years is rare at best. On the other hand, since the business's total inventory has increased, it is unlikely that anyone else will discover that the LIFO method is actually penalizing the business. If she just keeps quiet, she may avoid embarrassment and possible damage to her career.

What should Amy do?

When the value of inventory decreases below its cost, the business has incurred a loss. The loss is attributed to the decrease in the inventory's revenue-producing ability and the inability to recover its cost. Under GAAP, the business should report the loss in net income in the period that the decrease in value occurs. This means that a business should not wait until the period it sells the merchandise to report the loss in net income. The measurement of the loss, however, is different for decreases in value that are the result of damage or obsolescence and price decreases.

Damage or Obsolescence

The loss from damaged or obsolete goods is measured as the difference between the cost of the goods and their estimated net realizable value. For example, assume that Carol's Dress Shop has five dresses on display in the shop's window. The dresses originally cost $125 each and have a normal selling price of $250 each. The dresses are slightly faded from being in the window, and Carol's estimates that it can sell them for only $100 each. Additionally, Carol's pays its salesclerks a 10% commission on all sales. The estimated net realizable value of each dress is $90, as shown below:

Estimated selling price	$100
Less estimated costs of disposal:	
Sales commission	10
Estimated net realizable value	$ 90

For the five dresses, Carol's has incurred a loss of $175 [5 x ($125 − $90)] that should be reported in net income of the current period. The following entry recognizes the loss:

(Date)	Loss from Damaged Inventory	175	
	Merchandise Inventory		175
	To record estimated loss on damaged inventory.		

In the period that the dresses are sold, Carol's recognizes no income or loss on the sale unless the actual selling price is different from the estimated selling price.

Price Decreases

In the previous discussion, we have illustrated several methods of determining the cost of merchandise inventories. Under GAAP, inventories should be presented in the balance sheet at the lower of cost or market. *Cost*, in lower of cost or market, means the cost of the ending inventory as determined by one of the alternative methods—FIFO, LIFO, or weighted-average cost. When the market value of inventory falls below this cost because of price decreases, the business has incurred a loss that should be recognized immediately by reducing the inventory to market value. For example, in the first quarter of 1986, the price of crude oil decreased dramatically from approximately $35 per barrel to approximately $10 per barrel. This decrease in the price of crude oil caused many oil companies to write down their inventories of crude oil and to recognize a loss.

The loss recognized for some of the companies exceeded $100 million.[1] The term *market value*, as used in this context, means the cost of replacing the inventory item, or *replacement cost*. Reporting inventories at market value when the market value has fallen below cost is called the **lower-of-cost-or-market rule**. Raychem Corporation disclosed the following accounting policy in the notes to the financial statements:

Inventories

Inventories are stated at the lower of cost (principally the first-in, first-out method) or market. Market is determined on the basis of replacement cost or net realizable value. Appropriate consideration has been given to obsolescence and other factors in evaluating net realizable value.

Applying the Lower-Of-Cost-Or-Market Rule

The lower-of-cost-or-market rule is applied by comparing the cost of the inventory as determined by one of the methods previously discussed to the market value of the inventory. In the example that follows, Hi-Fi Electronics is a retail business that sells radios and televisions. Illustration 9-15 shows the application of the lower-of-cost-or-market rule to the inventories of radios and televisions for Hi-Fi Electronics.

ILLUSTRATION 9-15 Determination of Lower of Cost or Market

	Model	Units	Cost per Unit	Market per Unit	Total Cost	Total Market	Lower of Cost or Market
Radios							
	1	20	$ 27	$ 28	$ 540	$ 560	
	2	10	50	44	500	440	
	3	5	64	66	320	330	
Televisions							
	101	3	220	212	660	636	
	102	2	279	285	558	570	
	103	4	456	420	1,824	1,680	
					$4,402	$4,216	
Inventory at lower of cost or market							$4,216

For Hi-Fi Electronics, the market value of the inventory is lower than the cost by $186 ($4,402 − $4,216). Hi-Fi Electronics would make the following journal entry to write down the cost of the inventory to lower of cost or market and to recognize the decline in value:

(Date)	Loss from Decline in Market Value of Merchandise Inventory	186	
	Merchandise Inventory		186
	To record inventory at the lower of cost or market.		

Hi-Fi Electronics would make the entry above *after* recording cost of goods sold in the closing process as previously illustrated. However, if the market

[1]"Oil Firms Scramble to Restate Earnings In Wake of SEC Ruling on Write-Down," *The Wall Street Journal* (May 12, 1986), p. 8.

value of $4,216, instead of the cost of $4,402, were used in the closing process, cost of goods sold would include the $186 loss; and it would be double-counted in net income after the entry to reduce merchandise inventory to market. For the subsequent period, Hi-Fi Electronics would use the $4,216 (lower of cost or market) as the beginning inventory.

LO 7

Describe perpetual inventory systems and prepare the necessary entries.

PERPETUAL INVENTORY PROCEDURES

To this point, the discussions of inventory procedures have dealt with periodic inventory systems. With periodic inventory systems, businesses determine the current inventory only at the end of an accounting period by taking a physical inventory. Some businesses desire to know the amount of inventory on hand at any time during the period. With this information, they can respond more effectively to customer inquiries about merchandise availability and better avoid being out of stock. This information permits managers to have more control over the merchandise inventory and to determine cost of goods sold for periods shorter than a year, without the need of frequent physical inventories. Businesses use a perpetual inventory system to increase control and up-to-date information about inventory.

Recording Perpetual Inventory Transactions

Accounting under perpetual inventory procedures differs from that under periodic inventory procedures in that Merchandise Inventory is continually updated by recording purchases and sales as they occur. Recall that for the periodic method, Merchandise Inventory remains at the beginning amount until the end of the period when the business takes a physical inventory and updates the account balance. Accounts such as Purchases, Purchases Returns and Allowances, Purchases Discounts, and Freight-in that you saw for the periodic method are not used in the perpetual method. For the perpetual method Cost of Goods Sold is posted as sales occur for the cost of merchandise sold to customers.

To illustrate the differences between the two methods, consider the following information for stereo headsets of Don's Stereo Shop, which uses the FIFO method:

March	1	Beginning inventory is 20 units that cost $50 each.
	10	Sold 10 units at a price of $90 each.
	13	Purchased 20 units at a cost of $60 each.
	20	Sold 8 units at a price of $90 each.

Illustration 9-16 compares the recording in general journal form for both the perpetual and periodic methods.

As shown in Illustration 9-16, the difference between the perpetual and periodic methods is the continual updating of Merchandise Inventory and Cost of Goods Sold. At the end of a period, the entries that you saw for the periodic method to adjust Merchandise Inventory and to establish Cost of Goods Sold are not needed for the perpetual method. The balances of Merchandise Inventory and Cost of Goods Sold are updated when each purchase and sale transaction occurs.

Merchandise Inventory Card

In a perpetual inventory system, purchases of merchandise are *not* recorded in a separate Purchases account. Instead, businesses keep an inventory card simi-

ILLUSTRATION 9-16 Entries for Perpetual and Periodic Methods

Perpetual Method			Periodic Method		
To record sale of 10 units at $90 each:					
Mar. 10 Cash	900		Cash	900	
Sales		900	Sales		900
To record cost of 10 units sold at $50 each:					
10 Cost of Goods Sold	500		No Entry		
Merchandise Inventory		500			
To record purchase of 20 units at $60 each:					
13 Merchandise Inventory	1,200		Purchases	1,200	
Accounts Payable		1,200	Accounts Payable		1,200
To record sale of 8 units at $90 each:					
20 Cash	720		Cash	720	
Sales		720	Sales		720
To record cost of 8 units sold at $50 each:					
20 Cost of Goods Sold	400		No Entry		
Merchandise Inventory		400			

lar to the one in Illustration 9-17 for each type of merchandise in inventory. The **merchandise inventory card** records in both quantities and costs the beginning inventory for the item, purchases of the item and sales of the item. For each item, employees keep a continuous record on the inventory card of the quantity of the item on hand. At any time, the total of all the dollar balances of the inventory cards should agree with Merchandise Inventory (control) in the general ledger. Consider what is recorded in Illustration 9-17. First, there is a balance of 20 units on hand at March 1. These units cost $50 each, or a total of $1,000. On March 10, the business sold 10 units. The inventory card indicates that the 10 units sold have a cost of $50 each, or a total of $500. After the sale, the inventory card indicates that the remaining inventory is 10 units at $50 each, or a total of $500.

The next transaction recorded on the inventory card is a purchase of merchandise on March 13. On that date, Don's purchased 20 units at a cost of $60 each. The inventory card reflects that after the purchase the inventory consists

ILLUSTRATION 9-17 Perpetual Inventory Card

ITEM: Stereo Headsets

DATE	PURCHASED VOUCHER #	UNITS	COST	TOTAL	SOLD INVOICE#	UNITS	COST	TOTAL	BALANCE UNITS	COST	TOTAL
Mar. 1									20	50	1,000
10					S-2602	10	50	500	10	50	500
13	V-989	20	60	1,200					10	50	500
									20	60	1,200
20					S-2615	8	50	400	2	50	100
									20	60	1,200

of 10 units at a cost of $50 each, and 20 units at a cost of $60 each. The total cost of inventory after the purchase transaction is $500 + $1,200 = $1,700.

In Illustration 9-17, Don's is using the first-in, first-out inventory method and the cost of the eight units sold on March 20 is $50 per unit, which are the older costs. After the March 20 sale, the remaining inventory consists of 2 units at a per unit cost of $50 and 20 units at a per unit cost of $60, or a total cost of $1,300. Businesses with perpetual inventory systems also may use last-in, first-out and weighted-average cost methods.

The inventory card in Illustration 9-17 is for a business that does not have a computerized accounting system. Businesses that have computerized accounting systems have similar inventory records in their accounting systems, typically stored on magnetic tape or magnetic disks. Modern computers have greatly enhanced the ability of businesses to use perpetual inventory procedures. Consider the number of items of merchandise and the number of sale and purchase transactions of a supermarket or a retailer such as J.C. Penney Company. Without computers, perpetual inventory procedures would require considerable effort. Not only do computers enhance the accounting for merchandise inventory, they also enhance the management of merchandise inventory. With continually updated inventory information, management can be more effective in avoiding being out of stock of merchandise desired by customers. The timely information indicates when inventory on hand of an item is low and merchandise should be ordered. Some computerized inventory systems automatically reorder merchandise when the number of units on hand reaches a predetermined level.

The inventory card, as shown in Illustration 9-17, has columns to record the sales invoices and vouchers used to post increases and decreases in the inventory item. Periodically, the balances of all the inventory cards should be summed and reconciled to the balance of the Merchandise Inventory account in the general ledger. If the two figures do not agree, employees should undertake an investigation to determine the cause of the discrepancy and to make any necessary corrections. Such a reconciling and correcting process contributes to the completeness and accuracy of the recording of the changes in perpetual inventory.

Perpetual Inventories and the Need for Physical Inventories

Since businesses keep a continuous record of merchandise inventory with perpetual inventory systems, it may appear that physical inventories are not needed. The merchandise inventory records, however, only show what inventory *should* be on hand. A physical inventory is needed to determine what inventory actually is on hand. The perpetual inventory records may not show the actual inventory because of shrinkage, breakage, theft, and other causes. Also, employees may have made errors in recording inventory transactions. After the actual inventory on hand is determined by physical inventory, employees should adjust the merchandise inventory card to reflect the correct inventory on hand. After all inventory cards are corrected, the business adjusts Merchandise Inventory in the general ledger, the control account, to reflect the sum of the corrected inventory cards. For example, assume that the physical inventory determines a shortage of merchandise that cost $85. The entry in general journal form to record the loss is:

Dec. 31	Loss from Inventory Shortage	85	
	Merchandise Inventory		85
	To record loss from inventory shortage.		

Point-of-Sale Systems

Point-of-sale systems for the electronic transfer of funds from customers' bank accounts to the business's bank account are described in an earlier chapter. Some businesses also have point-of-sale systems for updating their inventory records. For example, consider a business that uses an electronic product code reader. Each item of merchandise has a unique code that the electronic reader recognizes. Such a product code is shown below.

The product code reader is connected to the cash register and to the business's computer. When a customer makes a purchase, the product code reader (scanner) identifies the merchandise being purchased. The computer contains information about the prices of merchandise and enters the proper amounts in the cash register. Simultaneously, the computer adjusts the perpetual inventory records of each item of merchandise sold. Some businesses have programmed their computers to order merchandise automatically from suppliers whenever inventory levels drop to a designated amount. Point-of-sale systems enhance the management of inventory levels by instantaneously adjusting the inventory records.

LO 8

Apply the two methods of estimating inventories.

ESTIMATING INVENTORIES

Businesses frequently must estimate the amounts of inventories to prepare interim financial reports and to file an insurance claim should the inventory be lost due to a disaster. Two methods businesses use to estimate inventories are the gross profit method and the retail method. To manage more effectively, retail merchandise businesses often need financial statements prepared more frequently than annually. Managers frequently desire financial statements at least monthly. Also, creditors may desire financial statements on a more frequent basis than annually, perhaps every three months or even monthly. Financial statements prepared for accounting periods shorter than one year are called *interim financial statements*.

Although interim financial statements are as valuable to retail businesses as to any other business, retail businesses often find that both perpetual inventory procedures and frequent periodic physical inventories are too costly. This is because of the varieties and quantities of retail inventories. Many retail businesses use periodic inventory systems and do not keep continuous track of the merchandise on hand and sold in their accounting records. At the end of the annual accounting period, they determine inventory by taking a physical inventory. To avoid the time and expense of a physical inventory when preparing interim financial statements, businesses may estimate the amount of inventory on hand by using the gross profit method or retail method.

Gross Profit Method

The **gross profit method** of estimating inventories relies on the formula for calculation of cost of goods sold:

> **Beginning inventory**
> **Add: Purchases**
> _____
> **Cost of goods available for sale**
> **Less: Ending inventory**
> _____
> **Cost of goods sold**

The gross profit method also assumes that the business's cost of goods sold/sales ratio is relatively stable over time. The steps in applying the gross profit method are as follows:

1. Calculate the cost of goods available for sale by summing the beginning inventory and purchases, both at cost.
2. Calculate *estimated* cost of goods sold by multiplying net sales by the cost of goods sold/sales ratio.
3. Calculate *estimated* ending inventory by subtracting the estimated cost of goods sold from the cost of goods available for sale.

Gross Profit Method Illustrated

Assume the accounting records at the end of a period show the following amounts:

Sales	$112,000
Sales returns and allowances	4,000
Inventory (beginning)	21,000
Purchases	70,000
Transportation-in	5,000

In recent years, the gross profit margin has been relatively stable at 25% of net sales; and nothing has occurred in the current period to indicate any change in that margin. A gross profit margin of 25% means that the cost of goods sold/sales ratio is 75% as shown by the following relationship:

Net sales (as a percent of net sales)	100%
Gross profit (as a percent of net sales)	25%
Cost of goods sold (as a percent of net sales)	75%

The cost of goods sold/sales ratio of 75% is used to estimate the ending inventory:

1. Beginning inventory		$21,000
Purchases	$ 70,000	
Add: Transportation-in	5,000	75,000
Cost of goods available for sale		$96,000
2. Sales	$112,000	
Less: Sales returns and allowances	4,000	
Net sales	$108,000	
Estimated cost of goods sold		
(75% x $108,000)		81,000
3. Estimated ending inventory		$15,000

Businesses use the gross profit method of estimating inventories in several ways. In estimating inventories when preparing interim financial statements or when estimating inventories destroyed by fires or storms, businesses use the gross profit method to determine the amount of inventory. Also, accountants often use the gross profit method to check the reasonableness of inventory amounts determined by physical inventories.

Retail Method

To use the **retail method** of estimating inventories, the records of the business should have information about the beginning inventory at cost and at retail. The term *at cost* means the cost of the beginning inventory as determined by one of the acceptable inventory methods previously discussed. The term *at retail* means the selling price of the merchandise. In addition to this information about the beginning inventory, the accounting records should show the purchases during the period at both cost and retail and the *net* sales at retail for the period. The net sales at retail consist of the amount of sales entered in Sales Revenue during the period less sales returns, allowances, and discounts for the period. The following section describes the steps involved in applying the retail method.

Steps in Applying the Retail Method

1. Calculate the amount of goods available for sale at both cost and retail. Goods available for sale at cost consist of (1) beginning inventory at cost, plus (2) net purchases at cost, plus (3) transportation-in related to the purchases, minus (4) purchase discounts, returns, and allowances. Goods available for sale at retail is the sum of beginning inventory at retail plus net purchases at retail.
2. Determine the cost/retail ratio by dividing the goods available for sale at cost by the goods available for sale at retail.
3. Calculate ending inventory at retail by subtracting net sales, which are at retail, from the goods available for sale at retail.
4. Determine ending inventory at cost by multiplying the ending inventory at retail by the cost/retail ratio determined in Step 2.

These steps in applying the retail method are shown in Illustration 9-18.

ILLUSTRATION 9-18 Applying the Retail Method

Step	Cost	Retail
1. Beginning inventory	$ 60,000	$ 96,000
Purchases	115,000	204,000
Transportation-in	5,000	
Goods available for sale	$180,000	$300,000
2. Cost/retail ratio: $180,000 ÷ $300,000 = 60%		
3. Net sales		250,000
Ending inventory, at retail		$ 50,000
4. Ending inventory, at cost		
($50,000 x 60%)	$ 30,000	

The example shown in Illustration 9-18 may be interpreted as follows:

1. The business had merchandise for sale during the period worth $300,000 at retail prices.
2. The average cost of each $1.00 of merchandise for sale is $.60.
3. Of the merchandise for sale at total retail prices of $300,000, merchandise with total retail prices of $250,000 was sold during the period, leaving $50,000 of merchandise at retail on hand at the end of the period.
4. Since each $1.00 of merchandise at retail has, on average, a cost of $.60, the merchandise on hand at the end of the period must have cost approximately $30,000 (i.e., $50,000 x 60%).

Although the retail method is acceptable for estimating inventory for interim financial statements, the business needs to take a physical inventory at least one time each year for purposes of preparing the annual financial statements. As with the perpetual inventory method, the retail method indicates the cost of inventory that *should* be on hand, not what is actually on hand.

Calculate and interpret the inventory turnover ratio.

INVENTORY TURNOVER

Inventory turnover indicates the rate at which inventory passes through a business. The measure compares the volume of inventory sold to the average amount of inventory on hand during the period. To analyze a business's performance, a commonly used measure—that includes the amount of merchandise inventory reported in the financial statements—is the inventory turnover ratio. This ratio is calculated as follows:

$$\text{Inventory Turnover Ratio} = \frac{\text{Cost of Goods Sold}}{\text{Average Inventory}}$$

where

$$\text{Average Inventory} = \frac{\text{Beginning Inventory} + \text{Ending Inventory}}{2}$$

If a business has cost of goods sold of $100,000 and average inventory of $25,000, the inventory would have *turned over* four times ($100,000 ÷ $25,000 = 4) in the period.

Interpreting Inventory Turnover Ratio

The inventory turnover ratio varies for different types of businesses. On the average, family clothing, sporting goods, and department stores have inventory turnover ratios of about four times per year. This implies that they turn over their inventories about once every season. Restaurants, on the other hand, deal mainly in fresh food and have inventory turnover ratios of about 60 times per year, or about once every six days.

The inventory turnover ratio allows financial statement readers to assess how efficiently management utilized its inventory. A business's merchandise inventory requires an investment of capital. To maintain the investment in inventory, a business incurs costs. These costs include: storage of the merchandise, insurance, property taxes, ordering, and handling. By maintaining a relatively low level (high turnover) of inventory, a business can minimize storage, insurance, and property tax costs. Conversely, a relatively high level (low turnover) of inventory tends to minimize ordering and handling costs. There is, however, an implicit cost to low levels of inventory. This implicit cost is lost sales and perhaps poor customer relations from not being able to meet customer demand. Management must often try to balance these inventory costs.

Analyzing Marie's Shoes Experience

In the scenario that opened this chapter, Marie's frustration with the shoe stores resulted from two different approaches to inventory management. European Shoe Boutique's approach is to maintain relatively high levels of inventory to avoid lost sales and to establish a clientele. These customers should provide repeat business because they know the store always has in stock what they want. This approach usually results in the business charging higher prices to cover the costs of maintaining high levels of inventory with low inventory turnover and low sales volume.

Conversely, Bob's Discount Shoe Mart's approach to inventory management involves a minimum level of inventory and high sales volume. The low level of inventory allows such businesses to charge lower prices because of the lower inventory maintenance costs. These businesses experience high inventory turnover. Under this approach, management expects the low prices to attract customers, even though the business often might not have in stock what the customer wants. If Marie were to examine the financial statements of the two stores and calculate their inventory turnover ratios, she would probably see these two approaches to inventory management reflected in their turnover ratios. Bob's Discount Shoe Mart's turnover ratio is probably much higher than that for European Shoe Boutique.

SUMMARY

Describe the process for determining inventory quantities at the end of an accounting period.   Businesses determine the number of units of merchandise that make up ending inventory by taking a physical inventory and by analyzing goods in transit at the end of an accounting period. Taking a physical inventory involves following strictly controlled procedures to count each item in the inventory. Businesses analyze goods in transit to ensure that the goods the business owns are included in ending inventory.

Calculate cost of goods available for sale and allocate it to units in ending inventory and to units sold during the period.   Cost of goods available for sale consists of the cost of the beginning inventory plus the cost of inventory purchases during the year. Businesses allocate cost of goods available for sale to the units in the ending inventory and to the units sold during the year. The allocation procedures are: (1) assign costs to the units in the ending inventory, and (2) calculate the cost of goods sold by subtracting the cost of the ending inventory from the cost of the goods available for sale.

Describe the importance of inventory errors. By incorrectly determining inventory quantities or by incorrectly assigning costs to the units in inventory, errors may occur in the process of determining the cost of the ending inventory. When an error occurs in determining the cost of the ending inventory, cost of goods sold, net income, owner's equity, and current assets are all misstated in the financial statements.

Apply the alternative methods of assiging costs to ending inventory.   The fact that prices of inventory items change over time complicates the assignment of costs to goods that are sold and to goods in the ending inventory. Businesses use four methods to assign costs to these two elements: (1) specific identification, (2) weighted-average cost, (3) first-in, first-out (FIFO), and (4) last-in, first-out (LIFO). The inventory methods, except for specific identification, assume some flow of the costs of the units rather than keeping track of the physical flow of units.

Discuss the factors management should consider in selecting an inventory method.   Management's decision about which inventory costing method to use depends on its expectations about future costs of inventory items and the relative amounts of net income and taxable income it desires to report. During periods of rising prices, the FIFO method will result in the highest net income and LIFO will result in the lowest taxable income.

Discuss when inventories should be valued at less than cost and calculate the relevant values.   Usually, inventories are shown on the balance sheet at cost. While items of inventory are held for resale their values may decline below assigned costs. The decline in value may be the result of damage or obsolescence or changes in consumer demand. When the value of inventory declines below cost, the business has incurred a loss that should be reported in net income in the period that the decline in value below cost occurs.

Describe perpetual inventory systems and prepare the necessary entries.   Some businesses desire to know the amount of inventory on hand at any time during the period. This allows greater control over inventory and the determination of cost of goods sold for a period shorter than a year. These businesses use the perpetual inventory system, which keeps a continuous record of merchandise inventory and permits summarizing cost of goods sold at any point in time.

Apply the two methods of estimating inventories.   For businesses that use the periodic inventory system, the preparation of interim financial statements using normal end-of-period inventory procedures is often too costly. These businesses prepare interim statements by estimating the cost of inventory at the end of an interim period. Two common methods businesses use to estimate the cost of inventories are the gross profit method and the retail method.

Calculate and interpret the inventory turnover ratio.   The inventory turnover ratio is the ratio of cost of goods sold to the average inventory for the period. The ratio shows the rate at which inventory passes through a business and how efficiently the business utilizes its inventory.

REVIEW PROBLEM

The data shown on the next page are given for the inventory transactions of Boutique Clothiers Company for the month of March.

REQUIRED:

a. Calculate cost of goods available for sale.
b. Calculate cost of goods sold for March and ending inventory for the month, assuming that Boutique Clothiers Company uses a periodic inventory system using the following methods: (1) FIFO, (2) LIFO, or (3) weighted-average cost.

Date	Purchases Units	Cost	Sales (Units)	Inventory (Units)
Beg. inventory	300	$5.00		300
Mar. 2	600	$5.25		900
6			400	500
10	250	$5.40		750
13			500	250
20	100	$5.45		350
22	700	$5.50		1,050
28			250	800
31	100	$5.60		900

SOLUTION:

Planning and Organizing Your Work

1. Find the cost of beginning inventory and the cost of each purchase by multiplying the quantity times the unit price.
2. Determine cost of goods available for sale by adding the cost of the beginning inventory plus purchases calculated in Step 1.
3. Determine the cost of the ending inventory for each method as shown in "Methods Used to Assign Costs to Inventories" in this chapter.
4. Determine the cost of goods sold for each method by subtracting the ending inventory, calculated in Step 3, from the cost of goods available for sale, calculated in Step 2.

(a) *Calculate cost of goods available for sale.*

Date		Units	Unit Cost	Total Cost
Mar. 1	Beg. inventory	300	$5.00	$ 1,500
2	Purchase	600	5.25	3,150
10	Purchase	250	5.40	1,350
20	Purchase	100	5.45	545
22	Purchase	700	5.50	3,850
31	Purchase	100	5.60	560
Cost of goods available for sale		2,050		$10,955

(b) *Calculate cost of goods sold and ending inventory.*

FIFO

Goods available for sale		$10,955
Ending inventory:		
100 x $5.60	$ 560	
700 x $5.50	3,850	
100 x $5.45	545	
Less: Total ending inventory		4,955
Cost of goods sold		$ 6,000

LIFO

Goods available for sale		$10,955
Ending inventory:		
300 x $5.00	$1,500	
600 x $5.25	3,150	
Less: Total ending inventory		4,650
Cost of goods sold		$ 6,305

Weighted-Average Cost

Goods available for sale	$10,955
Less: Ending inventory	
(900 x $5.344*)	4,810
Cost of goods sold	$ 6,145

*$10,955 ÷ 2,050 units

KEY TERMS

cost of goods available for sale, *365*

estimated net realizable value, *377*

first-in, first-out (FIFO), *371*

goods in transit, *365*

gross profit method, *384*

inventory turnover, *386*

inventory turnover ratio, *386*

last-in, first-out (LIFO), *372*

lower-of-cost-or-market rule, *379*

merchandise inventory card, *381*

retail method, *385*

specific identification method, *368*

weighted-average cost method, *370*

SELF-QUIZ

LO 1 1. Which of the following should *not* be included in ending inventory?
a. Goods sold F.O.B. shipping point that are in transit.
b. Goods sold F.O.B. destination point that are in transit.
c. Goods purchased F.O.B. shipping point that are in transit.
d. Goods purchased F.O.B. destination that have arrived on the loading dock.

LO 2 2. Which of the following is *not* a component of the cost of goods available for sale?
a. Purchases discounts
b. In-transit insurance costs
c. Beginning inventory
d. Transportation-out

LO 2 3. True or False? Cost of goods available for sale is equal to ending inventory plus cost of goods sold.

LO 3 4. Which of the following is *correct* if ending inventory is overstated in 19X1?
a. Beginning inventory is understated in 19X2.
b. Owner's equity is correctly stated at the end of 19X2.
c. Gross profit is understated for 19X1.
d. Cost of goods sold is overstated for 19X1.

LO 4 5. Which of the following is *not* an assumed cost flow method?
a. Specific identification   c. FIFO
b. Weighted-average cost   d. LIFO

LO 5 6. Supporters of the FIFO method argue that it produces the most realistic measurement of the _____ _____.

LO 5 7. Which of the following statements about inventory methods is *incorrect* if purchase prices are rising?
a. The LIFO method produces the lowest amount of ending inventory.
b. The FIFO method produces the lowest cost of goods sold.
c. The weighted-average cost method produces the highest gross profit.
d. The LIFO method produces the lowest gross profit.

LO 5 8. True or False? During periods of decreasing costs, the LIFO method minimizes the amount of income taxes paid.

LO 6 9. Reporting inventories at market value when the market value has fallen below cost is called the _____ - _____ - _____ - _____ - _____ rule.

LO 7 10. True or False? Businesses that use a perpetual inventory system record purchases of merchandise in Purchases.

LO 8 11. Which of the following is *not* a correct step in applying the retail method?
a. Dividing purchases at cost by purchases at retail to determine the cost/retail ratio
b. Subtracting net sales from goods available for sale at retail to determine ending inventory at retail
c. Calculating goods available for sale at both cost and retail
d. Multiplying ending inventory at retail by the cost/retail to determine ending inventory at cost

LO 8 12. Two methods used to estimate inventories are the _____ _____ method and the _____ method.

LO 9 13. True or False? The inventory turnover ratio is calculated by dividing cost of goods sold by average inventory.

SOLUTIONS TO SELF-QUIZ
1. a   2. d   3. True   4. b   5. a   6. ending inventory   7. c   8. False   9. lower-of-cost-or-market
10. False   11. a   12. gross profit, retail   13. True

QUESTIONS

Q9-1   What is the process for determining inventory quantities at the end of an accounting period?

Q9-2   What two allocations of cost of goods available for sale do businesses make at the end of the year?

Q9-3   Why is it important for the accountant to make sure each year's inventory is correctly stated even though most inventory errors automatically correct themselves within two years?

Q9-4   What are three inventory methods that assume a cost flow?

Q9-5   Which inventory flow method would result in net income being stated at the most current value and why?

Q9-6   Which inventory flow method would result in ending inventory on the balance sheet being stated at the most current value and why?

Q9-7   What factors should management consider when selecting an inventory method?

Q9-8   What are the two main reasons why the value of merchandise held for resale to customers may decrease below its assigned cost?

Q9-9   Why do businesses use perpetual inventory procedures?

Q9-10 Why do businesses need physical inventories if they use a perpetual inventory system?

Q9-11 What is the gross profit inventory method and when should it be used?

Q9-12 What is the retail inventory method and when should it be used?

Q9-13 What does the inventory turnover ratio measure?

EXERCISES

LO 2

E9-1   **Assign Inventory Costs**   The cost of goods available for sale for Kringle's Christmas Store is $189,000. The cost of the ending inventory is $23,000.

REQUIRED:

Determine cost of goods sold.

LO 2,3

E9-2   **Determining Ending Inventory**   Determined by a physical count at the end of 19X5, the ending inventory for Catherine's Jewelry Store is $139,200. The accounting records revealed that inventory on January 1, 19X5 equaled $105,600. The general ledger shows that Purchases and Transportation-In equal $992,500 and $9,100, respectively. In addition, Catherine's sold jewelry with a cost of $41,600 that was shipped F.O.B. shipping point, and it is still in transit. This shipment was not included in the physical count of ending inventory. Also not included in ending inventory was a $69,300 order in transit that Catherine's purchased from Diamond Wholesalers, F.O.B. destination.

REQUIRED:

Determine for 19X5 the cost of goods available for sale, ending inventory, and cost of goods sold for Catherine's Jewelry Store.

LO 3

E9-3 **Inventory Errors** A $14,500 overstatement of inventory occurred during a physical count and valuation of inventory at the end of 19X3. In addition, purchases during 19X4 were understated by $9,200.

REQUIRED:

Determine the effects of these errors on cost of goods sold, gross profit, net income, and ending owner's equity for 19X3 and 19X4.

LO 4

E9-4 **Calculating Ending Inventory and Cost of Goods Sold** The following information is given for the inventory transactions of Altman's Stereo Store for the month of May:

	Purchases		Total
Date	*Units*	*Cost*	*Cost*
Beg. inventory	60	$3.50	$210.00
May 4	42	3.60	151.20
11	84	3.65	306.60
16	55	3.75	206.25
21	40	3.70	148.00
30	50	3.80	190.00

Altman's sold 235 units during May.

REQUIRED:

Determine ending inventory and cost of goods sold for Altman's if it uses the following: (1) FIFO, (2) LIFO, and (3) weighted-average cost.

LO 6

E9-5 **Damaged Inventory** Heavy rains caused some flooding at Harold's Haberdashery. Unfortunately, 10 snakeskin Western hatbands that cost $160 each were damaged. Harold's estimates that it can sell each hatband for $120. In addition, Harold's pays a 5% commission on each hatband sold.

REQUIRED:

Determine the net realizable value of the inventory and record the journal entry to record the effects of the damage.

LO 6

E9-6 **Lower of Cost or Market** Appliance Warehouse is a discount store that sells major appliances. The inventory for Appliance Warehouse is given below:

Model	*Units*	*Cost per Unit*	*Market Price per Unit*
17	20	$ 98.50	$ 89.00
23	14	136.00	142.50
41	55	228.00	213.00
56	40	435.50	472.50
72	70	539.90	501.30
81	10	601.00	610.00

REQUIRED:

Determine the amount of the ending inventory by applying the lower-of-cost-or-market rule and record the journal entry (if any) to adjust the inventory.

LO 7

E9-7 **Perpetual Inventory**   The Scott Appliance Company began operations on June 1, 19X0. Following are some June transactions:

June 1 Purchased 50 television sets at a cost of $275 per set.
  8 Sold 5 television sets on credit at a price of $325 per set.
  15 Sold 9 television sets for cash at a price of $335 per set.

REQUIRED:

Journalize the transactions for the Scott Appliance Company if it uses a perpetual inventory system.

LO 8

E9-8 **Retail Inventory Method**   Jasmine's Sporting Goods uses the retail inventory method to estimate ending inventory. During the period, Jasmine's had sales of $130,000.

REQUIRED:

Estimate ending inventory at cost given the following information:

	Cost	Retail
Beginning inventory	$40,000	$ 68,000
Net purchases	98,000	142,000
Transportation-in	2,000	

LO 8

E9-9 **Gross Profit Method**   The accounting records of Stuart's Musicland show the following amounts:

Sales	$250,000
Sales returns and allowances	4,000
Inventory (beginning)	45,000
Purchases	205,000
Purchases returns	4,500
Purchases discounts	5,500
Transportation-in	5,000

Stuart's Musicland's percentage of gross profit to sales is 30%.

REQUIRED:

Using the gross profit method, determine the estimated ending inventory for Stuart's Musicland.

LO 9

E9-10 **Calculate the Inventory Turnover Ratio**   For 19X1, Singh's Carpet Warehouse has cost of goods sold of $400,000 and average inventory of $80,000.

REQUIRED:

Calculate the 19X1 inventory turnover ratio for Singh's Carpet Warehouse.

PROBLEM SET A

LO 1,2,3

P9-1A **Inventory Errors**   Maude's Tile Company's books were in a shambles; so, it hired Regina Bruce to put the books back in order. During her investigation, Regina found the following facts for the years 19X7 and 19X8:

(1) In-transit purchases of $5,000 shipped F.O.B. shipping point were not included in 19X7 ending inventory, and were recorded in 19X7 purchases.
(2) In-transit sales of merchandise that cost $8,000 shipped F.O.B. destination point were not included in 19X8 ending inventory.

(3) $3,500 of goods were included in the 19X8 ending inventory but were never record-ed as a purchase.

(4) In-transit purchases of $6,000 shipped F.O.B. destination point were included in 19X8 ending inventory, but were not recorded as purchases until 19X9.

REQUIRED:

a. Identify which, if any, of the above errors will not be self-correcting in the subse-quent year.

b. Determine the effect of each error on 19X7 and 19X8 ending inventory, cost of goods sold, gross profit, and owner's equity.

c. Determine the combined effects of all errors on 19X7 and 19X8 ending inventory, cost of goods sold, gross profit, and owner's equity.

LO 4   **P9-2A**   **Calculating Inventory**   The following inventory transactions of Ann's Dress Shop took place in 19X4 and 19X5:

	Purchases		*Total*
Date	*Units*	*Cost*	*Cost*
Beg. inventory	90	$62.00	$5,580.00
Mar. 7, X4	30	67.50	2,025.00
May 8, X4	40	71.25	2,850.00
Aug. 8, X4	20	69.50	1,390.00
Nov. 6, X4	50	67.75	3,387.50
Mar. 1, X5	25	71.50	1,787.50
Jun. 6, X5	30	70.00	2,100.00
Oct. 2, X5	60	72.50	4,350.00

Ann sold 180 dresses in 19X4 and 100 dresses in 19X5 and uses a periodic inventory system.

REQUIRED:

a. Calculate cost of goods sold and ending inventory for 19X4 and 19X5 if Ann's uses the FIFO inventory method.

b. Calculate cost of goods sold and ending inventory for 19X4 and 19X5 if Ann's uses the LIFO inventory method.

c. Calculate cost of goods sold and ending inventory for 19X4 and 19X5 if Ann's uses the weighted-average cost inventory method.

LO 6   **P9-3A**   **Lower of Cost or Market**   Dinettes Galore is a discount store that sells tables and chairs. The inventory for Dinettes Galore is given below:

	Model	*Units*	*Cost per Unit*	*Market Price per Unit*
Tables	15	20	$ 97.50	$ 86.00
	21	14	106.00	111.50
	46	35	207.00	203.00
Chairs	113	60	37.50	41.50
	129	80	40.25	38.00
	144	48	68.00	66.50
	162	32	88.50	97.00

REQUIRED:

Determine the amount of the ending inventory by applying the lower-of-cost-or-market rule and record the journal entry (if any) to adjust the inventory.

LO 8 **P9-4A** **Retail Inventory** Gunther's Pet Supply Store uses the retail inventory method to estimate ending inventory. Information relating to the estimation of inventory is as follows:

	Cost	Retail
Beginning inventory	$ 25,000	$ 48,000
Purchases	108,000	202,000
Transportation-in	5,000	
Purchases discounts	3,500	
Purchases returns and allowances	9,500	
Sales		190,400
Sales discounts		2,200
Sales returns and allowances		3,200

REQUIRED:

a. Calculate net purchases.
b. Calculate net sales.
c. Estimate ending inventory using the retail method.

LO 8 **P9-5A** **Gross Profit Method** The accounting records of Reid's Rare Books show the following amounts:

Sales	$153,600
Sales returns and allowances	1,100
Inventory (beginning)	65,500
Purchases	115,000
Purchases returns	2,700
Purchases discounts	1,300
Transportation-in	2,400

Reid's Rare Books has average annual sales of $140,000 and an average gross profit of $49,000.

REQUIRED:

a. Calculate the gross margin percentage.
b. Estimate the ending inventory.
c. Estimate the amount of the loss Reid would incur if a fire destroyed everything except for $22,000 of rare books in ending inventory.

LO 9 **P9-6A** **Inventory Turnover** The accounting records of Classic Stores provides the following information for 19X1:

Beginning inventory	$120,000
Purchases	790,000
Transportation-in	45,000
Purchases discounts	15,000
Purchases returns and allowances	10,000
Ending inventory	130,000

REQUIRED:

a. Calculate the inventory turnover ratio for 19X1.
b. If asked by management, how would you interpret the ratio that you calculated?

PROBLEM SET B

LO 1,2,3 **P9-1B** **Inventory Errors** Bubba's Plumbing Supply Company's books were disorganized; so, it hired Shirley Williams to put the books back in order. During her investigation, Shirley found the following facts for the years 19X8 and 19X9:

(1) In-transit sales of merchandise that cost $6,000 shipped F.O.B. destination point were not included in 19X8 ending inventory.

(2) In-transit purchases of $2,700 shipped F.O.B. shipping point were not included in 19X8 ending inventory, but were included in 19X8 purchases.

(3) $2,100 of goods were included in the 19X9 ending inventory but were never recorded as a purchase.

(4) In-transit purchases of $4,500 shipped F.O.B. destination point were included in 19X9 ending inventory, and were included in purchases in the following year.

REQUIRED:

a. Identify which, if any, of the above errors will not be self-correcting in the subsequent year.

b. Determine the effect of each error on 19X8 and 19X9 ending inventory, cost of goods sold, gross profit, and owner's equity.

c. Determine the combined effects of all errors on 19X8 and 19X9 ending inventory, cost of goods sold, gross profit, and owner's equity.

LO 4   **P9-2B**   **Calculating Inventory**   The following information is for the inventory transactions of Executive Suits for 19X2 and 19X3:

| | Purchases | | Total |
Date	Units	Cost	Cost
Beg. inventory	40	$ 97.50	$3,900.00
Feb. 2, X2	25	102.00	2,550.00
Apr. 13, X2	30	103.25	3,097.50
Sept. 2, X2	15	106.50	1,597.50
Oct. 30, X2	50	105.40	5,270.00
Feb. 15, X3	20	107.00	2,140.00
Jul. 7, X3	35	103.50	3,622.50
Sept. 28, X3	70	108.00	7,560.00

Executive Suits had sales of 90 suits in 19X2 and 95 suits in 19X3 and uses a periodic inventory system.

REQUIRED:

a. Calculate cost of goods sold and ending inventory for 19X2 and 19X3 if Executive Suits uses the FIFO inventory method.

b. Calculate cost of goods sold and ending inventory for 19X2 and 19X3 if Executive Suits uses the LIFO inventory method.

c. Calculate cost of goods sold and ending inventory for 19X2 and 19X3 if Executive Suits uses the weighted-average cost inventory method.

LO 6   **P9-3B**   **Lower of Cost or Market**   Modern Electronics is a discount store that sells stereos and televisions. The inventory for Modern Electronics is given below:

	Model	Units	Cost per Unit	Market Price per Unit
Stereos	18	46	$ 89.50	$ 98.00
	25	42	163.00	148.00
	48	60	197.90	187.50
Televisions	131	20	147.50	151.50
	149	32	159.25	138.00
	157	22	219.50	206.50
	173	36	288.50	298.00

REQUIRED:

Determine the carrying value of the ending inventory by applying the lower-of-cost-or-market rule and record the journal entry (if any) to adjust the inventory.

LO 8   **P9-4B**   **Retail Inventory**   Discount Lawn Furniture uses the retail inventory method to estimate ending inventory. Information relating to the estimation of inventory is given below:

	Cost	Retail
Beginning inventory	$ 37,500	$ 72,000
Purchases	162,000	303,000
Transportation-in	7,500	
Purchases discounts	5,250	
Purchases returns	14,250	
Sales		235,600
Sales discounts		1,200
Sales returns		4,400

REQUIRED:

a. Calculate net purchases.
b. Calculate net sales.
c. Estimate ending inventory using the retail method.

LO 8   **P9-5B**   **Gross Profit Method**   The accounting records of Napa River Wines show the following amounts:

Sales	$102,400
Sales returns and allowances	700
Inventory (beginning)	43,600
Purchases	79,000
Purchases returns	1,800
Purchases discounts	950
Transportation-in	1,650

Napa River Wines has average annual sales of $104,000 and an average gross profit of $41,600.

REQUIRED:

a. Calculate the gross margin percentage.
b. Estimate the ending inventory.
c. Estimate the amount of the loss Napa River Wines would incur if a fire destroyed everything except for $13,000 of wine in ending inventory.

LO 9   **P9-6B**   **Inventory Turnover**   Construction Supply Company is attempting to borrow funds from North National Bank. The bank has asked for information about the company's inventory, specifically the inventory turnover ratio. The accounting records of Construction Supply Company provide the following information for 19X2:

Beginning inventory	$350,000
Purchases	815,000
Transportation-in	20,000
Purchases discounts	10,000
Purchases returns and allowances	5,000
Ending inventory	410,000

REQUIRED:

a. Calculate the inventory turnover ratio for 19X2.
b. Assuming that the inventory turnover ratio has been averaging about 4:1 in previous years, how would you interpret the ratio that you calculated for 19X2?

CRITICAL THINKING AND COMMUNICATING

 C9-1   Special Chips is a newly formed company that specializes in semiconductors. George Castro, the owner and president, is trying to determine which inventory method to select. Since the inventory items are not unique, George has determined that he should not select the specific identification method. George decided he needed help in making the decision; so, he hired Teresa Iglesias to advise him on this matter. George particularly wanted to know what inventory methods are available as well as the effects of the different methods on his financial statements.

REQUIRED:

a. Identify the different inventory methods and explain how they work.
b. Pretend you are Teresa Iglesias and answer George's questions.

 C9-2   The Falcon Company has always used the weighted-average cost inventory method. Justine Falcon, the owner of the company, asked her bookkeeper to restate inventory under the FIFO and the LIFO methods for the last three years. The bookkeeper presented the following schedule of cost of goods sold under the two methods:

Date	FIFO	Weighted-Average Cost	LIFO
Dec. 31, X1	$13,300	$14,600	$16,200
Dec. 31, X2	13,500	15,200	16,400
Dec. 31, X3	14,210	16,740	18,320

Justine wondered why FIFO always had the lowest cost and LIFO always had the highest cost and the existing method always was in-between.

REQUIRED:

Explain in a written memo why the different methods result in this pattern of cost of goods sold.

 C9-3   Refer to the financial statements of J.C. Penney Company reprinted in Appendix B at the end of this text. J.C. Penney is a major retail merchandising company; therefore, merchandise inventory is critical to the company's performance.

REQUIRED:

a. Comment on J.C. Penney's method of accounting for merchandise inventories. Hint: Examine the *Summary of Accounting Policies* located immediately after the statement of cash flows.
b. Calculate the inventory turnover ratios for J.C. Penney for 1993 and 1992 (ignore the additional costs included with cost of goods sold).
c. Comment on the direction of fluctuation in the turnover ratios.
d. Determine the cause of the fluctuation in the turnover ratio. Hint: Calculate the percentage changes in the numerator and the denominator of the turnover ratio.

CHAPTER 10

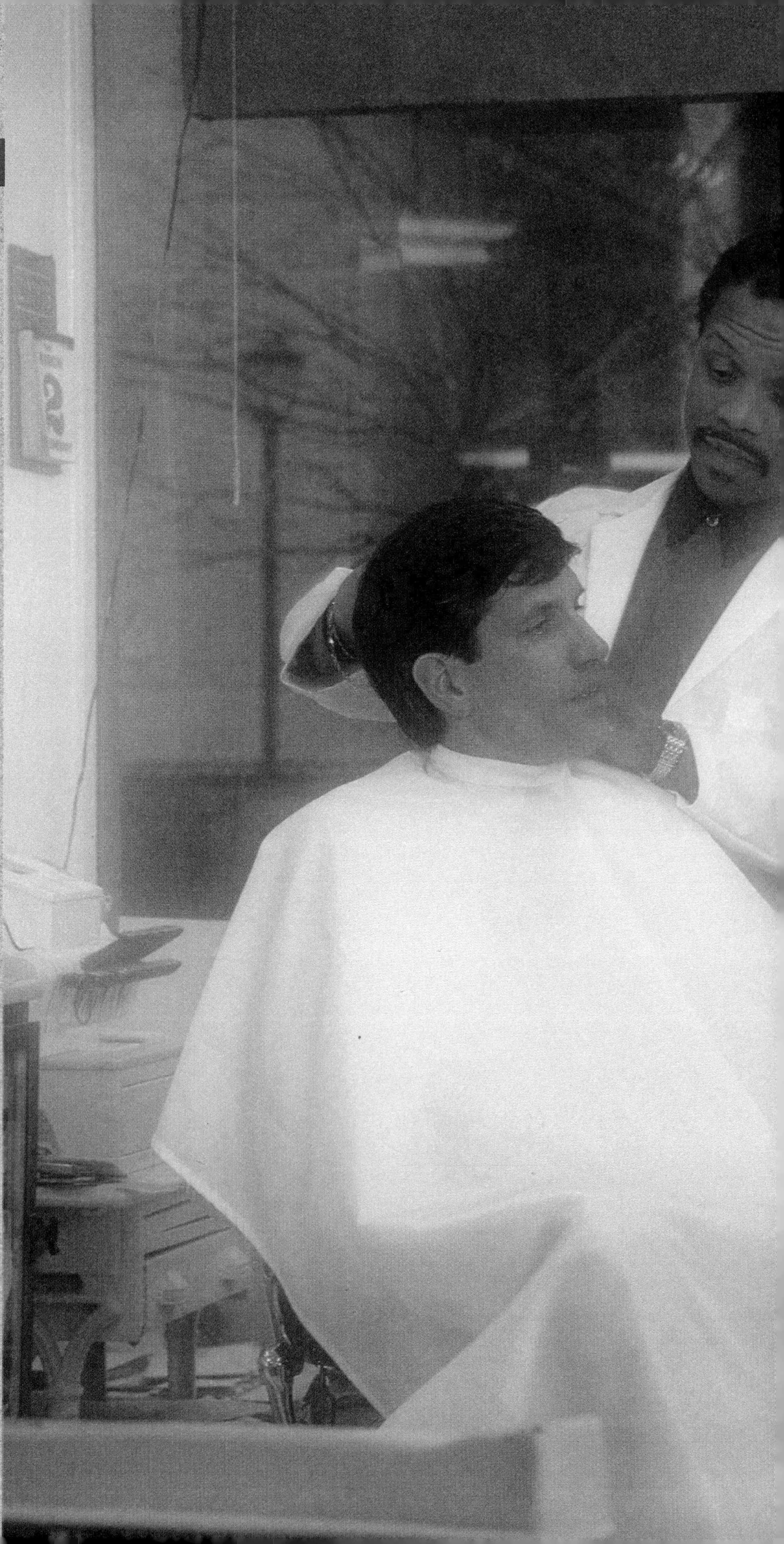

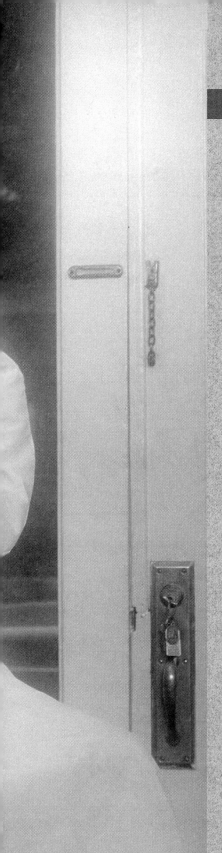

Plant Assets: Acquisition and Depreciation

The last time Chris Rader had his hair trimmed, the hair stylist asked his advice about an investment. The stylist, Jeff Foreman, is considering purchasing his own business. Jeff currently works in Red's Barber Shop, and the owner has offered to sell the business to Jeff. Also, Jeff is acquainted with the owner of Nouveau Hair Styling Salon who has offered to sell his business to Jeff. The two businesses have similar locations and have the same number of styling chairs, as well as other equipment used in the hair styling business. While the two businesses are similar in the services they provide, Red's is an old, established business and Nouveau is a relatively new business. Chris told Jeff that he needs to assess the relative profitability of the two businesses before making an investment decision.

This chapter and the following chapter present the accounting for the noncurrent, or long-term, productive assets a business uses in its operations. This chapter discusses the accounting for the acquisition and the expiration of the service potential through use of plant assets. You will learn one way to evaluate how well the business's assets are performing. Chris can use this approach to evaluate the productivity of assets and to help Jeff make his decision.

1. Identify the categories of plant assets.
2. Determine which costs are included in the recorded cost of plant assets.
3. Explain the concept of depreciation.
4. Identify the factors used in calculating depreciation.
5. Calculate depreciation expense using several alternative depreciation methods.
6. Compare the alternative depreciation methods and explain the factors that affect management's choice of depreciation methods.
7. Calculate depreciation for partial periods, account for revisions of depreciation rates, and calculate depreciation for income taxes.
8. Analyze and record expenditures related to plant assets during their useful lives.
9. Calculate and interpret the return on total assets.

LO 1

Identify the categories of plant assets.

CATEGORIES OF PLANT ASSETS

Most businesses own tangible productive assets called **plant and equipment**; **property, plant, and equipment**; or **plant assets**. The primary characteristics of plant assets are:

1. They are useful for a period of time exceeding a year.
2. They are acquired to be used in the business's operations and not to be resold to customers.

These assets also are commonly called **fixed assets** or **capital assets**. Although the term *fixed assets* implies that assets are permanent, they do in fact wear out or become obsolete and need to be replaced.

What a business classifies as plant assets depends on the business's nature and its operations. For example, a retail store's plant assets include land and building, merchandise display equipment, office equipment, and delivery equipment; whereas, a manufacturing business's plant assets include land and buildings, manufacturing equipment, delivery trucks, and office equipment. The plant asset classification would also include stand-by equipment that the business uses only during peak time or in case of an emergency. Once the business ceases to use plant assets in its operations, it should cease classifying them as plant and equipment. Unless the business plans to sell these assets within one year or less, it classifies them as long-term investments. If the business plans to resell the plant assets to customers, then it should classify them as inventory. Plant assets are often classified into the following four categories:

1. Land. Businesses often own land as a building site.
2. Land improvements. Examples of land improvements include driveways, sidewalks, parking lots, fences, and lighting.
3. Buildings. The types of buildings that a business owns varies according to the type of business—retail store, factory building, storage building, etc.
4. Equipment. The types of equipment a business owns depends on the nature of its operations. Examples include cash registers, computers, conveyor belts, drill presses, delivery trucks, and office equipment such as desks, chairs, and file cabinets. Illustration 10-1 shows the asset classifications found in the 1992 annual survey of the financial statements of 600 large businesses.

ILLUSTRATION 10-1 Asset Captions in Financial Statements for 1992

Land Captions	
Land	367
Land and improvements	128
Land and buildings	37
Land and other identified assets	17
No caption with term land	21
Buildings Captions	
Buildings	253
Buildings and improvements	210
Buildings and land or equipment	74
Buildings and other identified assets	5
No caption with term buildings	25
Other Asset Captions	
Machinery and/or equipment	454
Machinery and/or equipment with other assets	90
Construction in progress	254
Leasehold improvements	103
Automobiles, marine equipment, etc.	61
Leased assets	71
Furniture, fixtures, etc.	48
Assets leased to others	14

Source: *Accounting Trends and Techniques* (Jersey City, New Jersey: AICPA, 1993).

For many businesses, plant assets are a major portion of the assets reported in their balance sheets. Therefore, not only is the accounting for plant assets important, but management must also safeguard and maintain plant assets. Also, expanding investment in plant assets and replacing existing plant assets as needed are critical management responsibilities.

DETERMINING COSTS OF PLANT ASSETS

LO 2
Determine which costs are included in the recorded cost of plant assets.

Although a business may occasionally self-construct an asset such as a building or a specialized machine, businesses generally acquire plant assets by purchasing them. Regardless of how businesses acquire plant assets, accountants should record them according to the cost principle, which applies to the acquisition of *used* assets as well as to *new* assets. The total recorded cost of a plant asset includes all necessary costs a business incurs to acquire the asset, to put the asset in the proper condition for use, to prepare the site for the asset, and to move the asset to the location of its intended use. Necessary acquisition costs include such expenditures as the purchase price, transportation costs, and insurance while the asset is in transit. The purchase price used in recording the acquisition cost should be the cash outlay, which is the purchase price less any discounts the supplier offered. A business may not always use cash to purchase assets; rather, it may exchange other assets for the purchased asset. In these cases, we determine the purchase price by the fair value of the asset given or the asset received, whichever is more clearly evident. (We discuss the accounting for exchanges of noncash assets in more detail in the next chapter.)

Land

Land purchases commonly involve costs in addition to the purchase price. Such costs include real estate sales commissions, legal fees, title transfer and registration fees, and survey costs. Accountants should record these costs as part of the cost of the land. If a business acquires land for the site of a new building, all costs the business incurs in preparing the land for construction should also be debited to Land. When a building site already has an existing building, we include the cost of removing the old building, less the amount received as salvage for the materials from the old building, in the cost of the land. Also, we include the cost of clearing, draining, and grading land in the cost of the land. The rationale for including these costs is that they are necessary costs of preparing the land for its intended use—the site of a new building.

For example, assume that on January 4, 19X1, Paul's Print Shop incurs the following costs in purchasing land as the site of a new building:

Purchase price		$250,000
Real estate commissions		5,000
Legal and title fees		1,000
Removal of old building	$20,000	
Less: Salvage	7,500	12,500
Clearing and grading		8,000
		$276,500

The purchase of the land and the costs of site preparation are recorded in Land with the following summary entry:

Jan. 4	Land	276,500	
	Cash		276,500
	To record the purchase of land and the cost of site preparation.		

We record land and building costs in separate accounts because land does not deteriorate or become obsolete and, therefore, is not subject to depreciation. (We discuss depreciation later in this chapter.) A building deteriorates and becomes obsolete and, therefore, is subject to depreciation. Thus, we record the cost of a building in a separate account.

Land Improvements

Certain improvements to land—driveways, sidewalks, parking lots, fences, and lighting—have a limited life and are subject to depreciation. We record the cost of these land improvements in Land Improvements rather than in Land so that we may calculate depreciation without confusion. To illustrate the recording of land improvements, assume Paul's Print Shop constructs a new parking lot at a cost of $10,000 beside its office building. On April 27, 19X1, Paul's pays the construction company for the parking lot with a $2,000 cash down payment and an $8,000 interest-bearing note payable. Paul's entry to record the cost of the new parking lot is as follows:

Apr. 27	Land Improvements	10,000	
	Cash		2,000
	Notes Payable		8,000
	To record the cost of a new parking lot.		

Buildings

A business may acquire a building either by purchasing an existing structure or by constructing a new building. When a business purchases a building, the cost of the building includes the purchase price and other costs to prepare the building for occupancy such as renovation and repair costs. Repair costs a business incurs to maintain the building after it is put into use, however, are expenses because they are not necessary costs to acquire the building and get it ready for use.

When a business constructs its own building, the cost of the building should include all construction costs. Construction costs include architectural fees, building permits, legal fees, excavation, materials, labor, a portion of administration costs, and insurance during the period of construction—and the interest incurred on loans used to finance the construction of the building. After the building is put into use, such costs as insurance, interest, and repairs and maintenance are expenses, not additional costs of the building itself.

Assume Paul's Print Shop incurs the following costs in constructing a building that it will use in its operations:

Architectural fees	$ 60,000
Building permits and legal fees	5,000
Excavation	75,000
Materials	400,000
Labor	350,000
Administration costs	100,000
Insurance during construction	8,000
Interest on construction loans	96,000
Total cost	$1,094,000

The total cost of the building is $1,094,000, which we debit to Buildings with the following *summary* entry:

(Date)	Buildings	1,094,000	
	Cash, Accounts Payable, etc.		1,094,000
	To record the cost of self-constructed building.		

Equipment

The cost of equipment includes the net purchase price (purchase price less any discounts), freight, insurance during transit, installation, and testing. Assume that on October 31, 19X1, Paul's Print Shop purchases a new binding machine. The price of the machine is $10,000, and the terms are 2/10, n/30; freight cost incurred for shipping the machine is $125; insurance during transit is $25; and installation and testing of the machine is $275. We calculate the cost of the machine and debit it to Equipment as follows:

Purchase price	$10,000	
Less: 2% cash discount	200	
Net purchase price		$ 9,800
Freight		125
Insurance during transit		25
Installation and testing		275
Total cost		$10,225

Oct. 31	Equipment	10,225	
	Accounts Payable		10,225
	To record purchase of binding machine.		

If the equipment is damaged accidentally while in transit or when it is being installed, the cost of repairing the equipment is an expense, not a cost of the equipment, because the repairs are not necessary costs of acquiring the asset.

Group Purchases

Businesses commonly purchase plant assets as a group rather than individually. For example, in one transaction a business purchases a building and the land on which it is located. When a business purchases these assets as a group, we record the various assets separately. As previously discussed, the land is not subject to depreciation. However, the other assets purchased, such as building and equipment, are subject to different rates of depreciation. In recording group purchases, we allocate the purchase price to the individual assets in the group on the basis of their relative fair values. We determine the fair values of the assets by referring to any available price lists or by appraisal. The relative fair value assigned to an asset included in the group of assets purchased is the fair value of that asset as a percent of the total fair value of the group of assets:

$$\frac{\textbf{Fair Value of Asset}}{\textbf{Total Fair Value of Group of Assets}}$$

On November 24, 19X1, Paul's Print Shop purchases an existing printing operation that is located in a nearby city. The assets purchased in the transaction include land, building, and equipment. Paul's purchases the printing operation for $90,000 cash. An appraisal of the assets indicates the following fair values: land $25,000, building $60,000, and equipment $15,000—for a total of $100,000. Paul's is able to purchase the group of assets at less than their individual fair values because the former owner was anxious to sell. Based on this information, we assign the $90,000 group purchase price to the individual assets as follows:

	Proportion of Total Fair Value	Allocated Cost
Land	$ 25,000/$100,000 x $90,000	$22,500
Building	60,000/100,000 x 90,000	54,000
Equipment	15,000/100,000 x 90,000	13,500
Total	$100,000/$100,000 x $90,000	$90,000

The journal entry below shows how to record the group purchase:

Nov. 24	Land	22,500	
	Buildings	54,000	
	Equipment	13,500	
	Cash		90,000
	To record the group purchase of property, plant, and equipment.		

DEPRECIATION ACCOUNTING

A business purchases plant assets because they can provide useful services to its operations. In fact, an asset can be thought of as a bundle of benefits to be provided to a business as it uses the asset. For example, a delivery truck provides transportation services, and a computer provides computational and word processing services. Plant assets, however, generally have limited useful lives. In other words, except for land, these assets can only provide a limited amount of services. Over the entire useful life of the asset, the *cost of the services* it provides is the cost of the asset less the value received when the asset is sold or traded in on a new asset. **Depreciation** is the process of allocating the cost of the assets to the periods benefited from the services they provide.

In accordance with the matching principle, recording depreciation expense matches the cost of the services provided by plant assets with the related revenues in determining net income. The accounting profession describes depreciation as follows:

> The cost of a productive facility is one of the costs of the services it renders during its useful economic life. Generally accepted accounting principles require that this cost be spread over the expected useful life of the facility in such a way as to allocate it as equitably as possible to the periods during which services are obtained from the use of the facility. This procedure is known as depreciation accounting, a system of accounting which aims to distribute the cost or other basic value of tangible capital assets, less salvage (if any), over the estimated useful life of the unit ... in a systematic and rational manner. It is a process of allocation, not valuation.[1]

The profession's description includes an important distinction about depreciation in accounting—depreciation is a cost allocation process, not a valuation process. In particular, depreciation does *not* attempt to measure the asset's market value. The **current value** is the amount that the asset could be sold for at its current age and in its current condition. We do *not* determine the amount of depreciation expense by measuring the change in the asset's market value that occurs in the accounting period. Businesses acquire plant assets to be used in providing goods and services, not for resale to customers. Therefore, the accounting profession has decided that information about fluctuations in market values of these assets is not as important as information about the original cost sacrificed to use the asset.

Recording Depreciation

We record depreciation at the end of each accounting period by a debit to Depreciation Expense and a credit to Accumulated Depreciation. For example, assume that on January 2, 19X1, Paul's Print Shop purchases a new computerized printing machine at a cost of $40,000; and depreciation for 19X1 is determined to be $5,000. Paul's entries to record the purchase and the depreciation are as follows:

Jan. 1	Equipment	40,000	
	Cash		40,000
	To record purchase of printing machine.		

---

[1] *Financial Accounting Standards: Original Pronouncements as of July 1, 1992*, ARB No. 43, (Norwalk, Conn.: FASB, 1993), Chap. 9, Sec. C, par. 5.

Dec. 31	Depreciation Expense—Equipment	5,000	
	Accumulated Depreciation—Equipment		5,000
	To record depreciation for the year.		

     Businesses commonly have separate depreciation expense and accumulated depreciation accounts for groups of assets that serve similar functions or common uses. For example, several groupings of assets by function would include buildings, machinery, and equipment, which are usually depreciated at different rates. Groupings of assets by use could include store equipment, factory equipment, and office equipment. These groupings by use allow depreciation expense to be allocated among various organizational components such as manufacturing, sales, and administration.

Depreciation in the Financial Statements

In its December 31, 19X1, balance sheet, Paul's Print Shop displays the printing equipment as follows:

| Equipment | $40,000 | |
| Less: Accumulated depreciation | 5,000 | $35,000 |

     We call the $35,000 net amount the **carrying amount** or **net book value** of the asset, and it represents the undepreciated cost of the asset as of the balance sheet date. **Accumulated Depreciation** is a contra-asset account. Some accountants refer to Accumulated Depreciation as a **valuation account**. This usage does not mean that Accumulated Depreciation adjusts the asset to its market value. Rather, we adjust the asset to its undepreciated cost, which is the carrying amount or net book value. In this text, we use the term carrying amount instead of net book value.

LO 4
Identify the factors used in calculating depreciation.

FACTORS USED IN CALCULATING DEPRECIATION

In addition to the asset's recorded cost, accountants must know its estimated residual value and estimated useful life.

Estimated Residual Value

The **estimated residual value** is either the estimated net proceeds if the asset is sold or the trade-in value if the asset is traded in on a replacement asset. A business estimates, in the period it acquires the asset, the amounts to be received at the date of disposal. We base the estimate of the residual value generally on the company's experience and on other sources of information such as prices of used assets. If a business incurs costs in disposing of the asset, the residual value is the estimated proceeds less the estimated costs of disposing of the asset. We commonly refer to the estimated residual value as the **estimated salvage value**.

     Accountants call the cost of the asset minus the estimated residual value the **depreciable cost**. The depreciable cost of an asset is the total amount subject to depreciation and is the total amount allocated to depreciation expense over the asset's useful life.

Estimated Useful Life

An asset's **estimated useful life** is the estimated period of time that the business can *use* the asset in the business. As a business uses depreciable assets in its operations, they wear out. Eventually, the assets deteriorate to the point that the business can no longer use them; and the business has to replace the assets. For example, as a business uses a delivery truck, it begins to wear out. Eventually, the truck will be completely worn out; and the business will have to replace the old truck with a new truck.

Plant assets may have limited lives due to obsolescence or inadequacy as well as to physical wear. As society makes technological advances, new assets become available and are superior to those the business currently uses. These new assets may provide the same services as the old assets, but at a lower cost, or they may provide higher quality services. Some new assets may even provide higher quality services at a lower cost. For example, the rapid technological advances made in computers quickly rendered existing computers obsolete because the newer computers can process data faster and at a lower cost than the older models. Because of obsolescence, an asset's useful life may be less than its potential physical life. For example, a computer may have a potential physical life of ten years, but because of obsolescence, a business may replace its computers every five years. Consequently, the business should allocate the cost of its computers over five years.

Assets may become inadequate for the needs of a business as it grows or as the nature of its operations changes. For example, a rapidly growing business may become too large for its physical facilities and be forced to relocate its operations to larger facilities.

Useful life may be measured in time, in total units of service (such as machine hours), or in output (number of stampings or castings produced). In the next section on depreciation methods, we illustrate some of the alternative measures of useful life.

LO 5

Calculate depreciation expense using several alternative depreciation methods.

DEPRECIATION METHODS

Within GAAP, many alternative methods for allocating assets' depreciable costs to accounting periods are available. The following discussion illustrates four of the most commonly used methods: straight-line, units-of-production, sum-of-the-years'-digits, and double-declining-balance. Illustration 10-2 shows the use of the various depreciation methods in 1992 by 600 large businesses.

ILLUSTRATION 10-2 Number of Companies Using Various Depreciation Methods*

Straight-line	564
Declining-balance	26
Sum-of-the-years'-digits	12
Accelerated method—not specified	62
Units-of-production	47
Other	5

*The total exceeds 600 because some companies use different depreciation methods for different categories of assets.

Source: *Accounting Trends and Techniques* (Jersey City, New Jersey: AICPA, 1993).

Straight-Line Method

Virtually all types of businesses use the straight-line method, the most popular depreciation method in practice. The **straight-line method** of depreciation allocates an equal amount of depreciation expense to each period in the asset's estimated useful life. Accountants calculate the depreciation expense for each period by dividing the depreciable cost of the asset (cost less estimated residual value) by the number of periods in the asset's estimated useful life:

$$\text{Depreciation Expense Per Year} = \frac{\text{Depreciable Cost}}{\text{Estimated Useful Life (in years)}}$$

An equivalent method for computing straight-line depreciation is:

$$\text{Depreciable Expense Per Year} = \text{Depreciable Cost} \times \text{Straight-Line Rate}$$

The **straight-line rate** is defined as follows:

$$\text{Straight-Line Rate} = \frac{100\%}{\text{Estimated Useful Life}}$$

For example, assume Paul's Print Shop purchases a new packaging machine at a cost of $12,000. The machine has an estimated useful life of 4 years, and the residual value is $2,000. The straight-line rate for a useful life of 4 years is 25% (100% ÷ 4). Depreciable cost is $10,000 ($12,000 - $2,000). Depreciation expense per year for the machine using the straight-line method is calculated as follows:

$$\text{Depreciation Expense Per Year} = \frac{\$10,000}{4} = \$2,500$$

Or, equivalently,

$$\text{Depreciation Expense Per Year} = \$10,000 \times 25\% = \$2,500$$

A **depreciation schedule** that shows the allocation of depreciation expense over the machine's useful life is shown in Illustration 10-3. From the depreciation schedule, you can observe four characteristics of the straight-line depreciation method. First, as previously discussed, depreciation expense is an equal amount each period. Second, Accumulated Depreciation increases by an equal amount each time period. Third, the asset's carrying amount decreases by an equal amount each time period. Fourth, the carrying amount at the end of the machine's expected useful life is equal to the residual value expected at the time it was acquired.

ILLUSTRATION 10-3 Depreciation Schedule for Straight-Line Method

Period	Depreciable Cost	Depreciation Rate	Depreciation Expense	Accumulated Depreciation	Carrying Amount
At purchase	$10,000	——	——	——	$12,000
End of Year 1	10,000	25%	$2,500	$ 2,500	9,500
End of Year 2	10,000	25%	2,500	5,000	7,000
End of Year 3	10,000	25%	2,500	7,500	4,500
End of Year 4	10,000	25%	2,500	10,000	2,000

Units-Of-Production Method

The **units-of-production method** <u>allocates depreciation to time periods based on the asset's output</u>. While the straight-line method allocates an equal amount of depreciation to each time period, the units-of-production method allocates an equal amount of depreciation to each unit the asset produces. We calculate the amount of depreciation allocated to each unit of production by dividing the asset's depreciable cost by the estimated lifetime units of production. The equation for calculating depreciation for each unit of output is:

$$\text{Depreciation Expense Per Unit of Production} = \frac{\text{Depreciable Cost}}{\text{Estimated Total Units of Production}}$$

We calculate the depreciation expense for an accounting period by multiplying the units of production during the accounting period by the depreciation expense per unit of production, as follows:

$$\text{Depreciation Expense} = \frac{\text{Units of Production}}{\text{During the Period}} \times \frac{\text{Depreciation Expense}}{\text{Per Unit of Production}}$$

If Paul's Print Shop decides to use the units-of-production method to depreciate the new packaging machine, management must estimate how many packages the machine can wrap during its useful life. Management bases the estimate of total production on the manufacturer's specifications and any previous experience the business has had with similar machines. Based on the information available, management estimates that the machine can wrap 40,000 packages during its useful life. Using the units-of-production method, the calculation of depreciation expense per unit of output is as follows:

$$\text{Depreciation Expense Per Unit of Production} = \frac{\$10,000}{40,000 \text{ units}} = \$.25 \text{ per unit}$$

If the machine's actual production is 8,000 packages during Year 1, depreciation expense for Year 1 is:

$$\text{Depreciation Expense for Year 1} = 8,000 \text{ units} \times \$.25 \text{ per unit} = \$2,000$$

Assuming Paul's produces 10,000 units in Year 2, 14,000 units in Year 3, and 8,000 units in Year 4, the depreciation schedule for the machine using the units-of-production method is shown in Illustration 10-4. From the depreciation schedule, observe that depreciation expense varies directly in relation to the asset's pattern of production. Likewise, accumulated depreciation *increases* directly in relation to the pattern of production. Finally, the carrying amount *decreases* directly in relation to the pattern of production and, in the end, equals the original estimate of residual value.

ILLUSTRATION 10-4 Depreciation Schedule for Units-of-Production Method

Period	Units of Production	Depreciation per Unit	Depreciation Expense	Accumulated Depreciation	Carrying Amount
At purchase	——	——	——	——	$12,000
End of Year 1	$ 8,000	$0.25	$2,000	$ 2,000	10,000
End of Year 2	10,000	0.25	2,500	4,500	7,500
End of Year 3	14,000	0.25	3,500	8,000	4,000
End of Year 4	8,000	0.25	2,000	10,000	2,000

Accelerated Depreciation Methods

A group of depreciation methods, called **accelerated depreciation methods**, results in <u>depreciation expense that is higher in the earlier years but is lower during the later years of the asset's useful life</u>. Accelerated depreciation methods are based on the assumption that more of an asset's benefits are consumed during the earlier years than they are in the later years of its useful life. As assets age, they require more maintenance and are out of service more frequently. The following section discusses two commonly used accelerated depreciation methods: the sum-of-the-years'-digits method and the double-declining-balance method.

Sum-of-the-Years'-Digits.   The **sum-of-the-years'-digits (SYD) method** <u>allocates depreciation by multiplying the asset's depreciable cost by a fraction for each year</u>. The fraction is sometimes called the *SYD fraction.* The numerator of the fraction for each year is the number of periods in the asset's estimated remaining useful life as of the *beginning* of the period. The denominator of the fraction is the sum of the digits in the asset's estimated useful life. The calculation, expressed in the form of an equation, is as follows:

$$\text{Depreciation Expense} = \text{Depreciable Cost} \times \frac{\text{Periods Remaining in Useful Life}}{\text{Sum of the Years' Digits}}$$

In the example of the new packaging machine Paul's Print Shop purchased, the estimated useful life is 4 years and the sum of the years' digits is:[2]

$$1 + 2 + 3 + 4 = 10$$

Depreciation for the first year is calculated as follows:

$$\$10{,}000 \times 4/10 = \$4{,}000$$

The numerator in the fraction is 4 because the asset's estimated useful life remaining at the beginning of Year 1 is 4 years. Depreciation expense for Year 2 is:

$$\$10{,}000 \times 3/10 = \$3{,}000$$

At the beginning of Year 2, the asset's remaining estimated useful life 3 years; therefore, the fraction used is 3/10.

    A depreciation schedule for the machine using the sum-of-the-years'-digits method is shown in Illustration 10-5. The depreciation schedule illustrates that the sum-of-the-years'-digits method is an accelerated depreciation method. Depreciation expense is largest in the first year and decreases in each subsequent year. Also, the amounts of the increases in accumulated depreciation and the amounts of the decreases in the asset's carrying amount both decrease in each subsequent period.

Double-Declining-Balance.   Accountants calculate depreciation expense using the declining-balance method by *multiplying the asset's carrying amount by*

---

[2]For assets that have relatively long estimated useful lives, directly summing the years may be burdensome. The sum of the years may be calculated using the following formula:

$$\text{Sum} = N(N{+}1) \div 2$$

In the formula, N is equal to the asset's estimated useful life. For example, the sum of the years for a building that has an estimated useful life of 40 years is:

$$40(40 + 1) \div 2 = 820$$

ILLUSTRATION 10-5 Depreciation Schedule for the Sum-of-the-Years'-Digits Method

Period	Depreciable Cost	SYD Fraction	Depreciation Expense	Accumulated Depreciation	Carrying Amount
At purchase	$10,000	——	——	——	$12,000
End of Year 1	10,000	4/10	$4,000	$ 4,000	8,000
End of Year 2	10,000	3/10	3,000	7,000	5,000
End of Year 3	10,000	2/10	2,000	9,000	3,000
End of Year 4	10,000	1/10	1,000	10,000	2,000

some percentage of the straight-line depreciation rate. Common percentages of the straight-line rate used are: 125%, 150%, 175%, and 200%. The choice of which percentage to use depends on how rapidly management desires to depreciate the asset. When it chooses 200% of the straight-line rate, management uses the method called **double-declining-balance**. The term *declining-balance* originates from the fact that the asset's carrying amount, or "balance," declines each period as we record additional depreciation expense. We apply the depreciation rate to this declining balance to calculate each successive period's depreciation expense.

Continuing with the example of the new packaging machine Paul's Print Shop purchased, assume Paul's uses the double-declining-balance method to calculate depreciation. The first step is to determine the straight-line depreciation rate. We determine the straight-line rate by dividing 100% by the asset's estimated useful life (in years). The machine in the example has an estimated useful life of 4 years; therefore, the straight-line rate is 100% ÷ 4 = 25%. To calculate depreciation for the first year, multiply the asset's carrying amount by 200% times the straight-line rate, or 2 x 25% = 50%. For the first year, the carrying amount is the cost of the asset since accumulated depreciation is zero. Notice that, of the depreciation methods presented, *only the double-declining-balance method starts with the asset's cost* rather than with the depreciable cost. Depreciation expense for Year 1 is:

$$\text{\$12,000 x 50\% = \$6,000}$$

We determine depreciation for the second year by multiplying the asset's *carrying amount* at the beginning of the period by 50%. The carrying amount of the machine at the beginning of Year 2 is $6,000:

Machine (at cost)	$12,000
Less: Accumulated depreciation	6,000
Carrying amount (on balance sheet)	$ 6,000

We base depreciation for Year 2 on the carrying amount at the end of Year 1.

$$\text{\$6,000 x 50\% = \$3,000}$$

Illustration 10-6 presents a depreciation schedule for the machine using the double-declining-balance method.

Notice in the depreciation schedule that the depreciation expense for Year 3 is only $1,000, even though 50% x $3,000 = $1,500. Depreciation in Year 3 is limited to $1,000 because the machine has an estimated residual value of $2,000. *In recording depreciation, as a rule, we do not reduce an asset's carrying amount below its estimated residual value.* Therefore, the amount of depre-

ILLUSTRATION 10-6 Depreciation Schedule for the Double-Declining-Balance Method

Period	Depreciable Cost	Depreciation Rate	Depreciation Expense	Accumulated Depreciation	Carrying Amount
At purchase	——	——	——	——	$12,000
End of Year 1	$12,000	50%	$6,000	$ 6,000	6,000
End of Year 2	6,000	50%	3,000	9,000	3,000
End of Year 3	3,000	50%	1,000*	10,000	2,000
End of Year 4	2,000	50%	0**	10,000	2,000

*Adjusted to $1,000 so that carrying amount is not less than residual value.

**No depreciation is recorded so that carrying amount is not less than residual value.

ciation that we record in Year 3 is $1,000; and we record no depreciation in Year 4.

The depreciation schedule illustrates that the double-declining-balance method is an accelerated depreciation method. Similar to the sum-of-the-years'-digits method, depreciation expense is largest in the first year and decreases in each subsequent year. Also, the amounts of the increases in accumulated depreciation and the amounts of the decreases in the asset's carrying amount decrease in each subsequent period.

LO 6

Compare the alternative depreciation methods and explain the factors that affect management's choice of depreciation methods.

COMPARISON OF DEPRECIATION METHODS

Presented in Illustration 10-7 is a comparison of the amounts of depreciation expense for the packaging machine Paul's Print Shop purchased for each year under the four depreciation methods. The schedule shows that the amount of depreciation varies significantly among the depreciation methods. Each of the methods, however, is acceptable under GAAP.

ILLUSTRATION 10-7 Depreciation Expense Under Different Methods

Year	Straight-Line	Units-of-Production	Sum-of-the Years'-Digits	Double-Declining-Balance
1	$ 2,500	$ 2,000	$ 4,000	$ 6,000
2	2,500	2,500	3,000	3,000
3	2,500	3,500	2,000	1,000
4	2,500	2,000	1,000	—
	$10,000	$10,000	$10,000	$10,000

Choosing a Depreciation Method

When management chooses a depreciation method to use for an asset, it commonly considers several factors. One important factor is whether the asset's usefulness expires as a result of the amount of usage or of the passage of time. The units-of-production method results in the allocation of depreciation to periods based on the pattern of usage, and this method is particularly appropriate when the usage of the asset varies significantly from period to period.

The straight-line and accelerated depreciation methods assume that the asset's usefulness expires with the passage of time. The straight-line method assumes that an equal amount of the asset's benefits are used up each period. The accelerated methods, however, assume that more benefits expire in the earlier periods of the asset's useful life than they do in the later periods. For example, a machine may be more efficient when it is relatively new than when it becomes older. Therefore, accelerated depreciation results in a better matching of revenues and expenses since the machine produces more service per unit of time when it is new than after it becomes older and less efficient.

Advocates of accelerated depreciation methods also argue that these methods result in more accurate total expense for using the asset. As assets become older, they often require more maintenance and repairs. Since accelerated depreciation expense decreases in these later years, the sum of depreciation, maintenance, and repairs is relatively constant for each period of the asset's useful life.

Management is responsible for selecting the depreciation methods for assets. Managers may rely upon the advice of accountants in making this selection; but in any event, the ultimate responsibility rests with management. In addition to the causes of the expiration of the asset's usefulness, management may also consider the relative amounts of depreciation per year when choosing a method. As shown in Illustration 10-7, the selection among the alternative depreciation methods can significantly affect net income through different patterns of depreciation expense.

Disclosing Depreciation Methods in Financial Statements

In selecting depreciation methods, management should depreciate similar assets using the same method. When management adopts a method for a category of assets, it should use the method consistently to enhance the comparability of the financial statements from period to period. Also, because of the significance of depreciation, the financial statements should disclose the methods of depreciation used for the plant assets presented in the balance sheet.

LO 7
Calculate depreciation for partial periods, account for revisions of depreciation rates, and calculate depreciation for income taxes.

SPECIAL PROBLEMS IN DEPRECIATION ACCOUNTING

When certain events occur, the accountant must modify the normal depreciation accounting procedures. These special problems are:

1. Calculating depreciation when assets are purchased at times other than the beginning of the fiscal year
2. Revising depreciation rates because of new information
3. Calculating depreciation for income taxes

Depreciation for Partial Years

A business commonly purchases assets during a fiscal year so it can allocate only a partial year's depreciation to the first and last fiscal year within the asset's estimated useful life.

Partial Years for Straight-Line Method.   For example, assume that on April 1, 19X1, Paul's Print Shop purchases a machine for $5,600. The machine has an estimated useful life of 5 years and an estimated residual value of $600. Paul's uses the straight-line depreciation method for the machine, and the calendar year is its annual accounting period. Annual depreciation is $1,000, calculated as follows:

$$\frac{\$5{,}600 - \$600}{5 \text{ years}} = \$1{,}000$$

For 19X1, however, Paul's uses the machine for only 9 months (April through December); therefore, only 9/12 of the annual depreciation should be allocated to 19X1. The depreciation for 19X1 is 9/12 x $1,000 = $750.

For 19X6, the last year of the machine's useful life, we allocate $250 (3/12 x $1,000) of depreciation to that year. The $250 of depreciation for 19X6 reduces the machine's carrying amount to its estimated residual value.

When a business purchases assets during the month, accountants commonly calculate depreciation for the nearest whole month. For assets purchased in the first half of a month, we allocate a whole month's depreciation for that month. For assets purchased in the second half of a month, we allocate no depreciation for that month.

Partial Years for Sum-of-the-Years'-Digits Method.   When a business uses the sum-of-the-years'-digits method, a unique problem arises with purchases made during the year. The problem is due to the use of a different fraction for allocating depreciation for each year of the asset's useful life. Furthermore, each year of useful life overlaps two annual accounting periods. Accountants handle the problem by allocating each year's depreciation expense between the two accounting periods. Assume Paul's Print Shop purchases an asset on May 4, 19X1. The asset cost $4,000 and has an estimated residual value of $400 and an estimated useful life of 4 years. Illustration 10-8 shows the allocation of depreciation for the asset's 4-year estimated useful life to the annual accounting periods.

ILLUSTRATION 10-8 Allocation of Depreciation Among Annual Accounting Periods

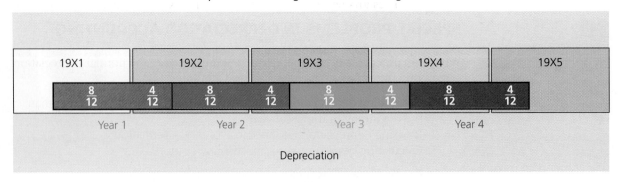

The asset was purchased on May 4, 19X1; therefore, we allocate the first year's depreciation 8/12 to 19X1 and 4/12 to 19X2. Depreciation expense related to the asset for 19X2 is the four months of the first year's depreciation and the eight months of the second year's depreciation.

Using the sum-of-the-years'-digits method, the depreciation for each year is calculated as follows:

Useful Life	Sum-of-the-Years'- Digits Depreciation	Allocation of Depreciation						
		8/12	4/12	19X1	19X2	19X3	19X4	19X5
1	$3,600 x 4/10 = $1,440	$960	$480	$960	$ 480			
2	3,600 x 3/10 = 1,080	720	360		720	$360		
3	3,600 x 2/10 = 720	480	240			480	$240	
4	3,600 x 1/10 = 360	240	120				240	$120
				$960	$1,200	$840	$480	$120

Revision of Depreciation Rates

Management's estimates in the period the business acquires the asset determine two factors involved in the calculation of depreciation—the useful life and residual value. Since these estimates involve forecasts of the future, it is not uncommon for the actual useful life or the actual residual value to be different from the earlier estimates of those amounts.

Revised Useful Life.   Under GAAP, if management receives new information indicating that the asset's estimated useful life or estimated residual value is different than the original estimates of those amounts, then management should revise the depreciation rates for the remaining estimated useful life. We apply the revised depreciation rate only to the current and future periods remaining in the asset's useful life. Under GAAP, the depreciation recorded in prior periods is *not* adjusted for the revised rate. The accounting profession adopted this rule to avoid the erosion of confidence in financial reporting that might occur if prior years' financial statements are revised as a result of future events.

Assuming the straight-line method, we determine the new annual depreciation expense by dividing the remaining depreciable cost at the time of the revision by the asset's revised remaining estimated useful life. For example, assume Paul's Print Shop purchases a machine on January 2, 19X1, for $14,000. Management estimates that the asset's useful life is 4 years and the estimated residual value is $2,000. Following the straight-line depreciation method, the annual depreciation is: ($14,000 - $2,000) ÷ 4 = $3,000. Based on the machine's condition at the beginning of 19X3, management revises the estimate of its useful life from 4 years to 6 years. At the end of 19X2, the accounts for the machine appear as follows:

Equipment		Accumulated Depreciation–Equipment	
Jan. 2, X1 14,000			Dec. 31, X1 3,000
			Dec. 31, X2 3,000
			Bal. 6,000

We calculate the revised *annual* depreciation as follows:

$$\frac{\text{Carrying Amount - Estimated Residual Value}}{\text{Revised Remaining Estimated Useful Life}} = \frac{\$8,000 - \$2,000}{4} = \$1,500$$

By depreciating the machine at the rate of $1,500 per year for the remaining 4 years of estimated useful life, we reduce the asset's carrying amount to the estimated residual value of $2,000 at the end of the sixth year, as follows:

Equipment		Accumulated Depreciation–Equipment	
Jan. 2, X1 14,000		Dec. 31, X1 3,000	
		Dec. 31, X2 3,000	
		Dec. 31, X3 1,500	
		Dec. 31, X4 1,500	
		Dec. 31, X5 1,500	
		Dec. 31, X6, 1,500	
		Bal. 12,000	

Revised Residual Value. If management revises the estimate of the asset's residual value, then we depreciate the revised remaining depreciable cost over the remaining estimated useful life to reduce the carrying amount to the revised estimated residual value. For example, Paul's acquires an asset on January 2, 19X1, for $1,400. The asset has an estimated useful life of 6 years and an estimated residual value of $200. Using the straight-line method, annual depreciation is $200 per year ($1,400 - $200) ÷ 6.

After two years have passed, management revises its estimate of the residual value from $200 to zero. The revised annual depreciation is calculated as follows:

Carrying amount of asset $1,400 - (2 x $200) =	$1,000
Revised estimated residual value	0
Remaining depreciable cost	$1,000
Remaining useful life	÷ 4
Revised annual depreciation	$ 250

The revised annual depreciation will reduce the asset's carrying amount to its revised estimated residual value of zero at the end of its useful life.

Depreciation and Income Taxes

For determining taxable income, a business is allowed a deduction for depreciation. The rules for depreciation for income tax purposes are called the **Accelerated Cost Recovery System (ACRS)**. The current ACRS rules were adopted as part of the Tax Reform Act of 1986 and apply to assets purchased since December 31, 1986. In practice, accountants call the current rules **Modified ACRS** or **MACRS**. The tax rules classify depreciable property as either real property (buildings) or personal property (equipment). MACRS requires that real property be depreciated using the straight-line method. Residential rental property must be depreciated over 27 1/2 years, and all other real property must be depreciated over 31 1/2 years—regardless of management's estimate of the asset's useful lives.

The tax rules classify personal property into several classes of depreciation periods that range from 3 years to 20 years. MACRS assigns assets to classes based on the type of asset, and the class lives are generally shorter than the asset's useful lives. Personal property may be depreciated using the straight-line method; however, accelerated depreciation is also available under MACRS. If a business elects accelerated depreciation, MACRS specifies the percentage of the asset's cost that the business can take as a depreciation deduction for each year of the asset's class life. The percentages assume that the assets were purchased in the middle of the tax year, regardless of when the assets were actually purchased. The depreciation percentages for 3, 5 and 7-year assets are as follows:

		CLASSES	
Year	3-Year	5-Year	7-Year
1	33.33%	20.00%	14.29%
2	44.45	32.00	24.49
3	14.81	19.20	17.49
4	7.41	11.52	12.49
5	—	11.52	8.93
6	—	5.76	8.92
7	—	—	8.93
8	—	—	4.46
	100.00%	100.00%	100.00%

Notice that the percentages extend for one more year than the class lives due to the mid-year acquisition assumed for MACRS. That is, a 3-year asset assumed to be acquired in the middle of Year 1 would be depreciated for 3 years, to the middle of Year 4. Also, MACRS ignores estimated residual value.

To illustrate the use of the percentages, assume Baker Corporation purchases a machine in the 5-year class on February 1, 19X1, at a cost of $10,000. Annual depreciation deductions for the 6 years are:

19X1	$10,000 x 20.00% =	$ 2,000
19X2	10,000 x 32.00% =	3,200
19X3	10,000 x 19.20% =	1,920
19X4	10,000 x 11.52% =	1,152
19X5	10,000 x 11.52% =	1,152
19X6	10,000 x 5.76% =	576
Total		$10,000

The advantage of accelerated depreciation for income tax purposes is that it results in higher depreciation expense and lower taxable income and taxes early in the asset's life. Deductions are larger in the early years of an asset's life under MACRS than they are for straight-line depreciation. However, the total deductions over the asset's life are always the same because for accelerated depreciation, the deductions are smaller in the later years than they are for straight-line depreciation. While the total deductions are the same for the two methods, the deferral of payments gives the business the "interest free" use of cash due to smaller tax payment for some period of time.

LO 8

Analyze and record expenditures related to plant assets during their useful lives.

EXPENDITURES DURING USEFUL LIFE OF PLANT ASSETS

In the periods after a business acquires plant assets, additional expenditures related to the upkeep, reconditioning, and improvement of them are not uncommon. Examples of such expenditures include the cost of replacing tires and engine tuneups on vehicles and the cost of painting and replacing damaged building components. An accounting issue arises concerning the proper classification of such expenditures. The possible classifications of the expenditures are either as assets, called capital expenditures, or as expenses, called revenue expenditures.

Capital expenditures are those expenditures subsequent to acquisition that extend the asset's useful life beyond its original useful life or those expenditures that enhance the asset's efficiency or effectiveness. Accountants record capital expenditures as assets because they increase the future benefits the asset provides. **Revenue expenditures**, on the other hand, merely maintain the asset's usefulness and keep it functioning at its original capacity. Since revenue expenditures do not create additional future benefits, we record them as expenses of the current period and match them with current revenue.

Repairs

Because they are ordinary and routine expenditures made to maintain the asset in good working order, **repairs** are revenue expenditures. For example, a delivery truck periodically needs tuneups, oil changes, and lubrication, as well as replacement of minor parts. A building needs painting, roofing repairs, plumbing repairs, and electrical repairs. These routine expenditures are necessary to maintain the asset's usefulness, and we record them as debits to an expense account called Maintenance Expense. For example, Paul's Print Shop pays $125 for an engine tuneup on one of its delivery trucks. Paul's entry to record the repair expense is:

(Date)	Maintenance Expense	125	
	Cash		125
	To record cost of engine tuneup.		

Replacements

Occasionally, a business makes a nonroutine, major expenditure that extends the asset's useful life beyond its original estimated useful life. These expenditures, which we call **replacements**, are capital expenditures. We record them as a reduction in the related accumulated depreciation account on the basis that the expenditures *recover* a portion of past depreciation by extending the asset's useful life. For example, Baker purchases a delivery truck for $22,000; it has an estimated useful life of 5 years and an estimated residual value of $2,000. Assuming straight-line depreciation, after 4 years, the truck's remaining depreciable cost is $4,000, as follows:

Cost	$22,000
Less: Accumulated depreciation of 4 years	16,000
Carrying amount	$ 6,000
Less: Estimated residual value	2,000
Remaining depreciable cost	$ 4,000

At the end of the fourth year, Baker performs a major engine overhaul costing $2,000. The overhaul extends the estimated useful life by 2 years to a total of 7 years. Baker records the cost of the overhaul as follows:

(Date)	Accumulated Depreciation-Delivery Equipment	2,000	
	Cash		2,000
	To record cost of engine overhaul.		

The remaining depreciable cost, which the above entry increases to $6,000, should be depreciated over the revised remaining useful life of 3 years. We calculate the revised annual depreciation as follows:

Remaining depreciable cost before replacement	$4,000
Add: Replacement	2,000
Revised remaining depreciable cost	$6,000
Remaining useful life	÷ 3
Revised annual depreciation expense	$2,000

Three years of depreciation at $2,000 per year exactly reduce the truck's carrying amount to its estimated residual value of $2,000.

Improvements

An **improvement,** a subsequent expenditure that makes an asset more efficient or effective, does not necessarily extend the asset's useful life. For example, a business converts a machine from manual operation to computer-controlled operation; and the change results in fewer flaws in the output. This type of expenditure enhances the machine's usefulness, and we consider it a capital expenditure.

Accountants debit the cost of an improvement either to the asset account or to Accumulated Depreciation, depending on whether the cost increases the asset's useful life. To illustrate, assume that on January 2, 19X4, Paul's Print Shop decides to replace the electric motor in a machine with a more powerful motor that will enhance the rate of output but not extend the machine's useful life. The cost of the new motor is $2,000. Paul's purchased the machine 3 years ago, and it has an estimated useful life of 6 years. When the improvement does not increase the asset's useful life, we debit the cost to the asset account as follows:

Jan. 2	Equipment	2,000	
	Cash		2,000
	To record cost of new motor.		

By increasing Equipment, this entry increases the machine's carrying amount and depreciable cost by $2,000. We allocate the machine's revised depreciable cost over its remaining useful life—which is 3 years. We account for the cost of improvements that increase the asset's useful life the same as we account for replacements—debiting the cost to Accumulated Depreciation. We allocate the revised remaining depreciable cost over the revised remaining useful life.

RETURN ON ASSETS

LO 9

Calculate and interpret the return on total assets.

At the beginning of this chapter, we introduced you to the investment decision that Jeff Foreman, the hair stylist, is considering. The owners of both Red's

Income Tax Treatment of Asbestos Removal Costs

For income tax purposes, the Internal Revenue Service (IRS) has developed rules for what expenditures may be deducted currently and, thereby, reduce current income taxes payable. Expenditures that cannot be deducted currently must be capitalized and deducted over the remaining life of the asset in the form of depreciation. To be deductible currently, the expenditure must be a repair. To be a repair, the expenditure must not extend the life of the asset, adapt it to a different use, materially increase its value, or create a separate asset.

For several years the federal government has been involved in requiring businesses (and others) to remove asbestos insulation because of its apparent link to cancer. A particular business had manufacturing equipment with asbestos as thermal insulation. Federal government regulations would have required the business to monitor continuously the air for asbestos particles, and totally encapsulate the equipment each time routine maintenance or repairs were required. These procedures would have been costly and resulted in loss of manufacturing time.

The business decided it would be less costly in the long run to replace the asbestos insulation on its manufacturing equipment with another thermal lining than to comply with the government regulations concerning the safety measures it would otherwise have to take. The business considered the cost of replacement to be a repair and treated it as a current deduction on its tax return.

The current deduction was disallowed by the IRS. The IRS took the position that the cost was a capital expenditure because the removal of the asbestos added to the value of the equipment because the equipment would be more readily salable with the non-asbestos insulation than with the asbestos in place. It apparently did not matter to the IRS that the business did not intend to sell the equipment, but to continue to use it in manufacturing.

Source: Grant Thornton, *National Tax Alert*, No. 92-40 (September 8, 1992).

Barber Shop and Nouveau Hair Styling Salon have offered Jeff the opportunity to purchase their businesses. Jeff wants to invest in the business that is the more profitable. He has asked Chris Rader to help him assess their profitability.

Jeff asked each current owner to provide him with the most recent financial statements. Jeff has shown these statements to Chris and has asked him what the statements show about the relative profitability of the two businesses. Illustration 10-9 shows the two sets of financial statements.

Calculating Return on Total Assets

We calculate the return on total assets using the following formula:

$$\text{Return on Total Assets} = \frac{\text{Net Income} + \text{Interest Expense}}{\text{Total Assets}}$$

The numerator of the ratio is income before interest expense. We add interest expense to net income because interest is a payment to creditors for the business's use of money to acquire assets. We want to calculate the return on assets without regard to how the business financed the acquisition of its assets.

ILLUSTRATION 10-9 Financial Statements for Red's and Nouveau

Red's Barber Shop Income Statement For the Year Ended December 31, 19X3		
Revenue		$86,000
Operating expenses:		
Wages and salaries	$58,000	
Taxes and fees	1,090	
Utilities	1,600	
Interest	240	
Depreciation	1,500	
Repairs	2,900	65,330
Net Income		$20,670

Nouveau Hair Styling Salon Income Statement For the Year Ended December 31, 19X3		
Revenue		$89,000
Operating expenses:		
Wages and salaries	$64,000	
Taxes and fees	1,200	
Utilities	1,400	
Interest	4,000	
Repairs	3,000	73,600
Net income		$15,400

Red's Barber Shop Balance Sheet December 31, 19X3		
Assets		
Cash		$ 500
Supplies		350
Equipment	$ 2,600	
Less: Accum. deprec.	2,100	500
Land		10,000
Buildings	$30,000	
Less: Accum. deprec.	15,000	15,000
Total assets		$26,350
Liabilities and Owner's Equity		
Accounts payable		$ 175
Notes payable		6,000
Owner's equity		20,175
Total liabilities and owner's equity		$26,350

Nouveau Hair Styling Salon Balance Sheet December 31, 19X3		
Assets		
Cash		$ 600
Supplies		375
Equipment	$3,700	
Less: Accum. deprec.	700	3,000
Land		12,000
Buildings	$70,000	
Less: Accum. deprec.	2,300	67,700
Total assets		$83,675
Liabilities and Owner's Equity		
Accounts payable		$ 200
Notes payable		75,000
Owner's equity		8,475
Total liabilities and owner's equity		$83,675

The calculations of the return on total assets for Red's and Nouveau are as follows:

$$\text{Red's:} \quad \frac{\$20,670 + \$240}{\$26,350} = 79\%$$

$$\text{Nouveau:} \quad \frac{\$15,400 + \$4,000}{\$83,675} = 23\%$$

Interpreting Return on Assets

In previous chapters, we discussed ratios used to assess the business's profitability such as return on equity. The return on total assets is another ratio that can be used to assess profitability. This ratio reflects the business's ability to utilize its assets to generate net income. By just looking at the two ratios, it appears that Red's is much more profitable than Nouveau. When using ratio analysis, however, you must be careful to assess whether the ratios may be misleading.

When we study the balance sheets of the two businesses, it becomes apparent that Red's has assets that are much older than Nouveau's assets. We see this by comparing the accumulated depreciation amounts to the assets' costs. For example, Red's building is 50% ($15,000 ÷ $30,000) depreciated as compared to Nouveau's building, which is 3% ($2,300 ÷ $70,000) depreciated. There are two implications for the ratios of return on total assets of this circumstance:

1. The carrying amounts of assets included in the measurement of total assets will be much smaller for older assets than for newer assets because accumulated depreciation is greater relative to the cost of the older assets.
2. Because of inflation, the cost of newer assets will be higher than the cost of assets acquired in earlier years.

Both of these implications result in the denominator being larger (and the ratio being smaller) for the business with newer assets. Also, the business with newer assets will record more depreciation expense than the business with older assets. This leads to lower net income and a smaller return on total assets for the business with the newer assets.

How should the ratios for Red's and Nouveau affect Jeff's decision? Obviously, Red's appears to be more profitable. However, Jeff should keep in mind that he may have to replace the older assets of Red's in the near future and the apparent profitability of Red's may be only a temporary situation. Chris probably should advise Jeff to investigate the replacement cost of Red's assets and assess what the affect of new assets would be on the relative profitability of the two businesses.

SUMMARY

Identify the categories of plant assets.   In financial statements, plant assets are often classified into four categories: land, land improvements, buildings, and equipment.

Determine which costs are included in the recorded cost of plant assets.   We record plant assets according to the cost principle. The total recorded cost of plant assets includes all necessary costs incurred to acquire the asset. The necessary costs include the purchase price, transportation costs, and insurance while in transit.

Explain the concept of depreciation.   Depreciation is the process of allocating the cost of assets to the periods benefited from the services they provide. The cost of an asset to be allocated over its useful live is the cost of the asset less the value received when the asset is sold or traded for another asset.

Identify the factors used in calculating depreciation.   The factors are:

1. *Cost*. The amount the business records as the cost of the asset at the time of acquisition.
2. *Estimated residual value*. Either the estimated net proceeds if the asset is sold or the trade-in value if the business trades in the asset on a replacement asset.

3. *Estimated useful life.* The estimated period of time that the business can use the asset.

Calculate depreciation expense using several alternative depreciation methods. The alternative depreciation methods include:

1. *Straight-line method.* Allocates a constant amount of depreciation to each period of the asset's estimated useful life.
2. *Units-of-production method.* Allocates depreciation to time periods based on the asset's output.
3. *Accelerated methods.* Allocates a higher amount of depreciation to the earlier periods of estimated useful life and a lower amount to the later periods. Two commonly used accelerated methods are the sum-of-the-years'-digits method and the double-declining-balance method.

Compare the alternative depreciation methods and explain the factors that affect management's choice of depreciation methods.   An important factor for management to consider is whether the asset's usefulness expires as a result of the amount of usage or of the passage of time. The units-of-production method allocates depreciation based on the amount of usage of the asset. Both the straight-line method and the accelerated methods allocate depreciation based on the passage of time. The straight-line method allocates the same amount of depreciation to each period, and the accelerated methods allocate a higher amount to the early years. Another factor management needs to consider is the relative effect on net income of the alternative depreciation methods.

Calculate depreciation for partial periods, account for revisions of depreciation rates, and calculate depreciation for income taxes.   Calculating depreciation for partial periods involves allocating a proportionate amount of depreciation to the first and last time periods in the asset's estimated useful life. For the sum-of-the-years'-digits method, special care must be taken because for each year two different fractions enter into the calculation of depreciation. If management revises its estimates of the asset's useful life or residual value, management should revise the depreciation rates for the remaining estimated useful life. We apply the revised rate only to the current and future periods remaining in the asset's useful life. Businesses calculate depreciation for income taxes according to the Modified Accelerated Cost Recovery System. This system classifies depreciable property as either personal property or as real property. MACRS classifies personal property into several classes of depreciation periods that range from 3 years to 20 years. MACRS depreciates real property using the straight-line method.

Analyze and record expenditures related to plant assets during their useful lives. We classify expenditures during the asset's useful life as capital expenditures or as revenue expenditures. Capital expenditures extend the asset's useful life beyond its original life or enhance the asset's efficiency or effectiveness. Capital expenditures include replacements and improvements. Accountants record capital expenditures as assets. Revenue expenditures such as repairs maintain the asset's usefulness. Accountants record revenue expenditures as expenses.

Calculate and interpret the return on total assets.   The return on total assets is the ratio of net income plus interest expense to total assets. The ratio can be used to assess the business's ability to utilize its assets to generate net income.

REVIEW PROBLEM

Allison Crib Company purchased a new lathe on January 2, 19X1, for cash of $145,000. In addition, Allison has to pay transportation costs of $3,500 and installation costs of $1,500. The estimated life is 5 years, and the lathe has an estimated salvage value of $30,000.

REQUIRED:

a. Determine the cost of the lathe.
b. Record the journal entry for the purchase of the lathe on January 2, 19X1.
c. Determine depreciation expense for each year using: (1) straight-line, (2) sum-of-the-years'-digits, and (3) double-declining-balance methods.
d. Determine depreciation expense for each year for tax purposes using MACRS, assuming that the lathe is classified as 5-year property.

SOLUTION:

Planning and Organizing Your Work

1. Determine the sum of all relevant costs in acquiring and installing the lathe.
2. Record the journal entry for the acquisition of the lathe, using the sum determined in Step 1.
3. Calculate the depreciation expense for each method, using the formulas given in the chapter under Depreciation Methods.
4. Calculate the depreciation expense for tax purposes using the percentages given for 5-year property in the table provided on page 419.

(a) *Determine the cost of the lathe.*

Purchase price	$145,000
Transportation	3,500
Installation	1,500
Total	$150,000

(b) *Record the purchase.*

Jan. 2	Equipment	150,000	
	Cash		150,000
	To record the acquisition of a lathe.		

(c) *Determine the depreciation expense.*

Straight-Line Method

($150,000 - 30,000) ÷ 5 = $24,000 per year

Sum-of-the-Years'-Digits Method

Year	Calculation	Depreciation Expense
1	5/15 x $120,000	$40,000
2	4/15 x 120,000	32,000
3	3/15 x 120,000	24,000
4	2/15 x 120,000	16,000
5	1/15 x 120,000	8,000

Double-Declining-Balance Method

Year	Calculation	Depreciation Expense	Carrying Value
			$150,000
1	40% x $150,000	$60,000	90,000
2	40% x 90,000	36,000	54,000
3	40% x 54,000	21,600	32,400
4	$32,400 - $30,000*	2,400	30,000
5		0	30,000

*An asset cannot be depreciated below its estimated residual value.

(d) *Determine the depreciation expense for tax purposes.*

MACRS Method

Year	Calculation	Depreciation Expense
1	20.00% x $150,000	$ 30,000
2	32.00% x 150,000	48,000
3	19.20% x 150,000	28,800
4	11.52% x 150,000	17,280
5	11.52% x 150,000	17,280
6	5.76% x 150,000	8,640
Total		$150,000

KEY TERMS

Accelerated Cost Recovery
  System (ACRS), *418*
accelerated depreciation
  methods, *412*
accumulated depreciation, *408*
capital assets, *402*
capital expenditures, *420*
carrying amount, *408*
current value, *407*
depreciable cost, *408*
depreciation, *407*
depreciation schedule, *410*
double-declining-balance
  method, *413*

estimated residual value, *408*
estimated salvage value, *408*
estimated useful life, *409*
fixed assets, *402*
improvements, *421*
Modified Accelerated Cost
  Recovery System (MACRS),
  418
net book value, *408*
plant and equipment, *402*
plant assets, *402*
property, plant, and
  equipment, *402*
repairs, *420*

replacements, *420*
return on total assets, *422*
revenue expenditures, *420*
straight-line method, *410*
straight-line rate, *410*
sum-of-the-years'-digits
  method, *412*
units-of-production method,
  411
valuation account, *408*

SELF-QUIZ

LO 1 1. Which of the following is *not* a plant asset
category?
  a. Land improvements
  b. Buildings
  c. Inventory
  d. Equipment

LO 2 2. Which of the following would *not* be included in the cost of land purchased as a site for
a new building?
  a. Real estate commissions
  b. Removal of old building

  c. Architectural fees
  d. Clearing and grading

LO 2 3. True or False? The cost of constructing a
driveway should be included in the cost of a
building.

LO 4 4. Which of the following is typically *not* used
when calculating depreciation?
  a. Estimated useful life
  b. Estimated benefit from using the asset
  c. Estimated residual value
  d. Depreciable cost

LO 5   5. The _____ depreciation method does *not* directly use the depreciable cost in the computation of depreciation expense.

LO 6   6. Which method would have the highest depreciation expense in the first year of an asset's life of 4 years (ignore residual value)?
   a. Sum-of-the-years'-digits method
   b. Pay-as-you-go method
   c. Double-declining-balance method
   d. Straight-line method

LO 7   7. True or False? Management should restate prior years' depreciation of an asset if they receive new information indicating that the asset's estimated useful life is different than the original estimate.

LO 7   8. The _____ _____ _____ _____ _____ is used to depreciate assets for tax purposes.

LO 8   9. Repairs are _____ expenditures, and replacements are _____ expenditures.

LO 8   10. True or False? While an improvement makes an asset more efficient or effective, it does not necessarily extend the asset's useful life.

LO 9   11. State the formula to calculate return on assets.

LO 9   12. True or False? Return on assets tends to be higher when a company has older assets rather than newer assets.

SOLUTIONS TO SELF-QUIZ

1. c   2. c   3. False   4. b   5. double-declining-balance   6. c   7. False   8. Modified Accelerated Cost Recovery System   9. revenue, capital   10. True   11. (Net Income + Interest Expense) ÷ Total Assets   12. True

---

QUESTIONS

Q10-1   What are four commonly used categories of plant assets?

Q10-2   What comprises the total recorded cost of a plant asset?

Q10-3   How should the cost of a group purchase be allocated to each item in the group?

Q10-4   Why do we depreciate an asset?

Q10-5   What factors are needed to calculate depreciation?

Q10-6   What are the basic differences between straight-line and accelerated depreciation methods?

Q10-7   What factors should be considered when choosing a depreciation method?

Q10-8   What action should management take if it receives new information indicating that the asset's estimated useful life or estimated residual value is different than the original estimates of these amounts?

Q10-9   What is the advantage of using accelerated depreciation for income tax purposes?

Q10-10   What are the differences between a capital expenditure and a revenue expenditure?

Q10-11   What are the differences between repairs, replacements, and improvements?

Q10-12   What is the interpretation of the return on total assets ratio?

EXERCISES

LO 1,2   **E10-1   Costs Included In Plant Assets**   Determine the capitalized cost of the land and studio building for Mo Yost's Commercial Art Service from the following expenditures:
   a. Purchased a tract of land with an unusable building for $287,500, which does not include a real estate commission of $12,500.
   b. Paid an architect $39,000 to design a studio.
   c. Delinquent taxes on the land of $3,900 were paid.
   d. Demolished the building at a cost of $19,000 and paid an additional $3,500 to clear and grade the land.
   e. Constructed a studio building at a cost of $457,200 excluding the cost of building permits and legal fees of $6,000.
   f. Interest expense during construction was $18,400.

LO 1,2   **E10-2**   **Costs Included in Plant Assets**   The Pep Twins bought a new hydraulic lift for their auto repair shop. The lift had a list price of $40,000, but the dealer gave the Pep Twins a 10% reduction. Pep Twins paid a shipping firm $1,000 to pick up and deliver the lift. Insurance during transit was $500. In addition, the twins had to pay $600 to reinforce the floor on which the lift would be placed. Normal installation fees on the lift were $750, but the installers broke a part and charged an additional $250. The Pep Twins paid the installers the full amount requested.

REQUIRED:

Determine the cost of the equipment.

LO 2   **E10-3**   **Group Purchases**   Billy Bob's Hardware bought land, building, and a parking lot for $210,000 to open a store in a new location. The following information relates to acquired assets:

Asset	Appraised Value	Book Value
Land	$140,000	$100,000
Building	100,000	60,000
Parking lot	40,000	40,000

REQUIRED:

Determine the amount of cost to be allocated to the land, building, and parking lot.

LO 5   **E10-4**   **Calculating Depreciation**   Denisha Higgins purchased a video camera for $22,000 for her video production company. The camera has an estimated residual value of $2,000 at the end of its useful life. It is estimated that the camera has an expected useful life of 4 years, or it can be used on 250 jobs.

REQUIRED:

Determine the annual depreciation expense for:
a. Straight-line depreciation method
b. Units-of-production method if 50 jobs are shot in the first year; 100 jobs in Year 2; 75 jobs in Year 3, and 25 jobs in Year 4

LO 5   **E10-5**   **Calculating Depreciation**   Frank's Canvas Factory purchased equipment for $165,000 with an estimated residual value of $15,000 on January 2, 19X1. The estimated useful life of the equipment is 5 years.

REQUIRED:

a. Determine the depreciation expense for each year if Frank's Canvas Factory uses the sum-of-the-years'-digits method.
b. Show how the equipment would appear on the December 31, 19X3, balance sheet.

LO 5   **E10-6**   **Calculating Depreciation Expense**   The Automated Laundry Company bought a triple-capacity washing machine for $8,000. The machine has an estimated life of 4 years, and it is to be depreciated using the double-declining-balance depreciation method.

REQUIRED:

Determine depreciation expense for each year if the estimated residual value is:
a. $0
b. $3,000

LO 7   **E10-7**   **Calculating Depreciation Expense for Partial Periods**   Wolf's Pet Supplies purchased $13,000 of store equipment on October 1, 19X3. The equipment has an estimated
residual value of $1,000 and an estimated useful life of 6 years.

REQUIRED:

Determine depreciation expense for 19X3 and the carrying amount of the equipment at
Wolf's year end on December 31, 19X4, using the straight-line method.

LO 7   **E10-8**   **Calculating Depreciation Expense for Partial Periods**   Hahn's Meat Packing
Company purchased a new conveyor belt on August 1, 19X5, at a cost of $20,000. The
belt has a 3-year useful life and will be depreciated using the sum-of-the-years'-digits
method. The estimated residual value is $2,000, and Hahn's accounting year-end is
December 31.

REQUIRED:

Determine depreciation expense for the machine for 19X5, 19X6, 19X7, and 19X8.

LO 7   **E10-9**   **Revision of Depreciation Rates**   Honey's Pancake House acquired a restaurant on
January 2, 19X2, for $220,000. The restaurant had an estimated residual value of $20,000
and an estimated useful life of 20 years when it was acquired. On January 2, 19X7, it was
determined that the restaurant would only have an estimated useful life of 10 more years
with $0 estimated residual value.

REQUIRED:

Determine the depreciation expense for 19X7 if Honey's uses the straight-line method.

LO 8   **E10-10**   **Capital versus Revenue Expenditures**   Determine if each of the following items are
capital (*C*) expenditures or revenue (*R*) expenditures:
___a.   A major overhaul was performed on a service vehicle that had broken down.
___b.   Purchased new tires for a delivery van.
___c.   A new wing was added to a store.
___   d.   The roof of a building is replaced with a new one. The roof extended the life of
the building.
___e.   Repaired a leaky roof.
___   f.   A machine was modified so that it will use 10 percent less energy after the
modification.
___   g.   A crumbling wall was plastered and painted.

LO 8   **E10-11**   **Replacements**   Ellis Print Shop has a printing press that it purchased on January 1,
19X6, at a cost of $20,000. The company uses the straight-line depreciation method. The
estimated residual value was $4,000, and the estimated useful life was 4 years. On
January 1, 19X8, Ellis replaced the press's motor at a cost of $6,000. This will extend the
life of the press by 3 years. The residual value is now estimated to be $3,000.

REQUIRED:

Record the journal entry on January 1, 19X8, for the replacement and the journal entry
on December 31, 19X8, to record 19X8's depreciation expense.

LO 9   **E10-12**   **Calculating Return on Total Assets**   Feliciano Company's net income for the year
ended December 31, 19X5, is $38,500. Interest expense was $140 for 19X5. Total assets
on December 31, 19X5, is $322,000.

REQUIRED:

Calculate Feliciano Company's return on total assets for 19X5.

PROBLEM SET A

LO 2,5

P10-1A   Purchase and Depreciation of Equipment   Metalwork International paid $190,000 on January 2, 19X4, for a computerized machine to fabricate metal machine parts. In addition, Metalwork incurred transportation costs of $3,000, installation fees of $11,000, testing costs of $2,500, and removal cost of the old equipment being replaced of $3,500. The machine has an estimated useful life of 5 years and no estimated residual value.

REQUIRED:

a. Record the journal entry for the asset's acquisition.
b. Calculate annual depreciation expense using the straight-line method.
c. Calculate the annual depreciation expense for all 5 years using the sum-of-the-years'-digits method.
d. Calculate the annual depreciation expense for all 5 years using the double-declining-balance method.
e. Show how the fabrication machine would appear on the December 31, 19X6, balance sheet if the double-declining-balance method is used.

LO 5

P10-2A   Depreciation Methods   On January 1, 19X2, Smithers Incorporated bought a high-speed production machine for $330,000. The machine has an estimated useful life of 5 years and an estimated residual value of $30,000. The machine should be able to produce 1,500,000 good units of output over its productive life. Estimated production is given below:

Year	Output
19X2	300,000
19X3	500,000
19X4	400,000
19X5	200,000
19X6	100,000

REQUIRED:

a. Prepare a depreciation schedule if Smithers uses the straight-line method.
b. Prepare a depreciation schedule if Smithers uses the units-of-production method and actual production equals estimated production.
c. Prepare a depreciation schedule if Smithers uses the sum-of-the-years'-digits method.
d. Prepare a depreciation schedule if Smithers uses the double-declining-balance method.

LO 7

P10-3A   Partial Period Depreciation   On April 1, 19X7, Microware Enterprises purchased a high-speed floppy disk copier for $9,000. The copier has an estimated useful life of 4 years and an estimated residual value of $1,000. Microware's fiscal year ends December 31.

REQUIRED:

a. Determine depreciation expense for 19X7 and 19X8 if Microware uses the straight-line depreciation method.
b. Determine depreciation expense for 19X7 and 19X8 if Microware uses the sum-of-years'-the-digits depreciation method.
c. Determine depreciation expense for 19X7 and 19X8 if Microware uses the double-declining-balance depreciation method.

LO 2,5,7

P10-4A   Group Purchase, Depreciation Methods, and Revision of Estimates   On January 2, 19X1, Joanne Bern opened a machining operation by buying an existing factory. The purchase price of the factory was $4,000,000 and included the land, the factory building, and equipment. Relevant information concerning all three assets is given below:

	Appraised Value	Estimated Useful Life	Estimated Residual Value
Land	$2,500,000		
Building	2,000,000	4 years	$200,000
Equipment	500,000	5 years	25,000

REQUIRED:

a. Record the journal entry for the group purchase on January 2, 19X1.
b. Record the journal entry for depreciation expense for 19X1, assuming the straight-line method is used.
c. Record the journal entry for depreciation expense for 19X1, assuming the double-declining-balance method is used.
d. Assume Bern uses straight-line depreciation for all assets. On January 2, 19X3, it becomes apparent that the equipment will last another 5 years and have no residual value. Record the journal entry for 19X3's depreciation of the equipment.

LO 8   **P10-5A   Capital versus Revenue Expenditures**   Atley Atwater purchased a delivery van on January 1, 19X4, at a total cost of $20,000. The van will be depreciated using straight-line depreciation over its estimated 4-year life. Residual value is estimated to be $2,000. On February 7, 19X5, Atley takes the truck to Phil's Repair Shop for a tuneup, oil change, belt replacement, and brake job. The total bill is $400. On January 4, 19X6, the van is taken back to Phil's for replacement of the engine at a cost of $1,500.

REQUIRED:

a. Record the journal entry for the asset's acquisition.
b. Record the journal entry for the work done on February 7, 19X5.
c. Record the journal entry on December 31, 19X5 for depreciation expense.
d. Record the journal entry on January 4, 19X6, for the replacement of the engine, assuming it will extend the life of the asset by 1 year but not change the estimated residual value. Also, record the journal entry for depreciation expense on December 31, 19X6.
e. Record the journal entry on January 4, 19X6, assuming that the engine replacement significantly improves the fuel economy of the truck but does not extend its useful life. Also record the journal entry for depreciation expense on December 31, 19X6.

LO 9   **P10-6A   Calculate and Interpret Return on Total Assets**   Denita's Hamburger Heaven has the following income statement for 19X1:

Denita's Hamburger Heaven
Income Statement
For the Year Ended December 31, 19X1

Revenues		$78,000
Cost of goods sold		41,000
Gross profit		$37,000
Expenses:		
Advertising	$ 2,700	
Depreciation	6,500	
Insurance	900	
Interest	2,400	
Wages and salaries	14,000	26,500
Net income		$10,500

Denita's balance sheet for December 31, 19X1, shows assets of $112,500, liabilities of $30,000, and owner's equity of $82,500.

REQUIRED:

a. Calculate the return on total assets for Denita's Hamburger Heaven.
b. While talking to owners of other restaurants in the area, Denita learns that most of them are experiencing returns on total assets of 18-20 percent. What could be the causes of Denita's return on total assets as compared to those of the other owners? What steps might Denita take to improve her return on total assets?

PROBLEM SET B

LO 2,5   **P10-1B   Purchase and Depreciation of Equipment**   Hardwood Furniture paid $105,000 for a computerized sawing station to fabricate parts for furniture on January 2, 19X1. In addition, Hardwood incurred transportation costs of $2,100, installation fees of $8,700, testing costs of $4,200, and removal cost of the old equipment being replaced of $10,000. The machine has an expected life of 4 years and an estimated residual value of $5,000.

REQUIRED:

a. Record the journal entry for the asset's acquisition.
b. Calculate annual depreciation expense using the straight-line method.
c. Calculate the annual depreciation expense for all 4 years using the sum-of-the-years'-digits method.
d. Calculate the annual depreciation expense for all 4 years using the double-declining-balance method.
e. Show how the sawing station would appear on the December 31, 19X3, balance sheet if the double-declining-balance method is used.

LO 5   **P10-2B   Depreciation Methods**   On January 1, 19X4, Cousins bought a high-speed production machine for $425,000. The machine has an estimated useful life of 5 years and an estimated residual value of $25,000. The machine should be able to produce 1,600,000 good units of output over its productive life. Estimated production is given below:

Year	Output
19X4	200,000
19X5	500,000
19X6	300,000
19X7	200,000
19X8	400,000

REQUIRED:

a. Prepare a depreciation schedule if Cousins uses the straight-line method.
b. Prepare a depreciation schedule if Cousins uses the units-of-production method and actual production equals estimated production.
c. Prepare a depreciation schedule if Cousins uses the sum-of-the-years'-digits method.
d. Prepare a depreciation schedule if Cousins uses the double-declining-balance method.

LO 7   **P10-3B   Partial Period Depreciation**   On April 1, 19X8, We Rentit All purchased a minicomputer system for $30,000 to account for its rentals. The computer has an estimated useful life of 4 years and an estimated salvage value of $5,000.

REQUIRED:

a. Determine depreciation expense for 19X8 and 19X9 if We Rentit All uses the straight-line depreciation method.
b. Determine depreciation expense for 19X8 and 19X9 if We Rentit All uses the sum-of-the-years'-digits depreciation method.
c. Determine depreciation expense for 19X8 and 19X9 if We Rentit All uses the double-declining-balance depreciation method.

LO 2,5,7　　**P10-4B**　**Group Purchase, Depreciation Methods, and Revision of Estimates**　On January 2, 19X6, Hank Stern opened a business by buying an existing radio station. The purchase price of the station was $12,000,000 and included the land, the building, and equipment. Relevant information concerning all three assets is given below:

	Appraised Value	Estimated Useful Life	Estimated Residual Value
Land	$ 4,000,000		
Building	10,000,000	10 years	$1,000,000
Equipment	2,000,000	5 years	100,000

REQUIRED:

a. Record the journal entry for the group purchase on January 2, 19X6.
b. Record the journal entry for depreciation expense for 19X6, assuming the straight-line method is used.
c. Record the journal entry for depreciation expense for 19X6, assuming the double-declining-balance method is used.
d. Assume Stern uses straight-line depreciation for all of his assets. On January 2, 19X8, it becomes apparent that the equipment will last another 5 years and have no residual value. Record the journal entry for 19X8's depreciation of the equipment.

LO 8　　**P10-5B**　**Capital versus Revenue Expenditures**　Mary Jones purchased a used bus to give guided tours on January 1, 19X4, at a total cost of $20,000. The bus will be depreciated using straight-line depreciation over its estimated 5-year life. Residual value is estimated to be $2,000. On February 7, 19X4, Mary takes the bus to Tony's Repair Shop to fix leaking windows and the air conditioner. The total bill is $500. On January 3, 19X5, the bus is taken back to Tony's for replacement of the engine at a cost of $2,200.

REQUIRED:

a. Record the journal entry for the asset's acquisition.
b. Record the journal entry for the work done on February 7, 19X4.
c. Record the journal entry on December 31, 19X4, for depreciation expense.
d. Record the journal entry on January 3, 19X5, for the replacement of the engine assuming it will extend the life of the asset by 1 year but not change the estimated residual value. Also, record the journal entry for depreciation expense on December 31, 19X5.
e. Record the journal entry on January 3, 19X5, assuming that the engine replacement significantly improves the fuel economy of the bus but does not extend its useful life. Also record the journal entry for depreciation expense on December 31, 19X5.

LO 9　　**P10-6B**　**Calculate and Interpret Return on Total Assets**　Assume you are a management consultant. One of your clients is unhappy with the performance of her business, Tigert's Tapes and CDs. Your client shows you the following income statement:

Tigert's Tapes and CDs Income Statement For the Year Ended December 31, 19X1		
Revenues		$320,000
Cost of goods sold		180,000
Gross profit		$140,000
Expenses:		
Advertising	$12,000	
Depreciation	26,000	
Insurance	3,000	
Interest	18,000	
Wages and salaries	60,000	119,000
Net income		$ 21,000

Tigert's balance sheet shows total assets of $840,000. The property, plant, and equipment section of the balance sheet is as follows:

Land		$ 80,000
Building	$560,000	
Less: Accumulated depreciation	30,000	530,000
Equipment	$ 96,000	
Less: Accumulated depreciation	6,000	90,000

REQUIRED:

a. Calculate the return on total assets for Tigert's Tapes and CDs.
b. Should your client be unhappy with the performance of her business? Why?
c. Suggest to your client some actions she might take in order to improve the performance of her business.

CRITICAL THINKING AND COMMUNICATING

C10-1   Ed Lohmann owns a chain of toy stores. Ed, having just acquired a new store, asked his auditor how the store should be depreciated. The accountant told Ed that there are several alternatives that could create significant differences on the balance sheet and income statement. Ed was confused about the many alternatives available and asked Hillary Karlinsky, the company accountant, to explain why different methods are acceptable and what factors should be considered when selecting a method.

REQUIRED:

Assuming the role of Hillary Karlinsky, write a memo explaining why different methods are acceptable and what factors Ed should consider.

C10-2   Helene Caudill owns a chain of discount office supply stores. Over the past 2 years, Helene has added 5 additional stores for a total of 9 stores. Helene purchased all the new stores and depreciates them using the sum-of-the-years'-digits method. The stores have an estimated useful life of 10 years. Selected financial information for her chain of stores for the last 2 years is given on the next page.

	19X4	*19X5*
Sales	$1,400,000	$2,325,000
Net income	$280,000	$320,000
Return on total assets	28%	21%

Helene is concerned about the decline in the return on total assets ratio and is considering slowing down or eliminating the expansion of her business.

REQUIRED:

Explain why the return on assets is declining and advise Helene if she should slow or eliminate the expansion.

C10-3   Refer to the financial statements of J.C. Penney reprinted in Appendix B at the end of this text. In considering the requirements of this case, remember that Penney's is a retail merchandising company.

REQUIRED:

a. Locate Penney's depreciation accounting policy in the *Summary of Accounting Policies* immediately after the statement of cash flows. Determine the estimated useful lives for the various categories of assets. Evaluate the depreciation method used by Penney's.

b. Calculate the return on total assets for 1993, 1992, and 1992. For net income in the ratio as discussed in the chapter, use the amount in Penney's income statements named "Income before extraordinary charge and cumulative effect of accounting changes."

c. Comment on the direction of fluctuation in the return on total assets ratios.

d. By analyzing the changes in the numerators and denominators of the ratios, determine the possible causes for the fluctuations in the ratios.

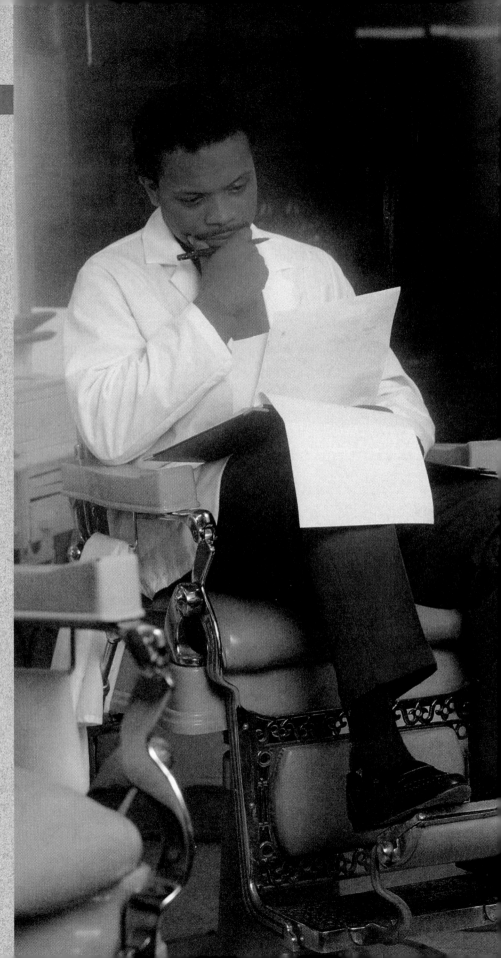

CHAPTER 11

Disposals of Plant Assets and Accounting for Other Assets

In the previous chapter, Jeff Foreman had asked Chris Rader for advice concerning the calculation and interpretation of the return on total assets of the two businesses he was considering purchasing. Jeff decided to purchase Red's Barber Shop and now has even more questions for Chris to answer.

Jeff's first question concerns how to record the net assets he acquired upon his purchase of Red's Barber Shop. In Red's accounts, the net assets have a carrying amount of $20,175. Jeff paid $50,000 for the business, and he wants to know the amount to record in his accounts for the assets and liabilities.

Jeff's second question for Chris concerns a transaction that Jeff is considering. Jeff would like to replace some of the older equipment he acquired with some newer models. A distributor that handles the equipment is willing to take the old equipment as a trade-in on the new equipment. Jeff wants to know how he should account for the trade-in in his financial statements. The question relates to whether he would have to recognize a gain or loss and at what amount he would report the new equipment in the balance sheet. He also wants to know how the trade-in would affect his income taxes.

This chapter continues the discussion of accounting for plant assets. In particular, we discuss the disposal of plant assets. In addition to plant assets, some businesses may have other noncurrent productive assets, such as intangible assets and natural resources. In this chapter, we discuss the accounting for both of these types of assets.

1. Explain how to record the disposal of plant assets by abandonment and by sale.
2. Record exchanges of plant assets for both dissimilar and similar assets.
3. Describe the role of accounting records in the control of plant assets.
4. Identify the accounting issues related to the acquisition and amortization of intangible assets.
5. Apply GAAP to the acquisition and depletion of natural resources.

LO 1

Explain how to record the disposal of plant assets by abandonment and by sale.

DISPOSAL OF PLANT ASSETS

When plant assets wear out or become technologically obsolete, a business commonly disposes of them. A business accomplishes disposal by ceasing to use the asset, by selling the asset, or by trading in the asset on the purchase of a new one. The following sections discuss how a business can use and account for different methods of disposal of plant assets.

Ceasing to Use

When an asset reaches the end of its estimated useful life, its carrying amount will equal its estimated residual value. At this point, since an asset should not be depreciated below its estimated residual value, a business should cease depreciation of the asset. If the business continues to use the asset, it should not remove the asset account and the related accumulated depreciation account from its accounting records. Thus, the accounting records continue to reflect all assets the business presently uses. However, if for any reason the business ceases to use the asset, it should remove the asset cost and the related accumulated depreciation from its records by a journal entry.

Assume that on January 2, 19X6, Paul's Print Shop ceases to use a machine because it is worn out. Paul's will discard the machine because the cost of transporting the machine is more than its scrap value. An examination of the accounting records reveals the account balances for the machine as shown in the T-accounts below:

Equipment		Accumulated Depreciation—Equipment	
Jan. 2, X1 5,000			Dec. 31, X1 1,000
			Dec. 31, X2 1,000
			Dec. 31, X3 1,000
			Dec. 31, X4 1,000
			Dec. 31, X5 1,000
			Bal. 5,000

The account balances indicate that the machine's carrying amount is zero. We depreciate the machine to zero, in this case, because its estimated residual value is zero. At the time it discards the machine, Paul's should remove the asset cost and the related accumulated depreciation from the accounting records with the entry shown below:

Jan. 2	Accumulated Depreciation—Equipment	5,000	
	Equipment		5,000
	To record discarding of fully depreciated machine.		

After the above entry, both Equipment and Accumulated Depreciation—Equipment have zero balances, as follows:

Equipment			
Jan. 2, X1	5,000	Jan. 2, X6	5,000
Bal.	0		

Accumulated Depreciation—Equipment		
	Dec. 31, X1	1,000
	Dec. 31, X2	1,000
	Dec. 31, X3	1,000
	Dec. 31, X4	1,000
	Dec. 31, X5	1,000
Jan. 2, X6 5,000		
	Bal.	0

Selling the Asset

When a business disposes of an asset by selling it, we record the difference between the asset's carrying amount and the proceeds from the sales transaction as a gain or loss. For example, assume that on January 2, 19X5, Paul's Print Shop sells a machine for $500. The accounting records contain the account balances for the machine as shown in the following T-accounts:

Equipment		
Jan. 2, X1	3,000	

Accumulated Depreciation—Equipment		
	Dec. 31, X1	600
	Dec. 31, X2	600
	Dec. 31, X3	600
	Dec. 31, X4	600
	Bal.	2,400

The carrying amount of the machine is $600, as follows:

Equipment (cost)	$3,000
Less: Accumulated depreciation	2,400
Carrying amount	$ 600

The proceeds from selling the machine, $500, are less than the machine's carrying amount. Therefore, Paul's incurs a loss from the sales transaction. The following entry records the sale:

Jan. 2	Cash	500	
	Accumulated Depreciation—Equipment	2,400	
	Loss from Sale of Equipment	100	
	Equipment		3,000
	To record sale of machine.		

The above entry records the receipt of cash (or a promise to pay from the buyer), reduces to zero the balances in Equipment and Accumulated Depreciation—Equipment, and recognizes the loss from the sale of the machine.

If, on the other hand, the proceeds from the sale of the machine are $850, then Paul's would recognize a gain of $250 on the sales transaction as follows:

Proceeds from sale	$850
Carrying amount of machine	600
Gain from sale	$250

The entry to record this transaction is shown below:

Jan. 2	Cash	850	
	Accumulated Depreciation—Equipment	2,400	
	Equipment		3,000
	Gain from Sale of Equipment		250
	To record sale of machine.		

The above entry records the receipt of cash (or a promise to pay from the buyer), reduces to zero the balances in Equipment and Accumulated Depreciation—Equipment, and recognizes the $250 gain from the sale of the machine. Gains and losses from the sale of plant assets are components of net income in the income statement.

Depreciation to the Date of Disposal

When a business disposes of plant assets, regardless of the method of disposal, we record the asset's depreciation expense for the period between the end of the preceding accounting period and the date of disposal. For example, assume Paul's Print Shop purchases a machine on January 2, 19X1, for $9,000. The machine has an estimated useful life of 4 years and an estimated residual value of $1,000, and Paul's uses the straight-line method of depreciation. We calculate annual depreciation expense as follows:

$$(\$9,000 - \$1,000) \div 4 = \$2,000$$

If Paul's sells the machine on June 30, 19X4, for cash of $2,200, we record depreciation for the 6-month period from January 1, 19X4, to June 30, 19X4, *before* we record the sale transaction. Depreciation expense for the 6-month period is 6/12 x $2,000 = $1,000. After recording the depreciation for 19X4, Accumulated Depreciation has a balance of $7,000 [(3 x $2,000) + $1,000]. The sale of the machine results in a $200 gain, calculated as follows:

Proceeds from sale	$2,200
Carrying amount of machine	
($9,000 – $7,000)	2,000
Gain from sale	$ 200

The entries to record the depreciation and the sales transaction are shown below:

Jun. 30	Depreciation Expense—Equipment	1,000	
	Accumulated Depreciation—Equipment		1,000
	To record depreciation on machine that was sold.		
30	Cash	2,200	
	Accumulated Depreciation—Equipment	7,000	
	Equipment		9,000
	Gain from Sale of Equipment		200
	To record sale of machine.		

Failure to record depreciation to the date of sale causes the financial statements to be incorrect in that depreciation expense would be understated and a gain (loss) from disposal would be understated (overstated).

Record exchanges of plant assets for both dissimilar and similar assets.

EXCHANGING ASSETS

Businesses frequently dispose of one asset and acquire another asset by exchanging the assets with another business or individual. The assets exchanged may be **similar**—meaning that the assets exchanged serve the same function—or **dissimilar**—meaning that the assets exchanged serve different functions. An exchange of a computer for another computer involves similar assets. An exchange of a computer for a drill press involves dissimilar assets. Frequently, an exchange also involves a cash payment by one of the parties to make equal the fair values of the assets exchanged. The accounting for the exchange of assets involves three steps on the date of the exchange:

1. Determine the value (cost) of the asset(s) acquired.
2. Determine any gain or loss from assets given, if applicable.
3. Record in a single entry the acquisition of a new asset, the disposal of the old asset, and any applicable gain or loss.

Whether there is a gain or loss from the disposal of the old asset—and the calculation of the cost of the new asset—depends on whether the exchange involves dissimilar or similar assets.[1]

Exchange of Dissimilar Assets

In an exchange involving dissimilar assets, the new asset's recorded cost is equal to the old asset's fair value plus the amount of any cash paid to the other party to the exchange. Also, we always recognize a gain or loss from an exchange involving dissimilar assets. The gain or loss is equal to the difference between the old asset's carrying amount and its fair value on the date of the exchange.

Assume that on January 4, 19X1, Paul's Print Shop exchanges a computer and $14,700 cash for a delivery truck. On the date of the exchange, the computer has a carrying amount of $3,000 (original cost of $4,500 and accumulated depreciation of $1,500). By appraisal, Paul's determines that the computer's fair value is $3,500.

Step 1: Based on this information, the acquisition cost of the truck is $18,200:

Fair value of computer	$ 3,500
Cash paid	14,700
Cost of truck	$18,200

Step 2: Paul's calculates a gain of $500 on the disposal of the computer, according to the following calculation:

Fair value of computer	$3,500
Carrying amount of computer	3,000
Gain from disposal	$ 500

---

[1]*Accounting for Nonmonetary Exchanges*, APB Opinion No. 29 (New York, NY: AICPA, 1973), para. 18–26.

Step 3: Paul's entry to record the exchange is shown below:

Jan. 4	Delivery Equipment	18,200	
	Accumulated Depreciation—Office Equipment	1,500	
	Office Equipment		4,500
	Cash		14,700
	Gain from Disposal		500
	To record exchange of computer for delivery truck.		

If, on the other hand, the computer's fair value is only $2,000, we apply the three steps as follows:

Step 1: The cost of the truck is $16,700, determined as follows:

Fair value of computer	$ 2,000
Cash paid	14,700
Cost of truck	$16,700

Step 2: In this case, Paul's would calculate a loss from the disposal of the computer of $1,000:

Fair value of computer	$2,000
Carrying amount of computer	3,000
Loss from disposal	$1,000

Step 3: Paul's entry to reflect these circumstances is:

Jan. 4	Delivery Equipment	16,700	
	Accumulated Depreciation—Office Equipment	1,500	
	Loss from Disposal	1,000	
	Office Equipment		4,500
	Cash		14,700
	To record exchange of computer for delivery truck.		

Exchange of Similar Assets

When a productive asset wears out, a business commonly trades in the old asset on the purchase of a new one. For example, when a delivery truck wears out, the business purchases a new delivery truck by trading in the old truck and paying cash to the truck dealer. The proper accounting for the exchange of similar assets depends on whether the transaction results in a loss or gain.

Loss Recognized When Incurred.   When a business exchanges one of its assets for a similar asset, the business incurs a loss if the asset's carrying amount exceeds the trade-in allowance received for the old asset. GAAP require that businesses recognize losses in the period they occur, regardless of whether similar or dissimilar assets are exchanged. For example, on July 1, Paul's Print Shop trades in a computer it owns toward the purchase of a new computer. The cost of the old computer is $10,000, and accumulated depreciation (including depreciation to the date of the exchange) is $8,800. The price of the new computer is $15,000, and Paul's receives a trade-in allowance of $1,000 for the old computer. So, Paul's must pay $14,000 in cash.

Step 1: Based on this information, the acquisition cost of the new computer is $15,000:

Fair value of computer	$ 1,000
Cash paid	14,000
Cost of new computer	$15,000

Step 2: Paul's calculates a loss of $200 from the disposal of the old computer:

Fair value of old computer	$1,000
Carrying amount of old computer	1,200
Loss from disposal	$ 200

Step 3: Paul's entry to record the exchange is as follows:

July 1	Office Equipment (new)	15,000	
	Accumulated Depreciation—Office Equipment	8,800	
	Loss from Disposal	200	
	Office Equipment (old)		10,000
	Cash		14,000
	To record trade-in of old computer on a new computer.		

The above entry accomplishes several things: it reduces old Office Equipment and the related Accumulated Depreciation—Office Equipment to zero; it records the new computer at its purchase price; it records the loss from the disposal; and it records the cash paid for the difference between the price of the new computer and the trade-in allowance received on the old computer.

Gain Not Recognized Immediately.   A gain on the exchange of similar productive assets occurs when the trade-in allowance received for the old asset exceeds its carrying amount at the date of exchange. In determining that a business has realized a gain, however, we must be careful that the indicated trade-in allowance is the old asset's fair value, not an inflated trade-in allowance resulting from a list price of the new asset that exceeds its normal selling price.

In the previous example of an exchange of computers, assume that instead of a trade-in allowance of $1,000, Paul's receives a trade-in allowance of $1,600, which represents the old computer's fair value. Therefore, the cash payment required is $13,400. With this new assumption, the exchange transaction results in a $400 gain because the trade-in allowance of $1,600 exceeds the old computer's $1,200 carrying amount by $400. In the case of a gain, GAAP provide that we do not recognize the gain at the time of the exchange. Instead, we record the new computer at the carrying amount of the old computer plus the cash payment. This amount is commonly called the **cost basis** of the new asset.

Step 1: We calculate the new computer's recorded amount as the old computer's carrying amount plus the cash payment:

Carrying amount of old computer ($10,000 − $8,800)	$ 1,200
Cash payment	13,400
Cost basis of new computer	$14,600

Step 2: We calculate the amount of the gain:

Fair value of old computer	$1,600
Carrying amount of old computer	1,200
Gain (unrecognized)	$ 400

In this case, the gain is not recognized at the time of the exchange because accountants consider the exchange of similar assets not to be the end of the old asset's earning process. In effect, the new asset's recorded cost is reduced from its fair value by the unrecognized gain. The new computer's recorded cost, calculated as $14,600, is the new computer's $15,000 fair value less the $400 unrecognized gain. By reducing the new computer's total recorded cost by the amount of the unrecognized gain, we recognize the gain in net income over the computer's estimated useful life through lower amounts of annual depreciation expense.

Step 3: Paul's entry to record the exchange transaction is:

July 1	Office Equipment (new)	14,600	
	Accumulated Depreciation—Office Equipment	8,800	
	Office Equipment (old)		10,000
	Cash ($15,000 – $1,600)		13,400
	To record trade-in of old computer on a new computer.		

Income Tax Treatment of Exchanges of Assets

For purposes of computing income taxes, special rules exist for exchanges of assets. The tax rules classify asset exchanges as either "like-kind exchanges" or "non-like-kind exchanges." These classifications are close to the similar and dissimilar classifications used for financial statements.

Like-kind exchanges do not result in the recognition of taxable gains or losses. The tax basis of the asset received is the tax basis of the asset given up in the exchange. **Non-like-kind exchanges** result in the recognition of taxable gains and losses. The amount of the gain or loss is the difference between the tax basis of the asset given up and the fair value of the asset received. The tax basis of the asset received is its fair value at the time of the exchange.

LO 3

Describe the role of accounting records in the control of plant assets.

CONTROL OF PLANT ASSETS

For most businesses, the amount of money paid for property, plant, and equipment represents a significant investment and requires that they maintain good control of the assets. Most businesses, except for some very small businesses, use identification numbers to identify the assets they own. Generally, businesses attach the identification numbers to the assets in the form of small decals that cannot be removed or altered easily.

The accounting records also play an important role in the control of property, plant, and equipment. Generally, a business has a general ledger asset account and a related accumulated depreciation general ledger account for each functional group of assets. For example, a hardware store has Buildings and Accumulated Depreciation—Buildings accounts; Equipment and Accumulated

Depreciation—Equipment accounts to record equipment in the store; and Office Equipment and Accumulated Depreciation—Office Equipment accounts. Related to these general ledger accounts is a plant asset subsidiary ledger. In manual accounting systems, the subsidiary ledger takes the form of a separate page or card for each asset. In a computerized accounting system, the same information is stored on some electronic data storage medium.

To illustrate a computer-based subsidiary ledger and general ledger accounts, assume Paul's Print Shop's office equipment consists of only two assets—a desk and a computer. Paul's acquired both assets on October 1, 19X1, and depreciated both assets for the remaining three months of 19X1 and for all of 19X2. Illustration 11-1 shows the subsidiary ledger printout and the general ledger accounts for the two assets as of December 31, 19X2. Notice that the system summarizes the information in the subsidiary ledger in the general ledger accounts. The $10,400 balance in Office Equipment is the total cost of the desk and the computer as shown in the subsidiary ledger asset records. Similarly, the amounts entered and the balance of Accumulated Depreciation—Office Equipment is the sum of the amounts in the subsidiary ledger depreciation records. The computer system satisfies the control objective of recording accuracy because the plant asset software ties the subsidiary ledger records directly to the general ledger account balances.

To maintain security over the assets, Paul's periodically counts and inspects the assets. The physical count, or inventory, should verify that all assets shown in the subsidiary ledger are still on hand and, conversely, that all assets on hand are listed in a subsidiary ledger. Paul's should resolve any discrepancies before preparing the financial statements. When doing the physical count of the assets, Paul's employees should inspect the assets for deterioration and obsolescence; and Paul's management should give consideration to discontinuing their use.

LO 4

Identify the accounting issues related to the acquisition and amortization of intangible assets.

INTANGIBLE ASSETS

Accountants generally describe **intangible assets** as noncurrent, or long-term, assets without physical existence. Examples of intangible assets are patents, copyrights, trademarks and trade names, franchises, and goodwill. Some current assets such as accounts and notes receivable also do not have physical existence; however in accounting, the term *intangible assets* refers only to noncurrent, nonphysical assets.

Because they grant a legal right or represent favorable economic circumstances, intangible assets have value to a business. An example of a legal right granted is the sole right to sell a product or to use a process. A favorable economic circumstance would be a unique business location. In accordance with the matching principle, we allocate the cost of intangible assets such as the cost of plant assets to the periods the assets benefit. **Amortization** is the process of allocating the cost to periods benefited and is the same process as depreciation of plant assets. GAAP require that the period of time over which a business amortizes intangible assets cannot exceed 40 years. Also, a business generally uses the straight-line method to calculate amortization expense. As shown in Illustration 11-2, we present intangible assets in the balance sheet in a separate section following plant assets. We present intangible assets at cost net of accumulated amortization.

ILLUSTRATION 11-1 Plant Asset Subsidiary Ledger and General Ledger Accounts

```
                Plant Asset and Depreciation Record
                                                        Asset ID # 269

Asset: Desk                                Serial #: None
General Ledger Acct: Office Equipment       Purchased From: Ace, Inc.
Location: Office
Person Responsible: Store Manager          Depr. Method: S/L
Estimated Life: 10 years                    Depr. per Year: $36
Residual Value: $40                         Depr. Per Mo.: $3
```

			Asset Record			Depreciation Record		
Date	Explan.	Post. Ref.	Dr.	Cr.	Bal.	Dr.	Cr.	Bal.
19X1								
10/01		GJ40	400.00		400.00			
12/31		GJ65					9.00	9.00
19X2								
12/31		GJ78					36.00	45.00

```
                Plant Asset and Depreciation Record
                                                        Asset ID # 270

Asset: Computer                            Serial #: 178456
General Ledger Acct: Office Equipment       Purchased From: Ace, Inc.
Location: Office
Person Responsible: Store Manager          Depr. Method: S/L
Estimated Life: 6 years                     Depr. per Year: $1,500
Residual Value: $1000                       Depr. Per Mo.: $125
```

			Asset Record			Depreciation Record		
Date	Explan.	Post. Ref.	Dr.	Cr.	Bal.	Dr.	Cr.	Bal.
19X1								
10/01		GJ40	10,000.00		10,000.00			
12/31		GJ65					375.00	375.00
19X2								
12/31		GJ78					1,500.00	1,875.00

```
                    General Ledger Account
```

Name: Office Equipment   Account No.: 242

Date	Description	Post. Ref.	Debit	Credit	Balance
10/01/X1		GJ40	10,400		10,400

```
                    General Ledger Account
```

Name: Accumulated Depreciation-Office Equipment   Account No.: 243

Date	Description	Post. Ref.	Debit	Credit	Balance
12/31/X1		GJ65		384	384
12/31/X2		GJ78		1,536	1,920

ILLUSTRATION 11-2 Partial Balance Sheet

Plant Assets:			
Land		$50,000	
Building	$125,000		
Less: Accumulated depreciation	30,000	95,000	
Equipment	$ 69,000		
Less: Accumulated depreciation	13,000	56,000	$201,000
Intangible Assets:			
Patents (at cost less amortization)		$24,000	
Goodwill (at cost less amortization)		18,000	42,000
			$243,000

Patents

The federal government grants patents through the U.S. Patent Office. A **patent** gives the holder the exclusive right to use the product or process for a period of 17 years. The government grants patents to encourage inventions of new products or processes. Consistent with the cost principle, we record patents at their acquisition costs. We amortize the cost of the patent over its legal life or useful life, whichever is shorter. Although the legal life of a patent is 17 years, its useful life is often shorter because of new inventions and other factors.

To illustrate the accounting for patents, assume Product Research purchased a patent for $9,000 on April 2, 19X1. Management estimates that the patent will be useful for only 6 years even though its legal life is 17 years. Product Research should record the patent at cost as shown in the following journal entry:

Apr. 2	Patents	9,000	
	Cash		9,000
	To record acquisition of patent.		

At the end of 19X1, the following entry records amortization for 9 months (April through December). Amortization for the 9 months is $1,125 ($9,000 x 1/6 x 9/12).

Dec. 31	Patent Amortization Expense	1,125	
	Patents		1,125
	To record patent amortization.		

By tradition, accountants record amortization directly to the asset account, as illustrated in the entry above, rather than to an accumulated amortization account.

Research and Development

Under GAAP, accountants do not record the costs of research and development activities as assets. Rather, we record these costs as expenses.[2] **Research and development** activities involve the search for and the application of knowledge to new products or processes. Although research and development does

---

[2]*Accounting for Research and Development Costs*, Statement No. 2 para. 12. (Stamford, Conn: FASB, 1974).

not result in recorded intangible assets, we discuss the costs of these activities in this section because they sometimes result in patents and copyrights.

Research and development costs are significant for many businesses. Large businesses such as DuPont and IBM spend billions of dollars annually on research and development. IBM's 1992 Annual Report contains the following note to the financial statements:

Research, Development and Engineering

Research, development and engineering expenses amounted to $6,522 million in 1992, $6,644 million in 1991, and $6,554 million in 1990.

Included in these amounts were expenditures of $5,083 million in 1992, $5,001 million in 1991, and $4,914 million in 1990 for a broad program of research and development activities covering basic scientific research in a variety of fields and the application of scientific advances to the development of new and improved products and their uses. In addition, expenditures for product-related engineering amounted to $1,439 million, $1,643 million, and $1,640 million for the same three years.

We do not record intangible assets for research and development costs because it is often virtually impossible to identify the costs of individual projects and the amounts (if any) and timing of the future benefits of these costs are highly uncertain. For these reasons, the FASB decided that all businesses should record the costs of research and development as expenses and disclose the amounts of the costs in their financial statements.

For example, assume Hi-Tech Labs incurred costs of $1,800,000 for research and development activities during 19X1. The *summary* entry to record these costs is:

(Date)	Research and Development Expense	1,800,000	
	Cash		1,800,000
	To record the costs of research and development for the year.		

In the notes to its 19X1 financial statements, Hi-Tech Labs should disclose that during the year it incurred costs of $1,800,000 related to research and development activities.

Copyrights

Similar to patents, the federal government grants **copyrights**. The government grants copyrights to authors, painters, musicians, sculptors, software engineers, and others. Copyrights give them and their heirs the exclusive right to their creative works for the lifetime of the creator plus 50 years. For example, composers of popular music obtain copyrights on the songs they compose to prohibit their work from being copied without their permission. When a business purchases a copyright, we record the cost as an intangible asset; and we amortize that cost over the useful life of the copyright, not to exceed 40 years.

Trademarks and Trade Names

Trademarks and **trade names** are words, symbols, or other devices that identify or distinguish a product or a business. Examples of trade names are Coke, Kleenex, and Chevrolet. The U.S. Patent Office grants the right of exclusive use of a registered trademark or trade name to the creator or original user for a

INSIGHTS INTO ACCOUNTING

WHAT'S IN A NAME? BILLIONS

Marlboro is the best-known brand on the face of the earth. But how much is it worth? About $31 billion, twice its annual revenue, says *Financial World*. The magazine takes on one of the toughest tasks in business: putting dollar values on brand names.

Conventional accounting doesn't have an accepted way to value the trade names businesses back with millions in marketing money. *Financial World* used its own complex formula to pin down brands' value.

The most valuable brands after Marlboro: Coca-Cola, worth $24.4 billion; Budweiser, $10.2 billion; Pepsi-Cola, $9.6 billion; and Nescafe instant coffee, $8.5 billion. Only eight brands—including megasellers Coke and Barbie and luxury names Hennessy, Hermes and Louis Vuitton—would sell for more than twice their annual revenue. "What it says is that the folks running these companies are very, very smart," says the Senior Editor of *Financial World*. "They have maximized whatever cachet the brand has."

Source: Martha T. Moore, "What's in a Name? Billions," *USA Today* (August 12, 1992), p. 1B.

period of 20 years. Additional 20-year registrations are granted so long as the business continuously uses the trademark or trade name.

If a business purchases a trademark or trade name, we record it at the acquisition cost. If a business develops a trademark or trade name internally, the recorded cost includes attorneys' fees, registration fees, costs of successful legal defense, and other costs related to developing and retaining the trademark or trade name. We amortize the cost of trademarks and trade names over the estimated period benefited, not to exceed 40 years.

Franchises

A **franchise** is a legal agreement in which one party (franchisor) grants the exclusive right to another party (franchisee) to market a product or provide a service within a designated geographical area. Examples of franchise businesses include Shell service stations, McDonald's restaurants, and General Motors dealers. In many franchise agreements, the franchisee must pay the franchisor an initial fee plus yearly fees that are based on some factor such as net sales revenue. The initial fee is the cost of the franchise that we record as the franchisee's intangible asset. We amortize the cost of the franchise over the term of the franchise, or over 40 years if the term of the agreement exceeds 40 years. We record the yearly fee the franchisee pays to the franchisor as an expense of the franchisee when incurred in accordance with the matching principle.

McDonald's 1992 Annual Report contains the following note to its financial statements:

Franchise Agreements

Franchise arrangements, with franchisees who operate in various geographical locations, generally provide for initial fees and continuing payments to the Company based upon a percent of sales, with minimum rent payments. Among other things, franchisees are provided the use of restaurant facilities, generally for a period of 20 years. They are required to pay related occupancy costs which include property taxes, insurance, maintenance and a refundable, noninterest-bearing security deposit. On a limited basis, the Company receives notes from franchisees. Generally the notes are secured by interests in restaurant equipment and franchises.

(In millions of dollars)	1992	1991	1990
Minimum rents:			
Owned sites	$ 538.7	$ 494.5	$ 439.8
Leased sites	353.3	303.7	250.0
	$ 892.0	$ 798.2	$ 689.8
Percentage fees	$1,120.6	$ 970.4	$ 914.0
Initial fees	18.2	17.9	16.0
Revenues from franchised restaurants	$2,030.8	$1,786.5	$1,619.8

Goodwill

In accounting terminology, **goodwill** refers to the business's ability to generate earnings at a higher rate than is normal for the industry in which the business operates. We attribute goodwill to such factors as superior management, unique location, superior work force, and monopolistic access to a scarce resource. Under GAAP, however, accountants record goodwill only when a business purchases another entire business or a major portion of the operating assets of another business. The amount of goodwill recorded in such cases is the measure of the excess of the purchase price over the fair value of the identifiable assets purchased.

Jeff's Purchase of Red's Barber Shop

In the beginning of this chapter, we discussed some questions that Jeff had concerning his purchase of Red's Barber Shop. The first question related to how he would account for the assets and liabilities he acquired when he purchased Red's. We show below the carrying amounts of the assets and liabilities from Red's balance sheet immediately before Jeff's purchase (except for cash, which the owner of Red's will keep). Also, the second column shows the fair values of the assets and liabilities at the time of the purchase. Jeff obtained the fair values from distributors' price lists and from an appraisal of the property's value.

Item	Carrying Amount	Fair Value
Sales supplies	$ 350	$ 350
Equipment (net)	500	1,825
Land	10,000	20,000
Buildings (net)	15,000	25,000
Accounts payable	(175)	(175)
Notes payable	(6,000)	(7,000)
Total net assets	$19,675	$40,000

Recall from the beginning of the chapter that Jeff paid $50,000 for Red's Barber Shop. In recording the purchase, Jeff records the assets and liabilities of Red's at their fair values, which net to $40,000. Jeff would allocate to goodwill

INTERNATIONAL PERSPECTIVES

ACCOUNTING FOR GOODWILL IN THE UNITED KINGDOM

The accounting for goodwill is not uniform around the world. U.S. businesses carry goodwill as an asset on their balance sheets and amortize the goodwill over its useful life, not to exceed 40 years. Businesses in the United Kingdom, however, have the option of accounting for the goodwill similar to the method followed by U.S. businesses or to write off immediately the cost of goodwill to owners' equity. The accounting standards in the U.K. express a preference for the immediate write off of goodwill. Many businesses prefer this method because it does not result in amortization expense in future periods.

Source: "Accounting for Goodwill," *Statements of Standard Accounting Practice 22* (United Kingdom, July 1989).

the $10,000 excess purchase price over the fair values of the purchased net assets. Jeff should record the purchase of Red's with the following entries:

(Date)	Cash	50,000	
	Jeff Foreman, Capital		50,000
	Cash investment by owner to begin new business.		
(Date)	Sales supplies	350	
	Equipment	1,825	
	Land	20,000	
	Buildings	25,000	
	Goodwill	10,000	
	Accounts Payable		175
	Notes Payable		7,000
	Cash		50,000
	To record purchase of Red's Barber Shop.		

Under GAAP, the "advantages" represented by goodwill are always assumed to have a finite life span. We amortize recorded goodwill, therefore, over the estimated period of benefit, not exceeding 40 years.

Apply GAAP to the acquisition and depletion of natural resources.

NATURAL RESOURCES

Natural resources consist of such things as oil and gas, mineral deposits, and standing timber. As businesses pump oil and gas, mine mineral deposits, and cut timber, the assets are depleted. For this reason, natural resources are commonly called "wasting" assets. When natural resources are pumped, mined, or cut, they become inventory to be sold. Under the cost principle, accountants record natural resources at cost. Generally, we allocate the cost to periods in accordance with the matching principle using the units-of-production method. Accountants call the process of allocating the cost of natural resources **depletion**, and it is similar to depreciation and amortization.

Assume that on January 2, 19X1, Southern Mines purchases a mineral deposit for $5,200,000. Southern's entry to record the purchase of the mineral deposit is:

Jan. 2	Mineral Deposits	5,200,000	
	Cash		5,200,000
	To record the purchase of a mineral deposit.		

Based on tests performed by geologists, the estimated deposit consists of 2,000,000 tons of ore. Furthermore, the estimated land value for the property after mining operations are completed is $200,000. As shown below, we calculate the depletion per ton by dividing the depletable cost (cost of the deposit less the estimated residual value) by the estimated tons of ore that can be mined from the deposit:

For Southern Mines, the depletion per ton is $2.50, calculated as follows:

$$(\$5,200,000 - \$200,000) \div 2,000,000 \text{ tons} = \$2.50 \text{ per ton}$$

We calculate the amount of depletion to be recorded for a period as shown below:

If, during the first year, Southern mines 300,000 tons of ore, we debit $750,000 (300,000 tons x $2.50/ton) to inventory as shown by the following *summary* entry:

Dec. 31	Mineral Inventory	750,000	
	Accumulated Depletion		750,000
	To record the cost of ore mined for the year.		

In the entry above to record the depletion, the credit is to the contra-asset account Accumulated Depletion. In the financial statements, Southern would show Mineral Deposits along with Accumulated Depletion as follows:

| Mineral deposits | $5,200,000 | |
| Less: Accumulated depletion | 750,000 | $4,450,000 |

Some businesses follow the practice of crediting the asset account directly for depletion, similar to recording amortization of intangible assets.

If Southern sells 200,000 tons of the ore, then we debit $500,000 (200,000 tons x $2.50/ton) to depletion expense as follows:

(Date)	Depletion Expense	500,000	
	Mineral Inventory		500,000
	To record depletion expense on ore sold during the year.		

The amount shown as Depletion Expense in the entry above is the cost of ore sold during the period.

SUMMARY

Explain how to record the disposal of plant assets by abandonment and by sale. When a business abandons a plant asset, we remove its cost and accumulated depreciation accounts from the accounting records. Also, the business recognizes a loss for any remaining carrying amount of the asset. When a business sells a plant asset, we recognize a gain or loss for the difference between the proceeds of the sale and the asset's carrying amount.

Record exchanges of plant assets for both dissimilar and similar assets. For exchanges of dissimilar assets, we record the new asset at the old asset's fair value plus any cash paid. The business recognizes a gain or loss for the difference between the old asset's carrying amount and its fair value. For exchanges of similar assets, the business recognizes a loss if the old asset's carrying amount exceeds its fair value; and we record the new asset at its purchase price. If the old asset's carrying amount is less than its fair value, the business does not recognize a gain. Rather, we record the new asset at its selling price less the amount of the gain not recognized.

Describe the role of accounting records in the control of plant assets. A business has a general ledger asset account and a related accumulated depreciation general ledger account for each group of assets. Related to the general ledger accounts is a plant asset subsidiary ledger. Periodically, the business performs a physical count of the plant assets to verify the accuracy of the items listed in the subsidiary ledger.

Identify the accounting issues related to the acquisition and amortization of intangible assets. Intangible assets are noncurrent productive assets without physical existence. We record intangible assets at the amount of cost incurred in acquiring the asset in accordance with the cost principle. Under the matching principle, we allocate the costs of intangible assets that are used up to the periods the assets benefit. The cost allocation process for intangible assets is similar to straight-line depreciation.

Apply GAAP to the acquisition and depletion of natural resources. In accordance with the cost principle, we record natural resources at the amount of costs incurred in acquiring the assets. Accountants call the cost allocation process for natural resources depletion, and it is similar to units-of-production depreciation.

REVIEW PROBLEM A

Gigantic Cleaners purchased a computer on January 2, 19X1, for $125,000. The computer had an estimated useful life of 5 years and an estimated salvage value of $25,000.

REQUIRED:

a. Record the journal entry for the sale of the computer if Gigantic sells it for $20,000 on December 31, 19X5.
b. Record the journal entry for the sale of the computer if Gigantic sells it for $40,000 on December 31, 19X5.
c. Record the journal entry for the sale of the computer if Gigantic sells it for $35,000 on December 31, 19X4.
d. Record the journal entry for the disposal of the computer if Gigantic exchanges it plus $5,000 cash for a truck on December 31, 19X4. The computer had a fair value of $18,000 when the exchange was made.

SOLUTION:

Planning and Organizing Your Work
1. Calculate the accumulated depreciation and the carrying amount for the asset that is sold.
2. Determine the gain or loss from the sale of the asset by subtracting the sold asset's carrying amount from the proceeds from the sale.
3. Record the disposition of the asset by removing the asset and the related accumulated depreciation and by recording the cash proceeds and the gain or loss calculated in Step 2 above.
4. For the exchange in Requirement d, record removing the asset and the related accumulated depreciation, the payment of cash, the asset received, and any gain or loss from the exchange.

(a) *Record the entry for the sale on December 31, 19X5, for $20,000.*

Accumulated depreciation: ($20,000 x 5 years)   = $100,000
Carrying amount ($125,000 – $100,000)   =   25,000

19X5			
Dec. 31	Cash	20,000	
	Accumulated Depreciation—Equipment	100,000	
	Loss from Sale of Equipment ($25,000 – $20,000)		
	Equipment		125,000
	To record sale of computer.		

(b) *Record the entry for the sale on December 31, 19X5, for $40,000.*

Accumulated depreciation: ($20,000 x 5 years)   = $100,000
Carrying amount ($125,000 – $100,000)   =   25,000

19X5			
Dec. 31	Cash	40,000	
	Accumulated Depreciation—Equipment	100,000	
	Equipment		125,000
	Gain from Sale of Equipment ($40,000 – $25,000)		15,000
	To record sale of computer.		

(c) *Record the entry for the sale on December 31, 19X4, for $35,000.*

Accumulated depreciation: ($20,000 x 4 years)   = $80,000
Carrying amount ($125,000 – $80,000)   = $45,000

19X4			
Dec. 31	Cash	35,000	
	Accumulated Depreciation—Equipment	80,000	
	Loss from Sale of Equipment ($45,000 – $35,000)	10,000	
	Equipment		125,000
	To record sale of computer.		

(d) *Record the exchange for the truck on December 31, 19X4.*

Accumulated depreciation: ($20,000 x 4 years)   = $80,000
Carrying amount ($125,000 – $80,000)   =   45,000

19X4			
Dec. 31	Delivery Equipment ($18,000 + $5,000)	23,000	
	Accumulated Depreciation—Equipment	80,000	
	Loss from Disposal ($45,000 – $18,000)	27,000	
	Cash		5,000
	Equipment		125,000
	To record exchange of computer for truck.		

REVIEW PROBLEM B

Star Company purchased a silver mine for $950,000 on January 2, 19X1. A geological survey company has estimated that 250,000 ounces of recoverable silver are in the mine. The estimated land value of the property after mining is $400,000.

REQUIRED:

a. Record the purchase of the silver mine.
b. Calculate the depletion per ounce.
c. Record depletion for the year ended December 31, 19X1, if 60,000 ounces of silver are mined and 50,000 ounces are sold.

SOLUTION:

Planning and Organizing Your Work
1. Record the purchase of the silver mine at cost.
2. Calculate depletion per ounce by dividing the cost by the estimated recoverable amount of silver.
3. Record the depletion for the silver that is mined and add the amount to inventory.
4. Record the sale of silver.

(a) *Record the purchase of the mine.*

19X1			
Jan. 2	Mineral Deposits	950,000	
	Cash		950,000
	To record the purchase of the silver mine.		

(b) *Calculate depletion per ounce.*

($950,000 – $400,000) ÷ 250,000 ounces = $2.20 per ounce.

(c) *Record the mining and sale of silver.*

19X1			
Dec. 31	Mineral Inventory (60,000 x $2.20)	132,000	
	Accumulated Depletion		132,000
	To record the cost of the silver ore mined for the year.		
	Depletion Expense (50,000 x $2.20)	110,000	
	Mineral Inventory		110,000
	To record depletion expense on silver ore sold.		

KEY TERMS

amortization, *447*
copyrights, *450*
cost basis, *445*
depletion, *453*
dissimilar assets, *443*
franchise, *451*

goodwill, *452*
intangible assets, *447*
like-kind exchanges, *446*
natural resources, *453*
non-like-kind exchanges, *446*
patents, *449*

research and development, *449*
similar assets, *443*
trademarks, *450*
trade names, *450*

SELF-QUIZ

LO 1 1. True or False? Disposal of an asset may be accomplished by ceasing to use it.

LO 1 2. When a business disposes of plant assets, we record the asset's depreciation expense for the period between the end of the preceding accounting period and the _____ ____ _____.

LO 2 3. Accounting for the exchange of assets involves three steps on the date of the exchange. Name these steps.

LO 2 4. What is the new asset's recorded cost in an exchange involving dissimilar assets?
 a. The new asset's fair value plus the amount of any cash paid.
 b. The old asset's fair value plus the gain recorded on the exchange.
 c. The new asset's fair value less the amount of cash paid.
 d. The old asset's fair value plus the amount of any cash paid.

LO 2 5. When does a gain occur on an exchange of similar productive assets?
 a. When the cash paid out is greater than the recorded loss.
 b. When the trade-in allowance received for the old asset exceeds its carrying amount.

 c. When the old asset's fair value exceeds the new asset's fair value and cash is received.
 d. When the old asset's fair value exceeds the new asset's fair value and cash is paid.

LO 3 6. True or False? When doing the physical count of assets, employees should inspect the assets for deterioration and obsolescence; and if these conditions are observed, management should give consideration to discontinuing their use.

LO 4 7. When a business purchases a copyright, we record the cost as an intangible asset and we amortize that cost over the useful life of the copyright, not to exceed _____ years.

LO 4 8. True or False? Goodwill is recorded anytime a business is able to generate earnings at a higher rate than is normal for the industry in which the business operates.

LO 5 9. Natural resources are commonly called _____ assets.

LO 5 10. Depletion, or the cost allocation process for natural resources, is similar to the _____-__-_____ depreciation method.

QUESTIONS

Q11-1   What is the effect on the financial statements if a company fails to record depreciation to the date of sale?

Q11-2   Why would a company abandon an asset with a carrying amount greater than zero?

Q11-3   When can a gain be recognized from an exchange of assets?

Q11-4   What is the tax treatment of like-kind exchanges of assets?

Q11-5   How does a company maintain security over its assets?

Q11-6   What are the differences among depreciation, amortization, and depletion?

Q11-7   Why do intangible assets have value to a business?

Q11-8   What is the difference between a patent and a copyright?

Q11-9   How do we account for research and development costs?

Q11-10 Why do companies record depletion for the cost of their natural resources?

EXERCISES

LO 1

E11-1   **Disposal of Plant Assets**   Barne's Manufacturing purchased equipment for $79,000 on January 2, 19X1, with an estimated life of 7 years and an estimated salvage value of $2,000. This asset is depreciated using the straight-line method.

REQUIRED:

Determine the gain or (loss) on disposal of the asset and record the journal entry on January 2, 19X5, if Barne's receives:
a. $0
b. $46,000

LO 1

E11-2   **Disposal of Plant Assets**   Ewing Supply Company purchased equipment for $320,000 on January 2, 19X2, with an estimated life of 5 years and an estimated salvage value of $20,000. The asset is depreciated using the sum-of-the-years'-digits method.

REQUIRED:

Determine the cash received if Ewing's disposed of the asset on December 31, 19X4, at a gain of $23,000.

LO 1

E11-3   **Disposal of Plant Assets**   Pam's Pancake House purchased a griddle on July 1, 19X0, at a cost of $20,000. The asset was depreciated using the straight-line method. The griddle had an estimated useful life of 5 years and an estimated residual value of $0. Pam's sold the griddle on October 1, 19X3. Pam's Pancake House has a June 30 fiscal year-end.

REQUIRED:

Record the necessary journal entries for the sale on October 1, 19X3, if the griddle is sold for:
a. $6,000
b. $15,000

LO 2

E11-4   **Disposal of Plant Assets by Exchange**   John's Delivery Service exchanged an old delivery truck for a new one. On the date of exchange, the old truck had a carrying amount of $7,000. The original cost was $16,000, and accumulated depreciation was $9,000. The new truck has a list price of $20,000. A trade-in allowance of $5,500 was allowed on the old truck. Therefore, John paid an additional $14,500 in cash to purchase the new truck.

REQUIRED:

Record the journal entry for the exchange.

LO 2

E11-5   **Disposal of Plant Assets by Exchange**   Marlin's Auto Sales exchanged a used service truck and paid cash of $6,000 for an air conditioning system. On the date of exchange, the accumulated depreciation on the truck was $14,000, and the original cost was $23,500 The fair value of the used truck is $11,000 and the fair value of the air conditioning system is estimated to be $17,000.

REQUIRED:

Determine the gain or (loss) on the disposal of the truck and record the journal entry.

LO 2

E11-6   **Disposal of Plant Assets by Exchange**   Abalone's Lunch Meats exchange a used refrigeration unit and paid cash of $35,000 for a new unit. On the date of exchange, the accumulated depreciation on the refrigeration unit was $53,000; and the original cost was $82,000. The trade-in on the old refrigeration unit was $39,000.

REQUIRED:

Record the exchange of assets.

LO 4

E11-7   **Amortization of Intangible Assets**   Determine the annual amortization for the following intangible assets:
a. A patent was purchased from another company for $80,000. The patent has an expected economic life of 10 years.
b. A copyright was acquired for $25,000. The copyright has an expected economic life of 45 years.
c. An artist developed a trademark. The artist was paid $12,000, and an additional $3,000 in legal fees were incurred to process the application for the trademark. The trademark has an expected economic life of 75 years.
d. A company with net assets having a fair value of $780,000 was purchased for $900,000. The goodwill is expected to have an economic life of 20 years.

LO 4

E11-8   **Amortization of Intangible Assets**   Bill Smythe bought a Burger Bun Franchise on January 2, 19X1. The franchise fee is $20,000 and gives Smythe the exclusive right to sell Burger Buns for 20 years.

REQUIRED:

a. Record the journal entry on January 2, 19X1, for the purchase of the franchise right.
b. Also, record the journal entry on December 31, 19X1, for the first year's amortization of the franchise right, using straight-line amortization.

LO 4

E11-9   **Research and Development**   During 19X1, Delta Computers spent $400,000 in cash to research and develop a line of software. On August 14, 19X1, the software was copyrighted and is expected to be profitable for 5 years.

REQUIRED:

Record the necessary journal entries in 19X1 relating to the new line of software.

LO 5   **E11-10   Depletion of Natural Resources**   Geo Exploration purchased an offshore tract for $360,000 on January 2, 19X5. Based on test wells, geologists estimate that 240,000 barrels of oil can be recovered.

REQUIRED:

If 50,000 barrels is pumped from the well and 40,000 barrels are sold during 19X5, determine the amount to be debited to inventory and the amount of depletion expense for the year ended 19X5.

PROBLEM SET A

LO 1   **P11-1A   Disposal of Assets**   Kennel Kare purchased a grooming station on September 1, 19X6, for $7,150. The grooming station has an estimated useful life of 5 years and an estimated residual value of $550. Kennel Kare uses the straight-line depreciation method. On June 30, 19X8, Kennel Kare disposed of the grooming station.

REQUIRED:

a. Determine the gain or (loss) on disposal if Kennel Kare received $4,700 for the grooming station.
b. Record the journal entry for the disposal of the grooming station.
c. Determine the gain or (loss) on disposal if Kennel Kare received $750 for the grooming station.

LO 1,2   **P11-2A   Disposal of Assets**   Martin Manufacturing purchased a stamping machine on January 3, 19X7. The machine had a cost of $20,000, an estimated useful life of 5 years, and an estimated residual value of $5,000. Martin uses straight-line depreciation and has a December 31 year-end. The machine was disposed of on April 30, 19X9. Four independent situations are given below for the disposal of the asset.

REQUIRED:

a. Record the necessary journal entries in 19X9 if Martin sold the asset for $16,000.
b. Record the necessary journal entries in 19X9 if Martin sold the asset for $5,000.
c. Record the necessary journal entries in 19X9 if Martin traded in the asset and $18,000 in cash for a truck. The estimated fair value of the old machine is $14,000.
d. Record the necessary journal entries in 19X9 if Martin traded in the asset for a similar machine. The new machine cost $30,000. Martin is being given a trade-in allowance of $10,000 and must pay $20,000 in cash.

LO 2   **P11-3A   Exchange of Assets**   Chico Company purchased a computerized checkout system to replace a group of cash registers by trading in the cash registers and paying $50,000. On the date of exchange, the accumulated depreciation for the cash registers was $28,000; and the original cost was $50,000. The fair value of the computerized checkout system is estimated to be $80,000.

REQUIRED:

a. Prepare the journal entry necessary to record this exchange if the assets are considered to be similar in nature.
b. Prepare the journal entry necessary to record this exchange if the asset exchanged for the checkout system is a building originally costing $50,000 and with accumulated depreciation of $28,000.

LO 4   **P11-4A** **Calculation and Amortization of Goodwill**
On January 2, 19X2, Janet Johnson purchased the assets of Texas International for $1,300,000. The fair value of the assets purchased are as follows:

Asset	Fair Value
Merchandise inventory	$190,000
Equipment	480,000
Land	290,000
Office equipment	35,000
Supplies	4,000

REQUIRED:

a. Calculate the amount of goodwill.
b. Record the entry for the purchase of the assets from Texas International.
c. Record the entry for the amortization of goodwill for 19X2.

LO 5   **P11-5A** **Depletion of Natural Resources**   On January 3, 19X4, Ironore Mining Company bought a mine in the Appalachian Mountains. Experts employed by the company estimated that the mine has deposits of 20,000,000 tons of coal. The mine cost $3,900,000, and an additional $200,000 was spent on legal fees to obtain necessary operating permits. The land is estimated to be worth $100,000 after all the ore has been mined. During 19X4, 4,000,000 tons were mined and 3,500,000 tons were sold for $.60 per ton cash. During 19X5, 5,000,000 tons were mined and sold for $.60 per ton cash. The mine ceased operations on June 4, 19X6, after an additional 1,000,000 tons had been mined since January 1, 19X6. All remaining coal was sold for $.50 per ton cash. Ironore sold the mine to a real estate developer for $200,000 on June 10, 19X6.

REQUIRED:

a. Record the journal entry for the purchase of the mine.
b. Record the journal entries in 19X4 for the mining and sale of coal.
c. Record the journal entries in 19X5 for the mining and sale of coal.
d. Record the journal entries in 19X6 for the mining and sale of coal.
e. Record the journal entry for the sale of the mine on June 10, 19X6.

PROBLEM SET B

LO 1   **P11-1B** **Disposal of Assets**   Auto Wash purchased an automated car wash on October 1, 19X7, for $21,850. The car wash has an expected life of 4 years and an estimated residual value of $1,850. Auto Wash uses the straight-line depreciation method. On April 1, 19X9, Auto Wash disposed of the automated car wash.

REQUIRED:

a. Determine the gain or (loss) on disposal if Auto Wash received $12,700 for the automated car wash.
b. Record the journal entry for the disposal of the automated car wash.
c. Determine the gain or (loss) on disposal if Auto Wash received $8,750 for the automated car wash.

LO 1,2   **P11-2B** **Disposal of Assets**   Marlin Boats purchased a mold injection machine on January 3, 19X2. The machine had a cost of $125,000, an estimated useful life of 8 years, and an estimated residual value of $5,000. Marlin uses straight-line depreciation and has a December 31 year-end. The machine was disposed of on April 30, 19X4. Four independent situations are given below for the disposal of the asset.

REQUIRED:

a. Record the necessary journal entries in 19X4 if Marlin sold the asset for $88,000.
b. Record the necessary journal entries in 19X4 if Marlin sold the asset for $92,000.
c. Record the necessary journal entries in 19X4 if Marlin traded in the asset and $98,000 in cash for a truck. The estimated fair value of the old machine is $80,000.
d. Record the necessary journal entries in 19X4 if Marlin traded in the asset for a similar machine. The new machine cost $130,000. Martin is being given a trade-in allowance of $60,000 and must pay $70,000 in cash.

LO 2 **P11-3B** **Exchange of Assets** Harpo Company purchased a crane to replace a block and tackle system by trading in the block and tackle system and paying $140,000. On the date of exchange, the accumulated depreciation for the block and tackle system was $39,000; and the original cost was $60,000. The fair value of the crane is estimated to be $175,000.

REQUIRED:

a. Prepare the journal entry necessary to record this exchange if the assets are considered to be similar in nature.
b. Prepare the journal entry necessary to record this exchange if the asset exchanged for the crane is a computer system originally costing $60,000 and with accumulated depreciation of $39,000.

LO 4 **P11-4B** **Calculation and Amortization of Goodwill** On January 2, 19X1, David Dakota purchased the assets of North Company for $890,000. The fair value of the assets purchased are as follows:

Asset	Fair Value
Merchandise inventory	$160,000
Equipment	195,000
Land	160,000
Delivery equipment	65,000
Supplies	15,000

REQUIRED:

a. Calculate the amount of goodwill.
b. Record the entry for the purchase of the assets from North Company.
c. Record the entry for the amortization of goodwill for 19X1.

LO 5 **P11-5B** **Depletion of Natural Resources** On January 3, 19X2, Geld Mining Company bought a mine in the Sierra Mountains. Experts employed by the company estimated that the mine has deposits of 10,000 ounces of gold. The mine cost $1,910,000, and an additional $5,000 was spent on legal fees to obtain necessary operating permits. The land is estimated to be worth $15,000 after all the gold has been mined. During 19X2, 2,000 ounces were mined and 1,750 ounces were sold for $240 per ounce cash. During 19X3, 2,500 ounces were mined and sold for $260 per ounce cash. The mine ceased operations on June 4, 19X4, after 5,000 ounces had been mined since January 1, 19X4. All remaining gold was sold for $280 per ounce cash. Geld sold the mine to a real estate developer for $290,000 on June 10, 19X4.

REQUIRED:

a. Record the journal entry to record the purchase of the mine.
b. Record the journal entries in 19X2 for the mining and sale of gold.
c. Record the journal entries in 19X3 for the mining and sale of gold.
d. Record the journal entries in 19X4 for the mining and sale of gold.
e. Record the journal entry for the sale of the mine on June 10, 19X4.

CRITICAL THINKING AND COMMUNICATING

C11-1   Todd Kesterson is a new accounting clerk for Compusoft, a computer software company.

His supervisors asked Todd to prepare a memo detailing the accounting treatment for two independent situations described below. His supervisors are not sure why the accountants do not treat these two similar situations the same.

Situation 1. Compusoft purchased the copyright on a new spreadsheet package for $1,000,000 from Number Crunching Incorporated. Number Crunching Incorporated is in the business of developing software packages, which it then sells to companies such as Compusoft to market. This package should have a useful life of 5 years before it becomes obsolete.

Situation 2. Compusoft's own research and development group has developed a new word processing package at a cost of $1,000,000. The company views the new software as superior to anything currently on the market. The average useful life of word processing packages is 5 years. After 5 years, newer improved packages usually replace existing ones.

REQUIRED:

a. Explain the appropriate accounting treatment for each of the two situations.
b. Draft the memo as if you were Todd.

C11-2   Gwyn Lopez was assigned to inspect physically the plant assets of Twyla Company.

During the inspection, Gwyn noticed a group of machines that were not in use. These machines were rusted and in very poor condition. Gwyn checked the numbers attached to the machines with the subsidiary ledger and determined that the machines were only partially depreciated. Gwyn scheduled a meeting with the controller of the plant and discussed the possibility of writing off the machines since they appeared to be obsolete. The controller told Gwyn that the company was already having a bad year and, therefore, writing off the machines would aggravate the situation and would cause him to receive a poor performance evaluation. The controller suggested that they should wait for a more profitable year to write off the equipment.

REQUIRED:

If you were Gwyn's friend, what would you advise her to do?

CHAPTER 12

Current Liabilities

Katherine Schmidt has just put her life savings and the proceeds of a loan from her parents into buying a women's apparel shop called Fashion Ready-Wear. As the name implies, the shop specializes in women's ready-to-wear clothes that are copies of high-fashion originals. Katherine, who did her college degree in "Textiles and Related Arts" at Western University, has been with a major department store for ten years and had progressed to buyer of women's fashions before leaving to run her own business. So, she feels very capable of competing in the retail market for women's off-the-rack apparel, including buying the best fashions and managing the inventory. However, she feels less capable to run the other important aspects of her newly acquired business. In the words of experienced businesspeople, "She's never met a payroll." And, payroll is one of Katherine's concerns. The previous owners of the business warned her that the Internal Revenue Service had shut them down for a week during the Christmas peak selling season last year for nonpayment of payroll taxes. They also warned Katherine about the difficulty of managing cash flows and credit during the three peak selling seasons (Christmas for gift and winter-spring fashions, spring for summer fashions, and summer for fall fashions).

Katherine knows that shutting the doors of a retail business, even for a few days, during one of the peak selling seasons can mean an unprofitable year and possible financial distress or failure (bankruptcy). So, now having purchased the business in September, she wants to be prepared to finance her first peak Christmas season; and she wants to know if the business is in good shape for utilizing the necessary sources of credit.

In this chapter, you will learn about the current liabilities that are used to finance a business and how their various features may make them more or less desirable as sources of funds. You will learn how to account for bank loans and notes payable. You will also learn about the payroll accounting and payment obligations of employers. Finally, you will learn some of the simple tools for evaluating the current liability position of a business.

1. Describe the various types of current liabilities businesses incur and the factors that affect which ones they utilize.
2. Calculate the interest rate implicit in losing discounts on accounts payable.
3. Account for short-term notes payable.
4. Account for short-term bank loans.
5. Describe payroll expense-payroll liability relationships.
6. Calculate the employee's gross pay, withholdings, deductions and net pay and an employer's payroll-related costs.
7. Prepare the payroll-related journal entries.
8. Calculate and interpret the number of days-purchases-in-payables and the percent utilization of a line of credit.
9. Describe the types of special journals and other records used by businesses to facilitate payroll accounting and reporting. (Appendix 12-A)
10. Describe the applications of computers to payroll accounting. (Appendix 12-A)

LO 1

Describe the various types of current liabilities that businesses incur and the factors that affect which ones they utilize.

CURRENT LIABILITIES

Liabilities are a business's obligations to provide assets or services to other businesses or individuals in the future. Liabilities arise out of present and past activities or transactions. For example, when a business employs a person to work a particular day, the business has an obligation to pay that person. Similarly, when a business purchases merchandise from another business on credit, it is obligated to pay for the merchandise at a later date. These obligations are liabilities because they require the business to provide assets to other entities for things that have already happened.

Estimated and Contingent Liabilities

Many liabilities are quite definite; a debtor owes a specific amount of money due at a specific time. However, two types of liabilities are not so definite—estimated liabilities and contingent liabilities.

Estimated liabilities are those whose exact amounts will not be known until future events take place. They require estimation whenever a business prepares a balance sheet. For example, Computer Sales Company sells personal computers and warrantees them for one-year periods, following expiration of the manufacturers' typical 90-day warranties. At any balance sheet date, Computer Sales has an obligation for repairs to or replacement of the computers it has sold within the last 15 months. However, Computer Sales does not know the exact amount of the obligation and must estimate an amount based on its past experience, modified for current conditions.

Contingent liabilities are potential obligations only. They depend on the outcomes of future events to determine *whether* the business must pay and, in some cases, how much the business must pay. For example, in the event that the maker of a promissory note does not pay, the endorser of the note must pay the holder (buyer). Until the maker actually defaults, the endorser's obligation is a liability *contingent* on the maker's future actions. Contingent liabilities also arise from disputed claims. Assume a customer sues Computer Sales for damages arising from the failure of computer equipment to perform adequately. Computer Sales maintains that the equipment performs properly and that it is the software the customer uses that is causing the problem. Whether an obligation exists in such a case depends on the outcome of a trial, arbitration, or settlement negotiations. Computer Sales would not even recognize such a potential obligation on its balance sheet as a liability unless it is *probable* that it will lose the suit *and* the amount awarded the plaintiff is *reasonably estimable.* Computer Sales would disclose other contingent liabilities in notes at the end of its financial statements, rather than recognizing them as specific amounts in its balance sheet.[1]

This chapter and a later chapter cover a variety of business liabilities. However, further discussion of contingent liabilities is beyond the text's scope.

Current and Long-Term Liabilities

A liability's **term to maturity** refers to the period of time until the liability must be paid. In accounting, we classify liabilities according to their terms to maturity. **Current liabilities** are those that must be satisfied within a short period by paying cash, providing other current assets, or incurring other current liabilities. According to GAAP, current liabilities generally include all liabilities due within one year or within one operating cycle, *whichever is longer.* In an earlier chapter, we defined a business's **operating cycle** as the average period of time it takes from committing of resources to provide goods or services to collecting cash from customers. In certain industries such as distilling, shipbuilding, high-rise construction, and research contracting, the operating cycle exceeds one year. In most other businesses, including virtually all merchandising businesses, the operating cycles are shorter than one year. When this is the case, we use one year to define what is "current." Liabilities that are not due within one year (or within one operating cycle, if longer) generally are referred to as **noncurrent liabilities, long-term liabilities,** or **long-term debts**.

TYPICAL CURRENT LIABILITIES

Before we begin discussion of some types of loans and notes payable, we list and describe the typical liabilities businesses incur. Not all of these liabilities are new to you. We briefly introduced such liabilities as accounts payable and wages and salaries payable in earlier chapters. Here, we include them in an expanded list, because it is possible to trade off the use of one type of liability for another in managing a business—as you will see very soon. In addition, several of the liabilities mentioned below will receive further coverage in subsequent chapters.

Current Liabilities

Businesses incur a variety of current liabilities, including the portion of noncurrent liabilities to be paid in the short term.

Accounts Payable.   Accounts payable consist of the amounts a business owes to outside suppliers of goods and services as of a point in time.

---

[1]"Accounting for Contingencies," *Statement of Financial Accounting Standards No. 5* (Stamford, Conn.: FASB, 1975), paras. 8–11 and 38.

Short-Term Notes Payable.   Notes payable represent written promises to pay specified amounts on specified dates at specified places to particular payees (or bearers of the notes). Short-term notes payable are due within one year (or within one operating cycle, if longer). A note payable of a debtor (maker of the note) is a note receivable to a payee. A previous chapter covers basic features common to both notes receivable and notes payable.

Short-Term Bank Loans.   Short-term bank loans are designed to help a business with short-term needs to finance assets such as accounts receivable and inventory.

Wages and Salaries Payable.   Wages and salaries payable consist of the amounts a business owes to employees for hours or periods already worked.

Payroll Taxes Payable.   Payroll taxes payable are the unpaid amounts of employee and employer payroll taxes and premiums a business owes to federal and state goverments. Employee taxes include federal, state, and local income taxes withheld from employees' pay, as well as the employees' portions of social security and Medicare taxes deducted from their pay. Employer taxes consist of the employer's share of social security taxes, state and federal unemployment tax (or premiums), and workers' compensation insurance premiums.

Income Taxes Payable.   Proprietorships and partnerships are not taxed on their incomes *per se*. Instead, the owners of proprietorships and partnerships are taxed on the incomes they derive from those types of businesses. Corporations, on the other hand, are generally required to pay estimated (accrued, but unpaid) income taxes to the respective governments at least quarterly. Until a business makes these payments, the balances due are liabilities.

Current Portion of Long-Term Liabilities.   Liabilities whose terms are more than one year are often paid in installments or portions that are due at shorter intervals of one or more months. At each balance sheet date, a business evaluates such liabilities, determines the portions that are due within the coming 12 months, and reclassifies them from noncurrent to current liabilities.

Liability Trade-Offs

Some liabilities such as accounts payable, wages and salaries payable, and taxes payable arise more or less spontaneously in the course of business. Businesses use other liabilities such as bank loans and notes payable more deliberately to satisfy specific financing objectives—for example, to minimize total interest costs. The factors that affect whether a firm should borrow from one source of credit versus another are interest costs and other terms, loan arrangement costs, collateral requirements, and creditor restrictions on the business. Katherine Schmidt needs to understand these factors and how she can use different types of liabilities to finance Fashion Ready-Wear through the peak season.

LO 2

Calculate the interest rate implicit in losing discounts on accounts payable.

FINANCING OF PURCHASES THROUGH ACCOUNTS PAYABLE

A business such as Fashion Ready-Wear that purchases goods and services on account, in effect, borrows from the supplier of those goods or services.

Fashion Ready-Wear's suppliers offer terms of 2/10, n/30. Based on these terms, Fashion Ready-Wear may effectively borrow funds to finance each purchase for ten days at no interest cost. However, if it takes longer to pay than ten days, the business incurs a cost to borrowing from the supplier—the loss of the 2% discount on every purchase. This can have a profound effect on Fashion Ready-Wear's profitability.

Advantage of Accounts Payable as a Financing Source

Borrowing by not taking discounts on accounts payable has one great advantage—virtually no arrangement costs or arrangement requirements. A purchaser who has established credit with a supplier does not have to notify the supplier if it does not intend to take discounts on its purchases. Therefore, the purchaser can borrow spontaneously—without any arrangement costs.

Katherine Schmidt will want to purchase $150,000 in new inventory from Southwest Distributors for the Christmas buying season. If she purchases the goods on November 15 under the usual terms, 2/10, n/30, she automatically has two payment plans.

First, in general journal format, Fashion Ready-Wear records the season's purchases as follows:

19X1			
Nov. 15	Purchases	150,000	
	Accounts Payable		150,000
	To record purchases.		

If Katherine pays for the purchases in ten days, her entry to record the cash disbursement is:

Nov. 25	Accounts Payable	150,000	
	Cash		147,000
	Purchases Discounts		3,000
	To record payment for purchases—		
	2% discount taken.		

She would not pay sooner, because the first ten days of credit are free (she keeps her money and does not lose the discount). On the other hand, she may merely wait and pay $150,000 on December 15:

Dec. 15	Accounts Payable	150,000	
	Cash		150,000
	To record payment for purchase after discount		
	period expired.		

In this latter case, she will have simply borrowed the supplier's money for an additional 20 days at a cost of $3,000—the loss of the discount. During the extra 20 days, Katherine can collect and accumulate receipts from sales to pay for the purchases and other costs of running the business. So, not taking discounts on accounts payable is a form of financing the business—a form of borrowing.

Equivalent Annual Interest Rate on Accounts Payable

The $3,000 discount lost in the above example seems like a minor amount compared to the purchases. However, borrowing from suppliers for longer than the discount period can be very costly, indeed. In the case above, the discount was 2% for payment in 10 days. For keeping the money for an additional 20 days,

Fashion Ready-Wear pays 2% interest. To find the *effective (equivalent) annual interest rate* for discounts lost, use the following formula:

$$\text{Effective Annual Rate} = \text{Discount Rate} \times \frac{365 \text{ days}}{\text{Additional Days to Payment}}$$

$$36.5\% = 2\% \times \frac{365 \text{ days}}{20 \text{ days}}$$

So, we see that not taking discounts in this case is effectively equivalent to paying 36.5% interest per year. Under most conditions, such a rate is exhorbitant and will have an adverse impact on profits.

Thus, despite the ease with which Katherine will be able to use her suppliers' money, the effective interest rate is high, as illustrated above. In addition, the terms of payment are fixed. Katherine must be able to sell the apparel purchased on November 15 and collect sufficient cash from her customers by December 15 to pay for the purchases and all the other costs of running the business during that period. This may be impossible if many of the sales are on credit and not collectible until later, say, after January 1.

Like other retailers, Katherine may wish to look to other forms of borrowing to get her business through its peak season. For example, she might offer negotiable notes payable to her suppliers at better terms (for her) than those for normal terms of accounts payable. Because the notes would be negotiable and the suppliers can discount (sell) them, they may be willing to accept better terms. Alternatively, she may arrange for a bank loan. The following sections describe the characteristics of and the accounting for these alternatives.

LO 3
Account for short-term
notes payable

SHORT-TERM NOTES PAYABLE

The important components of short-term promissory notes are covered in the earlier chapter on Accounts Receivable and Notes Receivable. But, some minor differences exist in how notes payable are handled relative to notes receivable. For example, the maker of a note does not change accounting for a note when a note is discounted (sold by the original payee to a subsequent holder). To the maker of the note, the liability is the same, regardless of who ultimately will be paid.

Here, we cover short-term notes that are written for single payments of both principal and interest at fixed dates 1 to 12 months from the date they are made. You will recall from the earlier chapter that the interest rate of a single-payment note is sometimes explicitly stated, for example, 10%. In such cases, the "face" amount of the note is the amount borrowed. In other cases, when no interest is stated, the face amount is more than the amount borrowed (the maker receives an amount discounted from face value). In such cases, the interest is implicit and is measured by the amount of the discount. In either case, the accounting requirements are to record the notes at the time they are made, recognize interest and properly value the notes at financial statement dates, and record payment of the notes at time of maturity.

Interest-Bearing Notes Payable

Suppose that on November 25, 19X1, Southwest Distributors agrees to accept Fashion Ready-Wear's note payable for $147,000 to pay its account payable for the November 15 purchase of inventory. The note matures in 75 days. Its purpose is to permit Fashion Ready-Wear to postpone payment for the large quantity of merchandise purchased in anticipation of the Christmas selling season until after it sells the inventory and collects cash from its customers. Also, the interest rate of 12% is much preferred to losing discounts by paying ordinary accounts payable late. Katherine's entry to record the note is:

Nov. 25	Accounts Payable	150,000	
	Notes Payable—Southwest Distributors		147,000
	Purchases Discounts		3,000
	To record issue of 12% note payable to Southwest Distributors in payment of accounts payable less 2% discount taken.		

Fashion Ready-Wear has a fiscal year-end of January 31. Therefore, Katherine would calculate the appropriate interest accrual for the 67 days from November 25 to January 31 as follows (Remember: PRT or Principal x Rate x Time)

$$\$3,238.03 = \$147,000 \times 12\% \times \frac{67 \text{ days}}{365 \text{ days}}$$

Katherine's entry is:

19X2			
Jan. 31	Interest Expense	3,238.03	
	Interest Payable		3,238.03
	To record interest through year-end on 12% note payable to Southwest Distributors.		

The note is due on February 8, 19X2. At that time, another 8 days' interest has accrued:

$$\$386.63 = \$147,000 \times 12\% \times \frac{8 \text{ days}}{365 \text{ days}}$$

Katherine's entry to record payment of the note and to record further interest for February is:

Feb. 28	Interest Expense	386.63	
	Interest Payable	3,238.03	
	Notes Payable—Southwest Distributors	147,000.00	
	Cash		150,624.66
	To record interest on and payment of 12% note payable to Southwest Distributors.		

The total cost of the note to Fashion Ready-Wear is $3,624.66, which is more than the $3,000 discount that was lost in the earlier example. However, under the note payable option, Katherine pays $3,624.66 to borrow $147,000 for 75 days; whereas, under the account payable option, she pays $3,000 to borrow $147,000 for only 20 days. Just as important, Fashion Ready-Wear probably needs the extra 55 days to generate the cash collections on its peak-season sales to pay for the loan. Thus, assuming its suppliers are willing to accept Katherine's notes, using the notes to finance purchases for the peak season is superior to losing discounts on purchases for postponed payments. The suppliers will accept the notes as payments for accounts payable, provided they are negotiable and can be discounted on favorable terms.

Noninterest-Bearing Notes Payable

All of the above advantages also apply to a note payable that carries no explicit interest rate. For example, suppose Fashion Ready-Wear gives Southwest Distributors a $150,750, 75-day note to pay its account payable of $147,000 on November 25. The key interest calculations are as follows:

$$\text{Total interest cost (discount)} = \$150{,}750 - \$147{,}000 = \$3{,}750$$

$$\text{Daily interest cost} = \$3{,}750 \div 75 \text{ days} = \$50$$

$$\text{Interest expense November–January} = \$50 \times 67 \text{ days} = \$3{,}350$$

$$\text{Interest expense for February} = \$50 \times 8 \text{ days} = \$400$$

Katherine's entry to record issue of this alternative note that carries *implicit* interest is:

Nov. 25	Accounts Payable	150,000	
	Discounts on Notes Payable	3,750	
	Notes Payable—Southwest Distributors		150,750
	Purchases Discounts		3,000
	To record issue of note payable to Southwest		
	Distributors in settlement of account.		

Notice that the discounted note is recorded at $150,750. However, the net account payable that it paid is only $147,000 ($150,000 less the purchase discount of $3,000). Thus, to complete its initial valuation, the $3,750 of implicit interest that ultimately will be paid is recognized as a discount on the note payable. The discount is recognized with a debit to a contra-liability account called Discounts on Notes Payable. If Katherine prepared a balance sheet as of November 25, she would use the contra-account to value the note properly on the balance sheet as follows:

Current liabilities:		
Notes payable—Southwest Distributors	$150,750	
Less: Discounts on notes payable	3,750	$147,000

No payments of interest are made on the discounted note. But, as of January 31, the end of Fashion Ready-Wear's fiscal year, Katherine records $3,350 of the total $3,750 discount as interest expense of the year ending on that date.

19X2			
Jan. 31	Interest Expense	3,350	
	Discounts on Notes Payable		3,350
	To record interest through year-end on note payable		
	to Southwest Distributors.		

The note would then appear as follows on the January 31, 19X2, balance sheet:

Current liabilities:		
Notes payable—Southwest Distributors	$150,750	
Less: Discounts on notes payable	400	$150,350

At the time the note is paid on February 8, Katherine recognizes the rest of the discount as interest.

Feb. 8	Interest Expense	400	
	Notes Payable—Southwest Distributors	150,750	
	Discounts on Notes Payable		400
	Cash		150,750
	To record interest on and payment of note payable to Southwest Distributors.		

LO 4
Account for short-term bank loans.

SHORT-TERM BANK LOANS

In the preceding example, the problem of the fixed term to payment and high effective interest rate on accounts payable is solved by issuing a note to the supplier. However, suppose Katherine purchased the inventory that needed to be financed for the peak season from several suppliers. These circumstances require Katherine to negotiate the acceptance of a note by each of the suppliers. Under these circumstances, Katherine will probably prefer to arrange a bank loan so that she can take discounts on all of the accounts payable. The bank loan requires effort to arrange, may require a loan origination fee, and probably will impose some restrictions on Fashion Ready-Wear. However, these disadvantages are offset by substantial savings in interest costs and the security of prearranged financing.

Short-Term Borrowing Needs

When a business approaches a bank for a loan, the bank typically requires the applicant to supply copies of current and past financial statements, along with information about its business history and plans. The bank will do a credit analysis of the business, including an investigation of its past record of paying its creditors. The bank will evaluate the applicant's plans, including its probable ability to repay a loan. The bank will also look at the specific purpose that the business has for the loan and will counsel the business about the more suitable type of loan for its needs. For example, if the business plans to grow and requires permanent additions to buildings and equipment, then a long-term loan may be more suitable. On the other hand, the business may have a short-term, seasonal need to expand its inventory and accounts receivable during its busy selling season, as in the case of Fashion Ready-Wear.

Revolving Lines of Credit.   A short-term, revolving line of credit is suitable for the latter type of need. **A short-term, revolving line of credit** is a bank's commitment to advance funds on demand to a borrower up to a limit and for a period it sets. If a bank approves a line of credit for a borrower, it usually sets an absolute limit on the loan and a flexible limit. A flexible limit is generally tied to something that reflects the customer's need to borrow the money. For example, a flexible limit might be set as an amount equal to "50% of the cost of inventory on hand *plus* 80% of accounts receivable that are less than ninety days old." The customer can then borrow up to the amount of the flexible limit but not more than the absolute limit. The absolute limit is the maximum amount the bank expects the customer will need or the maximum amount the customer can be expected to repay—whichever is less. The flexible limit escalates with the needs of the customer, thereby providing the customer with additional financing on an "as needed" basis.

When Katherine bought Fashion Ready-Wear, she understood that the previous owners had negotiated a line of credit with a bank. The bank had agreed to lend Fashion Ready-Wear amounts up to 50% of its inventory total and 50% of its accounts receivable—but not to exceed $200,000. On November 25, Fashion Ready-Wear has inventory of $200,000 and accounts receivable of $140,000. This means that it can borrow up to $170,000 [(.5 x $200,000) + (.5 x $140,000)] on its line of credit by simply calling its bank loan officer and requesting that the money be transferred to its account. However, after the busy season is over and inventory and accounts receivable resettle to off-season levels of $70,000 and $50,000, respectively, the maximum loan amount will be $60,000 [(.5 x $70,000) + (.5 x $50,000)]. If Fashion Ready-Wear borrows more than this during the busy time, it will have to repay at least part of the loan as its accounts receivable and inventory levels drop.

Other Short-Term Lending Terms.   Other customary terms are used for short-term bank loans such as the one described above. First, banks making such loans generally require that the customer pledge its inventory and accounts receivable as collateral for the loan, which means that the bank may take the assets in settlement if the customer does not repay the loan on time. Second, the loan is usually a "demand" loan, which means that the bank can *require that it be repaid in full at any time*. The bank usually requires that the customer pays the loan balance in full once each year (in the off-season). Third, the interest rate is often flexible; that is, it is tied to a "base" rate that fluctuates with the rate at which the Federal Reserve Bank makes loans to other banks, called the *rediscount rate*. Bank base rates vary with conditions in the economy and the Federal Reserve System's policy of either expanding or contracting the money supply. A business borrowing on a revolving line of credit is likely to be quoted "base plus one" or "base plus two."[2] If the base rate is 8%, the customer will pay an annual effective rate of 9% or 10%, respectively. Fourth, interest on the loan balance is payable each month or quarter. Fifth, the bank makes a commitment to provide funds to the borrower up to the applicable limit. If the borrower does not use the full credit available, the bank often charges a small rate on the unused portion of the commitment, say, 1% or 2%. Sixth, the bank may require that the borrower maintain a minimum balance in the borrower's accounts with the bank; or the bank may adjust the interest rate downward if the borrower maintains such a balance. Seventh, the bank may require the borrower to sign a special note (non-negotiable) agreeing to all the other required terms and conditions. If the borrower is required to pledge assets as collateral or to maintain a minimum balance, the borrower must disclose these facts in notes at the end of the financial statements.

Accounting for Short-Term Bank Loans

The bank agreed to charge Fashion Ready-Wear 10% per year with interest payable for each month on the tenth day of the following month. On November 25, Fashion Ready-Wear borrows $147,000 to pay its total accounts payable on

---

[2]The often quoted base rate that large banks charge their most creditworthy customers is called the *prime rate*.

its seasonal purchases in time to take the discounts. Katherine's entries to record the two transactions are:

19X1			
Nov. 25	Cash	147,000	
	Notes Payable—Bank		147,000
	To record borrowing against revolving line of credit.		
25	Accounts Payable	150,000	
	Cash		147,000
	Purchases Discounts		3,000
	To record payment for purchases less 2% discount taken.		

On December 10, 19X1, interest is due for the month of November. We calculate interest in this case in the same way that we do for short-term notes receivable as described earlier:

$$\$201.37 = \$147,000 \times 10\% \times \frac{5 \text{ days}}{365 \text{ days}}$$

Katherine would accrue this amount as of November 30, 19X1:

Nov. 30	Interest Expense	201.37	
	Interest Payable		201.37
	To record accrued interest on short-term bank borrowing.		

When payment is made, Katherine records it as follows:

Dec. 10	Interest Payable	201.37	
	Cash		201.37
	To record payment of accrued interest on short-term bank borrowing.		

Since interest costs are paid monthly, the entry to record repayment of the loan would include only interest not previously paid. For example, if Fashion Ready-Wear repays its loan on February 10, Katherine would remit the principal amount plus interest for January (which would have been accrued on January 31) plus interest for the 10 days in February:

$$\$1,248.49 = \$147,000 \times 10\% \times \frac{31 \text{ days}}{365 \text{ days}}$$

$$\$402.74 = \$147,000 \times 10\% \times \frac{10 \text{ days}}{365 \text{ days}}$$

19X2			
Feb. 10	Interest Payable	1,248.49	
	Interest Expense	402.74	
	Notes Payable—Bank	147,000.00	
	Cash		148,651.23
	To record repayment of short-term bank loan with accrued interest.		

The total interest cost of the loan would be:

November	$ 201.37
December	1,248.49
January	1,248.49
February	402.74
Total	$3,101.09

Thus, the bank loan alternative provides advantages over losing discounts on accounts payable similar to the advantages of issuing negotiable notes payable to individual suppliers—a longer, more flexible term and lower effective interest cost. The bank loan also provides the additional advantage of prearranged financing with only one entity—the bank.

PAYROLL

Katherine Schmidt not only wants to know how to finance her business through its peak selling seasons, but she also wants to understand her payroll obligations to her employees and to the government. She knows that the Internal Revenue Service will not tolerate failure to pay U.S. employer tax obligations promptly, and she wants to avoid difficulties. She needs to know how payroll accounting works.

Payroll accounting serves many objectives. First, it is necessary to account for all the costs of services employees perform for a business. Second, the business should recognize these costs as expenses in the appropriate period. For merchandising or service businesses, the appropriate periods for recognizing payroll-related expenses are those in which employees perform services. Third, the employer must withhold federal, state, and local taxes from employees' wages and salaries and remit appropriate payments to the taxing authorities. Fourth, the employer must pay certain taxes to the federal, state, and local governments, in addition to those withheld from employees' pay. Fifth, the employer may withhold amounts from employees' wages and salaries as employee contributions to group life insurance, group health insurance, and pension plans. Sixth, the employer may make contributions to both group insurance plans and pension plans. Seventh, the employer must typically accrue amounts of vacation and sick pay benefits that employees earn during pay periods when they are working. The accrued liabilities are reversed when employees take vacations or days off due to illness. Finally, the employer must keep cumulative wage and salary records for all employees—at a minimum to comply with federal tax requirements.

These eight objectives may seem formidable at first glance, but payroll accounting has evolved to handle these objectives efficiently and effectively. Moreover, payroll accounting lends itself very well to computer assistance and frequently is the first area of computer applications for many businesses. Because the payroll function is very similar from business to business, software manufacturers have developed flexible and reliable programs to handle the payrolls of small, medium, and large businesses. In addition, independent payroll processing firms have been formed to meet the payroll needs of other businesses. By specializing, these independent payroll processors become very expert in handling payroll problems; and they are able to afford larger computers and better software than their clients.

LO 5

Describe payroll expense-liability relationships.

PAYROLL EXPENSE-LIABILITY RELATIONSHIPS

Illustration 12-1 shows several important payroll relationships. One is the relationship between an employee's net pay and gross pay. Another is an employer's total payroll-related expense, composed of the employee's gross pay plus the employer's payroll taxes and benefits costs. A third is the relationship between total payroll-related expenses and total payroll-related liabilities.

ILLUSTRATION 12-1 Payroll Relationships

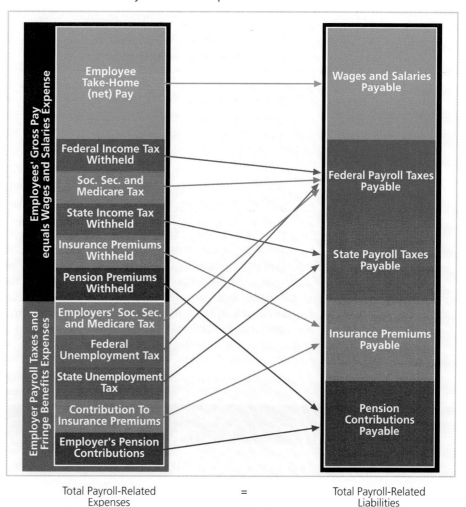

Total Payroll-Related   =   Total Payroll-Related
Expenses   Liabilities

Gross Pay and Net Pay

The first relationship appears in the upper left portion of the illustration: An employee's **gross pay** is equal to his/her total salary or wages for a period. **Net pay** is equal to gross pay minus

1. *Withholdings* for federal income taxes, federal social security and Medicare taxes, state income taxes, and local taxes (if any), and

2. *Deductions* for insurance premiums and employee contributions to pension programs.[3]

In effect, in payroll accounting, gross pay is broken down into net pay and the various withholdings and deductions from gross pay.

Payroll Taxes and "Benefits"

Another important relationship is depicted by the left column of Illustration 12-1. An employer's total payroll-related expenses consist of more than just the employees' gross pay. In addition, employers must pay payroll taxes such as the employer's share of social security and Medicare taxes, and they may contribute to their employees' insurance and pension programs. The latter contributions are called **employee benefits**.

Payroll Expenses Equal Credits to Payroll-Related Liabilities

Notice that the left and right columns of Illustration 12-1 are equal. Payroll expenses *for a period* equal the related credits to payroll liabilities *as of the end of the payroll period.* It is important to remember this equality since it can be used to check your work and to correct errors. Basically, as employees perform services for their employers, the employers are obligated to pay an amount equal to the employees' gross pay plus the additional employer expenses related to payrolls. These combined amounts technically are obligations that arise as the employee finishes each hour, or even minute or second, of work.

However, we usually recognize payroll expenses periodically at regular intervals of one week, two weeks, half a month, or one month. For hourly employees, we may need a tabulation period after the end of the work period to tabulate hours worked. Then, we calculate payroll expenses, record the expenses and obligations, issue payroll checks or cash pay envelopes, and pay the other payroll-related liabilities. The sequence looks like this in time line form:

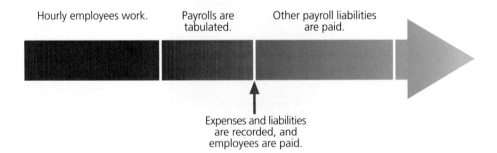

The sequence differs slightly for salaried employees because we do not use the specific hours worked to calculate the payroll. Instead, a fixed sum is paid for each interval. Since the fixed sum is known in advance, there is no tabulation period. Salary payrolls are generally prepared on or before the end of each

---

[3]Deductions are not limited to insurance premiums and pension contributions, but may also include savings deductions, United Way contributions, and other optional deductions. However, we illustrate the treatment and effects of all such deductions using only insurance and pension contributions.

work period, and payroll checks are typically issued to salaried workers on the last day of the work period or the first day of the next period.

In any case, liabilities exist until payroll checks are issued and payments are made for the various taxes, insurance premiums, etc. Comparing the left and right columns of Illustration 12-1, you will note there are fewer types of liabilities than there are payroll-related withholdings, deductions, and employer expenses. Many of the withholdings, deductions, and employer payroll obligations are payable to the same payees. For example, federal withholding tax, employee social security and Medicare taxes, employer social security and Medicare taxes, and federal unemployment tax all are payable to the federal government. Therefore, it is unnecessary to establish separate liabilities for each of them individually, although separate liabilities may be established for book-keeping convenience.

LO 6

Calculate an employee's gross pay, withholdings, deductions, and net pay and an employer's payroll-related costs.

CALCULATING PAYROLL EXPENSES AND LIABILITIES

A business must perform three broad categories of payroll expense and liabilty calculations for each payroll period. Employees' gross wages must be calculated for hourly workers. Various withholdings and deductions from employees' gross wages and salaries must be calculated—often based on the amount of gross wages and salary amounts. Also, the employer's various payroll-related expenses must be calculated.

Employee Gross Wages

We calculate an employee's gross wages by simply multiplying the employee's hourly rate of pay by the hours worked. However, overtime hours must be distinguished from regular hours and are compensated at a different rate than the employee's normal rate. The overtime rate is typically a multiple such as 1.5 or 2.0 times the regular hourly rate. Suppose, for example, that an employer pays overtime at a rate of 1.5 times the regular wage rate. Suppose further that a particular employee, Mary Johnson, was credited with working 40 hours of regular time and 4 hours of overtime during the week ended April 28, 19X1. Her regular hourly rate is $11.10 per hour. Her gross wages for the week would be calculated as follows:

Regular-time wages	40 hours x $11.10 =	$444.00
Overtime wages	4 hours x $11.10 x 1.5 =	66.60
Gross wages		$510.60

Different employers determine overtime hours in different ways. For example, some employers count as overtime any work performed in excess of 8 hours per day, regardless of how many or few hours are worked on other days of a work period. Others count as overtime only the hours in excess of 40 hours of work per week. Suppose an employee worked 7 hours one day, 10 hours another day, and 8 hours the remaining 3 days of a workweek. The employee would be credited with 2 hours of overtime under the former system, but with only 1 hour under the latter. Employers may also vary the multiple for determining the overtime rate. However, large employers, those covered by the Fair Employment Standards Act of 1938, must credit any hours worked in excess of 40 hours per week as overtime and must pay overtime at no less than 1.5 times the employee's regular rate for the job performed.

Employee Payroll Withholdings and Deductions

Persons employed in the United States incur certain federal tax obligations that arise from their earned wages and salaries. Employers are required by law to withhold estimated amounts of these taxes as the work year progresses and to remit them to the federal government on behalf of employees. The same holds for the income taxes of states and cities where applicable. In addition, many employers arrange group life and health insurance plans and group or individual pension programs. These plans are usually less costly or provide greater benefits to employees than those plans they could arrange for themselves. Some employers pay all of the costs of such employee benefits. In other cases, employers deduct some or all of the required insurance premiums and pension contributions from the employees' gross pay. The amounts deducted are remitted on behalf of the employees to insurance companies and pension funds.

Benefits such as health insurance premiums that the employer either pays or deducts from employees' wages and salaries are not, strictly speaking, tied to hours worked or wages and salaries earned. However, accounting for them is usually included in payroll accounting because:

1. They are part of the employer-employee relationship.
2. They are often part of the total compensation paid to employees.
3. It is convenient to lump them in with true payroll-related costs.

Individual Federal Withholding Taxes

Employers act as the collecting agents for the federal withholding tax on individuals' salaries, wages, and tips. The amount an employer withholds and remits for a given employee for a pay period is a function of two things:

1. The amount the employee earns for the pay period.
2. The number of "allowances" the employee claims on Form W-4, filed with the employer.

Fredrick A. Phillips, a married taxpayer, works on an hourly basis for Fashion Ready-Wear. Fredrick and Fashion Ready-Wear will serve as examples to illustrate the calculations of employees' withholdings and deductions and the calculation of employer taxes and fringe benefit costs. Fredrick (Fred) earns gross pay of $10.25 per hour, is paid weekly, and works 39.5 hours during the week of March 25-31, 19X1. He reported four allowances on his Form W-4 for 19X1, shown in Illustration 12-2. Illustration 12-3 gives the 19X1 deduction values of one allowance for pay periods of various lengths. The 19X1 withholding tables for weekly and monthly pay periods are shown in Illustration 12-4.

The withholding tax for Fred for this particular week is calculated as follows:

Gross pay (39.5 hours x $10.25 per hour)	$404.88
Less: Allowances (4 x $45.19)	180.76
Pay subject to withholding tax	$224.12
Withholding tax (.15 x ($224.12 – $119.00))	$ 15.77

ILLUSTRATION 12-2 Form W-4

Form **W-4**	**Employee's Withholding Allowance Certificate**		19**X**1
Department of the Treasury Internal Revenue Service	▶ For Privacy Act and Paperwork Reduction Act Notice, see reverse.		

1 Type or print your first name and middle initial Frederick A. Phillips	Last name	2 Your social security number
Home address (number and street or rural route) 123 4th Street	3 ☐ Single ☒ Married ☐ Married, but withhold at higher Single rate. **Note:** If married, but legally separated, or spouse is a nonresident alien, check the Single box.	
City or town, state, and ZIP code Anytown, Anystate 00000	4 If your last name differs from that on your social security card, check here and call 1-800-772-1213 for more information ▶ ☐	

5 Total number of allowances you are claiming (from line G above or from the worksheets on page 2 if they apply) . | **5** | 4
6 Additional amount, if any, you want withheld from each paycheck . . . . | **6** $ –0–
7 I claim exemption from withholding for 1993 and I certify that I meet **ALL** of the following conditions for exemption:
 • Last year I had a right to a refund of **ALL** Federal income tax withheld because I had **NO** tax liability; **AND**
 • This year I expect a refund of **ALL** Federal income tax withheld because I expect to have **NO** tax liability; **AND**
 • This year if my income exceeds $600 and includes nonwage income, another person cannot claim me as a dependent.
 If you meet all of the above conditions, enter "EXEMPT" here . . . . ▶ | **7** |

Under penalties of perjury, I certify that I am entitled to the number of withholding allowances claimed on this certificate or entitled to claim exempt status.

Employee's signature ▶ *Frederick A. Phillips*   Date ▶ January 10   , 19**X**1

8 Employer's name and address (Employer: Complete 8 and 10 only if sending to the IRS) ✓ | 9 Office code (optional) | 10 Employer identification number

ILLUSTRATION 12-3 Federal Withholding Allowances[4]

Payroll period	*One withholding allowance*
Weekly	45.19
Biweekly	90.38
Semimonthly	97.92
Monthly	195.83
Quarterly	587.50
Semiannually	1,175.00
Annually	2,350.00
Daily or miscellaneous (each day of payroll period)	9.04

After calculating his gross pay and deducting the dollar value of his allowances, Fashion Ready-Wear calculated Fred's withholding tax using the table shown in Illustration 12-4.

First, recognize that Fred is a married taxpayer and is paid weekly. Therefore, only the upper right-hand quarter of Illustration 12-4 applies. Now, find the pair of numbers in the left two columns of that quarter that contain $224.12 between them. The numbers are $119 and $784. That is, Mr. Phillips's eligible wages are more than $119 but less than $784. Reading to the right indicates that his withholding tax should be 15% of the excess of $224.12 over $119, or $15.77 (to the nearest cent).

Individual Social Security and Medicare Taxes

The Social Security System of the United States was originated with the Social Security Act of 1935. The System is intended to provide at least minimum old age, survivors, disability, and hospital insurance. The Medicare tax finances the

---

[4]"Employer's Tax Guide," *Circular E* (Department of the Treasury: Internal Revenue Service, Revised December, 1992), p. 24. The withholding allowances in this table, which we use here for illustration only, are the actual allowances that applied to payrolls of 1993. They should not be used for any other year. Request the most current information from the IRS to use in any actual payroll calculations that you perform. According to law, the employer is always liable for the full amounts of taxes that should have been withheld from an employee's pay, whether or not the employer withholds the correct amount.

ILLUSTRATION 12-4 Federal Withholding Tax Tables[5]

Table 1—WEEKLY Payroll Period

(a) SINGLE person (including head of household)—

If the amount of wages (after subtracting withholding allowances) is:		The amount of income tax to withhold is:	
Not over $49. . . . . . $0			
Over—	**But not over—**		**of excess over—**
$49	—$451 . . .	14%	—$49
$451	—$942 . . .	$60.30 plus 28%	—$451
$942 .	. . . . .	$197.78 plus 31%	—$942

(b) MARRIED person—

If the amount of wages (after subtracting withholding allowances) is:		The amount of income tax to withhold is:	
Not over $119. . . . . . $0			
Over—	**But not over—**		**of excess over—**
$119	—$784 . . .	15%	—$119
$784	—$1,563 . . .	$99.75 plus 28%	—$784
$1,563.	. . . . . .	$317.87 plus 31%	—$1,563

Table 4—MONTHLY Payroll Period

(a) SINGLE person (including head of household)—

If the amount of wages (after subtracting withholding allowances) is:		The amount of income tax to withhold is:	
Not over $210 . . . . . $0			
Over—	**But not over—**		**of excess over—**
$210	—$1,954 . . .	14%	—$210
$1,954	—$4,081 . . .	$261.60 plus 28%	—$1,954
$4,081	. . . . . .	$857.16 plus 31%	—$4,081

(b) MARRIED person—

If the amount of wages (after subtracting withholding allowances) is:		The amount of income tax to withhold is:	
Not over $517 . . . . . $0			
Over—	**But not over—**		**of excess over—**
$517	—$3,396 . . .	15%	—$517
$3,396	—$6,771 . . .	$431.85 plus 28%	—$3,396
$6,771.	. . . . . .	$1,376.85 plus 31%	—$6,771

hospital portion, and the separate social security tax finances the other benefits. The Federal Insurance Contributions Act (FICA) requires that both employees and employers pay separate social security and Medicare taxes to the System.

We will assume that for 19X1 employers must *withhold* and pay to the federal government 6.2% of the first $57,600 of wages and salaries earned by each of their employees for social security and 1.45% of the first $135,000 for Medicare.[6] The employer must also match both taxes. Reconsider the example of Fred Phillips who earned $404.88 in the last week of March, 19X1. Fashion Ready-Wear would withhold from his pay for the week $25.10 ($404.88 x .062) for social security and $5.87 ($404.88 x .0145) for Medicare. Fashion Ready-Wear would match these amounts but would not deduct them from Fred's pay.

To summarize the weekly payroll events recognized so far for Fred Phillips and Fashion Ready-Wear, we begin to keep a score card. As additional withholdings, payroll taxes, and employee benefits are introduced below, the score card will be updated until Fred's net pay and Fashion Ready-Wear's total expense are calculated.

---

[5]"Employer's Tax Guide," *Circular E* (Department of the Treasury: Internal Revenue Service, Revised December, 1992), p. 26. The withholding tax amounts and rates in this table, which we use here for illustration only, are the actual amounts and rates that applied to payrolls of 1993. They should not be used for any other year. Request the most current information from the IRS to use in any actual payroll calculations that you perform. According to law, the employer is always liable for the full amounts of taxes that should have been withheld from an employee's pay, whether or not the employer withholds the correct amount.

[6]"Employer's Tax Guide," *Circular E* (Department of the Treasury: Internal Revenue Service, Revised December, 1992), p. 14. These rates and limits, which we use here for illustration only, are the actual rates and limits that applied to payrolls of 1993. They should not be used for any other year. Request the most current information from the IRS to use in any actual payroll calculations that you perform. According to law, the employer is always liable for the full amounts of taxes that should have been withheld from an employee's pay, whether or not the employer withholds the correct amount.

Fred Phillips: Gross Pay, Withholdings, and Net Pay		Fashion Ready-Wear: Wages and Salaries Expense, Payroll Taxes, and Employee Benefits	
Gross pay	$404.88	Wages and salaries expense	$404.88
Federal withholding tax	15.77		
Employee's social security tax	25.10	Employer's social security tax	25.10
Employee's Medicare tax	5.87	Employer's Medicare tax	5.87

State and Local Income (Withholding) Tax

Forty-four of the 50 states and the District of Columbia have individual income taxes. Many cities such as New York and Detroit also levy income taxes. Thus, there is a variety of tax rates and methods of calculation of income tax liabilities and withholding taxes. For purposes of illustration, assume no local income taxes, the basis for withholding state income tax is the same as federal income tax, and the state tax rates are one-tenth of the federal rates. This implies that Fashion Ready-Wear should withhold $1.58 of state income tax from Fred Phillips' gross pay (.1 x $15.77).

Federal and State Unemployment Taxes

Both the states and the federal government have unemployment compensation programs to provide a period of minimum payments to eligible workers who are involuntarily unemployed. The tax rate under the Federal Unemployment Tax Act (FUTA) is 6.2% of the first $7,000 earned annually by each employee. It is a tax levied on the employer, not the employee. Therefore, it is not withheld from the employee's gross pay, but it is an additional expense of the employer. State unemployment tax (SUTA) rates vary. Up to 5.4% of a state tax rate may be offset against the federal tax, provided the state tax is levied on the employer, not deducted from employees' wages and salaries. For example, at this writing, the State of Texas charges a state unemployment tax rate of only 2.7%. Thus, the federal rate for Texas employers is 3.5% (6.2% − 2.7%). Many other states charge the full 5.4% allowed to be offset against the federal rate, making the effective federal rate .8%. Many of these same states charge even higher rates to employers (industries) with unstable employment histories. However, only the first 5.4% may be offset against the federal rate in such cases.

Fred Phillips and Fashion Ready-Wear are in a state that levies a SUTA rate of 5.4%. Assuming that Fred has not yet earned more than $7,000, Fashion Ready-Wear would accrue a SUTA expense for the last week in March, 19X1, of $21.86 ($404.88 x .054) and a FUTA expense of $3.24 ($404.88 x .008).

Workers' Compensation Insurance

All 50 states make employers responsible for the financial consequences (within limits) of injury to or death of workers on the job. Forty-seven of the 50 states require that employers insure their workers against the losses that may occur due to work-related injuries and deaths. Of these, 14 states have state workers' compensation funds within the state institutions. In the remaining 33 states, employers secure workers' compensation insurance from private insurance companies or group self-insurance funds.

In many cases, the workers' compensation insurance premiums involve a fixed charge per-employee-per-year plus a small percentage of each period's gross pay. For simplicity, however, we assume that Fashion Ready-Wear's insurance company charges a premium of 0.25% of gross pay for each employee for each weekly payroll period. The premium for Fred Phillips for the last week of March is $1.01 ($404.88 x .0025). Updated now for state withholding tax, SUTA, FUTA, and the workers' compensation insurance premium, the score card looks like this:

Fred Phillips: Gross Pay, Withholdings, Deductions, and Net Pay		Fashion Ready-Wear: Wages and Salaries Expense, Payroll Taxes, and Employee Benefits	
Gross pay	$404.88	Wages and salaries expense	$404.88
Federal withholding tax	15.77		
Employee's social security tax	25.10	Employer's social security tax	25.10
Employee's Medicare tax	5.87	Employer's Medicare tax	5.87
State withholding tax	1.58		
		SUTA	21.86
		FUTA	3.24
		Workers' compensation insurance	1.01

Group Insurance Benefits

Many employers, even small businesses, arrange with insurance companies for group life, accident, disability, medical, and dental insurance for their employees. The employer also often pays all or part of the insurance premiums. This transfers all or part of the premium cost from a deduction from the employee's gross pay to an employee benefit cost of the employer.[7]

To illustrate, suppose Fashion Ready-Wear has arranged the group insurance options displayed in Illustration 12-5. Assume that Fred Phillips elects Option 2 for medical insurance, Options 3 and 4 for life insurance (with $100,000 coverage on himself and $10,000 on his spouse), and Options 5 and 6 for disability and accident insurance, respectively. The costs to him and to Fashion Ready-Wear can be calculated as follows:

Option	Coverage	Cost	Fashion Ready-Wear's Share	Fred Phillips' Share
2	Employee and family	$25	$15.00	$10.00
3	$100,000 plus	100 x $.05 = $5.00	2.00	3.00
4	$10,000 (spouse)	10 x $.04 = $0.40	0.00	0.40
5	$15,000	15 x $.20 = $3.00	0.00	3.00
6	Accident insurance	$2/week	2.00	0.00
Totals			$19.00	$16.40

---

[7]Employer payments above certain limits for group life insurance and other benefits, while not part of the gross or net pay of the employee, are subject to income tax (and withholding), social security tax, and Medicare tax. Consult the IRS for documents detailing these tax provisions.

ILLUSTRATION 12-5 Fashion Ready-Wear—Benefits Summary

Option	Description	Coverage	Cost	Fashion Ready-Wear's Share
1	Medical insurance A	Employee only	$15/wk.	$15/wk.
2	Medical insurance B	Employee and family	$25/wk.	$15/wk.
3	Life insurance A	Employee—up to $100,000	$.05/wk./$1,000	first $2/wk.
4	Life insurance B	Spouse up to $10,000	$.04/wk./$1,000	-0-
5	Disability insurance	Up to 70% of previous year's income	$.20/wk./$1,000	-0-
6	Accident insurance	Varies, depending on injuries	$2/wk.	100%

Supplemental Pension Contributions

Employers have incentives to set up pension programs for their employees to supplement social security benefits upon retirement. Such programs, along with insurance programs and other benefits, may be negotiated with employers by labor unions. In other cases, the employers voluntarily set up pension plans to improve employee recruiting, retention, and morale.

Pension plans are almost as varied as the firms that set them up for their employees. Some are simply paternalistic plans in which the employers continue to pay employees after the employees retire—usually at some percentage of what they earned while still working. Others are more formal, providing specific rights to the employees. One version of a formal plan is a **defined-benefit pension plan**. Typically, such plans promise employees specific retirement benefits. The specific amounts of benefits are based on their lengths of service with the employer at retirement and their levels of earnings in a period prior to retirement. A simple, defined-benefit formula, for instance, might offer annual retirement incomes equal to 25% of employees' last two years' average earnings plus an additional 1% for each year worked with the employer. Under this plan, an employee who worked for the employer for 30 years and earned $25,000 in his/her second-to-last year and $29,000 in the last year would receive a pension of $14,850 per year:

Last year's earnings	$29,000
Previous year's earnings	25,000
Total	$54,000
	÷ 2
Average of last two years' earnings	$27,000
Retirement income percent 25% + (1% x 30 years)	x 55%
Retirement income	$14,850

An alternative to a defined-benefit plan is a **defined-contribution pension plan** in which the employer sets aside, or pays to an insurance or investment company, a specific amount each pay period, based on the employee's earnings. These amounts are invested and accumulated on behalf of the employee who then uses them at retirement to provide a retirement income.

Fashion Ready-Wear has a defined-contribution pension plan. It pays an amount equal to 5% of each employee's gross pay to an insurance company each pay period. The insurance company keeps a separate account for each employee and guarantees a minimum rate of interest on all contributions. The insurance company also permits employees to contribute fixed percentages of their earnings from their gross pay, provided Fashion Ready-Wear withholds and remits the amounts each pay period. Fashion Ready-Wear requires its employees to contribute 3% of their gross pay each week. For the last week of March 19X1, Fred's retirement contributions are $20.24 from Fashion Ready-Wear ($404.88 x .05) and $12.15 deducted from his gross pay ($404.88 x .03).

When the score sheet is updated for the various insurance coverages and pension contributions, the result is:

Fred Phillips: Gross Pay, Withholdings, Deductions, and Net Pay		Fashion Ready-Wear: Wages and Salaries Expense, Payroll Taxes, and Employee Benefits	
Gross pay	$404.88	Wages and salaries expense	$404.88
Federal withholding tax	15.77		
Employee's social security tax	25.10	Employer's social security tax	25.10
Employee's Medicare tax	5.87	Employer's Medicare tax	5.87
State withholding tax	1.58		
		SUTA	21.86
		FUTA	3.24
		Workers' compensation insurance	1.01
Medical insurance	10.00	Medical insurance	15.00
Life insurance	3.40	Life insurance	2.00
Disability insurance	3.00		
		Accident insurance	2.00
Pension contribution	12.15	Pension contribution	20.24

Vacation Pay and Sick Pay

Most employers provide their employees with incomes during vacations and brief illnesses when the employees do not perform services. Frequently, employees are credited in advance with vacation pay and sick pay in direct relationship to the services they perform and/or the gross pay they earn. For example, an employer may award salaried employees 1.75 vacation days and 1 sick day for each month worked. After working 12 months, an employee would have accumulated 21 working days of vacation (enough for one calendar month of fun) and 12 working days of sick pay. Hourly employees might be credited with vacation pay and sick pay equal to 5% and 4% of their gross pay, respectively, each payroll period. After working 50 weeks at 40 hours per week, an hourly worker would have accumulated vacation pay equal to more than 2 week's full-time earnings and would be protected with 8 full days of sick pay.

As these formulas imply, sick pay and vacation pay are part of the costs for the services that employees perform. Therefore, an employer should accrue the costs of vacation and sick pay as expenses as regular payrolls are tabulated and recorded, not when employees go on vacation or sick leave.

Assuming that Fashion Ready-Wear uses the 5%/4% vacation/sick pay formulas described above, the accruals for Fred Phillips for the last week of March would be $20.24 ($404.88 x .05) and $16.20 ($404.88 x .04), respectively. Illustration 12-6 shows the completed score card.

ILLUSTRATION 12-6 Fred Phillips Weekly Payroll Calculations

Fred Phillips: Gross Pay, Withholdings, Deductions, and Net Pay		Fashion Ready-Wear: Wages and Salaries Expense, Payroll Taxes, and Employee Benefits	
Gross pay	$404.88	Wages and salaries expense	$404.88
Federal withholding tax	15.77		
Employee's social security tax	25.10	Employer's social security tax	25.10
Employee's Medicare tax	5.87	Employer's Medicare tax	5.87
State withholding tax	1.58		
		SUTA	21.86
		FUTA	3.24
		Workers' compensation insurance	1.01
Medical insurance	10.00	Medical insurance	15.00
Life insurance	3.40	Life insurance	2.00
Disability insurance	3.00		
		Accident insurance	2.00
Pension contribution	12.15	Pension contribution	20.24
		Accrued vacation pay	20.24
		Accrued sick pay	16.20
		Employer payroll expense	$132.76
Net pay	$328.01		
		Total payroll-related expenses	$537.64

LO 7
Prepare the payroll-related
journal entries.

PAYROLL-RELATED JOURNAL ENTRIES

Having calculated Fred Phillips' gross pay (wages and salaries expense) and net pay and Fashion Ready-Wear's payroll-related expenses, we can now illustrate the entries to record them. Wages and salaries expense and the related liabilities can be recorded from the calculation of net pay on the left-hand side of Illustration 12-6:

19X1				
Mar. 31	Wages and Salaries Expense	404.88	
	Federal Withholding Taxes Payable		15.77
	Social Security Taxes Payable		25.10
	Medicare Taxes Payable		5.87
	State Withholding Taxes Payable		1.58
	Medical Insurance Premiums Payable		10.00
	Life Insurance Premiums Payable		3.40
	Disability Premiums Payable		3.00
	Pension Contributions Payable		12.15
	Wages and Salaries Payable		328.01
	To record wages and salaries expense and related liabilities for the week ended March 31.		

Fashion Ready-Wear's payroll-related expenses are recorded from the right-hand side of Illustration 12-6:

Mar. 31	Employer Payroll Expense	132.76	
	Social Security Taxes Payable		25.10
	Medicare Taxes Payable		5.87
	SUTA Taxes Payable		21.86
	FUTA Taxes Payable		3.24
	Workers' Compensation Insurance Payable		1.01
	Medical Insurance Premiums Payable		15.00
	Life Insurance Premiums Payable		2.00
	Accident Insurance Premiums Payable		2.00
	Pension Contributions Payable		20.24
	Accrued Vacation Pay		20.24
	Accrued Sick Pay		16.20
	To record employer payroll expense and related liabilities for the week ended March 31.		

While we have illustrated a single journal entry for all payroll-related expenses, many businesses record certain of these expenses—for example, pension expense and vacation and sick pay expenses—as separate expenses to track them individually. Assuming Fashion Ready-Wear followed this practice, the separate entries would be made as follows:

19X1			
Mar. 31	Employer Payroll Expense	76.08	
	Social Security Taxes Payable		25.10
	Medicare Taxes Payable		5.87
	SUTA Taxes Payable		21.86
	FUTA Taxes Payable		3.24
	Workers' Compensation Insurance Payable		1.01
	Medical Insurance Premiums Payable		15.00
	Life Insurance Premiums Payable		2.00
	Accident Insurance Premiums Payable		2.00
	To record employer payroll expense and related liabilities for the week ended March 31.		
31	Pension Expense	20.24	
	Pension Contributions Payable		20.24
	To record pension expense for the week ended March 31.		
31	Vacation Pay Expense	20.24	
	Accrued Vacation Pay		20.24
	To record vacation pay expense for the week ended March 31.		
31	Sick Pay Expense	16.20	
	Accrued Sick Pay		16.20
	To record sick pay expense for the week ended March 31.		

Employers pay payroll-related liabilities to employees and other entities owed at varying intervals. Employees are issued pay envelopes or payroll checks shortly after their pay is calculated and recored. Fashion Ready-Wear calculates and records its hourly payroll during the week immediately following each workweek and pays its employees at the end of that week. The entry to record payment of Fred Phillips for work performed in the last week of March would be as follows:

19X1			
Apr. 7	Wages and Salaries Payable	328.01	
	Cash		328.01
	To record issue of payroll check to Fred Phillips for work performed in the week ended March 31.		

Fashion Ready-Wear pays all other payroll-related liabilities when payments are due to the respective payees. The entries are similar to the entry to record the payment of the combined pension contribution of $32.39 ($20.24 employer's contribution plus $12.15 employee's contribution) for Fred Phillips for the last week of March:

Apr. 7	Pension Contributions Payable	32.39	
	Cash		32.39
	To pay pension contributions of Fred Phillips for work performed in the week ended March 31.		

As the opening scenario of this chapter implies, the Social Security Administration and the Internal Revenue Service expect employers to pay their withholding, social security, and Medicare tax payments on a timely basis. In general, the more an employer accumulates in taxes payable to these two agencies, the more promptly the amounts must be paid after the end of any given payroll period. For example, if on any day an employer has accumulated $100,000 or more of unpaid taxes, it must pay the taxes on the next day. At the other extreme, if an employer accumulates less than $500 at the end of a payroll period, it may carry over the amount to the next payroll period. All other employers must pay either semiweekly or monthly, depending on the size of their payments in the recent past.[8]

LO 8

Calculate and interpret the number of days-purchases-in-payables and the percent utilization of a line of credit.

ANALYZING AND INTERPRETING INFORMATION ABOUT CURRENT LIABILITIES

Let us now return to the basic problem that Katherine Schmidt faces. As she looks forward to the peak selling season, she needs:

1. Sufficient financing to purchase a large quantity of inventory and
2. Postponement of repayment over a sufficient period to recover cash from the sales of the seasonal inventory to repay the financing.

She believes the bank line of credit is her best source of financing because the terms fit her needs and the line of credit is already arranged. However, this special financing will allow her to meet her out-of-pocket expenses such as wages and salaries, payroll taxes, and employee benefits only if the business is in good financial condition going into the peak season. To determine Fashion Ready-Wear's short-term financial condition going into the peak season, Katherine wants some diagnostic tools to indicate whether the business is up-to-date in paying its bills and has borrowing power in its line of credit. Illustration 12-7 shows the financial statements of Fashion Ready-Wear for October 19X1.

---

[8]See the current version of "Employer's Tax Guide," Circular E, published by the Internal Revenue Service.

ILLUSTRATION 12-7 Fashion Ready-Wear's Financial Statements

Fashion Ready-Wear
Income Statement
For the Month Ended October 31, 19X1

Net sales	$150,000
Cost of goods sold	75,000
Gross profit	$ 75,000
Expenses	65,000
Net income	$ 10,000

Fashion Ready-Wear
Balance Sheet
September 30 and October 31, 19X1

	Sept. 30		Oct. 31	
Assets				
Cash		$ 10,000		$ 40,000
Accounts receivable		90,000		80,000
Inventory		75,000		70,000
Store equipment	$200,000		$200,000	
Less: Accumulated depreciation	122,000	78,000	125,000	75,000
Total assets		$253,000		$265,000
Liabilities and Owner's Equity				
Accounts payable		$ 30,000		$ 20,000
Notes payable—bank		20,000		10,000
Wages and salaries payable		6,000		5,000
Payroll taxes and employee benefits payable		3,000		2,000
Owner's capital		194,000		228,000
Total liabilities and owner's equity		$253,000		$265,000

Days-Purchases-in-Payables

Two indicators of short-term financial condition are **days-purchases-in-payables** and **percent utilization of a line of credit**. The former can be used to infer how promptly a business has been paying its accounts payable; the latter can be used to determine whether credit is available to the business when it needs it.

To calculate days-purchases-in-payables, you must first calculate purchases. This is often the case when businesses do not publish financial statements with the full detail of cost of goods sold included. To calculate purchases (cost of goods purchased), recall the following calculation of cost of goods sold from an earlier chapter:

INSIGHTS INTO ACCOUNTING

As we pointed out earlier, the payroll function is very similar from business to business. Thus, independent payroll processing firms have been formed to meet the payroll needs of other businesses. By specializing, these independent payroll processors become very expert in handling payroll problems and they are able to afford larger computers and better software than their clients. The following advertisement from the March 1994 *Journal of Accountancy* illustrates this point.

Beginning inventory (BI)
Add: Purchases (P)

Cost of goods available for sale
Less: Ending inventory (EI)

Cost of goods sold (COGS)

In symbol form, the relationship is:

$$P + BI - EI = COGS$$

We solve this equation for cost of purchases (P), thusly:

$$P = COGS - BI + EI, \text{ or}$$

$$P = COGS + (EI - BI), \text{ or}$$

$$P = COGS + \text{(Change in Inventory)}$$

In other words, since goods purchased are either sold during the period or remain in ending inventory at the end of the period, purchases equals cost of goods sold plus any increase in inventory. When purchases are less than cost of goods sold, the business draws down its inventory to make sales. Then, purchases equals cost of goods sold less the decrease in inventory. Thus, Ready-Wear's purchases for October must have been:

$$\text{Purchases} = \$75,000 + (\$70,000 - \$75,000)$$

$$\text{Purchases} = \$75,000 + (-\$5,000) = \$70,000$$

Now, using the calculated purchases figure, we determine the days-purchases-in-payables using the following equation:

$$\text{Days-Purchases-in-Payables} = \frac{\text{Accounts Payable Balance}}{\text{Purchases}} \times \text{Days in Period}$$

$$\text{Days-Purchases-in-Payables} = \frac{\$20,000}{\$70,000} \times 31 \text{ days} = 8.86 \text{ days}$$

The value of 8.86 days tells us that the Accounts Payable balance of $20,000 is equal to approximately 9 days purchases, or that the accounts are, on average, about 9 days old. Since Fashion Ready-Wear buys on terms of 2/10, n/30, accounts that are, on average, 9 days old are within the 10-day discount period. We interpret this information as favorable, since it implies that Fashion Ready-Wear has had the ability to pay its accounts on a timely basis and not lose purchases discounts.

As you can see, the days-purchases-in-payables is a useful diagnostic tool, especially when the terms of purchases are known. However, a word of caution is in order. Note that the number of days-purchases-in-payables and the age of the payables are average figures. Both are based on the average day's purchases for the period. They can be quite accurate when applied to one month's data. However, purchases may fluctuate significantly over a period as long as a year, especially in a seasonal business. Therefore, great caution should be used in making inferences from annual calculations.

Percent Utilization of a Line of Credit

The percent utilization of a line of credit is a straightforward indicator. We calculate it as follows:

$$\text{Percent Utilization} = \frac{\text{Loan Balance}}{\text{Maximum Available Loan}} \times 100\%$$

For a revolving line of credit such as Fashion Ready-Wear has arranged, the maximum available loan is the flexible loan limit or the absolute limit, whichever is less. Fashion Ready-Wear's bank has agreed to loan it amounts up to 50% of its inventory total and 50% of its accounts receivable—but not to exceed $200,000. We calculate the flexible limit on October 31 as follows:

$$(.5 \times \$70,000) + (.5 \times \$80,000) = \$75,000$$

Since the flexible limit is less than the absolute limit of $200,000, it is used in calculating the percent utilization:

$$\text{Percent Utilization} = \frac{\$10,000}{\$75,000} \times 100\% = 13.3\%$$

The value of 13.3% tells us that the revolving line of credit is not being heavily utilized as of October 31 and that a significant borrowing capacity is ready for utilization as the peak selling season approaches.

Together, the approximately 9 days-purchases-in-payables, the relatively low utilization of the line of credit, and the cash balance of $40,000 (up from $10,000 at the end of September) imply that Fashion Ready-Wear is in relatively good condition to enter the peak selling season. To achieve a more precise conclusion would require an analysis of expected cash inflows (including borrowings) and outflows (including interest and repayments).

SUMMARY

Describe the various types of current liabilities that businesses incur and the factors that affect which ones they utilize. Liabilities are a business's obligations to provide assets or services to other businesses or individuals in the future. They arise out of present and past activities or transactions. Many liabilities are quite definite—however, two types of liabilities are not so definite, estimated liabilities and contingent liabilities. Current liabilities are those that must be satisfied within one year or within one operating cycle, whichever is longer. Typical current liabilities include accounts payable, short-term notes payable, short-term bank loans, wages and salaries payable, payroll taxes payable, income taxes payable, and the current portion of long-term debt. The factors that affect whether a firm should borrow from one source of credit versus another are interest costs and other terms, loan arrangement costs, collateral requirements, and creditor restrictions on the business.

Calculate the interest rate implicit in losing discounts on accounts payable. To find the effective (equivalent) annual interest rate for discounts lost, use the following formula:

$$\text{Effective Annual Rate} = \text{Discount Rate} \times \frac{365 \text{ days}}{\text{Additional Days to Payment}}$$

Account for short-term notes payable. Accounting for short-term notes payable consists of three stages. First, record the liability at time of issue, including a discount for noninterest-bearing notes. Second, accrue interest or amortize the discount on financial statement dates that come before the note is paid. Finally, recognize payment of the note along with any accrued interest.

Account for short-term bank loans.   Accounting for short-term bank loans is comparable to accounting for short-term notes payable. However, bank loans often require monthly or quarterly payment of interest.

Describe payroll expense liability relationships.   You should keep three important payroll relationships in mind. First, net pay is equal to gross pay minus (a) *withholdings* for federal income taxes, federal social security and Medicare taxes, state income taxes, and local taxes (if any), and (b) *deductions* for insurance premiums and employee contributions to pension programs. Second, an employer's total payroll-related expenses consist of the employees' gross pay *plus* the employer's payroll taxes *plus* the employer's contributions to the insurance, pension, and other "benefit" programs of their employees *plus* accrued vacation and sick pay. Third, payroll expenses *for a period* equal the related credits to payroll liabilities *as of the end of the payroll period.*

Calculate an employee's gross pay, withholdings, deductions, and net pay and an employer's payroll-related costs.   We calculate an employee's gross wages by simply multiplying the employee's hourly rate of pay by the hours worked— using the overtime multiple for overtime hours. Net pay equals gross pay less withholdings and deductions. Employer payroll-related expenses consist of employer payroll taxes, employer contributions to employee benefits, and accrued vacation and sick pay.

Prepare the payroll-related journal entries.   Payroll related journal entries include: an entry to record wages and salaries expense (gross pay), withholdings, deductions, and the related liabilities; at least one entry to record employer payroll expense and the related liabilities for taxes payable, contributions payable to benefit programs, and accrued vacation and sick pay; and multiple entries to recognize the payment of the various liabilities when they are due.

Calculate and interpret the number of days-purchases-in-payables and the percent utilization of a line of credit.   Days-purchases-in-payables is calculated according to this formula:

$$\text{Days-Purchases-in-Payables} = \frac{\text{Accounts Payable Balance}}{\text{Purchases}} \times \text{Days in Period}$$

Where the cost of purchases (P) is calculated as follows, if it is not given directly in the income statement:

$$P = COGS + (\text{Change in Inventory})$$

The percent utilization of a line of credit is a straightforward indicator. We calculate it as follows:

$$\text{Percent Utilization} = \frac{\text{Loan Balance}}{\text{Maximum Available Loan}} \times 100\%$$

APPENDIX 12-A: PAYROLL RECORDS AND PROCESSING

LO 9
Describe the types of special journals and other records used by businesses to facilitate payroll accounting and reporting.

SPECIAL JOURNALS FOR PROCESSING PAYROLL EXPENSES

It should be obvious from the chapter that many calculations are required to prepare a typical payroll. The score card in Illustration 12-6 illustrates this point for just one hypothetical employee. Thus, it is necessary to have recording devices to organize the calculation of payroll expenses and payroll liabilities. Illustrations 12-8, 12-9, and 12-10, respectively, show a payroll register, an employer payroll expense register, and an employee earnings record. The **payroll register** is a special journal used to record employees' gross wages (salaries), withholdings, deductions, and net pay. The **employer payroll expense register** is the special journal used to record all the payroll expenses *other than* the employees' gross wages and salaries expense.

Besides these special journals (registers), employers must keep individual employee earnings records. An **employee earnings record** is a "history" or "diary" of the individual employee's earnings, withholdings, and deductions, recorded by pay period and often cumulatively from the beginning of the year. Illustration 12-10 is the 19X1 employee earnings record of Fred Phillips, with entries through March 31. Notice that each line records the facts of one week's wages, withholdings, and deductions. Also, beginning with gross wages, a column for the amount applicable to the particular week and a column for the cumulative or year-to-date (YTD) total are included.

An earnings record of this kind is essential for employers to comply with at least one legal requirement. Under the Internal Revenue Code, employers must supply each of their employees with a Form W-2 for each year by January 31 of the following year. These Forms W-2 report the employees' wages and salaries subject to withholding tax, the amounts withheld, the amounts of wages subject to social security tax (up to the applicable limit), the amounts of wages subject to Medicare tax (up to the applicable limit), and the amounts of social secutity and Medicare taxes withheld for the previous calendar year. Copies of the forms are filed with the Social Security Administration. Businesses must keep the backup information underlying the Forms W-2 for 4 years for possible IRS review. Moreover, employers covered by the Fair Labor Standards Act of 1938 must keep records on regular, overtime, and total wages and salaries on all employees for three years. These requirements are met or compliance is facilitated (at least in part) by keeping employee earnings records like the one in Illustration 12-10.

LO 10
Describe the applications of computers to payroll accounting.

APPLICATIONS OF COMPUTERS TO PAYROLLS

Because payrolls involve many repetitive calculations, some of which are complex, opportunities exist for using computers effectively. Just a glance at the detail in Illustrations 12-8, 12-9, and 12-10 and your knowledge of the many underlying calculations should tell you that such records would be difficult to maintain by hand, within reasonable cost and acceptable accuracy. In fact, Illustrations 12-8, 12-9, and 12-10 were prepared by computer.

ILLUSTRATION 12-8 Payroll Register

FASHION READY-WEAR
Payroll Register

DATE	EMPLOYEE	SOC. SEC. NO.	WORK-WEEK ENDED	TOTAL HOURS	HOURLY RATE	GROSS WAGES	WITHHOLDINGS AND DEDUCTIONS								NET PAY	CHECK NO.
							FEDERAL W/H TAX	SOC. SEC. TAX	MEDICARE TAX	STATE W/H TAX	MED. INS.	LIFE INS.	DISABILITY INS.	PENSION CONTRIB.		
03/31/X1	Year-to-Date Totals					45,856.13	2,746.42	3,330.89	664.99	274.98	639.00	225.78	336.54	1,375.98	37,263.08	
04/07/X1	Fredrick A. Phillips	555-66-7777	03/31/X1	39.5	10.25	404.88	15.77	25.10	5.87	1.58	10.00	3.40	3.00	12.15	328.01	40703
04/07/X1	Jane M. Frost	999-00-1111	03/31/X1	41.5	10.75	454.19	23.16	34.11	6.59	2.32	10.00	2.90	3.20	13.63	358.28	40704
04/07/X1	Mary K. Brown	111-22-3333	03/31/X1	40.0	8.33	333.20	35.85	25.02	4.83	3.59	0.00	0.50	2.40	10.00	251.01	40705
04/07/X1	Roberta F. Franklin	666-77-8888	03/31/X1	40.0	11.25	450.00	36.09	33.80	6.53	3.61	0.00	0.40	3.60	13.50	352.47	40706
04/07/X1	John J. Washington	444-55-6666	03/31/X1	44.0	11.10	510.60	18.07	38.35	7.40	1.81	10.00	3.40	3.60	15.32	412.65	40707
04/07/X1	Week Totals		03/31/X1			2,152.87	128.94	156.38	31.22	12.91	30.00	10.60	15.80	64.60	1,702.42	
04/07/X1	Year-to-Date Totals					48,009.00	2,875.36	3,487.27	696.21	287.89	669.00	236.38	352.34	1,440.58	38,965.50	

ILLUSTRATION 12-9 Employer Payroll Expense Register

FASHION READY-WEAR
Employer Payroll Expense Register

DATE	EMPLOYEE	SOC. SEC. NO.	WORK-WEEK ENDED	PAYROLL TAXES					BENEFITS						TOTAL
				SOC. SEC. TAX	MEDICARE TAX	SUTA	FUTA	WORK. COMP.	MED. INS.	ACCIDENT INS.	LIFE INS.	PENSION CONTRIB.	ACCRUED VAC. PAY	ACCRUED SICK PAY	
03/31/X1	Year-to-Date Totals			3,330.89	664.99	2,476.13	367.00	114.81	1,597.50	213.00	213.00	2,292.73	2,292.73	1,834.36	15,397.13
04/07/X1	Fredrick A. Phillips	555-66-7777	03/31/X1	25.10	5.87	21.86	3.24	1.01	15.00	2.00	2.00	20.24	20.24	16.20	132.76
04/07/X1	Jane M. Frost	999-00-1111	03/31/X1	34.11	6.59	24.53	3.63	1.14	15.00	2.00	2.00	22.71	22.71	18.17	152.59
04/07/X1	Mary K. Brown	111-22-3333	03/31/X1	25.02	4.83	17.99	2.67	0.83	15.00	2.00	2.00	16.66	16.66	13.33	116.99
04/07/X1	Roberta F. Franklin	666-77-8888	03/31/X1	33.80	6.53	24.30	3.60	1.13	15.00	2.00	2.00	22.50	22.50	18.00	151.36
04/07/X1	John J. Washington	444-55-6666	03/31/X1	38.35	7.40	27.57	4.09	1.28	15.00	2.00	2.00	25.53	25.53	20.42	169.17
04/07/X1	Week Totals		03/31/X1	156.38	31.22	116.25	17.23	5.39	75.00	10.00	10.00	107.64	107.64	86.12	722.87
04/07/X1	Year-to-Date Totals			3,487.27	696.21	2,592.38	384.23	120.20	1,672.50	223.00	223.00	2,400.37	2,400.37	1,920.48	16,120.01

ILLUSTRATION 12-10 Employee Earnings Record

Employee Earnings Record

Employee Name: Fredrick A. Phillips
Social Security Number: 555-66-7777

Address: 123 4th Street
Anytown, Anystate 00000

Department: Maintenance
Title: Operating Engineer

Authorized Wage Rate

Date	Rate	Initials
05/01/19X0	10.10	rak
03/01/19X1	10.25	rak

	EMPLOYEE PAY				WITHHOLDINGS AND DEDUCTIONS																	
			GROSS WAGES		FED. W/H TAX		SOC. SEC. TAX		MEDICARE TAX		ST. W/H TAX		MED INS.		LIFE INS.		DISAB'TY INS.		PENS. CONTR.		ACC. VAC. PAY		ACC. SICK PAY	
WEEK ENDED	REGULAR WAGES	OVER-TIME	WEEK	YTD	WEEK	YTD	WEEK	YTD	WEEK	YTD	WEEK	YTD	WEEK	YTD	WEEK	YTD	WEEK	YTD	WEEK	YTD	WEEK	YTD	WEEK	YTD
01/06/X1	404.00	10.10	414.10	414.10	17.15	17.15	25.67	25.67	6.00	6.00	1.72	1.72	10.00	10.00	3.40	3.40	3.00	3.00	12.42	12.42	20.71	126.76	16.56	420.56
01/13/X1	404.00	25.25	429.25	843.35	19.42	36.57	26.61	52.28	6.22	12.22	1.94	3.66	10.00	20.00	3.40	6.80	3.00	6.00	12.88	25.30	21.46	148.22	17.17	437.73
01/20/X1	404.00	20.20	424.20	1,267.55	18.67	55.24	26.30	78.58	6.15	18.37	1.87	5.53	10.00	30.00	3.40	10.20	3.00	9.00	12.73	38.03	21.21	169.43	16.97	454.70
01/27/X1	404.00	30.30	434.30	1,701.85	20.18	75.42	26.93	105.51	6.30	24.67	2.02	7.55	10.00	40.00	3.40	13.60	3.00	12.00	13.03	51.06	21.72	191.15	17.37	472.07
02/03/X1	393.90	0.00	393.90	2,095.75	14.12	89.54	24.42	129.93	5.71	30.38	1.41	8.96	10.00	50.00	3.40	17.00	3.00	15.00	11.82	62.88	19.70	210.85	15.76	487.83
02/10/X1	398.95	0.00	398.95	2,494.70	14.88	104.42	24.73	154.66	5.78	36.16	1.49	10.45	10.00	60.00	3.40	20.40	3.00	18.00	11.97	74.85	19.95	230.80	15.96	503.79
02/17/X1	404.00	50.50	454.50	2,949.20	23.21	127.63	28.18	182.84	6.59	42.75	2.32	12.77	10.00	70.00	3.40	23.80	3.00	21.00	13.64	88.49	22.73	253.53	18.18	521.97
02/24/X1	404.00	10.10	414.10	3,363.30	17.15	144.78	25.67	208.51	6.00	48.75	1.72	14.49	10.00	80.00	3.40	27.20	3.00	24.00	12.42	100.91	20.71	274.24	16.56	538.53
03/03/X1	404.00	15.15	419.15	3,782.45	17.91	162.69	25.99	234.50	6.08	54.83	1.79	16.28	10.00	90.00	3.40	30.60	3.00	27.00	12.57	113.48	20.96	295.20	16.77	555.30
03/10/X1	410.00	25.63	435.63	4,218.08	20.38	183.07	27.01	261.51	6.32	61.15	2.04	18.32	10.00	100.00	3.40	34.00	3.00	30.00	13.07	126.55	21.78	316.98	17.43	572.73
03/17/X1	410.00	5.13	415.13	4,633.21	17.31	200.38	25.74	287.25	6.02	67.17	1.73	20.05	10.00	110.00	3.40	37.40	3.00	33.00	12.45	139.00	20.76	337.74	16.61	589.34
03/24/X1	410.00	0.00	410.00	5,043.21	16.54	216.92	25.42	312.67	5.95	73.12	1.65	21.70	10.00	120.00	3.40	40.80	3.00	36.00	12.30	151.30	20.50	358.24	16.40	605.74
03/31/X1	404.88	0.00	404.88	5,448.09	15.77	232.69	25.10	337.77	5.87	78.99	1.58	23.28	10.00	130.00	3.40	44.20	3.00	39.00	12.15	163.45	20.24	378.48	16.20	621.94

Many payroll systems involve calculations such as those described in the chapter and records such as those illustrated in this Appendix, with the actual processing of payrolls being done by computer. Employee hours are entered onto a storage medium such as magnetic tape or disk to be read by a computer. The other inputs to the payroll-processing program are a file of all the up-to-date data about the employees, such as wage rates, withholding allowances, insurance choices, and a file of the most recent version of the employee earnings records—all on electronic tape or disk. The payroll-processing program reads these input files, calculates the payrolls, and produces the payroll register, employer payroll expense register, and the updated file of employee earnings records. The computer may also print the payroll checks and, in an "integrated system," may go so far as to post the payroll totals to the general ledger accounts.

In recent times, computers have been used to facilitate funds transfers as well. For example, employers may give their employees the option of having their net pay deposited directly in their checking accounts. To do this, the employer's payroll program creates an electronic tape or disk with employees' names, social security numbers, net pay amounts, banks, and checking account numbers. The electronic file is sent to the employer's bank. The bank's computer reads the file and transfers the appropriate amounts and account information to the employees' banks via the electronic funds transfer system and deducts from the employer's account the total net pay transferred.

Small employers have a choice about whether they use computers to prepare payrolls and transfer funds. However, large employers (with more than 250 employees) are required by the federal government to file Form W-2 information with the Social Security Administration on some form of computer-readable electronic medium.

REVIEW PROBLEM A:　SHORT-TERM NOTES PAYABLE

On May 1, 19X5, Mountain View Nursing Home borrowed $100,000 cash from the Colonial Bank and signed a $100,000, 90-day, 12% interest-bearing note dated May 1. On the same day, Mountain View Nursing Home purchased 50 special-care beds from Medical Technology for $200,000, paid $100,000 cash, and signed a 90-day, noninterest-bearing note dated May 1, with a face value of $102,958.90. Mountain View has a June 30 year-end.

REQUIRED:

a. Prepare journals entries to record the issue of the notes.
b. Prepare the necessary adjusting entries on June 30.
c. Show the presentation of the notes in the June 30 balance sheet.
d. Prepare the journal entries to record the payment of the notes.

SOLUTION:

Planning and Organizing Your Work

1. Determine what value you should assign to the notes in your entries to record them. Record interest-bearing notes in one account, Notes Payable, at their face values, which usually equal the values received in exchange for them. Record noninterest-bearing notes in two accounts. Record their face values, which equal their maturity values and include implicit interest, in Notes Payable. Record the difference between their face values and the values received in exchange for them in Discounts on Notes

Payable. Thus, in both cases, the initial carrying values of the notes equal the values received in exchange for them.

2. Write the journal entries to record the issuing of the notes.
3. Calculate interest accruals using the following formula for interest-bearing notes:

$$\text{Interest = Principal x Rate x Time}$$

or

$$\text{I = PRT}$$

where principal is the face amount of the note, rate the annual interest rate; and time the fraction of a year for which interest is being calculated.

Calculate interest accruals using the following formula for noninterest-bearing notes:

$$\text{Interest = Total Interest x } \frac{\text{Days}}{\text{Term}}$$

where total interest is the discount at issue or the difference between the face value of the note and the value exchanged for it, days the number of days for which you wish to calculate interest, and term the full term of the note in days.

4. Write the adjusting journal entries to accrue interest on the notes at June 30. Interest on interest-bearing notes is recorded in Interest Expense and Interest Payable; interest expense on noninterest-bearing notes reduces Discounts on Notes Payable.
5. Show the financial statement presentation of the notes. Show the notes' face values as notes payable in the current liabilities section of the balance sheet. In the case of an interest-bearing note, show the interest payable as a separate current liability. In the case of a noninterest-bearing note, offset the unamortized balance of the discount against the face value to show the carrying value of the note, which equals the original discounted value plus accrued interest to date.
6. Calculate the additional interest accruals through the maturity dates of the notes. Write journal entries to recognize the further (previously unaccrued) interest expense and the cash payment to pay off the notes in full.

(a) *Record the issue of notes.*

The issue of the May 1 note to Colonial Bank:

19X5			
May 1	Cash	100,000.00	
	Notes Payable		100,000.00
	To record issue of 90-day, 12%, $100,000 face value note to Colonial Bank.		

The interest on the Colonial note is not recorded on May 1 because no interest is owed at that date. Interest expense is incurred over the term of the note.

The issue of the May 1 note to Medical Technology:

May 1	Equipment	200,000.00	
	Discounts on Notes Payable	2,958.90	
	Cash		100,000.00
	Notes Payable		102,958.90
	To record issue of 90-day, $102,958.90 face value note to Medical Technology.		

The net amount of the note to Medical Technology is calculated as follows:

Cost of equipment	$200,000.00
Less: Cash paid	100,000.00
Net amount of note	$100,000.00

The difference between the face value of the note and the net amount of the note represents interest to be paid over the term of the note:

Face value of note	$102,958.90
Net amount of note	100,000.00
Interest to be paid over term of note	$ 2,958.90

Since the interest is not a liability at the time the note is issued (interest is incurred over the 90-day term of the note), the $2,958.90 is recorded in a contra-liability account, Discounts on Notes Payable, thus reducing the liability to the amount owed ($100,000) at the date the note is issued.

(b) *Prepare the adjusting entries on June 30.*
To adjust for the Colonial note:

19X5			
June 30	Interest Expense	1,972.60	
	Interest Payable		1,972.60
	To record accrual of interest expense.		
	[$100,000 x 12 x (60/365)] = $1,972.60		

To adjust for the Medical Technology note:

June 30	Interest Expense	1,972.60	
	Discounts on Notes Payable		1,972.60
	To record recognition of interest expense.		
	[$2,958.90 x (60/90)] = $1,972.60		

(c) *Show presentation of notes in balance sheet.*

Current Liabilities		
Notes payable—Colonial Bank		$100,000.00
Interest payable		1,972.60
Notes payable—Medical Technology	$102,958.90	
Less: Discounts on notes payable	986.30	101,972.60

The June 30 balance in Discounts on Notes Payable: $2,958.90 – $1,972.60 = $986.30.

(d) *Prepare journal entries for the payment of the notes.*
The payment of the Colonial note:

19X5			
July 30	Interest Expense (1)	986.30	
	Interest Payable (2)	1,972.60	
	Notes Payable	100,000.00	
	Cash		102,958.90
	To record payment of Colonial note.		

    (1) 100,000 x .12 x (30/365) = 986.30
    (2) 100,000 x .12 x (60/365) = 1,972.60
    (3) 100,000 + [100,000 x .12 x (90/365)] = 102,958.90

Due date of note: Count 90 days; do not include date of note (May 1); do include date of payment:

May	30 days (May 2 through May 31)
June	30 days (June 1 through June 30)
July	30 days (July 1 through July 30)
	90 days = July 30

The payment of the Medical Technology note:

July 30	Interest Expense (1)	986.30	
	Notes Payable	102,958.90	
	Discounts on Notes Payable (1)		986.30
	Cash		102,958.90
	To record payment of Medical Technology note.		

    (1) Amortize remaining amount of discount: $2,958.90 x (30/90)

REVIEW PROBLEM B: PAYROLL

Ann Clark, MD, is semiretired and maintains a part-time medical practice. Dr. Clark has one employee, Helen Rogers, a registered nurse who handles the nursing and administrative duties of the practice. Helen earns a salary of $2,500 per month and is paid monthly on the last day of the month. Dr. Clark has a paid vacation and sick pay plan that credits Helen with vacation pay and sick pay equal to 5% and 4% of her gross pay, respectively, each payroll period. Information related to the January 19X3, payroll is presented below:

Employee Withholdings:

Federal withholding tax	$250.00
State withholding tax	$75.00
Social security tax	6.2% of the first $57,600
Medicare tax	1.45% of the first $135,000
Medical insurance	$125
Pension	$150
Life insurance	$10

Employer Payroll Taxes and Employee Benefits:

State unemployment tax (SUTA)	5.4% of the first $7,000
Federal unemployment tax (FUTA)	.8% of the first $7,000
Social security tax	6.2% of the first $57,600
Medicare tax	1.45% of the first $135,000
Workers' compensation insurance	$6
Medical insurance	$125
Pension	$150
Vacation pay	5% of monthly salary
Sick pay	4% of monthly salary

REQUIRED:

a. Prepare the journal entry on January 31 to record the January salary expense and related liabilities for employee withholdings and employee net pay.
b. Prepare the journal entry on January 31 to record the employer payroll expenses for January. Use a single expense account for both employer payroll taxes and employer benefits.
c. Calculate the total cost of employer payroll taxes and employer benefits for January as a percentage of Helen's salary.

SOLUTION:

Planning and Organizing Your Work

1. Calculate the employee's required payments for social security and Medicare tax using the rates given times the gross salary. This is the payroll for the first month of the year, so the upper limits of the tax bases do not apply. Benefits deductions are given.
2. Write the journal entry to record the salary expense for the month and the related payroll liabilities.
3. Calculate the employer's social security, Medicare, SUTA, and FUTA taxes for January. Calculate the amounts of vacation pay and sick pay that should be accrued. The employer's contribution to benefits are given.
4. Write the journal entry to record the employer's payroll expense for the month and the related payroll liabilities.
5. You will have calculated the employer's total cost of payroll taxes and benefits in making the journal entry to record the employer's payroll expense for January. Divide that total (the debit to Employer Payroll Expense) by Helen's gross pay (the debit to Wages and Salaries Expense) to determine the percentage of the employer's other payroll costs to Helen's salary.

(a) *Prepare journal entry to record January salary.*

19X3			
Jan. 31	Wages and Salaries Expense (1)	2,500.00	
	Federal Withholding Taxes Payable (2)		250.00
	State Withholding Taxes Payable (3)		75.00
	Social Security Taxes Payable (4)		155.00
	Medicare Taxes Payable (5)		36.25
	Medical Insurance Premiums Payable (6)		125.00
	Pension Contributions Payable (7)		150.00
	Life Insurance Premiums Payable (8)		10.00
	Wages and Salaries Payable (9)		1,698.75

To record salary for January.

(1) given
(2) given
(3) given
(4) .062 x $2,500 = $155.00
(5) .0145 x $2,500 = $36.25
(6) given
(7) given
(8) given
(9) $2,500 - ($250 + $75 + $155 + $36.25 + $125 + $150 + $10) = $1,698.75

(b) *Prepare journal entry to record employer payroll taxes and benefits for January.*

19X3			
Jan. 31	Employer Payroll Expenses (1)	852.25	
	SUTA Taxes Payable (2)		135.00
	FUTA Taxes Payable (3)		20.00
	Social Security Taxes Payable (4)		155.00
	Medicare Taxes Payable (5)		36.25
	Workers' Compensation Premiums Payable (6)		6.00
	Medical Insurance Premiums Payable (7)		125.00
	Pension Contributions Payable (8)		150.00
	Accrued Vacation Pay (9)		125.00
	Accrued Sick Pay (10)		100.00

To record employer payroll taxes and benefits

(1) $135 + $20 + $155 + $36.25 + $6 + $125 + $150 + $125 + $100
    = $852.25
(2) .054 x $2,500 = $135
(3) .008 x $2,500 = $20
(4) .062 x $2,500 = $155
(5) .0145 x $2,500 = $36.25
(6) given
(7) given
(8) given
(9) .05 x $2,500
(10) .04 x $2,500

(c) (1) *Calculate cost of employer payroll taxes and employer benefits: $852.25*
    (2) *Calculate total cost of services of Helen Rogers:*

Salary	$2,500.00
Employer payroll taxes and benefits	852.25
Total	$3,352.25

   (3) *Calculate cost of employer payroll taxes and benefits as a percentage of Helen's salary:*

$$\frac{\text{Employer payroll taxes/benefits}}{\text{Salary}} \quad \frac{852.25}{2,500.00} = 34\%$$

KEY TERMS

contingent liabilities, *468*
current liabilities, *469*
days-purchases-in-payables, *492*
defined-benefit pension plan, *487*
defined-contribution pension plan, *487*
employee benefits, *480*
employee earnings record (Appendix), *497*

employer payroll expense register (Appendix), *497*
estimated liabilities, *468*
gross pay, *479*
liabilities, *468*
long-term debt, *469*
long-term liabilities, *469*
net pay, *479*
noncurrent liabilities, *469*
operating cycle, *469*

payroll register (Appendix), *497*
percent utilization of a line of credit, *492*
short-term, revolving lines of credit, *475*
term to maturity, *469*

SELF-QUIZ

LO 1   1.   An example of a contingent liability is
a. The obligation of a retailer of mountain bikes for a one-year product warranty
b. Social security taxes withheld from employees
c. A noninterest-bearing note payable
d. A lawsuit brought against us seeking $100,000 for breach of contract

LO 1   2.   An example of an estimated liability is
a. The obligation of the endorser of a note receivable sold to the bank
b. A lawsuit against us by the Internal Revenue Service seeking additional income taxes
c. Payments we will have to make related to the warranty on products sold
d. The amount of merchandise we expect to purchase on account during the next fiscal year

LO 1   3.   Current liabilities are
a. Liabilities due within 30 days
b. Liabilities that we expect to pay
c. Liabilities due within one year or within one operating cycle, whichever is shorter
d. Liabilities due within one year or within one operating cycle, whichever is longer

LO 2   4.   Berry Company purchases merchandise 2/5, n/30. The effective annual interest rate of not taking the purchase discount is
a. 2%
b. 29%
c. 40%
d. 24%

LO 2   5.   2/10, n/30 purchase discounts
a. Provide for the effective borrowing of funds for 30 days at no interest cost
b. Provide for the effective borrowing of funds for 20 days at no interest cost
c. Provide for the effective borrowing of funds for 10 days with no interest cost
d. Allow a 10% discount if paid within 2 days

LO 3   6.   Interest-bearing notes payable
a. Include the interest in the face (maturity) value of the note
b. Require the payment of the face value of the note plus interest
c. Are a more expensive way of borrowing than noninterest-bearing notes
d. Require the payment of only the face value of the note

LO 3   7.   Noninterest-bearing notes payable
a. Allow funds to be borrowed without an interest charge
b. Require the payment of the face value of the note plus an interest charge
c. Require payment of only the face value of the note
d. Are a less expensive way of borrowing than interest-bearing notes

LO 4   8.   Short-term, revolving lines of credit
a. Are good ways to finance permanent additions to buildings and equipment
b. Are good ways to finance short-term, seasonal needs to expand inventory and accounts receivable

c. Are commitments by banks to advance funds on demand up to the limits and periods in the agreement

d. Both b and c

LO 4 9. Customary terms for short-term bank loans include

a. The pledging of inventory and accounts receivable as collateral

b. The right of the bank to require that it be paid in full at any time

c. A flexible interest rate that fluctuates with the rate at which the Federal Reserve Bank makes loans to other banks

d. All of the above

LO 5 10. The total cost of the payroll to an employer is

a. Gross wages and salaries of the employees plus employee withholdings

b. Gross wages and salaries of the employees minus employee withholdings

c. Gross wages and salaries of the employees plus employer's payroll taxes and benefits

d. The net pay of the employees plus employee withholdings

LO 5 11. If the federal income tax withheld is increased

a. This will increase the total cost of the payroll to the employer

b. This will increase employer payroll taxes

c. This will increase the net pay of the employees

d. This will decrease the net pay of the employees

LO 6 12. Roger Johnson worked 40 hours of regular time and 2 hours of overtime during the week. He is paid overtime at the rate of 1.5 times the regular rate. His regular pay rate is $12 per hour. His gross wages for the week are: _____.

LO 6 13. Gordon Lee earns $1,000 for the first week of January 19X3. The amount of social security tax and Medicare tax that the federal government will receive (at the rates given in the chapter) as a result of this work is

a. $153.00

b. $76.50

c. $62.00

d. $14.50

LO 7 14. In the journal entry to record the wages and salaries of employees, the federal income taxes withheld is

a. Recorded in an expense account

b. Recorded in a liability account

c. Recorded in an asset account

d. None of the above

LO 7 15. Federal unemployment tax

a. Is withheld from the wages of employees

b. Reduces the employee's net pay

c. Is paid by both the employee and employer

d. Is paid only by the employer

LO 8 16. Warner Company had cost of goods sold of $100,000, beginning inventory of $15,000, and ending inventory of $20,000. Its purchases during the period were

a. $95,000

b. $120,000

c. $105,000

d. $100,000

LO 8 17. Matrix Company has a monthly (assume 30 days) accounting period. Purchases for the month were $200,000 and the balance in Accounts Payable at the end of the accounting period was $50,000. The days-purchases-in-payable were:

a. 120

b. 7.5

c. 4

d. .25

LO 9 18. (Appendix) The _____ _____ is a special journal used to record employees' gross salaries and wages, withholdings, and net pay.

LO 9 19. (Appendix) An employee earnings record is used to supply each employee with a Form _____ for the year.

SOLUTIONS TO SELF-QUIZ

1. d	2. c	3. d	4. b	5. c	6. b	7. c	8. d	9. d	10. c	11. d	12. $516	13. a	14. b
15. d	16. c	17. b	18. payroll register		19. W-2								

QUESTIONS

Q12-1   Do the liabilities included on a balance sheet dated December 31, 19X4, include the cost of purchases on account that the company will make in January 19X5? Explain.

Q12-2   What two conditions must exist to recognize a contingent liability in the balance sheet?

Q12-3   What is the operating cycle of a business?

Q12-4 How can the operating cycle of a business affect the classification of a liability as current or noncurrent?

Q12-5 List four typical current liabilities.

Q12-6 A company purchases merchandise, terms 2/10, n/30. Calculate the effective annual interest rate of failing to take the purchases discount.

Q12-7 A company borrows $100,000 cash and signs a 60-day noninterest-bearing note. Will the maturity value of the note equal $100,000? Explain.

Q12-8 On November 1, 19X7, a company purchases merchandise for $10,000 and signs a 90-day, 9%, interest-bearing note for $10,000. A company spokesperson says that the company will not incur any interest expense for the year ended December 31, 19X7, because the interest will not be paid until 19X8. Do you agree?

Q12-9 On November 1, 19X7, a company purchases merchandise for $10,000 and signs a 90-day, noninterest-bearing note for $10,221.92. Show how the note payable would be presented in a November 1, 19X7, balance sheet.

Q12-10 If a bank approves a line of credit for a borrower, it usually sets an absolute limit and a flexible limit on the loan. Briefly describe how a bank might determine each limit.

Q12-11 Will an increase in the federal income tax withheld from employees increase the cost of the payroll to the employer? Explain.

Q12-12 Jane Mason earns a salary of $6,000 per month. The social security tax rate on employees is 6.2%. Can we be sure that the amount withheld from Jane's current check is $372 ($6,000 x .062)? Explain.

Q12-13 Does the Social Security Taxes Payable account consist of the liability for social security taxes withheld from employees or the liability for the employer's tax? Explain.

Q12-14 (Appendix) Why is it necessary for a company to maintain employee earnings records for each employee?

Q12-15 (Appendix) Discuss why payroll is often the first accounting function computerized.

EXERCISES

LO 2

E12-1 **Implicit Interest Rate on Lost Discounts** The Brown Sage Company purchases merchandise from three suppliers. The terms offered by each supplier are:

Supplier A: 1/10, n/30
Supplier B: 2/15, n/30
Supplier C: 3/10, n/45

REQUIRED:

For each supplier, calculate the effective annual interest rate of failing to take purchases discounts.

LO 3

E12-2 **Short-Term Notes Payable, Interest-Bearing** Pepper Company records purchases at gross and its accounting period ends on December 31.

19X2
Oct. 15 Purchased $10,000 of merchandise from Turner Company, terms 2/10, n/30.
     25 Gave Turner a 90-day, 8%, interest-bearing note for $9,800.
Dec. 31 Accrued interest owed Turner.

19X3
Jan. 23 Paid the Turner note.

REQUIRED:

Record journal entries on the books of Pepper Company for the above events.

LO 3   **E12-3** **Short-Term Notes Payable, Noninterest-Bearing**   Pepper Company records purchases at gross and its accounting period ends on December 31.

19X2
Oct. 15 Purchased $10,000 of merchandise from Turner Company, terms 2/10, n/30.
      25 Gave Turner a 90-day, noninterest-bearing note for $9,993.32.
Dec. 31 Recognized interest expense.

19X3
Jan. 23 Paid the Turner note.

REQUIRED:

Record journal entries on the books of Pepper Company for the above events.

LO 3   **E12-4** **Presentation of Interest-Bearing and Noninterest-Bearing Notes on the Balance Sheet**   On December 1, 19X6, the Greenwich Company borrowed $50,000 cash from the Fidelity Trust Company and signed a note.

REQUIRED:

a. Show the presentation of the liability to Fidelity on the December 31, 19X6, balance sheet of Greenwich, assuming the note was a 60-day, 7%, $50,000 interest-bearing note.
b. Show the presentation of the liability to Fidelity on the December 31, 19X6, balance sheet of Greenwich, assuming the note was a 60-day, noninterest-bearing note for $50,575.34.

LO 4   **E12-5** **Short-Term Bank Loans**   The Industrial Bank agreed to loan Bargain Mart up to 40% of its inventory and 40% of its accounts receivable during the next 3 years, with the amount of the loan not to exceed $1,000,000. On June 15, 19X1, Bargain Mart exercised the line of credit and had the bank transfer $200,000 to its account. Interest on the loan, at the rate of 9%, is payable monthly on the 10th day of the following month.

REQUIRED:

a. Prepare a journal entry to record the loan on June 15, 19X1.
b. Prepare the journal entry to accrue interest on June 30, 19X1.
c. Prepare the July 10, 19X1, journal entry to record the payment of interest for June.
d. Assuming Bargain Mart has a July 31 year-end, prepare the adjusting entry necessary on July 31, 19X1.

LO 6   **E12-6** **Calculation of Gross Pay**   Hammer Data Company has 4 employees in its data entry department. The employees earn $9.80 per hour and are paid time and a half for work exceeding 40 hours during a workweek. Employee time cards for the week ending September 10, 19X3, show the following hours worked:

	Hrs.
Mary Kendel	49.2
Jason Giannati	40
Roy Jefferson	42
Gigi Wang	45.5

REQUIRED:

Calculate the gross wages for each employee.

LO 6   **E12-7** **Calculation of Social Security and Medicare Taxes**   The following information is available for the Kinder Consulting Company's November 19X8, payroll:

Name	Earnings Prior To November Payroll	November Earnings
M. Sukuzi	$ 55,000	$ 5,500
A. Adams	50,000	5,000
L. Cavika	130,000	13,000
J. Smith	57,000	5,700

The social security rate is 6.2% of the first $57,600 earned in a calendar year, and the Medicare rate is 1.45% of the first $135,000 earned in a calendar year.

REQUIRED:

a. For each employee, calculate the amount of November salary subject to the social security and Medicare taxes.
b. Calculate the social security tax and the Medicare tax assessed on each employee for the November payroll.
c. Calculate the total social security tax and Medicare tax assessed on the employer for the November payroll.

LO 6,7   **E12-8**   **Payroll-Related Journal Entries**   The Baxter Company has 2 employees. Information related to the February 7, 19X0, weekly payroll follows:

James Ballanger

Hours worked	40
Hourly rate	$8.60
Federal withholding taxes	$15.00
Medical insurance premiums withheld	$30.00

Judy Phillips

Hours worked	32
Hourly rate	$9.25
Federal withholding taxes	$14.00
Medical insurance premiums withheld	$25.00

The social security tax is 6.2% of the first $57,600, and the Medicare tax is 1.45% of the first $135,000 earned in the calendar year.

REQUIRED:

Prepare a journal entry to record the employee wages for the February 7, 19X0, payroll. Do not record the employer payroll tax and benefits expense.

LO 6,7   **E12-9**   **Payroll-Related Journal Entries**   Use the data presented in E12-8 to prepare a journal entry to record the employer payroll tax expense and the employer benefits expense. The employer matches the medical premiums paid by the employees, and the SUTA and FUTA rates are 5.4% and .8% of the first $7,000 earned in the calendar year. In addition, workers' compensation premiums are $3 for each employee. Use one expense account for employer payroll taxes and benefits.

LO 8   **E12-10**   **Number of Days-Purchases-in-Payables**   The following information is available for the Dryden Company for the accounting year ended December 31, 19X6.

Purchases	$25,000,000
Accounts payable, 12/31/X6	900,000

Dryden makes all purchases on account, terms 2/10, n/30.

REQUIRED:

a. Calculate the days-purchases-in-payables.
b. Comment on what the calculation in *a* tells us about Dryden.

LO 7,9   **E12-11   Payroll Related Journal Entries, Payroll Register (Appendix)**   Refer to the payroll register shown in Illustration 12-8 of the Appendix. Use the data in the payroll register to prepare a general journal entry to record employee wages and withholdings for the work week ending on March 31, 19X1.

LO 7,9   **E12-12   Payroll Related Journal Entries, Employer Payroll Expense Register (Appendix)** Refer to the employee payroll expense register shown in Illustration 12-9 of the Appendix. Use the data in the employer payroll expense register to prepare a general journal entry to record employer payroll taxes and benefits for the work week that ended on March 31, 19X1. Use one expense account for all payroll taxes and benefits.

▌PROBLEM SET A

LO 2,3   **P12-1A   Short-Term Notes Payable, Interest-Bearing; Implicit Interest Rate in Losing Discounts**   Selected transactions for the American Information Company are given below. American's annual accounting period ends on August 31.

19X1

May   1   Purchased merchandise from the Green Company for $100,000, terms 1/10, n/30.
      11 Gave the Green Company a $99,000, 10%, 180-day note in payment of the open account.
      12 Borrowed $250,000 from the Western Trust Company and gave Western a one-year, 9%, note for $250,000.

REQUIRED:

a. If American had elected to pay Green on May 31, calculate its implicit interest rate.
b. Prepare journal entries to record the transactions on May 1, 11, and 12.
c. Prepare necessary adjusting entries on August 31.
d. Show the presentation of the liabilities in the August 31, 19X1, balance sheet.
e. Prepare journal entries to record payment of the Green note on November 7, 19X1, and the Western note on May 12, 19X2.

LO 3   **P12-2A   Short-Term Notes Payable, Noninterest-Bearing**   Selected transactions for the American Information Company are given below. American's annual accounting period ends on August 31.

19X1

May   1   Purchased merchandise from the Green Company for $100,000, terms 1/10, n/30.
      11 Gave the Green Company a $103,882.19, 180-day, noninterest-bearing note in payment of the open account. The note has a net value of $99,000.
      12 Borrowed $250,000 from the Western Trust Company and gave Western a one-year, noninterest-bearing note for $272,500.

REQUIRED:

a. Prepare journal entries to record the transactions on May 1, 11, and 12.
b. Prepare necessary adjusting entries on August 31.
c. Show the presentation of the liabilities in the August 31, 19X1, balance sheet.
d. Prepare journal entries to record payment of the Green note on November 7, 19X1, and the Western note on May 12, 19X2.

LO 4   **P12-3A   Short-Term Bank Loans**   The Cascades Country Club arranged a line of credit with the Atlantic National Bank that provides for a loan of up to 40% of its pro-line golf club inventory and 50% of its most recent month's green fees (receivable). This line of credit extends over a one-year period. Interest on any loans made is payable monthly on the

15th day of the following month. The interest rate is 7.75%. The maximum loan available is $1,600,000.

On March 13, 19X2, Cascades had Atlantic transfer $300,000 to its account under the terms of the agreement. On May 5, 19X2, Cascades had Atlantic transfer another $200,000 to its account.

Cascades' accounting year ends on June 30.

REQUIRED:

a. List some other terms, in addition to the ones mentioned, that are customary for short-term loans like the one above.
b. Prepare all journal entries necessary in Cascades' records for the transactions related to the line of credit for the period March 13, 19X2, through June 30, 19X2.

LO 5,6   **P12-4A**   **Calculation of Employee Gross Pay, Deductions, and Net Pay; Payroll-Related Costs of Employer**   Information related to the December payroll of the Bradstreet Company follows:

Gross wages and salaries	$2,350,000
Wages and salaries subject to:	
Social security tax	2,100,000
Medicare tax	2,300,000
Federal unemployment tax	200,000
State unemployment tax	200,000
Federal income taxes withheld	270,000
State income taxes withheld	50,000
City income taxes withheld	47,000
Medical insurance premiums withheld	42,000
Medical insurance premiums paid by employer	42,000
Pension contributions withheld	141,000
Pension contributions paid by employer	141,000
Workers' compensation premiums paid by employer	3,000
Vacation pay accrued by employer	117,500
Sick pay accrued by employer	94,000
Social security tax rate	6.2%
Medicare tax rate	1.45%
SUTA rate	5.4%
FUTA rate	.8%

REQUIRED:

a. Prepare a list of the employee withholdings and deductions for December and their total.
b. Determine the employees' net pay for December.
c. Prepare a list of employer payroll taxes and benefits for December and total the items.
d. Calculate the total cost of the payroll for December.
e. Calculate the cost of employer payroll taxes and benefits as a percentage of gross wages and salaries.

LO 6,7   **P12-5A**   **Calculation of Employee Gross Pay, Deductions, and Net Pay; Payroll-Related Costs of Employer; Payroll-Related Journal Entries**   Information related to the November payroll of the Southwest Building and Loan follows:

Gross wages and salaries	$900,000
Wages and salaries subject to:	
Social security tax	875,000
Medicare tax	900,000

Federal unemployment tax	$ 20,000
State unemployment tax	20,000
Federal income taxes withheld	120,000
State income taxes withheld	45,000
City income taxes withheld	18,000
Medical insurance premiums withheld	30,000
Medical insurance premiums paid by employer	30,000
Pension contributions withheld	54,000
Pension contributions paid by employer	54,000
Workers' compensation premiums paid by employer	1,350
Vacation pay accrued by employer	45,000
Sick pay accrued by employer	36,000
Social security tax rate	6.2%
Medicare tax rate	1.45%
SUTA rate	5.4%
FUTA rate	.8%

REQUIRED:

a. Explain why the entire $900,000 in gross wages and salaries is not subject to the social security tax.
b. Prepare a journal entry to record the employee wages and salaries for November.
c. Prepare a journal entry to record the employer's payroll taxes and benefits for November. Use one expense account for all payroll taxes and benefits.
d. Calculate the total cost of the payroll for November.
e. Calculate the cost of employer payroll taxes and benefits as a percentage of gross wages and salaries.

LO 8   **P12-6A   Days-Purchases-in-Payables**   The Jackson Home Center has the following information available for the accounting year ended December 31, 19X8.

Jackson Home Center Income Statement For the Year Ended December 31, 19X8	
Sales	$6,000,000
Cost of goods sold	4,000,000
Gross profit	$2,000,000
Operating expenses	1,500,000
Net income	$ 500,000

On December 31, 19X7, and December 31, 19X8, Jackson's balance sheets report merchandise inventories of $400,000 and $450,000, respectively, and Accounts Payable balances of $100,000 and $110,000, respectively. All accounts payable are owed to merchandise vendors, and Jackson purchases nearly all of its merchandise under 2/10, n/30 terms.

REQUIRED:

a. Calculate the purchases for 19X8.
b. Calculate the days-purchases-in-payables on December 31, 19X8.
c. Discuss what you can infer from Jackson's days-purchases-in-payables.

PROBLEM SET B

LO 2,3   **P12-1B**   **Short-Term Notes Payable, Interest-Bearing; Implicit Interest Rate in Losing Discounts**   Selected transactions for the Data Management Company are given below. Data's annual accounting period ends on September 30.

19X4

Jun.   1   Purchased merchandise from the Hacker Company for $30,000, terms 2/10, n/30.
      11   Gave the Hacker Company a $29,400, 8%, 180-day note in payment of the open account.
      25   Borrowed $50,000 from the Future Bank and gave Future a one-year, 9.5%, note for $50,000.

REQUIRED:

a. If Data Management had elected to pay Hacker on July 1, calculate its implicit interest rate.
b. Prepare journal entries to record the transactions on June 1, 11, and 25.
c. Prepare necessary adjusting entries on September 30.
d. Show the presentation of the liabilities in the September 30, 19X4, balance sheet.
e. Prepare journal entries to record payment of the Hacker note on December 8, 19X4, and the Future note on June 25, 19X5.

LO 2,3   **P12-2B**   **Short-Term Notes Payable, Noninterest-Bearing**   Selected transactions for the Data Management Company are given below. Data's annual accounting period ends on September 30.

19X4

Jun.   1   Purchased merchandise from the Hacker Company for $30,000, terms 2/10, n/30.
      11   Gave the Hacker Company a $30,559.89, 180-day, noninterest-bearing note in payment of the open account. The note has a net value of $29,400.
      25   Borrowed $50,000 from the Future Bank and gave Future a one-year, noninterest-bearing note for $54,750.

REQUIRED:

a. Prepare journal entries to record the transactions on June 1, 11, and 25.
b. Prepare necessary adjusting entries on September 30.
c. Show the presentation of the liabilities in the September 30, 19X4, balance sheet.
d. Prepare journal entries to record payment of the Hacker note on December 8, 19X4, and the Future note on June 25, 19X5.

LO 4   **P12-3B**   **Short-Term Bank Loans**   The Highland Tennis Club arranged a line of credit with the Valley National Bank that provides for a loan of up to 50% of its tennis merchandise inventory and 60% of its most recent month's court fees (receivable). This line of credit extends over a one-year period. Interest on any loans made is payable monthly on the 10th day following the end of the month. The interest rate is 11%. The maximum loan available is $400,000.

On May 7, 19X1, Highland had Valley transfer $150,000 to its account under the terms of the agreement. On June 5, 19X1, Highland had Valley transfer another $200,000 to its account.

Highland's accounting year ends on August 31.

REQUIRED:

Prepare all journal entries necessary on Highland's books to record transactions related to the line of credit for the period May 7, 19X1, through August 31, 19X1.

LO 5,6 | **P12-4B** | **Calculation of Employee Gross Pay, Deductions, and Net Pay; Payroll-Related Costs of Employer**   Information related to the December payroll of the Ocean Products Company follows:

Gross wages and salaries	$325,000
Wages and salaries subject to:	
Social security tax	$310,000
Medicare tax	$310,000
Federal unemployment tax	$20,000
State unemployment tax	$20,000
Federal income taxes withheld	$30,000
State income taxes withheld	$6,000
City income taxes withheld	$3,250
Medical insurance premiums withheld	$15,000
Medical insurance premiums paid by employer	$15,000
Pension contributions withheld	6%
Pension contributions paid by employer	6%
Workers' compensation premiums paid by employer	$500
Vacation pay accrued by employer	$16,250
Sick pay accrued by employer	$13,000
Social security tax rate	6.2%
Medicare tax rate	1.45%
SUTA rate	5.4%
FUTA rate	.8%

REQUIRED:

a. Prepare a list of the employee withholdings and deductions for December and their total.
b. Determine the employees' net pay for December.
c. Prepare a list of employer payroll taxes and benefits for December and total the items.
d. Calculate the total cost of the payroll for December.
e. Calculate the cost of employer payroll taxes and benefits as a percentage of gross wages and salaries.

LO 6,7 | **P12-5B** | **Calculation of Employee Gross Pay, Deductions, and Net Pay; Payroll-Related Costs of Employer; Payroll-Related Journal Entries**   Information related to the November payroll of the Redbird Construction Company follows:

Gross wages and salaries	$175,000
Wages and salaries subject to:	
Social security tax	$169,000
Medicare tax	$175,000
Federal unemployment tax	$25,000
State unemployment tax	$25,000
Federal income taxes withheld	$16,000
State income taxes withheld	$3,000
City income taxes withheld	$3,500
Medical insurance premiums withheld	$7,875
Medical insurance premiums paid by employer	$7,875
Pension contributions withheld	5.5%
Pension contributions paid by employer	5.5%
Workers' compensation premiums paid by employer	$300
Vacation pay accrued by employer	$8,750
Sick pay accrued by employer	$7,000
Social security tax rate	6.2%
Medicare tax rate	1.45%
SUTA rate	5.4%
FUTA rate	.8%

REQUIRED:

a. Explain why the entire $175,000 in gross wages and salaries is not subject to the social security tax.

b. Prepare a journal entry to record the employee wages and salaries for November.

c. Prepare a journal entry to record the employer's payroll taxes and benefits for November. Use one expense account for both payroll taxes and benefits.

d. Calculate the total cost of the payroll for November.

e. Calculate the cost of employer payroll taxes and benefits as a percentage of gross wages and salaries.

LO 8 **P12-6B** **Days-Purchases-in-Payables** The Big Sky Building Supply Company has the following information available for the accounting year ended July 31, 19X6.

Big Sky Building Supply Company Income Statement For the Year Ended July 31, 19X6	
Sales	$9,000,000
Cost of goods sold	6,000,000
Gross profit	$3,000,000
Operating expenses	2,000,000
Net income	$1,000,000

On July 31, 19X5, and July 31, 19X6, Big Sky's balance sheets report merchandise inventories of $600,000 and $550,000, respectively, and Accounts Payable balances of $150,000 and $140,000, respectively. All accounts payable are owed to merchandise vendors, and Big Sky purchases nearly all of its merchandise under 2/10, n/30 terms.

REQUIRED:

a. Calculate the purchases for 19X6.

b. Calculate the days-purchases-in-payables on July 31, 19X6.

c. Discuss what you can infer from Big Sky's days-purchases-in-payables.

CRITICAL THINKING AND COMMUNICATING

C12-1 The Burger Grill is a fast-food chain that operates across the United States. BG's staffing comes mostly from part-time workers, made up of college students, retired individuals, and others who appreciate the flexible working hours offered by BG. The hourly pay rate ranges from $4.75 to $6.10 with an average rate, nationally, of $5.10. The hours worked by the staff range from as few as 10 hours per month to as many as 160, with a national average of 80 hours per month.

BG does not offer any benefits to these part-time employees, other than discounts on meals. Employer payroll costs currently are as follows:

Social security tax	6.2% of the first $57,600
Medicare tax	1.45% of the first $135,000
FUTA tax	.8% of the first $7,000
SUTA tax	5.4% of the first $7,000
Workers' compensation	$3 per worker per month

A national health care plan is being proposed and will require BG to provide health care for part-time employees. You have been hired as a consultant to provide BG with information about the impact of the proposed health care plan on its staffing costs.

Assume you are able to determine that coverage under the proposed health care plan will cost about $150 per month per employee and that BG will be able to pass about one-third of this cost on to the employee.

REQUIRED:

a. Using an average part-time employee as an example, calculate the current cost of employer payroll taxes and benefits per dollar of wages.
b. Using an average part-time employee as an example, calculate the cost of employer payroll taxes and benefits per dollar of wages under the proposed health care plan.
c. Write a letter to BG's management discussing the potential impact of the proposed health care plan on BG's operating costs.

C12-2 You are having coffee with Sally Edison, a local businesswoman who operates a data-entry business that employs about 150 keyboard operators through a large contract with the General Services Administration to maintain updated databases on certain GSA operations. Sally comments that she recently learned there might be a decrease in the employee withholding rates for federal income taxes.

Sally tells you she is confused as to how this reduction might affect the cost of operating her business, but she welcomes the decrease because she is currently paying a large amount of federal withholdings to the federal government for each payroll.

REQUIRED:

a. Use a hypothetical employee earning $300 per week and having $30 federal income tax withheld to illustrate the effect on Sally's costs of a 10% decrease in the withholding rate. For purposes of simplicity, assume federal income taxes are the only withholding from employee wages.
b. Explain to Sally the effect of changes in employee withholdings on her operating costs.

C12-3 Refer to the J.C. Penney Company, Inc. financial statements in Appendix B at the end of the text. Find the accounts payable and accrued expenses and merchandise inventory figures in the balance sheet. Find the cost of goods sold, occupancy, buying, and warehousing costs in the income statement.

REQUIRED:

a. Using these figures, *approximate* J.C. Penney's days-purchases-in-payables for 1991, 1992, and 1993. The 1990 ending merchandise inventory was $2,657 million.
b. Comment on any fluctuations or trends in J.C. Penney's days-purchases-in-payables and their implication for the company.

CHAPTER 13

Concepts of Financial Statements

Chris Rose recently inherited a substantial sum of money from a close relative. To finish her college education without additional student loans, Chris wants to invest her money to provide a steady stream of cash flows.

Chris has a close friend whose family owns DeAngelis Construction, and she is considering their offer of part ownership by investment of her inheritance. DeAngelis Construction appears to be very successful and prudently managed. It specializes in constructing regional mail distribution centers for the U.S. Postal Service. While interested in this investment, Chris has a reservation about the company's policy of cash withdrawals by owners. DeAngelis limits withdrawals to one-half of the net income of the current period. While Chris believes the policy is generally very prudent, she is concerned about the availability of a steady stream of cash flows to finance her education.

The construction projects that DeAngelis performs for the U.S. Postal Service take approximately three years to complete. Chris knows that DeAngelis only works on one project at a time. While a distribution center is under construction, DeAngelis incurs costs such as building materials, construction equipment, and the wages and salaries of employees. Chris knows that businesses normally only recognize revenue at the completion of the earning process, which she thinks would be at the time the construction project is completed.

Chris has asked to see DeAngelis's financial statements before she makes a final decision. Because of the nature of the company's operations, Chris expects to see a pattern of two years of large net losses, in the first two years of a project, and then a third year of large net income, at the completion of the project. DeAngelis's policy concerning cash withdrawals would mean that Chris would not have any cash flows for the two years of net losses. Clearly, this pattern of cash flows would not be acceptable given Chris' investment goal of steady cash flows for college.

This chapter presents a discussion of the concepts underlying financial statements. A conceptual framework for financial statements is necessary to develop generally accepted accounting principles that maximize the usefulness of the financial statements to those who read and use the information in them. Also, a conceptual framework enhances the consistency among the various Generally Accepted Accounting Principles.

Much of the discussion in this chapter is based on the FASB's Conceptual Framework. Other parts of the discussion are based on assumptions and principles that existed and were practiced before the FASB developed its Conceptual Framework and that continue to be an important part of financial accounting. Many of the concepts presented in this chapter have been discussed in previous chapters of this text. Some of the concepts will be new to you. In any event, an understanding of the conceptual framework that underlies generally accepted accounting principles should enhance your understanding of financial accounting.

LEARNING OBJECTIVES

1. Identify the objectives of financial statements.
2. Explain the qualitative characteristics of useful financial statement information.
3. Define the elements of financial statements.
4. Discuss financial statement recognition and measurement.
5. Describe the assumptions underlying financial statements.
6. Identify the modifying conventions that alter the application of GAAP.

THE FASB'S CONCEPTUAL FRAMEWORK

The Conceptual Framework began taking form in 1973, at the inception of the FASB, and its final piece was issued in December, 1984. Obviously, the framework's development was a time-consuming effort. Why was a conceptual framework needed? The FASB answers this with the following statement:

> A conceptual framework is a *constitution*, a coherent system of interrelated objectives and fundamentals that can lead to consistent standards and that prescribes the nature, function, and limits of financial accounting and financial statements. The objectives identify the goals and purposes of accounting. The fundamentals are underlying concepts of accounting, concepts that guide the selection of events to be accounted for, the measurement of those events, and the means of summarizing and communicating them to interested parties. Concepts of that type are fundamental in the sense that other concepts flow from them and repeated reference to them will be necessary in establishing, interpreting, and applying accounting and reporting standards.[1]

As shown in Illustration 13-1, the FASB's **Conceptual Framework** consists of: objectives of financial statements, qualitative characteristics of useful information, elements of financial statements, and recognition and measurement in financial statements.

---

[1]*Scope and Implications of the Conceptual Framework Project* (Stamford, Conn.: FASB, 1976), p. 2.

ILLUSTRATION 13-1 FASB's Conceptual Framework

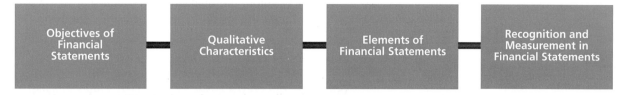

Objectives of Financial Statements	Qualitative Characteristics	Elements of Financial Statements	Recognition and Measurement in Financial Statements

LO 1
Identify the objectives of financial statements.

Objectives of Financial Statements

As you learned in previous chapters, the end product of the accounting process is the financial statements. Financial statements are the business's primary means of reporting information to owners, creditors, and other users about its financial position at the end of the period and about the results of its operations during the period. In developing the **objectives of financial statements**, the FASB considered issues such as the following:

Who are the users of financial statements?
What is the nature of the decisions users make?
What kinds of information are financial statements capable of communicating to these users for making their decisions?

In answering these questions, the FASB specified objectives in *SFAC No. 1*:

1. Financial [statements] should provide information that is useful to present and potential investors and creditors and other users in making rational investment, credit, and similar decisions. The information should be comprehensible to those who have a reasonable understanding of business and economic activities and are willing to study the information with reasonable diligence.
2. Financial [statements] should provide information to help present and potential investors and creditors and other users in assessing the amounts, timing, and uncertainty of future cash receipts from the business and the proceeds from the sale, redemption, or maturity of ownership interests or loans. Since investors' and creditors' cash flows are related to cash flows of the business, financial [statements] should provide information to help investors, creditors, and others assess the amounts, timing, and uncertainty of future cash inflows to the related business.
3. Financial [statements] should provide information about the assets of a business, the claims to those assets (liabilities and owners' equity), and other effects of transactions, events, and circumstances that change its assets and claims to those assets.[2]

The first objective states a broad concern that financial statements be useful to individual users in making investment, credit, and other similar decisions. The objectives then move to the more narrow concerns that financial statements provide information that is useful for assessing the amounts, timing, and uncertainty of future cash flows and information about the business's financial position and performance.

---

[2]"Objectives of Financial Reporting by Business Enterprises," *Statement of Financial Accounting Concepts No. 1* (Stamford, Conn.: FASB, 1978), p. 2. In this Statement, the FASB actually uses the more inclusive information set of financial reporting, rather than financial statements.

After the FASB reached its conclusions regarding the objectives of financial statements, its next step was to explore the qualitative characteristics that make financial statements useful for those making the types of decisions discussed.

LO 2

Explain the qualitative characteristics of useful financial statement information.

Qualitative Characteristics of Useful Information

In *SFAC No. 2*, the FASB established three levels of **qualitative characteristics** of useful financial statement information. The FASB intends for accountants to use the qualitative characteristics to answer questions concerning the amount of information to provide in the financial statements, the manner in which to present the information, and which alternative accounting methods to use in recording transactions and events. As presented in Illustration 13-2, the three levels of characteristics are decision usefulness, relevance and reliability, and comparability and consistency.[3]

ILLUSTRATION 13-2 Qualitative Characteristics

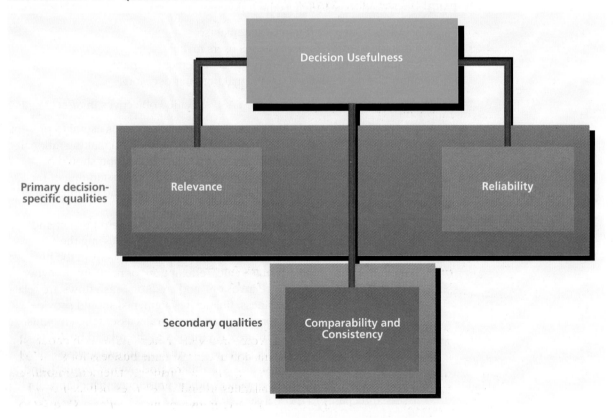

Decision Usefulness.   **Decision usefulness** is the primary qualitative characteristic of financial statement information. It requires that the information be useful in making investment, credit, and other decisions. If information is not useful, then it has no value; and any cost incurred in providing the information cannot be justified.

Relevance.   The characteristic of **relevance** means that the information is capable of making a difference in a decision. To be relevant, information must

---

[3]"Qualitative Characteristics of Useful Financial Reporting Information," *Statement of Financial Accounting Concepts No. 2* (Stamford, Conn.: FASB, 1980), par. 6–20.

have predictive value, feedback value, and timeliness. **Predictive value** is the ability to help users form predictions about the outcomes of events. Information has **feedback value** if it can improve decision makers' capabilities to predict by providing feedback about earlier expectations. The feedback may confirm that the prediction model the decision maker uses is appropriate, or the feedback may suggest changes in the prediction model that would improve subsequent predictions. **Timeliness** of information means that the information is available to the user before it loses its capacity to influence decisions. Delays in providing the information causes a loss in its ability to be useful in decision making and, therefore, a loss of any relevance that otherwise may have existed.

Reliability.   **Reliability** assures that the information is reasonably free from error and bias and faithfully represents what it intends to represent. To be reliable, information must have representational faithfulness, and it must be verifiable and neutral. **Representational faithfulness** is the degree of correspondence or agreement between financial statement numbers and the assets, liabilities, transactions, and events those numbers intend to represent. **Verifiability** is the quality that results in a high degree of agreement among independent measurers. For example, if 10 accounting students were asked to compute depreciation expense for an asset with a cost of $1,000, estimated useful life of 10 years, estimated residual value of zero, and using the straight-line method, hopefully, there would be a high degree of agreement (verifiability) among the 10 students' answers. On the other hand, if the 10 students were asked to estimate the useful life of a particular asset, there would probably be a wide range of answers and, therefore, less verifiability. **Neutrality** means that in choosing an accounting method, there is freedom from bias towards a predetermined result.

Relationship Between Relevance and Reliability.   To be useful, information cannot be completely void of either relevance or reliability. Both qualities must exist to some degree. For example, an estimate of a new business's net income for each of the next 10 years might be highly relevant to the owner. On the other hand, an estimate of that information would probably be unreliable; and, therefore, the information would have limited usefulness. While both qualities must exist to some degree, there are trade-offs; information that is highly relevant but has low reliability or information with high reliability but low relevance may still be decision useful.

Comparability and Consistency.   Information about a particular business becomes more useful if it can be compared with similar information about other businesses and with similar information about the same business for some other time period. **Comparability** is the quality of financial statement information that enables users to identify similarities in and differences between two businesses or within a single business between two or more periods. **Consistency** of financial statement information means using the same accounting methods for a business from period to period.

LO 3
Define the elements of financial statements.

Elements of Financial Statements

In previous chapters, you were introduced to many of the **elements of financial statements**. Below are the definitions presented in *SFAC No. 6.*[4] These definitions tend to be more technical than the ones we used to introduce the elements.

---

[4]"Elements of Financial Statements," *Statement of Financial Accounting Concepts No. 6 (SFAC No. 6* replaced *SFAC No. 3*). (Stamford, Conn.: FASB, 1985), p 1–2.

Assets are probable future economic benefits obtained or controlled by a particular entity as a result of past transactions or events.

Liabilities are probable future sacrifices of economic benefits arising from present obligations of a particular entity to transfer assets or provide services to other entities in the future as a result of past transactions or events.

Equity is the residual interest in the assets of an entity that remains after deducting its liabilities. In a business enterprise, the equity is the ownership interest.

Investments by owners are increases in equity of a particular business enterprise resulting from transfers to it from other entities of something valuable to obtain or increase ownership interests (or equity) in it. Assets are most commonly received as investments by owners, but that which is received may also include services or satisfaction or conversion of liabilities of the enterprise.

Distributions to owners are decreases in equity of a particular business enterprise resulting from transferring assets, rendering services, or incurring liabilities by the enterprise to owners. Distributions to owners decrease ownership interest (or equity) in an enterprise.

Comprehensive income is the change in equity of a business enterprise during a period from transactions and other events and circumstances from nonowner sources. It includes all changes in equity during a period except those resulting from investments by owners and distributions to owners.

Revenues are inflows or other enhancements of assets of an entity or settlement of its liabilities (or a combination of both) from delivering or producing goods, rendering services, or other activities that constitute the entity's ongoing major or central operations.

Expenses are outflows or other using up of assets or incurrences of liabilities (or a combination of both) from delivering or producing goods, rendering services, or carrying out other activities that constitute the entity's ongoing major or central operations.

Gains are increases in equity (net assets) from peripheral or incidental transactions of an entity and from all other transactions and other events and circumstances affecting the entity except those that result from revenues or investments by owners.

Losses are decreases in equity (net assets) from peripheral or incidental transactions of an entity and from all other transactions and other events and circumstances affecting the entity except those that result from expenses or distributions to owners.

Because many of the other elements are defined in their terms, assets and liabilities appear to be the primary definitions. For example, "Revenues are inflows or other enhancements of assets of an entity or settlement of its liabilities (or a combination of both)...," and "Losses are decreases in equity (net assets)...."

Recognition and Measurement in Financial Statements

LO 4
Discuss financial statement recognition and measurement.

The FASB presents the recognition and measurement concepts in *SFAC No. 5*.[5] Because the concepts adopted are consistent with accounting principles current-

[5]"Recognition and Measurement in Financial Statements of Business Enterprises," *Statement of Financial Accounting Concepts No. 5* (Stamford, Conn.: FASB, 1984).

ly used in practice and, therefore, do not imply changes in financial statements that some accountants and scholars strongly favor, this Statement was the most controversial. **Recognition** in accounting refers to recording the effects of events and transactions formally in the financial statements as assets, liabilities, revenues, expenses, etc.. A recognized item is shown in the financial statements in both words and amounts. **Measurement** in accounting refers to assigning a numerical amount to the information that is recognized. There are two aspects to measurement: choosing the characteristic to be measured and choosing the measurement scale. For example, many transactions are measured using the characteristic of the exchange price observed in the transaction and the measurement scale of the actual dollar amounts exchanged.

The recognition criteria presented in *SFAC No. 5* are divided into fundamental criteria that apply to all recognition decisions and additional guidance in applying the fundamental criteria to the elements of earnings.

Fundamental Recognition Criteria.   According to *SFAC No. 5*, a business should recognize information about an item when the following four criteria are met:

1. *Definitions*. The item meets the definition of an element of financial statements.
2. *Measurability*. The item has a relevant attribute measurable with sufficient reliability.
3. *Relevance*. The information about the item is capable of making a difference in user decisions.
4. *Reliability*. The information is representationally faithful, verifiable, and neutral.[6]

Notice that the recognition criteria rely heavily on the definitions of financial statement elements from *SFAC No. 6* and the qualitative characteristics from *SFAC No. 2*.

Additional Guidance for Applying the Fundamental Criteria to the Elements of Earnings. Because of the importance of net income in reporting on the business's performance, the FASB issued additional guidance for the recognition of revenues and gains and for expenses and losses.

Revenues and gains.   The additional guidance is intended to provide a higher level of assurance of the existence and amounts of revenues and gains. Recognition of revenues and gains involves consideration of two factors: Revenues must be realized and earned.

1. *Realized*. Revenues and gains are realized when merchandise, services, or other assets are exchanged for cash or claims to cash.
2. *Earned*. Revenues and gains are considered to have been earned when the entity has accomplished what it must do to be entitled to the revenues. Gains are the result of transactions that are not part of the normal operations of the business, such as the sale of an operating asset at a price that is more than the carrying amount of the asset. As a result, the realization and the earning of gains usually occur simultaneously[7]

The two criteria that revenues must be realized and earned are generally met at the time the business delivers merchandise to or performs services for cus-

---

[6]*Ibid.*, par. 63.
[7]*Ibid.*, par. 83.

tomers. There are, however, some exceptions to the "time of sale" recognition of revenues. These exceptions include the percentage-of-completion method and the installment method for recognition of revenue.

Percentage-of-completion method. Under the **percentage-of-completion method**, businesses that enter into long-term construction projects recognize revenue before they complete the contract. Recall from the beginning of this chapter that Chris Rose has the opportunity to invest in DeAngelis Construction. She is concerned that a business in long-term construction projects will not provide her with a steady stream of cash flows for her to use to finance her college education. Recall also DeAngelis Construction's policy of limiting withdrawals from the business to one-half of the current year's net income. Chris asked to see DeAngelis's financial statements to assess the cash flow potential. We present DeAngelis Construction's income statement for the last three years (19X1 – 19X3) in Illustration 13-3.

ILLUSTRATION 13-3 Income Statement of DeAngelis Construction

DeAngelis Construction Income Statement For the Years Ended December 31, 19X3, 19X2, and 19X1			
	19X3	*19X2*	*19X1*
Revenue from long-term contracts	$975,000	$850,000	$825,000
Costs of construction	682,500	595,000	577,500
Gross profit	$292,500	$255,000	$247,500
General and administrative expenses	125,000	115,000	109,000
Net income	$167,500	$140,000	$138,500

In reading the notes to the financial statements, Chris learned that DeAngelis uses the percentage-of-completion method to account for long-term construction projects. Chris does not really understand this method of accounting, so she asked the Chief Accountant of DeAngelis, Josh O'Neal, to explain how this method affects the financial statements.

Josh O'Neal pulled from the file cabinet a contract that DeAngelis Construction had just entered into. DeAngelis Construction received a contract from the U.S. Government to construct a mail distribution center in Atlanta. The contract is for $1,200,000. DeAngelis estimates that it will cost $900,000 to construct the building and that it will take 3 years to complete the project beginning in 19X4. If it follows normal revenue recognition procedures, DeAngelis will show no revenues or net income for 19X4 and 19X5 and revenues of $1,200,000 and gross profit of $300,000 in 19X6. If DeAngelis reports these amounts, the financial statements will imply that DeAngelis generated no revenues in 19X4 and 19X5. Assuming that DeAngelis incurs the $900,000 of estimated costs evenly throughout the 3 years it takes to complete the building, gross profit statements would appear as shown in Illustration 13-4.

This sort of financial reporting would not convey what really happened. (Using the language of *SFAC No. 2*, the information would not be representationally faithful.) Since its contract is with the federal government, DeAngelis will receive the contracted price when it completes the building and meets all

ILLUSTRATION 13-4 *Estimated* Partial Income Statements

DeAngelis Construction Partial Income Statements (Estimated) For the Years Ending December 31, 19X6, 19X5, and 19X4			
	19X6	19X5	19X4
Revenue from long-term contracts	$1,200,000	$0	$0
Costs of construction	900,000	0	0
Gross profit (loss)	$ 300,000	$0	$0

the specifications. Therefore, DeAngelis is earning revenue as it performs the tasks involved in constructing the distribution center.

To overcome the reporting problems of recognizing revenue for long-term construction contracts at their completion, businesses use the percentage-of-completion method when they can make reliable estimates of costs. Using this method, businesses recognize revenue and gross profit each period during the term of the construction as they make progress towards completion. We measure progress towards completion by the ratio of costs incurred in the period to the total estimated cost of the project. The calculation of the amount of revenue recognized in a period is shown in Illustration 13-5.

ILLUSTRATION 13-5 Percentage-of-Completion Method

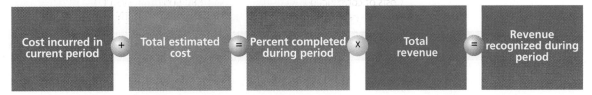

According to the calculation in Illustration 13-5, DeAngelis would recognize revenue in each period and arrive at gross profit by recognizing as expenses the actual costs incurred during the period. We present the application of the percentage-of-completion method for the new contract in Illustration 13-6.

ILLUSTRATION 13-6 Percentage-of-Completion Calculations

	Costs Incurred During Period	Total Costs	Percent Complete	Total Revenue	Revenue Recognized
19X4	$300,000	$900,000	33 1/3%	$1,200,000	$ 400,000
19X5	300,000	900,000	33 1/3%	1,200,000	400,000
19X6	300,000	Balance of contract price			400,000
Totals	$900,000				$1,200,000

The amounts of gross profit that DeAngelis would recognize each period is presented in Illustration 13-7.

Notice that, in this example, we assume actual total costs turned out to be exactly equal to estimated total costs. In an actual project, this is not likely to occur; and businesses that use the percentage-of-completion method periodically revised their accounting estimates. Also, if reliable estimates are not available,

ILLUSTRATION 13-7 Gross Profit—Percentage-of-Completion Method

	19X6	19X5	19X4
Revenue from long-term contracts	$400,000	$400,000	$400,000
Costs of construction	300,000	300,000	300,000
Gross profit (loss)	$100,000	$100,000	$100,000

businesses should not use the percentage-of-completion method because the measure of progress on the project is not sufficiently reliable to be used in recognizing revenue.

In reading the financial statements of DeAngelis Construction for 19X3, 19X2, and 19X1 presented in Illustration 13-3, Chris is pleased with the net income reported in the income statements, but what about cash flows? Josh O'Neal explained to Chris that the terms of the contracts require that the government must pay a portion of the contract price to DeAngelis each period. These are called *progress payments*, and they are based on the portion of the project that has been completed. Therefore, DeAngelis does have sufficient cash flow each period, and it can make distributions to owners.

Many businesses engage in projects with long-term production processes, and they use the percentage-of-completion method. The following quote is from the 1991 Annual Report of General Motors Corporation, and it describes GM's revenue recognition policy for part of its operations:

> Certain sales under long-term contracts, primarily in the defense business, are recorded using the percentage-of-completion method of accounting. Under this method, sales are recorded equivalent to costs incurred plus a portion of the profit expected to be realized on the contract, determined based on the ratio of costs incurred to estimated total costs at completion. Profits expected to be realized on contracts are based on the Corporation's estimates of total sales value and cost at completion. These estimates are reviewed and revised periodically throughout the lives of the contracts, and adjustments to profits resulting from such revisions are recorded in the accounting period in which the revisions are made.

Installment method. Another alternative to recognizing revenue, called the *cash basis*, recognizes revenue when cash is collected. Businesses use the cash basis to account for credit sales when there is significant uncertainty about whether the cash will be collected. The installment method is a form of the cash basis of revenue recognition. Under the **installment method**, each receipt of cash from a credit sale is considered to consist of a recovery of part of the cost of the goods sold and part of the gross profit from the sale. The installment method is implemented by first calculating the gross profit percentage of the sale. As shown in Illustration 13-8, each cash collection generates gross profit equal to the amount of cash collected x gross profit percentage. Implicitly, cost of goods sold is the remainder of the amount of cash collected. For example, if a sale has a gross profit percentage of 30%, each cash collection would be considered as 30% gross profit and 70% (100–30%) cost of goods sold.

Assume that Martinez Construction Machinery had credit sales of $2,000,000 in 19X1, its first year of operations. The cost of the goods sold on credit sales is $1,500,000. The total gross profit is, therefore, $500,000 ($2,000,000 – $1,500,000). The gross profit percentage is 25% ($500,000 ÷ $2,000,000), and the cost of goods sold percentage is 75% (100–25%). Martinez decided to use the installment method to recognize revenue because the construction industry is in

ILLUSTRATION 13-8 Installment Method

a recession and Martinez is uncertain about whether all the customers will be able to make cash payments for the machinery they purchased. Cash collections of the credit sales turn out to be as follows:

19X1	$800,000
19X2	600,000
19X3	600,000

The calculation of the gross profit recognized from the credit sales is presented in Illustration 13-9.

ILLUSTRATION 13-9 Calculation of Gross Profit—Installment Method

Year	Cash Collected	Gross Profit Percentage	Gross Profit Recognized
19X1	$ 800,000	25%	$200,000
19X2	600,000	25%	150,000
19X3	600,000	25%	150,000
Totals	$2,000,000		$500,000

As you can see from Illustration 13-9, we consider the installment method to be a cash basis of revenue recognition because the business recognizes gross profit in the period that it collects cash.

Expenses and losses *SFAC No. 5* also presents criteria for the recognition of expenses and losses. Accountants call the recognition criterion for expenses the **matching principle** because traditionally accountants try to "match" the timing of expense recognition with related revenue recognition. Therefore, under accrual accounting concepts, we recognize expenses when the business incurs them in its earning process. In other words, we recognize expenses when they contribute to the business's earning of revenues. The matching principle often leads to recognition of expenses at times different from those when costs are incurred. We present this concept in Illustration 13-10.

In many cases when there is no apparent direct relationship between some expenses and revenues, the process of matching expenses with revenues is difficult. For example, is there a direct link between costs incurred in repairing the business's roof and revenues earned? To deal with this problem, accountants recognize expenses based on the types of costs that the business incurs. Some costs provide future benefits by contributing to the earning of revenues in both the current and future periods. We record these costs as assets initially, and they represent unexpired costs. Merchandise inventory, prepaid insurance, and

ILLUSTRATION 13-10 Matching Principle

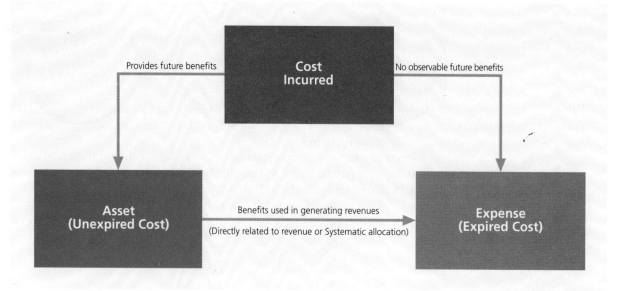

property, plant, and equipment are examples of costs that generate revenues in current and future periods. Other costs such as advertising, repairs, and salaries benefit the business in earning revenues only in the current period; and we record these costs as expenses in the period the business incurs them. Sometimes costs such as advertising indirectly benefit the business in earning future revenues as well, but the relationship between the costs and future revenues is so indirect or difficult to measure that we simply ignore it and recognize the costs as expenses in the period incurred.

We recognize some unexpired costs as expenses based on a direct relationship between the expiration of the costs and revenues that the business earns. The best example of this direct relationship is merchandise inventory. In the period the business sells merchandise, we recognize revenue; and we record the cost of the merchandise as cost of goods sold and match it with the related revenue in the income statement in the same period.

Other unexpired costs clearly contribute to the earning of revenues in both the current and future periods, but we cannot observe the same direct relationship to specific revenues. We recognize these costs as operating expenses of current and future periods, based on accepted allocation procedures. For example, we allocate the cost of a delivery van to current and future periods in the form of a systematic allocation of depreciation expense.

The following note is from the Annual Report of Santa Anita Operating Company:

> (The) Operating Company has adopted an accounting practice whereby the revenues associated with thoroughbred horse racing at Santa Anita Racetrack are reported as they are earned. Costs and expenses associated with thoroughbred horse racing revenues are charged against income in those periods in which the thoroughbred horse racing revenues are recognized. Other costs and expenses are recognized as they actually occur throughout the year.

When an asset (unexpired cost) is reduced or eliminated or a liability increased because of events and circumstances not related to the earning of revenue, the business recognizes a loss rather than an expense. For example, if a tornado destroys an uninsured building, the business will recognize a loss equal to the building's carrying amount (unexpired cost) on the date the tornado destroyed it.

LO 5
Describe the assumptions underlying financial statements.

UNDERLYING ASSUMPTIONS

The accounting profession developed generally accepted accounting principles over time. Underlying these principles are the following assumptions: business entity, going-concern, time periods, and stable-dollar unit.

Business Entity Assumption

We assume that information gathered and recorded in the accounts are for a specific business entity. As a result of this assumption, we can be confident that the financial statements report only the business entity's financial position and results of operations. Accountants have to be careful to distinguish the business's transactions from those of the owner. For example, if Rick Jones pays some of his personal living expenses with the cash of his business, Jones Cleaning Service, the accountant should not record these payments as business expenses. Rather, the accountant would record the payments as owner withdrawals.

Another result of the **business entity assumption** is that when one business owns other businesses, one set of financial statements may be prepared for the group of businesses. These financial statements are called *consolidated financial statements*, and they are discussed in a subsequent chapter. The assumption underlying consolidated financial statements is that even though several separate legal business entities exist under the same owner's control, they operate as though they are one economic business entity. Therefore, the consolidated financial statements report the financial position and results of operations of the single economic business entity.

Going-Concern Assumption

When accounting for a business entity, accountants assume that the business will continue to operate indefinitely, unless there is evidence that the business is about to cease operations. The **going-concern assumption**, as discussed in a previous chapter, records as assets, rather than expenses, costs that will generate revenues in both the current and future periods. For example, when a business purchases equipment that it expects to use for five years, it records the cost of the equipment as an asset. Through depreciation, the business allocates the cost of the equipment to expenses of the periods the equipment benefits.

Time Periods Assumption

Accountants assume that the life of a business can be divided into a series of equal time periods—or the **time periods assumption**. These time periods are generally years, quarters, or months. Although most businesses prepare financial statements annually, some may prepare them every three months, or quarterly. Recall from a previous chapter that financial statements for a period shorter than a year are called *interim financial statements*.

While accountants strive to report accurate financial statements for the time periods, this process requires management to make many estimates and to exercise considerable judgment. As you saw in previous chapters, the adjustment process at the end of an accounting period requires management to make estimates of the useful lives of depreciable assets and to exercise judgment about items such as the collectibility of receivables. The adjustment process is required because the business's transactions do not always fit nicely into the time periods the financial statements cover.

Stable-Dollar Assumption

When recording the effects of transactions in the accounts, accountants measure the amounts in dollars. Under the **stable-dollar assumption**, accountants assume the U.S. dollar is a reasonably constant unit of measure. As a result, accountants do not make adjustments in the financial statement amounts for the dollar's changing value.

Although accountants assume the dollar is reasonably constant, we know the value of the dollar does change. Over the past several decades, the value of the U.S. dollar has been declining because the prices of goods and services have been rising. This phenomenon is called *inflation*. Many accountants believe inflation has a significant impact on financial statements, and that we should adjust financial statement amounts for its effects. For example, compare the net incomes of two similar companies. One company purchased its building 10 years earlier than the other did. While both buildings may be identical in all aspects, except the date of purchase, the company that purchased the building at the earlier date will show a higher amount of net income. That is, the older building will cost less because of inflation; therefore, depreciation expense will be less, and the result is higher net income. (More on the effects of changing prices on financial statements is presented in a later chapter.)

LO 6

Identify the modifying conventions that alter the application of GAAP.

MODIFYING CONVENTIONS (CONSTRAINTS)

The application of accounting principles is sometimes altered by several **modifying conventions** that the accounting profession has adopted. These modifying conventions also are called *constraints*. The modifying conventions discussed below include cost/benefits, materiality, and conservatism.

Cost/Benefits

The **cost/benefits convention** requires that information presented in financial statements should provide benefits to the users that exceed the costs of preparing and using the information. The benefits of using information result in better decisions, and the costs of information include those of gathering and presenting the information. Also, users of information incur a cost in processing information through their decisions models.

The cost/benefits convention is difficult to apply in practice. Reasonable estimates for the cost of presenting information are available, but attempts to estimate the costs of using information are elusive at best. Quantitative esti-

533

mates of the benefits of using information are impossible to obtain. Neverthe-less, the convention of cost/benefits is frequently offered in practice as the rea-son for not providing some kinds of information in the financial statements.

Materiality

The **materiality convention** involves judgments about whether errors and omissions in financial statements are of sufficient size to cause the financial statements to be misleading. If an item is judged to be immaterial, then GAAP does not have to be followed in accounting for the item.

An example of how businesses use the materiality convention is their accounting policies to determine whether they will treat certain costs as expens-es in the current period or capitalize and depreciate them over their useful lives. Businesses commonly set some dollar level below which they merely expense purchases of assets in the period of purchases. They capitalize purchases of assets above that amount. This policy results in expensing small purchases such as pencil sharpeners, wastebaskets, and staplers. Large purchases such as com-puters, copying machines, and telephone systems are capitalized. Under GAAP, these businesses should technically capitalize and depreciate all of the purchas-es over their useful lives. The materiality convention, however, allows these businesses to expense the small purchases in the current period because the effects on the financial statements between expensing and capitalizing is not large enough to influence decisions—that is, are not *material*.

Conservatism

Conservatism in financial reporting is a means of dealing with uncertainty. When accountants make estimates and judgments about items such as the use-ful lives of assets, whether revenue should be recognized, and whether gains or losses should be recognized, they are often trying to predict what will happen in an uncertain future time period. For example, assume two estimates exist about the amount of a future payment the business will be required to make. The accountant believes that both estimates are equally likely to occur. The conservatism convention requires that the accountant use the less optimistic estimate in presenting the financial statements.

A popular misconception about conservatism is that accountants deliberate-ly understate net assets and net income. This sort of practice would cause the statements to be unreliable. As discussed earlier in this chapter, reliability is one of the primary qualitative characteristics of useful financial statement informa-tion. Therefore, the deliberate misstatement of financial statements amounts is an inappropriate interpretation of the conservatism convention.

In a previous chapter you saw an example of conservatism when we applied the lower-of-cost-or-market method to merchandise inventories. Under this method, we recognize as losses the decreases in the market values of mer-chandise in the period those decreases occur. We do not recognize increases in market values, however, until the increases are realized in the form of sales to outside parties. The justification given for recognizing losses when the value changes and not recognizing increases in value on the same basis is the con-vention of conservatism.

SUMMARY

Identify the objectives of financial statements. Financial statements should provide information that is useful in making rational investment, credit, and similar decisions. The information should help users in assessing the amounts, timing, and uncertainty of future cash flows. Also, financial statements should provide information about the business's financial position.

Explain the qualitative characteristics of useful financial statement information. There are three levels of qualitative characteristics of useful financial statement information: (1) decision usefulness, (2) relevance and reliability, and (3) comparability and consistency.

Define the elements of financial statements. The FASB defined ten elements of financial statements. These elements are assets, liabilities, equity, investments by owners, distributions to owners, comprehensive income, revenues, expenses, gains, and losses.

Discuss financial statement recognition and measurement. The fundamental recognition criteria include definitions, measurability, relevance, and reliability. Additional recognition criteria for revenues and gains are that they be realized and earned. Additional recognition criteria for expenses are included in the matching principle. Losses are recognized when unexpired costs are reduced or eliminated because of events and circumstances unrelated to the business's normal operations. Measurement in accounting involves choosing the characteristic to be measured and selecting the measurement scale. Generally, the actual exchange price related to a transaction is used for measurement in financial accounting.

Describe the assumptions underlying financial statements. The assumptions underlying financial accounting include business entity, going-concern, time periods, and stable-dollar.

Identify the modifying conventions that alter the application of Generally Accepted Accounting Principles. The conventions that alter the application of GAAP include cost/benefits, materiality, and conservatism.

REVIEW PROBLEM

1. A conceptual framework is
   a. A set of specific accounting rules
   b. A list of specific accounting procedures that are acceptable for reporting business transactions
   c. A theory developed to explain current accounting standards
   d. A coherent system of interrelated objectives and fundamentals of financial accounting and financial statements
2. The objectives of financial statements
   a. Have not yet been defined by the FASB
   b. Require straight-line depreciation for plant assets
   c. State that the objective of business is to earn a profit
   d. State that information provided in financial statements should be useful in making investment and credit decisions

3. In the FASB's *SFAC No. 2*, qualitative characteristics of financial statement information
   a. Require financial statement information to be relevant, reliable, and have the qualities of comparability and consistency
   b. Require that assets minus liabilities equal equity
   c. Are the basis for the going-concern assumption
   d. None of the above
4. The FASB's *SFAC No. 6*, "Elements of Financial Statements,"
   a. Defines consistency and comparability
   b. Defines the objectives of financial statements
   c. Defines assets, liabilities, equity, revenues, expenses, gains, and losses
   d. Defines the underlying assumptions of accounting
5. The FASB's *SFAC No. 5*, on recognition and measurement,
   a. Discusses the parties who use financial statements
   b. Requires revenue to be recognized when the cash is collected
   c. Establishes four criteria for recognition of items in financial statements
   d. Requires expenses to be recognized in the period they are paid
6. Underlying assumptions to accounting principles
   a. Include the business entity assumption, the going-concern assumption, the time periods assumption, and the stable-dollar assumption
   b. Assume financial statements are used primarily by creditors
   c. Assume revenues are recognized when cash is collected
   d. None of the above
7. Modifying conventions in accounting
   a. Include the going-concern assumption
   b. Establish the goals and objectives of financial statements
   c. Include the costs/benefits, materiality, and conservatism conventions
   d. None of the above

SOLUTION:

1. d (p. 520)   5. c (p. 524-5)
2. d (p. 521)   6. a (p. 531)
3. a (p. 522-3) 7. c (p. 532)
4. c (p. 523-4)

KEY TERMS

assets, *524*
business entity assumption, *531*
comparability, *523*
comprehensive income, *524*
Conceptual Framework, *520*
conservatism, *533*
consistency, *523*
cost/benefits convention, *532*
decision usefulness, *522*
distributions to owners, *524*
elements of financial statements, *523*
equity, *524*
expenses, *524*
feedback value, *523*

gains, *524*
going-concern assumption, *531*
installment method, *528*
investments by owners, *524*
liabilities, *524*
losses, *524*
matching principle, *529*
materiality convention, *533*
measurement, *525*
modifying conventions, *532*
neutrality, *523*
objectives of financial statements, *521*
percentage-of-completion method, *526*

predictive value, *523*
qualitative characteristics, *522*
recognition, *525*
relevance, *522*
reliability, *523*
representational faithfulness, *523*
revenues, *524*
stable-dollar assumption, *532*
time periods assumption, *531*
timeliness, *523*
verifiability, *523*

SELF-QUIZ

LO 1 1. The FASB's objectives of financial statements
 a. Were the next logical step to explore after identifying the qualitative characteristics that make financial statements useful
 b. State a broad concern that financial statements should be useful to individual users in making investment and credit decisions
 c. Provide definitions of expenses and revenues
 d. Establish criteria for the recognition of revenue

LO 1 2. The FASB's objectives of financial statements do not include the following objective
 a. Financial statements should provide information about assets, liabilities, and owners' equity.
 b. Financial statements should be useful to individual users in making investment and credit decisions.
 c. Financial statements should provide information useful in assessing the business's future cash flows.
 d. Financial statements be prepared on the cash basis of accounting.

LO 1 3. A conceptual framework
 a. Provides specific accounting rules outlining the proper treatment of specific transactions
 b. Functions as a "constitution" for financial reporting
 c. Is a coherent system of interrelated objectives and fundamentals
 d. Both b and c

LO-2 4. The *primary* qualitative characteristic of financial statement information is:
 a. Timeliness
 b. Decision usefulness
 c. Neutrality
 d. Conservatism

LO 2 5. Comparability of financial statement information
 a. Is the quality of financial statement information that enables users to identify similarities in and differences between two businesses
 b. Is a characteristic that makes financial statement information useful
 c. Refers to the process of matching revenues and expenses
 d. Both a and b

LO 2 6. Consistency of financial statement information
 a. Is the quality of financial statement information that enables users to identify similarities and differences between two businesses
 b. Means using the same accounting methods for a business from period to period
 c. Refers to the process of matching revenues and expenses
 d. Has the same meaning as comparability

LO 3 7. Examples of elements of financial statements, as defined in the FASB Concepts Statement, are
 a. Relevance and reliability
 b. Revenues and expenses
 c. Gains and losses
 d. Both b and c

LO 3 8. Comprehensive income, as defined in the FASB's elements statement, is
 a. Revenues − Expenses
 b. Assets − Liabilities
 c. Includes all changes in equity during a period, including those resulting from investments from owners and distributions to owners
 d. Includes all changes in equity during a period, except those resulting from investments from owners and distributions to owners

LO 4 9. Recognition in accounting refers to
 a. Assigning a numerical amount to accounting information
 b. Posting information from journals to ledgers
 c. Formally recording the effects of events and transactions in the financial statements
 d. None of the above

LO 4 10. Measurement in accounting refers to
 a. The difference between revenues and expenses
 b. Assigning a numerical amount to information that is recognized
 c. Formally recording the effects of events and transactions in the financial statements
 d. None of the above

LO 4 11. Two factors required for the recognition of revenue are
 a. Cash must be received and the revenue earned.
 b. Revenue must be earned, and it must be from a prior transaction or event.
 c. Revenue must be earned and realized.
 d. Both a and c

LO 4 12. Expenses are recognized
 a. In the period they are paid
 b. In the period they contribute to the earning of revenue
 c. In the period after they are paid
 d. Only if they provide future benefit to the business

LO 5 13. The owner of a business pays her house payment out of the business's cash. The accountant debits Withdrawals and credits Cash to record the transaction. This accounting treatment is based on what underlying assumption?
a. Business entity
b. Going-concern
c. Time period
d. Stable-dollar

LO 5 14. A company spends $100,000 to pay rent in advance, and the amount is not refundable. The accountant debits Prepaid Rent and credits Cash to record the transaction. This accounting treatment is based on what underlying assumption?
a. Business entity
b. Going-concern
c. Stable-dollar
d. None of the above

LO 5 15. A company makes an estimate of the amount of uncollectible accounts at year-end and prepares a journal entry debiting Uncollectible Accounts Expense and crediting Allowance for Uncollectible Accounts. This accounting treatment is based on what underlying assumption?
a. Business entity
b. Going-concern
c. Time periods
d. Stable-dollar

LO 6 16. The cost/benefits convention suggests that

a. Only information that does not involve a cost to prepare should be presented in financial statements.
b. Information about a business's costs and the benefits of these costs should be included in the financial statements.
c. Information should be presented in the financial statements only if the benefits of using the information exceed the costs of preparing and using the information.
d. None of the above

LO 6 17. A business computes the cost of the merchandise inventory at the end of the accounting period and does not include the small amount of transportation costs incurred when the items were purchased as part of the inventory cost. This accounting treatment is based on
a. Materiality
b. Stable-dollar assumption
c. Going-concern assumption
d. Matching principle

LO 6 18. Conservatism in accounting is
a. The deliberate understatement of net assets and net income
b. A reluctance to change current accounting standards
c. A tendency to select the least optimistic estimate from a set of estimates that are equally likely to occur
d. None of the above

SOLUTIONS TO SELF-QUIZ
1. b   2. d   3. d   4. b   5. d   6. b   7. d   8. d   9. c   10. b   11. c   12. b   13. a   14. b
15. c   16. c   17. a   18. c

QUESTIONS

Q13-1 Why is a conceptual framework for financial accounting and reporting needed?

Q13-2 In developing the objectives of financial statements, what important questions did the FASB consider?

Q13-3 The FASB specified three objectives of financial statements. Which is considered the broadest and most fundamental?

Q13-4 The characteristic of relevance in financial reporting means that the information is capable of making a difference in a decision. To be relevant, information must have _____ _____, _____ _____, and _____.

Q13-5 Reliability assures that the information is reasonably free from error and bias and faithfully represents what it intends to represent. To be reliable, information must have _____ _____; and it must be _____ and _____.

Q13-6 Is it possible for accounting information to be useful and be completely void of either relevance or reliability? Explain.

Q13-7 Distinguish between comparability and consistency, as these terms relate to qualitative characteristics of financial statement information.

Q13-8 Distinguish between revenues and gains.

Q13-9 Distinguish between expenses and losses.

Q13-10 Which two definitions contained in the FASB's "Elements of Financial Statements" can be viewed as the primary definitions? Why?

Q13-11 What four conditions should be met before accounting information is recognized? (1) _____, (2) _____, (3) _____, and (4) _____.

Q13-12 The recognition of revenue requires that the revenue be _____ and _____.

Q13-13 Two accounting methods that are exceptions to the "time of sale" recognition of revenues include: (1) _____ and (2) _____.

Q13-14 When a business incurs a cost, how does it determine if the cost is classified as an asset or an expense?

Q13-15 Many of the adjusting entries made in the business's accounting records are required because of the time periods assumption. Explain.

EXERCISES

LO 1

E13-1 **Objectives of Financial Statements** Identify several different parties who use financial statements.

LO 1

E13-2 **Objectives of Financial Statements** One objective of financial statements places a lot of importance on helping decision makers assess a business's cash flows. Does this mean the FASB is expressing a preference for the cash basis of accounting over the accrual basis of accounting? Discuss.

LO 2

E13-3 **Qualitative Characteristics** To be reliable, accounting information must have representational faithfulness, and it must be verifiable and neutral. Rate the following accounting items, as to their relative reliability, using the following scale:

ST = Strong
F   = Fair
WK = Weak

___ a. Cost of equipment
___ b. Amount of prepaid insurance at the end of the accounting period
___ c. Depreciation expense on equipment
___ d. Value of ending inventory determined by a physical count
___ e. Value of the ending inventory determined by an estimate based on the gross profit method
___ f. Liability related to the warranty of products
___ g. Uncollectible Accounts Expense determined under the allowance method of accounting
___ h. Uncollectible Accounts Expense determined under the direct write-off method
___ i. Liability to pay health care benefits to employees after they retire
___ j. Utility expense for the accounting period
___ k. Amount of cash

LO 2

E13-4 **Qualitative Characteristics** To be relevant, accounting information must be capable of making a difference in a decision. The information must have predictive value, feedback value, and timeliness. Rate the following accounting items, as to their degree of relevance to a potential creditor, using the following scale:

ST = Strong
F   = Fair
WK = Weak

___ a. Net income of a business
___ b. Organization costs of a business
___ c. Amount of purchases discounts lost
___ d. Current assets and current liabilities of a company
___ e. Projection of future cash flows for the next accounting year
___ f. Supplies on hand at the end of the period
___ g. Depreciation expense for the period

LO 3   **E13-5**   **Elements of Financial Statements**   Listed below are the elements of financial statements as defined by the FASB and their summarized definitions. Match the elements and
the definitions.

Elements

___ (1) Assets
___ (2) Liabilities
___ (3) Equity
___ (4) Investments by owners
___ (5) Distributions to owners
___ (6) Comprehensive income
___ (7) Revenues
___ (8) Expenses
___ (9) Gains
___ (10) Losses

Summarized Definitions

a. Increases in net assets from peripheral transactions
b. Increases in equity resulting from transfers to a business of something of value to
   obtain ownership interests
c. Includes all changes in equity during a period that result from transactions and other
   events and circumstances, *except* investments by owners and distributions to owners
d. Probable future economic benefits controlled by an entity as a result of past transactions or events
e. Residual interest in the assets of an entity, after deducting its liabilities
f. Outflows of net assets from activities that constitute the entity's ongoing major or central operations
g. Decreases in equity resulting from transferring assets, rendering services, or incurring
   liabilities to owners
h. Decreases in equity from peripheral transactions
i. Inflows of net assets from activities that constitute the entity's ongoing major or central operations
j. Probable future sacrifices of economic benefits arising from present obligations

LO 3   **E13-6**   **Revenues and Gains, Expenses and Losses**   Baxter Computer Warehouse sells computers and computer components through mail-order operations. Identify the following
items as revenues (*R*), gains (*G*), expenses (*E*), or losses (*L*).

___ a. Increases in equity resulting from the sale of computers
___ b. Increase in equity resulting from selling short-term investments at an amount
       above cost
___ c. Decrease in equity resulting from selling a copy machine Baxter uses in its own
       operations at an amount below book value
___ d. Decrease in equity resulting from payment of monthly phone bill
___ e. Decrease in equity from payment of a penalty to the federal government for the
       violation of an environmental code

___ f. Increase in equity resulting from cash awarded in litigation against a competitor
___ g. Decrease in equity resulting from the payment of advertising
___ h. Decrease in equity resulting from the payment of employee salaries

LO 4   **E13-7**   **Recognition and Measurement, Percentage-of-Completion**   In January 19X3, the Biaz Group was awarded a contract to install underground cables connecting the major structures of a large regional university. The contract was for $9,000,000. Biaz estimates that it will cost $8,000,000 and take 2 years to complete. Biaz incurs construction costs of $3,000,000 in 19X3 and $5,000,000 in 19X4. The contract is completed in 19X4.

REQUIRED:

Complete the following partial income statements showing Biaz's operating results, assuming; (1) traditional "time of completion" revenue recognition procedures and (2) the percentage-of-completion method.

Normal revenue recognition method:

	19X3	*19X4*
Revenue, long-term contracts	____	____
Costs of contracts	____	____
Gross profit (loss)	____	____

Percentage-of-completion method:

	19X3	*19X4*
Revenue, long-term contracts	____	____
Costs of contracts	____	____
Gross profit (loss)	____	____

LO 4   **E13-8**   **Recognition and Measurement, Installment Method**   In January 19X4, the Bradley Company sold the GGH Development Company a track of land for $9,000,000. The land cost Bradley $6,000,000. The GGH Company makes the following payments to Bradley, including interest at 10% on the unpaid balance.

	Principal	*Interest on Unpaid Balance*	*Total Payment*
12-31-X4	$5,000,000	$90,000	$5,090,000
12-31-X5	3,000,000	40,000	3,040,000
12-31-X6	1,000,000	10,000	1,010,000

Bradley Company uses the installment method to recognize gross profit because GGH has been experiencing financial trouble, and it is not certain that Bradley will collect the full amount of the contract. Bradley recognizes the interest received on the unpaid balance as interest revenue.

REQUIRED:

a. Complete the following table to show the total revenue Bradley recognized in each of the 3 years under the installment method.

	Principal Collected	*GP%*	*Gross Profit Recognized*	*Interest Revenue Recognized*
12-31-X4	____	____	____	____
12-31-X5	____	____	____	____
12-31-X6	____	____	____	____

b. Complete the following table to show the total revenue Bradley recognized in each of the 3 years, assuming the traditional "time of sale" method was used.

	Principal Collected	GP%	Gross Profit Recognized	Interest Revenue Recognized
12-31-X4	_____	_____	_____	_____
12-31-X5	_____	_____	_____	_____
12-31-X6	_____	_____	_____	_____

LO 5

E13-9   Underlying Assumptions   Listed below are four underlying assumptions of accounting principles and a set of items. Identify the assumption most directly related to each item.

Assumptions

Business entity assumption (*BE*)
Going-concern assumption (*G*)
Time periods assumption (*TP*)
Stable-dollar assumption (*SD*)

Items

___ a. Adjusting entries made at the end of the accounting period, accruing and deferring various items

___ b. Preparing a single income statement that includes the operations of both Ford Motor Company and Ford Credit Corporation

___ c. Classifying costs that will benefit future accounting periods as assets

___ d. A tract of land purchased in 1967 for $100,000 and a tract of land purchased in 1994 for $100,000 added together to show the total cost of land reported on the balance sheet

___ e. Classifying a payment out of the business's bank account for the personal living expenses of the owner as withdrawals

___ f. Reporting production equipment on the balance sheet at its carrying amount, although its fair market value is less

___ g. Selling land that cost $100,000 twenty years ago for $125,000, and reporting a gain of $25,000

LO 6

E13-10   Modifying Conventions   Listed below are three modifying conventions adopted by the accounting profession and a set of items describing a particular accounting treatment. Identify the modifying convention most closely related to each item.

Modifying Conventions

Cost/benefits (*CB*)
Materiality (*M*)
Conservatism (*C*)

Items

___ a. A company estimates the life of an asset to be from 4 to 6 years and elects to depreciate the asset over 4 years.

___ b. The lower-of-cost-or-market inventory valuation method is used.

___ c. A company has accounts payable to several hundred different suppliers and reports the total as a single amount on the balance sheet.

___ d. All items of supplies and equipment costing under $50 are expensed when purchased.

___ e. Transportation-in is ignored when valuing ending inventory.

___ f. A company uses the LIFO cost flow method for valuing ending inventory in a period of rising prices.

___ g. A company elects to depreciate its assets under the double-declining-balance method of depreciation.

___ h. The effect of purchases discounts are ignored when calculating the cost of the ending inventory.

___ i. Costs that may have future benefit are expensed in the year incurred.

___ j. The ending merchandise inventory is presented as a single number. The costs of distinct categories of items making up the total inventory are not disclosed.

PROBLEM SET A

LO 1

P13-1A **Objectives of Financial Statements** "Objectives of Financial Reporting by Business Enterprises" was the first concepts statement the FASB issued in the development of a conceptual framework of accounting.

REQUIRED:

a. Discuss why establishing objectives is a logical first step in a conceptual framework.
b. What process might the FASB have used to arrive at the objectives?

LO 2

P13-2A **Qualitative Characteristics** The primary qualitative characteristic of financial statement information is that it be useful in making investment, credit, and other decisions. Decision usefulness is based on the primary decision-specific qualities of relevance and reliability and the secondary qualities of comparability and consistency.

REQUIRED:

a. Identify some types of financial information that are not useful in making investment, credit, and other decisions.
b. Discuss what kinds of decisions might be included under the "other" category when classifying decisions as investment, credit, or other.
c. Discuss the relationship between relevance and reliability as to how they affect usefulness. Can information be useful if it is void of either relevance or reliability?
d. Distinguish between comparability and consistency and discuss how they affect usefulness.
e. Discuss how the establishment of qualitative characteristics can lead to better accounting standards.

LO 3

P13-3A **Elements of Financial Statements** Issues related to the elements of financial statements are presented below.

REQUIRED:

a. The Mountain Ski Resort regards the cable weather channel as a valuable resource in operating its business. Discuss whether this asset meets the definition of an asset for Mountain's financial accounting purposes.
b. A competitor is suing MicroSolutions Software Company for violation of a copyright. MicroSolutions is contesting the litigation but believes it has a reasonable chance of losing. Discuss whether this potential loss meets the definition of a liability.
c. Discuss why comprehensive income is not increased by investments by owners and decreased by distributions to owners.
d. Explain how distinguishing between expenses and losses and between revenues and gains might help a decision maker better project the business's future cash flows.

LO 4

P13-4A **Expense Recognition** Accountants match the timing of expense recognition with revenue recognition when it is practical. Two expenses of a merchandising company are presented below:

1. Cost of goods sold
2. Depreciation

REQUIRED:

a. Which expense is the easier to match against revenue? Discuss.
b. Which expense is the more difficult to match against revenue? Discuss.

LO 4   **P13-5A   Percentage-of-Completion Method**   In 19X4, the New England Construction Company enters into a contract to construct an oil storage facility in Saudi Arabia. The project is scheduled to take 4 years to complete at a cost of $12,000,000. New England is to be paid $15,000,000 for the contract. Information related to the contract during the 4-year period follows:

Year	Cost Incurred Current Period	Estimated Costs to Complete at End of Period
19X4	$3,000,000	$9,000,000
19X5	4,000,000	5,000,000
19X6	4,000,000	1,000,000
19X7	1,000,000	-0-

REQUIRED:

a. Prepare a partial income statement down to gross profit for the contract over the 4-year period, assuming the revenue is recognized in the period the contract is completed.
b. Prepare a partial income statement down to gross profit for the contract over the 4-year period, assuming the percentage-of-completion method is used.
c. Which method provides better information about New England's operating results? Discuss the circumstances under which each method should be used.

LO 1,2,3,4   **P13-6A   Conceptual Framework**   Four concepts statements the Financial Accounting Standards Board issued discuss issues fundamental to financial statements of business enterprises. These statements and the issues they represent are assigned the following identifying codes:

OBJ = "Objectives of Financial Reporting by Business Enterprises"
QC = "Qualitative Characteristics of Useful Financial Statement Information"
ELE = "Elements of Financial Statements"
R&M = "Recognition and Measurement in Financial Statements of Business Enterprises"

REQUIRED:

An assortment of items, consisting of comments, terms, questions, and statements that relate to the concepts statements are presented below. Using the appropriate identifying code, match each item to the appropriate concepts statement.

Items

___ a. If information is not useful, then it has no value; and any cost incurred in providing the information is not justified.
___ b. Assign a numerical amount to the information that is recognized.
___ c. Financial statements should help investors, creditors, and others to assess future cash flows from the business and from their interest in the business.
___ d. Assets are probable future economic benefits.
___ e. What kinds of information are financial statements capable of communicating to users?
___ f. Information in financial statements should be relevant.
___ g. Expenses are decreases in net assets from producing goods or services.
___ h. Information in financial statements should be reliable.
___ i. Information about a business is more useful if it can be compared with similar information about other businesses.
___ j. Financial statements should provide information about the assets of a business and the claims to the assets.
___ k. Determine when we formally record the effects of events and transactions in the financial statements as assets, liabilities, expenses, revenues, etc.
___ l. Liabilities are probable future sacrifices of economic benefits.

___ m. Equity is the residual interest in the assets of an entity.
___ n. What kinds of decisions do users of financial statements make?
___ o. Revenues are increases in net assets of an entity from providing goods or services.
___ p. Who are the users of financial statements?
___ q. Financial statements should provide information to investors, creditors, and others to help them make good investment and credit decisions.

PROBLEM SET B

LO 1

P13-1B **Objectives of Financial Statements** In developing the objectives of financial statements, one of the issues the FASB considered was the kinds of information financial statements are capable of communicating to users.

REQUIRED:

a. Discuss the types of information that financial statements are capable of communicating to users.
b. Discuss the types of information that financial statements are not capable of communicating to users.

LO 2

P13-2B **Qualitative Characteristics, Relevance and Reliability** Many investors believe that a projection of future operating results, based on the current information available to management, should be included in the financial statements.

REQUIRED:

a. Evaluate the relevance of such information.
b. Evaluate the reliability of such information.

LO 3

P13-3B **Elements of Financial Statements** Equity is one of the elements of financial statements the FASB defined.

REQUIRED:

a. Equity can essentially be defined in two ways. What are the two definitions?
b. List three elements of financial statements (excluding comprehensive income) that have the effect of increasing equity.
c. List three elements of financial statements that have the effect of decreasing equity.
d. Which of the elements in b and c are included in comprehensive income?

LO 4

P13-4B **Recognition of Revenues** The MegaSub Sandwich Shop has franchised its operations. It sells franchises for $50,000 each, which gives the franchisee the exclusive right to use the MegaSub logo and recipes in a specified territory for 10 years. The $50,000, which is payable at the contract signing date, also entitles the franchisee to free technical assistance from the MegaSub Home Office and to the benefits of a nationwide advertising program conducted by the Home Office.

REQUIRED:

a. What two factors are important to the recognition of revenue?
b. Apply these two criteria to determine if MegaSub should recognize the $50,000 as revenue in the period it signs the contract with the franchisee.

LO 4

P13-5B **Percentage-of-Completion-Method** In 19X6, the Hubbard Group entered into a contract with the Atlanta Center for Disease Control to study the effects of exposure to carbon dioxide among urban residents. Hubbard estimates the project will take 3 years.

The contract is for $2,500,000, and the estimated costs of the project are $2,000,000. Information related to the contract over the 3-year period follows:

Year	Cost Incurred Current Period	Estimated Costs to Complete at End of Period
19X6	$ 300,000	$1,700,000
19X7	400,000	1,300,000
19X8	1,300,000	-0-

REQUIRED:

a. Prepare a partial income statement down to gross profit for the contract for the 3-year period, assuming the revenue is recognized in the period the contract is completed.
b. Prepare a partial income statement down to gross profit for the contract for the 3-year period, assuming the percentage-of-completion method is used.
c. Which method provides better information about Hubbard's operating results? Discuss the circumstances under which each method should be used.

LO 5

P13-6B   **Going-Concern Assumption**   When accounting for a business entity, accountants assume the business will continue to operate indefinitely, unless there is evidence to the contrary.

REQUIRED:

a. Discuss how the going-concern assumption affects accounting principles.
b. If accountants were to assume that there is evidence to the contrary and that a business is not a going-concern, discuss how this might affect the way financial statements are prepared.

CRITICAL THINKING AND COMMUNICATING

C13-1   One of the traditional and long-debated issues in financial reporting centers around the primary qualitative characteristic of financial statement information: that it should be useful in making investment, credit, and other decisions.

   While everyone agrees with the idea of usefulness, the difficult choices emerge when the primary decision qualities of relevance and reliability are considered. The problem is that the two characteristics often conflict. Some types of information that are highly relevant may be difficult to present with the reliability normally considered necessary for inclusion in financial statements.

REQUIRED:

a. Discuss the relationship between relevance and reliability as these concepts apply to financial statements.
b. Use a brainstorming approach and attempt to identify financially related information that is highly relevant but low in reliability.

C13-2   Jokes can sometimes illustrate and identify important issues that are anything but funny. The following story has probably been told at more than one after-dinner speech:

   The CEO needed a new controller. She interviewed the short list of candidates. Her interview included the following question: "What is two plus two?" Most candidates, of course, responded: "Four." Not the candidate who got the job. He responded: "What do you want it to be?"

REQUIRED:

a. While this story may be amusing, discuss the importance of reliability of financial information.
b. Discuss forces that exist in the business environment which could pressure accountants to produce accounting information that is not neutral.
c. How should the accounting profession respond to such forces?

 C13-3   Comparability is the quality of financial statement information about a particular business that enables users to identify similarities in and differences between two businesses.

Although comparability is a characteristic that makes financial statement information useful, Generally Accepted Accounting Principles (GAAP) allow businesses to use different accounting methods. For example, one company might use straight-line depreciation to depreciate property, plant, and equipment; and another company might use double-declining-balance depreciation. Both depreciation methods are in accordance with GAAP. As another example, one company might use the FIFO cost flow assumption for inventory valuation, and another company might use the LIFO cost flow assumption.

REQUIRED:

a. Discuss how the quality of comparability improves the usefulness of financial statement information.
b. Why do you think GAAP allow different accounting methods?
c. Should GAAP require all businesses to use the same accounting methods?

 C13-4   In Appendix B at the end of the text, the financial statements of J.C. Penney Company, Inc. are reprinted. Immediately following the consolidated statements of cash flows, you will find the *Summary of Accounting Policies*. Read J.C. Penney's accounting policies for deferred charges and advertising.

REQUIRED:

a. Discuss J.C. Penney's accounting policies for deferred charges and for advertising. Include in your discussion how the policies relate to the matching principle.
b. Discuss how the policies are affected by the time periods and going-concern assumptions and by the materiality and conservatism modifying conventions.

CHAPTER 14

Partnerships

When Ray Johnson graduated from college five years ago, he began a business that sells compact discs and cassette tapes, as well as some related items. At first, business was slow. Recently, since he began advertising frequently on the local cable television system, Ray's business has grown rapidly. In fact, Ray's business is so good that he is considering expanding. A national developer of shopping malls is building a new mall across town from Ray's current location. Ray believes there is enough business to support another store, and he is considering renting space in the new mall.

However, Ray is concerned about finding financing for his new store. In the last year, the local banks have been hesitant to loan money to small businesses, and Ray is looking for alternative sources of financing. Ray's Uncle Hank recently took early retirement from a major business and has approached Ray about investing in the business. Hank has suggested that they form a partnership, but Ray has some concerns about the partnership form of business. Since Hank wants to be a passive investor, not involved in the day-to-day operations, Ray is uncertain about how he and Hank would divide the profits. Also, Ray has read in the newspapers about the increasing number of small businesses declaring bankruptcy, and he wants to know how a partnership would affect his personal finances if the business fails.

Previous chapters in this text use the sole proprietorship form of business to present and illustrate various accounting concepts, principles, and procedures that apply to business enterprises. The partnership form of business is an alternative to proprietorships. While partnerships offer certain advantages to other forms of business, they also have some disadvantages. This chapter discusses accounting procedures the partnership form of business uses. While GAAP for assets, liabilities, owners' equity, revenues, and expenses also apply to partnerships, this chapter presents some unique applications of those principles to partnerships.

1. Describe the advantages and disadvantages of the partnership form of business.
2. Record in the accounting records the formation of a partnership.
3. Calculate and record the allocation of partnership net income and losses to the partners according to the partnership agreement.
4. Prepare partnership financial statements.
5. Explain and record the various forms of partnership dissolution.
6. Record the transactions related to the liquidation of partnerships.

LO 1

Describe the advantages and disadvantages of the partnership form of business.

THE NATURE OF PARTNERSHIPS

State laws regulate partnerships, and most states have adopted the Uniform Partnership Act to regulate partnerships within their jurisdictions. Section 16 of the Uniform Partnership Act defines a **partnership** as "an association of two or more persons to carry on as co-owners a business for profit." The provisions of the Act apply to the formation, operation, and dissolution of partnerships. The following sections discuss certain unique characteristics of partnerships.

Voluntary Association

According to its definition, a partnership is not a legal entity, but an association of two or more individuals. In forming a partnership, individuals are free to choose with whom they wish to carry on a business and cannot be forced against their will into joining a partnership. The reasons for the voluntary association feature of partnerships are:

1. Each partner is responsible for the acts of his or her partners, so long as the acts are within the scope of the partnership.
2. Each partner is personally responsible for partnership liabilities.

For example, a partner can enter into a contract on behalf of the partnership. If the contract causes financial distress for the partnership, the law may require individual partners to satisfy partnership liabilities. Given the responsibilities partners assume, it is reasonable to give individuals such freedom to choose with whom to be associated in a business.

Partnership Agreement

A **partnership agreement**, the agreement between two or more persons, governs their association as partners and constitutes a contract that creates the partnership without additional legal formalities. A partnership may be formed by the oral agreement of two or more individuals. However, *written* partnership agreements are usually considered to be a better business practice because written agreements are less likely to be misunderstood. The partnership agreement is an important document to the business's smooth operation and to relations between the partners. A well-written agreement anticipates all important aspects of the partnership and, at a minimum, should include the following:

1. The nature of the business
2. Each partner's rights and duties
3. Each partner's initial investment
4. Subsequent additional investments and withdrawals
5. How partnership income and losses are to be shared
6. Procedures for dissolution of the partnership

Limited Life

Any event or act that terminates the partnership agreement also terminates the partnership. The admission of a new partner, the withdrawal or death of a partner, voluntary dissolution by the partners, and bankruptcy terminate partnerships. Also, some partnership agreements specify that the partnership is for a limited time, such as the time required for the completion of a project; and when the specified event occurs, the partnership terminates. For example, individuals may form a partnership for the purpose of developing new computer software. When the partnership completes development of the software, the partnership terminates.

Unlimited Liability

Under partnership law, each partner is personally liable for all partnership liabilities. If a partnership encounters financial difficulties and cannot pay all of its liabilities, the partnership's creditors must first satisfy their claims out of the partnership's assets. When the partnership's assets are insufficient, creditors may then satisfy their claims out of the partners' personal assets. If one or more partners are insolvent, then the creditors may call upon the remaining partners' assets to satisfy their claims. Also, the law could require any partner to satisfy all of the partnership's liabilities. Hence, each partner has unlimited liability for the partnership's obligations. This feature of partnerships is particularly important when considered in conjunction with the mutual agency feature discussed in the following section.

An exception to the unlimited liability of partnerships exists for limited partnerships. In a **limited partnership**, the liability of the limited partners is only for the amount of their investment in the partnership. However, limited partnerships must have at least one general partner who has unlimited liability.

Mutual Agency

Normally, each partner is an agent of the partnership. This characteristic, referred to as **mutual agency**, means that any partner can enter into a binding agreement on behalf of the partnership, provided the agreement relates to the scope of the partnership's business. For example, a partner in an office equipment business can enter into contracts to purchase and sell office equipment, lease store space, and hire salespersons. A partner could not, however, bind the partnership to the purchase of a sailing yacht because that sort of transaction is not within the scope of an office equipment business.

Co-Ownership of Partnership Property

When the partners admit an individual to a partnership, the new partner's investment may be cash or other property. Property that partners invest in a partnership becomes the partnership's property and is owned jointly by all of the partners. Thus, if the property invested in the partnership increases in value, all the partners share in the increase.

Participation in Partnership Income

Each partner has a right to share in partnership income. Likewise, each partner also shares in partnership losses. As previously indicated, the partnership agreement should specify how partners share income and losses. If the partnership agreement is silent about the sharing of income and losses, the Uniform Partnership Act requires that income and losses be shared equally. Also, if the partnership agreement specifies how income is shared but is silent about losses, the Act requires that losses be shared in the same way as income. Accounting for the distribution of partnership income and losses is discussed in a subsequent section of this chapter.

Summary of Advantages and Disadvantages

There are both advantages and disadvantages to the partnership form of business. The primary disadvantages are limited life, unlimited liability, and mutual agency. Also, the transfer of an ownership interest in a partnership is not as easy as it is for corporations (described in subsequent chapters). Some of the advantages of partnerships include the ability to pool the resources and talents of two or more persons, the ease of formation and dissolution, and the freedom of action afforded the partners. Also, because they are not legal entities, partnerships are not subject to income taxes. However, the individual partners are subject to income taxes on their shares of partnership income. Appendix A of this text discusses certain income tax aspects of the various forms of business organizations.

LO 2

Record in the accounting records the formation of a partnership.

FORMATION OF A PARTNERSHIP

The partnership agreement should specify the assets each partner is to invest at the time they form the partnership. The assets they invest may consist of either cash or noncash assets such as inventory and property, plant, and equipment. When partners invest noncash assets in the partnership, they must agree on the assets' valuation. The general rule is that partners should value noncash assets at their fair values at the dates of investment.

Investment of Noncash Assets

To give the investing partner proper credit for his or her investment in the partnership, we record the investment of noncash assets at fair value. The fair values of noncash assets fluctuate; and, therefore, the fair value of an asset at the date the partners form the partnership may be different than its previously recorded cost. The partners determine the fair value of noncash assets by checking current price lists or by having an appraisal performed. In any event, partners have to agree to the fair values assigned to noncash assets invested; and they should specify these amounts in the partnership agreement. We record additional investments by partners in the same way we do initial investments.

Accounting for Partnership Equity

In earlier chapters of this text, GAAP are discussed in the context of a sole proprietorship form of business. Those accounting principles also apply to the partnership form of business. Thus, the recording of assets, liabilities, revenues, and expenses is consistent for both proprietorships and partnerships. However, differences arise between the two forms of business concerning owners' equity. For a proprietorship, there is only a single owner. Therefore, there is only one capital account and one withdrawals account. On the other hand, since a partnership has two or more owners, separate capital and withdrawals accounts are established for each partner. Illustration 14-1 demonstrates the differences in owners' equity for a proprietorship owned by Jones and a partnership consisting of Roberts and Stewart.

ILLUSTRATION 14-1 Owners' Equity T-Accounts

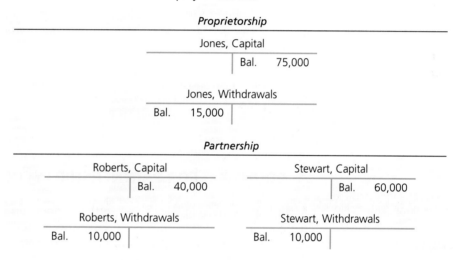

The balance in a partner's capital account on any date consists of the cumulative effect of the partner's initial investment in the partnership, plus any subsequent investments, plus the partner's share of partnership income, less the partner's share of losses, less withdrawals by the partner. In the balance sheet of a partnership, we display separately the balance of each partner's capital account in the partners' equity section, as shown in the partial balance sheet in Illustration 14-2.

We record the investment of assets in the partnership by debiting the appropriate asset account(s) and crediting the investing partner's capital account. For example, assume Lane and Morgan agree to form a partnership. The partnership agreement specifies that Lane is to invest cash of $25,000 and Morgan is to invest inventory. Current price lists for the merchandise indicate that the inventory's value is $30,000, and Lane and Morgan agree that $30,000 is the fair value. The following is the general journal entry to record the formation of the partnership:

(Date)	Cash	25,000	
	Merchandise Inventory	30,000	
	Lane, Capital		25,000
	Morgan, Capital		30,000
	To record initial investment of cash and inventory		
	by partners.		

ILLUSTRATION 14-2 Partial Balance Sheet

Liabilities and Partners' Equity		
Current liabilities	$15,000	
Noncurrent liabilities	50,000	
Total liabilities		$ 65,000
Partners' equity:		
Roberts, Capital	$30,000	
Stewart, Capital	50,000	
Total partners' equity		80,000
Total liabilities and partners' equity		$145,000

Partnerships may also assume liabilities in conjunction with an investment. For example, assume Lane makes an additional investment of a building that has a fair value of $100,000 at the date of investment and is subject to a $80,000 mortgage. We record Lane's additional investment in the partnership by the following general journal entry:

(Date)	Buildings	100,000	
	Mortgage Payable		80,000
	Lane, Capital		20,000
	To record additional investment by Lane.		

LO 3
Calculate and record the allocation of partnership net income and losses to the partners according to the partnership agreement.

ACCOUNTING FOR PARTNERSHIP INCOME AND LOSSES

According to the terms specified in the partnership agreement, partners share partnership net income and net losses. The income allocated to partners consists of compensation for services partners perform and a monetary return on the capital they invest in the partnership. Ideally, the basis for allocating partnership income to the partners should reflect these two elements of partnership income. The following sections discuss the several bases for allocating partnership income: specified ratio, ratio of invested capital, and allowances for salaries and interest with the remainder at a specified ratio.

Specified Ratio

When partners use a specified ratio to allocate partnership income, the ratio should reflect the relative contributions of the partners. If partners provide the same quantity and quality of services and invest equal amounts of capital, then an equal sharing of partnership income is appropriate. On the other hand, an unequal sharing of income is appropriate when partners provide different amounts of service to the partnership and when there are differences in the amounts of invested capital. Other factors that may result in an unequal sharing of income include superior managerial or technical skills, valuable business contacts, and an established customer base.

Assume the partnership agreement of Ames, Baker, and Cook specifies that income and losses are to be shared 40% by Ames, 30% by Baker, and 30% by Cook. This ratio reflects that Ames is assuming management responsibility for the partnership. At the end of 19X1, we close all partnership revenue and expense accounts to Income Summary. The balance of Income Summary is

$40,000, which is the income of the partnership for the year. We allocate the partnership income to the partners as follows:

Ames:	$40,000 x	40%	=	$16,000
Baker:	40,000 x	30%	=	12,000
Cook:	40,000 x	30%	=	12,000
	Total	100%		$40,000

The general journal entry to allocate income to the partners is as follows:

19X1			
Dec. 31	Income Summary	40,000	
	Ames, Capital		16,000
	Baker, Capital		12,000
	Cook, Capital		12,000
	To close Income Summary and to allocate		
	partnership income.		

Ratio of Invested Capital

For many businesses, the amount of invested capital is an important factor in their success. For these businesses, the allocation of partnership income based on the ratio of the partners' invested capital results in a fair allocation. For example, assume the partnership agreement of Banes's and Corbett specifies that they will share partnership income in the ratio of their capital accounts. Throughout 19X1, the balances of Banes' and Corbett's capital accounts are $50,000 and $75,000, respectively. Partnership net income for 19X1 is $30,000. We calculate each partner's share of partnership income by multiplying net income of $30,000 by the ratio of that partner's capital account balance to the total of the capital account balances of $125,000 ($50,000 + $75,000). The calculations for Banes and Corbett are shown below:

Banes:	$30,000 x ($50,000 / $125,000) =	$12,000
Corbett:	$30,000 x ($75,000 / $125,000) =	18,000
	Total partnership income	$30,000

The entry to record the allocation of partnership income is as follows:

19X1			
Dec. 31	Income Summary	30,000	
	Banes, Capital		12,000
	Corbett, Capital		18,000
	To close Income Summary and to allocate		
	partnership income.		

For purposes of calculating the ratio, invested capital may be the beginning balance of the partners' capital accounts, the ending balance, or, if partners expect their capital accounts to fluctuate, the weighted-average balance. The partnership agreement should specify how partners determine invested capital. Assume the partnership agreement of Davis and Edwards specifies that partners are to share partnership net income in the ratio of the weighted-average balances of the partners' capital accounts. Income for 19X1 is $60,000, and the partners have the following activities in their capital accounts during 19X1:

	Davis	Edwards
Beginning balance	$100,000	$60,000
Additional investment, April 1	40,000	
Additional investment, July 1		40,000
Withdrawals, October 1		(40,000)
Ending balance	$140,000	$60,000

We calculate the weighted-average capital account balances below. The fractions in the Portion of Year column are the number of months of the year that the specified capital account balance existed.

		Davis		
Dates	Balance		Portion of Year	Product
1/1 to 3/31	$100,000	x	3/12	$ 25,000
4/1 to 12/31	140,000	x	9/12	105,000
		Weighted-average balance		$130,000

		Edwards		
Dates	Balance		Portion of Year	Product
1/1 to 6/30	$ 60,000	x	6/12	$30,000
7/1 to 9/30	100,000	x	3/12	25,000
10/1 to 12/31	60,000	x	3/12	15,000
		Weighted-average balance		$70,000

We calculate each partner's share of partnership net income by multiplying income of $60,000 by the ratio of that partner's weighted-average capital balance to the total of the weighted-average capital balances of $200,000 ($130,000 + $70,000). We show the calculations for Davis and Edwards below:

Davis:	$60,000 x ($130,000 / $200,000) = $39,000
Edwards:	$60,000 x ($70,000 / $200,000) = 21,000
	Total partnership net income $60,000

The general journal entry to record the allocation of partnership net income is as follows:

19X1			
Dec. 31	Income Summary	60,000	
	Davis, Capital		39,000
	Edwards, Capital		21,000
	To close Income Summary and to allocate partnership income.		

Allowances for Salaries and Interest

When partners provide unequal services to the partnership, the partnership agreement may specify that partners use salary allowances in allocating net income to recognize the differences in the amount of services. Similarly, when partners' capital contributions are unequal, they may use allowances for interest on invested capital to recognize the differences. If both services and contributed capital are unequal, then the partners may use allowances for both salaries and interest to allocate partnership net income. When partners use salary and interest allowances, they allocate any residual income or loss according to the ratio specified in the partnership agreement. If the agreement does not specify a ratio, then partners share residual income and losses equally as required by the Uniform Partnership Act.

While salary and interest allowances are common provisions of partnership agreements, it is important to note that these distributions are not expenses of the partnership. Although called salaries and interest, they are merely means of allocating net income to the partners. The allowances are not partnership expenses because a partnership is not a legal entity but an association of persons; and the partners cannot pay themselves salaries and interest. Corporations, on the other hand, are legal entities; and salaries and interest paid to employees, who are also owners, are expenses of the corporation. When comparing the financial statements of partnerships and corporations, you should keep this difference in mind and adjust the analysis accordingly.

The following sections illustrate the allocation of partnership income using allowances for salaries and interest.

Allowance for Salaries and Specified Ratio. Assume the partnership agreement of Johnson and Key provides that Johnson is to receive a salary of $30,000 and Key is to receive a salary of $20,000. They are to share equally any residual income or loss. The partners agreed to the difference in the salary allowances because of Johnson's established contacts with customers. Partnership income for 19X1 is $85,000, and we show the allocation to Johnson and Key in Illustration 14-3.

ILLUSTRATION 14-3 Allocation of Partnership Income

	Johnson	Key	Total
Income to be allocated			$85,000
Salaries	$30,000	$20,000	(50,000)
			$35,000
Residual shared equally	17,500	17,500	(35,000)
Total income allocated to each partner	$47,500	$37,500	$ 0

Allowances for Interest and Specified Ratio. Assume the partnership agreement of Lowell and Morris provides that partners are to receive annually an allowance for interest of 12% of the weighted-average capital balances. They are to allocate the remainder, after the allowances for interest, 60% to Lowell and 40% to Morris. The balance of Lowell's capital account remained at $100,000 throughout 19X1. The balance of Morris's capital account is $80,000 on January 1, 19X1; and the only transaction affecting his capital account during 19X1 is an additional investment of $40,000 on October 1, 19X1. The weighted-average balance of Morris's capital account is $90,000, calculated as follows:

		Morris		
Dates	Balance		Portion of Year	Product
1/1 to 9/30	$ 80,000	x	9/12	$60,000
10/1 to 12/31	120,000	x	3/12	30,000
	Weighted-average balance			$90,000

Partnership net income is $32,800 for 19X1, and we show the allocation to the partners in Illustration 14-4.

ILLUSTRATION 14-4 Allocation of Partnership Income

	Lowell	Morris	Total
Income to allocate			$32,800
Interest:			
Lowell			
$100,000 x 12%	$12,000		(12,000)
Morris			
$90,000 x 12%		$10,800	(10,800)
			$10,000
Residual shared 60/40	6,000	4,000	(10,000)
Total income allocated to each partner	$18,000	$14,800	0

Allowances for Salaries and Interest and Specified Ratio. The partnership agreement of Newman and Owen provides for salaries of $24,000 for Newman and $20,000 for Owen. In addition, the partners are to receive interest at the rate of 12% on their weighed-average capital balances. For 19X1, the weighted-average capital balances for Newman and Owen are $100,000 and $120,000, respectively. Finally, the partners are to allocate the remainder, after the salaries and interest, 70% to Newman and 30% to Owen. We show the allocation of the partnership net income of $60,000 for 19X1 to the partners in Illustration 14-5.

ILLUSTRATION 14-5 Allocation of Partnership Income

	Newman	Owen	Total
Income to allocate			$60,000
Salaries	$24,000	$20,000	(44,000)
			$16,000
Interest:			
Newman			
$100,000 x 12%	12,000		(12,000)
Owen			
$120,000 x 12%		14,400	(14,400)
			$(10,400)
Residual shared 70/30	(7,280)	(3,120)	10,400
Total income allocated to each partner	$28,720	$31,280	$ 0

The allocation of income for Newman and Owen shown in Illustration 14-5 demonstrates an important point about allocating partnership income and losses. Notice that the partnership income of $60,000 is not sufficient to cover both the salaries and interest. Nevertheless, *the partners should follow the provisions of the partnership agreement and allocate the salaries and interest as planned, with the resulting negative remainder allocated to the partners as specified in the agreement.* Also, if a partnership incurs a net loss for the year, the partners should continue to allocate salaries and interest to the partners as specified in the agreement and the resulting larger negative remainder allocated according to the agreement.

PARTNERSHIP FINANCIAL STATEMENTS

LO 4
Prepare partnership
financial statements.

The financial statements of partnerships are similar to those of proprietorships illustrated in previous chapters. The differences arise from the fact that a proprietorship has only one owner, whereas a partnership has multiple owners. The partners' equity section of the partnership balance sheet reflects the multiple owners' capital accounts. Partnership income statements are the same as proprietorship income statements. We illustrated previously the partners' equity section of a partnership balance sheet in Illustration 14-2.

Accountants call the statement of owners' equity for a partnership a **statement of partners' capital**. We show a statement of partners' capital in Illustration 14-6. The purpose of the statement is to show the changes in each partner's capital account that occurred during the period. The statement starts with each partner's capital balance at the beginning of the period. Next, it shows increases in the capital account balances. Increases consist of additional investments by the partners and the allocation of net income. After the increases, the statement shows the decreases in the capital accounts. Decreases consist of withdrawals by the partners and allocations of net losses. Finally, the statement presents the capital account balances at the end of the period.

ILLUSTRATION 14-6 Statement of Partners' Capital

Newman and Owen Statement of Partners' Capital For the Year Ended December 31, 19X1			
	Newman	*Owen*	*Total*
Capital, January 1	$ 80,000	$100,000	$180,000
Add: Additional investments	40,000	40,000	80,000
Net income	28,720	31,280	60,000
	$148,720	$171,280	$320,000
Less: Withdrawals	20,000	24,000	44,000
Capital, December 31	$128,720	$147,280	$276,000

PARTNERSHIP DISSOLUTION

LO 5
Explain and record the
various forms of
partnership dissolution.

When a change in the association of partners occurs, the partnership is *legally* dissolved. Dissolution of a partnership occurs when the partners admit a new partner to the partnership, when a partner withdraws from the partnership, or upon the death of a partner. The admission of new partners and the withdrawal of existing partners can occur through a variety of transactions, all of which dissolve the existing partnership. Upon the dissolution of a partnership, partners must either wind up the affairs of the partnership or form a new partnership.

Admission of a New Partner

The admission of a new partner may occur in two ways:

1. One or more of the original partners may sell all or part of their partnership interests to the new partner.
2. The new partner may invest assets in the partnership.

In either case, the original partners must approve the admission of the new partner. Also, since a new association is formed, the partners should prepare a new partnership agreement that describes the features of the new association.

Sale of an Interest in the Partnership.
Assume the capital balances of Charles Stevens and Jay Tilton are $80,000 and $100,000, respectively. Stevens agrees to sell his $80,000 interest in the partnership to Karen Burns for $95,000. If Tilton agrees to the transaction, the following general journal entry records the transfer of Stevens's interest to Burns:

(Date)	Stevens, Capital	80,000	
	Burns, Capital		80,000
	To record the transfer of Stevens's equity to Burns.		

We show the effects of this transaction on the net assets and the partners' capital accounts in the T-accounts in Illustration 14-7.

ILLUSTRATION 14-7 Partnership T-Accounts

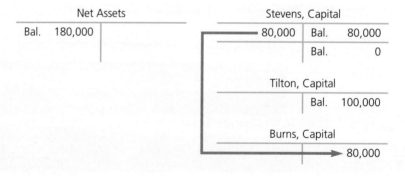

This transaction is external to the partnership and does not affect partnership net assets, which remain at $180,000. Therefore, the entry merely transfers Stevens's recorded equity in the partnership of $80,000 to Burns's capital account. The price negotiated by Stevens and Burns does not affect the entry because the exchange is between the two individuals and does not involve partnership assets. As a result, even though Burns paid Stevens $95,000 for the interest in the partnership, the entry only transfers the $80,000 recorded interest. The $15,000 Stevens received in excess of his capital account balance is, in effect, profit for Stevens from the sale of his partnership interest.

In the transaction above, Burns purchased all of Stevens's interest in the partnership; and, assuming Tilton agrees, they form a new partnership consisting of Tilton and Burns. Instead of completely buying out one partner, the partners may admit a new partner by selling a portion of each of the original partners' interests. Assume that instead of Burns purchasing all of Stevens's interest, Burns purchases one-half of each of the partners' interests, paying Stevens $47,500 and Tilton $65,000. Again, this transaction is external to the partnership; and the prices paid for the two interests do not affect the partnership assets. We show the entry to record this transaction as follows:

(Date)	Stevens, Capital	40,000	
	Tilton, Capital	50,000	
	Burns, Capital		90,000
	To record the transfer of one-half of the equity of Stevens and Tilton to Burns.		

We show the effects of this transaction on the net assets and partners' capital accounts in Illustration 14-8.

ILLUSTRATION 14-8 Partnership T-Accounts

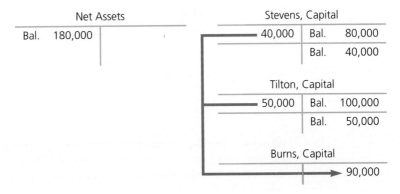

Since the transaction does not affect partnership assets, the transfer is for one-half of Stevens's recorded equity (1/2 x $80,000) and for one-half of Tilton's recorded equity (1/2 x $100,000). As a result of this transaction, the partners form a new partnership consisting of Stevens, Tilton, and Burns.

Investment of Assets in a Partnership.   As previously stated, the partners may admit a new partner to the partnership by having the new partner invest assets. In this case, the investment affects partnership assets. Therefore, the amount the new partner invests and the partners' shares of total equity agreed to affects the entry to record the transaction. Assume that Stevens and Tilton agree to admit Burns to the partnership. Under the agreement, Burns is to receive a one-fourth interest in exchange for investing $60,000 cash in the partnership. After Burns's investment, the net assets are $240,000 ($180,000 + $60,000) and partnership equity is as follows:

Stevens, Capital	$ 80,000
Tilton, Capital	100,000
Burns, Capital	60,000
Total	$240,000

In this case, the $60,000 Burns invested for a one-fourth interest is equal to one-fourth of the net assets after the investment and one-fourth of the new partnership equity (1/4 x $240,000 = $60,000). We show the entry to record Burns's investment below:

(Date)	Cash	60,000	
	Burns, Capital		60,000
	To record investment by Burns for a one-fourth		
	interest in the partnership.		

We show the effects of this transaction on the net assets and the partners' capital accounts in Illustration 14-9.

ILLUSTRATION 14-9 Partnership T-Accounts

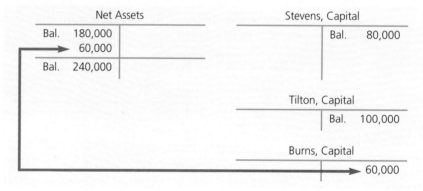

Although Burns receives a 25% interest for her investment, the income and loss sharing ratio may be different from the capital ratios. The new partnership agreement should specify the income and loss sharing ratio to which the partners agree.

Bonus to the Original Partners.   Because of the cost principle, the carrying amount of assets over time does not necessarily represent their fair value. For example, plant assets may have increased in value since the business purchased them; however, we do not record the increase in value. As a result, the recorded amount of partnership equity may be an amount that is less than the fair value of the partnership's net assets. In this case, when partners admit a new partner by having the new partner invest assets in the partnership, the amount invested may be more than the new partner's share of the partnership net assets and equity.

Assume Stevens and Tilton agree to admit Burns to the partnership. The agreement specifies that Burns is to receive a one-fourth interest in exchange for investing $80,000 cash in the partnership. After Burns's investment, the total partnership net assets and equity will be $260,000 as follows:

Stevens, Capital	$ 80,000
Tilton, Capital	100,000
Burns, investment	80,000
Total	$260,000

In this transaction, Burns is giving a bonus of $15,000 to Stevens and Tilton, calculated as follows:

Investment	$80,000
One-fourth interest (1/4 x $260,000)	65,000
Bonus to the old partners	$15,000

When the new partner gives a bonus, we allocate the bonus to the old partners based on their original income and loss sharing ratio. Because it represents income from the increases in the assets' fair values that have not been recorded, we use the income and loss sharing ratio to allocate the bonus to the old partners. If Stevens and Tilton share income and losses equally, we allocate the $15,000 bonus $7,500 to each. The following entry records the admission of the new partner and the allocation of the bonus to the old partners:

(Date)	Cash	80,000	
	Stevens, Capital		7,500
	Tilton, Capital		7,500
	Burns, Capital		65,000
	To record investment by Burns for a one-fourth interest in the partnership.		

Bonus to the New Partner.   As an inducement to join the partnership, the old partners may be willing to give a larger interest in the partnership than the amount of investment the new partner makes. The old partners are willing to give a bonus to a new partner because the individual may have some desirable talent, possess an established customer base, or the partnership may need additional capital to expand operations.

Assume Stevens and Tilton agree to admit Burns to the partnership. Burns is to receive a one-fourth interest in exchange for a cash investment of $40,000. After Burns's investment, the total partnership net assets and equity will be $220,000 as follows:

Stevens, Capital	$ 80,000
Tilton, Capital	100,000
Burns, investment	40,000
Total	$220,000

In this case, Burns receives a bonus of $15,000, calculated as follows:

One-fourth interest (1/4 x $220,000)	$55,000
Investment	40,000
Bonus to Burns	$15,000

We always allocate to the old partners in their original income and loss sharing ratio the bonus given to a new partner. Assume Stevens and Tilton share income and losses in the ratio of 1/3 – 2/3, respectively. We show the entry to record Burns's admission to the partnership below:

(Date)	Cash	40,000	
	Stevens, Capital	5,000	
	Tilton, Capital	10,000	
	Burns, Capital		55,000
	To record investment by Burns for a one-fourth interest in the partnership.		

Withdrawal from a Partnership

Because a partnership is a voluntary association of two or more individuals, a partner can withdraw at any time he or she chooses. A well-written partnership agreement should anticipate that partners may withdraw and should specify the procedures to be followed. In general, a partner can withdraw by two ways:

1. Selling his or her interest in the partnership (previously covered).
2. Withdrawing assets from the partnership.

As shown in the right side of Illustration 14-10, partners have several ways of withdrawing assets.

ILLUSTRATION 14-10   Forms of Partnership Withdrawals

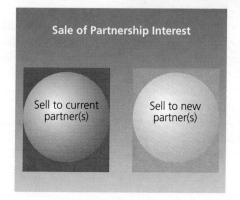

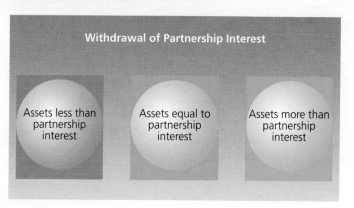

The following sections illustrate the accounting for each way of withdrawing from a partnership. For each of the examples, assume that partners Rhonda Addison, Jill Bailey, and Roy Carey have the capital balances listed below:

Addison, Capital	$ 80,000
Bailey, Capital	100,000
Carey, Capital	60,000
Total	$240,000

Withdrawal of Assets Equal to Recorded Equity. As previously mentioned, the partnership agreement should specify the procedures required when a partner withdraws. When a partner withdraws by taking partnership assets, a common procedure is to restate partnership assets and equity to their current fair values. Also, an audit may be performed to ensure that the partnership records are in order. An advantage of restating the assets to their current fair values is that the withdrawing partner's capital account reflects the current fair value of his or her equity. In such cases, the agreement usually provides that the withdrawing partner take assets equal to his or her restated capital account.

Assume that Carey decides to withdraw from Addison, Bailey, and Carey. The agreement specifies that at the time of withdrawal, a partner is to receive assets equal to the balance in his capital account after it is restated to reflect the current fair values of partnership assets. The partners agree that the present carrying amounts of the assets are equal to their current fair values. If Carey takes a promissory note, instead of cash, equal to the balance in his capital account of $60,000, the following entry is needed to record the withdrawal:

(Date)	Carey, Capital	60,000	
	Notes Payable (to Carey)		60,000
	To record the withdrawal of Carey from the partnership.		

The withdrawal of Carey reduces the partnership's net assets by $60,000. We show the effects of the transaction on the net assets and partners' capital accounts in the T-accounts in Illustration 14-11.

ILLUSTRATION 14-11 Partnership T-Accounts

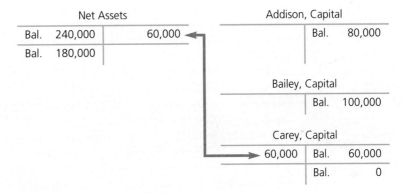

Withdrawal of Assets Worth More Than Recorded Equity. A partner may sometimes decide to withdraw, and the remaining partners may decide not to restate the partnership assets to their current fair values. If the recorded amounts of assets are less than their current fair values, then the withdrawing partner's recorded equity is less than its current fair value. To be fair, the withdrawing partner should receive assets worth more than his or her recorded equity and equal to his or her share of the net assets' fair value. Another reason why a withdrawing partner may receive assets worth more than his or her recorded equity is that the other partners are willing to give the partner a bonus to induce the withdrawal. When a partner withdraws and takes assets worth more than his or her recorded equity, the partners deduct the excess amount from the remaining partners' capital accounts according to their income and loss sharing ratio.

Assume in the partnership of Addison, Bailey, and Carey, the income and loss sharing ratio is 25/50/25, respectively. Carey decides to withdraw from the partnership, and the partners agree not to restate the assets to their current fair values. The partners also agree that the current fair value of partnership assets is $40,000 higher than their recorded amounts. If the partners restate assets, they would credit Carey's capital account for his share of the increase, or $10,000

(25% x $40,000). This means that the current fair value of Carey's equity is $70,000 ($60,000 + $10,000). The partners agree to giving Carey $70,000 cash when the withdrawal occurs. We allocate the additional amount given to a withdrawing partner to the remaining partners according to their relative income and loss sharing ratio. For Addison and Bailey, we calculate their relative ratio as follows:

$$\text{Addison:} \quad 25\% \div (25\% + 50\%) = 1/3$$

$$\text{Bailey:} \quad 50\% \div (25\% + 50\%) = 2/3$$

Therefore, we allocate Addison $3,333.33 (1/3 x $10,000) and Bailey $6,666.67 (2/3 x $10,000). The entry to record Carey's withdrawal is as follows:

(Date)	Carey, Capital	60,000.00	
	Addison, Capital	3,333.33	
	Bailey, Capital	6,666.67	
	Cash		70,000.00
	To record the withdrawal of Carey from the partnership.		

Withdrawal of Assets Worth Less Than Recorded Equity. A partner sometimes withdraws and takes assets that are worth less than his or her recorded equity. This situation may arise for two reasons. First, the carrying amount of partnership assets may be more than their current fair values, and the partners decide not to restate the assets. Second, the withdrawing partner may be so anxious to withdraw that he or she is willing to accept less than recorded equity. Assume that Carey is anxious to withdraw from the partnership of Addison, Bailey, and Carey and agrees to accept $54,000 cash even though his recorded equity is $60,000. We allocate the amount of the equity in excess of the assets Carey takes, $6,000, to the remaining partners in their relative income and loss sharing ratio. If the income and loss sharing ratio for the partnership is 25/50/25, then we allocate Addison $2,000 ($6,000 x 1/3) and Bailey $4,000 ($6,000 x 2/3). The entry to record Carey's withdrawal is as follows:

(Date)	Carey, Capital	60,000	
	Addison, Capital		2,000
	Bailey, Capital		4,000
	Cash		54,000
	To record the withdraw of Carey from the partnership.		

Death of a Partner

When a partner dies, a partnership terminates because the association is broken. The partnership agreement should specify the procedures partners will follow upon the death of a partner. Normal procedures include:

1. Determining the fair values of partnership assets
2. Closing the books to determine partnership income or loss since the end of the previous accounting period
3. Allocating partnership income or loss to the partners so that the partner capital accounts are stated at the appropriate balances as of the date of death
4. Having an audit performed to ensure that the partnership records are in order

The final disposition of the deceased partner's equity must be agreed to by his or her estate and by the remaining partners. The estate of the deceased partner may sell his or her interest to one or more of the remaining partners or to an outsider; or the estate may withdraw assets from the partnership. The entries for these transactions resulting from the decisions of the deceased partner's estate are the same as those discussed previously for withdrawals by living partners.

LO 6

Record the transactions related to the liquidation of partnerships.

PARTNERSHIP LIQUIDATION

Liquidating a partnership involves ending its operations, settling its debts, and either requiring additional contributions from partners to settle the debts or distributing assets to them. The procedures normally followed for liquidation include: closing the books and allocating partnership income or loss to the partners, selling partnership assets to convert them to cash, allocating gains and losses from selling the assets to partners in their income and loss sharing ratio, paying partnership creditors, and distributing cash to partners equal to the balances in their capital accounts. Although many situations can arise leading to partnership liquidation, we discuss only three:

1. Partners sell partnership assets for a gain.
2. Partners sell partnership assets for a loss, and there is sufficient partner equity.
3. Partners sell partnership assets for a loss, and one partner has insufficient equity.

Assets Sold for a Gain

Because of declining demand for their services, Rita Davis, Jackson Ewing, and Donald Fox decide to end operations. The income and loss sharing ratio for the partners is 25/50/25, respectively. After closing the accounts and allocating partnership net income, the partnership has the balance sheet shown in Illustration 14-12.

ILLUSTRATION 14-12 Partnership Balance Sheet

Davis, Ewing, and Fox **Balance Sheet** **October 1, 19X1**			
Assets		*Liabilities and* *Partners' Equity*	
Cash	$ 10,000	Accounts payable	$ 10,000
Accounts receivable	50,000	Davis, capital	80,000
Merchandise inventory	120,000	Ewing, capital	100,000
Equipment (net)	70,000	Fox, capital	60,000
		Total liabilities and	
Total assets	$250,000	partners' equity	$250,000

The next step in the liquidation is for the partners to convert all noncash assets to cash by selling them. When they sell the assets, partners normally incur a gain or loss. In the entry to record the sale of assets, we credit or debit the gain or loss to an account called Gain (Loss) from Realization. In the process of converting the assets to cash, assume: (1) The partners collect only $49,500 of the accounts receivable. (2) The partners sell the merchandise inventory for $125,000. (3) The partners sell the equipment for $77,500. We show the entries to record these transactions as follows:

(1) (Date)	Cash Gain (Loss) from Realization Accounts Receivable To record collection of accounts receivable.	49,500 500	 50,000

(2)
(Date)
	Cash
	  Merchandise Inventory
	  Gain (Loss) from Realization
	To record sale of merchandise inventory.
		125,000	
			120,000
			5,000

(3)
(Date)
	Cash
	  Equipment
	  Gain (Loss) from Realization
	To record sale of equipment.
		77,500	
			70,000
			7,500

Notice that we credit gains to Gain (Loss) from Realization, and we debit losses to the account. After the partners sell all of the assets, Gain (Loss) from Realization has either a debit balance, if there is a net loss incurred in selling the partnership assets, or a credit balance, if there is a net gain from selling the assets. The three transactions of the Davis, Ewing, and Fox partnership result in a net gain of $12,000. The T-account shown below presents the three entries in Gain (Loss) from Realization.

Gain (Loss) from Realization

(1)	500	(2)	5,000
		(3)	7,500
		Bal.	12,000

We then allocate the net gain to the partners according to their income and loss sharing ratio. The entry to allocate the gain is as follows:

| (Date) | Gain (Loss) from Realization
  Davis, Capital
  Ewing, Capital
  Fox, Capital
To close Gain (Loss) from Realization. | 12,000 |
3,000
6,000
3,000 |

We show the effects of the above entry on the partners' capital accounts in Illustration 14-13.

The next step in the liquidation process is for the partners to pay the creditors. Before the partners distribute any cash to themselves, they must first pay any creditors. By paying creditors before distributing cash to themselves, they avoid the risk of insufficient cash to pay the creditors. We show the entry to record the payment of creditors below:

| (Date) | Accounts Payable
  Cash
To record the payment of creditors. | 10,000 |
10,000 |

ILLUSTRATION 14-13 Partnership T-Accounts, Gain from Realization

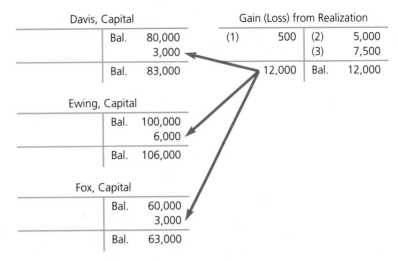

After the partners sell the assets and pay the creditors, the only balance sheet accounts with balances are Cash and the partners' capital accounts, as shown in Illustration 14-14.

ILLUSTRATION 14-14 Partnership Balance Sheet, Gain from Realization

Davis, Ewing, and Fox Balance Sheet December 1, 19X1			
Assets		**Partners' Equity**	
Cash	$252,000	Davis, capital	$ 83,000
		Ewing, capital	106,000
		Fox, capital	63,000
Total assets	$252,000	Partners' equity	$252,000

The final step in the liquidation process is for the partners to distribute the cash to themselves in the amount of their capital account balances. Notice that the capital account balances are not in the income and loss sharing ratio. Partners distribute the cash to themselves according to their capital balances. The entry to record the distribution of the cash to the partners is as follows:

(Date)	Davis, Capital	83,000	
	Ewing, Capital	106,000	
	Fox, Capital	63,000	
	Cash		252,000
	To record final distribution of cash to partners according to balances in their capital accounts.		

After this entry, all partnership accounts are closed, all partnership assets have been distributed, and the operations of the partnership have ceased.

Assets Sold for a Loss — Sufficient Partner Equity

In the previous example of a partnership liquidation, the partners sold their partnership assets for a net gain. However, the sale of assets sometimes results in a net loss. Assume that, instead of selling the assets for $252,000, the partnership of Davis, Ewing, and Fox only realizes $200,000 from the sale of the partnership assets. The carrying amount of the assets sold is $240,000, and the partners incur a loss of $40,000. The sale of the assets may be summarized in a single entry as follows:

(Date)	Cash	200,000	
	Gain (Loss) from Realization	40,000	
	Accounts Receivable		50,000
	Merchandise Inventory		120,000
	Equipment		70,000
	To record collection of accounts receivable and sale of merchandise inventory and equipment.		

After converting the assets to cash, the partners allocate the net loss incurred to the capital accounts according to their income and loss sharing ratio of 25/50/25. We show the entry to allocate the loss and to close Gain (Loss) from Realization below:

(Date)	Davis, Capital	10,000	
	Ewing, Capital	20,000	
	Fox, Capital	10,000	
	Gain (Loss) from Realization		40,000
	To close Gain (Loss) from Realization.		

We show the effects of the entry on the partners' capital balances in the T-accounts in Illustration 14-15.

ILLUSTRATION 14-15 Partnership T-Accounts, Loss from Realization

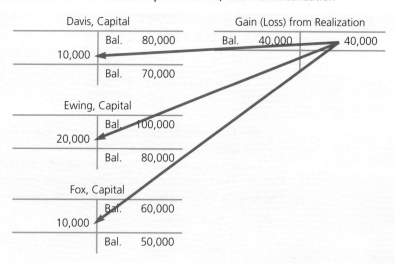

Before partners distribute any cash to themselves, they must pay the creditors. We show the entry to record the payment of the creditors below:

(Date)	Accounts Payable	10,000	
	Cash		10,000
	To record payment of creditors.		

The balance sheet shown in Illustration 14-16 presents the balances of the partnership accounts after creditors are paid.

ILLUSTRATION 14-16 Partnership Balance Sheet, Loss from Realization

Davis, Ewing, and Fox Balance Sheet December 1, 19X1			
Assets		*Partners' Equity*	
Cash	$200,000	Davis, capital	$ 70,000
		Ewing, capital	80,000
		Fox, capital	50,000
Total assets	$200,000	Partners' equity	$200,000

The balance sheet shows that even though converting the assets to cash results in a loss, all of the partners have sufficient equity to absorb their share of the loss. Therefore, the liquidation of the partnership may proceed by distributing the remaining cash to the partners according to the balances in their capital accounts. The entry to record the distribution of cash is as follows:

(Date)	Davis, Capital	70,000	
	Ewing, Capital	80,000	
	Fox, Capital	50,000	
	Cash		200,000
	To record final distribution of cash to partners according to their capital account balances.		

Assets Sold for a Loss — One Partner Has Insufficient Equity

In the previous example, all partners have sufficient equity to absorb the loss incurred in converting the partnership assets to cash. Sometimes, however, a partner may not have a large enough balance in his or her capital account to absorb the share of loss. In such cases, the partner with insufficient equity is liable to the other partners and must make up the deficit. Assume that, because of severely depressed economic conditions, the noncash assets of Davis, Ewing, and Fox can only generate $20,000 of cash. Since the assets have a carrying amount of $240,000, this results in a loss of $220,000. We show the entry to summarize the conversion of partnership assets to cash below:

(Date)	Cash	20,000	
	Gain (Loss) from Realization	220,000	
	Accounts Receivable		50,000
	Merchandise Inventory		120,000
	Equipment		70,000
	To record collection of accounts receivable and sale of merchandise inventory and equipment.		

The next entry allocates the loss to the partners in their income and loss sharing ratio:

(Date)	Davis, Capital	55,000	
	Ewing, Capital	110,000	
	Fox, Capital	55,000	
	Gain (Loss) from Realization		220,000
	To close Gain (Loss) from Realization.		

We show the effects of this entry on the partners' capital accounts in Illustration 14-17.

ILLUSTRATION 14-17 Partnership T-Accounts, Partner with Insufficient Equity

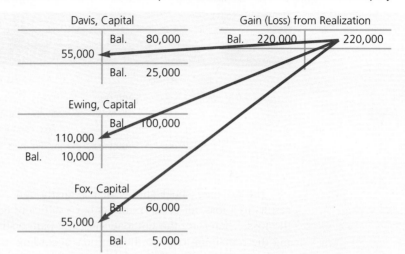

After the partners pay the accounts payable of $10,000, the account balances of the partnership are as shown in Illustration 14-18.

ILLUSTRATION 14-18 Partnership Balance Sheet, Partner with Insufficient Equity

Davis, Ewing, and Fox Balance Sheet December 1, 19X1			
Assets		*Partners' Equity*	
Cash	$20,000	Davis, capital	$ 25,000
		Ewing, capital	(10,000)
		Fox, capital	5,000
Total assets	$20,000	Partners' equity	$ 20,000

As the balance sheet shows, Ewing's capital account balance is insufficient to absorb his share of the loss. Ewing is responsible for investing additional assets in the amount of his capital account's deficit. Assuming Ewing has personal assets of $10,000, the entry to record the additional investment is as follows:

(Date)	Cash	10,000	
	Ewing, Capital		10,000
	To record additional investment by Ewing.		

After Ewing's additional investment, the partnership has cash of $30,000, which the partners distribute to Davis and Fox according to the balances in their capital accounts.

(Date)	Davis, Capital	25,000	
	Fox, Capital	5,000	
	Cash		30,000
	To record final distribution of cash to partners according to their capital account balances.		

After this entry, all partnership account balances are zero; and the partners have liquidated the partnership.

A partner who has insufficient equity to absorb his or her share of a loss realized from converting the partnership assets to cash is sometimes personally insolvent. Assume that, in the previous example, Ewing is personally insolvent and cannot contribute funds to eliminate his deficit. In such cases, we allocate the deficit in the insolvent partner's capital account to the other partners according to their relative income and loss sharing ratio. Davis and Fox share income and losses 25/25, respectively. Therefore, we allocate each one half of the $10,000 deficit in Ewing's capital account. The entry to allocate Ewing's deficit is as follows:

(Date)	Davis, Capital	5,000	
	Fox, Capital	5,000	
	Ewing, Capital		10,000
	To allocate Ewing's deficit to the remaining partners in their relative income and loss sharing ratio.		

Allocating Ewing's deficit to the other partners does not relieve Ewing of his liability for the deficit. In this case, Davis and Fox join Ewing's personal creditors with respect to rights to Ewing's personal assets.

After we allocate Ewing's deficit to Davis and Fox, the capital account balances of both Ewing and Fox are zero. The capital account balance of Davis is $20,000, which is equal to the amount of cash of the partnership. The final step is to record the distribution of the cash to Davis with the following entry:

(Date)	Davis, Capital	20,000	
	Cash		20,000
	To record final distribution of cash according to partners' capital account balances.		

Ray Johnson's Partnership Decision

At the beginning of this chapter, Ray Johnson considered forming a partnership with his Uncle Hank. The discussion in this chapter addresses the concerns that Ray had about the partnership. Keep in mind that one advantage of the partnership form of business over proprietorships is that it allows a business to grow by joining individuals who can provide more resources than just one individual. Hank's willingness to invest capital in the business is why Ray considers forming a partnership with Hank.

One of Ray's questions involved the division of profits. Since Hank wants to be a passive investor, not involved in daily management, Ray should structure the partnership agreement to provide a management salary for himself. On the other hand, the agreement should provide interest to Hank for the capital that he would invest. The division of any residual income (or losses) is a matter that Ray and Hank will have to negotiate. It is important that the partnership agreement accurately reflect what Ray and Hank agree to and that the agreement contemplates all contingencies. It is probably well worth the cost for Ray to engage an attorney experienced in partnership law to prepare the agreement.

Another concern Ray had was how the partnership would affect him personally if the business fails. One of the disadvantages of the partnership form of business is the partners' personal liability for the partnership's debts. Also, since individual partners can enter into business transactions on behalf of the partnership, Ray's decision may depend on how well he knows and trusts Hank. For instance, Ray's personal finances could be affected dramatically if Hank were to commit the partnership to debts and then the business fails. Ray might be called upon to pay some of the partnership debts with his personal assets.

Ultimately, Ray will have to weigh the advantages and disadvantages of partnerships relative to other forms of businesses. A corporation is another form of business that offers both advantages and disadvantages relative to proprietorships and partnerships. (We discuss corporations in subsequent chapters of this text.)

SUMMARY

Describe the advantages and disadvantages of the partnership form of business. A partnership is an association of two or more persons to carry on a business for profit as co-owners. The advantages of the partnership form of business include the ability to pool the resources and talents of more than one person, the ease of formation and dissolution, and the freedom of action afforded the partners. Disadvantages include limited life, unlimited liability, mutual agency, and restrictions on transferring an ownership interest.

Record in the accounting records the formation of a partnership. Individuals form partnerships by contributing cash and/or noncash assets to the partnership. We record the assets that the partners invest at their fair values at the time of the investment. At the same time, we record each partner's capital at the fair value of the assets that each invested in the partnership.

Calculate and record the allocation of partnership net income and losses to the partners according to the partnership agreement. A partner's capital account is increased by investments and his or her share of partnership income and is decreased by withdrawals and his or her share of partnership losses. Partnership net income and losses may be allocated to partners according to a specified ratio, the ratio of invested capital, or allowances for salaries and interest with the remainder at a specified ratio.

Prepare partnership financial statements. Accounting for partnerships differs from sole proprietorships only for partners' equity. A separate capital account is maintained for each partner. Other than displaying each partner's capital account in the partners' equity section of the balance sheet and the preparation of a statement of partners' capital, financial statements for partnerships are the same as for sole proprietorships.

Explain and record the various forms of partnership dissolution. Partners legally dissolve partnerships when a change in the association of the partners occurs. Partnership dissolution results from the admission of a new partner, the withdrawal of a partner, or the death of a partner. When dissolution occurs, partners must either wind up the affairs of the association and liquidate the partnership or form a new partnership.

Record the transactions related to the liquidation of partnerships. Partnership liquidations involve closing the books and allocating partnership income or loss to the partners, selling partnership assets, allocating gains and losses from selling assets to the partners, paying partnership creditors, and distributing cash to the partners.

REVIEW PROBLEM

Harold Gabris and Sarah Golaan form a partnership on January 1, 19X4, to provide household maintenance services in their local area. Gabris contributes $5,000 in cash and a carpet cleaner with a cost of $2,300 and a fair value of $1,500. Golaan contributes $4,000 in cash, a commercial vacuum cleaner worth $1,200, and a truck with a fair value of $2,500. During the first year of operations, they generated $95,000 in revenue and incurred $34,500 in expenses. Gabris and Golaan each withdrew $12,000 during the year. By the end of the year, business volume had grown high enough to need another partner to work in the business.

On January 2, 19X5, Stevesen is admitted to the partnership upon contributing $25,000 to the partnership assets. The partners agree to share profits 35%, 35%, 30% to Gabris, Golaan, and Stevesen, respectively. The revenues for the year total $165,000, and the expenses incurred total $66,000. During the year each of the partners withdrew $15,000.

REQUIRED:

a. Record the journal entries affecting capital accounts for 19X4 and prepare a statement of partners' capital. They operate on a calendar year basis.
b. Record the journal entries affecting capital accounts for 19X5 and prepare a statement of partners' capital.

SOLUTION:

Planning and Organizing Your Work

1. Analyze the formation of the partnership and prepare the journal entries. Remember that noncash assets contributed to a partnership are recorded at their fair values.
2. For 19X4, close the $60,500 balance in Income Summary to the partners' capital accounts according to their income and loss distribution agreement. Close the partners' withdrawals accounts to their capital accounts.
3. Prepare the 19X4 statement of partners' capital using the information from your journal entries.
4. Repeat the procedures (including the admission of the new partner) for 19X5 using the information provided.

(a) *Record journal entries for 19X4 and prepare a statement.*

19X4			
Jan. 1	Equipment	1,500	
	Cash	5,000	
	Gabris, Capital		6,500
	To record investment in partnership.		

The equipment is recorded at fair value.

Jan. 1	Equipment	1,200	
	Truck	2,500	
	Cash	4,000	
	Golaan, Capital		7,700
	To record investment in partnership.		

The equipment and the truck are both recorded at fair value.

(Date)	Gabris, Withdrawals	12,000	
	Golaan, Withdrawals	12,000	
	Cash		24,000
	To record partners' withdrawals during year.		

Dec. 31	Income Summary	60,500	
	Gabris, Capital		30,250
	Golaan, Capital		30,250
	To close Income Summary to Capital.		

The profits are shared equally under the Uniform Partnership Act because the partners made no mention of a ratio for sharing profits and losses.

Dec. 31	Gabris, Capital	12,000	
	Golaan, Capital	12,000	
	Gabris, Withdrawals		12,000
	Golaan, Withdrawals		12,000
	To close withdrawals to Capital.		

Gabris and Golaan
Statement of Partners' Capital
December 31, 19X4

	Gabris	Golaan	Total
Beginning capital, 1/1/X4	$ 0	$ 0	$ 0
Investments by partners	6,500	7,700	14,200
Income for 19X4	30,250	30,250	60,500
Subtotal	$36,750	$37,950	$74,700
Partners' withdrawals	12,000	12,000	24,000
Ending capital, 12/31/X4	$24,750	$25,950	$50,700

(b) *Record journal entries for 19X5 and prepare a statement.*

19X5 Jan. 2	Cash	25,000	
	Stevesen, Capital		25,000
	To record Stevesen's admission to partnership.		
(Date)	Gabris, Withdrawals	15,000	
	Golaan, Withdrawals	15,000	
	Stevesen, Withdrawals	15,000	
	Cash		45,000
	To record partners' withdrawals during year.		
Dec. 31	Income Summary	99,000	
	Gabris, Capital		34,650
	Golaan, Capital		34,650
	Stevesen, Capital		29,700
	To close Income Summary to Capital.		
	Gabris ($99,000 x .35 = $34,650)		
	Golaan ($99,000 x .35 = $34,650)		
	Stevesen ($99,000 x .30 = $29,700)		
31	Gabris, Capital	15,000	
	Golaan, Capital	15,000	
	Stevesen, Capital	15,000	
	Gabris, Withdrawals		15,000
	Golaan, Withdrawals		15,000
	Stevesen, Withdrawals		15,000
	To close withdrawals to Capital.		

Gabris, Golaan, and Steveson Statement of Partners' Capital December 31, 19X5				
	Gabris	*Golaan*	*Stevesen*	*Total*
Beginning capital, 1/1/X5	$24,750	$25,950	$ 0	$ 50,700
Investment by Stevesen			25,000	25,000
Subtotal	$24,750	$25,950	$25,000	$ 75,700
Income for 19X5	34,650	34,650	29,700	99,000
Subtotal	$59,400	$60,600	$54,700	$174,700
Partners' withdrawals	15,000	15,000	15,000	45,000
Ending capital, 12/31/X5	$44,400	$45,600	$39,700	$129,700

KEY TERMS

co-ownership of partnership
   property, *551*
limited life, *551*
limited partnership, *551*

mutual agency, *551*
partnership, *550*
partnership agreement, *550*

statement of partners' capital,
   559
unlimited liability, *551*

SELF-QUIZ

LO 1 1. Indicate which of the following items are part of the definition of the term *partnership*:
   ___ a. Amalgamation
   ___ b. Conglomeration
   ___ c. Association
   ___ d. Two or more persons
   ___ e. Three or more persons
   ___ f. Four or more persons
   ___ g. Business for profit
   ___ h. Legal entity
   ___ i. Limited liability
   ___ j. Mandatory
   ___ k. Voluntary
   ___ l. Regulatory
   ___ m. Shareholder
   ___ n. Co-owner
   ___ o. Co-resident
   ___ p. Co-director

LO 1 2. Indicate which of the following are among the minimum key elements of a partnership agreement:
   ___ a. Business nature
   ___ b. Projected cash flows
   ___ c. State of incorporation
   ___ d. Income sharing agreement
   ___ e. Chart of accounts
   ___ f. Trial balance
   ___ g. Original investments

   ___ h. Subsequent   investments   and withdrawals
   ___ i. Partner's previous business experience
   ___ j. Dissolution procedures

LO 1 3. Indicate which of the following are considered to be disadvantages of the partnership form of business organization:
   ___ a. Ease of formation
   ___ b. Unlimited liability
   ___ c. Freedom of action
   ___ d. Limited life
   ___ e. Pooling resources
   ___ f. Mutual agency

LO 1 4. A partnership agreement may be
   a. Oral
   b. Written
   c. a and b
   d. None of the above

LO 2 5. Assets invested in a partnership are recorded at
   a. the lower of depreciated cost or fair value
   b. the lower of cost or fair value
   c. fair value
   d. depreciated cost

LO 2 6. Partnership capital balances include the cumulative effect of
   a. Initial investments
   b. Subsequent investments

c. Shares of income
d. Shares of losses
e. Withdrawals
f. All of the above
g. None of the above

LO 2 7. Partner's investments may include which of
the following?
a. Cash assets
b. Noncash assets
c. Noncash assets subject to debt claims
d. Only a and b above
e. a, b, and c above

LO 3 8. In calculating the allocation of partnership
income to partners, where no mention is
made of income sharing in the partnership
agreement, which of the following ratios
would be used?
a. Ratio of beginning capital balances
b. Ratio of weighted-average capital balances
c. Ratio of ending capital balances
d. None of the above

LO 3 9. Indicate which of the following distributions
would be made last in allocating partnership
income to the partners, where interest on
capital balances and salary allowances to
partners are involved
a. Specified ratio
b. Salary allowance
c. Interest on capital balances
d. None of the above would be last.

LO 3 10. For the most equitable distribution of partnership income based on invested capital, the
partnership agreement should specify which
of the following is considered invested capital?
a. Beginning capital
b. Ending capital
c. Weighted-average capital
d. None of the above

LO 4 11. A statement of partners' capital should
include all of the following *except*:
a. Partners' beginning capital balances
b. Partners' investments during the period
c. Partners' share of income for the period
d. Partners' withdrawals during the period
e. Partners' ending capital balances
f. Partners' payments of loans

LO 5 12. Partnerships are dissolved when
a. A new partner is admitted
b. Partner withdraws
c. Partner dies
d. Partners agree to dissolve
e. All of the above
f. None of the above

LO 5 13. When partners agree to sell a portion of their
respective interests to a new partner, the journal entry to record the transaction on the
partnership books includes

a. Debiting Cash for the investment
b. Debiting the capital account of the new
partner
c. Debiting the capital accounts of the old
partners
d. None of the above

LO 5 14. When partners agree to admit a new partner
to the partnership in exchange for an investment of cash or other assets in the partnership, the new partner's capital account can
reflect an amount
a. Equal to the investment
b. Greater than the investment
c. Less than the investment
d. Any of the above
e. None of the above

LO 5 15. When a partner elects to withdraw, the
amount of cash or other assets paid in settlement of the partner's capital interest may
be
a. Worth more than the withdrawing partner's
recorded equity
b. Worth less than the withdrawing partner's
recorded equity
c. Worth an amount equal to the withdrawing
partner's recorded equity
d. Any of the above
e. None of the above

LO 5 16. When a partner dies, the partners should
a. Retire all partnership debt
b. Close the books of the partnership
c. Determine the fair value of the partnership
assets
d. b and c
e. None of the above

LO 5 17. Partnership dissolution (without liquidation)
results in
a. Closing the business and selling the assets
b. Creating a new partnership and replacing
the old one
c. Terminating the old partnership agreement
d. b and c
e. None of the above

LO 6 18. The liquidation of a partnership results in
a. Closing the business and selling the assets
b. Creating a new partnership and replacing
the old one
c. Terminating the old partnership agreement
d. b and c only
e. None of the above

LO 6 19. Which of the following is *not* associated with
the liquidation of a partnership?
a. Converting partnership assets to cash
b. Paying creditors
c. Admitting a new partner
d. Closing the books and allocating income or
losses to the partners' capital accounts

LO 6 20. In converting partnership assets to cash, any differences between the proceeds of sale and the carrying amount of the assets sold should be recorded as a
a. Debit to the partners' equity accounts
b. Debit to the partners' withdrawals accounts
c. Debit or credit to Gain (Loss) from Realization
d. Debit or credit to Income Summary
e. None of the above

SOLUTIONS TO SELF-QUIZ

1. c, d, g, k, n   2. a, d, g, h, k   3. b, d, and f   4. c   5. c   6. f   7. e   8. d   9. a   10. c   11. f   12. e
13. c   14. d   15. d   16. d   17. d   18. a   19. c   20. c

QUESTIONS

Q14-1   Define partnership.

Q14-2   List six important elements that should be included in a partnership agreement.

Q14-3   Match the following terms with the definitions below:
a. Limited life
b. Unlimited liability
c. Mutual agency
d. Co-ownership of partnership property

___ (1) Each partner is an agent of the partnership and has the ability to bind the partnership to business agreements within the scope of the business.
___ (2) The business will be terminated when a partner withdraws, a new partner is admitted, the partners voluntarily terminate the agreement, bankruptcy terminates the agreement, or the agreed life of the entity expires.
___ (3) Each partner risks not only the assets invested in the business but also personal assets.
___ (4) Specific assets a partner invests in a partnership business are not necessarily available to that partner upon withdrawal from the partnership.

Q14-4   If the partnership agreement sets a ratio for distribution of profits but ignores the topic of losses, any losses incurred will be shared
a. Equally
b. In the ratio of capital balances
c. In the same ratio as profits
d. None of the above

Q14-5   Which of the following is *not* an advantage of the partnership form of business organization?
a. Ability to pool the resources of several owners
b. Ease of formation and dissolution
c. Unlimited liability of the partners
d. Freedom of action afforded partners

Q14-6   How are partnership income and losses distributed if the partnership agreement is silent about the sharing of income and losses?

Q14-7   Explain how the assets invested in a partnership should be recorded.

Q14-8   Discuss why it might be appropriate to provide for interest on partners' capital balances and to distribute the remainder in a predetermined ratio.

Q14-9   Discuss why it might be appropriate to provide for salary allowances to partners and to distribute the remainder in a predetermined ratio.

Q14-10   Discuss why it might be appropriate to provide for interest on partners' capital balances, salary allowances, and for distributing the remainder of partnership income in a predetermined ratio.

Q14-11   List events that could alter the partnership agreement and terminate the partnership.

Q14-12   Does altering the partnership agreement and, hence, terminating the partnership necessarily mean that the assets will be disposed of and that the business will cease to exist as a going-concern? Explain.

Q14-13   When partners agree to sell a portion of their respective interests to an incoming partner, what happens to the cash the incoming partner pays?

Q14-14   Discuss what happens to the equity created when an incoming partner receives a capital interest that is less that the amount invested.

Q14-15   Discuss what happens when a new partner receives a capital interest that exceeds the amount invested in the partnership.

Q14-16   What could be the justification for paying a retiring partner more than the balance reflected in that partner's capital account?

Q14-17   Discuss the accounting procedures that would be followed when a partner dies.

Q14-18   Explain the difference between partnership dissolution and partnership liquidation.

Q14-19   Discuss what happens if in a partnership liquidation the cash realized from the sale of the partnership assets is insufficient to cover the claims of the partnership creditors.

Q14-20   In a partnership liquidation, after the allocation of losses from conversion of the partnership assets, one of the partners has a capital balance that is insufficient to absorb the partner's share of the loss. Discuss how the resulting debit balance in the deficient partner's capital account is disposed of.

EXERCISES

LO 2   **E14-1**   **Formation of a Partnership**   Abell, Babec, and Cadore agree to form a partnership to practice accounting. They agree to each contribute $10,000 to the partnership and to share profits and losses equally.

REQUIRED:

Prepare the journal entry or entries to record the partners' investments.

LO 2   **E14-2**   **Formation of a Partnership**   Martha Walters and Ivan Recuso form a partnership to provide computer repair services. Walters has been repairing computers part-time in her garage for the last several months. She brings to the partnership testing equipment that had cost her $8,000 last year and $3,000 in cash. Recuso is investing cash in an amount to make his investment equal to hers. They agree that the testing equipment has a fair value of $6,500.

REQUIRED:

Prepare the journal entries to record each partner's investment in the partnership.

LO 3   **E14-3**   **Partnership Income Distribution**   Clark and Clendenny had 19X8 beginning capital balances of $35,000 and $45,000, respectively. Income for 19X8 is $60,000.

REQUIRED:

Prepare the journal entries to distribute the income to Clark and Clendenny for the two following cases:
a. There is no written agreement as to the distribution of profits and losses.
b. Income is distributed in the ratio of beginning capital balances.

LO 3   **E14-4   Partnership Income Distribution**   Thibodeaux and Swafford share income and losses by allocating 6% interest on weighted-average capital balances for the year and dividing the remainder in the ratio of 3 to 2. The weighted-average capital balances were $80,000 and $40,000 for the year, respectively.

REQUIRED:

Prepare the journal entry to distribute income of $60,000 for the period. Show calculations.

LO 3   **E14-5   Partnership Income Distribution**   Hilliard and Hariman share income and losses by using a salary allowance of $5,000 and $10,000, respectively, with the remainder distributed 35/65.

REQUIRED:

Prepare the journal entry to distribute income of $14,000 for the period. Show calculations.

LO 3   **E14-6   Partnership Loss Distribution**   Califano and Christoffersen operate a retail store as partners. The partnership agreement calls for income and losses to be distributed with 8% interest on beginning capital balances, salaries of $10,000 and $12,000, respectively, and any remainder in the ratio of 40/60. The loss for the year was $6,000. Beginning capital balances were $20,000 and $30,000, respectively.

REQUIRED:

Prepare the journal entry to record the distribution of the loss to the partners. Show calculations.

LO 3,4   **E14-7   Partnership Income Distribution and Statement of Partners' Capital**   McCoy and Wade began 19X8 with January 1 capital balances of $35,000 and $45,000, respectively. McCoy's withdrawals for the year totaled $25,000, and Wade's withdrawals totaled $20,000. Net income for the year ended December 31, was $60,000. The partnership agreement is silent regarding the distribution of profits and losses.

REQUIRED:

Prepare a statement of partners' capital at year-end.

LO 5   **E14-8   Admission of a New Partner, Sale of Existing Interest**   Rice and Rhoades share profits and losses equally. On January 1, 19X9, when their capital balances are $40,000 and $60,000, respectively, they admit Reid to the partnership by each selling one-half of their interest to Reid. Reid pays a total of $60,000 for the interests acquired.

REQUIRED:

Prepare the journal entry to reflect Reid's admission to the partnership.

LO 5   **E14-9   Admission of a New Partner, Investment of Assets**   Secore and Seay admit Brown to a one-fourth interest in the partnership with an investment of $50,000 in cash. At the time of Brown's admission, the former partners had capital balances of $50,000 and $60,000, respectively. Secore and Seay's income and loss ratio was 50/50.

REQUIRED:

Prepare the journal entry to record the admission of Brown to the partnership. Show calculations.

LO 5   **E14-10** **Withdrawal of Assets Greater Than Recorded Equity**   Adam Mitchell, Colleen Grace, and Richard Mellon have worked together for many years. Mellon elects to retire and in accordance with the partnership agreement, Mellon is to receive cash equal to 125% of his capital account balance at the date of withdrawal. Capital balances at this time are $145,000, $155,000, and $100,000, respectively. The partners have always shared income and losses equally.

REQUIRED:

Prepare the journal entry to record Mellon's withdrawal from the partnership, assuming there is ample cash for settlement. Show calculations.

LO 5   **E14-11** **Withdrawal of Assets Less Than Recorded Equity**   Johansson, Brank, Wilson, and Isenhower share income and losses in the ratio 40%, 20%, 20%, 20%. Marcus Isenhower is withdrawing from the partnership and is to receive an amount of cash equal to 90% of his capital balance. The capital balances at the date of withdrawal are $100,000, $50,000, $60,000, and $40,000, respectively.

REQUIRED:

Prepare the journal entry to record Isenhower's withdrawal from the partnership, assuming there is ample cash for settlement. Show calculations.

LO 6   **E14-12** **Partnership Liquidation**   Barnes and Corbin have decided to terminate the operation of their partnership. Their assets consist of $5,000 in cash and inventory with a carrying amount of $95,000. Their only liability is an account payable of $10,000. Their capital balances are $40,000 and $50,000, respectively, and they share profits and losses equally.

REQUIRED:

a. Prepare the journal entries to record the sale of the inventory for $85,000, the distribution of the loss to the partners, and the final disposition of the cash.
b. Post the journal entries to T-accounts to illustrate the liquidation.

PROBLEM SET A

LO 1,2,4   **P14-1A** **Partnership Formation**   On April 1, 19X8, Pepin and Pentz agree to form a partnership to sell and install residential water-softening equipment. The partners agree that Pepin will invest tools and equipment, which cost $8,000, and have a current fair value of $6,000 together with cash of $14,000; and Pentz will invest a truck, which cost $15,500 and has a fair value of $9,500 together with sufficient cash to equal Pepin's investment.

REQUIRED:

a. Prepare the journal entry to record the partners investments.
b. Prepare a balance sheet for the Pepin and Pentz partnership at April 1, 19X8.

LO 3   **P14-2A** **Accounting for Partnership Income and Losses**   Freis, Fritag, and Friedlander own and operate a go-cart track. The business has been operating for 3 years; and the partners have beginning capital balances of $10,000, $15,000, and $25,000, respectively. The partners work part-time in the business and have different amounts of time available to work at the track. They have been sharing profits and losses equally and have decided that a different distribution of profits and losses may be more equitable.

The following plan has been adopted: salaries of $6,000, $4,000, and $3,000, respectively; interest of 8% on the beginning capital balances; and the remainder shared equally.

REQUIRED:

a. Calculate the distribution of income or loss to partners assuming income of $38,000.

b. Prepare the journal entry to close Income Summary to partners' capital accounts under Requirement a.

c. Calculate the distribution of income or loss to partners, assuming a loss of $10,000.

d. Prepare the journal entry to close Income Summary to partners' capital accounts under Requirement c.

LO 3,4   **P14-3A**   **Accounting for Partnership Income and Losses; Partnership Financial Statements** Cross-Bayou Nursery buys bedding plants and resells them to landscapers. The partners, B. Kinnear and G. King, have beginning capital balances of $35,000 each and share profits and losses by allowing interest of 5% on beginning capital balances, salaries of $15,000 and $20,000, respectively, and the remainder shared equally. During the fiscal year ended July 31, 19X9, Cross-Bayou reported revenues of $235,000 and expenses of $190,000.

REQUIRED:

a. Prepare the journal entries to close the revenue and expense accounts and to distribute the income to the partners' capital accounts. Show the calculation of the distribution of income.

b. Prepare a statement of partner's capital for the year ended July 31, 19X9. There were no withdrawals during the period.

LO 3,4,5   **P14-4A**   **Partnership Dissolution, Admission of a Partner with Sale of Existing Interests** On January 1, 19X1, Tiger and Tisdale, with capital balances of $45,000 and $55,000, respectively, have tired of working full-time in the Limousine Service and agree to admit Stiles to a one-fourth interest in the partnership by each selling Stiles one-fourth of their existing interests. Stiles pays a total of $40,000 for the interest, the cash being given to Tiger and Tisdale in proportion to their capital balances. They agree to share profits 40%, 40%, 20%. During 19X1, the business generates revenues of $400,000, while incurring expenses of $220,000. The partners withdrew $30,000 each during the year.

REQUIRED:

a. Prepare the journal entry to record Stiles's admission to the partnership.

b. Prepare the journal entries to close the accounts on December 31, 19X1.

c. Prepare a statement of partners' capital as of December 31, 19X1.

LO 3,4,5   **P14-5A**   **Partnership Dissolution, Withdrawal of a Partner with Bonus to Withdrawing Partner**   Crew, Mull, and Dray share profits 40%, 30%, 30% and have capital balances of $60,000, $80,000, and $80,000, respectively, on January 1, 19X2. During the year, revenues total $220,000, and expenses incurred total $110,000. Crew, Mull, and Dray each withdrew $25,000 during the year.

Roberta Crew has elected to retire. The other partners have agreed that she should receive an amount $5,000 higher than the reported capital balance at year-end because the fair value of the assets is greater than the carrying amount.

REQUIRED:

a. Prepare the journal entries to close the accounts of the partnership as of December 31, 19X2, and to distribute income to the partners.

b. Prepare the journal entry to record Crew's withdrawal from the partnership on December 31, 19X2.

c. Prepare a statement of partners' capital for the year ended December 31, 19X2.

LO 3,6   **P14-6A**   **Partnership Liquidation, Gain or Loss from Realization, Remaining Cash to Partners**   The Helms Family Store has been operated as a partnership for many years by Hal, Fred, and Doris. They have shared income equally over the years. Their current balance sheet is shown below:

Helms Family Store Balance Sheet December 31, 19X8			
Cash	$ 80,000	Accounts payable	$ 30,000
Supplies	25,000	H. Helms, capital	15,000
Inventory	125,000	F. Helms, capital	90,000
Equipment	140,000	D. Helms, capital	135,000
Accumulated depreciation	(100,000)		
	$270,000		$270,000

In the course of the liquidation, the supplies are sold for $29,000; inventory, for $100,000; and equipment, for $10,000, all at an auction on December 31, 19X8.

REQUIRED:

a. Prepare the entries to record the sale of the supplies, inventory, and equipment.
b. Prepare the entries to record the payment of the accounts payable and to distribute the gain or loss to the partners' capital accounts.
c. Assume any partner with a deficit balance in capital after the distribution of losses pays the amount of the deficit into the partnership. Prepare the journal entry to record this payment.
d. Prepare the entry to distribute the cash to the partners and to close the books.
e. Explain why the cash in Requirement d was not distributed equally to all the partners in view of their agreement to share profits equally.

PROBLEM SET B

LO 1,2,4   **P14-1B**   **Partnership Formation**   Salzano and Salzillo agree to form a partnership on August 5, 19X5, for the purpose of manufacturing and selling custom silver jewelry. Both are master crafters and have their own tools, which they will invest in the business. Salzano and Salzillo agree that their tools have fair values of $4,500 and $6,000 respectively. They further agree to invest sufficient cash such that each partner will have a beginning capital balance of $25,000.

REQUIRED:

a. Prepare the journal entry to record the partners' investments.
b. Prepare a balance sheet for the Salzano and Salzillo partnership at August 5, 19X5, immediately after formation.

LO 3   **P14-2B**   **Accounting for Partnership Income and Losses**   Bucca, Casho, and DeVita operate a car wash as partners. The partners have beginning capital balances of $15,000, $15,000, and $20,000, respectively. Each partner works part-time in the business. They are seeking a more equitable distribution of profits and losses.

The following plan has been adopted: salaries of $3,000, $4,000, and $5,000, respectively; interest of 6% on the beginning capital balances; and the remainder shared equally.

REQUIRED:

a. Calculate the distribution of income or loss to partners, assuming income of $24,000.
b. Prepare the journal entry to close Income Summary to partners' capital accounts under Requirement a.

    c. Calculate the distribution of income or loss to partners, assuming a loss of $6,000.

    d. Prepare the journal entry to close Income Summary to partners' capital accounts under Requirement c.

LO 3,4 **P14-3B** **Accounting for Partnership Income and Losses; Partnership Financial Statements**
Aldret and Arvey operate a carpet and rug cleaning service. The partners have beginning capital balances of $25,000 and $35,000, respectively. They share profits and losses by allowing interest of 8% on capital beginning balances, salaries of $8,000 and $12,000 respectively, with the remainder shared equally. During the fiscal year ended March 31, 19X6, Carpet Cleaners Company reported revenues of $190,000 and expenses of $95,000.

REQUIRED:

    a. Prepare the journal entries to close the revenue and expense accounts and to distribute the income to the partners' capital accounts. Show the calculation of the distribution of income.

    b. Prepare a statement of partners' capital for the year ended March 31, 19X6. There were no withdrawals during the period.

LO 3,4,5 **P14-4B** **Partnership Dissolution, Admission of a Partner with Investment of Assets and Bonus to Original Partners**   Panagos and Trainor have successfully operated a bowling alley for 3 years. They have capital accounts of $125,000 and $175,000, respectively, and share profits and losses equally. The need to add 12 lanes caused them to seek a new partner with ample funds. Sara Owle has indicated a willingness to invest $200,000 for a 35% interest in capital and a 1/3 share in the profits. The agreement was completed, and Sara invested the cash on January 4, 19X7, the beginning of the fiscal year. During 19X7, the business generates revenues of $485,000, while incurring expenses of $275,000. The partners withdrew $50,000 each during the year.

REQUIRED:

    a. Prepare the journal entry to record Owle's admission to the partnership.

    b. Prepare the journal entries to close the accounts on December 31, 19X7.

    c. Prepare a statement of partners' capital as of December 31, 19X7.

LO 3,4,5 **14-5B** **Partnership Dissolution, Withdrawal of a Partner with Bonus from Withdrawing Partner**   Borke, Radcliff, and Smart have capital balances of $45,000, $65,000, and $40,000, respectively, after closing the accounts on December 31, 19X8. During 19X9, revenues earned were $190,000, and expenses incurred were $120,000. Each of the partners withdrew $12,000 during the year. Smart has decided to retire as of December 31, 19X9, and the partners agree that Smart will receive $40,000 in settlement of the partnership interest because the assets are overvalued. The partners share profits and losses 30%, 50%, 20%, respectively.

REQUIRED:

    a. Prepare the journal entries to close the accounts of the partnership as of December 31, 19X9, and to distribute the income to the partners.

    b. Prepare the journal entry to record Smart's withdrawal from the partnership on December 31, 19X9.

    c. Prepare a statement of partners' capital for the year ended December 31, 19X9.

LO 3,6 **P14-6B** **Partnership Liquidation, Gain or Loss from Realization, Settlement with Capital-Deficient Partner**   Li, Ho, and Chin have decided to liquidate their partnership and retire. They share profits and losses in the ratio 40%, 40%, 20%, respectively. The balance sheet as of December 31, 19X6, after closing, is shown on the next page:

Li, Ho, and Chin Balance Sheet December 31, 19X6			
Cash	$ 7,000	Accounts payable	$20,000
Supplies	1,500	Li, capital	5,000
Inventory	22,500	Ho, capital	15,000
Equipment	69,000	Chin, capital	10,000
Accumulated depreciation	(50,000)		
	$50,000		$50,000

In the course of the liquidation, supplies are sold for $1600; inventory, for $15,000; and equipment, for $10,000. Assume that any partner with a deficit balance after the distribution of losses from the liquidation of assets is unable to pay the amount owed.

REQUIRED:

a. Prepare the entries to record the sale of the supplies, inventory, and equipment.
b. Prepare the entry to distribute the gain or loss to the partners' capital accounts.
c. Prepare the entry to pay the liabilities.
d. Prepare the entry to adjust the partners' capital balances to absorb the deficit balance of the deficient partner.
e. Prepare the entry to distribute the cash to the partners.

CRITICAL THINKING AND COMMUNICATING

C14-1 Rocker, Mellon, and Barche have operated a partnership for 15 years. They started on a handshake and have done business that way ever since. On August 14, this year, Barche died suddenly. Since there is no written agreement as to the means of settlement with Barche's estate or family, Rocker and Mellon have come to you, their accountant, to ask what needs to be done. You explain that you are not an attorney and advise them that they should retain one. They agree to retain an attorney and ask you what accounting procedures will be required and what questions they should ask the attorney since they wish to continue to operate the business.

REQUIRED;

Provide a written response in the form of a letter to Rocker and Mellon.

C14-2 Jody Ham and Gerald Ham, brothers, have decided to enter into a partnership. The two brothers are master mechanics who specialize in tuning racing motorcycles.

Jody, now 25 years old, has been tuning motorcycles since he was 5. He is known in racing circles as something of a genius. His services are highly sought-after on the racing circuit. Gerald, a skilled mechanic in his own right, does not have the reputation of brother Jody; but as an ex-racer, he is a valuable part of the team because he can test ride the bikes that Jody is tuning and give his brother accurate feedback about the bikes. Also, Gerald has the capital to finance the partnership. Together, Jody and Gerald plan to offer their services to factory racing teams.

They already have offers of contracts for the upcoming year, which could total as much as $400,000. The operation will require a $100,000 investment in equipment.

Gerald will provide the capital by investing $150,000 cash in the partnership. Jody will not make an investment.

REQUIRED:

The brothers come to you and ask for help with an equitable profit-sharing agreement. Propose a plan and show a projected distribution of profits, assuming a net income of $150,000.

CHAPTER 15

Introduction to Corporations

Josh Adams went home from college for the holidays to visit his parents and to see old friends from high school. During dinner one evening, between discussions of football games played the past weekend, Josh's father told the family about the terrific investments he had recently made. In particular, Josh's father seemed pleased that all stocks in which he had invested had shown increases in earnings per share. Josh's father even had an article from a financial magazine that summarized earnings per share and the change in earnings per share for several hundred companies. Josh's father had invested in the stocks of some of these companies.

As Josh considered his father's enthusiasm and excitement, he started to wonder about this number called earnings per share. Josh had seen financial statements before in his accounting course at school. He knew that net income was a measure of business performance. However, his father was excited about earnings per share, not net income, and the magazine article evaluated companies based solely on earnings per share. Josh wondered about the validity of ignoring all the other information that financial statements present and simply looking at earnings per share.

Of the three forms of business organizations—sole proprietorship, partnership, and corporation—the corporation is by far the primary form of business in the United States in terms of the numbers of transactions, the dollar amounts of transactions, total assets, and the numbers of employees. This dominance exists even though the number of businesses organized as proprietorships and partnerships exceeds the number of corporations. Some characteristics of corporations, such as ease of raising capital and ease of transferring ownership, encourage the development of large businesses. In fact, virtually all large businesses in the United States are organized as corporations. For example, General Electric had total assets of $193 billion at the end of 1992, and General Motors Corporation had total revenues of $133 billion for 1992. The Fortune 500 Companies as a group had total assets at the end of 1992 of over $2.5 trillion.[1]

[1]*Fortune* (April 19, 1993), p. 202.

This chapter presents a discussion of the characteristics of the corporate form of business and the fundamental transactions involving owners—issuing stock and paying dividends. A subsequent chapter completes the discussion of accounting for corporations by covering some of the more complex issues involving corporate transactions and financial statements.

LEARNING OBJECTIVES

1. Describe the organization and management of a corporation.
2. State the advantages and disadvantages of the corporate form of business organization.
3. Explain how a corporation is formed and account for organization costs.
4. Describe the characteristics of the components of stockholders' equity.
5. Account for the issuance of common stock in exchange for cash and noncash assets and account for stock subscriptions.
6. Account for the issuance of preferred stock.
7. Account for the declaration and payment of cash dividends.
8. Calculate the stated, cumulative, and participating dividends on preferred stock.
9. Define redemption, book, and market values of stock and calculate book value per share.
10. Calculate and interpret earnings per share.

LO 1

Describe the organization and management of a corporation.

THE CORPORATION

A **corporation** is a legal entity separate from its owners, created when a state government grants a **charter**. Thus, a corporation comes into existence in accordance with the applicable statutes and continues to exist as a legal entity only as permitted by those statutes. The separate legal status of corporations distinguishes them from sole proprietorships and partnerships and results in some differences in accounting that we discuss in this chapter. The state laws grant to a corporation most of the privileges persons possess. Exceptions include those privileges that only a person can exercise such as the rights to vote and to hold public office. Aside from these exceptions, corporations assume most of the duties and responsibilities of persons such as paying taxes and conducting their affairs in accordance with applicable laws.

One way to classify corporations is by the purpose for which they were created—profit and not-for-profit. Many corporations are organized to carry on a business to earn a **profit**. Examples include IBM and General Motors. Other organizations, however, are **not-for-profit**, yet are organized as corporations. These not-for-profit organizations are charitable, educational, and medical organizations. Examples include the United Way and the American Accounting Association.

Another way to classify corporations is by the nature of their ownership. Virtually all large corporations are **publicly-owned corporations**. These corporations, such as American Express and McDonald's, have thousands of owners (stockholders); and their stocks are traded on the national stock exchanges. Other corporations have only a few owners. Corporations with relatively few owners are called **privately-owned corporations**. A family business is often organized as a privately-owned corporation, and the members of the family are the owners of the corporation.

Organization of a Corporation

The stockholders, as owners of the corporation, collectively have the authority to appoint the manager of the business. The stockholders delegate their authority to an elected board of directors, which establishes the corporation's broad operating policies. Appointed by the board of directors, the corporate officers manage the day-to-day operations of the corporation. In managing the operations, the officers are responsible for implementing the policies the directors establish. We show the organizational structure of a corporation in Illustration 15-1.

ILLUSTRATION 15-1 Organization Chart of a Corporation

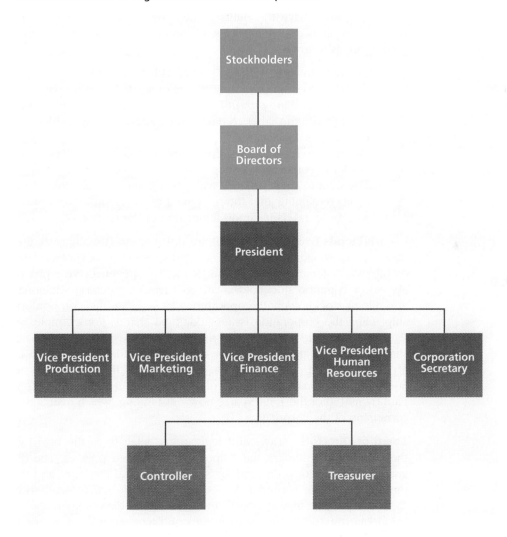

Stockholders.   The **stockholders** are the owners of the corporation. Technically, stockholders participate in management of a corporation only indirectly by electing the board of directors. However, individual stockholders may serve as directors if elected by the stockholders or as officers if appointed by the board of directors. Direct stockholder involvement in management is more typical in small, privately-owned corporations, but is less typical in large corporations. Stockholders also indirectly participate in management by voting on certain issues, including selection of an independent auditor, changes in the number of shares authorized, and proposed mergers and acquisitions at the annual stockholders' meeting.

State laws generally require corporations to hold annual meetings of the stockholders. At these meetings, stockholders elect directors and vote on other matters. Not all stockholders can attend the meeting, however. For large corporations, stockholders are located across the nation; and for some corporations, ownership is international. Stockholders who are unable to attend the stockholders' meeting may delegate their votes to an agent. By signing a legal document called a **proxy**, a stockholder allows the agent to cast the number of votes to which he or she is entitled. Typically, the agent is a current officer of the corporation.

Stockholders have the rights granted by the charter and specified by the various state laws and regulations. Generally, the rights of the common stockholders are as follows:

1. The right to vote in meetings of stockholders.
2. The right to dispose of their shares of stock as they please.
3. The right to share *pro rata* (meaning in proportion to their ownership shares) with the other common stockholders in any dividends the board of directors declare.
4. The right to have the *first* opportunity to purchase additional shares of stock the corporation issues.
5. The right to share *pro rata* with other common stockholders in any assets remaining after the settlement of the creditors' and preferred stockholders' claims upon liquidation of the corporation.

Dividends (Number 3, above) are distributions, usually cash, a corporation makes to its stockholders. Dividends distributed to stockholders are similar to withdrawals of partners and proprietors. The **preemptive right** (Number 4, above) of common stockholders allows them to purchase additional shares. It also allows stockholders the opportunity to maintain their proportion of ownership when the corporation issues additional shares. For example, assume that Paul Johnson owns 100 shares of the Southeast Design, Inc.'s 1,000 outstanding shares, or 10% of the shares. If the corporation undertakes to issue an additional 500 shares, the preemptive right gives Paul the first opportunity to purchase 50 of the additional shares. The purchase of the additional shares means that Paul owns 150 of the 1,500 shares now outstanding, which maintains Paul's 10% ownership of the corporation.

Board of Directors. Laws and regulations delegate to the board of directors the authority to establish the corporation's business policies. The directors are also responsible for protecting the stockholders and creditors, and they appoint the officers of the corporation to whom they delegate the authority to implement the policies they establish. In addition, the directors are also responsible for declaring dividends, approving contracts, approving major borrowing arrangements, and setting executive compensation.

Laws or regulations do not prescribe the exact composition of the board of directors. For most publicly-owned corporations, the board consists of several officers of the corporation, along with a number of outside directors who are not employees of the corporation. Outside director membership on the board is desirable because it allows the board to monitor independently the performance of management.

Management.   The board of directors appoints the corporation's managers and gives them the responsibility of implementing the business policies the board adopts and for carrying on the business's operations. The officers of a corporation generally include the president, vice president(s), controller, treasurer, and secretary. The president, or chief operating officer of the corporation, reports directly to the board. Many corporations have several vice presidents, each responsible for a specific function such as production, marketing, finance, and human resources (personnel). The controller is the chief accounting officer responsible for preparing financial statements, tax returns, other required regulatory reports, internal financial and operating reports, and budgets. The treasurer is responsible for managing the corporation's funds. In addition to maintaining the minutes of meetings of stockholders and the board of directors, the secretary is also responsible for the stockholder records.

LO 2

State the advantages and disadvantages of the corporate form of business organization.

Advantages of a Corporation

The corporate form of business offers several advantages over sole proprietorships and partnerships.

Separate Legal Entity.   A corporation is a legal entity and separate from its owners. Under U.S. law, a corporation has the rights and responsibilities of a person. Through its agents, a corporation conducts its affairs and can enter into contracts; purchase, own, and sell property; and hire and dismiss employees. It can also sue and be sued in the courts, independent of its owners.

Limited Stockholder Liability.   Since a corporation is a separate legal entity, it is responsible for its actions and debts. Laws limit creditors' claims against a corporation to the total amount of the corporation's assets. The stockholders are not liable for the claims of creditors of the corporation. That is, if the corporation's assets do not fully satisfy creditor claims, stockholders are *not* required to make up the difference. Laws limit the risk stockholders assume to losing their investments in the corporation. For investors in the corporation's stock, the limited liability aspect of the corporate form of business has great appeal. In contrast, proprietors and partners may be liable for debts of proprietorships and partnerships; and creditors may make claims against their personal assets to satisfy the debts of their businesses.

Lack of Mutual Agency.   In the corporate form of business, mutual agency does not exist. The stockholders, acting as owners, cannot bind the corporation to contracts. For example, a stockholder cannot purchase land in the name of the corporation. For partnerships, however, mutual agency does exist; and a partnership can be bound by the actions of any partner. Because of the lack of mutual agency, stockholders do not have to be as concerned as partners do about the other owners with whom they associate in a business enterprise.

Ease of Transferring Ownership.   Shares of stock represent the stockholders' ownership of the corporation. Stockholders can transfer shares of stock to others whenever they please. The transfer of ownership neither affects the corporation's operations nor requires the approval of other stockholders.

Ease of Raising Capital. Because of the previously discussed characteristics of a corporation, it is possible to raise large amounts of capital. In particular, limited stockholder liability, lack of mutual agency, and the ease of transferring ownership make it possible to have a large number of owners who each invest relatively small amounts of money. The only limit on a corporation's capital-raising potential is its ability to employ the invested capital profitably.

Continuity of Existence. The time specified in the charter and the state laws where it is incorporated define the life of a corporation. When the time specified in the charter expires, renewing the charter extends the life of the corporation. In contrast to a partnership, the death or withdrawal of an owner does not affect the life of the corporation.

Professional Management. Many corporations are owned by large numbers of stockholders. They have neither the skill nor the time to manage the corporation. To solve this problem, corporations hire professional managers to run the corporation's day-to-day operations. This situation creates a separation between the owners and management. While professional management is an advantage of corporations, the separation of owners and managers sometimes creates some disadvantages. For example, if there is a lack of communication between management and the owners, the owners may not be able to observe the managers' actions. Thus, managers may make decisions that are not in the best interests of the owners.

Disadvantages of a Corporation

When compared to proprietorships and partnerships, corporations also have the disadvantages of increased government regulation and certain aspects of income taxation.

Government Regulation. Corporations are subject to the control and regulation of the state where incorporated. Generally, state laws and regulations require corporations to submit numerous reports to state agencies. In addition, publicly-owned corporations that operate across state lines and have a relatively large number of stockholders are regulated under federal statutes administered by the Securities and Exchange Commission (SEC). Among other things, federal laws require that quarterly and annual financial statements, as well as other reports, be filed on a timely basis with the SEC. Fulfilling the requirements of the various laws and regulations imposes significant costs on corporations.

Taxation of Income. The owners of a special class of corporations, known as "S corporations," are taxed as if they are partners of a partnership. The S corporations themselves are not taxed. The incomes of all other corporations, known as "C corporations," are subject to both federal and state income taxes. (Refer to Appendix A of this text to learn about income taxation of corporations; and, henceforth, when we mention corporations, we refer to C corporations.) Together, state and federal income taxes can amount to more than 40% of a corporation's pre-tax earnings. Furthermore, when a corporation distributes after-tax earnings to the owners as dividends, the dividends are taxable income of the stockholders. This is called **double taxation of corporations**. First, the corporation's income is taxed and, when paid to the stockholders as dividends, the income is taxed again. In contrast to C corporations, the incomes of proprietorships, partnerships and S corporations are taxable only once as their owners' personal incomes.

Explain how a corporation is formed and account for organization costs.

FORMING A CORPORATION

In most states, corporations are formed by obtaining a charter from the state. To obtain a charter, at least three incorporators must submit an application to the appropriate state agency.

Articles of Incorporation and Bylaws

The application that incorporators submit contains a document called the **articles of incorporation**, which is a contract between the corporation and the state. The articles of incorporation contains information about the name and address of the corporation, the purpose of the corporation, the different classes and authorized shares of stock, the voting and dividend rights of each class of stock, and the life of the corporation.

Once the state agency approves the application and after the incorporators pay all fees, the state grants the charter; and the corporation comes into existence. The corporation is then able to sell stock to the incorporators and to others who become the owners (stockholders) of the corporation. The stockholders then hold a meeting to elect the board of directors. The directors adopt **bylaws** to govern the corporation's conduct and appoint officers of the corporation to manage the business's operations.

Organization Costs

Organization costs, those incurred in forming a corporation, include fees paid to the state to obtain a charter, legal fees incurred in preparing the application for a charter, promoters' fees, printing fees for stock certificates, and any other costs incurred. We record organization costs as intangible assets because they, at least conceptually, benefit the corporations throughout their lives.

When the business incurs organization costs, we debit the amount to an asset account called Organization Cost. We amortize the intangible asset over its useful life; but according to GAAP, the amortization period should not exceed 40 years. In practice, businesses usually amortize organization costs over 5 years. This practice developed because federal income tax laws and regulations permit amortization over 5 years. Since the amortization of organization costs is immaterial for many corporations, the 5-year amortization period is the easiest way to account for the organization costs. To illustrate accounting for organization costs, assume Home Furnishings, Inc. incurs $8,500 of organization costs on January 2, 19X1. The entry to record the intangible asset is as follows:

19X1			
Jan. 2	Organization Costs	8,500	
	Cash		8,500
	To record costs incurred in forming the corporation.		

If Home Furnishings elects to amortize the organization costs over 5 years, it would make the entry shown below on December 31, 19X1, to record the first year's amortization:

19X1			
Dec. 31	Organization Cost Amortization Expense	1,700	
	Organization Costs		1,700
	To record one year's amortization of organization cost: ($8,500 ÷ 5 = $1,700)		

Notice that we make the credit directly to Organization Costs account rather than to Accumulated Amortization. This treatment is consistent with the amortization of other intangible assets discussed in previous chapters.

STOCKHOLDERS' EQUITY

With the exception of the stockholders' equity section of the balance sheet, the financial statements of corporations are consistent with those of other forms of business enterprises. Also, the GAAP for assets, liabilities, revenues, and expenses are the same for corporations as they are for proprietorships and partnerships. We show the stockholders' equity section of a corporation's balance sheet in Illustration 15-2. It recognizes that, in general, there are two classes of corporate stock—common stock and preferred stock.

An important reporting objective of the stockholders' equity section is to distinguish the *sources of stockholders' equity*. The two principal sources, as presented in Illustration 15-2, are *contributed capital* and *retained earnings*. **Contributed capital** represents the stockholders' claim to the corporation's net assets due to the purchase of the corporation's capital stock. Contributed capital consists of the sum of the capital stock accounts (preferred and common) and the additional paid-in capital accounts for both preferred and common stock. The stockholders' equity section presents detailed information about contributed capital such as: classes of stock that the corporation has issued, par or stated values of the stock issued, total shares authorized of each class, and total shares issued of each class. The *par value* of stock represents the corporation's legal capital. We discuss par value and legal capital below in the section titled "Capital Stock."

ILLUSTRATION 15-2 Partial Balance Sheet

Stockholders' Equity	
Contributed capital:	
Preferred 8% stock, $100 par value, 50,000 shares authorized	
and issued	$ 5,000,000
Additional paid-in capital, preferred	800,000
Common stock, $1 par value, 100,000 shares authorized,	
80,000 shares issued	80,000
Additional paid-in capital, common	9,600,000
Total contributed capital	$15,480,000
Retained earnings	8,230,000
Total stockholders' equity	$23,710,000

A corporation's **retained earnings** consist of the cumulative net income from the business, less the cumulative dividends paid out to stockholders from the beginning of the corporation's life. Another way of describing retained earnings is that it represents the corporation's net income that is retained in the business. We discuss retained earnings more fully in a subsequent chapter. The following sections present a discussion of the components of contributed capital.

Capital Stock

When an investor purchases shares of stock, the stockholder receives from the corporation a stock certificate such as the one shown in Illustration 15-3. The **stock certificate** is evidence of ownership of shares in a corporation and indicates the name of the stockholder and the class and number of shares owned. When a stockholder decides to transfer ownership, usually by selling shares, he or she must endorse the stock certificate on the reverse side of the certificate and send it to the corporation secretary. The secretary will then cancel the old certificate and issue a new certificate to the new stockholder.

ILLUSTRATION 15-3 Stock Certificate

Corporations that have more than a few stockholders normally record information about stock ownership in a **stockholders' ledger**, a subsidiary ledger to the company's capital stock accounts. Each stockholder has a separate account in the ledger. The stockholders' ledger may be a book in a manual system or a file on an electronic data storage device in a computerized system. We show a stockholders' ledger account in Illustration 15-4. Each stockholder's account has information about the number of shares owned, the stock certificate numbers, and the dates of purchase and sale of shares by the stockholder.

Large corporations have millions of shares of stock outstanding, and investors transfer thousands of shares daily. Large corporations usually engage **registrars** and **transfer agents** to handle these tasks. The corporation gives its registrar and transfer agent (usually large banks or trust companies) the responsibilities of transferring the corporation's stock. In addition, the registrar is responsible for maintaining stockholder records and supplying the corporation with a list of stockholders for stockholders' meetings and for dividend payments.

ILLUSTRATION 15-4 Stockholders' Ledger

Angela Freeland
4518 Pecos Avenue
Austin, TX 78730-4518

CERTIFICATES ISSUED			CERTIFICATES CANCELLED			
DATE	CERTIFICATE NO.	NO. OF SHARES	DATE	CERTIFICATE NO.	NO. OF SHARES	SHARES OWNED
19X2						
Aug. 28	1012	500				500
Dec. 12	1532	100				600
			19X7			
			Oct. 16	1532	100	500

When a stockholder decides to transfer ownership of the shares, he or she endorses the stock certificate and sends the certificate to the transfer agent through a stockbroker. The transfer agent then cancels the old certificate, prepares a new certificate, and forwards it to the registrar. The registrar then updates the corporation's stockholder records and records the change in ownership of the shares. The registrar then sends the new certificate to the new stockholder.

Authorized and Issued Shares.   A corporation's **authorized shares** are the number of shares of stock the corporation can issue. The articles of incorporation include the number of shares of preferred and common stock that the state authorizes the corporation to issue. To increase the authorized shares, a corporation must amend its charter by making application to the state to change the number of authorized shares. Commonly, corporations apply for more authorized shares than they initially intend to issue. Then, in the future, if they decide to raise additional capital by selling more shares of stock, they have authorized shares available immediately without having to amend their charters. The partial balance sheet in Illustration 15-2 shows the number of authorized shares for each class of stock. Also, the balance sheet shows the number of shares of stock that the corporation has issued for each class of stock.

Par and No-Par Value Stock.   The shares of stock a corporation issues may be either par value stock or no-par value stock. If the stock has a par value, the corporation's charter specifies the amount of the par value, which is printed on the stock certificate. The corporation's organizers designate the par value of stock, which may be $100, $10, $1, $.10, $.01, or any other amount. Under the state incorporation laws, the **par value** of the stock issued determines the corporation's legal capital. The amount of **legal capital** is the minimum amount of contributed capital for the number of shares issued. In concept, the amount of legal capital is for the protection of creditors in that a corporation cannot pay dividends that would reduce stockholders' equity below legal capital. In practice, creditors are concerned more with the corporation's assets and earning power when evaluating its ability to pay interest and principal.

Usually, the par value of stock is set arbitrarily low and bears no relationship to the stock's market value. In determining the par value to specify, the organizers usually select an amount that is less than the stock's expected market value. In some states, if stock is sold at an amount below par value, the pur-

HISTORICAL PERSPECTIVES

STOCKS AS OBJET'S D'ART

In addition to representing ownership of a company, many stock certificates were exalted to the status of near-works of art. Numerous entrepreneurs did not hesitate to engage skilled painters, etchers, and both steel, and copper-plate engravers to provide the artistic embellishment of their stock certificates.

In the past, the collection of these documents was the hobby of only a few individual bankers and financiers. But its popularity is spreading. To an increasing extent, share certificates are being taken out of safe-deposit boxes and, once elegantly framed, hung as decorations on walls.

Source: Kristina Piwecki and George Alexander, "Stocks and Shares as Objets d'Art," *swiss Business*, No. 4 (July 1990): 61.

chasers may subsequently be assessed for the deficiency if corporation assets are not sufficient to satisfy creditor claims upon liquidation. Also, some state laws forbid the issuance of stock at an amount below par value.

Some corporations elect not to assign a par value to stock, and this results in stock, called **no-par value** stock. An advantage of no-par value stock is that the corporation can sell it at any price without creating a deficiency in legal capital. Also, the absence of a par value on the stock certificate avoids the possibility of investors mistakenly believing that the par value is the stock's market value. Some states allow a corporation to assign a **stated value** to no-par value stock, and the stated value is the corporation's legal capital. In other states, the entire amount received from selling no-par value stock is considered legal capital.

Common Stock

A corporation may issue two classes of stock: common stock and preferred stock. Common stockholders have all of the rights discussed previously in this chapter, including the right to vote at stockholders' meetings. **Common stock** represents the claims of the common stockholders to the corporation's net assets. However, when a corporation liquidates (goes out of business), it must satisfy all creditors' claims to corporate assets and the preferred stockholders before it can distribute any assets to common stockholders. Moreover, the corporation may not issue dividends to common stockholders unless a positive balance remains in Retained Earnings after the corporation meets the dividend preferences of preferred stockholders (described in a subsequent section). If a corporation is authorized to issue only one class of stock, it must be common stock.

Preferred Stock

Preferred stock has several characteristics that differ from those of common stock. **Preferred stock** is generally nonvoting stock, but it does entitle the stockholders to certain preferences relative to those of common stockholders. Preferred stock usually affords preferred stockholders preferences as to dividends and preferences as to assets upon liquidation. A corporation may issue several classes of preferred stock with each class having unique features such as different dividend rates.

LO 5
Account for the issuance
of common stock in
exchange for cash and
noncash assets and
account for stock
subscriptions.

ACCOUNTING FOR ISSUANCE OF COMMON STOCK

When a corporation sells common stock, it receives either cash or noncash assets. When the investor pays fully for the shares, the corporation issues stock certificates for the shares of stock purchased. The shares of stock the corporation sells may be either par value stock or no-par value stock.

Sale of Par Value Common Stock for Cash

When a corporation sells par value stock for cash, we credit the total par value of the stock to Common Stock. For example, assume that on April 1, 19X1, Scientific Products Co. sells 100 shares of $10 par value common stock for cash of $10 per share. We show Scientific's entry to record the sale and issuance of the stock as follows:

19X1			
Apr. 1	Cash	1,000	
	Common Stock		1,000
	To record the sale and issuance of common stock.		

When the corporation sells par value stock at an amount greater than par value, we credit the excess to **Paid-In Capital in Excess of Par**. Assume that, in the previous example, the corporation sells the 100 shares of stock for $25 cash per share instead of $10 per share. Scientific's entry to record the sale and issuance or the stock is as follows:

19X1			
Apr. 1	Cash	2,500	
	Common Stock		1,000
	Paid-In Capital in Excess of Par–Common		1,500
	To record the sale and issuance of common stock.		

The balance of Common Stock is Scientific Products Co.'s legal capital. The corporation's contributed capital, however, is the sum of the balances of Common Stock and Paid-In Capital in Excess of Par–Common.

Sale of No-Par Value Common Stock for Cash

The accounting for the issuance of no-par value stock depends on whether the directors assigned a stated value to the stock. Assume the directors of Home Furnishings, Inc. assign a stated value of $5 per share to its no-par value stock. We record the sale and issuance of 100 shares for $50 cash per share on August 10 as follows:

Aug. 10	Cash	5,000	
	Common Stock		500
	Paid-In Capital in Excess of Stated Value–Common		4,500
	To record the sale and issuance of common stock.		

Notice that the stated value assigned to the no-par value stock functions similarly to a par value. The stated value determines the amount credited to Common Stock, and the balance in that account is the corporation's legal capital. We credit proceeds from the sale of the stock that are in excess of the stated value to Paid-In Capital in Excess of Stated Value–Common. The sum of the balances of Common Stock and Paid-In Capital in Excess of Stated Value–Common is the corporation's total contributed capital.

If the directors do *not* assign a stated value to no-par value stock, we consider legal capital to be the entire amount of the proceeds from the sale of the stock. If the directors of Home Furnishings, Inc. do not assign a stated value to its no-par value stock, we record the sale and issuance of 100 shares for $50 per share as follows:

Aug. 10	Cash	5,000	
	Common Stock		5,000
	To record the sale and issuance of no-par value stock.		

Sale of Common Stock for Noncash Assets

In the previous examples, the corporation sells stock for cash. However, the corporation also may sell stock in exchange for noncash assets. For example, assume that on September 28, Appliance Sales Co. exchanges 10,000 shares of $10 par value stock for a parcel of land that the previous owner had offered to sell for $275,000. We record the purchase of the land and the sale of stock at the stock's fair value, or the land's fair value, whichever is more clearly evident. If the stock is traded actively, we can determine the stock's fair value by referring to the currently quoted price. In some cases, however, stock is not traded actively; and the fair value of the noncash asset is more clearly evident. In any event, the board of directors should approve the value assigned to the exchange of stock for noncash assets. Assume that the stock of Appliance Sales Co. is traded actively and the current market price per share is $25. We show Appliance's entry to record the transaction below:

Sept. 28	Land	250,000	
	Common Stock		100,000
	Paid-In Capital in Excess of Par–Common		150,000
	To record the issuance of 10,000 shares of $10 par value common stock in exchange for land.		

Stock Subscriptions

Corporations commonly sell stock for cash and immediately issue the shares of stock. However, corporations sometimes sell shares of stock on a subscription basis. When the corporation sells shares of stock through a **stock subscription**, the purchaser signs an agreement to pay a specified price for the shares at some future date(s). The purchaser may pay for the shares in a single payment or in installments.

In a stock subscription transaction, the purchaser enters into a contractual agreement to purchase the shares of stock. The promise to pay for the shares of stock creates a receivable for the corporation, and we debit it to an account called Subscriptions Receivable. Since the corporation may sell either common or preferred stock on a subscription basis, the account should specify to which it applies. Since the shares are not fully paid for at the time the corporation enters into the stock subscription agreement, the corporation does not issue the shares to the purchaser. At the time the corporation collects the stock subscription and the shares are fully paid for, the corporation issues the shares to the investor. At the time the corporation enters into the stock subscription, we credit the par value or stated value of the subscribed shares to a temporary stockholders' equity account called Stock Subscribed, designated as either common or preferred. When the shares are fully paid for and issued, we transfer the amount credited to Stock Subscribed to either Common Stock or to Preferred Stock.

Accounting for Stock Subscriptions.   To illustrate the accounting for stock subscriptions, assume that Ace Glass Co. receives subscriptions for 20,000 shares of common stock on April 1, 19X1. The common stock has a par value of $5 per share, and the subscription price is $12 per share. We show Ace's entry to record the stock subscription below:

19X1			
Apr. 1	Subscriptions Receivable–Common	240,000	
	Stock Subscribed–Common		100,000
	Paid-In Capital in Excess of Par–Common		140,000
	Received stock subscriptions for 20,000, $5 par-value shares of common stock at $12 per share.		

Notice that in the entry above, we credit only the par value of the subscribed shares to Stock Subscribed–Common. However, we credit the amount that the purchaser agrees to pay in excess of the par value to Paid-In Capital in Excess of Par–Common.

Assume that on June 1, 19X1, Ace Glass Co. receives the first installment of $60,000 for the subscribed shares. Ace's entry to record the receipt of the payment is as follows:

19X1			
Jun. 1	Cash	60,000	
	Subscriptions Receivable–Common		60,000
	To record receipt of cash for stock subscriptions.		

In most states, the corporation cannot issue the stock until all of the subscribed shares are paid fully. Therefore, even though the investor has paid for the equivalent of 5,000 shares ($60,000 ÷ $240,000 x 20,000 shares), the corporation does not issue any shares.

Stock Subscriptions in the Balance Sheet.   In the corporation's balance sheet, we display subscriptions receivable as an asset—usually a current asset since, in most cases, the corporation collects the receivable within one year of the date of the balance sheet. If Ace Glass Co. receives no additional payments during June, a balance sheet dated June 30, 19X1, would show subscriptions receivable of $180,000 ($240,000 − $60,000) in the current assets section. We display the account, Stock Subscribed–Common, in the stockholders' equity section of the balance sheet as part of contributed capital. We show the partial balance sheet sections for the example in Illustration 15-5.

ILLUSTRATION 15-5 Partial Balance Sheet

Assets	
Current assets	
Subscriptions receivable, common stock	$ 180,000
Stockholders' Equity	
Contributed capital:	
Common stock, $5 par value, 500,000 shares authorized,	
200,000 shares issued and outstanding	$1,000,000
Common stock subscribed but not issued, 20,000 shares	100,000
	$1,100,000
Paid-in capital in excess of par, common	640,000
Total contributed capital	$1,740,000

If Ace collects the remaining subscriptions in July, all of the subscribed shares would be paid for fully; and the corporation would issue the stock certificates. The following entries summarize Ace's collection of the remaining subscription price and the issuance of the shares:

19X1			
Jul. 31	Cash	180,000	
	Subscriptions Receivable–Common		180,000
	To record receipt of cash for stock subscriptions.		
31	Stock Subscribed–Common	100,000	
	Common Stock		100,000
	To record the issuance of 20,000 shares		
	of $5 par value common stock.		

We transfer only the par value of the shares issued from Stock Subscribed—Common to the permanent Common Stock. At the time of initially recording the stock subscription, we credit the agreed-upon price *in excess of par value* to Paid-In Capital in Excess of Par–Common. Therefore, it is unnecessary to record additional paid-in capital when the corporation issues the subscribed shares.

ACCOUNTING FOR ISSUANCE OF PREFERRED STOCK

LO 6

Account for the issuance of preferred stock.

The accounting for the sale and issuance of preferred stock is the same as for common stock, except account titles specify they are for preferred stock. For example, if Ace Glass Co. sells 1,000 shares of $100 par value preferred stock for $125 cash per share, its entry to record the sale and issuance is:

(Date)	Cash	125,000	
	Preferred Stock		100,000
	Paid-In Capital in Excess of Par–Preferred		25,000
	To record the sale of 1,000 shares of $100 par value		
	preferred stock.		

Similar to Common Stock, we credit Preferred Stock for the par value of the shares. State laws include the par value of preferred stock in the corporation's total legal capital. We credit the proceeds in excess of the par value to Paid-In Capital in Excess of Par–Preferred. Both Preferred Stock and Paid-In Capital in Excess of Par–Preferred are part of the corporation's contributed capital.

Corporations may also sell preferred stock on a subscription basis. The accounting for preferred stock subscriptions is the same as for common stock subscriptions, except the account titles are designated as preferred stock.

ACCOUNTING FOR DIVIDENDS

LO 7

Account for the declaration and payment of cash dividends.

Only the corporation's board of directors have the authority to declare dividends. Generally, state corporation laws require that a company have positive retained earnings, which means a credit balance in Retained Earnings, before the directors can declare dividends. To illustrate the accounting for cash dividends, assume that the board of directors of Vacation Travel Co. meets on December 1, 19X1, and declares a cash dividend of $2 per share to the common stockholders of record on December 15, 19X1. The dividend is payable on December 28,

19X1, and 10,000 shares of common stock are outstanding. Therefore, the total amount of the dividends declared is $20,000 ($2 x 10,000 shares).

Notice that the description of the dividend declaration indicates three dates—declaration, record, and payment. The **declaration date** is the date that the board of directors meets and declares the dividend. Similar to withdrawals by partners and proprietors, dividends are not expenses of the business, but distributions of earnings. When directors declare a dividend, the company is obligated legally to make the dividend payment. It is common for corporations to declare dividends more than one time a year, for example, quarterly. At the time the directors declare dividends, the company commonly follows the practice of debiting a temporary retained earnings account entitled Dividends. On the declaration date, Vacation Travel Co. records the dividend and the related liability as shown in the following entry:

19X1			
Dec. 1	Dividends	20,000	
	Dividends Payable		20,000
	To record the declaration of dividends.		

During the year, we accumulate the amounts of the several dividend declarations in Dividends. At the end of the fiscal year, we close Dividends directly to Retained Earnings. We do *not* close Dividends to Income Summary because it is *not* an expense. Assume Vacation Travel Co. declares the same amount of dividends each quarter of the fiscal year. The following entry shows Vacation's closing entry for Dividends:

19X1			
Dec. 31	Retained Earnings	80,000	
	Dividends		80,000
	To close Dividends to Retained Earnings.		

The second date indicated in the description of the dividend declaration is the record date. The **record date** is the date the board of directors designates for determining who owns what number of shares of stock and, therefore, who is entitled to receive the dividend. The company's stock registrar compiles the list of owners of shares of stock and the number of shares as of the record date and sends it to the company to use in paying the dividend. If a stockholder sells shares of stock between the declaration date and the record date, the new owner is entitled to receive the dividends. The new owner is the stockholder as of the designated record date. Conversely, if a stockholder sells shares after the record date, but before the corporation pays the dividend, the former owner is entitled to receive the dividends, because he or she is the owner as of the record date. When investors sell stock after the record date, the stock sells "ex dividend," meaning without the right to the dividend that the directors declared.

The third date indicated in the description of the dividend declaration is the **payment date**. The payment date is the date that the corporation actually pays the dividends. We record the dividend payment as a decrease in Dividends Payable and as a decrease in Cash, as shown in the following entry for Vacation Travel Co.:

19X1			
Dec. 28	Dividends Payable	20,000	
	Cash		20,000
	To record the payment of cash dividends.		

Occasionally, a company will declare dividends that are payable in noncash assets such as items of inventory or shares of another company's stock that the dividend-paying company owns. The accounting for noncash dividends is the same as for cash dividends except that at the time of payment, we decrease the noncash asset account rather than Cash. The amount at which the company records a noncash dividend is a complex issue that more advanced accounting texts discuss.

LO 8
Calculate the stated, cumulative, and participating dividends on preferred stock.

PREFERRED STOCK DIVIDENDS

The most common special feature of preferred stock is a preference as to dividends. Stock certificates specify the amount of dividends to which a class of preferred stock is entitled. They also express the amount of preferred dividends in two ways: as a stated dollar amount per share or as a percentage of par value per share. For example, $9 preferred stock, $100 par value, means that the *annual* dividend is $9 per share. If a certificate describes the stock as 10% preferred stock, $50 par value, the annual dividend is $5 per share (10% x $50 = $5 per share).

The preferred stock dividend preference does *not* give preferred stockholders an absolute right to dividends. The declaration of dividends by the board of directors entitles the preferred stockholders to dividends. In deciding to declare dividends, the board of directors takes into consideration such things as the company's current cash position, future cash requirements, and potential investment opportunities.

Cumulative and Noncumulative

With respect to dividend preference, preferred stock may be either noncumulative or cumulative. If preferred stock is **noncumulative**, in any single year that characteristic entitles preferred stockholders to the stated amount of dividends before the common stockholders can receive any dividends. If the board of directors decides not to declare dividends for a year, the preferred stockholders' right to receive a dividend for that year lapses. The dividend preference only means that preferred stockholders must receive their dividends before the common stockholders are entitled to any dividends *when dividends are declared*.

If preferred stock is **cumulative**, the right to receive the annual amount of the stated dividend does not expire when the board of directors fails to declare dividends in a given year. Rather, the right to receive the preferred dividends carries over to future years; and the undeclared dividends are called **dividends in arrears**. For example, assume Home Furnishings, Inc. has preferred stock outstanding as follows: 8% cumulative preferred stock, $100 par value, 10,000 shares outstanding. During 19X1, the board of directors does not declare dividends because the company has insufficient cash to pay dividends. At the end of 19X1, dividends in arrears on the preferred stock are $80,000 ($100 x 8% x 10,000 shares).

The general rule is that in any year, the cumulative characteristic entitles preferred stockholders to receive all of the dividends in arrears and the current year's dividends before the common stockholders receive any dividends. However, dividends in arrears are not a liability of the corporation. The corporation is not obligated to pay dividends until the board of directors declares them. Therefore, at the end of 19X1, Home Furnishings, Inc.'s balance sheet does *not* list a liability for the preferred dividends in arrears. However, to inform the users of the financial statements adequately, the corporation should disclose the fact that dividends are in arrears and the amount in either the notes to the financial statements or the body of the statements. The following footnote discloses the preferred dividends in arrears for the previous example:

> As of January 1, 19X2, the company is in arrears by $80,000, or $8 per share, on dividends to preferred stockholders. The company must pay all dividends in arrears, as well as current dividends, to preferred stockholders before dividends may be paid to common stockholders.

In 19X2, Home Furnishings, Inc.'s cash position has improved; and on December 15, 19X2, the board of directors declares dividends of $250,000. The corporation will distribute dividends to the preferred and common stockholders as follows:

Total dividends declared		$250,000
Preferred dividends in arrears from 19X1	$80,000	
19X2 preferred dividends	80,000	
Total preferred dividends		160,000
Remainder to the common stockholders		$ 90,000

Participating and Nonparticipating

When the stock certificate limits the dividends on preferred stock to the stated amount, as in the above example, the preferred stock is called **nonparticipating**. Most preferred stock is nonparticipating. However, a corporation may issue **participating preferred stock** that allows preferred stockholders to receive dividends in excess of the stated amount in certain circumstances. If preferred stock is fully participating, the corporation first allocates preferred stockholders their stated dividend amount. Next, the corporation allocates common stockholders dividends up to the percentage of par value represented by the stated preferred dividend. Finally, the preferred and common stockholders share any additional dividends on an equal percent of par values.

For example, during 19X1, assume Atlantic Distributing Co. has the following stock outstanding:

6% preferred stock, $100 par value, fully participating, 10,000 shares outstanding;
Common stock, $10 par value, 50,000 shares outstanding

At the end of 19X1, the board of directors declares dividends of $150,000. We allocate the dividends first to preferred stockholders according to the stated dividend amount:

$$6\% \times \$100 \times 10,000 \text{ shares} = \$60,000$$

Next, we allocate the common stockholders' dividends up to 6% of the par value of the common stock:

$$6\% \times \$10 \times 50,000 \text{ shares} = \$30,000$$

After these two initial allocations, we calculate the dividends remaining to be shared by the preferred and common stockholders as follows:

Dividends declared		$150,000
Allocated to preferred	$60,000	
Allocated to common	30,000	90,000
To be shared by preferred and common		$ 60,000

We allocate the $60,000 of dividends to preferred and common stockholders in proportion to the par values of their stock as follows:

Par value of preferred: 10,000 shares x $100 = $1,000,000
Par value of common: 50,000 shares x $10 =   500,000
Total $1,500,000

$$\text{Portion allocated to preferred} = \frac{\$1,000,000}{\$1,500,000} \times \$60,000 = \$40,000$$

$$\text{Portion allocated to common} = \frac{\$500,000}{\$1,500,000} \times \$60,000 = \$20,000$$

The total dividends allocated to preferred stockholders is $100,000 ($60,000 + $40,000); to common stockholders $50,000 ($30,000 + $20,000). As a percent of total par value, the preferred stockholders receive 10% ($100,000 ÷ $1,000,000), and the common stockholders receive the same percent of total par value, or 10% ($50,000 ÷ $500,000).

PREFERRED STOCK ASSETS UPON LIQUIDATION

Preferred stockholders generally have a preference as to the corporation's assets upon liquidation. When a corporation goes out of business and is liquidated, creditors' claims are settled first. Preferred stockholders have the next priority to any remaining assets. The amount of assets that the preferred stockholders are entitled to upon liquidation is the par value of the preferred stock or a larger stipulated liquidation value. The claim to assets of the cumulative preferred stockholders includes any dividends in arrears. No assets are distributed to the common stockholders until the preferred stockholders' claims are settled. After the creditors' and preferred stockholders' claims are settled fully, the common stockholders are then entitled to any remaining assets.

LO 9
Define redemption, book, and market values of stock and calculate book value per share.

STOCK VALUES

We often hear reference made to the "value" of corporate stock. There are several possible concepts of stock value, and we must exercise care to avoid misunderstandings. We discuss the terms *par value* and *stated value* previously in this chapter. They define a corporation's legal capital. Other concepts of stock value include redemption value, book value, and market value.

Redemption (or Call) Value

The term *redemption* (or *call*) *value* refers only to preferred stock. The terms of some preferred stock issues allow the issuing corporation to redeem (or call) the preferred shares by paying a specified amount, called the **redemption** (or **call**) **price**, to preferred stockholders. The redemption (or call) price is usually a small premium above the stock's par value. To redeem preferred stock, a corporation commonly must pay the redemption (or call) price and any cumulative dividends in arrears. Corporations usually redeem preferred stock to retire the shares. When the corporation retires preferred stock, we eliminate all amounts related to the stock from the accounts.

Book Value

The **book value** of common stock is the common stockholders' equity in the corporation's net assets. If the corporation only has common stock outstanding, the book value of the common stock is equal to stockholders' equity. The book value per share is the book value of the common stock divided by the number of shares of common stock outstanding and the number of shares that are subscribed but unissued. To illustrate the calculation of book value per share, assume Florida Export Co. has the stockholders' equity shown in Illustration 15-6.

ILLUSTRATION 15-6 Partial Balance Sheet

Stockholders' Equity

Contributed capital:	
Common stock, $1 par value, 100,000 shares authorized, 80,000 shares issued and outstanding	$ 80,000
Paid-in capital in excess of par, common	720,000
Total contributed capital	$ 800,000
Retained earnings	640,000
Total stockholders' equity	$1,440,000

Since the corporation has only common stock outstanding, we calculate book value per share (BV) using the following formula:

$$BV = \frac{\text{Stockholders' Equity}}{\text{Number of Shares Outstanding + Shares Subscribed}}$$

$$BV = \frac{\$1,440,000}{80,000 + 0}$$

$$BV = \$18.00 \text{ per share}$$

When a corporation has both preferred and common stock outstanding, the calculation of book value per share becomes more complex. First, we must allocate the stockholders' equity between the preferred and the common stocks. The stockholders' equity allocated to preferred stock is the redemption value of the preferred stock plus any dividends in arrears. The stockholders' equity allocated to the common stock is the residual left after subtracting the amount allocated to preferred stock from total stockholders' equity. To illustrate, assume Car Products Co. has the stockholders' equity section shown in Illustration 15-7.

ILLUSTRATION 15-7 Partial Balance Sheet

Stockholders' Equity

Contributed capital:	
Preferred $10 stock, noncumulative, $100 par value, 1,000 shares authorized and outstanding, redemption price $110	$ 100,000
Paid-in capital in excess of par, preferred	20,000
Common stock, $10 par value, 40,000 shares authorized and outstanding	400,000
Paid-in capital in excess of par, common	100,000
Total contributed capital	$ 620,000
Retained earnings	380,000
Total stockholders' equity	$1,000,000

Since the preferred stock is noncumulative, there are no dividends in arrears. Therefore, the amount of stockholders' equity allocated to the preferred is the redemption price of $110 per share.

The calculation of the stockholders' equity allocated to the common stock is as follows:

Total stockholders' equity	$1,000,000
Less: Equity allocated to preferred stock (1,000 shares x $110)	110,000
Equity allocated to common stock	$ 890,000

The book values per share of preferred and common stock are then calculated as follows:

$$\text{BV Preferred} = \$110,000 \div 1,000 \text{ shares} = \$110.00 \text{ per share}$$

$$\text{BV Common} = \$890,000 \div 40,000 \text{ shares} = \$22.25 \text{ per share}$$

To illustrate the calculation of book values when there are dividends in arrears, assume the same facts as in the example above, except that the preferred stock is cumulative and one year's dividends are in arrears. In this case, the allocation of stockholders' equity between preferred stock and common stock is as follows:

Stockholders' equity of preferred:	
Redemption Price x Number of Shares ($110 x 1,000)	$ 110,000
Dividends in arrears ($10 x 1,000 shares)	10,000
Total	$ 120,000
Stockholders' equity of common:	
Total stockholders' equity	$1,000,000
Amount allocated to preferred (above)	120,000
Residual allocated to common	$ 880,000

The calculation of book values per share are shown below:

$$\text{BV Preferred} = \$120,000 \div 1,000 \text{ shares} = \$120.00 \text{ per share}$$

$$\text{BV Common} = \$880,000 \div 40,000 \text{ shares} = \$22.00 \text{ per share}$$

Remember, carrying amounts are based on original values of assets and liabilities net of adjustments such as depreciation and amortization. Because the carrying amounts of assets and liabilities do not equal their fair values, caution should be used in interpreting book values of preferred and common stocks.

Market Value

The **market value** per share of a corporation's common stock is the price at which investors can sell and purchase shares. Investors' expectations about the business's future earnings, general economic conditions, and the prospects of the industry in which the company operates affect the market value of stock. There is often little relationship between the market value per share and the book value per share. If expectations about the future are favorable, the market value may be well above book value; but if expectations are unfavorable, the market value may be less than book value.

EARNINGS PER SHARE

LO 10
Calculate and interpret earnings per share.

At the beginning of this chapter, we introduced you to Josh Adam's uncertainty about using one number, earnings per share, to evaluate a company's performance. Now that we have introduced you to the corporate form of business, we will explain how to calculate earnings per share, how to interpret the number, and then discuss some limitations of using the ratio.

Calculating Earnings Per Share

Earnings per share (EPS) is the ratio of net income available to the common stockholders to the number of shares of common stock outstanding. We will use the stockholders' equity section of Southeast Products Co., presented in Illustration 15-8, to illustrate the calculation of earnings per share.

ILLUSTRATION 15-8 Partial Balance Sheet

Stockholders' Equity	
Contributed capital:	
Preferred 8% stock, $100 par value, 50,000 shares authorized and issued	$ 5,000,000
Additional paid-in capital, preferred	800,000
Common stock, $1 par value, 100,000 shares authorized, 80,000 shares issued	80,000
Additional paid-in capital, common	9,600,000
Total contributed capital	$15,480,000
Retained earnings	8,230,000
Total stockholders' equity	$23,710,000

In addition to the information about stockholders' equity, assume Southeastern Products' net income for 19X1 is $752,000. First, we must determine the amount of net income available to the common stockholders by subtracting preferred stock dividends from net income. The preferred dividends are $400,000 (8% x $100 x 50,000). The amount of net income available to the common stockholders is $352,000 ($752,000 − $400,000). Next, we divide net income available to common stockholders by the number of shares of common stock outstanding to calculate earnings per share as:

$$EPS = \frac{\$352,000}{80,000 \text{ shares}} = \$4.40 \text{ per share}$$

Interpreting Earnings Per Share

In the numerator of earnings per share, dividends of the preferred stockholders have been deducted from net income, and the result is the amount of net income available to common stockholders. Dividing by the number of shares of common stock outstanding produces earnings per common share. The usual interpretation of EPS is that the greater the amount of the ratio, the better the company's performance. EPS gives common stockholders a means of assessing the company's performance relative to the number of shares they own. When EPS increases, it means that the company has generated more resources with which to pay dividends (assuming cash is available), and/or invest in projects that will generate future earnings.

Limitations of Earnings Per Share

Relying solely on EPS to evaluate a company's performance may lead to misleading results. Investors should be concerned with what contributes to EPS, that is, with the components of net income (revenues, expenses, gains, and losses). Investors should evaluate whether the current magnitude of EPS is a long-term condition or merely temporary. For example, current EPS may be high because the company liquidated a portfolio of investments for a large gain. The large gain will not be a recurring item; and, therefore, future EPS would be expected to decline. On the other hand, current EPS may be depressed because the company decided to sell an unprofitable operation even though it would realize a large current period loss from the sale. Future EPS may increase as a result of this action, since the loss from the sale is not a recurring item, and the losses that the operation generated will not reduce future earnings. While the financial press focuses on EPS, the other information presented in the company's financial statements provides useful insight into its interpretation.

SUMMARY

Describe the organization and management of a corporation. A corporation is a legal entity that is separate from its owners. The separate legal status of a corporation results in accounting for owners' equity, different from that of proprietorships and partnerships. A corporation has most of the rights and duties of a person. Corporations may be classified as profit and not-for-profit corporations and as publicly-owned and privately-owned corporations.

The stockholders own a corporation, but their authority is exercised by a selected board of directors. The board of directors establishes the corporation's broad business policies and appoints the management to carry on the business's day-to-day operations.

State the advantages and disadvantages of the corporate form of business organization. The corporate form offers several advantages to business organizations, especially limited stockholder liability, lack of mutual agency, ease of transferring ownership, and ease of raising capital. The disadvantages of corporations include the double taxation of income and the extent of government regulation.

Explain how a corporation is formed and account for organization costs. A corporation is created when the state government grants a charter to the incorporators. We record the costs of forming the corporation as an intangible asset, called Organization Costs, that we amortize over its useful life, not to exceed 40 years.

Describe the characteristics and components of stockholders' equity.   The stockholders' equity of a corporation includes the major components of contributed capital and retained earnings. Contributed capital is the total proceeds received from selling preferred stock and common stock. The corporation's minimum legal capital is the par or stated value of common stock. Retained earnings is the cumulative earnings that the business has reinvested in itself.

Account for the issuance of common stock in exchange for cash and noncash assets and account for stock subscriptions.   A corporation sells common stock and receives either cash or noncash assets in exchange. The contributed capital that we record from the issuance of common stock is the amount of cash received or the fair value of noncash assets received. The corporation may sell common stock on a subscription basis, in which the investor agrees to pay for the stock at some future date(s). In this case, the stock in not issued until the investor pays the full purchase price.

Account for the issuance of preferred stock.   We account for the issuance of preferred stock the same as we account for common stock, except the account titles specify that the corporation has sold preferred stock.

Account for the declaration and payment of cash dividends.   The board of directors of a corporation has the authority to declare dividends. On the declaration date of a dividend, a liability is recorded for the amount of the dividend and the temporary retained earnings account Dividends is debited by the same amount. As part of the closing process, Dividends is closed to Retained Earnings. Ownership of stock on the record date determines the stockholders who are entitled to receive the dividend. On the payment date, the liability for the dividend is settled by the payment of the dividend.

Calculate the stated, cumulative, and participating dividends on preferred stock. The stock certificate states the amount of dividends that the preferred stockholders are entitled to receive. The preferred stock may be either cumulative or noncumulative. Cumulative preferred stockholders are entitled to receive the stated dividends each year. If the directors do not declare dividends for a year, those cumulative preferred dividends accumulate and must be satisfied before common stockholders receive any dividends. Participating preferred stockholders are entitled to participate with the common stockholders in dividends in excess of the stated amount.

Define redemption, book, and market values of stock and calculate book value per share.   The redemption value of preferred stock is the amount at which the corporation can redeem the shares of preferred stock. The book value per share is the stockholders' equity divided by the number of shares. Book value per share may be calculated for either common or preferred stock. Market value of stock is the price at which investors may sell and purchase shares.

Calculate and interpret earnings per share.   Earnings per share is the ratio of earnings available to the common shareholders (net income less preferred dividends) to the number of shares of common stock outstanding. EPS provides common stockholders a means of assessing the company's performance relative to the number of shares they own.

REVIEW PROBLEM

Great Graphics became a publicly-traded company on January 2, 19X1. It was authorized to issue 1,000,000 shares of common stock and 10,000 shares of preferred stock. Great Graphics had net income of $445,000 during 19X1 and the following transactions occurred:

19X1

Jan.   2   Issued 45,000 shares of $5 par value common stock for $30 per share.
       5   Issued 10,000 shares of cumulative, 8%, $100 par and redemption value preferred stock for $110 per share.

June 30   Exchanged 5,000 shares of common stock for a parcel of land with a market value of $165,000.

Sep.   1   Declared an 8% preferred stock dividend payable on December 30.
       1   Declared a $1.00 per share common stock dividend payable on December 30.
       30   Paid the preferred stock dividend declared on September 1.
       30   Paid the common stock dividend declared on September 1.

Oct. 19   Received a stock subscription for 20,000 shares of common stock at a price of $28 per share.

Dec.   1   Received cash payment in full for subscribed stock and issued the stock.

REQUIRED:

a. Prepare the journal entries for the transactions above.
b. Prepare the stockholders' equity section of the December 31, 19X1, balance sheet.
c. Calculate the book value per share for common stock and preferred stock.

SOLUTION:

Planning and Organizing Your Work

1. Analyze each transaction and prepare the journal entry.
2. Prepare the stockholders' equity section of the balance sheet using the information from Step 1. Remember that Dividends is closed to Retained Earnings at the end of the period.
3. Calculate the book value per share for preferred stock by summing the redemption value of preferred stock plus any dividends in arrears and dividing the amount by the number of preferred shares outstanding.
4. Calculate the book value per share for common stock by subtracting the summation in Step 3 from total stockholders' equity and dividing the remainder by the number of common shares outstanding.

(a) *Prepare journal entries.*

19X1			
Jan. 2	Cash ($30 x 45,000)	1,350,000	
	Common Stock ($5 x 45,000)		225,000
	Paid-In Capital in Excess of Par–Common		
	($30 – $5) x 45,000		1,125,000
	To record the issuance of common stock for $30 per share on January 2.		
5	Cash ($110 x 10,000)	1,100,000	
	Preferred Stock ($100 x 10,000)		1,000,000
	Paid-In Capital in Excess of Par–Preferred		
	($110 – $100) x 10,000		100,000
	To record the issuance of preferred stock for $110 per share.		
Jun. 30	Land	165,000	
	Common Stock ($5 x 5,000)		25,000
	Paid-In Capital in Excess of Par–Common		
	($165,000 – $25,000)		140,000
	To record the exchange of stock for a parcel of land.		
Sep. 1	Dividends (8% x $1,000,000)	80,000	
	Dividends Payable		80,000
	To record the declaration of an 8% preferred stock cash dividend.		
1	Dividends (45,000 + 5,000) x $1	50,000	
	Dividends Payable		50,000
	To record the declaration of a $1 per share common stock cash dividend.		
30	Dividends Payable	80,000	
	Cash		80,000
	To record the payment of the preferred dividend.		
30	Dividends Payable	50,000	
	Cash		50,000
	To record the payment of the common dividend.		
Oct. 19	Subscriptions Receivable–Common ($28 x 20,000)	560,000	
	Stock Subscribed–Common ($5 x 20,000)		100,000
	Paid-In Capital in Excess of Par–Common		
	($28 – $5) x 20,000		460,000
	To record common stock subscribed.		
Dec. 1	Cash	560,000	
	Subscriptions Receivable–Common		560,000
	To record cash received for subscribed stock		
1	Stock Subscribed–Common	100,000	
	Common Stock		100,000
	To record issuance of common stock.		

(b) *Prepare the stockholders' equity section.*

Stockholders' Equity

Contributed capital:	
Preferred 8% stock, $100 par value, 10,000 shares authorized and issued	$1,000,000
Paid-in capital in excess of par, preferred	100,000
Common stock, $5 par value, 1,000,000 shares authorized, 70,000 shares issued	350,000
Paid-in capital in excess of par, common	1,725,000
Total contributed capital	$3,175,000
Retained earnings*	315,000
Total stockholders' equity	$3,490,000

*$445,000 − $50,000 − $80,000

(c) *Calculate book value per share.*

BV Preferred = $1,000,000 ÷ 10,000 shares = $100.00 per share
BV Common = ($3,490,000 − $1,000,000) ÷ 70,000 shares = $35.57 per share

KEY TERMS

articles of incorporation, *595*	**earnings per share (EPS)**, *610*	**preferred stock**, *599*
authorized share, *598*	**legal capital**, *598*	**privately-owned corporation**, *590*
book value, *608*	**market value**, *610*	
bylaws, *595*	**noncumulative preferred stock**, *605*	**profit**, *590*
charter, *590*		**proxy**, *592*
common stock, *599*	**nonparticipating preferred stock**, *606*	**publicly-owned corporation**, *590*
contributed capital, *596*		
corporation, *590*	**no-par value**, *599*	**redemption (call) price**, *608*
cumulative preferred stock, *605*	**not-for-profit**, *590*	**registrar**, *597*
dividend declaration date, *604*	**organization costs**, *595*	**retained earnings**, *596*
dividend payment date, *604*	**Paid-In Capital in Excess of Par**, *600*	**stated value**, *599*
dividend record date, *604*		**stock certificate**, *597*
dividends, *592*	**participating preferred stock**, *606*	**stockholders**, *591*
dividends in arrears, *605*		**stockholders' ledger**, *597*
double taxation of corporations, *594*	**par value**, *598*	**stock subscription**, *601*
	preemptive right, *592*	**transfer agent**, *597*

SELF-QUIZ

LO 1 1. Corporations with thousands of owners are called _____ corporations, and corporations with relatively few owners are called _____ corporations.

LO 1 2. True or False? The preemptive right of common stockholders is the right to receive dividends.

LO 1 3. Which of the following is *not* typically a common stockholder's right?

a. To vote in meetings of stockholders
b. To have the first opportunity to purchase additional shares of stock
c. To run the daily operations of the company
d. To dispose of their shares of stock as they please

LO 2 4. Which of the following is *not* an advantage of a corporation?

a. Reduction of taxes
b. Limited stockholders' liability
c. Continuity of existence
d. Ease of raising capital

LO 3 5. Organization costs must be amortized over a period that should not exceed _____ years.

LO 4 6. Which of the following is *not* typically found in the stockholders' equity section of a corporation's balance sheet?
a. Net income
b. Common stock
c. Retained earnings
d. Paid-in Capital in Excess of Par

LO 4 7. True or False? Par value of stock is typically equal to the stock's market value.

LO 5 8. True or False? Common stock may be issued in exchange for noncash assets such as land.

LO 6 9. Both Preferred Stock and Paid-In Capital in Excess of Par–Preferred are part of the corporation's _____ capital.

LO 7 10. Which of the following events relating to dividends requires no journal entries?
a. Declaration of dividends
b. Date of record
c. Date of payment
d. Simultaneous declaration and payment

LO 8 11. If the preferred stock is _____, the right to receive the annual amount of the stated dividend does not expire when the board of directors fails to declare dividends in a given year.

LO 9 12. State the formula for computing the book value of common stock if a company has no preferred stock.

LO 10 13. _____ ___ _____ is the ratio of net income available to the common shareholders to the number of shares of common stock outstanding.

SOLUTIONS TO SELF-QUIZ

1. publicly-owned, privately-owned   2. False   3. c   4. a   5. 40   6. a   7. False   8. True   9. contributed
10. b   11. cumulative   12. Stockholders' Equity ÷ Number of Shares Outstanding   13. Earnings per share

QUESTIONS

Q15-1 What are the differences among a corporation, a partnership, and a sole proprietorship?

Q15-2 Describe the role of the board of directors of a corporation.

Q15-3 Describe the duties of the president, controller, and treasurer of a corporation?

Q15-4 What are the advantages and disadvantages of a corporation?

Q15-5 How is a corporation formed?

Q15-6 What are the advantages of no-par value stock compared to par value stock?

Q15-7 What are the differences between common stock and preferred stock?

Q15-8 How does a corporation sell shares of stock through a stock subscription?

Q15-9 Why do corporations pay dividends?

Q15-10 What is the difference between participating and nonparticipating preferred stock?

Q15-11 Explain the differences between cumulative and noncumulative preferred stock.

Q15-12 What are the implications of relying solely on current EPS to evaluate a company's performance?

EXERCISES

LO 3

E15-1 **Organization Costs** Yates Corporation incurred the following costs during formation:

Charter fees paid to the state	$1,900
Legal fees to prepare charter	4,300
Promoters' fees	3,700
Printing of stock certificates	1,100

REQUIRED:

Record the journal entry for the payment of organization costs and first-year amortization of organization costs if Yates Corporation amortizes these costs over 5 years. Assume a full year's amortization is appropriate for the first year.

LO 4 **E15-2** **Stockholders' Equity Section**   Prepare the stockholders' equity section in good form for the Castle Corporation given the following information:

a. Paid-in Capital in Excess of Par–Common and Preferred Stock are $268,000 and $400,000, respectively.
b. There is $189,000 of retained earnings.
c. There are 100,000 shares of $2 par value common stock authorized and 20,000 shares issued.
d. There are 50,000 shares of 8%, $100 par value preferred stock authorized and issued.

LO 5 **E15-3** **Common Stock**   Prepare journal entries for the following independent common stock transactions:

a. Sold 5,000 shares of $10 par value common stock for $48 per share.
b. Sold 10,000 shares of no-par value common stock with a stated value of $5 per share for $40 per share.
c. Sold 2,000 shares of no-par value common stock (no stated value) for $42 per share.
d. Exchanged 6,000 shares of $5 par value common stock for a parcel of land that the previous owner offered to sell for $125,000.

LO 5 **E15-4** **Stock Subscriptions**   Stone Concrete Company receives subscriptions for 50,000 shares of common stock on July 1, 19X2. The common stock has a par value of $2 per share, and the subscription price is $15 per share. On October 1, 19X2, Stone Company received payment of one-third of the total subscription price, and it received the balance on November 1, 19X2.

REQUIRED:

Prepare all journal entries for the stock subscription and subsequent receipts of cash.

LO 6 **E15-5** **Issuance of Preferred Stock**   Bilko Company sells 5,000 shares of $100 par value preferred stock for $110 per share.

REQUIRED:

Record the journal entry for the issuance of the preferred stock.

LO 7 **E15-6** **Cash Dividends**   On December 1, 19X1, the board of directors of Technology Incorporated declared a cash dividend of $2.50 per share to the common stockholders of record on December 20, 19X1. The dividend is payable on December 30, 19X1, and 20,000 shares of common stock are outstanding.

REQUIRED:

Prepare journal entries for the declaration and payment of dividends.

LO 8 **E15-7** **Stated and Cumulative Dividends**   Edwards Furniture, Incorporated has 50,000 shares of 8%, $100 par value, cumulative preferred stock. During 19X3, the board of directors did not declare dividends. In 19X4 and 19X5, Edward's board of directors decided to pay all dividends required.

REQUIRED:

Determine the total amount of dividends paid to preferred stockholders in 19X4 and in 19X5.

LO 8   **E15-8   Participating Dividends**   Texoma International Corporation has the following stock outstanding:

8% preferred stock, $100 par value, fully participating, 10,000 shares outstanding;
Common stock, $30 par value, 100,000 shares outstanding.

At the end of 19X6, the board of directors declared dividends of $400,000.

REQUIRED:

Determine the amount of dividends to be paid to preferred and common stockholders.

LO 9   **E15-9   Book Value Per Share**   Melody Company has 10,000 shares of $5 common stock outstanding that was originally issued for $20 per share as of December 31, 19X8, and a balance in Retained Earnings of $80,000.

REQUIRED:

Calculate the book value per share for the Melody Company on December 31, 19X8.

LO 10   **E15-10   Earnings Per Share**   Domingo company has 100,000 shares of $1 par value common stock and 50,000 shares of 6%, $100 par value preferred stock outstanding on December 31, 19X9. Net income during 19X9 for Domingo company is $790,000.

REQUIRED:

Determine earnings per share for Domingo's common stockholders for 19X9.

PROBLEM SET A

LO 4,5,6,7,8   **P15-1A   Stock Transactions**   Trans-International Company was formed on January 2, 19X2. The following stock transactions occurred during 19X2:

19X2
Jan.   2 Sold 50,000 shares of $5 par common stock for $35 per share (1,000,000 shares authorized).
        3 Sold 10,000 shares of $100 par, 6%, nonparticipating preferred stock for $122 per share (50,000 shares authorized).
June   1 Received subscriptions for 5,000 shares of the $5 par common stock at $37 per share.
July   31 Received cash for the full amount of the stock subscriptions of June 1.
Dec.   1 Declared the annual cash dividend to preferred stockholders of record on December 20.
        1 Declared a cash dividend of $2.00 per share to the common stockholders of record on December 20.
       30 Paid the preferred stock dividend declared on December 1.
       30 Paid the common stock dividend declared on December 1.

REQUIRED:

a. Prepare journal entries for the transactions listed above.
b. Prepare the stockholders' equity section of the balance sheet as of December 31, 19X2, if the ending balance in Retained Earnings is $49,000 (after Dividends and Income Summary are closed).

LO 4,5,6   **P15-2A**   **Determine Missing Values**   The stockholders' equity section for the Sunnie Company is presented below:

Contributed capital:

Preferred 8% stock, $50 par value, 50,000 shares authorized and _____ issued	$500,000
Paid-in capital in excess of par, preferred	150,000
Common stock, $5 stated value, 1,000,000 shares authorized, 100,000 shares issued	?
Common stock subscribed but not issued, 20,000 shares	100,000
Paid-in capital in excess of stated value, common	600,000
Total contributed capital	$?
Retained earnings	945,000
Total stockholders' equity	$?

REQUIRED:

a. Calculate the number of shares of preferred stock issued.
b. Calculate the issue price per share of preferred stock.
c. Calculate the issue price per share of common stock, assuming the price of the subscribed stock is the same as the common stock issued.
d. Calculate total stockholders' equity.

LO 7,8   **P15-3A**   **Preferred and Common Dividends**   The Musket Corporation paid $60,000 of dividends in 19X2, $450,000 in 19X3, and $600,000 in 19X4. During this time, there were 50,000 shares of 8%, $20 par preferred stock outstanding and 200,000 shares of $5 par common stock outstanding.

REQUIRED:

a. Calculate the dividends paid to common and preferred stockholders for each of the 3 years if the preferred stock is noncumulative and nonparticipating.
b. Calculate the dividends paid to common and preferred stockholders for each of the 3 years if the preferred stock is cumulative and nonparticipating (no dividends were paid in 19X0 and 19X1).
c. Calculate the dividends paid to common and preferred stockholders for each of the 3 years if the preferred stock is cumulative and fully participating (no dividends were paid in 19X0 and 19X1).

LO 9,10   **P15-4A**   **Book Value Per Share and Earnings per Share**   The stockholders' equity section for the Traymond Company is presented below:

Contributed capital:

Preferred 8% stock, $100 par value, 10,000 shares authorized and issued	$1,000,000
Paid-in capital in excess of par, preferred	200,000
Common stock, $5 par value, 1,000,000 shares authorized, 100,000 shares issued	500,000
Paid-in capital in excess of par, common	300,000
Total contributed capital	$2,000,000
Retained earnings	600,000
Total stockholders' equity	$2,600,000

REQUIRED:

a. Determine the book value per share for common and preferred stock if the preferred stock is noncumulative, nonparticipating, and has a redemption price of $110.
b. Determine the book value per share for common and preferred stock if the preferred stock is cumulative, nonparticipating, and has dividends in arrears for 4 years.

c. Determine earnings per share under the assumption of requirement a if net income is $250,000.

PROBLEM SET B

LO 4,5,6,7,8   **P15-1B**   **Stock Transactions**   The Montoya Corporation was formed on January 2, 19X6. The following stock transactions occurred during 19X6:

19X6
Jan.   2 Sold 40,000 shares of $1 par common stock for $20 per share (100,000 shares authorized).
        3 Sold 8,000 shares of $100 par, 8%, nonparticipating preferred stock for $115 per share (10,000 shares authorized).
June   3 Received subscriptions for 10,000 shares of common stock at $19 per share.
July   29 Received cash for the full amount of the stock subscriptions of June 3.
Dec.   2 Declared the annual cash dividend to preferred stockholders of record on December 21.
        2 Declared a cash dividend of $1.50 per share to the common stockholders of record on December 21.
       28 Paid the preferred stock dividend declared on December 2.
       29 Paid the common stock dividend declared on December 2.

REQUIRED:

a. Prepare journal entries for the transactions listed above.
b. Prepare the stockholders' equity section of the balance sheet as of December 31, 19X6, if the ending balance in Retained Earnings is $38,000 (after Dividends and Income Summary are closed).

LO 4,5,6   **P15-2B**   **Determine Missing Values**   The stockholders' equity section for the Wallack Company is presented below:

Contributed capital:
    Preferred 8% stock, $50 par value, 50,000 shares authorized
        and _____ issued $400,000
    Paid-in capital in excess of par, preferred   50,000
    Common stock, $4 stated value, 1,000,000 shares authorized,
        75,000 shares issued   ?
    Common stock subscribed but not issued, 20,000 shares   80,000
    Paid-in capital in excess of stated value, common   570,000
            Total contributed capital $?
Retained earnings   425,000
            Total stockholders' equity $?

REQUIRED:

a. Calculate the number of shares of preferred stock issued.
b. Calculate the issue price per share of preferred stock.
c. Calculate the issue price per share of common stock, assuming the price of the subscribed stock is the same as the common stock issued.
d. Calculate total stockholders' equity.

LO 7,8   **P15-3B**   **Preferred and Common Dividends**   The Fife Corporation paid $90,000 of dividends in 19X7, $600,000 in 19X8, and $500,000 in 19X9. During this time, there were 75,000 shares of 8%, $20 par preferred stock outstanding and 300,000 shares of $5 par common stock outstanding.

REQUIRED:

a. Calculate the dividends paid to common and preferred stockholders for each of the 3 years if the preferred stock is noncumulative and nonparticipating.

b. Calculate the dividends paid to common and preferred stockholders for each of the 3 years if the preferred stock is cumulative but not participating (no dividends were paid in 19X5 and 19X6).

c. Calculate the dividends paid to common and preferred stockholders for each of the 3 years if the preferred stock is cumulative and fully participating (no dividends were paid in 19X5 and 19X6).

LO 9,10   **P15-4B   Book Value Per Share**   The stockholders' equity section for the Crane Company is presented below:

Contributed capital:

Preferred 8% stock, $100 par value, 5,000 shares authorized and issued	$ 500,000
Paid-in capital in excess of par, preferred	150,000
Common stock, $4 par value, 500,000 shares authorized, 100,000 shares issued	400,000
Paid-in capital in excess of par, common	240,000
Total contributed capital	$1,290,000
Retained earnings	710,000
Total stockholders' equity	$2,000,000

REQUIRED:

a. Determine the book value per share for common and preferred stock if the preferred stock is noncumulative, nonparticipating, and has a redemption price of $120.

b. Determine the book value per share for common and preferred stock if the preferred stock is cumulative, nonparticipating, and has dividends in arrears for 4 years.

c. Determine earnings per share under the assumption of requirement b if net income is $175,000.

CRITICAL THINKING AND COMMUNICATING

C15-1   Mr. Spear, the sole owner of a small furniture manufacturer, was contemplating forming a corporation. Mr. Spear's company has experienced consistent sales growth in the past 5 years. As a result of the increase in sales, Mr. Spear was contemplating expansion of his factory, which would require a large capital investment. Mr. Spear's management style consists of running every aspect of the business himself.

Because of the complexity of the decision to incorporate, Mr. Spear hired Mr. Rodgers, a member of a major accounting firm, as a consultant to help determine whether or not to incorporate. If Mr. Spear does incorporate, he contemplates issuing stock to the public.

REQUIRED:

a. Explain to Mr. Spear the procedures necessary to incorporate.
b. Explain to Mr. Spear the advantages and disadvantages of forming a corporation.
c. What advice would you give Mr. Spear about incorporating his business? Defend your answer.

C15-2   Martha Borg is considering an investment in Cyclonics Corporation. Martha prefers to invest in companies that have strong potential for rapid growth. She has been extremely impressed by the large increases in earnings per share for Cyclonics over the last 3 years. Selected financial data for Cyclonics is given below:

	19X3	*19X4*	*19X5*
EPS	$1.07	$1.46	$2.33
Sales	$780,000	$792,000	$793,000
Shares outstanding	1,000,000	750,000	425,000

REQUIRED:

Examine the information above. Explain how Martha should interpret this information and how she might use it in making her investment decision.

C15-3   The financial statements of J.C. Penney Company, Inc. are reprinted in Appendix B at the end of this text. Examine J.C. Penney's balance sheet carefully. Note that in the stockholders' equity section, there are both preferred and common stock. In addition, presented below the preferred stock is something called "guaranteed LESOP obligation" that is shown as a negative amount. For purposes of responding to the requirements of this case, use the net amount of preferred stock and the LESOP obligation (i.e., for 1993 use $269 million for preferred stock).

REQUIRED:

a. Calculate the preferred stock book value per share at the end of the 1993 fiscal year.
b. Calculate the common stock book value per share at the end of the 1993 fiscal year.
c. Find the section entitled *Quarterly Data* located after the financial statements. In the schedule, locate the common stock price range for the fourth quarter of 1993. Compare the common stock price to the common stock book value per share that you calculated in Requirement b. Explain possible reasons for the difference in the amounts of the two items.

CHAPTER 16

Corporate Stock Transactions, Consolidations, and International Operations

Jennifer Johnson has money to invest, and she is studying her stockbroker's research reports on two companies that are possible investment opportunities. These two companies are Midwestern Industries, Inc. and Scientific Products, Inc.. Securities of both companies trade on a national stock exchange. Jennifer has two investment goals: current cash returns and long-term growth potential. With these goals in mind, she is comparing the two companies' current cash dividend policies. The research reports contained the following information about the companies:

	Midwestern Industries, Inc.	Scientific Products, Inc.
Current price of stock	$25 per share	$12 per share
Current dividend	$2 per share	$.30 per share
Earnings growth rate	10% per year	14% per year

Jennifer wants to know how to use this information to compare the two investment opportunities and to determine which one better meets her investment goals.

This chapter continues the discussion of accounting for corporations. In particular, we discuss transactions that affect retained earnings and transactions in the company's own equity securities. These transactions include cash dividends, stock dividends, and treasury stock transactions. This chapter also discusses accounting for transactions in the equity securities of another corporation. One corporation may purchase stock in another corporation to influence or control the other company or simply to make an investment that earns income. This chapter concludes with a discussion of how companies account for transactions with parties in other countries and for their own international operations.

1. Describe those events and transactions that increase and decrease retained earnings and prepare a retained earnings statement.
2. Describe the recording of stock dividends and stock splits.
3. Account for the purchase and reissuance of treasury stock.
4. Describe how businesses report the retirement of stock in their financial statements.
5. Discuss the accounting for appropriations of retained earnings.
6. Account for investments in stock using the market, cost, and equity methods.
7. Prepare consolidated balance sheets at the date of acquisition and for subsequent periods.
8. Record foreign currency transactions in the accounts.

LO 1

Describe those events and transactions that increase and decrease retained earnings and prepare a retained earnings statement.

RETAINED EARNINGS

A corporation's **retained earnings** is the cumulative net income of the business since its inception, less the total amount of dividends that the corporation distributed to the stockholders. Thus, net income increases a company's retained earnings, and net losses and dividends decrease retained earnings. The retained earnings statement of Quality Hardware Company, Inc., presented in Illustration 16-1, shows the change in retained earnings for the period that the heading of the statement indicates—the year 19X1. Similar to an income statement, we prepare a retained earnings statement for a period of time. As shown in Illustration 16-1, Quality's retained earnings increased by $25,000 during 19X1 because net income of $45,000 exceeded dividends of $20,000 by that amount.

Retained Earnings is increased by net income through the closing entries for a corporation. For Quality Hardware Company, Inc., revenues exceed expenses by $45,000. As for proprietorships and partnerships, we close a corporation's revenue and expense accounts to Income Summary. After closing the revenue and expense accounts, Income Summary has a credit balance of $45,000. Quality then closes Income Summary to Retained Earnings by the following entry:

19X1			
Dec. 31	Income Summary	45,000	
	Retained Earnings		45,000
	To close Income Summary and to record net income in Retained Earnings.		

ILLUSTRATION 16-1 Retained Earnings Statement

Quality Hardware Company, Inc. Retained Earnings Statement For the Year Ended December 31, 19X1	
Retained earnings, January 1, 19X1	$160,000
Add: Net income for 19X1	45,000
	$205,000
Less: Dividends declared during 19X1	20,000
Retained earnings, December 31, 19X1	$185,000

As you saw in a previous chapter, cash dividends decrease a corporation's retained earnings. In addition to cash dividends, stock dividends also affect retained earnings.

LO 2

Describe the recording of stock dividends and stock splits.

STOCK DIVIDENDS

If the board of directors decides not to pay cash dividends to conserve the company's assets for some purpose such as expansion or investment, the directors may decide to distribute a stock dividend. In this way, the directors are giving the stockholders something that represents their interest in the company's reinvested earnings. When a company issues common stock to its own common stockholders without receiving any assets in return, it gives a **stock dividend**.

While cash dividends reduce both the company's assets and stockholders' equity, stock dividends have no effect on assets or on the amount of total stockholders' equity because the company does not distribute assets to the stockholders. The accounting profession has decided to account for a stock dividend by transferring the market value of the shares issued from retained earnings to contributed capital. We call the procedure of transferring an amount from retained earnings to contributed capital **capitalizing retained earnings**.

Stockholders find stock dividends desirable because, although they own more shares, the market price per share is not often affected significantly.[1] This is especially true whenever the company maintains the cash dividend per share after the stock dividend. Therefore, many stockholders believe that a stock dividend represents a distribution of the company's retained earnings in the amount of the market price of the shares issued.[2] Actually, the common stockholders have the same equity in the company's net assets after the stock dividends as they did before the dividend. For example, Modern Office Supplies, Inc. has stockholders' equity as shown in Illustration 16-2; and Cindy Stepp owns 10,000 shares of the common stock.

ILLUSTRATION 16-2 Partial Balance Sheet

Contributed capital:	
Common stock, $1 par value, 200,000 shares authorized,	
100,000 shares issued and outstanding	$ 100,000
Paid-in capital in excess of par value	900,000
Total contributed capital	$1,000,000
Retained earnings	260,000
Total stockholders' equity	$1,260,000

The shares of stock Stepp owns represent a 10% ownership interest in the company (10,000 shares ÷ 100,000 shares outstanding = 10%). We calculate the book value per share of the stock as follows:

---

[1]"Restatement and Revision of Accounting Research Bulletins," *Accounting Research Bulletin No. 43* (New York, NY: AICPA, 1953), Chap. 7, Sec. B, par. 10.

[2]*Ibid.*

$$BV = \frac{\text{Total Stockholders' Equity}}{\text{Number of Shares Outstanding}}$$

$$BV = \frac{\$1,260,000}{100,000 \text{ shares}}$$

$$BV = \$12.60 \text{ per share}$$

The total book value of the shares Stepp holds is:

$$10,000 \text{ shares } \times \ \$12.60 \text{ per share } = \ \$126,000$$

Now, assume Modern Office Supplies, Inc. declares a 5% stock dividend on June 15. A 5% stock dividend means that stockholders receive an additional 5 shares of stock for each 100 shares they own. Stepp owns 10,000 shares and receives an additional 500 shares (5% x 10,000 shares = 500 shares). However, her ownership interest in Modern Office Supplies, Inc. remains at 10%, calculated as follows:

$$\frac{\text{Number of Shares Owned after Stock Dividend}}{\text{Number of Shares Outstanding}}$$

$$\frac{10,500 \text{ shares}}{105,000 \text{ shares outstanding}} = 10\%$$

After the stock dividend, we calculate the book value per share as follows:

$$BV = \frac{\text{Total Stockholders' Equity}}{\text{Number of Shares Outstanding}}$$

$$BV = \frac{\$1,260,000}{105,000 \text{ shares}}$$

$$BV = \$12.00 \text{ per share}$$

The book value of the 10,500 shares owned after the stock dividend is equal to $126,000 (10,500 shares x $12 per share = $126,000). Therefore, a stock dividend affects neither the ownership interests nor the book values of the total shares stockholders own.

If the market price per share of the stock at the time the company declares the stock dividend is $16, we record the stock dividend declaration by capitalizing $80,000 of retained earnings (100,000 shares x 5% x $16 = $80,000). In the entry to record the stock dividend that is shown below, we credit the *par value* of the stock to be issued to Stock Dividend Distributable; and we credit the market price in excess of par value to Paid-In Capital—Stock Dividend.

June 15	Retained Earnings	80,000	
	Stock Dividend Distributable		5,000
	Paid-In Capital—Stock Dividend		75,000
	To record 5% stock dividend when market price per share is $16.		

On June 30, when the company issues the shares of stock, it makes the following entry:

June 30	Stock Dividend Distributable	5,000	
	Common Stock		5,000
	To record distribution of stock dividend.		

If the company prepares financial statements between the declaration date and the distribution date of the stock dividend, we classify Stock Dividend Distributable as part of contributed capital in stockholders' equity. The account is not a liability because it is the result of an equity transaction; and it is satisfied by the company's issuance of the common stock, *not* by transferring assets or by incurring other liabilities. The stockholders' equity section of a balance sheet prepared between the declaration date and the distribution date is shown in Illustration 16-3.

ILLUSTRATION 16-3 Partial Balance Sheet

Contributed capital:	
Common stock, $1 par value, 200,000 shares authorized,	
100,000 shares issued and outstanding	$ 100,000
Stock dividend distributable	5,000
Paid-in capital in excess of par value	975,000
Total contributed capital	$1,080,000
Retained earnings	180,000
Total stockholders' equity	$1,260,000

After the stock dividend, total stockholders' equity remains at the amount of $1,260,000. However, the recorded amount of the stock dividend increases contributed capital and decreases retained earnings.

Large Stock Dividends

The board of directors may sometimes decide to distribute a large stock dividend to decrease the market price per share of its common stock. A **large stock dividend** is defined as greater than 20–25% of the outstanding shares. Over time, the market price per share of a successful corporation that reinvests some or all of its earnings increases. The price may become so high that many investors become hesitant to purchase shares. Thus, to encourage wider ownership of the company's stock, the directors may declare a large stock dividend to decrease the market price of the shares.

Because a large stock dividend significantly reduces the market price of the shares, stockholders do *not* perceive the dividend as a distribution of retained earnings as they do for small stock dividends. Therefore, the amount of retained earnings capitalized for large stock dividends is not equal to the market value of the shares issued. Instead, the amount of retained earnings capitalized is the amount required to satisfy state corporation laws concerning minimum legal capital. Usually, this amount is par value or stated value for no-par stock in some states.

Computer Supplies, Inc. has 10,000 shares of $100 par value common stock outstanding when it declares a 50% stock dividend. When the company declares the stock dividend, the market price per share of the stock is $150. However, we capitalize only the par value of $500,000 (50% x 10,000 x $100 = $500,000) of the stock to be issued. Computer Supplies records the declaration of the stock dividend as follows:

(Date)	Retained Earnings	500,000	
	Stock Dividend Distributable		500,000
	To record the declaration of a 50% stock dividend.		

Notice that the par value, not the market price per share, affects the retained earnings capitalized as shown in the above entry for a large stock dividend.

Stock Splits

The board of directors may also reduce the market price per share of the stock by declaring a stock split. In a **stock split**, the company calls in the outstanding shares and replaces them with a multiple of the number of shares previously outstanding. Common multiples are 2, 3, or 4 shares of new stock for each old share. Actually, the company may exchange any number of new shares for each old share. Companies describe stock splits by their exchange ratios. For example, a 2-for-1 stock split means that stockholders receive 2 shares of new stock for each share owned prior to the stock split.

Food Distributors, Inc. has 100,000 shares of $10 par value stock and declares a 2-for-1 stock split. The stock split declaration requires the company to amend the charter to reduce the par value of the stock from $10 to $5 per share and to double the number of shares authorized. The company calls in the old shares and replaces each $10 par value share with 2 of the new $5 par value shares. The company then cancels the old shares.

A stock split does not affect the corporation's net assets or stockholders' equity, and there is *no effect* on retained earnings. Therefore, we do not need a formal entry to record a stock split. However, the company should include information about the stock split in its stockholder records. Also, the company should modify the description of the stock in its balance sheet. The description of the common stock in the stockholders' equity section before and after the stock split is shown below. Notice that the stock split does not change the balance of Common Stock.

Before the stock split:

Common stock, $10 par value, 100,000 shares authorized, 100,000 shares issued and outstanding	$1,000,000

After the stock split:

Common stock, $5 par value, 200,000 shares authorized, 200,000 shares issued and outstanding	$1,000,000

ANALYSIS OF DIVIDEND POLICY

At the beginning of this chapter, we discussed Jennifer Johnson's investment decision. Investment analysts use two ratios to compare companies' dividend policies: dividend payout ratio and dividend yield ratio. In the following sections, we discuss how analysts compute and interpret these two ratios.

Computing Dividend Payout and Dividend Yield

Dividend payout is the ratio of dividends per share to earnings per share:

$$\text{Dividend Payout} = \frac{\text{Dividends Per Share}}{\text{Earnings Per Share}}$$

The income statements for the current year shows that earnings per share for Midwestern Industries and Scientific Products are $4 per share and $2 per share, respectively. Using the EPS information and the dividend information for the two companies at the beginning of this chapter, we compute dividend payout as follows:

Midwestern Industries: Dividend Payout $= \dfrac{\$2.00}{\$4.00} = 50\%$

Scientific Products: Dividend Payout $= \dfrac{\$.30}{\$2.00} = 15\%$

Dividend yield is the ratio of dividends per share to market price per share:

$$\text{Dividend Yield} = \dfrac{\textbf{Dividends Per Share}}{\textbf{Market Price Per Share}}$$

Using the information at the beginning of this chapter, we compute dividend yield for the two companies as follows:

Midwestern Industries: Dividend Yield $= \dfrac{\$2.00}{\$25} = 8\%$

Scientific Products: Dividend Yield $= \dfrac{\$.30}{\$12} = 2.5\%$

Now that we have computed the ratios for the investment opportunities, we next discuss the interpretation of the two ratios.

Interpretation of Dividend Payout and Dividend Yield

Investors receive income from investments in common stocks in two forms: current cash dividends and appreciation in the price of the stock (commonly called capital gains because of their treatment for income tax purposes). The dividend payout ratio shows what percentage of current earnings the company pays to its owners in the form of dividends. When companies pay dividends that are less than earnings, they have more net assets available to invest in projects that generate future income and future increases in the stock's value. Most companies have established dividend payout policies, and they are reluctant to deviate from those policies. In particular, stock market participants view downward deviations as a signal from management that future earnings will be depressed from historic levels. On the other hand, companies generally do not raise dividend payout levels unless they lack opportunities to efficiently invest the net assets generated by operations. Therefore, investors may not view news of an increase in the dividend payout for a company as positive information. Thus, management is careful to explain any change in dividend policy to avoid confusion.

The dividend payout ratio varies among companies, and there is no correct dividend payout. Companies that we consider to be growth firms have lower cash dividend payouts than do mature, slow-growing companies because growth companies usually have more attractive investment opportunities available to them. The cash dividend payouts for Midwestern Industries and Scientific Products are 50% and 15%, respectively. This information seems to indicate that Scientific Products is a growth firm that retains earnings for investment rather than paying out earnings as dividends.

The dividend yield shows the relationship between current dividends and the stock's market price. Dividend yield is analogous to the interest yield on a savings account at the bank—i.e., it represents the current earnings on the investment. As with dividend payout, there is no correct dividend yield. Growth companies tend to have lower dividends because they retain earnings to invest and this causes the stock's market price to rise. The dividend yields for Midwestern Industries and Scientific Products are 8% and 2.5%, respectively. These ratios reinforce the conclusion that Scientific Products is more of a growth firm than is Midwestern Industries. The retention of earnings to invest in profitable projects results in a low dividend payout and a low dividend yield.

Recall that Jennifer Johnson has two investment goals: current cash income and long-term growth potential. With the inverse relationship between current dividend yield and long-term growth, it may not be possible to invest in a single stock that satisfies both of Jennifer's goals. A possible investment strategy would be to invest some in each of the two companies since one (Midwestern Industries) has a relatively high dividend yield and the other (Scientific Products) appears to have long-term growth potential.

LO 3
Account for the purchase and reissuance of treasury stock.

TREASURY STOCK TRANSACTIONS

Corporations sometimes reacquire shares of their previously issued stock. We call the reacquired shares of stock **treasury stock**. The company may reacquire shares by purchase from the stockholders or by the stockholders donating the shares to the company. The distinction between treasury stock and unissued shares (authorized shares that have not been issued) is that the company has issued treasury stock but the shares are no longer outstanding, whereas the company has never issued unissued shares. Treasury stock is similar to unissued shares in that shares of treasury stock may be resold. Also, like unissued shares, shares of treasury stock do not carry the usual stockholder rights such as the rights to vote and receive dividends, as well as the preemptive right.

Corporations repurchase outstanding shares of stock for various reasons, including:

1. At some time in the future to distribute to executives as part of stock compensation plans
2. To use at a later date in acquiring other businesses
3. To increase the market price of the shares that remain outstanding. By keeping dividends constant and buying back shares, dividends per share increase, which may favorably affect the market price of a share.

In all but the last case, companies can accomplish the same purpose with authorized but previously unissued stock. However, sufficient unissued shares may not always be available.

Purchasing Treasury Stock

The purchase of treasury stock is similar to cash dividends in that each reduces both the corporations' assets and stockholders' equity. Also, the purchase of treasury stock results in a distribution of corporate assets to certain stockholders, similar to the payment of cash dividends. For this reason, the corporation laws of most states limit both treasury stock purchases and dividends to the amount of the corporation's retained earnings. The cost of the treasury stock reduces the amount of retained earnings available for dividends.

When a company purchases treasury stock, we generally record the stock at the cost of the reacquired shares. For example, on May 19, Atlantic Beverage Co. purchases 5,000 of the outstanding shares of its $10 par value common stock for $36 per share. We debit the total cost of the reacquired shares to Treasury Stock. The par or stated value of the stock or the amount at which the shares were previously issued does not affect the entry. Atlantic's entry to record the purchase is as follows:

May 19	Treasury Stock	180,000	
	Cash		180,000
	To record the purchase of 5,000 shares of treasury stock for $36 per share.		

Treasury Stock in the Financial Statements

As shown in Illustration 16-4, we classify Treasury Stock in the financial statements as a reduction in total stockholders' equity, *not* as an asset. Sometimes Treasury Stock is called a contra-stockholders' equity account. Notice that in the stockholders' equity section of the balance sheet in Illustration 16-4, we modify the description of common stock to indicate the number of previously outstanding shares that the company reacquired. While we modify the number of shares outstanding (from 40,000 to 35,000), the number of shares issued remains unchanged at 40,000 shares.

ILLUSTRATION 16-4 Partial Balance Sheet

Stockholders' Equity	
Contributed capital:	
Common stock, $10 par value, 50,000 shares authorized,	
40,000 shares issued, 35,000 shares outstanding	$ 400,000
Paid-in capital in excess of par value—common	1,200,000
Total contributed capital	$1,600,000
Retained earnings	600,000
Total	$2,200,000
Less: Treasury stock, 5,000 shares at cost	180,000
Total stockholders' equity	$2,020,000

Reissuing Treasury Stock

A company may reissue shares of treasury stock just as it may issue previously unissued stock. When a company reissues treasury stock, it increases the number of shares outstanding; and we should modify the description of the stock in the stockholders' equity section of the balance sheet. The reissuance of treasury stock increases both the corporation's assets and stockholders' equity. The company may reissue treasury stock for an amount equal to its cost, greater than its cost, or less than its cost.

Reissuing Treasury Stock at Cost.   Assume that on August 20, Atlantic Beverage Co. reissues for cash 2,000 of the shares of treasury stock at the original cost of $36 per share. Atlantic's entry to record the reissuance of the treasury stock is as follows:

Aug. 20	Cash	72,000	
	Treasury Stock		72,000
	To record the sale of 2,000 shares of treasury stock		
	for $36 per share.		

As a result of the reissuance, we should modify the stockholders' equity section of the balance sheet as shown in Illustration 16-5. By comparing Illustration 16-4 and Illustration 16-5, you will notice that while the number of shares issued remains at 40,000, the number of shares outstanding increases by the number of shares of treasury stock reissued. Also, stockholders' equity increases by $72,000 which is the amount of proceeds the corporation received from reissuing the treasury stock.

ILLUSTRATION 16-5 Partial Balance Sheet

Stockholders' Equity	
Contributed capital:	
Common stock, $10 par value, 50,000 shares authorized,	
40,000 shares issued, 37,000 shares outstanding	$ 400,000
Paid-in capital in excess of par value—common	1,200,000
Total contributed capital	$1,600,000
Retained earnings	600,000
Total	$2,200,000
Less: Treasury stock, 3,000 shares at cost	108,000
Total stockholders' equity	$2,092,000

Reissuing Treasury Stock at More Than Cost.   Assume Atlantic Beverage Co. reissues the 2,000 shares of treasury stock for $60 per share, instead of $36 per share. Although the reissuance price is in excess of the cost of the treasury stock, we do *not* recognize a gain. Under GAAP, a corporation may not recognize a gain or a loss in transactions involving its own equity securities.[3] Rather, we view the difference between the proceeds from reissuing the treasury stock and the original cost of the treasury stock as an increase or as a decrease in contributed capital or, in some cases, as a decrease in retained earnings. As a result of reissuing the 2,000 treasury shares at $60 per share, Atlantic Beverage would make the following entry:

Aug. 20	Cash	120,000	
	Treasury Stock		72,000
	Paid-In Capital—Treasury Stock Transactions		48,000
	To record the sale of 2,000 shares of treasury stock		
	for $60 per share; original cost of $36 per share.		

In the stockholders' equity section of the balance sheet, we classify Paid-In Capital—Treasury Stock Transactions as a component of total contributed capital, the same as Paid-In Capital in Excess of Par from the original issuance of the stock.

Reissuing Treasury Stock at Less Than Cost.   When the corporation reissues treasury stock at a price that is less than the original cost, it does not recognize

---

[3]"Reporting the Results of Operations," *Accounting Principles Board Opinion No. 9* (New York, NY: AICPA, 1966), par. 28.

a loss. We report the difference between the cost and the reissue price of the treasury stock as a reduction in Paid-In Capital—Treasury Stock Transactions. If the balance of the account is less than the amount needed to absorb the deficiency in the reissuance price, then we debit any excess to Retained Earnings. Assume that on October 12, Atlantic Beverage Co. reissues the remaining 3,000 shares of treasury stock at a price of $24 per share. It records the reissuance of the treasury stock with the following entry:

Oct. 12	Cash	72,000	
	Paid-In Capital—Treasury Stock Transactions	36,000	
	Treasury Stock		108,000
	To record the sale of 3,000 shares of treasury stock		
	at $24 per share. Cost of the shares is $36 per share.		

In this case, the $48,000 balance in Paid-In Capital—Treasury Stock Transactions (from the sale of treasury stock in the previous example) is sufficient to absorb the $36,000 deficiency in the reissuance price.

On the other hand, if the company reissues the 3,000 shares of treasury stock at a price of $16 per share, the $48,000 balance is not sufficient to absorb the $60,000 deficiency in the reissuance price. In this case, the following entry records Atlantic's reissuance of the treasury stock:

Oct. 12	Cash	48,000	
	Paid-In Capital—Treasury Stock Transactions	48,000	
	Retained Earnings	12,000	
	Treasury Stock		108,000
	To record the sale of 3,000 shares of treasury stock		
	at $16 per share. Cost of the shares is $36 per share.		

RETIREMENT OF STOCK

LO 4

Describe how businesses report the retirement of stock in their financial statements.

A corporation may reacquire some of its previously outstanding shares with no intention of reissuing the shares. The company may retire or cancel the reacquired shares, but only with the approval of the stockholders. When the company retires stock, we should remove from the accounts all amounts related to the original issuance of the shares. For example, assume that on January 22, Adams Corporation reacquires 500 shares of its outstanding common stock at a price of $20 per share. The common stock has a par value of $5 per share, and the company originally issued it at a price of $20 per share. Adams records the reacquisition and retirement of the shares with the following entry:

Jan. 22	Common Stock	2,500	
	Paid-In Capital in Excess of Par—Common	7,500	
	Cash		10,000
	To record the reacquisition and retirement of 500		
	shares of common stock at $20 per share.		

If the company reacquires the shares at a price that is less than the original issue price, we credit the difference to contributed capital in an account called Paid-In Capital—Retirement of Stock. For example, assume that Adams Corporation reacquires 500 shares of stock at a price of $16 per share. The following entry records Adams's reacquisition and retirement of the shares:

Jan. 22	Common Stock	2,500	
	Paid-In Capital in Excess of Par—Common	7,500	
	Cash		8,000
	Paid-In Capital—Retirement of Stock		2,000
	To record the reacquisition and retirement of 500 shares of common stock at $16 per share.		

Conversely, if the company reacquires the shares at a price that is more than the original issue price, we debit the difference first to Paid-In Capital—Retirement of Stock. If this account does not have a balance at least equal to the difference, we debit the excess to Retained Earnings. For example, assume that Adams Corporation reacquires 500 shares of stock at a price of $28 per share. Adams Corporation previously had not retired any shares of stock. Adams records the reacquisition and retirement of the shares with the following entry:

Jan. 22	Common Stock	2,500	
	Paid-In Capital in Excess of Par—Common	7,500	
	Retained Earnings	4,000	
	Cash		14,000
	To record the reacquisition and retirement of 500 shares of common stock at $28 per share.		

APPROPRIATIONS OF RETAINED EARNINGS

LO 5
Discuss the accounting for appropriations of retained earnings.

When a corporation has a contingency that may require a significant amount of assets at some future date, the board of directors may decide to restrict the payment of dividends to accumulate assets to meet the contingency. Examples of such contingencies include a possible loss from a lawsuit or future investments such as a plant expansion. In restricting the payment of dividends, the board of directors may segment retained earnings into appropriated and unappropriated amounts. We call the restriction on the amount of retained earnings available for dividends an **appropriation of retained earnings**. The amount of unappropriated retained earnings is available for dividend declaration. The existence of unappropriated retained earnings does not necessarily mean that sufficient cash is available to pay dividends. After the contingency is satisfied, the board of directors will generally remove the restriction on dividend payments. In the accounting records, we reclassify the appropriated retained earnings as unappropriated retained earnings.

Assume Western Supply Co. plans a future plant expansion that is anticipated to cost $800,000. To restrict dividend payments, the board appropriates retained earnings in the amount of $800,000. In the accounting records, Western records the appropriation as follows:

(Date)	Retained Earnings	800,000	
	Retained Earnings Appropriated		800,000
	To record resolution of board of directors appropriating retained earnings.		

The company presents the appropriation of retained earnings in the stockholders' equity section of the balance sheet as shown in Illustration 16-6.

Recently, the appropriation of retained earnings has become a rare practice. Rather, management discusses restrictions on dividend payments in the notes to

ILLUSTRATION 16-6 Partial Balance Sheet

Stockholders' Equity

Contributed capital:		
Common stock, $10 par value, 500,000 shares authorized		
and issued		$5,000,000
Paid-in capital in excess of par value—common		1,500,000
Total contributed capital		$6,500,000
Retained earnings:		
Appropriated for future plant expansion	$ 800,000	
Unappropriated	1,950,000	2,750,000
Total stockholders' equity		$9,250,000

the financial statements. By discussing the restrictions in the notes, the chances for misunderstanding the nature of appropriated retained earnings are reduced. Some users of financial statements may believe that appropriated retained earnings results in the accumulation of a fund of cash that the company can use. The amount of the dividend restriction, however, does not necessarily result in such a fund because the company may invest the cash not paid as dividends in assets such as inventories and plant assets or use the cash to pay off liabilities such as notes payable.

LO 6

Account for investments in stock using the market, cost, and equity methods.

INVESTMENTS IN STOCK

In a previous chapter and in this chapter, we discuss a corporation's dealings in its own equity securities. Corporations also invest in the equity securities of other corporations. Some of these investments are short-term, and we classify them as current assets on the balance sheet. Companies make short-term investments to generate income from cash that the companies currently do not need in their business operations. Such investments are part of their cash management programs.

Corporations intend for some investments in the equity securities of other corporations to be long-term, and we classify them as noncurrent assets in the balance sheet. Companies make these investments for various reasons, including: to earn a favorable rate of return on the investment and to influence or control the other corporation's policies. The reasons for wanting to invest in and control another corporation may be to expand, diversify, or enhance the production, marketing, and financing success of the investing corporation. For example, when General Motors Corporation acquired controlling ownership of Electronic Data Services (EDS), the purpose was to gain control of the computer-systems expertise of EDS. This expertise is valuable to General Motors not only because of the growing demand for computer services by other businesses, but also because GM could use the expertise to modernize its own operations.

Similar to other assets, long-term investments in corporate securities are initially recorded at cost. Cost includes the purchase price plus any other costs such as brokerage fees the company incurs in acquiring the securities. For subsequent periods, companies account for long-term investments in stocks by the market method, the cost method, the equity method, or with consolidated financial statements. The appropriate method for the company to use depends on the level of influence the investor company (company that owns the stock) is able to exert on the investee company (the company whose stock the investor owns) and, in some cases, whether quoted market prices are available. The level of influence may be insignificant, significant, or controlling. Illustration 16-7 presents the guidelines followed in selecting the appropriate accounting method.

ILLUSTRATION 16-7 Accounting Methods for Stock Investments

Ownership Percentage	Presumed Influence	Accounting Method
Less than 20%	Insignificant	Market or cost methods
20% to 50%	Significant	Equity method
More than 50%	Controlling	Consolidated financial statements

In applying the guidelines presented in Illustration 16-7, the accountant should use judgment. The relationship between the ownership percentages and the levels of influence are merely guidelines, and the accountant should assess the level of influence by considering the circumstances. For example, an investor may own 20% of the voting stock of a corporation but has no significant influence because another investor owns the remaining 80% of the voting stock. With such an ownership interest, the 80% investor is able to control the investee company's operations and to ignore the wishes of the 20% investor.

Insignificant Influence

When the level of ownership does not allow the investor to exert significant influence on the investee company's management decisions, the investor should account for the investments in stock using the market method or the cost method. These methods apply to investments in both common and preferred stocks. They also apply to both long-term and short-term investments in stocks.

Available Market Prices—Market Method.   If the investments are in stocks for which fair values are available, GAAP require the company to use the **market method**—that is, to present the investments in the balance sheet at the fair values of the stocks as of the balance sheet date. GAAP consider the stocks to have available fair values if sales prices or bid and ask prices are available currently on a national securities exchange (such as the New York Stock Exchange) or in the over-the-counter market.[4] The over-the-counter market refers to stocks that the public purchases and sells, but these transactions do not occur on an organized stock exchange. The National Association of Securities Dealers Automated Quotation systems (NASDAQ) or the National Quotation Bureau report price quotations for stocks traded over-the-counter.

 Long-term investments.   Long-term investments in stocks accounted for by the market method are called **available-for-sale securities**. To illustrate the application of the market method to long-term investments, assume the Oaks Company has the following transactions in 19X1, involving investments in long-term equity securities:

---

[4]"Accounting for Certain Investments in Debt and Equity Securities," *Statement of Financial Accounting Standards No. 115* (Norwalk, Conn.: FASB, 1993), pars. 3–14.

Stock Transactions in 19X1	
May 5	Purchased 500 shares of Sand Company common stock for $12,500 ($25 per share) and 800 shares of Stone Company common stock for $38,400 ($48 per share). These investments represent less than 20% of the outstanding voting stock of each company, and there is no possibility that Oaks Company will have any significant influence on either investee. (For simplicity, assume there are no commissions from the stock purchases.)
June 30	Stone Company paid dividends of $2 per share that it declared on June 15, 19X1.
Dec. 31	Market prices per share: Sand Company $27 per share and Stone Company $40 per share.

Investment in Stock.   On May 5, 19X1, Oaks records the investments at cost as shown in the following entry:

19X1			
May 5	Investment in Sand Company Stock	12,500	
	Investment in Stone Company Stock	38,400	
	Cash		50,900
	To record purchase of 500 shares of Sand Company common stock for $25 per share and 800 shares of Stone Company common stock for $48 per share.		

Dividends Received.   On June 30, 19X1, Oaks records the dividends received. Since the declaration date and the payment date are in the same accounting period, it may record the dividends earned on the payment date.

19X1			
June 30	Cash	1,600	
	Dividends Revenue		1,600
	To record dividends received from Stone Company of $2 per share.		

Year-End Adjustment.   At the end of an accounting period, we must calculate the market value of each investment to determine the amount to be presented in the balance sheet. On December 31, 19X1, the market price of Oaks' investments are calculated as follows:

Investment	Number of Shares	Market Prices	Market Value	Carrying Amount	Increase (Decrease)
Sand Company	500	$27	$13,500	$12,500	$ 1,000
Stone Company	800	40	32,000	38,400	(6,400)
			$45,500	$50,900	$(5,400)

The calculations indicate that the market prices of the investments have changed since the date of purchase (May 5). The market value of the investment in Sand Company's stock increased by $1,000, and the market value of the investment in Stone Company's stock decreased by $6,400. The market method requires that Oaks present investments on the balance sheet at a total amount of $45,500, the total market price. This results in the offsetting of the unrealized gains and losses of the two stocks. Oaks records the following entry to adjust the investments to their total market values:

19X1			
Dec. 31	Unrealized (Gain) Loss from Available-for-Sale		
	Securities	5,400	
	Investment in Sand Company Stock	1,000	
	Investment in Stone Company Stock		6,400
	To adjust long-term investments in stocks to current		
	market prices.		

The net effect of the above journal entry on long-term investments is to reduce them to the total market price at the balance sheet date of $45,500. Because the investments are long-term, we do *not* include Unrealized Loss from Available-for-Sales Securities in the calculation of net income. That is, it is *not* closed to Income Summary at the end of the accounting period. Rather, we present it as a contra-stockholders' equity account in the balance sheet, similar to Treasury Stock. We present the investments in the noncurrent asset section of the balance sheet and the unrealized loss in the stockholders'equity section of the balance sheet as follows:

Investments:	
Long-term investments in equity securities (at market)	$ 45,500
Stockholders' Equity:	
Contributed capital:	
Common stock	$130,000
Paid-in capital in excess of par	350,000
Retained earnings	270,000
Total paid-in capital and retained earnings	$750,000
Less: Unrealized loss from available-for-sale securities	5,400
Total stockholders' equity	$744,600

To continue the example, assume Oaks Company has the following transactions in 19X2, involving investments in long-term investments in equity securities:

Stock Transactions in 19X2	
June 18	Sold all the shares of Sand Company common stock for $14,000. The sale is entered into due to a change in investment policy by the management of Oaks.
Sept. 30	Received a cash dividend from Stone Company of $1 per share.
Oct. 15	Purchased 400 shares of Shale Company common stock for $12,000. The 400 shares represent 1% of the voting stock of Shale.
Dec. 31	Market prices per share: Stone Company $45 per share and Shale Company $31 per share.

Sale of Stock.   When a company sells a long-term investment in stock, *we record a realized gain or loss for the difference between the proceeds from the sale and the original cost of the shares sold.*

*Calculation of realized gain (loss) from sale
of Sand Company stock:*

Selling price	$14,000
Original cost	12,500
Gain	$ 1,500

The amount of the realized gain or loss recorded is not affected by the previously recorded unrealized gain or loss related to the stock sold. On June 18, 19X2, Oaks records the sale of the shares of Sand Company as follows:

19X2			
June 18	Cash	14,000	
	Unrealized (Gain) Loss from Available-for-Sale		
	Securities	1,000	
	Investment in Sand Company Stock		13,500
	Gain from Sale of Investments		1,500
	To record the sale of 500 shares of Sand Company		
	stock for $28 per share.		

Dividends Received. On September 30, 19X2, Oaks records the dividends received as follows:

19X2			
Sept. 30	Cash	800	
	Dividends Revenue		800
	To record the receipt of cash dividends from Stone		
	Company of $1 per share.		

Investment in Stock. Oaks records the purchase of the Shale Company stock at cost by the entry shown below:

19X2			
Oct. 15	Investment in Shale Company Stock	12,000	
	Cash		12,000
	To record the purchase of 400 shares of Shale		
	Company common stock for $30 per share.		

Year-End Adjustment. On December 31, 19X2, we calculate the total market price and the total cost of Oaks' investments on hand as follows:

Investment	Number of Shares	Market Prices	Market Value	Carrying Amount	Increase (Decrease)
Stone Company	800	$45	$36,000	$32,000	$4,000
Shale Company	400	31	12,400	12,000	400
			$48,400	$44,000	$4,400

The calculations indicate that the market price of both investments has increased. This means that Oaks should record the net gain of $4,400 in Unrealized (Gain) Loss from Available-for-Sale Securities. Oaks makes the following entry to record the change in market prices of the investments:

19X2			
Dec. 31	Investment in Stone Company Stock	4,000	
	Investment in Shale Company Stock	400	
	Unrealized (Gain) Loss from Available-for-Sale		
	Securities		4,400
	To adjust long-term investments to current market		
	prices.		

After the above entry, Unrealized (Gain) Loss from Available-for-Sale Securities that the company presents as a contra-stockholders' equity account in the balance sheet has a debit (loss) balance of $2,000. We can reconcile this amount by comparing the original cost of $50,400 ($38,400 + $12,000) of the two investments to the total current market value of $48,400. This comparison shows that there has been a net $2,000 unrealized loss on the two investments.

Short-term investments.   The application of the market method to short-term investments in stock is similar to that for long-term investments, which we discussed in the preceding section. However, there is one major exception. For short-term investments, we include the unrealized change in market value for each period in net income rather than accumulate it in the stockholders' equity valuation account. Also, when the investments are sold, we include in net income the change in market value from the beginning of the period to the date of sale. In other words, we make no distinction between realized and unrealized changes in the market value of short-term investments in stocks. We include changes in value in net income in the period they occur, whether or not the investments are sold.

Market Prices Not Available—Cost Method.   We use the cost method for investments in stocks where the investor is unable to exert significant influence on the investee company's decisions *and* where market prices for the stocks are not available. The application of the cost method is the same for both long-term and short-term investments. Under the **cost method**, the investment is initially recorded at cost; and the investment is carried at cost until the securities are sold. Any dividends received from the investment are recorded as dividend revenue. Because the investor has no significant influence on the investee's operating and financing decisions, the investor should recognize revenue when the investee declares dividends.

Investment in Stock.   On July 2, Dynamic Research, Inc. purchases 100 of the 2,500 outstanding shares of JJM Corporation's common stock. The market price of the stock is $49 per share, and the broker's commission is $215. Dynamic's purchase of the shares is recorded with the following entry:

July 2	Investment in JJM Corporation Stock	5,115	
	Cash		5,115
	To record the purchase of 100 shares of common		
	stock at $49 per share plus commission of $215.		

Notice that, in the above entry, the entire cost of the shares is debited to Investment in JJM Corporation Stock. The par or stated value of the stock is not relevant to the *investor* company's recording of the purchase.

When the investee company declares cash dividends, the investor company recognizes dividends earned. Since the dividend declaration by the investee's board of directors creates the right for stockholders to receive the dividends, under the realization concept, the investor should recognize dividends as revenue when declared rather than when received.

Dividends Declared. On December 10, 19X1, the directors of the JJM Corporation declare cash dividends of $4 per share, payable on January 5, 19X2, to owners of record on December 20, 19X1. If Dynamic does not intend to sell the stock before December 20, it should record the dividends on December 10 with the entry shown below:

19X1			
Dec. 10	Dividends Receivable	400	
	Dividends Revenue		400
	To record dividends of $4 per share on common stock of JJM Corporation.		

On December 31, 19X1, the end of Dynamic's annual accounting period, Dividends Revenue is closed to Income Summary. On January 5, 19X2, when the dividend is received, Dynamic makes the following entry:

19X2			
Jan. 5	Cash	400	
	Dividends Receivable		400
	To record the receipt of dividends from JJM Corporation.		

Stock dividends of JJM Corporation do *not* result in income for Dynamic Research; therefore no entry is required to record the stock dividend. Stock dividends do, however, reduce the cost per share of the stock owned. For example, assume JJM Corporation declares a 10% stock dividend. Before the stock dividend, the cost per share of the stock Dynamic Research, Inc. owned is $51.15 ($5,115 ÷ 100 shares). After the stock dividend, Dynamic owns 110 shares; and the cost per share is $46.50 ($5,115 ÷ 110 shares). Thus, Dynamic would calculate gains and losses on any subsequent sales of the shares by using the $46.50 cost per share amount.

Stock Sold. When all or part of an investment is sold, the difference between the cost of the shares and the proceeds from the sale is recorded as a gain or loss. For example, assume Dynamic Research sells 50 of the JJM Corporation's shares at $70 per share and pays a broker's commission of $175. The sale results in a gain of $1,000 calculated as follows:

Proceeds from sale:		
50 shares x $70 per share	$3,500	
Less: Commission	175	
	$3,325	
Cost (after stock dividend):		
50 shares x $46.50 per share	2,325	
Gain	$1,000	

Dynamic records the sale of the shares with the following entry:

(Date)	Cash	3,325	
	Investment in JJM Corporation Stock		2,325
	Gain from Sale of Investments		1,000
	To record sale of 50 shares of stock for $70 per share less $175 commission.		

On the other hand, if Dynamic sells the 50 shares for $40 per share, less a broker's commission of $150, it incurs a loss of $475, calculated as follows:

Proceeds from sale:		
50 shares x $40 per share	$2,000	
Less: Commission	150	
	$1,850	
Cost (after stock dividend):		
50 shares x $46.50 per share	2,325	
Loss	$ 475	

Dynamic's entry to record the sale is shown below:

(Date)	Cash	1,850	
	Loss from Sale of Investments	475	
	Investment in JJM Corporation Stock		2,325
	To record sale of 50 shares at $40 per share less commission of $150.		

Significant Influence — Equity Method

When the long-term investment in another company's common stock is large enough that the investor is able to exert significant influence on the investee company's operating and financial policies, we account for the investment using the **equity method**. Stock ownership may indicate the ability to exert significant influence on the investee company's policies in several ways, including: representation on the board of directors, participation in policy making, material intercompany transactions, interchange of managerial personnel, or technological dependency.[5]

Under the equity method, we initially record the investment at cost. Because of the influence the investor can exert on the investee's policies, however, the investor recognizes as income the earning of income by the investee. The investor has the ability to influence the investee's declaration of dividends. If the investor were to recognize income based on dividends, the investor would be able to influence the timing of the recognition of income from the investment.

The investee's net assets are increased by its net income and are decreased by its cash dividends. Therefore, the investment account is increased for the investor's share of the investee's net income and is reduced for the investor's share of the investee's cash dividends. As a result, conceptually, under the equity method of accounting for long-term investments in stock, the balance of the investment account represents the investor's equity (proportionate share as a stockholder) in the investee company's net assets.

Investment in Stock.   Assume Oaks Company purchases 10,000 shares of Water Company common stock for $250,000 cash on January 2, 19X1. The 10,000 shares represent 25% of Water Company's voting stock. Assuming Oaks can exert significant influence on Water Company's policies, Oaks should

---

[5]"The Equity Method of Accounting for Investments in Stock," *Accounting Principles Board Opinion No. 18* (New York, NY: AICPA, 1971), par. 17.

account for the investment using the equity method. Oaks' investment is recorded at cost as shown in the following entry:

19X1 Jan. 2	Investment in Water Company Stock	250,000	
	Cash		250,000
	To record the purchase of 10,000 shares of Water Company common stock for $25 per share.		

Dividends Declared.   Assume the Water Company declares cash dividends of $1 per share on August 15, 19X1. Under the equity method, Oaks Company records its share of the dividends with the following entry:

19X1 Aug. 15	Dividends Receivable	10,000	
	Investment in Water Company Stock		10,000
	To record the receipt of dividends of $1 per share.		

Recognition of Income.   For 19X1, Water Company reports net income of $84,000. Under the equity method, Oaks Company records its 25% share of Water Company's earnings as shown in the following entry:

19X1 Dec. 31	Investment in Water Company Stock	21,000	
	Income from Water Company		21,000
	To record share of net income of Water Company (25% x $84,000).		

At the end of the accounting period, Income from Water Company is closed to Income Summary and is included in Oaks Company's net income.

The relationship between the investor's investment account and the investee's net assets is shown in Illustration 16-8. When the 25% interest in Water Company is initially purchased for $250,000, Water Company's net assets are $1,000,000. The balance in the investment account represents the investor's 25% interest in Water Company's net assets. The dividends Water Company declares reduces its net assets by $40,000, and Oaks Company recognizes the decrease in the net assets by reducing the investment account by $10,000 ($40,000 x 25%). On the other hand, Water Company's net income increases its net assets by $84,000. Oaks Company recognizes this increase in the investee's net assets by increasing the investment account by $21,000 ($84,000 x 25%). Notice that the balance in the investment account of $261,000 is equal to 25% of the investee's net assets of $1,044,000.

ILLUSTRATION 16-8 Investee and Investor T-Accounts

Oaks Company				Water Company			
Investment in Water Company Stock				Net Assets			
Purchase	250,000	Dividends	10,000	Bal.	1,000,000	Dividends	40,000
Income	21,000			Net income	84,000		
Bal.	261,000			Bal.	1,044,000		

CONTROL—PARENT AND SUBSIDIARY RELATIONSHIPS

LO 7
Prepare consolidated balance sheets at the date of acquisition and for subsequent periods.

One corporation sometimes owns a majority (more than 50%) of another corporation's voting stock and is said to **control** the investee company. The investor company, called the **parent company**, is able to control the investee company, called the **subsidiary company**, by electing a majority of the members of the subsidiary's board of directors. In this way, the parent can control (not just influence) the subsidiary's operating, financing, and investing policies. Most large corporations in the United States are actually parent and subsidiary companies. The companies exist as separate entities because of certain economic, tax, and legal advantages. Many large, publicly-owned companies consist of a parent and numerous subsidiaries.

Parent and subsidiary companies are separate legal entities. This means that each company has the rights and duties of a corporation and that each company maintains its own accounting records and prepares its own financial statements. However, under GAAP, parent companies generally also must prepare consolidated financial statements. **Consolidated financial statements** are prepared as though the parent and subsidiary companies are one entity. This view represents the economic substance of the relationship, since the parent company can control the subsidiary companies' resources and operations. Preparing consolidated financial statements is a complex topic that is covered in advanced accounting texts. The next section, however, presents an overview of preparing consolidated balances sheets.

PREPARING CONSOLIDATED BALANCE SHEETS

In the consolidated balance sheet, the assets and liabilities of the parent and subsidiaries are combined so that, for example, cash is reported as the combined amount of the parent's and subsidiaries' cash. However, in preparing a consolidated balance sheet, duplicate balance sheet items are eliminated to avoid double-counting them. Duplicate balance sheet items exist because of transactions between the parent and the subsidiaries. A primary example of duplicate amounts is the investment in subsidiary account in the parent's accounting records and the assets and liabilities recorded in the subsidiary's accounting records. If the parent's investment account and the subsidiary's individual asset and liability accounts are both reported in the consolidated balance sheet, net assets would be double-counted. Also, since the parent company owns the subsidiary's common stock, stockholders' equity would be double-counted. To avoid the duplicate amounts from being reported, the parent's investment account and the subsidiary's stockholders' equity accounts are eliminated in the preparation of the consolidated balance sheet.

For example, Illustration 16-9 shows the balance sheets for Plant Co. and Simko, Inc. Plant owns 100% of Simko's common stock. The consolidated balance sheet for Plant Co. and its subsidiary (Simko) is also presented in Illustration 16-9. Notice that Investment in Simko Stock from Plant's individual balance sheet and Simko's stockholders' equity are not included in the consolidated balance sheet to avoid double-counting net assets and stockholders' equity.

Consolidated Balance Sheet at the Date of Acquisition

The process of preparing a consolidated balance sheet involves using a consolidation worksheet such as the one shown in Illustration 16-10. To illustrate the preparation of a consolidated balance sheet, assume that on January 2, 19X1, Plant Company purchases 100% of the 800 shares of $100 par value common

ILLUSTRATION 16-9 Consolidation of Balance Sheets

			Consolidated	
Plant Co. and Simko, Inc. Balance Sheets July 1, 19X1				
Assets		Plant Co.	Simko, Inc.	Balance Sheet
Current assets		$ 25,000	$ 17,000	$ 42,000
Investment in Simko		90,000		
Plant assets (net)		100,000	103,000	203,000
Total assets		$215,000	$120,000	$245,000
Liabilities and Stockholders' Equity				
Liabilities		$ 80,000	$ 30,000	$110,000
Stockholders' equity		135,000	90,000	135,000
Total liabilities and stockholders' equity		$215,000	$120,000	$245,000

stock of Simko, Inc. Simko's common stock has a carrying value of $126,000, and Plant paid that amount for the shares of stock. On the acquisition date, a consolidated balance sheet is prepared using the worksheet in Illustration 16-10.

In the worksheet, the first two columns present the two companies' separate balance sheets that are prepared from their separate ledger accounts after appropriate adjusting entries have been made. The next two columns, one for debits and one for credits, are for recording elimination entries needed to avoid double-counting amounts in the separate balance sheets resulting from intercompany transactions. Even though these are called "entries," they are *not* recorded in the journals or ledgers of either the parent or the subsidiary, both of which keep separate accounting records. The entries appearing in the consolidation worksheet are used solely to prepare the consolidated financial statements. The final column in the worksheet presents the consolidated balance sheet. The procedures for determining the consolidated amounts are also discussed below.

The elimination entry in the worksheet is labeled "(a)." In more complex consolidation examples, several elimination entries are required; and labeling the entries aids in interpreting the worksheet. In this example, the single entry is to eliminate Investment in Simko in Plant's balance sheet and Simko's stockholders' equity accounts. In preparing consolidated balance sheets, this elimination entry is always required. After these amounts are eliminated, combining the two balance sheets results, in effect, in the investment account being replaced by Simko's individual assets and liabilities.

The consolidated balance sheet in the worksheet in Illustration 16-10 is determined by summing the amounts in each row, including the debits and credits in the Eliminations columns. For example, cash of $42,000 in the consolidated balance sheet is determined by summing Plant's cash of $24,000 and Simko's cash of $18,000. Notice that Plant's Investment in Simko does not have a balance in the Consolidated Balance Sheet column because the $126,000 debit in the first column is exactly offset by the $126,000 credit in the third column. Also, Simko's Common Stock and Retained Earnings are eliminated in the same way. The consolidated balance sheet, therefore, shows only Plant's stockholders' equity accounts. This reflects the fact that the only "outside" stockholders of the combined entities are those of Plant.

ILLUSTRATION 16-10 Consolidation Worksheet

Plant Company and Subsidiary
Worksheet for Consolidated Balance Sheet
January 2, 19X1

	PLANT COMPANY	SIMKO, INC.	ELIMINATIONS		CONSOLIDATED BALANCE SHEET
			DEBITS	CREDITS	
Assets					
Cash	24,000	18,000			42,000
Accounts Receivable	30,000	26,000			56,000
Inventories	80,000	52,000			132,000
Investment in Simko	126,000			(a) 126,000	
Plant Assets (net)	120,000	100,000			220,000
	380,000	196,000			450,000
Liabilities and Stockholders' Equity					
Current Liabilities	26,000	10,000			36,000
Noncurrent Liabilities	129,000	60,000			189,000
Common Stock	150,000	80,000	(a) 80,000		150,000
Retained Earnings	75,000	46,000	(a) 46,000		75,000
	380,000	196,000	126,000	126,000	450,000

Once the consolidation worksheet is completed, it is used to prepare the consolidated balance sheet in the same format as the balance sheet of an individual company.

Less Than 100 Percent Acquisition

Recall that consolidated financial statements are required when the parent owns more than 50% of the investee company's voting stock. To illustrate the preparation of a consolidated balance sheet when less than 100% of the voting stock is purchased, assume that, rather than purchasing 100% of Simko, Inc., Plant Co. purchases 80% of the common stock. The carryng value of 80% of Simko's stock is $100,800 ($126,000 x 80%). Plant pays carrying value for the shares. The worksheet for preparing the consolidated balance sheet at the acquisition date based on the new assumption is presented in Illustration 16-11.

When a company purchases more than 50%, but less than 100%, of another company's voting stock, it purchases a **majority interest** in the investee's net assets. In these circumstances, the other stockholders are said to have a **minority interest** in the subsidiary company's net assets. In the worksheet in Illustration 16-11, when Investment in Simko Stock of $100,800 debit and Common Stock and Retained Earnings of Simko of $126,000 credit ($80,000 + $46,000) are eliminated, a residual credit of $25,200 remains to balance the elimination entry. The $25,200 credit is the minority interest of the other stockholders (20% x $126,000 = $25,200). The minority interest is presented in the consolidated balance sheet, but in practice the presentation is not uniform. Some companies present minority interest in the noncurrent liabilities section; other companies present minority interest as part of stockholders' equity; and

ILLUSTRATION 16-11 Consolidation Worksheet

Plant Company and Subsidiary
Worksheet for Consolidated Balance Sheet
January 2, 19X1

	PLANT COMPANY	SIMKO, INC.	ELIMINATIONS		CONSOLIDATED BALANCE SHEET
			DEBITS	CREDITS	
Assets					
Cash	49,200	18,000			67,200
Accounts Receivable	30,000	26,000			56,000
Inventories	80,000	52,000			132,000
Investment in Simko	100,800			(a) 100,800	
Plant Assets (net)	120,000	100,000			220,000
	380,000	196,000			475,200
Liabilities and Stockholders' Equity					
Current Liabilities	26,000	10,000			36,000
Noncurrent Liabilities	129,000	60,000			189,000
Common Stock	150,000	80,000	(a) 80,000		150,000
Retained Earnings	75,000	46,000	(a) 46,000		75,000
	380,000	196,000			
Minority Interest				(a) 25,200	25,200
			126,000	126,000	475,200

some companies present minority interest as a separate classification between noncurrent liabilities and stockholders' equity. In any case, two sets of outside stockholders are now represented in the consolidated balance sheet, the stockholders of Plant and the stockholders of Simko. Illustration 16-12 shows the liabilities and stockholders' equity section of the consolidated balance sheet with the minority interest presented in stockholders' equity. This approach is used throughout the remainder of this textbook.

ILLUSTRATION 16-12 Partial Consolidated Balance Sheet

Liabilities and Stockholders' Equity		
Liabilities:		
Current liabilities	$ 36,000	
Noncurrent liabilities	189,000	
Total liabilities		$225,000
Stockholders' equity:		
Common stock	$150,000	
Minority interest, Simko	25,200	
Retained earnings	75,000	
Total stockholders' equity		250,200
Total liabilities and stockholders' equity		$475,200

Acquisition at More Than Carrying Value

Companies do not always pay carrying value for the purchased shares of a subsidiary. Quite often the purchase price is in excess of the shares' carrying value. An investor has three reasons for paying more than carrying value for the stock:

1. The fair values of the investee company's assets are more than their recorded carrying values.
2. The fair values of the investee company's liabilities are less than their recorded carrying values.
3. The investor's expectations about the investee's future earnings justify paying more than carrying value.

When the cost of the investment is in excess of its carrying value, the accounting profession requires that any excess cost first be assigned to the investee company's assets and liabilities to recognize their fair values in the consolidated balance sheet. Any remaining excess of cost over carrying value is presented as goodwill in the consolidated balance sheet.

Assume Plant Company purchases 80% of Simko, Inc.'s common stock for $118,000 on January 2, 19X1. Consistent with the previous example, the carrying value of the stock is $100,800 ($126,000 x 80%). Also, assume that the carrying values of Simko's assets and liabilities are equal to their fair values. The worksheet for preparing the consolidated balance sheet is presented in Illustration 16-13. Notice that in the elimination entry, $17,200 of goodwill

ILLUSTRATION 16-13 Consolidation Worksheet

Plant Company and Subsidiary
Worksheet for Consolidated Balance Sheet
January 2, 19X1

	PLANT COMPANY	SIMKO, INC.	ELIMINATIONS DEBITS	ELIMINATIONS CREDITS	CONSOLIDATED BALANCE SHEET
Assets					
Cash	32,000	18,000			50,000
Accounts Receivable	30,000	26,000			56,000
Inventories	80,000	52,000			132,000
Investment in Simko	118,000			(a) 118,000	
Plant Assets (net)	120,000	100,000			220,000
	380,000	196,000			
Goodwill			(a) 17,200		17,200
					475,200
Liabilities and Stockholders' Equity					
Current Liabilities	26,000	10,000			36,000
Noncurrent Liabilities	129,000	60,000			189,000
Common Stock	150,000	80,000	(a) 80,000		150,000
Retained Earnings	75,000	46,000	(a) 46,000		75,000
	380,000	196,000			
Minority Interest				(a) 25,200	25,200
			143,200	143,200	475,200

emerges. This is the difference between the cost of the investment of $118,000 and the carrying value of the interest acquired in Simko's net assets of $100,800 ($126,000 x 80%). **Goodwill** is the excess of cost over the fair value of the net assets. Since the fair values and carrying values of Simko's assets and liabilities are equal, the excess of cost over carrying value is presented as purchased goodwill in the consolidated balance sheet.

Consolidated Balance Sheet Subsequent to Acquisition Date

For accounting periods subsequent to the acquisition date, the basic procedures for preparing a consolidated balance sheet are the same. Assume that for 19X1, Simko has net income of $12,000 and pays dividends of $10,000. Under the equity method of accounting for investments in stocks, Plant makes the following entries to (1) record its 80% share of the dividends and (2) record its 80% share of the net income:

19X1 (Date)	Cash	8,000	
	Investment in Simko		8,000
	To record dividends received from Simko (80% x $10,000).		
Dec. 31	Investment in Simko	9,600	
	Income from Simko		9,600
	To record share of net income of Simko (80% x $12,000).		

To simplify the example, assume Plant has only one other transaction in 19X1, which is a loan to Simko of $5,000. The loan is still owed on December 31, 19X1.

The worksheet to prepare the consolidated balance sheet at December 31, 19X1, is shown in Illustration 16-14. In the Plant Company column, cash increased by $3,000 from the previous Illustration 16-13. This increase is the $8,000 dividend received from Simko minus the $5,000 loan made to Simko. Also, Investment in Simko increased by $1,600, which is the excess of Plant's share of Simko's net income over its share of Simko's dividends. Retained Earnings of Plant increased by its $9,600 share of Simko's net income.

For Simko, cash increased by $7,000 from the previous example, which is the $2,000 excess of net income over dividends ($12,000 – $10,000) plus the $5,000 loan from Plant. For simplicity, it is assumed that all other asset accounts are unchanged. Current liabilities increased by $5,000 for the loan from Plant. Finally, Retained Earnings increased by $2,000, which is the excess of net income over dividends ($12,000 – $10,000).

In the Eliminations columns, the entry to Investment in Simko and Retained Earnings of Simko reflect the changed amounts as explained above. Minority interest has increased by $400, which is the minority interest's share of the increase in Simko's retained earnings [20% x ($12,000 – $10,000)]. A second elimination entry, labeled (b), is needed to eliminate Receivable from Simko of $5,000 in Plant's balance sheet and $5,000 of Current Liabilities in Simko's balance sheet. These amounts are eliminated because they are not an asset and a liability of the consolidated entity. To report them in the consolidated balance sheet would overstate both assets and liabilities because an entity cannot owe money to itself.

ILLUSTRATION 16-14 Consolidation Worksheet

Plant Company and Subsidiary
Worksheet for Consolidated Balance Sheet
January 2, 19X1

	PLANT COMPANY	SIMKO, INC.	ELIMINATIONS DEBITS	ELIMINATIONS CREDITS	CONSOLIDATED BALANCE SHEET
Assets					
Cash	35,000	25,000			60,000
Accounts Receivable	30,000	26,000			56,000
Receivable from Simko	5,000			(b) 5,000	
Inventories	80,000	52,000			132,000
Investment in Simko	119,600			(a) 119,600	
Plant Assets (net)	120,000	100,000			220,000
	389,600	203,000			
Goodwill			(a) 17,200		17,200
					485,200
Liabilities and Stockholders' Equity					
Current Liabilities	26,000	15,000	(b) 5,000		36,000
Noncurrent Liabilities	129,000	60,000			189,000
Common Stock	150,000	80,000	(a) 80,000		150,000
Retained Earnings	84,600	48,000	(a) 48,000		84,600
	389,600	203,000			
Minority Interest				(a) 25,600	25,600
			150,200	150,200	485,200

Other Consolidation Issues

In Illustration 16-14, Goodwill is shown in the consolidated balance sheet column at its original amount of $17,200. Under GAAP, goodwill is an intangible asset that should be amortized over its useful life, not exceeding 40 years.[6] For simplicity in the example, goodwill is not amortized.

For periods subsequent to the acquisition date, consolidated income statements also are prepared. In simplistic examples such as in the previous discussion, the consolidated income statement is prepared by summing the revenues and expenses of the separate companies. In practice, however, consolidated income statements are affected by complex intercompany transactions that must be eliminated. These complexities are discussed in advanced accounting texts.

Purchase Versus Pooling-of-Interests Accounting

The discussion of accounting for business combinations in this chapter has followed the purchase method, which treats the business combination as a pur-

[6]"Intangible Assets," *Accounting Principles Board Opinion No. 17* (New York, NY: AICPA, 1970), pars. 27–28.

chase of assets. Under the **purchase method**, the acquired company's assets and liabilities are reported at their fair values on the date of the business combination. Any excess of the cost of the purchase over the fair value of the net assets acquired is reported as goodwill. A business combination accounted for by the purchase method often involves the exchange of cash or other assets for the net assets acquired.

Another way of accounting for a business combination is the pooling-of-interests method (pooling). Under the **pooling-of-interests method**, the combining company's net assets are reported in the consolidated financial statements at their carrying values immediately preceding the combination. The pooling method is used for combinations that involve the exchange of common stock.

Alternative Methods.   While the purchase and pooling methods are alternative ways of accounting for business combinations, they are not alternative methods for the same business combination. *APB Opinion No. 16* specifies 12 criteria that must be met for the combination to be accounted for as a pooling.[7] If all 12 criteria are met, the combination *must* be accounted for as a pooling. Otherwise, the purchase method must be followed. Two of the criteria are:

1. The combination must be completed in a single transaction.
2. One company must exchange shares of its common stock for at least 90% of the other company's voting stock.

Comparison of the Balance Sheet Effects.   Because of inflation, the combining company's net assets reported under the purchase method will be greater than if the pooling method is used. Also, no goodwill is recognized under the pooling method because the net assets are reported at their carrying values.

Comparison of Income Statement Effects.   Under the purchase method, the acquired company's earnings are included in the combined company's net income only from the date of the combination. Under the pooling method, the combining company's earnings are included in the combined company's net income for the entire year in which the combination occurs, regardless of the date of the combination. Also, operating expenses will usually be greater under the purchase method because the net assets are reported at fair value rather than at carrying value. This affects expenses such as cost of goods sold and depreciation. Amortization expense will usually be greater under the purchase method because no goodwill is recognized under the pooling method.

Illustration 16-15 shows that both the purchase and pooling methods are used in practice, but the use of the purchase method is much greater.

ILLUSTRATION 16-15 Number of Purchases and Poolings

	1991	*1990*	*1989*	*1988*
Poolings	16	10	18	14
Purchases	160	190	219	216

Source: *1992 Accounting Trends and Techniques*, p. 62.

---

[7]"Business Combinations," *Accounting Principles Board Opinion No. 16,* (New York, NY: AICPA, 1970), pars. 45–48.

INTERNATIONAL OPERATIONS

In recent years, the level of foreign business activity has risen rapidly. This development is the result of governments' relaxation of trade restrictions and companies' search for new markets. Many businesses have operations in other countries, and some operate throughout the world. These companies are called multinational companies. Some companies sell to customers located in foreign countries. Similarly, some companies make purchases from suppliers located in foreign countries. These transactions are called import and export transactions. Other companies have subsidiaries that are located in foreign countries, while some companies have both import and export transactions and foreign subsidiaries. The following sections discuss accounting for both of these types of arrangements.

LO 8

Record foreign currency transactions in the accounts.

Foreign Currency Transactions

When a U.S. company sells to a foreign customer or purchases from a foreign supplier, the transaction may be settled in either U.S. dollars or in a foreign currency. The settlement currency depends on the agreement between the parties to the transaction. From the perspective of a U.S. company, a **foreign currency transaction** is a one that calls for settlement in a currency other than the U.S. dollar.

Foreign currency transactions affect accounting in the recording of the transactions. Foreign currency amounts have to be translated into U.S. dollar equivalents, and translation requires the use of exchange rates. An **exchange rate** is the value of one currency expressed in terms of another currency. Exchange rates change daily as the supplies of and demands for currencies change. Illustration 16-16 presents some examples of exchange rates.

ILLUSTRATION 16-16   Foreign Exchange Rates

Currency	Rates in U.S. dollars
British pound	$1.52
Canadian dollar	.76
French franc	.17
Japanese yen	.01
German mark	.60

Source: *The Wall Street Journal* (August 23, 1993), p. C15.

To see how exchange rates are used for translation, assume a U.S. citizen purchases a product from a French company. The price of the product is 500 francs. To pay for the purchase, the U.S. citizen must buy French francs. If the exchange rate between U.S. dollars and francs is $.17 per franc, it costs $85 ($.17 x 500) to purchase the 500 francs needed to settle the transaction. (Note: Included in this exchange rate is the fee the foreign currency dealer charges for handling the transaction.)

Foreign Currency Purchases Transactions.   To illustrate the accounting for a foreign currency purchases transaction, assume that on May 2, Southern Import Co., a U.S. corporation, purchases goods from a Japanese company. The invoice states that the price for the goods is 1,000,000 yen. On the date of the purchase, the exchange rate for yen is $.008 per yen. Southern should record the purchases on the date of the purchase at the U.S. dollar equivalent amount, which is $8,000 (1,000,000 x $.008). The following entry records the purchase:

May 2	Purchases	8,000	
	Accounts Payable		8,000
	To record the purchase of goods from Japanese		
	company for 1,000,000 yen (1,000,000 x $.008).		

On May 12, when the payment of the invoice is due, the exchange rate for yen has changed to $.0082. Therefore, to purchase the 1,000,000 yen to pay the invoice costs $8,200 (1,000,000 x $.0082). Southern's entry to record the payment is:

May 12	Accounts Payable	8,000	
	Exchange Loss	200	
	Cash		8,200
	To record payment of accounts payable		
	(1,000,000 yen x $.0082).		

Because the yen *increased* in value relative to the U.S. dollar between the date of purchase and the payment date, Southern incurred an exchange loss. If the yen had decreased in value during this time period, Southern would have realized an exchange gain. Accounting standards require that the net amount of exchange gains and losses for a period should be included in the determination of net income for the period.[8]

Foreign Currency Sales Transactions.   The accounting for a foreign currency sales transaction follows the same concepts as accounting for foreign currency purchases transactions. At the date of sale, the transaction is recorded using the exchange rate on that date. For example, assume that on June 5, Eastern Export Co., a U.S. corporation, sells merchandise to a British company. The sales price is 10,000 British pounds, and the exchange rate is $1.75 per pound. Eastern's entry to record the sale is as follows:

June 5	Accounts Receivable	17,500	
	Sales		17,500
	To record sales revenue (10,000 pounds x $1.75).		

The exchange rate on the date that Eastern receives payment is used to record the receipt of cash. The following entry records the receipt of cash, assuming that the exchange rate has changed to $1.80 per pound on July 15 when Eastern receives payment.

July 15	Cash	18,000	
	Accounts Receivable		17,500
	Exchange Gain		500
	To record receipt of cash (10,000 pounds x $1.80).		

An exchange gain is realized because the value of the British pound *increased* during the time period. If the value of the pound had *decreased*, Eastern would have incurred an exchange loss. Notice that the relationship between the direction of exchange rate changes and exchange gains and losses for sales transactions is opposite that of purchases transactions.

---

[8]"Foreign Currency Translation," *Statement of Financial Accounting Standards No. 52* (Stamford, Conn.: FASB, 1987), par. 15.

Intervening Financial Statement Date

At the end of an accounting period, accounts receivable and payable from foreign currency transactions may be unsettled. Accounting standards require that the receivables and payables should be adjusted to reflect the exchange rates at the end of the accounting period. The resulting exchange gains and losses should be recognized in net income for the period.[9]

In the previous example, assume that Eastern Export Co.'s fiscal year ends on June 30. The exchange rate on that date is $1.82 per pound. Eastern's entry at the end of the accounting period is as follows:

June 30	Accounts Receivable	700	
	Exchange Gain		700
	To record exchange gain at the end of the period.		
	[($1.82 – $1.75) x 10,000 pounds]		

On July 15, when Eastern receives payment, the exchange rate is $1.80; and the following entry is recorded:

July 15	Cash	18,000	
	Exchange Loss	200	
	Accounts Receivable		18,200
	To record receipt of cash (10,000 pounds x $1.80).		

Notice that the net exchange gain is $500 ($700 – $200), which is the same amount recorded previously when there is no intervening financial statement date. However, a $700 exchange gain is recorded in the year of sale; and a $200 exchange loss is recorded in the year of cash receipt. This method reflects fluctuations in exchange rates in the periods in which they occur.

Translation of Foreign Currency Financial Statements

U.S. foreign subsidiaries commonly keep their accounting records and prepare financial statements in terms of the currency of the country in which they operate. The financial statements of a foreign subsidiary should be consolidated with those of its U.S. parent. This requires that the subsidiary's statements be translated into U.S. dollars because consolidated financial statements prepared in different currencies yield meaningless results.

Accounting standards require that the assets and liabilities of foreign currency financial statements be translated into U.S. dollars using the exchange rates at the date of the financial statements. Stockholders' equity accounts are translated using the exchange rates at the dates the securities were issued, and revenue and expense accounts are translated at the average exchange rate for the period.[10]

SUMMARY

Describe those events and transactions that increase and decrease retained earnings and prepare a retained earnings statement. A corporation's retained earnings account is increased by net income and is decreased by dividends and net losses. The board of directors declare dividends, which may be either cash divi-

[9]*Ibid.*

[10]*Ibid.*, par. 12.

dends or stock dividends. Cash dividends reduce both the corporation's assets and retained earnings. Stock dividends do not affect the amount of the corporation's assets or the amount of total stockholders' equity.

Describe the recording of stock dividends and stock splits. Small stock dividends result in the capitalization of retained earnings equal to the stock's market price. For large stock dividends, retained earnings are capitalized in the amount necessary for minimum legal capital, which usually is par or stated value of the stock issued as a dividend. Stock splits do not result in any formal entry in the accounts of the corporation.

Account for the purchase and reissuance of treasury stock. Previously issued shares of stock that the corporation reacquires are called treasury stock. Treasury stock is recorded at cost and is presented as a reduction of stockholders' equity in the balance sheet. When treasury stock is reissued, an increase or decrease in contributed capital may result.

Describe how businesses report the retirement of stock in their financial statements. When the stockholders approve the retirement of stock, all amounts related to the original issuance of the stock are removed from the accounts.

Discuss the accounting for appropriations of retained earnings. Companies use appropriations of retained earnings to inform owners and others that a portion of retained earnings will not be paid out as dividends. We record appropriations of retained earnings by transferring the appropriated amount from Retained Earnings to Retained Earnings–Appropriated.

Account for investments in stock using the market, cost, and equity methods. An investment in another company's stock is accounted for by the equity method if the investor is able to exert significant influence on the investee's policies. Otherwise, the market or cost methods are used. Under the market method, the investments are presented in the balance sheet at their current market values. Unrealized changes in market values of long-term investments are accumulated in stockholders' equity. Unrealized changes in the market value of short-term investments are included in net income. Under both the market and cost methods, dividends earned are recognized when the investee company declares them. Under the cost method, the investments are presented in the balance sheet at their original cost. Under the equity method, the investment account is decreased for dividends received from the investee company. The investment account is increased and income is recorded for the investor's share of the investee's net income.

Prepare consolidated balance sheets at the date of acquisition and for subsequent periods. When a company controls another company through ownership of a majority of the voting stock, a parent and subsidiary company relationship exists and consolidated financial statements are prepared. The preparation of consolidated balance sheets involves the use of a consolidation worksheet. In the worksheet, duplicate amounts are eliminated; and the remaining amounts are summed to prepare the consolidated balance sheet.

Record foreign currency transactions in the accounts. Companies that have foreign currency transactions account for them by using the exchange rate at the date of the transaction. Exchange gains and losses that result from fluctuations in exchange rates are recognized in net income in the period the rates change.

◼ REVIEW PROBLEM A

The Stockholders' Equity section for Carol Ann Corporation is given below:

Carol Ann Corporation Partial Balance Sheet December 31, 19X0		
Stockholders' Equity		
Contributed capital:		
Common stock, $5 par value, 1,000,000 shares authorized,		
200,000 shares issued		$1,000,000
Paid-in capital in excess of par value		2,000,000
Total contributed capital		$3,000,000
Retained earnings		1,700,000
Total		$4,700,000
Less: Treasury stock, 10,000 shares at a cost of $12 per share		120,000
Total stockholders' equity		$4,580,000

REQUIRED:

Prepare journal entries for each of the following **independent events** in 19X1.

a. Declared a 10% stock dividend when the market price of stock is $18 per share.
b. Declared a 40% stock dividend when the market price of stock is $16 per share.
c. Declared a 2-for-1 stock split.
d. Distributed the stock dividend in (a) above.
e. Purchased 1,000 shares of treasury stock for $20 per share.
f. Sold 2,000 shares of treasury stock at $10 per share.
g. Sold 3,000 shares of treasury stock at $15 per share.
h. Retired 5,000 shares of common stock at $14 per share.

SOLUTION:

Planning and Organizing Your Work

1. Analyze each transaction.
2. Determine if the stock dividend is large or small.
3. If the stock dividend is small, use the stock's market value to determine the amount of retained earnings to capitalize.
4. If the stock dividend is large, use the stock's par or stated value to determine the amount of retained earnings to capitalize.
5. Record purchases of treasury stock at cost.
6. Record the difference between the reissuance price of treasury stock and its original cost as either an increase or a decrease in paid-in capital (or retained earnings if necessary).
7. Remove all amounts related to the original issuance of stock for retirement of stock.

(a) *Declared a 10 % stock dividend.*
Retained earnings: $18 x 200,000 shares x 10%

19X1	Retained Earnings	360,000	
	Stock Dividend Distributable*		100,000
	Paid-in Capital — Stock Dividend**		260,000
	To record the declaration of a 10% stock dividend.		
	*$5 x 200,000 shares x 10%		
	**($18 – $5) x (200,000 x 10%)		

(b) *Declared a 40% stock dividend.*
Retained earnings: $5 x 200,000 shares x 40%

19X1	Retained Earnings	400,000	
	Stock Dividend Distributable		400,000
	To record the declaration of a 40% stock dividend.		

(c) *Declared a 2-for-1 stock split.*

No entry required. Show Common Stock at $2.50 par ($5 ÷ 2) and 400,000 (200,000 x 2) shares issued.

(d) *Distributed stock dividend.*

19X1	Stock Dividend Distributable	100,000	
	Common Stock		100,000
	To record the distribution of the stock dividend.		

(e) *Purchased treasury stock for $20 per share.*

19X1	Treasury Stock	20,000	
	Cash		20,000
	To record the purchase of 1,000 shares of treasury stock for $20 per share.		

(f) *Sold treasury stock for $10 per share.*
Cash: $10 x 2,000 shares
Treasury Stock: $12 x 2,000 shares
Retained Earnings: $24,000 − $20,000

19X1	Cash	20,000	
	Retained Earnings	4,000	
	Treasury Stock		24,000
	To record the sale of 2,000 shares of treasury stock below cost.		

(g) *Sold treasury stock for $15 per share.*
Cash: $15 x 3,000 shares
Treasury Stock: $12 x 3,000 shares
Paid-In Capital—Treasury Stock Transactions: $45,000 − $36,000

19X1	Cash	45,000	
	Paid-In Capital—Treasury Stock Transactions		9,000
	Treasury Stock		36,000
	To record the sale of 3,000 shares of treasury stock above cost.		

(h) *Retired common stock for $14 per share.*
Common stock: $5 x 5,000 shares

19X1	Common Stock	25,000	
	Paid-In Capital in Excess of Par——Common*	50,000	
	Paid-In Capital—Retirement of Stock		5,000
	Cash		70,000
	To record the retirement of 5,000 shares of common stock.		
	*($2,000,000/200,000 shares) x 5,000		
	**($15-$14) x 5,000		

REVIEW PROBLEM B

Greer Corporation purchased 5,000 shares of Hogg Corporation's common stock for $30 per share on January 2, 19X1. During 19X1, Hogg Corporation declared and subsequently paid a dividend of $2 per common share. Hogg Corporation earned $5 per share during 19X1. The market price of Hogg Corporation stock on December 31, 19X1 is $33 per share. Greer considers the investment to be long-term.

REQUIRED:

a. Record Greer Corporation's purchase of Hogg Corporation stock.
b. Record the necessary entries if Greer Corporation uses the market method of accounting for the investment in Hogg Corporation stock.
c. Record the necessary entries if Greer Corporation uses the equity method of accounting for investment in Hogg Corporation stock.
d. Record Greer's sale of 2,000 shares of Hogg Corporation stock on June 30, 19X2, for $32.50 per share. Assume that Greer Corporation uses the cost method of accounting for the investment in Hogg. Hogg pays a broker's fee of $900.

SOLUTION:

Planning and Organizing Your Work

1. Record the purchase of Hogg Corporation stock at cost.
2. Calculate the dividends Greer received to determine dividends earned under the market method. Record the entries for the recognition and collection of dividends.
3. Record the entry to adjust Hogg stock to market value and record the unrealized gain or loss under the market method.
4. Record the entry to reduce Greer's Investment in Hogg Corporation Stock account for Greer's dividends from Hogg for the equity method.
5. Record the entry to recognize Greer's share of Hogg's income under the equity method.
6. Record cash received minus the broker's commission from the sale and recognize the appropriate gain or loss on the sale.

(a) *Record the purchase.*

19X1			
Jan. 2	Investment in Hogg Corporation Stock*	150,000	
	Cash		150,000
	To record the purchase of 5,000 shares of stock for $30 per share.		
	*($30 x 5,000 shares)		

(b) *Prepare market method entries.*

(Date)	Dividends Receivable	10,000	
	Dividends Revenue		10,000
	To record dividend revenue of $2 per share.		
(Date)	Cash	10,000	
	Dividends Receivable		10,000
	To record the receipt of dividends declared.		
(Date)	Investment in Hogg Corporation Stock*	15,000	
	Unrealized Gain (Loss) from Available-for-Sale Securites		15,000
	To adjust long-term investments in stocks to current market prices.		
	*($33 – $30) x 5,000 shares		

(c) *Prepare equity method entries.*

(Date)	Dividends Receivable	10,000	
	Investment in Hogg Corporation Stock		10,000
	To record the declaration of dividends by the investee of $2 per share.		
(Date)	Cash	10,000	
	Dividends Receivable		10,000
	To record the receipt of dividends declared.		
(Date)	Investment in Hogg Corporation Stock*	25,000	
	Income from Hogg Corporation		25,000
	To record share of income earned by the investee of $5 per share.		
	* ($5 x 5,000 shares)		

(d) *Record the sale of long-term investments.*
Cash: ($32.50 x 2,000 shares) – $900
Gain: $64,100 – $60,000

19X2 June 30	Cash [($32.50 x 2,000 shares) – $900]	64,100	
	Investment in Hogg Corporation Stock *		60,000
	Gain from Sale of Investments ($64,100 – $60,000)		4,100
	To record sale of 2,000 shares of stock for $32.50 per share less $900 commission.		
	*$30.00 x 2,000 shares		

KEY TERMS

appropriation of retained
  earnings, *636*
available-for-sale securities, *638*
capitalizing retained earnings,
  627
consolidated financial
  statements, *646*
control (of a corporation), *645*
cost method, *642*
dividend payout, *630*

dividend yield, *631*
equity method, *644*
exchange rate, *654*
foreign currency transaction,
  654
goodwill, *651*
large stock dividend, *629*
majority interest, *648*
market method, *638*
minority interest, *648*

parent company, *646*
pooling-of-interests method,
  653
purchase method, *653*
retained earnings, *626*
stock dividend, *627*
stock split, *630*
subsidiary company, *646*
treasury stock, *632*

SELF-QUIZ

LO 1   1. Which of following is a *true* statement about Retained Earnings?
    a. It is decreased by net income.
    b. It is increased by dividends.
    c. It is decreased by net losses.
    d. It is unaffected by stock dividends.

LO 2   2. Which of the following is a *correct* statement about stock dividends?
    a. They decrease assets when declared.
    b. They decrease assets when distributed.
    c. They do not require declaration by the board of directors.
    d. They cause the capitalization of retained earnings.

LO 2   3. True or False? A stock split reduces retained earnings.

LO 3   4. Which of the following is *not* a true statement about treasury stock?
    a. Treasury stock is shown at the end of the stockholders' equity section of the balance sheet.
    b. Treasury stock is always recorded at the stock's original par value.
    c. Treasury stock reduces stockholders' equity.
    d. Treasury stock reduces shares outstanding when it is acquired.

LO 3   5. If a company retires shares at a price less than their original issue price, we credit the difference to an account called _____ _____– _____ _____ _____.

LO 5 6. Which of the following is *not* a correct statement about the appropriation of retained earnings?
  a. Most corporations frequently practice it.
  b. It is used to restrict the payment of dividends in order to meet a future contingency.
  c. The decision to appropriate retained earnings is made by the board of directors.
  d. It is shown separately from unappropriated retained earnings on the balance sheet.

LO 6 7. Which of the following is *not* a method of accounting for long-term investments in stocks?
  a. Cost
  b. Equity
  c. Market
  d. Net realizable value

LO 6 8. For short-term investments, we include the unrealized change in market value for each period in _____ _____.

LO 6 9. When the level of ownership does not allow the investor to exert significant influence on the investee company's management decisions, the investor should account for the investments in stock using the _____ method or the _____ method.

LO 7 10. Which of following is *not* a reason why investors are willing to pay more than book value for another company's stock?
  a. The fair value of the assets of an investee company exceeds their recorded values.
  b. The fair value of the liabilities of an investee company are less than their recorded values.
  c. The par value of a company's stock is less than the issue price.
  d. Expected future earnings of the investee are optimistic.

LO 8 11. True or False? GAAP require that the receivables and payables for unsettled foreign currency transactions be adjusted to reflect the exchange rates at the end of the accounting period.

SOLUTIONS TO SELF-QUIZ
1. c   2. d   3. False   4. b   5. Paid-In Capital–Retirement of Stock   6. a   7. d   8. net income   9. market, cost   10. c   11. True

---

QUESTIONS

Q16-1   Why do corporations declare stock dividends?

Q16-2   What is the difference between the accounting treatment of a small stock dividend and a large stock dividend?

Q16-3   Why are small stock dividends accounted for differently than large stock dividends?

Q16-4   What is the difference between a stock dividend and a stock split?

Q16-5   What is the interpretation of the dividend yield ratio?

Q16-6   Why do firms acquire treasury stock?

Q16-7   What is the difference between acquiring treasury stock and retiring common stock?

Q16-8   Why do companies appropriate retained earnings?

Q16-9   What key factors are used to determine the appropriate accounting method for long-term investments in stocks?

Q16-10 Why do companies prepare consolidated financial statements?

Q16-11 What is the difference between a foreign currency transaction and foreign currency translation?

EXERCISES

LO 1   **E16-1   Retained Earnings Statement**   Evelyn and Meyer Corporation had a credit balance of $137,500 in Retained Earnings on January 1, 19X1. Net income for 19X1 was $47,200, and the December 31, 19X1, post-closing balance in Retained Earnings was $152,700.

REQUIRED:

Prepare a retained earnings statement for 19X1.

LO 2   **E16-2 Small Stock Dividend** Uncle Jimmy's has 20,000 shares of $2 par common stock outstanding on June 30, 19X2, when the market price is $24 per share. The board of directors declares a 10% stock dividend to be distributed on July 15, 19X2.

REQUIRED:

Record the necessary journal entries for the declaration and distribution of the stock dividend.

LO 2   **E16-3 Large Stock Dividend** Assume that Uncle Jimmy's board of directors declares a 50% stock dividend, instead of a 10% stock dividend, as given in E16-2.

REQUIRED:

Record the necessary journal entries for the declaration and distribution of the stock dividend.

LO 2   **E16-4 Stock Splits** Imelda's Shoes, Inc. has 1,000,000 shares authorized and 200,000 shares issued and outstanding of $15 par value common stock and declares a stock split.

REQUIRED:

Show how Common Stock would appear on the balance sheet:
a. Before the stock split
b. After a 2-for-1 stock split
c. After a 3-for-1 stock split.

LO 2   **E16-5 Dividend Ratios** Audionics Corporation reported $2,350,000 net income and paid $1,200,000 in dividends for 19X3. The market price per common share of stock and number of shares of common stock outstanding on December 31, 19X3, is $31.00 per share and 1,000,000 shares, respectively.

REQUIRED:

Calculate the dividend payout and dividend yield ratios for 19X3.

LO 3   **E16-6 Purchase of Treasury Stock** Moon Distillers, Inc. purchased 3,000 shares of its $5 par value common stock for $59 per share on October 31, 19X4.

REQUIRED:

Prepare the journal entry to record the purchase of treasury stock.

LO 3   **E16-7 Sale of Treasury Stock** The stockholders' equity section for Squire Corporation is given on the next page.

REQUIRED:

Record the necessary journal entry to record the sale of 4,000 shares of treasury stock in 19X6 at:
a. $35 per share
b. $50 per share

Squire Corporation Partial Balance Sheet December 31, 19X5	
Stockholders' Equity	
Contributed capital:	
Common stock, $10 par value, 1,000,000 shares authorized,	
150,000 shares issued	$1,500,000
Paid-in capital in excess of par—common	4,400,000
Paid-in capital—treasury stock	100,000
Total contributed capital	$6,000,000
Retained earnings	2,800,000
Total	$8,800,000
Less: Treasury stock, 10,000 shares at a cost of $38 per share	380,000
Total stockholders' equity	$8,420,000

LO 4

E16-8   **Retirement of Stock**   On March 13, 19X7, Cass Corporation retired 7,500 shares of its outstanding common stock at a price of $40 per share. The common stock has a par value of $10 per share and originally was issued at a price of $32 per share.

REQUIRED:

Record the journal entries for the retirement of the shares.

LO 6

E16-9   **Investments in Stock, Market Method**   Oklahoma Instruments, Inc. purchased 10% of the 10,000 shares of common stock of BMOC Corporation on January 3, 19X8, for $30 per share. Oklahoma Instruments intends to retain the investment in BMOC for more than one year. BMOC reported earnings of $3.50 per share and declared dividends of $1.25 per share for 19X8 on December 31. The dividends will be paid on January 15, 19X9. The market price of BMOC on December 31, 19X8, is $31.50 per share.

REQUIRED:

Record the purchase of BMOC, the recognition of income, the adjustment to current market price, and the receipt of dividends by Oklahoma Instruments.

LO 6

E16-10   **Investments in Stock, Equity Method**   Quick Express, Inc., purchased 40% of the 80,000 shares of common stock of Fax-It Corporation on January 3, 19X1, for $25 per share. Fax-It reported earnings of $2.50 per share and declared dividends of $1 per share for 19X1. The dividends will be paid on February 15, 19X2.

REQUIRED:

Record the purchase of the Fax-It stock, the recognition of income, and the recognition of dividends by Quick Express, Inc. using the equity method.

LO 6

E16-11   **Sale of Investments, Cost Method**   Outdoors Unlimited purchased 2,000 shares of Trailblazers Incorporated on February 24, 19X0, for $80.25 per share. Outdoors Unlimited intended to retain the stock for more than one year at the time of purchase. Outdoors Unlimited sold the 2,000 shares of Trailblazers Incorporated on March 13, 19X3, for $81.00 per share and paid a broker's fee of $600.

REQUIRED:

Record the sale of the Trailblazers Incorporated stock using the cost method.

LO 7   **E16-12**   **Consolidated Balance Sheet Worksheet**   Primo Company purchased 100% of the Segundo Company common stock on January 2, 19X2, for $196,000.

REQUIRED:

On a separate sheet of paper, complete the partially completed worksheet below to prepare a consolidated balance sheet for Primo and Segundo.

Primo Company and Subsidiary
Worksheet for Consolidated Balance Sheet
January 2, 19X1

	PRIMO COMPANY	SEGUNDO COMPANY	ELIMINATIONS DEBITS	ELIMINATIONS CREDITS	CONSOLIDATED BALANCE SHEET
Assets					
Cash	41,500	14,700			
Accounts Receivable	32,300	21,900			
Inventories	91,700	57,300			
Investment in Segundo	196,000				
Plant Assets (net)	379,600	167,200			
	741,100	261,100			
Liabilities and Stockholders' Equity					
Current Liabilities	117,800	51,700			
Noncurrent Liabilities	183,200	13,400			
Common Stock	300,000	50,000			
Retained Earnings	140,100	146,000			
	741,100	261,100			

LO 8   **E16-13**   **Foreign Currency Purchases Transactions**   Worldwide Imports purchased goods on December 1, 19X3, from a Swiss company for 80,000 Swiss francs. On February 15, 19X4, Worldwide Imports paid for the purchase. Worldwide has a December 31 fiscal year-end. The Swiss franc was worth $.55, $.60, and $.58 in terms of U.S. dollars on December 1, December 31, and February 15, respectively.

REQUIRED:

Record all necessary journal entries to record the purchase and payment.

LO 8   **E16-14**   **Foreign Currency Sale Transactions**   IBU Exports sold goods on October 1, 19X5, to a British company for 9,000 British pounds. On January 15, 19X6, IBU Exports collected for the sale. IBU has a December 31 fiscal year-end. The British pound was worth $1.75, $1.80, and $1.85 in terms of U.S. dollars on October 1, December 31, and January 15, respectively.

REQUIRED:

Record all necessary journal entries to record the sale and collection.

PROBLEM SET A

LO 1,2,3,4,5   **P16-1A**   **Stockholders' Equity Transactions**   The stockholders' equity section for Candee Corporation is given below:

Candee Corporation Partial Balance Sheet December 31, 19X0	
Stockholders' Equity	
Contributed capital:	
Common stock, $1 par value, 1,000,000 shares authorized,	
100,000 shares issued	$ 100,000
Paid-in capital in excess of par—common	1,400,000
Paid-in capital in excess of par—treasury	50,000
Total contributed capital	$1,550,000
Retained earnings	700,000
Total stockholders' equity	$2,250,000

The following events occurred during 19X1:

Jan. 15 Declared a 10% stock dividend when the market price was $20 per share.
     31 Distributed the stock dividend declared on January 15.
May 15 Purchased 3,000 shares of treasury stock at $18 per share.
July 10 Appropriated $150,000 of retained earnings to finance future plant expansion.
Aug. 15 Sold 1,000 shares of treasury stock at $16 per share.
Nov. 19 Retired 5,000 shares of common stock at $17 per share.
Dec. 2 Sold 750 shares of treasury stock at $20 per share.

REQUIRED:

a. Record the necessary journal entries for 19X1.
b. Prepare the stockholders' equity section on December 31, 19X1, assuming net income of $90,000 for the year.
c. Record the journal entry for January 15, assuming a 40% stock dividend, instead of a 10% stock dividend.

LO 6   **P16-2A**   **Investments in Stock**   Rose Corporation had never made any long-term investments in marketable equity securities. During 19X2, it decided to invest in Blackjack Company, Greta Company, and Harcor Company. All investments are classified as long-term. The following information relates to the stock of these companies and other 19X2 results.

	Blackjack	**Greta**	**Harcor**
Acquisition price	$45,000	$33,000	$90,000
Number of shares	1,000	1,500	4,500
Ownership percentage	10%	15%	30%
Earnings per share	$ 9.00	$ 6.00	$ 4.00
Dividends per share	$ 3.00	$ 2.50	$ 2.50
Market price per share on			
December 31, 19X2	$ 41.00	$ 22.50	$ 19.00

REQUIRED:

a. Prepare the journal entries for the purchases of the investments.
b. Prepare the journal entries to record the recognition of income and the receipt of dividends for the investments.

c. Prepare the journal entries to record the adjustment to the investment account if the market method is used for investments where the ownership percentage is less than 20%.

d. Show how these investments would appear on Rose Corporation's balance sheet and how they would affect the income statement.

LO 7   **P16-3A**   **Consolidated Balance Sheet**   Pop Company purchased 75% of Son Company's common stock on January 2, 19X3, for $216,000. Assume the carrying values of Son Company's assets and liabilities are equal to their fair values. Pop has a $5,000 account receivable from Son.

Pop Company and Subsidiary
Worksheet for Consolidated Balance Sheet
January 2, 19X3

	POP COMPANY	SON COMPANY	ELIMINATIONS DEBITS	ELIMINATIONS CREDITS	CONSOLIDATED BALANCE SHEET
Assets					
Cash	84,000	38,000			
Accounts Receivable	60,000	48,000			
Inventories	130,000	98,000			
Investment in Son	216,000				
Plant Assets (net)	270,000	208,000			
	760,000	392,000			
Goodwill					
Liabilities and Stockholders' Equity					
Current Liabilities	27,000	15,000			
Noncurrent Liabilities	263,000	125,000			
Common Stock	284,000	150,000			
Retained Earnings	186,000	102,000			
	760,000	392,000			
Minority Interest					

REQUIRED:

a. Calculate goodwill.

b. Calculate the minority interest.

c. On a separate piece of paper, complete the partially completed worksheet to prepare a consolidated balance sheet for Pop and Son.

LO 8   **P16-4A**   **Foreign Currency Transactions**   The Everything French Company buys and sells French merchandise in the United States on a regular basis and has a December 31 fiscal year-end. The following transactions took place during 19X4:

19X4

Jan. 26 Purchased merchandise from Conehead Inc., a French company, for 10,000 francs when the exchange rate for the franc was $0.18.

Mar. 17 Paid Conehead Inc. when the franc had an exchange rate of $0.19.

Apr.   2 Sold 19,000 francs of merchandise to Eiffel Company when the franc had an exchange rate of $0.17.

June 15 Sold 34,000 francs of merchandise to Bon Soir Company when the franc had an exchange rate of $0.16.

Aug. 17 Collected 19,000 francs from Eiffel Company for the April 2 sale when the franc had an exchange rate of $0.16.

Oct.   3 Purchased merchandise from Mirage, Inc. for 22,000 francs when the franc had an exchange rate of $0.17.

Dec.   1 Collected 34,000 francs from the Bon Soir Company when the franc had an exchange rate of $0.19.

REQUIRED:

a. Record all necessary journal entries. (The franc has an exchange rate on December 31 of $0.15.)
b. Calculate the net exchange gain or loss from entering into the foreign currency transactions.

PROBLEM SET B

LO 1,2,3,4,5   **P16-1B**   **Stockholders' Equity Transactions**   The Stockholders' Equity section for Leslie Corporation is given below:

Leslie Corporation Partial Balance Sheet December 31, 19X4	
Stockholders' Equity	
Contributed capital:	
Common stock, $2 par value, 1,000,000 shares authorized, 200,000 shares issued	$ 400,000
Paid-in capital in excess of par—common	800,000
Paid-in capital—treasury stock	70,000
Total contributed capital	$1,270,000
Retained earnings	420,000
Total stockholders' equity	$1,690,000

The following events occurred during 19X5:

Jan.   2 Declared a 15% stock dividend when the market value was $10 per share.
Feb.   5 Distributed the stock dividend declared on January 2.
June 15 Purchased 4,000 shares of treasury stock at $9.50 per share.
July 10 Appropriated $90,000 of retained earnings to finance future plant expansion.
Aug. 25 Sold 1,500 shares of treasury stock at $8 per share.
Nov.   9 Retired 6,000 shares of common stock at $7 per share.
Dec. 22 Sold 1,000 shares of treasury stock at $12 per share.

REQUIRED:

a. Record the necessary journal entries for 19X5.
b. Prepare the stockholders' equity section on December 31, 19X5, assuming net income of $80,000 for the year.
c. Record the journal entry for January 2, assuming a 50% stock dividend, instead of a 15% stock dividend.

LO 6   **P16-2B** **Investments in Stock**   Broccoli Corporation had never made any long-term investments in marketable equity securities. During 19X6, it decided to invest in Bush Company, Ranger Company, and Bean Company. All investments are classified as long-term. The following information relates to the stock of these companies and other 19X6 results.

	Bush	*Ranger*	*Bean*
Acquisition price	$60,000	$42,000	$81,000
Number of shares	2,000	1,500	4,500
Ownership percentage	10%	16%	40%
Earnings per share	$ 5.50	$ 5.00	$ 3.50
Dividends per share	$ 1.50	$ 1.20	$ 0.75
Market price per share on December 31, 19X6	$31.00	$24.50	$19.00

REQUIRED:

a. Prepare the journal entries for the purchases of the investments.
b. Prepare the journal entries to record the recognition of income and the receipt of dividends for the investments.
c. Prepare the journal entries to record the adjustment to the investment account if the market method is used for investments where the ownership percentage is less than 20%.
d. Show how these investments would appear on Broccoli Corporation's balance sheet and how they would affect the income statement.

LO 8   **P16-3B** **Consolidated Balance Sheet**   Plum Company purchased 85% of Seay Company's common stock on January 2, 19X7, for $324,000. Assume the book values of Seay Company's assets and liabilities are equal to their fair values. Plum has $8,000 of accounts receivable from Seay.

Plum Company and Subsidiary
Worksheet for Consolidated Balance Sheet
January 2, 19X7

	PLUM COMPANY	SEAY COMPANY	ELIMINATIONS DEBITS	ELIMINATIONS CREDITS	CONSOLIDATED BALANCE SHEET
Assets					
Cash	126,000	57,000			
Accounts Receivable	90,000	72,000			
Inventories	195,000	147,000			
Investment in Seay	324,000				
Plant Assets (net)	405,000	312,000			
	1,140,000	588,000			
Goodwill					
Liabilities and Stockholders' Equity					
Current Liabilities	41,000	22,000			
Noncurrent Liabilities	394,000	188,000			
Common Stock	426,000	225,000			
Retained Earnings	279,000	153,000			
	1,140,000	588,000			
Minority Interest					

REQUIRED:

a. Calculate goodwill.
b. Calculate the minority interest.
c. On a separate sheet of paper, complete the partially completed worksheet to prepare a consolidated balance sheet for Plum and Seay.

LO 8   **P16-4B   Foreign Currency Transactions**   Jewel Company buys and sells Japanese merchandise in the United States on a regular basis and has a December 31 fiscal year-end. The following transactions took place during 19X8:

19X8
Jan. 16 Purchased merchandise from Plume Inc., a Japanese Company, for 800,000 yen when the yen had an exchange rate of $0.018.
Mar.   7 Paid Plume Inc. when the yen had an exchange rate of $0.020.
Apr.   5 Sold 2,900,000 yen of merchandise to Hattari Company when the yen had an exchange rate of $0.016
June 25 Sold 2,400,000 yen of merchandise to Bon Soup Company when the yen had an exchange rate of $0.015.
Aug.   7 Collected 2,900,000 yen from Hattari Company for the April 5 sale when the yen had an exchange rate of $0.016.
Oct. 13 Purchased merchandise from Viscount, Inc. for 4,200,000 yen when the yen had an exchange rate of $0.019.
Dec.   4 Collected 2,400,000 yen from the Bon Soup Company when the yen had an exchange rate of $0.020.

REQUIRED:

a. Record all necessary journal entries. (The yen has an exchange rate on December 31 of $0.017.)
b. Calculate the net exchange gain or loss from entering into the foreign currency transactions.

CRITICAL THINKING AND COMMUNICATING

C16-1   The common stock of We-Haul, Incorporated is traded on a national stock exchange.

Barbara Coe, the CEO of We-Haul, is evaluating the company's dividend policy. For the past several years, the company's dividend payout ratio has been constant at 20%. Barbara is considering two options that she thinks might increase the market price of the stock:

1. Increasing the dividend payout ratio to 50%.
2. Supplementing the current dividend by also distributing a stock dividend.

REQUIRED:

a. Discuss Barbara's two dividend policy options. What are the possible investor reactions to the two alternative dividend actions?
b. What other actions might Barbara consider to increase the market price of We-Haul's stock?

C16-2   You are the auditor of Modern Electronics Company. You recently informed the chief

financial officer (CFO) that a new accounting standard will require that the company's portfolio of long-term investments in stocks will have to be accounted for by the market method (instead of the cost method) beginning with the next set of financial statements. The CFO was very upset at this development and replied: "These are long-term investments, why should the company's performance be judged on changes in the market price of the stocks when the company has no intention of selling the stocks?"

REQUIRED:

Write a letter to the CFO explaining the accounting for long-term investments in stocks and how the financial statements are affected. Be sure and respond to his concern about judging the company's performance when there is no intention to sell the stocks.

C16-3

The financial statements of J.C. Penney Company, Inc. are reprinted in Appendix B at the end of the text. On the income statement is the earnings per share information. Notice that the company reports numerous EPS numbers for each year. Discussion of the various EPS figures are the subject of more advanced accounting texts. For purposes of this case, use the EPS number called "Primary, Income before extraordinary charge and cumulative effect of accounting changes."

REQUIRED:

a. Calculate the dividend payout ratio for 1991–1993. You can find both the numerators and denominators for this ratio in the *Supplemental Information*, located after the financial statements, entitled Five Year Financial Summary.
b. Calculate the dividend yield for 1991–1993. You can find the market price of the stock in the *Supplemental Information* entitled Quarterly Data. For calculating this ratio, use the fourth quarter average market price (i.e., average of the high and low for the fourth quarter).
c. Analyze J.C. Penney's dividend policy using the ratios you calculated in Requirements a and b. Would you classify J.C. Penney as a growth company? Why?

CHAPTER 17

Long-Term Liabilities

The Chief Operating Officer has just informed Miklos Kronis, the chief financial officer (CFO) of Midwestern Alliance Corporation, that the company must replace some of its equipment immediately or stop essential operations. The equipment, which has an estimated useful life of 10 years is available from a supplier at a cash price of $100,000. The question is: How should the company finance its purchase?

The company has only enough cash to meet its regular bills, so it must raise new equity capital or borrow the necessary funds. Miklos faces two limiting factors, however. First, Mr. Conrad, who is the Chairman, Chief Executive Officer (CEO), and majority shareholder of the corporation, neither wishes to invest more equity in Midwestern nor to have new (or existing) owners dilute his majority share. Second, the bank that provides Midwestern with its revolving line of credit has placed restrictions, called debt covenants, on the corporation's ability to borrow from other sources. Specifically, Midwestern will default on its line of credit if its debt-equity ratio exceeds 1.0 (or 1-to-1).

Ordinarily, Miklos would feel free to choose among the various long-term financing (borrowing) plans available—for example, a long-term installment note payable, issuing bonds payable, leasing the equipment under a capital lease, or leasing under an operating lease. He would normally choose the financing plan that costs the least (had the lowest present value). Unfortunately, in this case, Miklos now has to worry more about the financing plan's impact on the corporation's debt-equity ratio.

In this chapter, you will learn about using present value methodology to establish the values of long-term liabilities and how various types of long-term debt work. You will learn to account for installment loans, bonds, and leases. You also will learn how to calculate the debt-equity ratio, how to interpret it, and how to apply it in the case of a debt restriction. Finally, you will be exposed to the controversial topic of off-balance-sheet financing.

1. Account for long-term notes with constant principal payments.
2. Find the present value of an amount to be received in some future period, calculate the present value of a long-term note, and account for the note from issue to maturity.
3. Find the amount of the constant payments required to pay off an installment note, and account for installment notes from issue to maturity.
4. Describe the important features of bonds businesses issue as a form of borrowing; explain why some bonds are issued at face value, some at discounts, and some at premiums and record issues of bonds.
5. Calculate total interest cost of bond issues and record interest expense, including amortization of discounts and premiums, using the straight-line and interest methods.
6. Accrue interest expense and amortize discounts and premiums between interest payment dates, account for bond issue costs, and account for bonds issues between interest payment dates.
7. Account for investments in bonds.
8. Explain the difference between capital leases and operating leases.
9. Account for the assets and liabilities recognized under capital leases.
10. Calculate and interpret the debt-equity ratio as an indicator of potential financial distress, and recognize its limitations when off-balance-sheet financing is used.

LONG-TERM NOTES AND LOANS PAYABLE

A business often arranges long-term loans when it requires additional financing for long-run expansions of its assets and when the necessary capital is not available from either the owners or internally from past earnings. Long-term borrowings may be in the form of long-term notes payable or bonds payable (described later in the chapter). A business may borrow money from a bank, giving a long-term note in exchange, and then spend the cash on needed assets. Or, the supplier of the assets may accept a long-term note in exchange for the assets.

LO 1

Account for long-term notes with constant principal payments.

Long-Term Notes With Constant Principal Payments

On January 1, 19X1, Centex Retail Store gave a $5,000, 5-year, 12% note payable to Quality Equipment in exchange for store equipment that is worth $5,000. The terms of the note call for semiannual interest payments and $500 semiannual payments of principal on June 30 and December 31 of 19X1 through 19X5. Illustration 17-1 shows the first-year history of the note.

In the same way that we illustrated for short-term notes in an earlier chapter, Centex accrues interest every 6 months on this note. However, Centex prefers to measure time in months, not days. For the first six months, it accrues $300:

$$I = PRT = \$5,000 \times 12\% \times \frac{6 \text{ months}}{12 \text{ months}} = \$300$$

ILLUSTRATION 17-1 First-Year History of a Long-Term Note Payable

	19X1
January 1, balance	$5,000
Accrued interest, Jan.–June	300
Payment on June 30	(800)
July 1, balance	$4,500
Accrued interest, July–Dec.	270
Payment on December 31	(770)
December 31, balance	$4,000

The two payments in Illustration 17-1 each consists of the $500 payment of principal plus the interest accrued since the previous payment—a total of $800 on June 30 and $770 on December 31. Because Centex pays $500 of the principal every 6 months, the principal amount of the note declines. As a result, the amount of interest accrued and paid at each date declines. Thus, Centex accrues $270 for the July-December period of 19X1, because the July 1 balance is $4,500 after the first principal payment. Because the principal payment remains constant, the total payment declines as the 6-month interest declines. Centex's entries for the first year of the note are representative of all the subsequent years:

19X1			
Jan. 1	Equipment	5,000	
	Notes Payable—Noncurrent		5,000
	To record purchase of equipment and issue of 5-year note to Quality Equipment.		
June 30	Interest Expense	300	
	Notes Payable—Noncurrent	500	
	Cash		800
	To record interest and semiannual payment on 5-year note payable to Quality Equipment.		
Dec. 31	Interest Expense	270	
	Notes Payable—Noncurrent	500	
	Cash		770
	To record interest and semiannual payment on 5-year note payable to Quality Equipment.		

Illustration 17-2 shows the complete history of the 5-year note. Notice that the above interest and payment pattern repeats every January-June and every July-December from 19X1 to 19X5. Interest is accrued on the beginning balance and is paid along with $500 of the principal amount of the note. Notice that the December 31 balance (last line) declines from $4,500 on December 31, 19X1, to $0 on December 31, 19X5, the maturity date of the note.

LO 2
Find the present value of an amount to be received in some future period, calculate the present value of a long-term note, and account for the note from issue to maturity.

Notes That Require Initial Valuation

Accounting for the note in the above example is straightforward because the principal payments are constant and the interest payments are simply added on. Conveniently, the note's face amount equaled the equipment's cash value at the time it was purchased. Thus, no question is raised about the proper valuation of the equipment or the liability. However, these conditions are not always met.

ILLUSTRATION 17-2 Five-Year History of Note Payable

	19X1	19X2	19X3	19X4	19X5
January 1, balance	$5,000	$4,000	$3,000	$2,000	$1,000
Accrued interest, Jan.-June	300	240	180	120	60
Payment on June 30	(800)	(740)	(680)	(620)	(560)
July 1, balance	$4,500	$3,500	$2,500	$1,500	$ 500
Accrued interest, July-Dec.	270	210	150	90	30
Payment on December 31	(770)	(710)	(650)	(590)	(530)
December 31, balance	$4,000	$3,000	$2,000	$1,000	$ 0

Sometimes, the cash value of an asset purchased with a note does not equal the note's face amount. At other times, the cash value of the asset acquired cannot be established, except implicitly from the terms of the note. To handle such situations, we use the concept of the "present value" of future cash payments.

Concept of Present Value.   The **present value** of an amount to be received in the future is the amount that a rational person would accept now in exchange for the right to receive the future amount. Intuitively, future values always exceed the equivalent present values:

Present Value < Future Value

Why do rational individuals attach smaller present values to future sums? Because they can invest the money they currently hold and earn additional funds during the time they would have to wait to receive the future funds. For example, if they can invest funds to earn 12% interest for one year, then $1 invested currently would be worth $1.12 one year from now. Thus, $1 is the present value of $1.12 to be received after one year. If the $1 is invested for two years, it will be worth $1.25 in two years; and $1 is the present value of $1.25 to be received in two years:

Beginning principal, Year 1	$1.0000	◄──── Present Value
Add interest at 12% per year	0.1200	
Beginning principal, Year 2	$1.1200	
Add interest at 12% per year	0.1344	
Ending principal, Year 2	$1.2544	
Ending principal rounded to nearest cent	$1.25	◄──── Future Value

Notice that the interest earned in Year 1, in turn, earns interest in Year 2. We call interest earned on principal *and* previous interest amounts **compound interest**. Compound interest calculations reduce to a simple mathematical formula:

$$FV = PV(1 + i)^n$$

FV stands for the future value of a current or present value (*PV*) invested. The term, *n*, is the number of periods for which the amount is invested; and the term, *i*, is the interest rate. Using the example above in which *n* = 2, *i* = 12%, and *PV* = $1:

$$FV = \$1(1 + .12)^2 = \$1.2544$$

Turning this relationship around gives us a formula for the present value of an amount to be received in the future.

$$PV = \frac{FV}{(1 + i)^n}$$

$$PV = \frac{\$1}{(1 + .12)^2} = \$.7972$$

This says that the present (cash) equivalent value of $1 to be received at the end of 2 years is $.7972. To prove that the present value formula is correct, we repeat our previous detailed interest calculations, beginning with a first-year principal amount of $.7972:

Beginning principal, Year 1	$0.7972	◀—— Present Value
Add interest at 12% per year	0.0957	
Beginning principal, Year 2	$0.8929	
Add interest at 12% per year	0.1071	
Ending principal, Year 2	$1.0000	◀—— Future Value

Earlier we said that $1 invested for two years at 12% will equal $1.2544. Therefore, we can say that $1 is the present value of $1.2544. We can get the same result by multiplying the $1.2544 times the present value of $1 to be received after two years:

$$PV = \$1.2544 \times .7972 = \$1.000$$

Thus, we can find the present value of any future amount by simply multiplying the future amount by the present value of $1 to be received after the same number of periods.

Present Value Tables.   Since the present-value-future-value relationship reduces to a mathematical formula, anyone who solves it for a particular interest rate and number of periods achieves the same result. However, the calculations can be tedious without a calculator or computer assistance. To save unnecessary effort, tables of present values are available. Table 1 in Appendix C to this text displays the present value of one dollar to be received after 1 to 25 periods at interest rates from 1% to 18%. To use the table, find the intersection of the column of the desired interest rate and the row of the relevant waiting period (n). For example, the present value of $1 to be received after 14 years at 11% interest is $.2320.

Valuing Notes Payable Using Present Values.   Quality Equipment offers merchants such as Centex Retail Store a special payment plan. The entire price charged for equipment is due in a lump sum at the end of two years. On July 1, 19X1, the first day of its fiscal year, Centex purchases equipment under the plan for an agreed-upon payment of $9,000 to be made on June 30, 19X3. Centex makes a noninterest-bearing note payable to Quality Equipment for $9,000. Quality custom-configured the equipment for Centex, so there is no market value of comparable equipment to refer to in establishing its value. In this case, the present value of the payment is a reasonable approximation of the equipment's value, assuming Centex is competent and rational in accepting the payment arrangement. Indeed, Centex probably should calculate the present value of the payment to determine whether the equipment is "worth" its equivalent cash price.

If the prevailing interest rate to Centex for borrowed funds is 9% per year, $.8417 is the present value of $1 to be received (paid) after two years (see the intersection of the $n=2$ row and the 9% column of Table 1, Appendix C). Therefore, $7,575.30 is the present value of $9,000 ($9,000 x .8417 = $7,575.30). $7,575.30 is the value of the liability at the date of purchase and the value to Centex of the equipment purchased in exchange for the liability. Centex would record the transaction thus:

19X1 Aug. 1	Equipment	7,575.30	
	Discount on Notes Payable	1,424.70	
	Notes Payable—Noncurrent		9,000.00
	To record purchase of equipment and issue of note payable to Quality Equipment.		

Notice that we record the note payable at face value, but we also record the difference between its face value and its present value in Discount on Notes Payable. Thus, the note's carrying value (face value less discount) is equal to its present value, the value of the liability and of the equipment.

Interest on Notes Valued Using Present Values.   By just knowing the implicit interest rate and the number of periods used to derive the note's present value, the note's entire history can be scheduled in advance as in Illustration 17-3. Only one terminal payment is required and, therefore, interest is compounded annually.

ILLUSTRATION 17-3 History of a Two-Year Discounted Note Payable

Balance, July 1, 19X1	$7,575.30
Fiscal 19X2 interest @ 9%*	681.78
Balance, June 30, 19X2	$8,257.08
Fiscal 19X3 interest @ 9%#	742.92
Balance, June 30, 19X3	$9,000.00

*Recall that Centex's fiscal year begins July 1.
#Compound interest calculations often lead to rounding differences. It is customary to "adjust" the final interest accrual to correct any difference and force the final value of the liability to the exact amount to be paid at maturity. In this case, the final interest accrual was reduced by $.22 to eliminate a rounding difference ($8,257.08 x .09 = $743.14).

Centex would record interest expense and the single payment as follows:

19X2 June 30	Interest Expense	681.78	
	Discount on Notes Payable		681.78
	To record interest on 2-year note payable to Quality Equipment.		
19X3 June 30	Interest Expense	742.92	
	Discount on Notes Payable		742.92
	To record interest on 2-year note payable to Quality Equipment.		

June 30	Notes Payable—Noncurrent	9,000.00	
	Cash		9,000.00
	To record payment of 2-year note payable to		
	Quality Equipment.		

Notice that Centex does not credit the amount of interest expense to an interest payable account. Instead, it deducts the accrued interest from (credits it to) Discount on Notes Payable. This process is called *amortizing the discount.* Interest is then calculated on the note's larger carrying value (face value less the unamortized remainder of the discount) in the second year. The second year's amortization of the discount reduces it to zero; and, thus, the note's carrying value equals its face value at the time it is paid:

	Note Payable	Discount	Carrying Value
Balance, July 1, 19X1	$9,000.00	$1,424.70	$7,575.30
Fiscal 19X2 interest (amortization) @ 9%		(681.78)	
Balance, June 30, 19X2	9,000.00	742.92	8,257.08
Fiscal 19X3 interest (amortization) @ 9%		(742.92)	
Balance, June 30, 19X3	9,000.00	0.00	9,000.00

We do not use the same straight-line methodology for amortizing the discount and recognizing interest that we use on short-term notes. Under the straight-line method, we would have divided the total discount of $1,424.70 ($9,000 − $7,575.30) by the number of days of the loan to get a daily interest accrual. Then, we would have multiplied the daily accrual times the number of days in each accrual period. That methodology would have allocated an equal amount of interest to both years in the life of the note:

	Note Payable	Discount	Carrying Value
Balance, July 1, 19X1	$9,000.00	$1,424.70	$7,575.30
Fiscal 19X2 interest @ 9%		(712.35)	
Balance, June 30, 19X2	9,000.00	712.35	8,287.65
Fiscal 19X3 interest @ 9%		(712.35)	
Balance, June 30, 19X3	9,000.00	0.00	9,000.00

However, the straight-line methodology ignores the compound interest *implicit* in the present value that permitted us to value the note initially. The difference between a "straight-line" allocation of the total interest cost to 19X2 and 19X3 and the allocation based on the interest rate times the note's increasing carrying value is not very great. Nevertheless, the interest rate method is considered to be more "correct." The difference is generally immaterial over periods shorter than a year, and the straight-line methodology illustrated earlier is widely used for short-term notes.

Find the amount of the constant payments required to pay off an installment note, and account for installment notes from issue to maturity.

Long-Term Installment Loans

Installment loans present some additional challenges, both in financing a business and in accounting for the liabilities. Many loans require multiple payments of interest and principal. Technically, they all could be called installment loans. However, it is customary to use the term **installment loan** only to describe a loan that is repaid with a *series of equally spaced payments of a constant amount*. One of the challenges is to determine the constant amount of the installment payments required to repay a loan at a particular interest rate over a particular number of installments. For example, what annual payment is required in each of 5 years to repay a $10,000 loan at 11% interest? To determine the answer, you first have to understand the concept of an annuity value.

Concept of an Annuity Value. An **annuity** is any series of equal payments to be paid or received at the ends of a series of fixed periods. Annuities are described by the amount of the payments and the number and length of the periods. For example, a $1,000, 5-year annuity is a series of $1,000 amounts to be paid or received at the end of each year for 5 years illustrated by this time line:

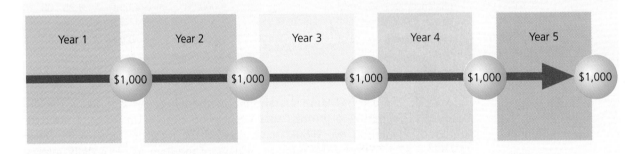

The first payment in the annuity series is paid or received at the end of the first year; the second payment, at the end of the second year, etc. A stream in which the amounts are paid or received at the beginnings of the periods is called an **annuity due**. However, most liabilities requiring constant payments fit the pattern of an annuity rather than an annuity due.

An **annuity value** is the *sum* of the present values of each of the individual $1 amounts paid or received at the end of each of a specified number of periods in a $1 annuity. *To calculate the annuity value of $1 to be received at the end of, say, each of 5 years at 11% interest, we add the present values of each of the individual payments:*

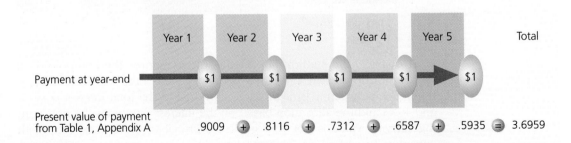

This calculation tells us that an individual who could earn 11% interest on money invested would be willing to pay $3.6959 for the right to receive $1 at the end of each year for 5 years. Note that the above total of the 5 present values, rounded to three decimal places (3.696), can be found at the intersection of the 11% column and the 5-period row of Table 2 in Appendix C. Table 2 contains the annuity values corresponding to $1 annuities for all the periods and at all the interest rates included in Table 1.

Present Value of an Annuity.   Since the annuity value from the table is the present value of an annuity of $1 payments, it can be multiplied by the amount of the payments of annuities of any sizes to get their present values:

$$PV = AV \times PMT$$

PV here represents the total present value of the entire annuity; *AV*, the annuity value factor from Table 2; and *PMT*, the amount of each payment in the annuity. The total present value at, say, 13% of the $1,000, 5-year annuity illustrated in the time line above is:

Amount of each payment	$1,000.00
Annuity value from Table 2	
for 5 periods at 13%	x 3.517
Present value of the payments	$3,517.00

Receiving the rights to the $1,000 annuity is the economic equivalent of having $3,517.00 invested at 13% interest today. Thus, we can interpret the $3,517.00 present value as the amount a rational individual would be willing to pay for $1,000 to be received at the end of each of 5 years, assuming the individual could earn 13% on money he or she invests.

Installments Required to Repay a Note Payable.   Now, by simply turning the above present value formula around (that is, solving for *PMT*), we have a relationship that will tell us the size of a series of payments required to repay a loan.

$$PMT = \frac{PV}{AV}$$

The required payment size is the present value (the amount borrowed or the value of the goods purchased with a note) *divided by* the appropriate annuity value factor. Now, we return to the problem posed earlier: How much must each of 5 equal annual payments be to repay a $10,000 loan at 11% interest? The appropriate annuity value of 3.696 is found in Table 2 at the intersection of the 5-period row and the 11% column. The payment (rounded to the nearest cent) is:

$$PMT = \frac{\$10,000}{3.696} = \$2,705.63$$

Accounting for Long-Term Installment Notes Payable.   Suppose the note in the above example is made payable to a bank in exchange for a loan of $10,000 on January 1, 19X1. The first-year history of the note is shown in Illustration 17-4.

Notice that interest is accrued at the interest rate on which the installment calculation was based, 11%, times the January 1 balance. Since the payment is

ILLUSTRATION 17-4 First-Year History of Installment Note

	19X1
January 1, balance	$10,000.00
Accrued interest, Jan.–Dec.	1,100.00
Payment on December 31	(2,705.63)
December 31, balance	$ 8,394.37
Implicit principal payment	$ 1,605.63

fixed at $2,705.63, we derive the **implicit principal payment** by subtracting the interest component from the total payment ($1,605.63 = $2,705.63 – $1,100.00). The implicit principal payment is the amount by which the first installment payment reduces the principal amount owed on the note. Here are the entries to record the issue of the note and to recognize interest expense and the first year's payment:

19X1			
Jan. 1	Cash	10,000.00	
	Notes Payable—Noncurrent		10,000.00
	To record issue of 5-year installment note payable to Bank.		
Dec. 31	Notes Payable—Noncurrent	1,605.63	
	Interest Expense	1,100.00	
	Cash		2,705.63
	To record interest and payment on 5-year installment note payable to Bank.		

The entry for interest and the annual payment for the first year is representative of the subsequent years' entries. However, because the principal amount of the loan declines with each payment, the subsequent year's interest expense declines; and the amount of each year's payment that reduces the principal amount increases. These patterns are reflected in the 5-year history of the note in Illustration 17-5.

ILLUSTRATION 17-5 History of an Installment Note Payable*

	19X1	19X2	19X3	19X4	19X5
January 1, balance	$10,000.00	$8,394.37	$6,612.12	$4,633.82	$2,437.91
Accrued Interest, Jan.–Dec.	1,100.00	923.38	727.33	509.72	267.72
Payment on December 31	(2,705.63)	(2,705.63)	(2,705.63)	(2,705.63)	(2,705.63)
December 31, balance	$ 8,394.37	$6,612.12	$4,633.82	$2,437.91	$ 0.00
Implicit principal payment	$ 1,605.63	$1,782.25	$1,978.30	$2,195.91	$2,437.91

*In multiple-period present value and annuity calculations, there is always some rounding difference. Rounding differences will prevent the calculations used in accounting for long-term debts to come out exactly even. Accountants commonly adjust the last interest accrual to make the numbers work out evenly. We follow this practice throughout this chapter, and you will need to do the same in solving some of the exercises and problems at the end of the chapter.

For example, interest for 19X2 is $923.38 ($8,394.37 x 11%), rather than the $1,100.00 of 19X1. Thus, $1,782.25 of 19X2's installment is a reduction of principal—in contrast to $1,605.63 in 19X1. The principal payments implicit in each year's installment in Illustration 17-5 reduce the liability's carrying value to zero after the fifth payment—as they should.

Balance Sheet Disclosure of Long-Term Obligations

Because long-term installment obligations generally have one or more remaining installments due within one year, a portion of the long-term obligation is a current liability. For example, in the case of the long-term installment note of Illustration 17-5, the carrying value of $8,394.37 as of December 31, 19X1, can be broken down into the following present values:

Installment due December 31, 19X2 ($2,705.63 x .9009*)	$2,437.50
Installments due after December 31, 19X2 ($8,394.37 – $2,437.50)	5,956.87
Total	$8,394.37

*Present value of $1 for one year at 11% interest.

The issuer of the installment note in this case would disclose the note in its December 31, 19X1, balance sheet as follows:

Current liabilities	
Current portion of noncurrent notes payable	$2,437.50
Noncurrent liabilities	
Notes payable—noncurrent	$5,956.87

Year-End Accrued Interest on Long-Term Installment Notes

If the installment note of Illustration 17-5 had been issued on July 1, 19X1, but the issuer's fiscal year ended on December 31 (as assumed above), accounting for the note would change slightly. The issuer would accrue one-half year's interest at December 31 each year and the other half at the time of the annual payment. The entries for the first year in the life of the note would be:

19X1			
July 1	Cash	10,000.00	
	Notes Payable—Noncurrent		10,000.00
	To record issue of 5-year installment note payable to Bank.		
Dec. 31	Interest Expense	550.00	
	Interest Payable—Installment Note		550.00
	To accrue interest expense on 5-year installment note payable to Bank.		
19X2			
June 30	Notes Payable—Noncurrent	1,605.63	
	Interest Expense	550.00	
	Interest Payable—Installment Note	550.00	
	Cash		2,705.63
	To record interest and payment on 5-year installment note payable to Bank.		

LO 4
Describe the important
features of bonds
businesses issue as a form
of borrowing; explain why
some bonds are issued at
face value, some at
discounts, and some at
premiums and record
issues of bonds.

BONDS

One of the many ways businesses can borrow is by selling or issuing bonds. **Bonds** are debt securities—meaning they are debts represented by transferable certificates. The borrower or debtor is called the **issuer of bonds**; the lenders or creditors are called **bondholders**. Bonds differ from negotiable notes (which are also transferable) in several respects:

1. The terms of bonds are usually longer than those for notes.
2. The total amount of debt or borrowing represented by an "issue" of bonds is broken down into separate debt securities of relatively small denominations (amounts).
3. Costs are associated with issuing bonds, and costs may be associated with retiring them.
4. All individual bonds are covered by one legal contract of indebtedness called a bond indenture.

The **bond indenture** for a bond issue contains all the debt's terms and conditions. Bond indentures include such things as: number of bonds that may be issued under the agreement, denomination of the bonds, interest rate paid on the bonds, term of the bonds, and any restrictions the debt imposes on the issuer of the bonds. Common restrictions limit the issuer's amount of total debt and the amount of dividends that may be paid to stockholders.

Bonds are most often issued in denominations of $1,000 each. So, if an issuer wishes to raise $3,000,000 by issuing bonds, it would issue 3,000 bonds at $1,000 each. The **denominations of bonds** are also referred to as their par values, face values, principal amounts, and maturity values. The interest rate stated in the indenture is usually called the **stated**, **nominal**, or **coupon rate**. It specifies the annual rate of interest to be paid on the bonds' face value. Frequently, interest on bonds is paid semiannually. So, for example, an issuer of $1,000 bonds that have a stated rate of 11% to be paid semiannually, pays two payments of $55 each year per bond.

The **full term** of a bond is the total number of years between the date it can be first issued and the date it matures. At any date subsequent to the first date a bond can be issued, the time remaining before it matures is referred as the **term to maturity**, or the remaining term of the bond.

Together, the face value, term (full or remaining), interest rate, and frequency of payment of a bond determine the stream of payments the issuer makes to the bondholder. Suppose, for example, that Ace Corporation issues a $1,000, 5-year, 9% bond, paying interest semiannually on June 30 and December 31 of each year. These terms imply that someone who buys such a bond on or after January 1, but before June 30 of the first year of its full term, will receive the following stream of payments from Ace:

Year 1	June 30	Interest	$ 45
	Dec. 31	Interest	45
Year 2	June 30	Interest	45
	Dec. 31	Interest	45
Year 3	June 30	Interest	45
	Dec. 31	Interest	45
Year 4	June 30	Interest	45
	Dec. 31	Interest	45

Year 5	June 30	Interest	45
	Dec. 31	Interest	45
	Dec. 31	Principal	1,000
Total			$1,450

Registered bonds are issued in the buyer's name. The issuer enters the buyer's name on the bond certificate and in a bond register. The issuer makes interest and principal payments only to the *registered* owners of the bonds and enters the payments in the bond register. The owners of registered bonds cannot transfer them directly to purchasers. They must turn the bond certificates in to the issuer, who then reissues certificates registered in the new owner's name. **Bearer** or **coupon bonds** are not registered. Instead, the bond certificates have detachable coupons that are redeemed for interest payments with the issuer or the issuer's agent (usually a bank). The bearer (owner) of the bonds surrenders them when they mature in exchange for payment of the principal amount.

Bonds differ from long-term notes payable in another way. Individual bonds are generally *not* structured on an installment basis. However, a special kind of bonds, called serial bonds, have the same effect. Borrowers issue **serial bonds** under indentures specifying that certain subsets of the total issue of bonds will be due at different maturity dates. Serial bond indentures identify by serial numbers which bonds in the issue are due at which maturity dates. For the issuer, the series of due dates for subsets of a serial bond issue has an effect similar to an installment loan arrangement. Bonds issued under indentures that specify that all the bonds are due at the same date are called **term bonds**. We cover only term bonds in this text.

Values of Bonds at Issue

Most bonds are sold for cash. However, they rarely are sold precisely for their face values. If they are sold for less than face value, we say they are sold at a **discount**. If they are sold for more than face value, we say they are sold at a **premium**. Discounts and premiums result from differences between the nominal (stated) rate of interest on the bond and the market rate (also called the prevailing rate) that investors can receive on other investments of about equal risk and duration.

To see this, consider 100 bonds Beta Corporation issued on April 1, 19X1. Each bond has a face value of $1,000, nominal interest rate of 10%, annual interest payments on March 31, and a 5-year term. Now, consider how much a buyer would be willing to pay Beta for the bond if the interest rate for comparable investments at the time of issue is 8%, 10%, or 12%. To determine these amounts, we find the present value of the bond's interest and principal payments at each of these interest rates as shown in Illustration 17-6.

The dates and payments implied by the terms of the bonds are shown in the first and second columns of Illustration 17-6. We find the present value factors in Table 1 of Appendix C at the intersections of the appropriate interest rate columns and the rows representing the numbers of years to payment. We multiply these factors times the payment amounts to derive the present values of the individual payments. Then, we sum the present values of the payments to get the present values of the bonds for each interest rate.

Now consider the middle case (the face-value case) in Illustration 17-6. Recall that interest payments are determined by the nominal rate of 10% and the

ILLUSTRATION 17-6 Present Value of a Bond

March 31	Bond Payments	8 % (Premium Case)		10 % (Par Value)		12 % (Discount Case)	
		Present Value Factor	Present Value	Present Value Factor	Present Value	Present Value Factor	Present Value
19X2	$ 100.00	0.9259	$ 92.59	0.9091	$ 90.91	0.8929	$ 89.29
19X3	100.00	0.8573	85.73	0.8264	82.64	0.7972	79.72
19X4	100.00	0.7938	79.38	0.7513	75.13	0.7118	71.18
19X5	100.00	0.7350	73.50	0.6830	68.30	0.6355	63.55
19X6	100.00	0.6806	68.06	0.6209	62.09	0.5674	56.74
19X6	1,000.00	0.6806	680.60	0.6209	620.93	0.5674	567.40
Total present values			$1,079.86		$1,000.00		$927.88

note's face value. If the prevailing rate for similar investments is the same as the nominal rate, then this investment pays the same rate on the face value as does any other comparable investment. The investor, therefore, would be willing to pay Beta face value of $1,000 for it.

However, if the prevailing rate is higher than 10%, then an investor would not be willing to pay Beta face value for the bond, but something less than face value. Illustration 17-6 shows that if the prevailing rate is 12%, the investor would be willing to pay $927.88. If the investor buys the bond for $927.88, it is equivalent to investing this amount in any other comparable investment that pays 12%. In other words, the bondholder will actually earn 12% on the bond if it is purchased at $927.88. The 12% is known as the effective interest rate of the bond purchased at this price. The **effective interest rate** is the interest rate at which the present value of all the payments due on a bond (or other long-term obligation) equal the proceeds from issuing the bond.

If the prevailing rate is lower than the nominal rate, investors will pay Beta more than face value for the bond. According to Illustration 17-6, if the prevailing rate is 8%, investors will pay $1,079.86 for the bond. At this price, the bond has an effective interest rate of 8%.

Recording Bond Issues

To illustrate the recording of bond issues, we assume that Beta issued 100 of the bonds described in Illustration 17-6 on April 1, 19X1 at each of the prices illustrated. When Beta issues the bonds, it receives assets and incurs a liability. If the bonds are issued at face value, for cash, Beta's entry to record the issue is very straightforward:

19X1			
Apr. 1	Cash	100,000	
	Bonds Payable		100,000
	To record issue of 100, $1,000 bonds at face.		

In Beta's balance sheet, bonds issued at face value are presented as follows:

Noncurrent liabilities	
10% bonds payable, due March 31, 19X6 issued at face value	$100,000

When bonds are issued at a lower price than face value, the difference is recorded in a separate contra-liability account, Discount on Bonds Payable. If Beta sold the 100 bonds at $927.88, the entry is:

19X1			
Apr. 1	Cash	92,788	
	Discount on Bonds Payable	7,212	
	Bonds Payable		100,000
	To record issue of 100 $1,000 bonds at $927.88.		

In Beta's balance sheet, bonds issued at a discount are presented as follows:

Noncurrent liabilities
10% bonds payable, due March 31, 19X6

Face value	$100,000	
Less: Unamortized discount	7,212	$92,788

When bonds are issued at a price higher than face value, the difference is recorded in a separate valuation account, Premium on Bonds Payable. If Beta sold the 100 bonds at $1,079.86, the entry is:

19X1			
Apr. 1	Cash	107,986	
	Bonds Payable		100,000
	Premium on Bonds Payable		7,986
	To record issue of 100, $1,000 bonds at $1,079.86.		

In Beta's balance sheet, bonds issued at a premium are presented as follows:

Noncurrent liabilities
10% bonds payable, due March 31, 19X6

Face value	$100,000	
Add: Unamortized premium	7,986	$107,986

Total Bond Interest Cost

LO 5
Calculate total interest cost of bond issues and record interest expense, including amortization of discounts and premiums, using the straight-line and interest methods.

When bonds are issued at face value, total interest cost over the term of the bonds equals the sum of the interest payments. Total interest cost also equals the difference between the total payments (principal and interest) and the proceeds from issuing the bonds. The interest cost for any period is the interest that applies to that period at the stated interest rate. For example, if Beta Corporation's 5-year, 10% bonds illustrated above are issued at face value, the total interest cost over the term of the bonds is $50,000, the sum of five, $10,000 annual interest payments. Total interest cost also equals the sum of the interest and principal payments, $150,000, less the proceeds of issue, $100,000.

However, when a bond is sold at a premium or discount, the premium or discount becomes part of the calculation of the bond's interest cost. The total interest costs of the premium and discount cases for Beta's bonds described in Illustration 17-6 are shown in Illustration 17-7.

When we add the discount of $7,212 to the interest payments of $50,000, we get a total interest cost of $57,212 over the term of the bonds. When we

ILLUSTRATION 17-7 Total Interest Cost Calculations

		Discount Case	Premium Case
Payments to be made:			
March 31,19X2	Interest	$ 10,000	$ 10,000
March 31,19X3	Interest	10,000	10,000
March 31,19X4	Interest	10,000	10,000
March 31,19X5	Interest	10,000	10,000
March 31,19X6	Interest	10,000	10,000
March 31,19X6	Principal	100,000	100,000
Total payments		$150,000	$150,000
Less: Proceeds of sale		92,788	107,986
Total interest cost—full term		$ 57,212	$ 42,014

subtract the premium of $7,986 from the $50,000 in interest payments, we get a net interest cost of $42,014 over the term of the bonds. These amounts for total interest cost agree with the figures in Illustration 17-7, found by subtracting total proceeds from total payments.

Interest Expense: Straight-Line Amortization of Discounts and Premiums

If bonds are issued at face value, recognizing interest expense is relatively straightforward. If Beta Corporation issues its 100, 10% bonds at face value on April 1, 19X1, it will pay $10,000 in interest payments on each subsequent March 31 for 5 years. Beta would make an entry like the following one on each interest payment date, starting with March 31, 19X2:

19X2			
Mar. 31	Interest Expense	10,000	
	Cash		10,000
	To record interest expense and annual interest payment on 10% bonds payable.		

If Beta issues the bonds at a discount or premium, it will recognize a greater or lesser amount of interest cost over the term of the bonds by the amount of the discount or premium. Thus, the amount of the discount or premium must be allocated (amortized) to the periods in the full term of the bonds. The simplest method of amortization is the straight-line method, which allocates an equal portion of the discount or premium to each period in the term of the bonds. In the case where the total discount at issue was $7,212, Beta would allocate $1,442 to each year ($7,210 ÷ 5). This allocation increases interest expense Beta recognizes and reduces the balance in Discount on Bonds Payable:

19X2			
Mar. 31	Interest Expense	11,442	
	Discount on Bonds Payable		1,442
	Cash		10,000
	To record interest expense, amortization of discount, and annual interest payment on 10% bonds payable.		

INSIGHTS INTO ACCOUNTING

Below is an advertisement, called a "tombstone," that appeared in *The Wall Street Journal* on May 23, 1994. It announces the issue of $100 million in senior subordinated debentures. Debentures are unsecured bonds. Holders of subordinated debentures have the usual rights of creditors to payments of their claims before owners receive any proceeds of liquidation of the assets of a corporation, but their claims come after the claims of other creditors. Notice that the advertisement contains a disclaimer that it is neither an offer to sell nor a solicitation of an offer to buy the debentures. Security regulations prevent sellers of new issues of securities from offering them for sale without providing the prospective buyers with a disclosure document, called a prospectus, that has been registered with the Securities and Exchange Commission. Notice that the offer price is quoted as 99.266% (of face or par value), which means that the debentures will be issued at a discount and the effective interest rate will be slightly higher than the stated interest rate of 11%. The four companies listed at the bottom of the advertisement are investment banking firms that are underwriting this issue of debentures. They will receive a percentage of the proceeds as a commission and they guarantee some minimum level of proceeds to the issuer.

This announcement is neither an offer to sell nor a solicitation of an offer to buy these securities.
The offer is made only by the Prospectus.

New Issue / May 23, 1994

$100,000,000

Santa Fe Energy Resources, Inc.

11% Senior Subordinated Debentures Due 2004

Price 99.266% and accrued interest, if any, from May 25, 1994

Copies of the Prospectus may be obtained in any State in which this
announcement is circulated only from such of the undersigned
as may legally offer these securities in such State.

Salomon Brothers Inc

Dillon, Read & Co. Inc.

Lazard Frères & Co.

Chemical Securities Inc.

After the first year's amortization of the discount, Beta would present the bonds issued at a discount in its balance sheet as follows:

Noncurrent liabilities		
10% bonds payable, due March 31, 19X6		
Face value	$100,000	
Less: Unamortized discount	5,770	$94,230

In the case where the total premium at issue was $7,986, Beta would allocate $1,597 per year ($7,986 ÷ 5). This allocation reduces Beta's interest expense and the balance in Premium on Bonds Payable thus:

19X2			
Mar. 31	Interest Expense	8,403	
	Premium on Bonds Payable	1,597	
	Cash		10,000
	To record interest expense, amortization of premium		
	and annual interest payment on 10% bonds payable.		

After the first year's amortization of the premium, Beta would present the bonds issued at a premium in its balance sheet as follows:

Noncurrent liabilities		
10% bonds payable, due March 31, 19X6		
Face value	$100,000	
Add: Unamortized premium	6,389	$106,389

In the case of both premiums and discounts, the straight-line method of amortization accomplishes two things. First, the sum of the interest expense amounts recognized in the periods in the term of the bonds equals the total interest cost over the term of the bonds. In Illustration 17-7, the total interest costs of bonds issued at a discount or at a premium is $57,212 or $42,014, respectively. The interest expense columns in Illustration 17-8 agree with these figures, based on adding the discount amortizations or subtracting the premium amortizations to interest paid, respectively.

Second, the discount or premium account balance is reduced to zero just at the time the principal amount is due. This is illustrated in the right-hand columns of the discount and premium panels of Illustration 17-8. As a consequence, whether bonds are issued at a premium, at a discount, or at face value, Beta's entry to record their retirement at full term is the same:

19X6			
Mar. 31	Bonds Payable	100,000	
	Cash		100,000
	To record payment at maturity of 10% bonds		
	payable.		

Interest Method of Amortization

The straight-line method not only is the simplest method of amortization, but for this reason, also is the most frequently used. However, it is not the most

ILLUSTRATION 17-8 Straight-Line Amortization of Bond Discount and Premium

		Discount Case		
Date	Interest Payment	Amortization	Interest Expense	Discount Balance
April 1, 19X1				$7,212
March 31, 19X2	$10,000	$1,442	$11,442	5,770
March 31, 19X3	10,000	1,442	11,442	4,328
March 31, 19X4	10,000	1,442	11,442	2,886
March 31, 19X5	10,000	1,442	11,442	1,444
March 31, 19X6	10,000	1,444	11,444	0
Totals	$50,000	$7,212	$57,212	

		Premium Case		
Date	Interest Payment	Amortization	Interest Expense	Discount Balance
April 1, 19X1				$7,986
March 31, 19X2	$10,000	$1,597	$ 8,403	6,389
March 31, 19X3	10,000	1,597	8,403	4,792
March 31, 19X4	10,000	1,597	8,403	3,195
March 31, 19X5	10,000	1,597	8,403	1,598
March 31, 19X6	10,000	1,598	8,402	0
Totals	$50,000	$7,986	$42,014	

theoretically correct or preferred method. The preferred method is called the effective interest method or just the "interest method." Under the **interest method of amortization**, all payments to bondholders are considered installments on a loan, whether they are interest or principal payments. *Interest expense is determined by applying the effective interest rate to the bonds' carrying value.* The difference between the interest payments and interest expense is the amount of amortization to be applied to bond discount or premium.

To illustrate, consider again Beta Corporation's 100, 5-year bonds with face values of $1,000 and interest of 10%, payable annually. Look at the numbers at the top of the Carrying Value columns of Panels A and B of Illustration 17-9. The numbers are the proceeds of issue or carrying values of the 10% bonds, assuming they were issued on April 1, 19X1, at a discount to yield 12% interest (carrying value of $92,788) or at a premium to yield 8% interest (carrying value of $107,986).

Panel A of Illustration 17-9 applies the interest method to the discount case. Under this method, Beta determines its interest expense for the year ended March 31, 19X2, by multiplying the effective interest rate of 12% times the carrying value of the bond liability as of April 1, 19X1. Thus, the first year interest expense is $11,135 ($92,788 x 12%). Since the interest payment is $10,000, more interest expense is recorded than is owed and paid. Beta recognizes the difference of $1,135 as the amount of the amortization of the discount for the first year. By reducing the discount by this amount, the carrying value of the debt is increased. In effect, the reduction of the discount adds *interest recorded but not paid* to the balance owed (carrying value) of the liability.

Beta then applies the 12% interest rate to the higher carrying value at March 31, 19X3, resulting in a higher interest expense ($11,271) in the second year. This pattern continues until the discount is fully amortized at the maturity date

ILLUSTRATION 17-9 Interest Method of Amortization

	Panel A: 10% Bonds Sold at a Discount to Yield 12%				
Date	Interest Expense	Interest Payment	Amortization of Discount	Unamoritized Discount	Carrying Value
April 1, 19X1				$7,212	$ 92,788
March 31, 19X2	$11,135	$10,000	$1,135	6,077	93,923
March 31, 19X3	11,271	10,000	1,271	4,806	95,194
March 31, 19X4	11,423	10,000	1,423	3,383	96,617
March 31, 19X5	11,594	10,000	1,594	1,789	98,211
March 31, 19X6	11,789	10,000	1,789	0	100,000
Total expense	$57,212				

	Panel B: 10% Bonds Sold at a Premium to Yield 8%				
Date	Interest Expense	Interest Payment	Amortization of Premium	Unamoritized Premium	Carrying Value
April 1, 19X1				$7,986	$107,986
March 31, 19X2	$ 8,639	$10,000	$1,361	6,625	106,625
March 31, 19X3	8,530	10,000	1,470	5,155	105,155
March 31, 19X4	8,412	10,000	1,588	3,567	103,567
March 31, 19X5	8,285	10,000	1,715	1,852	101,852
March 31, 19X6	8,148	10,000	1,852	0	100,000
Total expense	$42,014				

of the bonds. Total interest expense for the full term of the bonds ($57,212) is equal to the total payments less the proceeds of issue. Moreover, as the carrying value of the liability increases, interest expense increases commensurate with it.

Panel B illustrates the premium case. Beta determines its interest expense for the year ended March 31, 19X2, by multiplying 8% times the carrying value of the bond liability as of April 1, 19X1 ($8,639 = $107,986 x 8%). Since the interest payment is $10,000, Beta will accrue $1,361 less interest than is paid. The difference is the amount of the amortization of the premium for the first year. By reducing the premium by this amount, Beta decreases the debt's carrying value, reflecting the fact that a larger amount was paid than the interest expense recorded for the year.

Beta then applies the 8% interest rate to the lower carrying value at March 31, 19X3, resulting in a lower interest expense ($8,530) in the second year. This pattern continues until the premium is fully amortized at the maturity date of the bonds. Total interest expense for the full term of the bonds ($42,014) is equal to the total payments less the proceeds of issue. Moreover, as the carrying value of the liability decreases, interest expense decreases commensurate with it.

When the Straight-Line Method Is Acceptable

Although the interest method of expense recognition and discount amortization is preferred, it is sometimes acceptable to use the straight-line method. The straight-line method is acceptable unless the difference between the methods is material. A **material difference** in the amounts appearing in financial statements is one that could alter the decision of a qualified and informed individual who takes the care to analyze the financial statements. What is material in a particular case is a matter of judgment for those who prepare the business's financial statements. The differences between the two methods for the previous example are shown in Illustration 17-10. In this particular case, the maximum difference between the interest expense recognized in any given year under the two methods is $345—in the fifth year for the discount case. Since the total annual interest payment is $10,000, it appears unlikely that this difference would be judged material. Therefore, the straight-line method would probably be acceptable in this example.

ILLUSTRATION 17-10 Differences Between Straight-Line and Interest Methods of Amortization

Panel A: 10% Bonds Sold at a Discount to Yield 12%			
Year Ended	Interest Method*	Straight-Line*	Difference
March 31, 19X2	$1,135	$1,442	$307
March 31, 19X3	1,271	1,442	171
March 31, 19X4	1,423	1,442	19
March 31, 19X5	1,594	1,442	−152
March 31, 19X6	1,789	1,444	−345
Totals	$7,212	$7,212	$ 0

Panel B: 10% Bonds Sold at a Premium to Yield 8%			
Year Ended	Interest Method*	Straight-Line*	Difference
March 31, 19X2	$1,361	$1,597	$236
March 31, 19X3	1,470	1,597	127
March 31, 19X4	1,588	1,597	9
March 31, 19X5	1,715	1,597	−118
March 31, 19X6	1,852	1,598	−254
Totals	$7,986	$7,986	$ 0

*Minor differences due to rounding.

LO 6
Accrue interest expense and amortize discounts and premiums between interest payment dates, account for bond issue costs, and account for bonds issues between interest payment dates.

Accruing Interest Between Interest Payment Dates

To this point, we have considered only recognizing interest expense and amortizing discounts and premiums at the times interest payments are made. However, if financial statements are prepared at other dates in the bond issuer's fiscal year, we must accrue interest expense with an adjusting entry. Suppose, for example, that Beta Corporation, the issuer of the bonds described in Illustration 17-8, ends its fiscal year on December 31 instead of March 31. Beta will accrue interest for the first time on December 31, 19X1, for the 9-month period, April through December. Assuming straight-line amortization of the discount as in Illustration 17-8, interest expense for the 9-month period of $8,581.50 consists of two parts. First, Beta takes three-fourths of one year's interest payment, $7,500, and adds to it three-fourths of one year's amortization of discount, $1,081.50 ($1,442 x 3/4). Beta's adjusting entry is:

19X1			
Dec. 31	Interest Expense	8,581.50	
	Discount on Bonds Payable		1,081.50
	Interest Payable		7,500.00
	To accrue interest and amortize discount on		
	10% bonds payable.		

After the 9 month's amortization of the discount, Beta would disclose its bonds issued at a discount in its balance sheet as follows:

Noncurrent liabilities		
10% bonds payable, due March 31, 19X6		
Face value	$100,000.00	
Less: Unamortized discount	6,130.50	$93,869.50

For the period January through March, 19X2, Beta would recognize interest expense in two parts: one-fourth of the annual payment, $2,500, plus $360.50 ($1,442 x 1/4), for a total of $2,860.50. Beta's entry to recognize interest expense and the interest payment on March 31, 19X2, is:

19X2			
Mar. 31	Interest Expense	2,860.50	
	Interest Payable	7,500.00	
	Discount on Bonds Payable		360.50
	Cash		10,000.00
	To accrue interest, amortize discount, and record interest payment on 10% bonds payable.		

For the premium case, Beta would accrue interest on December 31 equal to three-fourths of the first year's interest payment less amortization of premium: $7,500 less $1,197.75 ($1,597 x 3/4), or $6,302.25. Beta's year-end accrual entry is:

19X1			
Dec. 31	Interest Expense	6,302.25	
	Premium on Bonds Payable	1,197.75	
	Interest Payable		7,500.00
	To accrue interest and amortize premium on 10% bonds payable.		

After the first year's amortization of the premium, Beta would show the bonds issued at a premium in its balance sheet as follows:

Noncurrent liabilities		
10% bonds payable, due March 31, 19X6		
Face value	$100,000.00	
Add: Unamortized premium	6,788.25	$106,788.25

For the period January through March, 19X2, Beta will recognize interest expense equal to the other one-fourth of its annual payment, $2,500, less $399.25, the remaining one-fourth of the first year's amortization of premium ($1,597 x 1/4), or $2,100.75. Beta's entry to recognize interest expense and the interest payment on March 31, 19X2, is:

19X2			
Mar. 31	Interest Expense	2,100.75	
	Interest Payable	7,500.00	
	Premium on Bonds Payable	399.25	
	Cash		10,000.00
	To accrue interest, amortize premium, and record interest payment on 10% bonds payable.		

Bond Issue Costs

Issuers usually incur some costs to issue bonds. These costs include costs of printing the bonds, registering them with the state or the Securities and Exchange Commission, advertising, etc. Issue costs represent part of the total cost of borrowing money from bondholders. Like interest costs, bond issue costs are recognized as expenses over the full term of the bonds. First, we record issue costs when they are incurred in a deferred expense account called Bond Issue Costs. A deferred expense account is a debit-balance account, customarily shown as an asset in the balance sheet. It is somewhat akin to prepaid expenses such as prepaid insurance. If, in the continuing example, Beta Corporation incurred issue costs of $6,600, it would record the costs initially with this entry:

19X1			
Apr. 1	Bond Issue Costs	6,600	
	Cash (or Vouchers Payable)		6,600
	To record issue costs on 10% bonds payable.		

Next, we recognize issue costs as expenses according to a simple rule of thumb: *Recognize issue costs as expense in the same periods and in proportion to interest expense.* Under the straight-line method of amortization, interest costs are recognized at a constant rate per year. Under this method, the bond issue costs would also be amortized on a straight-line basis. For the period from April through December, Beta should amortize three-fourths of one year's portion of its issue costs, or $990 (($6,600 ÷ 5) x 3/4). Beta's accrual entry is:

19X1			
Dec. 31	Bond Issue Expense	990	
	Bond Issue Costs		990
	To amortize issue costs on 10% bonds payable.		

Issuing Bonds Between Interest Payments

Because bonds are often issued in large numbers to many different buyers, it is inconvenient to make interest payments to different bondholders in unique amounts, covering different periods. This is especially true for coupon bonds, since the coupons are preprinted and are redeemable for uniform amounts of interest. Therefore, issuers customarily make the same interest payment on each payment date to each bondholder, regardless of whether the bondholder held the bonds for the full interval of payment. However, when bonds are issued between interest payments, the bondholder does not earn all the interest that will be paid at the first subsequent payment date. Thus, the issuer charges the bondholder at the time of bond purchase for any interest that has accrued from the last interest payment date.

Suppose Beta Corporation, whose bond indenture requires that it pay a full year's interest of $10,000 to its bondholders on March 31, 19X2, issues its bonds on July 1, 19X1, instead of April 1, 19X1. The bondholders should not receive $2,500 of the annual interest payment on March 31, 19X2—the amount that would have accrued for the period April through June, 19X1. To handle this difference between the annual interest payment and the amount to which the bondholders actually are entitled, Beta simply charges the bondholders in advance for interest through June 30, 19X1, at the time they buy the bonds (July 1). If the bondholders otherwise would have paid face value for the bonds, then they should actually pay face value plus accrued interest of $2,500. That is, the bondholders would pay $102,500 for the bonds, and Beta would record the transaction thus:

19X1			
July 1	Cash	102,500	
	Interest Expense		2,500
	Bonds Payable		100,000
	To record issue of 100, $1,000 bonds at face value plus accrued interest of $2,500.		

Notice that Beta credits the interest the bondholders paid to Interest Expense. At this point, the balance in Beta's Interest Expense, which is ordinarily a debit-balance account, is a credit of $2,500.

Beta's actual interest expense for the year ended December 31, 19X1, should be $5,000—interest on $100,000 at 10% for one-half year (July 1 to December 31). However, since the bondholders paid for $2,500 additional interest, Beta accrues a full three-fourths of one year's interest expense at December 31:

19X1			
Dec. 31	Interest Expense	7,500	
	Interest Payable		7,500
	To accrue interest expense on 10% bonds payable.		

The credit balance in Interest Expense of $2,500 from the previous entry is offset by this debit of $7,500. Between these two entries, Beta records $5,000 interest expense—the correct interest expense for 19X1. At the same time, Beta's Interest Payable balance is $7,500 from the entry above. This is composed of the $5,000 interest the bondholders earned plus the $2,500 of accrued interest they paid at the time of purchase. On March 31, 19X2, Beta accrues further interest expense and pays the bondholders their first interest payment, which is recorded as follows:

19X2			
Mar. 31	Interest Expense	2,500	
	Interest Payable	7,500	
	Cash		10,000
	To accrue interest expense and record the annual interest payment on 10% bonds payable.		

LO 7
Account for investments in bonds.

INVESTMENTS IN BONDS

The bonds of corporations and of certain government entities, including the federal government, are attractive investments because they provide fixed principal and interest payments to the investor. With the exception of so-called junk bonds, bonds as a class generally are less risky as investments than common stocks of corporations.

In general, businesses buy bonds for one of two reasons: as long-term investments or as short-term investments. Only by holding bonds to maturity can an investor realize the fixed schedule of interest or principal payments. If bonds are sold before maturity, the prices they bring—that is, their fair or market values—may be less or more than their carrying values, depending on whether current interest rates are higher or lower than the bonds' interest rates.

Thus, when bonds are bought and then sold before maturity, gains and losses usually arise.

Readily marketable bonds, such as those traded on the major securities exchanges, may be purchased as short-term or long-term investments. A controversy arises when such bonds are purchased and held while their market prices increase or decrease relative to their carrying values. Many accountants, financial analysts, and investors believe that, since ready market prices are available for such bonds, gains and losses should be recognized in each accounting period that the securities are held, as well as when they are finally sold or redeemed. Many companies that invest in bonds dispute this position, arguing that bonds can always be held to maturity and, therefore, the investor need not realize any gains or losses in market values over the terms of the bonds.

The FASB, in a recent pronouncement, basically recognized some merit in both arguments and struck a compromise between the two positions. The FASB's position requires investments in bonds to be classified into three categories that are accounted for by different methods:

1. Investments in bonds held to maturity
2. Investments in bonds available for sale
3. Short-term investments (trading securities)[1]

The accounting methods for bonds held to maturity and trading bonds represent two extremes. We will cover the two extremes first. Then, we will examine the way we account for bonds available for sale.

Investments in Bonds Held to Maturity

For bonds to be classified as **bonds held to maturity** the business must have a "positive intent and ability to hold those [bonds] to maturity."[2] That is, there must not be any foreseeable intent or need to sell the bonds to secure cash. Accounting for bonds that are held to maturity generally mirrors the issuing corporation's accounting.

Suppose Omega Corporation purchased all 100 of Beta Corporation's $1,000 face value, 10%, 5-year bonds on July 1, 19X1. Omega paid Beta $95,250 plus accrued interest of $2,500 for the bonds and recorded the transaction thus:

19X1			
July 1	Investment in Beta Bonds	95,250	
	Interest Revenue	2,500	
	Cash		97,750
	To record purchase of Beta Corporation bonds at a discount plus accrued interest.		

Unlike the issuer of bonds, the purchaser does not use a discount account but records the bonds in the investment account at net cost or carrying value (including brokerage fees or other costs, if any). The bonds would be shown in the investments section of Omega's balance sheet at carrying value:

Investments:
   Beta Corporation 10% bonds purchased at a discount $92,250

---

[1] "Accounting for Certain Investments in Debt and Equity Securities," *Statement of Financial Accounting Standards No. 115* (Norwalk, CT: FASB, May 1993), par. 6.

[2] *Ibid.*, par. 7.

The accrued interest Omega purchased at July 1 is not part of its cost of the long-term investment. Omega debits its Interest Revenue for $2,500, giving that normally credit-balance account a temporary debit balance.

Assuming Omega's fiscal year ends on December 31, 19X1, it would accrue additional interest revenue and amortize a portion of the discount on the bonds. The discount on the bonds is $4,750($100,000 − $95,250). Assuming the straight-line method of amortization is used, Omega should amortize $1,000 per year ($4,750 ÷ 4.75 years). Omega will accrue interest revenue through December at three-fourths of the annual interest payment (from April 1 to December 31), $7,500, plus one-half of the annual discount amortization, $500:

19X1			
Dec. 31	Interest Receivable	7,500	
	Investment in Beta Bonds	500	
	Interest Revenue		8,000
	To accrue interest revenue and amortize discount		
	through year-end on Beta Corporation bonds.		

This entry brings the Interest Revenue balance to $5,500:

Interest accrued through December 31	$7,500	
Less: Accrued interest paid at July 1	2,500	$5,000
Amortization of discount (July 1–December 31)		500
Interest revenue (July 1–December 31)		$5,500

On March 31, 19X2, when it receives the first interest payment from Beta, Omega makes the following entry to record the receipt and another one-fourth year's interest accrual ($2,500) and amortization ($250):

19X2			
Mar. 31	Cash	10,000	
	Investment in Beta Bonds	250	
	Interest Receivable		7,500
	Interest Revenue		2,750
	To accrue interest revenue, amortize discount and		
	record interest received on Beta Corporation bonds.		

Assuming Omega holds the Beta Corporation bonds to maturity, the discount will be fully amortized and the bonds' carrying value will be the face value of $100,000 at the receipt of the final payment from Beta. When the bonds held to maturity are within one year of maturity, Omega should reclassify them as current assets in the balance sheet.

Investments in Bonds as Trading Securities

Trading securities are those purchased and held for resale in the short-term. The objective of short-term investments in trading securities is not so much to earn interest (dividends) on these securities as to realize gains due to market price increases. Short-term investments are always classified as current assets in the balance sheet. Bonds purchased as short-term investments are initially recorded at their purchase costs, including brokerage fees and commissions. Interest revenue is recognized on the face amount of the bonds at the stated interest rate. The major difference in accounting for short-term investments in bonds is that at the end of each accounting period, their carrying values are compared to their current market values, and the unrealized gains and losses in value are recognized as if they are realized gains and losses.

Suppose Geneva Corporation buys the following bonds on July 1, 19X1, for purposes of holding them for a short period and reselling them for gains:

100, $1,000, 8% bonds of Paris, Inc., due December 31, 19X5, for $100,000
100, $1,000, 9% bonds of Rome Corp., due December 31, 19X3, for $97,107

Both of these companies' bonds pay interest semiannually on June 30 and December 31. Geneva could record the investments in one entry as follows:

19X1			
July 1	Investment in Paris, Inc. Bonds	100,000	
	Investment in Rome Corp. Bonds	97,107	
	Cash		197,107
	To record purchase of Paris, Inc. and Rome Corp. bonds as short-term investments.		

On December 31, 19X1, Geneva recognizes interest revenue with the following entries:

19X1			
Dec. 31	Cash	4,000	
	Interest Revenue		4,000
	To record interest received from Paris, Inc.		
	Cash	4,500	
	Interest Revenue		4,500
	To record interest received from Rome Corp. and amortization of discount at purchase of bonds.		

Now, assume interest rates have fallen slightly since July 1. Based on present value reasoning, if interest rates fall, the market values of bonds with fixed payment schedules should increase. Because increases and decreases in interest rates tend to affect all bonds in the same way, bond prices tend to rise and fall together—more so than stock prices. A comparison of the carrying values and current market values of the Paris, Inc. and Rome Corp. bonds as of December 31 shows the following:

	Carrying Value	Current Market Value	Increase (Decrease)
Paris, Inc. 10% bonds	$100,000	$101,632	$1,632
Rome Corp. 9% bonds	97,107	98,721	1,614
	$197,686	$200,353	$3,246

Geneva would record the unrealized holding gains with the following journal entry:

19X1			
Dec. 31	Investment in Paris, Inc. Bonds	1,632	
	Investment in Rome Corp. Bonds	1,614	
	Unrealized Gain (Loss) from Investments		3,246
	To record unrealized gains on trading securities.		

Unrealized Gain (Loss) from Investments is closed to Income Summary and, therefore, is included in the current period's income on the income statement. In addition, the bonds' carrying values are now their market values as of December 31, 19X1.

Now, assume that on February 1, 19X2, Geneva sells the Paris bonds for $103,000. It records the sale as follows:

19X2			
Feb. 1	Cash	103,000	
	Investment in Paris, Inc. Bonds		101,632
	Gain on Sale of Investments		1,368
	To record unrealized gains on trading securities.		

Notice that only the incremental amount above the December 31 market value of the bonds is recognized as an additional gain on the sale of the bonds.

Investments in Bonds Available for Sale

If bonds are not held to maturity or held for short-term trading, the FASB considers them to be **bonds available for sale**. That is, they could be liquidated at any time, but they may not be, depending on circumstances. Bonds available for sale should be classified as current if they will mature within a year (or longer operating cycle) or if management intends to sell them within that period. We account for investments in securities available for sale in a manner similar to short-term investments. However, we amortize discounts and premiums, and we do not include unrealized gains and losses in current income. Referring to Geneva's transactions in the Paris, Inc. and Rome Corp. bonds, assume Geneva did not purchase the bonds as short-term investments and is not holding them to maturity. Interest revenue from the Rome bonds would consist of $4,500 interest received plus $579 amortization of discount on a straight-line basis. The increase in the carrying value of the bonds from amortization of the discount decreases the unrealized gain. Geneva's December 31 entry to record the increase in their market values is:

19X1			
Dec. 31	Investment in Paris, Inc. Bonds	1,632	
	Investment in Rome Corp. Bonds	1,035	
	Unrealized Gain (Loss) from Available for Sale Securities		2,667
	To record unrealized gains on bond investments.		

Unlike the case of short-term investments, Unrealized Gain (Loss) from Available for Sale Securities is not a temporary account that is closed to Income Summary. Instead, it is a permanent (valuation) account in owners' equity. Thus, the unrealized gains and losses on securities available for sale are not included in current income.

When the Paris, Inc. bonds are sold on February 1, Geneva makes the following entry:

19X2			
Feb. 1	Cash	103,000	
	Unrealized Gain (Loss) from Available for Sale Securities	1,632	
	Investment in Paris, Inc. Bonds		101,632
	Gain from Sale of Investments		3,000
	To record unrealized gains on trading securities.		

Notice that we clear the previous gain in market value recorded in Unrealized Gain (Loss) with this entry (debit of $1,632). We also recognize the entire cumulative gain between cost and selling price at the time of sale, when the gain becomes a realized gain. This treatment contrasts to the inclusion in current income of previous unrealized holding gains in the case of short-term investments in bonds.

LO 8

Explain the difference between capital leases and operating leases.

LEASE OBLIGATIONS

Businesses often lease (rent) assets rather than purchasing them. Virtually any asset a business might use can be leased as well as purchased. Major airlines often lease the aircraft that are their primary means of providing services to their customers. Some businesses even lease the potted plants they use to decorate their premises.

By leasing assets, businesses may avoid some or all of the risks of ownership such as obsolescence and costs of maintenance. They also avoid the necessity of raising the funds required to purchase the assets.

Types of Leases

Leases may be short-term (less than one year) or long-term. They may also be operating leases or capital leases. **Operating leases** are short-term or long-term leases that involve strictly renting assets for use in the lessee's (renter's) business. No special rights or privileges are acquired, and the lessor (owner) bears all of the risks of ownership. **Capital leases** are long-term leases that involve the lessee's acquisition of at least some significant ownership rights and obligations, in addition to the use of the assets over the term of the lease.

Operating Leases.   An operating lease agreement does not represent many formidable challenges to accountants. The major problem is to allocate rent payments as expenses to the periods covered by the lease arrangement. Suppose, for example, that Gamma Corporation rents a computer for 2 years under a lease calling for advance rent of $1,800 plus rent payments of $150 per month. The computer's owner (lessor), Alpha Computers, agrees under the lease to maintain the computer and to pay for all parts and labor required to keep it in satisfactory working condition.

The total rent expense for the 2-year lease is $5,400 ($1,800 + $3,600), or an average of $225 per month. A key question in allocating a portion of the total rent expense to each month is the pattern of benefits expected from the rented asset(s). In this case, assume the computer is expected to benefit Gamma's business equally in each of the 24 months the lease covers. This implies that an equal amount of rent should be recognized as expense in each month.

First, Gamma recognizes the initial payment of $1,800 as prepaid rent, thus:

(Date)	Prepaid Rent	1,800	
	Cash		1,800
	To record prepayment of rent under operating lease agreement.		

Then, each month Gamma pays the monthly rent and amortizes the prepaid rent to recognize $225 of total rent expense. Gamma's entries for each month is of this form:

(Date)	Rent Expense	225	
	Cash		150
	Prepaid Rent		75
	To record rent expense and amortize prepaid rent.		

At the end of the 2 years, the operating lease will have expired, the Prepaid Rent balance will be zero, Gamma will return the computer to the owner and will have no further rights or obligations under the operating lease.

Capital Leases. Although many leases simply involve the lessees' renting of assets, accountants have long recognized that some leases are *in substance* purchases of assets.[3] Such leases, called capital leases, are effectively the same as the "rent-to-own" arrangements appliance and furniture stores offer to consumers. Instead of involving only the temporary use of assets for rental fees, the lessee (renter) also acquires some property rights over the course of the lease. Whether a particular lease is a rental agreement or a special kind of purchase is a matter of judgment. Thus, different accountants and managers might come to different conclusions about any given lease. As a result, the Financial Accounting Standards Board has set forth criteria, any one (or more) of which identify a lease as a capital lease. The criteria may be *paraphrased* as follows:[4]

1. The lease transfers the ownership of the property to the lessee by the end of the lease term.
2. The lease contains an option to purchase the assets at less than their expected fair value at the end of the term of the lease.
3. The lease term is equal to 75% or more of the estimated remaining economic life of the leased property.
4. At the beginning of the lease term, the present value of the minimum lease payments equals or exceeds 90% of the fair value of the leased property to the lessor at the start of the lease term.[5]

Accounting for Capital Leases

LO 9

Account for the assets and liabilities recognized under capital leases.

Now, suppose Gamma Corporation leases a computer on January 1, 19X1, for 5 years at an annual rental of $2,000. At the end of the lease term, the computer becomes Gamma's property. This lease arrangement conforms to Criterion 1 and must be accounted for as a capital lease. Accounting for capital leases roughly approximates the accounting that would be accorded an asset that is financed entirely with borrowed funds. Assume Gamma can borrow funds over 5 years at an interest rate of, say, 12%. From Table 2 in Appendix C, we see that the present value of each $1 paid annually for 5 years at 12% is 3.605. Thus, the lease is equivalent to borrowing $7,210 ($2,000 x 3.605) and spending the proceeds of the loan on the computer.

The capital lease treatment requires that the computer be recognized as an asset and the lease obligation be recognized as a liability. Gamma's journal entry to recognize initially both the asset and liability in this case is:

---

[3]"Accounting for Leases," *Statement of Financial Accounting Standards No. 13* (Stamford, CT: FASB, 1976), paras. 61 and 63.

[4]*Ibid.*, para. 7.

[5]Note: Criteria 3 and 4 apply only if more than 25% of the asset's estimated total economic life remains at the start of the lease term.

19X1			
Jan. 1	Equipment Under Capital Lease	7,210	
	Long-Term Lease Payable		7,210
	To record acquisition of a computer under a		
	long-term capital lease agreement.		

Assets Leased Under Capital Leases. Once Gamma makes the above entry, the computer is depreciated just as it would be if it had been purchased for cash. That is, depreciation is recognized according to the method Gamma uses for any similar asset. Assuming a useful life of 6 years, expected residual value of $1,000, and straight-line depreciation, Gamma recognizes depreciation expense of $1,035 (($7,210 − $1,000) ÷ 6) each year. At the end of the first year, the asset would appear in Gamma's balance sheet thus:

Property, plant, and equipment:
    Equipment leased under capital lease $7,210
    Less: Accumulated depreciation   1,035 $6,175

Capital Lease Liabilities. The lease obligation is treated just like other long-term installment obligations such as the long-term notes illustrated earlier in the chapter. Illustration 17-11 summarizes the history of the lease liability.

ILLUSTRATION 17-11 History of a Capital Lease Liability

Year	Balance Jan. 1	+	Annual Interest Expense	−	Annual Payment	=	Balance Dec. 31
19X1	$7,210.00		$865.20		$2,000.00		$6,075.20
19X2	6,075.20		729.02		2,000.00		4,804.22
19X3	4,804.22		576.51		2,000.00		3,380.73
19X4	3,380.73		405.69		2,000.00		1,786.42
19X5	1,786.42		213.58		2,000.00		0.00

At the beginning of 19X1, the lease liability equals $7,210, the present value of the payments of the five, $2,000 lease installments. The liability would be disclosed in two parts in the January 1 balance sheet as follows:

Current liabilities:
    Current portion of long-term lease $1,786.00
Noncurrent liabilities:
    Long-term lease $5,424.00

The current portion of the liability is the present value of the $2,000 payment due on December 31, 19X1 ($2,000 x .8929 = $1,786). The noncurrent portion is the present value of the remaining four payments ($7,210 − $1,786 = $5,424).

The interest in any year of the lease is equal to the beginning carrying value times the interest rate used to determine the liability's original present value (12%). During 19X1, Gamma accrues a total of $865.20 in interest expense

($7,210 x 12%). Gamma's entries to accrue the interest and pay the annual installment are:

19X1			
Dec. 31	Interest Expense—Long-Term Lease	865.20	
	Long-Term Lease Payable		865.20
	To accrue interest on long-term capital lease.		
31	Long-Term Lease Payable	2,000.00	
	Cash		2,000.00
	To record annual payment on long-term capital lease.		

According to the first line of Illustration 17-11, the net effect of these two entries is to reduce the principal amount of Gamma's liability by $1,134.80, the difference between the accrued interest and the lease payment. The reduction in principal leaves a new balance as of December 31, 19X1, of $6,075.20. To calculate approximately the same balance, we can multiply the payment amount times the annuity factor from Table 2 in Appendix C for 4 years at 12%: $2,000 x 3.037 = $6,074. This new balance would appear in the December 31, 19X1, balance sheet as follows:

Current liabilities	
Current portion of long-term lease	$1,786.00
Noncurrent liabilities	
Long-term lease	$4,289.20

LO 10

Calculate and interpret the debt-equity ratio as an indicator of potential financial distress, and recognize its limitations when off-balance-sheet financing is used.

DEBT-EQUITY RATIO AND OFF-BALANCE-SHEET FINANCING

Let us return to Miklos Kronis' problem of financing $100,000 of new equipment for Midwestern Alliance Corporation. Miklos has asked the supplier about the possibility of acquiring the equipment under either an operating or capital lease; he has talked to the company's commercial bank about a long-term installment loan, which will require $2,000 in various loan-origination costs; and he has consulted an investment banker about issuing bonds. He now focuses on financing the equipment over a 5-year period. Five years balances off the equipment's expected useful life (10 years) against the risk of early obsolescence. Miklos definitely dislikes still having to pay for assets after they are no longer useful.

Miklos rules out issuing bonds, because the registration process will take too long and the issuing costs will be high. Midwestern Alliance can borrow long-term funds at 9% annual interest. The cash payments for the other three options and their present values (at the 9% interest rate) are shown in Illustration 17-12. Payments in Illustration 17-12 on the line labeled End of Year 0 should be interpreted as payments at the beginning of Year 1. Notice that, in effect, the lease alternatives require that the major annual payments start immediately; whereas only the loan origination costs will be required immediately under the installment note alternative.

ILLUSTRATION 17-12 Comparative Cash Payments and Present Values

End of Year	Present Value of $1	Installment Note		Capital Lease		Operating Lease	
		Cash Payments	Present Value	Cash Payments	Present Value	Cash Payments	Present Value
0	1.0000	$ 2,000	$ 2,000	$ 24,000	$ 24,000	$ 21,000	$21,000
1	.9174	25,500	23,394	24,000	22,018	21,000	19,266
2	.8417	25,500	21,463	24,000	20,200	21,000	17,675
3	.7722	25,500	19,691	24,000	18,532	21,000	16,216
4	.7084	25,500	18,065	24,000	17,002	21,000	14,877
5	.6499	25,500	16,573		0		0
Totals		$129,500	$101,186	$120,000	$101,752	$105,000	$89,034

According to the calculations in Illustration 17-12, the operating lease has the lowest present value—meaning the lowest equivalent cost of the equipment in present cash-equivalent terms. However, Miklos expects the equipment to be worth at least $25,000 at the end of 5 years ($16,248 in present value terms) and to have perhaps as many as 5 additional years of useful life. Under the operating lease, the company will have to return the equipment to the supplier at the end of the 5-year lease. Thus, in pure economic terms, Miklos prefers either the installment note or the capital lease. Although either the note or capital lease will cost about $12,000 more than the operating lease in present value terms, at the end of 5 years, the company will own the equipment. Since the residual value of the equipment is over $16,000 in present value terms, the loan and capital lease are the better forms of financing. Miklos further prefers the loan, because it requires only $2,000 in "up-front" costs, whereas the capital and operating leases require a full year's payment of $24,000 and $21,000, respectively, upon delivery of the equipment.

However, before making a final decision on a financing plan, Miklos must consider the effects of the plans on Midwestern's debt-equity ratio. Therefore, as soon as he was faced with the equipment acquisition issue, he asked the Accounting Department to prepare the balance sheet in Illustration 17-13.

Debt-Equity Ratio

The **debt-equity ratio**, defined below, is one of the most popular financial indicators.

$$\text{Debt-Equity Ratio} = \frac{\text{Total Liabilities}}{\text{Total Stockholders' Equity}}$$

The debt-equity ratio most directly measures the relationship between the business's debt financing and equity financing. The more a business relies on debt, the higher its ratio will be. Also, the more a business relies on debt, the more fixed payment obligations it has and the higher the probability that it might not be able to pay all of its bills. Therefore, the debt-equity ratio is considered an indicator of potential financial distress or insolvency. Creditors often use the debt-equity ratio to restrict a borrower's tendency to overuse debt and to risk insolvency—as the bank has done to Midwestern Alliance Corporation.

Recall that under its revolving line of credit agreement with the bank, Midwestern may not let its debt-equity ratio exceed 1.0. Based on its balance

ILLUSTRATION 17-13 Midwestern Alliance Balance Sheet

Midwestern Alliance Corporation Balance Sheet		
Assets		
Current assets:		
Cash		$ 40,000
Accounts receivable		60,000
Inventory		50,000
Prepaid expenses		5,000
Total current assets		$155,000
Property, plant, and equipment	$900,000	
Less: Accumulated depreciation	400,000	500,000
Total assets		$655,000
Liabilities and Stockholders' Equity		
Current liabilities:		
Accounts payable		$ 30,000
Notes payable		80,000
Wages and salaries payable		10,000
Taxes payable		5,000
Total current liabilities		$125,000
Noncurrent liabilities		175,000
Total liabilities		$300,000
Stockholders' equity:		
Capital stock		$ 20,000
Paid-in capital in excess of par		200,000
Retained earnings		135,000
Total stockholders' equity		$355,000
Total liabilities and stockholders' equity		$655,000

sheet in Illustration 17-13, before the equipment acquisition, Midwestern's debt equity ratio is .845:

$$\text{Debt-Equity Ratio} = \frac{\$300,000}{\$355,000} = .845$$

However, if Midwestern acquires the equipment with the long-term installment loan or the capital lease, at least $77,752 of new debt will be recorded (the present value of the 4 remaining payments under the capital lease). That would change Midwestern's debt-equity ratio to 1.064.

$$\text{Debt-Equity Ratio} = \frac{\$377,752}{\$355,000} = 1.064$$

Thus, the installment loan and the capital lease arrangement are infeasible under Midwestern's line of credit agreement with its bank. Midwestern can acquire the equipment only through the operating lease arrangement under which no new debt will show up on its balance sheet.

Off-Balance-Sheet Financing

By acquiring the equipment under an operating lease, Midwestern is accepting an economically less favorable arrangement just to avoid having debt financing show up on its balance sheet (and be included in calculating its debt-equity ratio). This is an example of off-balance-sheet financing. **Off-balance-sheet financing** is any scheme or system through which a business effectively acquires or retains property rights in assets without showing the assets or a source of funds on its balance sheet. In the extreme form of off-balance-sheet financing, companies work with suppliers or other creditors specifically to structure leases and other arrangements so they need not be recognized as debt obligations. The purpose is to present to the world a balance sheet with less debt. If analysts of their financial statements are not careful, they will underestimate those companies' risks of financial distress. For example, is Midwestern Alliance Corporation less likely to have financial difficulty under the operating lease than under the installment loan or capital lease? Probably not. In fact, Midwestern must make annual rent payments that are only marginally less than those for the capital lease and installment loan payments. If it is unable to make a rent payment, Midwestern will lose the equipment, which is essential to its ongoing operations. Thus, because of off-balance-sheet financing, the debt-equity ratio is limited in its ability to measure a company's exposure to financial distress due to debt obligations.

SUMMARY

Account for long-term notes with constant principal payments. When a company issues a long-term note with constant principal payments, accounting for the note is straightforward. Interest payable and interest expense are accrued on financial statement dates, and further interest and payments are recorded on payment dates. Payments include a constant amount of principal and a declining interest component due to the effect of the principal payments.

Find the present value of an amount to be received in some future period, calculate the present value of a long-term note, and account for the note from issue to maturity. When a single-payment note is issued for an asset whose value cannot be determined independently, then the note's current cash equivalent value must be derived using present value calculations (or tables). If the note's term to maturity spans more than one year, interest should be accrued or amortized on a compound-interest basis rather than on a straight-line basis. Compound interest calculations lead to a pattern of increasing interest accruals. Interest is accrued in one period on the original principal plus all previously accrued interest. As the discount on a note is amortized, the carrying value increases, increasing the base for calculating subsequent interest and amortizations.

Find the amount of the constant payments required to pay off an installment note, and account for installment notes from issue to maturity. Installment notes present all the problems of multiple-year notes plus some. Specifically, it is necessary to determine the exact constant payment amount that will pay off the installment note in the specified period at the specified interest rate. It is also necessary to calculate the portion of each installment payment that is interest and the implicit amount of payment of the note's principal. With each payment, the principal portion reduces the note's principal. As a consequence, over the term to maturity of an installment note, the interest portion of each payment declines and the principal portion increases.

Describe the important features of bonds businesses issue as a form of borrowing; explain why some bonds are issued at face value, some at discounts, and some at premiums and record issues of bonds. Bonds are a major source of debt financing, especially for large corporations. Bonds are debt obligations represented by securities that holders can exchange. Bearer bonds can be exchanged without notifying the issuer; whereas registered bonds can be exchanged only by returning them to the issuer and having them reissued to the new owner. Serial bonds are paid off in a series of retirements over a period of years and have the characteristics of installment loans to the issuer. The bond indenture is the agreement between the issuer and all holders of a particular issue of bonds. The indenture sets forth the full term of the bonds and the stated, nominal, or coupon rate of interest. When the market rate is less than the coupon rate of interest, buyers are willing to pay more than face value for the bonds; and they sell at a premium such that they yield the market rate on the higher carrying value. When the market rate is greater than the coupon rate of interest, buyers are unwilling to pay face value for the bonds; and they sell at a discount such that they yield the market rate on the lower carrying value. Bonds are recorded in the bond liability account at face value, and the premium or discount is recorded in a separate valuation account or contra-liability account, respectively.

Calculate total interest cost of bond issues and record interest expense, including amortization of discounts and premiums using the straight-line and interest methods. When bonds are issued at a discount or premium, the bonds are valued at face value plus any premium or minus any discount. Total interest expense equals the interest payments plus any discount or minus any premium. The discount or premium is amortized—most commonly according to the straight-line method. To recognize interest expense in each period, the total discount or premium is divided by the number of periods to maturity of the bonds to determine the amount of amortization. Then the amount of amortization is added to or subtracted from the interest payment for a period to determine the interest expense for the period. Under the interest method, the effective interest rate is found by determining the rate that equates the present value of the bonds' interest and principal payments to the proceeds from issue. This rate is applied to the beginning-of-period carrying value of the bonds to determine interest expense for the period. The difference between interest expense and the interest payment is the amount of discount or premium amortized. If the difference between methods is immaterial, a business may use the simpler straight-line method to amortize discounts and premiums.

Accrue interest expense and amortize discounts and premiums between interest payment dates, account for bond issue costs, and account for bonds issues between interest payment dates. When financial statements fall between payment dates, proportional amounts of the payments and amortizations are accrued on the financial statement dates. Bond issue costs are recognized at issue as prepaid expenses and are amortized over the remaining term of the bonds in proportion to interest expense. When bonds are issued between interest payment dates, the issuer charges the buyers the interest that has accrued since the last payment, records this amount as a credit to interest expense, and then pays and debits interest expense for the full payment next due.

Account for investments in bonds. Accounting for investments in bonds differs, depending on the bonds' classification as: held to maturity, short-term, or available for sale. Buyers account for investments in bonds held to maturity in a way that virtually mirrors the issuers' recognition of interest payments and amortizations of premiums and discounts. The only exception is that buyers recognize the bonds' carrying value in a single account—no discount or premium accounts are used. Holders of short-term investments in bonds purchase them for short-term resale and short-term gains. They account for interest earned at face value of the bonds times the stated interest rate. However, in addition, they add (deduct) increases (decreases) in the market values of the bonds to their carrying values and recognize these unrealized gains (losses) as current income. In contrast, bonds available for sale (not bought for short-term trading or for holding to maturity) are accounted for in a third way. They are treated similarly to short-term investments. However, the unrealized gains and losses are not closed to Income Summary or included in current income. Instead, the unrealized gains and losses are accumulated in an owners' equity account. When the securities are sold, their previous unrealized gains (losses) are reversed from this account and included in an overall realized gain or loss that is included in current income.

Explain the difference between capital leases and operating leases. Leases have become increasingly popular as a means of acquiring needed assets. Assets are provided strictly for the lessee's temporary use under an operating lease in exchange for rent payments, possibly including advance payments. The only problem in accounting for such leases, known as operating leases, is to recognize rent paid as expense according to the benefits derived from the leased assets. This generally requires that advanced rent payments be set up in a prepaid rent account and amortized over the life of the lease. On the other hand, capital leases involve acquisition of at least some property rights in the leased assets.

Account for the assets and liabilities recognized under capital leases. When assets are acquired under a capital lease, the assets and the capital lease liability are valued at the present value of the lease payments. The asset is then amortized (depreciated) in the same way other similar assets in the business would be amortized (depreciated). And the lease is treated like other long-term, installment liabilities.

Calculate and interpret the debt-equity ratio as an indicator of potential financial distress, and recognize its limitations when off-balance-sheet financing is used. The debt-equity ratio is one of the most popular financial indicators.

$$\text{Debt-Equity Ratio} = \frac{\textbf{Total Liabilities}}{\textbf{Total Stockholders' Equity}}$$

The more a business relies on debt, the higher its ratio will be. Also, the more a business relies on debt, the more fixed payment obligations it has and the higher the probability that it might not be able to pay all of its bills. Therefore, the debt-equity ratio is considered an indicator of potential financial distress or insolvency. However, when companies work with suppliers or other creditors specifically to structure leases and other arrangements so they need not be recognized as debt obligations, the debt-equity ratio is limited in its ability to measure a company's exposure to financial distress. Analysts should, therefore, be aware of off-balance-sheet financing and take it into account separately.

◼ REVIEW PROBLEM A

J. M. Hobart Company has arranged to borrow $50,000 from a bank on October 1, 19X4 in exchange for an installment note payable to the bank. The note, repayable in 10 semi-annual installments over 5 years, carries an interest rate of 8%, compounded semiannually. Hobart's fiscal year-end is December 31.

REQUIRED:

a. Calculate the amount of each of Hobart's 10 semiannual note payments.
b. Prepare the journal entry to accrue interest expense as of December 31, 19X4.
c. Prepare the journal entry to recognize interest expense and payment when the first semiannual note payment is due.

SOLUTION:

Planning and Organizing Your Work

1. Find the amount of the installment payments by first finding the annuity factor for 10 periods at the appropriate interest rate. In this case, the stated interest rate is an *annual* rate of 8%, but the payments are due and interest is compounded *semiannualy*. Thus, you should divide the annual rate by 2 to get the appropriate semiannual rate of 4%. The annuity factor will be at the intersection of the row for 10 periods (n) and the column for 4% compound interest in Table 2, Appendix C. Then find the amount of an installment by dividing the amount of the loan by the annuity factor.

2. Find the interest expense for 6 months of the loan (one semiannual period) by multiplying the interest rate of 4% by the balance of the loan at the beginning to the period, in this case $50,000. For accrual purposes, the amount of the semiannual interest expense may be allocated proportionately to sub-periods within payment periods. Since the period from October 1, to December 31, is 3 months, accrue one-half of the 6-month interest amount at December 31, crediting Interest Payable.

3. Use one entry to accrue an additional 3-month's interest and recognize the first payment on March 31, 19X5. Credit Cash for the amount of the payment. Debit Interest Expense for the additional interest, Interest Payable for the previously accrued interest, and Note Payable—Noncurrent for the difference between the sum of the two interest amounts and the payment amount.

(a) *Calculate the amount of each of the payments.*

The annuity factor in Table 2, Appendix C, for 10 periods at a rate of 4% is 8.111. The amount of a payment is:

$$PMT = \frac{\$50,000}{8.111} = \$6,165$$

(b) *Prepare the journal entry to accrue interest expense as of December 31, 19X4.*

Interest expense=$50,000 x 4% ÷ 2=$1,000

19X4			
Dec. 31	Interest Expense	1,000	
	Interest Payable		1,000
	To accrue interest expense as of year end on installment note payable.		

(c) *Prepare the journal entry to recognize interest expense and payment when the first semiannual note payment is due.*

19X5			
Mar. 31	Interest Payable	1,000	
	Interest Expense	1,000	
	Notes Payable—Noncurrent	4,165	
	Cash		6,165
	To accrue interest expense and record payment on installment note payable.		

REVIEW PROBLEM B

On January 2, 19X1, Day Company issued 1,000, $1,000 face value, 8% bonds that pay interest annually on December 31 of each year for 5 years. Crandall Company purchased the entire bond issue with an effective interest rate of 10%.

REQUIRED:

a. Calculate the price of the bonds when issued.
b. Record Day Company's issuance of the bonds.
c. Record Day Company's interest expense and amortization of discount for 19X1 and 19X2, using the straight-line method.
d. Record the interest expense and amortization of discount for 19X1 and 19X2, using the interest method.
e. Record Crandall Company's investment in the bonds.
f. Record the interest revenue and amortization of discount for 19X1 if Crandall classified the bonds as held to maturity.
g. Assuming Crandall classifies the bonds as short-term investments, record the interest revenue, and unrealized holding gain for 19X1. The bonds have a market value of $945,000 on December 31, 19X1.
h. Assuming Crandall classifies the bonds as available for sale, record the interest revenue, amortization of discount, and unrealized holding gain for 19X1. The bonds have a market value of $945,000 on December 31, 19X1.

SOLUTION:

Planning and Organizing Your Work

1. Determine the bonds' annual cash flows and multiply the cash flows times 10% present value factors for the appropriate time periods. Sum the discounted cash flows.
2. Record the bonds' issuance by debiting cash for the amount determined in Step 1, crediting Bonds Payable at face value and debiting the difference to the discount account.
3. Calculate the annual amortization of the discount by dividing the total discount by the outstanding life of the bond issue. Record the amortization of the discount and the payment of interest. The amortization of the discount plus the cash paid for interest equals the debit to Interest Expense. The amounts are the same for both years since the straight-line method is used..
4. Multiply the bond's carrying value at the beginning of 19X1 and 19X2 by the effective interest rate of 10% to determine the interest expense for each year. Record the payment of interest for each year. The difference between interest expense and the interest payment is credited to the bond discount account for each year.
5. Record the investment in bonds. Debit Investments in Bonds and credit Cash for the amount computed in Step 1.
6. Compute interest revenue by the same procedure as in Step 4. Record interest revenue and the collection of interest. The difference between interest revenue and interest collected is added to the debit balance in Investments in Bonds.

712

PART 1 FINANCIAL ACCOUNTING

7. Follow the procedures in Step 6 for bond investments classified as short-term; but ignore amortization. Adjust (debit) the investment account by the increase in market value after you record interest and amortization. Credit Unrealized Gain (Loss) from Investments.
8. Follow the procedures in Step 6 for bond investments classified as available for sale. Adjust (debit) the investment account by the increase in market value after you record interest and amortization. Credit Unrealized Gain (Loss) from Available-for-Sale Securities (a component of stockholders' equity).

(a) *Calculate the price of the bonds.*

December 31	Payment*	10% Present Value Factor	Present Value
19X1	$ 80,000	0.9091	$ 72,728
19X2	80,000	0.8264	66,112
19X3	80,000	0.7513	60,104
19X5	80,000	0.6830	54,640
19X6	80,000	0.6209	49,672
19X6	1,000,000	0.6209	620,900
Total present value			$924,156

*1,000 bonds x $1,000 x 8%

(b) *Record the issuance of the bond on January 2, 19X1.*

Discount on bonds = $100,000 − $924,156 = $75,844

19X1			
Jan. 2	Cash	924,156	
	Discount on Bonds Payable	75,844	
	Bonds Payable		1,000,000
	To record issue of 1,000, $1,000 8% bonds		
	for $924,156.		

(c) *Record the interest expense and amortization of discount for 19X1 and 19X2, using the straight-line method (same entry for both years).*

Interest payment = $1,000,000 x 8% = $80,000
Amortization of discount = $75,844 ÷ 5 = $15,169

19X1–19X2			
Dec. 31	Interest Expense	95,169	
	Cash		80,000
	Discount on Bonds Payable		15,169
	To record interest expense, amortization of discount,		
	and annual interest payment on 8% bonds payable.		

(d) *Record the interest expense and amortization of discount for 19X1 and 19X2, using the interest method.*

Interest expense 19X1 = $924, 156 x 10% = $92,416
Amortization of discount = $92,416 − $80,000 = $12,416
Interest expense 19X2 = ($924,156 + $12,416) x 10% = $93,657
Amortization of discount = $93,657 − $80,000 = $13,657

19X1			
Dec. 31	Interest Expense	92,416	
	Cash		80,000
	Discount on Bonds Payable		12,416
	To record interest expense, amortization of discount,		
	and annual interest payment on 8% bonds payable.		

19X2 Dec. 31	Interest Expense	93,657	
	Cash		80,000
	Discount on Bonds Payable		13,657
	To record interest expense, amortization of discount, and annual interest payment on 8% bonds payable.		

(e) *Record Crandall Company's investment.*

19X1 Dec. 31	Investments in Bonds	924,156	
	Cash		924,156
	To record purchase of Day Company Bonds at a discount.		

(f) *Record the interest revenue and amortization of discount for 19X1 if Crandall classified the bond as held to maturity.*

19X1 Dec. 31	Cash	80,000	
	Investments in Bonds	12,416	
	Interest Revenue		92,416
	To record interest revenue, amortize discount, and record collection of interest.		

(g) *Record the interest revenue and unrealized holding gain for 19X1.*

Unrealized gain = $945,000 − $924,156 = $20,844

19X1 Dec. 31	Cash	80,000	
	Interest Revenue		80,000
	To record interest received from Day Company and amortization of discount.		
	Investments in Bonds	20,844	
	Unrealized Gain (Loss) from Investments		20,844
	To record unrealized gains on short-term investments.		

(h) *Record the interest revenue, amortization of discount, and unrealized holding gain for 19X1.*

19X1 Dec. 31	Cash	80,000	
	Investments in Bonds	12,416	
	Interest Revenue		92,416
	To record interest received from Day Company and amortization of discount.		
	Investments in Bonds	8,428	
	Unrealized Gain (Loss) from Available-for-Sale Securities		8,428
	To record unrealized gains on bond investment.		

REVIEW PROBLEM C

On January 1, 19X2, Hostettler Corporation acquired new equipment under a 5-year lease calling for annual payments of $10,000 starting immediately. Although the equipment will revert back to the owner at the end of the lease term, its expected useful life is

5 years, and it is expected to have no market value at the end of the lease term. Hostettler, whose fiscal year-end is Deember 31, can borrow funds to acquire such equipment at 11%. Hostettler uses straight-line depreciation for similar equipment it has purchased.

REQUIRED:

a. Prepare the journal entry to recognize the first lease payment, including any assets and liabilities, if appropriate.
b. Prepare a journal entry or entries to recognize any necessary accruals or adjustments of of December 31, 19X2.
c. Prepare a journal entry to recognize the lease payment of January 1, 19X3.
d. Demonstrate the relationship between the balance of any lease obligation that you have recognized and the remaining lease payments at January 1, 19X3.

SOLUTION:

Planning and Organizing Your Work

1. First, determine if the lease is an operating lease or a capital lease by comparing its terms to the 4 criteria for capital leases listed in the chapter. In this case, the lease term is more than 75% of the remaining economic life of the equipment. Therefore, the lease is a capital lease.
2. Next, determine the value of the lease liability and the cost of the equipment. In this case, the lease is an annuity due. The value of the liability on January 1, 19X2 is equal to the present value of the remaining annuity of $10,000 each year for 4 years at 11%. The cost of the equipment is the value of the lease plus the first payment of $10,000 on January 1, 19X2. Debit Equipment Under Capital Lease with the value of the equipment, credit Long-Term Lease Payable with the value of the lease, and credit Cash with the first payment.
3. Find the depreciation expense for the year by applying the straight-line method to the cost of the equipment less any salvage value (none). Prepare the adjusting entry, debiting Depreciation Expense and crediting Accumulated Depreciation—Equipment Under Capital Lease.
4. Find the interest expense for the year by multiplying the beginning balance of the lease liability by the effective interest rate. Prepare the adjusting entry, debiting Interest Expense and crediting Long-Term Lease Payable.
5. Recognize the payment by debiting Long-Term Lease Payable and crediting Cash for the amount of the payment.
6. Calculate the present value of the remaining annuity of 3 payments and compare them to the balance in Long-Term Lease Payable. Ignore a small rounding difference, if any.

(a) *Prepare the journal entry to recognize the first lease payment.*

Annuity value of $1 paid at the end of each of 4 years at 11% (from Table 2, Appendix C): 3.102. Value of the lease liability: $10,000 x 3.102 = $31,020. Cost of the equipment: $31,020 + $10,000 = $41,020.

19X2			
Jan. 1	Equipment Under Capital Lease	41,020	
	Long-Term Lease Payable		31,020
	Cash		10,000
	To record acquisition of equipment under a long-term capital lease agreement.		

(b) *Prepare a journal entry or entries to recognize any necessary accruals or adjustments as of December 31, 19X2.*

19X2 Dec. 31	Depreciation Expense	8,204	
	Accumulated Depreciation—Equipment Under Capital Lease		8,204
	To record depreciation of equipment under a long-term capital lease agreement.		
31	Interest Expense	3,412	
	Long-Term Lease Payable		3,412
	To record interest expense on a long-term capital lease.		

(c) *Prepare a journal entry to recognize the payment on January 1, 19X3.*

19X3 Jan. 1	Long-Term Lease Payable	10,000	
	Cash		10,000
	To record payment on a long-term capital lease		

(d) *Demonstrate the relationship between the balance of the lease obligation and the remaining lease payments at January 1, 19X3.*

Present value of remaining lease payments:
Lease payment	$10,000
Times annuity of $1 each year for 3 years at 11%	x 2,444
Present value of remaining payments	$24,440

Balance in Long-Term Lease Payable:
Lease balance, January 1, 19X2	$31,020
Interest for 19X2	3,412
Payment on January 1, 19X3	(10,000)
Lease balance, January 1, 19X3	$24,432

KEY TERMS

annuity, *680*
annuity due, *680*
annuity value, *680*
bearer or coupon bonds, *685*
bondholders, *684*
bond indenture, *684*
bonds, *684*
bonds available for sale, *700*
bonds held to maturity, *697*
capital leases, *701*
compound interest, *676*
debt-equity ratio, *705*

denominations of bonds, *684*
discount, *685*
effective interest rate, *686*
full term, *684*
implicit principal payment, *682*
installment loan, *680*
interest method of amortization, *691*
issuer of bonds, *684*
material difference, *692*
off-balance-sheet financing, *707*

operating leases, *701*
premium, *685*
present value, *676*
registered bonds, *685*
serial bonds, *685*
stated, nominal, or coupon rate, *684*
term bonds, *685*
term to maturity, *684*
trading securities, *698*

SELF-QUIZ

LO 1,4 1. Name two forms of long-term borrowing.

LO 2 2. If the cash value of an asset acquired cannot be established, except implicitly from a note's terms, we use the concept of the _____ _____ of future cash payments.

LO 2 3. True or False? Future values always exceed equivalent present values.

LO 3 4. If a long-term obligation has one or more installments due within one year, a portion of the long-term installment is a(n) _____ _____ .

LO 4 5. Which of the following is *not* a difference between bonds and negotiable notes?
   a. The terms of the bonds are usually longer than those of notes.
   b. The total amount of bond debt is broken down into relatively small denominations.
   c. More costs are associated with issuing notes than with issuing bonds.
   d. All individual bonds are covered by a bond indenture.

LO 4 6. Which of the following statements is *false*?
   a. If a bond sells for more than face value, it is sold at a premium.
   b. If the nominal interest rate exceeds the market interest rate for a comparable investment, a bond will sell at a discount.
   c. If the nominal interest rate equals the interest rate for a comparable investment, a bond will sell at face value.
   d. If a bond sells for less than face value, it is sold at a discount.

LO 5 7. Which of following represents total interest cost of a bond?
   a. The sum of the interest payments for any bond
   b. The sum of the interest payments for bonds issued at face value

   c. The sum of the interest payments plus the premium for bonds issued at greater than face
   d. The sum of the interest payments plus the discount for a bond issued at greater than face

LO 6 8. Which of the following statements is *not* correct about bond issue costs?
   a. These include costs of registering and printing the bonds.
   b. These costs should be included in a deferred expense account.
   c. The deferred expense account should be classified as a contra-liability on the balance sheet.
   d. The costs should be recognized as expenses over the full term of the bonds.

LO 7 9. The three classifications of investments in bonds are: _____ ___ _____, _____ ___ _____, and _____ _____.

LO 8 10. Which of the following is *not* a criterion for identifying a capital lease?
   a. The lease transfers the ownership of the property to the lessee by the end of the lease term.
   b. The lease contains an option to purchase the assets at less than their expected fair value at the end of the lease term.
   c. The lease term is equal to 75% or more of the leased property's estimated remaining economic life.
   d. The lessor agrees to perform all maintenance on the leased property and to pay all taxes and insurance relating to the property.

LO 10 11. State the formula for the debt-equity ratio.

SOLUTIONS TO SELF-QUIZ

1. notes payable, bonds payable   2. present value   3. True   4. current liability   5. c   6. b   7. b   8. c
9. held to maturity, available for sale, short-term investments   10. d   11. Total Liabilities ÷ Total Stockholders' Equity

QUESTIONS

Q17-1   What is the mathematical formula for calculating compound interest?

Q17-2   What is the process of amortizing the discount on a note payable?

Q17-3   What is an installment loan?

Q17-4   What is an annuity?

Q17-5   What are the differences between a registered bond and a coupon bond?

Q17-6   What are the differences between a serial bond and a term bond?

Q17-7   What is the difference between the interest method and the straight-line method of premium or discount amortization?

Q17-8   When is it acceptable to use the straight-line method of interest amortization?

Q17-9   What is the rule of thumb for recognizing bond issue cost expense?

Q17-10   Why are bonds attractive investments?

Q17-11   What are the requirements for bonds to be classified as held to maturity?

Q17-12   What are the differences between an operating lease and a capital lease?

Q17-13   What does the debt-equity ratio measure?

EXERCISES

LO 1

E17-1   Long-Term Notes with Constant Principal Payments   On January 1, 19X2, SuperPet Stores gave a $16,000, 4-year, 10% note to Rapid Construction Company in exchange for remodeling one of the company's stores. The remodeling is worth $16,000. The terms of the note call for semiannual interest payments and $2,000 semiannual payments of principal on June 30 and December 31 over the 4-year term of the note.

REQUIRED:

Prepare the journal entries for June 30 and December 31, 19X2.

LO 2

E17-2   Valuing Notes Payable Using Present Values   Fontasia exchanged a note payable for equipment from Computers Unlimited on January 1, 19X3. There is no market value for comparable equipment to refer to in establishing value. Fontasia agreed to pay $20,000 on December 31, 19X4. The prevailing interest rate to Fontasia for borrowed funds is 8%.

REQUIRED:

Determine the value of the note and prepare the journal entry to record the purchase of equipment.

LO 3

E17-3   Determining Installment Loan Payments   Boomer Corporation issued a 9% installment note payable to the bank in exchange for $30,000. Boomer is to repay the note in equal payments at the end of each year for 5 years.

REQUIRED:

Calculate the amount of each payment and the amount of implicit principal paid on the first installment.

LO 4

E17-4   Value of Bonds at Issue   Vernon Company sold an issue of 100, $1,000, 5-year, 8% bonds. The bonds pay interest annually.

REQUIRED:

Calculate the selling price of the bond issue if a comparable investment would yield:
a. 8%
b. 10%
c. 6%

LO 4

E17-5   Recording Bond Issues   Knight Company sold a $500,000, 5-year, 9% bond issue. The bonds pay interest annually.

REQUIRED:

Record the issuance of the bonds, assuming they were sold for:
a. $500,000
b. $485,000
c. $529,000

LO 5   **E17-6**   **Straight-Line Method of Amortization of Discounts**   Western Company sold a $100,000, 5-year, 7% bond issue for $94,000 on January 2, 19X5. The bonds pay interest annually on December 31 of each year, and the discount is amortized using the straight-line method.

REQUIRED:

Record the journal entry for the accrual of interest expense, amortization of discount, and payment of interest on December 31, 19X5 and 19X6.

LO 5   **E17-7**   **Straight-Line Method of Amortization of Premiums**   Eastern Company sold a $1,000,000, 10-year, 9% bond issue for $1,150,000 on January 2, 19X7. The bonds pay interest annually on December 31 of each year, and the premium is amortized using the straight-line method.

REQUIRED:

Record the journal entry for the accrual of interest expense, amortization of premium, and payment of interest on December 31, 19X7 and 19X8.

LO 5   **E17-8**   **Interest Method of Amortization of Discounts**   McBurger Company sold a $500,000, 10-year, 9% bond issue for $469,275 on January 2, 19X8. The bonds pay interest annually on December 31 of each year, and the discount is amortized using the interest method. The effective rate of interest is 10%.

REQUIRED:

Record the journal entry for the accrual of interest expense, amortization of discount, and payment of interest on December 31, 19X8 and 19X9.

LO 5   **E17-9**   **Interest Method of Amortization of Premiums**   Elise Company sold a $200,000, 5-year, 12% bond issue for $223,340 on January 2, 19X1. The bonds pay interest annually on December 31 of each year, and the premium is amortized using the interest method. The effective rate of interest is 9%.

REQUIRED:

Record the journal entry for the accrual of interest expense, amortization of premium, and payment of interest on December 31, 19X1 and 19X2.

LO 6   **E17-10**   **Accruing Interest Between Interest Payment Dates**   F.I.A. Company sold a $1,000,000, 10-year, 9% bond issue for $1,200,000 on April 1, 19X2. The bonds pay interest annually on March 31 of each year, and the premium is amortized using the straight-line method. F.I.A. Company's fiscal year ends on December 31.

REQUIRED:

Record the journal entry for the recognition of interest expense on December 31, 19X2, and the payment of interest on March 31, 19X3.

LO 6   **E17-11**   **Bond Issue Costs**   Alpha Corporation paid $24,000 in bond issue costs when issuing a 12-year, 10% bond on April 1, 19X3. Alpha Corporation uses the straight-line method of amortization. Alpha's fiscal year ends on December 31.

REQUIRED:

Record the issue costs for the bond on April 1, 19X3, and the amortization of the issue costs on December 31, 19X3.

LO 7   **E17-12**   **Investments in Bonds Held to Maturity**   Canseco Inc. purchased 1,000 of the $500 face value, 12%, 10-year bonds of Palmero Corporation on January 1, 19X4. The bonds pay interest annually beginning on December 31, 19X4. Canseco paid $524,000 for the bonds. Canseco classifies the bonds as bonds held to maturity. Canseco uses the straight-line amortization method to amortize premiums or discounts on bond investments.

REQUIRED:

Record the purchase of the bonds on January 1, 19X4, and the recognition of interest revenue on December 31, 19X4.

LO 7   **E17-13**   **Short-Term Investments in Bonds**   Jordan Inc. purchased 2,000 of the $100 face value, 10%, 5-year bonds of Harper Corporation on January 1, 19X5. The bonds pay interest annually beginning on December 31, 19X5. Jordan paid $192,000 for the bonds. Harper Corporation bonds had a market value of $92 per bond on December 31, 19X5. Jordan classifies the bonds as short-term investments.

REQUIRED:

Record the purchase of the bonds on January 1, 19X5, the recognition of interest revenue on December 31, 19X5, and the recognition of the unrealized gain or loss for 19X5.

LO 8   **E17-14**   **Operating Leases**   Price Company rents a private branch exchange telephone system for 3 years under a lease calling for advance rent of $3,600 plus monthly rent payments of $150 per month.

REQUIRED:

Record the initial payment of $3,600 and the payment of the first month's rent. Assume Price will receive equal benefits from the system each month.

LO 9   **E17-15**   **Capital Leases**   DeMaris Company leased a delivery truck for 5 years on January 1, 19X6. The estimated life of the truck is 5 years; and, therefore, the lease is considered a capital lease. The annual payments are $6,000 for 5 years, which, at DeMaris' borrowing rate of 9%, makes them equivalent to borrowing $23,340—the truck's fair value.

REQUIRED:

Record the initial entry for the lease and the first payment on December 31, 19X6.

LO 10   **E17-16**   **Calculating the Debt-Equity Ratio**   Audionics has total assets and total liabilities of $1,850,000 and $392,000, respectively.

REQUIRED:

Calculate the debt-equity ratio for Audionics.

PROBLEM SET A

LO 2, 3   **P17-1A**   **Long-Term Notes Payable**   Jet Technologies issued an 8% installment note payable to
United Bank on January 1, 19X1, in exchange for $200,000. Jet Technologies is to repay
the note in equal payments at the end of each year for four years. Jet Technologies also
exchanged a note payable for equipment from Turbine Corporation on July 1, 19X1.
There is no market value for comparable equipment to refer to in establishing value. The
terms of the note called for Jet Technologies to pay $150,000 on June 30, 19X4, to repay
the note. The prevailing interest rate to Jet Technologies for borrowed funds is 8%.

REQUIRED:

a. Determine the annual payment for the installment note issued to United Bank.
b. Determine the present value of the note issued to Turbine Corporation.
c. Record all necessary journal entries for 19X1 and 19X2.
d. Show the balance sheet disclosure of both notes as of December 31, 19X1.

LO 4,5   **P17-2A**   **Bond Transactions, Straight-Line Method**   The Maurro Company uses the straight-
line method for amortizing bond discounts and premiums. The following transactions
took place during 19X2 and 19X3:

19X2
Jan.   2 Issued 1,000, $1,000 face value, 8% bonds that pay interest annually on
           December 31 of each year for 5 years. The bonds sold for $1,100,000.
        3 Bond issue costs of $5,000 are paid.
July   1 Issued 500, $1,000 face value, 7% bonds dated January 1, 19X2, that pay inter-
           est annually on January 2 of each year for 10 years. The bonds sold for
           $481,000 (excluding accrued interest).
Dec. 31   Paid the interest due on the 8% bonds issued on January 2, 19X2.

19X3
Jan.   2 Paid the interest due on the 7% bonds issued on July 1, 19X2.
Dec. 31   Paid the interest due on the 8% bonds issued on January 2, 19X2.

REQUIRED:

a. Record all necessary journal entries for 19X2.
b. Record all necessary journal entries for 19X3.
c. Show the balance sheet presentation for bonds payable and bond issue costs as of
    December 31, 19X3.

LO 4, 6   **P17-3A**   **Bond Transactions, Interest Method**   On January 2, 19X4, Laddie Company issued
500, $1,000 face value, 9% bonds that pay interest annually on December 31 of each
year for 5 years. At the time of issue, comparable bonds pay interest at the rate of 8%.
Laddie Company uses the interest method of amortization.

REQUIRED:

a. Determine the bonds' selling price.
b. Record the issue of the bonds on January 2, 19X4.
c. Record the payment of interest on December 31, 19X4.
d. Record the payment of interest on December 31, 19X5.

LO 4,5,6   **P17-4A**   **Prepare a Bond Amortization Table**   On July 1, 19X2, Eagle Company issued
$100,000 of 12% bonds that pay interest annually on June 30 of each year for 5 years.
Eagle Company uses the interest method of amortization.

REQUIRED:

a. Prepare a table similar to that in Illustration 17-9 (page 692) if comparable bonds pay interest at the rate of 8%.
b. Prepare a table similar to that in Illustration 17-9 (page 692) if comparable bonds pay interest at the rate of 15%.
c. Record all necessary entries for 19X2 and 19X3 if the bonds are issued at a rate of 8%.
d. Record all necessary entries for 19X2 and 19X3 if the bonds are issued at a rate of 15%.

LO 7   **P17-5A**   **Investment in Bonds**   Transcontinental purchased 3 bond issues on January 1, 19X8. All bonds pay interest annually on December 31 of each year. Transcontinental uses the straight-line method of amortization. Information for these issues is given below:

Bond	*Interest Rate*	*Face Value*	*Purchase Price*	*Dec. 31, 19X8 Price*	*Dec. 31, 19X9 Price*	*Term*
Deer Corp.	8%	$100,000	$ 95,786	$ 97,152	$ 97,022	5-year
Clear Corp.	9%	50,000	51,162	50,894	50,912	10-year
Pappas Corp.	10%	180,000	194,200	199,400	200,120	10-year

Transcontinental classifies the investment in Deer Corp. and Clear Corp. bonds as available for sale and that in Pappas Corp. as bonds held to maturity. No additional purchases or sale of bond investments occurred after the purchase of the 3 bonds.

REQUIRED:

a. Record Transcontinental's purchase of the bonds.
b. Record the journal entries for recognition of interest and amortization of premium or discount for all 3 bond issues on December 31, 19X8.
c. Record the journal entries for unrealized gains or losses for 19X8 and 19X9.

LO 8, 9   **P17-6A**   **Operating and Capital Leases**   Lee Company leased equipment for 5 years from Lor Company on January 2, 19X3. Lee Company agreed to pay Lor Company $25,000 on December 31 of each year. The equipment will revert to Lor Company at the end of the lease. The equipment has an estimated useful life of 5 years. Lee uses the straight-line depreciation method for similar equipment. Assume Lee can borrow money from a bank at an interest rate of 10%.

REQUIRED:

a. Determine if this lease is an operating lease or a capital lease and explain your answer.
b. Assuming the lease is a capital lease, determine the initial value of the leased asset and liability.
c. Assuming the lease is a capital lease, record the inception of the lease on January 2, 19X3.
d. Assuming the lease is a capital lease, record the depreciation of the equipment, the lease payment, and the accrual of interest on December 31, 19X3, and December 31, 19X4.
e. Assuming the lease is an operating lease, record the lease payment on December 31, 19X3.

PROBLEM SET B

LO 2, 3   **P17-1B**   **Long-Term Notes Payable**   Kennel Corporation issued a 10% installment note payable to Partners Loan Corporation on January 1, 19X4, in exchange for $100,000. Kennel is to repay the note in equal payments at the end of each year for 4 years. Kennel Corporation also exchanged a note payable for equipment from K-9 Corporation on July

1, 19X4. There is no market value for comparable equipment to refer to in establishing value. The terms of the note called for Kennel Corporation to pay $300,000 on June 30, 19X8, to repay the note. The prevailing interest rate to Kennel Corporation for borrowed funds is 10%.

REQUIRED:

a. Determine the annual payment for the installment note issued to Partners Loan Corporation.
b. Determine the present value of the note issued to K-9 Corporation.
c. Record all necessary journal entries for 19X4 and 19X5.
d. Show the balance sheet disclosure of both notes as of December 31, 19X4.

LO 4,5   **P17-2B**   **Bond Transactions, Straight-Line Method**   The Richards Company uses the straight-line method for amortizing bond discounts and premiums. The following transactions took place during 19X5 and 19X6:

19X5

Jan.   2 Issued 500, $1,000 face value, 11% bonds that pay interest annually on December 31 of each year for 5 years. The bonds sold for $470,000.
        3 Bond issue costs of $2,500 are paid.

July   1 Issued 1,000, $1,000 face value, 8% bonds dated January 1, 19X5, that pay interest annually on January 2 of each year for 10 years. The bonds sold for $1,190,000 (excluding accrued interest).

Dec. 31 Paid the interest due on the 11% bonds issued on January 2, 19X5.

19X6

Jan.   2 Paid the interest due on the 8% bonds issued on July 1, 19X5.
Dec. 31 Paid the interest due on the 11% bonds issued on January 2, 19X5.

REQUIRED:

a. Record all necessary journal entries for 19X5.
b. Record all necessary journal entries for 19X6.
c. Show the balance sheet presentation of bonds payable and bond issue costs as of December 31, 19X6.

LO 4,6   **P17-3B**   **Bond Transactions, Interest Method**   On January 2, 19X3, Prince Company issued 1,000, $1,000 face value, 8% bonds that pay interest annually on December 31 of each year for 5 years. At the time of issue, comparable bonds pay interest at the rate of 10%. Prince Company uses the interest method of amortization.

REQUIRED:

a. Determine the bonds' selling price.
b. Record the issue of the bonds on January 2, 19X3.
c. Record the payment of interest on December 31, 19X3.
d. Record the payment of interest on December 31, 19X4.

LO 4,5,6   **P17-4B**   **Bond Amortization Table**   On October 1, 19X1, Buckeye Company issued $500,000 of 8% bonds that pay interest annually on September 30 of each year for 5 years. Buckeye Company uses the interest method of amortization.

REQUIRED:

a. Prepare a table similar to that of Illustration 17-9 (page 692) if comparable bonds pay interest at the rate of 6%.
b. Prepare a table similar to that of Illustration 17-9 (page 692) if comparable bonds pay interest at the rate of 10%.

c. Record all necessary entries for 19X1 and 19X2 if the bonds are issued at a rate of 6%.

d. Record all necessary entries for 19X1 and 19X2 if the bonds are issued at a rate of 10%.

LO 7   **P17-5B** **Investment in Bonds** PanEurope purchased 3 bond issues on January 1, 19X3. All bonds pay interest annually on December 31 of each year. PanEurope uses the straight-line method of amortization. Information for these issues is given below:

Bond	Interest Rate	Face Value	Purchase Price	Dec. 31, X3 Price	Dec. 31, X4 Price	Term
Steelman Corp.	8%	$200,000	$191,572	$194,304	$194,044	5-year
Hurwitz Corp.	9%	100,000	102,324	101,788	101,824	10-year
Menendez Corp.	10%	360,000	388,400	398,800	400,240	10-year

PanEurope classifies the investment in Steelman Corp. and Hurwitz Corp. as bonds as available for sale and that in Menendez Corp. as bonds held to maturity. No additional purchases or sale of bond investments occurred after the purchase of the 3 bonds.

REQUIRED:

a. Record PanEurope's purchase of the bonds.

b. Record the journal entries for recognition of interest and amortization of premium or discount for all 3 bond issues on December 31, 19X3.

c. Record the journal entries for unrealized gains or losses for 19X3 and 19X4.

LO 8,9   **P17-6B** **Operating and Capital Leases** See Company leased equipment for 5 years from Sor Company on January 2, 19X2. See Company agreed to pay Sor Company $15,000 on December 31 of each year. The equipment will revert to Sor Company at the end of the lease. The equipment has an estimated useful life of 5 years. See uses the straight-line depreciation method for similar equipment. Assume See can borrow money from a bank at an interest rate of 10%.

REQUIRED:

a. Determine if this lease is an operating lease or a capital lease and explain your answer.

b. Assuming the lease is a capital lease, determine the value of the leased asset and liability.

c. Assuming the lease is a capital lease, record the inception of the lease on January 2, 19X2.

d. Assuming the lease is a capital lease, record the depreciation of the equipment, the lease payment, and the accrual of interest on December 31, 19X2, and December 31, 19X3.

e. Assuming the lease is an operating lease, record the lease payment on December 31, 19X2.

CRITICAL THINKING AND COMMUNICATING

 C17-1 Leather Works Corporation is a conservative company that has always relied on contributed capital to finance expansion. There is no long-term debt on the balance sheet. Mary Shearling, the president of Leather Works Corporation, told the treasurer Herman Schwartz to investigate using long-term debt to finance an attractive business opportunity for Leather Works.

REQUIRED:

Write a memo for Herman Schwartz explaining the different types of long-term debt financing alternatives.

C17-2 Aerobics World is a national chain of fitness clubs. The following information is abstracted from Aerobics World's 19X7 and 19X8 balance sheet.

	19X7	19X8
Total liabilities	$4,500,000	$5,900,000
Total stockholders' equity	9,000,000	9,100,000

Aerobics World is considering a large expansion of its operation. It plans to lease several new fitness clubs in a series of strip shopping centers being opened in the coming year by a real estate investment company. The leases offered by the investment company do not meet any of the criteria for capital leases, so they can be treated as operating leases. However, Aerobics World does not have sufficient cash to buy the neccessary $500,000 of fitness equipment and other furnishings for the new clubs. Management does not want to incur the costs of issuing additional stock to raise capital from owners. Unfortunately, one of the existing long-term creditors of the company insisted on a debt covenant requiring Aerobics World's debt-equity ratio to remain below 65%. This rules out borrowing the $500,000. The equipment manufacturer offered to lease the equipment to Aerobics World, but the lease, when appropriately discounted, covered 90% of the fair value of the equipment. Thus, the lease would have to be capitalized and treated like debt, which would also violate the covenant.

At an officers meeting, Aerobics World's chief financial officer proposed a scheme. Aerobics World would ask the equipment manufacturer to customize the equipment by affixing to it Aerobics World's own nameplate with the company's logo. Then, they would ask the equipment manufacturer to raise the cash price of the equipment substantially, but adjust the required lease payments only slightly to cover the costs of customizing. Thus, the present value of the lease payments would be less than 90% of the new "fair value" of the equipment and the lease could be treated as an operating lease. The other officers at first objected to the plan, but when a phone call to the equipment manufacturer won easy cooperation, they approved the scheme and went ahead with it.

REQUIRED:

Comment on the CFO's scheme for financing the equipment for the fitness clubs. Do you see any way that the definitional criteria for capital leases could be changed to prevent such schemes? Do you see any way the long-term creditor could have written a debt covenant that might have prevented the scheme?

C17-3 Refer to the financial statements of J.C. Penney Company, Inc. in Appendix B at the end of the text. Find the balance sheet.

REQUIRED:

1. Calculate J.C. Penney's total debt and its debt-equity ratio for 1991, 1992, and 1993. Hint: Subtract total stockholders' equity from total liabilities and stockholders' equity to calculate total liabilities.
2. What are the implications of the changes in J.C. Penney's debt-equity rations over the 3 years?

CHAPTER 18

Statement of Cash Flows

Peter Chang owns 1,000 shares of Davis Company's common stock, which he purchased recently for $6,000. During the current year of 19X2, he knows that Davis Company declared cash dividends of $.25 per share. When Peter analyzed the company's balance sheet and income statement for 19X2 (shown in Illustration 18-1 on pages 729–730), he discovered that net income for the year was $14,400, or $1.20 per share. Puzzled about why dividends were less than 25% of earnings, Peter further studied the statements and noticed that cash declined from $8,000 at the beginning of the year to $1,000 at the end of the year. Peter wants to know what happened to the cash since net income was $14,400 and the cash dividends declared certainly did not use up all the cash. While doing his study, Peter noticed another financial statement called the statement of cash flows. Unfamiliar with this statement, he wonders if it might answer the mystery of the disappearing cash.

When a company prepares a *complete set of financial statements*, it includes a statement of cash flows with the income statement, balance sheet, and retained earnings statement.[1] A **statement of cash flows** is a financial statement that displays a business's cash receipts and cash disbursements for a period according to categories of business activities— operating activities, financing activities, and investing activities. The statement shows the reader the business's cash sources and how the business used the cash during the period. Readers use this information in answering such questions as: Why did the company pay little or no cash dividends when it had significant net income? or, How did the company finance the purchase of new plant assets? This chapter presents a discussion of the statement of cash flows, including its usefulness, and describes techniques for preparing the statement.

---

[1]"Statement of Cash Flows," *Statement of Financial Accounting Standards No. 95* (Stamford, Conn.: FASB, 1987), par. 3.

1. Explain the purpose of a statement of cash flows.
2. Describe the operating, investing, and financing classifications of cash flow activities.
3. Explain how to prepare a statement of cash flows.
4. Analyze accrual basis accounting information to determine the effects on cash flows.
5. Describe the indirect method of reporting cash flows from operating activities.
6. Prepare a statement of cash flows using a worksheet (Appendix 18-A).

LO 1

Explain the purpose of a statement of cash flows.

PURPOSE OF A STATEMENT OF CASH FLOWS

The accounting profession has identified information about a business's cash flows as an objective of financial reporting as indicated by the following paragraph:

> Financial reporting should provide information to help present and potential investors and creditors and other users in assessing the amounts, timing, and uncertainty of prospective cash receipts from dividends or interest and the proceeds from the sale, redemption, or maturity of securities or loans. The prospects for those cash receipts are affected by an enterprise's ability to generate enough cash to meet its obligations when due and its other cash operating needs, to reinvest in operations, and to pay cash dividends.[2]

Accountants designed the statement of cash flows to meet this objective by assisting investors, creditors, and other readers of the financial statements in assessing such factors as follow:

- The business's ability to generate positive cash flows in future periods
- The business's ability to meet its obligations and to pay dividends
- Reasons for differences between the amount of net income and the related cash flows from operations
- Both the cash and noncash aspects of the business's investing and financing activities for the period.[3]

Complete Set of Financial Statements

Illustration 18-1 presents a complete set of financial statements for the Davis Company. The financial statements presented include a comparative balance sheet for 19X1 and 19X2, an income statement for 19X2, a retained earnings statement for 19X2, and a statement of cash flows for 19X2.

The statement of cash flows shown in Illustration 18-1 classifies cash receipts and cash disbursements according to operating, investing, and financing activities. The general format of a statement of cash flows is depicted visually in Illustration 18-2.

---

[2]"Objectives of Financial Reporting by Business Enterprises." *Statement of Financial Accounting Concepts No. 1* (Stamford, Conn.: FASB, 1978), par. 37.

[3]*Ibid.*, par. 5.

ILLUSTRATION 18-1 Davis Company Financial Statements

Davis Company Comparative Balance Sheet December 31, 19X1 and 19X2		
	19X1	*19X2*
Assets		
Current assets:		
Cash	$ 8,000	$ 1,000
Accounts receivable	12,000	14,000
Rent receivable	0	400
Merchandise inventory	14,000	13,000
Prepaid insurance	2,000	1,800
Total current assets	$36,000	$30,200
Plant assets:		
Office equipment	$ 2,300	$ 2,700
Accumulated depreciation—office equipment	(1,000)	(1,250)
Buildings	40,000	45,000
Accumulated depreciation—buildings	(6,000)	(8,000)
Land	35,000	30,000
Total plant assets	$ 70,300	$68,450
Total assets	$106,300	$98,650
Liabilities and Stockholder's Equity		
Current liabilities:		
Notes payable	$ 5,000	$10,000
Accounts payable	8,000	2,300
Wages and salaries payable	500	750
Dividends payable	1,500	1,800
Income taxes payable	1,850	1,950
Total current liabilities	$16,850	$16,800
Noncurrent liabilities:		
Notes payable—noncurrent	40,000	15,000
Total liabilities	$56,850	$31,800
Stockholders' equity:		
Common stock, $1 par value	$ 10,000	$12,000
Paid-in capital in excess of par-common	25,000	30,000
Paid-in capital—stock dividend	0	4,000
Retained earnings	14,450	20,850
Total stockholders' equity	$ 49,450	$66,850
Total liabilities and stockholders' equity	$106,300	$98,650

Difference is net decrease in cash of $7,000 ← (annotation pointing to Cash 19X2 $1,000)

ILLUSTRATION 18-1 (Continued) Davis Company Financial Statements

Davis Company
Income Statement
For the Year Ended December 31, 19X2

Revenues:		
Sales	$84,800	
Rent	2,600	
Total revenues		$87,400
Cost of goods sold		44,000
Gross profit		$43,400
Expenses:		
Wages and salaries expense	$21,000	
Depreciation expense—office equipment	550	
Depreciation expense—buildings	2,000	
Interest expense	800	
Income tax expense	7,250	
Other operating expenses	400	
Total expenses		(32,000)
Gain from sale of property		3,000
Net income		$14,400

Davis Company
Statement of Cash Flows
For the Year Ended December 31, 19X2

Cash flows from operating activities:		
Collections from customers	$82,800	
Rent received	2,200	
Payments to suppliers	(48,700)	
Payments to employees	(20,750)	
Interest paid	(800)	
Income taxes paid	(7,150)	
Payments for other operating expenses	(200)	
Net cash flows from operating activities		$7,400
Cash flows from investing activities:		
Purchase of office equipment	$ (700)	
Building addition	(5,000)	
Sale of land	8,000	
Net cash flows from investing activities		2,300
Cash flows from financing activities:		
Payment of 10% note	$(25,000)	
Common stock issued	6,000	
Cash dividends paid	(2,700)	
Net proceeds from short-term notes	5,000	
Net cash used by financing activities		(16,700)
Net decrease in cash		$ (7,000)

ILLUSTRATION 18-1 (Continued) Davis Company Financial Statements

Davis Company Retained Earnings Statement For the Year Ended December 31, 19X2		
Balance, January 1		$14,450
Add: Net income for 19X2		14,400
Total		$28,850
Less: Cash dividends declared	$3,000	
Stock dividends declared	5,000	8,000
Balance, December 31		$20,850

ILLUSTRATION 18-2 Format of Statement of Cash Flows

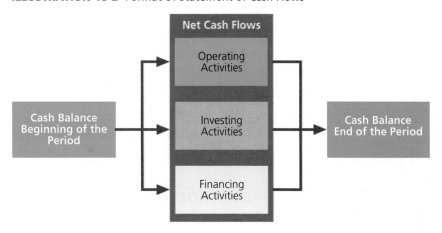

For each of the three activity classifications, we sum the cash receipts and cash disbursements and present a net cash inflow or outflow. Then, we sum the net cash flows for the three classifications and present the total as the change in cash for the period. The change in cash in the statement of cash flows ($7,000) equals the difference between the cash balances in the comparative balance sheet ($8,000 − $1,000).

A statement of cash flows plays a complementary role with a balance sheet and income statement in providing a *complete* picture of the business's assets and financial structure (liabilities and owners' equity) and how those assets, liabilities, and equities changed during a period. A balance sheet provides information about the assets, liabilities, and owners' equity of a business at a *moment in time.* However, the balance sheet provides an incomplete picture because it provides no information about how changes in those elements occur from period to period. Both an income statement and a statement of cash flows provide information about how changes in the business's net assets occurred during a period. The information an income statement provides is about changes in net assets resulting from revenue and expense transactions of the business. On the other hand, a statement of cash flows provides more detailed information about how particular assets, liabilities, and owners' equity elements changed as a result of cash receipts and cash disbursements from the business's operating, investing, and financing activities.

The statement of cash flows is useful for identifying the business's cash sources and how the business used that cash. Also, the statement of cash flows can be used in conjunction with other financial statements to explain changes in the business's financial position. While balance sheets and income statements provide information about these activities, they present only partial information. For example, a financial statement reader (such as Peter Chang who was introduced at the beginning of this chapter) might ask the following question concerning the Davis Company: "How is it possible that with net income of $14,400, cash on the comparative balance sheet *decreased* by $7,000 ($8,000 − $1,000) for the year even though the company declared only $3,000 of dividends?"

Interpreting the Statement of Cash Flows

An examination of the statement of cash flows reveals the following response to Peter Chang's question about the disappearing cash: Even though net income is $14,400, operating activities actually generated net cash flows of only $7,400. Also, investing activities generated net cash flows of $2,300, resulting from the sale of land less the purchase of new assets. Finally, financing activities used net cash of $16,700, resulting from the net effects of issuing common stock, paying off debt of $25,000, paying the $2,700 cash dividends, and increasing short-term borrowings. The net effect of these transactions is a $7,000 decrease in cash for the year. Overall, rather than paying greater dividends, Davis Company paid off a large portion of its long-term debt. Certainly, such a detailed analysis of Davis Company would be difficult without the statement of cash flows.

CLASSIFICATION OF CASH FLOWS

LO 2
Describe the operating, investing, and financing classifications of cash flow activities.

As you see in Illustration 18-1, the statement of cash flows classifies the business's cash receipts and cash payments according to the categories of operating, investing, and financing activities.

Operating Activities

A business's normal operations result in both cash receipts and cash disbursements. Cash receipts result from selling merchandise and providing services. The cost of goods sold and other operating expenses result in cash disbursements. The revenues and expenses reported in the income statement, however, do not coincide with the cash receipts and cash disbursements. Under GAAP, we prepare the income statement on an accrual basis, which means we record the revenues when earned and expenses when incurred. The receipts and payments of cash for these revenues and expenses may occur in either an earlier or later period than the period we report the revenues and expenses.

All transactions and events that are not classified as either investing or financing activities are classified as operating activities. Cash flows from operating activities generally are the *cash effects* of the transactions—selling or producing goods or providing services—included to determine net income. Illustration 18-3 presents a listing of the types of transactions that are classified as operating activities for the statement of cash flows.

In some cases, the classification of certain transactions depends on the business's nature. For example, it is generally assumed that property, plant, and

ILLUSTRATION 18-3 Cash Flows From Operating Activities

Cash Inflows	Cash Outflows
*Cash sales to customers *Collections of both short-term and long-term receivables from credit sales to customers *Cash receipts of interest and dividends Refunds from suppliers Cash collected from settlements of lawsuits	*Payments to suppliers for goods and services *Payments of both short-term and long-term payables resulting from the purchase of goods and services *Payments of taxes, fines, and other fees *Payments of interest Payments to settle lawsuits Refunds to customers Contributions to charities

*Illustrated in the statement of cash flows in Illustration 18-1.

equipment acquisitions and sales are part of the business's investing activities because the business uses such assets for a long time to produce revenue. Some businesses, such as a dealer in used construction equipment, earn net income by purchasing property, plant, and equipment and then, in a short period of time, reselling those assets at a profit. In the latter case, we classify the purchase and sale of property, plant, and equipment as an operating activity, rather than as an investing activity, because, in effect, those transactions are merely inventory transactions.

Direct Method of Calculating Cash Flows From Operating Activities. The statement of cash flows in Illustration 18-1 presents cash flows from operating activities using the direct method. The **direct method** of presenting cash flows from operating activities shows major classes of cash receipts and cash payments and their sum. The sum is net cash flows from operating activities.

Indirect Method of Calculating Cash Flows From Operating Activities. An alternative approach to reporting cash flows from operating activities is the indirect or reconciliation method. The **indirect method** begins with net income and shows the adjustments necessary to determine cash flows from operating activities. This chapter emphasizes the direct method because we believe it reports cash flows from operating activities more clearly. We illustrate the indirect method later in the chapter.

Investing Activities

Businesses enter into various kinds of investing activities that result in cash receipts and cash disbursements. These transactions involve purchasing and selling assets that are classified in the balance sheet as short-term and long-term investments, plant assets, and intangible assets. Also, lending and collecting loans are considered investing activities. Illustration 18-4 lists the kinds of transactions that are considered investing activities in the statement of cash flows.

In Illustration 18-4, the collection of loans listed as a cash inflow needs further explanation. Normally, we classify the collection of loan principal as a cash flow from an investing activity. If the loan is a receivable from the sale of goods or services, then the cash inflow is considered an operating activity as shown in Illustration 18-3. Also, all collections of interest and dividends are considered operating activities.

ILLUSTRATION 18-4 Cash Flows From Investing Activities

Cash Inflows	Cash Outflows
Collections of loans *Cash received from the sale of plant assets (including land) Cash received from the sale of intangible assets	Payments in the form of loans to others Payments to purchase stocks and bonds of other companies *Payments to purchase plant assets (including land) Payments to purchase intangible assets

*Illustrated in the statement of cash flows in Illustration 18-1.

Financing Activities

Various cash receipts and cash disbursements occur as a result of the business's financing activities. Financing activities include:

1. Obtaining assets from owners, repaying assets to owners, and providing owners with returns in the form of withdrawals or dividends
2. Obtaining loans from creditors and repaying the principal amount of the loans

Illustration 18-5 presents a listing of the kinds of transactions that are considered financing activities in the statement of cash flows.

ILLUSTRATION 18-5 Cash Flows From Financing Activities

Cash Inflows	Cash Outflows
*Proceeds from issuing common and preferred stock Proceeds from issuing bonds *Proceeds from other short-term and long-term borrowings	*Payments of common and preferred dividends Payments to purchase treasury stock *Repayments of principal amounts to creditors

*Illustrated in the statement of cash flows in Illustration 18-1.

Transactions involving repayments to creditors need further explanation. As you saw in the discussion of operating activities, repayments of borrowings from suppliers for the purchase of goods and services are considered operating activities. Repayments of other types of short-term and long-term borrowings are considered financing activities in the statement of cash flows. Examples of short-term borrowings classified as financing activities would include repaying amounts borrowed under lines of credit agreements with banks. Long-term borrowings classified as financing activities would include long-term notes payable and bonds payable.

LO 3

Explain how to prepare a statement of cash flows.

PREPARING THE STATEMENT OF CASH FLOWS

To prepare a statement of cash flows, accountants analyze the accounts to identify the cash receipts and cash disbursements associated with the three classifications of operating, investing, and financing activities. The framework for the analysis of accounts relies on the characteristics of the double-entry accounting system and the balance sheet equation. In particular, any change in Cash is associated with a change in another account. We know from the accounting equation (Assets = Liabilities + Owners' Equity) that if the amount of cash increases, either the other assets must decrease by an equal amount or liabilities and owners' equity must increase by an equal amount. Similarly, if the amount of cash decreases, either other assets must increase by an equal amount or liabilities and owners' equity must decrease by an equal amount.

The Accounting Equation

These relationships may be depicted by manipulating the accounting equation as follows:

$$\text{Assets = Liabilities + Owners' Equity}$$

$$\text{Cash + Other Assets = Liabilities + Owners' Equity}$$

$$C + OA = L + OE$$

Subtracting other assets (OA) from both sides of the equation results in the following expression of the accounting equation:

$$C = L + OE - OA$$

As we account for a business's transactions and other activities, change (Δ) in one side of the equation must be accompanied by an equal change in the other side of the equation or the balance will not be retained:

$$\Delta C = \Delta L + \Delta OE - \Delta OA$$

This final equation shows that a change in cash must be accompanied by an equal change in liabilities or owners' equity in the *same* direction, or an equal change in other assets in the *opposite* direction. For example, assume a business has the following balance sheet totals:

$$
\begin{array}{ccccccc}
C & = & L & + & OE & - & OA \\
\$10{,}000 & = & \$12{,}000 & + & \$38{,}000 & - & \$40{,}000
\end{array}
$$

The purchase of an asset for $3,000 cash results in a decrease in cash of $3,000 and an increase in other assets of $3,000 as follows:

$$
\begin{array}{ccccccc}
C & = & L & + & OE & - & OA \\
\$10{,}000 & = & \$12{,}000 & + & \$38{,}000 & - & \$40{,}000 \\
\underline{(3{,}000)} & = & & & & - & \underline{3{,}000} \\
\$\ 7{,}000 & = & \$12{,}000 & + & \$38{,}000 & - & \$43{,}000
\end{array}
$$

Notice that the equation remains in balance after including the effects of the transaction.

If the business borrows $6,000 from the bank, the effect is an increase in cash of $6,000 and an increase in liabilities of $6,000:

$$
\begin{array}{ccccccc}
C & = & L & + & OE & - & OA \\
\$\ 7{,}000 & = & \$12{,}000 & + & \$38{,}000 & - & \$43{,}000 \\
\underline{6{,}000} & = & \underline{6{,}000} & & & & \\
\$13{,}000 & = & \$18{,}000 & + & \$38{,}000 & - & \$43{,}000
\end{array}
$$

Again, the equation remains in balance after including the effects of the transaction.

Remember that Cash is a debit-balance account; therefore, increases in cash are accompanied by credits to a noncash account(s). For example, the issuance of common stock for cash results in a debit (increase) in Cash and a credit to Common Stock. On the other hand, decreases in cash are accompanied by debits to a noncash account(s). For example, the purchase of a plant asset for cash results in a credit to Cash and a debit to a plant asset account.

Accountants use these relationships in analyzing the accounts to prepare a statement of cash flows. The account analysis consists of *analyzing the changes in the noncash balance sheet accounts to explain the changes in cash for the period.* The account analysis is complicated by the fact that not all changes in noncash accounts result in a cash inflow or outflow. For example, the purchase of a building by incurring a mortgage payable does not have an immediate effect on cash. Also, depreciation expense does not involve an entry to Cash. To prepare the statement of cash flows, the accountant must sort through the changes in the noncash balance sheet accounts and *identify those transactions and events that change the noncash accounts and involve cash receipts and disbursements.*

Sources of Information

To perform the account analysis described in the previous section, the accountant should have the following sources of information:

- *Comparative balance sheet.* The accountant needs a balance sheet for the end of the current period and a balance sheet for the end of the previous period to determine the *net* change in Cash and the noncash balance sheet accounts for the period.
- *Income statement.* The accountant uses an income statement for the current period to determine the cash flows from operating activities. The income statement provides information about the revenue and expenses for the period, including noncash expenses such as depreciation.
- *Summary transaction data.* The accountant can obtain summary information about the components of changes in account balances by analyzing the general ledger accounts. The summary information about transactions is needed because the comparative balance sheet only shows the *net* changes in the various account balances. For example, a $1,000 increase in Equipment may be the result of a purchase of equipment costing $1,000, or the result of a $2,000 purchase and the disposal of equipment that originally cost $1,000. Acquisitions and dispositions of plant assets are shown as separate investment activities on a statement of cash flows.

LO 4
Analyze accrual basis accounting information to determine the effects on cash flows.

PREPARING A STATEMENT OF CASH FLOWS— AN ILLUSTRATION

In Illustration 18-1, the statement of cash flows for Davis Company is presented. Following is a discussion of how we developed that statement from the company's accrual basis records.

In addition to the company's financial statements, shown in Illustration 18-1, we derived the following information from analyzing Davis Company's accounts:

1. Prepaid Insurance is related to "Other operating expenses" shown on the income statement.
2. New office equipment was purchased at a cost of $700.
3. Worn-out and fully depreciated office equipment was discarded. The equipment cost $300 when purchased.
4. A new storage room was added to the building at a cost of $5,000.
5. Depreciation expense, office equipment, is $550.
6. Depreciation expense, building, is $2,000.
7. Land that cost $5,000 was sold for $8,000.
8. $25,000 of the 10% note payable was paid.
9. A 10% stock dividend was declared when the market price of the stock was $5 per share.
10. After the stock dividend, common stock was issued for $6 per share.
11. Cash dividends of $3,000 were declared.

Cash Flows From Operating Activities

The analysis of cash flows from operating activities consists of identifying relevant income statement amounts. We then adjust the income statement amounts for any changes in related balance sheet accounts. The result of the adjustment is the amount of cash flow from the identified activity.

Collections From Customers.   If a business has only cash sales, the amount of sales revenue it reports in the income statement is the amount of cash it collected from customers. However, when a business has credit sales, we adjust the amount of sales revenue for the change in accounts receivable. A decrease in accounts receivable for the period means that cash collections from customers for the period exceed sales revenue on the accrual basis. Conversely, an increase in accounts receivable means that cash collections from customers was less than sales revenue in the income statement.

Illustration 18-1 shows sales revenue in the income statement of $84,800 for 19X2 and accounts receivable in the comparative balance sheet increased from $12,000 at the beginning of the year to $14,000 at the end of the year. With this information, a summary of sales revenue transactions is:

Accounts Receivable			
Beg. Bal.	12,000		
Sales	84,800	**Collections**	**82,800**
End. Bal.	14,000		

The T-account summary shows that for accounts receivable to increase, cash collections from customers must be less than sales revenue recorded on the accrual basis. In other words, if we know that sales revenue, which increase accounts receivable, are $84,800, but that the Accounts Receivable balance increased by $2,000, then we know that collections must have been $82,800. In general, the following relationships exist:

Cash Collections from Customers = Sales Revenue
$$\begin{cases} - \text{ Increase in Accounts Receivable} \\ or \\ + \text{ Decrease in Accounts Receivable} \end{cases}$$

We show the $82,800 cash collections from customers in the statement of cash flows in Illustration 18-1 as a cash *inflow* from operating activities.

Rent Received. The analysis of rent received is similar to cash collected from customers. The analysis begins with rent revenue from the income statement. We then adjust the amount of rent revenue for any change in rent receivable in the comparative balance sheet. In general, we use the following relationships to calculate rent received:

$$\text{Rent Received} = \text{Rent Revenue} \begin{cases} - \text{ Increase in Rent Receivable} \\ or \\ + \text{ Decrease in Rent Receivable} \end{cases}$$

Illustration 18-1 shows that rent revenue in the income statement is $2,600 for 19X2 and that rent receivable in the comparative balance sheet increased by $400 during 19X2. The rent revenue transactions may be summarized as follows:

Rent Receivable			
Beg. Bal.	0		
Rent Revenue	2,600	**Receipts**	**2,200**
End. Bal.	400		

Rent revenue increases rent receivable, and receipts of rent payments decrease rent receivable. Since rent receivable increased by $400 for Davis Company during 19X2, rent revenue must exceed receipts of rent payments by $400. Therefore, to calculate rent received, we reduce rent revenue by the $400 increase in rent receivable. We show the rent received in the statement of cash flows in Illustration 18-1 as a cash *inflow* from operating activities.

Payments to Suppliers. The analysis of cash payments to suppliers begins with cost of goods sold from the income statement. Cost of goods sold is different from cash payments for purchases of merchandise inventory in two respects:

1. Cost of goods sold is different from purchases by the amount of the change in merchandise inventory for the period.
2. Purchases are different from cash payments to suppliers of merchandise by the change in accounts payable for the period.

The calculation of cash payments to suppliers involves the following two adjustments:

$$\text{Purchases} = \text{Cost of Goods Sold} \begin{cases} + \text{ Increase in Merchandise Inventory} \\ or \\ - \text{ Decrease in Merchandise Inventory} \end{cases}$$

$$\text{Cash Payments to Suppliers} = \text{Purchases} \begin{cases} + \text{ Decrease in Accounts Payable} \\ or \\ - \text{ Increase in Accounts Payable} \end{cases}$$

For Davis Company, cost of goods sold in the income statement is $44,000 for 19X2; and merchandise inventory in the comparative balance sheet decreased from $14,000 to $13,000 during 19X2. The merchandise inventory transactions may be summarized as follows:

Merchandise Inventory

Beg. Bal.	14,000		
Purchases	**43,000**	Cost of	
		goods sold	44,000
End. Bal.	13,000		

With the amount of purchases calculated as $43,000, the purchases transactions may be summarized thus:

Accounts Payable

		Beg. Bal.	8,000
Payments	**48,700**	Purchases	43,000
		End. Bal.	2,300

We show the cash payments to suppliers of $48,700 in the statement of cash flows in Illustration 18-1 as a cash *outflow* from operating activities.

Payments to Employees.   The income statement amount with which to begin the analysis of cash payments to employees is wages and salaries expense. The balance sheet account related to wages and salaries expense is Wages and Salaries Payable. The calculation of payments to employees is:

$$\text{Cash Payments to Employees} = \text{Wages and Salaries Expense} \begin{cases} + \text{ Decrease in Wages and Salaries Payable} \\ or \\ - \text{ Increase in Wages and Salaries Payable} \end{cases}$$

In Illustration 18-1, Davis Company reports wages and salaries expense in the income statement of $21,000 for 19X2. Wages and salaries payable in the comparative balance sheet increased $250 during 19X2. We summarize the wages and salaries transactions as follows:

Wages and Salaries Payable

		Beg. Bal.	500
Payments	**20,750**	Expense	21,000
		End. Bal.	750

We show the cash payments to employees of $20,750 in the statement of cash flows in Illustration 18-1 as a cash *outflow* from operating activities.

Interest Paid.   The analysis of interest paid begins with interest expense in the income statement. We then adjust the amount of interest expense for any change in interest payable as follows:

$$\text{Interest Paid} = \text{Interest Expense} \begin{cases} + \text{ Decrease in Interest Payable} \\ or \\ - \text{ Increase in Interest Payable} \end{cases}$$

In Illustration 18-1, Davis Company reports interest expense in the income statement of $800. Since no interest payable is shown in either the balance sheet at the beginning of the year or the balance sheet at the end of the year, interest paid must be equal to interest expense. We summarize the interest transactions thus:

Interest Payable

		Beg. Bal.	0
Payments	800	Expense	800
		End. Bal.	0

We show the cash payments of $800 for interest in the statement of cash flows in Illustration 18-1 as a cash *outflow* from operating activities.

Income Taxes Paid.   The analysis of income taxes paid is similar to the analyses of cash payments for wages and salaries and interest payments. We adjust the amount of income tax expense for any change in income taxes payable as follows:

$$\text{Income Taxes Paid} = \text{Income Tax Expense} \begin{cases} + \text{ Decrease in Income Taxes Payable} \\ or \\ - \text{ Increase in Income Taxes Payable} \end{cases}$$

For Davis Company, we summarize the income taxes transactions as follows:

Income Taxes Payable

		Beg. Bal.	1,850
Payments	7,150	Expense	7,250
		End. Bal.	1,950

We show income taxes paid of $7,150 in the statement of cash flows in Illustration 18-1 as a cash *outflow* from operating activities.

Payments for Other Operating Expenses.   The analysis of operating expenses begins with operating expenses shown in the income statement in Illustration 18-1. Included in other operating expenses are: rent, insurance, utilities, property taxes, etc. To calculate cash payments, the amount of operating expenses requires two adjustments for changes in related balance sheet accounts: prepaid expenses and expenses payable. These adjustments are:

$$\text{Cash Payments for Operating Expenses} = \text{Operating Expenses} \begin{cases} + \text{ Increases in Prepaid Expenses} \\ or \\ - \text{ Decreases in Prepaid Expenses} \\ and \\ + \text{ Decreases in Expenses Payable} \\ or \\ - \text{ Increases in Expenses Payable} \end{cases}$$

For Davis Company, the "Other operating expenses" shown in the income statement in Illustration 18-1 has a related prepaid expenses account. However, there is no related payable account. Therefore, we summarize the other operating expenses transactions as follows:

Prepaid Insurance

Beg. Bal.	2,000		
Payments	200	Expense	400
End. Bal.	1,800		

We show the cash payments of $200 for other operating expenses in the statement of cash flows in Illustration 18-1 as a cash *outflow* from operating activities.

Gain From Sale of Property (Land).   The income statement in Illustration 18-1 shows a gain from the sale of property (land) of $3,000. The gain from the sale of land is not analyzed in determining cash flows from operating activities because we classify cash received from the sale of plant assets as an investing activity (as shown in Illustration 18-4). We analyze the gain from the sale of land below in the discussion of investing activities.

Cash Flows From Investing Activities

The statement of cash flows in Illustration 18-1 shows that in 19X2, Davis Company had three cash flows resulting from investing activities.

Purchase of Office Equipment.   During 19X2, Davis Company purchased new office equipment at a cost of $700. In the statement of cash flows, this amount is shown as a cash *outflow* from investing activities. The listing of information obtained from analyzing the accounts, however, shows that office equipment was affected by three transactions described in Items 2, 3 and 5 on page 737. Transaction 2 is the purchase of new office equipment described above, and Transaction 3 is the discarding of worn-out and fully depreciated office equipment. At the time Davis discarded the equipment, it made the following entry:

(Date)	Accumulated Depreciation—Office Equipment	300	
	Office Equipment		300
	To record the disposal of fully depreciated office equipment.		

As you can see in this entry, no cash flows occurred as a result of this transaction. Therefore, this transaction is not included in the statement of cash flows because it does not result in either a cash inflow or a cash outflow.

Transaction 5 is for depreciation of the office equipment for 19X2. Recording depreciation expense also does not include cash flows, as shown in Davis's following entry to record depreciation expense:

19X2			
Dec. 31	Depreciation Expense—Office Equipment	550	
	Accumulated Depreciation—Office Equipment		550
	To record depreciation expense.		

The transactions affecting office equipment may be summarized as follows:

Office Equipment					Accumulated Depreciation—Office Equip.			
Beg. Bal.	2,300						Beg. Bal.	1,000
Purchase	**700**	Disposal	300	Disposal	300		Expense	550
End. Bal.	2,700						End. Bal.	1,250

Notice that the beginning and ending balances of the two accounts can be reconciled to the amounts in the comparative balance sheet. This reconciliation provides assurance that no transactions involving office equipment are omitted from the analysis.

Building Addition.   During 19X2, Davis Company added a new storage room at a cost of $5,000 to its building. We show this transaction as a cash *outflow* in the statement of cash flows. Transaction 6 on page 737 for depreciation expense is also related to the building. As you have seen, recording depreciation expense does not involve cash flows. The transactions related to the building may be summarized thus:

Building			Accumulated Depreciation—Building		
Beg. Bal.	40,000			Beg. Bal.	6,000
Addition	**5,000**			Expense	2,000
End. Bal.	45,000			End. Bal.	8,000

Sale of Land.   During 19X2, Davis Company sold land. In the statement of cash flows, we report the transaction as a cash *inflow* from investing activities in the amount of $8,000. The comparative balance sheet shows a decrease in land of $5,000. The difference is the gain from the sale of $3,000 that is shown in the income statement. The entry Davis made when it sold the land shows that the cash inflow is $8,000.

(Date)	Cash	8,000	
	Land		5,000
	Gain from Sale of Property		3,000
	To record the sale of property.		

The transaction involving land is shown in the accounts as follows:

Land			
Beg. Bal.	35,000	Sale	5,000
End. Bal.	30,000		

Cash Flows From Financing Activities

For 19X2, Davis Company reports four cash flow transactions from financing activities.

Payment of 10% Note.   Davis Company paid off $25,000 of the 10% note payable during 19X2. In the statement of cash flows, we show the transaction as a cash *outflow* from financing activities. In the accounts, the transaction is shown thus:

Notes Payable—Noncurrent			
		Beg. Bal.	40,000
Payment	**25,000**		
		End. Bal.	15,000

Common Stock Issued.   In 19X2, Davis Company had two transactions involving common stock. The first transaction is the 10% stock dividend Davis declared when the market price of the stock was $5 per share. The stock dividend is not a "large" stock dividend. Therefore, the stock dividend is recorded by capitalizing the market price of the stock issued as the dividend. As shown by the following entry, the stock dividend does not involve cash flow:

(Date)	Retained Earnings	5,000	
	Common Stock		1,000
	Paid-In Capital—Stock Dividend		4,000
	To record 10% stock dividend (10% x 10,000 x $5).		

The other transaction involving common stock is the issuance of 1,000 shares for $6 per share. In the statement of cash flows, we show this transaction as a cash inflow of $6,000 from financing activities. The effect on cash flows of this transaction can be seen by examining Davis's entry to record the issuance of the stock:

(Date)	Cash	6,000	
	Common Stock		1,000
	Paid-In Capital In Excess of Par–Common		5,000
	To record the issuance of $1 par value stock		
	for $6 per share.		

The common stock transactions for 19X2 may be summarized as follows:

Common Stock				Paid-In Capital In Excess of Par—Common		
	Beg. Bal.	10,000			Beg. Bal.	25,000
	Dividend	1,000			**Issuance**	**5,000**
	Issuance	**1,000**			End. Bal.	30,000
	End. Bal.	12,000				

Paid-In Capital—Stock Dividend		
	Beg. Bal.	0
	Dividend	4,000
	End. Bal.	4,000

Cash Dividends Paid.   The analysis of cash dividends paid begins with the amount of cash dividends declared. To calculate the amount of cash dividends paid, we adjust the amount declared for the change in dividends payable, as follows:

$$\text{Cash Dividends Paid} = \text{Cash Dividends Declared} \begin{cases} + \text{ Decrease in Dividends Payable} \\ or \\ - \text{ Increase in Dividends Payable} \end{cases}$$

The amount of cash dividends declared is $3,000 (from additional information Item 11 on page 737 or from the retained earnings statement in Illustration 18-1). The comparative balance sheet shows that dividends payable increased by $300 during 19X2. In the statement of cash flows, we show cash dividends paid of $2,700 as a cash *outflow* from financing activities. We summarize the cash dividends transactions as follows:

Dividends Payable			
		Beg. Bal.	1,500
Payments	**2,700**	Declared	3,000
		End. Bal.	1,800

Net Proceeds From Short-Term Notes.   Many businesses maintain lines of credit with banks as well as other sources of short-term credit such as commercial paper. Borrowings from these sources occur during the year as the business needs funds, and repayments occur within a relatively short period of time. During 19X2, Davis Company had net proceeds of $5,000 from these sources. That is, the borrowings exceeded repayments by $5,000. For this type of debt, the borrowings and repayments may be shown as a net cash inflow or a net cash outflow. Since Davis Company had net proceeds, in the statement of cash flows, we show $5,000 as a cash *inflow* from financing activities.

Additional Considerations in Preparing the Statement

The preparation of a statement of cash flows sometimes involves certain additional considerations that are discussed below.

Cash and Cash Equivalents. As discussed in an earlier chapter, businesses sometimes have cash on hand that is not temporarily needed in their daily operations. Rather than let the cash be idle, businesses invest it in short-term, highly liquid securities (e.g., U.S. Treasury bills) to earn income. These temporary investments of excess cash are called **cash equivalents**. In a statement of cash flows, cash should be combined with or include cash equivalents.[4] Cash plus cash equivalents is used because in evaluating a business's cash flows, it matters little to a reader whether the cash is on hand, on deposit in a bank, or invested temporarily in *highly liquid assets*. In preparing a statement of cash flows, cash and short-term investments that management designates as cash equivalents are combined and treated as a single item.

In the notes to its October 31, 1992, annual report, General Cinema Corporation describes cash and cash equivalents as follows:

Cash and equivalents

Cash equivalents consist of liquid investments which are readily convertible into cash. Cash and equivalents are stated at cost plus accrued interest, which approximates market. At October 31 cash and equivalents consisted of the following:

(In thousands)	1992	1991
Cash	$ 19,162	$ 18,189
Bank obligations	45,160	800,813
Corporate obligations	254,115	474,696
Other cash equivalents	112,291	325,270
Total cash and equivalents	$430,728	$1,618,968

Noncash Investing and Financing Activities. A statement of cash flows reports only the business's cash receipts and cash disbursements. For this reason, there may be some significant transactions that did not involve either receiving or paying cash. Some common examples of noncash investing and financing transactions include the following:

1. *Acquiring assets by assuming liabilities.* A business may purchase land and buildings by assuming a mortgage payable.
2. *Acquiring assets by issuing stock.* A company may purchase assets such as plant assets and intangible assets by issuing preferred or common stock directly to the seller.
3. *Exchanges of nonmonetary assets.* Companies commonly trade one asset to another company or individual for a more desirable asset.
4. *Issuance of stock to repay loans.* A company may repay a loan by issuing preferred or common stock to the creditor.

To present a complete picture of the business's investing and financing activities, significant noncash investing and financing transactions are presented

---

[4] *Ibid.,* par. 7.

in a separate schedule following the statement of cash flows or in the notes to the financial statements.[5] An example of a separate schedule of noncash investing and financing activities is shown in Illustration 18-6.

ILLUSTRATION 18-6 Schedule of Noncash Investing and Financing Activities

Preferred stock issued to settle noncurrent debt	$ 125,000
Purchase of land and building by assumption of mortgage payable	890,000
Exchange of land in Texas for land in Washington	100,000
	$1,115,000

Other noncash transactions such as stock dividends, stock splits, and appropriations of retained earnings are neither investing nor financing activities and are not reported in the schedule of noncash investing and financing activities. Information about these noncash transactions is generally reported in the retained earnings statement or in schedules and notes explaining changes in stockholders' equity.

LO 5
Describe the indirect method of reporting cash flows from operating activities.

ALTERNATIVE PRESENTATION OF CASH FLOWS FROM OPERATING ACTIVITIES

The indirect method of reporting cash flows from operating activities begins with net income and adjusts for items that are included in net income but did not affect cash flows from operating activities. There are three types of adjustments to net income.

Noncash Expenses

Certain expenses that are included in net income do not result in a cash outflow. The primary noncash expenses are depreciation and amortization. The offsetting entry for these expenses is to an accumulated depreciation account and to an intangible asset account, respectively. The cash flows associated with these transactions occur at the time of purchase and disposal of the related assets and are classified then as investing activities.

Adjustments to Convert Revenues and Expenses to the Cash Basis

Revenues and expenses are recognized on the accrual basis at times that may be different than the time of the related cash flows. The adjustments to net income for these items involve analyzing changes in receivables, inventories, prepaid expenses, and payables that are related to revenues and expenses.

Nonoperating Items

Gains and losses from investing and financing transactions are included in net income, but the transactions are not considered operating activities. These gains and losses are from disposals of plant assets and settlements of long-term liabili-

---

[5] *Ibid.*, par. 32.

ties. *These transactions are considered investing and financing activities.* Therefore, the gains and losses associated with these transactions should be removed from net income in calculating cash flows from operating activities.

The Indirect Method—An Illustration

Illustration 18-7 presents Davis Company's statement of cash flows following the indirect method of reporting cash flows from operating activities. Notice that only the operating activities section is different from the statement of cash flows in Illustration 18-1, which follows the direct method.

ILLUSTRATION 18-7 Statement of Cash Flows (Indirect Method)

Davis Company Statement of Cash Flows For the Year Ended December 31, 19X2			
Cash flows from operating activities:			
Net income		$ 14,400	
Noncash expense:			
Depreciation		2,550	
Adjustments to convert revenues and expenses to cash basis			
Increase in accounts receivable	$(2,000)		
Increase in rent receivable	(400)		
Decrease in merchandise inventory	1,000		
Decrease in prepaid insurance	200		
Decrease in accounts payable	(5,700)		
Increase in wages and salaries payable	250		
Increase in income taxes payable	100	(6,550)	
Adjustment for nonoperating item:			
Gain on sale of land		(3,000)	
Net cash flows from operating activities			$ 7,400
Cash flows from investing activities:			
Purchase of office equipment		$ (700)	
Building addition		(5,000)	
Sale of land		8,000	
Net cash flows from investing activities			2,300
Cash flows from financing activities:			
Payment of 10% note		$(25,000)	
Common stock issued		6,000	
Cash dividend paid		(2,700)	
Net proceeds from short-term notes		5,000	
Net cash used by financing activities			(16,700)
Net decrease in cash			$(7,000)

Although the FASB expressed a clear preference for the direct method of reporting cash flows from operating activities, most businesses use the indirect method. The reasons they usually offer for using the indirect method involve past practice and cost. Historically, they have used the indirect method. Also, changing their accounting systems to collect information to prepare the statement using the direct method would be too costly. Presented in Illustration 18-8 are the results of a survey of 600 large corporations about their reporting of cash flows.

ILLUSTRATION 18-8 Method of Reporting Cash Flows From Operating Activities

	1991	1990	1989
Indirect method	585	585	583
Direct method	15	15	17
Total	600	600	600

Source: *Accounting Trends and Techniques*, 1992, p. 392.

SUMMARY

Explain the purpose of a statement of cash flows. The primary purpose of a statement of cash flows is to provide information about the business's cash receipts and cash disbursements during a period. A secondary objective of the statement is to provide information about the business's investing and financing activities during a period. Classifying cash flows in the statement into categories of operating, investing, and financing activities serve these two purposes.

Describe the operating, investing, and financing classifications of cash flow activities. Cash receipts and cash disbursements from operating activities are the cash effects of revenue and expense transactions. Investing activities include transactions that involve acquiring and disposing of productive assets, investing in securities, and investing in intangible assets. Financing activities include transactions with stockholders (owners) and creditors.

Explain how to prepare a statement of cash flows. To prepare a statement of cash flows, accountants analyze the accounts to identify the cash receipts and cash disbursements associated with operating, investing, and financing activities. The information accountants use includes comparative balance sheets, income statements, and additional information from the business's accounts.

Analyze accrual basis accounting information to determine the effects on cash flows. In preparing the statement of cash flows, we adjust income statement amounts for the differences between the timing of related cash flows and the timing of revenue and expense recognition under accrual accounting.

Describe the indirect method of reporting cash flows from operating activities. The indirect method begins with net income and adjusts for items that are included in net income but did not affect cash flows from operating activities. These adjustments are for noncash expenses, adjustments to convert revenues and expenses to the cash basis, and nonoperating items.

APPENDIX 18-A: USING A WORKSHEET TO PREPARE THE STATEMENT OF CASH FLOWS

In earlier chapters, we discussed how accountants use a worksheet to prepare the income statement and balance sheet. For complex situations involving numerous adjustments, accountants also use a worksheet to facilitate the preparation of the statement of cash flows. In this Appendix, we give a comprehensive example to illustrate the use of a worksheet for preparing a statement of cash flows. The worksheet we demonstrate is for the indirect method for cash flows from operating activities. We chose this approach because of its widespread use in the business world. A similar worksheet method is available for the direct method.

LO 6
Prepare a statement of cash flows using a worksheet.

PREPARING THE WORKSHEET

The worksheet for preparing Davis Company's statement of cash flows is presented in Illustration 18-9. The worksheet consists of five columns. The first column is for listing the names of the accounts. The remaining four columns are for listing the dollar amounts of and changes in the account balances. We use the following steps in preparing the worksheet:

1. Enter the beginning balances of the balance sheet accounts in the first dollar column, and enter the ending balances in the fourth dollar column.
2. List the accounts with debit balances first, followed by the accounts with credit balances. This convention means that accumulated depreciation accounts are listed with the credit balances (such as liabilities) rather than as contra-asset accounts as presented in the balance sheet. Listing the accounts in this order facilitates the analysis of the changes in account balances. Recall that any credit change to an account balance is a possible increase in cash and any debit is a possible decrease in cash.
3. After entering the account balances, sum the debits and credits in each column to make sure that they are equal in each of the two columns. If the debits and credits are not equal, you have made an error in entering the data in the worksheet. Before proceeding, locate and correct the error(s).
4. Enter relevant components of the changes in accounts in the Account Analysis columns. These entries (1) represent changes in the account balances and (2) allow the determination of cash flows from operating, investing, and financing activities, which are listed at the bottom of the worksheet. For some changes in account balances, more than one entry is necessary to explain the change. For example, in Illustration 18-9, two entries are needed to explain the $400 increase in office equipment: (1) a $700 debit (Entry f) and (2) a $300 credit (Entry g). Notice that the two entries net to a $400 debit, which explains the $400 increase in office equipment from a balance of $2,300 at December 31, 19X1, to $2,700 at December 31, 19X2. *Remember: The data for the entries come from the income statement, statement of retained earnings, and analysis of the general ledger accounts.*

   The entries on the worksheet summarize the effects of the various transactions that changed the account balances during the period. For example, Entry (g) is a debit to Accumulated Depreciation—Office Equipment and a credit to Office Equipment. For every entry representing a component of the change in one account balance, there is an offsetting entry(ies) to other accounts of equal amount. Some of these offsetting entries involve an increase or a decrease in cash. However, we do not enter the changes in cash on the Cash line at the top of the worksheet. Instead, we enter them at the bottom of the worksheet in the proper activity category of the statement of cash flows. The statement substitutes for entries in the change columns of the Cash line. For example, the payment on the 10% note payable (Entry q) is a debit to Note Payable and a credit (decrease in cash) in the "Financing activities" category at the bottom of the worksheet.

Other entries explain changes in noncash accounts, but the related transaction(s) have no effect on cash. For example, the disposal of fully depreciated office equipment (Entry g) noted above results in a credit to Office Equipment and a debit to Accumulated Depreciation—Office Equipment. Since cash is not affected by the transaction, we make no entry to the statement of cash flows section of the worksheet.

The bottom portion of the worksheet allows the preparer to enter the change in cash as a cash inflow or outflow from operating, investing, or financing activities. The worksheet preparer must be knowledgeable about the classification of cash flows to complete the worksheet. The terms Increases and Decreases in the Account Analysis columns in the bottom portion of the worksheet represent cash inflows (increases) and cash outflows (decreases), respectfully. After fully explaining the changes in all noncash accounts with appropriate entries, the cash flows statement at the bottom of the worksheet is also complete and it (Entry u) explains the change in Cash at the top of the worksheet.

5. After analyzing all account balance changes, sum the Debits and Credits columns to make sure that the debits equal the credits.

Analyzing the Changes in Accounts

Presented below is an analysis of the selected transactions of Davis Company that we use in preparing the entries in the worksheet.

Net Income.   The worksheet presented prepares the cash flows from operating activities according to the indirect method. We begin the analysis of the accounts by analyzing net income. After the analysis of net income, we analyze the accounts in the order presented in the balance sheets in Illustration 18-1.

In the statement of cash flows, we classify net income as a source of cash inflow from operating activities. Note that the worksheet entries are used solely for preparing the statement of cash flows; they are *not* posted to the accounts. The worksheet entry is:

| (a) | Operating Activities, Net Income | 14,400 | |
| | Retained Earnings | | 14,400 |

Accounts Receivable.   The increase in accounts receivable means that the cash Davis collected from customers is $2,000 less than the revenue reported in the income statement. The change in accounts receivable is one adjustment required to convert net income to cash flows from operating activities. Therefore, to calculate cash flows from operating activities, we deduct the $2,000 increase in accounts receivable from net income. *Rule of thumb:* A debit change to any noncash account is offset by a credit (decrease) to cash. A credit change to any noncash account is offset by a debit (increase) to cash. The worksheet entry in the Account Analysis columns is:

| (b) | Accounts Receivable | 2,000 | |
| | Operating Activities, Increase in Accounts Receivable | | 2,000 |

ILLUSTRATION 18-9 Cash Flow Worksheet

Davis Company
Worksheet for Statement of Cash Flows
For the Year Ended December 31, 19X2

	ACCOUNT BALANCES 12/31/X1	ACCOUNT ANALYSIS DEBITS		ACCOUNT ANALYSIS CREDITS		ACCOUNT BALANCES 12/31/X2
Debits						
Cash	8,000			(u)	7,000	1,000
Accounts Receivable	12,000	(b)	2,000			14,000
Interest Receivable		(c)	400			400
Merchandise Inventory	14,000			(d)	1,000	13,000
Prepaid Insurance	2,000			(e)	200	1,800
Office Equipment	2,300	(f)	700	(g)	300	2,700
Buildings	40,000	(h)	5,000			45,000
Land	35,000			(i)	5,000	30,000
Total debits	113,300					107,900
Credits						
Accumulated Depr.–Off. Equip.	1,000	(g)	300	(j)	550	1,250
Accumulated Depr.–Buildings	6,000			(k)	2,000	8,000
Accounts Payable	8,000	(m)	5,700			2,300
Notes Payable	5,000			(l)	5,000	10,000
Wages and Salaries Payable	500			(n)	250	750
Dividends Payable	1,500			(o)	300	1,800
Income Taxes Payable	1,850			(p)	100	1,950
Notes Payable—Noncurrent	40,000	(q)	25,000			15,000
Common Stock	10,000			(r)	1,000	
				(s)	1,000	12,000
Paid-In Capital–Stock Dividend	0			(r)	4,000	4,000
Paid-In Capital in Excess of Par– Common	25,000			(s)	5,000	30,000
Retained Earnings	14,450	(r)	5,000			
		(t)	3,000	(a)	14,400	20,850
Total credits	113,300					107,900

Cash flows from:		**Increases**		**Decreases**	
Operating activities:					
Net income		(a)	14,400		
Increase in accounts receivable				(b)	2,000
Increase in interest receivable				(c)	400
Decrease in merchandise inventory		(d)	1,000		
Decrease in prepaid insurance		(e)	200		
Gain from sale of land				(i)	3,000
Depreciation expense–office equip.		(j)	550		
Depreciation expense–building		(k)	2,000		
Decrease in accounts payable				(m)	5,700
Increase in wages and salaries pay.		(n)	250		
Increase in income taxes payable		(p)	100		
Investing activities					
Purchased office equipment				(f)	700
Building addition				(h)	5,000
Sale of land		(i)	8,000		
Financing activities					
Increase in short-term notes pay.		(l)	5,000		
Increase in dividends payable		(o)	300		
Payment of notes payable				(q)	25,000
Issued common stock		(s)	6,000		
Cash dividend declared				(t)	3,000
Decrease in cash		(u)	7,000		
Totals			91,900		91,900

Rent Receivable.   The increase in rent receivable means that Davis's cash collections of rent are *less* than the rent revenue reported in the income statement. Therefore, to calculate cash flows from operating activities, we deduct the $400 increase in rent receivable from net income. The worksheet entry is:

| (c) | Rent Receivable | 400 | |
| | Operating Activities, Increase in Rent Receivable | | 400 |

Merchandise Inventory.   The decrease in merchandise inventory means that Davis's purchases are *less* than the cost of goods sold reported in the income statement. Therefore, to calculate cash flows from operating activities, we add the decrease in merchandise inventory to net income. The worksheet entry is:

| (d) | Operating Activities, Decrease in Merchandise Inventory | 1,000 | |
| | Merchandise Inventory | | 1,000 |

Prepaid Insurance.   The $200 decrease in prepaid insurance means that expenses Davis used in calculating net income are *more* than the cash payments for those expenses. Therefore, we add the $200 decrease in prepaid insurance to net income in calculating cash flows from operating activities. The worksheet entry is:

| (e) | Operating Activities, Decrease in Prepaid Insurance | 200 | |
| | Prepaid Insurance | | 200 |

Office Equipment.   The $400 increase in office equipment is the result of two transactions. A $700 increase is the result of Davis's purchase of new office equipment, and it is a cash outflow from investing activities. The worksheet entry is:

| (f) | Office Equipment | 700 | |
| | Investing Activities, Purchase of Office Equipment | | 700 |

Also, Davis discarded worn-out and fully depreciated office equipment that originally cost $300. This transaction does not affect cash flows. However, we make an entry in the worksheet so that all changes in account balances are analyzed. The worksheet entry is:

| (g) | Accumulated Depreciation—Office Equipment | 300 | |
| | Office Equipment | | 300 |

Buildings.   Davis's building addition of $5,000 is a cash outflow from investing activities. The worksheet entry is:

| (h) | Building | 5,000 | |
| | Investing Activities, Building Addition | | 5,000 |

Land.   The sale of land resulted in a gain of $3,000 as reported in the income statement. In the statement of cash flows, we classify the sale of a plant asset as an investing activity. Therefore, we deduct the gain from the sale of land from net income in determining cash flows from operating activities. We classify the entire amount of proceeds from the sale of $8,000 as a cash inflow from investing activities. The worksheet entry is:

(i)	Investing Activities, Sale of Land	8,000	
	Land		5,000
	Operating Activities, Gain from Sale of Land		3,000

Accumulated Depreciation—Office Equipment.   The recording of depreciation expense decreases net income, but there is no effect on cash flows. Therefore, to calculate cash flows from operating activities, we add the amount of depreciation expense to net income. The worksheet entry is:

| (j) | Operating Activities, Depreciation Expense—Office Equipment | 550 | |
| | Accumulated Depreciation—Office Equipment | | 550 |

Accumulated Depreciation—Buildings.   The analysis of the accumulated depreciation for the building is the same as for the office equipment. The worksheet entry is:

| (k) | Operating Activities, Depreciation Expense—Building | 2,000 | |
| | Accumulated Depreciation—Building | | 2,000 |

Notes Payable.   The increase in short-term notes payable is a cash inflow from financing activities. The worksheet entry is:

| (l) | Financing Activities, Increase in Notes Payable | 5,000 | |
| | Notes Payable | | 5,000 |

Accounts Payable.   The $5,700 decrease in accounts payable means that the purchases amount Davis used in the determination of net income is *less* than the cash payments to suppliers. Therefore, to calculate cash flows from operating activities, we deduct the decrease in accounts payable from net income. The worksheet entry is:

| (m) | Accounts Payable | 5,700 | |
| | Operating Activities, Decrease in Accounts Payable | | 5,700 |

Wages and Salaries Payable.   The $250 increase in wages and salaries payable means that the wages and salaries expense Davis deducted in the determination of net income is *more* than the cash payments made to employees. Therefore, to calculate cash flows from operating activities, we add the increase in wages and salaries payable to net income. The worksheet entry is:

| (n) | Operating Activities, Increase in Wages and Salaries Payable | 250 | |
| | Wages and Salaries Payable | | 250 |

Dividends Payable.   The $300 increase in dividends payable means that cash payments for dividends are less than the dividends Davis declared. In the statement of cash flows, we classify the payment of cash dividends as a financing activity. Therefore, we deduct the increase in dividends payable from dividends declared in the calculation of cash flows from financing activities. The worksheet entry is:

| (o) | Financing Activities, Increase in Dividends Payable | 300 | |
| | Dividends Payable | | 300 |

Income Taxes Payable.   The $100 increase in income taxes payable means that income taxes expense Davis deducted in the determination of net income is more than cash payments made to the government(s) for income taxes. Therefore, to calculate cash flows from operating activities, we add the increase in income taxes payable to net income. The worksheet entry is:

(p)	Operating Activities, Increase in Income Taxes Payable	100	
	Income Taxes Payable		100

Notes Payable—Noncurrent.   In the statement of cash flows, we classify the $25,000 decrease in the note payable as a cash outflow from financing activities. The worksheet entry is:

(q)	Notes Payable—Noncurrent	25,000	
	Financing Activities, Payment of Note Payable		25,000

Common Stock and Additional Paid-In Capital.   During 19X2, Davis had two transactions that affect common stock and additional paid-in capital. The first transaction is the stock dividend. The stock dividend does not involve cash flows, but we enter the effects on the accounts in the worksheet so that we include all changes in the accounts. The worksheet entry is:

(r)	Retained Earnings	5,000	
	Common Stock		1,000
	Paid-In Capital—Stock Dividend		4,000

The second transaction that affects common stock and additional paid-in capital is Davis's issuance of stock. The issuance of common stock results in a cash inflow from financing activities. The worksheet entry is:

(s)	Financing Activities, Issued Common Stock	6,000	
	Common Stock		1,000
	Paid-In Capital in Excess of Par—Common		5,000

Retained Earnings.   Retained earnings is affected by several transactions. We analyze the stock dividend above, and we analyze the net income effect at the beginning of this section. Davis's retained earnings is also reduced by the declaration of cash dividends. In the statement of cash flows, we classify cash dividends as a cash outflow from financing activities. The worksheet entry is:

(t)	Retained Earnings	3,000	
	Financing Activities, Cash Dividend Declared		3,000

Cash.   After the changes in all noncash accounts are analyzed, the final step to complete the worksheet is to enter the change in cash. The offsetting entry to the $7,000 credit to Cash is the last amount entered in the Debits column. This procedure results in the Debits and Credits columns being equal, assuming that no mistakes have occurred in preparing the worksheet. The worksheet entry is:

(u)	Decrease in Cash	7,000	
	Cash		7,000

Preparing the Statement

After the worksheet is complete, all the information needed to prepare the statement of cash flows is contained in the bottom portion of the worksheet. The statement prepared according to the indirect method is presented in Illustration 18-7 on page 746.

REVIEW PROBLEM

Prepare a statement of cash flows using the direct method for the Neeley Company from the financial statements and additional information that follow:

Neeley Company Comparative Balance Sheet December 31, 19X1 and 19X2		
	19X1	*19X2*
Assets		
Current assets:		
Cash	$ 18,000	$ 26,000
Accounts receivable	36,000	33,800
Interest receivable	3,500	6,000
Merchandise inventory	72,000	65,000
Prepaid insurance	2,700	2,500
Total current assets	$132,200	$133,300
Plant assets:		
Equipment	$ 53,000	$ 68,000
Accumulated depreciation—equipment	(2,500)	(2,800)
Buildings	80,000	123,500
Accumulated depreciation—buildings	(4,000)	(7,000)
Land	22,000	72,000
Total plant assets	$148,500	$253,700
Total assets	$280,700	$387,000
Liabilities and Stockholder's Equity		
Current liabilities:		
Accounts payable	$ 12,200	$ 3,100
Wages and salaries payable	14,300	6,900
Interest payable	1,300	1,000
Dividends payable	1,500	2,000
Income taxes payable	200	0
Total current liabilities	$ 29,500	$ 13,000
Noncurrent liabilities:		
Notes payable—noncurrent	0	20,000
Bonds payable	0	50,000
Total liabilities	$ 29,500	$ 83,000
Stockholders' equity:		
Common stock, $10 par	$150,000	$190,000
Paid-in capital in excess of par—common	50,000	60,000
Retained earnings	51,200	54,000
Total stockholders' equity	$251,200	$304,000
Total liabilities and stockholders' equity	$280,700	$387,000

Neeley Company
Income Statement
For the Year Ended December 31, 19X2

Revenues:		
Sales	$90,000	
Interest	4,200	
Total revenue		$94,200
Cost of goods sold		68,000
Gross profit		$26,200
Expenses:		
Wages and salaries expense	$10,100	
Depreciation expense—equipment	1,500	
Depreciation expense—buildings	3,000	
Interest expense	1,700	
Income taxes expense	1,000	
Insurance expense	2,800	
Total expenses		(20,100)
Loss from sale of equipment		(800)
Net income		$ 5,300

Neeley Company
Retained Earnings Statement
For the Year Ended December 31, 19X2

Balance, January 1	$51,200
Add: Net income for 19X2	5,300
Total	$56,500
Less: Cash dividends declared	2,500
Balance, December 31	$54,000

Additional Information:
(a) Equipment was purchased for $20,000 cash.
(b) Equipment with a cost of $5,000 and a book value of $3,800 was sold for $3,000.
(c) An addition to the building was added at a cost of $43,500. The addition was paid for in cash.
(d) Borrowed $70,000 cash by issuing a $20,000 10% note payable and $50,000 of bonds.
(e) Acquired land with a fair value of $50,000 by exchanging 4,000 shares of common stock for the land.

SOLUTION:

Planning and Organizing Your Work
1. Analyze the change in each balance sheet account to determine the cash inflows and cash outflows. You may find it helpful to analyze the account changes by using T-accounts as demonstrated in the chapter.
2. Make note of changes in balance sheet accounts resulting from noncash investing and financing activities.
3. Classify each cash flow as resulting from operating, investing, or financing activities.
4. Prepare the statement of cash flows in the proper format.
5. Prepare the supplementary schedule for noncash investing and financing activities.

Neeley Company		
Statement of Cash Flows		
For the Year Ended December 31, 19X2		

Cash flows from operating activities		
Collections from customers (1)	$92,200	
Interest received (2)	1,700	
Payments to suppliers (3)	(70,100)	
Payments to employees (4)	(17,500)	
Interest paid (5)	(2,000)	
Income taxes paid (6)	(1,200)	
Payments for insurance (7)	(2,600)	
Net cash flows from operating activities		$ 500
Cash flows from investing activities		
Purchase of equipment (8)	$(20,000)	
Sale of equipment (given)	3,000	
Building addition (9)	(43,500)	(60,500)
Net cash used from investing activities		
Cash flows from financing activities		
Issue of 10% note payable (10)	$20,000	
Issue of bond payable (11)	50,000	
Cash dividend paid (12)	(2,000)	
Net cash flows from financing activities		68,000
Net increase in cash		$ 8,000
Schedule of noncash investing and financing activities		
Purchase of land in exchange for common stock (13)		$50,000

(1)	Accounts Receivable			(2)	Interest Receivable		
Beg. Bal.	36,000			Beg. Bal.	3,500		
Sales	90,000	**Receipt**	**92,200**	Interest Rev.	4,200	**Receipt**	**1,700**
End. Bal.	33,800			End. Bal.	6,000		

(3)	Merchandise Inventory			(3)	Accounts Payable		
Beg. Bal.	72,000					Beg. Bal.	12,200
Purchases	**61,000**	Cost of		**Payments**	**70,100**	Purchases	61,000
		Goods Sold	68,000			End. Bal.	3,100
End. Bal.	65,000						

(4)	Wages and Salaries Payable			(5)	Interest Payable		
		Beg. Bal.	14,300			Beg. Bal.	1,300
Payments	**17,500**	Wages and		**Payments**	**2,000**	Interest Exp.	1,700
		Salary Exp.	10,100			End. Bal.	1,000
		End. Bal.	6,900				

(6)	Income Taxes Payable			(7)	Prepaid Insurance		
		Beg. Bal.	200	Beg. Bal.	2,700		
Payments	**1,200**	Income Taxes		**Payments**	**2,600**	Ins. Exp.	2,800
		Expense	1,000	End. Bal.	2,500		
		End. Bal.	0				

(8)	Equipment		
Beg. Bal.	53,000		
Purchases	**20,000**	Sold	5,000
End. Bal.	68,000		

(9)	Buildings		
Beg. Bal.	80,000		
Purchases	**43,500**		
End. Bal.	123,500		

(10)	Notes Payable—Noncurrent		
		Beg. Bal.	0
		Receipt	**20,000**
		End. Bal.	20,000

(11)	Bonds Payable		
		Beg. Bal.	0
		Receipt	**50,000**
		End. Bal.	50,000

(12)	Dividends Payable		
		Beg. Bal.	1,500
Payments	**2,000**	Declared	2,500
		End. Bal.	2,000

(13)	Land		
Beg. Bal.	22,000		
Acquired	50,000		
End. Bal.	72,000		

(13)	Common Stock		
		Beg. Bal.	150,000
		Issued for Land	40,000
		End. Bal.	190,000

(13)	Paid-In Capital in Excess of Par—Common		
		Beg. Bal.	50,000
		Issued for Land	10,000
		End. Bal.	60,000

KEY TERMS

cash equivalents, *744*
direct method, *733*

indirect method, *733*
statement of cash flows, *727*

SELF-QUIZ

LO 1   1. True or False? The statement of cash flows is not one of the statements included in a complete set of financial statements.

LO 1   2. True or False? The statement of cash flows should help the user assess a business's ability to meet its obligations and to pay dividends.

LO 2   3. Which of the following is *not* a cash flow from an operating activity?
a. Cash receipts of dividends
b. Payments of interests
c. Payments of dividends
d. Refunds to customers

LO 2   4. Which of the following is *not* a cash flow from an investing activity?
a. Payment of principal on bonds payable

b. Cash received from the sale of investments in stocks
c. Payments in the form of loans to others
d. Collections of loans

LO 2   5. Which of the following is *not* a cash flow from a financing activity?
a. Payment of dividends to stockholders
b. Payment to purchase treasury stock
c. Proceeds from sale of property, plant, and equipment
d. Proceeds from issuing bonds

LO 3   6. To perform account analysis in preparing a statement of cash flows, the accountant needs a _____ _____ _____, the_____ _____, and summary transaction data.

LO 4 7. True or False? Short-term notes payable can be included in cash equivalents.

LO 5 8. Which of the following is *not* a noncash investing and financing activity?
a. Purchase of land and building by assuming a mortgage payable
b. Declaring a stock dividend
c. Issuing stock to repay loans
d. Trading one asset for a similar asset of another company

LO 5 9. Which of the following would *not* be an adjustment to net income using the indirect method?
a. Increase in notes payable to bank
b. Decrease in accounts receivable
c. Depreciation expense
d. Loss from sale of land

SOLUTIONS TO SELF-QUIZ
1. False   2. True   3. c   4. a   5. c   6. comparative balance sheet, income statement   7. False   8. b   9. a

---

QUESTIONS

Q18-1 What are the purposes of a statement of cash flows?

Q18-2 What is the difference between the direct method and the indirect method of calculating cash flows from operating activities?

Q18-3 What are some examples of cash flows from operating activities?

Q18-4 What are some examples of investing activities?

Q18-5 What are some examples of financing activities?

Q18-6 How does the accountant use account analysis to help prepare the statement of cash flows?

Q18-7 What balance sheet account(s) and income statement items are analyzed to determine cash payments to employees?

Q18-8 How do we report noncash investing and financing activities?

Q18-9 (Appendix) What are the four steps in preparing a statement of cash flows using a worksheet?

EXERCISES

LO 2

E18-1 **Operating, Investing, and Financing Activities**   The following events occurred during 19X1. Determine if each event should be classified as an operating activity (*O*), investing activity (*I*), financing activity (*F*), or not on the statement of cash flows (*NS*).
___ a. Purchased property, plant, and equipment
___ b. Collected cash from customers
___ c. Sold land held for investment
___ d. Paid dividends
___ e. Issued common stock
___ f. Paid suppliers of merchandise
___ g. Collected interest
___ h. Distributed stock dividends
___ i. Paid wages and salaries due employees
___ j. Retired bonds payable

LO 2

E18-2 **Cash Flow Impact**   Determine if each of the items presented in E18-1 would be a cash inflow (*I*), a cash outflow (*O*), or have no effect (*NE*) on cash flow.

LO 3,4   **E18-3**   **Operating Cash Flows**   Determine the impact on cash flows from operating activities for each of the following items:

(1) Wages and Salaries Payable has a beginning balance of $3,200 and an ending balance of $1,100. Wages and salaries expense is $15,900.

(2) Prepaid Rent has a beginning balance of $2,800 and an ending balance of $1,600. Rent expense is $11,500.

(3) Accounts Receivable has a beginning balance of $5,900 and an ending balance of $6,300. Credit sales total $39,000.

(4) Income Taxes Payable has a beginning balance of $2,100 and an ending balance of $2,900. Income Taxes Expense is $6,900.

(5) Interest Receivable has a beginning balance of $1,900 and an ending balance of $1,600. Interest revenue is $3,700.

LO 3,4   **E18-4**   **Investing Cash Flows**   Determine the impact on cash flows from investing activities for each of the following items:

(1) Land held for investment has a beginning balance of $178,000 and an ending balance of $199,000. No land was sold.

(2) Notes receivable has a beginning balance of $28,000 and an ending balance of $44,000. No notes receivable were collected.

(3) Buildings has a beginning balance of $1,297,000 and an ending balance of $1,639,000. No buildings were sold.

(4) Equipment with a cost of $530,000 and accumulated depreciation of $210,000 is sold. The loss on sale of equipment is $45,000.

LO 3,4   **E18-5**   **Financing Cash Flows**   Determine the impact on cash flows from financing activities for each of the following items:

(1) Dividends Payable has a beginning balance of $9,200 and an ending balance of $3,800. Dividends declared is $18,500.

(2) Bonds Payable has a beginning balance of $470,000 and an ending balance of $770,000. No bonds were retired.

(3) Mortgage Payable has a beginning balance of $629,000 and an ending balance of $625,100. No additional mortgage loans were obtained.

(4) Notes Payable—Noncurrent has a beginning balance of $83,000 and an ending balance of $62,000. Additional cash of $30,000 was borrowed by issuing a long-term note payable.

(5) Common Stock has a beginning balance of $1,200,000 and an ending balance of $1,350,000. Paid-In Capital in Excess of Par-Common has a beginning balance of $4,700,000 and an ending balance of $5,150,000. No common stock was retired.

LO 3,4   **E18-6**   **Investment Account Analysis**   The account balances relating to equipment during 19X1 for the Taylor Company are as follows:

	Beginning balance	**Ending balance**
Equipment	$75,000	$145,000
Accumulated Depreciation	25,000	34,000

Equipment with an original cost of $16,000 and a book value of $12,000 was sold for $15,000.

REQUIRED:

Calculate the cash inflow from the sale of equipment and the cash outflow to purchase new equipment.

LO 4   **E18-7**   **Schedule of Noncash Investing, Financing Activities**   Prepare a schedule of non-cash investing and financing activities for the Stone Company if the following transactions occurred during 19X1:

(1) Issued $500,000 (fair value) of preferred stock in exchange for land and building.
(2) Acquired $175,000 of equipment with a capital lease.
(3) Traded $240,000 of land in California for land with an equivalent fair market value in Florida.
(4) Purchased a $300,000 parking garage by assuming a mortgage payable.

LO 5

E18-8   Operating Cash Flows, Indirect Method   For each of the following items, determine if they would be added (+), subtracted (−), or neither (N) when adjusting net income to derive cash flows from operating activities.

___ a. Increase in accounts payable
___ b. Gain from sale of equipment
___ c. Depreciation expense
___ d. Uncollectible accounts expense
___ e. Amortization of goodwill
___ f. Decrease in wages and salaries payable
___ g. Loss from sale of land
___ h. Decrease in interest receivable
___ i. Decrease in accounts receivable
___ j. Interest revenue

LO 3,4

E18-9   Operating Section of a Statement of Cash Flows   A partial comparative balance sheet and income statement for the Truax Company are presented below and on the next page.

REQUIRED:

Prepare the cash flow from operating activities section of Truax Company's statement of cash flows for the year ended December 31, 19X3. Use the direct method.

Truax Company Comparative Balance Sheet (Partial) December 31, 19X2 and 19X3		
	19X2	*19X3*
Current assets:		
Cash	$ 4,100	$ 3,800
Accounts receivable	13,300	14,900
Merchandise inventory	16,600	14,600
Prepaid rent	1,000	1,200
Total current assets	$35,000	$34,500
Current liabilities:		
Accounts payable	$ 2,100	$ 1,800
Wages and salaries payable	2,000	2,650
Interest payable	4,500	3,900
Income taxes payable	1,400	0
Total current liabilities	$10,000	$ 8,350

Truax Company
Income Statement
For the Year Ended December 31, 19X3

Sales		$66,400
Cost of goods sold		40,800
Gross profit		$25,600
Expenses:		
Wages and salaries expense	$12,900	
Depreciation expense—equipment	1,500	
Income taxes expense	1,000	
Interest expense	1,400	
Rent expense	2,300	
Total expenses		19,100
Net income		$ 6,500

LO 3,4   **E18-10**   **Investment Section of a Statement of Cash Flows**   A partial comparative balance sheet and additional information are as follows:

Truax Company		
Comparative Balance Sheet (Partial)		
December 31, 19X2 and 19X3		
	19X2	*19X3*
Assets		
Long-term investments	$13,500	$ 8,900
Plant assets:		
Equipment	23,000	28,000
Accumulated depreciation–equipment	(2,500)	(4,000)
Land	14,000	17,500
Total noncurrent assets	$48,000	$50,400

Additional Information:
(1) Long-term investments were sold at cost. No long-term investments were purchased.
(2) Equipment was purchased for $5,000 cash. No equipment was sold.
(3) Land was purchased for $3,500 cash. No land was sold.

REQUIRED:

Prepare the cash flow from investing activities section of Truax Company's statement of cash flows for the year ended December 31, 19X3.

LO 3,4   **E18-11**   **Financing Section of a Statement of Cash Flows**   A partial comparative balance sheet for Truax Company is shown on the next page.

Additional Information:
(1) Long-term notes payable of $5,000 were paid.
(2) Common stock was issued for $3,000.
(3) Net income was $6,500. All dividends declared were paid.

REQUIRED:

Prepare the cash flow from financing activities section of Truax Company's statement of cash flows for the year ended December 31, 19X3.

Truax Company		
Comparative Balance Sheet (Partial)		
December 31, 19X2 and 19X3		
	19X2	*19X3*
Noncurrent liabilities:		
Note payable—noncurrent	$20,000	$15,000
Stockholders' equity:		
Common stock, $10 par	$20,000	$22,000
Additional paid-in capital	10,000	11,000
Retained earnings	23,000	28,550
Total stockholders' equity	$53,000	$61,550

PROBLEM SET A

LO 2,3

P18-1A   **Determining the Change in Cash**   The Cash balance on January 1, 19X4, for the Pickens Company was $285,900. The following items occurred during 19X4:

(1)	Cash collected from customers	$493,800
(2)	Proceeds from issuing common stock	221,000
(3)	Purchase of equipment	79,100
(4)	Sale of building	99,300
(5)	Interest paid	29,900
(6)	Payments on long-term borrowings	129,400
(7)	Payments to suppliers	198,500
(8)	Dividends paid	87,700
(9)	Income taxes paid	41,200
(10)	Long-term borrowings	192,000
(11)	Interest collected	39,400
(12)	Wages and salaries paid	119,800

REQUIRED:

a. Determine the cash balance on December 31, 19X4.
b. Classify each item as either an operating (*O*), investing (*I*), or financing (*F*) activity.
c. Prepare a statement of cash flows for 19X4 using the direct method.

LO 3,4

P18-2A   **Cash Flow Information From Financial Statements**   Financial statements for Clarinda's Prime Rib Company are as shown on the next page.

REQUIRED:

Determine the following for 19X6:
a. Cash collected from customers
b. Interest collected
c. Wages and salaries paid
d. Payments to suppliers of merchandise
e. Interest paid
f. Income taxes paid
g. Dividends paid (Only cash dividends are declared.)
h. Proceeds from issue of common stock
i. Proceeds from issue of notes payable
j. Purchase of building and land (No building or land was sold.)

Clarinda's Prime Rib Company
Comparative Balance Sheet
December 31, 19X5 and 19X6

	19X5	19X6
Assets		
Current assets:		
Cash	$ 50,000	$ 75,000
Accounts receivable	145,000	210,000
Interest receivable	12,500	25,000
Merchandise inventory	105,000	165,000
Total current assets	$312,500	$475,000
Plant assets:		
Equipment	$ 20,000	$ 20,000
Accumulated depreciation—equipment	(6,500)	(13,500)
Buildings and land	130,000	282,500
Accumulated depreciation—building	(6,000)	(14,000)
Total plant assets	$137,500	$275,000
Total assets	$450,000	$750,000
Liabilities and Stockholders' Equity		
Current liabilities:		
Accounts payable	$110,000	$132,500
Wages and salaries payable	28,500	30,000
Interest payable	4,000	5,000
Dividends payable	0	17,500
Total current liabilities	$142,500	$185,000
Notes payable—noncurrent	0	125,000
Total liabilities	$142,500	$310,000
Stockholders' equity:		
Common stock, $10 par	$112,500	$150,000
Paid-in capital in excess of par—common	112,500	150,000
Retained earnings	82,500	140,000
Total stockholders' equity	$307,500	$440,000
Total liabilities and stockholders' equity	$450,000	$750,000

Clarinda's Prime Rib Company
Income Statement
For the Year Ended December 31, 19X6

Revenues:		
Sales	$1,550,000	
Interest	50,000	
Total revenue		$1,600,000
Cost of goods sold		1,250,000
Gross profit		$ 350,000
Expenses:		
Wages and salaries expense	$ 175,000	
Depreciation expense—equipment and buildings	15,000	
Interest expense	40,000	
Income taxes expense	20,000	
Total expenses		250,000
Net income		$ 100,000

LO 5   **P18-3A**   **Cash Flows From Operating Activities, Indirect Method**   An abbreviated income statement for Thomas Company for 19X7 is presented below:

Sales	$1,100,000
Cost of goods sold	(614,000)
Gross profit	$ 486,000
Operating expenses	(160,000)
Depreciation expense	(36,000)
Net income before taxes	$ 290,000
Income taxes expense	(130,000)
Net income	$ 160,000

Beginning and ending balances in Thomas Company's current asset and current liability accounts for 19X7 were as follows:

	Beg. Balance	*End. Balance*
Cash	$176,000	$190,000
Accounts Receivable	565,000	590,000
Merchandise Inventory	378,000	367,000
Dividends Payable	36,000	29,000
Prepaid Rent	89,000	86,000
Accounts Payable	277,000	272,800
Wages and Salaries Payable	57,700	59,900
Income Taxes Payable	62,000	42,000

REQUIRED:

a. Determine which of the current assets and current liabilities should be subtracted or added to net income in determining cash flows from operating activities.

b. Prepare the cash flows from operating activities section of the statement of cash flows for 19X7, using the indirect method.

LO 3,4,5   **P18-4A**   **Statement of Cash Flows**   Financial statements and additional information for the Atlas Company are as follows:

Atlas Company Comparative Balance Sheet December 31, 19X8 and 19X9		
	19X8	*19X9*
Assets		
Current assets:		
Cash	$ 4,500	$ 6,500
Accounts receivable	9,000	8,450
Interest receivable	875	1,500
Merchandise inventory	18,000	16,250
Prepaid insurance	675	625
Total current assets	$33,050	$33,325
Plant assets:		
Equipment	$13,250	$17,000
Accumulated depreciation—equipment	(625)	(700)
Buildings	20,000	30,875
Accumulated depreciation—buildings	(1,000)	(1,750)
Land	5,500	18,000
Total plant assets	$37,125	$63,425
Total assets	$70,175	$96,750

Liabilities and Stockholders' Equity

Current liabilities:		
Accounts payable	$ 3,050	$ 775
Wages and salaries payable	3,575	1,725
Interest payable	325	250
Dividends payable	375	500
Income taxes payable	50	0
Total current liabilities	$ 7,375	$ 3,250
Noncurrent liabilities:		
Notes payable—noncurrent	0	17,500
Total liabilities	$ 7,375	$20,750
Stockholders' equity:		
Common stock, $1 par	$12,500	$22,500
Paid-in capital in excess of par—common	37,500	40,000
Retained earnings	12,800	13,500
Total stockholders' equity	$62,800	$76,000
Total liabilities and stockholders' equity	$70,175	$96,750

Atlas Company
Income Statement
For the Year Ended December 31, 19X9

Revenues:		
Sales	$32,500	
Interest	1,050	
Total revenue		$33,550
Cost of goods sold		17,000
Gross profit		$16,550
Expenses:		
Wages and salaries expense	$ 2,525	
Depreciation expense—equipment	2,575	
Depreciation expense—building	750	
Interest expense	425	
Income taxes expense	250	
Insurance expense	700	
Total expenses		(7,225)
Gain from sale of equipment		1,000
Net income		$10,325

Atlas Company
Retained Earnings Statement
For the Year Ended December 31, 19X9

Balance, January 1	$12,800
Add: Net income for 19X9	10,325
Total	$23,125
Less: Cash dividends declared	9,625
Balance, December 31	$13,500

Additional Information:

(1) Equipment was purchased for $7,750 cash.

(2) Equipment with a cost of $4,000 and a carrying value of $1,500 was sold for $2,500.

(3) A small building was purchased at a cost of $10,875. The building was purchased for cash.

(4) Borrowed $17,500 cash by issuing a 10% note payable.

(5) Acquired land with a fair value of $12,500 by exchanging 10,000 shares of common stock for the land.

REQUIRED:

a. Prepare a statement of cash flows using the direct method.

b. Prepare a statement of cash flows using the indirect method.

LO 6 | **P18-5A**   **Statement of Cash Flows Worksheet (Appendix 18-A)**   Prepare a statement of cash flows for the Atlas Company. Use the five-column worksheet format presented in Illustration 18-9 (page 750). The Atlas Company data are presented in P18-4A.

PROBLEM SET B

LO 2,3 | **P18-1B**   **Change in Cash**   The Cash balance on January 1, 19X1, for the Staggs Company was $331,500. The following items occurred during 19X1:

(1)	Cash collected from customers	$673,800
(2)	Proceeds from issuing bonds	176,000
(3)	Purchase of building	97,100
(4)	Sale of equipment	149,300
(5)	Interest paid	29,900
(6)	Payments on note payable	219,400
(7)	Payments to suppliers	98,900
(8)	Dividends paid	57,700
(9)	Taxes paid	93,200
(10)	Proceeds from issuing common stock	122,000
(11)	Interest collected	63,400
(12)	Wages and salaries paid	215,100

REQUIRED:

a. Determine the cash balance on December 31, 19X1.

b. Classify each item as either an operating (*O*), investing (*I*), or financing (*F*) activity.

c. Prepare a statement of cash flows for 19X1 using the direct method.

LO 3,4 | **P18-2B**   **Cash Flow Information From Financial Statements**   Financial statements for Fazzio's Pizza Company are as shown on the next page.

REQUIRED:

Determine the following for 19X3:

a. Cash collected from customers

b. Interest collected

c. Wages and salaries paid

d. Payments to suppliers of merchandise

e. Interest paid

f. Income taxes paid

g. Dividends paid (Only cash dividends were declared.)

h. Proceeds from issue of common stock

i. Proceeds from issue of notes payable

j. Purchase of building and land (No building or land was sold.)

Fazzio's Pizza Company
Comparative Balance Sheet
December 31, 19X2 and 19X3

	19X2	19X3
Assets		
Current assets:		
Cash	$ 85,000	$ 127,500
Accounts receivable	246,500	357,000
Interest receivable	21,250	42,500
Merchandise inventory	178,500	280,500
Total current assets	$531,250	$ 807,500
Plant assets:		
Equipment	$ 34,000	$ 34,000
Accumulated depreciation—equipment	(11,050)	(22,950)
Buildings and Land	221,000	480,250
Accumulated depreciation—building	(10,200)	(23,800)
Total plant assets	$233,750	$ 467,500
Total assets	$765,000	$1,275,000
Liabilities and Stockholders' Equity		
Current liabilities:		
Accounts payable	$187,000	$ 225,250
Wages and salaries payable	48,450	51,000
Interest payable	6,800	8,500
Dividends payable	0	29,750
Total current liabilities	$242,250	$ 314,500
Notes payable—noncurrent	0	212,500
Total liabilities	$242,250	$ 527,000
Stockholders' equity:		
Common stock, $10 par	$191,250	$ 255,000
Paid-in capital in excess of par—common	191,250	255,000
Retained earnings	140,250	238,000
Total stockholders' equity	$522,750	$ 748,000
Total liabilities and stockholders' equity	$765,000	$1,275,000

Fazzio's Pizza Company
Income Statement
For the Year Ended December 31, 19X3

Revenues:		
Sales	$2,635,000	
Interest	85,000	
Total revenue		$2,720,000
Cost of goods sold		2,125,000
Gross profit		$ 595,000
Expenses:		
Wages and salaries expense	$ 297,500	
Depreciation expense—equipment and buildings	25,500	
Interest expense	68,000	
Income taxes expense	34,000	
Total expenses		425,000
Net income		$ 170,000

LO 5

P18-3B   **Cash Flows From Operating Activities, Indirect Method**   An abbreviated income statement for Carrera Company for 19X4 is presented below:

Sales	$1,650,000
Cost of goods sold	(921,000)
Gross profit	$ 729,000
Operating expenses	(240,000)
Depreciation expense	(54,000)
Net income before taxes	$ 435,000
Income taxes expense	(195,000)
Net income	$ 240,000

Beginning and ending balances of Carrera Company's current asset and current liability accounts for 19X4 were as follows:

	Beg. Balance	*End. Balance*
Cash	$264,000	$285,000
Accounts receivable	847,500	885,000
Merchandise inventory	567,000	550,500
Dividends payable	67,000	59,000
Prepaid rent	133,500	129,000
Accounts payable	415,500	409,200
Wages and salaries payable	86,550	89,850
Income taxes payable	93,000	63,000

REQUIRED:

a. Determine which of the current assets and current liabilities should be subtracted or added to net income in determining cash flows from operating activities.
b. Prepare the cash flows from operating activities section of the statement of cash flows for 19X4, using the indirect method.

LO 3,4,5

P18-4B   **Statement of Cash Flows**   Financial statements and additional information for the Hercules Company are as follows:

Hercules Company Comparative Balance Sheet December 31, 19X5 and 19X6		
	19X5	*19X6*
Assets		
Current assets:		
Cash	$ 27,000	$ 39,000
Accounts receivable	54,000	50,700
Interest receivable	5,250	9,000
Merchandise inventory	108,000	97,500
Prepaid insurance	4,050	3,750
Total current assets	$198,300	$ 199,950
Plant assets:		
Equipment	$ 79,500	$102,000
Accumulated depreciation—equipment	(3,750)	(4,200)
Buildings	120,000	185,250
Accumulated depreciation—buildings	(6,000)	(10,500)
Land	33,000	108,000
Total plant assets	$222,750	$380,550
Total assets	$421,050	$580,500

Liabilities and Stockholders' Equity

Current liabilities:

Accounts payable	$ 18,300	$ 4,650
Wages and salaries payable	21,450	10,350
Interest payable	1,950	1,500
Dividends payable	2,250	3,000
Income taxes payable	300	0
Total current liabilities	$ 44,250	$ 19,500

Noncurrent liabilities:

Notes payable—noncurrent	0	105,000
Total liabilities	$ 44,250	$124,500

Stockholders' equity:

Common stock, $5 par	$ 75,000	$135,000
Paid-in capital in excess of par—common	225,000	240,000
Retained earnings	76,800	81,000
Total stockholders' equity	$376,800	$456,000
Total liabilities and stockholders' equity	$421,050	$580,500

Hercules Company
Income Statement
For the Year Ended December 31, 19X6

Revenues:

Sales	$165,000	
Interest	6,300	
Total revenue		$171,300
Cost of goods sold		102,000
Gross profit		$ 69,300

Expenses:

Wages and salaries expense	$ 15,150	
Depreciation expense—equipment	15,450	
Depreciation expense—building	4,500	
Interest expense	2,550	
Income taxes expense	1,500	
Insurance expense	4,200	
Total expenses		(43,350)
Gain from sale of equipment		6,000
Net income		$ 31,950

Hercules Company
Retained Earnings Statement
For the Year Ended December 31, 19X6

Balance, January 1	$ 76,800
Add: Net income for 19X6	31,950
Total	$108,750
Less: Cash dividends declared	27,750
Balance, December 31	$ 81,000

Additional Information:

(1) Equipment was purchased for $46,500 cash.

(2) Equipment with a cost of $24,000 and a carrying value of $9,000 was sold for $15,000.

(3) A small building was purchased at a cost of $65,250. The building was purchased for cash.

(4) Borrowed $105,000 cash by issuing a 9% note payable.

(5) Acquired land with a fair value of $75,000 by exchanging 12,000 shares of common stock for the land.

REQUIRED:

a. Prepare a statement of cash flows using the direct method.

b. Prepare a statement of cash flows using the indirect method.

LO 6   **P18-5B**   **Statement of Cash Flows, Worksheet (Appendix 18-A)**   Prepare a statement of cash flows for the Hercules Company using the five-column worksheet format presented in Illustration 18-9 (page 750). The Hercules Company data is presented in P18-4B.

CRITICAL THINKING AND COMMUNICATING

C18-1

Sandberg Company is a large national chain of drug stores. It had the following reported net income for the past 5 years (000 omitted):

19X1	19X2	19X3	19X4	19X5
$100	$1,100	$2,200	$2,400	$6,800

During this period, most financial analysts thought Sandberg was a well-run company and represented a good investment. David Kirsten, a well-respected accounting professor, disagreed with the optimistic analysis of Sandberg Company. Professor Kirsten calculated the cash flow generated from operating activities (000 omitted) for 19X1 through 19X5 as follows:

19X1	19X2	19X3	19X4	19X5
$(1,900)	$(600)	$100	$1,100	$2,600

REQUIRED:

a. Explain how net income amounts could differ from the cash flows from operating activities by such a substantial amount.

b. Why was Professor Kirsten's analysis so pessimistic?

c. What mitigating factors could possibly make Sandberg Company a good investment?

C18-2

Bethany Benson, the president of Ampflo Corporation, is confused about why depreciation expense is added to net income and why gain from sale of land is subtracted from net income on Ampflo's indirect-method statement of cash flows.

REQUIRED:

Write a memo to Bethany Benson explaining why these two adjustments are made to net income.

C18-3

The financial statements of J.C. Penney Company reprinted in Appendix B at the end of this text present statements of cash flows for 1991, 1992, and 1993.

REQUIRED:

1. What method of preparing the operating activities section of the statements does J.C. Penney use?
2. Comment on the direction and magnitude of fluctuations in each of the operating, investing, and financing activities sections of the statements.
3. In the operating activities section, identify what you think were the major causes of the fluctuations that occurred.
4. What is your assessment of the overall cash flow performance of J.C. Penney for the three-year period?

CHAPTER 19

Financial Statement Analysis

Just over one year ago, Brian Boerne took over as Chief Executive Officer of Flatland Distributing Corporation, a distributor of auto parts. He promised the Board of Directors that he could turn around Flatland's downward trend in earnings. The Board entered into an agreement with Boerne to award him a bonus in 19X3, based on the increase in Flatland's earnings in 19X2 over 19X1. However, as a condition of the bonus agreement, the Board stipulated that Flatland's overall performance for 19X2 must receive a favorable evaluation from an independent analyst. The agreement states that the overall analysis will include relative profitability (rate of return on equity), earnings quality and persistence, cash flows, efficiency of asset utilization, reliance on and servicing of short-term and long-term debt, and financial condition and risk of financial distress. Boerne and the Chairperson of the Board jointly chose Deidre Washington as the independent analyst.

In this chapter, you will learn how to analyze a complete set of financial statements. You will learn about the concept of general purpose financial statements and about the other sources of information available to financial statement analysts. You will see the relationships between income statement components, accounting methods, and the important concepts of earnings quality and persistence. You will also learn about the tools of financial analysis and how to structure a written analysis.

1. Define financial statement analysis and describe the relationship between a business's net income and its future cash flows.
2. Define the various components of net income recognized under GAAP and relate them to the concepts of income persistence and quality.
3. Describe the tools of financial statement analysis, including the key questions underlying financial statement analysis.
4. Perform an analysis of a complete set of financial statements.
5. Organize and write an analysis of a set of financial statements.
6. Describe what an independent auditors' report adds to financial statements.
7. Describe the effects of general inflation and specific price changes on businesses, their owners, and financial statement users (Appendix 19-A).

LO 1

Define financial statement analysis and describe the relationship between a business's net income and its future cash flows.

FINANCIAL STATEMENT ANALYSIS

Financial statement analysis is the art of systematically utilizing (1) financial statement data, (2) ratios and other statistics calculated from financial statement data, and (3) information related to the financial statements to answer questions about a business and to make predictions about its future.

Future Cash Flow Orientation

As the FASB notes in the objectives of financial reporting quoted in an earlier chapter, users of financial statements generally want to make predictions about the business's future cash flows. Since financial statement data generally describe past events and conditions, they do not relate directly to the prediction of future cash flows. Nevertheless, the processes that a business has used in the recent past will tend to be the same ones that the firm will use in the future, perhaps with some modification, to continue to generate cash flows. Therefore, analysts use analysis of financial statement information as a basis for formulating predictions about the future.

How Accounting Net Income Relates to Future Cash Flows

Among the most analyzed aspects of any business are its net income and profitability (a measure of relative performance based on income). However, current net income does not measure current cash flows. So, how can the analysis of earnings satisfy the objective of predicting future cash flows? Earnings convey information about future cash flows by matching expenses (which are generally measured in terms of cash paid or promised to be paid for goods and services) with revenues earned (which are generally measured in terms of cash received or to be received). When we match expenses with revenues earned to determine accounting net income, we ignore the exact timing of the related cash flows. Thus, for any given period, income and cash flows are not the same. However, by systematically matching the flows according to the earning process, earnings convey the long-run (average) cash-generating ability of the current earning process.

In general, we can make the following assertions about cash flows and net income:

1. Over the life of a business, accounting net income equals cash flows from all sources, except borrowings and repayments of debt and transactions with owners. In other words, lifetime income approximately equals cash flows from operations and investment activities—the cash flows the business generates for itself (not from owners and creditors).
2. Therefore, over the life of the business, average income (per period) approximately equals average cash flows from operations and investment activities. In other words, average income is an approximation of average cash flows per period.
3. If a business continues in operation indefinitely, providing the same volume of goods and services at the same prices and using the same inputs at the same prices, current income is an approximation of the average net cash flows per period the business will generate *in the future*.

This latter concept may seem naive, since the future is never the same as the present or past. Yet, financial statement analysts can directly build on this concept to forecast the future. First, the analyst will want to evaluate net income to determine how well it approximates steady-state future cash flows. We call this the income persistence problem. Next, the analyst may wish to judge the net income for any bias—especially optimistic bias management introduces by choosing particular accounting principles and methods. We call this the income quality problem. Finally, the analyst must predict how a particular firm's future will be different from its past and adjust net income to achieve a better prediction of the actual (non-steady-state) future. Thus, successful analysts are the ones who have the best insight into the future.

PERSISTENCE AND QUALITY OF INCOME

LO 2
Define the various components of net income recognized under GAAP and relate them to the concepts of income persistence and quality.

In this course, we cannot cover all there is to know about forecasting a company's future. We can, however, teach you the concepts an analyst needs to form *the platform for a forecast* of future earnings and cash flows. **Income persistence** is the tendency for a component of income to continue in future periods under steady-state (no change) assumptions. **Income quality** is the degree to which management does not exercise or does not have the opportunity to manipulate the firm's income to paint an optimistic picture of ongoing income.

Income Persistence

Income statements are formatted to segregate income components or segments with regard to their persistence. Illustration 19-1 conceptually represents an income statement that contains at least one of every kind of income component recognized under GAAP. The components of overall net income in Illustration 19-1 that are preceded by a bullet (•) are intentionally separated from revenues and expenses under GAAP. These income components are believed to have different relationships to future cash flows than do revenues and expenses.

Revenues and Expenses.   From earlier chapters, you are aware that revenues and expenses are the increases and decreases in the business's assets and liabilities that relate to its *continuing* processes of supplying products or services to customers. As we mentioned earlier, revenues and expenses are representative of the business's ability to generate cash flows in the future under steady-state assumptions—that is, by continuing to do in the future what it has done in the current period.

ILLUSTRATION 19-1 Components of Net Income Under GAAP*

Revenues
Expenses
•Gains (losses) other than from providing products or services to customers
Income (loss) from continuing operations before taxes
Provision for income taxes (income tax expense)
Income (loss) from continuing operations
•Income (loss) from discontinued operations—net of taxes:
Income (loss) from operating discontinued segment(s)
Gain (loss) on disposition of discontinued segment(s)
Income before extraordinary items
•Extraordinary items (gains or losses) — net of taxes
Income before cumulative effects on prior years of changes in accounting principles
•Cumulative effects of changes in accounting principles—net of taxes
Net income

*Adapted from "Recognition and Measurement in Financial Statements of Business Enterprises," *Statement of Financial Accounting Concepts No. 5* (Stamford, Conn.: FASB, 1984), par. 34.

Gains and Losses.   Gains and losses are associated with the business's cash flows, and they are *normal* parts of doing business. For example, whenever a business retires or sells assets such as property, plant, or equipment, it generally recognizes a gain or loss. Similarly, whenever a business pays off debt before it is due, it generally incurs a gain or loss. However, gains and losses arise from events and transactions that are incidental to providing products and services to customers. Moreover, gains and losses usually occur less frequently and at less regular intervals than do revenues and expenses, especially in smaller businesses. Therefore, gains and losses, if material, are segregated from revenues and expenses in the income statement. With material gains and losses displayed in income statements separately, analysts can factor them into their predictions of future cash flows in a different way than routine revenues and expenses.

Income (Loss) From Continuing Operations.   Income from continuing operations before taxes equals revenues minus expenses plus gains minus losses. The income tax provision (expense) is subtracted to calculate income from continuing operations (after taxes).

Income (Loss) From Discontinued Operations.   Discontinued operations (including the gain or loss on discontinuing them) contribute to the net income of the current period. Therefore, income (loss) from discontinued operations belongs somewhere in the income statement. However, if operations are not continuing, they have no implications for future cash flows. Therefore, analysts interested in predicting the business's future cash flows would not want revenues, expenses, and gains or losses from discontinued operations mingled with those from continuing operations.

Extraordinary Items.   **Extraordinary items** are similar to gains and losses from a bookkeeping perspective, but here the similarity ends. The transactions or circumstances giving rise to extraordinary items are *not normal* parts of doing business and are not expected to repeat themselves in the foreseeable future.[1] For example, suppose that a business had property, plant, and equipment located in a foreign country. If a material amount of loss resulted from the sale of some or all of these assets, the result would be a loss on the income statement. The loss would be included in the income from the business's continuing operations because it is *normal* for any business occasionally to sell some of its assets. However, suppose a material amount of loss occurred because the government of the foreign country confiscated assets of the business that one of its executives used to commit an illegal act in that country. The loss would be considered extraordinary, because the rare illegal act of an executive is not a normal part of the firm's operations and should not recur in the foreseeable future.

Because extraordinary items are not a normal part of the business and are not expected to recur, they do not have implications for the business's future cash flows. Therefore, they are segregated from other income statement components.

Cumulative Effects of Changes in Accounting Principles.   The cumulative effects of changes in accounting principles are the effects on beginning retained earnings of using one method of accounting instead of another—for example, straight-line versus accelerated depreciation. When a firm changes from one accounting method to another there are two effects:

1. A current effect on net income of the change in accounting methods
2. An effect on the beginning balance in retained earnings, which should be adjusted as if the new method had always been in use.

This second (cumulative) effect of the change does not relate to future income or future cash flows; it is a measurement adjustment. However, in its *Opinion No. 20*, the Accounting Principles Board requires that cumulative effects of changes in accounting principles generally be shown in a separate category on the current income statement.[2] This reporting standard presumably discourages management from making inappropriate accounting changes or attempting to make changes to increase income artificially. Analysts always can pick out the effects of the changes and segregate them from ongoing income components.

Quality of Income

Quality of income is much spoken about among financial analysts, but it is difficult to describe concisely how to analyze it. One thing is clear, however. If management tries to manipulate the amount of net income, analysts cannot rely on the net income figure to the same extent that they could if management remained neutral. How can management manipulate income? In a surprising variety of ways. First, management can select among GAAP those principles that produce the desired effect on income but do not fit the circumstances as well as

---

[1] *Accounting Principles Board Opinion No. 30* (New York: AICPA, 1973), par. 20.

[2] *Ibid.*, par. 18. There are some categories of accounting changes for which an adjustment to prior years' financial statements are *required*. But they represent only a *few* exceptions to the rule, stated in par. 18 of *APB Opinion 30*.

other principles. For example, a growing business facing rising prices selects FIFO instead of LIFO, straight-line instead of accelerated depreciation, and point-of-sale recognition of revenue instead of the installment sales method for risky installment sales. Each of these choices, if not the most appropriate in the circumstances, will bias net income upward. Second, management makes numerous estimates and judgments in applying GAAP. For example, management ultimately is responsible for estimating the useful lives and residual values of assets, future warrantee costs, and future losses on uncollectible accounts. Management can systematically over- and underestimate these accounting variables in the directions that have desired effects on income. Finally, management can engage in outright fraud or deception. The most common intentional deception in financial reporting is overstating revenues. Methods range from recording the subsequent year's sales early—as revenue of the current year—to shipping goods before year-end to customers that did not order them (and recording the sales returns in the subsequent year when the goods are returned).

The difficulty in analyzing quality of income is that, if management is manipulating income, they do not openly disclose their actions. In the financial reports of companies, notes to the financial statements disclose the accounting methods and many of the estimates used—but often only in broad terms. However, professional analysts follow companies for years, observe the judgments that their managers make, and compare them to peer firms and their managers. Over time, companies gain reputations for high or low quality earnings and analysts make adjustments accordingly.

TOOLS OF FINANCIAL STATEMENT ANALYSIS

LO 3

Describe the tools of financial statement analysis, including the key questions underlying financial statement analysis.

The tools of financial statement analysis consist of common-size and percent-change financial statements and various financial ratios, many of which you are familiar with from earlier chapters. Common-size financial statements support a technique known as vertical analysis; while percent-change financial statements support horizontal analysis.

Common-Size Financial Statements

Common-size financial statements are those whose numerical amounts are re-expressed as percents of an important summary figure. In common-size balance sheets, all individual asset and liability balances are re-expressed as percents of total assets (total liabilities plus owners' equity). Illustration 19-2 is the common-size version of the Flatland Distributing Corporation's balance sheets for 19X1 and 19X2. In common-size income statements, all dollar amounts are re-expressed as percents of gross or net sales (whichever is the beginning figure in the particular income statement). Illustration 19-3 is the common-size version of Flatland's 19X1 and 19X2 income statements.

The common-size percents of financial statement component amounts are calculated according to the following formula:

$$\text{Common-Size Percent} = \frac{\text{Component Amount}}{\text{Base Amount}} \times 100\%$$

ILLUSTRATION 19-2 Comparative Balance Sheet With Common-Size Percents

	19X1 Amount	19X1 Percent	19X2 Amount	19X2 Percent
Flatland Distributing Corporation Comparative Balance Sheet December 31, 19X1 and 19X2				
Assets				
Cash	$ 155,000	3.6%	$ 85,250	1.6%
Accounts receivable (net of allowance of $35,000 and $50,000, respectively)	465,000	10.8%	720,750	13.4%
Inventory	850,000	19.8%	1,283,500	23.8%
Prepaid expenses	95,000	2.2%	109,250	2.0%
Total current assets	$1,565,000	36.5%	$2,198,750	40.8%
Land	1,125,000	26.2%	1,125,000	20.9%
Buildings	1,250,000	29.1%	1,500,000	27.8%
Accumulated depreciation	(300,000)	(7.0%)	(350,000)	(6.5%)
Equipment	750,000	17.5%	1,050,000	19.5%
Accumulated depreciation	(100,000)	(2.3%)	(130,000)	(2.4%)
Total assets	$4,290,000	100.0%	$5,393,750	100.0%
Liabilities and Stockholders' Equity				
Accounts payable	$ 250,000	5.8%	$ 382,628	7.1%
Notes payable	600,000	14.0%	900,000	16.7%
Wages and salaries payable	30,000	0.7%	40,000	0.7%
Taxes payable	52,000	1.2%	75,000	1.4%
Total current liabilities	$ 932,000	21.7%	$1,397,628	25.9%
Notes payable—noncurrent	750,000	17.5%	1,200,000	22.2%
Total liabilities	$1,682,000	39.2%	$2,597,628	48.2%
Common stock	$ 100,000	2.3%	$ 100,000	1.9%
Paid-in capital in excess of par	900,000	21.0%	900,000	16.7%
Retained earnings	1,608,000	37.5%	1,796,122	33.3%
Total stockholders' equity	$2,608,000	60.8%	$2,796,122	51.8%
Total liabilities and stockholders' equity	$4,290,000	100.0%	$5,393,750	100.0%

Thus, the base amounts in each statement are expressed as 100%. In Illustration 19-2, the percent next to 19X1 total current assets of $1,565,000 is calculated as follows:

$$36.5\% = \frac{\$1,565,000}{\$4,290,000} \times 100\%$$

Similarly, in Illustration 19-3, the percent next to selling expense of $687,470 for 19X2 is calculated as follows:

$$11.5\% = \frac{\$687,470}{\$5,978,000} \times 100\%$$

Vertical Analysis.   One application of common-size statements is vertical analysis. **Vertical analysis** of financial statements is the analysis of the percentage composition of the components of a particular statement for a particular year. Looking at Illustration 19-3, for instance, we note that in 19X2 Flatland's

ILLUSTRATION 19-3 Comparative Income Statement With Common-Size Percents

| | 19X1 | | 19X2 | |
	Amount	Percent	Amount	Percent
Net sales	$4,900,000	100.0%	$5,978,000	100.0%
Cost of goods sold	3,332,000	68.0%	4,065,040	68.0%
Gross profit	$1,568,000	32.0%	$1,912,960	32.0%
Selling expense	$ 539,000	11.0%	$ 687,470	11.5%
Depreciation expense	60,000	1.2%	80,000	1.3%
Interest expense	126,150	2.6%	189,902	3.2%
Other administrative expenses	514,500	10.5%	538,020	9.0%
Total expenses	$1,239,650	25.3%	$1,495,392	25.0%
Income before taxes	$ 328,350	6.7%	$ 417,568	7.0%
Income tax expense	95,222	1.9%	129,446	2.2%
Net income	$ 233,128	4.8%	$ 288,122	4.8%

Flatland Distributing Corporation
Comparative Income Statement
For the Years Ended December 31, 19X1 and 19X2

cost of goods sold and gross profit were 68% and 32% of net sales, respectively, and that net income was 4.8% of net sales. Vertical analysis can be coupled with comparing the percentages of various components of a statement in two successive years, which can reveal important changes. For example, we note from Illustration 19-2 that Flatland's total liabilities went from about 39% of total liabilities and stockholders' equity in 19X1 to about 48% in 19X2. From this change, it is clear that Flatland is relying more heavily on debt financing.

Common-Size Analysis.   Common-size analysis involves the analysis of the common-size percents of two or more entities. Analysts frequently want to compare one entity with another, but they would prefer not to let the different sizes of the entities interfere with their analyses. The common-size percents adjust all numbers in the entities' financial statements to the same scale, 100%. This focuses the analysts' attention on relevant relationships. For example, Illustration 19-4 compares Flatland's 19X2 common-size income statement with its industry averages. You can see immediately that Flatland has a higher cost-of-goods-sold percent, making its gross profit percent lower. Although its other expenses are a

ILLUSTRATION 19-4 Common-Size Analysis

	Flatland	Industry
Net sales	100.0%	100.0%
Cost of goods sold	68.0%	65.0%
Gross profit	32.0%	35.0%
Selling expense	11.5%	11.5%
Depreciation expense	1.3%	1.3%
Interest expense	3.2%	3.5%
Other administrative expense	9.0%	9.5%
Total expenses	25.0%	25.8%
Income before taxes	7.0%	11.0%
Income tax expense	2.2%	3.4%
Net income	4.8%	7.6%

smaller percent of net sales, they do not fully compensate for the higher cost-of-goods-sold percent. Thus, Flatland's percent of net income to net sales is lower than that of its industry in general. This quick analysis suggests that Flatland may have an opportunity to improve its profitability by improving its control of the costs of its purchases.

Percent-Change Financial Statements

Percent-change financial statements are simply conventional financial statements with changes and percents of changes added. Illustrations 19-5 and 19-6 contain the Flatland percent-change balance sheets and income statements, respectively. To calculate the amounts of changes, subtract the earlier year amount from the later year amount. Calculate the percents of changes as follows:

$$\text{Percent Change} = \frac{\text{Later Year Amount} - \text{Earlier Year Amount}}{\text{Earlier Year Amount}} \times 100\% = \frac{\text{Amount of Change}}{\text{Earlier Year Amount}} \times 100\%$$

For example, the percent change in net accounts receivable in Illustration 19-5 and the percent change in interest expense in Illustration 19-6, respectively, are calculated as follows:

$$55.0\% = \frac{\$720{,}750 - \$465{,}000}{\$465{,}000} \times 100\% = \frac{\$255{,}750}{\$465{,}000} \times 100\%$$

$$50.5\% = \frac{\$189{,}902 - \$126{,}150}{\$126{,}150} \times 100\% = \frac{\$63{,}752}{\$126{,}150} \times 100\%$$

Looking at the rates of change across periods in components of financial statements is termed **horizontal analysis.** The change percents represent rates of growth or decline in financial statement components and can provide many insights about the business's activities. For instance, we know from looking at Illustration 19-6 that Flatland's net sales, cost of goods sold, and gross profit all grew by about the same percent, 22%, in 19X2. While its other expenses grew at a slower rate, 20.6%, income tax expense grew by 35.9%. Thus, Flatland's net income grew by 23.6% on the net sales growth of 22%. Ordinarily, we would expect net income to grow by a larger percent than net sales, because some expenses do not increase, or increase very little, in the short run as sales are expanded.

Financial Ratios

Financial ratios are numerical statistics that represent important relationships between financial statement amounts. The debt-equity ratio, for example, reveals the relationship between debt and equity financing. It also measures the amount of financial risk (risk of insolvency or bankruptcy) the business is bearing. Although ratios may reveal some of the same insights that common-size and percent-change financial statements reveal, they are much more flexible. A financial ratio can be calculated to represent almost any relevant relationship between financial statement amounts. Ratios are not confined to information contained in any one financial statement. For example, rate-of-return ratios, such as rate of return on total assets, use numbers from the income statement in their numerators and numbers from the balance sheet in their denominators.

ILLUSTRATION 19-5 Comparative Balance Sheet With Percent Changes

Flatland Distributing Corporation Comparative Balance Sheet December 31, 19X1 and 19X2				
	19X1	*19X2*	*Change*	*Percent*
Assets				
Cash	$ 155,000	$ 85,250	$ (69,750)	(45.0%)
Accounts receivable (net of allowance of $35,000 and $50,000, respectively)	465,000	720,750	255,750	55.0%
Inventory	850,000	1,283,500	433,500	51.0%
Prepaid expenses	95,000	109,250	14,250	15.0%
Total current assets	$1,565,000	$2,198,750	$ 633,750	40.5%
Land	1,125,000	1,125,000	0	0.0%
Buildings	1,250,000	1,500,000	250,000	20.0%
Accumulated depreciation	(300,000)	(350,000)	(50,000)	16.7%
Equipment	750,000	1,050,000	300,000	40.0%
Accumulated depreciation	(100,000)	(130,000)	(30,000)	30.0%
Total assets	$4,290,000	$5,393,750	$1,103,750	25.7%
Liabilities and Stockholders' Equity				
Accounts payable	$ 250,000	$ 382,628	$ 132,628	53.1%
Notes payable	600,000	900,000	300,000	50.0%
Wages and salaries payable	30,000	40,000	10,000	33.3%
Taxes payable	52,000	75,000	23,000	44.2%
Total current liabilities	$ 932,000	$1,397,628	$ 465,628	50.0%
Notes payable—noncurrent	750,000	1,200,000	450,000	60.0%
Total liabilities	$1,682,000	$2,597,628	$ 915,628	54.4%
Common stock	$ 100,000	$ 100,000	$0	0.0%
Paid-in capital in excess of par	900,000	900,000	0	0.0%
Retained earnings	1,608,000	1,796,122	188,122	11.7%
Total stockholders' equity	$2,608,000	$2,796,122	$ 188,122	7.2%
Total liabilities and stockholders' equity	$4,290,000	$5,393,750	$1,103,750	25.7%

Although a ratio depicting any financial statement relationship may be calculated, certain ratios have the status of being time-honored. Many analysts employ them because they help answer important questions about the business's financial condition or performance. In earlier chapters, we have introduced you to many of these frequently used ratios and have showed you how to interpret and use them in decisions. In this chapter, we incorporate them into our analysis of Flatland's financial statements.

Key Questions Underlying Financial Statement Analysis

Because financial statement analysis is an art, rather than a science, there is no single best way to structure an analysis of a particular set of statements. However, we believe the analysis must answer the following key questions about the business and, therefore, the questions form a working framework to guide you:

ILLUSTRATION 19-6 Comparative Income Statement With Percent Changes

Flatland Distributing Corporation
Comparative Income Statement
For the Years Ended December 31, 19X1 and 19X2

	19X1	19X2	Change	Percent
Net sales	$4,900,000	$5,978,000	$1,078,000	22.0%
Cost of goods sold	3,332,000	4,065,040	733,040	22.0%
Gross profit	$1,568,000	$1,912,960	$ 344,960	22.0%
Selling expense	$ 539,000	$ 687,470	$ 148,470	27.5%
Depreciation expense	60,000	80,000	20,000	33.3%
Interest expense	126,150	189,902	63,752	50.5%
Other administrative expenses	514,500	538,020	23,520	4.6%
Total expenses	$1,239,650	$1,495,392	$ 255,742	20.6%
Income before taxes	$ 328,350	$ 417,568	$ 89,218	27.2%
Income tax expense	95,222	129,446	34,224	35.9%
Net income	$ 233,128	$ 288,122	$ 54,994	23.6%

- How profitable is the business?
- What is the composition of the business's current cash flows?
- Does the business utilize its assets efficiently?
- Is the business able to service (pay) its debts satisfactorily?
- How risky is the business?

In the next section, we present the analysis of the Flatland statements according to this framework. In each subsection of the analysis (corresponding to one of the key questions), we raise additional, more detailed questions to guide you.

Standards for Analyzing Financial Statements

To answer the key questions of financial statement analysis, some standards of comparison are useful. Many of the questions cannot be answered in absolute terms. For example, what level of profitability is satisfactory? In a market-based economy, the standard is a competitive standard. That is, *a business is earning satisfactory profits when it is earning as much as any firm could with the same amount invested in assets at the same risk.* If a firm cannot earn such profits, the owners will want to withdraw their investments and invest them elsewhere.

Some of the standards of comparison that are used in financial statement analysis are:

1. Prior years' financial statements
2. Industry comparisons
3. The plans of the business

We confine our analysis in the next section to the first standard primarily because basing the analysis on multiple standards would become too complex for this text. Comparing the current year to the immediate past year (and other prior years) indicates the direction that the business has taken and may reveal important trends that could persist into the future and influence future cash flows. To facilitate this type of analysis, most companies prepare comparative financial statements for at least two years. Because the standard of comparison for this type of analysis is so readily available, it is the type of analysis most frequently performed.

In contrast, outside analysts often experience problems obtaining information on industry statistics and the plans of a business. It is sometimes impossible to define the industry of a business. For example, at one time, Quaker Oats Company and its Subsidiaries operated in two major industries, groceries and toys (the latter through its Fisher-Price subsidiary). It would have been incorrect to compare the performance of Quaker to either the toy industry or to the grocery industry alone. Yet, there were few or no other companies operating in only those two industries.

Securing information about a business's plans may be equally frustrating. Managers rarely like to reveal their plans to outsiders, except in the sketchiest terms, because competitors may use the knowledge of the firm's plans to their advantage. Thus, outside analysts often find it difficult to secure useful information about plans at the level of detail they would like to have to compare to actual financial statements.

LO 4

Perform an analysis of a complete set of financial statements.

APPLICATION OF FINANCIAL STATEMENT ANALYSIS

In this section, we first list a set of detailed subquestions for each major question or category to guide the analysis. Then, we provide sets of observations derived from (1) the common-size financial statements (Illustrations 19-2 and 19-3); (2) the percent-change financial statements (Illustrations 19-5 and 19-6); and (3) the ratio values defined, calculated, and interpreted under the applicable questions.

Business Profitability

To judge a business's overall profitability from its comparative financial statements, you will want to address the following detailed questions:

- Is the business increasing or decreasing in profitability?
- What accounts for its increasing or decreasing profitability?
- Does it earn a satisfactory return on assets?
- Does it earn a satisfactory return on owners' investment?
- Are there questions about the quality of earnings?
- Are there questions about earnings persistence?

Common-Size and Percent-Change Evidence.   Illustration 19-6 (percent-change income statement) shows us that net sales increased by an impressive 22% in 19X2 (over 19X1). Cost of goods sold and, therefore, gross profit also increased by 22%. Net income increased by only slightly more than net sales (23.6%). With gross profit increasing by the same percent as net sales, the expenses other than cost of goods sold must explain how net income increased by a slightly higher percent. In Illustration 19-6, we note that selling expense, depreciation expense, and interest expense all increased by greater percents than did net sales and gross profit. However, other administrative expenses hardly increased at all; and, thus, income before and after taxes grew by larger percents than net sales.

Because cost of goods sold and gross profit increased in proportion to sales, they remained at 68% and 32% of net sales, respectively (Illustration 19-3). Net income also remained a constant 4.8% of net sales.[4]

Profitability Ratios. Illustration 19-7 defines and interprets the major **profitability ratios** and calculates them for Flatland's 19X1 and 19X2 financial statements. As we would expect from the common-size financial statements, the gross margin ratio (which is also the percent of gross profit to net sales) and the profit margin ratio (which is the percent of net income to net sales) did not change between 19X1 and 19X2. However, the return on assets improved from 11.4% to 12.5%, and return on equity improved from 9.2% to 10.7%. Thus, we conclude that while the profitability of each sales dollar did not change, Flatland did improve its rates of return by modest amounts.

Earnings Persistence and Quality. Flatland made no changes in accounting methods that would affect the quality of earnings. Moreover, it uses no accounting principles or estimates that suggest it is trying to bias the measurement of income upward. However, we will return later to the issues of quality and persistence of earnings.

Cash Flows

Profitability is the business's lifeblood. If a business can be profitable in the long run, it should survive and even grow. However, in the short run, the flow of cash through the business determines whether or not it is in a healthy financial position; that is, whether it is able to invest in all needed assets, pay its bills on time, and have reserve funds available to absorb unexpected demands for expenditures. In analyzing cash flows, we want to know:

- Are cash flows from operations positive or negative?
- Are cash flows from operations increasing or decreasing?
- Were cash flows from operations able to supply the necessary funds for investments in noncurrent assets?
- Did financing activities supply or use material amounts of cash?
- Did investing activities supply or use material amounts of cash?

Statement of Cash Flows Information. No customary ratios are designed specifically to answer the above questions. However, the statement of cash flows is tailor-made for this analysis. Flatland's statement of cash flows appears in Illustration 19-8.

Analysis of Cash Flows. Flatland's operations consumed net cash of $169,750 in 19X2 in contrast to net cash generated by operations of $52,628 in 19X1. Inventories increased by much more than accounts payable, requiring significantly higher payments for inventory purchases than for the cost of goods sold. Accounts receivable increased significantly, indicating that collections lagged significantly behind sales. These are the big contributing factors in the negative cash flows from operations in 19X2. Because of the negative cash flow from operations, Flatland apparently had to increase its short-term notes payable to banks.

---

[4]Actually, since net income grew by more than net sales, you would expect net income to be a larger percent of net sales in 19X2 than in 19X1. This is indeed the case. The percentages to two decimal accuracy are 4.82% and 4.75%, respectively. However, when rounded to one decimal place as in Illustration 19-3, the slight difference disappears.

ILLUSTRATION 19-7 Profitability Ratios

Ratio	Definition	19X1	19X2
Profit Margin *Interpretation:* Indicates net profitability of each dollar of sales.	$$\frac{\text{Net Income}}{\text{Net Sales}}$$	$$\frac{\$233,128}{\$4,900,000} = .048$$	$$\frac{\$288,122}{\$5,978,000} = .048$$
Gross Margin *Interpretation:* Indicates the amount of each sales dollar available to cover expenses and to provide a profit	$$\frac{\text{Gross Profit}}{\text{Net Sales}}$$	$$\frac{\$1,568,000}{\$4,900,000} = .32$$	$$\frac{\$1,912,960}{\$5,978,000} = .32$$
Return on Assets *Interpretation:* Rate of return earned on all resources used. When compared to other firms, indicates the business's competitiveness in employing assets; also indicates the business's ability to generate competitive returns to suppliers of capital.	$$\frac{\text{Before Tax Income + Interest Expense}}{\text{Average Total Assets}}$$	$$\frac{\$328,350 + \$126.150}{(\$3,679,872^a + \$4,290,000)/2} = .114$$ [a]The 19X1 beginning total assets amount of \$3,679,872 was reconstructed from the ending balance and the changes in assets recognized in the statement of cash flows for 19X1.	$$\frac{\$417,568 + \$189,902}{(\$4,290,000 + \$5,393,750)/2} = .125$$
Return on Owner's Equity *Interpretation:* This is the rate of return earned on resources owners provide. When compared to other firms of comparable risk to owners, it indicates the business's ability to earn competitive returns to owners. If the same ratio is calculated "before tax" and compared to return on assets, it indicates leverage effects from using debt to finance assets.	$$\frac{\text{Net Income}}{\text{Average Owners' Equity}}$$	$$\frac{\$233,128}{(\$2,474,872^b + \$2,608,000)/2} = .092$$ [b]The 19X1 beginning owner's equity amount of \$2,474,872 was derived from the ending balance plus 19X1 dividends less 19X1 income.	$$\frac{\$288,122}{(\$2,608,000 + \$2,796,122)/2} = .107$$

ILLUSTRATION 19-8 Comparative Statement of Cash Flows

Flatland Distributing Company Comparative Statement of Cash Flows For the Years Ended December 31, 19X1 and 19X2		
	19X1	*19X2*
Cash flows from operating activities:		
Net income	$ 233,128	$ 288,122
Depreciation expense	60,000	80,000
Increase in accounts payable	30,000	132,628
Increase in wages payable	2,000	10,000
Increase in taxes payable	5,000	23,000
Increase in accounts receivable	(125,000)	(255,750)
Increase in inventory	(150,000)	(433,500)
Increase in prepaid expenses	(2,500)	(14,250)
Net cash flows from operating activities	$ 52,628	$(169,750)
Cash flows from investing activities:		
Building improvements	$(125,000)	$(250,000)
Equipment purchases	(150,000)	(300,000)
Net cash used by investing activities	$(275,000)	$(550,000)
Cash flows from financing activities:		
Net proceeds of notes payable to banks	$ 100,000	$ 300,000
Proceeds of notes—noncurrent	350,000	550,000
Repayments of noncurrent notes	(150,000)	(100,000)
Dividends paid	(80,000)	(100,000)
Net cash used by financing activities	$ 220,000	$ 650,000
Net decrease in cash	$ (2,372)	$ (69,750)

Flatland invested in substantial amounts of noncurrent assets financed by additional long-term borrowings. It also paid $100,000 in dividends and repaid $100,000 in previous long-term borrowings.

On balance, net new borrowings (financing) were less than the investment in noncurrent assets and the negative cash flow from operations. Thus, cash declined by $69,750 in 19X2.

Utilization of Assets

Efficient utilization of assets is important to the long-run success of a company. If a business can earn the same income by investing in fewer assets and using them more efficiently, then its rates of return on assets and equity will be higher and more competitive. An analysis of asset utilization should answer these detailed questions:

• Are asset turnovers increasing or decreasing?
• Are receivables being collected more or less promptly?
• Are inventories becoming older on average and possibly obsolete?

Common-Size and Percent-Change Information.   From the percent-change balance sheets (Illustration 19-5), we note that the following assets increased by more than the increase in net sales (22%): accounts receivable (55%), inventory (51%), equipment (40%), and total assets (25.7%). On the other hand, cash, land, and buildings did not increase in proportion to net sales. However, with at least some assets and total assets increasing by substantially higher percents than net sales, we expect to see some decline in efficiency of utilization of assets.

Also, as we would expect, accounts receivable, inventory, and equipment all increased as percents of total assets from 19X1 to 19X2.

Asset Utilization Ratios.   Illustration 19-9 defines and interprets the major **asset utilization ratios** and calculates them for Flatland's 19X1 and 19X2 financial statements. Notice that total asset turnover increased slightly, meaning that, compared to 19X1, Flatland was able to generate marginally more net sales per dollar of investment in assets in 19X2. On the other hand, the turnovers of both receivables and inventory declined. The slower turnovers mean that Flatland increased its investment in accounts receivable and inventory per dollar of net sales generated. The increase in relative investment, in turn, means that these assets are not being used as efficiently. The age of receivables and days' supply of inventory express the inefficiency in another way. Assuming Flatland sells to its customers on terms requiring full payment in 30 days, the aging of receivables from 37 days at the end of 19X1 to 47 days at the end of 19X2 is particularly troubling. Flatland seems to have gone from having a moderate amount of accounts receivable past due to having a substantial amount past due.

Quality and Persistence Issues.   The slowdown of inventory turnover and increase in age of accounts receivable raise questions of quality and persistence of earnings. The slowdown in inventory, which is due to the large increase in ending inventory, may be due to inventory obsolescence. That is, Flatland may be stockpiling types of previously purchased merchandise that are not selling, while at the same time purchasing and stocking adequate supplies of the types that are selling. The effect causes inventory to grow more than in proportion to sales—just what we observe for 19X2. If Flatland has obsolete inventory, it should be written off or written down, resulting in a loss. To understand how sensitive Flatland's 19X2 results could be to this issue, consider that it would only require a write-off or write-down of 7% of December 31, 19X2, inventory to wipe out the entire $89,000 increase in income before taxes in 19X2.

The growth in accounts receivable relative to net sales and the corresponding increase in average age also raise valuation and income questions. The increase in age of receivables is an indicator of deterioration in collectibility of the accounts. Yet, the following analysis shows that the balance of the allowance for uncollectible accounts is actually a smaller percent of gross receivables (net receivables plus the allowance) at the end of 19X2 than it was at the end of 19X1.

	19X1	19X2
Allowance for Uncollectible Accounts	$\dfrac{\$35,000}{\$465,000 + \$35,000} = 7\%$	$\dfrac{\$50,000}{\$720,750 + \$50,000} = 6.5\%$
Gross Accounts Receivable		

Given the circumstances, it is safe to say that the allowance for uncollectible accounts should be larger than reported at December 31, 19X2. This would require an adjustment that would also increase uncollectible accounts expense for the year and decrease income before and after taxes.

ILLUSTRATION 19-9 Asset Utilization Ratios

Ratio	Definition	19X1	19X2
Asset Turnover *Interpretation:* Indicates efficiency with which total resources are utilized. Higher turnovers imply greater efficiency.	$$\frac{\text{Net Sales}}{\text{Average Total Assets}}$$	$$\frac{\$4,900,000}{(\$3,679,872^a + \$4,290,000)/2} = 1.23$$ [a]The 19X1 beginning total assets amount of \$3,679,872 was reconstructed from the ending balance and the changes in assets recognized in the statement of cash flows for 19X1.	$$\frac{\$5,978,000}{(\$4,290,000 + \$5,393,750)/2} = 1.24$$
Receivables Turnover *Interpretation:* Indicates efficiency of collection of trade accounts receivable.	$$\frac{\text{Net Credit Sales}^b}{\text{Average Net Trade Receivables}}$$ [b]All of Flatland's sales are made on credit.	$$\frac{\$4,900,000}{(\$340,000^c + \$465,000)/2} = 12.2$$ [c]The 1991 beginning net receivables amount was derived from the ending balance less the increase shown in the statement of cash flows.	$$\frac{\$5,978,000}{(\$465,000 + \$720,750)/2} = 10.1$$
Age of Accounts Receivables *Interpretation:* Average number of days to collect trade receivables. Indicates efficiency of collection of trade accounts. Also, indicates degree to which customers are past due in payment, if terms of credit are known.	$$\frac{\text{Gross Trade Receivables}}{\text{Net Credit Sales}} \times 365 \text{ days}$$	$$\frac{\$500,000^d}{\$4,900,000} \times 365 = 37.2$$ [d]Gross receivables was derived by adding the allowance for bad debts amount back to the net receivables amount in the balance sheet.	$$\frac{\$770,750^d}{\$5,978,000} \times 365 = 47.1$$ [d]Gross receivables was derived by adding the allowance for bad debts amount back to the net receivables amount in the balance sheet.
Inventory Turnover *Interpretation:* Number of times an amount equal to average inventory on hand was sold. Indicates frequency of conversion of inventory into sales or efficiency of utilization of inventory.	$$\frac{\text{Cost of Goods Sold}}{\text{Average Inventory}}$$	$$\frac{\$3,332,000}{(\$700,000^e + \$850,000)/2} = 4.3$$ [e]The 19X1 beginning inventory amount was derived from the ending balance less the increase shown in the statement of cash flows.	$$\frac{\$4,065,040}{(\$850,000 + \$1,283,500)/2} = 3.8$$
Days' Supply in Inventory *Interpretation:* Average number of days' supply in inventory. Indicates availability and efficiency of utilization of inventory; also possible overstocking, obsolescence, etc.	$$\frac{\text{Inventory}}{\text{Cost of Goods Sold}} \times 365 \text{ days}$$	$$\frac{\$850,000}{\$3,332,000} \times 365 = 93.1$$	$$\frac{\$1,283,500}{\$4,065,040} \times 365 = 115.2$$

After examining the above issues, we conclude that the earnings Flatland reported are probably overstated due to understatement of the allowance for uncollectible accounts and may also be overstated due to unrecognized inventory obsolescence (or other inventory valuation errors). Thus, we cannot rate highly the quality of the reported net income. Moreover, to the extent that net income contains overstatement errors, we cannot expect the overstated amounts to persist.

Servicing Debt

An important part of an analysis of a business is its debt-servicing record and its general financial condition. To have a healthy financial condition, the business should not only have paid all of its bills that have already become due, but it should also be in a position to continue to do so. A firm's continuing ability to pay its bills is a function of the degree to which it relies on debt financing, its liquidity, its profitability, and its reserve funds, if any. An analysis of debt servicing ability should answer these questions:

- What is the business's liquidity position?
- What is the business's solvency position?
- Is it relying on debt financing more or less?
- Does it have reserve funds to act as a cushion against cash inadequacy?

Common-Size and Percent-Change Information.   From the percent-change balance sheet in Illustration 19-5, we note that current liabilities and noncurrent liabilities increased by 50% and 60%, respectively, while total liabilities and stockholders' equity increased by only 25.7%. Thus, we expect to see in Illustration 19-2 that both current liabilities and noncurrent liabilities have increased as percents of total liabilities and stockholders' equity.

Liquidity Ratios.   Illustration 19-10 defines, interprets, and calculates the major **liquidity ratios** for Flatland for 19X1 and 19X2. All of the ratios have deteriorated except the working capital ratio, which remained relatively unchanged between December 31, 19X1, and December 31, 19X2. We note further that, if a substantial portion of Flatland's inventory should be written down or written off, or should its allowance for uncollectible accounts be increased significantly, all of its liquidity ratios, except the age of accounts payable, would worsen.

Solvency Ratios.   Illustration 19-11 defines and interprets the major **solvency ratios** and calculates them for Flatland's 19X1 and 19X2 financial statements. All of Flatland's solvency ratios have deteriorated between 19X1 and 19X2 because of its greater reliance on debt financing (and negative 19X2 cash flow from operations).

Reserve Funds.   **Reserve funds**, like cash flows, are not measured by ratios. Reserve funds represent the margin of protection a business has against sudden financial distress. Reserve funds consist of three components. First, a business may have assets in excess of what is required to produce its products or services for customers. This type of reserve funds is usually held in the form of cash reserves, certificates of deposit, or marketable securities. However, in some cases, other assets such as land not required for new facilities can be liquidated in time of need to meet short-run cash requirements. The second source of reserve funds consists of prearranged amounts of new debt or equity funds. For example, many businesses arrange lines of credit with banks that exceed what they expect to need, the excess being reserve funds in case plans do not work

ILLUSTRATION 19-10 Liquidity Ratios

Ratio	Definition	19X1	19X2
Working Capital Ratio *Interpretation:* Interpreted as an indicator of short-term liquidity or ability to pay short-term obligations with current assets.	$\dfrac{\text{Current Assets}}{\text{Current Liabilities}}$	$\dfrac{\$1,565,000}{\$932,000} = 1.68$	$\dfrac{\$2,198,750}{\$1,397,628} = 1.57$
Quick (Acid Test) Ratio *Interpretation:* Liquid current assets usually include cash, marketable securities, receivables, and other highly liquid assets. Therefore, this is a more severe test of immediate ability to pay short-term obligations than is the current ratio.	$\dfrac{\text{Liquid Current Assets}}{\text{Current Liabilities}}$	$\dfrac{\$620,000}{\$932,000} = .665$	$\dfrac{\$806,000}{\$1,397,628} = .577$
Working Capital to Total Assets *Interpretation:* Indicator of relative amount of current assets financed by long-term debt and owners' equity. May be interpreted as an indicator of short-term liquidity or ability to pay short-term obligations.	Total Current A - Total Current L. $\dfrac{\text{Working Capital}}{\text{Total Assets}}$	$\dfrac{\$633,000}{\$4,290,000} = .148$	$\dfrac{\$801,122}{\$5,393,750} = .149$
Age of Accounts Payable *Interpretation:* Indicates the apparent age of accounts payable in terms of an average day's purchases and, therefore, the timeliness of payment of payables.	$\dfrac{\text{Accounts Payable}}{\text{Purchases}} \times 365 \text{ days}$	$\dfrac{\$250,000}{\$3,482,000^*} \times 365 = 26.2$ *Purchases is derived by adding the increase in inventory (statement of cash flows) to the cost of goods sold.	$\dfrac{\$382,628}{\$4,498,540^*} \times 365 = 31.0$ *Purchases is derived by adding the increase in inventory (statement of cash flows) to the cost of goods sold.

ILLUSTRATION 19-11 Solvency Ratios

Ratio	Definition	19X1	19X2
Times Interest Earned *Interpretation*: Indicates the business's ability to generate sufficient funds to pay its minimum debt service requirements. The larger the ratio, the more comfortably the business is able to meet its obligations.	$\dfrac{\text{Pre-Tax Income + Interest Expense}}{\text{Interest Expense}}$	$\dfrac{\$328,350 + \$126,150}{\$126,150} = 3.60$	$\dfrac{\$417,568 + \$189,902}{\$189,902} = 3.199$
Cash Flows to Total Debt *Interpretation*: Indicates the business's ability to generate sufficient cash to pay its debt service requirements. The larger the ratio, the more comfortably the business is able to meet its obligations.	$\dfrac{\text{Cash Flows From Operations}}{\text{Year-End Total Debt}}$	$\dfrac{\$52,628}{\$1,682,000} = .031$	$\dfrac{\$(169,750)}{\$2,597,628} = ---^{*}$ *Cannot be calculated due to negative numerator.
Total Debt to Total Assets *Interpretation*: Proportion of assets provided by creditors. Indicates magnitude of debt service burden and potential for insolvency.	$\dfrac{\text{Year-End Total Liabilities}}{\text{Year-End Total Assets}}$	$\dfrac{\$1,682,000}{\$4,290,000} = .392$	$\dfrac{\$2,597,628}{\$5,393,750} = .482$
Total Debt to Owners' Equity *Interpretation*: Amounts of resources provided by creditors relative to owners. Indicates magnitude of debt service burden and potential for insolvency.	$\dfrac{\text{Year-End Total Liabilities}}{\text{Year-End Owners' Equity}}$	$\dfrac{\$1,682,000}{\$2,608,000} = .645$	$\dfrac{\$2,597,628}{\$2,796,122} = .929$

out as expected. The third source of reserve funds consists of completely new debt and equity funds that can be tapped when financial distress appears imminent. This last source of funds suffers a potentially serious drawback. When reserve funds are needed quickly—that is, when financial distress is imminent—the business may not look particularly attractive to new lenders or owners. Still, economically, if a business is able to earn competitive returns on assets invested in the long run, then it should be able to secure adequate funds to survive, even if temporarily it is in peril of financial failure.

In the case of Flatland, we have little hard evidence about reserve funds, except that its position has deteriorated. Its cash balance declined 45% in 19X2, and it has no marketable securities. It has land that may not be in use or needed for planned expansion, but there is no concrete evidence that it could be sold readily or without impairing current or planned operations. Total debt has increased by more than 50% in 19X2, and total debt to total equity is approximately 1:1 as a result. Thus, the only probable source of reserve funds would be new financing by existing or new owners. This is the most difficult form of reserve funds to raise in the short run. In summary, Flatland's reserve funds situation may not be critical, but it has clearly deteriorated in 19X2.

Risk Analysis

Investors and creditors are interested in the amount, timing, and risk associated with a business's future cash flows. Risk is the potential that future cash flows will be less than expected. Two components make up the overall risk of a business, business risk and financial risk.

Business Risk.   **Business risk** stems from the nature of the business and the markets in which it operates. Businesses operating in markets in which demand for products or services fluctuate widely face greater business risk than do those operating in more stable markets. Consider three industries that provide people with three essentials: the food products industry (food), the automobile industry (transportation), and the residential housing industry (shelter). The food products industry is generally considered to have more stable demand and less business risk than the automobile industry or the housing industry. Because the typical expenditure for a house or a car is greater than that for food, consumers often postpone expenditures for new houses and cars when they are pessimistic about the economic future. Food, on the other hand, is a daily necessity for everyone. Industries with less business risk tend to experience more stable net incomes and cash flows from operations.

Financial Risk.   **Financial risk** is the added risk that a business incurs when it uses debt financing. Debt financing does two things to the riskiness of a business. It increases the volatility of earnings and cash flows from operations through the leverage effect (explained below); and it introduces the risk of bankruptcy. Bankruptcy occurs when a business is forced to quit operating, liquidate its assets, and pay off its debts because it was not able to pay the principal and interest on its debts as a going concern.

Leverage Effects.   **Leverage** is the effect of using debt financing to complement owners' capital to provide the necessary funds to operate a business. Leverage has two effects—a beneficial effect and a risk effect. The beneficial aspect of leverage is the effect on the rate of return on owners' equity of borrowing to finance assets. The best way to describe this effect is by example. Suppose a business is considering investing $100,000 in required assets for a new operation that is expected to earn $10,000 per period, or a *rate of return on assets* of 10% ($10,000 ÷ $100,000). However, suppose the business borrows $50,000 of the required new investment and asks the owners to contribute the other $50,000. Suppose further that the interest rate required on the borrowed funds is 8%, or $4,000 per period. The rate of return to the creditor on the borrowed funds is obviously 8% ($4,000 ÷ $50,000). The rate of return to the owners on their investment of $50,000 (the rate of return on equity) is calculated as follows:

Total return on new operation	$10,000
Less: Required interest on debt	4,000
Net return on equity investment	$ 6,000

Rate of return on equity: $6,000 ÷ $50,000 = 0.12 = 12%

Notice that because the creditors in this case require an interest rate less than the expected rate of return on assets, the owners can expect a rate of return on equity greater than the expected rate of return on assets. This illustrates the beneficial leverage effect of liabilities on rate of return on owners' equity.

However, this same effect can be negative if the operation does not prove to be as profitable as expected. For example, if the operation earns only $5,000 (5%) on the total $100,000 investment, the creditors are still entitled to their $4,000. This leaves only $1,000 for the owners, which is a rate of return of only 2%. Moreover, if the operation earns less than 4% on assets (less than $4,000) overall, the creditors must still be paid $4,000; and the business must derive the funds from some other source. A simple comparison of several rates of return on assets and the related return on equity for the above example shows how the return to the owners becomes more volatile with leverage.

Return on Assets	Return on Equity
0%	−8%
2	−4
4	0
6	4
8	8
10	12
11	14
12	16

As you can see, a range of 0% to 12% in return on assets, which would also be the return on equity if the investment were funded entirely by owners' capital, corresponds to a range of returns on equity from −8% to 16% with 50% debt financing.

In summary, the financing of business operations with liabilities provides an opportunity for the rate of return on owners' investments to be enhanced. However, it also means that the rate of return on equity will be very low or negative if results of operations are less than expected and, in general, the rate of return on equity will be more volatile than otherwise. Therefore, one important decision for management is how extensively to utilize liabilities in the financing of the business.

Analyzing Risk.   Numerous techniques are available for analyzing the risk associated with the business's future operating cash flows and net income. They range from straightforward observation and logical analysis to sophisticated statistical techniques. The latter are beyond the scope of this text.

Applying simple observation and analysis to Flatland's situation indicates that its risk has increased during 19X2. Flatland's industry, wholesale auto parts, is relatively low risk from a demand perspective. That is, cars always need repairs; and when times are tough, people hang on to their cars longer and repair them rather than buying new cars. However, the auto parts business is very competitive. As a small distributor of auto parts, Flatland's chief source of business risk is that its customers, small independent auto parts retailers, will be driven out of business or taken over by the large chain auto parts stores. There is no evidence in the financial statements and no other information that would suggest that Flatland's business risk condition changed during 19X2.

Flatland's increased reliance on debt has, however, increased its financial risk. The proportion of its assets financed by debt (total debt to total assets ratio) went from 39% at December 31, 19X1, to 48% at December 31, 19X2. Thus, it will have higher fixed interest charges in the future, and its earnings will tend to be more volatile. Moreover, there is some greater probability of insolvency and bankruptcy.

WRITING AN ANALYSIS OF FINANCIAL STATEMENTS

LO 5
Organize and write an analysis of a set of financial statements.

Above all else, you should remember to be brief when writing an analysis of a set of financial statements. Financial statements contain many individual numbers and may be accompanied by many explanatory notes. You write an analysis to capture only the essentials from this potentially vast array of data. Thus, successful analysts must be able to recognize those things that are important and to ignore those that are unimportant. What is important is a matter of judgment, which is why financial statement analysis was defined earlier as an art. The beginner should look for significant changes in financial statement components and ratios from year-to-year. More sophisticated analysts with experience and knowledge of the business being analyzed will pick out more subtle cues. For example, experienced analysts will focus sometimes on components of financial statements and ratios that do not change significantly—because the analysts have reasons to expect that the ratios or components *should have changed* significantly. Illustration 19-12 is the brief analysis provided to the Board of Directors of Flatland as part of the performance review of Brian Boerne, the new chief executive officer.

AUDITORS' REPORTS

LO 6
Describe what an independent auditors' report adds to financial statements.

One aspect of an analysis of financial statements is the question of reliability. Even the best analysis cannot overcome significant errors in the financial statements or intentional misstatements or omissions. Audits of financial statements are conducted to enhance their trustworthiness and, thereby, their credibility. Management prepares and presents financial statements for use by outsiders. Management knows the most about the business and, therefore, is in the best

ILLUSTRATION 19-12 Financial Analysis

February 1, 19X3

To the Board of Directors, Flatland Distributing Corporation:

I have analyzed the comparative financial statements of Flatland Distributing Company for the years ended 19X1 and 19X2. The statements given to me for analysis are unaudited. Except as otherwise noted, I have assumed that the financial statements are accurate and have based my analysis solely on the information in the statements. My findings and recommendations are outlined below.

Profitability. Flatland's sales increased by 22% in 19X2. Cost of goods sold increased by the same percent as sales, and all other expenses increased by a greater percent, except other administrative expenses. Other administrative expenses increased by only 5%, permitting income before and after income taxes to increase by 27% and 24%, respectively. Gross margin remained constant and profit margin increased, but by less than a tenth of a percent of net sales. Thus, profitability per sales dollar remained unchanged. Rate of return on average assets and rate of return on average equity increased modestly from 11.4% to 12.5% and from 9.2% to 10.7%, respectively. However, as will be discussed below, the debt-equity ratio increased from 65% to 93% in 19X2. Had the proportion of equity remained constant, the rate of return on average equity would have been 9.8% in 19X2, cutting growth in return to one-half of the growth reported.[5]

Cash Flows. Because collections lagged and purchases apparently were accelerated relative to sales, receivables and inventory increased substantially and caused cash flows from operations to be a negative $170,000. Net increases in current and noncurrent borrowings totaling $750,000 were not sufficient to cover the negative operating cash flows, pay dividends of $100,000, and provide for new investments in buildings and equipment totaling $550,000. Thus, cash decreased by approximately $70,000.

Asset Utilization. Overall asset turnover improved marginally during 19X2. However, inventory turnover decreased, and the average age of receivables at year-end increased from 37 to 47 days. The decrease in inventory turnover and increase in age of receivables raise questions about the efficiency of investments in these assets. Moreover, inventory and receivables are commonly susceptible to realization problems. (See accounting issues below.)

Liquidity and Solvency. Flatland is relying more heavily on current debt at the end of 19X2, principally in the form of accounts payable and notes payable to banks, which together increased by more than 50%. Thus, in spite of the large increases in accounts receivable and inventory, both the working capital and quick ratios deteriorated, indicating a decline in liquidity. If receivables are omitted from the quick assets due to the slowdown in collections, the quick ratio would have dropped from .17 to .06. The average age of accounts payable went from 21 to 31 days. While this does not indicate any serious late payment problems, Flatland apparently is losing many more discounts on purchases at the end of 19X2 than at the end of the previous year.

---

[5]If the debt-equity ratio had remained at 64.5%, and assets grew to $5,393,750, equity would have been $3,278,875 at the end of 19X2 ($5,393,750 ÷ 1.645). The return on equity would have been .098 [$288,122 ÷ (($2,608,000 + $3,278,875) ÷ 2)].

Flatland also increased its long-term notes by a net amount of $450,000. Its debt increased by 54%, while total assets increased by 26%. Thus, Flatland is a much more heavily leveraged company at the end of 19X2 than it was at the end of the previous year. While the leverage effect was sufficient to cause a small improvement in the return on equity as noted above, Flatland is more financially risky as well. That is, all indicators point to a deterioration in solvency or, in other words, a higher probability of financial distress.

Summary. Flatland's net income increased by about 24% on an increase in sales of 22%, and the rates of return on assets and equity increased modestly. However, the investments in receivables and inventory ballooned by over 50%, causing cash flows from operations to be negative. As a result, financing through short-term and long-term debt increased by 50% or more; and both liquidity and solvency have deteriorated. The cash balance declined by 45%. In light of the increase in debt, the significant decline in available cash suggests that Flatland's sources of reserve funds are minimal, except for possible additional equity funds. Thus, in summary, the increase in income and the accompanying modest increase in return on equity were achieved at a cost of substantially increased financial risk for Flatland's stockholders. In other words, Flatland's performance in 19X2 was "mixed."

Accounting Issues. Analysis of the turnover of inventory and age of receivables suggests two common accounting valuation problems. First, the receivables are significantly older at the end of 19X2 than they were at the end of the previous year. Such deterioration in the age of receivables generally is associated with a deterioration in collectibility. Yet, the allowance for uncollectible accounts actually is a smaller percent of gross receivables at December 31, 19X2 than it was at December 31, 19X1. Thus, I conclude that the allowance and uncollectible account expense could be understated. Second, inventory increased by 51%, while sales grew by only 22%. Although no specific conclusions can be drawn from such a disparity in growth rates, commonly such a disparity implies obsolete inventory that may need to be written off. Either an increase in uncollectible account expense or a write-off of inventory, or both, would mean that net income is less than reported.

Recommendations. While income has increased and Mr. Boerne will be interested in claiming a bonus and stock options as his agreement with the Board provides. Flatland's overall performance, taking into account cash flow and financial risk, is actually mixed. If the Board sees these other aspects of performance to be of importance to the stockholders, perhaps a more detailed contract with Mr. Boerne should be written to include other indicators besides net income and profitability ratios. In addition, having an incentive contract with Mr. Boerne raises a conflict of interest issue. Mr. Boerne's performance is judged from financial statements based on his own decisions, estimates, and other judgments. The Board, therefore, should consider engaging an outside certified public accountant to audit the financial statements, thus reducing the effects of any management bias and the risk of errors.

Sincerely,

Deidre Washington
Financial Consultant

position to make choices about accounting systems, accounting principles, and the appropriate format for the enterprise's financial statements. However, many decisions outsiders make affect management's welfare. Financial statements may influence elections of boards of directors who, in turn, hire and fire managers. Boards often base management bonuses on accounting net income.

As a consequence, management may have incentives to bias information presented through financial statements. Managers have been known to go so far as to produce fraudulent financial statements. Even if management is not biased, they are often too close to the situation to see the potential for inadvertent errors; and they may not detect fraud perpetrated by employees.

For all of these reasons, an *independent* examination of the relationship between the financial statements and underlying events, transactions, and circumstances makes the financial statements more valuable to outside users. An independent audit involves a significant amount of testing, analyzing, and evaluating the financial statements and the underlying accounting system that produced them. Although audits are not exhaustive investigations for reasons of cost-effectiveness, they are designed to give reasonable assurance that financial statements are not materially in error or misleading.

Standard Auditors' Reports

The standard **independent auditors' report** appears in Illustration 19-13. Notice that the report consists of three paragraphs. The first paragraph identifies the financial statements and management's and the auditors' relative responsibilities for them. Notice that the auditors never accept the primary responsibility for the business's financial statements. Management must always retain that responsibility. The second paragraph, called the scope paragraph, indicates that the examination was conducted according to generally accepted auditing standards, which are broad standards that apply primarily to the quality of the auditor's conduct of an audit examination.

Notice that the auditors warn the users of the financial statements about certain limitations of audit examinations. For example, audits are planned to give *reasonable assurance* (not complete certainty) that the financial statements are not *materially* misstated (as opposed to free from *all* error). Therefore, audits involve examining evidence on a *test* basis (as opposed to exhaustive examination). The third paragraph, called the opinion paragraph, begins with the words, "in our opinion," which again emphasizes the lack of complete assurance or perfect certainty. It goes on to say that in the auditors' opinion the financial statements fairly present what they are supposed to present in all material respects in accordance with GAAP.

The particular wording of the report in Illustration 19-13 is called by several names, including a "clean opinion," an "unqualified opinion" and a "standard opinion." All of these names mean the same thing. The auditors, their examination, and the financial statements satisfied several criteria:

1. The auditors were independent of the firm whose financial statements were audited.
2. The audit was conducted according to generally accepted auditing standards, and no restrictions were placed on the scope of the auditors' examination by management or by circumstances that prevented examination of material elements of the financial statements.
3. There were no material misstatements or omissions in the financial statements relative to the requirements imposed by GAAP that were not corrected by management.
4. There were no changes in an accounting principle or method that had a material effect on the financial statements.
5. There were no major uncertainties that, if resolved one way or the other, would make the financial statements seem misleading after the fact.

ILLUSTRATION 19-13 Standard Auditors' Report

To the Board of Directors and Stockholders of ABC Company:

We have audited the accompanying balance sheets of ABC Company as of December 31, 19X1 and 19X0, and the related statements of income, retained earnings, and cash flows for the years then ended. These financial statements are the responsibility of the company's management. Our responsibility is to express an opinion on these financial statements based on our audits.

We conducted our audits in accordance with generally accepted auditing standards. Those standards require that we plan and perform the audit to obtain reasonable assurance about whether the financial statements are free of material misstatement. An audit includes examining, on a test basis, evidence supporting the amounts and disclosures in the financial statements. An audit also includes assessing the accounting principles used and significant estimates made by management, as well as evaluating the overall financial statement presentation. We believe that our audit provides a reasonable basis for our opinion.

In our opinion, the financial statements referred to above present fairly, in all material respects, the financial position of ABC Company as of December 31, 19X1 and 19X0, and the results of its operations and its cash flows for the years then ended in conformity with generally accepted accounting principles.

Count & Footes, CPAs

February 29, 19X2

6. There was no substantial doubt about the business's ability to continue as a going concern in the short run.
7. There were no other auditors for whose work on the audit the primary auditor will not take responsibility.
8. No other matters that, in the auditors' opinion, should be called to the attention of users of the financial statements.

Any departure from the above conditions requires a departure from the auditors' standard report. There are several different types of such departures. Users of financial statements should always read the auditors' report and note any nonstandard wording. It is helpful to know that most departures from the standard report result in extra paragraphs describing the departures or their causes.

Other Financial Statement Services and Reports by Accountants

Frequently, small businesses find audits too costly to be cost-effective. CPAs can perform two other levels of service for such businesses. Sometimes, CPAs *compile* financial statements from the business's basic records. This level of service is suited to very small businesses that do not have regular staff accountants qualified to prepare financial statements according to GAAP. Although compilation services do not involve any testing or analysis of the underlying data, banks and other users often prefer that CPAs prepare the financial statements of such firms. For more sophisticated businesses that do not require audits but want some assurance that their statements are not significantly in error, CPAs conduct financial statement *reviews*. Financial statement reviews involve studies of the business, inquiries of management, analyses of the financial statements, and other similar procedures. Although financial statement reviews offer some assurance that the financial statements are not significantly in error, they fall far short of the work performed and the assurance achieved in an audit. Therefore, it is important to read the auditors' report on a set of financial statements carefully to determine the level of assurance provided.

SUMMARY

Define financial statement analysis and describe the relationship between a business's net income and its future cash flows.   Financial statement analysis is the art of systematically utilizing (1) financial statement data, (2) ratios and other statistics calculated from financial statement data, and (3) information related to the financial statements to answer questions about a business and to make predictions about its future.

In general, we can make the following assertions about cash flows and net income:

1. Over the life of a business, accounting net income equals cash flows from all sources, except borrowings and repayments of debt and transactions with owners. In other words, lifetime income approximately equals cash flows from operations and investment activities—the cash flows the business generates for itself (not from owners and creditors).
2. Therefore, over the life of the business, average income (per period) approximately equals average cash flows from operations and investment activities. In other words, average income is an approximation of average cash flows per period.
3. If a business continues in operation indefinitely, providing the same volume of goods and services at the same prices and using the same inputs at the same prices, current income is an approximation of the average net cash flows per period the business will generate *in the future*.

Define the various components of net income recognized under GAAP and relate them to the concepts of income persistence and quality.   To help analysts build on earnings to predict future cash flows, the income statement is segregated into segments of income according to their relative persistence. Income from *continuing* operations is segregated from other, more transitory components of income. Within income from continuing operations, material gains and losses are isolated and reported separately. Gains and losses are normal in any business, but they only indirectly relate to the provision of products and services to customers and generally occur less frequently and at less regular intervals than do ordinary expenses and revenues. Income from *discontinued* operations and *extraordinary* gains and losses are totally separated from income from continuing operations because they clearly are not expected to be repeated. Finally, the cumulative effects of changes in accounting principles and methods are reported separately as components of current net income. These effects are not the results of any earning process *per se*. They only arise from the differences in methods of accounting for the same facts.

Describe the tools of financial statement analysis, including the key questions underlying financial statement analysis.   The tools of financial statement analysis consist of common-size and percent-change financial statements and various financial ratios. Common-size financial statements support a technique known as vertical analysis, while percent-change financial statements support horizontal analysis.

An analysis of financial statements should answer the following key questions about a business:

- How profitable is the business?
- What is the composition of the business's current cash flows?
- Does the business utilize its assets efficiently?
- Is the business able to service (pay) its debts satisfactorily?
- How risky is the business?

Perform an analysis of a complete set of financial statements.   An analysis of a complete set of financial statements requires using various tools of analysis selectively to answer the above key questions.

Organize and write an analysis of a set of financial statements.   Financial statements contain many individual numbers and may be accompanied by many explanatory notes. You write an analysis to capture only the essentials from this potentially vast array of data. Thus, successful analysts must be able to recognize those things that are important and to ignore those that are unimportant. What is important is a matter of judgment, which is why financial statement analysis was defined as an art. Above all else, you should remember to be brief when writing an analysis of a set of financial statements.

Describe what an independent auditors' report adds to financial statements. Management prepares and presents financial statements for use by outsiders. Management knows the most about the business and, therefore, is in the best position to make choices about accounting systems, accounting principles, and the appropriate format for the enterprise's financial statements. However, many decisions outsiders make affect management's welfare. As a consequence, management may have incentives to bias information presented through financial statements. *Independent* examinations, called audits, of the relationship between the financial statements and underlying events, transactions, and circumstances enhance the trustworthiness of the financial statements and, thereby, make them more valuable to outside users.

APPENDIX 19-A: THE EFFECTS OF CHANGING PRICES ON BUSINESSES AND FINANCIAL STATEMENTS

One of the important assumptions underlying financial accounting is that the monetary unit, the dollar in the U.S., is stable in size over time. The **stable monetary unit assumption** means that, even though prices change over time, assets, liabilities, revenues, and expenses are still recorded and reported in financial statements according to the cost principle. You will recall that the **cost principle** requires that the values assigned to assets and liabilities be the amounts paid for the assets and the amounts received for the liabilities in the original exchanges in which the assets are acquired and the liabilities are incurred. In many cases, the differences between current and historical prices existing at the times of the original transactions are negligible. However, over many years of price changes, the current prices of such long-lived assets as buildings and equipment depart significantly from original costs. Moreover, if most prices increase over time, each dollar currently buys less, in general, than the dollars a business paid many years earlier for assets that are still in service. Although these differences usually are ignored within the financial accounting process, changing prices affect businesses; and they affect how users should interpret financial statements. To understand these issues, you must first be able to distinguish between general price changes and specific price changes.

GENERAL PRICE CHANGES

LO 7
Describe the effects of general inflation and specific price changes on businesses, their owners, and financial statement users.

General price changes refer to the general trend in prices in the economy as a whole, in a major sector of the economy, or in a region of the country. General price changes popularly are referred to as **inflation** if prices are generally rising or as **deflation** if prices are generally declining. General price changes are measured by pricing specified bundles of goods and services at different times. The aggregate price of the specified bundle is then compared between points in time to determine whether the prices of the goods and services have generally increased or declined. For example, suppose the total price of a broad cross-section of consumer goods (houses, cars, food, fuel, clothing, etc.) had the following aggregate prices at the ends of the years 19X0–19X9.

19X0	$20,454	19X5	$24,682
19X1	20,949	19X6	26,227
19X2	21,696	19X7	28,101
19X3	22,817	19X8	30,219
19X4	23,768	19X9	31,299

To find out the percent change in prices between any base year (say, 19X4) and any subsequent year (say, 19X5), we perform the following calculation:

$$\left(\frac{\text{Total Price in Subsequent Year}}{\text{Total Price in Base Year}} - 1 \right) \times 100\%$$

$$\left(\frac{\$24,682}{\$23,768} - 1 \right) \times 100\% = 3.85\%$$

This calculation tells us that, on average, prices of consumer goods at the end of 19X5 were 3.85% higher than prices of consumer goods at the end of 19X4. One obvious consequence of this increase in average prices is that a given amount of money would buy less in 19X5 than it did in 19X4.

For ease of expression, the prices of the bundles of goods are commonly expressed in index numbers instead of money. For example, 19X4 can be selected as a "base year"; and its price index number is arbitrarily set equivalent to a value of 100. Then, all of the other years' prices can be expressed relative to this base with the formula:

$$\left(\frac{\text{Total Price in Other Year}}{\text{Total Price in Base Year}} \right) \times 100$$

Using this method, the price index numbers of the specified bundle of goods at the ends of years 19X0–19X9 are re-expressed as:

19X0	86.06	19X5	103.85
19X1	88.14	19X6	110.35
19X2	91.28	19X7	118.23
19X3	96.00	19X8	127.14
19X4	100.00	19X9	131.69

SPECIFIC PRICE CHANGES

While prices may generally rise or fall together creating general trends of inflation or deflation, respectively, not all prices follow the trends. **Specific price changes** are changes in the prices of particular goods or services, irrespective of general trends. The prices of some goods and services fall in periods of inflation, while the prices of some goods may rise in times of deflation. Moreover, the prices of various goods do not rise or fall at the same rates. For example, during the 1970s, a period of relatively high general inflation, the price of crude oil rose faster than the general trend; whereas, in the 1980s, a period of relatively low but persistent inflation, the price of crude oil actually dropped substantially. During both decades, the prices of certain electronic products such as color television sets, personal computers, and compact tape and disc players tended to drop. The point is that, while prices may generally be inflating or deflating, the prices of specific products or services may behave quite differently from the average trend.

CONSEQUENCES OF PRICE CHANGES

To see the consequences of price changes for businesses, consider a simple example of a small business, ItemStore, that buys and sells Items. ItemStore starts at the beginning of 19X1 with an investment of $50,000, $20,000 of which it borrows on a 2-year, 10% note, payable at the end of 19X2. The $50,000 is invested in an inventory of 1,000 items at a cost of $10 each and $40,000 worth of equipment with an expected life of 2 years. During its first two years, ItemStore experiences the following operations and other events:

a. The firm sells 10,000 Items (inventory "turns over" 10 times) each year.
b. The purchase price and selling price of an Item are $10 and $15, respectively.
c. The firm depreciated the equipment on a straight-line basis.
d. The firm accrued interest payable of $2,000 on the note each year.
e. The firm paid income taxes on its income before taxes at 30%.
f. The firm paid cash dividends equal to its net income.
g. At the end of 19X2, the firm liquidated its inventory (did not replace inventory sold as year-end approached), retired its fully depreciated equipment (no gain or loss), and repaid the note with interest.

ItemStore's income statements for 19X1 and 19X2 are as follows:

	19X1	19X2
Net sales revenue	$150,000	$150,000
Cost of goods sold	(100,000)	(100,000)
Depreciation expense	(20,000)	(20,000)
Interest expense	(2,000)	(2,000)
Income before taxes	$ 28,000	$ 28,000
Income tax expense	(8,400)	(8,400)
Net income	$ 19,600	$ 19,600

Illustration 19-14 presents ItemStore's 2-year history in accounting-equation format.[6]

ILLUSTRATION 19-14 Two-Year Accounting History of ItemStore

Transactions and Events	Cash	+ Inventory	+ Equipment	– Accumulated Depreciation	= Note	+ Contributed Capital	+ Retained Earnings
19X1:							
Owners invest	30,000					30,000	
Borrowing	20,000				20,000		
Investment	(50,000)	10,000	40,000				
Sales	150,000						150,000
Purchases	(100,000)	100,000					
Cost of sales		(100,000)					(100,000)
Depreciation				(20,000)			(20,000)
Interest					2,000		(2,000)
Taxes	(8,400)						(8,400)
Dividends	(19,600)						(19,600)
Balances	22,000	10,000	40,000	(20,000)	22,000	30,000	0
19X2:							
Sales	150,000						150,000
Purchases	(90,000)	90,000					
Cost of sales		(100,000)					(100,000)
Depreciation				(20,000)			(20,000)
Interest					2,000		(2,000)
Taxes	(8,400)						(8,400)
Dividends	(19,600)						(19,600)
Repay note	(24,000)				(24,000)		
Retire equipment			(40,000)	40,000			
Balances	30,000	0	0	0	0	30,000	0

Illustration 19-14 shows us some of the business implications of financial accounting. Notice that when a firm follows a policy of paying dividends equal to net income, its Retained Earnings balance remains zero and its contributed capital remains intact. Moreover, if a firm goes through its life cycle following such a policy and then liquidates its assets and pays its liabilities, it will end its life with cash and contributed capital equal to the owners' cumulative invest-

---

[6]For convenience in presenting a single picture capturing ItemStore's 2-year history, several shortcuts are taken in Illustration 19-14. Increases and decreases in accounts are expressed algebraically instead of as debits and credits. Revenues and expenses are entered directly into Retained Earnings instead of to temporary accounts that would be closed to Retained Earnings. Finally, all sales and purchases are assumed to be for cash.

ments—in this case $30,000. In the case illustrated, the owners would have a choice between:

1. Withdrawing the $30,000 and having ItemStore go out of business
2. Borrowing $20,000 again, combining it with the $30,000 remaining investment of the owners, reinvesting in new inventory and equipment, and continuing the business as before

Some Consequences of General Inflation

When general inflation or deflation take place, owners of businesses and creditors experience purchasing power gains and losses. Constant dollar accounting can be used to measure these effects of changes in general prices.

Purchasing Power Gains and Losses.   Assume that prices did not change during the 2 years of ItemStore's existence. The owners will be as well off at the end of 19X2, if their $30,000 is returned to them, as they were when they invested that amount. Moreover, they will have enjoyed total dividends of $19,600 in each of the 2 years. Under this assumption, accounting net income measures the amount of benefits the owners enjoy as a result of investing in ItemStore. However, suppose the general price level rose from 86.06 at the time of the owners' investment at the beginning of 19X1 to 91.28 at the end of 19X2. This means that it would take $91.28 to purchase at the end of 19X2 what could be purchased at the beginning of 19X1 for $86.06. By extension, the $30,000 returned to the owners at the end of 19X2 would only have the purchasing power of $28,284.40 in 19X1:

$$\$30,000 \ \times \ \frac{86.06}{91.28} \ = \ \$28,284.40$$

The owners, therefore, have lost some of the purchasing power of their original investments while they enjoyed the dividends they received. Thus, in times of inflation, net income alone does not measure the benefits of ownership. To measure the owners' net benefits, it is necessary to offset the loss in purchasing power of their investments against the income recognized (or, in this case, the dividends paid).

Constant Dollar Accounting.   If the owners in the above example wanted to know just how well off they have been made over 2 years as a result of their investments, they would face a problem of nonconstant dollars. That is, their investment of $30,000, the first dividend of $19,600, the second dividend of $19,600 and the return of their investment of $30,000 occurred at times of different-sized dollars (different purchasing power). Adding and subtracting these amounts is like "adding and subtracting apples and oranges"—to quote the classic complaint about the stable monetary unit assumption. Logically, the amounts measured in different-sized dollars must be re-expressed in the same-sized units. To do this, the dollars of one point in time are converted to dollars of another point in time that would have the same purchasing power. The conversions are made according to the following formula:

$$\text{Transaction Amount} \ \times \ \frac{\textbf{Base Price Index}}{\textbf{Price Index at Time of Transaction}}$$

The base price index is the price index for the point in time whose dollars are used as the constant monetary units to express all other amounts. The investment history of the investors in ItemStore is re-expressed in constant, end-of-19X2 dollars as follows:

19X2 Return of investment	$30,000 x (91.28 ÷ 91.28) =	$30,000.00
19X2 Dividends	$19,600 x (91.28 ÷ 91.28) =	19,600.00
19X1 Dividends	$19,600 x (91.28 ÷ 88.14) =	20,298.25
Less: Original investment	$30,000 x (91.28 ÷ 86.06) =	(31,819.66)
Constant-dollar income (in 19X2 dollars)		$38,078.59

The owners of ItemStore received dividends for 19X1 and 19X2 totaling $39,200. However, the above calculation tells us that the net effect of the owners' investment in ItemStore for 2 years was $38,078.59 as expressed in 19X2 dollars. Thus, the owners lost purchasing power equivalent to $1,121.41 in 19X2 dollars ($39,200.00 − $38,078.59).

Debtor Gains From Inflation. One aspect of the above example is the business's use of debt to finance some of its investment in assets. Because the owners did not invest all the necessary funds to run the business, they transferred some of the purchasing power loss on the total required investment to the creditors. ItemStore borrowed $20,000 at the beginning of 19X1. At the end of 19X2, it paid back $20,000 plus $4,000 of accrued interest. However, the amount borrowed is the equivalent of $21,213.11 in end-of-19X2 dollars [$20,000 x (91.28 ÷ 86.06)]. Therefore, the creditors lost $1,213.11 in purchasing power. This is a benefit to the owners because they had the use of the assets purchased with the creditors' money without suffering a purchasing power loss on that portion of ItemStore's total investment in assets.

As a general rule, debtors gain and creditors lose purchasing power in times of inflation. However, since businesspeople, bankers, and investors are generally aware of this effect of general inflation, interest rates are higher when higher inflation is expected and lower when lower inflation (or deflation) is expected. Therefore, only unexpected inflation leads to *real gains* for debtors and *real losses* for creditors.

Some Consequences of Specific Price Changes

While general inflation and deflation affect the owners' purchasing power, specific price changes affect the business. Specific price changes can affect the business's ability to carry on future operations at the same level physically and they disrupt the relationship between current income and future cash flows.

Let us now *suppose there was no general inflation* from the beginning of 19X1 to the end of 19X2. Assume, also, that there were no specific price changes either. If the owners wish to continue the business, ItemStore may simply borrow $20,000 again, combine it with the owners' remaining investment of $30,000, reinvest in inventory and equipment, and carry on the business as usual. However, let us suppose that the specific cost of Items was increased to $12 each just at the end of 19X2 and the cost of the equipment used in the business had increased to $50,000. If the owners decide to withdraw their investment of $30,000 at the end of 19X2 and discontinue the business, these specific price changes are irrelevant. However, if the business is to continue, the specific price changes are significant.

Erosion of Capital.   The required total investment in assets has increased from $50,000 to $62,000—$50,000 for equipment plus $12,000 for inventory (1,000 Items x $12). If the debt-to-equity investment proportions are held constant, the business would borrow 40% of $62,000, or $24,800. This leaves a required equity investment of $37,200, or $7,200 more than the owners' remaining investment. Some would say, therefore, that the dividends paid in 19X1 and 19X2 were excessive, because they jeopardized the business's ability to continue its activities at the same volume. By extension, net income did not measure income because the income could not be spent on dividends to the owners without requiring new investment to continue the same volume of business. This tends to violate our intuition that income is disposable—that is, income may be withdrawn or distributed without diminishing the business's ability to continue.

Prediction of Future Operating Flows.   The specific price changes also mean that analysts may be missing information that is relevant for predicting future cash flows. The 19X1 and 19X2 income statements are based on old prices that definitely do not apply to the future. Unless analysts know that the replacement equipment will cost $50,000 in early 19X3 and that Items will cost $12 each, they might forecast different costs based on the 19X1 and 19X2 income statements. In addition, the firm will have to raise its selling price to maintain its profitability. This may or may not be possible, depending on aggregate demand and competition in its industry. If they do not know about the specific price changes, analysts may not anticipate these issues.

Supplemental Inflation and Current Cost Information

For many years, the limitations of the stable monetary unit assumption in times of changing prices were debated. The SEC and FASB were keenly aware of the implications of inflation and specific price changes for businesses, owners, creditors, and analysts of financial statements. Their awareness was particularly acute during the 1970s when inflation was high and significant specific price changes took place. The FASB issued *Statement of Financial Accounting Standards No. 33* in September 1979, *requiring* large, publicly-held corporations to provide supplemental information with their financial statements.[7] The supplements are too intricate to define and explain here, but they revealed certain aspects of the effects on the business of both general and specific price changes. However, in 1984, the FASB issued *SFAS No. 82*, making the general-inflation information voluntary.[8] Then, in 1986, the FASB issued *SFAS No. 89*, making the specific-price information voluntary.[9]

---

[7]"Financial Reporting and Changing Prices," *Statement of Financial Accounting Standards No. 33* (Stamford, Conn.: FASB, 1979).

[8]"Financial Reporting and Changing Prices: Elimination of Certain Disclosures," *Statement of Financial Accounting Standards No. 82* (Stamford, Conn.: FASB, 1984).

[9]"Financial Reporting and Changing Prices," *Statement of Financial Accounting Standards No. 89* (Stamford, Conn.: FASB, 1986).

REVIEW PROBLEM

The Bluegrass Distribution Company specializes in grass seeds. It sells a large variety of seeds to accommodate differing climates and conditions. Most of its business is with state highway departments and large contractors, and all sales are on credit. Bluegrass's financial statements for the years 19X2 and 19X3 are as follows:

Bluegrass Distribution Company
Comparative Balance Sheet (Unaudited)
December 31, 19X2 and 19X3

	19X2	19X3
Assets		
Cash	$110,000	$130,000
Accounts receivable	95,000	125,000
Allowance for uncollectible accounts	(3,000)	(2,500)
Inventory	205,000	290,000
Supplies	2,000	2,500
Prepaid expenses	4,000	3,000
Total current assets	$413,000	$548,000
Land	60,000	60,000
Buildings and equipment	250,000	400,000
Accumulated depreciation	(100,000)	(125,000)
Total assets	$623,000	$883,000
Liabilities and Stockholders' Equity		
Accounts payable	$ 52,000	$ 61,000
Notes payable	40,000	50,000
Wages and salaries payable	5,000	5,000
Taxes payable	4,000	5,000
Total current liabilities	$101,000	$121,000
Notes payable—noncurrent	0	100,000
Total liabilities	$101,000	$221,000
Common stock	$100,000	$110,000
Paid-in capital in excess of par	300,000	340,000
Retained earnings	122,000	212,000
Total stockholders' equity	$522,000	$662,000
Total liabilities & stockholders' equity	$623,000	$883,000

Bluegrass Distribution Company
Comparative Income Statement (Unaudited)
For the Years Ended December 31, 19X2 and 19X3

	19X2	19X3
Net sales	$1,200,000	$1,400,000
Cost of goods sold:		
Beginning inventory	$ 180,000	$ 205,000
Purchases (net)	720,000	900,000
Cost of goods available	$ 900,000	$1,105,000
Ending inventory	205,000	290,000
Cost of goods sold	$ 695,000	$ 815,000
Gross profit	$ 505,000	$ 585,000

Continued

Selling expenses	$150,000	$175,000
Depreciation expense	15,000	25,000
Administrative expenses	160,000	170,000
Total operating expenses	$325,000	$370,000
Operating income before taxes	$180,000	$215,000
Interest expense	4,000	15,000
Income before taxes	$176,000	$200,000
Income tax expense	52,800	60,000
Net income	$123,200	$140,000

Bluegrass Distribution Company
Comparative Statement of Retained Earnings (Unaudited)
For the Years Ended December 31, 19X2 and 19X3

	19X2	*19X3*
Retained earnings, beginning	$ 48,800	$122,000
Net income	123,200	140,000
Dividends declared	(50,000)	(50,000)
Retained earnings, ending	$122,000	$212,000

Bluegrass Distribution Company
Comparative Statement of Cash Flows
For the Years Ended December 31, 19X2 and 19X3

	19X2	*19X3*
Cash flows from operating activities:		
Net income	$123,200	$ 140,000
Depreciation expense	15,000	25,000
Increase in accounts payable	5,000	9,000
Increase in taxes payable	200	1,000
Decrease in prepaid expenses	100	1,000
Increase in accounts receivable (net)	(6,000)	(30,500)
Increase in inventory	(25,000)	(85,000)
Increase in supplies	0	(500)
Net cash flows from operating activities	$112,500	$ 60,000
Cash flows from investing activities:		
Purchase of building and equipment	(25,000)	(150,000)
Net cash flows from investing activities	$ (25,000)	$(150,000)
Cash flows from financing activities:		
Payment of dividends	(50,000)	(50,000)
Net proceeds from short-term notes	5,000	10,000
Noncurrent note issued	0	100,000
Common stock issued	0	50,000
Net cash flows from financing activities	$ (45,000)	$ 110,000
Net increase in cash	$ 42,500	$ 20,000

Additional Information:
Beginning 19X2 balances:

Total assets	$539,600
Receivables (net)	86,000
Owners' equity	448,800

REQUIRED:

a. Calculate the following profitability ratios for 19X2 and 19X3: profit margin, gross margin, return on assets, and return on owners' equity. Comment briefly about Bluegrass's profitability.

b. Analyze the statement of cash flows and comment on the health of Bluegrass's cash flows for 19X3.

c. Calculate the following asset utilization ratios for 19X2 and 19X3: asset turnover, receivables turnover, age of accounts receivable, inventory turnover, and days' supply in inventory. Comment briefly about Bluegrass's asset utilization.

d. Calculate the following liquidity ratios for 19X2 and 19X3: working capital ratio, quick ratio, working capital to total assets, and age of accounts payable. Comment briefly about Bluegrass's liquidity.

e. Calculate the following solvency ratios for 19X2 and 19X3: times interest earned, cash flows to total debt, total debt to total assets, and total debt to owners' equity. Comment briefly about Bluegrass's solvency.

f. Based on the limited information you have about Bluegrass, evaluate the persistence and quality of Bluegrass's income.

SOLUTION:

Planning and Organizing Your Work

1. For each of the ratio (key question) categories recall the ratio definitions or review them in Illustrations 19-7, 9, 10, or 11. Calculate the ratios for 19X2 and 19X3 and comment on their individual and collective implications.

2. Examine the statement of cash flows. Consider the cash flows for operating, investing, and financing activies. Comment of their individual and collective implications.

3. Examine the contents of the income statement and review your analyses of all of the previous categories. Consider whether there appear to be any transitory components of net income that will not persist at some level in the future and comment on them. Consider whether there appear to be overstatements or understatements of assets and liabilities and related income statement components that suggest that net income is biased relative to steady-state future cash flows. Comment.

(a) *Calculate profitability ratios.*

$$\text{Profit Margin} = \frac{\text{Net Income}}{\text{Net Sales}}$$

19X2	*19X3*
$\dfrac{\$123,200}{\$1,200,000} = .103$	$\dfrac{\$140,000}{\$1,400,000} = .100$

$$\text{Gross Margin} = \frac{\text{Gross Profit}}{\text{Net Sales}}$$

19X2	*19X3*
$\dfrac{\$505,000}{\$1,200,000} = .421$	$\dfrac{\$585,000}{\$1,400,000} = .418$

$$\text{Return on Assets} = \frac{\text{Before-Tax Income} + \text{Interest Expense}}{\text{Average Total Assets}}$$

19X2	*19X3*
$\dfrac{\$176,000 + 4,000}{(\$539,600 + \$623,000)/2} = .310$	$\dfrac{\$200,000 + 15,000}{(\$623,000 + \$883,000)/2} = .286$

$$\text{Return on Owners' Equity} = \frac{\text{Net Income}}{\text{Average Owners' Equity}}$$

19X2

$$\frac{\$123,200}{(\$448,800 + \$522,000)/2} = .254$$

19X3

$$\frac{\$140,000}{(\$522,000 + \$662,000)/2} = .236$$

Comment on profitability: Bluegrass has very strong profitability. The two years are nearly identical with a very slight downward movement in 19X3.

(b) *Analyze the statement of cash flows.*
Cash flow from operating activities for 19X2 is a healthy $60,000, but it is down from $125,000 in 19X2, primarily because of significant increases in the investments in accounts receivable and inventory. Investment in new plant and equipment of $150,000 and dividends of $50,000 were sufficiently greater than cash flows from operating activities to require issue of a noncurrent note for $100,000 and new owner contributions of capital totaling $50,000. The additional debt financing, however, did put the company in a weaker solvency position (see part e).

(c) *Calculate asset utilization ratios.*

$$\text{Asset Turnover} = \frac{\text{Net Sales}}{\text{Average Total Assets}}$$

19X2

$$\frac{\$1,200,000}{(\$539,600 + \$623,000)/2} = 2.06$$

19X3

$$\frac{\$1,400,000}{(\$623,000 + \$883,000)/2} = 1.86$$

$$\text{Receivables Turnover} = \frac{\text{Net Credit Sales}}{\text{Average Net Trade Receivables}}$$

19X2

$$\frac{\$1,200,000}{(\$86,000 + \$92,000)/2} = 13.5$$

19X3

$$\frac{\$1,400,000}{(\$92,000 + \$122,500)/2} = 13.1$$

$$\text{Age of Accounts Receivable} = \frac{\text{Gross Trade Receivables}}{\text{Credit Sales}} \times 365$$

19X2

$$\frac{\$95,000}{\$1,200,000} \times 365 = 28.9 \text{ days}$$

19X3

$$\frac{\$125,000}{\$1,400,000} \times 365 = 32.6 \text{ days}$$

$$\text{Inventory Turnover} = \frac{\text{Cost of Goods Sold}}{\text{Average Inventory}}$$

19X2

$$\frac{\$695,000}{(\$180,000 + \$205,000)/2} = 3.6$$

19X3

$$\frac{\$815,000}{(\$205,000 + \$290,000)/2} = 3.3$$

$$\text{Days' Supply in Inventory} = \frac{\text{Inventory}}{\text{Cost of Goods Sold}} \times 365 \text{ days}$$

19X2

$$\frac{\$205,000}{\$695,000} \times 365 = 107.7 \text{ days}$$

19X3

$$\frac{\$290,000}{\$815,000} \times 365 = 129.9 \text{ days}$$

Comment on asset utilization: Some downward trend is noted in the utilization of assets. Asset turnover has decreased; the age of receivables has increased; and inventory turnover has decreased. When viewed in the context of Bluegrass's outstanding profitability, the moderate downward trend in asset utilization is not a cause for concern; but the causes of the increased age of receivables and increased days' supply in inventory should be determined.

(d) *Calculate liquidity ratios.*

$$\text{Working Capital Ratio} = \frac{\text{Current Assets}}{\text{Current Liabilities}}$$

19X2
$$\frac{\$413,000}{\$101,000} = 4.09$$

19X3
$$\frac{\$548,000}{\$121,000} = 4.53$$

$$\text{Quick (Acid Test) Ratio} = \frac{\text{Liquid Current Assets}}{\text{Current Liabilities}}$$

19X2
$$\frac{\$110,000 + \$92,000}{\$101,000} = 2.00$$

19X3
$$\frac{\$130,000 + \$122,500}{\$121,000} = 2.09$$

$$\text{Working Capital to Total Assets} = \frac{\text{Working Capital}}{\text{Total Assets}}$$

19X2
$$\frac{\$413,000 - \$101,000}{\$623,000} = .50$$

19X3
$$\frac{\$548,000 - \$121,000}{\$883,000} = .48$$

$$\text{Age of Accounts Payable} = \frac{\text{Accounts Payable}}{\text{Purchases}} \times 365 \text{ days}$$

19X2
$$\frac{\$52,000}{\$720,000} \times 365 = 26.4 \text{ days}$$

19X3
$$\frac{\$61,000}{\$900,000} \times 365 = 24.7 \text{ days}$$

Comment on liquidity: The liquidity ratios show a very strong liquidity. Bluegrass's strong position of current assets to current liabilities combined with its profitability make it a good credit risk for short-term creditors.

(e) *Calculate solvency ratios.*

$$\text{Times Interest Earned} = \frac{\text{Pre-Tax Income} + \text{Interest Expense}}{\text{Interest Expense}}$$

19X2
$$\frac{\$176,000 + \$4,000}{\$4,000} = 45.00$$

19X3
$$\frac{\$200,000 + \$15,000}{\$15,000} = 14.33$$

$$\text{Cash Flows to Total Debt} = \frac{\text{Cash Flows From Operations}}{\text{Year-End Total Debt}}$$

19X2
$$\frac{\$112,500}{\$101,000} = 1.11$$

19X3
$$\frac{\$60,000}{\$221,000} = .27$$

$$\text{Total Debt to Total Assets} = \frac{\text{Year-End Total Liabilities}}{\text{Year-End Total Assets}}$$

19X2   *19X3*

$$\frac{\$101,000}{\$623,000} = .16 \qquad \frac{\$221,000}{\$883,000} = .25$$

$$\text{Total Debt to Owners' Equity} = \frac{\text{Year-End Total Liabilities}}{\text{Year-End Owners' Equity}}$$

19X2   *19X3*

$$\frac{\$101,000}{\$522,000} = .19 \qquad \frac{\$221,000}{\$662,000} = .33$$

Comment on solvency: Although Bluegrass's solvency ratios have weakened somewhat, the reason is clear. They issued a $100,000 long-term note and increased their short-term borrowing. As a result, the solvency ratios weakened from the very strong 19X2 levels. They remain strong with a sound debt to equity ratio and coverage of interest. The 19X3 ratios, combined with profitability, give Bluegrass strong solvency.

(f) *Evaluate the persistence and quality of income.*

The persistence of Bluegrass's income looks good. It did not have any extraordinary items, discontinued operations, accounting changes, or even any gains or losses on the income statements. It would be important to evaluate the impact of certain economic conditions on Bluegrass's customers' demands for grass seed.

The quality of income is difficult to evaluate from the information given. We would evaluate this by looking at the accounting methods Bluegrass is using to see if there appears to be a bias toward maximizing income. We would want to evaluate receivables in view of their increase in age to be sure the allowance account is adequate and look at the inventory for obsolete seed or spoilage because of the significant increase in inventory. We would be more comfortable with the quality of earnings issue if Bluegrass had its financial statements audited by an independent CPA firm.

KEY TERMS

asset utilization ratios, *788*
business risk, *793*
common-size financial
   statements, *778*
cost principle, *801*
deflation, *802*
extraordinary items, *777*
financial ratios, *781*
financial risk, *793*
financial statement analysis,
   774

general price changes, *802*
horizontal analysis, *781*
income persistence, *775*
income quality, *775*
independent auditor's report,
   798
inflation, *802*
leverage, *793*
liquidity ratios, *790*
percent-change financial
   statements, *781*

profitability ratios, *785*
reserve funds, *790*
solvency ratios, *790*
specific price changes, *803*
stable monetary unit
   assumption, *801*
vertical analysis, *779*

SELF-QUIZ

LO 1 1. The item that best describes financial statement analysis is
a. Analysis of a transaction to determine the best way to record it in the financial statements
b. Art of using financial statement data and information to answer questions about a business and to make predictions about its future
c. Analysis of documentation supporting business transactions
d. None of the above

LO 1 2. In general, which of the following statements about cash flows and net income is correct?
a. Net income will always be less than cash flows.
b. Net income will always be greater than cash flows.
c. Over the life of a business, average income per period approximately equals average cash flows from operations and investment activities.
d. Net income has no relationship to cash flows.

LO 2 3. Income persistence is
a. Tendency for a component of income to continue in future periods under steady-state assumptions
b. Very low for extraordinary gains
c. Higher for revenues than it is for gains
d. All of the above

LO 2 4. A high quality of income means
a. High net income
b. Absence of extraordinary transactions or discontinued operations in the income statement
c. Degree to which management does not manipulate the firm's income to present an optimistic picture of ongoing income
d. All of the above

LO 2 5. Which of the following component(s) of the income statement is (are) highest in income persistence?
a. Revenues and expenses
b. Extraordinary items
c. Cumulative effect of an accounting change
d. Gains and losses

LO 3 6. The tools of financial statement analysis consist of
a. Common-size and percent-change financial statements and various financial ratios
b. Trial balance
c. Journals and ledgers
d. None of the above

LO 3 7. Common-size financial statements
a. Express all financial statement numbers as a percent of the company's retained earnings
b. Support a technique known as vertical analysis
c. Support a technique known as horizontal analysis
d. Both a and b

LO 3 8. Vertical analysis
a. Refers to the evaluation of financial information for different years; for example, 19X1, 19X2, and 19X3
b. Refers to calculating financial ratios and presenting them in a vertical format
c. Refers to the analysis of the percentage composition of the components of a particular statement for a particular year
d. None of the above

LO 3 9. Percent-change financial statements
a. Are a form of horizontal analysis
b. Involve only one year's financial statements
c. Show rates of growth or decline in financial statement components
d. Both a and c

LO 3 10. Financial ratios
a. Can be calculated to represent almost any relevant relationship between financial statement amounts
b. Are more flexible than common-size financial statements
c. Are numerical statistics that represent important relationships between financial statement amounts
d. All of the above

LO 3 11. Once ratios and percents are computed in financial statement analysis, they are usually compared with other information. The standard of comparison used in this chapter is
a. Prior years' ratios and percents
b. Industry comparisons
c. Plans of the business
d. None of the above

LO 4 12. Select the group of profitability ratios
a. Asset turnover, receivables turnover, inventory turnover
b. Profit margin, gross margin, return on assets
c. Working capital ratio, quick ratio, age of accounts payable
d. Times interest earned, cash flows to total debt, total debt to owners' equity

LO 4 13. Select the group of asset utilization ratios
  a. Days' supply in inventory, inventory turnover, asset turnover
  b. Return on owners' equity, return on assets, profit margin
  c. Total debt to total assets, times interest earned, cash flows to total debt
  d. Quick ratio, working capital ratio, working capital to total assets

LO 5 14. A well-written analysis of a set of financial statements
  a. Comments about each item contained in the statements
  b. Captures only the essentials from the vast array of data included in the statements
  c. Is brief
  d. Both b and c

LO 6 15. An unqualified opinion in the independent auditors' report provides assurances that
  a. Management of the company is effective
  b. Financial statements are free of errors
  c. Financial statements probably are not materially misstated
  d. All transactions of the company have been verified

LO 7 16. (Appendix) Excluding the effect of interest, during a period of inflation, the party that owes money (debtor)
  a. Incurs a purchasing power loss
  b. Incurs a purchasing power gain
  c. Has neither a purchasing power gain nor loss
  d. None of the above

LO 8 17. (Appendix) Excluding the effect of interest, during a period of inflation, the party that is owed money (creditor)
  a. Incurs a purchasing power loss
  b. Incurs a purchasing power gain
  c. Has neither a purchasing power gain nor loss
  d. None of the above

SOLUTIONS TO SELF-QUIZ

| 1. b | 2. c | 3. d | 4. c | 5. a | 6. a | 7. b | 8. c | 9. d | 10. d | 11. a | 12. b | 13. a | 14. d |
| 15. c | 16. b | 17. a | | | | | | | | | | | |

QUESTIONS

Q19-1 How does the analysis of the income statement, which is prepared under the accrual method, help predict future cash flows?

Q19-2 Define financial statement analysis.

Q19-3 Explain why gains and losses are lower in income persistence than are revenues and expenses.

Q19-4 Explain how a company having an audit by an independent CPA firm can improve income quality.

Q19-5 Give two examples of ways that the management of a company might manipulate income.

Q19-6 Explain how a common-size income statement is prepared.

Q19-7 Give an example of how a common-size income statement can be used to identify important information.

Q19-8 The usual base figure (the important summary figure) in the common size balance sheet is: _____.

Q19-9 What is vertical analysis?

Q19-10 What is horizontal analysis?

Q19-11 Explain how a percent-change balance sheet is prepared.

Q19-12 Is financial statement analysis an art or a science? Discuss.

Q19-13 As part of analyzing the financial statements of Green Company, you compute a working capital ratio of 1:8 and a quick ratio of 1:1. Describe the possible implications of this information.

Q19-14 Five key questions, which can act as a framework, must be answered in the analysis of financial statements. List them.

Q19-15 Does an analyst who is primarily interested in a business's solvency have any interest in its profitability? Discuss.

Q19-16 What is meant by the term *utilization of assets*?

Q19-17 Distinguish between liquidity and solvency.

Q19-18 What are three components of reserve funds?

Q19-19 Distinguish between business risk and financial risk.

Q19-20 What is leverage? Give an example of the beneficial effect and the risk effect of leverage.

Q19-21 (Appendix) Describe how a purchasing power loss occurs. Is such a loss recognized in income statements prepared under GAAP?

EXERCISES

LO 2,3,4   **E19-1**   **Concepts of Income Persistence and Quality, Tools of Financial Statement Analysis, Performing Analysis**   Match the terms and the definitions.

___ a. Income persistence
___ b. Income quality
___ c. Common-size financial statements
___ d. Vertical analysis
___ e. Percent-change financial statements
___ f. Horizontal analysis
___ g. Financial ratios
___ h. Business risk
___ i. Financial risk
___ j. Beneficial leverage effect
___ k. Risk leverage effect
___ l. Reserve funds

(1) Risk associated with the nature of the business and the markets in which it operates
(2) Tendency for a component of income to continue in future periods under steady-state assumptions
(3) Statements whose numerical amounts are re-expressed as percents of an important summary figure
(4) Rate of return on assets: 15%; interest rate on borrowed funds: 12%
(5) Rate of return on assets: 8%; interest rate on borrowed funds: 12%
(6) Numerical statistics that represent important relationships between financial statement amounts
(7) Looking at rates of change in gross profit from 19X1 to 19X2
(8) Conventional financial statements with changes and percents of changes added
(9) Line of credit with a bank that exceeds what the business is expected to need
(10) Degree to which management does not manipulate the firm's income to paint an optimistic picture of ongoing income
(11) Analysis of the percentage composition of the components of a particular statement for a particular year
(12) Added risk that a business incurs when it uses debt financing

LO 3,4,5   **E19-2**   **Common-Size Income Statement**   Prepare a common-size comparative income statement for the Diaz Company for 19X5 and 19X6 and briefly comment on any significant trends that are identified.

Diaz Company **Comparative Income Statement** **For the Years Ended December 31, 19X5 and 19X6**		
	19X5	*19X6*
Net sales	$287,000	$350,000
Cost of goods sold	206,000	262,500
Gross profit	$ 81,000	$ 87,500
Selling and administrative expenses	60,000	64,000
Income before taxes	$ 21,000	$ 23,500
Income tax expense	6,300	7,050
Net income	$ 14,700	$ 16,450

LO 3,4,5 **E19-3 Common-Size Balance Sheet** Prepare a common-size comparative balance sheet for the Canner Company for 19X3 and 19X4 and briefly comment on any significant trends that are identified.

Canner Company **Comparative Balance Sheet** **June 30, 19X3 and 19X4**		
	19X3	*19X4*
Assets		
Cash	$ 60,000	$ 35,000
Accounts receivable (net)	100,000	140,000
Inventory	125,000	140,000
Prepaid expenses	10,000	10,000
Total current assets	$295,000	$325,000
Land	50,000	50,000
Buildings and equipment	400,000	400,000
Accumulated depreciation	(200,000)	(240,000)
Total assets	$545,000	$535,000
Liabilities and Stockholders' Equity		
Accounts payable	$210,000	$205,000
Wages and salaries payable	2,000	2,000
Total current liabilities	$212,000	$207,000
Contributed capital	$200,000	$200,000
Retained earnings	133,000	128,000
Total stockholders' equity	$333,000	$328,000
Total liabilities and stockholders' equity	$545,000	$535,000

LO 3,4,5 **E19-4 Percent-Change Income Statement** A comparative income statement for the Jefferson Supply Company for 19X1 and 19X2 is presented on the next page

REQUIRED:

Prepare a percent-change comparative income statement and briefly comment on any significant changes.

Jefferson Supply Company Comparative Income Statement For the Years Ended December 31, 19X1 and 19X2		
	19X1	*19X2*
Net sales	$600,000	$582,000
Cost of goods sold	420,000	419,000
Gross profit	$180,000	$163,000
Selling and administrative expenses	100,000	100,000
Income before taxes	$ 80,000	$ 63,000
Income tax expense	24,000	18,900
Net income	$ 56,000	$ 44,100

LO 3,4,5

E19-5   Percent-Change Balance Sheet   Prepare a percent-change comparative balance sheet for the Cross Walk Company and briefly comment on any significant changes that are identified.

Cross Walk Company Comparative Balance Sheet July 31, 19X8 and 19X9		
	19X8	*19X9*
Assets		
Cash	$ 51,450	$ 28,000
Accounts receivable (net)	75,000	72,000
Inventory	95,550	130,000
Prepaid expenses	4,000	5,000
Total current assets	$226,000	$235,000
Land	20,000	20,000
Buildings and equipment	250,000	260,000
Accumulated depreciation	(100,000)	(120,000)
Total assets	$396,000	$395,000
Liabilities and Stockholders' Equity		
Accounts payable	$110,000	$140,000
Wages and salaries payable	1,000	1,000
Total current liabilities	$111,000	$141,000
Capital stock	$150,000	$150,000
Retained earnings	135,000	104,000
Total stockholders' equity	$285,000	$254,000
Total liabilities and stockholders' equity	$396,000	$395,000

LO 4

E19-6   Financial Ratios   Use the codes presented below to classify the listed ratios as profitability ratios, asset utilization ratios, liquidity ratios, or solvency ratios.

PR = profitability ratio
AR = asset utilization ratio
LR = liquidity ratio

SR = solvency ratio

Ratios

___ a. Times interest earned
___ b. Asset turnover
___ c. Age of accounts payable
___ d. Profit margin
___ e. Quick (acid test) ratio
___ f. Total debt to total assets
___ g. Working capital ratio
___ h. Return on assets
___ i. Total debt to owners' equity
___ j. Age of accounts receivable
___ k. Gross margin
___ l. Inventory turnover
___ m. Days' supply in inventory
___ n. Working capital to total assets
___ o. Cash flow to total debt
___ p. Receivables turnover
___ q. Return on owners' equity

LO 4,5   **E19-7   Calculation of Profitability Ratios**   The income statement and additional financial information for the Orange Grove Company is presented below for the years 19X6 and 19X7.

Orange Grove Company Comparative Income Statement For the Years Ended December 31, 19X6 and 19X7		
	19X6	*19X7*
Net sales	$850,000	$890,000
Cost of goods sold	552,500	596,300
Gross profit	$297,500	$293,700
Selling and administrative expenses*	200,000	200,000
Income before taxes	$ 97,500	$ 93,700
Income tax expense	29,250	28,110
Net income	$ 68,250	$ 65,590

*Includes $10,000 interest expense in 19X6 and $20,000 interest expense in 19X7.

Additional Information:

	19X6	*19X7*
Average total assets	$700,000	$900,000
Average owners' equity	300,000	325,000

REQUIRED:

Use the information to calculate the profit margin, gross margin, return on assets, and return on owners' equity for 19X6 and 19X7. Briefly comment about what the ratios reveal about Orange Grove's profitability.

LO 4,5   **E19-8   Asset Utilization Ratios**   The Danzen Company has a local customer base in an area where a large military complex has been closed down. Danzen has been experiencing cash flow problems.

REQUIRED:

Use the following selected information to calculate the receivables turnover, age of accounts receivables, inventory turnover, and days' supplies in inventory for 19X3 and 19X4. Comment on what the ratios reveal.

	19X3	19X4
Net credit sales	$4,650,000	$4,200,000
Cost of goods sold	3,255,000	3,024,000
Average inventory	500,000	550,000
Ending inventory	500,000	600,000
Average net receivables	387,500	450,000
Ending gross receivables	425,000	475,000

LO 4

E19-9   Liquidity Ratios   Selected information from the balance sheet and income statement of Med Help is provided below:

Cash	$ 15,700
Accounts receivable (net)	88,000
Marketable securities	11,000
Supplies	36,000
Prepaid expenses	9,000
Land, buildings, and equipment (net)	450,000
Total assets	$609,700
Accounts payable	$125,000
Notes payable–current	40,000
Notes payable–noncurrent	200,000
Purchases of supplies	300,000

REQUIRED:

a. Use the information to calculate the following liquidity ratios: working capital ratio, quick (acid test) ratio, working capital to total assets, and age of accounts payable.
b. Based on the limited information from these ratios, would you, as a seller of medical supplies, extend credit to Med Help? Explain your reasoning.

LO 4,5

E19-10   Solvency Ratios   Selected information from the balance sheet and income statement of Cable Tech is presented below:

Total liabilities	$ 6,000,000
Owners' equity	9,000,000
Total assets	15,000,000
Pre-tax income	1,200,000
Interest expense	300,000
Cash flows from operations	1,500,000

REQUIRED:

a. Use the information to calculate the following solvency ratios: times interest earned, cash flows from operations to total debt, total debt to total assets, and debt-equity.
b. Briefly comment about what these ratios reveal about Cable's solvency.

LO 7

E19-11   Effects of General Inflation (Appendix)   Judy Morris paid $15,000 for a 5-acre tract of land in 19X2 when the general price index was 125. She sold the land in 19X7 for $16,500 when the general price index was 150.

REQUIRED:

Calculate the gain from the sale of the land, assuming a stable dollar, and calculate the gain or loss in constant 19X7 dollars.

PROBLEM SET A

LO 1   **P19-1A**   **Relationship of Net Income to Cash Flows and Future Cash Flows**   The graph presented below shows the net income and the net cash flows for Northeast Digital Company over a 10-year period. Digital is a growth company; and over this period, it has not paid dividends or made other distributions to shareholders. It has not engaged in any significant financing activities.

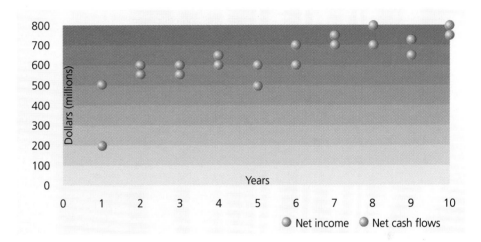

REQUIRED:

a. Speculate as to the cause of the cash flows being less than net income in years X1 and X5 and higher than net income in the other years.
b. Assuming any items between the $100 million increments on the Y axis represent $50 million increments, add the net income over the 10-year period and divide by 10 to compute average income.
c. Add the cash flows over the 10-year period and divide by 10 to compute average cash flows.
d. Compare the averages in c and d and discuss the income persistence exhibited by Northeast's income figures.

Financial Statements to be Used with Problems 2A through 6A

The American Apple Company (AAC) buys and exports apples, pears, oranges, and grapefruits to Japan, South Korea, and Thialand. All sales are in U.S. dollars. AAC's financial statements for the years 19X8 and 19X9 are presented on the following pages.

Additional Information (in Thousands):
Beginning 19X8 balances:

Total assets	$56,555
Receivables (net)	24,500
Owners' equity	11,250

American Apple Company
Comparative Balance Sheet
September 30, 19X8 and 19X9

	(Thousands)	
	19X8	19X9
Assets		
Cash	$ 6,500	$ 5,480
Investment in securities	2,000	2,000
Accounts receivable	26,000	32,000
Allowance for uncollectible accounts	(1,000)	(1,000)
Inventory	15,000	18,000
Supplies	100	125
Prepaid expenses	200	175
Total current assets	$48,800	$56,780
Land	1,500	1,800
Buildings and equipment	10,000	15,000
Accumulated depreciation	(2,000)	(2,500)
Total assets	$58,300	$71,080
Liabilities and Stockholders' Equity		
Accounts payable	$10,500	$14,000
Notes payable	7,000	9,000
Wages and salaries payable	50	60
Taxes payable	500	600
Total current liabilities	$18,050	$23,660
Bonds payable	24,000	24,000
Notes payable—noncurrent	4,000	8,000
Total liabilities	$46,050	$55,660
Common stock	$ 5,000	$ 5,000
Paid-in capital in excess of par	3,000	3,000
Retained earnings	4,250	7,420
Total stockholders' equity	$12,250	$15,420
Total liabilities & stockholders' equity	$58,300	$71,080

American Apple Company
Comparative Income Statement
For the Years Ended September 30, 19X8 and 19X9

	(Thousands)	
	19X8	19X9
Net sales	$90,000	$ 98,000
Cost of goods sold:		
Beginning inventory	$14,000	$ 15,000
Purchases (net)	80,000	86,000
Cost of goods available	$94,000	$101,000
Ending inventory	15,000	18,000
Cost of goods sold	$79,000	$83,000
Gross profit	$11,000	$15,000

Continued

	19X8	19X9
Selling expenses	$3,300	$3,000
Depreciation expense	400	500
Administrative expenses	2,000	2,500
Total operating expenses	$5,700	$6,000
Operating income before taxes	$5,300	$9,000
Interest expense	(2,600)	(3,200)
Interest revenue	160	160
Income before taxes	$2,860	$5,960
Income tax expense	860	1,790
Net income	$2,000	$4,170

American Apple Company
Comparative Statement of Retained Earnings
For the Years Ended September 30, 19X8 and 19X9

	(Thousands)	
	19X8	19X9
Retained earnings, beginning	$3,250	$4,250
Net income	2,000	4,170
Dividends declared	(1,000)	(1,000)
Retained earnings, ending	$4,250	$7,420

American Apple Company
Comparative Statement of Cash Flows
For the Years Ended September 30, 19X8 and 19X9

	(Thousands)	
	19X8	19X9
Cash flows from operating activities:		
Net income	$ 2,000	$ 4,170
Depreciation expense	400	500
Increase in accounts payable	200	3,500
Increase in taxes payable	50	100
Increase (decrease) in wages payable	(5)	10
Decrease in prepaid expenses	0	25
Increase in accounts receivable (net)	(500)	(6,000)
Increase in inventory	(1,000)	(3,000)
Increase in supplies	0	(25)
Net cash flows from operating activities	$ 1,145	$ (720)
Cash flows from investing activities:		
Purchase of land	$ 0	$ (300)
Purchase of building and equipment	(1,000)	(5,000)
Net cash flows from investment activities	$(1,000)	$(5,300)
Cash flows from financing activities:		
Payment of dividends	$(1,000)	$(1,000)
Net proceeds from current notes	500	2,000
Noncurrent note issued	0	4,000
Net cash flows from financial activities	$ (500)	$ 5,000
Net increase in cash	$ (355)	$(1,020)

LO 3,4,5   **P19-2A**   **Common-Size and Percent-Change Analysis of Income Statements**   Refer to American Apple Company's (AAC's) financial statements (pages 822-823).

REQUIRED:

a. Perform a vertical analysis of AAC's income statements by preparing a common-size comparative income statement for 19X8 and 19X9.
b. Comment on information the common-size income statement reveals.
c. Perform a horizontal analysis of AAC's income statements by preparing a percent-change comparative income statement from 19X8 to 19X9.
d. Comment on information the percent-change comparative income statement reveals.

LO 3,4,5   **P19-3A**   **Common-Size and Percent-Change Analysis of Balance Sheets**   Refer to American Apple Company's (AAC's) financial statements (pages 822-823).

REQUIRED:

a. Perform a vertical analysis of AAC's balance sheets by preparing a common-size comparative balance sheet for 19X8 and 19X9.
b. Comment on information the common-size comparative balance sheet reveals.
c. Perform a horizontal analysis of AAC's balance sheets by preparing a percent-change comparative balance sheet from 19X8 to 19X9.
d. Comment on information the percent-change comparative balance sheet reveals.

LO 3,4,5   **P19-4A**   **Analysis of Cash Flows Statements**   Refer to American Apple Company's (AAC's) financial statements (pages 822-823).

REQUIRED:

a. Evaluate AAC's cash flows from operating activities for 19X8 and 19X9.
b. Evaluate AAC's cash flows from investing activities for 19X8 and 19X9.
c. Evaluate AAC's cash flows from financing activities for 19X8 and 19X9.

LO 3,4,5   **P19-5A**   **Profitability and Asset Utilization Ratios**   Refer to American Apple Company's (AAC's) financial statements (pages 822-823).

REQUIRED:

a. Calculate AAC's profit margin, gross margin, return on assets, and return on owners' equity for 19X8 and 19X9. Summarize what they indicate about AAC's profitability.
b. Calculate AAC's asset turnover, receivables turnover, age of receivables, inventory turnover, and days' supply in inventory. Summarize what they indicate about AAC's asset utilization.

LO 3,4,5   **P19-6A**   **Liquidity and Solvency Ratios**   Refer to American Apple Company's (AAC's) financial statements (pages 822-823).

REQUIRED:

a. Calculate AAC's working capital ratio, quick ratio, working capital to total assets, and age of accounts payable. Summarize what they indicate about AAC's liquidity.
b. Calculate AAC's times interest earned, cash flows to total debt, total debt to total assets, and debt-equity. Summarize what they indicate about AAC's solvency.

PROBLEM SET B

LO 1   **P19-1B**   **Relationship of Net Income to Cash Flows and Future Cash Flows**   The graph
below shows the net income and the net cash flows for the Texas Communications
Company over a 10-year period.

TCC has not paid dividends or made other distributions to shareholders. It has,
however, engaged in some other significant financing activities.

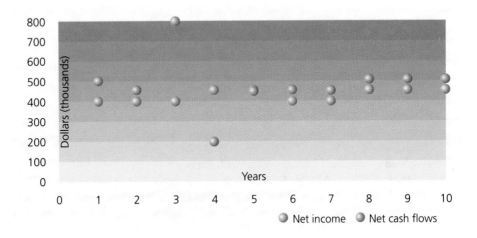

REQUIRED:

a. Speculate as to the cause of the cash flows being slightly above net income for all
   years except 19X3 and 19X4. Indicate possible events that could account for the 19X3
   and 19X4 disparities.
b. Assuming any items between the $100 thousand increments on the Y axis represent
   $50 thousand increments, add the net income over the 10-year period and divide by
   10 to compute average income.
c. Add the cash flows over the 10-year period and divide by 10 to compute average
   cash flows.
d. Compare the averages in c and d and discuss the income persistence evidenced by
   TCC's income figures.

Financial Statements to be Used with Problems 2B through 6B

Ohio Laser Supply (OLS) carries a complete supply of toner imaging cartridges and font
cartridges for all popular laser printers. It supplies large companies and government
agencies on a just-in-time basis and ships anywhere in the United States overnight. Its
sales have expanded significantly; but it is experiencing some problems stocking the
rapidly expanding line of laser cartridges. OLS's financial statements for the years 19X0
and 19X1 are presented on the following pages.

Additional Information (in Thousands):
Beginning 19X0 balances:

Total assets	$34,625
Receivables (net)	6,100
Owners' equity	5,610

Ohio Laser Supply
Comparative Balance Sheet
October 31, 19X0 and 19X1

	(Thousands) 19X0	(Thousands) 19X1
Assets		
Cash	$ 4,000	$ 1,000
Investment in securities	5,000	1,000
Accounts receivable	7,000	10,000
Allowance for uncollectible accounts	(300)	(400)
Inventory	4,000	8,000
Supplies	200	90
Prepaid expenses	100	110
Total current assets	$20,000	$19,800
Land	2,000	2,000
Buildings and equipment	20,000	35,000
Accumulated depreciation	(4,000)	(6,800)
Total assets	$38,000	$50,000
Liabilities and Stockholders' Equity		
Accounts payable	$ 6,500	$11,500
Notes payable	5,000	7,000
Wages and salaries payable	10	15
Taxes payable	290	185
Total current liabilities	$11,800	$18,700
Bonds payable	10,000	10,000
Notes payable—noncurrent	8,000	9,000
Total liabilities	$29,800	$37,700
Common stock	$ 1,000	$ 1,000
Paid-in capital in excess of par	6,000	6,000
Retained earnings	1,200	5,300
Total stockholders' equity	$ 8,200	$12,300
Total liabilities & stockholders' equity	$38,000	$50,000

Ohio Laser Supply
Comparative Income Statement
For the Years Ended October 31, 19X0 and 19X1

	(Thousands) 19X0	(Thousands) 19X1
Net sales	$80,000	$120,000
Cost of goods sold:		
Beginning inventory	3,500	4,000
Purchases (net)	56,500	95,000
Cost of goods available	$60,000	$ 99,000
Ending inventory	4,000	8,000
Cost of goods sold	$56,000	$ 91,000
Gross profit	$24,000	$ 29,000

Continued

Selling expenses	$ 6,000	$ 7,000
Depreciation expense	1,500	2,800
Administrative expenses	8,000	8,000
Total operating expenses	$15,500	$17,800
Operating income before taxes	$ 8,500	$11,200
Interest expense	(2,300)	(2,600)
Interest revenue	300	60
Income before taxes	$ 6,500	$ 8,660
Income tax expense	1,950	2,600
Net income	$ 4,550	$ 6,060

Ohio Laser Supply
Comparative Statement of Retained Earnings
For the Years Ended October 31, 19X0 and 19X1

	(Thousands)	
	19X0	*19X1*
Retained earnings, beginning	$(1,390)	$1,200
Net income	4,550	6,060
Dividends declared	(1,960)	(1,960)
Retained earnings, ending	$ 1,200	$5,300

Ohio Laser Supply
Comparative Statement of Cash Flows
For the Years Ended October 31, 19X0 and 19X1

	(Thousands)	
	19X0	*19X1*
Cash flows from operating activities:		
Net income	$ 4,550	$ 6,060
Depreciation expense	1,500	2,800
Increase in accounts payable	500	5,000
Increase (decrease) in taxes payable	290	(105)
Increase (decrease) in wages payable	(5)	5
Decrease (increase) in prepaid expenses	10	(10)
Decrease in supplies	0	110
Increase in accounts receivable (net)	(600)	(2,900)
Increase in inventory	(500)	(4,000)
Net cash flows from operating activities	$ 5,745	$ 6,960
Cash flows from investing activities:		
Sale of marketable securities	$ 0	$ 4,000
Purchase of building and equipment	(1,000)	(15,000)
Net cash flows from investment activities	$(1,000)	$(11,000)
Cash flows from financing activities:		
Payment of dividends	$(1,000)	$ (1,960)
Net proceeds from current notes	500	2,000
Noncurrent note issued	0	1,000
Net cash flows from financial activities	$ (500)	$ 1,040
Net increase in cash	$ (355)	$ (3,000)

LO 3,4,5   **P19-2B**   **Common-Size and Percent-Change Analysis of Income Statements**   Refer to Ohio Laser Supply's (OLS's) financial statements (pages 826-827).

REQUIRED:

a. Perform a vertical analysis of OLS's income statements by preparing a common-size comparative income statement for 19X0 and 19X1.
b. Comment on information the common-size income statement reveals.
c. Perform a horizonal analysis of OLS's income statements by preparing a percent-change comparative income statement from 19X0 to 19X1.
d. Comment on information the percent-change comparative income statement reveals.

LO 3,4,5   **P19-3B**   **Common-Size and Percent-Change Analysis of Balance Sheets**   Refer to Ohio Laser Supply's (OLS's) financial statements (pages 826-827).

REQUIRED:

a. Perform a vertical analysis of OLS's balance sheets by preparing a common-size comparative balance sheet for 19X0 and 19X1.
b. Comment on information the common-size comparative balance sheet reveals.
c. Perform a horizontal analysis of OLS's balance sheets by preparing a percent-change comparative balance sheet from 19X0 to 19X1.
d. Comment on information the percent-change comparative balance sheet reveals.

LO 3,4,5   **P19-4B**   **Analysis of Cash Flows Statements**   Refer to Ohio Laser Supply's (OLS's) financial statements (pages 826-827).

REQUIRED:

a. Evaluate OLS's cash flows from operating activities for 19X0 and 19X1.
b. Evaluate OLS's cash flows from investing activities for 19X0 and 19X1.
c. Evaluate OLS's cash flows from financing activities for 19X0 and 19X1.

LO 3,4,5   **P19-5B**   **Profitability and Asset Utilization Ratios**   Refer to Ohio Laser Supply's (OLS's) financial statements (pages 826-827).

REQUIRED:

a. Calculate OLS's profit margin, gross margin, return on assets, and return on owners' equity for 19X0 and 19X1. Summarize what they indicate about OLS's profitability.
b. Calculate OLS's asset turnover, receivables turnover, age of receivables, inventory turnover, and days' supply in inventory. Summarize what they indicate about OLS's asset utilization.

LO 3,4,5   **P19-6B**   **Liquidity and Solvency Ratios**   Refer to Ohio Laser Supply's (OLS's) financial statements (pages 826-827).

REQUIRED:

a. Calculate OLS's working capital ratio, quick ratio, working capital to total assets, and age of accounts payable. Summarize what they indicate about OLS's liquidity.
b. Calculate OLS's times interest earned, cash flow to total debt, total debt to total assets, and debt-equity. Summarize what they indicate about OLS's solvency.

CRITICAL THINKING AND COMMUNICATING

C19-1   Kathleen Gordon is the chief accountant of Microtech, a newly organized company that makes speakers for personal computers. Kathleen and her assistant are in the process of recommending to management the accounting methods that the new company will use, and she has come to you for advice.

She explains that the new company will be applying for a substantial loan soon, and management is interested in presenting the financial statements "in the best possible light" to improve its chances of getting a loan under favorable terms.

She tells you she is considering recommending the use of straight-line depreciation and the adoption of "reasonably optimistic estimated asset lives and salvage values."

Kathleen explains to you that she places a high value on her integrity as an accountant and asks you if you believe that her proposal is "an ethically proper recommendation."

REQUIRED:

Write Kathleen a letter expressing your views about her proposal.

C19-2 A large and well-known steel company in the United States uses the last-in, first-out (LIFO) method of inventory valuation. It has been using LIFO for many years; and as a result, the value of its steel inventory is measured in very old (World War II era) and, therefore, very low prices. The value of its steel inventory, reported in the balance sheet at the low LIFO prices, is about $1 billion less than the current cost of the inventory, an amount representing more than a third of the company's total assets.

REQUIRED:

a. Discuss how the inventory valuation of the steel company would affect the company's financial ratios.
b. What would you recommend to financial analysts calculating financial ratios for the steel company?

C19-3 Refer to the financial statements of J.C. Penney Company, Inc. in Appendix B at the end of the text. Find the balance sheet and income statement.

REQUIRED:

1. Calculate J.C. Penney's profitability ratios for 1991, 1992, and 1993. 1990 year-end total assets and stockholders' equity were $12,325 million and $4,394 million, respectively. In calculating gross margin, ignore the fact that J.C. Penney includes certain other costs with cost of goods sold.
2. What are the implications of the changes in J.C. Penney's profitability ratios over the 3 years?

PART 2

MANAGERIAL
ACCOUNTING

CHAPTER 20

Managerial Accounting and Cost Information

You may someday manage a department store, an advertising agency, or an automobile manufacturing plant. As a manager you will have to plan operations, evaluate subordinates, and make a variety of decisions using accounting information. In some cases you will find accounting information from the balance sheet, the income statement, the statement of retained earnings, and the statement of cash flows to be useful. However, much of the information in these statements is more relevant to *external* users of accounting information such as stockholders, creditors, and government agencies. In addition, you will need information prepared specifically for *internal* users of accounting information such as firm managers. This type of information is referred to as managerial accounting information.

Previous chapters introduced financial accounting which stresses accounting concepts and procedures that relate to preparing reports for external users of accounting information. In comparison, **managerial accounting** stresses accounting concepts and procedures needed to prepare reports for internal users of accounting information. The remainder of this book is devoted to the subject of managerial accounting. This chapter on managerial accounting provides an overview and illustrates the role of managerial accounting in planning, evaluation, and decision making. The chapter also introduces a number of cost terms and concepts that are critical to the understanding of managerial accounting.

LO 1

State the primary goal of managerial accounting.

INTRODUCTION TO MANAGERIAL ACCOUNTING

The primary goal of managerial accounting is to provide information that helps managers plan and evaluate company activities and make business decisions. Providing information for *planning, evaluation, and decision making* is the purpose of managerial accounting.

LO 2

Describe how budgets are used to plan and how performance reports are used to evaluate.

Planning and Evaluation

Planning is a key activity for all companies. A plan provides financial direction much like a road map provides directions and distances to specific locations. A map helps you avoid wrong turns and wasted time; likewise, a financial plan guides a company toward its objectives. With such a plan, employees focus on company goals and follow the most efficient route to achieve them Plans also aid evaluation. Managers can compare actual results to planned results and decide if corrective action is necessary. If actual results differ from those in the plan, then the company may not have followed the plan properly or the plan itself may have been deficient.

Illustration 20-1 presents the major steps in the planning and evaluation process. Managers take actions to implement the plan. Their actions lead to results that are compared to those of the original plan. Based on this evaluation, managers take necessary corrective action. Corrective action may consist of training employees to do a better job, changing a production process, or even firing a manager who is responsible for deviating from the plan. It may also consist of revising an unrealistic plan.

Budgets for Planning.   Managerial accountants prepare financial plans called **budgets**. A wide variety of budgets may be prepared. For example, a *profit budget* indicates planned income; a *cash flow budget* planned cash inflows and outflows; and a *production budget* the planned quantity of production and the expected cost.

Consider the production budget for Marie's Pie Company. In the coming year, the company plans to produce 200,000 pies. The company estimates it will use $225,000 of ingredients and pay factory workers $200,000. It also expects to pay $25,000 for rent, incur $20,000 of depreciation of equipment, and pay $15,000 for other costs. The production cost budget presented in Illustration 20-2 summarizes this information.

The production cost budget informs the managers of Marie's Pie Company how many pies the company intends to produce and what the needed

ILLUSTRATION 20-1 Planning and Evaluation Process

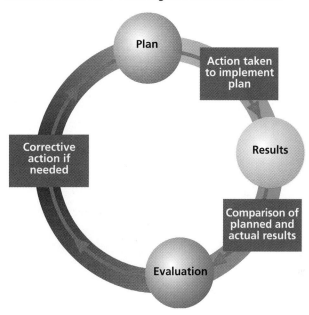

resources will cost. With this information, managers can implement the plan. For example, managers must purchase ingredients sufficient to produce 200,000 pies.

ILLUSTRATION 20-2 Production Cost Budget

Marie's Pie Company Budgeted Production Costs For the Year Ended December 31, 19X1	
Budgeted production	200,000 pies
Production costs:	
Ingredient cost	$225,000
Labor cost	200,000
Rent	25,000
Depreciation	20,000
Other	15,000
Total budgeted production costs	$485,000

Performance Reports for Evaluation.   Besides communicating company plans to managers, budgets are used to *evaluate* how well managers have implemented the plans. The evaluation compares the budget with actual results. The report comparing actual and budgeted performance is a **performance report**. If actual results are consistent with the budget, managerial performance is judged to be acceptable. If actual results deviate significantly from the budget, however, it is necessary to determine if the deviation is the result of good or bad managerial performance. By identifying good and poor performance, the company can maintain control of its operations. Managers who perform exceptionally well should be rewarded to encourage further high levels of job performance. The poor performance of other managers should be corrected.

Suppose that during 19X1, Marie's Pie Company actually produced 200,000 pies and incurred the following costs:

Ingredient cost	$265,000
Labor cost	195,000
Rent	25,000
Depreciation	20,000
Other	14,000
Total production cost	$519,000

A performance report comparing these actual costs to the budgeted costs is presented in Illustration 20-3.

ILLUSTRATION 20-3 Performance Report

Marie's Pie Company Performance Report, Production Costs For the Year Ended December 31, 19X1			
	Budget	Actual	Budget minus Actual
Production	200,000 pies	200,000 pies	
Production costs:			
Ingredient cost	$225,000	$265,000	$(40,000)
Labor cost	200,000	195,000	5,000
Rent	25,000	25,000	0
Depreciation	20,000	20,000	0
Other	15,000	14,000	1,000
Total production costs	$485,000	$519,000	$(34,000)

Typically, performance reports indicate only those areas that should be investigated. They do not provide definitive information on performance. For example, the performance report presented in Illustration 20-3 indicates that something may be amiss in the control of ingredient cost. Actual costs are $40,000 more than budgeted. There are many potential reasons why the cost is greater than the amount budgeted. Perhaps the price of fruit or sugar increased. Perhaps an oven malfunction resulted in wasted ingredients. Such explanations must be investigated before taking appropriate corrective action. While performance reports may not provide definitive answers, they are still extremely useful. Managers can use them to "flag" areas that need closer attention and to avoid areas that are under control. It would not seem necessary, for example, to investigate labor, rent, depreciation, or other costs since these costs are either equal to or relatively close to the planned level of cost. Typically, managers follow the principle of **management by exception** when using performance reports. Management by exception means they investigate departures from the plan that appear to be exceptional; they do not investigate minor departures from the plan.

Decision Making

In addition to providing information for planning and evaluation, managerial accounting information helps managers make nonroutine decisions, which address problems that do not occur regularly. For example, should the firm add a new product? Should it drop an existing product? Should it manufacture a component used in assembling its major product or contract with another company to produce the component? What price should the firm charge for a new product? While ways to solve these problems exist, the necessary cost information is not always readily available. In these cases, the managerial accountant must develop the needed information.

Differences Between Financial and Managerial Accounting

Important differences exist between financial and managerial accounting. In contrast to financial accounting, managerial accounting

1. Is directed at internal rather than external users of accounting information.
2. May deviate from GAAP.
3. May present more detailed information.
4. May present more nonmonetary information.
5. Places more emphasis on the future.

Internal Versus External Users.   As already discussed, financial accounting is aimed primarily at external users of accounting information while managerial accounting is aimed primarily at internal users. External users such as investors, creditors, and government agencies need information to make investment, lending, and regulation decisions. Thus, their information needs differ from those of internal managers who need information for routine planning and evaluation of the firm's internal operations and for making a number of other less routine decisions.

Need to Use GAAP.   Much of financial accounting information is required. The Securities and Exchange Commission (SEC) requires large, publicly traded companies to prepare reports in accordance with GAAP. Even companies that are not under the jurisdiction of the SEC prepare financial accounting information in accordance with GAAP to satisfy creditors. Managerial accounting, on the other hand, is completely optional. It stresses information that is *useful* to internal managers for planning, evaluation, and decision making. If a managerial accountant believes that deviating from GAAP will provide more useful information to internal managers, GAAP should not be followed.

Detail of Information.   Financial accounting presents information in a highly summarized form. Net income, for example, is presented for the company as a whole. To run a company, however, managers need the more detailed information that the managerial accountant can supply. For example, managers need information about the cost of operating individual departments, in addition to the cost of operating the company as a whole.

Emphasis on Nonmonetary Information.   Both managerial and financial accounting reports generally contain monetary information. Managerial accounting reports can also contain a substantial amount of nonmonetary information. The quantity of material consumed in production, the number of hours worked by the office staff, and the number of units produced are examples of important nonmonetary data that appear in managerial accounting reports.

Emphasis on the Future.   Financial accounting is primarily concerned with presenting the results of past transactions. Managerial accounting, on the other hand, places considerable emphasis on the future. As indicated previously, one of the primary purposes of managerial accounting is planning. Thus, managerial accounting information often involves estimates of the costs and benefits of future transactions.

Similarities Between Financial and Managerial Accounting

We do not want to overstate the differences between financial accounting and managerial accounting in terms of their respective user groups. Financial accounting reports are aimed *primarily* at external users, and managerial accounting reports are aimed *primarily* at internal users. However, managers also make significant use of financial accounting reports, and external users occasionally request financial information that is generally considered appropriate for internal users. For example, creditors may ask management to provide them with detailed cash flow projections.

EMPHASIS ON COST INFORMATION

Consider the following questions that a manager may need to address.

> *Planning*   What will our material *cost* be next month if we increase production by 20 percent?
>
> *Evaluation*   Did the night-shift supervisor do a good job of controlling labor *costs* last month?
>
> *Decision Making*   Does the labor *cost* savings justify purchasing a computer-controlled assembly line?

To answer these and other important questions, managers must understand a number of cost terms and concepts. The remainder of this chapter considers the classification of costs for manufacturing firms, the use of cost information by service organizations, and cost classifications in planning, evaluation, and decision making.

INSIGHTS INTO ETHICS

Bob Jakes is the chief financial officer of Suncamp Corporation. Last week he had lunch with one of the major shareholders of the company, Bruce Kemper, who is considering buying additional shares from other shareholders. Kemper indicated that while he was generally pleased with the company's performance, he had reservations about how the company plans to deal with increased foreign competition. Bob, of course, has access to all company information, including budgets for new product development and advertising campaigns. Bob knows this information, if shared with Kemper, will convince him that the company is well positioned for the coming year. Also, it will demonstrate to Kemper that Bob is "on top of" his important financial planning responsibilities. In his position as a major shareholder, Kemper could recommend Bob for the position of president, a position that will open in the next year following the current president's retirement.

Should Bob disclose how Suncamp Corporation plans to deal with increased foreign competition? What do you think most managers would do if they were in Bob's position?

LO 3
Distinguish between
manufacturing and
nonmanufacturing costs
and between product and
period costs.

COST CLASSIFICATIONS FOR MANUFACTURING FIRMS

Determining the cost of items a merchandising firm purchases from a supplier is relatively easy. The cost of the items is the purchase cost net of returns, allowances, and discounts plus related shipping costs. Determining the cost of items a manufacturing firm produces is more complex. Using both labor and machinery, a manufacturing firm converts raw materials into finished goods. Complexity arises because the costs of the resources used in production must be assigned to units produced. Merchandising and manufacturing firms are compared in Illustration 20-4. This section discusses the broad classification of manufacturing and nonmanufacturing costs. These classifications are based on whether the costs are associated with the production of goods. It also discusses product and period cost classifications that are related to the timing of expensing costs.

ILLUSTRATION 20-4 Comparison of Merchandising and Manufacturing Firms

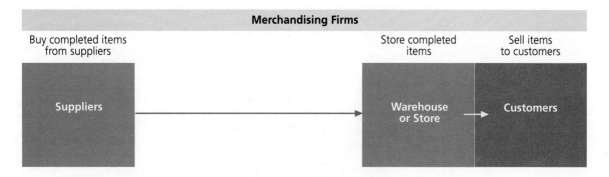

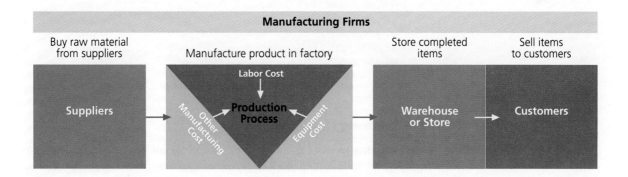

Manufacturing Costs

Manufacturing costs include all those associated with the production of goods. They include three cost categories: direct material, direct labor, and manufacturing overhead.

Direct Material. **Direct material** includes the cost of all materials and parts that are directly traced to items produced. For The Wooden Boat Company, a manufacturer of rowboats, direct material includes the cost of wood and fittings. Tracing these costs directly to individual boats is easy. Direct material probably does not include the cost of minor materials such as glue and nails. While such minor material costs could be traced to a particular boat, it probably is not worth the time to do so. Materials that are not directly traced to a product are referred to as **indirect materials**.

Direct Labor. **Direct labor** includes the cost of labor that is directly traced to items produced. The Wooden Boat Company's direct labor would include the labor cost of the workers directly involved in constructing a rowboat. It probably does not include the cost of managers or supervisors. Although it is theoretically possible to trace the time each supervisor spends on a particular boat, it is generally not worthwhile to do so. Labor costs that are not traced directly to products produced are referred to as **indirect labor costs**.

Manufacturing Overhead. **Manufacturing overhead** includes the costs of all manufacturing activities other than direct material and direct labor. It includes indirect material, indirect labor, and a wide variety of other cost items. For the Wooden Boat Company example, manufacturing overhead includes the costs of glue, nails, salaries of supervisors, depreciation of tools, depreciation of the building where manufacturing takes place, utilities, and a number of other items. Illustration 20-5 lists some common manufacturing overhead costs.

ILLUSTRATION 20-5 Common Manufacturing Overhead Costs

Indirect factory labor
Indirect material
Overtime premium
Night-shift premium
Vacation and holiday pay for factory workers
Social Security and Medicare taxes for factory workers
Health insurance for factory workers
Power, heat, and light in the factory
Depreciation of factory equipment
Depreciation of plant
Insurance on plant and factory equipment
Repair of factory equipment
Maintenance of factory building and grounds
Property taxes related to the factory

Nonmanufacturing Costs

Nonmanufacturing costs can be defined simply as all costs that are not associated with the production of goods. Nonmanufacturing costs typically include selling and general and administrative costs.

Selling Costs. Selling costs include all those associated with securing and filling customer orders. Thus, selling costs include advertising, sales personnel salaries, depreciation of automobiles and office equipment the sales force uses and costs of storing and shipping finished goods.

General and Administrative Costs. General and administrative costs include all those associated with the firm's general management. Thus, general and administrative costs include the salaries of the company president and accounting personnel, depreciation of the general office building, depreciation of office equipment general managers use, and the cost of supplies clerical employees use.

In many cases, a cost is classified by its use rather than by its specific nature. Consider janitorial costs. Janitorial costs associated with maintaining a production area are classified as a manufacturing cost (specifically, manufacturing overhead). On the other hand, janitorial costs associated with maintaining the general office building are classified as a nonmanufacturing cost (specifically, general and administrative cost).

Product and Period Costs

A distinction is made in regard to the timing of when costs are recognized as expenses. Product costs are identified with goods produced and expensed when goods are sold. Period costs are identified with accounting periods and expensed in the period incurred.

Product Costs.   **Product costs** are those assigned to goods produced. Thus, product costs and manufacturing costs are terms that are often used interchangeably. Both include direct material, direct labor, and manufacturing overhead. Product costs are considered an asset (inventory) until the finished goods are sold. When the goods are sold, the product costs are expensed. This ensures a proper matching of revenue with the costs necessary to produce it. Direct labor cost incurred in 19X1 to produce goods sold in 19X2 becomes an expense in 19X2, the year of the sale when revenues are recognized.

Period Costs.   **Period costs** are costs identified with accounting periods rather than with goods produced. Selling and general and administrative costs (nonmanufacturing costs) are period costs. We recognize period costs as expenses in the period incurred. Rent paid on an *office building* is a period cost and becomes an expense in the period incurred. In contrast, the rent paid on a *factory building* is a product cost and becomes an expense when goods are sold. Differences between product and period costs are summarized in Illustration 20-6.

ILLUSTRATION 20-6 Relationship Among Cost Categories

	Type of Cost	When Expensed
Manufacturing Costs	**Product Cost** Direct material Direct labor Manufacturing overhead	Expensed when goods are sold
Nonmanufacturing Costs	**Period Cost** Selling cost General and administrative cost	Expensed in period they are incurred

BALANCE SHEET PRESENTATION OF PRODUCT COSTS

Product costs may appear on the balance sheet as assets in three inventory accounts: raw materials, work in process, and finished goods. **Raw Materials Inventory** includes the cost of materials on hand that are used to produce a company's products. Returning to the Wooden Boat Company, wood and fittings are included in Raw Materials Inventory. **Work in Process Inventory** is the inventory account for the cost of goods that are only partially completed. For example, if at the end of the year The Wooden Boat Company has one partially completed boat, the cost of all direct labor, direct material, and manufacturing overhead incurred to bring the boat to its current state of partial completion would be included in Work in Process Inventory. **Finished Goods Inventory** is the account for the cost of all items that are complete and ready to sell. If, at the end of the year, The Wooden Boat Company has two boats that are completed and ready to sell, Finished Goods Inventory would include the cost of all direct material, direct labor, and manufacturing overhead incurred to bring the boats to their finished state. A simplified balance sheet showing the three inventory accounts is presented in Illustration 20-7.

ILLUSTRATION 20-7 Balance Sheet Presentation of Inventory Accounts

The Wooden Boat Company Balance Sheet For Year Ended December 31, 19X1				
Assets			*Liabilities and Stockholders' Equity*	
Cash		$ 1,000	Accounts payable	$ 1,000
Accounts receivable		2,000	Notes payable	2,000
Inventory:			Long-term debt	2,000
Raw materials	**$2,000**		Common stock	5,000
Work in process	**3,000**		Retained earnings	8,000
Finished goods	**4,000**	9,000		
Equipment (net)		6,000	Total liabilities and	
Total assets		$18,000	stockholders' equity	$18,000

LO 4
Describe the flow of product costs in a manufacturing firm's accounts.

FLOW OF PRODUCT COSTS IN ACCOUNTS

In an accounting system, product costs flow from one inventory account to another. Illustration 20-8 demonstrates the flow of product costs in the accounts.

The cost of *direct* material used reduces the Raw Material Inventory account and increases Work in Process Inventory. *Indirect* material used, however, is not added directly to Work in Process Inventory—it is accumulated in Manufacturing Overhead. The amount of direct labor used increases Work in Process Inventory, but indirect labor is not added directly to Work in Process Inventory. Instead, like indirect material, it is accumulated in Manufacturing Overhead. The cost accumulated in Manufacturing Overhead, which includes indirect material, indirect labor, and a variety of other overhead costs, is also added to Work in Process Inventory.

Once items are finished, the cost of the completed items is transferred from Work in Process Inventory and into Finished Goods Inventory. The cost of items completed is referred to as **cost of goods manufactured**. When the completed items are sold, the cost of the items sold is transferred from Finished Goods Inventory into Cost of Goods Sold.

ILLUSTRATION 20-8 Flow of Product Costs in Accounts

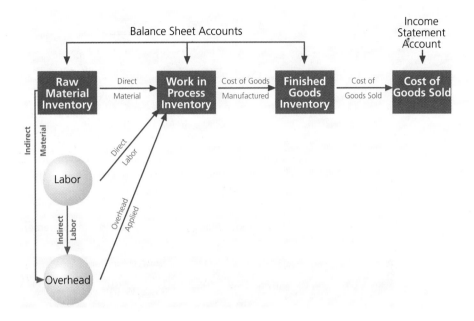

INCOME STATEMENT PRESENTATION OF PRODUCT COSTS

When finished goods are sold, the cost of the inventory sold is considered an expense and must be removed from inventory and charged to cost of goods sold. This provides a matching of revenue (sales dollars) with the cost of producing the revenue (the cost of goods sold). Before cost of goods sold can be calculated, however, we must first calculate cost of goods manufactured. Recall that cost of goods manufactured is the cost associated with all goods completed during a period. Cost of goods manufactured can be calculated using a simple formula. It is equal to the beginning balance in Work in Process Inventory plus current manufacturing costs (direct material, direct labor, and manufacturing overhead incurred in the current period) minus the ending balance in Work in Process Inventory.

Cost of Goods Manufactured:

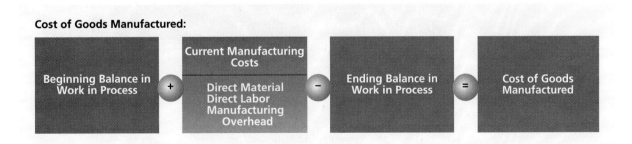

Once cost of goods manufactured is known, cost of goods sold can also be calculated using a simple formula. It is equal to the beginning balance in Finished Goods Inventory plus cost of goods manufactured minus the ending balance in Finished Goods Inventory.

Cost of Goods Sold:

| Beginning Balance in Finished Goods | + | Cost of Goods Manufactured | − | Ending Balance in Finished Goods | = | Cost of Goods Sold |

Illustration 20-9 presents a schedule of cost of goods manufactured and a simplified income statement showing cost of goods sold for the Wooden Boat

ILLUSTRATION 20-9 Schedule of Cost of Goods Manufactured and an Income Statement Showing Cost of Goods Sold

The Wooden Boat Company
Schedule of Cost of Goods Manufactured
For the Year Ended December 31, 19X1

Beginning balance in work in process			$ 2,000
Add current manufacturing costs:			
Direct material:			
Beginning balance	$10,000		
Purchases	20,000		
Ending balance	(5,000)	$25,000	
Direct labor		15,000	
Manufacturing overhead:			
Heat, light, and power	$ 1,000		
Depreciation of equipment	15,000		
Other	5,000	21,000	61,000
Total			$63,000
Less: Ending balance in work in process			3,000
Cost of goods manufactured			$60,000

The Wooden Boat Company
Income Statement
For the Year Ended December 31, 19X1

Sales		$150,000
Less cost of goods sold:		
Beginning finished goods	$20,000	
Add: Cost of goods manufactured	60,000	
Cost of goods available for sale	$80,000	
Less: Ending finished goods	4,000	76,000
Gross profit		$74,000
Less nonmanufacturing expenses:		
Selling expenses	$ 3,000	
General and administrative expenses	52,000	55,000
Net income		$19,000

Company. Note that in the schedule of cost of goods manufactured, the calculation of direct material cost is indicated (beginning balance, plus purchases, minus ending balance). Also, note that in the income statement, the sum of the beginning balance in finished goods plus cost of goods manufactured is referred to as the **cost of goods available for sale**.

Comparison of Financial Statements of Merchandising and Manufacturing Firms

The financial statements of a merchandising firm differ from those of a manufacturing firm. The main differences relate to the inventory accounts and cost of goods sold. Illustration 20-10 shows that the typical merchandising firm has a single inventory account—Merchandise Inventory. A manufacturing firm, on the other hand, has three inventory accounts: Raw Materials Inventory, Work in Process Inventory, and Finished Goods Inventory. Also, note that while cost of goods sold in a merchandising firm includes only the net cost of items purchased from suppliers, cost of goods sold in a manufacturing firm includes direct material, direct labor, and manufacturing overhead.

ILLUSTRATION 20-10 Comparison of Merchandising and Manufacturing Firms

Balance Sheet—Inventory Accounts

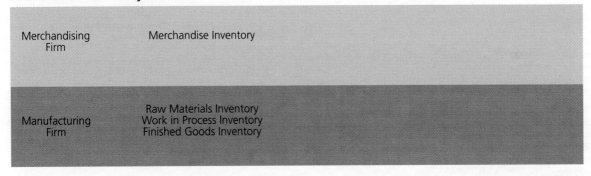

Income Statement—Cost of Goods Sold

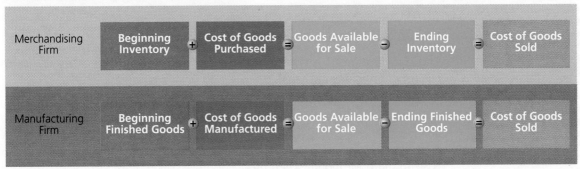

COST OF SERVICES

Just as accountants at manufacturing firms are asked to determine product costs, accountants at service companies are asked to determine the costs of various service activities. A bank may want to know the cost of processing customer checks, a firm of certified public accountants may want to know the cost of performing an audit or a hospital may want to know the cost of an x-ray. Managerial accounting procedures can provide this information. Suppose, for example, the owner of Lakeside Bicycle Shop wants to know the average cost, excluding parts, of repairing bicycles in the month of June for purposes of setting repair prices. The report presented in Illustration 20-11 provides the desired cost information.

ILLUSTRATION 20-11 Cost of Repair Services

Lakeside Bicycle Shop Cost of Repair Services For Year Month of June 19X1	
Repair salaries	$2,800
Supplies	500
Depreciation of tools	200
Miscellaneous costs	100
Total repair costs	$3,600
Number of repairs	240
Average cost per repair	$15
Number of labor hours	180
Average cost per labor hour	$20

LO 5
Distinguish between fixed and variable costs, direct and indirect costs, and controllable and noncontrollable.

COST CLASSIFICATIONS FOR PLANNING, EVALUATION, AND DECISION MAKING

Earlier, we distinguished between manufacturing and nonmanufacturing costs and between product and period costs. In addition to these cost terms, a number of cost classifications are also important for planning, evaluation, and decision making.

Variable and Fixed Costs

The classification of a cost as variable or fixed depends on whether the cost changes or remains the same in relation to business activity.

Variable Costs. **Variable costs** are those that increase or decrease in response to increases or decreases in business activity. Material and direct labor are variable costs because they fluctuate with changes in production (business activity). Suppose the Redmond Manufacturing Company incurred the following variable costs in the prior month when production was 1,000 units:

	1,000 Units	Cost per Unit
Variable costs:		
Direct material	$25,000	$25
Direct labor	50,000	50
Power costs	5,000	5
Total variable cost	$80,000	$80

How much cost should the company plan on for the current month if production is expected to increase by 10 percent to 1,100 units? Assuming the costs change in proportion to changes in activity, if production increases by 10 percent, the cost would be expected to increase by 10 percent. Thus, direct material should increase to $27,500; direct labor to $55,000; and power to $5,500.

	1,100 Units	Cost per Unit
Variable costs:		
Direct material	$27,500	$25
Direct labor	55,000	50
Power costs	5,500	5
Total variable cost	$88,000	$80

Note that while the *total variable cost* increases from $80,000 to $88,000 when production changes from 1,000 to 1,100 units, the *variable cost per unit* does not change. It remains $80 per unit. With an $80 per unit variable cost, variable cost (in total) increases by $8,000 (i.e., $80 x 100) when production increases by 100 units.

Fixed Costs. **Fixed costs** are those that do not change when there are changes in business activity. Depreciation, rent, and insurance are costs that typically do not change with changes in business activity. Suppose that in the prior month, Redmond Manufacturing Company incurred $6,000 of fixed costs, including $2,000 of depreciation, $3,000 of rent, and $1,000 of insurance. If the Redmond Manufacturing Company increases production to 1,100 units in the current month, the levels of depreciation, rent cost, and insurance cost incurred should remain the same as when production was only 1,000 units. However, with fixed costs, the cost per unit does change when there are changes in production. When production increases, the constant amount of fixed cost is spread over a larger number of units. This drives down the fixed cost per unit. With an increase in production from 1,000 to 1,100 units, *total fixed cost* remains at $6,000. Note, however, that *fixed cost per unit* decreases from $6 per unit to $5.46 per unit.

	Prior Month		Current Month	
	1,000 Units	Cost Per Unit	1,100 Units	Cost Per Unit
Fixed costs:				
Depreciation	$2,000	$2	$2,000	$1.82
Rent	3,000	3	3,000	2.73
Insurance	1,000	1	1,000	.91
Total fixed cost	$6,000	$6	$6,000	$5.46

848

Direct and Indirect Costs

A **direct cost** is one that is directly traceable to a product, activity, or department. **Indirect costs** are those that either cannot be directly traced to a product, activity, or department, or are not worth tracing. As discussed above, indirect product costs are referred to as manufacturing overhead. The distinction between a direct and an indirect cost depends on the object of the cost tracing. For example, The General Manufacturing Company has production facilities in Memphis and Houston and incurs separate insurance costs for each facility. The insurance cost related to the Memphis facility is obviously a direct cost of the Memphis plant. However, the insurance cost is an indirect cost of the individual products produced in the Memphis plant because *direct* tracing of the insurance cost to each product is not possible. This situation is presented in Illustration 20-12.

ILLUSTRATION 20-12 Insurance as Both a Direct and Indirect Cost

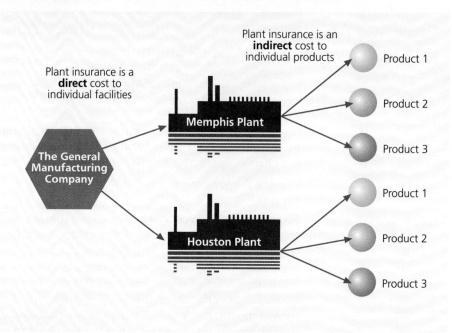

Controllable and Noncontrollable Costs

A manager can influence a **controllable cost** but cannot influence a **noncontrollable cost**. The distinction between controllable and noncontrollable costs is especially important when evaluating manager performance. Managers should not be evaluated unfavorably if a cost not under their control increases.

As an example of controllable and noncontrollable costs, consider a plant supervisor. This individual influences labor and material costs by scheduling workers and assuring an efficient production process. Thus, labor and material costs are a supervisor's controllable costs. However, the supervisor cannot determine insurance for a plant. A plant manager or an insurance specialist makes decisions regarding insurance. Therefore, insurance cost is a supervisor's noncontrollable cost but a plant manager's or an insurance specialist's controllable cost.

SUMMARY

State the primary goal of managerial accounting.   The primary goal of managerial accounting is to provide information that helps managers plan and evaluate company activities and make business decisions.

Describe how budgets are used to plan and how performance reports are used to evaluate.   Managerial accountants prepare financial plans referred to as budgets. These plans help employees understand company goals and follow the most efficient route to achieve them. Performance reports compare actual performance to the budget. Actual results that deviate significantly from the plan signal the need to determine the cause of the deviation.

Distinguish between manufacturing and nonmanufacturing costs and between product and period costs.   Manufacturing costs include all those associated with the production of goods. They include direct material, direct labor, and manufacturing overhead. Nonmanufacturing costs are all those not associated with the production of goods. Selling and general and administrative costs are nonmanufacturing costs. Costs can also be classified as either product costs or period costs. Product costs are identical to manufacturing costs and include direct labor, direct material, and manufacturing overhead. Period costs, on the other hand, are expensed in the period they are incurred. Period costs include both selling and general and administrative costs, which are also referred to as nonmanufacturing costs.

Describe the flow of product costs in a manufacturing firm's accounts.   As they are incurred, product costs are assigned to Work in Process Inventory. When the items in work in process are completed, the cost of the completed items is removed from Work in Process Inventory and added to Finished Goods Inventory. When the finished goods are sold, the cost of the items sold is removed from Finished Goods Inventory and added to Cost of Goods Sold. Thus, product costs become an expense when completed items are sold.

Distinguish between fixed and variable costs, direct and indirect costs, and controllable and noncontrollable costs.   Variable costs are those that increase or decrease in response to changes in business activity. Fixed costs remain constant when there are changes in business activity. Direct costs are those that are directly traceable to a product, activity, or department. Indirect costs either cannot be directly traced or they are not worth tracing. Controllable costs are those a manager can influence. On the other hand, a cost that a manager cannot influence is a noncontrollable cost.

REVIEW PROBLEM

The management of Cutter Saw Blade Company is reviewing the results of operations for the calendar year 19X2, for the purpose of evaluating the efficiency of their operations and the performance of their factory supervisor. The review is also the first step in preparing the manufacturing budget for the 19X3 operating year. The company accountant prepared the following information for the production of saw blades.

Cutter Saw Blade Company
Manufacturing Activity
For the Year Ended December 31, 19X2

	Budgeted	Actual
Production (units)	250,000	250,000
Production costs:		
Direct material	$ 375,000	$ 385,000
Direct labor	500,000	535,000
Indirect material	75,000	72,000
Indirect labor	300,000	320,000
Payroll taxes	57,500	60,700
Heat, light, & power	80,000	78,000
Depreciation on plant assets	50,000	50,000
Insurance & taxes	20,000	21,000
Total production costs	$1,457,500	$1,521,700

The manager knew the causes of some of the differences between budgeted and actual costs were due to the following items:

1. The cost of raw materials went up 5 percent on May 1.
2. The new three-year labor contract, signed July 1, 19X2, increased the hourly rate for direct labor from $10 per hour to $12 per hour and for indirect labor from $6 per hour to $7 per hour.
3. Property taxes increased in July 19X2, while the 5 year insurance policy continued at the same rate.

REQUIRED:

a. Prepare a performance report for 19X2 by adding a variance column (difference between budget and actual) to the Manufacturing Activity Report.
b. Calculate a budgeted unit cost and the actual unit cost for saw blades during 19X2.
c. Evaluate the variances identified in the performance report.

SOLUTION:

(a) *Prepare a performance report.*

Cutter Saw Blade Company
Performance Report, Production Costs
For the Year Ended December 31, 19X2

	Budgeted	Actual	Budget Minus Actual
Production (units)	250,000	250,000	0
Production costs:			
Direct material	$ 375,000	$ 385,000	$(10,000)
Direct labor	500,000	535,000	(35,000)
Indirect material	75,000	72,000	3,000
Indirect labor	300,000	320,000	(20,000)
Payroll taxes	57,500	60,700	(3,200)
Heat, light, & power	80,000	78,000	2,000
Depreciation on plant assets	50,000	50,000	0
Insurance & taxes	20,000	21,000	(1,000)
Total production cost	$1,457,500	$1,521,700	$(64,200)

(b) *Calculate budgeted and actual unit costs.*

Budgeted cost per unit:

$1,457,500 ÷ 250,000 = $5.83 per unit
Actual cost per unit: $1,521,700 ÷ 250,000 = $6.09 per unit

(c) *Evaluate the variances found in a.*

1. The production activity variance of zero indicates that production for the year equals the level planned.
2. The direct material cost variance is unfavorable. However, when the increase in the cost of material is considered, the expected cost of the material is $385,938 [(375,000 x 5/12) + (375,000 x 7/12 x 1.05)]. Therefore, what at first appears unfavorable becomes slightly favorable when examined more carefully. This could imply that management was effective in controlling material usage or it could relate to effective purchasing.
3. The direct labor cost variance is unfavorable. The increase in the labor rate in the middle of the year from $10 to $12 per hour gives an expected cost of the direct labor of $550,000 [(500,000 x 6/12) + (500,000 x 6/12 x 12/10)]. This means that the actual cost of $535,000 is less than expected in light of the wage increase and is actually favorable by $15,000. Management was apparently effective in controlling labor.
4. The indirect material variance is $3,000 favorable. This implies either control over material use or effective purchasing, or both.
5. The indirect labor variance is $20,000 unfavorable. The increase in the wage rate in the middle of the year from $6 to $7 per hour gives an expected cost for the indirect labor of $325,000 [(300,000 x 6/12) + (300,000 x 6/12 x 7/6)]. This means that the actual cost of $320,000 is less than would be expected in light of the wage increase.
6. The payroll taxes variance is $3,200 unfavorable. It was budgeted at 7.1875% (57,500 ÷ 800,000) for direct labor plus indirect labor. It would have been expected to be $62,891 [(550,000 + 325,000) x .071875)] in light of the wage increases in mid-year and is actually favorable by $2,191 (62,891 − 60,700).
7. The heat, light, & power variance is $2,000 favorable. This may be due to less demand for heat or air conditioning due to weather or it may be the result of management's actions to reduce the use of electrical power.
8. The depreciation of plant assets variance is zero, implying that there were no changes in the plant asset holdings during the year.
9. The insurance & taxes variance is $1,000 unfavorable. The July 19X2 increase in property taxes could explain part or all of this variance.

KEY TERMS

budgets, *834*
controllable cost, *848*
cost of goods available for sale, *845*
cost of goods manufactured, *842*
direct cost, *848*
direct material, *839*
finished goods inventory, *842*
fixed costs, *847*
indirect costs, *848*

indirect labor costs, *840*
indirect materials, *840*
management by exception, *836*
managerial accounting, *833*
manufacturing costs, *839*
manufacturing overhead, *840*
noncontrollable cost, *848*
nonmanufacturing costs, *840*
performance report, *835*
period costs, *841*
product costs, *841*

raw materials inventory, *841*
variable costs, *846*
work in process inventory, *842*

SELF-QUIZ

LO 1 1. The primary goal of managerial accounting is to:
  a. Provide information for potential and current investors in the company.
  b. Provide information for both current and prospective investors as well as for creditors.
  c. Provide information for current and prospective investors, current and prospective creditors, and for the several taxing agencies.
  d. Provide information for planning, evaluation, and decision making.

LO 1 2. Match the following terms with the management activities described below.
LO 2
  ___ a. Planning
  ___ b. Evaluation
  ___ c. Decision Making
  (1) This management activity involves the process of reviewing all the available data relative to a pressing question which requires a decision between alternative actions. This activity may involve routine operating items or one-time major choices.
  (2) This management activity provides both direction for the firm and a defined goal against which performance may be measured.
  (3) This activity relates actual results with planned outcomes as a basis for corrective action.

LO 2 3. Which of the following statements about budgets is incorrect?
  a. Budgets may be expressed in dollars, quantities, or both.
  b. Budgets may reflect projected revenues, projected expenses, projected cash flows, or projected quantities of inputs or outputs.
  c. Budgets must be prepared in accordance with GAAP.
  d. Budgets are used both for planning and for evaluating performance.

LO 2 4. Which of the following is not a basic element of a performance report?
  a. Assets, liabilities, and owner's equity.
  b. Budget data for the period.
  c. Actual cost results for the period.
  d. Variances of actual cost data from budget data.

LO 1 5. Which of the following statements is incorrect?
LO 2
  a. Managerial accounting statements do not necessarily comply with GAAP.
  b. Financial accounting statements normally reflect more detail than would be found in managerial accounting statements.
  c. Managerial accounting statements emphasize future activities and future costs.
  d. Financial accounting data is directed primarily at external users rather than internal users.

LO 3 6. Which of the following is not a manufacturing cost?
  a. Raw materials
  b. Freight out
  c. Direct labor
  d. Manufacturing overhead

LO 3 7. Which of the following inventory accounts found in the general ledger of a manufacturing firm would be equivalent to the Merchandise Inventory account of a retail establishment?
  a. Supplies Inventory
  b. Raw Materials Inventory
  c. Work in Process Inventory
  d. Finished Goods Inventory

LO 3 8. Which of the following does not describe direct materials in a manufacturing environment?
  a. Identifiable in the product
  b. Not material in amount
  c. Traceable to the product
  d. Material in amount

LO 3 9. Which of the following activities best represents direct labor in a manufacturing environment?
  a. Moving the product from one work station to another.
  b. Cleaning up around the machinery.
  c. Delivering raw materials to the work stations.
  d. Welding a component to the product.

LO 3 10. List three expenses that could be properly classified as manufacturing overhead.

LO 3 11. List three nonmanufacturing costs normally classified as selling expenses.

LO 3 12. List three nonmanufacturing costs normally classified as administrative expenses.

LO 3 13. Which of the following costs would be classified as a product cost?
  a. Transportation out
  b. Insurance expense—administrative
  c. Direct materials
  d. Sales salaries
  e. None of the above

LO 3 14. Which of the following costs would be classified as a period cost?
  a. Direct labor
  b. Indirect labor
  c. Direct materials
  d. Sales salaries

LO 3 15. Which of the following accounts would not appear in a balance sheet?
a. Raw Materials Inventory
b. Work in Process Inventory
c. Cost of Goods Sold
d. Finished Goods Inventory

LO 4 16. Which of the following reduces the work in process inventory account?
a. Cost of goods sold
b. Cost of goods manufactured
c. Cost of direct materials used
d. Cost of direct labor put into production

LO 4 17. The calculation of cost of goods manufactured does not include:

a. Work in process inventory, beginning
b. Cost of goods sold
c. Work in process inventory, ending
d. Direct materials
e. None of the above

LO 5 18. The total amount of _____ cost varies with changes in activity while the total amount of _____ cost remains unchanged with changes in activity.

LO 5 19. _____ costs are directly traceable to a product, activity, or department while _____ costs are not.

LO 5 20. A cost is _____ if a particular manager can influence it and _____ if he or she cannot.

SOLUTIONS TO SELF-QUIZ
1. d   2. a. (2) b. (3) c. (1)   3. c   4. a   5. b   6. b   7. d   8. b   9. d   10. Indirect materials, indirect labor, depreciation on factory plant and equipment (Note: Other examples are shown in the list in Table 20-5 on page 840).   11. Sales salaries and commissions, freight out, advertising (Note: Other sales expenses are shown on page 840).   12. Salaries of accounting personnel, salaries of administrative personnel, bad debt expense (Note: Administrative expenses are shown on page 840.)
13. c   14. d   15. c   16. b   17. b   18. variable, fixed   19. direct, indirect   20. controllable, noncontrollable

---

QUESTIONS

Q20-1   Discuss the purpose of managerial reports.

Q20-2   Briefly describe the planning and evaluation process.

Q20-3   Explain how budgets serve both the planning and evaluation process.

Q20-4   Describe the elements of a performance report and explain how it is useful to management.

Q20-5   How do managerial accounting reports differ from financial accounting reports?

Q20-6   Do GAAP-based financial statements serve the needs of both the external users and the internal users equally well? Discuss.

Q20-7   What kinds of non-monetary information might typically be found in managerial accounting reports?

Q20-8   Do managers normally use GAAP-based financial statements in performing their managerial functions? Discuss.

Q20-9   Explain what is meant by the statement: "Managerial accounting looks forward in time while financial accounting looks backward in time."

Q20-10 Are all material costs entered into production classified as direct materials? Explain.

Q20-11 Distinguish between direct labor and indirect labor.

Q20-12 List five costs which would typically be found in a manufacturing overhead account.

Q20-13 Explain the term *nonmanufacturing costs* and list the two general types of nonmanufacturing costs.

Q20-14 Define the term *product costs* and explain how product costs differ from period costs.

Q20-15 When are product costs charged to expense?

Q20-16 Explain how the costs of production flow through the accounting records.

Q20-17 How do the costs of a merchandising business differ from the costs of a manufacturing business?

Q20-18 Discuss how cost of service information may be used in a nonmanufacturing business.

Q20-19 Explain why fixed costs are called "fixed" and variable costs are called "variable."

Q20-20 Why are certain traceable costs not treated as direct costs?

EXERCISES

LO 1,2

E20-1 **Managerial Accounting, Budgets, Performance Reports** Match the following terms with the definitions that appear below.

___ a. Budgets

___ b. Evaluation

___ c. Planning

___ d. Decision making

___ e. Performance reports

___ f. Management by exception

(1) Looking forward in time to map out the activities that should take place to move the firm toward its objectives.

(2) Outputs of the planning process that will normally be monetary in nature but which may include nonmonetary data as well.

(3) Managements' review of the company's activities, on an after-the-fact basis, to see if the results are appropriate in light of the plans.

(4) One of management's main functions for which accountants may prepare a variety of reports to help management select between alternatives.

(5) The direction of management's attention to items that seem to be out of control or offer opportunities for benefits, minimizing management's time on activities under control.

(6) Show the actual results of the activities of a business and the planned results for comparative purposes by management.

LO 2

E20-2 **Budgets** Which of the following statements related to budgets are true? Explain why the false statements are not true.

a. Budgets are written plans, prepared by management, for the purpose of guiding future business activity.

b. Budgets may be expressed in dollars, in quantities such as pounds of materials or hours of direct labor, or both.

c. Budgets must be prepared in accordance with GAAP.

d. Budgets may be prepared for periods of less than a year, i.e., a week, month, or quarter.

e. The mandated use of budgets insures that some planning will take place but they have no value after the planning process is completed.

f. Budgets are useful to communicate the objectives and goals of the business.

LO 2

E20-3 **Performance Reports** Which of the following statements related to performance reports are true? Explain why the false statements are not true.

a. Performance reports provide a comparison of actual performance with planned performance.

b. Unfavorable variances in a performance report would indicate that the responsible manager did not exercise adequate control over his or her area of authority.

c. Performance reports should only be prepared annually.

d. Performance reports are prepared according to Generally Accepted Accounting Principles.

LO 3

E20-4 **Manufacturing Costs** Match the managerial accounting terms with the definitions shown on the next page.

___ a. Direct materials
___ b. Indirect materials
___ c. Direct labor
___ d. Indirect labor
___ e. Manufacturing overhead
___ f. Work in process

(1) All costs of production other than direct materials and direct labor.
(2) Those materials that are essential in the production of a firm's product but which either are not traceable to the product or are not in the product in material amounts.
(3) The costs associated with products that have entered the production process but which have not yet been completed.
(4) The costs of labor that are directly traceable to the product.
(5) Those materials that are essential in the production of a firm's products which are traceable to the products.
(6) The costs of labor that are essential to the production process but which cannot be directly traced to the product.

LO 3   **E20-5**   **Manufacturing Costs**   The three elements of manufacturing costs are (1) direct materials, (2) direct labor, and (3) manufacturing overhead. Define each of the three terms and include three examples of overhead costs in the definition of manufacturing overhead.

LO 3   **E20-6**   **Manufacturing Costs and Nonmanufacturing Costs**   Identify each of the following accounts as direct material (*DM*); direct labor (*DL*); manufacturing overhead (*MOH*); selling expense (*SE*); or administrative expense (*AE*).

___ a. Supervisors' salaries
___ b. Machine operators' salaries
___ c. Factory supplies used
___ d. Depreciation on machinery
___ e. Office supplies used
___ f. Raw materials used that are traced to products
___ g. Sales office electricity
___ h. Sales salaries
___ i. Factory rent
___ j. Freight out
___ k. Advertising
___ l. Factory electricity
___ m. Freight in
___ n. Office overhead

LO 3   **E20-7**   **Product and Period Costs**   Indicate which of the following statements regarding product and period costs are true and which are false and explain why the false statements are incorrect.

a. Product costs are includable in the cost of inventory of a firm prior to the sale of the items to which they relate.
b. Period costs are expensed in the period in which the goods produced are sold.
c. Product costs are expensed in the period in which they are incurred.
d. Period costs are matched with revenue on a period basis rather than on a product basis.
e. Product costs may include costs which expire over time rather than being directly traceable to the product.
f. All product costs are traceable to the product directly and involve material amounts.

LO 4

E20-8   **Flow of Product Costs**   Product costing involves the accumulation of the production-related costs temporarily in one inventory account and then transferring costs to another inventory account upon completion.

a. The first inventory account is _____.
b. The second inventory account is _____.
c. Which inventory account of a manufacturer is essentially equivalent to the merchandise inventory account of a retailer or wholesaler?

LO 4

E20-9   **Flow of Product Costs**   Which of the following statements are correct with regard to product cost flows? Explain why each incorrect statement is wrong.

a. Direct labor cost is added to the work in process account.
b. Manufacturing overhead cost includes selling and administrative expenses.
c. Materials issued into production increase Raw Materials Inventory and reduce Work in Process Inventory.
d. Delivery expense is an item includable in manufacturing overhead.
e. The cost of goods manufactured is the total of the additions to the work in process account.
f. The cost of units sold during the period increase Finished Goods Inventory and decrease Cost of Goods Sold.
g. Indirect labor and indirect materials are both part of manufacturing overhead.
h. The depreciation on factory equipment is a period cost because depreciation occurs relative to the passage of time.

LO 5

E20-10   **Cost Classifications**   Identify each of the following statements as being related to fixed costs or to variable costs.

a. A cost that varies in total with changes in the activity level.
b. A cost that varies on a per unit basis with changes in the activity level.
c. A cost that remains fixed per unit with changes in the activity level.
d. A cost that remains fixed in total with changes in the activity level.

LO 5

E20-11   **Identifying Costs**   Indicate whether each of the following costs is: (1) *Fixed* or *Variable*, and (2) *Direct* or *Indirect*.

a. Direct labor
b. Direct material
c. Factory supplies
d. Factory rent
e. Depreciation—machinery
f. Utilities expense

LO 5

E20-12   **Identifying Costs**   Explain how a cost can be controllable at one administrative level and noncontrollable at another administrative level.

PROBLEM SET A

LO 1,2

P20-1A   **Budgets in Managerial Accounting**   Ye Olde Forge makes hand-wrought iron mailbox posts which are marketed through monthly ads in three national magazines. The following production cost budget was prepared for 19X3.

Ye Olde Forge Budgeted Production Costs For the Year Ended December 31, 19X3	
Budgeted production	10,000 posts
Iron bar stock (direct material, variable)	$ 8,000
Direct labor (variable)	24,000
Fuel and flux (indirect material, variable)	3,600
Building rent (fixed)	12,000
Depreciation on forge and tools (fixed)	4,800
Utilities & other expenses (variable)	2,400
Total budgeted production costs	$54,800

REQUIRED:

Answer the following:
a. What is the budgeted cost of each mailbox post?
b. Use the budget information as a basis and prepare a new budget for a revised production output of 15,000 posts.
c. What is the budgeted cost of each mailbox post at the 15,000-unit production level?
d. Why is the new budgeted cost for each mail box post in part c less than under the budget in part a?

LO 2   **P20-2A   Performance Reports**   Crystal Line Co. manufactures a water filter insert that removes sediment and other small particles from residential water systems. The insert fits most brands of water filters currently available and can be washed and reused several times. It is marketed through several chain drug stores. The budget data and operating results shown below and on the next page are for the month of May 19X6.

REQUIRED:

a. Prepare a performance report. (Use Illustration 20-3 as a guide.)
b. Explain why the fixed costs did not generate a variance.
c. What might explain the unfavorable variances in the variable costs?
d. Does the high dollar amount of unfavorable variance indicate that management has a cost control problem?

Crystal Line Company Budgeted Production Costs For the Month Ended May 31, 19X6	
Budgeted production (units)	20,000
Production costs:	
Direct materials (variable)	$ 80,000
Direct labor (variable)	40,000
Indirect materials (variable)	20,000
Utilities (variable)	2,000
Factory rent (fixed)	4,000
Depreciation on equipment (fixed)	8,000
Total budgeted production costs	$154,000

Crystal Line Company Actual Production Costs For the Month Ended May 31, 19X6	
Actual production (units)	30,000
Production costs:	
Direct materials	$120,000
Direct labor	65,000
Indirect materials	29,000
Utilities	3,000
Factory rent	4,000
Depreciation on equipment	8,000
Total actual production costs	$229,000

LO 3,4   **P20-3A   Manufacturing and Nonmanufacturing Costs, Financial Statements**   The following selected data are from the records of Accountants Paper Products, Inc., for the month of February 19X3. They manufacture columnar pads and sell them directly to CPAs using direct mail advertising.

Advertising expense	$ 3,600
Factory payroll (70% direct labor)	20,000
Factory supplies used	3,000
Factory taxes	900
Factory utilities	400
Finished goods inventory (2/1/X3)	8,200
Finished goods inventory (2/28/X3)	5,200
Freight in	1,200
Freight out	2,400
Insurance expense (80% to factory)	500
Office salaries	2,400
President's salary	4,800
Raw materials inventory (2/1/X3)	3,700
Raw materials inventory (2/28/X3)	4,400
Raw material purchases (February)	13,200
Sales	92,600
Sales salaries	4,000
Factory supervisor's salary	2,400
Work in process inventory (2/1/X3)	3,800
Work in process inventory (2/28/X3)	2,800

REQUIRED:

a. Prepare a schedule of cost of goods manufactured for February 19X3, following Illustration 20-9 in the chapter.

b. Prepare an income statement for February 19X3.

LO 4   **P20-4A   Product Cost Flows**   Dyno Electric Company builds a small electric motor which is used as a component in the production of medical equipment by their customers. It is a very high-quality motor that is designed to operate for extended periods at variable speeds, with an unusually long time between failures. Special high-tech machines are used to wind the copper wire on the armatures and to wind the field coils. The armature shafts and the motor cases are purchased ready for use. The following information is available from the April 19X5 accounting records. Note that 80% of the motors produced during the period were sold.

Purchase of copper wire (25 spools)	$ 12,500
Ending inventory of copper wire	7,500
Beginning inventory of copper wire	0
Purchases of armature shafts	8,500
Ending inventory of armature shafts	700
Beginning inventory of armature shafts	1,200
Purchases of motor cases	3,000
Ending inventory of motor cases	800
Beginning inventory of motor cases	400
Direct labor costs	22,000
Overhead costs incurred and charged to production this period	33,000
Beginning inventory of work in process	2,000
Ending inventory of work in process	3,000
Beginning inventory of finished goods	16,000

REQUIRED:

a. Prepare T-accounts for Inventory of Copper Wire, Inventory of Armature Shafts, Inventory of Motor Cases, Inventory of Production Supplies, Manufacturing Overhead, Work in Process Inventory, Finished Goods Inventory, and Cost of Goods Sold.

b. Enter the given amounts as appropriate in the T-accounts to reflect the flow of product costs in the accounts of the firm.

c. Prepare a schedule of cost of goods manufactured.

LO 3,5   **P20-5A**   **Classification of Costs**   The costs shown in the following schedule are typical of a manufacturing environment.

Costs	a	b	c	d	e
1. Direct materials	____	____	____	____	____
2. Freight out	____	____	____	____	____
3. Freight in	____	____	____	____	____
4. Depreciation on equipment	____	____	____	____	____
5. Office salaries	____	____	____	____	____
6. Interest expense	____	____	____	____	____
7. Supervisors' salaries	____	____	____	____	____
8. Factory utilities	____	____	____	____	____
9. Office supplies	____	____	____	____	____
10. Factory supplies	____	____	____	____	____

REQUIRED:

Complete the schedule to classify the costs as:

a. Manufacturing or Nonmanufacturing (*Mfg* or *Non*)

b. Product or Period (*Pro* or *Per*)

c. Fixed or Variable as to production or sales (*Fix* or *Var*)

d. Direct or Indirect as to the product (*Dir* or *Ind*)

e. Controllable or Noncontrollable (*Con* or *NoC*) at the production department level.

LO 2,3,5   **P20-6A**   **Evaluation, Cost Identification, and Control**   The following data are from the general ledger and other records of the Highlander Pillow Corporation for the month ended June 19X4.

	Budget	Actual
Production quantities (pillows)	6,000	6,000
Polyfoam used (direct material)	$6,000	$6,200
Pillow ticking used (direct material)	$1,000	$900
Direct labor	$8,200	$8,300
Factory insurance	$750	$750

	Budget	**Actual**
Indirect labor	$4,100	$4,150
Indirect materials	$600	$700
Depreciation on factory machinery	$2,400	$2,400
Depreciation on factory buildings	$1,800	$1,800
Interest expense	$750	$775
Sales salaries	$1,600	$1,600

REQUIRED:

Identify the variances (differences between budget and actual) for each production cost and indicate at what managerial level (production supervisor, plant manager, or company president) you would expect control over the cost to exist. Explain your choice of the managerial level selected.

PROBLEM SET B

LO 1,2   **P20-1B   Managerial Accounting and Budgets**   Flexi-mold Company, of South Hampton, Virginia, produces a line of flexible molds for ceramic shops. These are sold domestically and abroad. The only direct material is a rubber-like plastic which results in a mold that can be reused many times. They are planning on producing 30,000 molds during 19X8. The direct material is expected to cost $1.50 per mold. The labor requirement, all direct, is 1/4 hour of labor per mold at $8.00 per hour. Utilities average $.40 per mold and supplies are expected to cost $.24 per mold. Depreciation is expected to be $8,000 per year for machinery and $12,000 per year for the factory building. The factory insurance premium is contracted at $2,400 for the year.

REQUIRED:

a. Develop the 19X8 production budget and expected unit cost for the Flexi-mold Company.
b. Calculate the per unit cost of molds.
c. Calculate the per unit cost of molds if the production volume were 25% higher.

LO 2   **P20-2B   Performance Reports**   Daly Book Binding Company does high-quality book binding for limited edition art books. The following budget and actual manufacturing data are for the month of August 19X9.

	Budget	**Actual**
Books bound	100	100
Bindery materials	$2,500	$2,600
Bindery labor	5,000	4,800
Utilities	150	75
Insurance	75	75
Depreciation expense	200	200
Rent	250	250

REQUIRED:

a. Prepare a performance report for Daly Book Binding Company, using Illustration 20-3 as a guide.
b. Discuss probable causes for each of the variances.
c. Why do some of the costs have no variances?
d. How should management react to the variances?

LO 3,4   **P20-3B**   **Cost Classifications**   Celtic Production Co. manufactures cabers (similar to small telephone poles) which are used for the caber toss at Scottish games around the world. They use spruce logs, purchased from suppliers in several western states, as their raw material. The cabers must be of uniform size and weight and require a considerable amount of hand labor in their production. The following information was taken from the records of Celtic Production Co. for the month of March 19X7.

Finished goods inventory, 3/1/X7	$12,000
Accounts payable	14,000
Factory supervision	4,000
Direct labor	30,000
Factory insurance	250
Factory depreciation	500
President's salary	5,000
Sales commissions	1,200
Sales revenue	93,000
Raw material inventory, 3/1/X7	400
Material purchases	16,750
Raw material inventory, 3/31/X7	800
Factory utilities	2,000
Factory supplies used	600
Work in process inventory, 3/1/X7	1,200
Work in process inventory, 3/31/X7	1,000
Sales salaries	3,600
Office salaries	2,400
Taxes on plant	300
Office insurance (one-third to sales)	300
Finished goods inventory, 3/31/X7	10,500

REQUIRED:

a. Prepare a schedule of cost of goods manufactured for the month ended March 31, 19X7.

b. Prepare an income statement for the month ended March 31, 19X7, classifying the selling expenses and administrative expenses in separate groups.

LO 4   **P20-4B**   **Product Cost Flows**   Vista Lighting Products Company produces a motion sensitive, automatic, external light fixture which is popular as both a residential and commercial lighting device. Ninety percent of the October production was sold during the month. The following information is available for operations during the month of October 19X6.

Fixture parts inventory, 10/1/X6	$11,500
Fixture parts inventory, 10/31/X6	9,500
Purchases of fixture parts	68,000
Work in process inventory, 10/1/X6	22,500
Work in process inventory, 10/31/X6	20,000
Finished goods inventory, 10/1/X6	16,000
Finished goods inventory, 10/31/X6	29,300
Direct labor costs	12,000
Indirect labor costs	6,000
Factory supplies used	14,500
Utilities expense—factory	1,100
Depreciation on machinery and factory buildings	22,000
Factory insurance	900
Factory supervision	4,000

REQUIRED:

a. Prepare T-accounts for Fixture Parts Inventory, Work in Process Inventory, Finished Goods Inventory, Manufacturing Overhead, and Cost of Goods Sold.
b. Enter the given amounts as appropriate in the T-accounts to reflect the flow of product costs for the month of October 19X6.
c. Prepare a schedule of cost of goods manufactured.

LO 3,5   **P20-5B**   **Classification of Costs**   The costs shown in the following schedule are typical of a manufacturing environment.

Costs	a	b	c	d	e
1. Administrative salaries	____	____	____	____	____
2. Direct material cost	____	____	____	____	____
3. Depreciation of plant assets	____	____	____	____	____
4. Depreciation of office equipment	____	____	____	____	____
5. Freight out	____	____	____	____	____
6. Plant utility costs	____	____	____	____	____
7. Cost of goods sold	____	____	____	____	____
8. Indirect labor cost	____	____	____	____	____
9. Factory insurance	____	____	____	____	____
10. Sales commissions	____	____	____	____	____

REQUIRED:

Complete the schedule to classify the costs as:
a. Manufacturing or Nonmanufacturing (*Mfg* or *Non*)
b. Product or Period (*Pro* or *Per*)
c. Fixed or Variable as to production or sales (*Fix* or *Var*)
d. Direct or Indirect as to the product (*Dir* or *Ind*)
e. Controllable or Noncontrollable (Con or NoC) at the production department level.

LO 2,3,5   **P20-6B**   **Performance Evaluation, Cost Identification, and Control**   You are in the process of preparing a performance report and a new budget for the Cabinet Corner, a manufacturer of bathroom base cabinets for mobile homes. The budgeted and actual production data for 19X7 are shown below:

	Budget	Actual
Production quantities (units)	4,000	4,000
Production costs:		
Cabinet plywood used	$ 32,000	$ 33,000
Direct labor	36,000	35,800
Indirect labor	18,000	21,000
Glue, nails and screws	4,200	4,450
Plant utilities	1,800	1,950
Insurance	2,400	2,500
Depreciation on plant assets	4,600	4,600
Supervision	20,000	20,000
Total production costs	$119,000	$123,300

REQUIRED:

Identify the variances (differences between budget and actual) for each production cost and indicate the managerial level (production supervisor, plant manager, or company president) at which you would expect to find control over the cost to exist. Explain your choices.

CRITICAL THINKING AND COMMUNICATING

C20-1

A spokesperson for a large U.S. auto maker made a statement in 1971 that the cost of the base model of one of their popular compact cars was $1,850. At the time the suggested retail price, before freight and dealer preparation, was $1,919. Around that same time, a union official involved in the negotiation of a labor contract with the auto maker made a public statement suggesting that the cost of producing that particular model was about $1,200.

REQUIRED:

a. Discuss how two responsible individuals could cite such different cost figures.
b. Do you feel, from the information presented, that one of the individuals was citing an incorrect cost? Discuss.

C20-2

A senior accounting professor at State University asked his students the following question on an exam: "Can depreciation expense be carried on the balance sheet as an asset?"

REQUIRED:

Provide a response to the question.

CHAPTER 21

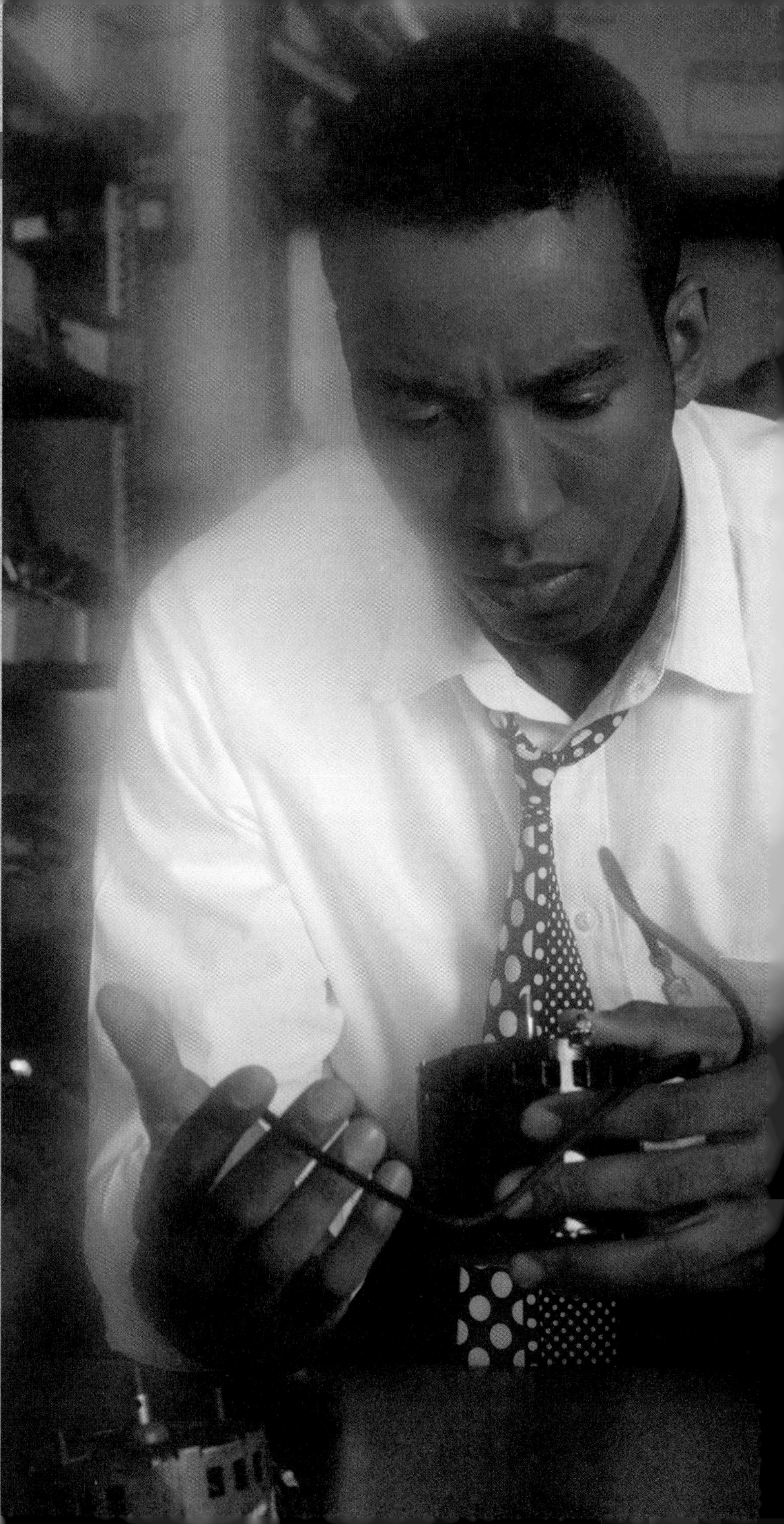

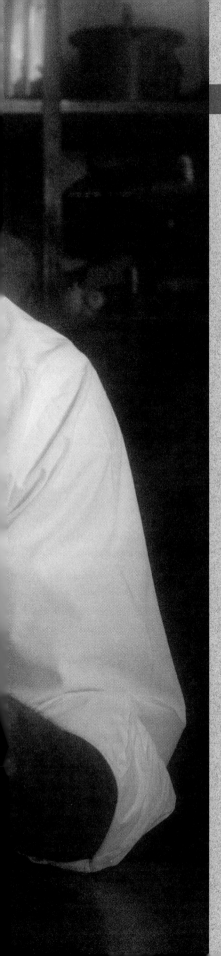

Job-Order Costing and Changes in the Manufacturing Environment

Ryan Spence, Ph.D., has recently designed a highly adjustable surgical table. To develop a prototype for marketing to hospitals, he needs several components, including five custom-built electric motors. Spence asks Eastern Electric to manufacture the motors and Eastern is interested because, based on projected demand, it knows Spence may ultimately order 10,000 motors per year. Eastern also knows Spence cannot afford to pay a high price for the motors at this stage and offers to sell them for just 10 percent over cost. But, how can Eastern determine the cost of the motors? For this determination, Eastern will use a **product costing system**, which is an integrated set of documents, ledgers, accounts, and accounting procedures used to measure and record the cost of manufactured products.[1]

In this chapter, we present a particular type of product costing system referred to as a job-order costing system. Most product costing systems develop product cost information that reflects the total cost of manufacturing a product. Because the product cost information is comprehensive (including both fixed and variable manufacturing costs), it is often referred to as **full cost** information.

In this chapter, we also address changes in the manufacturing environment and how these changes help companies survive in a competitive global economy. Management accountants need to keep abreast of these changes, which affect the type and amount of costs and, to some extent, the design of the product costing system.

[1]Product costing systems are also referred to as *cost accounting systems*.

1. Discuss the types of product costing systems.
2. Explain the relationship between the cost of jobs and Work in Process Inventory, Finished Goods Inventory, and Cost of Goods Sold.
3. Describe how direct material, direct labor, and manufacturing overhead are traced to jobs.
4. Explain how a predetermined overhead rate is used to apply overhead to jobs.
5. Discuss the accounting treatment of the difference between actual overhead and overhead allocated to jobs using a predetermined rate.
6. Discuss changes in the manufacturing environment of U.S. companies and how they affect product costing.

USE OF PRODUCT COST INFORMATION

Product cost information is used for a variety of purposes. Two of its most common uses are in financial reporting and in managerial decision making.

Financial Reporting and Product Costs

Manufacturing companies need product cost information to prepare financial statements in accordance with GAAP. To be consistent with GAAP, the inventory balance on the balance sheet must accurately reflect the cost of producing the goods that remain in inventory at the end of the accounting period. Also, the cost of goods sold amount presented on the income statement must accurately reflect the cost of the items sold during the accounting period. Because product cost information is necessary for external financial reporting, all manufacturing companies must have some type of product costing system. These systems generally produce full cost information, which GAAP requires.

Managerial Decision Making and Product Costs

Product cost information also is needed for a variety of managerial decisions. For example, Eastern Electric needs product cost information for its pricing decision. Sometimes the product cost information needed for management decision making is different from that produced for external financial reports. For external financial reports, product cost information mixes both fixed and variable manufacturing costs. Many internal management decisions, however, require information with separate fixed and variable cost components. The information needed for management decisions will be examined in detail later in the text. For now, you should simply understand that product cost information produced for external reporting purposes may not be appropriate for management decisions unless it is modified or adjusted.

LO 1
Discuss the types of product costing systems.

TYPES OF COSTING SYSTEMS

There are two major product costing systems: job-order and process. Which system to use depends on the type of manufacturing.

Job-Order Costing Systems

Companies that use a job-order costing system generally produce individual products or batches of unique products. This is the case when a company manufactures goods to a customer's specifications. A **job** is an individual product or batch for which a company needs cost information. When the items that make up the job are completed and sold, the company can match the cost of the job with the revenue it produced and obtain an appropriate measure of gross profit. Companies using job-order costing systems include construction companies, equipment and tool producers, ship building companies, and printing companies.

Process Costing Systems

In contrast, companies using a process costing system generally produce large quantities of identical items that pass through uniform and continuous production operations. Costs are accumulated by each operation, and the unit cost of items produced is determined by dividing the costs of the production operations by the number of identical items produced.

$$\text{Unit Cost of Items Produced} = \frac{\text{Total Cost of Production}}{\text{Total Number of Units Produced}}$$

In a process costing system, costs are not traced to specific items produced since each item is identical. It is sufficient to assign to each item its average unit cost of production. Companies using process costing systems include producers of metals, chemicals, paints, and plastics.

LO 2

Explain the relationship between the cost of jobs and Work in Process Inventory, Finished Goods Inventory, and Cost of Goods Sold.

OVERVIEW OF JOB COST AND FINANCIAL STATEMENT ACCOUNTS

As previously discussed, product costs include three items: direct material, direct labor, and manufacturing overhead. In a job-order costing system, the cost of a job is the sum of these three cost items. Thus, a job-order system must be able to trace these costs to specific jobs. (See Illustration 21-1.)

ILLUSTRATION 21-1 Relating Product Costs to Jobs

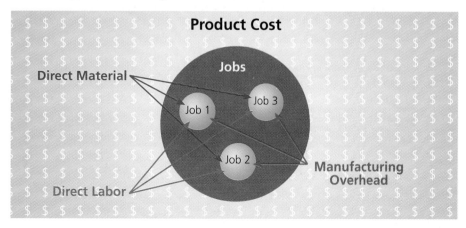

Also, recall that product costs are reflected in Work in Process Inventory and Finished Goods Inventory on the balance sheet and in Cost of Goods Sold on the income statement. In a job-order costing system, Work in Process Inventory will include the cost of all jobs that are currently being worked on (i.e., those that are in process). Finished Goods Inventory will include the cost of all jobs that are completed but not yet sold. Cost of Goods sold will include the cost of all jobs that are sold during the accounting period. (See Illustration 21-2.)

ILLUSTRATION 21-2 Job Costs and Financial Statement Accounts

Costs flow through a job-order costing system based on the status of jobs. First, direct material, direct labor, and manufacturing overhead costs related to jobs being worked on are added to Work in Process Inventory. When specific jobs are completed, the costs of those jobs (referred to as the costs of goods manufactured) are deducted from Work in Process Inventory and added to Finished Goods Inventory. When specific jobs are sold, the costs of those jobs are removed from Finished Goods Inventory and added to Cost of Goods Sold. These cost flows are indicated in Illustration 21-3.

As you read the following discussion, remember these components of a job-order costing system:

1. The items making up the costs of a job (direct material, direct labor, and manufacturing overhead).
2. The way the status of jobs triggers the flow of costs through the accounts (Work in Process Inventory, Finished Goods Inventory, and Cost of Goods Sold). These are the basic structural elements that we build on in our discussion of job-order costing system procedures.

ILLUSTRATION 21-3 Flow of Costs in a Job-Order Costing System

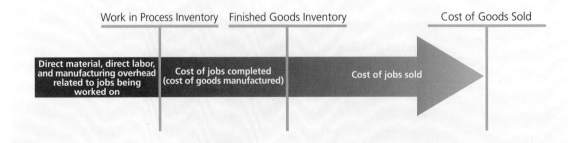

LO 3
Describe how direct material, direct labor, and manufacturing overhead are traced to jobs.

JOB-ORDER COSTING SYSTEM

A company begins its job-order costing operations when it decides to produce a specific product for a customer's order or for stock. For example, an electric motor manufacturer receives an order for five custom-designed motors, a print shop receives an order for 20,000 spring catalogs from a clothing manufacturer, or a residential construction company receives an order to build a summer home. If the company decides to accept the order, it prepares a **job cost sheet**, a form used to accumulate the cost of producing the item or items ordered (i.e., the cost of the job). An example of a job cost sheet is presented in Illustration 21-4. How specific numbers are entered on the job cost sheet will be explained later. For now, simply note that the job cost sheet contains detailed information on the three categories of product costs: direct material, direct labor, and manufacturing overhead.

ILLUSTRATION 21-4 Job Cost Sheet

 Eastern*Electric*

25 E. Hill Street, Columbus, Ohio 43268

Job number 2574 _____   Date needed 3/20 _____   Date started 3/12 _____   Date completed 3/16 _____
Customer   Spence Development Company, 628 Meridian, Columbus, OH 43205-1182
Description Five compact motors for use in medical equipment

| | Direct Material | | | Direct Labor | | | Manufacturing Overhead |
Date	Requisition Number	Cost	Labor Report Number	Hours	Cost	*$16.25 per direct labor hour*
3/12	7556	238.53	108	14	163.50	227.50
3/13	7642	5,480.30	109	22	250.25	357.50
3/14	7731	325.67	110	26	287.63	422.50
3/15	7805	1,683.50	111	43	485.60	698.75
3/16	7860	750.90	112	41	562.82	666.25
	Total	8,478.90		Total 146	1,749.80	Total 2,372.50

Cost summary:

Direct Material	$ 8,478.90
Direct Labor	1,749.80
Manufacturing Overhead	2,372.50
Total	$12,601.20

Direct Material Cost

A **material requisition form** (Illustration 21-5) is used to request the release of materials from a company's storage. The form lists the type, quantity, and cost of material, as well as the number of the job requiring the materials. Because the form includes the job number, it can be used to trace material cost to specific jobs. Requiring a supervisor's signature helps prevent the unauthorized issuance of material.

Each material requisition form is listed in summary form on the job cost sheet. For example, on material requisition form number 7556, presented in

Illustration 21-5, the total cost of items requested amounts to $238.53. When these items are released from storage, the total cost is posted to the job cost sheet (see Illustration 21-4) and cross-referenced by the material requisition number.

ILLUSTRATION 21-5 Material Requisition Form

Eastern*Electric*

Material Requisition Number __7556__   Job Number __2574__   Date __3/12__

Item	Quantity	Unit Cost	Total
A2763	2	10.25	$ 20.50
A5438	10	12.04	120.40
D3760	1	80.10	80.10
D3658	1	17.53	17.53
		Total	$238.53

Approved by: _____ *K. Dawson* _____

When a company purchases materials, it includes their costs in the raw materials inventory account. Removing materials from storage for a specific job decreases Raw Materials Inventory and increases Work in Process Inventory. Periodically (daily, weekly, or monthly), the company calculates and records in the general journal the total cost of materials issued to jobs. Suppose a company purchases $60,000 of materials and issues $50,000 of materials to specific jobs. The entries to record these transactions are:

(Date)	Raw Materials Inventory	60,000	
	Accounts Payable		60,000
	To record purchase of raw materials.		
(Date)	Work in Process Inventory	50,000	
	Raw Materials Inventory		50,000
	To record requisition of raw materials.		

Direct Labor Cost

In a job-order costing system, workers complete **time tickets** (also called *job tickets* or *work tickets*) to keep track of the amount of time spent on each job (Illustration 21-6). If many workers are assigned a particular job, individual time tickets may not be posted directly to job cost sheets since that would produce too much detail. Illustration 21-7 presents a daily labor cost summary by job. As you can see, Number 687 is just one of the tickets completed and submitted for Job 2574 on March 12. Time ticket 687 might represent 3 hours spent wiring motors, while time ticket 689 might represent 6 hours spent assembling components. On March 12, a total of 14 hours were spent on Job 2574 and cost $163.50. The total labor cost traced to Job 2574 ($163.50) is the amount posted to the job cost sheet. (See Illustration 21-4.)

Periodically, the amount of direct labor cost attributed to current jobs must be debited to Work in Process Inventory. Suppose a company incurs $30,000 of direct labor cost. The appropriate journal entry is:

(Date)	Work in Process Inventory	30,000	
	Wages and Salaries Payable		30,000
	To record direct labor cost.		

ILLUSTRATION 21-6 Labor Time Ticket

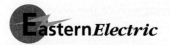

Eastern *Electric*

Date___3/12___

Time Ticket Number___687___   Employee Number___7843___   Grade___3___

Job	Time Start	Time Stop	Total Hours
2574	2:00 p.m.	5:00 p.m.	3.00

ILLUSTRATION 21-7 Daily Labor Cost Summary

Eastern *Electric*

Daily Labor Report Number: 108   Date: 3/12

Job	Time Ticket	Hours	Grade	Rate	Cost
2574	687	3.00	3	12.50	$ 37.50
2574	689	6.00	3	12.50	75.00
2574	690	2.50	2	11.80	29.50
2574	693	2.50	1	8.60	21.50
		14.00			$ 163.50
2580	688	5.00	3	12.50	$ 62.50
2580	692	6.00	3	12.50	75.00
2580	737	1.00	2	11.80	11.80
		12.00			$ 149.30

Various Additional Labor Charges by Job $2,254.50

Total Daily Labor Cost $2,567.30

Manufacturing Overhead

So far, we have traced raw materials and direct labor costs to jobs. The final and most complex cost component to trace is manufacturing overhead, which we will discuss in a general way before going into more detail later in the chapter.

Manufacturing overhead costs cannot be traced directly to goods produced. Thus an alternative method of assigning overhead costs to jobs is needed. The basic approach involves assigning overhead to jobs based on some common characteristic that jobs share, such as direct labor hours or cost. The common characteristic is referred to as an allocation base. Once an allocation base is selected, an **overhead allocation rate** can be developed by dividing estimated overhead costs by the estimated quantity of the allocation base. The terms *allocation base* and *overhead allocation rate* will be discussed further later in this chapter. Suppose Eastern Electric anticipates $325,000 of manufacturing overhead and 20,000 labor hours during the year. With these estimates, it calculates and assigns $16.25 of overhead for every direct labor hour worked ($325,000 ÷ 20,000). Of course, the more labor hours a job requires, the more overhead will be assigned to it. The amount of overhead assigned to jobs is referred to as **overhead applied**. Note that in Illustration 21-4, overhead is assigned to jobs on the basis of labor hours. With an overhead rate of $16.25 and 146 labor hours, $2,372.50 of manufacturing overhead is assigned to Job 2574.

Recording manufacturing overhead is a two-step process. First, when a company incurs actual overhead costs, it debits these costs to Manufacturing Overhead. Second, in applying overhead to jobs, the company credits Manufacturing Overhead and debits Work in Process Inventory.

Step 1.   Overhead costs include depreciation, utilities, and a variety of other costs. Therefore, the credit side of the entry to record manufacturing overhead can include a large number of accounts. Suppose a company incurs $10,000 of depreciation, $1,000 of utilities cost, and $55,000 of various other overhead costs that we will not specify for the sake of brevity. The journal entry to record these costs is:

(Date)	Manufacturing Overhead	66,000	
	Accumulated Depreciation		10,000
	Utilities Payable		1,000
	Various other accounts		55,000
	To record overhead costs incurred.		

Step 2.   The company periodically calculates the total amount of estimated overhead costs applied to jobs and makes an entry to credit Manufacturing Overhead and debit Work in Process Inventory. Suppose $60,000 of overhead is applied to jobs. The journal entry is:

(Date)	Work in Process Inventory	60,000	
	Manufacturing Overhead		60,000
	To record overhead costs applied to jobs.		

Tracing Costs to Jobs: A Summary   Material requisition forms are used to trace direct material costs to jobs while time tickets are used to trace direct labor costs to jobs. Since manufacturing overhead costs cannot be directly traced to jobs, they are indirectly traced by using an overhead rate multiplied by each job's measure of the allocation base. Illustration 21-8 summarizes the methods used to trace manufacturing costs to jobs.

ILLUSTRATION 21-8 How Manufacturing Costs Are Traced to Jobs

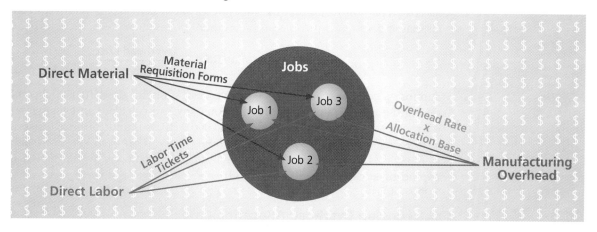

FLOW OF COSTS IN WORK IN PROCESS INVENTORY, FINISHED GOODS INVENTORY, AND COST OF GOODS SOLD

When a company begins work on a job, it records production costs in Work in Process Inventory using journal entries such as those illustrated earlier. When jobs are completed, the company reduces Work in Process Inventory by the cost of the completed jobs and increases Finished Goods Inventory by the same amount. When the company sells completed jobs it reduces Finished Goods Inventory by the cost of the completed jobs sold and increases Cost of Goods Sold. Suppose the cost of jobs completed is $80,000 and the cost of jobs sold is $70,000. The journal entries are:

(Date)	Finished Goods Inventory	80,000	
	Work in Process Inventory		80,000
	To record cost of jobs completed.		
(Date)	Cost of Goods Sold	70,000	
	Finished Goods Inventory		70,000
	To record cost of goods sold expense.		

ALLOCATING OVERHEAD TO JOBS

We have seen how direct material, direct labor, and manufacturing overhead are accumulated in a job-order costing system. However, the process of assigning manufacturing overhead to specific jobs and recording overhead in the accounts, referred to as **overhead allocation**, needs to be examined in more detail.

Overhead Allocation Rates

Because overhead costs are related only indirectly to jobs being produced, a company must develop some means of allocating or assigning overhead costs to current jobs. It does so by means of an overhead allocation rate. The rate is calculated as the ratio of overhead costs to activity. Common measures of activity include direct labor hours, direct labor cost, machine hours, and direct material cost. You will recall that the measure of these activities is referred to as the allocation base.

$$\text{Overhead Allocation Rate} \ = \ \frac{\text{Overhead Cost}}{\text{Activity}}$$

Suppose a company had $50,000 of overhead cost and used 10,000 labor hours during the year. In this example, the company can calculate an average *actual* overhead cost per labor hour of $5 ($50,000 ÷ 10,000) and can assign overhead to jobs based on the amount of labor hours worked on each job. For example, if a particular job required 100 labor hours, the company would assign it an overhead allocation of $500 (100 x $5).

Selecting an Overhead Allocation Base

The measure of activity (the denominator in the equation shown above) used to calculate an overhead rate is the **allocation base**. The allocation base is used to spread the overhead among various jobs, all of which have some quantity of activity associated with them. In choosing among alternative allocation bases (such as direct labor hours, direct labor cost, machine hours, and direct material cost), keep in mind that jobs with greater quantities of an allocation base will receive larger allocations of overhead. For example, suppose machine hours are used as an allocation base and an overhead rate is calculated as $10 per machine hour. If one job uses 40 machine hours and another job uses 20 machine hours, the first job will receive an allocation of $400 and the second job will receive an allocation of only $200. This would be appropriate if greater activity, as measured by machine time, requires the firm to incur more overhead cost.

The allocation base a company uses should be strongly associated with its overhead cost. That is, increases in overhead cost should coincide with increases in the allocation base. If increases in overhead are more closely associated with increases in machine hours rather than labor hours, the company should allocate overhead on the basis of machine hours. In selecting the allocation base, a company should consider whether the production process is labor intensive or machine intensive. If an operation is labor intensive (i.e., large quantities of labor are used to produce most jobs), then direct labor hours or direct labor cost might be a reasonable allocation base. If an operation is highly mechanized, then machine hours might be a reasonable allocation base.

Activity-Based Costing (ABC) and Multiple Overhead Rates

Many companies allocate overhead to jobs using a single overhead rate with an allocation base of direct labor. However, overhead costs are caused by a variety of factors; allocating costs just on the basis of labor, or any single allocation base, may seriously distort product costs. **Activity-based costing (ABC)** is a method of assigning overhead costs to products using a number of different allocation bases. In the ABC approach, the company first identifies the major activities that create overhead costs and then groups these costs into so-called **cost pools**. By dividing the amount of each cost pool by a measure of its corresponding activity (referred to as a **cost driver**), the company calculates multiple overhead rates. The company then assigns overhead to a product based on how much of each activity (cost driver) it caused.

Illustration 21-9 presents examples of typical cost pools and cost drivers. In the traditional approach to allocation, the allocation base or cost driver is a measure of production volume, such as direct labor or machine hours. In the ABC approach, the cost drivers include activities that are not necessarily related to production volume. Since many costs are not dependent on production volume, the ABC approach is more accurate. For example, consider the cost driver *number of setups*. *Setups* are activities involved in organizing and adjusting equipment in preparation for a production run. In the ABC approach, two products that require the same number of setups will receive the same allocation of setup cost. This is not the case when overhead is allocated only on the basis of a measure of production volume such as direct labor. If one of the products is a high-volume product, then it will have more labor and receive a greater allocation of setup cost than a low-volume product that requires little labor—even if both products require one setup.

ILLUSTRATION 21-9 Examples of Cost Pools and Cost Drivers

Cost Pools	Cost Drivers
Cost of setting up equipment	Number of setups
Material ordering costs	Number of purchase orders
Material receiving costs	Number of shipments received
Cost of electricity	Number of machine hours
Health insurance for workers	Number of workers

A simplified example with only two products and two cost pools illustrates how ABC results in more accurate cost information. Suppose the Wilson Manufacturing Company Produces two products, A and B, and has two major cost pools. The first cost pool is $600,000, and the related driver is labor cost. The second cost pool is $400,000, and the related driver is number of setups.

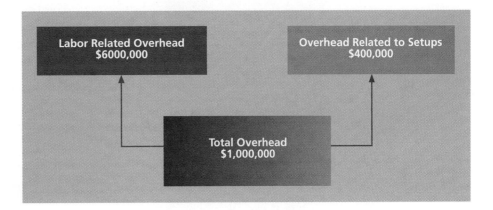

In the current year, Wilson Manufacturing expects $200,000 of labor and 40 setups. Product A, a high-volume product with annual production of 40,000 units, requires $150,000 of labor and 20 setups. Product B, a low-volume product with annual production of only 1,000 units, requires only $50,000 of labor but, as with Product A, also requires 20 setups.

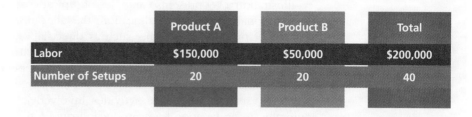

	Product A	Product B	Total
Labor	$150,000	$50,000	$200,000
Number of Setups	20	20	40

How much cost will Wilson Manufacturing assign to Products A and B if it uses an ABC system with labor and setups as the cost drivers? The analysis required to answer this question is presented in Illustration 21-10. The overhead rate for labor-related costs is $3 per dollar of labor ($600,000 overhead ÷ $200,000 labor). The overhead rate for setup-related costs is $10,000 per setup ($400,000 overhead ÷ 40 setups). With these overhead rates, Wilson assigns Product A $650,000 of total overhead ($450,000 of labor-related overhead and $200,000 of setup-related overhead) and product B $350,000 of total overhead ($150,000 of labor-related overhead and $200,000 of setup-related overhead).

ILLUSTRATION 21-10 Simplified Example Comparing ABC and Traditional Approaches to Allocation

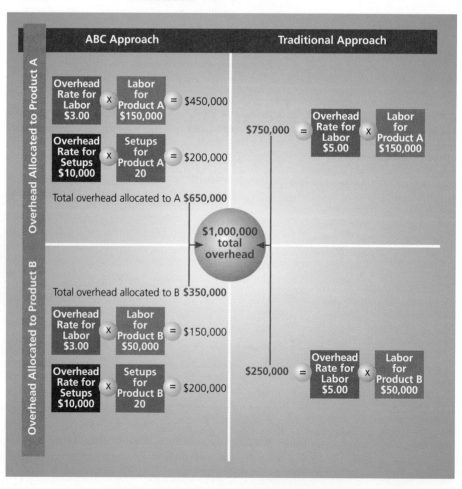

Since costs are allocated based on the factors that actually caused them, allocations under the ABC approach can be more accurate. Compare in Illustration 21-10 the allocations under ABC with those Products A and B would receive if overhead was allocated by taking a traditional approach with labor cost as the allocation base. Under the traditional approach, the overhead rate would be $5 per dollar of labor ($1,000,000 of total overhead ÷ $200,000 of total labor). Product A would thus receive an allocation of $750,000 and Product B an allocation of $250,000.

Note that when only a single allocation base (labor cost) is used, Product A receives a much larger allocation ($750,000 versus $650,000 using ABC). The reason: Product A, a high-volume product, uses a lot of labor, which is the only allocation base for overhead. However, this allocation is not accurate. Much of overhead is due to setting up the production lines. Product A requires no more setups than Product B and should, therefore, receive the same allocation of these costs. The ABC approach recognizes this important fact. With more accurate product cost information, managers can make better product pricing decisions. For example, managers might decide to decrease the price of Product A and increase the price of Product B.

In the real world, overhead costs are due to a variety of different factors; thus, they should be allocated using a number of different allocation bases or cost drivers. How many cost pools and cost drivers should a company use? The managerial accountant must make a cost/benefit tradeoff. The more cost pools and cost drivers used, the more accurate the product cost information. However, recordkeeping costs increase with the number of different allocation bases; beyond a certain point, the recordkeeping cost will exceed the benefit of more accurate information.

While multiple allocation rates generally should be used, you will see several examples in this chapter and elsewhere in the text where overhead costs are allocated using only a single allocation base such as labor hours, labor cost, or machine hours. This is done for simplicity, not because it is good practice in the real world.

Predetermined Overhead Rates

LO 4

Explain how a predetermined overhead rate is used to apply overhead to jobs.

Companies can develop overhead rates by dividing *actual* overhead by the *actual* level of the allocation base. Most companies do not follow this practice, however, because total actual overhead cost and the total actual level of the allocation base are not known until the end of the accounting period. It is impossible to determine the actual overhead rate until the end of the accounting period. However, until this rate is developed, no overhead can be applied to jobs. Companies want to know the cost of jobs before their accounting periods end. In many cases, the price companies charge for a job depends on its cost. Thus, companies need an immediate cost figure to determine the price to charge a customer and to determine the profitability of jobs.

Typically, overhead rates are based on *estimates* of overhead cost and *estimates* of the level of the allocation base rather than on *actual* costs and quantities. Overhead rates calculated by estimation are referred to as **predetermined overhead rates**. Once the estimated overhead cost and estimated allocation base are established, the company can calculate the predetermined overhead rate by dividing the estimated overhead by the estimated level of the allocation base.

$$\textbf{Predetermined Overhead Rate} = \frac{\textbf{Estimated Total Overhead Cost}}{\textbf{Estimated Level of Allocation Base}}$$

Consider our example of Eastern Electric. Management estimates that $325,000 of total manufacturing overhead will be incurred in the coming year and that 20,000 labor hours will be required. Thus, the predetermined overhead rate is $16.25 per labor hour ($325,000 ÷ 20,000), and a job requiring 100 direct labor hours to complete would be allocated $1,625 of overhead (i.e., $16.25 x 100 labor hours).

The estimated or budgeted overhead cost and the estimated level of the allocation base generally are estimated for a year so that the overhead allocation rate stays the same from month to month. If a shorter period such as one month were used, the overhead rate would fluctuate from month to month, causing identical jobs produced in different months to have different costs. This results because some overhead charges only occur in certain months. For example, in summer months a company may incur extra power costs because the plant is air-conditioned. Another reason for fluctuations in a shorter period of time is that overhead includes both variable and fixed cost items. When *expected* levels of the allocation base decrease, the *expected* amount of variable overhead also decreases. However, the expected amount of fixed overhead does not decrease. Thus, the overhead rate is likely to be higher in slower months.

LO 5

Discuss the accounting treatment of the difference between actual overhead and overhead allocated to jobs using a predetermined rate.

Eliminating Over- or Underapplied Overhead

As indicated earlier, recording manufacturing overhead is a two-step process. First, the company accumulates *actual* costs of various overhead items in the manufacturing overhead account. Second, the company applies overhead to individual jobs using the predetermined overhead rate. This increases Work in Process Inventory and decreases Manufacturing Overhead. Thus, a company makes two types of entries to the manufacturing overhead account: the debit entries record actual overhead costs incurred; the credit entries record the amount of overhead applied to jobs in process.

Manufacturing Overhead

Actual Overhead Costs Incurred	Overhead Costs Applied to Jobs

Unless the estimates for overhead and the level of the allocation base equal their actual amounts, the amount of overhead a company applies to jobs using a predetermined overhead rate will not equal actual overhead cost incurred. Because estimates are seldom perfectly accurate, there is likely to be a difference between the debits to Manufacturing Overhead (recording actual overhead costs) and the credits to Manufacturing Overhead (recording the amount of overhead applied to jobs using the predetermined overhead rate). The difference is referred to as **underapplied overhead** if actual overhead is greater than the amount of overhead applied, or as **overapplied overhead** if actual overhead is less than the amount applied. At the end of the accounting period, the amount of under- or overapplied overhead is equal to the balance in Manufacturing Overhead and the company must close the account eliminating the balance. If the company has done a reasonable job of estimating its predetermined overhead rate, the amount of over- or underapplied overhead will not be large. In this case, the company simply would close the account and adjust Cost of Goods Sold. For example, suppose a company had $50,000 of actual overhead and applied $48,000 to jobs using a predetermined overhead rate. In this case, overhead is underapplied by $2,000, the debit balance in the manufacturing overhead account. To close the account, the company makes the following journal entry:

(Date)	Cost of Goods Sold	2,000	
	Manufacturing Overhead		2,000
	To close out Manufacturing Overhead and eliminate underapplied overhead.		

Theoretically, the company should apportion the amount of under- or overapplied overhead among Work in Process Inventory, Finished Goods Inventory, and Cost of Goods Sold. This follows from the fact that use of a predetermined rate results in job costs that differ from their actual costs by the amount of over- or underapplied overhead. Because the costs of jobs are reflected in Work in Process Inventory, Finished Goods Inventory, and Cost of Goods Sold, the company should adjust all these accounts to reflect actual overhead costs. Apportioning costs among Work in Process Inventory, Finished Goods Inventory, and Cost of Goods Sold can be accomplished based on the relative cost recorded in these accounts. For example, suppose a company has Work in Process Inventory of $10,000, Finished Goods Inventory of $10,000, Cost of Goods Sold of $20,000, and underapplied overhead of $2,000. The apportionment rate would be $.05 for each dollar in the accounts (i.e., $2,000 ÷ $40,000). Thus, Work in Process Inventory would receive $500; Finished Goods Inventory, $500; and Cost of Goods Sold, $1,000. The company would make the following journal entry:

(Date)	Work in Process Inventory	500	
	Finished Goods Inventory	500	
	Cost of Goods Sold	1,000	
	Manufacturing Overhead		2,000
	To apportion underapplied overhead.		

Whether the amount of over- or underapplied overhead is applied to Cost of Goods Sold or apportioned among Work in Process Inventory, Finished Goods Inventory, and Cost of Goods Sold depends on the dollar value of over- or underapplied overhead. If the amount is immaterial, it is sufficient for practical purposes for the company to simply debit (for underapplied overhead) or credit (for overapplied overhead) the amount to Cost of Goods Sold. If the amount is material, the company should apportion it among Work in Process Inventory, Finished Goods Inventory, and Cost of Goods Sold.

LO 6

Discuss changes in the manufacturing environment of U.S. companies and how they affect product costing.

CHANGES IN THE MANUFACTURING ENVIRONMENT AND PRODUCT COSTING SYSTEMS

In the last two decades, U.S. companies have experienced stiff foreign competition. To compete effectively in a global economy, many U.S. manufacturers have made fundamental changes in their operations and business philosophies. These changes in the manufacturing environment affect the types of costs that are incurred and, to some extent, the way the costs are recorded in the product costing system. We will discuss four of the major changes: just-in-time manufacturing, computer-controlled manufacturing, flexible manufacturing systems, and total quality management.

Just-in-Time (JIT) Manufacturing

Many U.S. and Japanese companies use an innovative manufacturing system variously referred to as a **just-in-time (JIT) system**, a Kanban system, or a zero-inventory production system (ZIPS). One important goal of such manufacturing systems is to minimize inventories of raw materials and work in process. Companies with JIT systems make arrangements with suppliers to deliver materials just before they are needed in the production process. Also, when products need to be manufactured on multiple production lines (e.g., a product may need to be manufactured on a production line that involves welding before moving on to a production line that involves machining), production on one line is scheduled so that operations are completed just in time to meet the requirements of the next production line. With such a system, work in process inventory does not build up and clog the factory floor.

Survey data indicate that approximately 13 percent of U.S. companies have adopted JIT systems.[2] Dramatic improvements in manufacturing performance have been reported. Some companies report 90 percent reductions in production lead time, 90 percent reductions in work in process, and 80 percent reductions in space required for production.

The approach to product costing when JIT systems are adopted can be quite different from the job-order costing systems described in this chapter. For example, some companies have combined the raw materials inventory and work in process inventory accounts into a new account called Raw-and-in-Process (RIP). When a company uses the RIP account, Work in Process Inventory is not tracked since the balance (held down by the JIT approach to minimizing inventory) is not material. Detailed information on the way product costing systems are adapted to JIT, Kanban, or ZIPS can be found in most cost accounting texts.

Computer-Controlled Manufacturing

Another major change: more and more companies are using highly automated **computer-controlled manufacturing systems**. Using computers to control equipment, including robots, generally increases the flexibility and accuracy of the production process. While state-of-the-art equipment and computer-controlled systems may help U.S. firms meet the challenge of global competition, they also have a significant effect on the composition of product costs. Survey data indicate that, on average, product costs consist of 53 percent material, 15 percent direct labor, and 32 percent overhead.[3] However, some highly automated companies such as Hewlett Packard report that direct labor accounts for as little as 3 percent of total production costs.[4] Decreasing labor costs are causing many companies to reconsider their overhead allocation bases. Currently, the most commonly used allocation bases for assigning overhead to jobs are direct labor hours and direct labor cost. However, in highly mechanized companies where direct labor is a small part of total manufacturing costs, using labor as an allocation base generally is not appropriate. Investing in state-of-the-art equipment also changes the company's mix of fixed and variable

---

[2]See R. A. Howell, J. D. Brown, S. R. Soucy, and A. H. Seed, III, *Management Accounting in the New Manufacturing Environment*, (National Association of Accountants, 1987), p. 126.

[3]Howell, et al., op. cit., p. 39.

[4]See B. R. Neumann, and P. R. Jaouen, "Kanban, Zips and Cost Accounting: A Case Study," *Journal of Accountancy* (August, 1986), pp.133–138.

costs. When equipment is substituted for labor, fixed costs generally increase and variable costs decrease.

Flexible Manufacturing Systems

Many companies hope to gain a competitive advantage by developing **flexible manufacturing systems**. Such systems, which generally are highly automated and often involve computer-controlled equipment, are configured so that machines easily can be adjusted to produce a number of different products or variations of standard products. With a flexible manufacturing system, companies easily can respond to custom orders. Flexible manufacturing systems also improve delivery times on orders and allow companies to introduce new products quickly.

Flexible manufacturing can be costly. In many cases, it requires a substantial investment in equipment and software to coordinate computer-controlled production processes. Additionally, more white-collar workers such as engineers may be needed. In 1985, General Electric Company developed a "factory of the future" with a flexible manufacturing system for $52 million. To justify this investment, the plant has to keep its machines working at substantially higher activity levels. In spite of the high cost, expenditures on flexible manufacturing systems are growing rapidly.[5]

Flexible manufacturing systems also impact product costing since costs must be traced to each of the potentially large number of custom products. However, the additional effort in accounting for custom products will not be significant if computerized accounting systems are used.

Total Quality Management

To survive in an increasingly competitive environment, firms realize they must produce high-quality products. An increasing number of companies have instituted **total quality management (TQM)** programs to insure high-quality products and efficient production processes. Currently, no generally agreed-upon "right" way to institute a TQM program exists. However, most companies with TQM develop philosophies that stress listening to the needs of customers, making products right the first time and reducing defective products that must be reworked, and encouraging workers to improve their production processes continuously. Indeed, some TQM programs are referred to as Continuous Quality Improvement programs. At Marlow Industries, a manufacturer of thermoelectric cooling devices, workers sign a Quality Pledge that reads: "I pledge to make a constant, conscious effort to do my job right today, better tomorrow, recognizing that my individual contribution is critical to the success of Marlow Industries."[6]

The results of an effective TQM program can be impressive. At Sundstrand Data Control, a manufacturer of electronic instruments, statistics show that its TQM program has reduced rework on some instrument production lines by 66 percent and has reduced scrap costs by 60 percent. Its cycle time (the time it

---

[5]See Mark Trumball "Manufacturing in Small Batches," *Christian Science Monitor*, Vol. 83, No. 186, (August 20, 1991), Sec. 1, p. 8.

[6]"Charting a New Course: Marlow Industries Sets Its Sights on Quality and Shoots for the Coveted Baldrige on the Way," *Dallas Business Journal*, Vol. 15, Issue 4, September 27, 1991, Sec. 1, p. 15.

takes to produce a product from beginning to end) also has decreased by 90 percent.[7]

How does TQM affect product costing systems? Strong advocates would argue that unless there is TQM, there is no need for product costing since companies without TQM will not survive! Undoubtedly, there is some truth to this position. To survive, companies must have high-quality products. Additionally, TQM affects product costing by reducing the need for tracking the cost of scrap and rework related to each job. If TQM is able to reduce these costs to an insignificant level, the benefit of tracking the costs far outweighs the cost to the accounting system.[8]

We have touched on some of the significant changes in the environment of manufacturing firms. Our purpose has been to make sure you have a basic understanding of the setting in which management accountants calculate product costs. Management accountants must "speak the language" of top management and operating personnel if they want to have a significant impact on important decisions. Increasingly, the language includes references to TQM, flexible manufacturing, computer-controlled manufacturing, and JIT. These topics are discussed in much more detail in courses in operations management and production. If you plan on a career in management accounting, study of these topics should be a priority.

REVISITING THE EASTERN ELECTRIC EXAMPLE

At the start of the chapter, we presented a scenario where Eastern Electric agreed to sell Ryan Spence five motors for 10 percent over cost. Now you know

INSIGHTS INTO ETHICS

Andover Equipment Company manufactures compressors for both private companies and the Department of Defense. The compressors produced for the Department of Defense require more than average labor because of the hand finishing needed to insure that the units will function under extreme conditions. For example, the model 240 compressor normally requires 10 machine hours and 4 labor hours to produce. The model produced for the Department of Defense (model 240B) requires 10 machine hours and 6 labor hours.

Brad Stevens, the cost accountant for Andover, proposes that the company change its overhead allocation base from machine hours to labor hours. The result of this change will be that compressors produced for the Department of Defense will show a substantially higher cost than compressors produced for the general public. Brad thinks this is a good idea because the compressors sold to the Department of Defense are sold on a cost-plus basis. That is, the selling price is a fixed markup over cost.

Discuss the appropriateness of using the allocation system to justify charging higher prices to the Department of Defense.

---

[7]Steve Wilhelm, "Quality Program Keeps Spreading at Sundstrand," *Puget Sound Business Journal*, Vol. 11, Issue 52 (May 13, 1991), Sec. 1, p. 17.

[8]We should point out that many service firms such as banks, insurance companies, and hospitals have adopted the TQM programs initially developed by manufacturers. TQM is especially popular in the health-care field.

how Eastern could use a job-order costing system to determine its cost and the price to charge Spence. The job cost sheet for the example was presented in Illustration 21-4. Total cost was $12,601.20. The selling price, therefore, will be $13,861.32.

Total cost of five motors	$12,601.20
Plus markup of 10 percent	1,260.12
Selling price	$13,861.32

If Spence's product "takes off," Eastern Electric most likely will renegotiate the selling price of the motors—a 10 percent markup is generally considered to be low. Also, Eastern will be able to continue using its product costing system to analyze the profitability of future orders.

SUMMARY

Discuss the types of product costing systems.   There are two types of product costing systems: job-order systems and process costing systems. Companies using job-order systems generally produce individual products or batches of products that are unique. Companies using process costing systems generally produce large quantities of identical items in a continuous production operation.

Explain the relationship between the cost of jobs and Work in Process Inventory, Finished Goods Inventory, and Cost of Goods Sold.   Work in Process Inventory includes the cost of all jobs currently being worked on. Finished Goods Inventory includes the cost of all jobs that are completed but not yet sold. Cost of Goods Sold includes the cost of all jobs that are sold during the accounting period.

Describe how direct material, direct labor, and manufacturing overhead are traced to jobs.   Job cost sheets track the direct material, direct labor, and manufacturing overhead cost of each job. Direct material cost is traced to jobs by means of material requisition forms. Direct labor is traced to jobs by means of labor time tickets. Manufacturing overhead is applied to jobs using an overhead rate.

Explain how a predetermined overhead rate is used to apply overhead to jobs.   Most companies apply overhead to jobs using a predetermined, rather than an actual, overhead rate. Actual overhead cannot be determined until the end of the accounting period, and companies cannot wait until the end of the period before applying overhead to jobs.

Discuss the accounting treatment of the difference between actual overhead and overhead allocated to jobs using a predetermined rate.   If the amount of overhead applied to inventory does not equal actual overhead, the company must apportion the difference among Work in Process Inventory, Finished Goods Inventory, and Cost of Goods Sold. This adjusts the accounts to reflect actual overhead costs. If the amount of under- or overapplied overhead is immaterial, the company can close it to Cost of Goods Sold.

Discuss changes in the manufacturing environment of U.S. companies and how they affect product costing.   U.S. companies are facing stiff competition from foreign manufacturers. In response, many companies have adopted manufacturing systems that minimize inventories of raw materials and work in process. Also, many companies are developing total quality management programs and are becoming highly automated. Generally, highly automated companies should not use labor hours or labor cost as an overhead allocation base because labor is a relatively small part of their product cost.

REVIEW PROBLEM

Andre's Cabinetry Shop, Incorporated, manufactures and installs a wide variety of household cabinets built to customers' design from top quality lumber. The prices of the cabinets vary with the cost of woods selected by the customers and the complexity of the design.

Andre started with an investment of $30,000 in equipment and a building rented four years ago for $3,600 per year. The equipment has an estimated useful life of 24 years with no expected salvage value. 19X2 costs included: utilities, $1,200; maintenance, $600; shop supplies, $1,800; paint and varnish, $800; and insurance and taxes, $2,750. All of these costs are considered to be production costs and are assigned to jobs as overhead.

Job 524 was the only job in process at the end of 19X2. It had been charged with direct materials of $800, direct labor of $1,200, and overhead of $500, using an overhead allocation rate of 25 percent of direct costs (direct material plus direct labor). Costs are not expected to change in 19X3.

Andre works an average of 2,400 hours per year, and is paid at $20 per hour. The major difference in the jobs is the time required to build the designs.

Additional information is as follows:
1. Andre feels that his overhead allocation rate needs to be adjusted as he is not getting a reasonable share of the more expensive jobs he bids on.
2. During January 19X3, Andre completed Job 524, adding direct material costing $600 and 20 labor hours. Two other jobs, numbers 525 and 526, were started and completed. All completed jobs were installed and billed at cost plus 10%. Jobs 527 and 528 were started but not completed. Information related to jobs for January is as follows:

	525	526	527	528
Direct material	$1,100	$750	$900	$600
Direct labor cost	1,000	700	500	600
Direct labor hours	50	35	25	30

REQUIRED:

a. Select an appropriate overhead allocation base and calculate an overhead application rate for use in 19X3.
b. What is the total cost that will appear on the job cost sheets for Jobs 524 through 528 at the end of January 19X3?
c. Prepare summary journal entries to record the issuance of the materials to the jobs, to charge the jobs with the direct labor involved, and to apply the manufacturing overhead using the overhead rate determined above.
d. Prepare T-accounts for Work in Process Inventory, Finished Goods Inventory, and Cost of Goods Sold, including the beginning and ending balances of the accounts.
e. Reconcile Work in Process Inventory and Cost of Goods Sold balances with the totals on the appropriate job cost sheets.

SOLUTION:

Planning and Organizing Your Work

1. Costs making up manufacturing overhead are primarily related to labor hours and space utilization. Material cost does not seem to be a causal factor. Labor hours may be a better base.
2. Apply overhead to the jobs completed, including Job 524, and to jobs in process.

(a) *Select an appropriate overhead allocation base.*

Andre's expected overhead in 19X3 is:

Depreciation of equipment ($30,000 ÷ 24)	$ 1,250
Rent	3,600
Utilities	1,200
Maintenance	600
Shop supplies	1,800
Paint and varnish	800
Insurance and property taxes	2,750
Total expected overhead	$12,000

$$\frac{\text{Expected Overhead Cost}}{\text{Expected Direct Labor Hours}} \quad \frac{\$12,000}{2,400} = \$5.00 \text{ per Direct Labor Hour}$$

Direct labor hours were selected as the appropriate basis for the application of manufacturing overhead to the jobs because the major difference in the jobs was related to the number of labor hours worked. There should be a strong relationship between the total overhead cost incurred and the number of direct labor hours worked.

(b) *Prepare job cost sheets.*

Job 524	
Beg. Bal.	2,500
DM	600
DL	400
OH	100
End. Bal.	3,600

Job 525	
DM	1,100
DL	1,000
OH	250
Bal.	2,350

Job 526	
DM	750
DL	700
OH	175
Bal.	1,625

Job 527	
DM	900
DL	500
OH	125
Bal.	1,525

Job 528	
DM	600
DL	600
OH	150
Bal.	1,350

(c) *Prepare summary journal entries.*

Work in Process Inventory	3,950	
Raw Materials Inventory		3,950
To record material requisitions as follows:		

Job 524	$ 600
Job 525	1,100
Job 526	750
Job 527	900
Job 528	600
	$3,950

Work in Process Inventory		3,200	
Wages and Salaries Payable			3,200

To record labor time tickets as follows:

Job 524 20 hours @ $20	$ 400
Job 525 50 hours @ $20	1,000
Job 526 35 hours @ $20	700
Job 527 25 hours @ $20	500
Job 528 30 hours @ $20	600
	$3,200

Work in Process Inventory		800	
Manufacturing Overhead			800

To apply overhead to jobs as follows:

Job 524 20 hours @ $5.00	$ 100
Job 525 50 hours @ 5.00	250
Job 526 35 hours @ 5.00	175
Job 527 25 hours @ 5.00	125
Job 528 30 hours @ 5.00	150
	$ 800

(d) *Prepare T-accounts.*

Work in Process Inventory

Bal.	2,500	Job 524	3,600
Jan. Dir. Mat.	3,950	Job 525	2,350
Dir. Lab.	3,200	Job 526	1,625
Appl. OH	800		
Bal.	2,875		

Finished Goods

Bal.	0	Job 524	3,600
Job 524	3,600	Job 525	2,350
Job 525	2,350	Job 526	1,625
Job 526	1,625		
Bal.	0		

Cost of Goods Sold

Job 524	3,600	
Job 525	2,350	
Job 526	1,625	
Bal.	7,575	

(e) *Reconciliation of account balances and job cost sheets.*

Andre's Cabinetry Shop, Incorporated **Reconciliation of Job Cost Sheets to Work in Process Inventory** **January 31, 19X3**	
Job 527	$1,525
Job 528	1,350
Total Work in Process Inventory	$2,875

Andre's Cabinetry Shop, Incorporated **Reconciliation of Job Cost Sheets to Cost of Goods Sold** **January 31, 19X3**	
Job 524	$3,600
Job 525	2,350
Job 526	1,625
Total cost of goods sold	$7,575

KEY TERMS

activity-based costing (ABC), *874*

allocation base, *874*

computer-controlled manufacturing systems, *880*

cost driver, *874*

cost pools, *874*

flexible manufacturing systems, *881*

full cost, *865*

job, *867*

job cost sheet, *869*

just-in-time (JIT) system, *880*

material requisition form, *869*

predetermined overhead rates, *877*

product costing system, *865*

overapplied overhead, *878*

overhead allocation, *873*

overhead allocation rate, *872*

overhead applied, *872*

time tickets, *870*

total quality management (TQM), *881*

underapplied overhead, *878*

SELF-QUIZ

LO 1 1. Two common types of product costing systems are _____ _____ _____ and _____ _____.

LO 1 2. Product cost information is used for _____ _____ and _____ _____ _____.

LO 1 3. GAAP reporting of inventories in financial statements requires the use of _____ _____

LO 1 4. The components of a product costing system include which of the following?
a. Documents and ledgers
b. Sales invoices
c. Accounts and accounting procedures
d. a and b only
e. a and c only

LO 1 5. The best example of an entity using a job-order costing system would be:
a. Textile production
b. Concrete block production
c. Petroleum refining
d. Antique automobile restoration
e. None of the above

LO 1 6. Full costing includes which of the following in the determination of product cost?
a. Only variable costs of production
b. Only fixed costs of production
c. Direct fixed and variable costs of production
d. All fixed and variable costs of production
e. None of the above

LO 1 7. Product costs are necessary to report:
a. Production efficiency in the annual report
b. Product cost in inventory on the balance sheet
c. Product cost in cost of goods sold on the income statement
d. a and b only
e. b and c only

LO 1 8. The two most common uses of product cost information are for:
a. Financial reporting and managerial decision making
b. Controlling product quantity and quality
c. Setting management goals and objectives
d. Evaluation of management control skills
e. None of the above

LO 2 9. The costs of all jobs still in process will be found in the _____ _____ _____ account.

LO 2 10. The costs of all jobs completed and not yet sold will be found in the _____ _____ _____ account.

LO 2 11. The costs of all jobs completed and sold this period will be found in the _____ _____ _____ _____ account.

LO 3 12. A _____ _____ _____ _____ is used to accumulate the labor hours worked on each job from the time tickets.

LO 4 13. The overhead application rate is determined from:

a. Estimated overhead costs ÷ estimated activity base
b. Actual overhead costs ÷ estimated activity base
c. Estimated overhead costs ÷ actual activity base
d. Actual overhead costs ÷ actual activity base

LO 4 14. Three common activity bases are _____ _____ _____, _____ _____ _____, and _____ _____.

LO 4 15. A _____ _____ is a major activity used in activity-based costing (ABC) as the basis for assigning costs to a cost pool.

LO 4 16. _____ _____ _____ tends to provide more accurate allocation of costs and better information for decision making.

LO 5 17. Under- or overapplied overhead is theoretically allocated to _____ _____ _____ _____, _____ _____ _____, and _____ _____ _____ _____ unless the amounts are not material in amount.

LO 5 18. When under- or overapplied overhead is not material in amount, it is assigned to _____ _____ _____ _____.

LO 6 19. Total quality management (TQM) involves all of the following except:
a. Listening to customers and their needs
b. Very close supervision of all employees
c. "Get it right the first time" philosophy
d. Encouraging workers' continuous improvement.

SOLUTIONS TO SELF-QUIZ

1. job order costing, process costing   2. financial reporting, managerial decision making   3. full costing   4. e   5. d
6. d   7. e   8. a   9. work in process inventory   10. finished goods inventory   11. cost of goods sold
12. daily labor cost summary   13. a   14. direct labor hours, direct labor cost, machine hours   15. cost driver
16. Activity-based costing   17. Work in Process Inventory, Finished Goods Inventory, and Cost of Goods Sold   18. Cost of
Goods Sold   19. b

QUESTIONS

Q21-1   Is a product costing system necessary for a manufacturing company? Discuss.

Q21-2   What product costs are properly included in inventory according to Generally Accepted Accounting Principles (GAAP)?

Q21-3   Explain how product cost information is used in external financial reports.

Q21-4   Discuss how product cost information is used by management for internal purposes.

Q21-5   Identify the two most common types of product costing systems and discuss the manufacturing environment conducive to each system.

Q21-6   Identify the form used to withdraw materials from the storeroom for the production of a job and the information normally shown on that form.

Q21-7   What is the purpose of a job cost sheet and what information does it include?

Q21-8   What information is normally shown on a time ticket?

Q21-9   How can a large number of labor time tickets be handled efficiently?

Q21-10 Discuss the relationship between the job cost sheets and the work in process inventory account found in the general ledger.

Q21-11 Explain the rationale for applying overhead using a predetermined application rate instead of applying actual overhead to jobs.

Q21-12 Compare the traceability of costs in a job-order costing system and a process costing system.

Q21-13 Describe the content of the work in process inventory account, the finished goods inventory account, and the cost of goods sold account in a job-order costing system.

Q21-14 Describe the development of an overhead allocation rate.

Q21-15 Identify an important characteristic of a good overhead allocation base. Explain.

Q21-16 Trace the flow of costs through a job-order costing system from inception to the financial statements.

Q21-17   The manufacturing overhead account is debited for actual costs and is credited for the estimated overhead amounts applied to production. It is unlikely that the two amounts will be exactly equal, leaving a balance in the account at the end of the period. What is the difference between these two amounts called and how is it disposed of?

Q21-18   In modern, capital-intensive, production facilities, new approaches to manufacturing systems have reduced the proportion of direct labor cost to total production cost significantly. Discuss the effect this might have on the selection of an allocation base for the application of overhead.

EXERCISES

LO 1

E21-1   Product Costing Systems   For the list of product manufacturers below, indicate whether a job-order cost system (*JO*) or a process cost system (*P*) would be most appropriate.
___ a. Drink bottler
___ b. Pharmaceutical firm
___ c. Appliance manufacturer
___ d. Home builder
___ e. Printing shop
___ f. Ship builder

LO 2

E21-2   Cost System Accounts in Job-Order Costing   Place a YES beside the general ledger accounts utilized as inventory-related accounts in a job-order cost system and a NO by those which are not.
___ a. Raw Materials Inventory
___ b. Wages and Salaries Payable
___ c. General and Administrative Expenses
___ d. Work in Process Inventory
___ e. Finished Goods Inventory
___ f. Merchandise Inventory
___ g. Cost of Goods Sold
___ h. Manufacturing Overhead

LO 3

E21-3   Direct Materials in Job-Order Costing   Five material requisitions were received by the materials storeroom of the Saint Louis Foundry during the first week of 19X4. M.R. 101-C was for direct materials for Job 1501, $750.00. M.R. 102-C was for direct materials issued to Job 1502, $550.00. M.R. 103-C was for indirect materials issued to the factory supervisor $110.00. M.R. 104-C was for direct materials issued to Job 1501, $450.00. M.R. 105-C was for direct materials issued to Job 1503, $600.00.

REQUIRED:

Prepare a summary journal entry to record the issuance of these materials. Calculate the amount of direct materials assigned to each job.

LO 3

E21-4   Direct Labor in Job-Order Costing   Wolk Products Company had the following labor time tickets for the month of February 19X3.

Ticket Number	Employee Number	Pay Rate	Hours Worked	Job Number
2101	011	$ 8.00	120	201
2102	008	15.00	80	201
2103	011	8.00	40	202
2104	008	15.00	30	203
2105	008	15.00	50	204

REQUIRED:

a. Summarize the labor time tickets and prepare a journal entry to record the direct labor for the month.
b. Calculate the amount of direct labor assigned to each job.

LO 3,4   **E21-5   Overhead Allocation Bases**   The Muffler Repair Shop expects to incur total overhead of $24,000 during 19X6. They have 5 employees who each work 2,000 hours per year. Two of the employees earn $8 per hour and three earn $7 per hour. The only machines in the shop are three automobile lifts which together are used a total of 1600 hours per year and a gas welder which is used an average of 200 hours per year. Each job is billed for the materials, direct labor, and overhead, plus 20 percent of the total cost.

REQUIRED:

Calculate overhead allocation rates based on direct labor hours, direct labor cost, and automobile lift hours.

LO 2,3,4   **E21-6   Job-Order Costing Terminology**   Match the following cost accounting terms with the definitions shown below.
___ a. Full costing
___ b. Allocation base
___ c. Job cost sheet
___ d. Labor time ticket
___ e. Overhead allocation
___ f. Underapplied overhead
___ g. Overapplied overhead

(1) The systematic assignment of overhead costs to production, through the work in process inventory account, at a predetermined rate.
(2) A written record of time spent on a particular job by an individual worker.
(3) A measure of activity, highly correlated with overhead cost, which is used as the denominator in establishing an overhead allocation rate.
(4) A form used to accumulate the direct and indirect costs of production. It serves as a subsidiary ledger for Work in Process Inventory.
(5) A cost method which includes in product cost both the variable and fixed costs associated with the production process.
(6) A debit balance in Manufacturing Overhead remaining after all overhead applications to Work in Process Inventory have been made.
(7) A credit balance in Manufacturing Overhead remaining after all overhead applications to Work in Process Inventory have been made.

LO 4   **E21-7   Manufacturing Overhead in Job-Order Costing**   Franklin Machine Shop does a variety of automotive machine work for local repair businesses. The machinery used is a major cost factor in overhead and Franklin applies overhead on a machine hour basis. The average job requires less than one day and several jobs are completed each day.

REQUIRED:

Discuss why a predetermined overhead rate might be preferred by Franklin Machine Shop as opposed to applying actual overhead costs. Consider whether the use of two overhead rates, one based on labor hours and one based on machine hours, might provide more accurate costing.

LO 4,5   **E21-8   Allocating Manufacturing Overhead to Jobs**   Crankey Fabricators provided the following data for 19X1:

Expected annual direct labor hours	20,000
Expected annual direct labor cost	$250,000
Expected machine hours	15,000
Expected material cost for the year	$400,000
Expected overhead	$300,000

REQUIRED:

a. Prepare a computation of 19X1 overhead allocation rates using each of the four possible bases shown.

b. Determine the cost the following job (number 253) under each of the four overhead allocation rates.

Direct materials	$2,500
Direct labor (140 hours @ $11.00)	1,540
Machine hours used	100

LO 2,3,4   **E21-9**   **Job Cost Sheets**   Renko Company is a steel fabricator. Prepare a job cost sheet for Job 300, consisting of the production of 900 welded steel basement supports for Mickey Deeb Construction Company. The overhead is applied on the basis of direct labor hours, using a predetermined overhead rate of $15. The direct costs associated with Job 300 are: direct materials, $3,000; direct labor, 150 hours at $9.50 per hour. Use Illustration 21-4 in the text as an example. The job was started May 4, due May 21, and completed May 14.

LO 4   **E21-10**   **Predetermined Overhead Rates**   Arra Saunooke has operated a welding shop for a number of years, and the business always has generated ample cash to live on. Most jobs have been small and the charges made have been cash amounts set arbitrarily considering the needs of the customers and their ability to pay. This year, when calculating the year's profits, Arra has determined that net income amounted to only about $4.00 per hour for the hours worked. You have suggested that a job-cost system would allow Arra to better understand his costs and price his work accordingly. Additional information is as follows:

Hours worked totaled 2,100. The utility bills for the shop amounted to $2,800. Welding rods and other supplies cost $4,650. The equipment in the shop cost $25,000 three years ago and has an estimated life of 10 years and no salvage value. The building was built 6 years ago at a cost of $44,000 and has an estimated life of 20 years with no residual value. Both the building and equipment are depreciated on a straight-line basis. Direct materials used last year totaled $26,500.

REQUIRED:

Determine an appropriate overhead rate to be used.

LO 5   **E21-11**   **Under- and Overapplied Manufacturing Overhead**   Quest Manufacturing uses a job-order costing system. The account balances at the end of the period for the product-cost-related accounts are:

Raw Materials Inventory	$20,000
Work in Process Inventory	40,000
Finished Goods Inventory	60,000
Cost of Goods Sold	80,000
Manufacturing Overhead	9,000 (credit)

REQUIRED:

Prepare the journal entries to close the manufacturing overhead account assuming the overapplied amount is material.

LO 2,3   **E21-12**   **Tracing Production Inputs to Jobs**   Smith's Body Shop does collision damage repair and painting of automobiles and small trucks. Smith's billings reflect a markup of 15% over job cost.

During August 19X7, Smith bid $2,300 for the repair of a severely damaged automobile. He purchased replacement parts from a junkyard for $325 and a front windshield from Hour Glass Co. for $225. He bought the paint and hardener at Taylor's for $135. The job required six hours labor to strip the auto interior, seven hours of cutting and welding, two hours to replace the rear wiring (using the old harness), six hours of sanding and priming, five hours to re-install the interior, one hour to replace the windshield and eight hours to paint, trim and finish the job. Labor is paid at $24 per hour. Overhead is applied at $15 per labor hour. Apex Insurance company was billed directly for the job.

REQUIRED:

Prepare a job cost sheet for the repair job. Use the above information to prepare the journal entries to record the repair job in the accounting records of Smith's Body Shop. Prepare all entries through the recognition of revenue from the job.

◼ PROBLEM SET A

LO 2, 3   **P21-1A**   **Tracing Production Costs to Jobs**   Waterford Metal Shop makes a variety of parts for other manufacturers on an order basis. The following job cost sheets reflect the activity for the week ending October 15, 19X3. There was no beginning work in process inventory at the start of the week.

For: Regis Products			**Job** 302
Quantity: 300	**Item:** 713-R		
Number	**Direct Material**	**Direct Labor**	**Applied Overhead**
MR22	$1,200		
L116		$900	
L118		750	
Completed 10/13/X3			$825

For: White Sheetmetal			**Job** 303
Quantity: 1000	**Item:** 880-C		
Number	**Direct Material**	**Direct Labor**	**Applied Overhead**
MR23	$2,800		
L119		$1,800	
Completed 10/15/X3			$900

For: Quinto Primo Co.			**Job** 304
Quantity: 2,500	**Item:** 4992-D		
Number	**Direct Material**	**Direct Labor**	**Applied Overhead**
MR25	$1,450		
L117		$2,200	
MR27	1,220	850	
L120			
Completed 10/15/X3			$1,525

For: Mixweld, Inc.			**Job** 305
Quantity: 4200	**Item:** 1020		
Number	**Direct Material**	**Direct Labor**	**Applied Overhead**
MR26	$960		
L121		$410	$205

For: Brink Brakes			**Job** 306
Quantity: 200	**Item:** 2650		
Number	**Direct Material**	**Direct Labor**	**Applied Overhead**
MR28	$750		
L122		$500	$250

REQUIRED:

a. Reconstruct the journal entries in summary form to record the issuance of direct materials, to record direct labor, and to apply overhead for the week.
b. Prepare the journal entry to record the completion of Jobs 302 – 304.
c. Compute the balance in Work in Process Inventory and reconcile this balance with the job cost sheets.

LO 3,4

P21-2A   Calculating Predetermined Overhead Rates   Wilkes Manufacturing Company, a maker of furniture frames for furniture manufacturers, is reviewing the application of overhead in its job-order costing system. The expected activity levels for 19X3 are:

Direct material costs	$ 542,000
Direct labor hours	104,000
Direct labor cost	$1,248,000
Machine hours	2,080,000

Overhead expected for 19X3 includes:

Indirect material	$ 68,000
Indirect labor	624,000
Utility expense	48,000
Depreciation of equipment	140,000
Depreciation of factory building	24,000
Payroll taxes	140,000
Property and liability insurance	48,000
Total expected manufacturing overhead	$1,092,000

Most of the indirect labor is related to operating and maintaining machinery.

REQUIRED:

a. Determine the overhead application rate under each of the allocation bases for which you have information.
b. Select the overhead allocation base that you would recommend and justify your selection in one paragraph.

LO 3,4

P21-3A   Job Costs Under Different Overhead Rates   Highland Innovative Parts Co. manufactures parts to order for antique automobiles. Highland has a complete foundry and metal shop and makes everything from fenders to engine blocks. Each customer order is treated as a separate job. They currently have two jobs, 1523 and 1524, which are complete except for the application of overhead. They want to know what each job's cost would be under three different overhead application rates: (1) direct labor cost, (2) direct labor hours, and (3) machine hours. Projections for 19X3 are as follows:

Direct labor cost	$120,000
Direct labor hours	8,000
Machine hours	5,000
Overhead costs	$ 86,000

Depreciation on machinery and equipment accounts for 75 percent of the overhead costs.

The job cost sheets show the following:

	Job 1523	Job 1524
Direct material	$ 855	$1,650
Direct labor	$1,020	$1,020
Direct labor hours	85	68
Machine hours	100	200

REQUIRED:

a. Determine the overhead application rate under three suggested allocation bases.
b. Calculate the cost of Job 1523 and Job 1524 using each of the three bases.
c. Discuss which allocation base appears preferable.

LO 5

P21-4A   **Under- or Overapplied Overhead**   Atrium Door and Window Company produces metal doors and windows to order for architects. At the end of their accounting period, March 31, 19X3, their account balances reflected the following:

Raw Materials Inventory, 3/31/X3	$ 84,000
Work in Process Inventory, 3/31/X3	42,000
Finished Goods Inventory, 3/31/X3	84,000
Cost of Goods Sold (March)	290,000
Manufacturing Overhead	24,000 (credit)

REQUIRED:

a. Determine the adjusted balances of the above accounts if the balance of Manufacturing Overhead is considered material in amount.
b. Determine the adjusted balances of the above accounts if the balance of Manufacturing Overhead is considered immaterial in amount.

LO 2,3,4,5

P21-5A   **Inventory Accounts and Cost of Goods Sold under Job-Order Costing**   The following T-accounts represent transactions of the Seagrave Equipment Company, builders of large industrial machinery. During the month of October 19X8, Job 101 was completed and transferred to finished goods, Jobs 102 and 103 were started, completed, and transferred to finished goods, and Job 104 was started but incomplete by the end of the month.

Raw Materials Inventory				Work in Process Inventory		
Bal.	21,000	79,000		Bal.	32,000	232,000
	88,000	11,000			79,000	
					96,000	
					48,000	

Accounts Payable				Finished Goods Inventory		
		88,000		Bal.	38,500	105,500
					232,000	

Manufacturing Overhead				Cost of Goods Sold		
	11,000	48,000			105,500	
	28,000					
	4,000					
	2,500					

Indirect material	$ 50,000
Indirect labor	300,000
Depreciation of equipment	40,000
Other costs	10,000
Total manufacturing overhead	$400,000

Most of the indirect labor is related to ordering and moving material.

REQUIRED:

a. Determine the overhead application rate under each of the allocation bases for which you have information.
b. Select the overhead application base that you would recommend and justify your selection in one paragraph.

LO 3,4   **P21-3B**   **Different Overhead Application Rates for Job-Order Costing**

1. Millikan Company has expected manufacturing overhead consisting of:

Indirect material	$ 25,000
Indirect labor	40,000
Depreciation of machinery	100,000
Depreciation of building	20,000
Repair and maintenance on machinery	125,000
Utilities and taxes	35,000

They expect to use 15,000 direct labor hours at a cost of $330,000 and 10,000 machine hours during the year.

2. Acme Shoe Company has expected overhead costs of $1,200,000. The majority of the overhead costs are incurred providing production support to the direct labor force. The direct labor rates vary from $10 to $20 per hour for employees depending on the complexity of their task. Acme projects direct labor costs of $1,000,000 and 60,000 direct labor hours. The more complex tasks require proportionally more support than do the less complex tasks.

3. Moultre Metal Works fabricates steel on order. There exists a strong relationship between the weight of the materials handled and the overhead support required. Moultre expects production to require 280 tons of materials costing $280,000 in 19X3. They expect to incur $60,000 of direct labor costs, 6,000 direct labor hours, and overhead of $120,000.

REQUIRED:

a. Determine appropriate overhead allocation bases for each of the independent cases above.
b. Justify the selection of each allocation base.
c. Calculate the overhead application rate in each case.

LO 5   **P21-4B**   **Under- or Overapplied Overhead**   Ranger Custom Boots had total revenue of $120,000 for 19X3 with cost of goods sold of $50,000, administrative expenses of $24,000, and selling expenses of $12,000, before allocating a debit balance in the manufacturing overhead account of $22,000. The account balances are:

Raw Materials Inventory	$24,000
Work in Process Inventory	60,000
Finished Goods Inventory	30,000

REQUIRED:

a. Calculate net income treating the difference in the manufacturing overhead account as immaterial.

b. Calculate net income treating the difference in the manufacturing overhead account as material.

c. Discuss the significance of the alternative treatments.

LO 2,3,4,5   **P21-5B**   **Job-Order Costing Systems**   The following T-accounts represent one week of transactions in a typical large job shop.

Raw Materials Inventory			Insurance Payable	
Bal.	25,000	15,000		100
		5,000		

Work in Process Inventory			Finished Goods Inventory	
Bal.	15,000	55,000	Bal.	55,000	45,000
	25,000			
	25,000			

Manufacturing Overhead			Accumulated Depreciation	
	5,000	25,000		14,000
	10,000			
	14,000			
	900			
	100			

Utilities Payable			Accounts Payable	
		900		25,000

Cost of Goods Sold			Wages and Salaries Payable	
	45,000			35,000

REQUIRED:

a. Identify each of the several transactions from the ledger accounts and prepare a journal entry with an explanation for each. There were no beginning balances in the inventories.

b. Prepare the journal entry to close the under- or overapplied manufacturing overhead if:
   1. The difference is not deemed material.
   2. The difference is deemed material.

LO 2,3,4,5,6   **P21-6B**   **Accounting for a Job-Order Cost System**   Ellie Ford and Marti Wilson have both retired after 30 years in the food industry. Having been active for so many years, they found retirement boring and began catering wedding receptions on a limited basis. The primary costs involved in setting up in business included the purchase of appropriate linens, $1,000; two complete silver services (high quality silver plate), $800; glass plates and cups, $1,200; and cake decorating tools and accessories, $400. It is expected that all of the above equipment will last 10 years with no salvage value. They do all of the food preparation in their apartment and found that in an average month the utility bill is $100 higher than when they did not cater. All baking and cooking supplies are treated as direct materials and the only other cost incurred is liability insurance at $1,200 per year. All direct materials are purchased at a local grocery for cash, and they pay themselves an hourly wage of $25 per hour.

During the month of June, they catered 5 weddings.

	Direct Materials	*Labor Hours*
Boroski wedding	$ 350	20
Miller wedding	700	35
Walker wedding	425	18
Redfern wedding	1,500	80
Litchford wedding	550	28

The overhead allocation base is labor hours based on an estimated 1,000 hours per year, and the billings are at 120 percent of job cost. Overhead allocations and markups are rounded to the nearest dollar.

REQUIRED:

a. Journalize the month's activities.
b. Post the entries in T-accounts for Work In Process and Cost of Goods Sold.
c. Prepare the job cost sheets for each of the five June catering jobs.
d. Prepare a partial income statement (just through gross margin) for the month of June.

CRITICAL THINKING AND COMMUNICATING

C21-1 Two companies, A and B, manufacture identical products and use job-order costing systems. The materials handled by A and B are extremely heavy. While A uses a considerable amount of labor to move and process materials, B has recently automated. Thus, B has substituted a considerable amount of machinery for most of the direct labor that they formerly employed. The following information relates to the two companies:

Items Listed in *Manufacturing Overhead*	*(A)*	*(B)*
Indirect materials	$ 22,800	$ 22,000
Indirect labor	56,100	39,000
Depreciation on plant & equipment	22,200	122,800
Material handling costs	123,500	2,200
Supervision	18,000	9,000
Factory insurance	4,800	20,000
Factory property taxes	9,600	38,000
Payroll taxes	25,000	16,000
Utility expense	18,000	31,000
Total overhead costs	$300,000	$300,000
Direct material cost	$200,000	$200,000
Direct labor cost	$160,000	$ 80,000
Direct labor hours	16,000	8,000
Machine hours	10,000	20,000

REQUIRED:

Decide on an appropriate overhead application rate for each of the two companies and prepare a memo justifying the rate selected.

C21-2 Wall Well Drillers have been drilling domestic water supply wells for three years. Ed and Denise Wall, the owners, have accounted for all revenues and expenses properly from a tax standpoint but have simply closed the books once each year to determine profitability. They have priced their drilling based on $8.00 per foot, which is a rate they heard was prevalent in several nearby communities. Due to the mountainous terrain in their county they have found that some wells take much longer to drill than others and feel that there has to be a better way to price their work than simply by the foot. They ask you what could be done to better determine the cost of wells drilled in different areas of the county so they could price more appropriately and earn a fair return on each well drilled. You suggest that a job-order costing system would collect the type of information they need. Denise explains that she and Ed have to meet with two potential customers and ask if you can prepare a written explanation of how they could collect the cost information by job and mail your report to them. You agree.

REQUIRED:

Write the letter and explain job-order costing to Ed and Denise Wall in terms of their well drilling operation.

CHAPTER 22

Process Costing

Stacy Brannen was just finishing a plant tour at Kent Chemical Company's Midwest plant. Only two weeks ago, she had graduated from State University in mechanical engineering. Now, she was nearing the end of her first day on the job at Kent. The assistant plant manager, Bill Merton, conducted the tour and pointed out the steps involved in processing paints, stains, and wood preservatives. While the tour concentrated on the equipment used in the production processes, Stacy found herself wondering how the cost of products was determined. "Bill, can you give me a rough idea of how you calculate product costs?" she asked. "I noticed, for example, that to end up with a gallon of wood preservative ready to ship, both mixing and packaging operations must be performed. With labor, material, and overhead added in these separate operations, is tracing costs to wood preservative a difficult job?"

"Well," Bill replied, "let's see if we can catch Walter Hunt before he goes home for the night. He's the plant controller, and no one can do a better job than Walt of explaining how product costing is done at Kent Chemical."

Kent Chemical Company uses a process costing system. Companies that produce large numbers of homogeneous items—such as paints, plastics, cereals, cosmetics, and metals—in a continuous production process commonly use process costing. Thus, well-known companies like DuPont, the Quaker Oats Company, and the Ralston Purina Company use process costing. In this chapter, we introduce you to the essential elements of a process costing system.

DIFFERENCE BETWEEN JOB-ORDER AND PROCESS COSTING SYSTEMS

Manufacturing firms use one of two primary systems to calculate the cost of inventory: a job-order system or a process costing system. In a job-order system, each unique product or batch is a "job" for which the company needs cost information. Therefore, manufacturing costs are traced to specific jobs. When jobs are completed, the firm removes the cost of the jobs from Work in Process Inventory and debits it to Finished Goods Inventory. When it sells the completed jobs, the firm removes the cost of the jobs from Finished Goods Inventory and debits it to Cost of Goods Sold.

Process costing, on the other hand, is essentially a system of averaging. Dividing production costs by the total number of homogeneous items produced results in an average unit cost. When items are completed, multiplying the number of units completed by the average unit cost determines the cost the firm removes from Work in Process Inventory and debits to Finished Goods Inventory. When items are sold, multiplying the number of units sold by the average unit cost determines the cost the firm removes from Finished Goods Inventory and debits to Cost of Goods Sold. Illustration 22-1 compares job-order and process costing systems.

Describe product flows through departments and record cost flows in accounts.

PRODUCT AND COST FLOWS

Just as a product passes through several departments before it is completed, costs flow through several accounts before the firm can record the cost of the product in Finished Goods Inventory.

Product Flows Through Departments

In the typical production operation of process costing companies, the product must pass through two or more departments. The Kent Chemical Company, for example, manufactures wood preservative in two departments: Mixing and Packaging. After the mixing department blends chemical materials, it transfers the liquid preservative to the packaging department where it is placed in metal containers of various sizes.

Materials, labor, and overhead are added at different stages in each processing department. Generally, identifying the stage when materials enter the pro-

ILLUSTRATION 22-1 Comparison of Job-Order and Process Costing Systems

Job-Order System—Use Cost of Specific Jobs

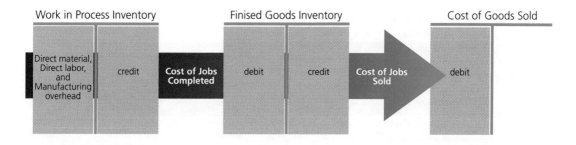

Process Costing System—Use Average Unit Cost Information

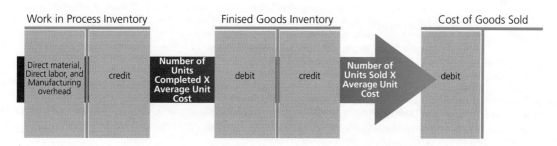

duction process is easy. The mixing department adds chemical materials at the start of the process. Determining exactly when labor and overhead are added to the process is more difficult. Labor and overhead are often grouped together and are referred to as **conversion costs**. Conversion costs are often assumed to be added evenly throughout the process. Illustration 22-2 shows how items flow through the two processing departments and how costs are incurred. As indicated, materials enter both processing departments at the start. However, conversion costs (labor and overhead) are assumed to enter each of the processes evenly.

Cost Flows Through Accounts

The product costs accumulated in a process costing system are essentially the same costs considered in job-order costing: direct material, direct labor, and manufacturing overhead. Additionally, a processing department may have a cost called **transferred-in cost**. This is the cost a prior processing department incurs and transfers to the next processing department. Each processing department accumulates product costs in a separate departmental work in process inventory account. The sum of the departmental work in process inventory accounts is the amount in Work in Process Inventory for the whole company. The following journal entries record product costs in a process costing system and illustrate the flow of costs between processing departments.

ILLUSTRATION 22-2 Flow of Items Through Processing Departments

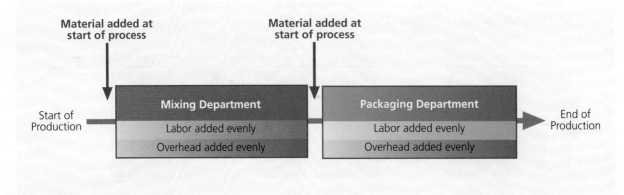

Direct Material.   Suppose the mixing department of Kent Chemical Company uses $142,000 of raw materials during April. The following journal entry would be appropriate:

(Date)	Work in Process Inventory, Mixing	142,000	
	Raw Materials Inventory		142,000
	To record use of raw material.		

Direct Labor.   Suppose the mixing department incurs $62,200 of direct labor costs during April. The following journal entry would be appropriate:

(Date)	Work in Process Inventory, Mixing	62,200	
	Wages and Salaries Payable		62,200
	To record direct labor cost.		

Manufacturing Overhead.   To assign overhead to products in a process costing system, a company may use either actual overhead costs or a predetermined overhead rate. Unless the amount of overhead cost and the level of production are fairly constant from month to month, using actual overhead costs results in substantial fluctuations in the unit cost of goods produced. For this reason, most companies use a predetermined overhead rate. Suppose that at the start of the year, the mixing department estimates it will incur $2,160,000 of overhead cost and $720,000 of direct labor cost. Using direct labor as an allocation base, the department calculates a predetermined overhead rate of $3 for each dollar of direct labor cost. Assuming the department incurs $62,200 of direct labor cost in the month of April, it would assign $186,600 of overhead to Work in Process Inventory that month.

(Date)	Work in Process Inventory, Mixing	186,600	
	Manufacturing Overhead		186,600
	To record manufacturing overhead applied		
	to Work in Process Inventory.		

Transferred-in Cost.   When one processing department completes its work, it transfers the items to the next department along with the related cost (referred to as *transferred-in cost*.) Suppose that during April, the mixing department

INSIGHTS INTO ACCOUNTING

HYBRID COSTING SYSTEMS

In many cases, product costing systems combine aspects of both process and job-order costing. Such a hybrid system is used by Kunde Estate Winery, a small wine producer in California's Sonoma Valley. At Kunde Estate Winery, costs are accumulated by various production processes as in a process costing system. The processes include crushing, fermenting, tank aging, barrel aging, and bottling. However, each lot of wine in a given vintage may be processed somewhat differently, requiring each lot to be treated as a separate job as in a job-order costing system.

Source: John Y. Lee and Brian Gray, "Kunde Estate Winery: A Case Study in Cost Accounting," CMA Magazine, Vol. 67, Issue 3 (April 1993): 15–19.

completes units with a cost of $360,000. It transfers the completed units to the packaging department and the related cost becomes a transferred-in cost to Packaging. The journal entry to record the transfer is:

(Date)	Work in Process Inventory, Packaging	360,000	
	Work in Process Inventory, Mixing		360,000
	To record transfer of units from Mixing to Packaging.		

The flow of costs between the departmental work in process inventory accounts is presented in Illustration 22-3.

ILLUSTRATION 22-3 Flow of Costs Between Processing Departments

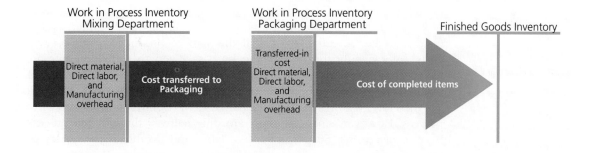

CALCULATING UNIT COST

We have said that process costing is essentially a system of averaging. This section shows how to calculate an average unit cost in a process costing system.[1] First, however, we must explain an essential concept in process costing—the concept of equivalent units.

---

[1]The approach we take is the so-called weighted-average method. Other approaches such as the FIFO method are possible but are not covered here.

Discuss the concept of
equivalent units.

Equivalent Units

In a process costing system, the number of partially completed units in work in
process are expressed in terms of an equivalent number of whole units. When
the units are converted to a comparable number of completed units, they are
referred to as **equivalent units**. In Illustration 22-4, if 100 units in work in
process are 50 percent completed, then they are equivalent to 50 completed
units (100 x 50%).

ILLUSTRATION 22-4 How Equivalent Units Are Calculated

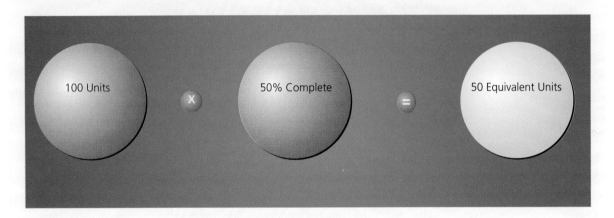

The number of equivalent units in work in process may be different for
material and conversion costs as shown in Illustration 22-5. The reason is that
material and conversion costs enter the production process at different times.
For example, suppose that at the end of July, the mixing department at Kent
Chemical has 100 gallons (units of production) of wood preservative in work in
process that are 50 percent through the mixing process. Further, assume that
materials enter into the process at the start of production, while conversion
costs enter evenly throughout the process. Even though the units are only
halfway through the process, they have received 100 percent of material since
material was added immediately at the start of the process. (See Illustration 22-
2.) Therefore, with respect to material cost, 100 equivalent units are in work in
process. However, since the units are only halfway through the process, they
have received only 50 percent of the labor and overhead needed for completion. Since the 100 gallons are only 50 percent complete with respect to conversion costs, there are 50 equivalent units for labor and overhead.

Calculate the cost per
equivalent unit.

Cost per Equivalent Unit

The unit cost in a process costing system is often referred to as a **cost per
equivalent unit**. The formula for the unit cost calculation is:

$$\text{Cost per Equivalent Unit} = \frac{\text{Cost in Beginning WIP} \ + \ \text{Cost Incurred in Current Period}}{\text{Units Completed} + \text{Equivalent Units in Ending WIP}}$$

The numerator contains the cost in beginning work in process plus the cost
incurred in the current period. This is the total cost that a processing department is responsible for each period. The total cost is divided by the units com-

ILLUSTRATION 22-5 Differences in Equivalent Units for Material and Conversion Costs (Assuming Material Added at Start of Process)

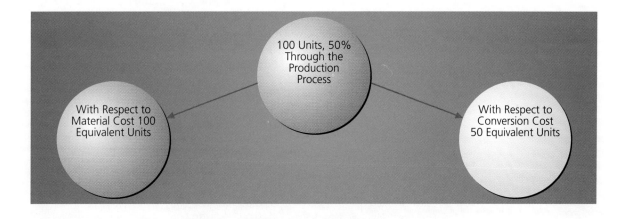

pleted plus the equivalent units in ending work in process. Thus, a cost per equivalent unit amount spreads the cost at the start of the period and the cost incurred during the period over the units in process at the end of the period and the units completed.

LO 4
Calculate the cost of goods completed and the ending work in process balance in a processing department.

CALCULATING AND APPLYING COST PER EQUIVALENT UNIT: MIXING DEPARTMENT EXAMPLE

The cost per equivalent unit calculations for the mixing department of Kent Chemical Company follow. At the start of April, the mixing department has on hand beginning work in process inventory consisting of 10,000 gallons of wood preservative that are 80 percent complete. During the month, 70,000 gallons are started, 60,000 are completed, and 20,000 are on hand at the end of April that are 50 percent complete with respect to conversion costs. The cost in beginning work in process consists of $18,000 of material cost, $7,800 of labor cost, and $23,400 of overhead cost. During April, the mixing department incurs $142,000 of material cost and $62,200 of labor cost. Since the mixing department's predetermined overhead rate is $3 for each dollar of labor cost, it applies $186,600 of overhead to production during the month.

The cost per equivalent unit calculations for the mixing department are presented in Illustration 22-6. The cost of material includes the $18,000 in beginning work in process and the $142,000 of material cost incurred during April. The total of $160,000 is divided by the sum of the number of units completed (60,000 gallons) and the equivalent units in ending work in process (20,000 gallons). Dividing total cost by the total number of units yields a cost per equivalent unit for materials of $2.

Note that there are 20,000 units on hand at the end of April that are only 50 percent through the mixing process. However, since material enters at the start of the mixing process, the 20,000 units are 100% complete with respect to material cost. Thus, there are 20,000 equivalent units in ending work in process for materials. However, for both labor and overhead, the 20,000 units on hand are only 50 percent complete, so they correspond to only 10,000 equivalent units. The total cost per equivalent unit is $6, consisting of $2 of material cost, $1 of labor cost, and $3 of overhead cost. These unit cost figures can be used to calculate the cost of goods completed and transferred out of the mixing department and the cost of ending work in process.

ILLUSTRATION 22-6 Calculation of Cost per Equivalent Unit—Mixing Department

	Material	Labor	Overhead	Total
Cost:				
Beginning WIP	$ 18,000	$ 7,800	$ 23,400	$ 49,200
Cost incurred during April	142,000	62,200	186,600	390,800
Total (a)	$160,000	$70,000	$210,000	$440,000
Units:				
Units completed	60,000	60,000	60,000	
Equivalent units, ending WIP	20,000	10,000	10,000	
Total (b)	80,000	70,000	70,000	
Cost per equivalent unit (a ÷ b)	$2 +	$1 +	$3 =	$6

Cost Transferred Out

The mixing department completed 60,000 gallons during April and transferred them to the packaging department. The unit cost is $6. Therefore, $360,000 of cost is related to the units completed and transferred. The journal entry at the end of April to record the transfer was presented earlier, but we repeat it here:

(Date)	Work in Process Inventory, Packaging	360,000	
	Work in Process Inventory, Mixing		360,000
	To record transfer of units from Mixing to Packaging.		

Ending Work in Process

The Mixing Department's ending balance in Work in Process Inventory is $80,000. This balance is made up of 20,000 equivalent units for material at $2 per equivalent unit, 10,000 equivalent units for labor at $1, and 10,000 equivalent units for overhead at $3.

Ending Balance in Work in Process Inventory, Mixing	
Material (20,000 equiv. units at $2)	$40,000
Labor (10,000 equiv. units at $1)	10,000
Overhead (10,000 equiv. units at $3)	30,000
Total	$80,000

The T-account for Work in Process Inventory summarizes the cost activity for the mixing department, resulting in the $80,000 ending balance.

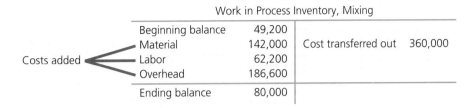

Work in Process Inventory, Mixing			
Beginning balance	49,200	Cost transferred out	360,000
Material	142,000		
Labor	62,200		
Overhead	186,600		
Ending balance	80,000		

Costs added → (Material, Labor, Overhead)

LO 5
Describe a production cost report.

PRODUCTION COST REPORT

A **production cost report**, an end-of-the-month report for a process costing system, provides reconciliations of units and costs as well as the details of the cost per equivalent unit calculations. A production cost report for the mixing department of Kent Chemical Company is provided in Illustration 22-7. The unit cost calculations in the production report are identical to the ones just presented. We will concentrate now on the reconciliations of units and costs.

Reconciliation of Units

Assuming no units are lost (due to evaporation, damage, or theft), the number of units in beginning work in process inventory plus the number of units started during the period should be equal to the number of units completed plus the number of units in work in process at the end of the period. For the mixing department, 10,000 units were in beginning inventory, and 70,000 units were started during the period. This means that 80,000 units must be accounted for. Since 60,000 units were completed and 20,000 units are in work in process at the end of the period, all of the units are accounted for.

Reconciliation of Costs

For each period, the total cost that must be accounted for is the sum of the costs in beginning Work in Process Inventory and the costs incurred during the period. In the mixing department, this amounts to $440,000. The cost must be either transferred out with the completed units or remain in ending work in process inventory. The amount transferred out is $360,000, and the amount in ending work in process inventory is $80,000. Since they sum to $440,000, the total amount of cost is accounted for.

BASIC STEPS IN PROCESS COSTING

Unless process cost problems are approached in a systematic way, it is easy to get lost in the calculations. Here is a summary of the basic steps we have presented above. As you can see, each of the steps is performed when the production cost report is prepared.

Step 1   Account for the number of physical units. The number of units at the start of the period plus the number of units started during the period should equal the number of units completed plus the number of units in ending work in process.

ILLUSTRATION 22-7 Production Cost Report, Mixing Department

Production Cost Report	
Mixing Department	
April 19X1	

Step 1

Quantity Reconciliation:

Units in beg. WIP (100% material, 80% conversion costs)	10,000
Units started during April	70,000
Units to account for	80,000
Units completed and transferred to Packaging	60,000
Units in ending WIP (100% material, 50% conversion costs)	20,000
Units accounted for	80,000

Step 2

Cost Per Equivalent Unit Calculation:

	Material	Labor	Overhead	Total
Cost:				
Beginning WIP	$ 18,000	$ 7,800	$ 23,400	$ 49,200
Costs incurred during April	142,000	62,200	186,600	390,800
Total	$160,000	$70,000	$210,000	$440,000
Units:				
Units completed	60,000	60,000	60,000	
Equivalent units, ending WIP	20,000	10,000	10,000	
Total	80,000	70,000	70,000	
Cost per equivalent unit	$2 +	$1 +	$3 =	$6

Step 4

Cost Reconciliation:

Total cost to account for	$440,000

Step 3

Cost of completed units transferred to Packaging		
(60,000 x $6)		$360,000
Cost of ending WIP:		
Material (20,000 equivalent units x $2)	$40,000	
Labor (10,000 equivalent units x $1)	10,000	
Overhead (10,000 equivalent units x $3)	30,000	80,000
Total cost accounted for		$440,000

Step 2 Calculate the cost per equivalent unit for material, labor, and overhead. Remember that cost (numerator in the calculation) includes both beginning costs and costs incurred during the period. The number of equivalent units (denominator in the calculation) includes both the number of units completed and the number of equivalent units in ending work in process.

Step 3 Assign cost to items completed and items in ending work in process. The cost of items completed is simply the product of the total cost per equivalent unit and the number of units completed. The cost of items in work in process is the sum of the products of equivalent units in process and cost per equivalent unit for material, labor, and overhead.

Step 4 Account for the amount of product cost. The cost of beginning inventory plus the costs incurred during the period should equal the amount of cost assigned to completed items plus the amount of cost assigned to items in ending work in process.

ANSWERING STACY'S QUESTION

Recall that in the scenario at the start of the chapter, Stacy Brannen asked how Kent Chemical Company calculates the cost of products such as wood preservative. At this point, you should be able to answer a similar question. Essentially, material, labor, and overhead costs are accumulated in each processing department. In each department, the cost per equivalent unit is calculated for material, labor, and overhead (Step 2). Then, the costs per equivalent unit are used to determine the cost of items completed and the cost of ending work in process (Step 3).

TRANSFERRED-IN COST

As noted earlier, companies using process costing systems generally use several processes to produce their product. When one processing department completes items, it transfers the cost of the completed units to the next processing department. This procedure is repeated until the units are completed in the last process. At that point, the firm transfers the cost of the items to Finished Goods Inventory. The method of dealing with cost transfers is presented in the following example of the packaging department of Kent Chemical Company. To calculate product costs in the packaging department, we will use the same procedures already used to calculate product costs in the mixing department. Thereby, you are provided with another opportunity to enhance your understanding of the procedures.

TRANSFERRED-IN COST: PACKAGING DEPARTMENT EXAMPLE

In working through the packaging department example, examine the information provided in the production cost report for the packaging department (Illustration 22-8). At the start of April, the packaging department has 15,000 gallons that are 50 percent through the packaging operation. During the month of April, the department receives 60,000 gallons from the mixing department. There are now 75,000 gallons to account for. At the end of April, 5,000 gallons are 40 percent complete, and 70,000 gallons are completed and transferred to finished goods, which accounts for the total of 75,000 gallons. Reconciling the physical number of units is the first of the four steps in solving a process costing problem and is shown in the Quantity Reconciliation section of the production cost report (Illustration 22-8).

The second step is to calculate the cost per equivalent unit. The beginning balance in work in process includes $10,500 of material cost, $4,500 of labor, $9,000 of overhead, and $92,250 of cost transferred-in from the mixing department. In addition, the packaging department incurred $49,500 of material cost, $27,900 of labor cost, $55,800 of overhead, and $360,000 of cost transferred-in from the mixing department during the month of April. The costs are divided by the number of completed units plus the equivalent units in ending work in

ILLUSTRATION 22-8 Production Cost Report, Packaging Department

Production Cost Report
Packaging Department
April 19X1

Quantity Reconciliation:

Units in beg. WIP (100% material, 50% conversion costs)	15,000
Units received from Mixing during April	60,000
Units to account for	75,000
Units completed and transferred to Finished Goods	70,000
Units in ending WIP (100% material, 40% conversion costs)	5,000
Units accounted for	75,000

Cost Per Equivalent Unit Calculation:

	Material	Labor	Overhead	Trans.-in	Total
Cost:					
Beginning WIP	$10,500	$ 4,500	$ 9,000	$ 92,250	$116,250
Costs incurred during April	49,500	27,900	55,800	360,000	493,200
Total	$60,000	$32,400	$64,800	$452,250	$609,450
Units:					
Units completed	70,000	70,000	70,000	70,000	
Equivalent units, ending WIP	5,000	2,000	2,000	5,000	
Total	75,000	72,000	72,000	75,000	
Cost per equivalent unit	$0.80 +	$0.45 +	$0.90 +	$6.03 =	$8.18

Cost Reconciliation:

Total cost to account for		$609,450
Cost of completed units transferred to Finished Goods (70,000 x $8.18)		$572,600
Cost of ending WIP:		
Material (5,000 equivalent units x $0.80)	$ 4,000	
Labor (2,000 equivalent units x $0.45)	900	
Overhead (2,000 equivalent units x $0.90)	1,800	
Transferred-in (5,000 equivalent units x $6.03)	30,150	36,850
Total cost accounted for		$609,450

process for each cost category. As the production cost report shows, this yields cost per equivalent unit values of $.80 for material, $.45 for labor, $.90 for overhead, and $6.03 for transferred-in cost. Because it has not been covered in the previous example, note especially the calculation of cost per equivalent unit for transferred-in cost. The sum of transferred-in cost in beginning work in process ($92,250) plus the transferred-in cost during April ($360,000) is the numerator of the calculation ($452,250). The denominator (75,000 units) is the sum of the units completed (70,000) plus the equivalent units in ending work in process

(5,000). The result is a cost per equivalent unit for transferred-in cost of $6.03. One aspect of the calculation may be confusing: the equivalent units in ending work in process. The 5,000 units in process at the end of April are only 40 percent through the packaging process. However, these units are 100 percent complete with respect to transferred-in cost since they were transferred in with all of the mixing department cost that they will receive. Therefore, there are 5,000 equivalent units in ending work in process with respect to transferred-in cost.

The third step in solving the process costing problem is to assign cost to items completed and items in ending work in process. The cost of the completed items is $572,600. As indicated in the production cost report, this is computed as the cost per equivalent unit ($8.18) times the number of units completed (70,000). Once the packaging department completes the units, Kent includes the cost of both the mixing operation and the packaging operation in the units transferred to finished goods. The entry to record the transfer is:

(Date)	Finished Goods Inventory	572,600	
	Work in Process Inventory, Packaging		572,600
	To record cost of units completed and transferred to Finished Goods Inventory.		

The cost of ending work in process is composed of material, labor, overhead, and transferred-in cost. For each cost category, the equivalent units in ending work in process is multiplied by the cost per equivalent unit. As indicated in the production cost report, the sum of the cost categories is the ending balance of $36,850.

The fourth, and final, step is to account for the amount of product cost. The cost of beginning inventory ($116,250) plus the amount of costs incurred during the period ($493,200) is the total cost that must be accounted for ($609,450). As indicated in the production cost report, this is accounted for by the cost of the completed items ($572,600) plus the cost of ending work in process ($36,850).

SUMMARY

Describe product flows through departments and record cost flows in accounts. Companies that produce large numbers of identical items use process costing systems to accumulate the cost of inventory. Typically, companies use several distinct processes to produce the items. When units are completed in one process, the cost of the units is transferred to the next process. This procedure is repeated until the units are completed in the last process. Along with transferred-in costs, each process may add its own material, labor, and overhead cost.

Discuss the concept of an equivalent unit. Units in work in process are not equal to fully completed units. Therefore, these partially completed units are expressed in terms of equivalent whole units.

Calculate the cost per equivalent unit. Process costing is essentially a system of averaging. The average cost is referred to as the cost per equivalent unit. It equals the sum of beginning work in process costs and current period costs divided by the sum of units completed and equivalent units in ending work in process.

Calculate the cost of goods completed and the ending work in process balance in a processing department. To calculate the cost of completed items, the total

INSIGHTS INTO ETHICS

Right after graduation, Carol Owens began working in the cost accounting department of Aktron Chemical Company. She's been employed by the company for five months and is beginning to feel comfortable with her job. Last week she completed a production cost report for the month of January, which assumed that the 10,000 units in process at the end of the month were 10 percent complete with respect to labor and overhead. The plant engineer in charge of production provided the 10 percent estimate. Her supervisor, Otis Atkins, reviewed the report and asked her to redo the analysis using a completion percentage of 80 percent. He explained that the engineers are often careless in estimating completion percentages, and he believed his figure was more accurate. However, he did not tell Carol how he determined his estimate. Further, Carol knows that the effect of this change will be to shift more cost to work in process and less cost to the finished units. Since the finished units will be sold in February, their lower cost will tend to boost net income during a month that is typically a low income month for the company.

What should Carol do? Should she confront her supervisor and ask him to justify the 80 percent figure?

cost per equivalent unit is multiplied by the number of units completed. To calculate the cost of units in work in process, the number of equivalent units in process is multiplied by the cost per equivalent unit separately for each cost category (i.e., material, labor, overhead, and transferred-in cost). This is necessary because the units in work in process at the end of the period may be completed to different degrees with respect to each of these costs.

Describe a production cost report. A production cost report provides a reconciliation of units in beginning inventory and units started to units in ending inventory and units completed. It also provides a reconciliation of costs in beginning inventory and costs added during the period to costs in ending inventory and costs transferred out.

REVIEW PROBLEM

Omega Files Company manufactures a single, five-drawer file cabinet for accounting and legal offices. They have 15-inch wide drawers and are insulated for fire survival of two hours. The production occurs in two departments, Forming and Assembly & Painting. The metal materials for the cabinets are introduced into production as the beginning step in the forming department.

The first process consists of cutting and forming cabinet housing and drawer parts from sheet metal, which is acquired in 50-yard rolls. The drawer rails and slide latches are stamped out of a heavier gauge steel alloy.

The completed parts are transferred to Assembly & Painting where the drawers and cabinets are assembled and painted, and the fire insulation and locking mechanisms are added. As units are transferred into the assembly & painting department from the forming department, the appropriate materials to complete those units are immediately issued to the assembly & painting department.

The completed units are transferred to a finished goods warehouse. The following information is available for April 19X3:

Unit Information:	Forming Dept.	Assembly & Painting Dept.
Beginning WIP Inventory, 4/1/X3:		
(100% material, 40% conversion costs)	750	
(100% material, 60% conversion costs)		1,000
Units started into production during April	6,000	
Units transferred in during April		?
Ending WIP inventory 4/30/X3:		
(100% material, 50% conversion costs)	600	
(100% material, 75% conversion costs)		800

Note: Transferred-in units are always 100% complete as to prior department costs. It is normally assumed that there are no spoiled or lost units unless specified.

Cost Information:	Forming Dept.	Assembly & Painting Dept.
Beginning WIP:		
Direct materials	$ 60,000	$ 20,000
Direct labor	6,000	36,000
Manufacturing overhead applied	6,000	12,000
Transferred-in costs	N/A	120,000
Total beginning WIP	$ 72,000	$188,000
Costs added during the period:		
Direct materials	$480,000	$123,000
Direct labor	123,000	381,000
Manufacturing overhead applied	123,000	127,000
Transferred-in costs	N/A	?
Total costs added during the period	$726,000	?

REQUIRED:

a. Prepare a production cost report for April for each of the departments.
b. Prepare journal entries to record the April transactions of the Forming Department.
c. Prepare journal entries to record the April transactions of the Assembly & Painting Department.

SOLUTION:

(a) *Prepare production cost reports.*

Production Cost Report
Forming Department
April 19X3

Quantity Reconciliation:

Units in beginning WIP	750
Units started during April	6,000
Units to account for	6,750
Units completed and transferred to Assembly & Painting	6,150
Units in ending WIP (100% material, 50% conversion costs)	600
Units accounted for	6,750

Cost Per Equivalent Unit Calculation:

Cost:	Material	Labor	Overhead	Total
Beginning WIP	$ 60,000	$ 6,000	$ 6,000	$ 72,000
Costs incurred during April	480,000	123,000	123,000	726,000
Total	$540,000	$129,000	$129,000	$798,000

Units:	Direct Material	Direct Labor	Mfg. Overhead
Units completed	6,150	6,150	6,150
Equivalent units, ending WIP	600	300	300
Total	6,750	6,450	6,450

Cost per equivalent unit	$80	+	$20	+	$20	=	$120

Cost Reconciliation:

Total cost to account for	$798,000

Cost of completed units transferred to Assembly & Painting (6,150 units x $120)		$738,000
Cost of ending WIP:		
Material (600 equivalent units x $80)	$48,000	
Labor (300 equivalent units x $20)	6,000	
Overhead (300 equivalent units x $20)	6,000	60,000
Total cost accounted for		$798,000

Production Cost Report
Assembly & Painting Department
April 19X3

Quantity Reconciliation:

Units in beginning WIP	1,000
Units received from Forming during April	6,150
Units to account for	7,150
Units completed and transferred to Finished Goods	6,350
Units in ending WIP (100% material, 75% conversion costs)	800
Units accounted for	7,150

Cost Per Equivalent Unit Calculation:

Cost:	Material	Labor	Overhead	Trans.-In	Total
Beginning WIP	$ 20,000	$ 36,000	$ 12,000	$120,000	$ 188,000
Costs incurred during April	123,000	381,000	127,000	738,000	1,369,000
Total	$143,000	$417,000	$139,000	$858,000	$1,557,000

Units:				
Units completed	6,350	6,350	6,350	6,350
Equivalent units, ending WIP	800	600	600	800
Total	7,150	6,950	6,950	7,150

Cost per equivalent unit	$20	+	$60	+	$20	+	$120	=	$220

Cost Reconciliation:

Total cost to account for		$1,557,000
Cost of completed units transferred to Finished Goods (6,350 units x $220)		$1,397,000
Cost of ending WIP:		
Material (800 equivalent units x $20)	$16,000	
Labor (600 equivalent units x $60)	36,000	
Overhead (600 equivalent units x $20)	12,000	
Transferred-in (800 equivalent units x $120)	96,000	160,000
Total cost accounted for		$1,557,000

(b) *Prepare journal entries for the forming department.*

These entries can be reconstructed from the information in the production cost report for the department for April.

(1)	Work in Process Inventory, Forming		726,000	
	Raw Materials Inventory			480,000
	Wages and Salaries Payable			123,000
	Manufacturing Overhead			123,000
	To record inputs to production for April.			
(2)	Work in Process Inventory, Assembly & Painting		738,000	
	Work in Process Inventory, Forming			738,000
	To record transfer of costs from Forming to Assembly & Painting.			

(c) *Prepare journal entries for the assembly & painting department.*

These entries can be reconstructed from the information in the April production cost report for the department.

(1)	Work in Process Inventory, Assembly & Painting		631,000	
	Raw Materials Inventory			123,000
	Wages and Salaries Payable			381,000
	Manufacturing Overhead			127,000
	To record inputs to production for April.			
	(Note: the entry for the costs transferred in from Forming has been made in entry b.(2) above.)			
(2)	Finished Goods Inventory		1,397,000	
	Work in Process Inventory, Assembly & Painting			1,397,000
	To record cost of units completed and transferred to Finished Goods Inventory.			

KEY TERMS

conversion costs, *905*

cost per equivalent unit, *908*

equivalent units, *908*

production cost report, *911*

transferred-in costs, *905*

SELF QUIZ

LO 1 1. Indicate which of the following characteristics are associated with a process costing system. (Yes/No)
   ___ a. Heterogeneous products
   ___ b. Homogeneous products
   ___ c. Continuous production
   ___ d. Discontinuous production
   ___ e. Costs are traced to jobs
   ___ f. Costs are traced to processing departments

LO 1 2. The best example of a business requiring a process cost system would be a(n):
   a. Custom cabinet shop.
   b. Antique furniture restorer.
   c. Soap manufacturer.
   d. Home builder.
   e. Automobile repair shop.

LO 1 3. The costs in a process cost system are traced to:
   a. Specific jobs.
   b. Specific customers.
   c. Specific company administrators.
   d. Specific production departments.
   e. None of the above.

LO 1 4. The transfer of indirect materials into production would include a debit to:
   a. Materials Inventory
   b. Manufacturing Overhead
   c. Work in Process Inventory
   d. Finished Goods Inventory

LO 1 5. Match the following cost accounting terms with the definitions shown below.
   ___ a. Conversion costs
   ___ b. Equivalent units of production
   ___ c. Transferred-in costs
   ___ d. Cost per equivalent unit
   (1) The costs associated with units received from a preceding department within the company for further processing.
   (2) The unit cost in a process costing system.
   (3) The costs associated with changing units of direct materials into finished products; they include both direct labor and manufacturing overhead.
   (4) Hypothetical units of output, which assume that a number of partially completed units may reasonably be treated as a proportionally smaller number of completed units with respect to any factor of production, i.e., direct materials, direct labor, etc., when calculating average unit cost in a process costing system.

LO 1 6. Determine the amount of conversion cost in the following list of costs.
   1. Direct material $25,000
   2. Direct labor 35,000

   3. Manufacturing overhead 45,000
   4. Selling expenses 10,000
   5. Administrative expenses 50,000

LO 1 7. When units completed in one processing department are received by another department for further processing, the related costs are called _____ _____ by the receiving department, and debited to the _____ _____ _____ of the receiving department.

LO 2
LO 3 8. If raw material A is introduced into a production department at the beginning of the production process, which statement is correct about the equivalent units of production respect to material A?
   a. All the units in the department are 100% complete as to materials.
   b. All the units in the department are on the average 50% complete as to materials.
   c. Equivalent units of materials is not a function of when the materials are entered into the process.
   d. All of the above statements are incorrect.

LO 2
LO 3 9. If raw material B is introduced into a production department at the very end of the production process as they are transferred to the next department, what statement can you make about the equivalent units of product in the ending work in process inventory account with respect to material B?
   a. All of the units in work in process are complete with respect to material B.
   b. All of the units in work in process are on average 50% complete as to material B.
   c. Equivalent units of materials is not a function of when the materials are entered into the process.
   d. All of the above statements are incorrect.

LO 1 10. A transfer of production goods from the first producing department to the second producing department would include a:
   a. Debit to Finished Goods Inventory.
   b. Debit to Cost of Goods Sold.
   c. Debit to Work in Process, Department One.
   d. Debit to Work in Process, Department Two.

LO 1 11. The application of manufacturing overhead to work in process would include which of the following?
   a. A debit to Manufacturing Overhead.
   b. A credit to Manufacturing Overhead.
   c. A credit to Work in Process Inventory.
   d. A debit to Finished Goods Inventory.

LO 5 12. The Quantity Reconciliation portion of a production cost report includes all of the following except:

a. Beginning units in process.

b. Ending units in process.

c. Units started and completed during the period.

d. Units completed and transferred out.

e. Units started during the period.

LO 5 13. The units as shown in the Quantity Reconciliation portion of a production cost report are:

a. Equivalent units of production.

b. Units without regard to stage of completion.

c. Units complete as to materials.

d. Units complete as to prime costs.

LO 3 14. The elements in the cost per equivalent unit calculation include all of the following except:

a. Cost of goods sold.

b. Total costs for each input.

c. Equivalent units for each input.

d. Unit cost for each input.

LO 2 15. The number of equivalent units of production

LO 3   for an input are:

a. The number of units placed into production and completed during the period.

b. The number of units placed into production during the period.

c. The comparable number of whole units.

d. None of the above.

LO 2 16. A company has beginning work in process of 10,000 units, 60% complete as to conversion costs. They start 50,000 units during the peri-

od and have 20,000 in ending work in process, 30% complete as to conversion cost. The denominator in the cost per equivalent unit calculation for conversion is:

a. 56,000.

b. 46,000.

c. 40,000.

d. 64,000.

LO 2 17. Transferred-in costs are:

LO 3   a. Always recalculated by the receiving

LO 4   department.

LO 5   b. Not considered further by the receiving department.

c. Related to 100% complete equivalent units.

d. None of the above.

LO 2 18. Transferred-in costs occur in:

LO 3   a. All production departments.

LO 4   b. The first and last production departments.

LO 5   c. All production departments after the first.

d. None of the above is correct.

LO 5 19. Production cost reports are:

a. Essential external financial reports.

b. Essential internal financial reports.

c. Useful to management but not essential.

d. None of the above.

LO 2 20. A key to solving process costing problems

LO 5   is:

a. Tracing costs to individual jobs.

b. Calculating equivalent units of production.

c. Having only one work in process inventory account.

d. None of the above.

QUESTIONS

Q22-1 What are the two primary systems used by manufacturing firms to calculate production costs?

Q22-2 Identify the fundamental difference in the assignment of costs in a process costing system and a job-order costing system.

Q22-3 The accounts used to track the flow of costs through either a job-order cost system or a process costing system are essentially the same, except that a process system may have a separate work in process account for each department. Explain how the flow of costs through the ledger accounts differs between the two systems.

Q22-4 Discuss the relationship between product flows and cost flows in a process costing manufacturing environment.

Q22-5 What factors must be considered in calculating equivalent units of work in process for direct materials when the direct materials are introduced into a production process at some point other than at the beginning of the process?

Q22-6 Costs are transferred into departments subsequent to the first department in a process costing system. Discuss how these costs are treated by the receiving departments.

Q22-7 Explain the concept of "equivalent units."

Q22-8 Why are units often in a different stage of completion with respect to raw materials and conversion costs?

Q22-9 Why do we usually calculate separate equivalent units in work in process for materials, labor, and manufacturing overhead?

Q22-10 What items of production cost make up the "costs to account for" in a production cost report?

Q22-11 Identify where the "costs to account for" on a production cost report would appear in the financial statements at the end of the period.

Q22-12 Discuss what is accomplished by preparing a reconciliation of the physical units as a part of the production cost report.

Q22-13 How does the production cost report provide the information for recording costs transferred out of a department?

Q22-14 A work in process inventory account has no beginning balance. 1,000 units are introduced into production, 900 units are completed and transferred out, and 100 units are in process at the end of the period. Is it logical to assume that 10% of the costs in the work in process account should be assigned to the ending balance in Work in Process Inventory? Discuss.

Q22-15 Do transferred-in costs occur in all departments of a manufacturer using a process costing system? Explain.

EXERCISES

LO 1

E22-1 **Flow of Process Costs Through Accounts**   Wilton Mfg. Co. produces one product in a single department on a process basis. Present the following information as it would appear in Wilton's ledger. Use T-accounts.

		Production Dept.
WIP, 5/1/X5		$ 13,800
Costs added during May:		
Direct material	$26,500	
Direct labor	34,000	
Manufacturing overhead	68,000	128,500
WIP, 5/31/X5		11,800

LO 1

E22-2 **Flow of Process Costs Through Accounts**   Chiapa Corporation uses a process costing system with only one work in process inventory account and completed its first year of manufacturing operations on December 31, 19X8. The cost of completed goods transferred to the finished goods warehouse during the period was $138,000. Direct material purchases totaled $45,000 with $5,000 remaining in ending inventory. Overhead applied to production during the year was $55,000.

REQUIRED:

Use T-accounts to determine the amount of direct labor used during the period assuming the ending Work in Process Inventory balance was $15,000.

LO 2   **E22-3**   **Equivalent Units**   A company has 25 units of product in beginning work in process which are 100% complete as to materials and 40% complete as to direct labor and manufacturing overhead. During the period, 150 additional units of product are started into production and at the end of the period 40 units are still in ending work in process, 100% complete as to materials, and 60% complete as to direct labor and manufacturing overhead.

REQUIRED:

Calculate the denominator to be used in determining the cost per equivalent unit for direct materials, direct labor, and manufacturing overhead.

LO 2   **E22-4**   **Equivalent Units**   Department B, which had no beginning work in process, received 25,000 units from Department A during the period. There were 5,000 of those units still in work in process at the end of the period.

REQUIRED:

What is the denominator Department B would use in calculating its cost per equivalent unit for transferred in cost?

LO 2   **E22-5**   **Calculation of Equivalent Units**   Arapaho Toy Company produces one model of a doll in a single department. The month ended with 500 dolls in process 80% complete as to direct materials and 50% complete as to conversion costs. 27,000 dolls were transferred to finished goods during the month and 25,000 were started during the month. The beginning inventory was 60% complete as to direct materials and 40% complete as to conversion costs.

REQUIRED:

Determine the denominators to be used in the calculations of cost per equivalent unit for materials and conversion costs.

LO 2   **E22-6**   **Calculation of Equivalent Units**   Marlin Reel Company produces heavy duty saltwater fishing reels in two departments, Stamping and Assembly. During 19X4, 2,800 reels were completed and shipped to customers. There were no beginning inventories in either department. The stamping department had an ending inventory of 420 units, 100% complete as to direct materials and 50% complete as to conversion costs. They started 3,500 units into production during the period. The ending inventory of the assembly department was 100% complete as to transferred-in costs and direct materials, and 60% complete as to conversion costs.

REQUIRED:

Determine the denominators to be used in the calculations of cost per equivalent units for the cost items in each department.

LO 3   **E22-7**   **Cost per Equivalent Unit**   The beginning balance in Work in Process Inventory at Maco Manufacturing included $4,000 for direct labor. During the period, $50,000 of direct labor costs were incurred. During the period, 8,000 units were completed, and 2,000 units, 50% complete with respect to direct labor, remained in work in process.

REQUIRED:

Calculate the cost per equivalent unit for direct labor.

LO 2,3,4   **E22-8**   **Cost per Equivalent Unit, Costs Transferred Out**   Bimini Beach Wear manufactures one popular model swimsuit in a single production department. All materials are added at the beginning of the process. 5,000 units were started into production during May. 2,000 units were in beginning work in process (100% DM, 80% CC) and 1,000 units were in ending work in process (100% DM, 60% CC). The May production costs were:

	Direct Materials	Conversion Costs
Beginning work in process	$ 6,000	$ 6,400
Costs added in May	15,000	20,000

REQUIRED:

Compute the cost per equivalent unit for May and the cost transferred to Finished Goods Inventory.

LO 4

E22-9   **Costing Ending Work in Process**   Wachovia Parts Co. had 2,400 units in ending work in process at May 31. The units are 100% complete with respect to materials and 40% complete with respect to conversion costs. Their equivalent units of production and costs for May were:

	Cost per Equivalent Unit
Direct materials	$6
Direct labor	$2
Manufacturing overhead	$1

REQUIRED:

Calculate the cost of the ending work in process inventory at May 31.

LO 4

E22-10   **Costing for Goods Completed and Ending Work in Process**   Howell Hang-Gliders produces a single model, HM24, in a process system. At the end of October 19X7, there were four gliders in process, 60% complete as to labor and overhead. Eighty percent of the materials are added at the beginning of production and the other twenty percent is added immediately before transfer to the finished goods warehouse. Eighty-five gliders were completed during the month. Assume that direct materials cost per equivalent unit during October was $250 and the conversion cost per equivalent unit was $400.

REQUIRED:

Determine the cost of the ending work in process inventory and the cost transferred to Finished Goods Inventory.

LO 5

E22-11   **Production Cost Report for a Single Department Firm**   Dolphin Products Company manufactures swimfins in a single department. Use the following information to prepare a production cost report for Dolphin.

	Units
WIP, October 1, 19X9	
(100% D.M., 80% D.L., 60% MOH)	800
Units started into production in October	2,600
WIP, October 31, 19X9	
(100% D.M., 60% D.L., 40% MOH)	600
Cost Data:	
Beginning WIP:	
Direct material (100%)	$3,200
Direct labor	1,920
Manufacturing overhead	960

Costs added during October:

Direct material	$11,080
Direct labor	7,876
Manufacturing overhead	5,728

LO 5

E22-12   Production Cost Reports With Two Departments   Beta Products produces school desk tops which are sold for further manufacturing use. Production occurs in two departments, Cutting and Laminating. There were no beginning inventories in either department.

REQUIRED:

Prepare a January production cost report for each department using the following unit information for January 19X8.

Unit information:	*Cutting*	*Laminating*
Started into production	12,000	
Transferred in		11,500
Ending WIP (100% direct materials,		
80% conversion cost in each department.)	?	500
Cost entering production in January 19X8:	*Cutting*	*Laminating*
Direct materials	$24,000	$17,250
Direct labor	17,850	18,240
Applied overhead	8,925	9,120

PROBLEM SET A

LO 1

P22-1A   Product Cost Flows   Whitmor Bag produces a heavy kraft paper mailing package in a single department for the U.S. Postal Service. Activity for February 19X6, resulted in the production and shipment of 30,000 packaging bags at a cost of $.60 per bag. The cost consisted of 30% material cost, 50% labor cost, and 20% manufacturing overhead. There were no beginning or ending inventories of raw material, work in process, or finished goods. Whitmor uses a process costing system with a single work in process inventory account.

REQUIRED:

Trace the product costs through Whitmor's accounts with journal entries.

LO 1

P22-2A   Flow of Process Costs through Departments and Accounts   Apex Manufacturing produces a single homogeneous product in a continuous process which involves two departments. The following cost information was available for the two departments for March 19X4:

	Dept. I	*Dept. II*
WIP, 3/1/X4	$ 0	$ 0
Costs added during March:		
Direct material	14,000	6,000
Direct labor	4,000	10,000
Manufacturing overhead applied	28,000	18,000
Transferred-in costs	N/A	45,200
WIP, 3/31/X4	800	12,400

REQUIRED:

Trace the costs for Apex through the accounts by preparing the accounting entries directly into T-accounts to record the issue of direct materials, the cost of direct labor (paid in cash), the application of manufacturing overhead, and the transfer of the costs associated with completed products, for both departments.

LO 2,3,4   **P22-3A**   **Equivalent Units, Cost per Equivalent Unit, and Valuation of Ending Work in Process Inventory for a Single Department Manufacturer**   Marquita Manufacturing produces one type of air filter for use in jet aircraft in a single department. Parts are added at many points throughout the heavily automated process. August 19X2, production began with 600 filters in work in process, 80% complete as to materials and 70% complete as to conversion costs. During the month, an additional 3,200 units were started into process. Eight hundred filters were still incomplete at the end of the month, which were on average 60% complete as to materials and 50% complete as to conversion costs.

Department cost information for August:

	Beginning Work in Process	Added in August
Raw materials	$48,000	$317,400
Direct labor	12,600	94,500
Manufacturing overhead	84,000	590,900

REQUIRED:

In the format used in a production cost report:

a. Calculate the cost per equivalent unit for each of the three factors of production and in total.
b. Calculate the costs remaining in Work in Process Inventory on August 31, 19X2.
c. Discuss possible reasons as to why the cost of manufacturing overhead is high relative to the other two inputs.

LO 2,3,4   **P22-4A**   **Equivalent Units, Cost per Equivalent Unit, and Cost of Goods Completed for Two Departments**   Classi-Craft, Ltd. builds a high quality ski-board that it markets in the southeastern U.S. at $125. During March 19X0, information about inventory production to be sold in the summer market was as follows:

Unit information:

	Laminating	Finishing
Beginning WIP	2,000	3,000
Started into production	12,000	
Transferred-in		?
Ending WIP (100% DM, 60% DL, 60% MOH in each department)	1,800	1,500

Costs in beginning WIP, March 1, 19X0:

	Laminating	Finishing
Direct material	$80,000	$ 30,000
Direct labor	42,000	42,000
Manufacturing overhead	36,000	36,000
Transferred-in costs	N/A	300,000

Costs incurred in March 19X0:

	Laminating	Finishing
Direct materials	$480,000	$152,400
Direct labor	356,400	381,400
Manufacturing overhead	362,400	299,800
Transferred-in costs	N/A	?

REQUIRED:

a. Calculate the cost per equivalent unit for each of the two departments during the month of March.

b. Calculate the costs assigned to the units transferred to the finishing department from the laminating department during March and prepare the journal entry to record the transfer.

c. Calculate the costs assigned to the units transferred from the finishing department to Finished Goods Inventory during March and prepare the journal entry to record the transfer.

LO 3,4,5   **P22-5A   Production Cost Report for One Department**   Lo-tech is a laminator of cross-country skis. The production process is primarily highly skilled hand labor working with high quality hardwoods. Work in process is always large because each pair of skis is in process for three to three and one-half months. Each craftsperson must allow considerable time for drying adhesives in lamination as well as between coats of the high-gloss finish.

September 19X1 began with 3,000 units in process which were on average 60% complete as to direct materials and conversion costs. Four thousand units were started in process during the month and ending inventory consisted of 5,000 units which were on average 50% complete as to direct materials and conversion costs.

Cost information:

	Beginning Work in Process	**Costs Added in September**
Direct material	$144,000	$216,000
Direct labor	288,000	432,000
Manufacturing overhead	36,000	54,000

REQUIRED:

a. Prepare a production cost report for Lo-Tech for the month of September 19X1.

b. Prepare the journal entry to show the transfer of the units completed during September.

LO 3,4,5   **P22-6A   Production Cost Report for Two Departments**   Bellrite Statuary manufactures bronzed statues in two departments, Casting and Finishing. Materials are added at the start of the production process in each department while direct labor and manufacturing overhead are incurred evenly over the processes. Information for production activity and related costs for July 19X3 include:

Unit information:

	Casting Dept.	**Finishing Dept.**
Beginning WIP	1,000	800
Started during July	24,000	?
Ending WIP:		
(55% complete as to conversion)	1,100	
(80% complete as to conversion)		1,000

Cost information:

	Casting Dept.	**Finishing Dept.**
Beginning WIP:		
Direct material	$30,000	$ 8,000
Direct labor	22,500	4,000
Manufacturing overhead	11,250	2,000
Transferred-in costs		59,200

	Casting Dept.	Finishing Dept.
Costs added in July 19X3:		
Direct material	$745,000	$246,410
Direct labor	688,145	216,500
Manufacturing overhead	331,820	122,950

REQUIRED:

Prepare a production cost report for each of the two departments for July 19X3.

PROBLEM SET B

LO 1

P22-1B   **Product Cost Flows**   Alamo Corp. manufactures a model of the famous Texas shrine from which it takes its name. They are sold as souvenirs at the historic site. Activity for February 19X5 resulted in the production of 5,000 models at a cost of $1.20 each. The cost consisted of 45% direct material cost, 45% direct labor cost, and 10% manufacturing overhead. There were no units in the work in process or finished goods at the beginning or at the end of the month and there was no beginning or ending balance in the raw materials inventory account. Eighty percent of the units were sold during the month. Alamo uses a process costing system with a single work in process inventory account.

REQUIRED:

Use the above information to reconstruct journal entries related to production for February.

LO 1

P22-2B   **Flow of Process Costs through Departments and Accounts**   Toren Chemical Company produces a single product in two departments. The following costs relate to April 19X7.

	Dept. I	Dept. II
WIP, 4/1/X7	$ 26,000	$ 46,000
Costs added during April:		
Direct material	180,000	80,000
Direct labor	45,000	55,000
Manufacturing overhead	230,000	110,000
Transferred-in costs	N/A	?
WIP, 4/30/X7	0	36,000

REQUIRED:

Trace the April costs for Toren through the accounts by posting entries directly into T-accounts to record the issue of direct materials, the cost of direct labor (paid in cash), the application of manufacturing overhead, and the transfer of the costs associated with completed products, for both departments.

LO 2,3,4

P22-3B   **Equivalent Units and Cost per Equivalent Units, Transferred Cost and Ending Work in Process for One Department**   Chip's Chips, a producer of jumbo bags of potato chips, began the month of August 19X9, with 5,000 units in process that were 100% complete as to materials and 60% complete as to labor and overhead. They started 25,000 units into production during the month of which 4,000 remained in ending inventory 80% complete as to materials and 40% complete as to conversion costs. The costs included:

Beginning WIP:

Direct materials	$ 4,000
Direct labor	1,050
Manufacturing overhead	2,100

Costs added during the period:

Direct materials	$22,280
Direct labor	9,990
Manufacturing overhead	11,700

REQUIRED:

a. Calculate the cost per equivalent unit for each element of production cost and the total cost per equivalent unit for the month of August.
b. Calculate the cost of the units transferred to Finished Goods Inventory during August.
c. Calculate the cost of Work in Process Inventory at the end of August.

LO 2,3,4   **P22-4B**   **Equivalent Units, Cost per Equivalent Unit, and Cost of Goods Completed for Two Departments**   Production information is shown below for the Corinth Column Company for August 19X8. Corinth manufactures decorative columns used in residential construction. The columns are produced in two departments, Cutting and Assembly. The cutting department saws the eight identical parts for each column and routes interlocking slots on each side. The assembly department assembles and glues the eight sides and routes decorative patterns on the completed column. The units are delivered unfinished as some contractors prefer to paint them while others use a stain finish.

Unit information:

	Cutting	*Assembly*
Beginning WIP	200	300
Started into production	1,000	
Transferred-in		?
Ending WIP:		
(100% DM, 60% DL, 60% MOH)	100	
(80% DL, 80% MOH)		200

Costs in beginning WIP, August 1, 19X8:

	Cutting	*Assembly*
Direct material	$10,000	N/A
Direct labor	4,700	$ 3,660
Manufacturing overhead	3,550	2,600
Transferred-in costs	N/A	36,000

Costs incurred in August 19X8:

	Cutting	*Assembly*
Direct materials	$50,000	N/A
Direct labor	41,700	$37,140
Manufacturing overhead	31,250	24,600
Transferred-in costs	N/A	?

REQUIRED:

a. Calculate the cost per equivalent unit for each of the departments during the month of August.
b. Calculate the costs assigned to the units transferred to the assembly department from the cutting department during August and prepare the journal entry to record the transfer.
c. Calculate the costs assigned to the units transferred from the assembly department to Finished Goods Inventory during August and prepare the journal entry to record the transfer.

LO 3,4,5   **P22-5B**   **Production Cost Report for One Department**   Ferrous Fabricators manufactures steel studs for residential construction from steel sheets. The steel sheet material is cut, punched, and folded in a single department using heavy machinery with a minimum of labor. The steel is brought into the production department directly from the trucks which deliver it as it is needed. The work in process inventory is kept relatively small at all times. The finished studs are loaded directly into the customers' trucks for shipment from the production department. No inventories of raw materials or finished goods are kept on hand. Consequently, the only manufacturing accounts used are Work in Process Inventory and Cost of Goods Sold.

       The plant operated three weeks in December 19X6, closing for the holidays during the last week.

       There were 500 units in process which were 100% complete as to direct material and 60% complete as to conversion costs. Thirty-six thousand units were started in process during the month and ending inventory consisted of 100 units which were 100% complete as to direct materials and 50% complete as to conversion costs.

Cost information:

	Beginning Work in Process	Costs Added in December
Direct material	$350	$25,200
Direct labor	32	3,613
Manufacturing overhead	96	10,839

REQUIRED:

a. Prepare a production cost report for Ferrous for the month of December 19X6.
b. Prepare the journal entry to show the transfer of the units completed during December.

LO 3,4,5   **P22-6B**   **Production Cost Report for Two Departments**   HydraProducts, Inc., produces a sports beverage in two departments: Blending and Bottling. In each department, material is added at the start of the process while labor and overhead are assumed to be incurred evenly throughout the process.

       The following costs were incurred during April 19X4:

Unit information:	*Mixing*	*Bottling*
Beginning WIP	1,000	2,000
Started during April	100,000	?
Ending WIP		
(50% complete for conversion costs)	11,000	4,000

Cost information:	*Mixing*	*Bottling*
Beginning WIP:		
Direct material	$ 500	$ 400
Direct labor	400	200
Manufacturing overhead	200	100
Transferred-in cost	N/A	1,000
Costs added in April 19X4:		
Direct material	$60,000	$40,000
Direct labor	50,000	22,000
Manufacturing overhead	25,000	11,000
Transferred-in cost	N/A	?

REQUIRED:

Prepare a production cost report for each of the two departments of HydraProducts for April 19X4.

CRITICAL THINKING AND COMMUNICATING

C22-1 Vermont Production Company has been operating successfully for several years in the manufacture and sale of folding boat seats. The seats are marketed to both manufacturers of boats and as after-market products for boat owners. The manufacturing costs in the first of its two production departments, Framing, have increased noticeably over the first six months of 19X2. The costs in the second department, Upholstery, have remained relatively constant except for the costs transferred in from the framing department. The following costs per equivalent unit were incurred in the framing department during the period.

Framing Department Cost per Equivalent Unit:

	Direct Material	Direct Labor	Mfg. Overhead	Total Cost
January 19X2	$46.20	$24.00	$12.00	$82.20
February 19X2	45.10	24.40	12.20	81.70
March 19X2	46.05	24.70	12.35	83.10
April 19X2	46.25	25.80	12.90	84.95
May 19X2	46.40	26.40	13.20	86.00
June 19X2	46.50	27.70	13.85	88.05

There have been no changes in the design of the production process or in the production layout. Output has remained constant per month over the period as has the number of direct labor hours worked. Material price increases have been very low. The labor contract, which includes a provision for time and one-half pay for overtime, is still in force through October 19X2, with the wage rate constant. The overapplied manufacturing overhead figure has increased each month throughout the six-month period. This has not occurred in the prior years.

REQUIRED:

a. Comment on the manufacturing overhead applied during the period. Consider what has caused the increase and what might be observed concerning the application base.
b. Comment on the change in the cost per equivalent unit for labor. Discuss a possible cause and an approach for management to seek a solution.
c. Comment on the change in the material cost during the period.

C22-2   Thermo Chemical, a company that produces paint stripper, is considering ways to treat the costs of "wasted units." At the start of December, there were 150,000 gallons in beginning work in process. During December, 600,000 gallons were started. Of the 750,000 units to account for, 150,000 gallons remained in process at the end of December. These units were 100% complete with respect to material and 20% complete with respect to conversion costs. 300,000 gallons were completed during April and, unfortunately, 300,000 gallons were wasted due to worker error. On two separate occasions, incorrect quantities of chemicals were added and batches of paint stripper were ruined.

Top management at Thermo has suggested that the cost associated with the production errors should be buried in the cost of the units completed and the units in process. This would result in cost of units completed of $1,528,182 and cost of ending work in process of $292,818 calculated as shown on the following page.

REQUIRED:

Assume you are the controller. Write a brief memo to Milton Stone, CEO at Thermo Chemical, commenting on the appropriateness of the proposed approach.

Thermo Chemical
Production Cost Report
December 19X1

Quantity Reconciliation:

Units in beginning WIP	150,000
Units started	600,000
Units to account for	750,000
Units completed	300,000
Units in ending WIP (100% material, 20% conversion costs)	150,000
Wasted units	300,000
Units accounted for	750,000

Cost Per Equivalent Unit Calculation:

Cost:	Material	Labor	Overhead	Total
Beginning WIP	$105,000	$ 45,000	$ 90,000	$ 240,000
Cost incurred during April	420,000	387,000	774,000	1,581,000
Total	$525,000	$432,000	$864,000	$1,821,000

Units:				
Units completed	300,000	300,000	300,000	
Equivalent units, ending WIP	150,000	30,000	30,000	
Total	450,000	330,000	330,000	

Cost per equivalent unit $1.16667 + $1.30909 + $2.61818 = $5.09394

Cost Reconciliation:

Total cost to account for		$1,821,000
Cost of completed units transferred to finished goods ($300,000 x $5.09394)		$1,528,182
Cost of ending WIP:		
Material (150,000 equivalent units x $1.16667)	$175,000	
Labor (30,000 equivalent units x $1.30909)	39,273	
Overhead (30,000 equivalent units x $2.61818)	78,545	292,818
Total cost accounted for		$1,821,000

CHAPTER 23

Cost-Volume-Profit Relationships

Mary Stuart, vice president of marketing for Union Skate Company, anticipates the company can increase sales of its deluxe in-line skates by 1,000 pairs if it launches an advertising campaign costing $80,000. The skates sell for $150 per pair. In the past year, the company produced and sold 20,000 pairs at a total cost of $2,940,000. Thus, last year's volume was 20,000 pairs; revenue, $3,000,000; costs, $2,940,000; and profit related to this model, $60,000. Should Union Skate launch the advertising campaign? The answer depends on how cost and profit will change in response to the 1,000-unit increase in volume.

Mary knows that advertising costs and revenues will increase by $80,000 and $150,000 (1,000 x $150), respectively. If no other costs change (i.e., all other costs are fixed), additional profits will be $70,000 ($150,000 – $80,000). This means profits would more than double as a result of the advertising. However, Mary believes some other costs will increase in response to the increase in volume. Suppose the costs are completely variable and increase in proportion to increases in volume. Last year, costs were $2,940,000 for 20,000 pairs of skates or $147 per pair. Thus, costs might be expected to increase by $147,000 if Union Skates produces and sells 1,000 additional pairs. Together with the $80,000 advertising cost, total costs will increase by $227,000. Since revenue will only increase by $150,000, profits would decrease by $77,000 as a result of the advertising campaign. Thus, if costs are completely variable, Mary should recommend that the advertising campaign not be implemented.

	Assume All Costs Fixed	Assume All Costs Variable
Additional revenue	$150,000	$150,000
Additional costs:		
Advertising	80,000	80,000
Other	0	147,000
Total additional costs	$ 80,000	$227,000
Effect on profit	$ 70,000	$ 77,000

Mary knows that neither analysis is appropriate because the costs of manufacturing the skates are neither 100 percent fixed nor 100 percent variable. How can she determine how costs and profit change in response to changes in volume? The method managerial accountants use to understand how costs and profits change when a company's volume changes is referred to as **cost-volume-profit (C-V-P) analysis**. In this chapter, we develop the tools to analyze cost-volume-profit relationships. These tools will help you solve the type of problem Mary faces.

LEARNING OBJECTIVES

1. Identify the common cost behavior patterns.
2. Estimate the relationship between cost and activity using account analysis, the high-low method, and scattergraphs.
3. Perform cost-volume-profit analysis for single products.
4. Perform cost-volume-profit analysis for multiple products.
5. Discuss differences between variable and full costing (Appendix 23-A).
6. Discuss how income will differ between variable and full costing when the number of units produced does not equal the number of units sold (Appendix 23-A).

LO 1

Identify the common cost behavior patterns.

COMMON COST BEHAVIOR PATTERNS

To perform C-V-P analysis, you need to know how costs behave when volume changes. In this section, some common patterns are presented. While these patterns may not provide exact descriptions of how costs behave in response to changes in volume or activity, they are reasonable approximations. The common cost behavior patterns discussed are *variable costs*, *fixed costs*, and *mixed costs*. Variable and fixed costs were briefly introduced earlier in the text. A more complete discussion is provided here.

Variable Costs

Variable costs are those that change in response to changes in volume or activity. Managerial accountants typically assume that variable costs change *in proportion* to changes in activity. Thus, if activity increases by 10 percent, then variable costs will also increase by 10 percent. Some common variable costs are direct and indirect materials, direct labor, energy, and sales commissions. Exactly how activity should be measured in analyzing a variable cost depends on the situation. At McDonald's restaurants, food costs vary with the number of customers served. At United Airlines, fuel costs vary with the number of miles flown. In these situations, number of customers and number of miles are good measures of activity.

Suppose Union Skate Company's variable costs equal $100 per pair of skates. In this case, total variable costs at a production level of 5,000 pairs (the measure of activity) are equal to $500,000 ($100 x 5,000), while total variable costs at 25,000 pairs are equal to $2,500,000 ($100 x 25,000). A graph of the relationship between total variable costs and production is provided in Illustration 23-1. Note that while total variable costs increase with production, variable costs per pair remain at $100.

ILLUSTRATION 23-1 Variable Cost Behavior

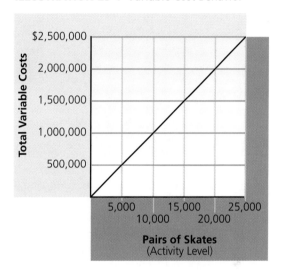

Fixed Costs

Fixed costs are those that do not change in response to changes in activity levels. Some typical fixed costs are depreciation, supervisory salaries, and building maintenance. Suppose Union Skate Company's fixed costs per year are $940,000. A graph of the relationship between fixed costs and production is provided in Illustration 23-2. Irrespective of the number of skates produced, the amount of total fixed costs remains at $940,000. However, the amount of fixed costs per pair does change with changes in the level of activity. When activity increases, the amount of fixed costs per pair decreases because the fixed costs are spread over more units. For example, at 5,000 pairs of skates, the fixed costs per pair are $188 ($940,000 ÷ 5,000), while at 25,000 pairs, the fixed costs per pair are only $37.60 ($940,000 ÷ 25,000).

Mixed Costs

Mixed costs are those that contain both variable cost and fixed cost elements. These costs are sometimes referred to as *semivariable costs*. Accountants often work with cost information that results from summing fixed and variable cost items. For example, total production cost is composed of material, labor, and both fixed and variable overhead cost items. Therefore, total production cost is a mixed cost. Some individual costs are also mixed costs. For example, a salesperson may be paid $30,000 per year (fixed amount) plus commissions equal to

ILLUSTRATION 23-2 Fixed Cost Behavior

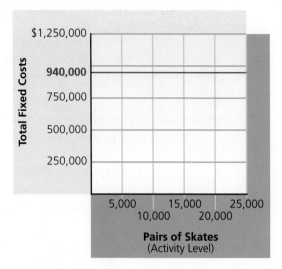

1 percent of sales (variable amount). In this case, the salesperson's total compensation is a mixed cost.

Suppose Union Skate Company's total manufacturing cost is composed of $940,000 of fixed costs per year and $100 of variable costs per pair of skates. In this case, total manufacturing cost is a mixed cost. A graph of the cost is presented in Illustration 23-3. Note that the total cost line intersects the vertical axis at $940,000 (just below the $1,000,000 point). This is the amount of fixed costs per year. From this point, total cost increases by $100 for every pair of skates produced. Thus, at 25,000 pairs the total cost is $3,440,000, or $940,000 of fixed costs and $2,500,000 of variable costs ($100 x 25,000).

ILLUSTRATION 23-3 Mixed Cost Behavior

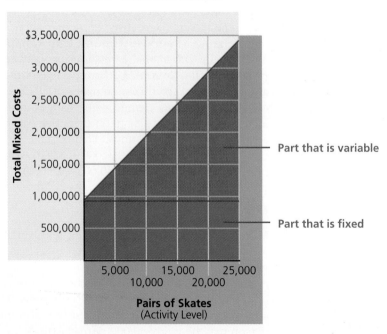

Estimate the relationship between cost and activity using account analysis, the high-low method, and scattergraphs.

COST ESTIMATION METHODS

To predict how much cost a company will incur at various activity levels, the managerial accountant must know how much of the total cost is fixed and how much is variable. In many cases, cost information is not broken down into fixed and variable cost components. Therefore, the accountant must know how to estimate fixed and variable costs from available information. In this section, we present four techniques for estimating the amount of fixed and variable costs: account analysis, scattergraph approach, high-low method, and regression analysis.

Account Analysis

One of the most common approaches to estimating fixed and variable costs, **account analysis** requires that the accountant use his or her professional judgment to classify cost accounts as either fixed or variable. The total of the costs classified as variable can be divided by a measure of activity to calculate the variable costs per unit of activity. The total of the costs classified as fixed provides the estimate of fixed costs. Return to the Union Skate Company example. For the past year, the cost of producing 20,000 pairs of deluxe in-line skates was $2,940,000. Account analysis would require a detailed analysis of the accounts that comprise the $2,940,000 of production costs. Suppose last year's costs were as follows:

Production Cost Report	
Deluxe In-Line Skates	
Production Costs	**20,000 Pairs**
Materials	$1,095,000
Direct labor	1,005,000
Supervisor salaries	350,000
Rent	60,000
Utilities	50,000
Depreciation	380,000
Total	$2,940,000

Using professional judgment, the accountant may decide that materials and direct labor are variable costs and all other items are fixed costs. In this case, variable and fixed costs are estimated as in Illustration 23-4. The accountant estimated total production costs as $840,000 of fixed costs per year, plus $105 of variable costs for each pair of skates produced.

An individual cost item does not need to be classified as either 100 percent fixed or 100 percent variable. For example, part of supervisor salaries and part of utilities may also be variable. In this case, the accountant can use his or her judgment to refine estimates using account analysis. Suppose the accountant believes that approximately 50 percent of supervisor salaries and utilities are variable. As indicated in Illustration 23-5, the revised estimate of total variable costs would then amount to $2,300,000, or $115.00 per pair of skates, while the revised estimate of fixed costs would amount to $640,000.

ILLUSTRATION 23-4 Estimate of Variable and Fixed Costs

	Variable Cost Estimate	
Materials	$1,095,000	
Direct labor	1,005,000	
Total	$2,100,000	(a)
Production	20,000	(b)
Variable cost per unit	$105	(a) ÷ (b)

	Fixed Cost Estimate	
Supervisor salaries	$350,000	
Rent	60,000	
Utilities	50,000	
Depreciation	380,000	
Total per year	$840,000	

ILLUSTRATION 23-5 Revised Estimate of Variable and Fixed Costs

	Variable Cost Estimate	
Materials	$1,095,000	
Direct labor	1,005,000	
Supervisor salaries (50% of $350,000)	175,000	
Utilities (50% of $50,000)	25,000	
Total	$2,300,000	(a)
Production	20,000	(b)
Variable cost per unit	$115.00	(a) ÷ (b)

	Fixed Cost Estimate	
Supervisor salaries (50% of $350,000)	$175,000	
Rent	60,000	
Utilities (50% of $50,000)	25,000	
Depreciation	380,000	
Total per year	$640,000	

With these estimates, how much cost would Union Skate Company expect to incur if it produced 22,000 pairs of skates? With 22,000 pairs, variable costs are estimated as $2,530,000; fixed costs as $640,000. Therefore, total cost of $3,170,000 would be expected.

Expected Annual Cost of 22,000 Pairs of Deluxe In-Line Skates	
Variable costs (22,000 x $115.00)	$2,530,000
Fixed costs per year	640,000
Total	$3,170,000

The account analysis method is somewhat subjective. That is, different accountants who view the same set of facts might reach different conclusions regarding which costs are fixed and which costs are variable. In spite of the method's limitation, most accountants view it as an important tool for estimating fixed and variable costs.

Scattergraph Approach

In some cases, an accountant may use cost information from several reporting periods to estimate how costs change in response to changes in activity. Weekly, monthly, or quarterly reports are particularly useful sources of cost information. However, annual reports are not very useful because the relationship between costs and activity generally is not consistent or stable over several years. Suppose the monthly production and cost information provided in Illustration 23-6 is available for the Union Skate Company.

ILLUSTRATION 23-6 Monthly Production Cost Information

Month	Skate Production (Pairs)	Cost
January	750	$ 170,000
February	1,000	175,000
March	1,250	205,000
April	1,750	250,000
May	2,000	265,000
June	2,250	275,000
July	3,000	400,000
August	2,750	350,000
September	2,500	300,000
October	1,250	210,000
November	1,000	190,000
December	500	150,000
Total	20,000	$2,940,000

One way to gain insight into the relationship between production cost and activity is by plotting the costs and activity levels. The plot of the data is referred to as a **scattergraph** and the scattergraph for these data is presented in Illustration 23-7. Typically, scattergraphs are prepared with cost measured on the vertical axis and activity level measured on the horizontal axis. Each point on the scattergraph represents one pair of cost and activity values.

The scattergraph in Illustration 23-7 provides a picture of what costs might be at different activity levels. For example, suppose Union Skate Company needed to estimate costs for 1,500 pairs of skates. The graph shows that costs will be approximately $225,000 when the company produces 1,500 pairs of skates.

High-Low Method

If multiple observations of cost and activity are available, **the high-low method** can estimate fixed and variable cost components. This method fits a straight line to the data points representing the highest and lowest levels of activity. The slope of the line is the estimate of variable costs and the intercept is the estimate of fixed costs. Using the data in Illustration 23-6, the highest level of production activity is 3,000 pairs in July with a corresponding cost of $400,000; the lowest level is 500 pairs in December with a corresponding cost of $150,000.

ILLUSTRATION 23-7 Scattergraph of Cost and Product Information

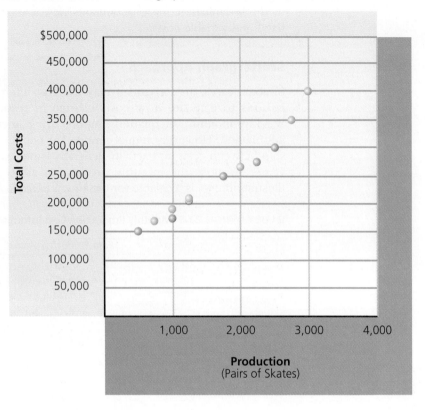

The slope is equal to the change in cost divided by the change in activity. In moving from the lowest to the highest levels of activity, cost changes by $250,000 and activity changes by 2,500 pairs. Thus, the estimate of variable costs (the slope) is $100.

$$\text{Estimate of Variable Costs} = \frac{\$400,000 - \$150,000}{3,000 - 500} = \$100 \text{ per pair}$$

Once obtained, an estimate of variable cost can be used to calculate an estimate of fixed costs. The amount of fixed costs is calculated as the difference between total costs and estimated variable costs. For example, at the lowest level of activity (500 pairs), total costs are $150,000. Since variable costs are $100 per pair, variable costs are $50,000 of the total costs. Thus, the remaining cost of $100,000 must be the amount of fixed costs. As indicated in the following calculation, the same estimated fixed costs amount ($100,000) works with either the lowest or the highest level of activity.

Estimate Using Lowest Activity		*Estimate Using Highest Activity*	
Total costs	$150,000	Total costs	$400,000
Less: Estimated variable costs (500 x $100)	50,000	Less: Estimated variable costs (3,000 x $100)	300,000
Estimated fixed costs per month	$100,000	Estimated fixed costs per month	$100,000

Be careful to note that since monthly data are used in this example, the fixed costs calculated are the fixed costs *per month*. If annual data were used, the fixed costs calculated would be the fixed costs *per year*.

Using the estimates from the high-low method, the straight-line cost equation is:

Total Costs = $100,000 of Fixed Costs + ($100 x Level of Activity)

Using this equation, Union Skate can predict total costs for various activity levels. For example, at an activity level of 1,500 pairs, Union Skate would expect to incur $250,000 of total cost.

$250,000 = $100,000 of Fixed Costs + ($100 x 1,500)

Illustration 23-8 presents a graph of the straight-line cost equation that is estimated using the high-low method. Notice that the cost line passes through the high-low data points but no others because only these two data points (and no others) were used to estimate the slope and intercept. The high-low estimate in Illustration 23-8 does not adequately fit the available data. Most of the data points lie below the high-low straight line. A significant weakness of the high-low method is that it uses only two data points when additional data may be available. Furthermore, the two data points may not represent the general relationship estimated between cost and activity. By definition, these two points represent unusually high and unusually low levels of activity, and costs at these levels may also be unusual. For example, at its highest level of activity, Union Skate may hire part-time workers to supplement its normal work force. These workers may not be as efficient as other workers, and Union Skate's costs may be unusually high.

ILLUSTRATION 23-8 High-Low Estimate of Production Costs

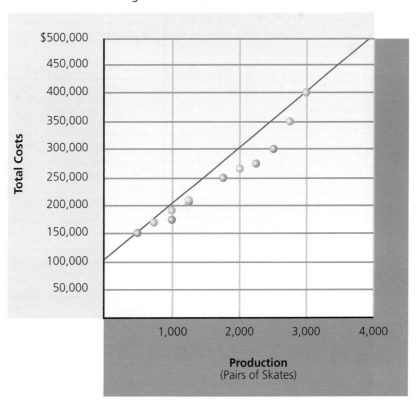

Regression Analysis

Regression analysis is a statistical technique that uses all available data points to estimate the intercept and slope of a cost equation. The line fitted to the data by regression analysis is the best straight-line fit to the data. Regression analysis programs are widely available, and many have been written for microcomputers or are built-in to some hand-held calculators. The topic of regression analysis is covered in introductory statistics classes and in cost accounting classes. For our purposes, we simply note that application of regression analysis to the data in Illustration 23-8 yields the following equation:

Total Costs = $93,619 of Fixed Costs + ($90.83 x Level of Activity)

At a production level of 1,500 units, the amount of total cost estimated is $229,864.

$229,864 = $93,619 of Fixed Costs + ($90.83 x 1,500)

This is less than the $250,000 estimated using the high-low cost equation. A graph of the regression analysis estimate of cost is presented in Illustration 23-9. Notice that the regression line better fits the data than does the line estimated with the high-low method. Because the regression line is more consistent with Union Skate's past data, it will probably provide more accurate predictions of future costs.

ILLUSTRATION 23-9 Regression Analysis Estimate of Production Cost

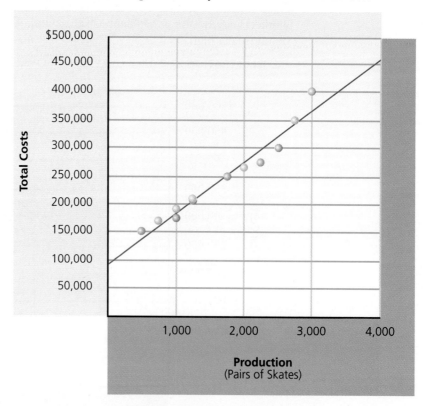

The Relevant Range

When working with estimates of fixed and variable costs, remember they are only valid for a limited range of activity. The **relevant range** is the range of activity for which estimates and predictions are likely to be accurate. Outside the relevant range, estimates of fixed and variable costs may not be very useful.

In some cases, actual costs behave differently from the common cost behavior patterns that we have discussed. All of those patterns imply linear (straight-line) relationships between cost and activity. In the real world, some costs behave as curves rather than straight lines. For example when companies produce unusually large quantities, production may not be as efficient and costs would increase more rapidly than the rate implied by a straight line. This may not be a serious limitation for a straight line approach as long as the predictions and estimates are restricted to the relevant range. Consider Illustration 23-10. Note that while the relationship between cost and activity is a curve, a straight line would closely approximate the relationship between cost and activity within the relevant range.

ILLUSTRATION 23-10 Relevant Range

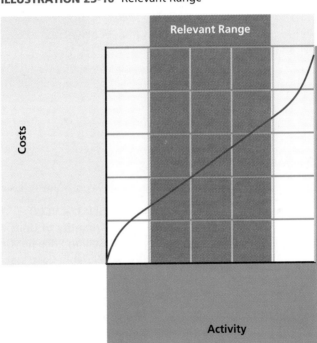

COST-VOLUME-PROFIT ANALYSIS

LO 3
Perform cost-volume-profit analysis for single products.

Once a company determines its fixed and variable costs, it can then conduct cost-volume-profit analysis (C-V-P). Basically, *C-V-P analysis* explores the relationships among costs, volume or activity levels, and profit.

Break-Even Point

One of the primary uses of C-V-P analysis is to calculate the break-even point. The **break-even point** is the number of units a company must sell to earn a zero profit (i.e., break-even). The break-even point is indicated in the profit graph presented in Illustration 23-11. At the point where sales revenue equals total costs (composed of fixed and variable cost) the company "breaks even."

ILLUSTRATION 23-11 Profit Graph and Break-Even Point

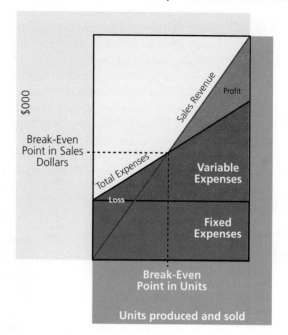

Profit Equation

The calculation of the break-even point relies on the following profit equation:

$$\text{Profit} = SP(x) - VC(x) - TFC$$

where

$$x = \text{Quantity of Units Produced and Sold}$$
$$SP = \text{Selling Price per Unit}$$
$$VC = \text{Variable Costs per Unit}$$
$$TFC = \text{Total Fixed Costs}$$

As stated in the equation, profit is equal to revenues (Selling Price per unit times Quantity) minus variable costs (Variable Costs per Unit times Quantity) minus total fixed costs. To calculate the break-even point, simply set profit to zero, insert the appropriate selling price, variable costs, and fixed costs and solve for the quantity (x).

Suppose Union Skate Company sells its deluxe in-line skates for $150 per unit (a pair of skates). Variable costs are estimated to be $100 per unit, and total fixed costs are estimated to be $100,000 per month. How many units must Union Skate sell to break even in a given month? To answer this question, solve the equation above for a particular value of x.

$$0 = \$150\,(x) - \$100\,(x) - \$100,000$$
$$0 = \$50\,(x) - \$100,000$$
$$\$50\,(x) = \$100,000$$
$$x = 2,000$$

Solving for x yields a break-even quantity of 2,000 pairs of skates. If management prefers the break-even quantity expressed in dollars of sales, rather than in units, the quantity is simply multiplied by the selling price of $150 to yield $300,000.

Margin of Safety

Obviously, managers want a level of sales greater than break-even sales. To express how close they expect to be to the break-even level, managers may calculate the **margin of safety**, which is the difference between the expected level of sales and break-even sales. For example, Union Skate Company's break-even level of sales is $300,000. If it expects to have sales of $420,000, the margin of safety is $120,000.

Contribution Margin

The profit equation can be rewritten by combining the terms with x in them.

$$\text{Profit} = (SP - VC)(x) - TFC$$

The difference between the selling price and variable costs per unit is referred to as the **contribution margin**. Each unit sold contributes this amount to cover fixed costs and increase profits. Consider what happens when sales increase by one unit. The firm benefits from revenue equal to the selling price, but it also incurs increased costs equal to the variable costs per unit. Since fixed costs are unaffected by changes in volume, they do not enter into the analysis.

If we solve the profit equation for the sales quantity in units (x), we get the following expression:

$$x = \frac{\text{Profit} + TFC}{\text{Contribution Margin}}$$

This is a handy formula for calculating the break-even point and solving for the quantity needed to earn various profit levels. Union Skate Company's amount of fixed costs is $100,000 per month. With a selling price of $150 and variable costs of $100, the contribution margin is $50. Using the formula implies that Union Skate must sell 2,000 units to break even each month.

$$2,000 = \frac{0 + \$100,000}{\$50}$$

Now Union Skate Company's management wants to know how many units the company must sell to achieve a profit of $40,000 in a given month. Using the formula implies that Union Skate must sell 2,800 units to achieve a profit of $40,000.

$$2,800 = \frac{\$40,000 + \$100,000}{\$50}$$

Contribution Margin Ratio

The **contribution margin ratio** is equal to the contribution margin per unit divided by the selling price.

$$\text{Contribution Margin Ratio} = \frac{SP - VC}{SP}$$

It measures the contribution of every sales dollar to covering fixed costs and generating a profit. Consider a company whose product has a selling price of $20 and requires variable costs of $15. In this case, the contribution margin ratio is 25 percent. Since its contribution margin per dollar of sales is 25 percent, the company will earn $.25 for every additional dollar of sales.

$$\text{Contribution Margin Ratio} = \frac{\$20 - \$15}{\$20} = 25\%$$

We can express the profit equation in terms of the contribution margin ratio as:

$$\textbf{Sales (in dollars)} = \frac{\textbf{Profit + TFC}}{\textbf{Contribution Margin Ratio}}$$

Union Skate Company can use this formula to calculate the amount of sales needed to earn a profit of $40,000 in a given month. Its contribution margin ratio is $.3333 (Contribution Margin of $50 ÷ Selling Price of $150). Thus, sales of $420,000 are needed.

$$\$420,000 = \frac{\$40,000 + \$100,000}{.3333}$$

"What If" Analysis

The profit equation can also show how profit will be affected by various options management is considering. Such analysis is sometimes referred to as **"what if" analysis** because it examines *what* will happen *if* a particular action is taken.

Change in Fixed and Variable Costs.   Suppose Union Skate Company currently is selling 3,200 pairs of skates per month at a unit price of $150. Variable costs per unit are $100 and total fixed costs are $100,000 per month. Management is considering a change in the production process that will increase fixed costs per month by $50,000 but decrease variable costs to only $80 per unit. How would this change affect the company's monthly profit? Using the profit equation and assuming there will be no change in the selling price or the quantity sold, monthly profit under the alternative will be $74,000.

$$\text{Profit} = \$150\,(3,200) - \$80\,(3,200) - \$150,000 = \$74,000$$

Without the change, profit will equal only $60,000.

$$\text{Profit} = \$150\,(3,200) - \$100\,(3,200) - \$100,000 = \$60,000$$

Thus, it appears that the change in the production process is advisable. However, before making a decision, management may wish to consider how the action affects the company's break-even point. With the new production process, Union Skate will face a higher level of fixed costs and a higher break-even level. Before the change, its break-even point was 2,000 units. If Union Skate implements the new production process, its break-even point will change to 2,143 units. Since there is no significant difference in these break-even points, the change in the production process appears appropriate.

Old Break-Even Point	New Break-Even Point
$\frac{\$100,000 \text{ Fixed Costs}}{\$50 \text{ Contribution Margin}} = 2,000$ Units	$\frac{\$150,000 \text{ Fixed Costs}}{\$70 \text{ Contribution Margin}} = 2,143$ Units

Change in Selling Price.   Any one of the variables in the profit equation can be considered in light of changes in the other variables. For example, suppose Union Skate's management wanted to know what the selling price would have to be to earn a profit of $80,000 if it sells 3,000 units in a given month. To answer this question, all of the relevant information is organized in terms of the profit equation and the equation then is solved for the selling price.

$$\$80,000 = SP\,(3,000) - \$100\,(3,000) - \$100,000$$
$$SP\,(3,000) = \$480,000$$
$$SP = \$160$$

LO 4
Perform cost-volume-profit analysis for multiple products.

MULTIPRODUCT ANALYSIS

The preceding examples have illustrated C-V-P analysis for a single product. C-V-P analysis can be extended to cover multiple products. In the following sections we demonstrate the use of the contribution margin and the contribution margin ratio in performing C-V-P analysis for a company with multiple products.

Contribution Margin Approach

If the products a company sells are similar (various flavors of ice cream, various types of calculators, various types of boats), the weighted average contribution margin per unit can be used in C-V-P analysis. For example, suppose the Hightech Calculator Company produces two types of calculators. Model A sells for $30 and requires $15 of variable cost per unit. Model B sells for $50 and requires $20 of variable costs per unit. Further, Hightech typically sells two Model A's for one Model B. To calculate the weighted average contribution margin, Hightech must first consider the fact that twice as many A's as B's are sold. Since two Model As are sold for each Model B, the contribution margin of A is multiplied by 2 and the contribution margin of B is multiplied by 1. The sum is then divided by 3 units to yield the weighted average contribution margin per unit of $20. (See Illustration 23-12.)

ILLUSTRATION 23-12 Calculation of Weighted Average Contribution Margin

	Contribution Margin Model A	Contribution Margin Model B
Selling price	$30	$50
Variable cost	15	20
Contribution margin	$15	$30

$$\text{Weighted Average Contribution Margin} = \frac{2\,(\$15) + 1\,(\$30)}{3} = \$20 \text{ per unit}$$

Now, suppose Hightech Company's fixed costs equal $100,000. How many calculators must it sell to break even? Working with the weighted average contribution margin, Hightech calculates its break even point as 5,000 calculators.

$$5{,}000 \text{ units} = \frac{0 + \$100{,}000}{\$20} \quad \begin{array}{l}\text{(Profit + Total Fixed Costs)}\\ \text{(Weighted Average Contribution Margin)}\end{array}$$

The 5,000 units sold to break even would be made up of the typical two-to-one mix. Thus, Hightech must sell 3,333 Model As (2/3 of 5,000) and 1,667 (1/3 of 5,000) Model Bs to break even.

Contribution Margin Ratio Approach

If a company sells very different products, it should perform C-V-P analysis using the contribution margin ratio. Consider a large department store such as

Sears. Sears sells literally thousands of different products. In this setting, it does not make sense to ask how many *units* Sears must sell to break even or how many *units* Sears must sell to generate a profit of $100,000. Because the costs and selling prices of the various items sold are considerably different, analyzing these types of questions in terms of number of units is not useful. Instead, these questions are addressed in terms of sales dollars. It is perfectly reasonable to ask how much must *sales* be to break even or how much must *sales* be to generate a profit of $100,000. To answer these questions, the contribution margin ratio, rather than the contribution margin per unit, is used.

Suppose Price-Low Drug Store is interested in using C-V-P analysis to analyze its operations. The company has three major departments—drugs, cosmetics, and household products—each of which sells a large number of different products. After performing a detailed study of fixed and variable costs in the prior year, the company prepared the analysis of departmental profitability indicated in Illustration 23-13.

ILLUSTRATION 23-13 Profitability Analysis of Departments

Price-Low Drug Store Profitability Analysis For the Year Ended December 31, 19X1				
	Drugs	*Cosmetics*	*Household Products*	*Total*
Sales	$1,000,000	$700,000	$460,000	$2,160,000
Less variable costs:				
Merchandise	$ 600,000	$550,000	$260,000	$1,410,000
Wages	100,000	70,000	40,000	210,000
Total variable costs	$ 700,000	$620,000	$300,000	$1,620,000
Contribution margin	$ 300,000	$ 80,000	$160,000	$ 540,000
Contribution margin ratio	.30	.1143	.3478	.25
Less fixed costs:				
Utilities				$ 40,000
Rent				80,000
Management salaries				180,000
Total fixed costs				$300,000
Company profit				$240,000

Given the information in the report, what is Price-Low Drug Store's break-even level of sales? To answer this question, the total amount of fixed costs is divided by the contribution margin ratio for the store. The contribution margin ratio can be calculated by dividing the total contribution margin for the store by total store sales. Since the contribution margin is $540,000 and sales are $2,160,000, this yields a contribution margin ratio of .25. Thus, Price-Low's break-even sales are $1,200,000.

$$\$1,200,000 \ = \ \frac{\$300,000 \ \text{(Total Fixed Costs)}}{.25 \quad \text{(Contribution Margin Ratio)}}$$

The contribution margin ratio can also be used to analyze the effect on net income of a change in total company sales. Suppose in the coming year, Price-Low's management believes total company sales will increase by 20 percent and is interested in assessing the effect of this increase on overall company profitability. If sales increase by $432,000 (i.e., 20 percent), the contribution margin and net income will increase by $108,000 (i.e., .25 x $432,000).

Note that this approach makes one very important assumption: The increase in sales will result in increases in drugs, cosmetics, and household products in the same proportion as current sales. If this assumption is not warranted, then the contribution margin ratios of the three departments must be weighted by their share of the increase. For example, suppose the company believes sales will increase by $432,000 but expects the increase will be made up of a $200,000 increase in drug sales, a $200,000 increase in cosmetics sales, and a $32,000 increase in sales of household products. To calculate the effect on net income, Price-Low must use the contribution margin ratios of the specific departments. The expected increase in profit is $93,989.60.

Department	Increase in Sales	Contribution Margin Ratio	Increase in Profit
Drugs	$200,000	.3000	$60,000.00
Cosmetics	200,000	.1143	22,860.00
Household products	32,000	.3478	11,129.60
Total increase in profit			$93,989.60

Why did this analysis yield a smaller increase in net income than the preceding analysis? The preceding analysis assumed the increase in sales would be proportionate to the current mix of drugs, cosmetics, and household products. The current analysis assumes that of the $432,000 increase in sales only $32,000 is due to household products. Since household products is the product line with the highest contribution margin ratio, profit will be less if proportionately less of this profitable product line is sold.

ASSUMPTIONS IN C-V-P ANALYSIS

Whenever C-V-P analysis is performed, managers make a number of assumptions that affect the validity of the analysis. Perhaps the primary assumption is that costs can be accurately separated into their fixed and variable components. For some companies, this a very difficult and costly task. An additional assumption is that fixed costs remain fixed and variable costs per unit do not change over the activity levels of interest. With large changes in activity, this assumption may not be valid. In spite of these assumptions, most managers use C-V-P analysis to explore various profit targets and to perform "what if" analysis.

Union Skate Company

At the beginning of the chapter, Mary Stuart was considering whether to spend $80,000 to increase sales of the deluxe in-line skates by 1,000 units. The skates sell for $150 per pair. Suppose Mary used account analysis, and determined that variable costs per pair are $100. Using the techniques developed in the chapter and the information above, would you recommend that Mary start the advertising campaign? Hopefully, you concluded that the advertising campaign should *not* be started because profit will decrease by $30,000.

(Contribution Margin x Increase in Units) – Increase in Fixed Costs = Change in Profit
($50 x 1,000)   – $80,000   =   ($30,000)

SUMMARY

Identify the common cost behavior patterns. Several common cost behavior patterns exist: variable, fixed, and mixed. Variable costs are those that change in response to changes in volume or activity. Fixed costs remain constant across activity levels. Mixed costs contain both variable and fixed cost components.

Estimate the relationship between cost and activity using account analysis, the high-low method, and scattergraphs. Accountants use account analysis, the scattergraph approach, and the high-low method to estimate the relationship between cost and activity. Account analysis requires that the accountant use his or her judgment to classify expense accounts as either fixed or variable costs. A scattergraph is prepared by plotting cost and activity levels. It presents a picture of what costs might be at different activity levels. The high-low method fits a straight line to the costs at the highest and the lowest activity levels. Accountants also use regression analysis to estimate the relationship between cost and activity. Regression analysis is an advanced approach, however, and the chapter provided only a brief introduction to the method.

Perform cost-volume-profit analysis for single products. Once a company estimates its fixed and variable costs, it can perform cost-volume-profit analysis. C-V-P analysis makes use of the profit equation:

$$\text{Profit} = \text{Sales} - \text{Variable Cost} - \text{Fixed Cost}$$

Managers can use the profit equation to perform "what if" analysis. The effect of changing various components of the equation can be explored by solving the equation for the variable affected by the change. Specific examples include solving for the break-even point or solving the equation to determine the level of volume required to achieve a certain level of profit. Managers can determine the number of units that must be sold or the sales dollars needed to achieve a specified profit level using the following formulas:

$$\text{Number of Units} = \frac{\text{Fixed Cost} + \text{Profit}}{\text{Contribution Margin}} \qquad \text{Sales Dollars} = \frac{\text{Fixed Cost} + \text{Profit}}{\text{Contribution Margin Ratio}}$$

Perform cost-volume-profit analysis for multiple products. C-P-V analysis of multiple products is easily addressed by using the weighted average contribution margin per unit or the weighted average contribution margin ratio.

APPENDIX 23-A: VARIABLE AND FULL COSTING

Many accounting reports fail to distinguish between fixed and variable costs. For example, almost all manufacturing companies prepare income statements for external purposes using full costing (also called absorption costing). In full costing, inventory and cost of goods sold include direct material, direct labor, and all manufacturing overhead. While direct material and direct labor are generally variable costs, manufacturing overhead includes both variable and fixed cost elements. Thus, fixed and variable costs are commingled or combined, and it is very difficult to untangle the costs to perform "what if" analysis that requires separating fixed and variable costs.

LO 5

Discuss differences between variable and full costing.

VARIABLE COSTING

An alternative to full costing is variable costing. In **variable costing**, only variable production costs are included in inventory and cost of goods sold. All fixed production costs are treated as period costs and expensed in the period incurred. Variable costing is also referred to as **direct costing** although this name is not very accurate. Inventory costs under variable costing include variable overhead costs; these costs are indirect, not direct. GAAP requires that fixed production costs be included in inventory and cost of goods sold for external financial reporting purposes. However, variable costing still can be used for internal purposes. Survey data indicate that 17 percent of U.S. companies use variable costing.[1]

As shown in Illustration 23-14, the only difference between the two methods is their treatment of fixed manufacturing overhead costs. Under the full costing method, these costs are included in inventory and are entered as expense only when the inventory is sold. Under the variable costing method, fixed manufacturing costs are entered as expense in the same way as other nonmanufacturing period costs. Consider depreciation, which usually is a fixed-cost component of manufacturing overhead. Under full costing, some portion of depreciation for the period remains in ending inventory when not all of the items produced are sold. However, under the variable costing method, the total amount of depreciation is treated as an expense of the period.

VARIABLE COSTING INCOME STATEMENT

If variable costing is used, a company can prepare an income statement that classifies all expenses in terms of their cost behavior—either fixed or variable. With variable expenses separated from fixed expenses, a contribution margin can be presented. With the contribution margin information, readers of the income statement can make reasonable estimates of how much profit will change for a change in sales. Income statements prepared using variable costing

---

[1]See R.A. Howell, J.D. Brown, S.R. Soucy, and A.H. Seed, III, *Management Accounting in the New Manufacturing Environment*, (National Association of Accountants, 1987), p. 131.

ILLUSTRATION 23-14 Comparison of Full and Variable Costing

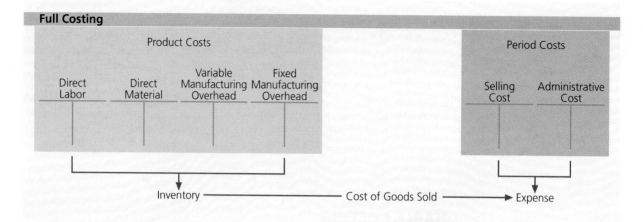

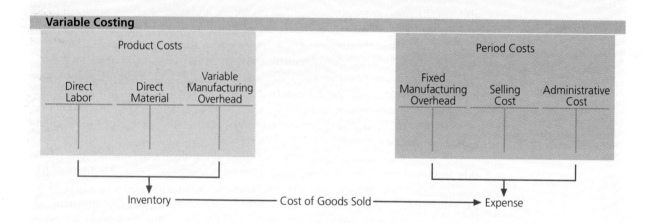

and then full costing are compared in Illustration 23-15. Suppose Federal Manufacturing Company expects its sales to increase by $10,000. What is the expected increase in profit? Using the variable costing income statement, we easily can calculate the contribution margin ratio as the contribution margin divided by sales, or 65 percent. If sales increase by $10,000, profit should increase by $6,500.

LO 6
Discuss how income will differ between variable and full costing when the number of units produced does not equal the number of units sold.

EFFECT OF FULL AND VARIABLE COSTING ON INCOME

To examine in detail the differences between full and variable costing, consider the following example. Miller Heating Company is a small manufacturer of auxiliary heaters. The units sell for $100 each. The variable production cost of each unit includes: direct material, $18; direct labor, $12; and variable manufacturing overhead, $10. In addition, Miller Heating incurs $200,000 of fixed manufactur-

ILLUSTRATION 23-15 Comparison of Income Statements Prepared Using Variable and Full Costing.

Income Statement Prepared Using Variable Costing

Federal Manufacturing Company
Income Statement
For the Period Ended December 31, 19X1

Sales		$100,000
Less variable costs:		
Variable cost of goods sold	$20,000	
Variable selling expense	10,000	
Variable administrative expense	5,000	
Total variable costs		35,000
Contribution margin		$ 65,000
Less fixed costs:		
Fixed manufacturing expense	$10,000	
Fixed selling expense	8,000	
Fixed administrative expense	7,000	
Total fixed costs		25,000
Net income		$ 40,000

Income Statement Prepared Using Full Costing

Federal Manufacturing Company
Income Statement
For the Period Ended December 31, 19X1

Sales		$100,000
Less cost of goods sold		30,000
Gross margin		$ 70,000
Less selling and administrative expense:		
Selling expense	$18,000	
Administrative expense	12,000	
Total selling and administrative expense		30,000
Net income		$ 40,000

ing overhead each period. Selling and administrative costs are fixed costs amounting to $50,000 and $100,000, respectively.

Selling price		$100
Variable production costs:		
Direct material	$18	
Direct labor	12	
Variable overhead	10	
Total variable production costs		40
Contribution margin per unit		$ 60
Fixed manufacturing overhead		$200,000
Fixed selling cost		50,000
Fixed administrative cost		100,000

Suppose that in 19X1 there is no beginning inventory of finished goods, 15,000 units are produced, and 10,000 units are sold. Illustration 23-16 provides a full costing income statement for this situation. The full cost of production is $800,000. This includes $600,000 of variable production cost ($40 per unit x 15,000 units) and $200,000 of fixed manufacturing overhead. With 15,000 units produced, Miller Heating's unit cost is $53.3333.

$$\text{Unit Cost Under Full Costing} = \frac{\text{Total Production Cost}}{\text{Number of Units Produced}}$$

$$\$53.3333 = \frac{\$800,000}{15,000}$$

Since Miller Heating sells 10,000 units, its cost of goods sold is $533,333. Net income amounts to $316,667.

ILLUSTRATION 23-16 Full Costing Income

Miller Heating Company Income Statement For the Year Ended December 31, 19X1		
Sales		$1,000,000
Less cost of goods sold:		
Beginning inventory	$ 0	
Plus production costs:		
Variable	600,000	
Fixed	200,000	
	$800,000	
Less ending inventory:	266,667	
Cost of goods sold		533,333
Gross profit		$ 466,667
Less selling and administrative expense:		
Selling expense	$ 50,000	
Administrative expense	100,000	150,000
Net income		$ 316,667

Note: Units produced were 15,000; units sold were 10,000; ending inventory equals 5,000 units x $53.3333.

Illustration 23-17 presents Miller Heating's income statement for the same situation using variable costing. Under variable costing, each unit contains only the $40 of variable production cost. Note that the ending inventory amount in the cost of goods sold calculation is only $200,000 (5,000 units x $40 per unit), compared to $266,667 under full costing, because under variable costing, none of the $200,000 of fixed production cost was included in inventory. Under full costing, part of the $200,000 of fixed cost remains in ending inventory. Since Miller Heating produced 15,000 units, the fixed cost of each unit is $13.3333 ($200,000 ÷ 15,000). Thus the cost of the 5,000 units in ending inventory includes $66,667 of fixed cost. This accounts for the difference in income under variable and full costing.

If the quantity produced exceeds the quantity sold, full costing yields a higher income than variable costing because some of the fixed costs remain in ending inventory under full costing. If the quantity sold exceeds the quantity

ILLUSTRATION 23-17 Variable Costing Income

Miller Heating Company Income Statement For the Year Ended December 31, 19X1		
Sales		$1,000,000
Less variable cost of goods sold:		
Beginning inventory	$ 0	
Plus variable production costs	600,000	
Less ending inventory	200,000	
Variable cost of goods sold		400,000
Contribution margin		$ 600,000
Less fixed costs:		
Fixed production costs	$200,000	
Fixed selling expense	50,000	
Fixed administrative expense	100,000	350,000
Net income		$ 250,000

Note: Units produced were 15,000; units sold were 10,000.

produced, however, the situation reverses. That is, variable costing results in the higher income because, under full costing, the units sold out of beginning inventory have a higher cost since they include fixed overhead. If the quantity sold is equal to the quantity produced, both methods result in the same level of income.

Condition	Result
Units produced exceed units sold	Full costing has the higher income
Units sold exceed units produced	Variable costing has the higher income
Units sold equal units produced	No difference in income

BENEFITS OF VARIABLE COSTING FOR INTERNAL REPORTING

Since variable costing separates fixed and variable costs, users of internal financial reports can more easily perform C-V-P analysis. Suppose a manager of Miller Heating Company is interested in forecasting profit in 19X2. Further, suppose the manager believes that sales in 19X2 will be 17,000 units. How much profit should the manager forecast? Ideally, to answer this question, the manager would multiply the 17,000 units by the contribution margin per unit and then subtract fixed cost. Unfortunately, the full costing income statement does not provide contribution margin information. Thus, the manager may be tempted to calculate net income per dollar of sales and multiply it by expected sales. This would result in an *incorrect* forecast of profit of $538,334 [i.e., ($316,667 ÷ $1,000,000) x (17,000 x $100)]. On the other hand, the manager could easily calculate the contribution margin per unit of $60 by using the variable costing income statement (i.e., $600,000 ÷ 10,000 units sold). Thus, expected profit is $670,000.

Expected Profit = (Contribution Margin x Units Sold) – Fixed Cost
$$\$670,000 = (\$60 \times 17,000) - \$350,000$$

Another reason why variable costing may be preferred for internal purposes is that it does not allow managers to inflate profit artificially by producing more than they can sell. Suppose a manager expects sales to be 1,000 units. The selling price is $100 per unit, variable costs are $50 per unit, and fixed costs are $45,000. If the manager produces 1,000 units, profit would be equal to $5,000 [i.e., 1,000 x ($100 – $50) – $45,000] under both the full costing and the variable costing methods. The manager may realize, however, that if the full costing method is used, part of the fixed costs can be assigned to ending inventory, thereby transferring the expense to a future period. Thus, if the manager produces 2,000 units, profit will be $22,500 higher because half of the fixed costs will be included in the 1,000 units remaining in ending inventory. Of course, this is a short-run strategy because eventually the inventory buildup will be noticed. However, by the time excess inventory is noted the manager may to be working for a different company and have a great "track record" as a manager at the former company. Note that the strategy of producing more than you can sell will not increase income under the variable costing method, since under that method, none of the fixed costs can be included in ending inventory.

REVIEW PROBLEM

The Dream Baking Company has a contract with a local military base to provide the base with dinner rolls. Dream receives $1.20 per dozen rolls. The costs of producing 4,000 dozen rolls for the month of January 19X3 were as follows:

Ingredients	$1,000
Labor	1,250
Depreciation of equipment	200
Rent, baking shop	400
Utilities (50% variable, 50% fixed)	300

REQUIRED:

a. Use the account analysis approach to estimate the total fixed and total variable costs of baking the 4,000 dozen rolls. Also calculate the variable costs per dozen rolls.

b. Calculate how many dozen rolls Dream must sell to the base in February to break-even. Also calculate the break-even point in dollars.

c. If Dream expects to sell 6,000 dozen rolls in February, calculate the margin of safety for February operations.

d. Calculate the contribution margin per dozen rolls.

e. Using the contribution margin, calculate how many dozen rolls must be sold in February to earn a $600 profit. Also calculate the dollar sales needed to earn a $600 profit.

f. Calculate the contribution margin ratio.

g. Using the contribution margin ratio, calculate the dollar sales in February necessary to earn a $600 profit.

h. Suppose Dream gets an order for 6,000 dozen rolls for February. Calculate the expected profit.

i. Construct a profit graph. Label the following: total revenue, total expenses, variable expenses, fixed expenses, break-even point, and margin of safety.

j. Suppose Dream has the opportunity to purchase a new oven that is more efficient. If the oven had been used in January, Dream estimates the variable utility cost would have been reduced from $150 to $40 and labor would have been reduced from $1,250 to $1,000. The monthly depreciation after the acquisition of the new oven would be $600 per month. Calculate the new break-even point. Calculate the expected profit assuming sales of 6,000 dozen rolls.

k. Should Dream purchase the new oven?

SOLUTION:

(a) *Calculate fixed and variable costs.*

The ingredients are clearly variable. The labor could be all fixed, all variable, or some combination of fixed and variable (i.e., mixed or semivariable). Direct labor is usually considered variable while indirect labor often is fixed or mixed. For our solution we will assume the labor is all variable. The depreciation and rent are assumed to be fixed, and the utilities are as given, 50% variable and 50% fixed.

The account analysis approach would provide the following results:

Variable costs:		Fixed costs:	
Ingredients	$1,000	Depreciation	$200
Labor	1,250	Rent	400
Utilities	150	Utilities	150
	$2,400		$750

The variable cost per dozen rolls is:

$$\$2,400 \div 4,000 = \underline{\underline{\$.60}}$$

(b) *Calculate the break-even point.*

The following profit equation yields the break-even point:

$$\text{Profit} = \text{SP}(x) - \text{VC}(x) - \text{TFC}$$

where

$$
\begin{aligned}
x &= \text{Quantity of units produced and sold} \\
\text{SP} &= \text{Selling price per unit} \\
\text{VC} &= \text{Variable cost per unit} \\
\text{TFC} &= \text{Total fixed costs}
\end{aligned}
$$

To find the break-even point, let profit = 0 and solve the equation:

$$
\begin{aligned}
0 &= \$1.20(x) - .60(x) - \$750 \\
0 &= .60(x) - \$750 \\
.60\,(x) &= \$750 \\
x &= 1,250 \text{ dozen}
\end{aligned}
$$

The break-even point in dollar sales is 1,250 x $1.20 = $\underline{\underline{\$1,500}}$

(c) *Determine the margin of safety.*

In units:	Expected sales	6,000
	Break-even point	1,250
	Margin of safety	4,750

In dollars:	Expected sales	$7,200
	Break-even point	1,500
	Margin of safety	$5,700

(d) *Determine the contribution margin.*

The difference between the selling price and the variable cost per unit is the contribution margin:

$$\$1.20 - \$.60 = \underline{\underline{\$.60}}$$

(e) *Calculate required sales using contribution margin.*

When the profit equation is solved for units (x), we get the following expression:

$$x = \frac{\text{Profit} + \text{TFC}}{\text{Contribution Margin}}$$

The contribution margin can be used with this expression to calculate how many units must be sold in February to earn a $600 profit.

$$x = \frac{\$600 + \$750}{\$.60}$$

$$x = \underline{\underline{2{,}250}} \text{ dozen rolls}$$

The dollar sales needed to earn the $600 profit are:

$$2{,}250 \times \$1.20 = \underline{\underline{\$2{,}700}}$$

(f) *Determine the contribution margin ratio.*

$$\text{Contribution margin ratio} = \frac{\text{SP} - \text{VC}}{\text{SP}}$$

$$= \frac{\$1.20 - \$.60}{\$1.20}$$

$$= .50 \text{ or } \underline{\underline{50\%}}$$

(g) *Calculate target sales using contribution margin.*

We can express the profit equation in terms of the contribution margin ratio as:

$$\text{Sales (in dollars)} = \frac{\text{Profit} + \text{TFC}}{\text{Contribution Margin Ratio}}$$

$$\text{Sales (\$)} = \frac{\$600 + \$750}{.50}$$

$$\text{Sales (\$)} = \underline{\underline{\$2{,}700}}$$

(h) *Calculate expected profit.*

$$\text{Profit} = \text{SP}(x) - \text{VC}(x) - \text{TFC}$$
$$\text{Profit} = \$1.20(6{,}000) - .60(6{,}000) - \$750$$
$$\text{Profit} = \$7{,}200 - \$3{,}600 - \$750$$
$$\text{Profit} = \underline{\underline{\$2{,}850}}$$

(i) *Create a profit graph.*

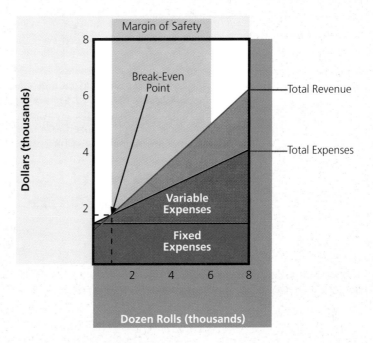

(j) *Determine the break-even point and projected profit if the new oven is purchased.*

The purchase of the oven changes Dream's cost behavior:

Variable costs:		Fixed costs:	
Ingredients	$1,000	Depreciation	$ 600
Labor	1,000	Rent	400
Utilities	40	Utilities	150
	$2,040		$1,150

The variable cost per dozen changes to:

$$\$2,040 \div 4,000 = \underline{\$.51}$$

Solving the profit equation to find the break-even point:

$$\text{Profit} = \text{SP}(x) - \text{VC}(x) - \text{TFC}$$

To find the break-even point, let profit = 0 and solve the equation:

$$0 = \$1.20(x) - .51(x) - \$1,150$$
$$0 = .69(x) - \$1,150$$
$$.69(x) = \$1,150$$
$$x = \underline{1,667 \text{ dozen}} \text{ (rounded)}$$

The break-even point in dollar sales is 1,667 x $1.20 = $2,000 (rounded)

The new break-even point is higher (1,667 dozen rolls) than the old break-even point (1,250 dozen rolls). To calculate the expected profit for a sales level of 6,000 dozen rolls, use the new cost data in the profit equation:

$$\text{Profit} = \text{SP}(x) - \text{VC}(x) - \text{TFC}$$
$$\text{Profit} = \$1.20(6,000) - .51(6,000) - \$1,150$$
$$\text{Profit} = \$7,200 - \$3,060 - \$1,150$$
$$\text{Profit} = \underline{\$2,990}$$

(k) *Determine if Dream should purchase the oven.*

The new oven increases Dream's fixed costs, and compensates for this by decreasing variable costs. At high production levels the savings in variable costs will at some point become greater than the increase in fixed costs. At the level of 6,000 dozen rolls the savings in variable costs (9 cents per dozen rolls x 6,000 = $540) is greater than the increase in fixed costs ($400). This results in a $140 projected increase in profit. Dream therefore will benefit from the purchase of the oven, but only at high production levels. At production levels of less than 4,444 dozen rolls (i.e., $400 ÷ .09) the increase in fixed costs will be greater than the savings in variable costs.

KEY TERMS

account analysis, *939*
break-even point, *945*
contribution margin, *947*
contribution margin ratio, *947*
cost-volume-profit (C-V-P) analysis, *936*

direct costing, *953*
fixed costs, *937*
high-low method, *941*
margin of safety, *947*
mixed costs, *937*
regression analysis, *944*

relevant range, *944*
scattergraph, *941*
variable costing, *953*
variable costs, *936*
"what if" analysis, *948*

SELF-QUIZ

LO 1 1. Variable costs:
   a. Decrease per unit of activity as activity decreases.
   b. Increase per unit of activity as activity decreases.
   c. Remain constant per unit of activity as activity decreases.
   d. None of the above.

LO 1 2. Fixed costs:
   a. Decrease per unit of activity as activity decreases.
   b. Increase per unit of activity as activity decreases.
   c. Remain constant per unit of activity as activity decreases.
   d. None of the above.

LO 1 3. Mixed costs:
   a. Are costs that are part selling and part manufacturing.
   b. Are costs that are part product and part period.
   c. Are costs that are part fixed and part variable.
   d. None of the above.

LO 3 4. One key to C-V-P analysis is determining how _____ behave when volume changes.

LO 1 5. In order to determine the effect that changes in volume have on costs, we classify costs as _____, _____, or _____.

LO 1 6. An example of a fixed cost for a company which manufactures automobiles is:
   a. Automobile tires
   b. Depreciation on the production plant

   c. Wages of production line workers
   d. None of the above

LO 1 7. Listed below are costs for a company which paints and sells custom designed T-shirts. Identify the costs as fixed (*F*) or variable (*V*). For possible mixed costs, label them *F and V*.
   ___ a. Depreciation of the air brush equipment
   ___ b. Rent on the store
   ___ c. Insurance
   ___ d. Paint
   ___ e. T-shirts
   ___ f. Advertising
   ___ g. Wages of artist employed to paint the shirts
   ___ h. Salary of cashier
   ___ i. Utilities
   ___ j. Monthly fee paid to accountant for bookkeeping
   ___ k. Solvents to clean air brush

LO 2 8. Four methods to estimate the fixed and variable components of total costs are: _____, _____, _____, and _____.

LO 3 9. The break-even point is:
   a. The activity level where total costs and total revenues are equal.
   b. The activity level where fixed costs are equal to variable costs.
   c. The activity level where revenue is equal to variable costs.
   d. None of the above.

LO 3 10. The profit equation is stated as:
   Profit = SP(*x*) – VC(*x*) – TFC.
   Identify the terms in the equation:

SP _____

x   _____

VC _____

TFC _____

LO 3 11. A company has the following:

Sales price per unit: $10

Variable cost per unit: $6

Total fixed cost: $1,000

The break-even point is:

a. 1,000 units.

b. 250 units.

c. 400 units.

d. None of the above.

LO 2 12. A company has the following cleaning solvent costs and activity levels for the past six months:

	Solvent Costs	Units Produced
March	$400	50
April	350	40
May	425	55
June	460	65
July	320	30
August	410	50

Using the high-low method to analyze the total cleaning solvent costs, the variable cost *per unit* and the *total* fixed costs are:

a. $4 and $200.

b. $5 and $200.

c. $3.50 and $300.

d. $3 and $500.

LO 1
LO 2
LO 3 13. Key terms and their definitions are listed below. Match the definitions with the key terms.

___ a. Account analysis

___ b. Fixed costs

___ c. Relevant range

___ d. Margin of safety

___ e. Contribution margin

___ f. High-low method

___ g. Cost-volume-profit analysis

(1) A method of estimating the fixed and variable components of total costs, based on costs at two activity levels.

(2) Explores the relationships among costs, volume or activity levels, and profit.

(3) The range of activity for which estimates of fixed and variable costs are likely to be accurate.

(4) The accountant uses his or her judgment to classify expenses as fixed or variable.

(5) The difference between selling price and variable cost per unit.

(6) Costs that do not change in response to changes in activity levels.

(7) The difference between the expected level of sales and break-even sales.

LO 3 14. A company has the following data:

Unit sales price: $20

Unit variable cost: $14

Calculate: (1) the contribution margin, and (2) the contribution margin ratio.

LO 2 15. A scattergraph:

a. Graphically illustrates total revenue, total costs, and profit or loss.

b. Plots total revenues.

c. Plots costs and activity levels to gain insight into the relationship between cost and activity.

d. None of the above.

LO 3 16. A company has the following data:

Unit sales price: $200

Unit variable cost: $150

Total fixed costs: $5,000

The contribution margin ratio is:

a. $50.

b. 3%.

c. 33.3%.

d. 25%.

LO 3 17. The break-even point on a profit graph is the point where the total revenue line intersects:

a. The fixed expense line.

b. The margin of safety.

c. The relevant range.

d. The total cost line.

LO 4 18. For a company selling more than one product:

a. C-V-P analysis cannot be used.

b. A separate C-V-P analysis must be performed for each product the company sells.

c. C-V-P is performed using the weighted average contribution margin approach or the weighted average contribution margin ratio approach.

d. None of the above.

LO 5 19. (Appendix) The difference between variable and full costing is:

a. Their treatment of variable manufacturing costs.

b. Their treatment of fixed manufacturing costs.

c. Their treatment of direct labor.

d. None of the above.

LO 6 20. (Appendix) Match the following:

___ a. Sales exceed production

___ b. Production exceeds sales

___ c. Production and sales are equal

(1) Full costing profit is greater than variable costing profit.

(2) Full costing profit is less than variable costing profit.

(3) Full costing profit and variable costing profit are equal.

QUESTIONS

Q23-1 To perform C-V-P analysis, we must (1) be able to estimate revenues at different volume levels, and (2) estimate expenses at different volume levels. Which is probably easier to estimate, revenues or expenses? Why?

Q23-2 Variable costs are normally a fixed amount per unit of activity. Why then are such costs referred to as variable?

Q23-3 Fixed costs vary on a per-unit basis in relation to changes in volume. Why then are such costs referred to as fixed?

Q23-4 In many businesses, expenses may not behave in a strict fixed and variable pattern. Does this mean that C-V-P is not a practical and useful analysis? Discuss.

Q23-5 Do total fixed costs ever increase or decrease? Discuss.

Q23-6 Give two examples of variable costs.

Q23-7 What is a mixed cost?

Q23-8 Account analysis is a common approach to estimating the fixed and variable components of costs. Why do you suppose this method is so popular?

Q23-9 A widely acclaimed accounting professor once said, "For the manager of a business, C-V-P is the single most important decision-making tool there is. Period." Do you agree with this or is it an exaggeration? Discuss.

Q23-10 A hospital administrator is performing C-V-P analysis. Activity level is measured in number of patient days. Would nursing salaries be a fixed, variable, or mixed cost? Discuss.

Q23-11 This statement was made by an experienced financial executive, "A lot of variable costs are fixed in the short run." Discuss the meaning of this statement.

Q23-12 The high-low method is one technique used to estimate the fixed and variable components of a total cost. It has some problems. What are they?

Q23-13 Why is the concept of relevant range so important to C-V-P? Discuss.

Q23-14 Comment on the following statement made by a business owner. "My accountant says that total fixed costs are $500,000 per year. I am using that number in my C-V-P analysis and I like the results. My calculations show that if we triple our business volume, something I think we can do, I am going to make a heck of a lot of money."

Q23-15 (Appendix) The difference between full costing and variable costing is in the amount of fixed manufacturing costs that are expensed during an accounting period. Explain how fixed manufacturing costs become an expense under full costing. Explain how fixed manufacturing costs become an expense under variable costing.

Q23-16 (Appendix) Those who support variable costing as a method of reporting income argue that the variable costing income statement is more useful to a decision maker who is trying to use the statement to project a company's future income. Explain how the variable costing statement assists in projecting income.

EXERCISES

LO 1

E23-1   Cost Behavior   Information for three costs incurred in a typical manufacturing company follows:

	Period	Amount	Units produced
Depreciation:	Jan.	$500,000	3,000
	Feb.	$500,000	4,500
	Mar.	$500,000	6,000
Direct labor:	Jan.	$120,000	3,000
	Feb.	$180,000	4,500
	Mar.	$240,000	6,000
Utilities:	Jan.	$25,000	3,000
	Feb.	$32,500	4,500
	Mar.	$40,000	6,000

REQUIRED:

For each cost plot the cost on a two dimensional graph, making the vertical axis dollars and the horizontal axis activity, and label it fixed, variable, or mixed.

LO 2

E23-2   High-Low Method   The Rough River Rafting Company wants to identify the behavior of their raft repair expense so that they will be able to project the expense at different levels of activity. The following data has been gathered:

Period	Repair Expense	Number of Customers
May	$ 8,000	2,000
June	$12,000	4,000
July	$20,000	8,000
Aug.	$16,000	6,000
Sept.	$10,000	3,000

REQUIRED:

Determine the fixed and variable components of raft repair expense using the high-low method.

LO 2

E23-3   Scattergraph   Ocean Rentals is interested in learning about the behavior of their utility costs in relation to the rental activity of one of their typical Ocean side condominiums. The climate is similar year-round and seasons do not materially influence utility cost. Activity level is measured in rental days per month. Use the following information to prepare a scattergraph of the utility costs. Based on the scattergraph, are the utility costs fixed, variable or mixed?

Period	Utility Expense	Rental Days
May	$150	10
June	$165	12
July	$120	4
August	$190	20

LO 2

E23-4   Account Analysis   Sunshine Tee Shirt Company has the following information available regarding the costs of operating their business, which consists of purchasing plain shirts, painting them with various designs and logos, and selling them to tourists.

Cost Information for May
2,000 shirts sold

Rent	$ 400
Insurance	100
Utilities	200
Artist salary	1,500
Cashier salary	800
Paint	500
Cost of plain shirts sold	10,000
Depreciation	900

REQUIRED:

Use the account analysis method to determine:
a. total fixed costs.
b. total variable costs.
c. variable costs per shirt.

For expenses which could be either fixed or variable, assume they are fixed.

LO 3

E23-5   C-V-P Analysis, Profit Equation   A single-product company has the following information for a particular accounting period.

Unit sales price	$500
Unit variable costs	$200
Fixed costs	$75,000

REQUIRED:

Calculate the break-even point in units using the profit equation.

LO 3

E23-6   C-V-P Analysis, Contribution Margin   A single-product company has the following information for its current accounting period.

Unit sales price	$500
Unit variable costs	$200
Fixed costs	$75,000

REQUIRED:

a. Calculate the contribution margin.
b. Use the contribution margin to calculate the break-even point in units.

LO 3

E23-7   C-V-P Analysis, Contribution Margin Ratio   A single-product company has the following information for a particular accounting period.

Unit sales price	$500
Unit variable costs	$200
Fixed costs	$75,000

REQUIRED:

a. Calculate the contribution margin ratio.
b. Use the contribution margin ratio to calculate the break-even point in sales dollars.

LO 3

E23-8   C-V-P Analysis, Margin of Safety   A single-product company has the following information for a particular accounting period. They expect to sell 5,000 units.

Unit sales price	$100
Unit variable costs	$70
Fixed costs	$100,000

REQUIRED:

a. Calculate the break-even point in units using the contribution margin method.
b. Calculate the margin of safety in units.
c. Calculate the projected profit in dollars.

LO 3

E23-9   C-V-P Analysis   A single-product company has the following information for a particular accounting period.

Unit sales price	$100
Unit variable costs	$70
Fixed costs	$100,000

REQUIRED:

a. Use the contribution margin method to calculate the unit sales needed to produce a $25,000 profit.
b. Use the contribution margin method to calculate the dollar sales needed to produce a $25,000 profit.

LO 3

E23-10   C-V-P Analysis, "What If" Analysis   A single-product company has the following information for its current accounting period.

Unit sales price	$25
Unit variable costs	$15
Fixed costs	$50,000

The company expects to sell 7,000 units. They are considering increasing advertising by $10,000 and feel the additional promotion would sell an additional 500 units.

REQUIRED:

a. Calculate the expected profit from the sale of 7,000 units.
b. Calculate the expected profit if they increase advertising.

LO 3

E23-11   C-V-P Analysis, "What If" Analysis   A single- product company has the following information for its current accounting period.

Unit sales price	$25
Unit variable costs	$15
Fixed costs	$50,000

The company expects to sell 7,000 units. They are considering purchasing more modern and efficient production equipment. The new equipment would increase their fixed costs by $15,000, but the increased efficiency would reduce variable labor costs by $3 per unit.

REQUIRED:

a. Calculate the expected profit without the new equipment
b. Calculate the expected profit with the new equipment.

LO 4

E23-12   C-V-P Analysis, Multiproduct, Contribution Margin Approach   The Head Gear Helmet Company produces two helmets, Model A for kayaking and rockclimbing, and model B for motorcycling. Model A sells for $35 and has a variable cost of $20; Model B sells for $150 and has a variable cost of $75. Head Gear typically sells three Model Bs for every one Model A. Their annual fixed costs are $250,000.

REQUIRED:

a. Calculate the weighted average contribution margin.
b. Use the weighted average contribution margin to calculate the break-even point in total helmets.
c. Break the total helmet sales into Model A and Model B helmets.

LO 4   **E23-13   C-V-P Analysis, Multiproduct, Contribution Margin Ratio Approach**   Assume the same set of facts as in E23-12. That is, the Head Gear Helmet Company produces two helmets, Model A for kayaking and rockclimbing, and Model B for motorcycling. Model A sells for $35 and has a variable cost of $20; Model B sells for $150 and has a variable cost of $75. Head Gear typically sells three Model Bs for every one Model A. Their annual fixed costs are $250,000.

REQUIRED:

a. Calculate the weighted average contribution margin ratio.
b. Use the weighted average contribution margin ratio to calculate the break-even point in dollar sales.

LO 5,6   **E23-14   Variable and Full Costing (Appendix)**   A manufacturing company began operations on January 1, 19X3. Information for their first year of operations is as follows:

Units produced	100,000
Units sold	80,000
Units in ending inventory	20,000
Fixed manufacturing costs	$500,000

REQUIRED:

a. Calculate the amount of fixed manufacturing costs that would be expensed for 19X3, assuming an income statement based on full costing.
b. Calculate the amount of fixed manufacturing costs that would be expensed for 19X3 assuming an income statement based on variable costing.
c. Calculate the difference in profit reported by the two methods.

PROBLEM SET A

LO 1,2   **P23-1A   Cost Behavior Patterns, Account Analysis**   The Beach Party Tanning Salon is interested in investigating the behavior patterns of their operating costs so that they can make better projections of their costs and profits. Beach Party caters to an exclusive clientele and provides the following services which are included in the basic tanning fee: tanning oil, towels, hot tub, sauna, shower facilities, soap, shampoo, body lotion, and the morning newspaper. Coffee, tea, and exotic non-alcoholic tropical drinks are provided as are hors d'oeuvres.

REQUIRED:

Selected Beach Party costs follow. Label each cost as fixed (*F*), variable (*V*), or mixed (*M*).

___ a. Building rental (rent is $400 per month plus 5% of gross tanning fees)
___ b. City occupational tax (2% of gross tanning fees)
___ c. Chlorine, PH +, PH –, other miscellaneous chemicals for operation of the hot tub
___ d. Depreciation of computer
___ e. Depreciation of typewriter
___ f. Depreciation of cash register
___ g. Salaries of two attendants
___ h. Salary of one janitorial worker

___ i.   Water
___ j.   Electricity
___ k.   Repairs and maintenance—tanning beds
___ l.   Insurance
___ m. Professional fees (accountant is paid a monthly fee to keep books, prepare monthly financial statements and all required tax returns)
___ n.   Towel service (a company provides clean towels and laundry service, monthly fee is $100 plus $.025 for each towel provided)
___ o.   Newspapers (A subscription to 12 copies of the local newspaper, 6 copies of the *New York Times*, and 6 copies of the *Wall Street Journal*)
___ p.   Soap, shampoo, body lotion
___ q.   Beverages and hors d'oeuvres (provided by a local caterer, fee $150 per month plus a charge for food and beverages provided).
___ r.   Radio commercials
___ s.   Office supplies
___ t.   Depreciation of tanning beds

LO 1,2   **P23-2A   Estimating Costs**   The Wildwood Country Club operates a swimming pool for its members. Records are kept of the number of people who enter the pool area. Wildwood is interested in learning about the behavior of their pool operating costs in relation to pool usage. Operating costs and usage data for last season are as follows:

	June	*July*	*August*
Admissions	2,600	4,000	2,000
Depreciation	$1,000	$1,000	$1,000
Life guard wages	1,600	2,000	1,500
Water	200	300	200
Chemicals	1,000	1,500	800
Total costs	$3,800	$4,800	$3,500

REQUIRED:

a. Use the high-low method to determine the fixed and variable components of the total pool operating costs.
b. Estimate the total monthly costs of operating the pool if the admissions are 5,000.
c. Draw a scattergraph plotting admissions on the horizontal axis and total costs in dollars on the vertical axis.

LO 1,2,3   **P23-3A   Cost Behavior Patterns, Estimating Costs, C-V-P, Margin of Safety, "What If" Analysis**   Nancy Adams has the opportunity to operate a refreshment stand at the state fair. The fair operates from August 1 through August 12. Nancy plans to sell a single item, a 16-ounce cola. It is served with six ounces of finely ground ice, similar to the consistency of a snow cone. She has named the drink "Cola Cooler." She has obtained the following information about the costs of operating the refreshment stand for the 12-day period.

License fee from the state fair board	$250
Rental of a 20 ft x 20 ft space	$500
Sales price of the Cola Cooler	$1.50
Cost of 16-ounce cola	$0.21
Cost of cup with special Cola Cooler label	$0.02
Cost of 6 ounces of ice	$0.01
Wages, (2 employees will be on hand for 8 of the days, 3 employees on hand for 4 of the days; hours 11 a.m. to 12 midnight, rate $4.25 per hour); 364 hrs. x $4.25	$1547
Employer's social security	$121

| Rental of concession stand, coolers, cash registers, ice making machine | $ 600 |
| Promotional signs | $ 300 |

REQUIRED:

a. Use the account analysis approach to calculate: (1) the total fixed costs, and (2) the variable costs per drink.
b. Calculate: (1) the contribution margin per Cola Cooler, and (2) the contribution margin ratio per Cola Cooler.
c. Calculate the break-even point three ways: (1) using the profit equation, (2) using the contribution margin, and (3) using the contribution margin ratio. Express the break-even point in both the number of drinks sold and in dollars.
d. Suppose Nancy is expecting to sell 5,000 Cola Coolers, assuming normal weather, and 7,000 if it is abnormally hot. Calculate the expected profit under: (1) normal weather, and (2) abnormally hot weather.
e. Calculate the margin of safety in units assuming normal weather.
f. Assuming normal weather, Nancy feels that she could sell 40% more Coolers if she drops the price to $1.00. Should she drop the price?

LO 3   **P23-4A**   **C-V-P, Profit Graph**   The Redline Oil Company was organized to produce and distribute a single product, a high-grade blended synthetic racing oil that is used in high-performance sport bikes and racing bikes. The oil is expensive and is targeted to a narrow market. Redline purchases the petroleum and chemical agents, blends them, packages the oil, and distributes the product to retail outlets (motorcycle dealers and parts shops). Information about Redline's expected costs of operations is as follows:

Wholesale price of quart of Redline	$9
Variable production costs:	
Chemical and petroleum ingredients	$3
Labor in mixing process	$0.40
Fixed production costs:	
Depreciation of production facilities (plant and equipment)	$50,000
Other fixed production costs	$50,000
Selling and administrative costs (fixed)	$100,000

REQUIRED:

a. Calculate: (1) the total fixed costs, and (2) the variable costs per quart of oil.
b. Calculate: (1) the contribution margin, and (2) the contribution margin ratio.
c. Calculate the break-even point three ways: (1) using the profit equation, (2) using the contribution margin, and (3) using the contribution margin ratio. Express the break-even point in both dollars and units.
d. Calculate the number of quarts Redline must sell to earn a $50,000 profit.
e. Draw a profit graph. Label sales revenue, total expenses, variable expenses, fixed expenses, the profit area, the loss area, and the break-even point.

LO 4   **P23-5A**   **C-V-P, Multiproducts**   The Redline Oil Company was organized to produce and distribute a single product, a high-grade blended synthetic racing oil that is used in high-performance sport bikes and racing bikes. Last year they added a second product, a high-performance chain lubricant. The oil is expensive and is targeted to a narrow market; the chain lubricant is more competitively priced and is targeted to a broader market. Redline purchases the petroleum and chemical agents for both products, blends, packages, and distributes them to retail outlets (motorcycle dealers and parts shops). Information about Redline's expected costs of operations is as follows:

Wholesale price of quart of Redline synthetic racing oil		$9
Wholesale price for 12-ounce tube of Redline chain lubricant		$3

	Racing Oil	Chain Lubricant
Variable production costs:		
Chemical and petroleum ingredients	$3.00	$1.50
Labor in mixing process	$0.40	$0.40
Fixed production costs:		
Depreciation of production facilities (plant and equipment)		$60,000
Other fixed production costs		$60,000
Selling and administrative costs (fixed)		$120,000

Redline expects to sell three tubes of chain lubricant for every one quart of racing oil.

REQUIRED:

a. Calculate the weighted average contribution margin ratio.
b. Use the weighted average contribution margin ratio to calculate the dollar sales necessary to earn a $50,000 profit.
c. Suppose Redline's actual product mix is four tubes of chain lubricant to every one quart of racing oil. Calculate: (1) the weighted average contribution margin ratio for this mix, and (2) the dollar sales needed to earn a $50,000 profit. Comment on how the changed product mix affects Redline's operations.

LO 5,6 — **P23-6A** **Full Costing and Variable Costing (Appendix)**   The following information relates to BingoBird Seed Company for the past three years. Ignore selling and administrative costs.

	19X3	19X4	19X5
Pounds produced	100,000	100,000	100,000
Pounds sold	100,000	90,000	110,000
Fixed overhead	$50,000	$50,000	$50,000
Variable production cost per pound	$1.50	$1.50	$1.50
Selling price per pound	$3.00	$3.00	$3.00

REQUIRED:

a. Prepare an income statement each year under variable costing.
b. Prepare an income statement each year under full costing.
c. Calculate the amount of fixed overhead expensed each year under: (1) variable costing, and (2) full costing.
d. What relationship do you see between variable and full costing profits when: (1) production and sales are equal, (2) production is greater than sales, and (3) production is less than sales?

PROBLEM SET B

LO 1,2 — **P23-1B** **Cost Behavior Patterns, Account Analysis**   The Tri-City Manufacturing Company is interested in investigating the behavior pattern of their operating costs so that they can make better profit projections. Tri-City manufactures condensers for large industrial grade heat pumps.

REQUIRED:

Selected Tri-City costs follow. Label each cost as fixed (*F*), variable (*V*), or mixed (*M*).

___ a. Depreciation of factory building and warehouses

___ b. Raw materials

___ c. Cleaning supplies for factory

___ d. Lubricants for factory machinery

___ e. Depreciation of computer

___ f. Depreciation of factory machinery (depreciation is based on machine hours, because the wear and tear of machine usage is the primary cause of decline in asset utility)

___ g. Wages of production line workers

___ h. Wages of machine operators

___ i. Wages of factory machine mechanics

___ j. Salaries of factory security officers

___ k. Salaries of factory production supervisors

___ l. Wages of factory maintenance workers

___ m. Salaries of accounting and bookkeeping department

___ n. Salaries of sales department (salespersons are paid a monthly salary plus commissions)

___ o. Electricity (about 75% to 90% of the electricity bill relates to the factory. The machinery used in the production process uses a large amount of electricity.)

___ p. Administrative salaries

___ q. Advertising in trade journals

___ r. Office supplies

___ s. Excess of cafeteria costs over revenues (the company provides meals to all employees for $1 per meal as a company benefit)

LO 1,2   **P23-2B**   **Estimating Costs**   The Slick Wheels Go-Cart Track provides go-cart rides on a highly banked quarter-mile course which simulates a NASCAR race track. Slick is interested in learning about the behavior of their track operation costs in relation to track usage. Operating costs and usage data for last season are as follows:

	June	July	August
Rides	30,000	35,000	46,000
Depreciation of carts	$ 1,500	$ 1,500	$ 1,500
Depreciation of track	1,200	1,200	1,200
Depreciation of building	250	250	250
Pit crew wages	9,600	12,000	14,400
Cashier wages	2,400	2,400	2,400
Gas and oil	9,400	10,900	12,500
Cart repairs and maintenance	1,300	1,350	1,400
Total costs	$25,650	$29,600	$33,650

REQUIRED:

a. Use the high-low method to determine the fixed and variable components of the total track operating costs.

b. Estimate the total monthly costs of operating the track assuming 37,000 rides.

c. Draw a scattergraph plotting rides on the horizontal axis and total costs in dollars on the vertical axis.

LO 1,2,3   **P23-3B**   **Cost Behavior Patterns, Estimating Costs, C-V-P, Margin of Safety, "What If"**
Analysis   Richard Glass has made arrangements to operate a parking service at the
Kentucky Derby. The business will operate two days, Friday for the Kentucky Oaks and
Saturday for the Derby. Richard plans to attract additional customers by providing a mint
julep glass to each driver. He has obtained the following information about the costs of
operating the parking service for the two days.

Rental of nine vacant lots for two days: $1,800 plus $2 for each car parked
Parking fee: $10
Total wages of parking attendants: $720 plus $1 for each car
Cost of mint julep glass: $1
Employer's social security: 7% of wages
Parking receipts: 3 cents per receipt
Promotional signs: $500
City business license: $100 plus 5% of gross

REQUIRED:

a. Use the account analysis approach to calculate: (1) the total fixed costs, and (2) the
   variable costs per car.
b. Calculate: (1) the contribution margin, and (2) the contribution margin ratio per car.
c. Calculate the break-even point three ways: (1) using the profit equation, (2) using the
   contribution margin, and (3) using the contribution margin ratio. Express the break-
   even point in both the number of cars parked and in dollars.
d. Suppose Richard is expecting to fill all lots to capacity. Each lot holds 100 cars, providing a total capacity of 900 cars. Calculate the expected profit.
e. Calculate the margin of safety in units.
f. Richard estimates he could charge $12 and park 25% less cars. Should he increase the
   price?

LO 3   **P23-4B**   **C-V-P, Profit Graph**   The Matrix Chemical Company was organized to produce and
distribute a single product, a highly toxic compound used in home and industrial pest
control treatments. The Matrix compound is used by about a dozen manufacturers of
pest treatment products, and goes by the name Matrix Seven. Information about Matrix's
expected costs of operations is presented below.

Wholesale price of quart of Matrix Seven	$90
Variable production costs:	
Ingredients	$28
Labor in mixing process	$5
Disposal of hazardous waste material	$2
Fixed production costs:	
Depreciation of production facilities (plant and equipment)	$800,000
Other fixed production costs	$200,000
Selling and administrative costs (fixed)	$100,000

REQUIRED:

a. Calculate: (1) the total fixed costs, and (2) the variable costs per quart of Matrix
   Seven.
b. Calculate: (1) the contribution margin, and (2) the contribution margin ratio.
c. Calculate the break-even point three ways: (1) using the profit equation, (2) using the
   contribution margin, and (3) using the contribution margin ratio. Express the break-
   even point in both dollars and units.
d. Calculate the number of quarts Matrix must sell to earn a $100,000 profit.
e. Draw a profit graph. Label sales revenue, total expenses, variable expenses, fixed
   expenses, the profit area, the loss area, and the break-even point.

LO 4

P23-5B **C-V-P, Multiproducts** The First Environment Chemical Company produces and markets three products; FEC 1, a chemical used in producing household pest control products; FEC 1 Plus, a chemical used in producing industrial pest control products; and FEC 2, a chemical used in producing agricultural pest control products. Information about First's operations is as follows:

Wholesale price of quart of FEC 1	$15
Wholesale price of quart of FEC 1 Plus	$20
Wholesale price of quart of FEC 2	$12

	FEC 1	FEC 1 Plus	FEC 2
Variable production costs:			
Ingredients	$4	$6	$5
Labor in mixing process	$1	$2	$2
Hazardous waste disposal costs	$1	$1	$1

Fixed production costs:	
Depreciation of production facilities (plant and equipment)	$1,000,000
Other fixed production costs	$300,000
Selling and administrative costs (fixed)	$400,000

First expects sales to reflect the following product mix: FEC 1, one quart; FEC 1 Plus, five quarts; FEC 2, four quarts.

REQUIRED:

a. Calculate the weighted average contribution margin.
b. Use the weighted average contribution margin to calculate the total units that must be sold to earn a $100,000 profit. Break the total units into quarts of FEC 1, FEC 1 Plus, and FEC 2.
c. Calculate the weighted average contribution margin ratio.
d. Use the weighted average contribution margin ratio to calculate the dollar sales necessary to earn a $100,000 profit.
e. Suppose First's actual product mix for FEC 1, FEC 1 Plus, and FEC 2 is 2:5:3. Calculate: (1) the weighted average contribution margin ratio for this mix, and (2) the dollar sales needed to earn a $100,000 profit. Comment on how the changed product mix affects First's operations.

LO 5,6

P23-6B **Full Costing and Variable Costing (Appendix)** The following information relates to the New River Coal Company for the past three years. Ignore selling and administrative costs.

	19X1	19X2	19X3
Tons produced	250,000	250,000	250,000
Tons sold	250,000	230,000	270,000
Fixed overhead	$5,000,000	$5,000,000	$5,000,000
Variable production cost per ton	$8	$8	$8
Selling price per ton	$30	$30	$30

REQUIRED:

a. Prepare an income statement each year under variable costing.
b. Prepare an income statement each year under full costing.
c. Calculate the amount of fixed overhead expensed each year under: (1) variable costing, and (2) full costing.
d. What relationship do you see between variable and full costing profits when: (1) production and sales are equal, (2) production is greater than sales, and (3) production is less than sales?

CRITICAL THINKING AND COMMUNICATING

C23-1 You are considering investing in a newly started business, called Freedom Freeze, which produces and sells a recently developed frozen dessert that is low in cholesterol and fat and is sugar free. The desserts are sold in five company-operated outlets, similar in their concept to several national franchises. The founder of the company tells you that they expect to open new stores at a rapidly increasing pace, doubling their sales and the number of stores each year for the next three years. The company has 100,000 shares of common stock outstanding and does not plan to issue additional stock during the three-year expansion period, planning instead to obtain expansion funds through internally generated capital.

Naturally, you are very interested in projecting the company's earnings for the next three years, assuming the owner's growth projections are realistic. An income statement for Freedom Freeze's first year of operations, prepared under Generally Accepted Accounting Principles, is as follows:

Freedom Freeze Income Statement For the Year Ended December 31, 19X5	
Sales	$5,000,000
Cost of goods sold	3,000,000
Gross profit	$2,000,000
Selling and administrative expenses	1,500,000
Income before taxes	$ 500,000
Income taxes	200,000
Net income	$ 300,000
Earnings per share	$3

REQUIRED:

a. The above income statement, in accordance with Generally Accepted Accounting Principles, is prepared under full costing. What problems are you going to encounter as you attempt to project income at sales of $10,000,000, $20,000,000, and $40,000,000?

b. Suppose you are able to obtain an income statement prepared under variable costing. Explain how this format would assist you in projecting income for the next three years.

c. What problems are you going to have in projecting income, even with the availability of a variable costing statement?

C23-2 **Krog's Metalfab**   John Krog is President, Chairman of the Board, Production Supervisor, and majority shareholder of Krog's Metalfab, Inc. He formed the company in 1978 to manufacture custom-built aluminum storm windows for sale to contractors in the greater Chicago area. Since that time the company has experienced tremendous growth and currently operates two plants: one in Chicago, the main production facility and a smaller plant in Moline, Illinois. The company now produces a wide variety of metal windows, framing materials, ladders, and other products related to the construction industry. Recently, the company developed a new line of bronz-finished storm windows and initial buyer reaction has been quite favorable. The company's future seemed bright but on January 3, 1994, a light fixture overheated causing a fire which virtually destroyed the entire Chicago plant. Three days later, Krog had moved 50% of his Chicago work force to the Moline plant. Workers were housed in hotels, paid overtime wages and provided with bus transportation home on weekends. Still, the company could not meet delivery schedules due to reduced operating capacity and total business began to decline. At the end of 1994, Krog felt that the worst was over. A new plant had been leased in Chicago and the company was about back to normal.

Finally, Krog could turn his attention to a matter of considerable importance: settlement with the insurance company. The company's policy stipulated that the building and equipment loss be calculated at replacement cost. This settlement had been fairly straight forward and the proceeds had aided the rapid rebuilding of the company. A valued feature of the insurance policy was "lost profit" coverage. This coverage was to "compensate the company for profits lost due to reduced operating capacity related to fire or flood damage." The period of "lost profit" was limited to twelve months. Interpreting the exact nature of this coverage proved to be difficult. The insurance company agreed to reimburse Krog for the overtime premium, transportation and housing costs related to emergency operations in the Moline plant. These expenses obviously minimized the damages related to the 12 months of lost or reduced profits. But, was the company entitled to any additional compensation?

Krog got out the latest edition of *Construction Today*. According to this respected trade journal, sales of products similar to products produced by Krog's Metalfab had increased by 7% during 1994. Krog felt that were it not for the fire, his company could also have increased sales by this percentage.

Income statement information is avaliable for 1993 (the year prior to the fire) and 1994 (the year during which the company sustained "lost profit"). The expenses in 1994 include excess operating costs of $240,000, which include overtime costs, hotel costs, meals, etc. related to emergency operations in Moline.

The chief accountant at Krog, Peter Newell, has estimated lost profit to be only $34,961. Thus, he does not feel that it's worthwhile spending a lot of company resources trying to collect more than the $240,000. Peter arrived at his calculation as follows.

	Sales in 1993	$5,079,094
	Predicted sales in 1994 with 7% increase	5,434,630
	Actual sales in 1994	3,845,499
(A)	Lost sales	$1,589,131
(B)	Profit in 1993 as a percent of 1993 sales ($111,928 ÷ $5,079,094)	.0220
	Lost profit (A x B)	$ 34,961

REQUIRED:

Mr. Krog is not convinced by Peter's analysis and has turned to you, an outside consultant, to provide a preliminary estimate of lost profit over and above the $240,000 amount. Using the limited information contained in the financial statements for 1993 and 1994, estimate lost profit. What is the fundamental flaw in Peter Newell's analysis? (Hint: Consider using account analysis or the high-low method to estimate fixed and variable costs.)

Krog's Metalfab **Income from Operations** **1993–1994**					
1993	*1st Quarter*	*2nd Quarter*	*3rd Quarter*	*4th Quarter*	*Total*
Sales	$1,208,770	$1,247,985	$1,583,045	$1,039,294	$5,079,094
Less:					
Cost of goods sold	$1,164,665	$1,095,630	$1,230,701	$1,016,502	$4,507,498
Selling expense	52,370	53,076	66,283	44,939	216,668
Administrative expense	60,750	60,750	60,750	60,750	243,000
Total expense	$1,277,785	$1,209,456	$1,357,734	$1,122,191	$4,967,166
Income from operations	$ (69,015)	$ 38,529	$225,311	$ (82,897)	$ 111,928
1994	*1st Quarter*	*2nd Quarter*	*3rd Quarter*	*4th Quarter*	*Total*
Sales	$971,984	$ 807,871	$1,171,679	$ 893,965	$3,845,499
Less:					
Cost of goods sold	$1,034,623	$ 968,950	$1,112,708	$1,001,738	$4,118,019
Selling expense	43,229	36,666	51,217	40,108	171,220
Administrative expense	69,575	73,035	70,787	68,340	281,737
Total expense	$1,147,427	$1,078,651	$1,234,712	$1,110,186	$4,570,976
Income from operations	$ (175,443)	$ (270,780)	$ (63,033)	$ (216,221)	$ (725,477)

CHAPTER 24

Cost Allocation and Activity-Based Costing

Gardenrite Manufacturing Company produces garden tools and lawn maintenance products that are sold through a national chain of hardware stores. More than 60 products are manufactured, and approximately 80 percent of revenue comes from selling small home garden tools such as rakes, pruners, and spades. The company also manufactures high-quality lawn mowers, edgers, and blowers that are popular with professional lawn service companies. However, sales of these products have been relatively small. In recent months, Ben Jakes, the CFO at Gardenrite, has become concerned about the apparent profitability of several products. In particular, some high-volume products such as the Model 250 spade are barely breaking even. On the other hand, low-volume products such as the new Model 900 mower are selling for much more than the cost of production. The high profit that the Model 900 mower generates is particularly surprising since the company only recently began manufacturing mowers. Ben expected production inefficiencies, associated with any new product line, to keep profit margins low for at least three years. Ben knows that manufacturing overhead is allocated to products based on labor cost. The approach is simple, but he suspects it may be causing allocations of cost that are too high for spades and too low for mowers.

Firms that produce more than one product or provide more than one type of service invariably have substantial indirect costs. Because indirect costs cannot be directly traced to products or services, firms must develop some means of assigning these costs. The process of assigning indirect costs is referred to as **cost allocation**. Unfortunately, cost allocation frequently results in problems similar to the one Ben Jakes faces. To prepare yourself to deal with them, you need a good understanding of why and how costs are allocated. Providing you with that understanding is the purpose of this chapter. One of the key points of the chapter is that costs are allocated for a variety of purposes. Also, allocations that are adequate for one purpose may not be adequate for another purpose. Thus, it is important to remember the maxim "Different costs for different purposes."

Many managers have expressed concern that the way overhead is typically allocated may seriously distort product cost for manufacturing firms. The problem arises because most product costing systems allocate overhead using measures related to production volume. This is the case at Gardenrite where manufacturing overhead is allocated based on labor cost. However, many overhead costs are not proportional to volume. Activity-based costing (ABC) is an approach to allocating overhead costs that addresses this problem. We briefly discussed ABC in the chapter on job order costing. Here, you will gain a better understanding of the general process of cost allocation, which allows for a more detailed treatment of ABC.

LEARNING OBJECTIVES

1. Explain why indirect costs are allocated.
2. Describe the cost allocation process.
3. Discuss allocation of service department costs.
4. Discuss allocation of joint costs.
5. Identify potential problems with cost allocation.
6. Discuss activity-based costing and cost drivers.

LO 1

Explain why indirect costs are allocated.

PURPOSES OF COST ALLOCATION

Reasons to allocate cost include:

1. To provide information for important decisions.
2. To calculate the "full cost" of products for financial reporting purposes and for determining cost-based prices.
3. To reduce the frivolous use of common resources.
4. To encourage managers to evaluate the efficiency of internally provided services.

We discuss each of these purposes below.

To Provide Information for Decision Making

As we have seen in previous chapters, information on variable costs is crucial for making appropriate business decisions. Because some indirect costs are variable costs, allocating them may provide useful information. Consider a company that manufactures several different wood stoves, including the Yukon model. The Yukon requires $600 of direct material and $400 of direct labor per unit. In addition, the company incurs a variety of indirect costs to produce the stove. Suppose the company receives an offer from a customer to purchase 2,000 Yukons for $1,500 each. This is $500 more than the direct costs of producing the stove. Should management accept the offer? Acceptance of the offer depends in part on whether the *variable* indirect costs of the stove exceed $500. Examples of indirect variable costs include indirect material, the variable portion of indirect labor, and the variable portion of maintenance cost.

If indirect costs are allocated to the Yukon model, management will have the information required to evaluate the customer's order. Suppose the indirect variable costs allocated to the stove amount to $200. In this case, the total variable costs of the Yukon are $1,200 per unit, which is less than the $1,500 revenue generated from selling each unit. Therefore, management would be inclined to accept the customer's offer.

To Provide "Full Cost" Information

Since GAAP requires full costing, firms must allocate indirect production costs to goods produced for external financial reporting. In addition to the GAAP requirement, full cost information is required when companies have agreements whereby the amount of revenue received depends on the amount of cost incurred. For example, defense contractors with the federal government often have contracts that specify they will be paid the cost of production plus some fixed amount or percentage of cost. Such contracts are commonly called "cost-plus" contracts. An interesting feature of these contracts is that the cost of production specified in the contract often includes not only manufacturing costs but also a share of general and administrative costs. Thus, a substantial amount of cost allocation is required to assign indirect manufacturing costs and indirect general and administrative costs to the contract work.

Cost-plus contracts have a major problem. They create an incentive for firms to allocate as much cost as possible to goods produced on a cost-plus basis but little cost to those goods not produced on a cost-plus basis. The more cost companies allocate to cost-plus contracts, the larger the total amount they receive. In spite of this limitation, cost-plus contracts serve a useful purpose. Without assurances that they will be reimbursed for their costs and that they will earn some profit, many manufacturers would not be willing to bear the financial risks associated with producing state-of-the-art products for the government. For example, since such products often require use of untried technologies, only a few companies would be willing to produce a new fighter aircraft without assurance of reimbursement for all production costs incurred.

To Reduce Frivolous Use of Common Resources

Allocated costs also serve as a charge or fee for using internal resources or services. Consider a company that purchases a computer that each of its three divisions will use. Further, assume that almost all of the costs associated with running the computer are fixed and amount to $100,000 per year. Some accountants argue that if costs are fixed, no cost should be allocated to the user divisions because their use causes no incremental costs. However, if the three divisions are not charged for using the computer, they may use the computer for frivolous or nonessential purposes (e.g., playing computer games or requesting unnecessary computer-prepared reports).

This situation may not seem that detrimental to the company's welfare. After all, the costs associated with the computer are primarily fixed. If frivolous use does not cause additional costs, why discourage it? The reason is that frivolous use may have some hidden costs. The primary hidden cost in the example would be slower service to departments that need to use the computer when another department is using it. For example, reports that usually take minutes to prepare may take hours to produce when the computer is being used to prepare unnecessary reports.

One common way to eliminate frivolous use of centrally provided services is to allocate their costs. For example, suppose Division 1 planned to use the computer for 1,000 hours, Division 2 for 1,000 hours, and Division 3 for 2,000 hours. In this case, a charge of $25 per hour ($100,000 ÷ 4,000 hours) could be assessed. Note that this rate would allocate the entire cost of the computer ($100,000) among the three users, assuming their plans worked out as expected. Divisions 1 and 2 would each be charged $25,000; Division 3 would be charged $50,000. If this method of cost allocation is used, then each division would reduce its frivolous use of the computer because such use would reduce its reported profit.

To Encourage Evaluation of Services

Cost allocation also encourages managers to evaluate carefully the services for which they are being charged. If no costs are charged for use of centrally administered services such as computer or janitorial services, then users have no incentive to evaluate these services carefully. After all, the services are free. However, if users are charged for the services (i.e., they receive an allocation of the cost), then they have a strong incentive to evaluate them and to consider lower-cost alternatives. If lower-cost alternatives exist, and if users bring them to the company's attention, then the company can evaluate whether the services are provided in an efficient manner.

For example, suppose the manager of Division 3 determines that similar computer services can be purchased outside the company for less than the $50,000 currently being allocated to Division 3. After the manager brings this matter to management's attention, management can consider alternatives. In this case, it could encourage the manager of the computer system to lower that operation's costs. If the costs cannot be lowered, then management might consider replacing the computer system with separate computers for the divisions or buying computer services outside the company.

LO 2
Describe the cost allocation process.

PROCESS OF COST ALLOCATION

The cost allocation process consists of three steps:

1. Identify the cost objectives.
2. Form cost pools.
3. Select an allocation base and allocate the cost pools to the cost objectives.

Once in place, the allocation process operates as shown in Illustration 24-1.

ILLUSTRATION 24-1 The Cost Allocation Process

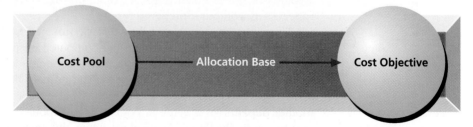

Determining the Cost Objectives

In designing the cost allocation process, the first step is determining the product, service, or department to receive the allocation. The object of the allocation is referred to as the **cost objective**. For example, if a company allocates depreciation of a drilling press to products such as flanges and brackets, the products are the cost objectives. If computer processing costs are allocated to the contracts a computer-aided design group works on, then contracts are the cost objectives (See Illustration 24-2.)

ILLUSTRATION 24-2 Cost Objectives

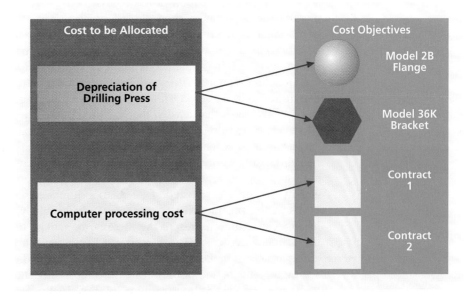

Forming Cost Pools

The second step in designing the cost allocation process is to form cost pools. A **cost pool** is a grouping of individual costs whose total is allocated using one allocation base. For example, all maintenance department costs could be treated as a cost pool. In this case, the cost pool would include the wages of workers in the maintenance department, supplies, small tools, and a variety of additional cost items. Cost pools are commonly formed along departmental lines (e.g., maintenance department costs in one cost pool and personnel department costs in another) or by major activities (costs related to equipment setups—a major activity in most manufacturing firms—in one cost pool and costs related to inspecting products for defects—another major activity—in another cost pool). However, they may also be formed in terms of cost behavior (e.g., fixed costs in one cost pool and variable costs in another).

In forming a cost pool, the overriding concern is to ensure that the costs in the pool are homogeneous or similar. One way to determine this is to compare the allocations with those that result from breaking the pool into smaller pools and using a variety of allocation bases. If there is no substantial difference in the allocations, then, for practical purposes, the costs in the pool are considered homogeneous.

Some manufacturing companies include all manufacturing overhead (including power costs, computing costs, material handling costs, etc.) in a single cost pool. Allocations from a large pool containing costs related to very different activities will not be accurate. While use of a single cost pool for overhead seems too broad, the exact number of appropriate cost pools is not clear. Managers must make a cost/benefit decision. More pools involve more record keeping, which is costly. However, more pools ensure more accurate information.

Selecting an Allocation Base and Allocating Costs

In designing the allocation process, the third step is selecting an allocation base that relates the cost pool to the cost objectives. The allocation base must be some characteristic that all of the cost objectives share. If the cost objectives are manufactured products, then direct labor hours, direct labor cost, and machine hours are characteristics that a company could use as allocation bases. If the cost objectives are the divisions of a multi-divisional firm, then sales dollars, total assets, and divisional profit could be used as allocation bases.

Deciding which of the possible allocation bases to use is not easy. Ideally, a department should select an allocation base that results in costs being allocated to cost objectives that *caused* the costs to be incurred. This is referred to as an allocation based on a **cause-and-effect** relationship. For example, if additional activity in a production department causes an increase in the costs the maintenance department incurs, then an allocation base that will result in the additional costs being allocated to the production department when there is additional activity should be selected. Direct labor hours, direct labor cost, or machine hours in the production department would be likely choices for the allocation base because they represent the increase in activity that leads to the increase in the maintenance cost. However, it would be difficult to argue that one of these allocation bases is better than another on cause-and-effect grounds. As we will see below, this is one of the problems of cost allocation. A number of allocation bases may appear to be equally valid, but they may also result in substantially different costs being assigned to the cost objectives.

Suppose Pratt Equipment company has two producing departments, Assembly and Finishing, that receive allocations of indirect costs from the maintenance department. In the coming year, the maintenance department expects to incur $200,000 of variable costs. These costs are related to both labor and machine hours incurred in the producing departments. The quantity of labor and machine hours are indicated below. With labor hours as the allocation base, the allocation rate is $4 per labor hour, and the assembly department receives an $80,000 allocation of cost from the maintenance department. However, with machine hours as the allocation base, the allocation rate is $10, and the assembly department receives a $110,000 allocation of cost from the maintenance department. The $30,000 difference in the allocations occurs in spite of the fact that both labor and machine hours are reasonable allocation bases to use.

	Labor Hours	Allocations	Machine Hours	Allocations
Assembly	20,000	$ 80,000	11,000	$110,000
Finishing	30,000	120,000	9,000	90,000
Total	50,000	$200,000	20,000	$200,000
Allocation Rate	$4 per labor hour		$10 per machine hour	

In many cases, establishing a cause-and-effect relationship between costs and cost objectives is not feasible. In these cases, accountants use other criteria such as relative benefits, ability to bear costs, and equity. Unfortunately, these terms are rather vague and difficult to implement. The **relative benefits** notion suggests that the allocation base should result in more costs being allocated to the cost objectives that benefit most from incurring the cost. This might suggest that computer costs should be allocated to departments based on time each spends using the computer. More use implies greater benefit. However, this could result in fixed computer costs being allocated to departments that did not exist (and could not have caused the cost of the computer to be incurred) when the computer was acquired. The **ability to bear costs** notion suggests that the allocation base should result in more costs being allocated to products, services, or departments that are more profitable. Because they are more profitable, they can *bear* the increased costs from the higher allocations. The **equity** notion suggests that the allocation base should result in allocations that are perceived to be fair or equitable. Obviously, this is a difficult criterion to apply because different individuals have different perceptions of what is equitable.

LO 3

Discuss allocation of service department costs.

ALLOCATING SERVICE DEPARTMENT COSTS

The organizational units in most manufacturing firms can be classified as either production departments or service departments. Production departments engage in direct manufacturing activity, while service departments provide indirect support. For example, in a furniture manufacturing company the assembly and finishing departments are production departments, while maintenance, janitorial, personnel, cafeteria, cost accounting, and power are service departments.

Service department costs are allocated to production departments that, in turn, allocate the costs to specific products. Two approaches are commonly used to allocate service department costs to production departments: the direct method and the sequential method. Both approaches are discussed below.

Direct Method of Allocating Service Department Costs

In the **direct method of allocating costs**, a company allocates service department costs to production departments but not to other service departments. Thus, even though the janitorial department provides a service to the personnel department, the company would not allocate janitorial costs to the personnel department. Instead, it would allocate these to the production departments. The process is presented in Illustration 24-3. Note the absence of an arrow between janitorial costs and personnel costs; there is no allocation of costs between the janitorial and the personnel departments.

Suppose janitorial costs at Bradley Furniture Company are $100,000. The company decides to allocate these costs to Assembly and Finishing based on the number of square feet in each of the production departments. Since Assembly has 20,000 square feet and Finishing has 30,000 square feet, the allocation rate is $2 per square foot ($100,000 ÷ 50,000 square feet). Assembly receives an allocation of $40,000 (20,000 square feet x $2) and Finishing receives an allocation of $60,000 (30,000 square feet x $2).

Suppose Bradley's personnel costs are $200,000. Bradley allocates these costs based on the number of employees in each production department. The assembly department has 60 employees and the finishing department has 40 employees. Thus, the allocation rate for personnel costs is $2,000 per employee

ILLUSTRATION 24-3 Allocating Service Department Costs to Production Departments and then to Products with the Direct Method

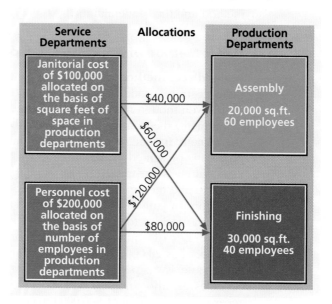

($200,000 ÷ 100 employees). The assembly department receives an allocation of $120,000 (60 employees x $2,000) and the finishing department receives an allocation of $80,000 (40 employees x $2,000). The allocations are presented in Illustration 24-4.

ILLUSTRATION 24-4 Direct Allocations of Service Department Costs for Bradley Furniture

Service Departments	Allocations	Production Departments
Janitorial cost of $100,000 allocated on the basis of square feet of space in production departments	$40,000 / $60,000	Assembly 20,000 sq.ft. 60 employees
Personnel cost of $200,000 allocated on the basis of number of employees in production departments	$120,000 / $80,000	Finishing 30,000 sq.ft. 40 employees

Sequential Method of Allocating Service Department Costs

Typically, service departments as well as producing departments consume the services a service department provides. For example, the personnel department may use the services of the janitorial department. The **sequential method of allocating costs** takes into account the fact that service departments make use of each other's services. However, to implement the method, the company must establish a hierarchy or order of services. At the top of the hierarchy is the service department that provides the greatest amount of service to the other service departments. At the bottom of the hierarchy is the service department that provides the least amount of service to the other service departments. Service departments that are lower in the order do not allocate costs to service departments that are higher in the order. For this reason, the method is sometimes referred to as the *step-down method*.

Suppose Bradley Furniture's janitorial department provides more service to the personnel department than the personnel department provides to the janitorial department. This is consistent with the hierarchy in Illustration 24-5.

ILLUSTRATION 24-5 Sequential Method of Cost Allocation

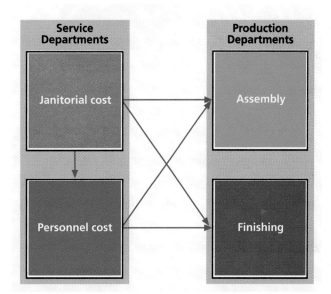

At Bradley Furniture, the personnel department occupies 1,282 square feet of space. In this case, the allocation of janitorial department cost will be at a rate of $1.95 per square foot.

Janitorial department cost		$100,000
Divided by square feet of space:		
Personnel	1,282	
Assembly	20,000	
Finishing	30,000	÷ 51,282
Cost per square foot		$1.95

With a rate of $1.95 per square foot, the personnel department will receive an allocation of $2,500 (1,282 square feet x $1.95); the assembly department, $39,000 (20,000 square feet x $1.95); and the finishing department, $58,500 (30,000 square feet x $1.95). (See Illustration 24-6).

ILLUSTRATION 24-6 Allocation of Janitorial Department Costs to Personnel, Assembly, and Finishing

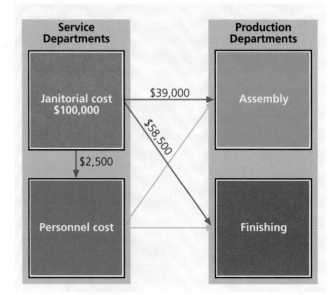

At this point, the personnel department has costs of $202,500, or $200,000 of its own cost and $2,500 allocated from the janitorial department. Its allocation rate will be $2,025 per employee.

Personnel department cost:		
Own cost	$200,000	
From Janitorial	2,500	$202,500
Divided by number of employees:		
Assembly	60	
Finishing	40	÷ 100
Cost per employee		$2,025

Thus, $121,500 of personnel department cost will be allocated to Assembly (60 employees x $2,025) and $81,000 of personnel department cost will be allocated to Finishing (40 employees x $2,025). (See Illustration 24-7).

In applying the sequential method, a company exercises considerable judgment in determining an appropriate order of service departments. Thus, the results of the method are somewhat arbitrary. However, the method often yields similar allocations to producing departments irrespective of the order chosen. Thus, the choice of the order may not present an important practical problem.

As a logical extension of the sequential method, a company could use a reciprocal allocation method to allow for allocations back and forth among its service departments. Such an approach requires solving simultaneous equations and is not presented here. It is covered in more advanced treatments of cost accounting topics.

ILLUSTRATION 24-7 Allocation of Personnel Department
Costs to Assembly and Finishing

LO 4
Discuss allocation of joint
costs.

ALLOCATING JOINT COSTS

Joint products, which arise when two or more products always result from common inputs, present an interesting cost allocation problem. The costs of the common inputs are referred to as **joint costs**, and these costs are common in the food processing, extractive, and chemical industries. For example, in the dairy processing business the common input of raw milk is converted into cream, skim milk, and whole milk. For lumber companies, the common input of a log is converted into various grades of lumber. For fuel companies, the common input of crude oil is converted into a variety of fuels and lubricants.

A graphic treatment of the joint costing problem is presented in Illustration 24-8. The incurred joint costs lead to two joint products. The stage of production when individual products are identified is referred to as the **split-off point**. Beyond this point, each product may undergo further separate processing, and the company incurs additional costs. However, these further processing costs do not present a cost allocation problem because they are directly attributable to individual products.

For financial reporting purposes, the company must allocate the cost of the common inputs to the joint products. However, managers must review carefully the resulting information about the profitability of the joint products. For example, suppose a lumber company spends $600 for an oak log and $20 to saw it into two grades of lumber. The process results in 500 board feet of Grade A lumber that sells for $1.00 per board foot and 500 board feet of Grade B lumber that sells for $.50 per board foot. How should the $620 joint cost be allocated to the joint products? The lumber company could use one approach to allocate the cost based on the physical quantity of output. Since the production process results in equal quantities of physical output, the company would allocate an equal share of the joint cost to each of the grades of lumber. In this case, both Grades A and B lumber would show a cost of $310. With this allocation, man-

ILLUSTRATION 24-8 Joint Costs and Joint Products

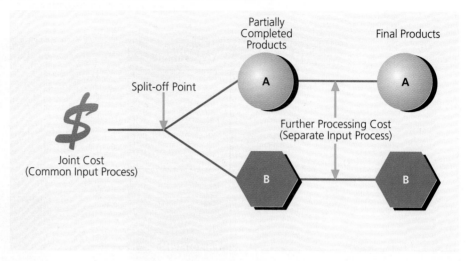

agers might think that Grade B lumber is not profitable and should be scrapped. After all, its cost is $310, while revenue from its sale is only $250. However this logic is not correct. If the Grade B lumber was scrapped, the company would loose $250 that helped cover the joint cost of $620. Remember: The company will incur total joint cost, regardless of what it does with the joint products beyond the split-off point. Therefore, the joint cost is largely irrelevant to any decision regarding a single joint product. However, the joint cost is relevant to decisions involving all of the joint products. If the total revenue from the sale of the joint products is less than the joint cost, then the company should cease production of all of the joint products.

A company can better allocate joint cost by using the **relative sales value method**. With this method, the amount of joint cost the company allocates to products depends on the relative sales values of the products at the split-off point. In the example below, the relative sales values are .333 for A and .667 for B.

Sales value of A at split-off	$500	Relative sales value of A ($500 ÷ $750)	.667
Sales value of B at split-off	250	Relative sales value of B ($250 ÷ $750)	.333
Total	$750	Total	1.000

Thus the company would assign an allocation of $413.33 (i.e., $620 x .667) to the Grade A lumber and an allocation of $206.67 (i.e., $620 x .333) to the Grade B lumber. One of the good features of this method is that the amount of joint cost a company allocates to a product cannot exceed its sales value at the split-off point. Thus, products that make a positive contribution to covering joint cost will not look unprofitable.

The costs allocated to the two grades of lumber using the physical quantity and the relative sales value approaches are compared in Illustration 24-9. In particular, note that for Grade B lumber, the physical quantity approach yields a negative gross margin of $60, while the relative sales value approach yields a positive gross margin of $43.33.

ILLUSTRATION 24-9 Comparison of Physical Quantity and Relative Sales Value Approaches to Allocation of Joint Costs

Joint cost:	
Cost of log	$600.00
Cost of sawing	20.00
Total	$620.00

Joint process yields:
  500 board feet of Grade A lumber selling for $1.00 per board foot
  500 board feet of Grade B lumber selling for $.50 per board foot

Results using physical quantities to allocate joint costs:

	Grade A	Grade B
Sales revenue:		
500 bf x $1.00	$500.00	
500 bf x $.50		$250.00
Cost:		
$620 x (500 bf ÷ 1,000 bf)	310.00	
$620 x (500 bf ÷ 1,000 bf)		310.00
Gross margin	$190.00	$ (60.00)

Results using relative sales values to allocate joint costs:

	Grade A	Grade B
Sales revenue:		
500 bf x $1.00	$500.00	
500 bf x $.50		$250.00
Cost:		
$620 x .667	413.33	
$620 x .333		206.67
Gross margin	$ 86.67	$43.33

LO 5

Identify potential problems with cost allocation.

PROBLEMS WITH COST ALLOCATION

There are a number of problems associated with the way costs are allocated in practice. In this section, we discuss four problems brought about by:

1. Allocations of costs that are not controllable.
2. Arbitrary allocations.
3. Allocations of fixed costs that make the fixed costs appear to be variable costs.
4. Allocations of manufacturing overhead to products using too few overhead cost pools.

Responsibility Accounting and Controllable Costs

Previous chapters have stressed that a primary use of managerial accounting is to evaluate the performance of managers and the operations under their control. Performance evaluation is facilitated by a system of accounting that traces revenues and costs to organizational units (e.g., departments and divisions) and individuals (e.g., plant manager, supervisor of assembly workers, vice president of operations) with related responsibility for generating revenue and controlling costs. Such a system is referred to as a **responsibility accounting system**.

Consider a company that produces tennis rackets and tennis clothes in two separate plants. The company could prepare monthly production cost reports that list the total amount of material, labor, and overhead costs for the two plants combined. However, this would *not* be consistent with responsibility accounting because the reports would not trace the production costs to the plants responsible for controlling them. A responsibility accounting system would require not only that the costs of producing the tennis rackets and tennis clothes be traced to their respective plants, but also that the costs in each plant be traced to the departments or other units responsible for those costs. For example, within the plant producing the tennis rackets, labor costs should be traced to each supervisor responsible for an identifiable group or team of workers (e.g., assembly workers and finishing workers).

Cost allocation is generally required in a responsibility accounting system because one organizational unit is often responsible for the costs another organizational unit incurs. For example, activity in a production department increases the costs the machine repair department incurs. Therefore, the production department's performance reports should reflect some share of the machine repair department cost. This can be achieved by allocating machine repair department costs to the production department.

However, some allocations of costs are not consistent with a responsibility accounting system. Most accountants believe that managers should be held responsible only for costs they can control. These costs, called **controllable costs**, are those that are affected by the manager's decisions. Allocating the cost of a building to the performance report of a supervisor responsible for controlling labor costs is not appropriate because the supervisor cannot control building costs. If allocated costs beyond their control appear on their performance reports, managers may experience considerable frustration. Managers want their performance evaluations to reflect their own strengths and weaknesses. However, in some cases, managers are allocated costs beyond their control simply to make them aware that the costs exist and that the firm's revenue must cover them. In such situations, the costs clearly should be labeled noncontrollable. This way managers know that company officials are aware the items are not the managers' responsibility. In labeling the costs as uncontrollable, the company will minimize possible resentment from their managers.

Arbitrary Allocations

In practice, cost allocations are the topic of numerous and often heated discussions. Managers may believe their departments receive unnecessarily large allocations of indirect costs, causing their departments to appear less profitable. Government agencies that have cost-plus contracts may believe products produced by contractors on a cost-plus basis receive unfairly high allocations of indirect costs. Unfortunately, such discussions will continue. The reason is that allocations of costs are inherently arbitrary. In almost all cost allocation situations, determining the one "true," "correct," or "valid" allocation is not possible. As noted earlier in the chapter, various allocation bases (e.g., labor hours, labor cost, and machine hours) may be equally justifiable but will result in substantially different allocations. Managers will naturally support allocations that make

INSIGHTS INTO ACCOUNTING

THE $7 ASPIRIN

In a recent Ann Landers column, a former patient complained about being charged $7 for a single aspirin tablet received during his hospitalization. How can a hospital justify such a charge? Look to the allocated costs. The product cost of that aspirin likely included allocations for: (1) the prescribing physician's time, (2) the dispensing pharmacist's time, (3) the administering nurse's time, (4) costs of the medical records department, and (5) a new cost category referred to as "shifted costs." This last classification includes such factors as unreimbursed Medicare costs, the cost to provide care to indigent and impoverished patients, and the cost of malpractice insurance. On top of these costs hospitals add a charge for other overhead costs not included in previous allocations.

After various costs have been added to the aspirin through cost-shifting and straightforward cost allocation, the aspirin has a cost basis of about $3.50. Add profit, and presto—the $7 aspirin. (See photo.)

Source: David W. McFadden, "The Legacy of the $7 Aspirin," published in *Management Accounting* (April 1990), pp. 38–41, copyright by the Institute of Management Accountants, Montvale, NJ.

County Community Hospital
Production Cost Sheet

	Unit	Unit Cost	Total Units	Total Cost
Raw material				
Aspirin	ea.	$0.006	2	$0.012
Direct labor				
Physician	hr.	60.000	0.0083	0.500
Pharmacist	hr.	30.000	0.0200	0.603
Nurse	hr.	20.000	0.0056	0.111
Indirect labor				
Orderly	hr.	12.000	0.0167	0.200
Recordkeeping	hr.	12.000	0.0167	0.200
Supplies				
Cup	ea.	0.020	1	0.020
Shared & shifted costs				
Unreimbursed Medicare		0.200	1	0.200
Indigent care		0.223	1	0.223
Uncollectible receivables		0.084	1	0.084
Malpractice insurance		0.034	2	0.068
Excess bed capacity		0.169	1	0.169
Other operating costs		0.056	1	0.056
Other administrative costs		0.112	1	0.112
Excess time elements		0.074	1	0.074
		Product cost		$2.632
		Hospital overhead costs @32.98%		.868
		Full cost (including overhead)		$3.500
		Profit		3.500
		Price (per dose)		$7.000

their performance look best and reject those that cast an unfavorable light on their performance.

Unitized Fixed Costs and Lump-Sum Allocations

One significant problem with cost allocation is the fact that the allocation process may make fixed costs appear to be variable costs. This happens when fixed costs are **unitized**, that is, stated on a per-unit basis. To illustrate the problem, suppose the Jones Tool Co. has several divisions. One of the divisions, referred to as the carpenter division, produces a variety of carpenter tools (e.g., hammers, saws, and drills). At the start of each year, Jones Tool Co. estimates the amount of general and administrative costs that are incurred centrally on behalf of the operations of the divisions. Such costs include administrative salaries, clerical costs, central accounting costs, and a variety of other costs, all of which are essentially fixed in the short run. In the current year, Jones expects these costs to be $2,000,000. Jones decides to let the divisions know these costs are being incurred on their behalf and, therefore, allocates them among the divisions based on their relative sales. In the current year, divisional sales are expected to be $50,000,000. Thus, Jones decides to allocate general and administrative costs to the divisions at a rate of $.04 per dollar of sales (i.e., $2,000,000 ÷ $50,000,000). Here general and administrative costs are unitized by sales dollar.

While the general and administrative costs are fixed, how will the manager of the carpenter division perceive them? This manager observes that as divisional revenue increases, the allocated costs increase. Thus, the manager perceives the costs as variable and may make decisions to maximize divisional profitability at the expense of the company's best interest. For example, suppose the carpenter division considers producing a new hammer that will sell for $20. At this price, the division expects to sell 100,000 units. Production of the hammer will require $12 of direct material cost, $6 of direct labor cost, and an increase in fixed manufacturing costs of $130,000. An analysis of the effect on the carpenter division's profit is presented in Illustration 24-10.

As indicated, sale of the hammer will result in an increase of $2,000,000 in sales. There will also be a $1,800,000 increase in variable costs (direct material and direct labor) and a $130,000 increase in fixed manufacturing cost. Thus, production and sale of the hammer will result in a $70,000 increase in profit. From this information, production of the hammer appears to be a profitable addition to the division's product line. However, will the manager be motivated to produce the hammer? Probably not. The reason is that, with the increase in sales, the division will receive a larger allocation of central general and administrative costs. With an allocation rate of $.04 per dollar of sales and an expected increase in sales of $2,000,000, the manager expects allocated costs to increase by $80,000. Since the manager perceives the additional allocated costs as variable when, in fact, they are fixed (that is, central administrative salaries, clerical costs, and accounting costs will not increase if the hammer is produced), the manager concludes that production of the hammer will result in the division losing $10,000 (i.e., $70,000 − $80,000).

To remedy the problem described above, firms need to allocate *fixed costs* in such a way that they *appear fixed* to the managers whose departments receive the allocation. This is achieved by **lump-sum allocations** of fixed costs, which allocate predetermined amounts not affected by changes in the activity levels of the organizational units receiving the allocation. Firms acquire resources based on the long-run needs of users. Thus, firms should also base

ILLUSTRATION 24-10 Problems of Unitized Fixed Costs

Sales of hammers (100,000 x $20)		$2,000,000
Less additional costs:		
Direct material (100,000 x $12)	$1,200,000	
Direct labor (100,000 x $6)	600,000	
Additional fixed manufacturing cost	130,000	
		1,930,000
Real increase in profit		$ 70,000
Less allocated fixed costs ($2,000,000 increase in sales x $.04)		80,000
Perceived loss on sale of hammers		$ (10,000)

allocations of fixed costs on the projected long-run needs that lead managers to incur the costs. For example, suppose Dyer Company purchases a computer to serve each of its two divisions. Purchase of the computer results in annual fixed costs of $40,000. In deciding what type of computer to purchase, management estimates that Division A would use the computer for 2,000 hours per year and Division B for 3,000 hours per year. Thus, allocating $16,000 to Division A (i.e., $40,000 x 2/5) and $24,000 to Division B ($40,000 x 3/5) is appropriate.

Although the activity of the two departments may deviate from expectations, lump-sum allocations should generally remain the same year after year. Suppose that Division A expanded and required 3,000 hours per year while Division B lost business and required only 2,000 hours. Should Dyer reverse the lump-sum allocations of the two divisions? Probably not. If Dyer reversed the allocations, the managers of the two divisions would perceive their allocations as based on their activity levels. In other words, they would view the fixed costs as variable. Thus, if lump-sum allocations of *fixed* costs are to *appear fixed*, the amount of the allocation must not depend on changes in activity.

Suppose the activity of Division A stayed at 2,000 hours, but Division B's activity level decreased from 3,000 hours to 2,000 hours. If the cost of the computer is allocated based upon current activity levels, the amount allocated to Division A would increase from $16,000 to $20,000, in spite of the fact that its use of the computer did not change. Obviously, the manager of Division A would be dissatisfied. Also, planning would be more difficult because the costs of the division would depend on the activity of the other division. This is not the case with a lump-sum allocation because, once the amount of the lump sum is determined, it does not vary in response to changes in activity.

How can lump-sum allocations improve a manager's decisions? Consider the Jones Tool Co. example presented earlier. Suppose Jones allocated the general and administrative costs on a lump-sum basis and assigned the carpenter division an allocation of $80,000. Note that this is the same amount allocated on the basis of revenue. However, when allocated as a lump-sum basis, the amount does not adversely affect the manager's decisions. The manager of the carpenter division now perceives the lump-sum allocation as a fixed cost. Thus, in the interest of maximizing divisional profit, the manager decides to produce the hammer because it contributes $70,000 toward covering the allocated costs that would be incurred whether or not the hammer is produced.

The Problem of Too Few Cost Pools

As you know from previous chapters, product costs consist of direct labor, direct material, and manufacturing overhead. Direct material and direct labor

INSIGHTS INTO ETHICS

Balsom Corporation has an informal policy of paying divisional managers a bonus that historically has amounted to 2% of the growth in divisional profit. Last year, the consumer products division had profit of $15,000,000. This year, preliminary figures show a profit of $20,000,000. This profit figure implies a bonus of $100,000, which the president of Balsom believes is excessive. (The manager of the consumer products division, no doubt, believes the bonus is well-deserved.) Accordingly, the president instructs the controller of Balsom to revise the allocation of centrally administered cost (e.g., administrative salaries, interest, and advertising) in such a way that the consumer products division will receive higher charges and have reduced profit. "After all," the president argues, "that division can stand to absorb more of these costs than our less profitable operations."

   Would a change in the allocation system be fair to the manager of the consumer products division? Would a change violate GAAP?

are traced directly to the products produced, and overhead is assigned to products using an overhead allocation rate. Many companies assign overhead to products using only one or two overhead cost pools. While this approach is simple and easy to use, product costs may be seriously distorted when a company uses only a small number of cost pools. Consider the problem in the context of the Electra Manufacturing Company, which manufactures products in two departments: Assembly and Finishing. Electra has total manufacturing overhead of $1,000,000 and each year the company incurs 50,000 labor hours. Thus, if the company includes all overhead in one cost pool and allocates overhead using labor hours, the overhead rate will be $20 per labor hour. Now, suppose that of the $1,000,000 of overhead, $600,000 is due to Assembly and $400,000 is due to Finishing. Further, Assembly has 40,000 labor hours; Finishing, only 10,000 labor hours. You can see that overhead per labor hour is much more expensive in the Finishing Department: overhead is $15 per labor hour in Assembly and $40 per labor hour in Finishing. (See Illustration 24-11.)

ILLUSTRATION 24-11 Overhead Rates Using One Versus Two Cost Pools

One Cost Pool

$$\frac{\text{Total Overhead}}{\text{Total Labor Hours}} = \frac{\$1,000,000}{50,000} = \$20 \text{ per labor hour}$$

Two Cost Pools (one for Assembly and one for Finishing)

$$\frac{\text{Assembly Overhead}}{\text{Assembly Labor Hours}} = \frac{\$600,000}{40,000} = \$15 \text{ per assembly labor hour}$$

$$\frac{\text{Finishing Overhead}}{\text{Finishing Labor Hours}} = \frac{\$400,000}{10,000} = \$40 \text{ per finishing labor hour}$$

   Now, assume that Electra has two products (A and B) that both require 10 labor hours. Product A requires 2 hours of assembly time and 8 hours of finishing, while Product B requires 8 hours of assembly time and 2 hours of finishing.

How much overhead will Electra allocate to each product if all overhead is included in a single cost pool and allocated on the basis of labor hours? The answer is that both products will receive the same allocation. They both require 10 hours of total labor, and use of a single cost pool allocates the average cost per labor hour. Both will receive $200 of overhead ($20 x 10 labor hours).

Which product is being under-costed and which product is being over-costed? Product A is under-costed because it requires relatively more production time in Finishing, which is a high-cost department in terms of overhead cost. Product B is over-costed because it requires relatively more production time in Assembly, which is a low-cost department in terms of overhead. Still, Product B receives the same charge per labor hour as Product A when only a single cost pool is used. Electra can easily solve this problem by setting up separate cost pools for overhead in each department. In general, product costs will be more accurate when a company uses more overhead cost pools. Also, decisions such as product pricing decisions that rely on product cost information will be improved. However, the more pools a company forms, the more costly will be its record keeping. The company must make a cost-benefit trade-off. Is the cost of forming more cost pools worth the benefit of improved information? This is a question a company must always address when considering improvements in accounting information.

LO 6

Discuss activity-based costing and cost drivers.

ACTIVITY-BASED COSTING

In the previous section, we discussed four potential problems with allocations of costs. Manufacturing companies face another problem when they use only measures of production volume as allocation bases to assign overhead to products. The problem and its solution, *activity-based costing* (ABC), are presented here.[1] A relatively recent development in managerial accounting, ABC has received a tremendous amount of attention from both academics and practitioners interested in improving managerial accounting information.[2] We briefly discussed ABC in Chapter 21; the discussion here is more detailed.

The Problem of Using Only Measures of Production Volume to Allocate Overhead

Manufacturing companies commonly use direct labor hours, direct labor cost, and machine hours as allocation bases when assigning overhead to products. Each of these items is a measure of production volume. Because most companies continue to allocate overhead using only measures of production volume as allocation bases, we refer to this as the "traditional approach." The problem with the traditional approach is that it assumes all overhead costs are proportional to production volume. (By "proportional," we mean that when volume

---

[1] Our discussion of activity-based costing is in a manufacturing context. However, banks, hospitals, insurance companies, and other service companies also have adopted an activity-based costing approach. See Yee-Ching Lilian Chan, "Improving Hospital Cost Accounting with Activity-Based-Costing," *Health Care Management Review*, Vol. 18 (Winter, 1993), pp. 71–77, for an example of activity-based costing in a service company context.

[2] Credit for developing activity-based costing is usually given to Robin Cooper and Robert Kaplan. See R. Cooper, "The Rise of Activity-Based Costing—Part One: What is an Activity-Based Cost System?" *Journal of Cost Management* (Summer, 1988), pp. 45–54, and R. Cooper, and R. Kaplan, "How Cost Accounting Distorts Product Costs," *Management Accounting* (April, 1988), pp. 20–27.

increases by 20 percent, overhead increases by 20 percent; when volume increases by 50 percent, overhead increases by 50 percent, etc.) However, many overhead costs (such as the cost of setting up equipment for a production run, the cost of inspecting raw materials, and the cost of handling materials) are not proportional to volume. Thus high-volume products often are over-costed, while low volume products are under-costed.

Consider the overhead costs a company incurs when starting a production line. Both a high-volume product (which is associated with a large amount of labor and machine time) and a low-volume product (which is associated with a small amount of labor and machine time) may require the same amount of setup time and setup cost. However, since the company allocates setup costs (along with all other overhead) only on the basis of production volume, the high-volume product will receive a larger *allocation* of setup cost. Thus, the high-volume product is over-costed. Let's see how the ABC approach avoids this problem.

The ABC Approach

In the ABC approach, companies identify the major activities that cause over-head costs to be incurred. Some of these activities are related to production volume, while others are not. Companies group the costs of the resources consumed performing these activities into cost pools. Finally, companies assign the costs to products using a measure of activity referred to as a *cost driver*. The steps involved in the ABC approach are:

1. Identify major activities.
2. Group costs of activities into cost pools.
3. Identify measures of major activities (called cost drivers).
4. Relate cost pools to products using cost drivers.

Some common activities and associated cost drivers are listed in Illustration 24-12. Note that some of the cost drivers are volume related (such as machine hours and assembly labor hours). Other cost drivers such as number of inspections and number of setups are not related to production volume. Some low-volume products that involve complex or fragile parts may need a large number of inspections, while some high-volume products that involve simple or rugged parts may need relatively few inspections. Also, both low-volume and high-volume products may require the same number of setups.

Each firm must decide how many separate activities (and related cost pools and cost drivers) to identify. If a company identifies too many activities, its system will be unnecessarily costly and confusing. For example, consider a company that produces 200 products and identifies 100 key activities. In this case, there are 20,000 (200 x 100) product-activity relationships. On the other hand, if a company uses too few activities the ABC system will not produce accurate data. Most companies that design ABC systems use 25 to 100 distinct activities.[3]

Relating Cost Pools to Products Using Cost Drivers

Before pursuing a comprehensive example, we will examine the last step in the ABC approach relating cost pools to products using cost drivers. Lacet

---

[3]See R. Cooper, R. Kaplan, L. Maisel, E. Morrissey and R. Oehm, *Implementing Activity-Based Cost: Management Moving From Analysis to Action*, (Institute of Management Accountants, 1992), p. 13.

ILLUSTRATION 24-12 Common Activities and Associated Cost Drivers

Major Activities	Associated Costs	Cost Drivers
Processing purchase orders for materials and parts	Labor cost for workers determining order quantities, contacting vendors, and preparing purchase orders	Number of purchase orders processed
Handling material and parts	Labor cost for workers handling material and parts, depreciation of equipment used to move material and parts (e.g, depreciation of fork-lift trucks), etc.	Number of material requisitions
Inspecting incoming material and parts	Labor cost for workers performing inspections, depreciation of equipment used to test strength of materials, tolerances, etc.	Number of orders received
Setting up equipment	Labor cost for workers involved in setups, depreciation of equipment used to adjust equipment	Number of setups
Producing goods using manufacturing equipment	Depreciation on manufacturing equipment	Number of machine hours
Supervising assembly workers	Salary of assembly supervisors	Number of assembly labor hours
Inspecting finished goods	Labor cost for finished goods inspectors, depreciation of equipment used to test whether finished goods meet customer specifications, etc.	Number of inspections
Packing customer orders	Labor cost for packing workers, cost of packing materials, etc.	Number of boxes shipped

Electronics produces a variety of electronic products ranging from simple hand-held calculators to hard disk drives. Inspection to ensure that products are of high quality is a major activity at Lacet. In the coming year, the company expects to incur inspection costs of $2,500,000. Forty workers are employed in the inspection process, and they are expected to perform 1,000,000 product inspections in the coming year. Using inspection cost as a cost pool and number of inspections as a cost driver, the company determines a rate of $2.50 per inspection for purposes of allocating inspection costs to products.

Lacet produces 20,000 Model ZX disk drives. Each drive is inspected three times during the production process, and workers test various functions for conformance with rigorous standards set by the company. How much of the total $2,000,000 inspection cost will Lacet allocate to the Model ZX? With 20,000 disk drives and three inspections per drive, a total of 60,000 inspections will be performed. A rate of $2.50 per inspection implies that $7.50 of inspection cost will be allocated to each disk drive ($2.50 rate x 3 inspections) for a total of $150,000 ($7.50 x 20,000). Lacet would take a similar approach to determine the amount of inspection cost to allocate to the other products it produces.

Comprehensive Example of the ABC Approach

In this section, we pursue a comprehensive example of the ABC approach using the situation Gardenrite Manufacturing Company faced at the start of the chapter. As you read the example, make sure you can explain why Gardenrite's

INSIGHTS INTO ACCOUNTING

ACTIVITY-BASED COSTING AT CAL ELECTRONIC CIRCUITS

Cal Electronic Circuits, Inc. (CECI) manufactures printed circuit boards (PCBs), which are sold to microcomputer manufacturers. Manufacturing involves a capital-intensive process that is partially automated. Historically, direct labor represented only 8% of total manufacturing costs while overhead accounted for 79%. Overhead allocations had been made on the basis of direct labor hours.

With direct labor contributing less than 10% of total production costs, CECI accountants felt they could not justify the allocation of overhead on the basis of direct labor hours. The solution was to implement an activity-based costing (ABC) system. The new system, like the old, was a full cost absorption approach to costing. Implementation of the new ABC system involved identification of multiple manufacturing and support processes. These were grouped into cost centers and a cost driver was assigned to each cost center (see below).

The accountants believe their new ABC system will assist in identifying the costs of various processes, incorporate the complexities of PCB production into their cost accounting system, and identify cost-volume-profit relationships more clearly for different products.

Cost Center ⟶	Driver
Engineering	Engineering hours
Prototype/tooling	Piece/panel volume
Site services and administration	Number of workers
Quality assurance	Number of setups
Waste treatment	Chemical dollar volume
Procurement	Piece/panel volume
Tab plate option	Number of sides
Soldermask	Number of sides
Component legend	Number of sides
Maintenance	Work hours

Source: John Y. Lee, "Activity-Based Costing at Cal Electronic Circuits," published in *Management Accounting* (October 1990), pp. 36–38, copyright by the Institute of Management Accountants, Montvale, NJ.

use of the ABC approach reduced the cost of the high-volume product (the Model 250 spade) and increased the cost of the low-volume product (the Model 900 Mower).

For product costing purposes, Gardenrite traces labor and material costs directly to products produced. The company allocates manufacturing overhead to products based on labor cost. At the start of 19X1, the company estimated manufacturing overhead at $40,000,000 and labor cost at $8,000,000. Thus, the overhead application rate was $5 per dollar of labor.

For 19X1, Gardenrite expected certain costs and revenues from sale of the Model 250 spade and the Model 900 mower (shown on the next page). Note that the overhead allocated to the Model 250 spade of $459,000 is equal to the overhead rate of $5 per dollar of labor times the $91,800 of direct labor incurred in production of the spade.

The production process for spades is fairly simple. The company uses one supplier for the metal handle and blade. The company produces shafts on an

	Model 250 Spade	Model 900 Mower
Number of units	85,000	800
Sales revenue	$765,000	$240,000
Direct labor	$ 91,800	$ 12,000
Direct material	153,000	48,000
Overhead	459,000	60,000
Total cost	$703,800	$120,000
Gross profit	$ 61,200	$120,000
Cost per unit	$8.28	$150.00
Gross profit per unit	$ .72	$150.00
Profit as a % of sales	8.00%	50.00%

automatic lathe and the workers assemble the handles, blades, and shafts by hand at a single workstation.

Two years ago, the company began manufacturing lawn mowers. The production process for lawn mowers is more complicated than the process used in spade production. The company uses 20 suppliers to provide the 50 components involved in production of the Model 900 mower. Further, assembly of mowers uses 15 separate assembly workstations.

Recall that Ben Jakes, the CFO at Gardenrite, suspects the low profit margin (less than 10% of sales) for spades may be due to problems with the current costing system. Further, he is somewhat surprised that the company is able to earn such a high margin on mowers (50%). Since the company only recently began manufacturing mowers, he expected production inefficiencies to keep profit margins low for at least three years.

Ben should be concerned about the product costing system at Gardenrite. The approach to allocating overhead assumes that all overhead is proportional to a single measure of production volume—labor cost. However, overhead is caused by several key activities. Suppose Ben authorizes a study of how the costs of the Model 250 spade and the Model 900 mower will change if Gardenrite takes an ABC approach. The study determines that the $40,000,000 of overhead cost is related to the four cost drivers identified in Illustration 24-13. As indicated, setup costs are related to the number of setups; material handling costs, to the number of material requisitions; and depreciation of equipment, to the number of machine hours required to produce products. All other overhead is categorized in a cost pool simply referred to as "Other."

ILLUSTRATION 24-13 Overhead Cost Items and Cost Drivers

Overhead Cost Items	Annual Cost	Cost Driver	Estimated Annual Value	Cost per Unit
Setup costs	$ 4,000,000	Number of setups	1,000 setups	$4,000 per setup
Material handling requisitions	$ 2,000,000	Number of material requisitions	$2,000 requisitions for all products produced	$1,000 per requisition
Depreciation of equipment	$10,000,000	Machine hours	20,000 machine hours	$500 per machine hour
Other	$24,000,000	Number of work-stations used in production of a product	3,000 workstations used for all products	$8,000 per workstation

Gardenrite has decided that "manufacturing complexity" is a major factor contributing to the incurrence of other overhead costs. The cost driver for complexity is the number of workstations required to produce a product. Products that require many workstations to produce are more complex products and cause more overhead.

Manufacturing spades requires two setups and three material requisitions. Forty machine hours are used to produce the 85,000 Model 250 spades. Assembly of spades requires one workstation. Production of the 800 Model 900 mowers requires 5 setups and 50 material requisitions. One hundred machine hours are used to produce the 800 mowers. Assembly of mowers requires 15 workstations. This information is summarized in Illustration 24-14.

ILLUSTRATION 24-14 Production Information for 85,000 Spades and 800 Mowers

	Model 250 Spade	Model 900 Mower
Number of setups	2	5
Number of material requisitions	3	50
Number of machine hours	40	100
Number of workstations	1	15

Using the information above, Ben can calculate the costs per unit of Model 250 spades and Model 900 mowers, assuming the company changes to an ABC system. The calculations are presented in Illustration 24-15. With the ABC approach, the cost of the Model 250 Spade drops from $8.28 to $3.34 per unit, while the cost of the Model 900 mower increases from $150.00 to $375.00 per unit.

	Model 250 Spade	Model 900 Mower
Cost per unit using traditional approach to allocating overhead	$8.28	$150.00
Cost per unit using ABC approach to allocating overhead	$3.34	$375.00

Recall that the Model 250 spades sold for $9.00 per unit; thus, the ABC approach reveals that this high-volume product is very profitable. However, the Model 900 mower sells for only $300 per unit. The ABC approach reveals that the selling price is not even covering the full cost of this low-volume product.[4] The CFO's intuition that the traditional product costing system at Gardenrite might be providing misleading information was correct. Because the traditional system only allocated costs using a volume-related allocation base, the high-volume product (spades) was over-costed and did not appear to be particularly profitable. The low-volume product (mowers) was under-costed and appeared to be highly profitable when, in fact, it was not covering its costs. This example has a clear message. Namely, companies should consider taking an ABC approach to product costing and use a variety of cost drivers in addition to dri-

---

[4]The fact that costs exceed revenue for the Model 900 mower does not *necessarily* imply that the product should be immediately dropped. Some of the costs included in the cost of the mower (such as depreciation) will exist whether or not the mower is produced. See the discussion in the chapter dealing with cost information and management decisions.

vers that measure only production volume. Otherwise, they run the risk of making poor product pricing decisions and continuing to produce products that are not profitable in the long run.

ILLUSTRATION 24-15 Costs of Model 250 Spade and Model 900 Mower Using an ABC Approach

Model 250 Spade			Model 900 Mower		
Number of units		85,000	Number of units		800
Direct labor		$ 91,800	Direct labor		$ 12,000
Direct material		153,000	Direct material		48,000
Overhead:			Overhead:		
Setup cost ($4,000 x 2)	$ 8,000		Setup cost ($4,000 x 5)	$ 20,000	
Material handling cost			Material handling cost		
($1,000 x 3)	3,000		($1,000 x 50)	50,000	
Depreciation of equipment			Depreciation of equipment		
($500 x 40)	20,000		($500 x 100)	50,000	
Other ($8,000 x 1)	8,000		Other ($8,000 x 15)	120,000	
Total overhead		39,000	Total overhead		240,000
Total cost		$283,800	Total cost		$300,000
Cost per unit		$3.34	Cost per unit		$375.00
Selling price per unit		$9.00	Selling price per unit		$300.00
Gross profit per unit		$5.66	Gross profit (loss) per unit		$(75.00)
Gross profit as a % of sales		63%	Gross profit (loss) as a % of sales		(25%)

Different Costs for Different Purposes

Allocations of costs that are quite suitable for one purpose may be inappropriate for another purpose. In particular, allocations that are satisfactory from a product costing standpoint may not provide useful information for decision making. For example, using a single overhead rate may result in product costs that are quite acceptable from a financial reporting standpoint. However, for decision-making purposes, an ABC approach may be more appropriate. Thus, when making an allocation, companies must carefully consider the purpose of the allocation and decide whether the allocated cost serves the particular purpose.

SUMMARY

Explain why indirect costs are allocated.   Indirect costs are allocated to provide information for decision making, to calculate the full cost of products, to reduce the frivolous use of common resources, and to encourage managers to evaluate the efficiency of internally provided services.

Describe the cost allocation process.   The cost allocation process has three steps: (1) identify the cost objectives, (2) form cost pools, and (3) select an allocation base and allocate the cost pools to the cost objectives.

Discuss allocation of service department costs.   Service department costs are allocated to production departments that, in turn, allocate these costs to products. The direct method allocates service department costs to production departments but not to other service departments. The sequential method considers the fact that service departments make use of each other's services.

Discuss allocation of joint costs.   The costs of common inputs that result in multiple products are referred to as joint costs. Companies may allocate these costs by using a physical measure of output. However, such an approach may make one or more of the joint products appear to be unprofitable when, in fact, they contribute to covering common costs. Allocating joint costs using the relative sales value of the joint products is a better approach. With this method, products that make a positive contribution to covering joint cost will not look unprofitable.

Identify potential problems with cost allocation.   Generally, managers should not receive allocations of costs they cannot control. This is a central idea of responsibility accounting, which is a system of accounting that traces revenues and costs to organizational units with related responsibility.

Companies must exercise care when they allocate fixed costs on a per unit basis (i.e., the fixed costs are unitized). Unitized fixed costs appear to be variable to the manager who receives the allocation. In many cases, it is better to allocate fixed costs with lump-sum allocations. Managers need to be aware that problems arise because allocations are often arbitrary. Also, accurate costs are seldom obtained when companies allocate costs using only one or two cost pools.

Discuss activity-based costing and cost drivers.   Activity-based costing is a product costing method that recognizes that costs are caused by activities. Measures of the key activities that cause costs to be incurred are referred to as cost drivers. The cost drivers are used as the allocation bases to relate indirect costs to products. Unlike traditional systems, ABC does not focus solely on volume-related cost drivers.

REVIEW PROBLEM

The Expeditions Food Company has three service departments (maintenance, personnel and security) and three production departments (cooking, freezing, and vacuum packing). Costs for the service departments are collected in cost pools and are allocated to the producing departments. The costs are then re-allocated to the company's products as part of the overhead of the production departments. Maintenance and security department costs are allocated on the basis of square footage, and personnel department costs allocated on the basis of the number of employees.

Selected data for Expeditions are as follows:

	Costs	Square Footage	Number of Employees
Service departments:			
Maintenance	$600,000	5,000	30
Personnel	$300,000	3,000	10
Security	$200,000	2,000	10
Production departments:			
Cooking		25,000	100
Freezing		10,000	50
Vacuum packing		5,000	50

REQUIRED:

a. Allocate the costs for each service department to the production departments using the direct method.

b. Allocate the costs for the service departments to the production departments using the sequential method. Assume maintenance is allocated first, then personnel, then security.

c. Using the information from a and b above, tabulate the total service department costs allocated to each production department under: (1) the direct method and (2) the sequential method. Comment on which method seems appropriate.

d. Expeditions is unsure of what allocation base to select for the allocation of security costs. The controller wants to use square footage and the chief cost accountant wants to use the number of employees. They settled on square footage after a full discussion of the merits of each allocation base. Do you think they made a good choice? Discuss.

SOLUTION:

(a) *Allocation of service department costs to production departments, direct method.*

$600,000 maintenance department costs:

To cooking: $600,000 x $\dfrac{25,000}{40,000}$ = $375,000   (See note)

To freezing: $600,000 x $\dfrac{10,000}{40,000}$ = $150,000

To vacuum packing: $600,000 x $\dfrac{5,000}{40,000}$ = $75,000

$300,000 personnel department costs:

To cooking: $300,000 x $\dfrac{100}{200}$ = $150,000

To freezing: $300,000 x $\dfrac{50}{200}$ = $75,000

To vacuum packing: $300,000 x $\dfrac{50}{200}$ = $75,000

$200,000 security department costs:

To cooking: $200,000 x $\dfrac{25,000}{40,000}$ = $125,000

To freezing: $200,000 x $\dfrac{10,000}{40,000}$ = $50,000

To vacuum packing: $200,000 x $\dfrac{5,000}{40,000}$ = $25,000

Note: The calculation could be performed as follows:

(1) Determine cost per unit of activity:

$\dfrac{\$600,000}{40,000}$ = $15 per square ft.

(2) Multiply cost per unit of activity by the activity level for the department:

$15 x 25,000 square ft. = $375,000

(b) *Allocation of service department costs, to production departments, sequential method (rounded to nearest dollar).*

$600,000 maintenance department costs:

To personnel: $600,000 x $\dfrac{3,000}{45,000}$ = $40,000

To security: $600,000 x $\dfrac{2,000}{45,000}$ = $26,667

To cooking: $600,000 x $\dfrac{25,000}{45,000}$ = $333,333

To freezing: $600,000 x $\dfrac{10,000}{45,000}$ = $133,333

To vacuum packing: $600,000 x $\dfrac{5,000}{45,000}$ = $66,667

$340,000 personnel department costs ($300,000 + $40,000 from maintenance):

To security: $340,000 x $\dfrac{10}{210}$ = $16,190

To cooking: $340,000 x $\dfrac{100}{210}$ = $161,905

To freezing: $340,000 x $\dfrac{50}{210}$ = $80,952

To vacuum packing: $340,000 x $\dfrac{50}{210}$ = $80,952

$242,857 security department costs ($200,000 + $26,667 from maintenance + $16,190 from personnel):

To cooking: $242,857 x $\dfrac{25,000}{40,000}$ = $151,786

To freezing: $242,857 x $\dfrac{10,000}{40,000}$ = $60,714

To vacuum packing: $242,857 x $\dfrac{5,000}{40,000}$ = $30,357

(c) *(1) Service department costs allocated under the direct method.*

	Costs Allocated	Cooking	Freezing	Vacuum Packing
Maintenance	$ 600,000	$375,000	$150,000	$ 75,000
Personnel	300,000	150,000	75,000	75,000
Security	200,000	125,000	50,000	25,000
Total	$1,100,000	$650,000	$275,000	$175,000

(2) Service department costs allocated under the sequential method.

	Costs Allocated	Personnel	Security	Cooking	Freezing	Vacuum Packing
Maintenance	$ 600,000	$ 40,000	$ 26,667	$333,333	$133,333	$ 66,667
Personnel	340,000		16,190	161,905	80,952	80,953
Security	242,857			151,786	60,714	30,357
Total	$1,182,857	$(40,000)	$(42,857)	$647,024	$274,999	$177,977

Comment: Although conceptually the sequential method reflects a more logical allocation of costs than the direct method, the sequential method is more complex, and in Expeditions' case does not result in a substantially different allocation of costs to the producing departments. Therefore, the direct method seems preferable.

(d) *Discuss the accountants' choice of allocation base.*

Ideally, an allocation base should result in costs being allocated to cost objectives (the three production departments in this instance) on a cause-and-effect basis. For example, in evaluating square footage as a basis of allocating security costs, cause-and-effect is present if a department with twice the square footage generates twice the costs in the security department. In other words, security cost should be a function of square footage. The relationship between the number of employees and security can be studied in the same manner, to determine if security costs are in some way a function of the number of employees. Many times a strong cause-and-effect relation to an allocation base cannot be found, and the selection of the base is determined by other criteria. Without being familiar with Expeditions' security operations, it is difficult to determine which allocation base, square footage or number of employees, represents the best cause and effect characteristics.

KEY TERMS

ability to bear costs, *985*
cause-and-effect, *984*
controllable costs, *992*
cost allocation, *979*
cost objective, *983*
cost pool, *983*
direct method of allocating costs, *985*
equity, *985*

joint costs, *989*
joint products, *989*
lump-sum allocations, *994*
relative benefits, *985*
relative sales value method, *990*
responsibility accounting system, *992*
split-off point, *989*

sequential method of allocating costs, *987*
unitized fixed cost, *994*

SELF QUIZ

LO 1   1. Costs are allocated:
   a. To provide information for important decisions.
   b. To calculate the "full cost" of products for financial reporting purposes.
   c. To reduce the frivolous use of common resources.
   d. To encourage managers to evaluate the efficiency of internally provided services.
   e. All of the above

LO 2   2. In the cost allocation process, the cost objective is:
   a. The allocation base used to allocate costs.
   b. A grouping of individual costs whose total is allocated using one allocation base.
   c. The product, service, or department that is to receive the allocation.
   d. None of the above.

LO 2   3. There are, in order, three steps in the cost allocation process. List them: (1) _____, (2) _____, and (3) _____.

LO 2   4. The overriding concern in forming a cost pool is to:
   a. Avoid placing similar costs in a pool.
   b. Limit the number of costs which make up the pool.
   c. Insure that the costs in the pool are homogeneous or similar.
   d. None of the above.

LO 2   5. The third step in the allocation process is to select an allocation base to allocate cost pools to the cost objectives. An allocation base:
   a. Must have some characteristic that is common to all cost objectives.
   b. Ideally, should result in costs being allocated based on a cause-and-effect relationship.
   c. Both a and b.
   d. None of the above.

LO 3   6. The direct method of allocating costs:
   a. Allocates service department costs to other service departments.

b. Allocates only direct costs.

c. Allocates service department costs to producing departments only.

d. Both b and c.

LO 3 7. X Company has three service departments and three production departments. They use the sequential method of allocating costs.

a. Each service department will allocate its costs to the other two service departments.

b. The production departments receive a smaller allocation of service department costs because some service department costs are allocated to other service departments.

c. All service department costs are allocated directly to production departments.

d. None of the above.

LO 4 8. The Southern Meat Packing Company pays $160 for a hog. The hog is slaughtered and processed into: hams, tenderloins, sausage, pork chops, and pigs feet. The cost of the hog is referred to as a _____ cost. The products are referred to as _____ products.

LO 4 9. The Southern Lumber Company pays $1,000 for a walnut log. They saw the log into boards totaling 500 board feet. There are two grades of boards. Grade A sells for $3 per board foot and grade B sells for $2 per board foot. The best method to allocate the cost of the log to the grade A and B lumber is the _____ _____ _____ _____ .

LO 4 10. The joint costs incurred in a joint product situation:

a. Are incurred before the split-off point.

b. Are incurred after the split-off point.

c. Should never be allocated.

d. None of the above.

LO 4 11. A joint product has a cost of $18, which includes $6 of allocated joint costs, and a sales price of $16.

a. Profit would improve if the company discontinued production of the product.

b. The company should sell as few of the products as possible to minimize the loss on product sales.

c. The data is misleading because the $6 allocated joint cost will have to be incurred even if the product is eliminated.

d. Both a and b.

LO 5 12. When fixed costs are stated on a per unit basis:

a. Fixed costs are said to be "unitized."

b. Fixed costs appear to be variable to managers receiving allocations.

c. Decision making is improved.

d. Both a and b.

LO 5 13. A way to avoid the problems of unitized fixed costs is to:

a. Not allocate fixed costs.

b. Use a lump-sum method of allocating fixed costs.

c. Combine fixed and variable costs in a single cost pool.

d. None of the above.

LO 5 14. Allocation of indirect costs:

a. Can be done with great accuracy and precision, if one applies the proper techniques.

b. Is an inherently arbitrary process, a characteristic that can lead to problems.

c. Can often be justified a variety of ways, leading to substantially different costs being allocated.

d. Both b and c.

LO 5 15. In allocating costs to products, more accurate
LO 6   costing is obtained by:

a. Having only one cost pool.

b. Having more than one cost pool.

c. Always using allocation bases that are based on production volume.

d. None of the above.

LO 5 16. Controllable costs for the manager of department A are:

a. Costs of the controller's department which are allocated to department A.

b. Costs of supplies used in department A.

c. All costs related to the final product.

d. All the above.

LO 6 17. Cost drivers in activity-based costing are:

a. Always related to production volume.

b. Often assign more costs to low-volume production than traditional allocation methods.

c. Often assign less costs to low-volume production than traditional allocation methods.

d. None of the above.

LO 2 18. Terms and their definitions are listed below.
LO 3   Match the definitions with the terms.
LO 4   ___ a. Ability to bear costs
LO 5   ___ b. Joint products
LO 6   ___ c. Cause-and-effect
           ___ d. Controllable costs
           ___ e. Cost allocation
           ___ f. Cost objective
           ___ g. Cost pool
           ___ h. Direct method of allocating costs
           ___ i. Equity
           ___ j. Activity-based costing
           (1) A grouping of individual costs whose total is allocated using one allocation base.

(2) Two or more products arising from common inputs.

(3) A concept of cost allocation which suggests that the allocations should be fair.

(4) The concept of an allocation base resulting in allocations to cost objectives that caused the costs to be incurred.

(5) The object of the cost allocation: usually a product, service, or department.

(6) An approach in managerial accounting that uses cost pools related to activities and cost drivers to assign costs to products.

(7) Costs which a manager can control.

(8) A cost allocation concept which suggests that the allocation base should result in more costs being allocated to products, services, or departments that are more profitable.

(9) The process of assigning indirect costs.

(10) Allocating costs from service departments directly to producing departments without any intermediate allocations among the service departments.

LO 2
LO 3
LO 4
LO 5
LO 6

19. Key terms and their definitions are listed below. Match the definitions with the key terms.

___ a. Cost pool
___ b. Cost drivers
___ c. Lump-sum allocations
___ d. Relative benefits
___ e. Relative sales value method
___ f. Responsibility accounting system
___ g. Split-off point
___ h. Sequential method of allocating costs
___ i. Unitized fixed costs
___ j. Joint products

(1) The stage of production when individual joint products are identified.

(2) Two or more products result from common inputs.

(3) A system of accounting which traces costs and revenues to organizational units and individuals responsible for the revenues and costs.

(4) Stating fixed costs on a per unit basis.

(5) A concept of cost allocation which allocates costs based on the amount of benefit the cost objective receives from the incurrance of the cost.

(6) Measures of activity used to allocate cost pools in activity-based costing.

(7) A grouping of individual costs whose total is allocated using one allocation base.

(8) Allocations of fixed costs in such a way that the costs appear to be fixed to the managers whose departments receive the allocations.

(9) A method of allocating service department costs which takes into account service departments using each other's services.

(10) A way of allocating joint costs based on the sales price of the joint products at the split-off point.

QUESTIONS

Q24-1   List four reasons why indirect costs are allocated.

Q24-2   "All variable costs are direct, and all fixed costs are indirect." Is this a true statement? Discuss.

Q24-3   A defense contractor has been awarded a contract to produce a submarine that includes a lot of high-cost electronic surveillance equipment. The contract is on a "cost plus" basis. The contractor is entitled to allocate indirect administrative costs to the submarine. Accordingly, the administrative costs are allocated to the submarine and to other jobs the contractor is working on using direct material costs as the allocation base. Is direct material a good allocation base? Discuss.

Q24-4   Allocated costs can serve as the basis for charging for the use of internal resources or services. What are the possible advantages obtained from charging for internal resources and services?

Q24-5   Explain what a cost objective is and give two examples.

Q24-6   Explain one possible advantage of having two cost pools for each service department, one for variable costs and one for fixed costs.

Q24-7   If a company is allocating the cafeteria costs to all departments within the company, what allocation base might result in a good cause-and-effect relationship?

Q24-8   If direct cause-and-effect relationships cannot be established when choosing an allocation base, accountants use other criteria. Name three such criteria.

Q24-9   How do controllable costs relate to a responsibility accounting system?

Q24-10   Should noncontrollable costs ever be allocated to a department?

Q24-11   "Unitizing" fixed costs might cause a manager to elect not to produce a product on the grounds that it is unprofitable, when, in fact, production of the product would be profitable. How can a company avoid this problem?

Q24-12   Explain the difference in the direct method of allocating service department costs and the sequential method of allocating service department costs.

Q24-13   A company has a joint product with allocated joint costs of $10 using a physical quantity method of allocation. They are only able to sell the product for $8. Should they discontinue the product? Discuss.

Q24-14   Why is the relative sales value a more logical way to allocate joint costs than is physical quantity? Discuss.

Q24-15   What is a cost driver?

Q24-16   Briefly explain how traditional methods of allocating overhead to products might underallocate costs to low-production-volume products.

EXERCISES

LO 1

E24-1   **Reasons for Allocating Indirect Costs**   The Quest Production Company operates a security department that provides protection to all departments within the company. Departmental managers are responsible for working with the head of security to ensure that their departments are protected. Briefly explain why Quest might want to allocate the security department costs to departments.

LO 2

E24-2   **Basic Allocation Process**   Quick Company's copy department, which does all of the bulk photocopying for the company, budgets the following costs for the year, based on expected activity of 5,000,000 copies.

Salaries (fixed)	$60,000
Depreciation of copy machines (fixed)	15,000
Employee benefits (fixed)	15,000
Utilities (fixed)	2,000
Paper (variable, 1 cent per copy)	50,000
Toner (variable, 1 cent per copy)	50,000

The costs are assigned to two cost pools, one for fixed costs and one for variable costs. The copy costs are then assigned to the sales department and the administrative department. Fixed costs are assigned on a lump-sum basis, 30 percent to sales and 70 percent to administration. The variable costs are assigned at a rate of 2 cents per copy.

REQUIRED:

Assuming 4,000,000 copies were made during the year, 1,500,000 by sales and 2,500,000 by administration, calculate the copy department costs allocated to Sales and Administration.

LO 2

E24-3   Basic Allocation Process, Selecting Allocation Bases   Following is a list of cost pools which must be allocated to two cost objectives: (1) general and administrative and (2) sales.

Cost Pools	Allocation Base
a. Maintenance	_____
b. Cafeteria	_____
c. Security	_____
d. Copying	_____
e. Child care	_____
f. Car fleet	_____
g. Nursing Station	_____
h. Career Counseling	_____
i. Utilities	_____

REQUIRED:

For each cost pool identify a cost allocation base.

LO 2,3

E24-4   Basic Allocation Process, Problems with Allocations   The maintenance department for the Wells Distribution Company budgets annual costs of $3,000,000 based on the expected operating level for the next year. The costs are assigned to two production departments using the direct method of allocation and a single cost pool. Wells is considering two allocation bases for the departmental assignments of cost: (1) square footage and (2) direct labor hours. The following data relate to the bases.

	Production Dept. 1	Production Dept. 2
Square footage	20,000	30,000
Direct labor hours	30,000	20,000

REQUIRED:

Calculate the costs allocated to the production departments using each allocation base. Comment on: (1) the problem that the significantly different allocation bases present, and (2) which base might be preferable.

LO 3

E24-5   Allocation of Service Department Costs, Direct Method   Ryan Company has three service departments (S1, S2, S3) and two production departments (P1, P2). The following data relate to Ryan's cost allocations.

	Budgeted Costs	Number of Employees
S1	$3,000,000	75
S2	$2,000,000	50
S3	$1,000,000	25
P1		150
P2		225

The service department costs are allocated by the direct method. The number of employees is used as the allocation base for service department costs.

REQUIRED:

a. Allocate service department costs to production departments.
b. Calculate the total service department costs allocated to each production department.

LO 3

E24-6   Allocation of Service Department Costs, Sequential Method   Ryan Company has three service departments (S1, S2, S3) and two production departments (P1, P2). The following data relate to Ryan's cost allocations.

	Budgeted Costs	*Number of Employees*
S1	$3,000,000	75
S2	$2,000,000	50
S3	$1,000,000	25
P1		150
P2		225

The service department costs are allocated by the sequential method, S1 first, S2 second, S3 third. The number of employees are used as the allocation base for service department costs.

REQUIRED:

a. Allocate service department costs to production departments.
b. Calculate the total service department costs allocated to each production department.

LO 4

E24-7 Allocating Joint Costs   The Western Produce company purchased a truckload of watermelons for $600. The load weighed 6,000 pounds. Western separated the melons into two grades: superior and economy. The superior grade melons had a total weight of 4,000 pounds and the economy grade melons totaled 2,000 pounds. Western sells the superior grade at 25 cents per pound and the economy grade at 10 cents per pound.

REQUIRED:

Calculate the allocation of the $600 cost of the truckload to the superior grade and economy grade melons, assuming (1) the physical quantity method of allocation, and (2) the relative sales value method of allocation.

LO 5

E24-8 Problems Associated with Cost Allocation   Qualla Company's outdoor wear division receives an offer from a motorcycle company to purchase 1,000 rainproof riding suits for $175 each. Qualla's accountants determine that the following costs apply to the production of the rain suit.

Direct material	$80
Direct labor	40
Variable overhead	10
Allocation of fixed Production department overhead	10
Allocation of fixed Service department costs	40

Although the manager, Cindy Brown, of the outdoor wear division questions the allocation of fixed service department costs to the rainwear, she is told that the fixed service department costs are allocated using an allocation base of direct labor dollars and that the $1 overhead rate must be applied to the $40 of direct labor in the rainsuit. The manager's performance is evaluated based on division profits.

REQUIRED:

a. Explain how "unitized" fixed costs may be creating a problem for Qualla.
b. Suggest a way to correct the problem.
c. Calculate the change in income from accepting the motorcycle company's offer.

LO 5

E24-9 Responsibility Accounting, Controllable Costs   David Mott, the manager of the service department at the Dirt Bike Sales and Service Company, is evaluated based on the profit performance of his department. The profit of the service department is down this year because the service department's share of the allocated cost of the accounting and bookkeeping department is much higher than last year. Discuss how this situation relates to a responsibility accounting system and controllable costs.

LO 6

E24-10   Activity-Based Costing   The following are six cost pools established for a company using activity-based costing. The pools are related to the company's products using cost drivers.

Cost Pools:
(1) Raw materials quality control
(2) Production equipment repairs and maintenance
(3) Raw materials storage
(4) Plant heat, light, water, and power
(5) Finished product quality control
(6) Production line setups

REQUIRED:

For each cost pool, identify a possible cost driver.

PROBLEM SET A

LO 1,2,5

P24-1A   Reasons Indirect Costs are Allocated; Basic Allocation Process; Problems with Cost Allocation   Railroads have been a regulated industry in the past with the rates set to transport coal based on the railroad's cost per mile of hauling a carload of coal. The president of a large coal company was reported to have said, "God in heaven, in all of His wisdom, cannot calculate a railroad's cost of hauling a carload of coal from Eastern Kentucky to Hampton Roads."

REQUIRED:

a. In reference to the situation above, why does the railroad allocate indirect costs?
b. Identify several indirect costs that the railroad would have to allocate.
c. In reference to the above situation, identify the cost objective.
d. Suggest some possible allocation bases that might be used by a railroad.
e. What do you think the president of the coal company is implying in his statement?

LO 2,3

P24-2A   Allocating Service Department Costs, Direct Method   New-World Airlines has three service departments: (1) tickets/booking, (2) baggage and handling, and (3) maintenance. The service department costs are collected in separate cost pools for each department and are allocated to the two revenue-producing departments—(1) domestic flights and (2) international flights. New-World does not differentiate between fixed and variable costs in making allocations. The following data relate to the allocations.

	Budgeted Costs	*Budgeted Air Miles*
Tickets/booking	$4,000,000	
Baggage/handling	$2,000,000	
Maintenance	$6,000,000	
Domestic flights		5,000,000
International flights		20,000,000

REQUIRED:

a. Allocate the service department costs to the revenue producing departments using air miles as the allocation base and the direct allocation method.
b. Evaluate the cause-and-effect relationship resulting from the use of air miles as the allocation base. In which of the cost pools do you think the cause and effect is the strongest? In which pool is it probably the weakest? Suggest an alternative allocation base for the cost pool with the weakest cause-and-effect relationship.

LO 2,5

P24-3A   **Choice of Allocation Base, Problems with Cost Allocation**   Smith Manufacturing has two production departments, molding and finishing, which are served by one service department, maintenance. Smith's accountants are trying to select an allocation base to allocate the service department costs to the production departments. Possible allocation bases identified are: (1) square footage of space occupied, (2) direct labor hours, (3) machine hours, and (4) cost of equipment. The following data relate to the allocation.

Budgeted maintenance department costs $500,000

	Molding	Finishing
Square footage of space occupied	20,000	30,000
Budgeted direct labor hours	200,000	400,000
Budgeted machine hours	50,000	50,000
Cost of equipment	3,000,000	2,000,000

REQUIRED:

a. Prepare a schedule showing the maintenance costs allocated to the production departments under each of the four possible allocation bases.
b. Do all of the allocation bases appear to have a good cause-and-effect relationship with maintenance department costs? What type of information is needed to answer this question?
c. Why are allocations sometimes considered arbitrary?
d. Suppose that the large majority of maintenance costs results from upkeep and repair of the equipment. Which allocation base appears to have the best cause-and-effect relationship with maintenance costs?
e. Discuss why it might be advantageous to separate the maintenance department costs into fixed and variable and allocate the fixed costs using a lump-sum allocation.

LO 3

P24-4A   **Allocating Service Department Costs, Direct and Sequential Methods**   Blair Industries produces electronic equipment for the aviation industry. Blair has two service departments, maintenance and computing, and two production departments, assembly and testing. Maintenance costs are allocated on the basis of square footage occupied and computing costs are allocated on the basis of the number of computer terminals. The following data relate to the cost allocations of the service departments.

	Maintenance	Computing	Assembly	Testing
Service department costs	$400,000	$600,000		
Square footage		20,000	70,000	30,000
Terminals			5	10

REQUIRED:

a. Allocate the service department costs using the direct method.
b. Allocate the service department costs using the sequential method. Start with the maintenance department.
c. When using the sequential method, what should have been the basis for selecting maintenance as the first service department allocated?

LO 4

P24-5A   **Allocation of Joint Costs**   The Cannon Petroleum Company purchases raw crude oil and refines the crude into petroleum products. The refining process produces three petroleum products that require no further processing and are sold at the split-off point to other petroleum refiners in bulk quantities. The products are labeled Product A, Product B, and Product C. The following information relates to Cannon's operations.

Crude oil and refining costs	$10,000,000	
Petroleum products produced:		
Product A	2,000,000 gallons	
Product B	3,000,000 gallons	
Product C	5,000,000 gallons	
Sales price per gallon:		
Product A	$4.00	
Product B	3.00	
Product C	0.50	

REQUIRED:

a. What is meant by the term "split-off point?"
b. Allocate the joint costs to Products A, B, and C using physical quantity as the basis of allocation. Calculate the cost per gallon and the profit or loss on the sale of a gallon of each product.
c. Based on your calculations in b, is Cannon loosing money on the sale of Product C? Would they be better off to eliminate product C? Discuss.
d. Allocate the joint costs to Products A, B, and C using the preferable method, which is the relative sales value method. Calculate the cost per gallon and the gross margin on the sale of a gallon of each product.
e. Compare the costs allocated under the two methods and discuss why the relative sales value method seems to be a more logical way to allocate joint costs.

LO 6   **P24-6A   Activity-Based Costing**   The Western Edge Manufacturing company produces two products. One is a recreational whitewater kayak molded from a cross link plastic and designed to perform as a durable whitewater playboat. The other product is a high-performance competition kayak molded with high-tech, fiberglass-like materials which are very light. The recreational boat is uniform in its dimensions and style. However the competition boat is custom designed to fit the paddler and his or her taste in certain features, such as rocker and cockpit size.

   Most of the sales come from the recreational boat, but recently sales of the competition boat have been increasing. The following information relates to the products for the most recent accounting year.

	Recreational Kayak	*Competition Kayak*
Sales and production (boats)	900	100
Sales price	$600	$650
Unit costs:		
Direct materials	$150	$200
Direct labor	100	100
Overhead	135	135
Total unit costs	$385	$435

Overhead costs:	
Building depreciation and maintenance	$ 25,000
Equipment depreciation and maintenance	25,000
Materials ordering	15,000
Quality control	10,000
Maintenance and security	10,000
Setup and drafting	20,000
Supervision	30,000
Total	$ 135,000

Overhead rate based on direct labor dollars:

$$\frac{\text{Total overhead}}{\text{Total direct labor}} \quad \frac{\$\ 135,000}{\$\ 100,000^*} = \begin{array}{l}\$1.35 \text{ overhead per}\\ \text{dollar of direct labor}\end{array}$$

*(900 x $100) + (100 x $100)

Victor Mason, the president, is concerned that the traditional cost accounting system used by Western may not be providing accurate costing information and that the sales price of the competition boat might not be enough to recover its true costs.

REQUIRED:

a. The traditional system that Western is using assigns 90% of the $135,000 total overhead to the recreational boat because 90% of the direct labor dollars were spent on the recreational boat. Discuss why this might not be an accurate way to assign overhead to the boats.

b. Discuss how Western might be able to improve their cost allocations by adapting more than one cost pool.

c. Assume Western retains a consultant to create an activity-based costing system, and the consultant develops the following data. Determine the overhead allocated to each model of boat using the activity-based costing information and compute the total unit costs for each boat.

Cost Pool	Amount	Cost Driver	Driver Activity Rec. Boat	Driver Activity Comp. Boat
Building	$25,000	square footage	6,000	1,000
Equipment	25,000	machine hours	3,400	600
Materials ordering	15,000	number of orders	200	100
Quality control	10,000	number of inspections	300	150
Maintenance and security	10,000	square footage	6,000	1,000
Set up and drafting	20,000	number of setups	20	40
Supervision	30,000	direct labor $	$90,000	$10,000

d. Discuss why the activity-based allocations are different than the traditional allocation method used by Western.

PROBLEM SET B

LO 1,2,5

P24-1B   Reasons Indirect Costs are Allocated; Basic Allocation Process; Problems with Cost Allocation   The president of a bank comes to the chief accountant and states. "I need some information for the board of directors meeting next week. A couple of the directors are on our case. They think everything we do is old-fashioned and inefficient. Now they are questioning the efficiency of our preparation and mailing of monthly bank statements. What I need from you is a report showing what it costs us to prepare and mail a bank statement each month. Let's show them we are not throwing money away around here."

REQUIRED:

a. Briefly discuss the concept of different costs for different purposes and how it relates to this problem.

b. Identify several direct costs of preparing a bank statement.

c. Identify several indirect costs that possibly could be allocated as part of the cost of preparing the statements.

d. For each indirect cost you identify, suggest an allocation base.

e. For each cost and its allocation base identified in d, rate the cause and effect relationship as: (1) good, (2) acceptable, or (3) poor.

f. Does the chief accountant face something of an ethical dilemma in this situation? Explain how the arbitrary nature of cost allocations exacerbates the accountant's problems. If you were the chief accountant, what approach would you take to preparing the report?

LO 3

P24-2B **Allocating Service Department Costs, Sequential Method**   The Water Wonder Park has three service departments: (1) maintenance, (2) security, and (3) parking. Wonder has two revenue-producing departments: (1) olympic pool and (2) water slides. The following data relate to the cost allocations.

Cost Pool	Budgeted Costs	Square Footage	Ticket Sales
Maintenance	$500,000		
Security	100,000	5,000	
Parking	50,000	100,000	
Olympic pool	600,000	50,000	180,000
Water slides	900,000	75,000	300,000

REQUIRED:

a. Allocate the service department costs using the sequential method and square footage as the allocation base. The order of allocation is maintenance, security, and parking.
b. Assuming the budgeted costs for the revenue-producing departments represent their projected operating costs, compute a projected cost per ticket which includes all allocated costs.
c. What is the basis for selecting the order of service departments for sequential allocation?

LO 3,5

P24-3B **Allocating Service Department Costs, Separate Allocations of Fixed and Variable Costs, Direct Method**   The American Washing Machine Company has two service departments, equipment maintenance and grounds keeping, and two production departments, assembly and packing. Fixed and variable service department costs are collected in separate cost pools and are allocated using different allocation bases. Fixed costs are allocated based on the percentages given, which represent the expected long term usage by each service department. Variable costs are allocated using labor hours. The following relates to the allocations.

	Equipment Maintenance	Grounds Keeping	Assembly	Packing
Costs:				
Fixed	$190,000	$150,000		
Variable	60,000	78,000		
Allocation bases:				
Equipment maintenance —fixed			60%	40%
Grounds keeping—fixed			70%	30%
Labor hours			40,000	40,000

REQUIRED:

a. Allocate the service department costs using the direct method of allocation.
b. What advantage might result from allocating fixed and variable service costs separately?

LO 3

P24-4B **Allocating Service Department Costs, Sequential Method**   Quick Stop makes brake pads for heavy trucks. They have two producing departments, cutting and finishing, and three service departments, maintenance, cafeteria, and environmental monitoring. The service department allocations are square footage for Maintenance, and number of employees for Cafeteria and Monitoring. The following data relate to the cost allocations.

	Maint.	*Cafeteria*	*Monitoring*	*Cutting*	*Finishing*
Budgeted costs	$80,000	$125,000	$130,000		
Square footage	3,000	2,000	1,000	35,000	25,000
Employees	5	6	4	35	25

The budgeted costs represent all direct operating costs for the service departments.

REQUIRED:

a. Allocate the service department costs to production departments using the sequential method. Use the order: maintenance, cafeteria, and monitoring.
b. What criteria should Quick Stop consider in selecting the order of allocation? Discuss.

LO 4   **P24-5B**   **Joint Cost Allocations**   Coal Products uses a common process to make coal into fireplace logs which are used in residential homes, and coal pellets, which are used in industry to fuel boilers. As raw material, Coal Tech purchases coal fines from several large industrial users of coal. Coal fines are essentially coal dust left in the coal storage areas of the industrial users. Coal Products then combines the coal fines with a special bonding agent in a patented process which yields small bonded chunks that are compressed into the fireplace logs and the pellets in a single process. In May 1993, 100,000 tons of coal fines were purchased at $3 per ton. The fines were processed with the bonding agent and compressed for an additional cost of $450,000. The yield was 100,000 tons of pellets and 50,000 tons of fire place logs. The pellets are sold for $7 per ton and the logs are sold for $20 per ton.

REQUIRED:

a. Allocate the joint costs to the pellets and logs using tons as the allocation base and calculate the cost per ton of each product.
b. Allocate the joint costs to the pellets and logs using the relative sales value method and calculate the cost per ton of each product.
c. Calculate the profit margins per ton on the pellets and logs based on (1) allocations of joint costs using tons as the allocation base, and (2) allocations of joint costs using the relative sales value as the allocation base.

LO 6   **P24-6B**   **Activity-Based Costing**   The Electronic Rodent Company manufactures mouse devices for computers. They make 12 different models of mouse devices, as well as several other types of computer components. They have recently adopted an activity-based costing system to assign manufacturing overhead to their products. The following data relates to one of their products, the wireless Field Mouse, and the ABC system cost pools.

Field Mouse:

Annual production	20,000 units
Direct material per unit	$31
Direct labor per unit	$6

Manufacturing overhead cost pools:

Pool	*Costs in Pool*	*Cost Driver*
Materials ordering	$ 800,000	number of purchase orders
Materials inspection	400,000	number of receiving reports for fragile materials
Equipment setup	2,000,000	number of setups
Quality control	900,000	number of inspections
Other	15,000,000	Direct labor dollars
Total annual manufacturing overhead	$19,100,000	

Activity information related to cost drivers:

Pool	Annual Activity All Products	Annual Activity Field Mouse
Materials ordering	100,000 (orders)	1,000
Materials inspection	2,000 (receiving reports)	300
Equipment setup	100 (setups)	0*
Quality control	4,000 (inspections)	400
Other	$10,000,000 (direct labor $)	$120,000

*Field mouse production utilizes machinery which does not require significant setup activity.

REQUIRED:

a. Calculate the overhead rate per unit of activity for each of the five cost pools.
b. Calculate the *total* overhead assigned to the production of the Field Mouse.
c. Calculate the *overhead costs per unit* for the Field Mouse.
d. Calculate the *total unit cost* for the Field Mouse.
e. Assume Rodent allocates overhead by a traditional production volume based method using direct labor dollars as the allocation base and one cost pool. Determine: (1) the overhead rate per direct labor dollar, (2) the per unit overhead assigned to the field mouse, and (3) discuss the differences in cost allocations between the traditional method and activity-based costing.

CRITICAL THINKING AND COMMNICATING

C24-1   A group of students toured the production facilities of a large well-known steel manufacturer located in the eastern United States. The production process involved manufacturing steel ingots and then rolling the ingots into rolls of steel of different widths, lengths, and thicknesses.

After the tour, the plant controller discussed with the group the problems the company was having in determining the costs of the different rolls of steel manufactured at the plant. In fact, it was learned that although the company had operated the plant for many years, they did not have a satisfactory way of allocating common costs to different rolls of steel. A study was currently under way to identify a way of allocating common costs that would be based on a strong cause-and-effect relationship. The controller stated that the preliminary results of the study indicate "that in fact, we have miscalculated the costs of the different types of steel under the old methods of allocation, and we have been establishing sales prices that have not reflected the true costs of producing the steel. I must tell you that management is disappointed that it has taken the company this long to get the bookkeeping to the point that we know what our product costs us to produce." Further discussion with the controller revealed that the old way of allocating common costs was based on the quantity of steel in each roll.

REQUIRED:

a. Discuss what problems, if any might result from the steel company's lack of information about the true cost of each type of steel.
b. Identify several common costs that would need to be allocated to the different types of steel.
c. Can you identify a major problem with using the quantity of steel as an allocation base?
d. Suggest an allocation base that would have a better cause-and-effect relationship.

C24-2   Buy-Mart is a small chain of discount department stores similar to several national
chains, although Buy-Mart is a regional operation. They have a policy of preparing
departmental income statements for all revenue-producing departments within each
store. The departmental statements use the following format.

Department _____ Operating Statement for Month Ended _____	
Direct departmental sales	$XXXXXX
Less cost of goods sold	XXXXXX
Departmental gross margin	$XXXXXX
Less other direct departmental expenses	XXXXXX
Departmental contribution to indirect expenses and profits	$XXXXXX
Less allocation of indirect costs	XXXXXX
Departmental income before taxes	$XXXXXX

A typical Buy-Mart store assigns all local store indirect costs to one of three local cost
pools: (1) general and administrative, (2) maintenance and security, and (3) advertising
and promotion. All home office common costs are also assigned to similar cost pools
and are in turn allocated to local store cost pools. All local store cost pools, including the
pool's share of home office costs, are allocated to the eight revenue-producing departments within the local store.

   A Buy-Mart store normally has the following revenue-producing departments: (1)
housewares, (2) sporting goods, (3) automotive, (4) hardware, (5) appliances, (6) adult
apparel, (7) children's apparel, and (8) lawn and garden shop.

REQUIRED:

a. If Buy-Mart uses the departmental statements as part of a responsibility accounting
   system, which part of the departmental statement should be used for the purpose of
   evaluating managers of the revenue-producing departments?
b. Suggest a possible allocation base to allocate local store maintenance and security
   costs to the eight revenue-producing departments.
c. Suggest a possible allocation base to allocate the home office general and administrative expenses to each local store.
d. Suppose, in reality, Buy-Mart allocates all cost pools based on sales, i.e., the home
   office costs are allocated to stores based on total store sales, and the local cost pools
   are allocated to departments based on departmental sales. Is this a good method of
   allocation? Discuss.
e. Suggest a reason why Buy-Mart might allocate all indirect costs to stores and finally to
   each revenue department.

CHAPTER 25

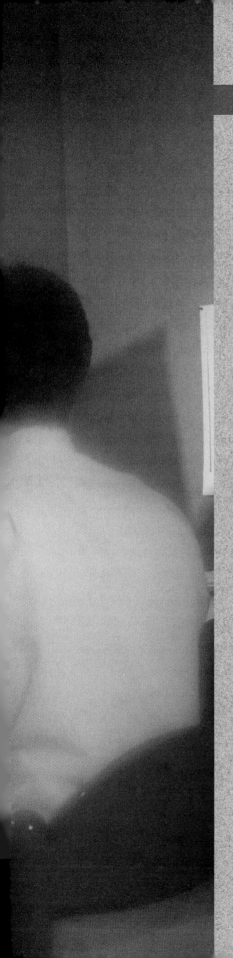

Budgetary Planning and Control

Preston Manufacturing Company produces metal containers that are designed to protect sensitive electronic equipment in shipment. At a meeting of key managers, Alan Renton, president of Preston Manufacturing, reviewed the past successes and failures of his firm. "As you know," he concluded, "we've begun a new marketing campaign, and I am confident that next year sales will increase by at least 15 percent." Jack North, the production manager, seemed caught off guard by this good news. "Look, Alan," he said, "If you really think sales are going to take off, we've got to plan for the increase. I'll have to hire additional workers, and the people in Purchasing will need to make larger purchases of materials so we don't run out." Pam Smith, vice president of Finance, chimed in, "Also, more sales means more inventory, and more inventory means we'll have to borrow additional funds to finance the expansion. I'll need some lead time to arrange the loan."

The meeting ended with everyone agreeing that more attention needed to be devoted to planning company activities. Alan returned to his office convinced that without a plan to guide and coordinate company activities, the coming year would be a series of "near disasters." He concluded, "The marketing, production, and financing groups must know what is anticipated so we can produce the right quantities of the right stuff."

In business, **budgets** are the formal documents that quantify a company's plans for achieving its goals. The entire planning and control process of many companies is built around budgets. This chapter illustrates the preparation of several different budgets that are in common use. The role of budgets in the performance evaluation process is presented, and a number of issues associated with budgets are discussed.

1. Discuss how budgets are used in planning and control.
2. Prepare the individual budgets that make up the master budget.
3. Describe why flexible budgets are needed for performance evaluation.
4. Discuss the conflict between the planning and control uses of budgets.

LO 1

Discuss how budgets are used in planning and control.

USE OF BUDGETS IN PLANNING AND CONTROL

Budgets are used by many companies to both plan and control operations.

Planning

Budgets are useful in the planning process because they enhance *communication* and *coordination*. The process of developing a formal plan (i.e., a budget) forces managers to consider carefully their goals and objectives and to specify means of achieving them. Budgets are the vehicle for communicating information about where the company is heading. They also aid coordination of managers' activities. For example, the marketing department may prepare a budget that includes estimates of sales for each month of a future year. The production department may use the information contained in this budget to schedule workers and material deliveries. Thus, the necessary coordination of product sales and product production is achieved.

Control

In the control process, budgets are useful because they provide a basis for *evaluating performance*. To control a company, and to ensure it is heading in the proper direction and operating efficiently, assessing the performance of managers and the operations for which they are responsible is essential. Generally, performance evaluation is best carried out by comparing actual performance to planned or budgeted performance. Significant deviations from planned performance indicate a need to consider corrective action. A graphic presentation of the role of budgets in the evaluation of performance is presented in Illustration 25-1.

DEVELOPING THE BUDGET

The group responsible for preparing budgets is often referred to as the **budget committee**. Members of the committee do not simply impose a budget on a particular department. Rather, they work with each department to develop realistic plans that are consistent with overall company goals. A distinction is often made between top-down and bottom-up approaches to the development of a budget. In a top-down approach, budgets are developed at higher organizational levels without substantial input from lower-level managers. In a bottom-up approach, lower-level managers are the primary source of information used in setting the budget. Most managers believe a successful budgeting process requires a bottom-up approach. After all, lower-level managers often have the

ILLUSTRATION 25-1 Role of Budgets in Performance Evaluation

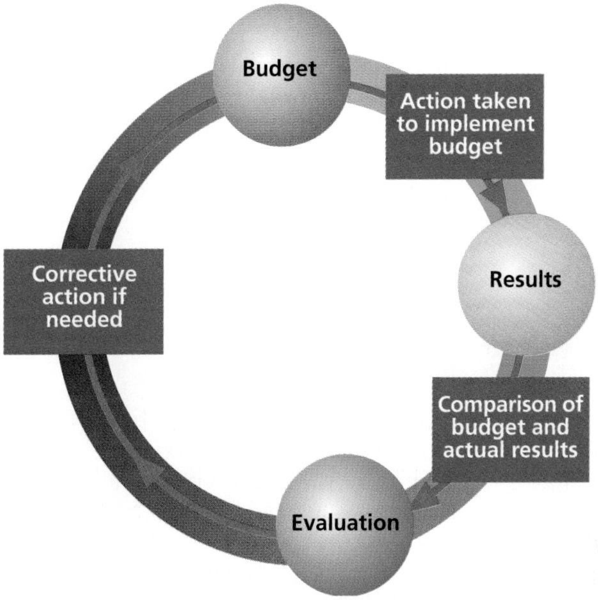

best information regarding business conditions affecting their departments. If this is the case, their input is critical in developing realistic financial plans.

Budget Time Period

Before preparing budgets, managers must decide on an appropriate budget period. Budgets are prepared for a variety of time periods, depending on a company's needs. In some cases, long-run budgets are prepared for a five- or even a ten-year period. Short-run budgets may cover a month, a quarter, or a year. Generally, the longer the time period, the less detailed the budget.

Zero Base Budgeting

A common starting point in developing a budget is the costs and revenues of the previous period. These amounts are adjusted up or down based on current information and assumptions or estimates of what will happen in the future. However, this approach may *not* lead to a fresh consideration of activities. So-called **zero base budgeting**, a method of budget preparation, requires each department to justify budgeted amounts at the start of each budget period, even if the amounts were supported in prior budget periods. That is, managers must start from zero in developing their budgets. This results in a fresh consideration of the budget's validity. However, the technique is time-consuming and expensive. While zero base budgeting has gained considerable support in governmental budgeting, business enterprises do not widely practice it.

LO 2
Prepare individual budgets that make up the master budget.

THE MASTER BUDGET

The **master budget**, a comprehensive planning document, incorporates a number of individual budgets. Typically, it includes budgets for sales, production, direct materials, direct labor, manufacturing overhead, selling and administrative expenses, capital acquisitions, and cash receipts and disbursements, as well as a budgeted income statement and a budgeted balance sheet. In this section we present examples of each of these components of a master budget. For purposes of the example, budgetary information is prepared by quarter for the Preston Manufacturing Company. We assume that the company produces only a single product (metal shipping containers) and does not have a material amount of work in process inventory. Thus, any complications work in process inventory introduces can be ignored. Monthly budgets for a multiproduct firm with work in process inventory require more computations, but these budgets are not conceptually more difficult.

Sales Budget

In the budget process, the first step involves preparation of sales forecasts and development of a sales budget. This budget comes first because other budgets cannot be prepared without an estimate of sales. For example, the production budget requires an estimate of future sales before production necessary to meet demand can be determined. A company can use numerous methods to estimate sales. Very large companies may hire economists to prepare sales forecasts using sophisticated mathematical models that consider the rate of inflation, national capital expenditures, and other economic data. Smaller companies may develop forecasts based on an analysis of the trend in their own sales data.

Trade journals or magazines exist for almost every industry and may provide useful information for developing sales forecasts. Typically, these journals contain information on past industry sales and make predictions about the industry's growth. Sales personnel may be another good source of information for forecasting sales. Some companies periodically ask all of their salespeople to estimate sales in their territories for the coming year. These estimates may be highly accurate if the salespeople base their estimates on thorough knowledge of their customers' needs. In general, forecasts of sales are part science and part art. The forecasts of even the most sophisticated mathematical models are often adjusted based on the professional judgment of experienced managers.

Based on the trend of sales and consideration of a planned marketing campaign, Alan Renton, president of Preston Manufacturing, predicts unit sales of its product, metal shipping containers, will increase by 15% in the coming year. Sales personnel generally agree that this level of increase is realistic, provided the company maintains a price per unit of $45. Accordingly, the company budgets sales for each quarter simply by increasing prior year sales in units by 15%. The result is the sales budget presented in Illustration 25-2.

Production Budget

Once the sales budget has been prepared, the company can develop a production budget. In deciding how much to produce, managers must consider how much they expect to sell, how much is in beginning inventory, and how much they want in ending inventory. The quantity that must be produced can be calculated from the following formula:

Finished Units to be Produced	=	Expected Sales in Units	+	Desired Ending Inventory of Finished Units	–	Beginning Inventory of Finished Units

ILLUSTRATION 25-2 Sales Budget

	First Quarter	Second Quarter	Third Quarter	Fourth Quarter	Year
Preston Manufacturing Company **Sales Budget** **For the Year Ended December 31, 19X2**					
Prior year sales in units	18,261	21,739	20,000	19,130	79,130
Projected at 115% of prior year (units)	21,000	25,000	23,000	22,000	91,000
Sales price per unit	x $45	x $45	x $45	x $45	x $45
Budgeted sales revenue	$945,000	$1,125,000	$1,035,000	$990,000	$4,095,000

Preston Manufacturing Company would like the ending inventory of finished goods to be equal to 10% of next quarter's sales. In the first quarter, Preston estimates that 21,000 units will be sold. Two thousand five hundred units are needed in ending inventory (i.e., 10% of 25,000 units expected to be sold in the second quarter). Thus, a total of 23,500 units are required. However, the company has 2,100 units in beginning inventory; thus, only 21,400 units must be produced. The production budget for Preston Manufacturing Company is presented in Illustration 25-3.

ILLUSTRATION 25-3 Production Budget

	First Quarter	Second Quarter	Third Quarter	Fourth Quarter	Year
Preston Manufacturing Company **Production Budget** **For the Year Ended December 31, 19X2**					
Unit sales[1]	21,000	25,000	23,000	22,000	91,000
Plus: Desired ending inventory of finished units[2]	2,500	2,300	2,200	2,400[3]	2,400
Total units needed	23,500	27,300	25,200	24,400	93,400
Less: Beginning inventory of finished units	2,100	2,500	2,300	2,200	2,100
Units to be produced	21,400	24,800	22,900	22,200	91,300

[1]Information from sales budget, Illustration 25-2.
[2]Equals 10% of next quarter's sales.
[3]Based on estimate of sales in the first quarter of the following year.

Direct Material Purchases Budget

The quantity of direct materials that must be purchased depends on the amounts needed for production and ending inventory. Obviously, a company needs some direct materials on hand at the end of the period for use in production at the start of the subsequent period. The quantity that must be purchased can be calculated from the following formula:

$$\begin{array}{c} \text{Required} \\ \text{Purchases of} \\ \text{Direct Materials} \end{array} = \begin{array}{c} \text{Quantity} \\ \text{Required for} \\ \text{Production} \end{array} + \begin{array}{c} \text{Desired Ending} \\ \text{Quantity of} \\ \text{Direct Materials} \end{array} - \begin{array}{c} \text{Beginning} \\ \text{Quantity of} \\ \text{Direct Materials} \end{array}$$

Preston Manufacturing Company has established a policy of maintaining direct materials inventory equal to 10% of the amount required for production in the subsequent quarter. In the first quarter, the company plans on producing 21,400 units. Each unit requires 2 pounds of direct material. Thus, 42,800 pounds of direct material are required for production. In addition, 4,960 pounds must be on hand at the end of the quarter (i.e., 10% of the quantity required for next quarter's production), but 4,280 pounds are on hand at the start of the quarter. Thus, 43,480 pounds must be purchased. The cost per pound is $3. Therefore, the cost of purchases of direct material in the first quarter is budgeted to be $130,440. This information is presented in the purchases budget, Illustration 25-4.

ILLUSTRATION 25-4 Purchases Budget

	Preston Manufacturing Company **Direct Material Purchases Budget** **For the Year Ended December 31, 19X2**				
	First Quarter	*Second Quarter*	*Third Quarter*	*Fourth Quarter*	*Year*
Units to be produced[1]	21,400	24,800	22,900	22,200	91,300
Pounds of direct material per unit of finished product	x 2	x 2	x 2	x 2	x 2
Number of pounds required for production	42,800	49,600	45,800	44,400	182,600
Plus: Desired ending quantity of direct material[2]	4,960	4,580	4,440	4,900[3]	4,900
Total pounds needed	47,760	54,180	50,240	49,300	187,500
Less: Beginning quantity of direct material	4,280	4,960	4,580	4,440	4,280
Number of pounds to be purchased	43,480	49,220	45,660	44,860	183,220
Cost per pound	x $3	x $3	x $3	x $3	x $3
Cost of purchases	$130,440	$147,660	$136,980	$134,580	$549,660

[1]Information from production budget, Illustration 25-3.
[2]Equals 10% of quantity required for next quarter's production.
[3]Based on estimate of quantity required for production in the first quarter of next year.

Direct Labor Budget

The direct labor budget for Preston Manufacturing Company (Illustration 25-5) presents direct labor cost by quarter. Direct labor cost is easily calculated by multiplying the number of units produced each quarter by the labor hours per unit and the rate per hour. In the first quarter, the company expects to produce 21,400 units and 1.5 labor hours per unit are required. In total, 32,100 labor hours are needed. At a rate of $10 per labor hour, this amounts to $321,000. Preston estimates that, on average, each employee works 520 hours per quarter. Preston can use this information to estimate the approximate number of employees needed each quarter. In the first quarter, 32,100 labor hours are required. Since an average employee works 520 hours per quarter, approximately 62 employees will be needed for production. Note that the direct labor budget indicates that 72 employees are needed in the second quarter, while only 62 are needed in the first quarter. With this information, the company may decide to adjust its production plans to keep employment stable. The new employees hired in the second quarter may not be efficient. Also, if several of these employees are fired in the third quarter when only 66 employees are needed, morale may suffer.

ILLUSTRATION 25-5 Direct Labor Budget

Preston Manufacturing Company Direct Labor Budget For the Year Ended December 31, 19X2					
	First Quarter	*Second Quarter*	*Third Quarter*	*Fourth Quarter*	*Year*
Units to be produced[1]	21,400	24,800	22,900	22,200	91,300
Direct labor hours per unit	x 1.5	x 1.5	x 1.5	x 1.5	x 1.5
Total hours	32,100	37,200	34,350	33,300	136,950
Labor rate per hour	x $10	x $10	x $10	x $10	x $10
Direct labor cost	$321,000	$372,000	$343,500	$333,000	$1,369,500
Total hours	32,100	37,200	34,350	33,300	
Average hours per quarter per employee	÷ 520	÷ 520	÷ 520	÷ 520	
Approximate number of employees needed	62	72	66	64	

[1]Information from production budget, Illustration 25-3.

Manufacturing Overhead Budget

Preston Manufacturing Company separates variable and fixed costs in the budget for manufacturing overhead. The cost per unit of production of each variable cost item is multiplied by the quantity produced each quarter. The fixed costs are identical each quarter, except for the amount of depreciation. This cost increases in the third and fourth quarters due to planned acquisitions of equipment that increase the level of depreciation. The manufacturing overhead budget is presented in Illustration 25-6.

Selling and Administrative Expense Budget

To this point, we have presented only production-related budgets. However, budget information is also necessary for selling and administrative expenses. Preston Manufacturing Company estimates that these expenses are all fixed. The 19X2 selling and administrative expense budget is presented in Illustration 25-7.

Budgeted Income Statement

The company uses much of the information contained in the previous budgets to prepare a **budgeted income statement**. Preston Manufacturing Company prepares its budgeted income statement using the *variable costing* method. With this method, only variable manufacturing costs are included in inventory. Fixed manufacturing costs are treated as period costs and deducted from the contribution margin to derive net income.

ILLUSTRATION 25-6 Manufacturing Overhead Budget

	First Quarter	Second Quarter	Third Quarter	Fourth Quarter	Year
Preston Manufacturing Company Manufacturing Overhead Budget For the Year Ended December 31, 19X2					
Units to be produced[1]	21,400	24,800	22,900	22,200	91,300
Variable costs:					
Indirect material ($2/unit)	$ 42,800	$ 49,600	$ 45,800	$ 44,400	$182,600
Indirect labor ($1.50/unit)	32,100	37,200	34,350	33,300	136,950
Power and light ($1/unit)	21,400	24,800	22,900	22,200	91,300
Total variable costs	$ 96,300	$111,600	$103,050	$ 99,900	$410,850
Fixed costs:					
Supervisory salaries	$ 90,000	$ 90,000	$ 90,000	$ 90,000	$360,000
Depreciation of plant and equipment[2]	20,000	20,000	26,000	28,000	94,000
Other	5,000	5,000	5,000	5,000	20,000
Total fixed costs	$115,000	$115,000	$121,000	$123,000	$474,000
Total overhead	$211,300	$226,600	$224,050	$222,900	$884,850

[1]Information from production budget, Illustration 25-3.
[2]Increase in third and fourth quarters due to acquisition of additional equipment. See capital acquisition budget, Illustration 25-9.

ILLUSTRATION 25-7 Selling and Administrative Expense Budget

	First Quarter	Second Quarter	Third Quarter	Fourth Quarter	Year
Preston Manufacturing Company Selling and Administrative Expense Budget For the Year Ended December 31, 19X2					
Salaries	$160,000	$160,000	$160,000	$160,000	$ 640,000
Advertising	70,000	70,000	70,000	70,000	280,000
Depreciation of office equipment	5,000	5,000	5,000	5,000	20,000
Other	15,000	15,000	15,000	15,000	60,000
Total	$250,000	$250,000	$250,000	$250,000	$1,000,000

The variable costs per unit are $25.50. This amount is derived as follows:

Direct materials	$ 6.00	(2 units at $3.00. See the direct material purchases budget, Illustration 25-4.)
Direct labor	15.00	(1.5 hours at $10. See the direct labor budget, Illustration 25-5.)
Variable overhead	4.50	($2.00 indirect material; $1.50 indirect labor; and $1.00 power and light. See the manufacturing overhead budget, Illustration 25-6.)
Total	$25.50	per unit

The budgeted income statement is presented in Illustration 25-8. As you know, the contribution margin is equal to sales minus variable expenses (including variable cost of goods sold, variable selling, and variable administrative expenses). However, to simplify presentation, the only variable expense for Preston Manufacturing Company is variable cost of goods sold. Therefore, the contribution margin is equal to sales minus variable cost of goods sold. Fixed production overhead and fixed selling and administrative expenses are deducted from the contribution margin to derive at net income.

ILLUSTRATION 25-8 Budgeted Income Statement

Preston Manufacturing Company Budgeted Income Statement (Variable Costing Method) For the Year Ended December 31, 19X2					
	First Quarter	Second Quarter	Third Quarter	Fourth Quarter	Year
Sales[1]	$945,000	$1,125,000	$1,035,000	$990,000	$4,095,000
Less: Variable cost of goods sold	535,500[2]	637,500	586,500	561,000	2,320,500
Contribution margin	$409,500	$ 487,500	$ 448,500	$429,000	$1,774,500
Less: Fixed production overhead[3]	(115,000)	(115,000)	(121,000)	(123,000)	(474,000)
Fixed selling and administrative expense[4]	(250,000)	(250,000)	(250,000)	(250,000)	(1,000,000)
Net income	$ 44,500	$ 122,500	$ 77,500	$ 56,000	$ 300,500

[1]Information from sales budget, Illustration 25-2.
[2]First quarter calculation is: 21,000 units sold x $25.50 = $535,500.
[3]Information from manufacturing overhead budget, Illustration 25-6.
[4]Information from selling and administrative expense budget, Illustration 25-7.

Management should evaluate the budgeted income statement to ensure that anticipated profit is consistent with company goals. If budgeted profit is less than the amount management considers satisfactory, then the company can take steps to increase sales and reduce costs. For example, the company may undertake an expanded advertising campaign to increase sales, or it can reduce overhead costs through more efficient use of part-time labor. If management decides to take steps to increase profit, then it must adjust the previous budgets to reflect the anticipated changes.

Capital Acquisitions Budget

The company must carefully plan acquisitions of capital assets (i.e., property, plant, and equipment) since they may substantially reduce cash reserves in the period of acquisition. The budget for capital assets is referred to as the capital acquisitions budget. Preston Manufacturing Company anticipates purchases of office equipment and machinery during the coming year, and this is reflected in the capital acquisitions budget presented in Illustration 25-9.

Cash Receipts and Disbursements Budget

In the cash receipts and disbursements budget, managers plan the amount and timing of cash flows. The information in this budget is a necessary supplement to the information presented in the budgeted income statement. It is quite possible for a company to project a substantial amount of net income and still face financial distress because its entire set of plans implies more cash outflows than

ILLUSTRATION 25-9   Capital Acquisitions Budget

	First Quarter	Second Quarter	Third Quarter	Fourth Quarter	Year
Preston Manufacturing Company **Capital Acquisitions Budget** **For the Year Ended December 31, 19X2**					
Office equipment (5-year life)	$10,000	$ 0	$ 0	$ 0	$ 10,000
Machinery (5-year life)	0	0	120,000¹	40,000²	160,000
Total	$10,000	$ 0	$120,000	$40,000	$170,000

¹Increases depreciation by $6,000 in third quarter [i.e., ($120,000 = 5 year life) x 1/4 for third quarter]. See manufacturing overhead budget, Illustration 25-6.
²Increases depreciation by $2,000 in fourth quarter [i.e.,($40,000 = 5 year life) x 1/4 for fourth quarter]. See manufacturing overhead budget, Illustration 25-6.

cash inflows. For example, the company may recognize a substantial amount of income when it makes a major sale. However, the cash received in payment for the sale may not arrive for many months. Or, consider a company that makes a substantial purchase of equipment. While cash reserves may be reduced immediately by the *total* cost of the equipment, current period income will only be reduced by a *fraction* of the cost of the equipment (i.e., by the amount of depreciation). By carefully planning cash receipts and disbursements, a company can anticipate cash shortages and arrange to borrow funds to enhance its cash positions. Or, if cash surpluses are anticipated, a company can seek additional investment opportunities or consider paying higher dividends to shareholders.

To prepare an estimate of cash collections, management must determine the percent of credit sales revenue that is collected in the period of sale and the percent collected in the subsequent period. The percentages can usually be estimated based on past collection experience. Preston Manufacturing Company has only credit sales, with 50% of the sales revenue collected in the quarter of sale and the other 50% collected in the next quarter.

To prepare an estimate of cash disbursements, management must determine the percent of material purchases paid in the period of purchase and the percent paid in the subsequent period. Preston Manufacturing Company determines that 70% is paid in the quarter of purchase and 30% is paid in the subsequent quarter. The company has determined that, for practical purposes, all other disbursements are made in the quarter the related cost is incurred.

In preparing a cash receipts and disbursements budget, it is important to remember that some expenses do not require cash outlays. For example, depreciation is part of manufacturing overhead, but it does not require a current outlay of cash. Cash is disbursed when an asset is purchased, not when depreciation is recorded. Another example of a noncash expense is the amortization of prepaid insurance. Cash is disbursed when the insurance is purchased, not when the expense is recognized through amortization of prepaid insurance.

In the cash receipts and disbursements budget for Preston Manufacturing Company, Illustration 25-10, note that cash disbursed for manufacturing overhead in the first quarter is only $191,300. This is $20,000 less than the $211,300 of overhead cost planned for the first quarter in the manufacturing overhead budget, Illustration 25-6. The $20,000 is the amount of depreciation in the first quarter.

ILLUSTRATION 25-10 Cash Receipts and Disbursements Budget

	Preston Manufacturing Company Cash Receipts and Disbursements Budget For the Year Ended December 31, 19X2				
	First Quarter	Second Quarter	Third Quarter	Fourth Quarter	Year
Cash receipts:					
Collection of credit sales:					
4th quarter prior year ($860,870)	$430,435				$ 430,435
1st quarter ($945,000)[1]	472,500	$ 472,500			945,000
2nd quarter ($1,125,000)		562,500	$ 562,500		1,125,000
3rd quarter ($1,035,000			517,500	$ 517,500	1,035,000
4th quarter ($990,000)				495,000	495,000
Total cash receipts	$902,935	$1,035,000	$1,080,000	$1,012,500	$4,030,435
Cash disbursements:					
Purchase of materials:					
4th quarter prior year ($120,600)	$ 36,180				$ 36,180
1st quarter ($130,440)[2]	91,308	$ 39,132			130,440
2nd quarter ($147,660)		103,362	$ 44,298		147,660
3rd quarter ($136,980)			95,886	$ 41,094	136,980
4th quarter ($134,580)				94,206	94,206
Total payments for purchases	$127,488	$ 142,494	$ 140,184	$ 135,300	$ 545,466
Direct labor[3]	321,000	372,000	343,500	333,000	1,369,500
Manufacturing overhead[4]	191,300	206,600	198,050	194,900	790,850
Selling and administrative expense[5]	245,000	245,000	245,000	245,000	980,000
Capital acquisitions[6]	10,000	0	120,000	40,000	170,000
Total cash disbursements	$894,788	$ 966,094	$1,046,734	$ 948,200	$3,855,816
Excess of receipts over disbursements	$ 8,147	$ 68,906	$ 33,266	$ 64,300	$ 174,619
Plus beginning cash balance	20,000	28,147	97,053	130,319	20,000
Ending cash balance	$ 28,147	$ 97,053	$ 130,319	$ 194,619	$ 194,619

[1]See Illustration 25-2 for sales information. Fifty percent collected in quarter of sale and 50% collected in subsequent quarter.
[2]See Illustration 25-4 for purchase information. Seventy percent paid in quarter of purchase and 30% paid in subsequent quarter.
[3]See Illustration 25-5 for labor cost information.
[4]Does not include depreciation indicated in manufacturing overhead budget, Illustration 25-6, since depreciation does not require a cash outlay.
[5]Does not include depreciation indicated in selling and administrative expense budget, Illustration 25-7, since depreciation does not require a cash outlay.
[6]See capital acquisitions budget, Illustration 25-9.

As indicated in the cash budget, the anticipated cash flows fluctuate significantly from quarter to quarter. The result is that at the end of the first quarter, Preston expects the cash balance to be only $28,147, but it expects the cash balance at the end of the fourth quarter to be $194,619. Obviously, a low cash balance is dangerous because the company may not have enough funds to pay employees and suppliers. Thus, Preston Manufacturing company may wish to consider borrowing money to improve the cash position in the first quarter. The cash budget is useful because it alerts management to a potential problem well in advance. This gives management sufficient time to arrange a loan on favorable terms. As the budget indicates, the loan can easily be repaid in the fourth quarter when cash reserves are high.

Excessively large cash balances should generally be avoided since they earn little, if any, interest. If a company is building up financial reserves for expansion (purchasing a major piece of equipment or even another company), then it should invest excess cash in low-risk, highly marketable securities. The return on these securities will most likely exceed interest earned from a bank on the cash balance. If the company is not building up reserves to expand, then it should distribute the excess cash to shareholders as dividends.

Budgeted Balance Sheet

The last component of the master budget we consider is the **budgeted balance sheet**, which is simply a planned balance sheet (sometimes called a *pro-forma balance sheet*). Managers can use this budget to assess the effect of their planned decisions on the firm's future financial position. The budgeted balance sheet for Preston Manufacturing Company is presented in Illustration 25-11.

ILLUSTRATION 25-11 Budgeted Balance Sheet

Preston Manufacturing Company Budgeted Balance Sheet (Partial) December 31, 19X2	
Current assets:	
Cash[1]	$ 194,619
Accounts receivable[2]	495,000
Raw materials inventory[3]	14,700
Finished goods inventory[4]	61,200
Property, plant, and equipment (net)	620,000
Total assets	$1,385,519
Current liabilities:	
Accounts payable[5]	$ 40,374
Stockholders' equity:	
Common stock	894,000
Retained earnings	451,145
Total liabilities and stockholders' equity	$1,385,519

---

[1] Ending balance from cash receipts and disbursements budget, Illustration 25-10.

[2] From cash receipts and disbursements budget, Illustration 25-10, 50% of 4th quarter sales not yet collected.

[3] 4,900 units at $3.00 = $14,700. See direct material purchases budget, Illustration 25-4.

[4] From production budget, Illustration 25-3, 2,400 units of finished goods are required. Variable cost per unit equals $25.50. Only variable costs are included in inventory since the company uses the variable costing method.

[5] From the cash receipts and disbursements budget, Illustration 25-10, 30% of 4th quarter purchases of materials not yet paid.

USE OF COMPUTERS IN THE BUDGET PLANNING PROCESS

As pointed out previously, during the budget process, management may review a budget and decide it is inconsistent with company goals. This may lead management to explore a variety of actions that affect future costs and revenues. If changes are anticipated, the budgets must be revised. Since the budgets are highly interdependent, a change in one budget can affect several other budgets. Computers are very useful in this regard. Many companies define the budget relationships in a computer model using spreadsheet programs such as Lotus 1-2-3™ and Excel,™ or custom programs specifically designed for them. With computerized budget information, an item in a budget can be changed; the computer can then recalculate that budget and any other budget affected by the change. Obviously, this results in a substantial savings in time and managerial effort.

"What if" analysis is also facilitated when budgets are prepared using a spreadsheet program. Suppose the management of Preston Manufacturing Company wants to know *what* the cash balance will be in the fourth quarter *if* sales in the first quarter are 22,000 units instead of the 21,000 units budgeted. If all budgetary relationships have been properly specified in a spreadsheet, the answer can be found by simply changing the sales figure in the first quarter sales budget from 21,000 to 22,000 and letting the computer recalculate the cash balance in the fourth quarter cash receipts and disbursements budget.

BUDGETARY CONTROL

The examples above indicate how budgets are used in the planning process to communicate company goals and coordinate diverse activities. Budgets also facilitate *control* of operations because they provide a standard for evaluating performance. Differences between budgeted and actual amounts are referred to as **budget variances**, and reports that indicate budget variances are referred to as **performance reports**. If budgeted and actual costs are approximately equal, management needs to take no action because results are consistent with its expectations. However, if actual costs differ from budgeted costs by a material amount, management should launch an investigation to determine the cause of the difference.

How would a company evaluate performance if budgets were not prepared? Most likely, actual performance in the current period would be compared to actual performance in the prior period. This is obviously an inferior approach since conditions may change significantly from one period to the next, making a comparison of the two periods meaningless. For example, suppose Preston Manufacturing Company evaluates the performance of the marketing department by comparing sales in the current year to sales in the past year. Further, suppose sales in the prior year are 79,130 units and actual sales in the current year are 85,000 units. An evaluation of performance based on a comparison with the prior year would lead to a favorable evaluation of the marketing department since sales increased by approximately 7%. However, suppose the overall market for Preston's product had grown by 15%. If this increase was forecasted at the start of the period, the company would have budgeted sales of 91,000 units (i.e., 79,130 x 1.15). A comparison of actual sales to budgeted sales indicates that, rather than receiving a favorable evaluation, the marketing department should be asked to explain why actual sales are only 85,000 units instead of the 91,000 units forecasted.

LO 3

Describe why flexible
budgets are needed for
performance evaluation.

Static and Flexible Budgets

In evaluating performance using budgets, a company must take care to ensure that the level of activity used in developing the budget is equal to the *actual* level of activity. Suppose the manager responsible for manufacturing overhead at Preston Manufacturing Company was evaluated at the end of the first quarter by comparing the actual level of overhead cost to the overhead costs budgeted at the start of the year. This comparison is presented in Illustration 25-12.

ILLUSTRATION 25-12   Performance Evaluation with a Static Budget

	Static Budget	Actual	Variance
Preston Manufacturing Company Performance Report, Manufacturing Overhead Static Budget Comparison First Quarter, 19X2			
Units produced	21,400	25,000	3,600
Variable costs:			
Indirect materials (budgeted at $2 per unit)	$ 42,800	$ 49,000	$ (6,200)
Indirect labor (budgeted at $1.50 per unit)	32,100	38,000	(5,900)
Power and light (budgeted at $1 per unit)	21,400	24,600	(3,200)
Total variable costs	$ 96,300	$111,600	$(15,300)
Fixed costs:			
Supervisory salaries	$ 90,000	$ 90,200	$ (200)
Depreciation on plant and equipment	20,000	20,300	(300)
Other	5,000	5,000	0
Total fixed cost	$115,000	$115,500	$ (500)
Total overhead	$211,300	$227,100	$(15,800)

( ) denotes unfavorable variance

The analysis implies that the manager responsible for overhead costs has not done a good job of cost control. After all, total variable overhead costs are $15,300 higher than planned, and total fixed overhead costs are $500 higher than planned. However, careful consideration of the comparison reveals that actual production was 25,000 units, while planned production was only 21,400 units. The extra production may be due to an unexpected increase in sales necessitating increased production. With the increase in production, an increase in variable costs is expected. Fixed costs, however, would be expected to remain the same. Since changes in cost are expected when actual production is different from planned production, the analysis presented is not very useful for evaluating performance.

The budget presented in Illustration 25-12 is referred to as a **static budget** because it is not adjusted for the actual level of production. A more appropriate analysis of performance would make use of a **flexible budget**, which is a budget adjusted for the actual level of production. Flexible budgets take into account the fact that when production increases or decreases, variable costs change. Fixed costs, however, stay the same. Consider a company that anticipates variable production costs of $10 per unit and fixed production costs of $500,000. With this cost structure, flexible budgets for production levels of 20,000 units, 30,000 units and, 40,000 units can be prepared as in Illustration 25-13.

ILLUSTRATION 25-13 Flexible Budgets for Various Production Levels

Flexible Budgets for Production Levels of 20,000, 30,000, and 40,000 Units			
Units produced	20,000	30,000	40,000
Variable costs ($10 per unit)	$200,000	$300,000	$400,000
Fixed costs	500,000	500,000	500,000
Total	$700,000	$800,000	$900,000

In Illustration 25-14, a flexible budget evaluates the performance of the manager responsible for manufacturing overhead at Preston Manufacturing Company. Note that the variable costs are adjusted to the actual level of units produced. Since they are not expected to change when production increases or decreases, the fixed costs are at the same level as in the static budget. Comparison of actual overhead costs to the overhead costs in a flexible budget reveals more about the manager's ability to control costs. Actual variable costs are $900 less than the *flexible* budget amount. This contrasts sharply with the $15,300 amount by which actual costs were greater than the *static* budget amount for variable costs. The variance with respect to fixed costs is still $500 more than budgeted—the same as in the static budget comparison.

ILLUSTRATION 25-14 Performance Evaluation with a Flexible Budget

Preston Manufacturing Company
Performance Report, Manufacturing Overhead
Flexible Budget Comparison
First Quarter, 19X2

	Flexible Budget	Actual	Variance
Units produced	25,000	25,000	0
Variable costs:			
Indirect materials (budgeted at $2 per unit)	$ 50,000	$ 49,000	$1,000
Indirect labor (budgeted at $1.50 per unit)	37,500	38,000	(500)
Power and light (budgeted at $1 per unit)	25,000	24,600	400
Total variable costs	$112,500	$111,600	$ 900
Fixed costs:			
Supervisory salaries	$ 90,000	$ 90,200	$ (200)
Depreciation on plant and equipment	20,000	20,300	(300)
Other	5,000	5,000	0
Total fixed cost	$115,000	$115,500	$ (500)
Total overhead	$227,500	$227,100	$ 400

( ) denotes unfavorable variances.

INVESTIGATING BUDGET VARIANCES

A budget variance may exist for several reasons. Budget variances are sometimes due to inefficiencies resulting from poor management techniques or decisions. In this case, top management may adjust the compensation of the manager responsible for attaining the budget (e.g., reduce or eliminate his or her bonus compensation) and suggest ways the manager can improve the performance of his or her operation. In some cases the company may even have to fire the manager if he or she is incapable of improving. On the other hand, if the budget is not carefully developed with reasonable estimates of cost, the company should not be surprised if actual costs are not equal to the budgeted amounts. In this case, management cannot blame budget variances on the manager responsible for attaining the budget. Even if the budget is carefully developed, the company may nonetheless experience unforeseen price increases that result in actual costs being different from budgeted costs.

While they may indicate inefficiencies, in some cases budget variances indicate only that the budget needs to be adjusted. The cause of the variance cannot be determined without an investigation. However, because of the cost of investigation, a company cannot investigate all budget variances. Rather, **a management by exception** approach is more economical. That is, only the exceptional variances are investigated. Generally, variances that are large in absolute dollars or relative to budgeted amounts are considered exceptional. It is important to point out that both exceptional "unfavorable" *and* exceptional "favorable" variances should be investigated. For example, in the performance report (Illustration 25-14), there is a $1,000 favorable variance for indirect materials, indicating that actual costs are less than budgeted costs. This seems to indicate a favorable state of affairs. However, it may be that cheap, low-quality materials are being used. This could result in substandard products that damage the company's reputation.

LO 4
Discuss the conflict between the planning and control uses of budgets.

CONFLICT IN PLANNING AND CONTROL USES OF BUDGETS

Conflict is inherent in the planning and control uses of budgets. On the one hand, top management would like the managers responsible for carrying out plans to participate in the development of budgets. After all, these managers have the best knowledge of the technology and costs of their operations. However, since their performance is evaluated in comparison to the budget, they have an incentive to make sure that the budget contains some **slack**. That is, managers want budgeted costs that they can easily achieve. To have slack, managers may suggest budgeted costs that are too high; thus, their actual costs will be lower than the budgeted amounts. Or they may suggest revenue levels that are too low; thus, their actual revenues will be higher than the budgeted amounts. If this happens, the company's budgets will not be plans for achieving maximum firm profit. There is no ready solution to this problem. Perhaps the best that can be done is to assure managers that their performance in comparison to the budget will be fairly evaluated. Managers should be confident that they will be allowed to comment on the real causes of budget variances and tell their side of the story. The problem is minimized, we believe, in organizations that foster open communication among all levels of employees.

EVALUATION, MEASUREMENT, AND MANAGEMENT BEHAVIOR

Managers pay great attention to those aspects of their jobs that are measured and evaluated. Thus, it is important to quantify in budgets key "success factors"

INSIGHTS INTO ETHICS

As manager of the waste treatment facility for Chemtron Industries, Ann Paxton is in the process of preparing an annual expense budget. "Next year, my department will probably be asked to process some 80,000 gallons of waste. Our variable costs are about $10 per gallon, and our fixed costs are about $1,000,000. So, the total cost should be somewhere around $1,800,000. I better submit a budget of around $2,300,000. Top management will probably reduce my budget. After all, when was the last time they ever approved a higher budget than the one submitted? And, what if I end up incurring higher expenses than anticipated? A new labor contract, for instance, could increase costs by more than $100,000. The last thing I want is to incur more costs than budgeted. My annual bonus would likely be reduced, and I could kiss any chance for promotion next year good-bye."

Is it ethical to submit a budget for an amount higher than the cost expected to be incurred? Explain.

for the company. Historically, budgets have primarily included dollar amounts. However, including some nonmonetary measures of performance in the budget may be advantageous. For example, if a key aspect of a company's success is high-quality, defect-free products, budgeting the number of defects and the number of customer complaints at levels consistent with high quality is useful. This way, the company can compare the actual number of defects and complaints with the budgeted quantities to evaluate performance. Or, if a company is experiencing problems with employee absenteeism, it may budget an acceptable number of days missed and compare actual days missed to the target.

THE PRESTON MANUFACTURING COMPANY CASE

At the start of the chapter, Alan Renton, President of Preston Manufacturing, noted that "The marketing, production, and financing groups must know what is anticipated so we can produce the right quantities of the right stuff." How can Alan plan and coordinate the activities of his company? As you know from reading the material above, the answer lies in developing budgets. Once a sales budget is produced, the production group can develop budgets for labor, material, and overhead that are consistent with the production level needed to meet expected sales. Once these budgets are produced, the finance group can prepare budgets that take into account the cash inflows and outflows anticipated in the sales and production budgets.

SUMMARY

Discuss how budgets are used in planning and control. Budgets are useful in the planning process because they enhance communication and coordination. Budgets are also useful in the control process because they provide a standard for evaluating performance.

Prepare the individual budgets that make up the master budget. The master budget is a comprehensive planning document and usually includes budgets for sales, production, direct materials, direct labor, manufacturing overhead, selling and administrative expenses, capital acquisitions, and cash receipts and disbursements, as well as a budgeted income statement and a budgeted balance sheet. These budgets are highly interrelated in that the amounts presented in one budget may be dependent on the amounts in one or more other budgets.

Describe why flexible budgets are needed for performance evaluation.   In evaluating performance, companies should use flexible budgets because they present amounts adjusted to the actual level of production. Comparing actual performance to a static budget is not very useful because variable costs are expected to differ from the budget if actual production is different from the production level indicated in the static budget.

Discuss the conflict between the planning and control uses of budgets.   The fact that budgets are used for both planning and performance evaluation presents a difficulty. Managers who participate in the development of their own budgets may tend to understate budgeted revenues and overstate budgeted expenses. The result is budgets that are easy to achieve and contain budget slack. However, this problem is minimized in companies that foster open communication among all levels of employees. In such organizations, managers are less likely to feel the need to build slack into budgets because they know their performance will be evaluated fairly.

REVIEW PROBLEM

Jimbo Manufacturing Company reported the following net income for the fourth quarter of 19X0:

Sales		$860,000
Less: Variable cost of goods sold		516,000
Contribution margin		$344,000
Less: Fixed production costs	$ 82,000	
Fixed selling and administrative expense	130,000	212,000
Income before taxes		$132,000
Less income taxes		52,800
Net income		$ 79,200

Note: Jimbo Manufacturing Company uses the variable costing method. Thus, only variable production costs are included in inventory and cost of goods sold. Fixed production costs are charged to expense in the period incurred.

Additional Information:
1. Sales and variable cost of sales are expected to increase by 10% in the next quarter.
2. Jimbo expects that 20% of all sales will be for cash. Of the remaining credit sales, 40% will be collected in the quarter of sale and 60% will be collected in the quarter following sale.
3. Variable cost of sales consists of 50% materials, 30% direct labor, and 20% variable overhead. Materials are purchased on credit and 70% are paid for in the quarter of purchase and the remaining amount is paid for in the quarter after purchase. Direct labor and variable overhead are paid for in the quarter incurred.
4. Fixed production costs are expected to increase by 5% in the next quarter. The fixed production costs consist of 75% depreciation and 25% other fixed costs. Fixed production costs requiring payment are paid in the quarter they are incurred.

5. Fixed selling and administrative expenses are expected to increase by 8%. Ten percent of selling and administrative costs consists of depreciation of the administrative building and equipment. Remaining costs are paid in the quarter they are incurred.
6. The tax rate is expected to be 40%. All taxes are paid in the quarter they are incurred.
7. The cash balance on January 1, 19X1, is $107,670.

REQUIRED:

a. Prepare a budgeted income statement for the first quarter of 19X1.
b. Prepare a cash receipts and disbursements budget for the first quarter of 19X1.

SOLUTION:

(a) *Prepare a budgeted income statement.*

Jimbo Manufacturing Company Budgeted Income Statement (Variable Costing Method) For the Quarter Ending March 31, 19X1		
Sales[1]		$946,000
Less: Variable cost of goods sold[2]		567,600
Contribution margin		$378,400
Less: Fixed production costs[3]	$ 86,100	
Fixed selling and administrative expense[4]	140,400	226,500
Income before taxes		$151,900
Less income taxes[5]		60,760
Net income		$ 91,140

[1]110% x $860,000.   [3]105% x $82,000.   [5]40% x $151,900.
[2]110% x $516,000.   [4]108% x $130,000.

(b) *Prepare a Cash receipts and disbursements budget.*

Jimbo Manufacturing Company Cash Receipts and Disbursement Budget For the Quarter Ending March 31, 19X1		
Cash receipts:		
Collection of cash sales (20% x $946,000)		$189,200
Collection of credit sales:		
4th quarter prior year (80% x $860,000 x 60%)	$412,800	
1st quarter (80% x $946,000 x 40%)	302,720	715,520
Total cash receipts		$904,720
Cash disbursements:		
Purchase of material:		
4th quarter prior year ($516,000 x 50% x 30%)	$ 77,400	
1st quarter ($567,600 x 50% x 70%)	198,660	$276,060
Direct labor ($567,600 x 30%)		170,280
Variable overhead ($567,600 x 20%)		113,520
Fixed production costs ($86,100 x 25%)		21,525
Selling and administrative expense ($140,400 x 90%)		126,360
Income taxes		60,760
Total cash disbursements		$768,505
Excess of receipts over disbursements		$136,215
Plus beginning cash balance		107,670
Ending cash balance		$243,885

KEY TERMS

budget committee, *1024*
budgeted balance sheet, *1034*
budgeted income statement, *1029*
budgets, *1023*
budget variances, *1035*

flexible budget, *1036*
management by exception, *1038*
master budget, *1025*
performance reports, *1035*
slack, *1038*

static budget, *1036*
zero base budgeting, *1025*

SELF QUIZ

LO 1 1. Which of the following is not a true statement about budgets?
  a. They are formal documents that quantify a company's plans.
  b. They enhance communication and coordination.
  c. They should be prepared infrequently.
  d. They provide a basis for evaluating performance.

LO 1 2. Budgets are useful in the planning process because they enhance _____ and _____.

LO 1 3. The group within the company that is responsible for preparing budgets is usually called the _____ _____.

LO 2 4. Which of the following is *not* a true statement about the sales budget?
  a. Input from the sales force may be useful in predicting sales.
  b. Very large companies may hire economists to help prepare sales budget.
  c. The first step in the budget process is to develop this budget.
  d. The production budget is developed before this budget.

LO 2 5. Which of the following is the correct formula to determine required purchases of direct materials?
  a. Quantity required for production + Desired ending quantity – Beginning quantity.
  b. Quantity required for production – Desired ending quantity + Beginning quantity.
  c. Quantity required for production + Desired ending quantity + Beginning quantity.
  d. Beginning quantity + Purchases – Desired ending quantity.

LO 2 6. True or False? A primary purpose of the budgeted income statement is to insure that anticipated profit is consistent with company goals.

LO 2 7. Which of the following items do *not* require a cash outflow?
  a. Wage expense.
  b. Purchase of raw materials.
  c. Selling expense.
  d. Depreciation expense.

LO 2 8. Differences between budgeted and actual amounts are referred to as _____ _____.

LO 3 9. The _____ budget is not adjusted for the actual level of production whereas a _____ budget is adjusted for the actual level of production.

LO 3 10. Which of the following is true about management by exception?
  a. Only large favorable variances are investigated.
  b. Management by exception is an economical approach to cost control.
  c. Management by exception can only be used with computers.
  d. Large unfavorable variances should not be investigated.

LO 4 11. True or False? Management should encourage subordinates to include a lot of slack in their budgets.

LO 4 12. True or False? The number of defects in a process is an example of a nonmonetary measure of employee performance.

SOLUTIONS TO SELF-QUIZ

1. c   2. communication, coordination   3. budget committee   4. d   5. a   6. true   7. d   8. budget variances   9. static, flexible
10. b   11. false   12. true

QUESTIONS

Q25-1   Why are budgets useful in the planning process?

Q25-2   Why are budgets useful in the control process?

Q25-3   What is the difference between the top-down and bottom-up approach to developing a budget?

Q25-4   What is meant by a *zero base budget*?

Q25-5   What are the typical components of a master budget?

Q25-6   What are the main purposes of preparing a cash receipts and disbursements budget?

Q25-7   How do computers assist in the budget planning process?

Q25-8   What are some possible causes for an unfavorable budget variance?

Q25-9   What are some nonmonetary performance measures that could be included in a budget?

Q25-10   Why is there an inherent conflict between the planning and control uses of budgets?

EXERCISES

LO 2

E25-1   **Order of Budgets**   Determine the order in which each of the following budgets are generally prepared.
   a. Materials purchase budget
   b. Sales budget
   c. Budgeted income statement
   d. Production budget
   e. Budgeted balance sheet

LO 2

E25-2   **Sales Budget**   The Locktight Company manufactures burglar-resistant commercial door locks. Due to a recent increase in burglaries, Locktight expects sales to dramatically increase compared to the prior year. Prepare a sales budget for Locktight Company using the following information. Locktight Company had sales of locks for 19X0 as follows:

First quarter   21,000
Second quarter   26,000
Third quarter   25,000
Fourth quarter   30,000

Assume that sales for each quarter in 19X1 are expected to be 10% higher than they were in 19X0 and the selling price per lock is $20.

LO 2

E25-3   **Production Budget**   Prepare the production budget for Powerhouse Computer Company for the months of January, February, and March using the following information:
      Powerhouse expects sales to be 15,600 computer workstations in January, 16,500 computer workstations in February, 16,000 computer workstations in March, and 18,500 workstations in April. There are 9,200 computer workstations on hand on January 1. Powerhouse desires to maintain monthly ending inventory at 40% of next month's expected sales.

LO 2

E25-4 **Direct Materials Purchases Budget** Prepare quarterly direct materials purchases budgets for Ajax Chemical Company for 19X2 using the following information. Expected unit production for each quarter is as follows:

First quarter	47,000
Second quarter	42,000
Third quarter	50,000
Fourth quarter	39,000
First quarter (19X3)	48,000

Finished units of production require three pounds of raw material per unit. The raw material cost is $4 per pound. There are 45,000 pounds of raw material on hand at the beginning of the first quarter. Ajax desires to keep 40% of next quarter's material requirements on hand at the end of each quarter.

LO 2

E25-5 **Direct Labor Budget** Prepare quarterly direct labor budgets for Ajax Chemical Company for 19X2 using the production information from E25-4. It takes 2.5 hours of direct labor to produce each finished unit of product. Direct labor costs are $7 per hour. Each employee can work 500 hours per quarter.

LO 2

E25-6 **Manufacturing Overhead Budget** Prepare quarterly manufacturing overhead budgets for Ajax Chemical Company for 19X2 using the production information from E25-4. Ajax has overhead costs as follows:

Variable Costs		*Fixed Costs Per Quarter*	
Indirect material	$2.25/unit	Supervisory salaries	$80,000
Indirect labor	1.50/unit	Factory depreciation	30,000
Utilities	1.00/unit	Other	4,100

LO 2

E25-7 **Cash Receipts Budget** Prepare cash receipts budgets for Duncan Company for the months of April, May, and June using the following expected sales information:

	April	*May*	*June*
Budgeted sales	$85,000	$70,000	$98,000

Prior experience has indicated that 40% of a month's sales are collected in the month of sale, 50% in the month following sale, and the remaining 10% in the second month following sale. February and March sales were $80,000 and $90,000 respectively.

LO 2

E25-8 **Cash Disbursements Budget for Purchases** Prepare cash disbursements budgets for the Mayper Company for the months of April, May, and June using the following expected sales information:

	April	*May*	*June*
Budgeted purchases	$65,000	$70,000	$58,000

Prior experience has indicated that 30% of a month's purchases are paid in the month of purchase, 45% in the month following purchase, and the remaining 25% in the second month following purchase. February and March purchases were $60,000 and $55,000 respectively.

LO 3

E25-9 **Flexible Budget** Determine Bedding Unlimited Company's expected total cost for production of 8,000 mattresses, 10,000 mattresses, and 12,000 mattresses given the following information:

Variable Costs		*Fixed Costs*	
Direct material	$5.50/unit	Supervisory salaries	$14,000
Direct labor	2.50/unit	Factory depreciation	8,500
Variable overhead	1.20/unit	Other factory costs	1,100

LO 3　**E25-10**　**Performance Report**　Prepare a performance report from the following information for Bookbinder Manufacturing Company. During the period, Bookbinder produced 12,000 units and incurred the following costs:

Variable Costs		Fixed Costs	
Direct material	$71,900	Supervisory salaries	$13,750
Direct labor	28,250	Factory depreciation	8,500
Utilities	15,300	Other factory costs	1,260

Bookbinder budgeted the following costs:

Variable Costs		Fixed Costs	
Direct material	$5.30/unit	Supervisory salaries	$12,900
Direct labor	2.60/unit	Factory depreciation	8,500
Utilities	1.40/unit	Other factory costs	1,390

PROBLEM SET A

LO 2　**P25-1A**　**Combined Production and Purchases Budget**　BugAway, Inc. produces and sells exterminating products in liquid form. Information about the budget for the second quarter, 19X1, is as follows:

(1) The company expects to sell 60,000 bottles of BugAway in the second quarter, 93,000 in the third quarter, and 42,000 in the fourth quarter.
(2) A bottle of BugAway requires 6 oz. of Chemical A and 10 oz. of Chemical B.
(3) The desired ending inventory of finished goods is 35% of next quarter's sales whereas the desired ending inventory for material is 25% of next quarter's production requirements.
(4) There are 21,000 bottles of BugAway, 117,000 oz. of Chemical A, and 197,000 oz. of Chemical B on hand at the beginning of the second quarter.
(5) The cost of Chemical A is 12 cents per oz., the cost of Chemical B is 9 cents per oz., and the selling price of BugAway is $9.95 per bottle.
(6) The cost of direct labor is 60 cents per bottle and the cost of variable overhead is 90 cents per bottle. Fixed manufacturing overhead is $28,000 per quarter.
(7) Variable selling and administrative expense is 4% of sales and fixed selling and administrative expenses are $39,000 per quarter.

REQUIRED:

a. Prepare a production budget for the second and third quarter, 19X1.
b. Prepare a material purchases budget for the second quarter, 19X1.
c. Prepare a budgeted income statement (variable costing method) for the second quarter, 19X1.

LO 2　**P25-2A**　**Integrating Budgets**　CycleEase Corporation has a policy of keeping 30% of next quarter's sales in ending finished goods inventory and 25% of raw materials needed for next quarter's production in ending raw materials inventory. It takes 2 units of raw materials to make one unit of finished goods. The cost of raw material is $2.50 per unit. Unit information for the budget of CycleEase Corporation is as follows:

	1st Quarter	2nd Quarter	3rd Quarter	4th Quarter
Sales	26,000	?	?	36,000
Production	?	35,000	?	?
Beginning finished goods	7,000	?	?	?
Ending finished goods	12,000	?	?	?
Beginning raw materials	13,600	?	?	12,600
Ending raw materials	?	?	?	13,800
Material purchases	?	76,280	?	67,200

REQUIRED:

a. Fill in the missing information for 19X2.
b. Prepare a production budget for 19X2.
c. Prepare a material purchases budget for 19X2.

LO 2

P25-3A   Cash Budget   Estimated data for Casey Corporation for 19X1 is as follows:

	1st Quarter	2nd Quarter	3rd Quarter	4th Quarter
Sales	$84,100	$80,800	$108,600	$96,200
Purchases	21,600	19,800	23,400	22,900
Direct labor	14,400	13,300	17,300	16,500
Manuf. overhead	39,400	35,600	37,800	36,200
Selling and administrative expense	21,800	23,400	24,300	23,500
Income taxes	11,200	9,800	10,100	8,800

(1) Prior experience has indicated that 60% of a quarter's sales are collected in the quarter of sale, 30% in the quarter following sale, and the remaining 10% in the second quarter following sale.

(2) Prior experience has indicated that 60% of a quarter's purchases are paid in the quarter of purchase, 25% in the quarter following purchase, and the remaining 15% in the second quarter following purchase.

(3) Casey pays 90% of its direct labor in the quarter incurred and 10% in the following quarter.

(4) Manufacturing overhead includes $30,000 depreciation per quarter. The remainder is paid in the quarter incurred.

(5) Selling and administrative expense includes $20,000 depreciation per quarter. The remainder is paid in the quarter incurred.

(6) A capital expenditure for $62,000 is planned for the fourth quarter.

(7) There is an expected beginning balance of cash of $49,330 at the beginning of the third quarter.

REQUIRED:

a. Prepare a cash receipts and disbursements budget for the 3rd quarter of 19X1.
b. Prepare a cash receipts and disbursements budget for the 4th quarter of 19X1.

LO 2

P25-4A   Master Budget   The results of operations for the Washington Manufacturing Company, a sole proprietorship, for the fourth quarter of 19X5 are as follows:

Sales		$688,000
Less: Variable cost of goods sold		412,800
Contribution margin		$275,200
Less: Fixed production expense	$ 65,600	
Fixed selling and administrative expense	104,000	169,600
Income before taxes		$105,600
Less income taxes		42,200
Net income		$ 63,400

Note: Washington Company uses the variable costing method. Thus, only variable production costs are included in inventory and cost of goods sold. Fixed production costs are charged to expense in the period incurred.

Additional Information:

1. Sales and variable cost of sales are expected to increase by 10% in the next quarter.
2. It is expected that 30% of all sales will be for cash. Of the remaining credit sales, 65% will be collected in the quarter of sale and 35% will be collected in the quarter following sale.

3. Variable cost of sales consists of 50% materials, 30% direct labor, and 20% variable overhead. Materials are purchased on credit and 60% are paid for in the quarter of purchase and the remaining amount is paid for in the quarter after purchase. Direct labor and variable overhead are paid for in the quarter incurred. Ending raw materials inventory is expected to equal $56,000 at the end of the first quarter. Finished goods inventory is expected to equal $136,000 at the end of the first quarter. Raw materials purchases equal materials used in production. Finished goods produced equal units sold.

4. Fixed production costs are expected to increase by 5% in the next quarter. The fixed production costs consist of 70% depreciation and 30% other fixed costs. Fixed production costs requiring payment are paid in the quarter they are incurred.

5. Fixed selling and administrative expenses are expected to increase by 6%. Ten percent of these costs consist of depreciation of administrative buildings and equipment. Fixed selling and administrative expenses (excluding depreciation) are paid in the quarter that they are incurred.

6. The tax rate is expected to be 40%. All taxes are paid in the quarter they are incurred.

7. The cash balance on January 1, 19X6, is $107,670.

8. Property, plant, and equipment has a cost of $1,900,000 on January 1, 19X6. Accumulated depreciation of $385,000 is expected at the end of the first quarter. No purchases or retirements of property, plant, and equipment are expected.

9. There is an expected noncurrent note payable of $180,000 at the end of the first quarter, 19X6.

10. Land held for investment has a cost of $375,000 at the end of the first quarter, 19X6.

11. Common stock is $1,250,000 on January 1, 19X6. No issue or purchase of stock and no stock dividends are expected for the first quarter.

REQUIRED:

a. Prepare a budgeted income statement for the first quarter of 19X6.
b. Prepare a cash receipts and disbursements budget for the first quarter of 19X6.
c. Prepare a budgeted balance sheet for the end of the first quarter of 19X6.

LO 3   **P25-5A   Performance Report**   The Toast-R Manufacturing Corporation has expected production costs as follows:

Variable Costs		Fixed Costs	
Direct material	$4.50/unit	Supervisory salaries	$15,600
Direct labor	1.50/unit	Factory depreciation	7,500
Indirect material	0.80/unit	Factory insurance	3,900
Indirect labor	1.20/unit	Other factory costs	2,100
Power and light	1.25/unit		

Actual costs for 18,000 units of production for the first quarter of 19X7 are as follows:

Variable Costs		Fixed Costs	
Direct material	$81,540	Supervisory salaries	$15,750
Direct labor	26,640	Factory depreciation	7,500
Indirect material	13,500	Factory insurance	4,500
Indirect labor	21,960	Other factory costs	2,260
Power and light	24,300		

REQUIRED:

a. Prepare a flexible budget for 18,000, 20,000 and 22,000 units of production.
b. Prepare a performance report for the first quarter of 19X7.

PROBLEM SET B

LO 2 **P25-1B** **Combined Production and Purchases Budget**   Grow-Up, Inc. produces and sells plant growth products in liquid form. Information about the budget for the third quarter, 19X2, is as follows:

(1) The company expects to sell 90,000 bottles of Grow-Up in the third quarter and 139,500 in the fourth quarter of 19X2, and 63,000 in the first quarter of 19X3.

(2) Each bottle of Grow-Up requires 4 oz. of Chemical A and 9 oz. of Chemical B.

(3) The desired ending inventory of finished goods is 40% of next quarter's sales whereas the desired ending inventory for material is 30% of next quarter's production requirements.

(4) There are 31,500 bottles of Grow-Up, 175,500 oz. of Chemical A and 295,500 oz. of Chemical B on hand at the beginning of the third quarter.

(5) The cost of Chemical A is 14 cents per oz., the cost of Chemical B is 7 cents per oz., and the selling price of Grow-Up is $9.95 per bottle.

(6) The cost of direct labor is 50 cents per bottle and the cost of variable overhead is $1.00 per bottle. Fixed manufacturing overhead is $37,000 per quarter.

(7) Variable selling and administrative expense is 5% of sales and fixed selling and administrative expenses are $36,000 per quarter.

REQUIRED:

a. Prepare a production budget for the third and fourth quarter, 19X2.

b. Prepare a material purchases budget for the third quarter, 19X2.

c. Prepare a budgeted income statement (variable costing method) for the third quarter, 19X2.

LO 2 **P25-2B** **Integrating Budgets**   Nonex Corporation has a policy of keeping 30% of next quarter's sales in ending finished goods inventory and 25% of raw materials needed for next quarter's production in ending raw materials inventory. It takes 2 units of raw materials to make one unit of finished goods. The cost of raw material is $2.50 per unit. Unit information for the budget of Nonex Corporation is as follows:

	1st Quarter	2nd Quarter	3rd Quarter	4th Quarter
Sales	65,000	100,000	?	90,000
Production	?	87,500	?	?
Beginning finished goods	17,500	?	?	?
Ending finished goods	?	?	?	?
Beginning raw materials	34,000	?	?	31,500
Ending raw materials	?	?	?	34,500
Material purchases	?	190,700	?	168,000

REQUIRED:

a. Fill in the missing information for 19X1.

b. Prepare a production budget for 19X1.

c. Prepare a material purchases budget for 19X1.

LO 2 **P25-3B** **Cash Budget**   Estimated data for the Drexin Corporation for 19X4 follows:

	January	February	March	April
Sales	$67,280	$64,640	$86,880	$76,960
Purchases	17,280	15,840	18,720	18,320
Direct labor	11,520	10,640	13,840	13,200
Manuf. overhead	31,520	28,480	30,240	28,960
Selling and admin. exp.	17,440	18,720	19,440	18,800
Income taxes	8,960	7,840	8,080	7,040

(1) Prior experience has indicated that 50% of a month's sales are collected in the month of sale, 40% in the month following sale, and the remaining 10% in the second month following sale.

(2) Prior experience has indicated that 55% of a month's purchases are paid in the month of purchase, 30% in the month following purchase, and the remaining 15% in the second month following purchase.

(3) Drexin pays 90% of its direct labor in the month incurred and 10% in the following month.

(4) Manufacturing overhead includes $24,000 depreciation per month. The remainder is paid in the quarter incurred.

(5) Selling and administrative expenses include $12,000 depreciation per month. The remainder is paid in the quarter incurred.

(6) A capital expenditure for $49,600 is planned for April.

(7) There is an expected beginning balance of cash of $102,400 at the beginning of March.

REQUIRED:

a. Prepare a cash receipts and disbursements budget for March of 19X4.

b. Prepare a cash receipts and disbursements budget for April of 19X4.

LO 2   **P25-4B**   **Master Budget**   The results of operations for the Suhm Manufacturing Company, a sole proprietorship, for the fourth quarter of 19X8 are as follows:

Sales		$1,204,000
Less: Variable cost of goods sold		722,400
Contribution margin		$ 481,600
Less: Fixed production expense	$114,800	
Fixed selling and administrative expense	182,000	296,800
Income before taxes		$ 184,800
Less income taxes		73,850
Net income		$ 110,950

Note: Suhm Manufacturing Company uses the variable costing method. Thus, only variable production costs are included in inventory and cost of goods sold. Fixed production costs are charged to expense in the period incurred.

Additional Information:

1. Sales and variable cost of sales are expected to increase by 15% in the next quarter.

2. It is expected that 40% of all sales will be for cash. Of the remaining credit sales, 75% will be collected in the quarter of sale and 25% will be collected in the quarter following sale.

3. Variable cost of sales consists of 60% materials, 25% direct labor, and 15% variable overhead. Materials are purchased on credit and 70% are paid for in the quarter of purchase and the remaining amount is paid for in the quarter after purchase. Direct labor and variable overhead are paid for in the quarter incurred. Ending raw materials inventory is expected to equal $112,000 at the end of the first quarter. Finished goods inventory is expected to equal $272,000 at the end of the first quarter. Raw materials purchases equal materials used in production. Finished goods produced equal units sold.

4. Fixed production costs are expected to increase by 2% in the next quarter. The fixed production costs consist of 80% depreciation and 20% other fixed costs. Fixed production costs requiring payment are paid in the quarter they are incurred.

5. Fixed selling and administrative expenses are expected to increase by 5%. Fifteen percent of these costs consist of allocated depreciation of administrative buildings and equipment. Fixed selling and administrative expenses (excluding depreciation) are paid in the quarter that they are incurred.

6. The tax rate is expected to be 40%. All taxes are paid in the quarter they are incurred.
7. The cash balance on January 1, 19X9, is $269,200.
8. Property, plant, and equipment has a cost of $5,230,000 on January 1, 19X9. Accumulated depreciation of $962,500 is expected at the end of the first quarter. No purchases or retirements of property, plant, and equipment are expected.
9. There is a noncurrent note payable of $280,000 at the end of the first quarter, 19X9.
10. Land held for investment has a cost of $575,000 at the end of the first quarter, 19X9.
11. Common stock is $2,500,000 on January 1, 19X9. No issue or purchase of stock and no stock dividends are expected for the first quarter.

REQUIRED:

a. Prepare a budgeted income statement for the first quarter of 19X9.
b. Prepare a cash receipts and disbursements budget for the first quarter of 19X9.
c. Prepare a budgeted balance sheet for the first quarter of 19X9.

LO 3

P25-5B   **Performance Report**   The Cantrell Manufacturing Company has expected production costs as follows:

Variable Costs		Fixed Costs	
Direct material	$2.25/unit	Supervisory salaries	$23,400
Direct labor	0.75/unit	Factory depreciation	11,250
Indirect material	0.40/unit	Factory insurance	5,850
Indirect labor	0.60/unit	Other factory costs	3,150
Power and light	1.10/unit		

Actual costs for 18,000 units of production for the first quarter of 19X4 are as follows:

Variable Costs		Fixed Costs	
Direct material	$40,770	Supervisory salaries	$25,750
Direct labor	13,320	Factory depreciation	11,200
Indirect material	6,750	Factory insurance	5,500
Indirect labor	10,980	Other factory costs	3,260
Power and light	20,700		

REQUIRED:

a. Prepare a flexible budget for 14,000, 16,000 and 18,000 units of production.
b. Prepare a performance report for the first quarter of 19X4.

CRITICAL THINKING AND COMMUNICATING

C25-1   Amy Schwartz is the divisional manager of the candy bar division of Universal Food. Every year, Amy has to submit an annual budget to Barney Strange, the chief financial officer of Universal Food. Amy's bonus, salary, and promotion opportunities are based on how her performance compares to budgeted net income. Barney and Amy negotiate the budget each year. Barney always insists that Amy is underestimating revenues and overestimating expenses, whereas Amy tells Barney that he is expecting too much from her department.

During 19X0, the candy bar division had a record year. Barney insisted that the budget for 19X1 be at least at last year's level of performance. Amy stated that last year was an exception and could not be repeated. After getting into a rather heated argument, they scheduled a meeting with the president of Universal Food to resolve their conflict.

REQUIRED:

a. Explain why Barney and Amy had conflicting opinions.
b. If you were the president of Universal Food, how would you resolve the argument between Barney and Amy?
c. How would you modify Universal's budget system to reduce future conflict between Barney and Amy?

C25-2 The Athletic Equipment Division of Physique International had a very poor year in 19X2. Sales were down and there were quality problems with the manufactured products. Also, manufacturing output was 30% below the amount forecasted. A performance report based on a static budget comparison for the athletic equipment division was sent to the John Martinez, the president of Physique International. John was puzzled by the number of highly favorable variances because he heard that the division was having difficulty with its manufacturing operations.

REQUIRED:

Write a memo to John Martinez explaining why the variances were positive. Suggest how the performance report may be modified and some additional performance measures to improve the performance report.

CHAPTER 26

Standard Costs and Variance Analysis

At the start of the year, Frosty Ice Cream Company budgeted material costs at $2 per gallon. During the year, the company produced 1,000,000 gallons; the material cost was $2,200,408. After receiving year-end information, Linda Evert, director of operations, immediately called a meeting with the plant manager and the production supervisor.

Linda's opening statement grabbed their undivided attention. "What's going on? Our actual costs are 10 percent higher than budgeted."

Both managers assured her that the increased costs were not due to waste in the use of materials. The plant manager was confident that the increased costs were due to a sudden jump in sugar and milk prices. "And", he added, "Price changes are beyond our control. Talk to Purchasing; they'll back me up on the price increase."

Linda returned to her office and continued thinking about the situation. "What would really be useful," she concluded, "is a report that broke down the material cost increase into two parts: the part due to using more material than planned and the part due to paying a higher price than planned. I wonder if Jane in the accounting department can help with these calculations."

Fortunately, Linda is on the right track. A trained accountant can help her with the needed calculations. Frosty Ice Cream Company needs a standard costing system. In such systems, a company does not record manufactured goods at their actual product cost but rather at the cost that *should have been incurred* to produce the items. This cost is referred to as the *standard cost*. A primary benefit of a standard costing system is that it allows a company to compare differences between standard and actual costs. Such differences are referred to as *standard cost variances*.

For material costs, the standard cost variances distinguish between variances due to the actual price and the actual quantity of raw material being different from standard. Standard costing systems also generate variances for direct labor and manufacturing overhead. Management can then investigate large or unusual variances to determine if production is inefficient. If problems exist, management can take corrective action. Thus, standard costs play an important role in *controlling operations* as well as in determining *product costs*. This chapter illustrates both of these uses of standard costs.

LEARNING OBJECTIVES

1. Explain how standard costs are developed.
2. Calculate and interpret variances for direct material.
3. Calculate and interpret variances for direct labor.
4. Calculate and interpret variances for manufacturing overhead.
5. Discuss how the management by exception approach is applied to investigate standard cost variances.
6. Record standard costs in a manufacturing firm's accounts.

STANDARD COSTS AND BUDGETS

The term **standard cost** refers to the cost management believes *should be incurred* to produce a good or service under anticipated conditions. A tool manufacturing company may set a standard cost for the production of a hammer, while a bank may set a standard cost for processing a check. In the following examples, we concentrate on standard costing in a manufacturing setting. However, much of the discussion also applies to service companies that use standard costs.

Some accountants use the terms "budgeted cost" and "standard cost" interchangeably. However, standard cost often refers to the cost of a single unit, while budgeted cost often refers to the cost, at standard, of the total number of budgeted units. The cost information contained in budgets must be consistent with standard costs. For example, suppose the standard cost of a unit of production is:

Standard cost per unit:	
Direct material (2 pounds x $5 per pound)	$10.00
Direct labor (3 hours x $10 per hour)	30.00
Manufacturing overhead ($5 per labor hour)	15.00
Standard cost per unit	$55.00

If the direct material purchases budget calls for 5,000 pounds of raw material, it would show an expected cost of $25,000 (i.e., 5,000 pounds x $5 per pound). Likewise, if the direct labor budget is prepared for an expected production level of 1,000 units, it would indicate 3,000 hours of labor costing $30,000.

Explain how standard costs are developed.

DEVELOPMENT OF STANDARD COSTS

Standard costs for material, labor, and overhead are developed in a variety of ways. The standard quantity of material may be specified in engineering plans that provide detailed lists of raw materials needed in production. For some companies, the standard quantity of raw material is actually specified in recipes. This would be the case in large commercial bakeries and other companies that produce food products. The standard price of the materials is often determined from price lists that suppliers provide.

Industrial engineers can perform time and motion studies to determine the standard quantity of direct labor. In time and motion studies, engineers observe workers under simulated or actual working conditions to determine standard labor hours. A company also can estimate standard labor hours from an analysis of past data. For example, suppose a company developed the following information on production and labor hours:

	Production in Units	Labor Hours
First quarter, 19X1	2,025	6,500
Second quarter, 19X1	2,500	7,400
Third quarter, 19X1	2,100	6,800
Fourth quarter, 19X1	2,600	7,900
Total	9,225	28,600

Based on these data, the average time to produce one unit is approximately 3.10 hours (28,600 hours ÷ 9,225 units). If the company does not anticipate any major changes in the production process, it could use this average as the standard quantity of labor. However, if the company had operated inefficiently in the past, and now bases its standards on past performance, its standards will not reflect efficient production practices. The standard labor wage rates are usually set at the rates management expects to pay the various categories of workers. In many cases, the wage rates are set equal to the rates specified in labor contracts.

Developing standard costs for overhead involves procedures similar to those used to develop the predetermined overhead rates discussed earlier in the text. Dividing the amount of anticipated overhead by the standard quantity of the allocation base results in a standard cost of overhead. For example, suppose a company anticipates it will incur $60,000 of overhead if workers perform 5,000 standard labor hours. In this case, the standard overhead rate would be $12 per standard labor hour. Companies that use activity-based costing develop standard costs for a number of overhead cost drivers such as the numbers of setups, purchase orders, and shipments received.

IDEAL AND ATTAINABLE STANDARDS

In developing standard costs, some managers emphasize **ideal standards**, while others emphasize **attainable standards**. Ideal standards are developed under the assumption that no obstacles to the production process will be encountered. Thus, they do not allow for equipment breakdown that would increase the quantity of labor hours or for defects in raw material that would increase the quantity of material required for production. Ideal standards are sometimes referred to as *perfection standards* because they emphasize production in a "perfect" environment. However, if a company expects occasional equipment failure, occasional substitution of inexperienced for experienced workers, and some raw material defects, then it should set standards at a level that allows for the cost of these events. Currently attainable standards are standard costs that take into account the possibility that a variety of circumstances may lead to costs that are greater than "ideal."

Managers who support ideal standards believe these standards motivate employees to strive for the best possible control over production costs. Such managers argue that if the cost of defects and breakdowns are built into the standards, the result will be an acceptance of defects and breakdowns rather than an effort to eliminate them. However, because they do not allow for *expected* deviations, ideal standards may not be useful for planning. If equipment breakdowns and defects are a "fact of life," then it makes sense to plan for their associated costs. Most managers support the use of attainable standards.

GENERAL APPROACH TO VARIANCE ANALYSIS

Companies that have standard costing systems can analyze the difference between a standard and an actual cost, referred to as a **standard cost variance**, to determine if operations are being performed efficiently. The analysis—referred to as *variance analysis*—involves dividing the total variance between standard and actual cost for material, labor, and overhead into two components. By breaking down the total variance, managers gain insight into the specific areas that need attention. For example, suppose the standard cost of materials per unit of production is 2 pounds at $5 per pound. During the year, the company produces 1,000 units and uses 2,010 pounds of material costing $6 per pound. In this case, the standard cost of materials is $10,000, and the actual cost is $12,060. Thus, the total variance is $2,060, which is labeled "unfavorable" since the actual cost is greater than standard.

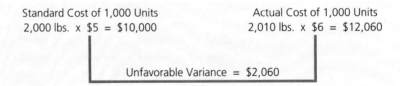

Standard Cost of 1,000 Units
2,000 lbs. x $5 = $10,000

Actual Cost of 1,000 Units
2,010 lbs. x $6 = $12,060

Unfavorable Variance = $2,060

This total variance provides information that material costs may be out of control and in need of management attention, but it does not suggest the nature of the problem. The actual cost may be greater than standard because too much material was used or because the price paid for material was greater than standard. A close look at the facts reveals that the actual quantity of material used is very close to the standard quantity of material—2,010 pounds were used, and the standard quantity is 2,000 pounds. However, the actual price per pound is $6, while the standard price per pound is only $5. We demonstrate in the next section how to divide the total material variance into the part due to the price paid for material and the part due to the use of material. Similar procedures for labor and overhead are presented later in the chapter.

Calculate and interpret variances for direct material.

MATERIAL VARIANCES

The total material variance can be divided into a material price variance and a material quantity variance.

Material Price Variance

The **material price variance** equals the difference between the standard and actual prices per unit of material times the actual quantity of material used.[1]

$$\text{Material Price Variance} = \left(\begin{array}{c} \text{Standard Price per} \\ \text{Unit of Material} \end{array} - \begin{array}{c} \text{Actual Price per} \\ \text{Unit of Material} \end{array} \right) \times \begin{array}{c} \text{Actual Quantity of} \\ \text{Material Used} \end{array}$$

Suppose Acme Manufacturing Company actually paid $9.50 per pound, rather than the standard price of $10, for 6,500 pounds of material it used in July. In this case, there would be a favorable $3,250 material price variance.

$$\$3,250 \text{ Favorable} = (\$10.00 - \$9.50) \times 6,500$$

Note that the material price variance is labeled favorable because the actual price per pound is less than the standard price.[2]

Material Quantity Variance

The **material quantity variance** equals the difference between the standard quantity of material allowed for the number of units produced and the actual quantity of material used times the standard price of material.

$$\begin{array}{c} \text{Material Quantity} \\ \text{Variance} \end{array} = \left(\begin{array}{c} \text{Standard Quantity of Material Allowed} \\ \text{for the Number of Units Produced} \end{array} - \begin{array}{c} \text{Actual Quantity of} \\ \text{Material Used} \end{array} \right) \times \begin{array}{c} \text{Standard} \\ \text{Price} \end{array}$$

Suppose Acme Manufacturing Company produces 3,000 units during July. The standard quantity of material is 2 pounds per unit with a standard price of $10 per pound. The standard quantity of material for 3,000 units is 6,000 pounds (3,000 units x 2 pounds per unit). During the month, Acme actually uses 6,500 pounds of material. Thus, the material quantity variance is $5,000 unfavorable.

$$\$5,000 \text{ Unfavorable} = (6,000 - 6,500) \times \$10$$

Note that the material quantity variance is labeled unfavorable. Acme actually used more material than required by its standards. This is considered an unfavorable outcome since it has a negative effect on company profit.

Reconciling the Material Price and Quantity Variances to the Total Material Variance

The total variance for materials is the difference between the standard and actual costs of materials. You can check the accuracy of your material price and quantity variance calculations by making sure they equal the total material variance. This check is performed for Acme Manufacturing Company in Illustration 26-1.

---

[1]An alternative approach calculates the material price variance with the actual quantity of material *purchased* rather than *used.*

[2]Using the variance formulas presented in this chapter, positive variances will be favorable and negative variances will be unfavorable. However, rather than concentrating on the sign of the variance, you should understand that prices or quantities greater than standard are labeled unfavorable and actual prices or quantities less than standard are labeled favorable.

ILLUSTRATION 26-1 Reconciliation of the Material Price and Quantity Variances to the Total Material Variance

Total Variance	
Standard cost for 3,000 units (6,000 pounds x $10)	$60,000
Actual cost (6,500 pounds x $9.50)	61,750
Excess of actual over standard cost	$(1,750) Unfavorable

Material Price Variance	
Paid $.50 less per pound on all 6,500 pounds used	$3,250 Favorable

Material Quantity Variance	
Used an extra 500 pounds at standard price of $10	(5,000) Unfavorable
Total of material price and quantity variances	$(1,750) Unfavorable

LO 3

Calculate and interpret variances for direct labor.

DIRECT LABOR VARIANCES

The difference between the standard and actual costs of direct labor can be separated into labor rate and labor efficiency variances using formulas similar to those used to calculate material variances.

Labor Rate Variance

The **labor rate variance** equals the difference between the standard and actual wage rates times the actual number of labor hours worked. This variance is very similar to the material price variance.

Labor Rate Variance = (Standard Wage Rate − Actual Wage Rate) x Actual Number of Labor Hours Worked

Suppose Acme Manufacturing Company's standards call for a standard wage rate of $8.00 per hour. During July, the actual wage rate was $8.25 and 9,400 actual hours were worked. In this case, the labor rate variance is an unfavorable $2,350.

$$\$2{,}350 \text{ Unfavorable} = (\$8.00 - \$8.25) \times 9{,}400$$

Labor Efficiency Variance

The **labor efficiency variance** equals the difference between the standard labor hours allowed for the number of units produced and the actual number of labor hours worked times the standard labor wage rate. This variance is very similar to the material quantity variance.

Labor Efficiency Variance = (Standard Labor Hours Allowed for the Number of Units Produced − Actual Number of Labor Hours Worked) x Standard Wage Rate

Acme Manufacturing Company uses 9,400 hours to produce 3,000 units. Standards call for 3 hours per unit at a standard wage rate of $8 per hour. The standard number of hours for 3,000 units is 9,000 (3,000 units x 3 hours per unit). In this case, the labor efficiency variance is $3,200 unfavorable.

$$\$3{,}200 \text{ Unfavorable} = (9{,}000 - 9{,}400) \times \$8$$

Reconciling the Labor Efficiency and Labor Rate Variances to the Total Labor Variance

The total labor variance equals the difference between the standard and actual costs of labor. As with the material variance, it is a good practice to reconcile the labor rate and efficiency variances to the total labor variance. The reconciliation for Acme Manufacturing Company is presented in Illustration 26-2.

ILLUSTRATION 26-2   Reconciliation of the Labor Rate and Efficiency Variances to the Total Labor Variance

Total Variance	
Standard cost for 3,000 units (9,000 hours x $8)	$72,000
Actual cost (9,400 hours x $8.25)	77,550
Excess of actual over standard cost	$ (5,550) Unfavorable

Labor Rate Variance	
Paid $.25 more per hour on all 9,400 actual hours	$(2,350) Unfavorable

Labor Efficiency Variance	
Used an extra 400 hours at standard rate of $8	(3,200) Unfavorable
Total of labor efficiency and rate variances	$(5,550) Unfavorable

LO 4
Calculate and interpret variances for manufacturing overhead.

OVERHEAD VARIANCES

The total variance for manufacturing overhead is the difference between standard and actual overhead costs. The total overhead variance can be separated into overhead volume and controllable overhead variances.

Overhead Volume Variance

The **overhead volume variance** equals the difference between the amount of overhead applied to production at standard and the amount of overhead included in the flexible budget.

$$\text{Overhead Volume Variance} = \text{Overhead Applied to Production at Standard} - \text{Flexible Budget Amount of Overhead}$$

Suppose Acme Manufacturing Company budgets $40,000 of fixed overhead and $5 per unit of variable overhead cost. Recall that a flexible budget is a budget restated for the actual level of production. For Acme Manufacturing, the flexible budget for overhead would be:

$$\$40,000 + (\$5 \times \text{Number of Units Produced})$$

Acme expects to produce 2,500 units. In this case, the standard overhead rate would be $21 per unit, which is calculated as follows:

Expected amount of overhead [$40,000 + ($5 x 2,500 units)]	$52,500
Expected production	÷2,500 units
Standard overhead rate	$ 21 per unit

Note that the standard overhead rate in this example is expressed on a per unit basis. This is because Acme only produces a single product. When multiple products are produced, a company must base the overhead rate on labor hours, machine hours, or some other measure of activity that is common to the various products.

If Acme actually produces 3,000 units, it would apply $63,000 of standard overhead to production (i.e., 3,000 x $21). However, the flexible budget amount for 3,000 units of production is $55,000. Thus, the overhead volume variance is $8,000 favorable.

Overhead Volume Variance	=	**Overhead Applied to Production at Standard**	−	**Flexible Budget Amount of Overhead**
$8,000 favorable	=	$21 x 3,000 units	−	$40,000 + ($5 x 3,000)

Interpreting the Overhead Volume Variance.   Volume variances do not signal that overhead costs are in or out of control. The controllable overhead variance, discussed in the next section, provides this signal. An overhead volume variance simply signals that the quantity of production was greater or less than anticipated when the standard overhead rate was developed. When a company produces more units than anticipated, the amount of overhead it applies to inventory exceeds the flexible budget because the amount of fixed cost per unit is being applied to more units than anticipated. Consider the standard overhead rate for Acme Manufacturing Company. The rate of $21 per unit is composed of $5 per unit of variable costs and $16 of fixed costs. The $16 of fixed costs per unit results from dividing the expected amount of fixed costs ($40,000) by the anticipated production of 2,500 units.

Standard overhead rate:	
Variable costs per unit	$ 5.00
Fixed costs per unit ($40,000 ÷ 2,500 expected units)	16.00
Total	$21.00

When this rate is applied to 3,000 units, Acme applies fixed costs of $48,000 to inventory. This exceeds the $40,000 of fixed costs in the flexible budget (which is not affected by the level of activity) by $8,000.

	Standard Cost Applied to 3,000 Units	Flexible Budget for 3,000 Units	Difference
Variable costs	$15,000 ($5 x 3,000)	$15,000 ($5 x 3,000)	0
Fixed costs	48,000 ($16 x 3,000)	40,000	$8,000
Total	$63,000	$55,000	$8,000

If Acme had anticipated 3,000 units would be produced, the fixed costs per unit would have been $13.3333 and the standard overhead rate would have been set at $18.3333.

Standard overhead rate:	
Variable costs per unit	$ 5.0000
Fixed costs per unit ($40,000 ÷ 3,000 expected units)	13.3333
Total	$18.3333

With a rate of $18.3333 per unit, Acme would have applied $55,000 of overhead to the 3,000 units produced, and the volume variance would be zero. The usefulness of the volume variance is limited. It only signals that more or less units have been produced than planned when the company set its standard overhead rate. If more units are produced than were originally planned, the company has a favorable variance; if less units are produced, the company has an unfavorable variance.

Controllable Overhead Variance

The **controllable overhead variance** is the difference between the amount of overhead that would be included in a flexible budget for the actual level of production and the actual amount of overhead. The variance is referred to as "controllable" because managers should be able to control costs to keep them in line with the amount included in the flexible budget.

Controllable Overhead Variance = Flexible Budget Amount of Overhead – Actual Overhead Cost

Suppose Acme Manufacturing Company has the flexible budget noted above ($40,000 of fixed overhead and $5 per unit of variable overhead). During the month of July, Acme produces 3,000 units and incurs $52,000 of overhead. Thus, it has a $3,000 favorable controllable overhead variance.

Controllable Overhead Variance = Flexible Budget Amount of Overhead – Actual Overhead Cost

| $3,000 Favorable | = | $ 40,000 + ($5 x 3,000) | – | $52,000 |

The variance is labeled favorable because the actual cost is less than the amount indicated in the flexible budget.

Reconciling the Overhead Volume Variance and the Controllable Overhead Variance to the Total Overhead Variance

In a standard costing system, the amount of overhead applied to production is based on standard costs rather than on actual costs. The total overhead variance equals the difference between the amount of overhead applied to production at standard and the actual amount of overhead. The reconciliation of the overhead volume variance and the controllable overhead variance to the total overhead variance for Acme Manufacturing Company is presented in Illustration 26-3.

COMPREHENSIVE EXAMPLE

In this section, a comprehensive example of standard cost variances is presented for Frosty Ice Cream Company. Recall from the scenario at the start of the chapter that Linda Evert, director of operations for Frosty, was concerned about a 10 percent increase in material cost. The plant manager assured her that the increase was not due to waste in the use of raw materials. The material variances we will calculate provide insight into the validity of the plant manager's statement.

At the start of the year, Frosty Ice Cream Company planned to produce 900,000 gallons of ice cream. Production of ice cream requires various raw materials (e.g., milk, cream, sugar, and flavorings), and Frosty would most likely develop separate standards for each. However, to simplify the setting, we assume Frosty uses only one raw material. Each gallon of ice cream requires .8

ILLUSTRATION 26-3 Reconciliation of the Overhead Volume Variance and the Controllable Overhead Variance to the Total Overhead Variance

Total Variance		
Standard overhead applied (3,000 units x $21)		$63,000
Actual overhead cost		52,000
Excess of standard over actual cost		$11,000 Favorable

Overhead Volume Variance		
Applied overhead (3,000 x $21)	$63,000	
Flexible budget overhead ($40,000 + $5 x 3,000 units))	55,000	$ 8,000 Favorable

Controllable Overhead Variance		
Flexible budget overhead ($40,000 + $5 x 3,000 units)	$55,000	
Actual overhead	52,000	3,000 Favorable
Total of overhead volume and controllable overhead variance		$11,000 Favorable

gallons of raw material costing $2.50 per gallon. (A gallon of ice cream does not require a gallon of raw material since air is incorporated in the production process.) Each gallon of ice cream also requires .125 hours of direct labor costing $12.00 per hour.

The company estimates that fixed production costs will equal $450,000 per year and variable production costs will equal $.25 per gallon. Thus, Frosty sets its standard overhead rate at $.75 per gallon.

Standard Overhead Rate = Expected Amount of Overhead at Standard ÷ Expected Production

$.75 per gallon   =   [$450,000 + ($.25 x 900,000 gallons)]   ÷   900,000 gallons

In summary, the standard cost per unit is:

	Standard Cost Per Unit
Direct material (.8 gallons x $2.50)	$2.00
Direct labor (.125 hours x $12)	1.50
Manufacturing overhead	.75
Total	$4.25

Actual demand during the year is somewhat greater than anticipated, necessitating production of 1,000,000 gallons. Frosty uses 809,000 gallons of material, costing $2.72 per gallon, to produce the 1,000,000 gallons of ice cream. Frosty incurs actual direct labor costs of $1,573,000 for 130,000 actual hours. Thus, the actual wage rate is $12.10 per hour ($1,573,000 ÷ 130,000). Finally, Frosty incurs actual overhead costs of $680,000.

At this point, you should attempt to calculate the standard cost variances for the Frosty Ice Cream Company data. For your convenience in working through the example and in solving problems at the end of the chapter, a summary of the variance formulas is presented in Illustration 26-4. Some key figures needed in the calculation of the variances for Frosty Ice Cream Company are summarized in Illustration 26-5.

ILLUSTRATION 26-4 Standard Cost Variance Formulas

$$\text{Material Price Variance} = \left(\text{Standard Price per Unit of Material} - \text{Actual Price per Unit of Material} \right) \times \text{Actual Quantity of Material Used}$$

$$\text{Material Quantity Variance} = \left(\text{Standard Quantity of Material Allowed for the Number of Units Produced} - \text{Actual Quantity of Material Used} \right) \times \text{Standard Price}$$

$$\text{Labor Rate Variance} = (\text{Standard Wage Rate} - \text{Actual Wage Rate}) \times \text{Actual Number of Labor Hours Worked}$$

$$\text{Labor Efficiency Variance} = \left(\text{Standard Labor Hours Allowed for the Number of Units Produced} - \text{Actual Number of Labor Hours Worked} \right) \times \text{Standard Wage Rate}$$

$$\text{Overhead Volume Variance} = \text{Overhead Applied to Production at Standard} - \text{Flexible Budget Amount of Overhead}$$

$$\text{Controllable Overhead Variance} = \text{Flexible Budget Amount of Overhead} - \text{Actual Overhead Cost}$$

ILLUSTRATION 26-5 Summary of Data for Production of 1,000,000 Gallons of Ice Cream

	Standard Cost Information	Actual Cost Information
Direct material	800,000 gallons x $2.50 per gallon	809,000 gallons x $2.72 per gallon
Direct labor	125,000 hours x $12 per hour	130,000 hours x $12.10 per hour
Overhead:		
Applied at standard	$.75 x 1,000,000 gallons	
Flexible budget	$450,000 + ($.25 x 1,000,000 gallons)	
Actual		$680,000

Material Variances

The standard price of material is $2.50 per gallon, and the actual price is $2.72 per gallon. The actual quantity of material used is 809,000 gallons. Thus, the material price variance is:

$$\$177,980 \text{ Unfavorable} = (\$2.50 - \$2.72) \times 809,000$$

Since 1,000,000 gallons of ice cream were produced and the standard quantity of material per gallon is .8 gallons, the standard quantity of material for the total units produced is 800,000 gallons. The actual quantity used is 809,000 gallons, and the standard price is $2.50 per gallon. Thus, the material quantity variance is:

$$\$22,500 \text{ Unfavorable} = (800,000 - 809,000) \times \$2.50$$

Reconciliation of Material Variances

Total Variance

Standard cost for 1,000,000 units (800,000 gallons x $2.50 per gallon)	$2,000,000
Actual cost (809,000 gallons x $2.72 per gallon)	2,200,480
Excess of actual over standard cost	$ (200,480) Unfavorable

Material Price Variance

Paid $.22 more per gallon on all 809,000 gallons used	$(177,980) Unfavorable

Material Quantity Variance

Used an extra 9,000 gallons at standard price of $2.50 per gallon	(22,500) Unfavorable
Total of material price and quantity variances	$(200,480) Unfavorable

Note that the material variances support the plant manager's contention that the large material variance was not due to wasting materials. Of the total $200,480 unfavorable variance, only $22,500 is due to using more material than planned. Most of the variance is due to paying more per gallon for raw material than planned.

Labor Variances

The standard wage rate is $12.00 per hour, and the actual wage rate is $12.10 per hour. Since 130,000 actual hours are worked, the labor rate variance is:

$$\$13,000 \text{ Unfavorable} = (\$12.00 - \$12.10) \times 130,000$$

The standard quantity of labor for the 1,000,000 gallons produced is 125,000 hours (1,000,000 gallons x .125 hours per gallon). The actual quantity of labor is 130,000 hours, and the standard wage rate is $12.00 per hour. Thus, the labor efficiency variance is:

$$\$60,000 \text{ Unfavorable} = (125,000 - 130,000) \times \$12.00$$

Reconciliation of Labor Variances	
Total Variance	
Standard cost for 1,000,000 gallons (125,000 hours x $12)	$1,500,000
Actual cost (130,000 hours x $12.10 per hour)	1,573,000
Excess of actual over standard cost	$ (73,000) Unfavorable
Labor Rate Variance	
Paid $.10 more per hour on all 130,000 actual hours	$(13,000) Unfavorable
Labor Efficiency Variance	
Used an extra 5,000 hours at standard rate of $12 per hour	(60,000) Unfavorable
Total of labor efficiency and rate variances	$(73,000) Unfavorable

Overhead Variances

The amount of overhead applied to production equals the standard overhead rate of $.75 per gallon times the 1,000,000 gallons produced. This amounts to $750,000. The flexible budget amount of overhead is $700,000 (i.e, $450,000 + $.25 x 1,000,000 gallons). The difference between the amount of overhead applied and the flexible budget amount of overhead is the overhead volume variance.

$$\$50,000 \text{ Favorable} = \$750,000 - \$700,000$$

The flexible budget amount of overhead for 1,000,000 gallons is $700,000, while the actual amount of overhead is $680,000. Thus, the controllable overhead variance is:

$$\$20,000 \text{ Favorable} = \$700,000 - \$680,000$$

Reconciliation of Overhead Variances		
Total Variance		
Standard overhead applied (1,000,000 gallons x $.75 per gallon)		$750,000
Actual overhead cost		680,000
Excess of standard over actual cost		$ 70,000 Favorable
Overhead Volume Variance		
Applied overhead (1,000,000 gallons x $.75 per gallon)	$750,000	
Flexible budget overhead ($450,000 + $.25 per gallon x 1,000,000 gallons)	700,000	$50,000 Favorable
Controllable Overhead Variance		
Flexible budget overhead ($450,000 + $.25 per gallon x 1,000,000 gallons)	$700,000	
Actual overhead	680,000	20,000 Favorable
Total of overhead volume and controllable overhead variances		$70,000 Favorable

INVESTIGATION OF STANDARD COST VARIANCES

All of the standard cost variances computed in the preceding comprehensive example are presented in Illustration 26-6.

ILLUSTRATION 26-6 Variance Summary

Frosty Ice Cream Company Variance Summary For the Period Ended December 31, 19X1		
Material price variance	$(177,980)	Unfavorable
Material quantity variance	(22,500)	Unfavorable
Labor rate variance	(13,000)	Unfavorable
Labor efficiency variance	(60,000)	Unfavorable
Overhead volume variance	50,000	Favorable
Controllable overhead variance	20,000	Favorable
Total	$(203,480)	Unfavorable

Standard cost variances do not provide definitive evidence that costs are "in or out of control" or that managers are performing effectively or ineffectively. Rather, they should be viewed as indicators of *potential* problem areas. Whether costs are being effectively controlled can only be determined by investigating the facts behind the variances. For example, as indicated in Illustration 26-6, there is a $177,980 unfavorable material price variance. Does this imply that the purchasing department is not doing a good job of searching for the lowest cost material consistent with desired quality levels? Not necessarily. Subsequent investigation may reveal that unavoidable price increases have taken place. Obviously, there is not much the purchasing department can do if all suppliers increase their prices.

As another example, consider the $60,000 unfavorable labor efficiency variance indicated in Illustration 26-6. What factors might account for this unfavorable variance? The first logical explanation may be that the manager responsible for supervising the production work force has not done a competent job. However, this is just one possibility. Perhaps workers went on strike and Frosty had to hire inexperienced substitutes. These substitutes would have a difficult time meeting standard allowable production times even if they were properly supervised. Another possibility is that Frosty may have placed a new piece of equipment into production during the period. Workers may simply require additional time to become familiar with the new equipment. Which of these, or other possible explanations, is correct can only be determined by an investigation to determine the real cause of the variance.

LO 5

Discuss how the management by exception approach is applied to investigate standard cost variances.

Management by Exception

Since investigation of standard cost variances is itself a costly activity, management must decide which variances to investigate. Most managers take a **management by exception** approach and investigate only those variances they deem are exceptional. Of course, this implies that managers must develop some criteria for determining what is meant by "exceptional." The absolute dollar value of the variance or the variance as a percent of actual or standard is often used as a criterion. Suppose Frosty Ice Cream Company decides to investigate any variance in excess of $40,000. This implies that Frosty should investigate the material price, labor efficiency, and overhead volume variances. However, the cause of the overhead volume variance is quite obvious—more units were produced than anticipated when Frosty developed its standard overhead rate. Thus, management need only investigate the material price and labor efficiency variances.

"Favorable" Variances May Be Unfavorable

The fact that a variance is "favorable" does not mean it should not be investigated. Indeed, a favorable variance may be indicative of poor management decisions. For example, suppose the price of raw materials increases. To avoid an unfavorable material price variance, a manager could order the purchase of cheap, inferior materials. This could generate a favorable material price variance if the price of the inferior goods is less than the standard price of materials. However, the inferior materials may result in undetected product defects and cause the company to lose its reputation as a high-quality producer. If the defects are detected, items would be scrapped or "reworked." This would lead to an unfavorable material quantity variance since the company would use additional materials to replace or rework defective items.

INSIGHTS INTO ETHICS

Bill Clayton is the CEO of Textile Products, Inc. At the end of last quarter, he received a performance report that listed the material, labor, and overhead variances of each of the company's ten production facilities. Bill wrote congratulatory memos to the seven plant managers whose reports indicated large favorable variances. He wrote negative memos to the three plant managers whose reports indicated large unfavorable variances, and he plans to reduce their annual bonuses. Bill doesn't believe in letting managers comment on their variances. As he explained to his assistant, Steve Olson, "If I ask them to explain the variances, the plant managers always find an excuse as to why their costs are so high. I don't want excuses. I want good cost control."

Does Bill have an ethical responsibility to allow the plant managers to explain why variances are unfavorable? Is Bill's policy a good business practice?

RESPONSIBILITY ACCOUNTING AND VARIANCES

As noted previously, the central idea of responsibility accounting is that managers should only be held responsible for costs they can control. The implication for variances is that managers and workers should only be held responsible for variances they can control. Thus, a supervisor who can control material usage but has no control over the price paid for materials should be held responsible for the material quantity variance but not for the material price variance. The purchasing agent responsible for buying material at the lowest price consistent with quality considerations should be held responsible for the price variance.

LO 6

Record standard costs in a manufacturing firm's accounts.

RECORDING STANDARD COSTS IN ACCOUNTS

Manufacturing companies use standard costing systems to control their operations and to determine product costs. We have previously illustrated the calculation of standard cost variances and discussed how managers can use them to evaluate operations. In this section, we illustrate how a manufacturing company records product costs at standard in its accounts. In a standard costing system, the costs a company adds to the work in process inventory, finished goods inventory, and cost of goods sold accounts are all recorded at standard rather than actual cost. In the process of recording inventory at standard cost, variances also are calculated and recorded for management's use in performance evaluation. As a concrete example, we will present the entries for recording material, labor, and manufacturing overhead using the information presented for Frosty Ice Cream Company. (See Illustration 26-5.)

Recording Material Costs

Frosty Ice Cream Company used 809,000 gallons of material in production. The material cost $2.72 per gallon, or $2,200,480 in total. The standard quantity of material was 800,000 gallons. At the standard price of $2.50 per gallon, the standard material cost is $2,000,000. Frosty records the standard amount as a debit in Work in Process Inventory; the actual amount is recorded as a credit in Raw Materials Inventory. The difference between the debit and the credit is due to the material quantity variance and the material price variance. Variance accounts are temporary cost accounts and are always closed before a company prepares its financial statements. We demonstrate the closing process below. Note that in this example, both the material price and material quantity variances are unfavorable and are recorded as debits. Unfavorable variances are associated with increases in a company's expenses and have debit balances like expense accounts. Favorable variances are associated with reductions in a company's expenses and have credit balances.

(Date)			
	Work in Process Inventory	2,000,000	
	Material Price Variance	177,980	
	Material Quantity Variance	22,500	
	Raw Materials Inventory		2,200,480
	To record material cost.		

Recording Labor Cost

During the year, 130,000 actual labor hours are worked at a rate of $12.10 per hour or a total cost of $1,573,000. The standard number of hours is 125,000 and the standard wage rate is $12 per hour. Thus, the total standard cost of labor Frosty must add to Work in Process Inventory is $1,500,000. The difference between the total actual labor cost payable and the total standard labor cost assigned to Work in Process Inventory equals the labor rate and labor efficiency variances.

(Date)	Work in Process Inventory	1,500,000	
	Labor Rate Variance	13,000	
	Labor Efficiency Variance	60,000	
	Wages and Salaries Payable		1,573,000
	To record labor cost.		

Recording Manufacturing Overhead

Recording manufacturing overhead in a standard costing system is a three-step process. First, a company records actual overhead in the Manufacturing Overhead account. Second, it applies overhead to Work in Process Inventory at the standard cost. Third, the company closes the difference between actual overhead and overhead applied at standard and identifies overhead variances. These three steps are illustrated below.

Frosty incurs actual overhead during the year of $680,000. Frosty would credit various accounts (e.g., Wages and Salaries Payable, Utilities Payable, and Accumulated Depreciation) to record this amount, and it would debit the actual cost of overhead in the manufacturing overhead account.

(Date)	Manufacturing Overhead	680,000	
	Various Accounts		680,000
	To record actual overhead cost.		

Frosty assigns to Work in Process Inventory the standard cost of overhead, which is equal to the standard overhead rate times the number of units produced. In the example, this amounts to $750,000 (i.e., 1,000,000 gallons x $.75 per gallon). When Frosty applies this amount to Work in Process Inventory, it reduces Manufacturing Overhead by the same amount.

(Date)	Work in Process Inventory	750,000	
	Manufacturing Overhead		750,000
	To apply overhead cost to inventory at standard.		

At this point, Frosty has debited Manufacturing Overhead for the actual amount of overhead and has credited it for the amount of overhead applied to Work in Process Inventory at the standard overhead rate. The difference between the actual overhead cost and the standard overhead applied to inventory ($70,000) equals the sum of the overhead volume and controllable overhead variances. These two variances are identified when Frosty records the journal entry to close Manufacturing Overhead.

(Date)	Manufacturing Overhead	70,000	
	Overhead Volume Variance		50,000
	Controllable Overhead Variance		20,000
	To close Manufacturing Overhead and record overhead variances.		

Recording Finished Goods

At this point, Work in Process Inventory contains the following costs:

Raw material	$2,000,000
Direct labor	1,500,000
Overhead	750,000
Total	$4,250,000

The total of $4,250,000 equals the 1,000,000 gallons produced at a standard cost per gallon of $4.25. When the units are completed, Frosty transfers the cost from Work in Process Inventory to Finished Goods Inventory.

(Date)	Finished Goods Inventory	4,250,000	
	Work in Process Inventory		4,250,000
	To record completed units in Finished Goods Inventory.		

Recording Cost of Goods Sold

When it sells units, Frosty reduces the Finished Goods Inventory and increases Cost of Goods Sold by the standard cost of the units sold. Assume Frosty sells all 1,000,000 gallons of ice cream produced. The standard cost is $4.25 per gallon. Therefore, Frosty's entry to record the cost of goods sold is:

(Date)	Cost of Goods Sold	4,250,000	
	Finished Goods Inventory		4,250,000
	To record cost of goods sold.		

CLOSING VARIANCE ACCOUNTS

At the end of the accounting period, a company must close its temporary variance accounts. As a practical matter, this is usually accomplished by debiting or crediting the variances to Cost of Goods Sold. Before closing the variance accounts, a company records Cost of Goods Sold at standard cost. Thus, closing the variances results in the account being adjusted to approximately actual cost. It would be more accurate to adjust Work in Process Inventory and Finished Goods Inventory (as well as Cost of Goods Sold) to actual cost by allocating part of the total variance to these accounts. However, unless the variances are material and the balances in Work in Process Inventory and Finished Goods Inventory are large relative to Cost of Goods Sold, closing the total variance to Cost of Goods Sold is convenient and not misleading. For Frosty Ice Cream, there is no Work in Process or Finished Goods Inventory at the end of the year. (It sold all of the ice cream produced.) Therefore, it closes the variances to Cost of Goods Sold.

Frosty's journal entry to close the variance accounts is as follows. Note that a favorable variance reduces the amount of Cost of Goods Sold, while an unfavorable variance increases the account.

(Date)	Cost of Goods Sold	203,480	
	Overhead Volume Variance	50,000	
	Controllable Overhead Variance	20,000	
	Material Price Variance		177,980
	Material Quantity Variance		22,500
	Labor Rate Variance		13,000
	Labor Efficiency Variance		60,000
	To close variance accounts to Cost of Goods Sold.		

SUMMARY

Explain how standard costs are developed.   Standard costs are developed in a variety of ways. Engineering studies may determine standard material quantities. Companies may use supplier price lists to determine standard prices of materials and time and motion studies to determine standard labor hours.

Calculate and interpret variances for direct material.   The total material variance can be divided into material price and material quantity variances.

Calculate and interpret variances for direct labor.   The total labor variance can be divided into labor rate and labor efficiency variances.

Calculate and interpret variances for manufacturing overhead.   The total overhead variance can be divided into overhead volume and controllable overhead variances.

Discuss how the management by exception approach is applied to investigate standard cost variances.   Since investigation of variances is costly, managers only investigate exceptional variances. Variances that are large in absolute dollar value or as a percent of actual or standard cost are generally considered exceptional.

Record standard costs in a manufacturing firm's accounts.   Journal entries are required to record material, labor, and overhead at standard cost. At the end of the accounting period, a firm must record a journal entry to close the variance accounts to Cost of Goods Sold.

▌REVIEW PROBLEM

The Long Company uses a standard cost system. The standard cost for producing one unit of finished goods is:

Materials (2 lbs. @ $2.25)	$ 4.50
Direct labor (0.5 hours @ $8.00)	4.00
Standard overhead	10.00
Total standard cost per unit	$18.50

The flexible budget amount of variable overhead is $5.50 per unit and the fixed overhead per year is $90,000. Expected production is 20,000 units. During 19X1, Long Company produced 21,000 units. The costs incurred for production in 19X1 are:

Materials (43,000 lbs @ $2.20)	$ 94,600
Direct labor (10,300 hours @ $8.05)	82,915
Actual overhead	208,000
Total cost	$385,515

REQUIRED:

a. Calculate the material variances.
b. Calculate the labor variances.
c. Calculate the overhead variances.
d. Prepare a variance summary.
e. Prepare the journal entries for 19X1.

SOLUTION:

Planning and Organizing Your Work

1. Insert the actual and standard cost information into the formulas for variances given in Illustration 26-4.
2. List each of the variances in a variance summary.
3. Record journal entries using a standard cost system.

(a) *Calculate the material variances.*

Material price variance   = ($2.25 – $2.20) x 43,000   = $2,150 Favorable
Material quantity variance = (42,000[1] – 43,000) x $2.25 = $2,250 Unfavorable

[1]21,000 units x 2 lbs. per unit

(b) *Calculate the labor variances.*

Labor rate variance   = ($8.00 – $8.05) x 10,300   = $ 515 Unfavorable
Labor efficiency variance = (10,500[2] – 10,300) x $8.00 = $1,600 Favorable

[2]21,000 units x 0.5 hours per unit

(c) *Calculate the overhead variances.*

Controllable overhead variance = $205,500[3] – $208,000 = $2,500 Unfavorable
Overhead volume variance   = $210,000[4] – $205,500 = $4,500 Favorable

[3]$90,000 + ($5.50 x 21,000)
[4]$10 x 21,000

(d) *Prepare a variance summary.*

Long Company Variance Summary For the Year Ended December 31, 19X1		
Material price variance	$2,150	Favorable
Material quantity variance	(2,250)	Unfavorable
Labor rate variance	(515)	Unfavorable
Labor efficiency variance	1,600	Favorable
Controllable overhead variance	(2,500)	Unfavorable
Overhead volume variance	4,500	Favorable
Total	$2,985	Favorable

(e) *Prepare the journal entries.*

Work in Process (42,000 x $2.25)	94,500	
Material Quantity Variance	2,250	
Material Price Variance		2,150
Raw Materials		94,600
To record material variances and the use of materials in production.		
Work in Process (10,500 x $8.00)	84,000	
Labor Rate Variance	515	
Labor Efficiency Variance		1,600
Wages and Salaries Payable		82,915
To record labor variances and the use of labor in production.		

Manufacturing Overhead	208,000	
Various Accounts		208,000
To record actual overhead cost.		
Work in Process Inventory	210,000	
Manufacturing Overhead		210,000
To apply overhead cost to inventory at standard.		
Manufacturing Overhead	2,000	
Controllable Overhead Variance	2,500	
Overhead Volume Variance		4,500
To close manufacturing overhead and record overhead variance.		
Material Price Variance	2,150	
Labor Efficiency Variance	1,600	
Overhead Volume Variance	4,500	
Material Quantity Variance		2,250
Labor Rate Variance		515
Controllable Overhead Variance		2,500
Cost of Goods Sold		2,985
To close the variance accounts.		

KEY TERMS

attainable standards, *1055*
controllable overhead variance,
  1061
ideal standards, *1055*
labor efficiency variance, *1058*
labor rate variance, *1058*
management by exception,
  1066

material price variance, *1057*
material quantity variance,
  1057
overhead volume variance,
  1059
standard cost, *1054*
standard cost variance, *1056*

SELF-QUIZ

LO 1   1.   What is the primary benefit of a standard costing system?
     a. It records costs at what should have been incurred.
     b. It allows the comparison of differences between actual and standard costs.
     c. It is easy to implement.
     d. It is inexpensive and easy to use.

LO 1   2.   Which of the following is *not* a way to develop a standard cost?

     a. By using a fixed rate that is higher every period.
     b. By performing time and motion studies.
     c. By analyzing past data.
     d. By using what is specified in engineering plans.

LO 2   3.   The total material variance can be divided into a material _____ variance and a material _____ variance.

LO 2   4.   Which statement below correctly describes an unfavorable material price variance?

a. Too much material was purchased.
b. Too much was paid for material used in production compared to the standard cost.
c. More material was used than called for by the standard.
d. Less material was used than called for by the standard.

LO 3 5. True or False? The labor rate variance is equal to the difference between the standard wage rate and the actual wage rate times the standard number of labor hours worked.

LO 3 6. What does a favorable labor efficiency variance mean?
a. Labor rates were higher than called for by the standard.
b. Inexperience labor was used causing the rate to be lower than standard.
c. More labor was used than called for by the standard.
d. Less labor was used than called for by the standard.

LO 4 7. What does an unfavorable overhead volume variance mean?
a. Overhead costs are out of control.
b. Overhead costs are in control.
c. Production was greater than anticipated.
d. Production was less than anticipated.

LO 4 8. State the formula for calculating the controllable overhead variance.

LO 5 9. True or False? Standard cost variances provide definitive evidence that costs are "out of control" and managers are not performing effectively.

LO 5 10. True or False? A favorable variance may be indicative of poor management decisions.

LO 6 11. For a standard cost accounting system, a journal entry must be made at the end of the accounting period to close the variance accounts to _____ ___ _____ _____.

QUESTIONS

Q26-1 What role do standard costs play in a business?
Q26-2 What is the difference between a budgeted cost and a standard cost?
Q26-3 How could the standard quantity of material be developed?
Q26-4 What is the difference between an ideal standard and an attainable standard?
Q26-5 What is the meaning of an unfavorable material quantity variance?
Q26-6 What action should management take if there is a large unfavorable variance?
Q26-7 What factors should be considered when investigating variances?
Q26-8 What is management by exception?
Q26-9 What is the central idea of responsibility accounting as it relates to variances?
Q26-10 What are the alternative methods to close variance accounts?

EXERCISES

LO 2 **E26-1 Calculating Material Variances** Crown Company produced 1300 rings during March 19X1. The standard cost of each ounce of gold used in the rings is $400 per ounce. The standard quantity of material for each ring is one-half ounce of gold per ring. The cost incurred for March production was $266,625 at $395 per ounce. Determine the material price variance and the material quantity variance for March 19X1. Indicate whether each variance is favorable or unfavorable.

LO 3

E26-2 **Calculating Labor Variances** Texas Electronics produced 1,428,000 calculators during August 19X2. The standard cost of each direct labor hour is $7.00 and the standard output is 80 calculators per labor hour. The cost incurred for August production was $137,088 for 19,040 actual direct labor hours. Determine the labor rate variance and the labor efficiency variance for August 19X2. Indicate whether each variance is favorable or unfavorable.

LO 2,3

E26-3 **Calculating Material and Labor Variances** J. A. Bootery uses a standard costing system. The standard cost for producing each pair of boots is as follows:

Materials (1.5 yards @ $9.00) $13.50
Direct labor (0.5 hours @ $7.00)   3.50

During May 19X3, Bootery company produced 7,000 pairs of boots. The material and labor costs incurred during May are $96,250 and $26,790, respectively. The actual cost of material was $8.75 per yard. During May there were 3,800 direct labor hours worked. Calculate all material and labor variances.

LO 4

E26-4 **Calculating Overhead Variances** Aquapit Company produced 15,200 aquariums during 19X4. The flexible budget amount of variable overhead is $8.50 per unit and the fixed overhead per year is $59,200. Expected production is 16,000 aquariums. Actual overhead incurred is $186,200. Determine the overhead volume variance and the controllable overhead variance.

LO 3,4

E26-5 **Calculating Labor and Overhead Variances** At the start of 19X1, U.S.A. Threads determined its standard labor cost to be $5.50 per hour. The budget for variable overhead was $6.00 per unit and budgeted fixed overhead was $135,000 for the year. Expected production was 30,000 units. During 19X1, the actual cost of labor was $5.75. U.S.A. Threads produced 32,500 units requiring 52,000 direct labor hours. Actual overhead for the year was $326,800. Determine labor and overhead variances.

LO 2,6

E26-6 **Calculating Material Variances and Recording Material Costs** Leahnka Company produced 2,200 cabinets during May 19X6. Leahnka uses a standard costing system. The standard cost of wood used in the cabinets is $25 per linear foot. The standard quantity of material for each cabinet is 30 linear feet. The cost incurred for March production was $1,601,600 at $26 per foot. Determine the material price variance, the material quantity variance, and record all necessary journal entries for May 19X6.

LO 6

E26-7 **Recording Labor Variances** LapTop Company uses a standard costing system. During 19X7, 93,280 actual labor hours were worked at a rate of $11.75 per hour. The standard number of hours is 94,000 and the standard wage rate is $11.90 per hour. Prepare the journal entry to record labor cost during 19X7.

LO 6

E26-8 **Recording Manufacturing Overhead** Krell Cosmetics uses a standard costing system. During 19X8, Krell incurred actual overhead of $381,000. The standard overhead rate is $2.25 per unit and 180,000 units were produced in 19X8. One-third of the total overhead variance is attributed to the volume variance and the remainder is attributed to the controllable overhead variance. Prepare the journal entries to record overhead.

LO 6

E26-9 **Closing Variance Accounts** The variance summary for Reasonable Facsimile is as follows:

Reasonable Facsimile Variance Summary For the Year Ended December 31, 19X9		
Material price variance	$ 4,150	Favorable
Material quantity variance	(3,250)	Unfavorable
Labor rate variance	115	Favorable
Labor efficiency variance	(2,600)	Unfavorable
Controllable overhead variance	(2,500)	Unfavorable
Overhead volume variance	(4,500)	Unfavorable
Total	$(8,585)	Unfavorable

Close the variance accounts presented for Reasonable Facsimile.

PROBLEM SET A

LO 1,2,3,4   **P26-1A   Calculating Material, Labor, and Overhead Variances**   The Short Company uses a standard costing system. The standards per unit produced for material and labor are 0.5 gallons and 1.5 hours, respectively. The standard cost per gallon of material is $6.50. The standard cost per hour for labor is $9.00. Overhead is applied at the rate of $10.50 per unit. Expected production is 15,000 units with fixed overhead per year of $30,000 and variable overhead of $8.50 per unit. Total overhead at expected production is $157,500. During 19X1, 17,500 units of finished goods were produced. The cost of 9,100 gallons of material used was $59,605. The cost of direct labor incurred in 19X1 was $229,643.75 based on an average wage rate of $9.05 per hour. Actual overhead for 19X1 was $169,750.

REQUIRED:

a. Determine the standard cost per unit.
b. Calculate and reconcile material variances.
c. Calculate and reconcile labor variances.
d. Calculate and reconcile overhead variances.

LO 2,3   **P26-2A   Calculating Material and Labor Variances With Missing Information**   Barnes Corporation produces bottles of liquid fertilizer. Partial information for June 19X2 is as follows:

Standard material per bottle	3 liters
Standard cost of material per liter	$0.40
Standard labor hours per bottle	0.2 hours
Actual production for June	10,000 bottles
Total material cost for June	$12,390
Total liters used in production	29,500
Material price variance	$590 Unfavorable
Total labor cost for June	$12,980
Actual cost per labor hour	$5.90
Labor rate variance	$220 Favorable

REQUIRED:

Determine the following:

a. Actual cost of material per liter.
b. Total standard liters of material for actual production.
c. Material quantity variance.

d. Total standard material cost for actual production.
e. Labor hours worked.
f. Standard cost per labor hour.
g. Labor efficiency variance.
h. Total standard labor cost for actual production.

LO 1

P26-3A   Determining Standard Costs   Computochair manufactures special chairs for use by data input personnel. They have decided to initiate a standard cost system to help improve planning and control. The president of the company assigned the task of developing standards to the company controller and the plant engineer. They came up with the following estimates:

Amount per Chair	Average Amount	Best Amount
Steel	1.5 lbs. @ $6.30	1.2 lbs. @ $5.95
Fabric	2.5 yds. @ $9.50	2.1 yds. @ $9.20
Direct labor	1.2 hrs. @ $7.50	1.0 hrs. @ $7.45
Variable overhead	$11.52	$9.40

In addition, the controller and engineer determined that fixed overhead has averaged $49,680 per year in the past and the lowest amount of fixed overhead incurred was $40,500. Expected production is 18,000 chairs per year. The company controller believes that the standard should be set using the average amounts whereas the plant engineer believes that they should be set at the best amounts. In a meeting with the controller and the plant engineer, the president decided to set the standard at the midpoint between the average and the best amount.

REQUIRED:

a. Determine the controller's standard cost per unit.
b. Determine the plant engineer's standard cost per unit.
c. Determine the president's standard cost per unit.

LO 3,4

P26-4A   Calculating Labor Variances With Missing Information   Noble Corporation produces dental crowns. Partial information for 19X4 is as follows:

	Labor
Actual cost	$208,950
Actual cost per hour	$10.50
Standard cost per hour	?
Total standard hours	?
Total actual hours	?
Labor rate variance	$9,950 Favorable
Labor efficiency variance	$9,900 Unfavorable
Standard hours per crown	?

REQUIRED:

Determine the unknown amounts listed as "?" in the information provided.

LO 2,3,4,5

P26-5A   Comprehensive Variance Problem   The VanPro Company uses a standard costing system. The standards per unit produced for material and labor are 3.5 pounds and 0.5 hours, respectively. The standard cost per pound of material is $3.50. The standard cost per hour of labor is $7.50. Standard overhead is $3.15 per unit. For 19X5, expected production is 104,000 units wih fixed overhead of $91,000 per year and variable overhead of $2.275 per unit. During 19X5, 99,000 units of finished goods were produced. The total cost of material used was $1,222,650 with each pound costing $3.25. The cost of direct labor incurred in 19X5 was $403,072 based on an average wage rate of $7.52 per hour. Actual overhead for 19X5 was $299,750.

REQUIRED:

a. Determine the standard cost per unit.
b. Calculate the material, labor, and overhead variances.
c. Prepare a variance summary.
d. Prepare journal entries for 19X5 including the closing entry.

PROBLEM SET B

LO 1,2,3,4   **P26-1B**   **Calculating Material, Labor, and Overhead Variances**   The Lopez Company uses a standard costing system. The standards per unit produced for material and labor are 0.25 gallons and 0.75 hours, respectively. The standard cost per gallon of material is $11.60. The standard cost per hour for labor is $7.40. Overhead is applied at a rate of $13.20 per unit. Expected production is 20,000 units with fixed overhead per year of $70,000 and variable overhead of $3.10 per unit. The total overhead at expected production is $132,000. During 19X6, 21,500 units of finished goods were produced. The cost of 5,600 gallons of material used was $65,520. The cost of direct labor incurred in 19X6 was $116,070 based on an average wage rate of $7.30 per hour. Actual overhead for 19X6 was $139,750.

REQUIRED:

a. Determine the standard cost per unit.
b. Calculate and reconcile material variances.
c. Calculate and reconcile labor variances.
d. Calculate and reconcile overhead variances.

LO 2,3   **P26-2B**   **Calculating Material and Labor Variances With Missing Information**   Loren Corporation produces economy size bottles of bath oil. Partial information for June 19X6 is as follows:

Standard material per bottle	3 liters
Standard cost of material per liter	$0.80
Standard labor hours per bottle	0.2 hours
Actual production for June	10,000 bottles
Total actual material cost for June	$24,780
Total liters of material used in production	29,500
Material price variance	$1,180 Unfavorable
Total labor cost for June	$6,490
Actual labor cost per labor hour	$2.95
Labor rate variance	$110 Favorable

REQUIRED:

Determine the following:

a. Actual cost of material per liter.
b. Total standard liters for actual production.
c. Material quantity variance.
d. Total standard material cost for actual production.
e. Labor hours worked.
f. Standard cost per labor hour.
g. Labor efficiency variance.
h. Total standard labor cost for actual production.

LO 1   **P26-3B**   **Determining Standard Costs**   Quiver International manufactures archery bows. They have decided to initiate a standard costing system to help improve planning and control.

The president of the company assigned the task of developing standards to the company controller and the plant engineer. They came up with the following estimates:

Amount per Bow	Average Amount	Best Amount
Wood	1.4 ft. @ $9.25	1.1 ft. @ $8.90
Aluminum	0.6 lbs. @ $7.50	0.5 lbs. @ $7.40
Direct Labor	2.4 hrs. @ $9.50	2.1 hrs. @ $9.45
Variable Overhead	$21.12	$17.85

In addition, the controller and engineer determined that fixed overhead has averaged $74,880 per year in the past and the lowest amount of fixed overhead incurred was $63,882. Expected production is 7,800 bows per year. The company controller believes that the standard should be set using the average amounts whereas the plant engineer believes that they should be set at the best amounts. In a meeting with the controller and the plant engineer, the president decided to set the standard at the midpoint of the average and the best amount.

REQUIRED:

a. Determine the controller's standard cost per unit.
b. Determine the plant engineer's standard cost per unit.
c. Determine the president's standard cost per unit.

LO 3,4   **P26-4B**   **Calculating Labor Variances With Missing Information**   Wheelie Corporation produces bicycles. Partial information for 19X8 is as follows:

	Labor
Actual cost	$313,425
Actual cost per hour	?
Standard cost per hour	?
Total standard hours	?
Total actual hours	29,850
Labor rate variance	$14,925 Favorable
Labor efficiency variance	$14,850 Unfavorable
Standard hours per bicycle	?

REQUIRED:

Determine the unknown amounts listed as "?" in the information provided.

LO 1,2,3,4,6   **P26-5B**   **Comprehensive Variance Problem**   The Manahawkin Company uses a standard costing system. The standards per unit produced for material and labor are 10.5 pounds and 1.5 hours, respectively. The standard cost per pound of material is $2.50. The standard cost per hour for labor is $7.60. Standard overhead is $9.00 per unit. For 19X9, expected production is 312,000 units with fixed overhead per year of $624,000 and variable overhead of $7.00 per unit. The total overhead at expected production is $2,808,000. During 19X9, 297,000 units of finished goods were produced. The total cost of material used was $8,030,880 with each pound costing $2.60. The cost of direct labor incurred in 19X9 was $3,704,778 based on an average wage rate of $7.56 per hour. Actual overhead for 19X9 was $2,799,250.

REQUIRED:

a. Determine the standard cost per unit.
b. Calculate the material, labor, and overhead variances.
c. Prepare a variance summary.
d. Prepare journal entries for 19X9 including the closing entry.

CRITICAL THINKING AND COMMUNICATING

C26-1 The Griffin Company manufactures bumper stickers. During the past four months they have found that, on average, they have been able to manufacture the following number of bumper stickers per hour:

Month	Output
January	240
February	260
March	300
April	240
Average	260

Brenda Griffin, the plant engineer, said that if everyone did what they were supposed to do, 320 bumper stickers per hour could be produced and therefore the standard should be set at 320 per hour. John Lewis, the controller, said that the standard should be set at 295 units, whereas Michael Levy, the plant supervisor, suggested that the standard should be set at 260.

REQUIRED:

a. Determine the advantages of each position.
b. Select a standard that would best accomplish the purpose of motivation, control, and planning.

C26-2 Will Simmons, the chemical division controller for Gulf and Eastern Corporation, was reviewing the variance summary for the Southside Chemical Plant. The variance summary revealed a large favorable material price variance and large unfavorable material quantity and labor efficiency variances. All other variances were immaterial. Will Simmon's initial instinct was to request a large bonus for Al Putnam, the purchasing manager and to give no bonus to Patty Smith, the plant supervisor.

REQUIRED:

a. Determine if Will Simmons should act in accordance with his initial instincts.
b. What other procedures should Will Simmons perform before requesting bonuses?
c. Explain a scenario other than "good performance in purchasing and poor performance in manufacturing" that would lead to the same variances.

CHAPTER 27

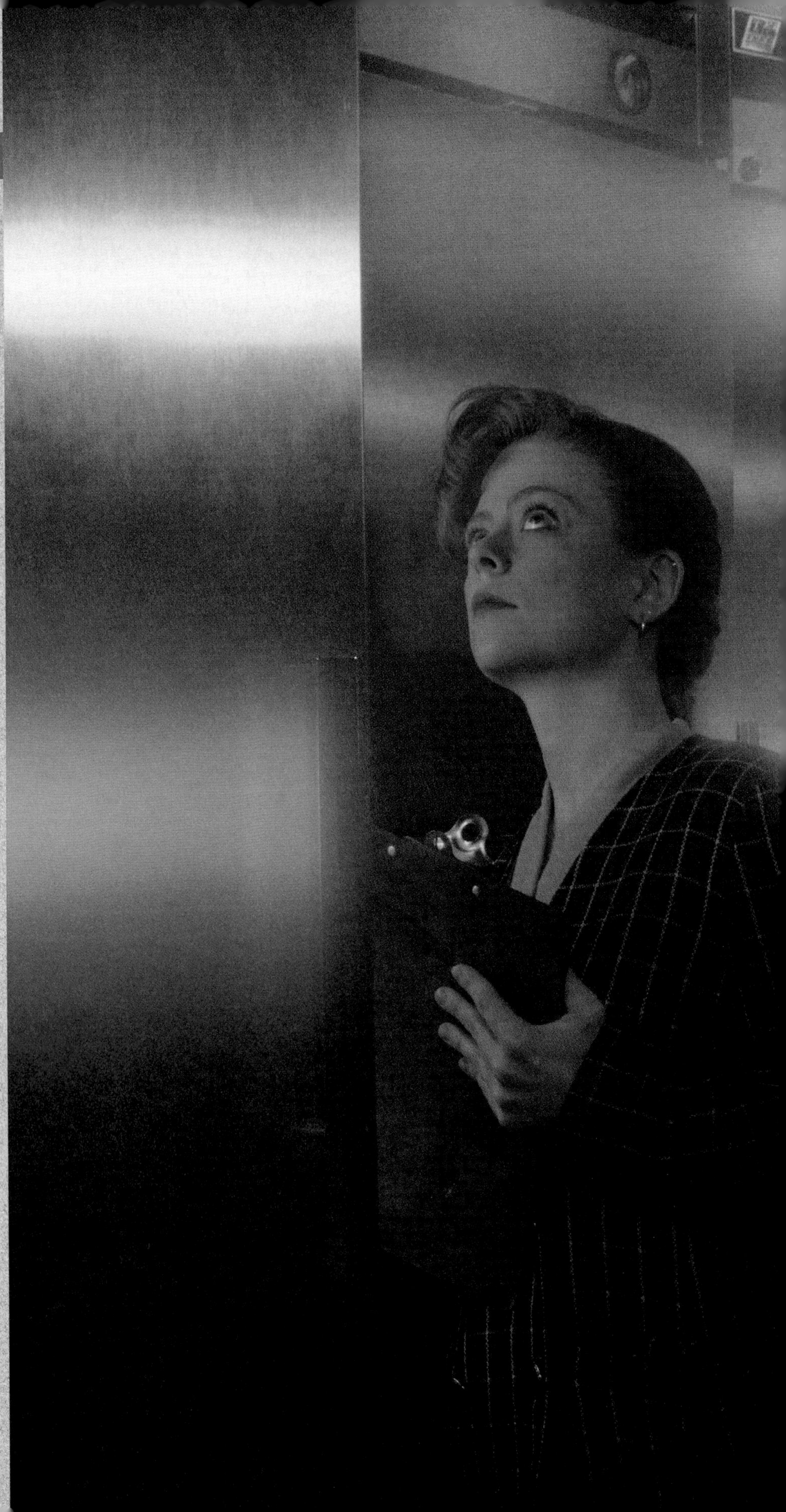

Cost Information and Management Decisions

At the start of the year, the president of General Refrigeration Company asked his three plant managers to examine their operations and search for ways to cut costs and improve profitability. The president also promised substantial bonuses to managers who achieved cost savings in excess of $1,000,000.

Wendy Grant, manager of the plant in Tennessee, thought she had a sure-fire way to save money. Her plant manufactures refrigeration units used by food processors and retail food stores. One main component of the refrigeration units is a compressor. Wendy anticipates producing 50,000 compressors in the coming year at a cost per unit of $345. Concerned that General's production of compressors is not efficient, Wendy asked Dillard Compressor Corporation to bid on supplying the 50,000 units. After studying the specifications of the compressor, Dillard indicated it is willing to supply the compressors at $310 per unit.

"Look," Wendy explained to Ed Anderson, the plant accountant, "if we close the compressor operation and buy compressors from Dillard, we'll save about $1,750,000 a year! That kind of cost saving should really grab the president's attention."

Ed seemed skeptical. "Wendy, let's look at the costs of producing the compressors. More than $1,000,000 of the cost is depreciation on plant and equipment purchased years ago. Another $500,000 represents the salaries of production supervisors. I don't think all of those costs will go away just because we shut down the compressor operation and turn to an outside supplier. I think you better let me analyze the cost information in some detail before you make a recommendation."

Ed's point is well taken. Before making a decision, managers must gain a thorough understanding of relevant cost information.

Cost information is necessary for planning, evaluation, and for making *nonroutine decisions*. The primary emphasis in previous chapters has been on how manufacturing companies record cost information in their accounts (using job and process costing systems) and on how they use cost information to plan and evaluate operations (using budgets and standard costing systems). While several examples of using cost information for decision making have already been presented, this chapter presents a more complete analysis of how management uses cost information in making decisions. The decision situations covered are referred to as nonroutine decisions because they are *not* the type of decisions that managers face daily. Decisions involving making or buying a component or discontinuing a product are critical to a company's success, but they are not everyday occurrences. Careful consideration of the decision examples presented here should help you gain insight into the cost information needed to solve a number of important problems that managers confront.

LEARNING OBJECTIVES

1. Explain the role of differential costs and revenues in management decisions.
2. Define sunk cost, avoidable cost, and opportunity cost.
3. Explain why the contribution margin per unit of a constrained resource is more important than the contribution margin per unit produced when there are production constraints.
4. Discuss how managers use cost information for product pricing decisions.
5. Discuss the important role of qualitative considerations in management decisions.

LO 1

Explain the role of differential costs and revenues in management decisions.

DIFFERENTIAL COSTS AND REVENUES

All decisions involve a choice between two or more alternatives. Managers must identify which of the alternatives is best for their company. Many business decisions can be approached by comparing the alternatives in terms of their differential costs and revenues. As the name implies, **differential costs and revenues** are cost and revenue items that differ among alternatives. Differential costs are sometimes referred to as **relevant costs** because they are the only relevant cost items managers need to consider when analyzing decision alternatives. In evaluating differential costs and revenues, managers decide which alternative will have the most positive impact on company profitability. This approach, referred to as differential analysis, is demonstrated here for a variety of decision settings.

Additional Processing Decision

Occasionally, manufacturers must decide whether to sell a product in a partially completed stage or to incur additional processing costs required to complete the product. Dandy Electronics has decided to discontinue manufacturing its Model 250 computer. Currently, it has 5,000 partially completed units on hand. To date, the company has spent $800 per unit or $4,000,000 to bring the computers to their current stage of completion. The company estimates it will incur additional costs of $400 per unit to complete the computers.

Dandy Electronics *Costs of Model 250 Computer*		
	Costs Per Unit *Incurred to Date*	*Costs Per Unit* *to Complete*
Material	$300	$200
Labor	200	100
Variable overhead	100	100
Fixed overhead	200	
	$800	$400

Because the company has announced that the Model 250 will be discontinued, the price of the computer has fallen. If the units are completed, they can be sold for only $1,000 per unit, which is less than the $1,200 per unit ($800 cost to date plus $400 of additional cost) total cost of producing the computers. On the other hand, a rival computer company is willing to buy the partially completed units for $500 per unit.

Which action should Dandy take? Should it sell computers in their current state of completion or should it incur the additional processing costs? Without a thorough understanding of accounting information and differential analysis, a manager at Dandy Electronics might conclude that further processing is not appropriate. After all, with further processing, total costs will amount to $1,200 per unit, which is more than the selling price of $1,000 per unit. The error of this analysis is revealed by analyzing the problem in terms of differential costs and revenues. The differential analysis is presented in Illustration 27-1. Compared to selling the units in their current state, revenue from selling completed units will be $500 more per unit. Since the costs of completing the units is only $400 more per unit, the company is better off by $100 per unit if it completes the computers. The differential analysis indicates that the $800 per unit costs incurred to date are not relevant to the further processing decision. Whether Dandy sells the units "as is" or processes them further, the costs incurred to date will not change.

Sunk Costs.   Costs incurred in the past are irrelevant to present and future decisions and are referred to as **sunk costs**. Sunk costs are not differential costs because they do not differ among decision alternatives. Because Dandy incurred the expenditures in the past to bring the Model 250 computers to their current state of completion, these costs cannot be reversed. Thus, they have no economic relevance to decisions affecting future periods.

Make or Buy Decisions

Most manufactured goods have numerous components. In some cases, a company may purchase one or more of the components from another company. This may lead to considerable savings if the outside supplier is particularly efficient at manufacturing the component and can offer it at a reasonable price. Two decision alternatives are presented in this situation: either make or buy the component. No differential revenues are involved. Therefore, to analyze this decision, managers concentrate solely on differential costs.

ILLUSTRATION 27-1 Differential Analysis of Further Processing Decision

Dandy Electronics Differential Analysis of Further Processing			
	Sell in Current State of Completion	Complete Processing	Differential Revenues and Costs
Revenue	$ 500	$1,000	$500
Less prior production costs:			
Material	$ 300	$ 300	$ 0
Labor	200	200	0
Variable overhead	100	100	0
Fixed overhead	200	200	0
Total	$ 800	$ 800	$ 0
	$(300)	$ 200	$500
Less additional processing costs:			
Material	$0	$ 200	$200
Labor	0	100	100
Variable overhead	0	100	100
Total	$0	$ 400	$400
Gain (loss) per unit	$(300)	$ (200)	$100

Recall that Wendy Grant, manager of the Tennessee plant of General Refrigeration Company, is considering Dillard Compressor Corporation's offer to supply 50,000 compressors at $310 per unit. Last year, when her plant produced 50,000 compressors, the company incurred the following costs:

General Refrigeration Company Cost of Manufacturing 50,000 Compressors	
Variable costs:	
Direct material ($100 per unit)	$ 5,000,000
Direct labor ($120 per unit)	6,000,000
Variable overhead ($80 per unit)	4,000,000
Total variable costs	$15,000,000
Fixed costs:	
Depreciation of building	$ 600,000
Depreciation of equipment	800,000
Supervisory salaries	500,000
Other	350,000
Total fixed costs	$ 2,250,000
Total costs	$17,250,000

Additional analysis reveals the following: (1) The market value of the machinery used to produce the compressors is approximately zero. (2) Five of the seven production supervisors will be fired if General discontinues production of compressors. However, two of the supervisors, who each has more than ten years of service, are protected by a clause in their union contract. They will be reassigned to other duties although their services will not really be needed. Their salaries total $110,000.

At first, you might assume that General should buy the compressors rather than manufacture the units internally. After all, the company can buy the units for $310 each while the cost of manufacturing them is $345 each (i.e., $17,250,000 ÷ 50,000 units). However, careful consideration of the differential costs reveals that it is cheaper to manufacture the compressors internally.

As indicated in Illustration 27-2, General will incur none of the $15,000,000 of variable manufacturing costs if it purchases the compressors outside the company. Thus, this is a differential cost between the two alternatives. However, the fixed costs associated with depreciation on the building and equipment do not represent a cost savings. General incurred the costs of purchasing the building and the pieces of equipment in prior periods. Remember: The approach to analyzing decisions requires consideration of only the differential revenues and costs of decision alternatives. The sunk costs related to purchasing the building and the pieces of equipment are not differential costs because General has already incurred them and they will not change, no matter what decision alternative General selects. The example assumes that fixed costs classified as "other" are also irrelevant sunk costs.

Avoidable Costs.   Not all fixed costs are irrelevant sunk costs. Some fixed costs are **avoidable costs** or costs that can be avoided if a company takes a particular action. If General purchases the compressors outside the company, it will save the salaries of five production supervisors. This totals $390,000 (total supervisory salaries of $500,000 less the $110,00 that must still be paid to supervisors with seniority). Supervisory salaries of $390,000 is an avoidable cost. That is, General will no longer incur this cost if it purchases the compressors outside the company. Avoidable costs are also differential costs.

While General can eliminate $15,000,000 of variable costs and $390,000 of fixed costs if it purchases the compressors from Dillard Compressor Corporation, this cost savings of $15,390,000 is exceeded by the $15,500,000 cost of purchasing the compressors from Dillard (50,000 units x $310). In total, General would be $110,000 worse off if it decided to buy rather than to make the compressors.

ILLUSTRATION 27-2 Differential Analysis of Make or Buy Decision

General Refrigeration Company Differential Cost Analysis			
	Cost of Manufacturing 50,000 Compressors	Cost of Buying 50,000 Compressors	Differential Costs
Variable costs:			
Direct material	$ 5,000,000	$ 0	$ 5,000,000
Direct labor	6,000,000	0	6,000,000
Variable overhead	4,000,000	0	4,000,000
Total variable cost	$15,000,000	$ 0	$15,000,000
Fixed costs:			
Depreciation of building	$ 600,000	$ 600,000	$ 0
Depreciation of equipment	800,000	800,000	0
Supervisory salaries	500,000	110,000	390,000
Other	350,000	350,000	0
Total fixed costs	$ 2,250,000	$ 1,860,000	$ 390,000
Cost of buying compressors	0	15,500,000	(15,500,000)
Total costs	$17,250,000	$17,360,000	$ (110,000)

In Illustration 27-2, we present a three-column approach to differential analysis. The first two columns present the costs of the two alternatives, while the third column presents the differential costs. However, once the concept of differential analysis is understood, it is easier to present the analysis in a single-column format that concentrates only on the differential costs. A single-column analysis of the make or buy decision that General Refrigeration Company faces is presented in Illustration 27-3.

As indicated, it will cost General $15,500,000 to buy the units outside. However, the company will only save $15,390,000 of internal manufacturing costs if it purchases the compressors. General will not incur the $15,000,000 of variable manufacturing costs if it purchases the compressors; thus, this item represents a major cost saving. However, the only fixed cost savings is the $390,000 of supervisory salary, which is avoidable if General purchases the compressors. Because the cost of buying the compressors exceeds the cost savings by $110,000, it appears the company should continue manufacturing the compressors. Before reaching a final decision, General should also consider qualitative factors, which we discuss later.

ILLUSTRATION 27-3 Single-Column Format for Differential Analysis

General Refrigeration Company Differential Cost Analysis		
Cost of buying compressors outside (50,000 units x $310)		$15,500,000
Cost savings (avoidable if purchase compressors outside):		
Variable costs	$15,000,000	
Supervisory salaries (salaries of 5 of 7 supervisors)	390,000	15,390,000
Excess cost of buying compressors outside		$ 110,000

Opportunity Costs.   **Opportunity costs** are the values of benefits foregone by selecting one decision alternative over another. For example, if you choose to purchase a $1,000 stereo system rather than investing in a certificate of deposit (CD), the potential interest that you could have earned on the CD is an opportunity cost associated with buying the stereo. Since opportunity costs differ,

INSIGHTS INTO ACCOUNTING

"MAKE VERSUS BUY" DECISIONS FACING BANKS
To gain cost savings, many manufacturing companies buy components from outside suppliers rather than making them internally. Smart car companies don't make steel, glass, or radios anymore. And, smart bankers are following the lead of auto and other manufacturers. They critically evaluate whether they can outsource processing operations. For bankers, it's not a "make or buy" decision—it's a "purchase outside or process internally" decision. Some services that banks may decide to purchase outside include building management, security, check processing, data processing, and printing.

Source: Charles H. Nobs, "Tracking the True Costs of Outsourcing." *The American Banker* (September 2, 1992), p. 4.

depending on which decision alternative is selected, they are also differential costs and are relevant in evaluating decision alternatives.

The opportunity cost concept can also be illustrated using the General Refrigeration example. Suppose the Tennessee plant is currently spending $500,000 per year to rent space for manufacturing metal shelving units that are used in the refrigeration units. If it discontinues production of compressors, the company will move the shelving operation to space currently occupied by the compressor operation. Thus, an opportunity cost of continuing to produce the compressors is the $500,000 in rent savings that is foregone. If General considers this opportunity cost, then the analysis presented in Illustration 27-4 indicates that purchasing the compressors outside is the best alternative because it results in a net $390,000 annual cost savings to the firm.

ILLUSTRATION 27-4 Make or Buy Analysis With Opportunity Costs Considered

General Refrigeration Company Differential Cost Analysis		
Cost of buying compressors outside (50,000 units x $310)		$15,500,000
Cost savings (avoidable if purchase compressors outside):		
Variable costs	$15,000,000	
Supervisory salaries (salaries of 5 of 7 supervisors)	390,000	
Opportunity cost of using the plant to produce compressors (foregone rent savings)	**500,000**	$15,890,000
Net savings resulting from buying the compressors outside		$ 390,000

Dropping a Product Line

Dropping a product line is a very significant decision and one that receives a great deal of attention. The proper approach to analyzing the problem is to calculate the change in income that will result if the company drops the product line. If income will increase, the company should drop the product line. If income will decrease, the company should keep the product line. This amounts to comparing the differential costs and revenues that result from dropping the product line.

Magnolia Hardware has three product lines: Tools, Hardware Supplies, and Garden Supplies. Illustration 27-5 presents a product line income statement for the prior year. To arrive at net income for each product line, both direct and allocated fixed costs are deducted from each product line's contribution margin. Direct fixed costs are fixed costs that are directly traceable to a product line. For example, the salary of a worker who spends 100% of his or her time working in the tool section of the hardware store would be a direct fixed cost to the Tools product line. Allocated fixed costs are those fixed costs that are not directly traceable to an individual product line. These costs are also referred to as **common costs** because a company incurs them for the common benefit of all product lines. An example of an allocated fixed cost would be the salary of the owner/manager of the hardware store. Magnolia Hardware allocates common fixed costs to product lines based on their relative sales revenues. Thus, of the

$80,000 of common costs, 43.373% (i.e., $180,000 tool sales ÷ $415,000 total sales) or $34,699 is allocated to Tools.

ILLUSTRATION 27-5 Product Line Income Statement for Magnolia Hardware

		Magnolia Hardware Product Line Income Statement For the Year Ended December 31, 19X1		
	Tools	Hardware Supplies	Garden Supplies	Total
Sales	$180,000	$160,000	$75,000	$415,000
Cost of goods sold	108,000	90,000	60,000	258,000
Gross margin	$ 72,000	$ 70,000	$15,000	$157,000
Other variable costs	2,000	4,000	1,000	7,000
Contribution margin	$ 70,000	$ 66,000	$14,000	$150,000
Direct fixed costs	$ 8,000	$ 5,000	$ 3,500	$ 16,500
Allocated fixed costs	34,699	30,843	14,458	80,000
Total fixed costs	$ 42,699	$ 35,843	$17,958	$ 96,500
Net income	$ 27,301	$ 30,157	$(3,958)	$ 53,500

The owner of Magnolia Hardware observes that the Garden Supplies line is currently showing a loss of $3,958. Would dropping this product line increase the profitability of the hardware store? To answer this question, we turn again to differential analysis. As indicated in Illustration 27-6, sales revenue will decline by $75,000 if Magnolia drops Garden Supplies. However, some costs will decrease or be eliminated altogether. Cost of goods sold will decrease by

ILLUSTRATION 27-6 Analysis of Dropping a Product Line

	Income With Garden Supplies				Income Without Garden Supplies			Difference[3]
	Tools	Hardware Supplies	Garden Supplies	Total	Tools	Hardware Supplies	Total	
Sales	$180,000	$160,000	$75,000	$415,000	$180,000	$160,000	$340,000	$(75,000)
Cost of goods sold	108,000	90,000	60,000	258,000	108,000	90,000	198,000	60,000
Gross margin	$ 72,000	$ 70,000	$15,000	$157,000	$ 72,000	$ 70,000	$142,000	$(15,000)
Other variable costs	2,000	4,000	1,000	7,000	2,000	4,000	6,000	1,000
Contribution margin	$ 70,000	$ 66,000	$14,000	$150,000	$ 70,000	$ 66,000	$136,000	$(14,000)
Direct fixed costs	$ 8,000	$ 5,000	$ 3,500	$ 16,500	$ 8,000	$ 5,000	$ 13,000	$ 3,500
Allocated fixed costs	34,699	30,843[1]	14,458[1]	80,000	42,353[2]	37,647[2]	80,000	0
Total fixed costs	$ 42,699	$ 35,843	$17,958	$ 96,500	$ 50,353	$ 42,647	$ 93,000	$ 3,500
Net income	$ 27,301	$ 30,157	$ (3,958)	$ 53,500	$ 19,647	$ 23,353	$ 43,000	$(10,500)

---

[1]Allocation of common costs based on percentage of total sales with Garden Supplies
($180,000 ÷ $415,000) x $80,000 = $34,699
($160,000 ÷ $415,000) x $80,000 = $30,843
($75,000 ÷ $415,000) x $80,000 = $14,458
[2]Allocation of common costs ased on percentage of total sales without Garden Supplies
($180,000 ÷ $340,000) x $80,000 = $42,353
($160,000 ÷ $340,000) x $80,000 = $37,647
[3]Differences with a favorable effect are reported as positive numbers. Differences with an unfavorable effect are shown in parentheses.

$60,000, and other variable costs will decrease by $1,000. These variable costs can be avoided by dropping the Garden Supplies product line. Whether the direct fixed costs will decrease depends on the nature of these costs.

For purposes of this example, assume that the direct fixed costs of $3,500 for Garden Supplies represents the salary paid a part-time employee. If Magnolia drops the Garden Supplies product line, this employee will not be retained. In this case, the direct fixed costs of $3,500 are avoidable and represent a cost savings achieved by dropping Garden Supplies. Allocated fixed costs are generally not avoidable and, thus, Magnolia achieves no cost savings with respect to the $14,458 of fixed costs allocated to Garden Supplies. For example, one component of the allocated fixed costs is rent of the hardware store. The rent will not decrease simply because one product line is eliminated. Another allocated fixed cost is electricity. This cost is also not likely to decrease if Magnolia drops Garden Supplies since the store still needs approximately the same amount of heat and light. Rather than being eliminated, the share of fixed costs allocated to Tools and Hardware Supplies will simply increase if the company drops Garden Supplies.

To summarize, the analysis of differential costs and revenues indicates that Magnolia will lose income of $10,500 if it drops Garden Supplies.

Differential Analysis Dropping Garden Supplies	
Lost revenue	$(75,000)
Cost savings:	
Cost of goods sold	$ 60,000
Other variable costs	1,000
Direct fixed costs	3,500
Total cost savings	$ 64,500
Net loss from dropping	$(10,500)

SUMMARY OF DIFFERENTIAL, AVOIDABLE, SUNK, AND OPPORTUNITY COSTS

LO 2
Define sunk cost, avoidable cost, and opportunity cost.

We have used a number of costs terms in this chapter; in this section, we briefly summarize them. Recall that the basic approach to decision making is to analyze the costs and revenues that differ among decision alternatives. These items are referred to as *differential* or *relevant* costs and revenues. Costs that can be *avoided* by taking a particular course of action are always differential costs and, therefore, relevant to the analysis of a decision. Costs that are *sunk*, (i.e., already incurred and not reversible) are never differential costs since they do not differ among the decision alternatives. Therefore, they are not relevant in making a decision.

Students of managerial accounting often assume that fixed costs are equivalent to sunk costs and irrelevant (i.e., they are not differential costs). This is not always the case. Fixed costs may be sunk and, therefore, irrelevant; or they may not be sunk but still be irrelevant. Finally, fixed costs may not be sunk but relevant. Examples of these three possibilities are presented in Illustration 27-6.

ILLUSTRATION 27-6 Fixed Costs and Decision Relevance

Fixed Costs	Classification
Depreciation on equipment already purchased	Sunk and irrelevant (not differential)
President's salary, which will not change for both Action A and Action B	Not sunk but still irrelevant (not differential)
Salary of supervisor who will be retained if Action A is taken and fired if Action B is taken	Not sunk and relevant (differential)

When making a decision, managers must consider *opportunity costs*. Opportunity costs represent the benefit foregone by selecting a particular decision alternative. To illustrate opportunity costs, consider the Magnolia Hardware example. In this example, the company considers dropping its Garden Supplies product line. Suppose that if Magnolia drops Garden Supplies, it can devote more space to selling tools. Sales of tools will increase, and the contribution margin associated with Tools will increase by $15,000. In this case, Magnolia has a $15,000 opportunity cost associated with its decision to keep the Garden Supplies product line. Considering this opportunity cost would make dropping the product line desirable rather than undesirable. Recall that our previous analysis indicated a $10,500 decrease in income from dropping the product line. However, considering the $15,000 opportunity cost representing forfeiture of tools sales, it appears that Magnolia will be better off by $4,500 (i.e., $15,000 − $10,500) if it drops Garden Supplies.

LO 3

Explain why the contribution margin per unit of a constrained resource is more important than the contribution margin per unit produced when there are production constraints.

DECISIONS INVOLVING PRODUCTION CONSTRAINTS

For products with a positive contribution margin (i.e., the selling price is greater than the variable cost of the product), a company would like to produce and sell as many units as possible. The reason is that company income increases with the sale of each unit. However, in most cases, there are limits or constraints on the number of items a company can produce. The number of hours of machine time available to produce an item may be limited by the number of machines a company has. Or, a company may have a limited number of skilled workers—at least in the short run. If a company faces production constraints, then how many units should it produce? If only one product is involved, the

INSIGHTS INTO ETHICS

Pat Smith, president of Regal Apparel, is considering closing a plant in Michigan that manufactures cotton uniforms (one of Regal's major product lines). Regal can purchase the uniforms from a firm in Korea at a cost savings of $2,000,000 per year. However, closing the plant will put 200 employees out of work in an area that already has substantial unemployment.

Does Smith have an ethical responsibility to consider the hardship imposed on employees from a plant closure? What is Smith's ethical responsibility to shareholders who will lose $2,000,000 per year if the plant is not closed?

answer is to produce as many units as allowed by the constraint. However, if more than one product is involved, the analysis becomes more complicated.

Consider a company that produces two products (Products A and B) that have the following selling prices and production costs per unit:

	Product A	Product B
Selling price	$100	$80
Variable costs	50	60
Contribution margin	$ 50	$20

Suppose 10 machine hours are needed to produce each unit of Product A, 2 machine hours are needed to produce each unit of Product B, and 1,000 machine hours are available. Which product should the company concentrate on producing? At first, it may appear that Product A should be produced because it has the higher contribution margin per unit. However, since production of Product A requires much more machine time than does Product B, fewer units of A can be produced. In fact, if just Product A is produced, the company can produce only 100 units in total (1,000 hours ÷ 10 hours per unit). The company's contribution margin will be $5,000 (i.e., $50 per unit x 100 units). On the other hand, with 1,000 available machine hours, the company can produce 500 units of Product B. Product B's contribution margin is $20 per unit, and if just Product B is produced, the company's contribution margin will be $10,000. Thus, the company is much better off producing the product with the smaller contribution margin per unit because it uses much less of the constrained resource (machine hours).

To decide which product to produce, one can perform a differential total contribution margin analysis. However, the same result is obtained by calculating the *contribution margin per unit of the constrained resource*. Product A's contribution margin is $50 per unit. However, each unit requires 10 hours of machine time (the constrained resource). Therefore, the contribution margin per unit of the constrained resource is $5. On the other hand, Product B's contribution margin is $20 per unit. However, since each unit only requires 2 hours of machine time, the contribution margin per unit of the constrained resource is $10. Multiplying the contribution margin per unit of the constrained resource by the amount of the resource available yields the available contribution margin. Thus, producing the product with the largest contribution per unit of the constrained resource ensures that the company will maximize total contribution margin and income.

	Product A	Product B
Selling price	$ 100	$ 80
Variable costs	50	60
Contribution margin	$ 50	$ 20
Machine hours per unit	÷ 10	÷ 2
Contribution margin per machine hour	$ 5	$ 10
Available machine hours	x 1,000	x 1,000
Feasible contribution margin	$ 5,000	$10,000

PRICING DECISIONS

Pricing decisions play a very important role in a company's success. If products are priced either too low or too high, the company may not maximize income or may sustain significant losses. While setting appropriate prices is a crucial business activity, the process of price setting is quite complex; most managers consider it to be more of an art than a science. Economic theory suggests an approach to pricing that requires knowledge of the relationship between price and the quantity demanded (the so-called "demand function"). However, estimating demand functions with reasonable accuracy can be very difficult.

Full Cost Pricing

Recognizing the difficulty of estimating demand functions, many companies have turned to so-called cost-based pricing approaches. With a cost-based approach, companies mark up an estimate of cost to a price that allows a reasonable level of profit. When the cost marked up is the full cost of an item (including fixed and variable cost), the approach is referred to as **full cost pricing**. To illustrate full cost pricing, suppose Ajax Pump Company produces three different models of fuel pumps: Model A, Model B, and Model C. The company's approach to pricing is to mark up the standard full cost of each pump by 30%. As indicated in Illustration 27-7, the full cost of the Model A pump is $100. With a 30% markup, the selling price is $130.

ILLUSTRATION 27-7 The Full Cost Pricing Approach

	Model A	Model B	Model C
Standard variable costs:			
Direct labor	$ 10.00	$ 20.00	$ 35.00
Direct material	20.00	25.00	40.00
Variable overhead ($2 per $1 of direct labor)	20.00	40.00	70.00
Total variable costs	$ 50.00	$ 85.00	$145.00
Standard fixed costs ($5 per $1 of direct labor)	50.00	100.00	175.00
Total production cost	$100.00	$185.00	$320.00
Profit markup (30% of total cost)	30.00	55.50	96.00
Selling price	$130.00	$240.50	$416.00

The obvious advantage of a full cost pricing approach is that it is simple to apply. Also, if a sufficient quantity can be sold at the specified price, the company will earn a reasonable profit. However, the approach has an obvious limitation. What markup percent should a company use? Is 30% an appropriate markup, or should a company use 10%, 20%, or 40%? Determination of an appropriate markup requires considerable judgment and experimentation with different markups before a company can make a final decision.

Contribution Approach to Pricing

A further problem with the full cost approach to pricing is that it focuses managers' attention on the full cost of production. Companies that use full cost pricing generally believe that no product should be sold for a price less than full cost. However, in some circumstances, the companies may benefit from charging a price that is less than full cost. This is often the case when companies face special orders from customers. If the products under consideration are somewhat unique or the customers' markets are different from the companies' normal markets, then companies need not charge the "normal" prices of the products.

Quality Lens Company manufacturers camera lenses. Their lenses are sold through camera shops with a variety of mounting adapters to fit most popular 35 millimeter cameras. Recently, Kanic Camera Company has asked them to produce 20,000 lenses for their compact 35 millimeter camera. The lens is identical to the Model A lens that Quality currently sells for $85. However, the model to be produced for Kanic will substitute the Kanic name for the Quality name stamped on the lens.

In the past year, Quality sold 280,000 units of the Model A. However, the company has been operating at only 75% of normal productive capacity and can easily accommodate production of the 20,000 additional units. The standard cost of producing Model A is $75.

Model A Standard Unit Cost	
Direct material	$30.00
Direct labor	15.00
Variable overhead	10.00
Fixed overhead	20.00
Total	$75.00

Kanic Camera Company has offered to buy the 20,000 lenses for $73 each. Since the total standard cost is $75, it appears that Quality should turn down the special order. However, the differential analysis presented in Illustration 27-8 indicates that the special order will make a substantial contribution to company income.

ILLUSTRATION 27-8 Analysis of Special Order

Differential Revenues and Costs of Special Order		
Differential revenue (20,000 x $73)		$1,460,000
Less differential costs:		
Direct material (20,000 x $30)	$600,000	
Direct labor (20,000 x $15)	300,000	
Variable overhead (20,000 x $10)	200,000	
		1,100,000
Net benefit of special order		$ 360,000

The special order decision presents two alternatives: either accept or reject the special order. Since the income from the main business is the same under both alternatives, it is not *differential*, and Quality need not consider this in the decision. The most obvious differential item is the revenue associated with the special order. If Quality accepts the order, its revenue will increase by $1,460,000. In addition, direct material, direct labor, and variable overhead will increase by $1,100,000 if Quality accepts the special order. These costs are differential. They will be incurred if Quality accepts the special order, and not incurred if Quality rejects it. Since the differential revenues exceed the differential costs by $360,000, it appears to be quite beneficial to accept the special order.

Note that in the calculation of the net benefit of accepting the special order, none of the fixed costs of production are considered as differential costs. This is because these costs will be incurred whether or not Quality accepts the special order. This assumption seems reasonable given that Quality Lens Company has excess capacity. However, suppose the management of Quality anticipates some increase in fixed costs if it accepts the special order. By how much could fixed costs increase before acceptance of the special order would not be advisable? As long as fixed costs increase by less than $360,000, the excess of differential revenues over differential costs, acceptance of the special order will increase company income.

The **contribution approach** to pricing basically suggests that a company should accept any order as long as it has a positive contribution margin. Acceptance of the special order would be consistent with the contribution approach. Kanic Camera Company offered $73 for each lens, while the variable cost is only $55. Thus, at a price of $73, each lens has an $18 contribution margin. Opponents of this approach argue that no company can stay in business unless it sells its products at a price greater than the full cost of production, including some share of fixed overhead. The contribution approach, they suggest, will lead to prices that are too low to sustain the business.

As you probably suspect, some validity exists for both full cost and contribution margin approaches to pricing. Obviously, companies need to charge prices that in the *long run* are greater than their total costs, including fixed costs. However, it is equally true that in some cases a company will be better off selling a product in the *short run* for less than its full cost as long as the price yields a positive contribution toward covering fixed costs. Probably the best approach is to make sure that a company does not implement any full cost pricing formula too rigidly. If sales are lagging or if special orders are received and a company has excess capacity, then management must consider the contribution margin that will be achieved with various prices. Also, it is important to remember that cost is just half of the product pricing equation. Demand is the other half. Thus a company should not set prices based only on a consideration of cost. Managers also need to consider the prices that competitors charge and the quantities consumers will demand at various prices.

QUALITATIVE CONSIDERATION IN DECISION ANALYSIS

LO 5

Discuss the important role of qualitative considerations in management decisions.

The solutions to the problems presented have concentrated on the *quantitative* features of the decision situations. In particular, we have concentrated on quantitative differences in costs and revenues among decision alternatives. However, most important problems have one or more features that are very difficult, if not impossible, to quantify. These *qualitative* aspects must receive the same careful attention as do the quantitative components.

The importance of qualitative considerations can be illustrated in the context of the make or buy decision discussed earlier. Recall that General Refrigeration Company was considering whether to continue producing compressors or to purchase them from another firm. Our analysis in Illustration 27-3 indicated that it would cost General $110,000 more to buy the compressors from an outside supplier. However, our analysis only considered the easily quantifiable differences in costs between the two decision alternatives. In addition, qualitative benefits and costs are associated with using an outside supplier.

Perhaps the primary benefit of using an outside supplier is that the adverse effect of a downturn in business is less severe. Suppose there is a temporary downturn in the demand for refrigeration units. In this case, General can simply order fewer compressors from its outside supplier, thus avoiding a major cost. On the other hand, if General continues to manufacture the compressors and a temporary downturn in business is experienced, it will have more difficulty eliminating some of the fixed costs associated with manufacturing the compressors. For example, the company probably could not eliminate the fixed costs of the supervisor's salary if the downturn was thought to be only temporary. Experienced supervisors are difficult to find, and they cannot be hired and fired based on temporary fluctuations in business.

Using an outside supplier also leads to a loss of control over the production process. Purchased items may not be of sufficiently high quality and delivery schedules may not be honored. The outside supplier may also believe it has the company "over a barrel" (i.e., it would be too costly to restart an internal operation), and may raise prices significantly in the future. Also, if a company decides to purchase a component outside, employee morale may suffer if the reduction in productive activity results in employees being fired or transferred. The cost to the firm of reduced morale is difficult to quantify, but it may have a significant effect on the quantity and quality of the products the remaining employees produce.

SUMMARY

Explain the role of differential costs and revenues in management decisions. Decisions involve a choice between two or more alternatives. Management can make the best decision by comparing alternatives in terms of the cost and revenue items that differ among them. These costs and revenues are referred to as differential costs and revenues.

Define sunk cost, avoidable cost, and opportunity cost.   Costs that companies have incurred in the past are irrelevant to present and future decisions. These costs are referred to as sunk costs. Avoidable costs are those that companies can avoid by taking a particular action. The term opportunity costs refers to the benefits companies forfeit by selecting a particular decision alternative.

Explain why the contribution margin per unit of a constrained resource is more important than the contribution margin per unit produced when there are production constraints.   When a production constraint exists, a company can earn the largest contribution margin by producing the product with the highest contribution margin per unit of the constrained resource.

Discuss how managers use cost information for product pricing decisions. Pricing products is one of the most important and challenging decisions businesses face. In practice, companies often use full cost pricing. With this approach, companies mark up the full cost of an item by a fixed profit percentage. This approach is simple to apply, but it is difficult to determine the appropriate profit percentage. The contribution approach to pricing recognizes that, in the short run, prices that are greater than variable cost will lead to increases in income. However, in the long run and if companies are to survive, they must sell products for amounts greater than their total costs (including fixed costs).

Discuss the important role of qualitative considerations in management decisions. When making decisions, management must consider a variety of qualitative factors (e.g., quality of goods, employee morale, and customer service). Qualitative factors are often even more important than costs and benefits which are easy to quantify.

REVIEW PROBLEM A

Clear Sounds manufactures compact disc players. During 19X0, Clear Sounds manufactured 5,000 players. In the past, Clear Sounds has manufactured the lasers that are an integral part of the players. In order to determine if it is efficient to manufacture their own lasers, they found out it would cost $61.50 to purchase each laser from an outside supplier. From past information, the following costs are associated with producing 5,000 units.

Clear Sounds
Cost of Manufacturing 5,000 Lasers

Variable costs:	
Direct material ($18.75 per unit)	$ 93,750
Direct labor ($8.30 per unit)	41,500
Variable overhead ($24.60 per unit)	123,000
Total variable costs	$258,250
Fixed costs:	
Insurance (lasers only)	$ 17,900
Depreciation of equipment (lasers only)	21,700
Engineer's salary (lasers only)	36,000
Miscellaneous administrative costs	8,700
Total fixed costs	$ 84,300
Total costs	$342,550

REQUIRED:

Prepare a differential cost analysis to determine if the lasers should be manufactured or purchased in 19X1.

SOLUTION:

Planning and Organizing Your Work

1. Determine the cost of buying lasers.
2. Determine the cost savings from buying the lasers for variable and fixed costs.
3. Subtract the cost savings from buying the lasers from the cost of buying the lasers.
4. If the result of step 3 is positive, purchase the lasers; if it is negative, produce the lasers.

Clear Sounds Differential Cost Analysis		
Cost of buying lasers (5,000 x $61.50)		$307,500
Cost savings:		
Variable costs [5,000 x ($18.75 + $8.30 + $24.60)]	$258,250	
Engineers salary	36,000	
Insurance	17,900	312,150
Excess cost of producing lasers internally		$ 4,650

Therefore, Clear Sounds would be better off to buy the lasers from the outside. This ignores qualitative factors that may favor buying the lasers.

REVIEW PROBLEM B

Seaside Incorporated manufactures sailboards. Pricelow, a large discount chain, has offered to purchase 1,000 sailboards at a cost of $365 each as a one-time special purchase. The discount chain was willing to have their own logo on the sailboards. The standard cost of producing a sailboard is as follows:

Sailboard Standard Cost

Direct material	$168.00
Direct labor	57.50
Variable overhead	82.50
Fixed overhead	72.75
Total	$380.75

The cost of putting the Pricelow logo on the sailboard is estimated to be $13.00 per unit. Seaside Incorporated's current production is near capacity, making it necessary to rent additional equipment for $10,950. Also, overtime premiums of $121,460 will have to be paid in order to complete the special order.

REQUIRED:

Determine if Seaside Incorporated should accept the special order from Pricelow.

SOLUTION:

Planning and Organizing Your Work
1. Determine the differential revenue from the special order.
2. Determine the differential variable costs and fixed costs from the special order.
3. Subtract the differential costs from the differential revenue.
4. If the result of step 3 is positive, accept the special order; if it is negative, reject the special order.

Differential Revenue and Costs of Special Order

Differential revenue (5,000 x $365)		$1,825,000
Less differential costs:		
Direct material (5,000 x $168)	$840,000	
Direct labor (5,000 x $57.50)	287,500	
Variable overhead (5,000 x 72.75)	363,750	
Rental equipment	10,950	
Overtime premiums	121,460	1,623,660
Net benefit of special order		$ 201,340

Therefore, Seaside Incorporated should accept the special order from Pricelow unless there are qualitative factors that would change the decision.

KEY TERMS

avoidable costs, *1085*	**differential costs and revenues,** *1082*	**opportunity costs,** *1086*
common costs, *1087*		**relevant costs,** *1082*
contribution approach, *1094*	**full cost pricing,** *1092*	**sunk costs,** *1083*

SELF-QUIZ

LO 1 1. Differential costs are sometimes referred to as _____ costs.

LO 1 2. Which of the following costs should not be
LO 2 taken into consideration when making a decision?
   a. Opportunity costs.
   b. Sunk costs.
   c. Relevant costs.
   d. Differential costs.

LO 1 3. Which of the following is often not a differential cost?
   a. Material.
   b. Labor.
   c. Variable overhead.
   d. Fixed overhead.

LO 4 4. True or False? For products with a positive contribution margin a company would like to produce and sell as many units as possible.

LO 4 5. When the cost marked up for pricing is the full cost of an item (including fixed and variable cost) the approach is referred to as _____ _____.

LO 4 6. True or False? Fixed costs of production may not be differential costs when accepting a special order.

LO 4 7. An approach to pricing known as the _____ approach basically suggests that any order should be accepted as long as it has a positive contribution margin.

LO 4 8. Which of the following should not be considered when accepting a special order?
   a. The contribution margin.
   b. The impact on the price regular customers are willing to pay.
   c. Available manufacturing capacity.
   d. Allocated common costs.

LO 5 9. Which of the following is not a qualitative benefit of using an outside supplier?
   a. The supplier lessens the impact of business downturns.
   b. A working relationship is established with the supplier that may prove useful in the future.
   c. There is more control over the production process and availability of components.
   d. There is greater flexibility to order the number of components needed.

LO 5 10. True or False? Qualitative aspects of a decision should receive the same careful attention as the quantitative components.

SOLUTIONS TO SELF-QUIZ
1. relevant   2. b   3. d   4. true   5. full cost pricing   6. true   7. contribution   8. d   9. c   10. true

QUESTIONS

Q27-1   What are differential costs and revenues?

Q27-2   Why are sunk costs irrelevant to present and future decisions?

Q27-3   What are avoidable costs?

Q27-4   Why are opportunity costs relevant when making decisions?

Q27-5   What is the proper approach to analyzing whether or not a product line should be dropped?

Q27-6   Give an example of a fixed cost that is not sunk but still irrelevant.

Q27-7   What factors other than cost should be considered in a product ___ ___ ___ng decision?

Q27-8   What are the qualitative disadvantages of buying instead of making a component?

EXERCISES

LO 1,2

E27-1   Identification of Relevant Costs   The Tisch Company manufactures tables. In the past, they produced their own metal angle brackets that were used in the production of tables. Char Reid, the chief financial officer of Tisch, initiated an investigation to determine if it may be cheaper to buy the part rather than to make it themselves. Identify which of the following items are relevant to her decision by stating that the item is relevant or irrelevant.

a. The original cost of the bracket machine.
b. The cost of buying the brackets.
c. Variable factory overhead.
d. Salvage value of the bracket machine.
e. Space created from no longer manufacturing brackets.
f. Material used in manufacturing brackets.
g. The salary of the president of Tisch Company.
h. Available capacity.
i. The quality of the bracket manufactured.
j. The quality of the bracket purchased.
k. Fixed factory overhead.
l. Shipping costs incurred in buying the bracket.
m. Material and labor to manufacture the bracket.
n. Depreciation on the bracket machine.
o. A contract with the labor union.

LO 1,2

E27-2   Identification of Relevant Costs   The Teller Company manufactures porcelain dinnerware along with other products. Don Lyon, the controller of Teller Company, wants to determine whether to drop the fancy dinnerware product line. Identify which of the following items are relevant to his decision.

a. The original cost of the machinery used to manufacture the fancy dinnerware.
b. The reduction in labor cost.
c. Depreciation of the machinery used to manufacture the fancy dinnerware.
d. The president's salary.
e. The floor space used by the fancy dinnerware manufacturing equipment.
f. The fancy dinnerware production manager's salary.
g. Estimated salvage value of the fancy dinnerware manufacturing equipment.
h. The cost of retraining personnel to use in another part of the company.
i   Material used in manufacturing the fancy dinnerware.
j. Electricity used to manufacture the dinnerware.
k. Fixed overhead allocated to fancy dinnerware.

LO 1

E27-3   Additional Processing Decision   Electronic World has decided to discontinue manufacturing its Electronic Elite mobile telephone. Currently, the company has a number of partially completed phones on hand. To date, the company has spent $189 per unit to manufacture these phones. Another manufacturer is interested in purchasing the partially completed phones for $235 per unit. On the other hand, if Electronic World completes the phones, they can sell them for $495 per unit. To complete the mobile telephones, Electronic World will incur $30 of additional material, $55 of direct labor, $29 of variable overhead and $150 of allocated fixed overhead, all stated on a per unit basis. The allocated overhead relates primarily to depreciation of plant and equipment. Determine if Electronic World should complete the mobile telephones by preparing a differential analysis of further processing.

LO 1

E27-4 **Make or Buy Decision**   Hot Dip Corporation produces whirlpool tubs for the home. In the past, Hot Dip manufactured their own pumps to power the water jets. Hot Dip has found that 40% of the pumps have burned out within the warranty period, causing them to incur large warranty costs. Because of the difficulty of manufacturing the pumps, Hot Dip investigated the possibility of purchasing the pumps from a reputable manufacturer rather than making the pumps themselves. The outside manufacturer agreed to pay any warranty costs caused by the pumps. It costs $83.75 to manufacture each pump which includes an allocation of $17.25 of fixed overhead. Also, Hot Dip has spent an average of $22.00 repairing each pump returned. Hot Dip can purchase pumps for $79.50, not including freight of $3.00 per pump. During 19X1, Hot Dip plans to sell 12,800 whirlpool tubs. Determine if Hot Dip should make or buy the pumps and the amount of cost savings of the best alternative by preparing a differential cost analysis.

LO 1,2

E27-5 **Dropping a Product Line**   Computer Warehouse sells computer hardware and computer furniture. Because computer furniture requires a lot of floor space, the president of Computer Warehouse is considering discontinuing sales of computer furniture. The following monthly costs relate to operating the store.

Store rent	$2,100
Utilities	880
Insurance	320
Cleaning	250
Total	$3,550

The monthly costs are allocated by floor space. It was determined that 70% of cleaning costs and 10% of the insurance and utilities could be saved if the furniture line is discontinued. Also, $3,500 of additional hardware could be sold with a cost of goods sold of $1,400 if the furniture line is discontinued. In the past, $5,300 of furniture and $11,000 of hardware were sold per month with cost of goods sold of $2,915 and $4,400, respectively. Determine if Computer Warehouse should discontinue the furniture line and the financial benefit of the best alternative.

LO 3

E27-6 **Production Constraints**   Power Vac produces two models of vacuum cleaners. It takes 3 machine hours to produce the regular model and 4 machine hours to produce the deluxe model. There is a total of 1,200 machine hours available. Determine the maximum feasible contribution margin for each model given the following price and cost data applicable to the two models.

	Regular Model	*Deluxe Model*
Selling price	$85.20	$125.00
Variable costs	61.50	99.00
Contribution margin	$23.70	$26.00

LO 5

E27-7 **Full-Cost Pricing**   Garth Incorporated produces Globes and uses full cost pricing. Each globe has the following standard costs:

Direct material	$9.50
Direct labor	6.75
Variable overhead	8.85
Fixed cost	3.40

Determine the selling price if Garth desires a markup on full cost of: (a) 10%, (b) 25%, (c) 30%, and (d) 40%.

LO 4   **E27-8   Special Orders**   Stuckie Manufacturing produces industrial glue. Each gallon of glue has the following standard cost:

Direct material	$ 3.50
Direct labor	1.25
Variable overhead	2.25
Fixed overhead	3.65
Total standard cost	$10.65

Box's unlimited has offered to purchase 5,000 gallons for $9.50 per gallon. Stuckie normally sells the glue for $14.25. Determine the net benefit or (loss) to Stuckie if the special order is accepted.

PROBLEM SET A

LO 1,2   **P27-1A   Complex Make or Buy Decision**   Breath-Away is a new mouthwash in a small spray container to be manufactured by Hy-Gene Corporation. The product will be sold to wholesalers and large drugstore chains in packages of 30 containers for $18.00 per package. Management allocates $200,000 of fixed production overhead costs to Breath-Away. The manufacturing cost per package of Breath-Away for expected production of 100,000 packages is:

Direct material per package	$ 6.50
Direct labor per package	3.50
Overhead per package (fixed and variable)	3.00
Total per package	$13.00

Hy-Gene has contacted packaging suppliers to determine if it would be better to buy the spray container rather than manufacture it. The lowest quote for the spray containers was $1.75 per 30 bottles. It is estimated that purchasing the sprayers from a supplier would save 10% of direct materials, 20% of direct labor, and 15% of variable overhead. Hy-Gene's manufacturing space is highly constrained. By purchasing the spray containers, Hy-Gene will not have to lease additional manufacturing space that is estimated to cost $15,000 per year. If the spray containers are purchased, Hy-Gene estimates that one supervisory position can be eliminated. Salary plus benefits for this position are $32,500 per year.

REQUIRED:

a. Calculate the variable overhead per package.
b. Prepare a differential cost analysis of the make or buy decision.
c. Should Hy-Gene make or buy the sprayer?

LO 1,2,3   **P27-2A   Additional Processing Decision With Production Constraints**   Mega Chemical produces Zilcron and a new and improved version called Flypex, along with other products. Flypex, which sells for $13.50 per gallon is manufactured from Zilcron plus additional ingredients. It takes 20 minutes to manufacture a gallon of Zilcron and an additional 10 minutes to manufacture a gallon of Flypex. Zilcron sells for $8.55 per gallon. The cost per gallon of manufacturing Zilcron and the additional costs to manufacture Flypex are as follows:

	Zilcron	*Additional Cost of Flypex*
Material	$2.25	$ .90
Labor	1.80	1.75
Variable overhead	2.60	1.10
Fixed overhead	1.75	3.95

Both products have been successful and demand for Zilcron and Flypex is strong. However, Mega's other products are also in demand and Mega is approaching full capacity. Since it takes longer to manufacture Flypex, the vice president of production is trying to determine if Flypex should continue to be manufactured.

REQUIRED:

Which product makes the largest contribution to company profit given a capacity constraint measured in terms of production time?

LO 1,2,3   **P27-3A   Dropping a Product Line**   Esoteric Electronics, a high-end consumer electronics specialist, has three product lines: audio, video, and laser discs. Common costs are allocated by percentage of sales. The income statement for Esoteric Electronics is as follows:

Esoteric Electronics Product Line Income Statement For the Year Ended December 31, 19X1			
	Audio	*Video*	*Laser Discs*
Sales	$118,000	$96,000	$73,000
Cost of goods sold	70,800	52,800	60,100
Gross margin	$ 47,200	$43,200	$12,900
Other variable costs	2,500	3,100	1,100
Contribution margin	$ 44,700	$40,100	$11,800
Direct fixed costs	$ 4,200	$ 2,100	$ 2,600
Common fixed costs	17,700	14,400	10,950
Total fixed costs	$ 21,900	$16,500	13,550
Net income	$ 22,800	$23,600	$ (1,750)

Since the profit on laser discs is negative, the owner of Esoteric Electronics is considering discontinuing their sale.

REQUIRED:

a. Determine the impact on profit of dropping laser discs.
b. Discuss the potential qualitative effects of discontinuing the sale of laser discs.

LO 3   **P27-4A   Sales Mix With Constrained Resources**   Jeff Choi, the chief financial officer of Fibers Unlimited, is reviewing the profitability of the three products sold in the carpet division. The division manager prepared the following summary of the products.

	Economy	*Standard*	*Deluxe*
Selling price per yard	$9.50	$13.25	$19.00
Variable cost per yard	$5.00	$7.50	$9.25
Fixed cost per yard	$3.00	$4.00	$5.00
Yards produced annually	21,000	16,000	10,000
Total machine hours used	3,150	3,360	3,300

REQUIRED:

a. Calculate the number of machine hours required to produce each yard.
b. Determine the contribution margin per yard for each product.
c. Determine the contribution margin per machine hour for each product.
d. Suppose only 3,000 machine hours are available. Which product should be produced?

LO 3,4

P27-5A   **Special Order with Production Constraints**   Cheap Skates ρ produces inexpensive ice skates which are primarily marketed through discount departmen. stores and sporting goods stores. It takes 0.50 machine hours to manufacture each pair of skates. During the current year, the factory is expected to produce 45,000 pairs which entails the factory producing at 90% of capacity. The standard costs of a pair of skates are as follows:

Direct material (1.5 lbs x $4.00)	$ 6.00
Direct labor (0.4 hours x $6.00)	2.40
Variable overhead (0.4 hours x $9.00)	3.60
Fixed costs (0.4 hours x $11.00)	4.40
Total costs	$16.40

Ice Rinks of America offered Cheap Skate the one-time opportunity to sell them 4,500 pairs of skates at $12.00 per pair.

REQUIRED:

a. Calculate the impact the order will have on Cheap Skates' net income.
b. Determine if Cheap Skates should accept the special order if it were for 7,500 pairs of skates.

PROBLEM SET B

LO 1,2

P27-1B   **Complex Make or Buy Decision**   Goopy-Glue is a new non-toxic glue in a bottle to be manufactured by Stickum Corporation. The product will be sold to wholesalers and large hardware stores in packages of 25 bottles for $21.00 per package. Management has determined that $120,000 of fixed production overhead costs should be allocated to Goopy-Glue. The cost per package of Goopy-Glue for expected production of 80,000 packages is:

Direct material per package	$ 7.00
Direct labor per package	4.50
Overhead per package (fixed and variable)	4.00
Total per package	$15.50

Stickum has contacted packaging suppliers to determine if it would be better to buy the bottle rather than manufacture it. The lowest quote for the bottles was $2.85 per 25 bottles. It is estimated that purchasing the bottles from a supplier would save 15% of direct materials, 10% of direct labor, and 20% of variable overhead. Stickum's manufacturing space is highly constrained. By purchasing the bottles, Stickum will not have to lease additional manufacturing space that is estimated to cost $12,000 per year. If the bottles are purchased, Stickum estimates that two supervisory positions can be eliminated. Salary plus benefits for each position are $18,500 per year.

REQUIRED:

a. Calculate the variable overhead per package.
b. Prepare a differential cost analysis of the make or buy decision.
c. Determine if Stickum should make or buy the bottles.

LO 1,2,3

P27-2B   **Additional Processing Decision With Production Constraints**   Fiberific produces Nyloron and a new and improved version called Superon, along with other products. Superon, which sells for $10.80 per meter is manufactured from Nyloron plus additional ingredients. It takes 10 minutes to manufacture a meter of Nyloron and an additional 5 minutes to manufacture a meter of Superon. Nyloron sells for $6.80 per meter. The cost per meter of manufacturing Nyloron and the additional costs to manufacture Superon are as follows:

	Nyloron	*Additional Cost of Superon*
Material	$1.80	$0.70
Labor	1.44	1.40
Variable overhead	2.08	0.90
Fixed overhead	1.75	3.15

Both products have been successful and demand for Nyloron and Superon is strong. However, Fiberific's other products are also in demand and Fiberific is approaching full capacity. Since it takes longer to manufacture Superon, the vice president of production is trying to determine if Superon should continue to be manufactured.

REQUIRED:

Which product makes the largest contribution to company profit given a capacity constraint measured in terms of production time?

LO 1,2,3   **P27-3B**   **Dropping a Product Line**   Music Village has three product lines: records, compact discs, and cassettes. Common costs are allocated by percentage of sales. The income statement for Music Village is as follows:

Music Village Product Line Income Statement For the Year Ended December 31, 19X1			
	Compact Discs	*Cassettes*	*Records*
Sales	$47,200	$38,400	$29,200
Cost of goods sold	27,800	22,600	23,100
Gross margin	$19,400	$15,800	$ 6,100
Other variable costs	1,500	1,300	700
Contribution margin	$17,900	$14,500	$ 5,400
Common fixed costs	$ 2,100	$ 2,100	$ 1,900
Allocated fixed costs	7,080	5,760	4,380
Total fixed costs	$ 9,180	$ 7,860	$ 6,280
Net income	$ 8,720	$ 6,640	$ (880)

Since the profit on records is negative, the owner of Music Village is considering discontinuing their sale.

REQUIRED:

a. Determine the impact on profit of dropping records.
b. Discuss the potential qualitative effects of discontinuing the sale of records.

LO 3   **P27-4B**   **Sales Mix With Constrained Resources**   Martha Lopez, the chief financial officer of Grasses Galore, is reviewing the profitability of the three products sold in the sod division. The division manager prepared the following summary of the products.

	Fescue	*Bermuda*	*St. Augustine*
Selling price per yard	$1.90	$2.65	$3.40
Variable cost per yard	$1.00	$1.50	$1.45
Fixed cost per yard	$0.60	$0.80	$1.00
Yards produced annually	4,200	3,200	2,580
Total machine hours used	630	672	860

REQUIRED:

  a. Calculate the number of machine hours required to produce each yard.
  b. Determine the contribution margin per yard for each product.
  c. Determine the contribution margin per machine hour for each product.
  d. Suppose only 3,000 machine hours are available. Which product should be produced?

LO 3,4   **P27-5B**   **Special Order with Production Constraints** Subtracto Corporation produces inexpensive calculators which are primarily marketed through discount department stores and discount drug stores. It takes 0.10 machine hours to manufacture each calculator. During the current year, the factory is expected to produce 225,000 calculators which entails the factory producing at 90% of capacity. The standard costs of a calculator are as follows:

Direct material (0.2 lbs x $4.00)	$0.80
Direct labor (0.1 hours x $5.00)	0.50
Variable overhead (0.1 hours x $14.00)	1.40
Fixed costs (0.1 hours x $24.00)	2.40
Total costs	$5.10

Clearance Stores offered Subtracto the one-time opportunity to sell them 14,500 calculators at $3.25 each.

REQUIRED:

  a. Calculate the impact the order will have on Subtacto's net income.
  b. Determine if Subtracto should accept the special order if it were for 30,000 calculators.

CRITICAL THINKING AND COMMUNICATING

C27-1

The Tennis Pro Shop handles four lines of products that include rackets, clothes, shoes, and tennis balls. Because of intense competition from discount stores, tennis balls are sold at variable cost and at a loss if fixed costs are included. However, the other product lines are all profitable. Because of the lack of profitability, Boris Evert (the store manager) asked Chris Becker (the owner) if they should discontinue the sale of tennis balls. Boris argued that the space and selling effort could be applied to the other product lines. Chris Becker vehemently objected, and told Boris he is not to discontinue the sale of tennis balls.

REQUIRED:

Decide if the Tennis Pro Shop should carry tennis balls and support your decision.

C27-2

Monroe Nurseries provides wholesale plants and shrubs to retail nurseries in the greater Cleveland area. Cromwell Construction proposed that Monroe supply a very large order of shrubs so that Cromwell could landscape an entire housing development. The price Cromwell was willing to pay was greater than Monroe's variable cost but less than the full cost. This price is also less than the price Monroe charges its regular customers.

REQUIRED:

Write a memo to the owner of Monroe Nurseries explaining the qualitative considerations that should be considered if the special order is accepted.

CHAPTER 28

Capital Budgeting Decisions

After several years of operating a successful charter business, Steve Wilson, president of Island Air, thought it was time to add to his "fleet" of three, 7-passenger aircraft. "Look," he explained to his chief accountant, Ellen Smith, "with another plane, we can service 3,000 additional passengers a year. At an average fare of $200, that's $600,000!"

"But don't forget," Ellen pointed out, "a new plane will cost around $1,000,000; operating costs will be nearly $400,000 per year; and after five years, that $1,000,000 plane will only be worth $500,000. It's not clear that buying another plane is a good business decision."

In this chapter, we extend the discussion of decision making to include decisions requiring an investment in long-lived assets. The goal of the chapter is to provide you with the tools to solve problems like the one Steve Wilson faces.

1. Define capital expenditure decisions and capital budgets.
2. Evaluate investment opportunities using the net present value approach.
3. Evaluate investment opportunities using the internal rate of return approach.
4. Calculate the depreciation income tax shield and explain why depreciation is only important in investment analysis because of income taxes.
5. Use the payback period and the accounting rate of return methods to evaluate investment opportunities.
6. Explain why managers may concentrate erroneously on the short-run profitability of investments rather than their net present values.
7. Explain how the internal rate of return is calculated when there are uneven cash flows. (Appendix 28A)

LO 1

Define capital expenditure decisions and capital budgets.

CAPITAL BUDGETING DECISIONS

Individuals make "investments" in their homes, automobiles, major appliances, furniture, and other long-lived assets. Companies must also make investments in long-lived assets. Examples of some common investment decisions are presented in Illustration 28-1. In each example, a firm considers making an investment in one or more assets that will affect the firm's operations for several years.

ILLUSTRATION 28-1 Common Investment Decisions

1. A firm of architects considers buying a computer-aided design system.
2. A restaurant considers buying a new refrigeration system.
3. A moving company considers replacing its old fleet of trucks with new diesel-powered trucks.
4. A bottling company considers opening a new plant in Texas.
5. An accounting firm considers purchasing a microcomputer for preparation of client reports.
6. A furniture manufacturer considers purchasing a new lathe.
7. A car repair company considers purchasing the building it currently rents.
8. A grain processor considers converting a coal-powered boiler to natural gas.
9. A newspaper considers buying a new printing press.
10. A computer company considers purchasing patent rights to an operating system.

Investment decisions are extremely important because they have a major, long-term effect on a firm's operations. For example, when Mazda decided to build some of its cars in Flat Rock, Michigan, it made an investment in additional productive capacity that will affect its labor and transportation costs for many years to come. U.S., rather than Japanese, workers supply labor to build the cars; therefore, labor costs are largely determined by business conditions in the United States rather than those in Japan. Transportation costs are greatly reduced because Mazda can ship by rail directly from Michigan to various U.S. cities rather than from the West Coast (after a long trans-Pacific crossing). The investment decisions of small companies are also extremely important. Consider a small print shop that decides to make an investment in a computerized printing machine. The machine's cost may represent 50% or more of the company's total assets. Also, the cost savings from the investment in new technology may make the difference between the company being a solid competitor in its market versus being on the verge of financial failure.

Investment decisions involving the acquisition of long-lived assets are often referred to as **capital expenditure decisions** because they require expenditure of capital (company funds) to acquire additional resources. Alternatively, investment decisions are called **capital budgeting decisions**. Most firms carefully analyze the potential projects in which they may invest. The process of evaluating the investment opportunities is referred to as *capital budgeting*, and the final list of approved projects is referred to as the **capital budget**.

EVALUATING INVESTMENT OPPORTUNITIES
TIME VALUE OF MONEY APPROACHES

Crucial to capital budgeting decisions is an understanding of the *time value of money*. In evaluating an investment opportunity, you must know not only *how much* cash is received from (paid for) an investment, but also *when* the cash is received (paid). The time value of money concept states that it is better to receive a dollar today than to receive a dollar next year or any other time in the future. The reason, of course, is that you can invest the dollar received today so that at the end of the year it amounts to more than a dollar.

In an investment decision, a company invests money today in the hopes of receiving more money in the future. Obviously, one would not invest money in a project unless the total amount of funds received in the future exceeded the amount of the original investment. But, by *how much* must the future cash flows exceed the original investment? Since money in the future is not equivalent to money today, we need to develop a way of converting future dollars into their equivalent current or present value. The method developed to equate future dollars to current dollars is referred to as **present value analysis**. Present value techniques were explained earlier in the text in connection with the valuation of long-term debt. In this section, we present two approaches for evaluating investments that take into account the time value of money: the *net present value method* and the *internal rate of return method*.

LO 2

Evaluate investment opportunities using the net present value approach.

The Net Present Value Method

The first step in using the net present value method is to identify the amount and time period of each cash flow associated with a potential investment. Investment projects have both cash inflows (which are positive) and cash outflows (which are negative). The second step is to discount the cash flows to their present values using a required rate of return. How to estimate the required rate of return will be discussed later. For now, you should simply assume that the required rate of return is the minimum return top management wants to earn on investments. The third and final step is to evaluate the net present value.

The sum of the present values of all cash flows (inflows and outflows) is the **net present value** (NPV) of the investment. If zero, the NPV implies that the investment is generating a rate of return exactly equal to the required rate of return. Thus, management should undertake the investment. If the NPV is positive, management should also undertake the investment because it is generating a rate of return that is greater than the required rate of return. On the other hand, management should not accept investment opportunities that have negative NPVs because their rates of return are less than the required rates of return. A graphical presentation of the NPV approach to evaluating investments is presented in Illustration 28-2.

ILLUSTRATION 28-2 NPV Approach to Evaluating Investments

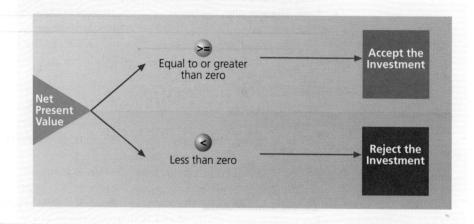

An Example of the NPV Approach.   Suppose an auto repair shop considers purchasing automated paint spraying equipment. The company estimates that the equipment will last 5 years, save $2,000 annually in paint wasted in the current manual spraying operation, and reduce labor costs by $20,000. The equipment's estimated maintenance costs are $1,000 per year. The equipment costs $70,000 and has an expected residual value of $5,000. If the required rate of return is 12%, should the company invest in the new equipment?

The cash flows related to the investment opportunity are presented on the time line in Illustration 28-3. In analyzing the cash flows, we make the assumption that all cash inflows and outflows (other than the cash outflow of $70,000 for purchasing the equipment) occur at the end of a year. To simplify analysis, managers commonly make this assumption, which is unlikely to introduce significant error even though cash flows actually take place throughout the year (not just at year-end).

Consider the $70,000 cash outflow due to purchasing the spraying equipment. Note that the present value factor associated with the $70,000 purchase price is 1.0000. Because this amount is to be spent immediately, it is already expressed in terms of its present value. Now, consider the cash flows in Year 1. In this year, the net cash inflow is $21,000. The present value factor for an amount received at the end of Year 1 using a 12% rate of return is .8929. (See Table 1 in Appendix C, Present Value of $1.) Multiplying the present value factor by the cash inflow of $21,000 indicates that the present value of the net cash inflow in Year 1 is $18,751. The net present value of the investment in spraying equipment is found by summing the present values of the cash flows in each year. This amounts to $8,538. Since the net present value is positive, the company should purchase the equipment.

In the problem, the $20,000 labor savings, the $2,000 paint savings, and the $1,000 maintenance expense are identical in each of the five years. Thus, the net amount of $21,000 can be treated as a five-year annuity in calculating the present value. This treatment is presented in Illustration 28-4. The present value factor, using a 12% rate of return, for an annuity lasting five years is 3.605. (See

ILLUSTRATION 28-3 Evaluation of Automated Paint Spraying Equipment

Time Period	Present 0	Year 1	Year 2	Year 3	Year 4	Year 5	
Cash Flow:							
Purchase Price	$(70,000)						
Labor Saving		$20,000	$20,000	$20,000	$20,000	$20,000	
Paint Saving		2,000	2,000	2,000	2,000	2,000	
Maintenance		(1,000)	(1,000)	(1,000)	(1,000)	(1,000)	
Salvage Value						$5,000	
Total Cash Flow	$(70,000)	$21,000	$21,000	$21,000	$21,000	$26,000	
PV Factor	1.000	.8929	.7972	.7118	.6355	.5674	
Total	$(70,000) +	$18,751 +	$16,741 +	$14,948 +	$13,346 +	$14,752 =	$8,538

Table 2 in Appendix C, Present Value of Annuity of $1.) Multiplying this factor by the $21,000 annuity indicates a present value of $75,705. The present value of the $5,000 residual value in Year 5 is calculated using a factor from the Present Value of $1 table. Note that the total net present value, $8,542, is $4 more than the amount calculated in Illustration 28-3. The $4 difference is due to rounding in development of the present value tables.

ILLUSTRATION 28-4 Evaluation of Automated Paint Spraying Equipment Using Present Value of an Annuity Approach

Item	Cash Flow	Present Value Factor	Present Value
Purchase price	$(70,000)	1.0000	$(70,000)
Labor, paint, and maintenance	21,000	3.6050	75,705
Residual value	5,000	.5674	2,837
		Net present value	8,542

LO 3
Evaluate investment opportunities using the internal rate of return approach.

The Internal Rate of Return Method

The internal rate of return method is an alternative to net present value for evaluating investments possibilities.[1] Like net present value, it takes into account the time value of money. The **internal rate of return** (IRR) is the rate of return that equates the present value of future cash flows to the investment outlay. If the IRR of a potential investment is greater than the required rate of return, management should undertake the investment. The IRR approach to evaluating investments is presented in Illustration 28-5.

Consider a simple case where someone invests $100 to yield $60 at the end of Year 1 and $60 at the end of Year 2. What rate of return equates the two-year, $60 annuity to $100? Recall that when we performed present value analysis for annuities, we multiplied an annuity value factor by the annuity to solve for a present value. That is:

Present Value = Annuity Value Factor x Annuity

[1]The internal rate of return method is also referred to as the *time-adjusted rate of return* method.

ILLUSTRATION 28-5 IRR Approach to Evaluating Investments

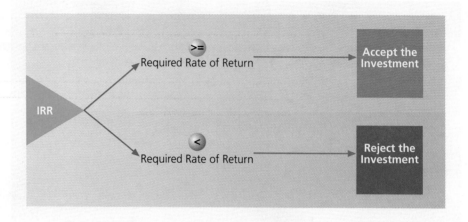

In the current case, we set the present value equal to the initial outlay for the investment. Then, we can solve for the annuity value factor and use it to look up the rate of return implicit in the investment.

$$\textbf{Annuity Value Factor} = \frac{\textbf{Cost of Investment}}{\textbf{Annuity Amount}}$$

With a $100 cost and a $60 annuity, the investment's annuity value factor is 1.667.

$$1.667 = \frac{\$100}{\$60}$$

Since the $60 is to be received in each of two years, we use the annuity table (Table 2 in Appendix C) to look up the internal rate of return. In the row in Table 2 for 2 periods, we find an annuity value factor of 1.668 (very close to 1.667) in the column for a 13% rate of return. Thus, the IRR on this investment is approximately 13%. If the required rate of return is 13% or less, then the investor should undertake the investment.

You can gain insight into the IRR by using it to calculate the net present value of the project. If we evaluated the project using a 13% required rate of return, what would be the net present value? The answer is *zero* since the internal rate of return equates the present value of future cash flows to the investment outlay.

Item	Cash Flow	Present Value Factor	Present Value
Cash flow	$ 60	1.668	$100.08
Initial investment	$(100)	1.000	(100.00)
		Difference (due to rounding)	$ .08

Summary of Net Present Value and Internal Rate of Return

While both the net present value and the internal rate of return methods take into account the time value of money, they differ in their approach to evaluating investment alternatives. In using net present value, management should

Henry Spellman, vice president of operations for Union Manufacturing, is preparing a presentation for the board of directors. Henry hopes to convince the board that the company should invest in a highly mechanized production line that makes extensive use of robotics. As part of his presentation, Henry will present a net present value analysis of the potential investment in equipment. In preparing this analysis, Henry discovers that the present value of the cash flows directly attributable to the investment is a negative $25,000.

Henry feels that investing in an automated production line is essential if the company is to remain competitive over the next ten years. However, the NPV doesn't capture the strategic importance of the new technology. If he "fudges" the operating expenses in his analysis, he will be able to show that the project has a positive NPV.

Should Henry "fudge" the numbers in the NPV analysis if this is the only way he can convince the board to make an investment decision that Henry feels is in the long-run interest of company? Explain.

undertake any investment with a zero or positive net present value. In using the internal rate of return method, management should undertake any investment with an internal rate of return equal to or greater than the required rate of return.[2]

ESTIMATING THE REQUIRED RATE OF RETURN

In the problems presented, we simply stated a required rate of return that could be used to calculate an investment's net present value or that could be compared to an investment's internal rate of return. In practice, management must estimate the required rate of return. Under certain conditions, the required rate of return should be equal to the cost of capital for the firm.

The **cost of capital** is the weighted average of the costs of debt and equity financing used to generate capital for investments. The cost of debt arises because the firm must pay interest to individuals, to banks, and to other companies that lend it money. Essentially, the cost of equity is the return shareholders demand for the risk they bear in supplying capital to the firm. Estimating the cost of capital, especially the cost due to equity capital, is a challenge even to sophisticated financial managers. Because of this difficulty, many managers take a judgmental approach to determine the required rate of return following the general principle that the more risky the investment, the higher the required rate of return.

FURTHER CONSIDERATION OF CASH FLOWS

To be useful in investment analysis, both the net present value and the internal rate of return methods require a proper specification of cash flows. It is particu-

---

[2]Under some circumstances, the net present value and the internal rate of return methods may be inconsistent with one another in evaluating the desirability of an investment opportunity. This potential problem is discussed in introductory texts on financial management.

larly important to remember that *only cash inflows and outflows, not revenues and expenses*, are discounted back to present value. Thus, if a firm expects a sale to occur in Period 1 but does not anticipate the collection of cash from the sale until Period 2, the cash flow it discounts back to present value is a Period 2 cash flow even though the related revenue will be recorded in Period 1. Likewise, if a firm anticipates a cash payment in Period 1 to purchase an asset, and records related depreciation in Periods 1 through 5, it uses only the Period 1 cash outflow in the net present value analysis. Depreciation is a legitimate business cost, but it does not require a cash outflow in the period in which it is recorded. Present value analysis is concerned only with cash flows.

LO 4
Calculate the depreciation income tax shield and explain why depreciation is only important in investment analysis because of income taxes.

Cash Flows, Taxes, and the Depreciation Income Tax Shield

In all of the examples given, we ignored the effect of income taxes on cash flows. However, tax considerations play a major role in capital budgeting decisions, and we discuss them here. If an investment project generates taxable revenue, cash inflows from the project will be reduced by the taxes that the firm must pay on the revenue. Likewise, if an investment project generates tax-deductible expenses, cash inflows from the project will be increased by the tax savings resulting from the decrease in income taxes payable.

We previously stated that depreciation is not relevant in a present value analysis of an investment opportunity because it is not a cash flow. While depreciation does not *directly* affect cash flow, it *indirectly* affects cash flow because it reduces the amount of tax a company must pay. That is, it acts to shield income from taxes. The term **depreciation income tax shield** is used to refer to the tax savings resulting from depreciation.

As an example, suppose a firm considers producing and selling a new product. Production of the product will require an investment in equipment costing $100,000. Each year, the company expects sales to amount to $70,000 and expenses (other than depreciation on the equipment) to amount to $40,000. Depreciation calculated on a straight-line basis for the expected 10-year life of the equipment is $10,000 per year. The company has a 40% tax rate.[3] Assume the company collects revenue in the period earned and pays expenses in the period incurred. Thus, net income and cash flows related to the investment are as follows:

Revenue		$70,000
Less: Operating expenses other than depreciation	$40,000	
Depreciation	10,000	50,000
Income before taxes		$20,000
Income taxes (40% tax rate)		8,000
Net income		$12,000
Add back: Depreciation		10,000
Cash flow each period		$22,000

Note that the firm deducts depreciation to arrive at income before taxes and thus reduces the amount of income taxes it must pay. However, depreciation is

---

[3]Our discussion and examples assume a 40% tax rate. This assumption ignores complexities in tax rates and rules in practice which may change from year to year. However, the assumption allows us to more clearly convey the essential role of taxes in investment decisions.

not itself a cash outflow. Therefore, the firm must add back depreciation to net income to arrive at its cash flow.

Because the project is fairly risky, the company has set a required rate of return of 16%. The net present value calculation for the investment under consideration is presented in Illustration 28-6. Note that because the amounts of revenue, expense, and tax are the same each year, we can work with the net amount and treat it as a 10-year annuity with a required rate of return of 16%. Since the net present value is a positive $6,326, the firm should undertake investment in the equipment.

ILLUSTRATION 28-6 NPV Analysis Taking Taxes Into Account

Item		Cash Flow	Present Value Factor	Present Value
Initial investment		$(100,000)	1.000	$(100,000)
Revenue	$70,000			
Operating expenses (other than depreciation)	(40,000)			
Taxes	(8,000)	22,000	4.833	106,326
Net present value				$ 6,326

The fact that depreciation reduced taxes had a significant effect on the value of the investment project. With depreciation of $10,000 and a 40% tax rate, the firm saves $4,000 in taxes each year due to depreciation. The present value of this "tax shield" over 10 years at 16% is $19,332 ($4,000 x present value factor of 4.833). Thus, it is apparent that without the tax shield afforded by depreciation, the investment would not have a positive net present value and would not be worth undertaking.

Adjusting Cash Flows for Inflation

An additional topic that must be addressed in estimating the cash flows of investments is how to handle inflation. During the 1970s and early 1980s, we experienced double-digit inflation in the U.S. High rates of inflation are still common in many foreign countries. Thus, it may be quite important to consider inflation when estimating the cash flows associated with investment opportunities. Inflation can be taken into account by multiplying the current level of cash flow by the expected rate of inflation. For example, if an investment is expected to yield a cash flow in Period 1 of $100 and the rate of inflation is expected to be 5% per year in the foreseeable future, then a reasonable estimate of the cash flow would be $105 (i.e., $100 x 1.05) in Period 2, $110.25 (i.e., $105 x 1.05) in Period 3, $115.76 in Period 4, etc. Financial journals publish estimates of inflation, and some firms that specialize in economic forecasts provide them for a fee.

If inflation is ignored in net present value analysis, firms may reject many worthwhile investment opportunities. Current rates of return for debt and equity financing already include estimates of future inflation. For example, when they estimate that inflation will be high, banks charge higher rates of interest on loans to companies. Suppose a company uses its current costs of debt and equity financing (which are high because a high rate of inflation is expected) to determine its required rate of return. Now, if the company does not take inflation into account in estimating future cash flows, the cash flows will be relatively low, while the required rate of return will be relatively high. The result may be that suitable projects will appear to have negative net present values.

LO 5
Use the payback period and the accounting rate of return methods to evaluate investment opportunities.

SIMPLIFIED APPROACHES TO CAPITAL BUDGETING

Companies often use the net present value and the internal rate of return methods to evaluate capital projects. Since the 1960s, their use has increased greatly. However, many companies continue to use other, more simple, approaches to evaluating capital projects. Two of these approaches, the *payback period method and the accounting rate of return method*, are discussed in this section. As you will see, both of these methods have significant limitations in comparison to net present value and internal rate of return.

Payback Period Method

The **payback period** is the length of time it takes to recover the initial cost of an investment. Thus, if an investment opportunity costs $1,000 and yields cash flows of $500 per year, it has a payback period of 2 years. If an investment costs $1,000 and yields cash flows of $300 per year, it has a payback period of 3-1/3 years. All things equal, a company would like to have projects with short payback periods.

One approach to using the payback method would be to accept investment projects that have a payback period less than some specified requirement. However, this can lead to extremely poor decisions. For example, suppose a company has two investment opportunities both costing $1,000. The first investment yields cash flows of $500 per year for 3 years and has a payback period of 2 years. The second investment yields no cash flows in the first two years but has cash flows of $1,000 in the third year and $4,000 in the fourth year. Thus, it has a payback period of 3 years. Obviously, the second investment is preferable. However if the company has a 2-year payback requirement, it would select the first investment and reject the second. The problem is that the payback method *does not take into account the total stream of cash flows related to an investment*. It only considers the stream of cash flows up to the time the investment is paid back. Thus, in this example, the payback period method ignores the $4,000 cash flow in the fourth year of the second investment.

A further limitation of the payback method is that it *does not consider the time value of money*. Consider two investments that both cost $1,000. The first investment yields cash flows of $700 in the first year, $300 in the second year, and $300 in the third year. Thus, it has a payback of 2 years. The second investment yields cash flows of $300 in the first year, $700 in the second year, and $300 in the third year. Thus, it also has a payback of 2 years. While both investments have the same payback (implying they are equally valuable), the first investment is really more favorable because the $700 cash inflow is received in the first year rather than in the second year. In fact, the first investment has an internal rate of return of 17%, while the second investment has an internal rate of return of only 14%.

While the payback method has significant limitations, some companies may find it useful, particularly if they have cash flow problems. Companies with cash flow problems may need to focus on investments that quickly return cash in order to avoid bankruptcy.

Accounting Rate of Return

The **accounting rate of return** equals the average after-tax income from a project divided by the average investment in the project.

$$\textbf{Accounting Rate of Return (ARR)} = \frac{\textbf{Average Net Income}}{\textbf{Average Investment}}$$

Companies can use the accounting rate of return to evaluate investment opportunities by comparing their accounting rates of return to a required accounting rate of return. The primary limitation of this approach is that, like the payback method, it ignores the time value of money. For example, a firm that has a cost of capital of 15% and a 40% tax rate considers two investment alternatives. Both alternatives require investments in equipment costing $100,000 and generate cash flows for two years as indicated in Illustration 28-7. Both investments are identical except that, while both have total revenue over two years of $180,000, Project 1 has $90,000 of revenue in the first year, while Project 2 has $70,000. In the second year, Project 1 has $90,000 of revenue, while Project 2 has $110,000. Illustration 28-7 presents the net incomes and cash flows of the two alternatives for the two years. We assume the firm collects all revenue items in the period earned and pays all expense items (other than depreciation) in the period incurred. Thus, the difference between net income and cash flow is simply the amount of depreciation.

ILLUSTRATION 28-7 Net Income and Cash Flow Data for Alternative Projects

	Project 1	Project 2
Year 1		
Revenue	$90,000	$ 70,000
Less: Operating expenses other than depreciation	20,000	20,000
Depreciation	50,000	50,000
Income before taxes	$20,000	$ 0
Taxes	8,000	0
Net income	$12,000	$ 0
Add back: Depreciation	50,000	50,000
Cash flow	$62,000	$ 50,000
Year 2		
Revenue	$90,000	$110,000
Less: Operating expenses other than depreciation	20,000	20,000
Depreciation	50,000	50,000
Income before taxes	$20,000	$ 40,000
Taxes	8,000	16,000
Net income	$12,000	$ 24,000
Add back: Depreciation	50,000	50,000
Cash flow	$62,000	$74,000

Based on the information, it is easy to calculate the accounting rate of return for each project as indicated in Illustration 28-8.

ILLUSTRATION 28-8 Comparison of ARRs for Alternative Projects

$$\text{Accounting Rate of Return (ARR)} = \frac{\text{Average Net Income}}{\text{Average Investment}}$$

$$\text{ARR for Project 1} = \frac{(\$12,000 + \$12,000) \div 2}{\$100,000 \div 2} = .24$$

$$\text{ARR for Project 2} = \frac{(\$0 + \$24,000) \div 2}{\$100,000 \div 2} = .24$$

Both have identical accounting rates of return of 24%, indicating that the two projects are equally desirable. However, when we take into account the time value of money, it is clear that Project 1 is more desirable than Project 2. As indicated in Illustration 28-9, using a cost of capital of 15%, the net present value of project 1 is $793.40, while Project 2 has a negative net present value of $568.60. Thus, taking into account the time value of money, Project 1 is an acceptable investment, while Project 2 is not acceptable.

ILLUSTRATION 28-9 NPV Comparison of Alternative Projects

Project 1

Time Period	Cash Flow	Present Value Factor	Present Value
0	$(100,000)	1.0000	$(100,000.00)
1	62,000	.8696	53,915.20
2	62,000	.7561	46,878.20
		Net present value	$ 793.40

Project 2

Time Period	Cash Flow	Present Value Factor	Present Value
0	$(100,000)	1.0000	$(100,000.00)
1	50,000	.8696	43,480.00
2	74,000	.7561	55,951.40
		Net present value	$ (568.60)

LO 6
Explain why managers may concentrate erroneously on the short-run profitability of investments rather than their net present values.

CONFLICT BETWEEN PERFORMANCE EVALUATION AND CAPITAL BUDGETING

In some companies, managers may be discouraged from using present value techniques for evaluating investments because of the way their own performance is evaluated. The reason for this is that some investments result in high amounts of depreciation in early years. In these early, start-up years, revenues may be quite low, resulting in low profits or even losses. However, revenues in later years may be large enough to ensure that the investments have positive net present values. If managers know that job performance is evaluated in terms of reported accounting income, they may fear being fired because of low initial profits. If this is the case, managers would likely ignore the fact that a project had a positive net present value and concentrate, instead, on reported income.

Suppose a manager considers producing a new product that requires an investment of $1,000,000 in equipment. Depreciation on the equipment will be recorded using the straight-line method. Based on a 10-year life, depreciation will be $100,000 per year. The product is not expected to sell well in the early years. (For example, expected first year revenue is only $40,000). However, by the end of the seventh year, expected revenue is up to $700,000 per year. In addition to depreciation, the company will incur $40,000 of other expenses each year. The company has a 10% required rate of return. Illustration 28-10 is a net present value analysis of the investment.

The net present value of the investment is $26,998, indicating that the manager should undertake the project. However, will the manager be motivated to do what is in the best interest of the company? Note that the project shows a

ILLUSTRATION 28-10 Net Present Value Analysis of New Product[1]

	Year 1	Year 2	Year 3	Year 4	Year 5
Revenue	$ 40,000	$ 60,000	$100,000	$150,000	$200,000
Less: Operating expenses other than depreciation	40,000	40,000	40,000	40,000	40,000
Depreciation	100,000	100,000	100,000	100,000	100,000
Net income	$(100,000)	$ (80,000)	$ (40,000)	$ 10,000	$ 60,000
Add back: Depreciation	100,000	100,000	100,000	100,000	100,000
Cash flow	$ 0	$ 20,000	$ 60,000	$110,000	$160,000

	Year 6	Year 7	Year 8	Year 9	Year 10
Revenue	$ 300,000	$400,000	$400,000	$400,000	$400,000
Less: Operating expenses other than depreciation	40,000	40,000	40,000	40,000	40,000
Depreciation	100,000	100,000	100,000	100,000	100,000
Net income	$ 160,000	$260,000	$260,000	$260,000	$260,000
Add back: Depreciation	100,000	100,000	100,000	100,000	100,000
Cash flow	$ 260,000	$360,000	$360,000	$360,000	$360,000

Time Period	Cash Flows	Factor for 10%	Present Value
0	$(1,000,000)	1.0000	$(1,000,000)
1	0	0.9091	0
2	20,000	0.8264	16,528
3	60,000	0.7513	45,078
4	110,000	0.6830	75,130
5	160,000	0.6209	99,344
6	260,000	0.5645	146,770
7	360,000	0.5132	184,752
8	360,000	0.4665	167,940
9	360,000	0.4241	152,676
10	360,000	0.3855	138,780
	Net present value		$ 26,998

[1]Note that the example is simplified and ignores taxes. Therefore, there is no depreciation tax shield. Also, the example assumes the company collects revenue in the period earned and pays other expenses in the period incurred.

substantial loss in each of the first three years. The manager may fear that this will reflect badly on his or her performance, perhaps leading to dismissal. If this is the case, the manager may opt to pass up this valuable investment opportunity. The solution to this potential problem is to make sure managers realize that, if they approve projects with positive net present values that lower reported income in the shortrun, evaluations of their performance will take the expected *future* benefits into account. Managers must be confident that their performance will be evaluated with respect to the firm's long-run profitability, or they will not take a long-run perspective in evaluating capital projects.

INTERNATIONAL PERSPECTIVES

EVALUATING CAPITAL PROJECTS: COMPARISON OF PRACTICES IN THE U.S., KOREA, AND JAPAN
Are approaches to evaluating capital projects the same in different countries? A survey comparing practices in the U.S., Korea, and Japan reveals interesting similarities and differences. One survey question asked companies to rate the role of intuition in evaluating investments. Only 5% of Japanese companies indicated that intuition was extremely important or very important while the percentage was 25% in the U.S. and 22% in Korea. Thus, it appears that qualitative factors taken into account in a manager's intuition, are less important in Japan.

Respondents in all three countries considered the payback method to be important with 71% of U.S. companies, 88% of Japanese companies and 75% of Korean companies rating payback as an extremely or very important criterion for justifiying investment in capital projects. A surprising result is the low percentage of Japanese companies who consider the net present value (NPV) approach to be a useful technique for evaluating capital projects. Only 28% of the Japanese companies rated NPV as extremely or very important while the percentages in the U.S. and Korea were 60% and 64%.

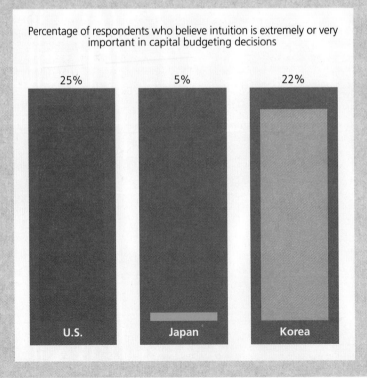

Percentage of respondents who believe intuition is extremely or very important in capital budgeting decisions

25%   5%   22%

U.S.   Japan   Korea

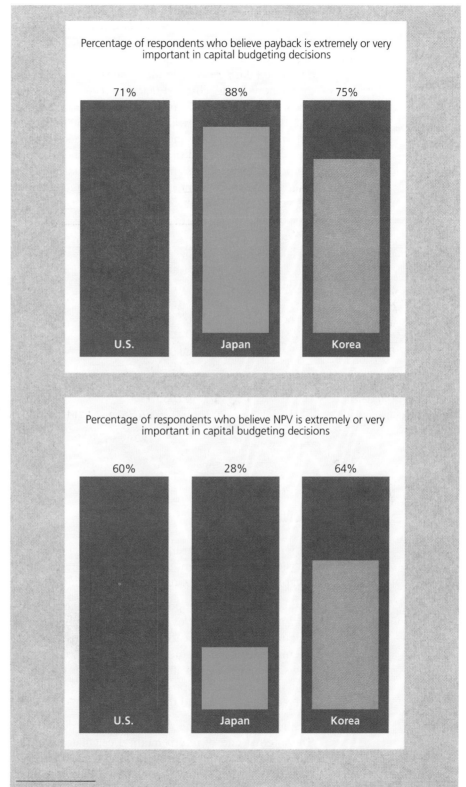

Percentage of respondents who believe payback is extremely or very important in capital budgeting decisions

71%   88%   75%

U.S.   Japan   Korea

Percentage of respondents who believe NPV is extremely or very important in capital budgeting decisions

60%   28%   64%

U.S.   Japan   Korea

Source: Il-Woon Kim and Ja Song, "U.S., Korea, & Japan: Accounting Practices in Three Countries," published in *Management Accounting* (August 1990), pp. 26–30, copyright by the Institute of Management Accountants, Montvale, N.J.

ISLAND AIR REVISITED

At the start of the chapter, Steve Wilson, president of Island Air, was trying to decide whether he should purchase another plane. At this point, we have developed the tools needed to analyze problems like the one Steve faces. Recall that a new plane costs $1,000,000. The residual value of the plane after five years will be $500,000, and annual depreciation using the straight-line method is $100,000. Revenue will increase by $600,000 per year, and operating costs (ignoring depreciation and taxes) will be $400,000. Revenue will be collected in the period earned and operating costs, other than depreciation, will be paid in the period incurred. Assume the income tax rate is 40%. What is the net present value of the investment in the plane if the required rate of return is 10%? The answer is ($82,990). Since the amount is negative, Island Air should reject the investment.

Item	Cash Flow	Present Value Factor	Present Value
Purchase price	$(1,000,000)	1.0000	$(1,000,000)
Revenue	$600,000		
Less: Operating expenses other than depreciation	400,000		
Deprecation	100,000		
Income before income taxes	$100,000		
Income taxes	40,000		
Net income	$ 60,000		
Add back: Depreciation	100,000		
Annual cash flow	160,000	3.7910	606,560
Residual value	500,000	.6209	310,450
		Net present value	$ (82,990)

SUMMARY

Define capital expenditure decisions and capital budgets.   Capital expenditure decisions are investment decisions involving the acquisition of long-lived assets. A capital budget is the final list of approved acquisitions.

Evaluate investment opportunities using the net present value approach.   Two primary methods for evaluating investment opportunities, which take into account the time value of money, are the net present value method and the internal rate of return method. The net present value method reduces all cash flows to their present values. If the sum of the present values (i.e., the net present value) is zero or positive, the return on the investment equals or exceeds the required return, and the company should make the investment.

Evaluate investment opportunities using the internal rate of return approach.   The internal rate of return method calculates the rate of return that equates the percent value of future cash flows to the initial investment. If this rate of return is equal to or greater than the required rate of return, then investment is warranted.

Calculate the depreciation income tax shield and explain why depreciation is only important in investment analysis because of income taxes.   In analyzing cash flows for a net present value analysis or an internal rate of return analysis, remember that depreciation is not a cash flow. However, the tax savings generated by depreciation is relevant to the analysis. The tax savings due to depreciation is referred to as the depreciation income tax shield.

Use the payback period and the accounting rate of return methods to evaluate investment opportunities. The payback method evaluates capital projects in terms of how quickly the initial investment is recovered by future cash inflows. The accounting rate of return method evaluates capital projects in terms of the ratio of average after-tax accounting income to the average investment. Both of these methods' major limitation is that they ignore the time value of money.

Explain why managers may concentrate on the short-run profitability of investments rather than their net present values. From a theoretical standpoint, managers should evaluate investment opportunities using the net present value method or the internal rate of return method. However, in some cases, projects with a positive net present value or with an internal rate of return greater than required may have a negative effect on short-run income. While these projects may be quite valuable to the firm's long-run success, managers may not approve them because they fear that their own job performance will receive negative evaluations if short-run income is reduced.

LO 7
Explain how the internal rate of return is calculated when there are uneven cash flows.

APPENDIX 28-A: THE INTERNAL RATE OF RETURN WITH UNEQUAL CASH FLOWS

In the chapter, the use of the IRR method is presented for the case where cash flows are equal each year. For cases where cash flows are not equal, the approach presented in the chapter cannot be implemented because we cannot divide the initial investment by a single cash flow annuity to yield an annuity value factor. Instead, we must estimate the internal rate of return and use the estimate to calculate the net present value of the project. If the net present value is greater than zero, the estimate of the internal rate of return should be increased. If the net present value is less than zero, the estimate should be decreased. By estimating the internal rate of return in this trial-and-error fashion, it is possible to arrive eventually at the actual internal rate of return.

Suppose a company considers changes in its production process that will involve purchasing several pieces of equipment costing a total of $120,000. The changes are expected to yield cost savings of $49,500 in Year 1, $45,000 in Year 2, $35,000 in Year 3, $22,000 in Year 4 and $19,600 in Year 5.

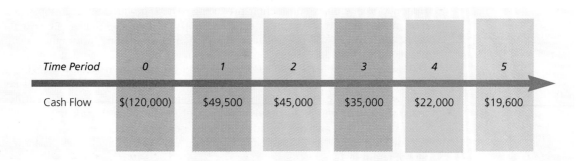

Time Period	0	1	2	3	4	5
Cash Flow	$(120,000)	$49,500	$45,000	$35,000	$22,000	$19,600

The company wants to evaluate the potential project in terms of its internal rate of return. Since the cash flows are fairly large in relation to the initial investment, a reasonable "guess" as to the internal rate of return might be 14%. However, when we use 14% to calculate the net present value of the investment as in Illustration 28-11, we see that the present value is a positive $4,880. Thus, the true internal rate of return is greater than 14%. As a next approximation, we can try 18%. However, with this rate of return, the present value is a negative $4,514. This indicates that our second estimate of the internal rate of return was too high. At this point, we know that the internal rate of return is somewhere between 14% and 18%. Thus, as a further attempt, we might try 16%. The net present value using a rate of 16% is $26. This is sufficiently close to zero to conclude that the internal rate of return is approximately 16%. If management believes that a return of 16% is sufficient, then the company should go ahead with the project.

ILLUSTRATION 28-11 Calculating the IRR When Cash Flows Are Unequal

Time Period	Cash Flows	14% Factor for 14%	Present Value	18% Factor for 18%	Present Value	16% Factor for 16%	Present Value
0	$(120,000)	1.0000	$(120,000)	1.0000	$(120,000)	1.0000	$(120,000)
1	49,500	0.8772	43,421	0.8475	41,951	0.8621	42,674
2	45,000	0.7695	34,268	0.7182	32,319	0.7432	33,444
3	35,000	0.6750	23,625	0.6086	21,301	0.6407	22,425
4	22,000	0.5921	13,026	0.5158	11,348	0.5523	12,151
5	19,600	0.5194	10,180	0.4371	8,567	0.4761	9,332
		Total	4,880		$ (4,514)		$ 26

It may appear that estimating the internal rate of return by using a trial-and-error approach is difficult and presents a significant obstacle to using the IRR approach. Actually, this is not the case. Many spreadsheet programs for microcomputers and even some pocket calculators contain functions that easily estimate the internal rate of return of a project. The user simply inputs the cash flow information and the IRR is calculated automatically.

REVIEW PROBLEM

Horton Corporation is considering producing a new product, Super Goop. Marketing data indicate that the demand for Super Goop will be 15,000 units per year for five years. The product will be produced in a section of an existing factory that is currently not in use. To produce Super Goop, Horton must buy a machine that costs $250,000. The machine has an expected life of 5 years and will have no residual value. Horton will depreciate the machine over 5 years using the straight-line method for both tax and financial reporting purposes. Horton has a tax rate of 30%. It is anticipated that no additional fixed costs will be incurred as a result of producing and marketing Super Goop, other than $22,200 annually for advertising the new product. Super Goop is expected to sell for $21 per unit and variable production cost is $15 per unit. Horton has a required rate of return of 14%.

REQUIRED:

a. Compute the net present value.
b. Compute the internal rate of return.
c. Compute the payback period.
d. Compute the accounting rate of return.

SOLUTION:

Planning and Organizing Your Work

1. Determine cash flow for each period by calculating after-tax income and adding back depreciation expense.
2. Apply present values to the annual cash flows and the initial investment to determine the net present value.
3. Divide the investment by the annual cash flows to determine the present value of an annuity table factor.
4. Look up the table factor in the present value of an annuity table to determine the internal rate of return.
5. Determine the payback period by dividing the initial investment by the annual cash flows.
6. Calculate the accounting rate of return by dividing the average net income by the average investment.

(a) *Compute the net present value.*

The net income and cash flows related to the investment are as follows:

Revenue ($21 x 15,000)		$315,000
Less: Production expenses ($15 x 15,000)	$225,000	
Advertising expense	22,200	
Depreciation expense (250,000 ÷ 5 years)	25,000	272,200
Income before taxes		$ 42,800
Taxes (30% tax rate)		12,840
Net income		$ 29,960
Add back: Depreciation		50,000
Cash flow each period		$ 79,960

The net present value is calculated as follows:

Item	*Cash Flow*	*Factor*	*Present Value*
Initial investment	$(250,000)	1.000	$(250,000)
Cash flow each period for 5 years	79,960	3.433	274,503
Net present value			$ 24,503

Since the net present value is positive, Super Goop should be produced.

(b) *Compute the internal rate of return.*

Present value factor = cost of investment ÷ annual cash flow
Present value factor = $250,000 ÷ $79,960 = 3.127

Use the annuity table (Table 2 in the Appendix C) to look up the internal rate of return. In the row in Table 2 for 5 periods we find a present value factor of 3.127 in the column for a 18% rate of return. Since the rate of return exceeds the required rate of return of 14%, the Super Goop should be produced.

(c) *Compute the payback period.*

The payback period for even cash flows can be calculated as follows:

Payback period = cost of investment ÷ annual cash flow
Payback period = $250,000 ÷ $79,960 = 3.127 years

(d) *Compute the accounting rate of return.*

ARR = average net income ÷ average investment

ARR = $29,960[1] ÷ ($250,000 ÷ 2) = 24%

---

[1]See calculation in NPV analysis above.

KEY TERMS

accounting rate of return, *1117*

capital budget, *1109*

capital budgeting decision, *1109*

capital expenditure decision, *1109*

cost of capital, *1113*

depreciation income tax shield, *1114*

internal rate of return, *1111*

net present value, *1109*

payback period, *1116*

present value analysis, *1109*

SELF-QUIZ

LO 1 1. Which of the following is *not* a common investment decision?
   a. Building a new factory.
   b. Accepting a special order.
   c. Purchasing a new piece of equipment.
   d. Purchasing a computer system.

LO 2 2. List the two factors about cash flows you need to know when evaluating investment alternatives using time value of money approaches.

LO 2 3. Which of the following is *not* a true statement about the net present value method?
   a. It uses time value of money concepts.
   b. The result is computed by calculating the present value of the inflows minus the initial investment.
   c. It is consistent with generally accepted accounting principles.
   d. It requires the user to know a required rate of return.

LO 3 4. Which of the following is *not* a true statement about the internal rate of return method?
   a. It uses time value of money concepts.
   b. It equates the present value of future cash flows to the investment outlay.
   c. It yields a rate of return that can be compared to a required rate.
   d. It will lead to the same investment decisions as the accounting rate of return.

LO 3 5. True or False? When the internal rate of return exceeds the required rate of return the investment should be rejected.

LO 3 6. Depreciation expense is only relevant to a capital budgeting decision because of _____.

LO 3 7. Which of the following is true about the cost of capital?
   a. It is the weighted average of the costs of debt and equity financing.
   b. It is the interest rate of borrowing an additional $1 of debt.
   c. It is easy to estimate.
   d. It is important to know when calculating the payback of an investment.

LO 4 8. True or False? If inflation is ignored in net present value analysis, many worthwhile investment opportunities may be rejected.

LO 5 9. Which of the following is *not* a limitation of the payback period method?
   a. It is difficult to calculate.
   b. It does not take into account the total stream of cash flows related to an investment.
   c. It does not consider the time value of money.
   d. It ignores the timing of cash flows.

LO 5 10. State the formula for calculating the accounting rate of return.

SOLUTIONS TO SELF-QUIZ

1. b   2. how much cash is received or paid, when the cash is received (paid)   3. c   4. d   5. false   6. taxes   7. a   8. true

9. a   10. ARR = average net income ÷ average investment

QUESTIONS

Q28-1   What is a capital expenditure?

Q28-2   Why it is important to include time value of money concepts when making capital budgeting decisions?

Q28-3   What are the two approaches for evaluating investments that take into account the time value of money?

Q28-4   How do net present value and internal rate of return differ in their approach to evaluating investment alternatives?

Q28-5   Why do managers often take a judgmental approach to determine the required rate of return rather than using the cost of capital?

Q28-6   How are cash flows affected as a result of the tax consequences of depreciation?

Q28-7   What are the advantages of evaluating projects using the net present value and internal rate of return methods instead of the payback and accounting rate of return methods?

Q28-8   Why do managers often concentrate on the short run profitability of investments rather than their net present values?

Q28-9   (Appendix) How is the internal rate of return (IRR) determined if there are uneven cash flows?

EXERCISES

LO 2   **E28-1**   **Determine Present Values**   Suppose you face the prospect of receiving $200 per year for the next 5 years plus an extra $500 payment at the end of 5 years. Determine how much this prospect is worth today if the required rate of return is 10%.

LO 2   **E28-2**   **Determine Present Values**   Juanita Martinez is ready to retire and she has a choice of three pension plans. Plan A provides for the immediate cash payment of $100,000. Plan B provides for the payment of $10,000 per year for ten years and the payment of $100,000 at the end of year 10. Plan C will pay $20,000 per year for 10 years. Juanita Martinez desires a rate of return of 8%. Determine the present value of each plan and select the best one.

LO 2   **E28-3**   **Calculate the Net Present Value**   An investment that costs $10,000 will return $4,000 per year for 4 years. Determine the net present value of the investment if the required rate of return is 12%. Ignore income taxes. Should the investment be undertaken?

LO 2   **E28-4**   **Calculate the Net Present Value**   Fancy Florist is considering replacing an old refrigeration unit with a larger unit to store flowers. Because the new refrigeration unit has a larger capacity, Fancy estimates that they can sell another $6,000 of flowers a year that cost $3,500. In addition, the new unit is energy efficient and should save $950 in electricity each year. It will cost an extra $150 per month for maintenance. The new refrigeration unit costs $20,000 and has an expected life of 10 years. The old unit is fully depreciated and can be sold for an amount equal to disposal cost. At the end of 10 years, the new unit has an expected residual value of $5,000. Determine the net present value of the investment if the required rate of return is 14%. Should the investment be undertaken? Ignore income taxes.

LO 2   **E28-5**   **Choosing Among Alternative Investments**   Walker Shoe Corporation is considering investing in one of two heeling machines that attach heels to shoes. Machine A costs $50,000 and is expected to save the company $15,000 for six years. Machine B costs $75,000 and is expected to save the company $20,000 for six years. Determine the net present value for each machine and which machine should be purchased if the required rate of return is 10%. Ignore income taxes.

LO 3   **E28-6**   **Calculate the Internal Rate of Return**   An investment that costs $79,100 will return $14,000 per year for 10 years. Determine the internal rate of return of the investment and whether or not to make the investment if the required rate of return is 18%. Ignore income taxes.

LO 4   **E28-7**   **Calculate the Net Present Value with Taxes**   Smokey Salmon Corporation is contemplating the purchase of a new smoker. The smoker will cost $21,000 but will create additional revenue of $15,500 per year for 7 years. Additional costs other than depreciation will equal $8,000 per year. The smoker has an expected life of 7 years at which time it will have no residual value. Smokey uses the straight-line method of depreciation for tax purposes. Determine the net present value of the investment if the required rate of return is 12% and the tax rate is 40%.

LO 5   **E28-8**   **Calculate the Payback Period**   The Lower Valley Wheat Cooperative is considering the construction of a new silo. It will cost $41,000 to construct the silo. Determine the payback period if the expected cash inflows are $5,000 per year.

LO 5   **E28-9**   **Calculate the Accounting Rate of Return**   The Deaton Company is considering the purchase of a new service vehicle for $20,000. It is expected that this vehicle will increase net income by $7,000 a year for 5 years. The vehicle will be depreciated over a five-year period using straight-line depreciation with no residual value. Determine the accounting rate of return of the new service vehicle.

PROBLEM SET A

LO 2,5   **P28-1A**   **Net Present Value, Payback, and Accounting Rate of Return with Even Cash Flows**   Walter Leland, the owner of Quality Motors, is considering the addition of a paint and body shop to his automobile dealership. The construction of the building and the purchase of the necessary equipment is estimated to cost $678,000 and will be depreciated over 10 years using the straight-line method. The building and equipment have zero estimated residual value at the end of 10 years. Leland's required rate of return for this project is 10%. The shop is expected to generate $195,000 in revenues for 10 years. Ignore income taxes. The annual cost of operating the paint and body shop is as follows:

Item	Cash Flow
Materials	$(18,000)
Labor	(53,000)
Direct overhead	(17,000)
Miscellaneous	(4,500)

REQUIRED:

a. Determine the net present value of investing in the paint and body shop.
b. Determine if the project should be undertaken.
c. Calculate the payback period of the investment.
d. Calculate the accounting rate of return.

LO 2   **P28-2A**   **Choosing Among Alternative Investments With Uneven Cash Flows**   Clean-M-Up Corporation, a chain of dry cleaning stores, has the opportunity to invest in one of two new dry-cleaning machines. Machine A has a 4-year expected life and a cost of $43,000. It will cost an additional $4,500 to have the machine delivered and installed and the expected residual value at the end of 4 years is $3,200. Machine B has a 4-year expected life and a cost of $73,000. It will cost an additional $5,000 to have the machine delivered and installed and the expected residual value at the end of 4 years is $5,200. Clean-M-Up has a required rate of return of 14%. Ignore income taxes. Additional cash flows related to the machines are as follows:

Machine A

Item	Year 1	Year 2	Year 3	Year 4
Labor saving	$21,000	$21,000	$21,000	$21,000
Power saving	1,300	1,300	1,300	1,300
Chemical saving	2,900	2,900	2,900	2,900
Maintenance	(1,000)	(1,300)	(1,600)	(2,500)
Miscellaneous	(2,200)	(2,700)	(3,200)	(3,700)

Machine B

Item	Year 1	Year 2	Year 3	Year 4
Labor saving	$29,000	$29,000	$29,000	$29,000
Power saving	1,900	1,900	1,900	1,900
Chemical saving	3,200	3,200	3,200	3,200
Maintenance	(1,200)	(1,400)	(1,600)	(2,700)
Miscellaneous	(2,300)	(2,800)	(3,500)	(3,800)

REQUIRED:

a. Determine the net present value of investing in machine A.
b. Determine the net present value of investing in machine B.
c. Determine which machine should be purchased (if any).

LO 2,4   **P28-3A**   **Net Present Value and Tax Effects**   On Time Charters plans to expand operations by acquiring another aircraft. They have a bid of $828,000 from an airplane manufacturer to provide a 12-passenger commuter aircraft. The airplane has an expected life of 8 years with an expected residual value for financial reporting and tax purposes of $62,000. On Time has a tax rate of 40% and uses straight-line depreciation for tax purposes. The required rate of return is 12%. The following annual cash flows relate to the investment in the new aircraft.

Item	Cash Flow
Passenger revenues	$263,000
Labor cost	(54,000)
Fuel cost	(15,800)
Maintenance cost	(26,700)
Miscellaneous cost	(3,500)

REQUIRED:

a. Determine the net present value of investing in the airplane if taxes are ignored.
b. Determine the net present value of investing in the airplane considering taxes.

LO 2,4,5   **P28-4A**   **Comprehensive Capital Budgeting Problem**   Clayton Corporation is considering producing a new product, Autodial. Marketing data indicate that the demand for Autodial will be 35,000 units per year for five years. The product will be produced in a section of an existing factory that is currently not in use. To produce Autodial, Clayton must buy a machine that costs $300,000. The machine has an expected life of 4 years and will have an ending residual value of $20,000. Clayton will depreciate the machine over 4 years using the straight-line method for both tax and financial reporting purposes. Clayton has a tax rate of 30%. It is anticipated that no additional fixed costs will be incurred as a result of producing and marketing Autodial, other than $129,500 annually for advertising the new product. Autodial is expected to sell for $35 per unit and direct production costs (including depreciation of the new machine) are $27 per unit. The required rate of return is 14%.

REQUIRED:

a. Compute the net present value.
b. Compute the payback period.
c. Compute the accounting rate of return.

LO 2,7 | **P28-5A**   **Internal Rate of Return with Uneven Cash Flows (Appendix)**   Luigi's Pizza Parlor is considering the purchase of another pizza oven. The oven will cost $39,503 including installation and is expected to last 5 years. The oven will be depreciated using the straight-line method. The cash flows associated with the extra oven are as follows:

Item	Year 1	Year 2	Year 3	Year 4	Year 5
Revenue	$15,000	$16,000	$18,000	$19,000	$20,000
Power	(1,200)	(1,200)	(1,300)	(1,300)	(1,400)
Labor	(2,200)	(2,200)	(2,400)	(2,400)	(2,600)
Ingredients	(2,100)	(2,100)	(2,200)	(2,200)	(2,200)
Residual value					4,100

REQUIRED:

a. Calculate the internal rate of return for the pizza oven. (Hint: Try a range of rates between 12% and 18%.)
b. Determine if Luigi's should invest in the pizza oven if the required rate of return is 15%.

PROBLEM SET B

LO 2,5 | **P28-1B**   **Net Present Value, Payback, and Accounting Rate of Return with Even Cash Flows**   Dana Walentsky, the owner of Ritzy Yachts, is considering the addition of a dry dock facility to his yacht dealership. The construction of the building and the purchase of the necessary equipment is estimated to cost $585,000 and will be depreciated over 15 years using the straight-line method. The dry dock and equipment have zero estimated residual values at the end of 15 years. Walentsky's required rate of return for this project is 12%. The dry dock is expected to generate $195,000 in revenues for 15 years. Ignore income taxes. The annual cost of operating the dry dock is as follows:

Item	Cash Flow
Materials	$(26,000)
Labor	(47,000)
Direct overhead	(13,500)
Miscellaneous	(5,500)

REQUIRED:

a. Determine the net present value of investing in the dry dock.
b. Determine if the project should be undertaken.
c. Calculate the payback period of the investment.
d. Calculate the accounting rate of return.

LO 2 | **P28-2B**   **Choosing Among Alternative Investments With Uneven Cash Flows**   Kar Klean Corporation, a chain of automated car washes, has the opportunity to invest in one of two new machines. Machine A has a 4-year expected life and a cost of $153,000. It will cost an additional $6,500 to have the machine delivered and installed and the expected residual value at the end of 4 years is $12,000. Machine B has a 4-year expected life and a cost of $161,000. It will cost an additional $7,000 to have the machine delivered and installed and the expected residual value at the end of 4 years is $15,000. Kar Klean has a required rate of return of 12%. Ignore income taxes. Additional cash flows related to the machine are as follows:

Machine A

Item	Year 1	Year 2	Year 3	Year 4
Labor saving	$51,000	$52,000	$54,000	$55,000
Power saving	3,300	3,300	3,400	3,400
Detergent saving	4,100	4,200	4,200	4,400
Maintenance	(4,000)	(4,300)	(5,600)	(5,500)
Miscellaneous	(5,200)	(5,700)	(4,200)	(5,700)

Machine B

Item	Year 1	Year 2	Year 3	Year 4
Labor saving	$54,000	$55,000	$56,000	$58,000
Power saving	3,800	3,800	3,900	3,900
Detergent saving	4,200	4,300	4,300	4,500
Maintenance	(4,400)	(4,700)	(6,000)	(5,900)
Miscellaneous	(5,100)	(5,800)	(4,100)	(5,800)

REQUIRED:

a. Determine the net present value of investing in machine A.
b. Determine the net present value of investing in machine B.
c. Determine which machine should be purchased (if any).

LO 2,4

P28-3B   Net Present Value and Tax Effects   Airport Shuffle plans to expand operations by acquiring another bus. They have a bid of $157,000 from a bus manufacturer to provide an 80-passenger bus. The bus has an expected life of 6 years with an expected residual value for financial reporting and tax purposes of $19,000. Airport Shuffle has a tax rate of 40% and uses straight-line depreciation for tax purposes. The required rate of return is 10%. The following annual cash flows relate to the investment in the new bus.

Item	Cash Flow
Passenger revenues	$ 78,000
Labor cost	(21,000)
Fuel cost	(6,300)
Maintenance cost	(5,900)
Miscellaneous cost	(1,300)

REQUIRED:

a. Determine the net present value of investing in the bus if taxes are ignored.
b. Determine the net present value of investing in the bus considering taxes.

LO 2,4,5

P28-4B   Comprehensive Capital Budgeting Problem   Denton Corporation is considering producing a new product, Electroduck Call. Marketing data indicate that the demand for Electroduck Call will be 15,000 units per year for six years. The product will be produced in a section of an existing factory that is currently not in use. To produce Electroduck Call, Denton must buy a machine that costs $190,000. The machine has an expected life of 6 years and will have an ending residual value of $10,000. Denton will depreciate the machine over 6 years using the straight-line method for both tax and financial reporting purposes. Denton has a tax rate of 40%. It is anticipated that no additional fixed costs will be incurred as a result of producing and marketing Electroduck Call, other than $48,500 annually for advertising the new product. Electroduck Call is expected to sell for $30 per unit and the direct production costs (including depreciation of the new machine) are $22 per unit. Denton's required rate of return is 12%.

REQUIRED:

a. Compute the net present value.
b. Compute the payback period.
c. Compute the accounting rate of return.

LO 2,7

P28-5B **Internal Rate of Return with Uneven Cash Flows (Appendix)** Athena's Greek Restaurant is considering the addition of another dining room. The dining room will cost $55,837 and is expected to last 5 years, which is when the restaurant's lease expires. The addition will be depreciated using the straight-line method. The cash flows associated with the addition are as follows:

Item	Year 1	Year 2	Year 3	Year 4	Year 5
Revenue	$23,000	$25,000	$28,000	$29,000	$30,000
Power	(1,400)	(1,400)	(1,600)	(1,700)	(1,900)
Labor	(3,100)	(3,100)	(3,400)	(3,600)	(3,600)
Food	(5,200)	(5,700)	(6,100)	(6,200)	(6,400)
Residual value					3,100

REQUIRED:

a. Calculate the internal rate of return for the dining room. (Hint: Try a range of rates between 12% and 18%.)
b. Determine if Athena's should invest in the dining room if the required rate of return is 15%.

CRITICAL THINKING AND COMMUNICATING

C28-1 Amanda Li is the manager of the Communications Division of United Conglomerate Corporation. Her bonuses and promotions are based on accounting income. Amanda was trying to decide between two alternative capital investments. The following information was tabulated by Amanda's assistant.

	Project A	Project B
Net present value	$107,000	$32,000
Internal rate of return	19%	11%
Expected life	10 years	10 years
Payback	4 years	1.5 years

Amanda decided to choose Project B.

REQUIRED:

a. Why did Amanda select Project B?
b. Which project should Amanda have selected and why?
c. How could United Conglomerate encourage Amanda to select Project A?

C28-2 Grinders International manufactures a large variety of industrial grinders. Grinders has always used payback and accounting rate of return to evaluate their capital investments. You have just been promoted to corporate controller and you believe that net present value should be used as the primary method to evaluate capital projects.

REQUIRED:

Write a memo to Stan Kawalski, the president of Grinders International, explaining why the net present value method should be used.

CHAPTER 29

1134

Control of Decentralized Organizations

Brian Adams, president and chief operating officer, rose to address the board of directors of Action Industries. "As you all know," he began, "last year we split the company into two divisions—the Tool Division and the Auto Parts Division. We gave Steve Carson, the vice president of Tools, and Ann Harris, the vice president of Auto, a lot of responsibility and the authority to run these operations independently. And, I think our strategy has paid off. Steve and Ann have been able to respond quickly to market opportunities, and the result is a 25 percent increase in corporate income."

Brian then compared the performance of the two divisions using the following financial information:

Action Industries
Comparison of Divisions

	Tool Division	Auto Parts Division	Corporate
Total assets as of 12/31/X0	$25,000,000	$10,000,000	$35,000,000
Profit in 19X0	3,000,000	1,500,000	4,500,000
Total assets as of 12/31/X1	30,000,000	11,000,000	41,000,000
Profit in 19X1	3,855,000	1,760,000	5,615,000
Increase in income	855,000	260,000	1,115,000
Percentage increase	29%	17%	25%

"In summary," Brian concluded, "the Tool Division had the largest income in 19X1 ($3,855,000 vs. only $1,760,000 for the Auto Parts Division). Further, the Tool Division had increased income by 29%, while the Auto Parts Division had an increase of 17%. In the coming year, we will be expanding and investing in equipment for both operations.

I suggest, however, that since the Tool Division is more profitable, we should focus our attention on that operation and budget more funds for its expansion."

At this point, Alister Hurd, the founder and chairman of the board of Action Industries, spoke up. "Brian, I agree we made a good decision when we decentralized and formed the two divisions. However, I don't think that in comparing the two operations we should focus solely on income or the increase in income. After all, the Tool Division is much larger than the Auto Parts Division. We're comparing apples to oranges if we don't make some sort of size adjustment."

"You've got a good point there," Brian responded. He turned to Peter Dunn, the controller of the company. "Pete, any suggestions on how we can compare the two divisions?" Pete assured Brian and the rest of the board that, after the lunch break, he would have just the information they were needing.

As firms increase in size and complexity, business segments or subunits are organized. The managers of these segments must be granted decision-making authority for the firm to function effectively. Firms that grant substantial decision-making authority to the managers of segments are referred to as **decentralized organizations**. Most firms are neither one hundred percent centralized nor one hundred percent decentralized. Decentralization is a matter of degree. To the extent that more decision-making authority is delegated to subunit managers, a firm is more decentralized. Action Industries is a decentralized organization in that substantial decision-making authority has been given to Steve and Ann, the managers of the two divisions. In this chapter, we examine the way subunits in a decentralized organization may be formed. We also illustrate how a company can use accounting information to control the behavior of subunit managers. The goal is to ensure that subunit managers make decisions that are in the best interest of the entire firm. We also discuss how to compare the profitability of two divisions. This discussion addresses the specific problem Action Industries faces.

LEARNING OBJECTIVES

1. List and explain the advantages and disadvantages of decentralization.
2. Identify cost centers, profit centers, and investment centers.
3. Calculate and interpret return on investment (ROI).
4. Calculate and interpret residual income (RI).
5. Discuss the use of market price, variable costs, full cost plus profit, and negotiation in setting transfer prices.
6. Explain how companies can use market-based transfer prices to treat service centers as profit centers.

LO 1

List and explain the advantages and disadvantages of decentralization.

WHY FIRMS DECENTRALIZE

Firms decentralize for a number of reasons. A primary reason is that subunit managers have *better information* than top management and these managers can *respond more quickly* to changing circumstances. Consider an electronics firm that has two primary divisions: a Copier Division and a Camera Division. Division managers report to top management responsible for both divisions. As shown in Illustration 29-1, each division operates in a unique environment.

ILLUSTRATION 29-1 Firm and Subunit Environments

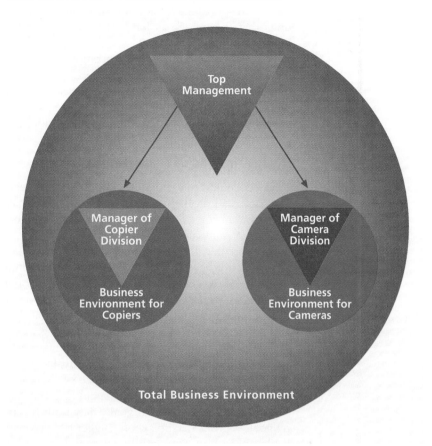

Competition, customer needs, and the supply of workers and raw materials are different for each of these product lines. Suppose a new personal copier is to be introduced in the coming year, and managers must make a pricing decision. Who has better information as to what will be an appropriate price to charge—the manager of the Copier Division or top management? Because of his or her daily involvement with the market for copiers, the manager of the Copier Division probably has a better understanding of how the market will react to a particular price. If this is the case, then the divisional manager should make the pricing decision which will further enhance the decentralization of the electronics firm.

Suppose the manager of the Camera Division learns that a supplier of camera lenses is facing excess capacity and is willing to supply the division with lenses at a bargain price. In a decentralized organization, the manager can react quickly to this opportunity and increase the profitability of both the division and the firm. However, if the firm is more centralized, the manager of the division may have to present the facts to top management who will then make the decision as to whether the lenses should be purchased. This is a more time-consuming process, and by the time top management makes a decision the supplier may no longer have excess capacity. Worse, other camera companies may have taken advantage of the situation and have gained a competitive edge.

Some firms decentralize because they believe managers who are given significant decision-making authority are *more motivated* and work harder than do managers in centralized organizations. If managers are given broad decision-making responsibility, they are thought to identify so strongly with their sub-units that they work as hard as they would work if they actually owned the business.

Finally, decentralized organizations provide excellent *training* for future top-level executives. Managers in decentralized organizations are accustomed to making important decisions and taking responsibility for their actions. Thus, when high-level positions in the firm need to be filled, the firm has a ready supply of managers with the required decision-making experience.

Disadvantages of Decentralization

While decentralization has several beneficial features, it may create problems. One potential problem is that decentralization may result in a costly *duplication of activities*. For example, two subunit managers may each decide to develop their own purchasing department when one purchasing department would be more economical. Or, each major subunit may have a separate sales force when a single, coordinated sales force would be more effective.

A second problem with a decentralized organization is that managers of subunits may take actions to achieve their own goals, which may be incompatible with the goals of the company as a whole. This problem is referred to as a *lack of goal congruence*. An example of a goal congruence problem is "empire building." Some managers derive substantial satisfaction from running a large subunit (their empires). Perhaps this satisfaction comes from impressing friends and business associates with the size of their staff and the size of the facilities under their control. However, maximizing the size of the subunits, which satisfies the managers' personal goals, may be incompatible with the overall company goal of profit maximization. Bigger operations are not necessarily more profitable operations. To control goal congruence problems in decentralized organizations, companies evaluate the performance of subunits. As we will see later in this chapter, the evaluation process should encourage managers of subunits to take actions that are in the interest of the company as a whole. That is, performance evaluation should encourage managers to behave as if their own personal goals were congruent with the goals of the company as a whole.

HISTORICAL PERSPECTIVES

DECENTRALIZATION IN CORPORATE AMERICA

Long before the rest of Corporate America made "empowerment" a management buzzword, Johnson and Johnson was practicing it. As early as the 1930s, longtime Chairman Robert Wood Johnson pushed the idea of decentralization. Believing that smaller, self-governing units were more manageable, quicker to react to their markets, and more accountable, the son of a J&J co-founder encouraged managers to operate independently. The J&J approach "provides a sense of ownership and responsibility for a business that you simply cannot get any other way," says chief Executive Ralph S. Larsen.

Source: Joseph Weber, "A Big Company That Works," Business Week, (May 4, 1992) p. 124.

A summary of the advantages and disadvantages of decentralization is presented in Illustration 29-2.

ILLUSTRATION 29-2 Summary of Advantages and Disadvantages of Decentralization

Advantages of Decentralization
1. Better information leading to superior decisions.
2. Faster response to changing circumstances.
3. Increased motivation of managers.
4. Excellent training for future top-level executives.

Disadvantages of Decentralization
1. Costly duplication of activities.
2. Lack of goal congruence.

RESPONSIBILITY ACCOUNTING AND DECENTRALIZATION

The discussion of cost allocation in an earlier chapter introduced the topic of *responsibility accounting*, a technique that holds managers responsible for costs and revenues that they can control. This idea should play a prominent role in the design of accounting systems used to evaluate the performance of managers in a decentralized organization. To implement responsibility accounting in a decentralized organization, management must first trace costs and revenues to the organizational level where they can be controlled.

For example, consider the information presented for the Jones Tool Co. in Illustration 29-3. Jones Tool Co. produces a variety of small tools in two plants: an Eastern plant and a Western plant. Each plant has a plant manager who is responsible for operations. Currently, two production shifts are run daily and individuals with the title of *production supervisor* supervise the work. A vice president of manufacturing is responsible for production in both the Eastern and Western plants. The illustration indicates, in a simplified setting, how implementation of responsibility accounting would suggest that costs be accumulated for assessing the performance of the production supervisors, the plant managers, and the vice president of manufacturing. Only labor costs and material costs are traced to the individual shift supervisors. This follows because at Jones Tool Co., the production supervisors make numerous decisions that affect the amount of labor and material costs incurred. However, plant overhead costs are not traced to the supervisors because they are not involved in decisions that affect the amount of overhead incurred at each plant. Overhead costs, however, are traced to the individual plant managers who can control overhead costs. The manager of the Eastern plant is responsible for $500,000 of labor costs ($300,000 from the first shift and $200,000 from the second shift), $400,000 of material costs ($250,000 from the first shift and $150,000 from the second shift), and $600,000 of overhead costs incurred in the Eastern plant.

The vice president of manufacturing is responsible for all costs incurred at both the Eastern and Western plants. Therefore, all production costs are traced to the vice president. For example, the overhead costs traced to the vice president are $1,400,000, which include $600,000 from the Eastern plant and $800,000 from the Western plant.

ILLUSTRATION 29-3 Tracing Costs to the Organizational Level Where They Can Be Controlled

Eastern Plant			Western Plant		
Controllable by supervisor on Shift 1 at Eastern plant	Labor cost	$ 300,000	Labor cost	$ 400,000	**Controllable by supervisor on Shift 1 at Western plant**
	Material cost	250,000	Material cost	350,000	
	Total	$ 550,000	Total	$ 750,000	
Controllable by supervisor on Shift 2 at Eastern plant	Labor cost	$ 200,000	Labor cost	$ 300,000	**Controllable by supervisor on Shift 2 at Western plant**
	Material cost	150,000	Material cost	250,000	
	Total	$ 350,000	Total	$ 550,000	
Controllable by Eastern plant manager	Labor cost	$ 500,000	Labor cost	$ 700,000	**Controllable by Western plant manager**
	Material cost	400,000	Material cost	600,000	
	Overhead	600,000	Overhead	800,000	
	Total	$1,500,000	Total	$2,100,000	
Controllable by vice president of manufacturing			Labor cost	$1,200,000	
			Material cost	1,000,000	
			Overhead	1,400,000	
			Total	$3,600,000	

Responsibility accounting also implies that if one segment of a business causes another segment to incur costs, the costs should be assigned to the operation that causes them to be incurred. For example, suppose the consumer credit department of a bank engages in promotional activities that result in the bank's central printing department incurring $10,000 of costs to print a promotional brochure. Since the manager of consumer credit made the decision that caused the incurrence of the cost, responsibility accounting suggests that the $10,000 cost be traced to his or her department.

LO 2
Identify cost center, profit centers, and investment centers.

COST CENTERS, PROFIT CENTERS, AND INVESTMENT CENTERS

Business segments are identifiable collections of related resources and activities.[1] A segment may be a department, a subsidiary, or a division. Business segments are sometimes referred to as **responsibility centers**, which are organizational units responsible for the generation of revenue or for the incurrence of costs. Responsibility centers are typically classified as either cost centers, profit centers, or investment centers.

Cost Centers

A **cost center**, a type of business segment, has responsibility for controlling costs, not for generating revenue. Most service departments (e.g., machine maintenance, janitorial services, and computer services) would be classified properly as cost centers. The managers of these departments are responsible for

[1]"Statement on Management Accounting Number 2," *Management Accounting Terminology* (National Association of Accountants, June, 1983).

making sure that their services are provided at a reasonable cost to the company, but they typically do not have responsibility for generating firm revenue. Production departments also may be classified as cost centers. As an example, consider a department that assembles electronic components into micro- computers. The manager of the assembly department certainly is responsible for making sure that the computers are assembled at the lowest cost consistent with acceptable quality standards. However, the manager probably has little input into how the computers will be marketed and what price will be charged for them. Because the manager has little direct control over the quantity sold or the price charged, the assembly department would be considered a cost center.

A common approach to controlling cost centers is to compare their actual costs to standard or budgeted costs. If variances from standard are significant, management should investigate the cost center's activities to determine if costs are out of control or, alternatively, if cost standards need to be revised.

Profit Centers

A **profit center**, another type of business segment, has responsibility for generating revenue as well as for controlling costs. Consider our earlier example of the electronics firm that has a Copier Division and a Camera Division. Each of these divisions could be classified as profit centers because each has responsibility for generating revenue through sales and controlling costs associated with producing and marketing its products.

Because both revenue and costs (the two elements that determine income) are under the control of the profit center manager, the performance of the profit center can be evaluated in terms of profitability. Evaluation in terms of profitability is extremely useful because it motivates managers to focus their attention on ways of maximizing profit center profitability.

Companies use a variety of methods to evaluate the profitability of profit centers. Income earned in the current year may be compared to an income target or budget. Or, income earned may be compared to income earned in the prior year. Some firms evaluate profit centers using **relative performance evaluation**, which involves evaluating the profitability of each profit center relative to the profitability of other, similar profit centers. For example, the Chicken King Company operates ten fast-food restaurants in a major Midwestern city. Each outlet (restaurant) is treated as a profit center because it is responsible for generating revenue (sales of chicken sandwiches, sodas, ice cream, etc.) and for controlling costs (food costs, labor, heat and light, etc.). If each outlet is *reasonably* similar in terms of size, appearance, and menu, comparing the income earned by each outlet to the income earned by other outlets may be a useful means of assessing the effectiveness of outlet managers.

Investment Centers

An **investment center**, still another type of business segment, has responsibility for generating revenue, controlling costs, and investing in assets. Because it has responsibility for revenue, costs, and investment, an investment center has responsibility for earning income consistent with the amount of assets invested in the segment. Most divisions of a company can be treated as either profit centers or investment centers. If the division manager can significantly influence decisions affecting investment in divisional assets, the division should be considered an investment center. If the division manager cannot influence investment decisions, the division should be considered a profit center. Subsidiaries generally are treated as investment centers.

Investment center managers generally play a major role in determining the level of inventory, the level of accounts receivable, and the investment in equipment and other assets the investment center holds. Thus, it seems reasonable to hold them responsible for earning a return on these assets. However, while investment center managers play a major role, they generally are not given complete autonomy in making investments in assets. Typically, central management has final approval of all major investments. Guidelines may be set such that investment center managers must have approval for all investments greater than some specified dollar amount (e.g., investments greater than $200,000) but may make their own decisions for smaller amounts (e.g., investments less than or equal to $200,000) unless the total exceeds a total budget amount.

EVALUATING INVESTMENT CENTERS

Approaches to evaluating investment centers are discussed in the following sections. Two approaches are presented: return on investment and residual income.

LO 3

Calculate and interpret return on investment (ROI)

Return on Investment

One of the primary tools for evaluating the performance of investment centers is **return on investment (ROI)**. ROI is calculated as the ratio of investment center operating income to investment in assets. **Operating income** is usually defined as income from continuing operations before interest and taxes.[2]

$$ROI = \frac{Operating\ Income}{Total\ Assets}$$

Thus, if investment center operating income is $200,000 and total assets of the investment center (the investment) are $2,000,000, ROI would be 10%.[3] DuPont (known then as The Du Point Powder Company) developed the idea of evaluating performance using ROI in the early part of the twentieth century. It has now gained widespread acceptance.[4]

ROI has a distinct advantage over income as a measure of performance. It focuses managers' attention not only on income (the numerator of ROI), but also on investment (the denominator of ROI). Suppose two business units earn the same income—$100,000. A performance measure based solely on income would rate the two units as equally successful. However, suppose the first business unit required an investment in assets of $1,000,000, while the second busi-

[2]This measure of income is useful because it facilitates comparisons of investment centers without the added complication of considering their tax rates and the effect of financing the investment center with debt (resulting in interest expense) as opposed to equity.

[3]Exactly how ROI is calculated varies from company to company. Some use total assets to measure investment as suggested above. Others use net assets (i.e., total assets minus total liabilities) or operating assets. The amount of investment is sometimes calculated as the average investment in assets, and sometimes it is taken to be the end of period value. Some companies use net income of the investment center rather than operating income. These various alternative measures cannot be explained in any depth in an introductory text. Cost accounting textbooks can be consulted for a more complete treatment.

[4]See Chapter 4, H. Thomas Johnson and Robert S. Kaplan, *Relevance Lost: The Rise and Fall of Management Accounting* (Harvard Business School Press, 1987.)

ness unit required only $500,000. The second unit has performed much better than the first because it required only half the investment to earn the same level of income. This allows the company to invest the funds not required by the second unit in another project and to earn additional income. Note that, unlike income, ROI does not rate the two units as equally successful. The first unit has an ROI of only 10%, while the second unit has a much higher ROI of 20%.

Some companies break ROI down into two components: margin and turnover.

$$\underbrace{\frac{\text{Operating Income}}{\text{Revenue}}}_{\textit{Margin}} \times \underbrace{\frac{\text{Revenue}}{\text{Total Assets}}}_{\textit{Turnover}} = \frac{\text{Operating Income}}{\text{Total Assets}} = \text{ROI}$$

Margin is the ratio of operating income to revenue, while *turnover* is the ratio of revenue to total assets. Breaking ROI into these components clearly indicates to managers that they can improve ROI in two ways. Managers can take actions to improve the income earned on each dollar of sales (i.e., increase the margin), or they can take actions to generate more sales for each dollar of total assets (i.e., increase turnover).

Evaluating Investment Centers and Managers with ROI

We must be careful to distinguish between using ROI in decisions involving expanding or contracting investment centers and using ROI to evaluate the performance of investment center managers. Suppose a company has three investment centers with the following ROIs:

Investment Center 1:	7%
Investment Center 2:	15%
Investment Center 3:	20%

Based on these ROIs, it appears that if the company has limited dollars to spend on assets for investment centers, it would be wiser to invest those dollars in Investment Center 3. After all, the ROI indicates that the center earns $.20 of income for every dollar invested. On the other hand, it may be a good idea to abandon Investment Center 1 since it earns only $.07 for every dollar invested. While the ROI of Investment Center 1 may indicate that additional investment is not wise, the relatively low ROI does not necessarily imply that the manager of Investment Center 1 has performed poorly. Suppose Investment Center 1 has historically had an ROI of only 5%. Under a new manager, the ROI has risen to 7%. Should the company give this manager an unfavorable evaluation simply because the investment center has the lowest ROI? The answer is no. While we may believe that a 7% ROI is not high enough to warrant additional investment, the manager has done well in improving the performance of the investment center.

Problems with Using ROI

A major problem with ROI is that investment in assets is typically measured using historical costs. Recall that under historical cost, the carrying amount (also called *book value*) of total assets is affected by depreciation of plant and equipment. As assets become fully depreciated, the measure of investment becomes very low and ROI becomes quite large. This makes comparison of investment centers using ROI quite difficult.

Consider two investment centers that are alike in all respects, except Investment Center 1 was started five years ago and its investment in fixed assets is substantially depreciated. Investment Center 2 was started in the current year. Both earn exactly the same level of income, which is $100,000. As indicated in Illustration 29-4, the ROI of Investment Center 1 is 29.41%, while the ROI of Investment Center 2 is 23.81%. The difference of 5.6% is due to the fact that the fixed assets of Investment Center 1 are substantially depreciated. Thus, the investment base of Investment Center 1 is much lower than the investment base of Investment Center 2. However, suppose additional funds became available to invest in either of the two business segments. Would Investment Center 1 earn a higher return than Investment Center 2 on the incremental investment? While Investment Center 1 has the highest ROI, the two business segments are identical in all respects except for the age of their equipment. Thus, we would probably be indifferent as to where the funds were invested since we would expect both segments to generate the same income with the funds. The point is that using ROI to rank the attractiveness of investment centers can be difficult if the remaining useful lives of the depreciable assets are very different.

ILLUSTRATION 29-4 Comparison of Investment Centers Affected by Carrying Value of Property and Equipment

	Investment Center 1		Investment Center 2	
Income		$100,000		$100,000
Investment:				
Cash		$ 20,000		$ 20,000
Accounts receivable		70,000		70,000
Inventory		150,000		150,000
Plant and equipment:				
Cost	$200,000		$200,000	
Less: Accumulated depreciation	100,000		20,000	
Carrying amount of equipment		100,000		180,000
Total investment		$340,000		$420,000
Return on investment (ROI)		29.41%		23.81%

Some critics of ROI have suggested that undue emphasis on ROI may lead managers to delay the purchase of modern equipment needed to stay competitive. Old equipment has a low carrying value because it is substantially depreciated. Thus, the denominator of ROI (total assets) is low and ROI is high. If new equipment is purchased, it may significantly raise the level of investment and reduce ROI. If managers are evaluated in terms of ROI, they may fear that the decline in ROI will lead to low ratings of their job performance. In situations like this, managers may fail to purchase equipment that is needed for the company's long-run success.

In an earlier chapter, we recommended that investment alternatives should be evaluated in terms of their net present values. Managers should undertake investment opportunities with positive net present values, while they should reject those with negative net present values. However, if their performance is evaluated using ROI, managers may *not* be motivated to invest in projects with positive net present values. The reason is that, in the short run, projects with positive net present values may have low levels of income and correspondingly low ROIs. If evaluated in terms of ROI, managers will be quite concerned about how ROI will be affected by additional investments. The result is that managers may consider the effect on ROI instead of net present value in evaluating investment alternatives.

A related problem with ROI is that managers of investment centers with high ROIs may be unwilling to invest in assets that will earn a return that is satisfactory to central management if that return is less than the current ROI. As illustrated in the next section, this problem can be minimized through the use of residual income.

Before turning to a discussion of residual income, recall the situation presented at the start of the chapter where Brian Adams, president of Action Industries, was presenting an evaluation of the company's two divisions: the Tool Division and the Auto Parts Division. Brian concluded that since the Tool Division is more profitable, the company should focus attention on that operation and budget more funds for its expansion. Do you agree? As you now know, Brian ignored the relative size of the two divisions, which is taken into account in the calculation of ROI. The ROI of the Tool Division is only 12.85%, but the ROI of the Auto Division is 16.00%. Thus, it appears that the Auto Division may be able to earn a higher return, and the company should perhaps focus on expanding its operations.

LO 4

Calculate and interpret residual income (RI).

Residual Income

Another measure of investment center performance is residual income. **Residual income (RI)** is the investment center's operating income in excess of that required for the level of its assets. To calculate residual income, management must first specify its required rate of return. The **required rate of return** is the rate of return that a company believes *should be* earned on investments. A formula for calculating residual income is:

$$\text{Residual Income of Investment Center} = \text{Investment Center Operating Income} - \left(\text{Required Rate of Return} \times \text{Investment Center Assets} \right)$$

Consider an investment center that has operating income of $200,000 and total assets of $1,500,000. The company has specified a required rate of return of 10% for investment centers. In this case, residual income is calculated as:

$$\text{Residual Income of Investment Center} = \text{Investment Center Operating Income} - \left(\text{Required Rate of Return} \times \text{Investment Center Assets} \right)$$

$$\$50,000 = \$200,000 - (10\% \times \$1,500,000)$$

While the investment center had operating income of $200,000, the company required the investment center to have a minimum return of 10%. Taking into account the level of investment, the investment center should have operating income of at least $150,000 (10% of investment center assets of $1,500,000). Thus, the investment center has residual income of $50,000.

Using residual income to evaluate investment center managers can minimize one of the problems of ROI. Managers of investment centers with relatively high ROIs may be unwilling to invest in assets that will earn a reasonable return, *if that return is less than the current ROI.* Consider an investment center that has operating income of $125,000 and total assets of $500,000. Thus, its ROI is 25%. Suppose the manager of the investment center considers a project that will require an additional investment in assets of $100,000 and will increase income by $16,000. Further, suppose the company's central management believes a return of 10% is acceptable for the investment center. Should the investment center manager invest in the project? *Yes.* The project will yield a return of 16%, which is greater than the required return of 10%. However, will the manager be willing to make the investment? Perhaps not. The investment will lower the already high ROI of 25% to 23.5% as illustrated below:

	Without New Project	*With New Project*
Operating income	$125,000	$141,000
Investment	$500,000	$600,000
ROI	25%	23.5%

On the other hand, if the investment center manager is evaluated in terms of residual income, the manager will be motivated to invest in the new project. The reason is that the new project has a higher rate of return (16%) than the required rate of return (10%). Whenever this is the case, residual income will be increased. In the example, residual income increases from $75,000 to $81,000.

	Without New Project	*With New Project*
Operating income	$125,000	$141,000
Investment	$500,000	$600,000
Required return	10%	10%
Required income	$50,000	$60,000
Residual income	$75,000	$81,000

While residual income is an intriguing concept, it is not as widely used as ROI. Some top-level managers note that stockholders and financial analysts evaluate companies using ROI. These managers believe that the evaluation of investment center managers should be consistent with the way these parties evaluate the company as a whole. Therefore, they are reluctant to use residual income as a measure of performance. Also, residual income shares some of the limitations of ROI. Like ROI, residual income requires a measure of investment in assets. Historical cost accounting is used to measure the asset base in residual income calculations as well as in calculations of ROI. To the extent that using historical cost information results in misleading ROI calculations, it will also result in misleading residual income calculations.

Perhaps the most significant limitation of residual income is that it cannot be used to compare investment centers. Generally, large investment centers will be able to generate a much higher level of residual income than will small investment centers, even if their return on invested assets is lower. Consider the situation where Investment Center 1 has operating income of $100,000 and total assets of $500,000, while Investment Center 2 has operating income of $360,000 and total assets of $3,000,000. The required rate of return is 10%. As indicated in Illustration 29-5, Investment Center 1 is generating a return on invested assets of 20%, while Investment Center 2 is only generating a return of 12%. However, Investment Center 2 has a higher level of residual income ($60,000 versus $50,000). The reason, of course, is that Investment Center 2 has a much larger asset base than does Investment Center 1. In spite of the fact that Investment Center 2 has the larger residual income, if a company invested additional funds, it would probably earn the highest return in Investment Center 1.

ILLUSTRATION 29-5 Limitations in Using Residual Income to Compare Investment Centers

	Investment Center 1	Investment Center 2
Operating income	$100,000	$360,000
Investment	$500,000	$3,000,000
ROI	20%	12%
Required return	10%	10%
Required income	$50,000	$300,000
Residual income	$50,000	$60,000

LO 5

Discuss the use of market price, variable costs, full cost plus profit, and negotiation in setting transfer prices.

TRANSFER PRICING

In many cases, profit or investment centers "sell" goods or services to other profit or investment centers within the same company. For example, a university print plant may sell printing services to other university departments. As another example, consider a car manufacturing company that has one division producing cars and another division producing a variety of auto and marine batteries. Most likely the Car Division will use auto batteries the Battery Division produces. The price used to value internal transfers of goods is referred to as a **transfer price**. If the Battery Division transfers 10,000 batteries to the car division at a transfer price of $15, the battery division will have revenue of $150,000. However, this revenue is only recognized for internal reporting purposes. For external financial reporting purposes, a company cannot recognize revenue on the sale of goods between responsibility centers within the firm because the revenue has not been realized. For financial reporting purposes, a company realizes revenue when it sells goods or services to customers outside the firm. Sales within a company are not "arm's-length" transactions. Without this restriction, companies could inflate sales and income by engaging in numerous unnecessary internal sales transactions.

Opportunity Costs and Transfer Prices

In practice, companies take a number of different approaches to setting transfer prices. The primary alternatives they practice are transfer prices based on: (1) market price, (2) variable cost, (3) full cost plus profit, and (4) negotiated price. These alternatives are discussed in the following sections. Which transfer price is most appropriate depends on the circumstances. What companies desire is a transfer price that will motivate division managers to make good decisions that maximize the firms' income. The transfer price that motivates the best decisions is the *opportunity cost of producing an item and transferring it inside the company to the buying division.* Recall that an opportunity cost is the foregone benefit or increased cost of selecting one alternative over another. Opportunity costs as transfer prices will be explained below.

Market Price as the Transfer Price

In some cases, the producing division transfers a product internally to a buying division and also sells the same product outside the firm. For example, the Battery Division of the car manufacturing company may sell batteries to various auto supply companies and also "sell" batteries internally to the Car Division. When the company or division sells a product outside the firm, that market price can be used as the transfer price. The external market price is an excellent internal transfer price because it allows both the buying division and the selling division to be treated as stand-alone, independent companies. Generally, both the buying and the selling divisions perceive market prices as fair and reasonable. The buying division cannot complain that the transfer price is too high because it represents the same price it would have to pay in the open market. Likewise, the selling division cannot complain that the transfer price is too low because it is the same price it receives in the open market.

In some cases, the selling division has cost savings from selling its product internally to the buying division rather than selling it externally. This may be due to reduced shipping costs if the buying division is close to the selling division. Advertising costs may also be lower, and production costs may be reduced if the selling division finds it easier to schedule production for internal sales versus production for external sales. If cost savings exist, the selling division should reduce the market price by the cost savings to arrive at the transfer price.

For example, suppose the Processor Division of Tectron Manufacturing Co. produces a micro-processor that it sells to a large number of companies at a market price of $300 each. The Computer Division of Tectron produces personal computers that utilize the micro-processor the Processor Division produces. By selling the micro-processor internally, the Processor Division saves approximately $2 per unit in shipping costs, $.50 per unit in advertising costs, and $1 per unit in manufacturing costs. In this case, a reasonable transfer price would be $296.50 (i.e., $300 market price − $3.50 cost savings).

Market price	$300.00
Savings due to reduced shipping costs	2.00
Savings due to reduced advertising costs	.50
Savings due to reduced manufacturing costs	1.00
Adjusted transfer price	$296.50

Market Price and Opportunity Cost

We have suggested that the best transfer price should be the *opportunity cost of producing an item and transferring it to the buying division.* When a market price exits, it is a good transfer price because it equals the opportunity cost. Suppose the Sweet Company is composed of two divisions. The Syrup Division produces corn syrup, and the Candy Division produces a variety of candies using corn syrup as a sweetener. The Syrup Division can sell corn syrup to outside buyers for $8 per gallon. If the Syrup Division uses the market price as a transfer price for sales of corn syrup to the Candy Division, it will set the transfer price at $8. However, is $8 the opportunity cost of transferring the corn syrup from the Syrup Division to the Candy Division? Since an opportunity cost is the foregone benefit or increased cost of selecting one alternative over another, what benefit is foregone by transferring corn syrup internally? The answer: the $8 that could have been earned by selling the corn syrup externally is foregone when the product is transferred to the Candy Division. Thus, the opportunity cost equals the market price of the transferred product.

Suppose one gallon of syrup is used to produce every 10 pounds of rock candy the Candy Division manufactures. The rock candy sells for $50 for a 10-pound container. Variable costs are as follows:

10-Pound Container	
Variable production cost, excluding corn syrup	$43
Transfer price of corn syrup	8
Total variable cost per container	$51

In this situation, the Candy Division has a negative contribution margin of $1 per 10-pound container and would not be willing to produce rock candy. Suppose the Candy Division argues that if the Syrup Division reduced the transfer price of corn syrup to $5 (the variable cost of producing corn syrup), then its variable costs would only be $48 and rock candy would have a positive contribution margin. Should the Syrup Division lower the transfer price? The answer is *no*. The Syrup Division's income and the Sweet Company's total income would be reduced if the Candy Division was subsidized by a transfer price lower than the market price. If the Candy Division cannot earn a profit by paying a transfer price equal to what it would pay if it had to purchase the syrup in the open market, then Sweet Company should consider eliminating the division.

The effect on the company's contribution margin of lowering the transfer price and transferring the syrup inside to the Candy Division is presented in Illustration 29-6. If the transfer price is the market price of $8, the Candy Division will not find production of rock candy to be profitable. Thus, the Candy Division will not demand syrup, and the Syrup Division will sell all syrup in the marketplace. In this case, the Syrup Division earns $3 of contribution margin on every gallon of syrup, the Candy Division earns no contribution margin, and the contribution margin of the company as a whole is $3. However, if the Syrup Division transfers syrup to the Candy Division at a transfer price of $5, the Syrup Division will earn no contribution margin because the transfer price equals its variable costs of producing the syrup. However, for each gallon of syrup the Candy Division can produce a 10-pound container of rock candy that sells for $50. The Candy Division will have $43 of variable costs, in addition to the $5 transfer price it must pay for each gallon of syrup. Thus, the Candy Division will earn a contribution margin of $2. The contribution margin to the company will also be $2 because the Syrup Division will have a contribution margin of zero.

Note that while the Candy Division is certainly better off with a transfer price of $5, the Syrup Division is worse off, and the company as a whole is worse off by $1 for each gallon of syrup transferred at the $5 transfer price.

ILLUSTRATION 29-6 Analysis of Lowering the Transfer Price Below the Market Price

Sell Syrup at Market Price		
Contribution Margin of Syrup Division per Gallon of Syrup	*Contribution Margin of Candy Division per 10-Pound Container*	*Contribution Margin of Company*
Selling price $8	0	
Variable costs 5	0	
Contribution margin $3	0	$3*

Transfer Syrup to Candy Division at $5		
Contribution Margin of Syrup Division per Gallon of Syrup	*Contribution Margin of Candy Division per 10-Pound Container*	*Contribution Margin of Company*
Transfer price $5	Selling price $50	
Variable costs 5	Own variable costs 43	
Contribution margin $0	Transfer price 5	
	Contribution margin $ 2	$2*

*Note that a gallon of syrup is required to produce a 10-pound container of candy. Thus, a gallon of syrup is equivalent to a 10-pound container of candy.

Variable Costs as the Transfer Price

When, the transferred product is unique, the producing division may not sell it in an open market. Obviously, no market price exists, and the division must choose some other transfer price. The variable costs of producing the transferred good may be the best choice of transfer price in this situation. The reason for selecting the variable costs of production as the transfer price is that it conveys accurate opportunity cost information. When no external market exists, the opportunity cost of producing and selling an item internally is simply the variable costs of producing that item.[5] Each time it produces an additional unit, the company must incur additional costs equal to the variable costs of production.

When it knows the opportunity cost of the transferred product, the buying division can make well-informed decisions. For example, suppose the buying division considers a special order from a customer. To produce the product, the buying division must use a component that another division of the firm (the selling division) will supply. Suppose the buying division will incur variable production costs, excluding the transfer price, of $50 per unit. Further, suppose the variable costs of producing the component are $25. What is the minimum price that the buying division could accept for the special order? The answer is $75, which is equal to the $50 of variable costs the buying division incurs and the $25 of variable costs the selling division incurs. Any price above $75 will increase the overall contribution margin of the company and its income.

However, suppose the selling division sets the transfer price at an amount greater than its variable costs. For example, suppose it sets the transfer price at

---

[5]This assumes that the selling division has excess capacity. If not, the opportunity cost must include the income lost on items that cannot be produced when capacity is used to produce goods for internal transfer.

$40. In this case, the manager of the buying division will perceive that the minimum acceptable selling price for the special order is $90, not $75. The $90 equals the $40 transfer price the selling division pays for each unit plus the other variable costs the selling division incurs that are equal to $50. The manager of the buying division would turn down the special order at prices between $75 and $90 at a definite loss of income for the company as a whole. In not knowing the real opportunity cost of production, the buying division manager may make poor decisions.

Full Cost Plus Profit as the Transfer Price

A very significant problem with using variable costs as the transfer price is that the selling division cannot earn a profit on production of the transferred product. In fact, if the transfer price equals the variable costs and if there are any fixed production costs, the selling division will have a loss equal to the amount of fixed costs. Thus, division managers may not find variable costs acceptable as transfer prices. For this reason, many companies add a profit margin to the full cost of an item and use the resulting amount as the transfer price.

For example, suppose the variable costs of producing an item for internal sale to a buying division is $100 per unit. Further, the producing division expects 1,000 units will be transferred in the coming year and its fixed costs will amount to $200,000 per year. Assume the fixed costs relate primarily to depreciation of equipment. Thus, they are fixed and sunk. The full cost per unit is $300 ($100 variable cost + $200 fixed cost). At a transfer price of $300, the selling division will just break even on the internal transfer. However, if the company utilizes a transfer pricing policy such that the transfer price equals the full cost plus 10%, the transfer price will be $330. Thus, the selling division will earn income of $30 on each item produced.

While full cost plus profit may be more acceptable as a transfer price to division managers, the information conveyed by the transfer price may not measure the opportunity cost of producing the transferred product. As we saw earlier, this can result in decisions that do not maximize the profitability of the whole company. Suppose the buying division must incur $400 of variable costs, in addition to the costs the selling division incurs. The market price for the item the buying division produces is $690. The buying division will not continue producing the product unless it makes a positive contribution toward covering its fixed costs. With a transfer price of $330, the contribution margin the buying division faces is a negative $40 (i.e., $690 selling price – $400 variable costs – $330 transfer price). Thus, the buying division will be inclined to drop the product. However, the product does, in fact, make a positive contribution to firm income. The selling price of $690 is greater than the variable costs of both the buying division ($400) and of the selling division ($100) by $190. Thus, the company as a whole will actually be better off by $190 for each unit it sells.

	Transfer Price Equals Full Cost Plus Profit	Transfer Price Equals Variable Costs
Selling price of final product	$690	$690
Less: Variable costs of the buying division, except for the transfer price	(400)	(400)
Transfer price	(330)	(100)
Contribution margin of buying division	$ (40)	$190

Negotiated Transfer Prices

As discussed at the start of this chapter, one benefit of decentralization is that managers who are delegated significant decision-making responsibility tend to be highly motivated. To encourage the sense of autonomy, some companies allow division managers to negotiate transfer prices. The subunit managers then face the same situation as an independent business that must negotiate a price for specialized items. However, the resulting transfer price may reflect the relative negotiating skill of the subunit managers and fail to reflect the underlying opportunity cost associated with producing a good and transferring it internally.

Service Centers Turned Into Profit Centers with Transfer Prices

LO 6
Explain how companies can use market-based transfer prices to treat service centers as profit centers.

Earlier in this chapter we noted that most service centers (e.g., janitorial services and computer services) are treated as cost centers and are controlled by comparing their actual costs to budgets. However, some companies treat service centers as profit centers. They accomplish this by assigning transfer prices that value the services these centers provide to other segments of the business. Attributing both revenue and expenses to their service centers, companies can calculate income and treat their service centers as profit centers. Companies have implemented this approach because they believe that evaluation in terms of income (rather than just cost) improves the efficiency of service center operations.

The transfer price companies typically use is an estimate of what the services would cost if they were purchased externally. Thus, transfer prices are based on market prices. For example, suppose the computer services department provides computer support to three operating departments at Jones Tool Company. The computer services department keeps track of how many hours of central processing unit (CPU) time is required for processing each department's work. In September, CPU time required for the three departments is:

	CPU Time in Hours
Department 1	100
Department 2	200
Department 3	150
Total	450

If the market value of similar computer services is estimated to be $50 per CPU hour, then Jones Tool could use $50 as the transfer price for computer services. With $50 as a transfer price, the computer services department would have $22,500 of revenue (i.e., 450 hours x $50). Of course, Jones Tool would not include this revenue in the annual income statement because it represents internal sales transactions between units of the same company. However, Jones Tool would include the revenue in the performance report of the computer services department. If the computer services department incurred $20,000 of expenses during the month of September, then it would have income of $2,500 for the month.

Companies must exercise care in treating service centers as profit centers. The approach works best when both the service centers and the departments that utilize their services are allowed to obtain or sell services externally. For example, if a user department believes that the $50 per CPU hour the computer services department charges is too high, the user should be allowed to obtain computer services externally at a lower price. Also, if Jones Tool holds the computer services department responsible for earning income, it should allow the department to sell its services to buyers willing to pay the highest price, even if those buyers are outside the company. It would not be appropriate to hold service center managers responsible for earning income and then restrict their opportunities for earning income to internal sales only. As a general rule, the more closely a service center resembles an autonomous business, the more appropriate it is to treat the service center as a profit center.

Transfer Prices and Income Taxes in an International Context

When goods are transferred between profit centers in different countries, the income tax situations in these countries may create incentives for relatively high or relatively low transfer prices. For example, suppose the tax rate in Country A is 10%, while the tax rate in Country B is 40%. Holding everything else constant, this creates an incentive to have high transfer prices when goods are transferred from a profit center in Country A to a profit center in Country B. With this approach, the profit center in Country A will have relatively high income (which is taxed at a low rate), and the profit center in Country B will have relatively low income (which is taxed at a high rate). Thus, overall taxes of company income for the two profit centers will be reduced. If goods were to be transferred from a profit center in Country B to a profit center in Country A, there would be an incentive for a relatively low transfer price. The Internal Revenue Service in the United States and the taxing authorities in other countries are aware of these incentives and try to make sure that transfer prices are not unreasonably high or low in response to the incentives created by differences in income tax rates between countries.

SUMMARY

List and explain the advantages and disadvantages of decentralization. Decentralization may lead to better information, faster responses to changing circumstances, and better motivation for managers. Decentralized organizations also may provide excellent training for future top-level executives. On the other hand, decentralization may lead to costly duplication of activities and problems of goal congruence.

INTERNATIONAL PERSPECTIVES

DODGING U.S. CORPORATE INCOME TAXES WITH HIGH TRANSFER PRICES

Economic advisors of President Clinton have alleged that some Japanese companies charge their U.S. subsidiaries high prices for the parts shipped from their factories in Japan. The U.S. subsidiaries avoid showing a profit within the U.S. and tax revenues are shifted back to Japan. Clintonites estimate that the loss from transfer pricing abuses runs up to $15 billion yearly.

Source: Paul Magnusson, "Why Corporate Nationality Matters," *Business Week* (July 12, 1993), p. 142.

Identify cost centers, profit centers, and investment centers.   Managers of cost centers are responsible only for controlling costs. Managers of profit centers are responsible for generating revenue as well as for controlling costs. Investment center managers are responsible for generating income and for the level of assets used to generate income.

Calculate and interpret return on investment (ROI).   Return on investment is calculated as the ratio of investment center operating income to investment center assets. Operating income is income before interest and taxes.

Calculate and interpret residual income (RI).   Residual income equals an investment center's operating income in excess of that required for the level of its assets.

Discuss the use of market price, variable costs, full cost plus profit, and negotiation in setting transfer prices.   If available, a market price is the best transfer price. If no market price exists, variable costs are a potential measure of the opportunity cost of producing the transferred good. However, use of variable costs will not allow the selling division (the subunit that produces the transferred item) to earn income. Thus, many managers do not find variable costs to be an acceptable transfer price. Some firms use full cost plus profit as a transfer price. While managers may find this more acceptable, it does not measure the opportunity cost of producing the transferred item; and managers may make poor decisions from using transfer prices based on full cost plus profit. Finally, some firms allow subunit managers to negotiate transfer prices.

Explain how companies can use market-based transfer prices to treat service centers as profit centers.   Service centers (e.g., janitorial services and computer services) that are normally treated as cost centers can be treated as profit centers if the company can determine a market value transfer price for the services they provide. Treatment as profit centers may be appropriate if service centers are allowed to *market* their services externally, and if internal users are allowed to *purchase* the services externally.

REVIEW PROBLEM

Watch-While-You-Sleep Alarm Company manufactures, sells, and installs residential alarm systems. The alarm systems include smoke and heat detection, motion detection, and window and door movement detection. They include high decibel internal and external alarms and automatic 911 dialing. Production is done in a single factory building with the completed units transferred to a storeroom located in the same building as the sales and installation departments and the administrative offices. Chin Hui, the company president, designed the original units which have remained basically unchanged. The company has operated successfully since 19X3. Chin, concerned that profits were not as high as they should be, divided the operation into two divisions at the end of 19X6. The Production Division operates the factory and the Sales/Installation Division works from the administrative building. Transfers of product to inventory are made at wholesale market price. As of the end of 19X8, the following data were made available for analysis.

Watch-While-You-Sleep Alarm Company
Divisional Data for 19X7 and 19X8

	Production Division	Sales/ Installation
Revenues, 19X7	$3,600,000	$10,600,000
Revenues, 19X8	5,200,000	12,400,000
Total assets (net) 12/31/X7	1,200,000	1,120,000
Total assets (net) 12/31/X8	1,400,000	1,125,000
Net income 19X7	240,000	420,000
Net income 19X8	320,000	510,000
Taxes 19X7	120,000	210,000
Taxes 19X8	150,000	312,000
Interest expense 19X7	25,000	4,000
Interest expense 19X8	35,000	2,000

REQUIRED:

a. Calculate operating income (before interest and taxes) for both divisions in 19X7 and 19X8.
b. Calculate the return on investment for both divisions to reflect margin and turnover in 19X7 and 19X8.
c. Calculate the residual income for both divisions in 19X7 and 19X8, assuming a required rate of return of 25%.
d. Mark Holland, the manager of the Sales/Installation Division, has suggested that since his division has a much higher return and requires a much lower investment, the company should consider phasing out the production unit and purchasing the alarm systems. Evaluate his idea.

SOLUTION:

(a) *Calculate operating income for both divisions for 19X7 and 19X8.*

	Production Division	Sales/ Installation
Net income, 19X7	$240,000	$420,000
Taxes, 19X7	120,000	210,000
Interest, 19X7	25,000	4,000
Income from operations before income and taxes	$385,000	$634,000
Net income, 19X8	$320,000	$510,000
Taxes, 19X8	150,000	312,000
Interest expense, 19X8	35,000	2,000
Income from operations before income and taxes	$505,000	$824,000

(b) *Calculate return on investment for both divisions, 19X7 and 19X8.*

Margin	Turnover	Return on Investment
$\dfrac{\text{Operating Income}}{\text{Revenue}}$ x	$\dfrac{\text{Revenue}}{\text{Total Assets}}$ =	$\dfrac{\text{Operating Income}}{\text{Total Assets}}$

Production Division:

19X7: $\dfrac{\$385{,}000}{\$3{,}600{,}000}$ x $\dfrac{\$3{,}600{,}000}{\$1{,}200{,}000}$ = $\dfrac{\$385{,}000}{\$1{,}200{,}000}$

.10694   x   3.0   =   .3208

19X8:
$$\frac{\$505,000}{\$5,200,000} \times \frac{\$5,200,000}{\$1,400,000} = \frac{\$505,000}{\$1,400,000}$$

$$.09712 \times 3.71429 = .3607$$

Sales/Installation Division:

19X7:
$$\frac{\$634,000}{\$10,600,000} \times \frac{\$10,600,000}{\$1,120,000} = \frac{\$634,000}{\$1,120,000}$$

$$.05981 \times 9.46429 = .5661$$

19X8:
$$\frac{\$824,000}{\$12,400,000} \times \frac{\$12,400,000}{\$1,125,000} = \frac{\$824,000}{\$1,125,000}$$

$$.06645 \times 11.02222 = .7324$$

(c) *Calculate residual income for both divisions, 19X7 and 19X8*

$$\text{Investment Center Operating Income} - \left(\text{Required Rate of Return} \times \text{Investment Center Asset} \right)$$

Production Division:

19X7	$385,000 − (.25 x $1,200,000) =	$85,000
19X8	$505,000 − (.25 x $1,400,000) =	$155,000

Sales/Installation Division:

19X7	$634,000 − (.25 x $1,120,000) =	$354,000
19X8	$824,000 − (.25 x $1,125,000) =	$542,750

(d) *Discuss the option of phasing out the production unit and purchasing the alarm systems.*

Both divisions of the company have done very well. Both reflect significant increases in their ROI and RI figures. These indicate improvement over the preceding year. The fact that residual income exists, and has increased over 19X7, indicates that the returns are greater than the minimum established by corporate management. The Sales/Installation Division manager's suggestion would imply that the same resources now employed in the Production Division could be invested at a higher return in the Sales/Installation Division. This is not necessarily true. There is no indication of production holding back the sales and installation activities. Finally, the whole issue of production versus purchasing the alarm systems involves many factors not included in this problem. Product quality, product availability, and future opportunities associated with each option would have to be considered. It is quite possible that the alarm company would elect to retain the manufacturing operation because of the opportunities associated with manufacturing capabilities, as well as increased quality control and product availability.

KEY TERMS

business segments, *1140*
cost center, *1140*
decentralized organizations, *1136*
investment center, *1141*
operating income, *1142*

profit center, *1141*
relative performance evaluation, *1141*
required rate of return, *1145*
residual income (RI), *1145*
responsibility center, *1140*

return on investment (ROI), *1142*
transfer price, *1147*

SELF QUIZ

LO 1 1. Which of the following is *not* a reason for having decentralized organizations?
a. Better information at the local level leads to superior decisions.
b. Goal congruence is enhanced.
c. Quicker response to changing circumstances.
d. Increased motivation of managers.

LO 1 2. Which of the following is an advantage to having decentralized organizations?
a. Suboptimization through local goals in decisions.
b. Tendency toward empire building.
c. Provides a training ground for future top executives.
d. Goal congruence is impaired.

LO 1 3. Which of the following is most indicative of a decentralized organization?
a. The physical facilities of the firm are widely dispersed geographically.
b. The organization is divided into several operating divisions.
c. Accounting is performed, in part, in the several operating divisions.
d. The entity grants substantial decision making authority to the heads of each of its several operating divisions.

LO 1 4. Identify which of the following should *not* be used to evaluate the performance of a plant manager in a decentralized organization:
a. Direct labor expense in the manager's plant.
b. Depreciation expense on equipment the manager authorized.
c. Variable overhead expenses in the manager's plant.
d. Fixed overhead allocated by the central office.

LO 1 5. Responsibility accounting suggests that a cost should be charged against a department other than the one actually incurring the costs, for:
a. Costs incurred for overhead in a production department.
b. Costs incurred by a department for services provided to another department.
c. Costs incurred for direct labor in a production department.
d. None of the above.

LO 2 6. Identify which of the following is *not* a cost center.
a. An accounting department.
b. A production department.
c. A retail sales outlet.
d. A maintenance department.

LO 2 7. An investment center is responsible for:
a. Investing in assets.
b. Controlling costs.
c. Generating revenues.
d. All of the above.

LO 2 8. A profit center is responsible for all of the following except:
a. Investing in assets.
b. Controlling costs.
c. Generating revenues.
d. None of the above.

LO 2 9. A cost center is responsible for which of the following?
a. Investing in assets.
b. Controlling costs.
c. Generating revenues.
d. None of the above.

LO 2 10. Which of the following is a responsibility center?
a. Cost center.
b. Profit center.
c. Investment center.
d. All of the above.

LO 3 11. Return on investment is calculated as:
a. Revenue ÷ Total assets.
b. Operating income ÷ Total assets.
c. Operating income ÷ Revenue.
d. None of the above.

LO 2 12. Cost centers are evaluated by:
a. Variance analysis.
b. Relative performance evaluation.
c. Return on investment.
d. Residual income.

LO 3 13. Profit centers are evaluated using:
a. Variance analysis.
b. Income budgets or targets.
c. Return on investment.
d. Residual income.

LO 3 14. Investment centers are evaluated by which of the following?
a. Variance analysis.
b. Relative performance evaluation.
c. Return on investment.
d. Residual income.
e. Both c and d.

LO 3 15. One drawback to the use of return on investment in evaluating investment centers and managers is:
a. Income from continuing operations before interest and taxes may be easily misstated by management.
b. Operating income does not take into account the other gains and losses which may have occurred.

c. The historical cost method and depreciation method may provide a misleading asset basis for the denominator.

d. None of the above.

LO 3 16. Which of the following is a problem in using return on investment to evaluate managers?

a. Managers could elect not to invest in projects yielding less than current ROI.

b. Managers could elect not to invest in projects yielding less than the minimum rate of return.

c. Managers' morale may suffer from being evaluated.

d. None of the above.

LO 4 17. Identify which of the following is *not* a part of the calculation of residual income.

a. Operating income.

b. Total assets.

c. Required rate of return.

d. Market rate of interest.

LO 4 18. One drawback to the use of residual income in evaluating investment centers and managers is:

a. Income from continuing operations before interest and taxes may be easily misstated by management.

b. Operating income does not take into account the other gains and losses which may have occurred.

c. It does not offer a good comparison of investment centers in a number of circumstances.

d. None of the above.

LO 4 19. In comparing investment centers:

a. Return on investment can be greater because of older, more depreciated assets.

b. Residual income often does not provide a good basis of comparison.

c. Both a and b.

d. None of the above.

LO 5 20. When a ready market exists, the best transfer price will probably be the:

a. Market price.

b. Variable cost.

c. Full cost plus profit.

d. Negotiated transfer price.

SOLUTIONS TO SELF-QUIZ

1. b   2. c   3. d   4. d   5. b   6. c   7. d   8. a   9. b   10. d   11. b   12. a   13. b   14. e
15. c   16. a   17. d   18. c   19. c   20. a

QUESTIONS

Q29-1 List four advantages frequently occurring because of decentralization of an entity's operations.

Q29-2 List two disadvantages normally associated with the decentralization of an entity's operations.

Q29-3 Discuss how decentralization of an entity's operations is a matter of degree rather than an absolute condition.

Q29-4 Discuss how decentralization can improve the motivation of managers.

Q29-5 What is empire building?

Q29-6 How could costly duplication of activities occur in a decentralized operating environment?

Q29-7 How does a decentralized operating environment provide an excellent training ground for future top-level executives?

Q29-8 Discuss goal congruence and how it impacts the decision to decentralize.

Q29-9 Explain how responsibility accounting is implemented.

Q29-10 Under the concept of responsibility accounting, discuss what is done when one segment causes another segment to incur costs.

Q29-11 Distinguish between cost centers, profit centers, and investment centers.

Q29-12 Discuss business segments and how they relate to responsibility centers.

Q29-13 What is the formula for return on investment?

Q29-14 What is the formula for residual income?

Q29-15 Identify two ways of evaluating investment centers.

Q29-16   Explain the advantages of using market value as a transfer price.

Q29-17   Discuss the advantages and disadvantages of using variable cost as a transfer price.

Q29-18   Explain why a division manager might want to use full cost plus profit as the transfer price.

Q29-19   Describe the disadvantage of using negotiated transfer prices.

Q29-20   In an international context, transfer price will be set at a high dollar amount when:
a. The goods are moving from a high tax economy to a low tax economy.
b. The goods are moving from a low tax economy to a high tax economy.
c. The goods are moving to an economy with taxes comparable to the those in the sending economy.
d. None of the above.

EXERCISES

LO 1

E29-1   Why Firms Decentralize   Malcort Corporation is a manufacturer of automobile bumpers and is highly centralized in its decision making. The four operating divisions are located in Atlanta, St. Louis, Detroit, and Los Angeles, each serving the large automobile manufacturers in its area. Discuss some advantages that might be gained by Malcort if it grants a greater degree of autonomy to each of its four plants in the form of decentralization.

LO 1

E29-2   Disadvantages of Decentralization   Marke Products has three operating divisions. They have been operating under a highly decentralized model for several years. Top management has allowed the three managers near autonomy in operating over that time period, but is now very concerned that depreciation and other overhead costs have grown significantly faster than in other firms within the industry. Discuss possible decisions by the division managers which could account for the higher than average costs.

LO 1,2

E29-3   Responsibility Accounting and Decentralization   Rutland Manufacturing Company has two operating divisions, Shaping and Joining, both of which are cost centers. They are nearing the end of the first year of decentralized operation. Describe how responsibility accounting could be implemented in the two divisions to provide a control mechanism.

LO 2,3

E29-4   Cost Centers and Profit Centers   Melrose Tool Company manufactures several lines of tools in two geographically separated plants that operate as cost centers, and feed their output into a finishing plant, a profit center, which polishes, packages, and sells the tools. As the management of Melrose finds it easier to control the one profit center than either of the two cost centers, you have been asked how they could convert the two cost centers to profit centers. Write a brief explanation to Melrose's management.

LO 2

E29-5   Profit Centers and Investment Centers   Brunswick Tents has two operating divisions that operate as profit centers. Top management has found the high degree of autonomy given the managers has resulted in performance at a level even better than hoped for and they now want to shift further responsibility to the two divisions. This would involve scaling down some of the activities at the corporate office, which is also appealing to management. Identify activities that might be shifted to the two operating divisions which would in essence convert them from profit centers to investment centers.

LO 3

E29-6   Evaluating Investment Centers, ROI   Lowery Mill is a division of Mharum, Inc., operating as an investment center. The mill reported income of $250,000 after taxes of

$150,000 and interest expense of $100,000. The assets totaled $4,000,000 with accumulated depreciation of $2,500,000. Calculate the return on investment for Lowery Mill.

LO 4   **E29-7**   **Evaluating Investment Centers, RI**   Modern Mill is an investment center and a division of Abacus Manufacturing. The mill reported income of $300,000 after taxes of $250,000, and interest expense of $100,000. The assets of the plant totaled $3,500,000 with accumulated depreciation of $1,000,000. Abacus has established a required rate of return of 20% of assets. Calculate the residual income of Modern Mill.

LO 3,4   **E29-8**   **Evaluating Investment Centers, ROI Versus RI**   Vassian Valves operates two investment centers of approximately the same size. Use the following information to compare the two centers under return on investment and residual income and comment on the results.

	Commercial Valves	Residential Valves
Operating income (before taxes and interest)	$1,200,000	$1,600,000
Total assets net of accumulated depreciation	6,000,000	7,500,000
Required rate of return	16%	16%

LO 5   **E29-9**   **Transfer Pricing, Market Price**   The market price of a sub-assembly produced in the Brockton plant is used as the transfer price charged to the Boston plant. Explain why the managers of both plants will tend to support such a transfer price in the absence of any special cost savings to the Brockton plant resulting from intra-company sales.

LO 2,5   **E29-10**   **Transfer Pricing, Variable Cost**   The variable cost of a sub-assembly produced in the Amherst plant is used as the transfer price charged to the Winston plant. The manager of the Amherst plant is very concerned that the operation of the plant always reports a loss. Explain to the Amherst plant manager why the corporation finds it advantageous to use variable cost as the transfer price and why it would not affect the method under which the plant's operation is evaluated.

LO 5   **E29-11**   **Transfer Pricing, Full Cost Plus Profit**   Four Seasons Paint Company has a plant that manufactures containers used by their paint-producing plants. Margaret Tignor, the manager of the container plant, has been operating this cost center for several years. The containers are transferred to paint plants at variable cost. She has approached the corporate executive committee concerned that her plant is the only one in the corporate group which is not a profit center and that it may affect the evaluation of her performance compared with other plant managers. She suggests that containers be transferred from her plant at full cost plus a ten percent profit. Discuss the disadvantages to the corporate group of treating this cost center as a profit center under this option.

LO 6   **E29-12**   **Turning Service Centers into Profit Centers**   Roberta McCoy, the manager of the vehicle maintenance service department for a large distribution and delivery company, has indicated a desire for some degree of autonomy in operating the service unit. She proposes billing each operating unit served using labor rates and part prices comparable to local repair shops. Discuss how this proposal could benefit the business.

PROBLEM SET A

LO 1,2   **P29-1A**   **Decentralization, Cost Centers, Profit Centers**   Gutierrez Guttering Company manufactures metal and plastic guttering for use in both commercial and residential construction. Production occurs in two separate plants. Distribution is from a central warehouse through a central sales office. Both production plants are currently treated as cost centers with the budgets prepared in close consultation with the central office and variance analysis as the control mechanism.

REQUIRED:

a. Explain how budgets and variance analysis provide a means of controlling cost.
b. Describe how the plants could be treated as profit centers in a decentralized model and the advantages of such a change.
c. Explain what control mechanisms would be available in a decentralized model operating as profit centers.

LO 3

P29-2A **Return on Investment, Effect of Depreciation** The manager of the Baldwin Corporation has heard that the ROI as a measure of effectiveness for investment centers will be distorted as assets age. The following data are available:

Total facility assets (gross)	$4,000,000
Operating income for the period before interest and taxes	900,000

REQUIRED:

Calculate the return on investment for Baldwin assuming the assets are:
a. 20% depreciated.
b. 50% depreciated.
c. Explain the difference in the results of a and b.

LO 3

P29-3A **Evaluating Investment Centers, Return on Investment** Gammon Company produces game machines in two plants for casinos. Each plant functions as an investment center serving different geographical regions. Data for the year of 19X8 are as follows:

	Reno Plant	*Atlantic Plant*
Total assets at plant	$1,900,000	$2,600,000
Accumulated depreciation on plant assets	800,000	500,000
After tax income	400,000	450,000
Tax on income	280,000	320,000
Interest expense	120,000	180,000
Revenue for the period	3,800,000	4,200,000

REQUIRED:

a. Calculate the return on investment for the Reno plant for 19X8, showing both the margin and the turnover ratios.
b. Calculate the return on investment for the Atlantic plant for 19X8, showing both the margin and the turnover ratios.

LO 3,4

P29-4A **Evaluating Investment Centers, Residual Income** Aphid Pest Control Corporation manufactures ecologically safe chemicals to control plant pests in its Due East plant. Plant fertilizers are produced in its Due West plant. Management is trying to compare the results of the Due East plant and the Due West plant. Both plants were built in the mid 80's and are approximately the same size.
Consider the following data:

	Due East Plant	*Due West Plant*
Reported income after taxes and interest	$ 400,000	$ 300,000
Taxes on income	280,000	210,000
Interest expense	30,000	20,000
Total assets (net)	1,600,000	1,520,000

REQUIRED:

a. Calculate the residual income for the Due East plant assuming a required rate of return of 20%.
b. Calculate the residual income for the Due West plant assuming a required rate of return of 20%.
c. Comment on the relative performance of the two plants.

LO 5   **P29-5A** **Transfer Pricing, The Alternatives** MacAllin Wool Products manufactures kilts and other Scottish wear from imported woolen yarns. The yarns are woven into tartan patterns in one plant and the various articles of clothing are cut and sewn in two other plants. Currently, the goods are transferred from the weaving plant to the sewing plants at full cost. The managers of the sewing plants have expressed concern that the weaving plant is inefficient and the prices which they pay for the yard goods are excessive compared to goods available on the open market. The weaving plant manager, on the other hand, has complained that the sewing plants reflect a profit which is used to justify salary increases to the sewing plants above that received by the weaving plant.

REQUIRED:

a. Discuss four possible transfer prices which could be reasonably used in the company.
b. Select and defend one of the four transfer prices from the standpoint of dealing with the objections of both the weaving and sewing managers.

LO 6   **P29-6A** **Turning Service Centers into Profit Centers with Transfer Prices** The City of Portal operates a plumbing and electrical maintenance department which is charged with maintaining all water and electric service functions in buildings owned by the city. Marie Esposito, the manager of the service department, is concerned that many of the service calls are strictly nuisance calls which would be avoided if the departments using the various facilities were billed for the services at regular plumbing and electrical rates. She cites examples of numerous calls for defective electrical outlets which turn out to be unplugged equipment, burned out light bulbs in lamps which could easily be changed by the users, and drains plugged up by coffee grounds. She suggests that her department could in fact function effectively with fewer employees if the city would establish the department as a profit center.

REQUIRED:

a. Discuss how the plumbing and electric maintenance department could be set up as a profit center.
b. Discuss how the plumbing and electric maintenance department could be set up as an investment center.

PROBLEM SET B

LO 1,2   **P29-1B** **Decentralization, Cost Centers, Investment Centers** The Century Steel Company mines coal for use in steel-making operations. The coal is mined in West Virginia and shipped to Century's three steel foundries located in the east.

REQUIRED:

Discuss the options Century might consider to generate accounting information which can be used to evaluate and control the mining operation.

LO 3   **P29-2B** **Return on Investment, Effect of Depreciation** Aaron Gest Inc. has two divisions that operate as profit centers. Division 1 and Division 2 have the same dollar total cost of assets, but Division 1 assets are 6 years old and Division 2 assets are only 3 years old. Both divisions reported income of $120,000 after taxes of $80,000 and interest expense of $60,000. Cost of facilities at gross historical cost (10 yr. life and no residual value) were $1,000,000 for each division.

REQUIRED:

a. Calculate the return on investment for Division 1.
b. Calculate the return on investment for Division 2.
c. Explain the effect the different ages of the assets have on the ROI for the two divisions.

LO 3

P29-3B **Evaluating Investment Centers, Return on Investment** Markwatt Manufacturing produces transformers and generators for electric utility companies. Production occurs in two operating divisions, the Transformer Division and the Generator Division, which are investment centers. The following data are from the first quarter of 19X7.

	Transformer Division	*Generator Division*
Total assets at division	$6,000,000	$10,000,000
Accumulated depreciation on plant assets	600,000	1,200,000
After tax income	500,000	850,000
Tax on income	320,000	510,000
Interest expense	400,000	550,000
Revenue for the period	6,000,000	9,000,000

REQUIRED:

a. Calculate the return on investment for the Transformer Divison for 19X7, showing both the margin and the turnover ratios.
b. Calculate the return on investment for the Generator Divison for 19X7, showing both the margin and the turnover ratios.

LO 3,4

P29-4B **Evaluating Investment Centers, Residual Income** The Happy Gardener Seed Company grows seeds in two facilities. The Grass Seed plant is located in Long Creek, South Carolina and the Plant Seed plant is located in Havre, Montana. Both plants have an extensive investment in enclosed propagation facilities to avoid the intrusion of unwanted seed strains into the process. Both plants are relatively new. The following information is from the accounting records of the two plants.

	Grass Seed	*Plant Seed*
Total revenue	$1,140,000	$1,600,000
Net income	250,000	280,000
Tax expense	180,000	195,000
Interest expense	40,000	60,000
Total assets (net)	2,070,000	2,100,000

REQUIRED:

a. Calculate the residual income for the Grass Seed plant given a required rate of return of 18%.
b. Calculate the residual income for the Plant Seed plant given a required rate of return of 18%.
c. Identify further analyses which could be performed.

LO 5

P29-5B **Transfer Pricing, The Alternatives** MacAbee Modern Parts produces automotive replacement parts in two plants. The Stamping plant stamps all of the parts from metals appropriate for the product and transfers the parts to the Finishing plant, which deburrs the parts, bores, threads, polishes and paints as required. Twenty percent of the production is sold to other finishers outside the corporate group and eighty percent are transferred to the Finishing plant. The corporate offices set the transfer price based on the variable costs incurred in the Stamping plant. Corporate management has had second thoughts about the transfer price selected. They believe that the Stamping plant might operate more efficiently if another transfer pricing policy were established.

REQUIRED:

a. Discuss briefly alternative transfer prices which could be considered in view of the concerns of corporate management.
b. Suggest and defend your choice of a transfer pricing method.

LO 5   **P29-6B**   **Turning Service Centers into Profit Centers with Transfer Prices**   Johnson Medical Center has a computer assistance group whose job is to solve computer problems in Johnson's fifteen administrative offices. The chief financial officer of Johnson is concerned because the cost of the computer assistance group has increased dramatically in the last three years. The senior employee of the computer assistance group, Mary Pelton, contends that the administrative offices have made unreasonably high demands for computer support and, to meet their demands, she has had to expand her staff. Mary points to a recent case where an administrative office requested assistance because a computer was malfunctioning—the problem turned out to be an unplugged machine.

Currently, the computer assistance group is treated as a cost center and user offices are not charged for services rendered by the group.

REQUIRED:

a. Why are the administrative offices "overusing" the services of the computer assistance group?
b. Recommend one or more solutions to the problem using transfer prices to charge for computer assistance.

CRITICAL THINKING AND COMMUNICATING

C29-1   Raz Corporation, a regional metal products company, has historically functioned in a centralized environment. The new chairperson of the board of directors is considering the implementation of some degree of decentralization of the operations. There are five operating plants. Four produce individual products which are sent to a central warehouse for distribution and the fifth produces components which are used in the other four. All five plants and the warehouse are located within five miles of the Middleground Community.

REQUIRED:

Prepare a letter to the chairperson of the board which explains the advantages and disadvantages of decentralization and includes descriptions of cost centers, profit centers, and investment centers as possible models for implementation.

C29-2   Santoriello Electric, S.A., an electric utility in a Central American country burns coal for generating power. The entity has acquired a high sulphur coal mine in central Tennessee and will ship the coal to its power generation facility via rail to northern Mexico and then by tractor trailer to its plant. In planning for profits, they found that they must file federal income tax returns in the U. S. at an average rate of 35% on the profits of the coal mine. The domestic tax rate for the power facility is 15%.

REQUIRED:

What steps may Santoriello take to minimize its total tax burden and thereby maximize its profits? What legal and ethical considerations should enter into the decision?

Tax Aspects of Business Decisions

One of the significant factors that any business decision-maker must consider is the impact that the United States federal income tax will have on business decisions. Over the years since the enactment of the first income tax law in 1913, the U.S. tax system has become so complex that no business decision-maker can hope to make effective decisions without considering a wide range of tax factors. Only a tax expert can be expected to really understand the complexities and interrelationships of the various areas of tax law. Not only has the law become exceedingly complicated, but it has also become extremely dynamic, with changes being enacted by Congress every year. Nevertheless, the decision-maker, while not a tax expert, must have a grasp of the fundamental concepts of the tax laws in order to formulate alternatives in making business decisions. The purpose of this appendix is to introduce you to some of the fundamental tax aspects of business decisions. Specific business decisions discussed include:

1. The form of business decision
2. The method of accounting decision
3. Capital expenditure decisions
4. Various other decisions.

Before making a final decision on any business plan, the conscientious decision-maker should consult a professional tax advisor in order to insure that no tax factor has been overlooked.

THE FORM OF BUSINESS DECISION

One of the first decisions faced by a manager is the decision as to which form of business to adopt:

1. Sole proprietorship
2. Partnership
3. Special corporation known as an S corporation
4. Regular corporation known as a C corporation.

What are the tax aspects of this decision? For example, will more taxes be paid if the business is a corporation? Does any tax apply upon formation of a business? What about the tax aspects of withdrawing money from the business? If the business has losses, is there any tax benefit? We discuss each of the forms of business separately in the following paragraphs.

Sole Proprietorship Taxation

A sole proprietorship is *not* a separate, taxable entity. Rather, all the income and deduction items for the business are simply included on the personal tax return of the individual who owns the business. A personal tax return consists of a Form 1040 (along with several supporting forms and schedules) that is filed with the Internal Revenue Service (IRS). Income from all sources is taxable unless some specific statute exempts it. For example, interest income earned on bonds that are issued by municipalities (cities, counties, states, or state agencies) is specifically exempt from federal income taxation. No expense item is deductible unless some specific statute authorizes the deduction. However, there is a far-reaching tax statute that authorizes deductions for all expenses that are related to a profit-seeking business. In addition to business-related expenses, individuals may deduct certain *personal* expenses such as medical expenses (to the extent that the medical expenses exceed a Congressionally-determined threshold or "floor" amount), contributions made to certain charitable organizations, interest paid on home mortgages, property taxes paid to local governments, and certain other personal expenses. Finally, every individual taxpayer is allowed to deduct an amount called the "personal exemption," which is an amount that is arbitrarily determined by Congress. To determine the tax liability for a particular tax year, all the income items minus all the deduction items produce an amount called "taxable income," which is multiplied by the tax rates that apply for that year.

As an example of determining personal tax liability, assume that taxpayer Glen Berg, a professor in the College of Engineering at a large university, had the following items of income and expense for the year 19X1:

University salary	$50,000
Gain from selling antique clock purchased two months ago	500
Dividend income on Microsoft, Inc. stock	275
Interest income on municipal bonds	2,000
Interest payments on his home mortgage	(8,000)
Food and clothing expenses	(5,000)
Contribution to United Way	(300)
Other allowable personal deductions and the personal exemption	(3,500)

Based on the above data, Professor Berg's taxable income would be $38,975, computed as follows:

Gross income:		
Salary	$50,000	
Gain on property sale	500	
Dividend income	275	
Interest income on municipal bonds	0*	$50,775
Deductions:		
Interest payments on his home mortgage	(8,000)	
Food and clothing expenses	0*	
Contribution to United Way	(300)	
Other allowable personal deductions and the personal exemption	(3,500)	(11,800)
Taxable income		$38,975

*Interest income on municipal bonds is exempt, and no statute authorizes deductions for personal living expenses.

Congress changes the tax rates almost every year.[1] For the sake of example, we will assume that the tax rates applicable to single taxpayers are 20% on the

---

[1]In 1993, the lowest tax rate for a single, individual taxpayer was 15% of the first $22,100 of taxable income. As taxable income increases, the rate becomes 28%, then 31%, then 36%, and finally 39.6%.

first $20,000 of income and 30% on all amounts above that. Professor Berg's tax liability would be $9,693, computed as follows:

		Taxable Income		Tax Amount
20%	X	$20,000	=	$4,000
30%	X	18,975	=	5,693
		$38,975		$9,693

If Professor Berg were to start a sole proprietorship business, the results of that business would be added to his personal tax return. Assume that early in 19X1, Professor Berg decides to start a business called CompuCar and operate it as a sole proprietorship. He contributes $8,000 to a bank account set up for the business. He has invented a voice-activated computer device that monitors automobile mileage and keeps records of which category of travel the driver has dictated to the device. The driver simply gets into the car, says "business" or "personal," and the device keeps track of the mileage in each category. At the end of the year, the driver asks for a printout of the number of miles in each category. During 19X1, Professor Berg successfully manufactured and marketed the device to several car manufacturers and earned $20,000 in sales revenue. He also incurred $3,000 of business-related expenses. From the $17,000 of extra income (net of expenses), Professor Berg withdrew $10,000 and spent it on a vacation trip to Australia. The facts are summarized as follows:

University salary	$50,000
Gain from selling antique clock purchased two months ago	500
Dividend income on Microsoft, Inc. stock	275
Interest income on municipal bonds	2,000
Interest payments on his home mortgage	(8,000)
Food and clothing expenses	(5,000)
Contribution to United Way	(300)
Other allowable personal deductions and the personal exemption	(3,500)
Payment to bank account to start CompuCar business	(8,000)
Sales revenue for CompuCar	20,000
Business expenses for CompuCar	(3,000)
Withdrawal of cash from CompuCar	10,000

The contribution of the $8,000 cash to a bank account to start the business has no tax impact. For tax purposes, Professor Berg simply adds $20,000 to his gross income and increases his deductions by $3,000, so his taxable income becomes $55,975. In addition, the fact that he withdrew $10,000 for his personal use is of no tax consequence. He had $17,000 of additional taxable profit ($20,000 revenue less $3,000 expense), and whether he spent that profit or left it in the business does not affect his tax liability.

Professor Berg has already calculated his tax liability (without the business income) to be $9,693 (as shown in the previous example). The quick way to calculate the new liability is to realize that, at a taxable income level of $38,975, the tax rate on the *next* dollar of income is 30%. In other words, his *marginal tax rate* is 30%. The **marginal tax rate** is the tax rate that would apply if the taxpayer were to receive an additional dollar of taxable income. The extra income of $17,000 (net of expenses) can be multiplied by the marginal tax rate to produce $5,100 of additional taxes. His new tax liability is $14,793 ($9,693 + $5,100). Alternatively, he could calculate his liability in the same manner as shown in the previous example:

		Taxable Income		Tax Amount
20%	x	$20,000	=	$ 4,000
30%	x	35,975	=	10,793
		$55,975		$14,793

As shown by the above examples, the taxpayer who wants to consider the tax factors of operating a business as a sole proprietorship need only be concerned with what the marginal tax rate is for his or her personal tax return. Whether any cash is withdrawn from the business is irrelevant for tax purposes. There is no tax upon *forming* the business, only on the profits generated after the business is operating. But, what if the business incurs losses instead of profits? Assuming that the owner of the business is actively involved in the business and that the business is truly a profit-seeking business, these losses can be used to offset other income on the personal tax return, thus reducing the tax liability.[2]

Assume that Professor Berg's CompuCar business incurred $7,000 in losses during 19X1 (instead of $17,000 of profits). Without the business, his taxable income was $38,975. When the loss from the business is applied to his personal tax return, the taxable income is reduced to $31,975. The tax liability is reduced to $7,593 as shown below:

		Taxable Income		Tax Amount
20%	x	$20,000	=	$4,000
30%	x	11,975	=	3,593
		$31,975		$7,593

An alternative way of calculating the tax effect of the $7,000 loss is simply to realize that the $7,000 loss will offset income that is being taxed at a marginal rate of 30%. Thus, the loss will produce *tax savings* of $2,100 ($7,000 x 30%). Without CompuCar, the tax liability was $9,693 (as shown in our first example). With CompuCar producing a $7,000 loss, the new tax liability is $9,693 minus $2,100 of tax savings, or $7,593.

To summarize, if a taxpayer wants to form a sole proprietorship, such a business, if profitable, will cause additional taxes to be paid at the taxpayer's personal marginal tax rate. Money withdrawn from the business will have no tax effect. If the business incurs losses, the amount of the loss will produce tax savings at the taxpayer's personal marginal tax rate.

---

[2]If the owner does *not* play a significant role in the management of the business, the loss is called a "passive activity loss" and can only be deducted against other "passive" activities that have profits. In this appendix, the owners always play a significant role in the management of the business, so that none of the business ventures are passive activities.

Partnership Taxation

Partnerships are quite similar to sole proprietorships, with the major difference being that there is more than one owner. Like sole proprietorships, partnerships are not separate taxable entities. Rather, each owner of the business simply reports to the IRS his or her share of the income and deduction items from the business.

S Corporation Taxation

The owners of corporations can make a special election to be treated in a manner similar to partnerships for tax purposes. The tax laws that provide these special rules are in Subchapter S of the Internal Revenue Code. Hence, these corporations are called S corporations. Each owner of an S corporation reports his or her share of the income and deduction items on his or her personal tax return.

The net income from the business flows through the S corporation or through the partnership to the individual tax returns of the owners. Thus, the tax liability is the same whether the business is operated as a partnership or as an S corporation. Given this fact, should the taxpayer be indifferent as to which form of business is chosen? No, because there are restrictions placed on S corporations that partnerships do not have. S corporations are limited to 35 shareholders, while partnerships may have any number of partners. Furthermore, only individuals may be S corporation shareholders, while partners may be individuals, other partnerships, or corporations.

In spite of the restrictions placed on S corporations, there is a nontax reason that may convince owners to operate the business as an S corporation rather than as a partnership. All corporations have "limited liability." That is, if the corporate business is sued, the owners' potential losses are limited to the amount of their original investments in the business. On the other hand, partnerships have unlimited liability. If the partnership is sued, the partners could lose their original investment in the business and their personal assets as well.[3]

C Corporation Taxation

Unlike proprietorships, partnerships, and S corporations, the C corporation is a taxable entity separate from its owners.[4] Because of its separate entity status, "double taxation" may apply. **Double taxation** means that the same income is taxed twice, once at the corporate level and once at the shareholder level. When a C corporation earns taxable income, it must pay tax based on its own set of tax rates. If the income earned by the corporation is distributed to the shareholders, this income is treated as dividend income to them, and the shareholders must pay another tax on this same income.

Assume that Professor Glen Berg had items of income and expense for the year 19X1 exactly as shown in the first example in this appendix. He decides to operate CompuCar as a C corporation, and he convinces one of his colleagues,

---

[3]There is a special form of partnership called a limited partnership where the so-called limited partners risk only the amount of their original investment. However, even a limited partnership must have at least one "general" partner who has unlimited liability.

[4]The laws that govern the taxation of regular corporations come from Subchapter C of the Internal Revenue Code, hence the name C corporations.

Professor Debra Seymour, to be a 40% owner in the business. She contributes $3,200 in return for 40% of the stock, and Professor Berg contributes $4,800 in return for 60% of the stock. Neither of the two shareholders will be paid a guaranteed salary, but each will withdraw money from the business if it is profitable. For the year 19X1, CompuCar had $20,000 in revenues and $3,000 in business expenses. Professor Berg withdrew $6,000 and Professor Seymour withdrew $4,000.

For the sake of example, assume that the tax rates for corporations are 15% on the first $25,000 of taxable income and 35% on all amounts above that.[5] CompuCar has taxable income of $17,000. The $10,000 in cash that was distributed to the two shareholders would be classified as a dividend payment. Dividend payments are not deductible by the corporation that pays them. CompuCar's tax liability would be $2,550.

For the C corporation:

		Taxable Income		Tax Amount
15%	x	$17,000	=	$2,550
35%	x	0	=	0
		$17,000		$2,550

Professor Berg received $6,000 in dividend income and the tax could be calculated by adding the $6,000 to the $38,975 of taxable income that Professor Berg had without CompuCar, producing taxable income of $44,975, as shown below:

For Professor Berg:

		Taxable Income		Tax Amount
20%	x	$20,000	=	$ 4,000
30%	x	24,975	=	7,493
		$44,975		$11,493

Alternatively, the $6,000 of dividend income could be multiplied by the marginal tax rate of 30%, to yield an *additional* tax of $1,800. Since his tax liability without CompuCar was $9,693, his tax liability with the dividend from CompuCar is $11,493 ($9,693 + $1,800).

Assuming that Professor Seymour's marginal tax rate is also 30%, she would pay *additional* taxes of $1,200 ($4,000 dividend income x 30%). Thus, double taxation results in $5,550 of taxes being paid. A comparison of the total tax that results when CompuCar is a C corporation versus when CompuCar is a partnership or S corporation follows:

[5]The tax rates for corporations change occasionally. In 1993, the actual rates were 15% on the first $50,000 of taxable income, 25% on the next $25,000, 34% on the next $25,000, 39% on the next $235,000, back to 34% on additional amounts of taxable income up to $10,000,000, 35% on the next $5,000,000, 38% on the next $3,333,333, then back to 35% on all additional amounts of taxable income above $18,333,333.

Form of Business	Tax on CompuCar Business	Additional Tax on Prof. Berg	Additional Tax on Prof. Seymour	Total
C corporation	$2,550	$1,800	$1,200	$5,550
S corporation or partnership	N/A	3,060[a]	$2,040[b]	5,100
Difference				$ 450

[a]($17,000 business profit) x (60% ownership interest) x (30% marginal tax rate) = $3,060.
[b]($17,000 business profit) x (40% ownership interest) x (30% marginal tax rate) = $2,040.

Thus, operating the business as a C corporation would cost an additional $450 in taxes compared to operating as a partnership or as an S corporation.

Does the fact that double taxation applies mean that there is never any tax advantage in choosing to operate a business as a C corporation? No, sometimes it may be advantageous tax-wise to operate as a C corporation because there are ways to avoid double taxation or to reduce its effects. The most straightforward way to reduce double taxation is to reduce the taxes on the corporation. This can be done by structuring the payments to the shareholders in such a way that they are deductible by the corporation. Payments that qualify as business expenses are deductible; whereas payments that qualify as dividends are not. Three common examples of deductible business expenses are salary payments, interest payments, and rental payments. Thus, paying the shareholder a salary rather than dividends would avoid double taxation.

Rather than reducing the tax paid by the corporation, another way to reduce the effects of double taxation is to reduce the tax paid by the shareholders. This can be done by reducing, or completely eliminating, the cash distributions paid to the shareholders. That is, the shareholders must agree to leave their money inside the corporation. The corporation would be taxed, but not the shareholders.

The Appropriate Decision on the Form of Business

If you were a decision-maker trying to decide what form of business to adopt, just what would the previous discussion tell you? Basically, there is no clear-cut rule as to which form of business is the most advantageous from a tax planning perspective. The decision-maker must be able to make accurate predictions about the future in order to make the appropriate choice. For example, will the business earn profits from its operations or are losses likely? How many owners will there be? Will the owners need to withdraw cash from the business? What are the relative tax rates on individuals versus corporations? Is Congress likely to change these rates in the future? If you, as the decision-maker, can make accurate predictions, then some guidelines can be given. In considering the following guidelines, assume that there will be more than one owner so the decision is between operating the business as a partnership, an S corporation, or a C corporation. Also assume that there will be no more than 35 owners and none of the owners will be partnerships or corporations, so the S election is always allowable.

1. First, assume that losses will occur during the first years of the business. In this case, the decision-maker should reject the C corporation form because the losses cannot be passed through to the owners' individual tax returns. Either an S corporation or partnership would allow losses to

be passed through, and these losses would offset income from other sources, thus saving taxes. If the owners want to have limited liability, choose the S corporation form.

2. Next, assume that profits will occur during the first years of the business, and the owners will not make cash withdrawals of these profits. In this case the decision turns on the relative tax rates that apply to C corporations and to individuals. If the rates are higher on individuals, then reject the partnership or S corporation form and choose the C corporation. The examples and discussion given in this appendix show that, at low levels of taxable income, the rates are higher on individuals, but as income level increases, the C corporation rates become higher. Congress could change this situation at any time, so the decision-maker needs to keep tabs on potential changes in tax rates.

3. Finally, assume that profits will occur during the first years of the business, and the owners will make at least some cash withdrawals of these profits. Now the choice becomes more complicated because withdrawals from C corporations *might* be treated as taxable dividend income to the recipient shareholders (and as nondeductible dividend payments by the C corporation), but withdrawals from S corporations and partnerships are not taxable to the recipients. On the other hand, the withdrawals might be deductible by the C corporation if they can be characterized as salary, interest, or rental payments to the shareholders. To make a tax-advantageous decision, the decision-maker must predict the amount of the withdrawals, as well as the tax rates that apply to the owners and to C corporations.

The above guidelines represent only a cursory overview of the tax aspects of choosing a form of business. There are many other factors to be considered that are beyond the scope of this appendix.[6]

THE METHOD OF ACCOUNTING DECISION

In accounting for routine transactions, individual taxpayers, S corporations, and partnerships are allowed to choose between the cash method and the accrual method of accounting. C corporations are also allowed to choose between these two methods unless the C corporation is "too large," in which case the C corporation must use the accrual method. The tax law currently defines a C corporation as too large to elect the cash method if it has more than five million dollars in gross receipts. In addition to these two methods, a taxpayer who sells a non-inventory asset (e.g., a machine that was used in production or land that was held for investment purposes) under a deferred-payment contract (i.e., one where at least some part of the sales price is collected in a year after the year of sale) is allowed to use the installment method of accounting for that particular sale, regardless of whether the cash or accrual method is used for the more routine transactions.

---

[6]Some of these factors are (a) the impact of the personal holding company tax, (b) the impact of the accumulated earnings tax, (c) the taxes that apply at the state level, (d) the power of the IRS to treat certain C corporations as if they were partnerships, etc.

The Cash Method

In general, the cash method of accounting requires the recognition of taxable income when cash is received and the recognition of deductions when cash is paid. However, there are some major exceptions to this general rule. One exception is that borrowing money does not cause taxable income, and repaying the principal does not produce a deduction. This rule makes intuitive sense because borrowing increases both an asset and a liability, so the taxpayer's net worth is not increased. Another exception to the general rule is that a payment for an asset that will continue to exist past the end of the year is not deductible when paid. Rather, the amount paid for such an asset (e.g., the amount paid for a building or for prepaid insurance) is deductible over several periods as depreciation or amortization. A third exception is that taxpayers with inventory for sale to customers must use the accrual method for the inventory. That is, no deduction is allowed when inventory is purchased, but only when the inventory is sold. If the inventory is sold on credit, the revenue from the sale must be recognized at the point of sale, not deferred until the cash is collected.

The tax law also provides that the receipt of anything with a fair market value (except accounts receivable arising from the sale of inventory) causes taxable income. For example, if a plumber received some shares of stock with a fair market value of $1,000 in return for his plumbing services, he would have taxable income even though he uses the cash method of accounting. This principle even applies when the taxpayer does not receive an asset. For example, if a taxpayer borrowed $1,000 in cash, there would be no taxable income at the time of borrowing the money. But, if this taxpayer were later to be released from the obligation to repay the debt, the release from the obligation would be treated as $1,000 of taxable income. The taxpayer's total liabilities would decrease as a result of the release from the debt, but total assets would not change. Therefore, the release from the obligation would increase the taxpayer's net worth.

Suppose that on January 1, 19X1, taxpayer Buddy Hamilton opened a sole proprietorship business known as Southern Landscape Enterprises. Southern Landscape Enterprises sold landscaping services and lawn maintenance equipment. Mr. Hamilton's cash receipts and disbursements for the year were as follows:

Receipts:	
Cash sales of inventory and landscaping	$ 50,000
Cash collections for sales of landscaping made on credit (credit sales for the year totaled $85,000)	40,000
Cash borrowed from the bank	100,000
	$190,000
Disbursements:	
Purchases of delivery trucks (only 15% of the cost is deductible as depreciation)	$100,000
Wages paid to employees ($1,500 is owed for work performed at the end of the year)	20,000
Rent for office space, paid in advance for two years on January 1, 19X1	45,000
Inventory purchased ($25,000 of the inventory was sold during the year)	60,000
	$225,000

In addition to the above cash receipts and disbursements, Mr. Hamilton accepted the use of a sail boat for one day in return for landscaping services. The fair market value of the one day's use of the sail boat was $300. The taxable income for Southern Landscape Enterprises determined under the cash basis would be $7,800, determined as follows:

Gross income:		
Cash sales of inventory and landscaping	$50,000	
Collections for sales of landscaping on credit	40,000	
Fair market value of sail boat use	300	$90,300
Deductions:		
Depreciation on delivery trucks	$15,000	
Wages	20,000	
Rent	22,500	
Cost of inventory sold	25,000	82,500
Taxable income		$ 7,800

The Accrual Method

Under the accrual method of accounting for tax purposes, amounts are included in gross income when they are earned, without regard to when cash is collected. Amounts are deducted when expenses are incurred, without regard to when cash is paid. These rules are basically the same rules used by accountants in financial reporting to investors.[7]

Assume that Mr. Hamilton, of the previous example, incurred all the same receipts and disbursements, but Mr. Hamilton uses the accrual method of accounting in calculating his taxable income. His taxable income would be $51,300, determined as follows:

Gross income:		
Cash sales of inventory and landscaping	$50,000	
Sales of landscaping on credit	85,000	
Fair market value of sail boat use	300	$135,300
Deductions:		
Depreciation on delivery trucks	$15,000	
Wages	21,500	
Rent	22,500	
Cost of inventory sold	25,000	84,000
Taxable income		$ 51,300

Obviously, the most significant difference between Mr. Hamilton's taxable income under the cash method and under the accrual method is in accounting for the landscaping sales made on credit. Under the accrual method, all these sales count as taxable income, while under the cash method only the collections on these sales produce taxable income. The examples show clearly why the cash method is frequently the better choice for tax purposes. The cash

---

[7]There are several differences between accrual accounting for tax purposes and generally accepted accounting principles. These differences are beyond the scope of this appendix.

method allows more flexibility in the timing of income recognition. Although Mr. Hamilton sold $85,000 of landscaping services on credit, under the cash method he only recognized $40,000 of taxable income from these sales because he only collected $40,000 in cash. Under the cash method Mr. Hamilton can control how much taxable income he wants to recognize in a particular year by controlling how much effort he puts into collecting on credit sales of his landscaping services. He can control his deductions by accelerating or delaying his cash payments for wages or rent.

The Installment Sales Method

The installment sales method is a special accounting method that allows taxpayers to spread over more than one year the recognition of gain on the sale of non-inventory assets if the sale is under a "deferred-payment contract." A **deferred-payment contract** provides that some or all of the sales price will be collected *after* the end of the year of sale. If the taxpayer uses the cash method or the accrual method to account for a deferred-payment sale of a non-inventory asset at a gain, the entire gain would have to be recognized in the year of sale. It may not be obvious why this is true for the cash method. The following example shows a deferred-payment contract accounted for under the cash method.

In 19X1, taxpayer Michelle Prater, who uses the cash method of accounting for tax purposes, sold land used in her business to Bradford Brown for a price of $10,000, to be collected as follows: (1) $4,000 in 19X1 and (2) $6,000 (plus interest at a market rate) in 19X2. Ms. Prater had a cost in the land of $8,000. Consequently, the realized gain for 19X1 amounted to $2,000 ($10,000 − $8,000). Were it not for the tax statute allowing the installment method, this entire $2,000 gain would have to be recognized when realized in 19X1. To understand the transaction, observe the diagram that follows, where P represents taxpayer Prater, B represents taxpayer Brown, and FMV represents fair market value:

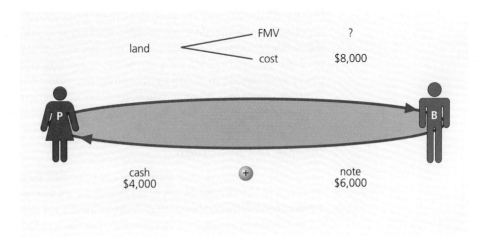

The FMV of the land must be $10,000; otherwise, why would the two parties agree to the exchange? Taxpayer Prater could calculate her realized gain as follows: FMV of property given up ($10,000) less cost of property given up ($8,000) = gain realized ($2,000). Taxpayer Prater would like to argue that she should not have to include the entire $2,000 gain in taxable income because she has not yet collected the entire sales price in cash. However, the cash method requires that anything with a fair market value must be counted in determining receipts. Since the $6,000 note presumably has a $6,000 market value, she is considered to have collected the entire $10,000 sales price in the year of sale and must recognize the $2,000 gain.

Even though the taxpayer in the above example is using the cash method for her normal, routine transactions, she is allowed to use the installment method for this particular transaction. A summary statement of the installment method would be this: if only a portion of the sales price is collected during the year, then only a portion of the total gain is recognized for that year. The following example shows how to apply the installment method.

Assume the same facts as the previous example, except that Ms. Prater elects to use the installment method in accounting for the sale for tax purposes. Although the total realized gain is $2,000, to calculate the amount of realized gain to recognize on the tax return, set up a ratio where the numerator is the amount of cash collected in one year and the denominator is the total amount of cash that will be collected over all years. Then multiply this ratio by the total realized gain. If the ratio is 25%, then 25% of the total cash has been collected, and 25% of the total realized gain should be recognized. In this example, the formula for 19X1 is:

($4,000 cash collected ÷ $10,000 total cash to be collected) x ($2,000 realized gain)

The ratio is 40%, so 40% of $2,000, or $800, should be recognized as gain in 19X1. In 19X2, the formula would be:

($6,000 cash collected ÷ $10,000 total cash to be collected) x ($2,000 realized gain)

Thus, 60% of $2,000, or $1,200, should be recognized as gain in 19X2. In short, as each portion of the cash is collected, a like portion of the gain is recognized. (In addition to the $6,000 cash, taxpayer Brown will pay interest accrued on the note and this amount must be recognized by Prater as ordinary interest income.)

In most instances, taxpayers benefit from using the installment method of reporting for deferred-payment sales for two reasons. First, this method permits the seller to delay the payment of tax. Second, it sometimes results in a lower total tax on the realized gain, since the spreading of the gain over a number of years may result in a lower marginal tax rate. Thus, when given a choice between reporting income when realized versus spreading the recognition of that income over the period cash is collected, most taxpayers prefer the latter.

Income Tax Allocation

Accounting revenues and expenses and taxable income and deductions often differ. The differences are classified as either permanent or temporary. **Permanent differences** include certain revenues and expenses that are included in the determination of net income, but are excluded in the determination of taxable income. An example of a permanent difference is tax-exempt interest earned on investments in bonds issued by state and local governments. The interest earned is included as interest revenue in the determination of accounting net income. However, such interest earned is not subject to federal income taxes and is not included in the determination of taxable income. Permanent differences are included in a corporation's income before deducting taxes. But, they are excluded from the calculation of the corporation's taxable income and, therefore, from the calculation of the income tax expense reported in the income statement.

Temporary differences are certain revenues and expenses that are included in the determination of *accounting* net income either in a later or an earlier period than the period in which they are included in the determination of *taxable* income. The installment sale example above is a case in point. A corporation may use the installment sales method for tax purposes, but recognize the entire realized gains from installment sales in the period of sale for accounting purposes. These choices lead to a difference in accounting for transactions in any given period, but eventually the transactions have the same effect on accounting income and taxable income over the life of the business. Hence, they are called temporary differences. Consider the example of the installment sale and how it would affect the accounting and taxable incomes of the business in the two periods and in total.

	Installment Sale		
	Period of Sale	Period Following Sale	Two-Period Total
Accounting treatment:			
Income from installment sale	$2,000	$ 0	$2,000
Income tax expense @ 40%	800	0	800
After-tax effect	$1,200	$ 0	$1,200
Tax treatment:			
Income from installment sale	$ 800	$1,200	$2,000
Income tax owed @ 40%	320	480	800
After-tax effect	$ 480	$ 720	$1,200

Notice that the effect of the installment sale transaction is the same over two periods for both tax and accounting purposes. However, the income and related tax expense are recorded entirely in the period of sale for accounting purposes, but are spread over two periods for tax purposes. These differences are completely legitimate because the accounting and tax systems serve different purposes. The objectives of financial accounting include presenting information about a) the financial position and b) changes in the financial position, including revenues and expenses resulting from events and transactions of the period. This information is designed to be relevant for making investment, credit, and other economic decisions about businesses. On the other hand, the income tax laws are intended primarily to generate funds for governments and may be modified to achieve social, political and administrative objectives. For example, one reason to allow taxpayers to use the installment sales method is to improve collection of taxes because they are levied in the period in which cash is collected from customers and is available to pay taxes.

Management has an obligation to choose the best methods for both accounting and tax purposes, leading to the kind of disparities illustrated above between income tax expense and the taxes actually owed for the period. How do we handle the disparity within financial accounting? We recognize differences between income tax expense and taxes owed for a period in deferred tax asset and liability accounts. In the case above, the journal entries recording income tax expense for the two years for the installment sale are as follows:

Year of Sale			
	Income Tax Expense	800	
	Income Taxes Payable		320
	Deferred Income Tax Liability		480
	To record income tax expense, taxes payable and deferred taxes on installment sale.		
Following year	Income Tax Expense	0	
	Deferred Income Tax Liability	480	
	Income Taxes Payable		480
	To record taxes payable on income previously recognized but not subjected to income tax in the period realized.		

In the above journal entries we ignore income and expenses from all other sources and even make a zero entry to income tax expense just to illustrate a point. Notice that in the year of sale the full tax consequences of realizing $2,000 of income from the installment sale are recognized. However, because the taxpayer corporation uses the installment sale method for tax purposes, only $320 is actually currently owed to the IRS in that year. We say that the other $480 is deferred to the future and will be due in the following year, when the second installment of $6,000 is received. At that time, $480 is owed to the IRS. However, since the full income from the sale was previously recognized for accounting purposes, no further income tax expense is recognized in the following year. Instead, the income taxes previously deferred are now currently due and the second journal entry above moves them from the deferred category to the current liability "income taxes payable."

Occasionally, corporations have the opposite problem from a deferred tax liability. That is, deductions are postponed for tax purposes that are recognized currently as expenses. Or, revenues are recognized currently for tax purposes that will be recognized for accounting purposes in some future period. These conditions lead to higher current taxes and lower future taxes. Most corporations do not adopt such patterns as conscious strategies. They occur because of unavoidable differences between tax law and generally accepted accounting principles.

If a corporation experiences such a pattern, it may result in a deferred tax asset—a kind of long-term prepaid expense. Generally accepted accounting principles permit corporations to recognize such an asset, but only if the benefits of lower future tax bills are virtually guaranteed.[8]

CAPITAL EXPENDITURE DECISIONS

A taxpayer's capital expenditure decision will be affected by the tax laws if that expenditure will produce a tax deduction for the taxpayer at some time. A tax deduction produces tax savings, and the tax savings reduce the cost of the expenditure. Depending on the type of asset purchased, the tax laws might allow (a) an immediate tax deduction for the full cost of the asset (this is called "expensing"), (b) tax deductions that are spread out over several years as

---

[8]"Accounting for Income Taxes," *Statement of Financial Accounting Standards No. 96* (Stamford, Conn.: FASB, 1987), Summary.

depreciation, or (c) no tax deduction at all (if the asset is not depreciable under the law). If the purchase price of several assets is the same, the asset that produces tax deductions the fastest has the lowest net cost. This is true because tax savings that are spread out far into the future are not worth as much in a present value sense as tax savings that come immediately. Thus, other things being equal, the decision-maker should choose to purchase the asset with the lowest net cost, meaning the asset that provides the earliest deductions.

Assume that taxpayer Vickie Mays owns a sole proprietorship, and she is considering the purchase of an asset for the business. The business generally has a rate of return on invested capital of 12% per year, and her marginal tax rate is 30%. She is considering the purchase of either Machine #1, which can be depreciated over 10 years using the straight-line method, or Machine #2, which is eligible for immediate expensing under the tax laws. Both machines cost $10,000. Assuming that she is indifferent about the qualities of the two machines, the analysis in Illustration A-1 indicates that she should purchase Machine #2 because it has the lowest net cost (using present value analysis).

The example in Illustration A-1 demonstrates the basic principle that the faster an asset can be written off (depreciated) for tax purposes, the less expen-

ILLUSTRATION A-1 Analyses of After-Tax Machine Costs

Machine #1

Year	1 Cost	2 Tax Savings	3 Present Value of Tax Savings	4 Net Cost (1 – 3)
1	$10,000	$ 300[1]	$ 300[2]	$9,700
2	0	300	268[3]	(268)
3	0	300	239[3]	(239)
4	0	300	214[3]	(214)
5	0	300	191[3]	(191)
6	0	300	170[3]	(170)
7	0	300	152[3]	(152)
8	0	300	133[3]	(133)
9	0	300	121[3]	(121)
10	0	300	108[3]	(108)
	$10,000	$3,000	$1,896	$8,104

[1]Tax deduction for the year of $10,000 x 30% marginal tax rate.
[2]Since the tax savings come immediately, no discounting is required.
[3]The present value of $300 discounted at 12% for N years, where N = the year – 1. For example, the present value factor from Appendix C for year 2 at 12% is .8929. $300 x .8929 = $267.87, or approximately $268.

Machine #2

Year	1 Cost	2 Tax Savings	3 Present Value of Tax Savings	4 Net Cost (1 – 3)
1	$10,000	$3,000[1]	$3,000[2]	$7,000
2–10	0	0	0	0
	$10,000	$3,000	$3,000	$7,000

[1]($10,000 tax deduction for the year) x (30% marginal tax rate).
[2]Since the tax savings come immediately, no discounting is required.

sive that asset is. How fast an asset can be written off is a function of (a) what type of property it is and (b) what the tax laws allowed in the year the asset was purchased. Every few years, Congress changes the rate at which assets can be written off. In general, there are three broad categories of depreciation rules. We present these broad categories below. However, space does not permit us to go into all the details that apply to each category.

For assets put into service before the beginning of 1981, acceptable methods of depreciation included straight-line, sum-of-the-years'–digits, and various declining balance methods. The period over which these assets could be written off was based on the taxpayer's estimate of the useful life of the asset. Up to $4,000 of certain assets could have been expensed in the year of purchase.

For assets put into service during the years 1981 through 1986, depreciation was based on the Accelerated Cost Recovery System (ACRS). Instead of the taxpayer estimating the useful life of an asset (which led to frequent arguments with the IRS), all assets were divided into categories (e.g., 3-year, 5-year, 10-year, or 15-year assets) depending on what type of property they were. For example, automobiles were assigned to the 3-year class and computers were assigned to the 5-year class, etc. For each class, the IRS published tables that indicated the amount of depreciation that was allowed for each year. The cost of an automobile used for business was written off over three years at the rate of 25% for the first year, 38% for the second year, and 37% for the third year. Up to $5,000 of the costs of certain assets could have been expensed in the year of purchase.

For assets put into service during 1987 and later years, the Modified Accelerated Cost Recovery System (MACRS) applies. Basically, the categories of assets were redefined so that there were more classes, slower depreciation rates were required, and tables were issued for the new classes. Up to $10,000 of the costs of certain assets could be expensed in the year of purchase.[9]

The ACRS and MACRS rules make no attempt to match the cost of purchasing an asset against the revenues produced by that asset over its useful life. However, even though the matching concept is no longer present, the rules have reduced the number of arguments with the IRS. The taxpayer making capital expenditure decisions no longer needs to estimate the useful life of assets but needs access to the tables showing how much depreciation is available for the assets under consideration.

OTHER IMPLICATIONS FOR DECISION-MAKING

In planning for the effect of taxes on income in general, every business decision-maker should have some familiarity with capital gains and losses and the alternative minimum tax. We discuss each of these topics briefly below.

Capital Gains and Losses

For many, many years Congress gave preferential tax treatment to gains on the sale of capital assets. Basically, capital assets are those assets that taxpayers buy to hold as investments (e.g., stocks and bonds, land, etc.) instead of those assets that are part of a business (e.g., inventory, accounts receivable). The preferential treatment was in the form of a significantly lower rate of tax. For exam-

---

[9]Starting in 1993, the $10,000 amount increased to $17,500.

ple, as recently as 1986, an individual taxpayer could be in the 50% marginal tax bracket for ordinary forms of income but the tax on capital gain income was only 20%. So much tax planning effort went into trying to convert ordinary income into capital gain income that some tax commentators called this activity "the second most popular indoor sport in America." Congress had granted the preferential treatment because it felt that it was unfair to tax such gains at the highest rates applicable. For example, if a taxpayer bought stock in 1950 for $1,000 and sold it in 1980 for $20,000, the entire $19,000 gain would be taxed in 1980, even though the appreciation in the market value of the stock took place gradually over a 30-year period. With the graduated tax rates of the U.S. tax system, the bunching of all the income into one year could put the taxpayer into a high marginal tax bracket. A lower rate of tax was a method to compensate the taxpayer for the fact that the income was all bunched into one year. Congress also thought that taxing capital gain income at ordinary income rates impaired the mobility of capital. That is, if a taxpayer who holds stock with $19,000 of appreciation thinks that he or she will have to pay a 50% tax on the sale of this stock, the taxpayer will simply continue to hold the stock instead of selling it and using the money to re-invest in some other asset. A lower rate of tax would encourage taxpayers to sell more often, and the money that was channeled into other investments would stimulate the economy.

However, in 1986 Congress passed a massive tax reform act that changed the relative difference in tax rates on ordinary income versus capital gain. Currently, the tax rate on capital gains for an individual is the same as the rate applied to ordinary income at low levels of taxable income, but the capital gain tax rate cannot exceed 28%. So, some taxpayers may be paying 15% on ordinary income and 15% on capital gains because their total income does not exceed the 15% bracket. Other taxpayers may have more total income that forces them into higher brackets, so they pay 39.6% on ordinary income and 28% on capital gains.

As part of this tax reform act, Congress left in the law the statutory web of rules dealing with capital gains and losses. In particular, Congress left in the law the provision that capital losses could only be deducted against the total of capital gains plus up to $3,000 of ordinary income. If a taxpayer had capital losses of, say, $10,000, but no capital gains, then only $3,000 of the capital losses could be deducted in the year they were incurred (assuming that the taxpayer had at least $3,000 of ordinary income). The remaining $7,000 of capital losses could be carried forward to the next year and matched against all capital gains plus up to $3,000 of ordinary income in that year. Thus, whenever a taxpayer has capital losses in excess of $3,000, an incentive exists for the income to be capital gain rather than ordinary income, as shown in the following example.

Assume that taxpayer Kathleen Kelly has ordinary income of $50,000 in Year 1. During the year she sold 100 shares of stock for $12,000. The stock had a cost of $21,000, so she has a capital loss of $9,000. She also sold another block of stock at a gain of $2,000. Of the $9,000 capital loss, she can deduct $2,000 against her capital gain income and another $3,000 against her ordinary income. The other $4,000 of the net capital loss can be carried forward to Year 2 and matched against any capital gains she has in Year 2. If she has no capital gains in Year 2, she can deduct another $3,000 of the capital loss carryover amount against ordinary income, leaving $1,000 to carry forward to Year 3. If Kathleen could convert $4,000 of her Year 1 ordinary income into capital gain, she would have a total capital gain of $6,000. In that case, she could deduct $6,000 of her capital loss against her capital gain and $3,000 of the capital loss against ordinary income. This would be preferable because the entire $9,000 capital loss would reduce taxes in Year 1 rather than in later years. Because of the time value of money, an immediate reduction in tax liability is worth more than an equal reduction in the liability for a later year.

In the above example, the key to a successful tax planning strategy was the ability of the taxpayer to convert what would have been ordinary income into capital gain income. The following example illustrates one way to accomplish this.

Taxpayer Bill Nelson has a $10,000 capital loss that he incurred this year, in addition to his $100,000 salary (ordinary income). If he has no capital gains, then he will only be able to deduct the capital loss at the rate of $3,000 per year. He also has an antique automobile (held for investment purposes, with a cost of $12,000) that he wants to sell, but it is in need of some repairs. The auto has a market value of $17,000 without any repairs but could be sold for $21,000 if Mr. Nelson incurs $4,000 of repair work. The repair work would be deductible as an investment expense. The results of Mr. Nelson's selling the auto with or without doing the repair work are shown below:

	Seller Does Repairs	Seller Does Not Do Repairs
Selling price of asset	$21,000	$17,000
Less: cost of asset	12,000	12,000
Capital gain	$ 9,000	$ 5,000
Less: repair expense	4,000	0
Net cash flow before taxes	$ 5,000	$ 5,000

Although Mr. Nelson would be just as well off cash-wise under either alternative before considering taxes, the choice of incurring the repair expense (and increasing the selling price by a like amount) leads to increasing his capital gain by $4,000. Thus, of his $10,000 capital loss, he could deduct all of it in the current year ($9,000 of the loss would be deducted against the capital gain and the other $1,000 would be deducted against ordinary income). If he does not incur the repair expense, his capital gain is only $5,000, meaning that, of his $10,000 capital loss, he could deduct $5,000 of it against his capital gain and $3,000 of it against his ordinary income, but $2,000 of the loss would have to be carried over to the next year. Thus, there is an incentive for Mr. Nelson to generate a larger discretionary capital gain.

It may not seem obvious that Mr. Nelson in the above example has *converted* ordinary income into capital gain by incurring the repair expense, but effectively that is the result. By deducting the repairs, Mr. Nelson has reduced his ordinary income. But, because these repair costs will result in a higher selling price for the auto, the reduction in ordinary income is *replaced* by an increase in capital gain.[10] Thus, what would have been ordinary income has been converted to capital gain.

---

[10]One proviso is in order, however. The repair expenses must be allowable as ordinary deductions for this strategy to work. If the IRS were to decide that the $4,000 really represented *improvements,* rather than repairs, then the $4,000 repair expense would be added to the cost of the auto and the capital gain would still be $5,000 [$21,000 − ($12,000 + $4,000)].

Alternative Minimum Tax

Historically, some taxpayers having very sizable economic incomes have been able to arrange their affairs so as to incur little, if any, regular income tax. Examples of how they have been able to do this include (a) arranging for a large part of their income to be in an excluded category (such as interest income from municipal bonds) or (b) claiming large amounts of accelerated depreciation deductions. In an effort to insure that such individuals would still be required to pay a minimum amount of tax, Congress enacted a provision called the "alternative minimum tax." This tax applies only if it exceeds a taxpayer's regular tax. In other words, taxpayers are subject to a dual tax system: the regular tax system and the alternative minimum tax (AMT) system.[11] The AMT system does not apply if it results in a lower tax than the regular tax system. This is often the case because the AMT system has lower rates and a larger exemption amount. However, sometimes the AMT system produces a larger tax than the regular tax system because the AMT system does not allow as many income exclusions or deferrals (such as accelerated depreciation). The following example demonstrates the type of situation to which the alternative minimum tax is intended to apply.

Sally Harris, a single business executive, received a salary of $75,000 in 19X8 (a year when she claimed $3,000 of cash charitable contribution deductions and personal exemptions were $2,000). In addition to this salary, she exercised some of her "incentive stock options (ISOs)." These ISOs allowed her to purchase the stock of her employer for $10,000 even though the stock's actual fair market value was $75,000. The $65,000 excess of the fair market value over the purchase price represents economic income since it is an increase in her wealth. However, this economic income is not reflected in her regular taxable income calculations. Assume that regular tax rates are 20% of the first $20,000 of taxable income and 30% on all amounts above that.

Gross income			$75,000
Less:			
Charitable contributions in cash			(3,000)
Personal exemption			(2,000)
Regular taxable income			$70,000

		Taxable Income		*Tax Amount*
20%	x	$20,000	=	$ 4,000
30%	x	50,000	=	15,000
		$70,000		$19,000

As illustrated below, however, Sally's liability to the IRS will actually be much higher than this because of the application of the alternative minimum tax.

The computational structure for the alternative minimum tax is as follows:

---

[11]The alternative minimum tax applies to C corporations as well as to individuals. In this appendix, we discuss its impact only on individuals.

Regular Taxable Income
± Tax Preference Adjustments

= Alternative Minimum Taxable Income (AMTI)
– Exemption Amount

= Alternative Minimum Tax Base
x AMT rates

= Alternative Minimum Tax (AMT)

Whereas "taxable income" is the name given to the base for the regular income tax, the base for the alternative minimum tax is alternative minimum taxable income less the exemption amount. The Internal Revenue Code does not have a name for this, but for convenience, we can call it the "AMT base." The starting point in its determination is taxable income (TI) computed in the regular way. Regular TI is then adjusted as shown in the above formula. Like any tax, the alternative minimum tax is computed by multiplying a rate times a base. For this tax, the rate is 26% when the base is less than $175,000 and 28% when the base equals or exceeds $175,000.

Because of the exemption amount, the alternative minimum tax can never apply to low-income taxpayers. Exemption amounts vary from $33,750 for single taxpayers to $45,000 for married couples.[12]

The adjustments to regular taxable income are specified in the Code and are called "tax preference items." In a general sense, you could say that a tax preference occurs anytime that a taxpayer's economic income escapes (regular) taxation because of a Code provision, administrative practice, or judicial doctrine. Congress felt that some tax preferences were being overused. Those that Congress designates as overused are listed in the Code as tax preference items and must be added back to or subtracted from regular taxable income in calculating AMTI.

One of the items that Congress designated as a tax preference item was the bargain element in incentive stock options. For regular TI purposes, a taxpayer who exercises an incentive stock option at a time when the fair market value of the stock exceeds the exercise price need not include this "bargain element" in income. However, since this bargain element does represent economic income, it must be added to regular TI in calculating AMTI.

Another tax preference item is the adjustment for the personal exemption. Under the AMT system, the exemption amount is $33,750 for single taxpayers and $45,000 for married couples. The much smaller personal exemption (around $2,000, with the exact amount depending on the particular year) allowed under the regular tax system must be added back to regular TI and the AMT exemption amount subtracted in order to arrive at the AMT base.

Consider the case of Sally Harris of the previous example. She calculated her 19X8 regular tax liability to be $19,000. However, Sally will have to pay more than this because her alternative minimum tax is $22,470, determined as follows:

---

[12]As AMTI increases in size, the exemption amount is phased out. This phase-out is ignored for purposes of this discussion.

Regular TI	$ 70,000
Adjustments:	
Bargain element in ISOs	65,000
Personal exemption	2,000
AMTI	$137,000
AMT exemption	(33,750)
AMT base	$103,250
AMT rate	26%
AMT	$ 26,845

Perhaps a more intuitive understanding of the AMT can be reached by calculating the AMT base in a "direct" manner (rather than by making adjustments to regular TI) and comparing the result to the calculation of regular TI:

	Regular Tax System	AMT System
Salary	$75,000	$ 75,000
Economic income from stock options	N/A	65,000
Less:		
Charitable contributions in cash	(3,000)	(3,000)
Personal exemption	(2,000)	N/A
AMT exemption	N/A	(33,750)
Tax base	$70,000	$103,250

For planning purposes, taxpayers need to be aware of the impact of both the regular tax and the alternative minimum tax. The following example illustrates the tax aspects of making a choice between alternative investments and demonstrates clearly that being aware of the basic concepts of the alternative minimum tax is necessary in order to make appropriate investment decisions.

Assume that taxpayer Chris Young received a large inheritance in 19X2. Inherited money is not taxable, but he was drawing a salary and expected to have taxable income of $42,000 for tax year 19X2, excluding the income from some investments he was considering purchasing with his inheritance. He was considering two potential investments, each costing the same amount. Investment #1 consisted of some standard municipal bonds that paid $64,000 in interest income per year. Under the regular tax system, interest income on municipal bonds is not taxable. Investment #2 consisted of some municipal bonds that qualified as "private activity bonds" because the city that issued them would turn the proceeds over to private developers to build a stadium for the city. Under the regular tax system, interest income on private activity bonds is not taxable. These bonds paid $68,000 in interest income per year. Mr. Young felt that he should purchase Investment #2 because these bonds paid more and because the interest income on both investments was tax-exempt. However, he was wise enough to consult his tax advisor about his decision.

His tax advisor informed Mr. Young that both investments were indeed tax-exempt, but only from the regular tax. The income from the private activity bonds of Investment #2 would be subject to the alternative minimum tax (while the income from Investment #1 was exempt from both the regular tax and the AMT). Assuming that Mr. Young chose investment #2 and had no other tax preference adjustments, his regular tax and his alternative minimum tax could be determined as follows:

	Regular Tax System	AMT System
Gross income:		
From salary	$42,000	$42,000
From private activity bonds	N/A	68,000
Less:		
Personal exemption	(2,000)	N/A
AMT exemption	N/A	(33,750)
Tax base	$40,000	$76,250
Tax liability	$10,000[1]	$19,825[2]

[1](20% x first $20,000) + (30% x next $20,000) = $10,000
[2]26% x $76,250 = $19,825.

By investing in the private activity bonds of Investment #2, Mr. Young would have an additional $9,825 of tax liability ($19,825 – $10,000) because he would have to pay the AMT instead of the regular tax. The after-tax income from his investment would thus be $58,175 ($68,000 interest income – $9,825 additional tax). On the other hand, Investment #1 would produce no additional tax liability because these bonds were not subject to either the regular tax or the alternative minimum tax. Therefore, the after-tax income from Investment #1 would be $64,000, and Mr. Young would be better off selecting Investment #1.

SUMMARY

This appendix has introduced some of the fundamental tax aspects of some important business decisions. Deciding on the form of business requires (a) knowledge of how sole proprietorships, partnerships, S corporations, C corporations, and their owners are taxed and (b) predictions about how much income will be earned and retained by the business. Deciding on the method of accounting in general requires recognition of (a) the flexibility that results from the cash method and (b) the tax deferral opportunities available with the use of the installment method. Making capital expenditure decisions requires (a) knowledge of the available tax depreciation methods and (b) recognition of the effect these depreciation methods have on the after-tax cost of the assets. Finally, tax planning for the effect of taxes on income in general requires an understanding of (a) the distinction between ordinary income and capital gain and (b) the effect of the alternative minimum tax.

J.C. Penney Company, Inc. 1993 Annual Report

To the Stockholders and Board of Directors of J.C. Penney Company, Inc.:

We have audited the accompanying consolidated balance sheets of J.C. Penney Company, Inc. and Subsidiaries as of January 29, 1994, January 30, 1993, and January 25, 1992, and the related consolidated statements of income, reinvested earnings, and cash flows for the years then ended. These consolidated financial statements are the responsibility of the Company's management. Our responsibility is to express an opinion on these consolidated financial statements based on our audits.

We conducted our audits in accordance with generally accepted auditing standards. Those standards require that we plan and perform the audit to obtain reasonable assurance about whether the financial statements are free of material misstatement. An audit includes examining, on a test basis, evidence supporting the amounts and disclosures in the financial statements. An audit also includes assessing the accounting principles used and significant estimates made by management, as well as evaluating the overall financial statement presentation. We believe that our audits provide a reasonable basis for our opinion.

In our opinion, the consolidated financial statements referred to above present fairly, in all material respects, the financial position of J.C. Penney Company, Inc. and Subsidiaries as of January 29, 1994, January 30, 1993, and January 25, 1992, and the results of their operations and their cash flows for the years then ended in conformity with generally accepted accounting principles.

As discussed on page 25, the Company adopted the provisions of the Financial Accounting Standards Board's Statement of Financial Accounting Standards No. 106, Employers' Accounting for Postretirement Benefits Other Than Pensions, in 1991. Also, as discussed on page 27, the Company adopted the provisions of the Financial Accounting Standards Board's Statement of Financial Accounting Standards No. 109, Accounting for Income Taxes, in 1993.

KPMG Peat Marwick

KPMG Peat Marwick
200 Crescent Court, Dallas, Texas 75201
February 24, 1994

The Company is responsible for the information presented in this Annual Report. The consolidated financial statements have been prepared in accordance with generally accepted accounting principles and are considered to present fairly in all material respects the Company's results of operations, financial position, and cash flows. Certain amounts included in the consolidated financial statements are estimated based on currently available information and judgment of the outcome of future conditions and circumstances. Financial information elsewhere in this Annual Report is consistent with that in the consolidated financial statements.

The Company's system of internal controls is supported by written policies and procedures and supplemented by a staff of internal auditors. This system is designed to provide reasonable assurance, at suitable costs, that assets are safeguarded and that transactions are executed in accordance with appropriate authorization and are recorded and reported properly. The system is continually reviewed, evaluated, and where appropriate, modified to accommodate current conditions. Emphasis is placed on the careful selection, training, and development of professional managers.

An organizational alignment that is premised upon appropriate delegation of authority and division of responsibility is fundamental to this system. Communication programs are aimed at assuring that established policies and procedures are disseminated and understood throughout the Company.

The consolidated financial statements have been audited by independent auditors whose report appears above. This audit was conducted in accordance with generally accepted auditing standards, which includes the consideration of the Company's internal controls to the extent necessary to form an independent opinion on the consolidated financial statements prepared by management.

The Audit Committee of the Board of Directors is composed solely of directors who are not officers or employees of the Company. The Audit Committee's responsibilities include recommending to the Board for stockholder approval the independent auditors for the annual audit of the Company's consolidated financial statements. The Committee also reviews the audit plans, scope, fees, and audit results of the auditors; internal audit reports on the adequacy of internal controls; non-audit services and related fees; the Company's ethics program; status of significant legal matters; the scope of the internal auditors' plans and budget and results of their audits; and the effectiveness of the Company's program for correcting audit findings. Company personnel, including internal auditors, meet periodically with the Audit Committee to discuss auditing and financial reporting matters.

William R. Howell
Chairman of the Board
and Chief Executive Officer

Robert E. Northam
Executive Vice President
and Chief Financial Officer

MANAGEMENT'S

DISCUSSION

AND ANALYSIS

OF FINANCIAL

CONDITION AND

RESULTS OF

OPERATIONS

Results of operations (In millions except per share data)	1993	1992	1991
Retail sales, per cent increase (decrease)	5.4	11.2	(1.0)
Gross margin, per cent of retail sales[1]			
FIFO	31.3	31.5	30.9
LIFO	31.5	31.7	31.5
Selling, general, and administrative expenses, per cent of retail sales[1]	23.7	24.7	25.6
Pre-tax income of other businesses	$ 149	$ 125	$ 91
Effective income tax rate	39.3	38.3	43.5
Net income[2,3]	$ 940	$ 777	$ 80
Per share[2,3]	$ 3.53	$ 2.95	$ .20

[1]Ratios for 1992 and 1991 reflect the reclassifications made to conform with 1993, as described on page 18.
[2]Excluding the effects of an extraordinary charge and the cumulative effect of an accounting change, after tax income was $944 million, or $3.55 per share, in 1993.
[3]Excluding the effects of nonrecurring items and the cumulative effect of an accounting change, after tax income was $528 million, or $2.00 per share, in 1991.

Net income was $940 million in 1993, an increase of 20.9 per cent from $777 million in 1992. Fully diluted earnings per share improved to $3.53 per share from $2.95 per share in 1992. Net income in 1993 was reduced by an extraordinary charge, net of tax, of $55 million, or 21 cents per share, for the premium and unamortized issuing costs related to retired debt. Net income was increased by $51 million, or 19 cents per share, for the cumulative effect of implementing Financial Accounting Standards Board Statement No. 109, *Accounting for Income Taxes*. Excluding the impact of the extraordinary charge and the cumulative effect of the accounting change, net income was $944 million, or $3.55 per share. 1993 net income also included a charge of $14 million, or 5 cents per share, for the impact of the tax rate increase on deferred taxes. Increased sales volume in both stores and catalog, resulting from the Company's strategy of offering fashion, quality, and price to its customers, as well as an aggressive national advertising campaign, were largely responsible for the improvement. Contributing to increased profits were well managed selling, general, and administrative expenses. These expenses, as a per cent of retail sales, declined significantly in 1993.

Net income was $777 million in 1992, an increase of 47.2 per cent from $528 million in 1991, excluding the impact in 1991 of nonrecurring items and the cumulative effect of an accounting change. On a comparable basis, fully diluted earnings per share improved to $2.95 per share from $2.00 per share in 1991. Higher sales volume due to increased unit sales, resulting from the shift in the Company's strategy to more affordable pricing, was largely responsible for the improvement. Selling, general, and administrative expenses, as a per cent of retail sales, declined significantly in 1992.

Net income was $80 million in 1991 and fully diluted earnings per share was 20 cents. Net income in 1991 was reduced by a provision for nonrecurring items and the cumulative effect of an accounting change. Nonrecurring items in 1991 amounted to $395 million before income taxes, and reflected certain changes in strategy. The Company made a strategic business decision in 1991 to hold only regional shopping center joint ventures in its real estate investment portfolio and to dispose of all other projects as soon as practicable. As a result of this decision, a provision of $220 million was made to record the costs to dispose of the properties the Company planned to exit. Also, in 1991, a decision was made to downsize or discontinue several non-core retail operations. This decision reflected a change in business strategy to deemphasize experimental businesses and to focus on the Company's core business, resulting in a provision of $115 million. In addition, nonrecurring items included a provision of $60 million for the costs associated with consolidating and streamlining various Company activities. In 1993, the Company completed the disposition of all its non-regional shopping center properties, and continued to close unproductive stores and implement cost cutting measures. The restructuring was substantially complete at the end of 1993. In 1991, the Company adopted Financial Accounting Standards No. 106, Employers' Accounting for Postretirement Benefits Other Than Pensions, that resulted in a one-time charge to earnings of $184 million, net of taxes, or 79 cents per share.

Excluding the effects of the nonrecurring items and the cumulative effect of the accounting change in 1991, income declined 8.5 per cent to $528 million from $577 million in 1990. The decline in 1991 was due to a 1.0 per cent decline in sales volume and an increase in the income tax rate. On a comparable basis, earnings per share declined from $2.16 in 1990 to $2.00 in 1991.

Revenue (In millions)	1993	Per cent increase (decrease)	1992	Per cent increase (decrease)	1991
JCPenney stores	$14,056	4.4	$13,460	12.1	$12,007
Catalog	3,514	11.0	3,166	5.5	3,002
Drug stores	1,413	2.2	1,383	16.0	1,192
Total retail sales*	18,983	5.4	18,009	11.2	16,201
JCPenney Insurance	475	22.5	388	18.3	328
JCPenney National Bank	120	2.0	118	(1.1)	119
Total revenue	$19,578	5.7	$18,515	11.2	$16,648

1993 and 1991 comprised 52 weeks, and 1992 comprised 53 weeks.

*On a comparable 52-week basis, total retail sales increased 6.9 per cent in 1993 and 9.8 per cent in 1992.

Sales of all JCPenney stores in 1993 increased 4.4 per cent while comparable store sales increased 4.0 per cent. The sales gain was primarily the result of the Company's strategy of offering fashion and quality merchandise to its customers at competitive, affordable prices; a new national television advertising campaign; and the increased emphasis on developing its private brands. On a comparable 52 week basis, sales of JCPenney stores increased 5.8 per cent in 1993, and comparable store sales increased 5.3 per cent. JCPenney store sales increased approximately 6 per cent in each of the merchandise divisions (women's, men's, children's and family shoes, and home and leisure). Sales of all JCPenney stores, on a 52 week basis, increased 10.9 per cent in 1992, and comparable store sales increased 9.7 per cent.

Catalog sales increased 11.0 per cent in 1993 to a record $3,514 million. The results were impacted by significant growth in the number of new customers, gains from specialty catalogs, and improved synergy with JCPenney stores' merchandise mix. The Company's decision to accept the Discover Card in April 1993 contributed to 1993's growth in attracting new customers.

Drug store sales increased 2.2 per cent in 1993. On a comparable 52 week basis, drug store sales increased 4.2 per cent in 1993, primarily as a result of higher mail order pharmacy sales.

Gross margin on a FIFO basis, as a per cent of retail sales, declined in 1993 to 31.3 per cent from 31.5 per cent in 1992, due to a more promotional environment during the holiday season. This ratio increased in 1992 as compared with 1991 due to lower markdowns. The decline in this ratio in 1991 as compared with 1990 was due to increased markdowns in the first half of 1991.

In 1991, based on its strategy to lower retail prices, the Company elected to apply an internally developed LIFO index (rather than one prepared by the U.S. Government for all department stores) to measure more accurately increases and decreases in JCPenney retail prices. Because of the continued decline in retail prices, there was deflation in the Company's LIFO index in 1993, 1992, and in 1991. As a result, there was a LIFO credit of $36 million in 1993, as compared with a credit of $32 million in 1992 and a $91 million credit in 1991.

Gross margin on a LIFO basis, as a per cent of retail sales, was 31.5 per cent in 1993, as compared with 31.7 per cent in 1992 and 31.5 per cent in 1991.

SG&A expenses increased in 1993 by 1.4 per cent from 1992's level. As a per cent of sales, SG&A expenses declined in 1993 to 23.7 per cent from 24.7 per cent in 1992, reflecting the Company's continuing efforts to control costs across all operating and support areas.

SG&A expenses increased in 1992 by 7.0 per cent, reflecting higher salaries and personnel related costs resulting from increased sales volume and planned increases in advertising associated with a national television advertising campaign and increased distribution of circulars. SG&A expenses declined in 1991 by 3.1 per cent, reflecting the Company's efforts to reduce costs across all operating and support areas. In 1992, the SG&A expense ratio declined to 24.7 per cent from 25.6 per cent in 1991 and 26.2 per cent in 1990, as a result of higher sales volume and well managed expenses.

Net interest expense and credit costs (In millions)	1993	1992	1991
Finance charge revenue	$ (523)	$ (509)	$ (567)
Interest expense, net	241	258	308
Credit costs			
Bad debt expense	95	122	175
Operating expenses (including third party credit costs)	260	261	260
Net interest expense and credit costs	$ 73	$ 132	$ 176

Net interest expense and credit costs declined 44.7 per cent in 1993 to $73 million, primarily as a result of lower bad debt and interest expense. Interest expense declined as a result of the debt restructuring program (described on page 13) initiated by the Company to take advantage of declining interest rates. Net interest expense and credit costs was $132 million in 1992, a decline of 25.0 per cent from $176 million in 1991. The decline in 1992 was also due to lower bad debt and interest expense.

The effective income tax rate for 1993 was 39.3 per cent as compared with 38.3 per cent in 1992 and 43.5 per cent in 1991. The 1993 rate included a one-time, non-cash charge of $14 million for the revaluation of deferred taxes, as required by Statement No. 109, Accounting for Income Taxes. Excluding the adjustment for deferred taxes, the 1993 effective income tax rate was 38.3 per cent, which approximates the expected rate for 1994. The 1993 rate increased from 1992's rate due to the legislated Federal income tax rate increase from 34 per cent to 35 per cent. The 1993 rate was reduced by the tax effect of dividends on allocated leveraged employee stock ownership plan (LESOP) shares, in accordance with Statement No. 109. The 1992 effective income tax rate declined from 1991's rate primarily due to the $21 million charge to income tax expense in 1991 for prior years' tax audit adjustments.

Pre-tax income of other businesses (In millions)	1993	1992	1991
JCPenney Insurance	$ 120	$ 101	$ 78
JCPenney National Bank	29	24	13
Total	$ 149	$ 125	$ 91

JCPenney Insurance, which markets life, accident and health, and credit insurance, continued its growth trend which began in 1989. Pre-tax income was $120 million, an increase of $19 million or 19.3 per cent over 1992. This growth resulted from favorable trends in both premiums earned and lower loss ratios. Premium income for 1993 was $416 million, an increase of $83 million or 25 per cent over 1992. The growth in premium income resulted from an increase of 1.2 million policies, 25 per cent more than in 1992. Increases in renewal premiums of $59 million resulted from the increased sales over the past three years coupled with favorable policy retention. Pre-tax income was $101 million in 1992, an increase of 27.9 per cent over 1991, primarily due to increased premiums. During the past two years, JCPenney Insurance has expanded its market share through relationships with other credit card issuers in both the United States and Canada to solicit their customers. These relationships included 17 companies in the United States and three companies in Canada.

JCPenney National Bank offers Visa and MasterCard credit cards. At the end of the year, about 403 thousand credit cards were active. Pre-tax income improved in both 1993 and 1992, as a result of lower interest rates and a reduction in bad debt expense.

Financial position. The Company generated $286 million in cash from operating activities in 1993 as compared with $1,574 million in 1992 and $911 million in 1991. The change in 1993 was due to an increase in customer accounts receivable, particularly in the fourth quarter when the utilization of the JCPenney credit card increased to 47.5 per cent of sales from 46.6 per cent in 1992's comparable period. Additionally, $425 million of securitized accounts receivable were amortized. The primary contributions to increased cash flow in 1992 were higher net income and declines in customer accounts receivable.

Total customer receivables serviced by the Company were $4.4 billion at the end of 1993, $352 million or 8.8 per cent higher than the level at the end of 1992. The increase in customer receivables was due to the higher sales volume in 1993. In 1993, the Company established the JCPenney Card Bank, National Association, which issues JCPenney credit cards to customers in five states. The customer accounts receivable owned by the Card Bank are fully consolidated for reporting purposes in the total customer receivables serviced by the Company. Customer receivables serviced totaled $4.0 billion at the end of 1992, $411 million or 9.3 per cent below the level at the end of 1991. The decline in 1992 customer receivables serviced reflected a reduction in the utilization of the JCPenney credit card, increased usage of third party credit cards, as well as faster repayments by customers. Customer receivables serviced were $4.4 billion at the end of 1991, or 8.6 per cent below the level at the end of 1990.

Merchandise inventories, on a FIFO basis, increased to $3.8 billion in 1993, up 7.1 per cent from 1992 and are in line with recent sales volumes. FIFO inventories increased 10.2 per cent in 1992 and 4.9 per cent in 1991.

Net property, plant, and equipment, at $3.8 billion, was $63 million above the level of the preceding year. Cash requirements for capital expenditures in 1993 were $480 million, $26 million above 1992. Capital expenditures were $516 million in 1991. The Company presently expects capital expenditures of approximately $500 million in each of the next three years.

Investments, at $1.2 billion, increased $191 million in 1993, primarily due to growth in JCPenney Insurance investments.

Accounts payable and accrued expenses increased 5 per cent to $2.1 billion in 1993 primarily as a result of the increase in trade accounts payable due to the $287 million increase in merchandise inventories. Accounts payable and accrued expenses were $2.0 billion in 1992 and $1.6 billion in 1991.

During 1993, the Company continued a program to restructure its debt and securitized accounts receivable portfolio to take advantage of the lower interest rate environment. The program, which was initiated in 1992, restructured and refinanced $2.6 billion of high cost debt, including both on and off-balance-sheet debt, through various methods including calls, open market purchases, defeasance, and scheduled retirements. Additionally, in February 1994, $350 million of zero coupon notes yielding 13 per cent matured. The restructured debt was financed with operating cash flow and lower cost debt. The weighted average annual interest rate on the restructured and refinanced debt was 10 per cent. In connection with the program, the Company issued $1.25 billion of fixed rate debt in 1993 and 1992 with maturities of five, 10, and 30 years, with a weighted average annual interest rate of 6.1 per cent. As a result, the program will produce annual financing cost savings in excess of $120 million.

Total debt at year end 1993 included $379 million of borrowings by the LESOP, which is guaranteed by the Company. The source of funds to repay the LESOP debt will be dividends from the Series B preferred stock and cash contributions by the Company, totaling approximately $50 million semi-annually through July 1998.

Stockholders' equity was $5.4 billion at the end of 1993, an increase of $660 million from the previous year due primarily to the increase in net income.

On March 9, 1994, the Board of Directors declared an increase in the regular quarterly dividend to 42 cents per share, or an indicated annual rate of $1.68 per share. The regular quarterly dividend on the Company's outstanding stock was payable on May 1, 1994, to stockholders of record on April 8, 1994. The Board also approved on March 9, 1994, the purchase of up to 10 million shares of the Company's common stock to offset dilution caused by the issuance of common shares under the Company's equity compensation and benefit plans. The shares will be purchased from time to time on the open market or through privately negotiated transactions. On March 10, 1993, the Board of Directors declared a two-for-one split of the Company's common stock and increased the quarterly dividend to 36 cents per share from 33 cents per share, or an indicated annual rate of $1.44 compared with $1.32 per share in 1992.

The Company anticipates that the major portion of its cash requirements during the next few years to finance its operations, update its stores, and expand will continue to be generated internally from operations. The Company will continue to review all expenditures to maximize financial returns and maintain financial flexibility.

Impact of inflation and changing prices. The impact of inflation on the Company has lessened in recent years as the rate of inflation has declined. Inflation causes increases in the cost of doing business, including capital expenditures. The effect of rising costs cannot always be passed along to customers by adjusting prices because of competitive conditions. By striving to control costs, the Company attempts to minimize the effects of inflation on its operations.

INDEPENDENT

AUDITORS'

REPORT

To the Stockholders and Board of Directors of J.C. Penney Company, Inc.:

We have audited the accompanying consolidated balance sheets of J.C. Penney Company, Inc. and Subsidiaries as of January 29, 1994, January 30, 1993, and January 25, 1992, and the related consolidated statements of income, reinvested earnings, and cash flows for the years then ended. These consolidated financial statements are the responsibility of the Company's management. Our responsibility is to express an opinion on these consolidated financial statements based on our audits.

We conducted our audits in accordance with generally accepted auditing standards. Those standards require that we plan and perform the audit to obtain reasonable assurance about whether the financial statements are free of material misstatement. An audit includes examining, on a test basis, evidence supporting the amounts and disclosures in the financial statements. An audit also includes assessing the accounting principles used and significant estimates made by management, as well as evaluating the overall financial statement presentation. We believe that our audits provide a reasonable basis for our opinion.

In our opinion, the consolidated financial statements referred to above present fairly, in all material respects, the financial position of J.C. Penney Company, Inc. and Subsidiaries as of January 29, 1994, January 30, 1993, and January 25, 1992, and the results of their operations and their cash flows for the years then ended in conformity with generally accepted accounting principles.

As discussed on page 25, the Company adopted the provisions of the Financial Accounting Standards Board's Statement of Financial Accounting Standards No. 106, Employers' Accounting for Postretirement Benefits Other Than Pensions, in 1991. Also, as discussed on page 27, the Company adopted the provisions of the Financial Accounting Standards Board's Statement of Financial Accounting Standards No. 109, Accounting for Income Taxes, in 1993.

KPMG Peat Marwick

KPMG Peat Marwick
200 Crescent Court, Dallas, Texas 75201
February 24, 1994

COMPANY

STATEMENT

ON FINANCIAL

INFORMATION

The Company is responsible for the information presented in this Annual Report. The consolidated financial statements have been prepared in accordance with generally accepted accounting principles and are considered to present fairly in all material respects the Company's results of operations, financial position, and cash flows. Certain amounts included in the consolidated financial statements are estimated based on currently available information and judgment of the outcome of future conditions and circumstances. Financial information elsewhere in this Annual Report is consistent with that in the consolidated financial statements.

The Company's system of internal controls is supported by written policies and procedures and supplemented by a staff of internal auditors. This system is designed to provide reasonable assurance, at suitable costs, that assets are safeguarded and that transactions are executed in accordance with appropriate authorization and are recorded and reported properly. The system is continually reviewed, evaluated, and where appropriate, modified to accommodate current conditions. Emphasis is placed on the careful selection, training, and development of professional managers.

An organizational alignment that is premised upon appropriate delegation of authority and division of responsibility is fundamental to this system. Communication programs are aimed at assuring that established policies and procedures are disseminated and understood throughout the Company.

The consolidated financial statements have been audited by independent auditors whose report appears above. This audit was conducted in accordance with generally accepted auditing standards, which includes the consideration of the Company's internal controls to the extent necessary to form an independent opinion on the consolidated financial statements prepared by management.

The Audit Committee of the Board of Directors is composed solely of directors who are not officers or employees of the Company. The Audit Committee's responsibilities include recommending to the Board for stockholder approval the independent auditors for the annual audit of the Company's consolidated financial statements. The Committee also reviews the audit plans, scope, fees, and audit results of the auditors; internal audit reports on the adequacy of internal controls; non-audit services and related fees; the Company's ethics program; status of significant legal matters; the scope of the internal auditors' plans and budget and results of their audits; and the effectiveness of the Company's program for correcting audit findings. Company personnel, including internal auditors, meet periodically with the Audit Committee to discuss auditing and financial reporting matters.

William R. Howell
Chairman of the Board
and Chief Executive Officer

Robert E. Northam
Executive Vice President
and Chief Financial Officer

For the Year	1993	1992	1991
Revenue			
Retail sales..	**$ 18,983**	$ 18,009	$ 16,201
Other revenue	**595**	506	447
Total revenue	**19,578**	18,515	16,648
Costs and expenses			
Cost of goods sold, occupancy, buying, and warehousing costs	**12,997**	12,297	11,099
Selling, general, and administrative expenses	**4,508**	4,446	4,154
Costs and expenses of other businesses	**446**	381	356
Net interest expense and credit costs	**73**	132	176
Nonrecurring items	**—**	—	395
Total costs and expenses	**18,024**	17,256	16,180
Income before income taxes, extraordinary charge, and cumulative effect of accounting changes	**1,554**	1,259	468
Income taxes	**610**	482	204
Income before extraordinary charge and cumulative effect of accounting changes	**944**	777	264
Extraordinary charge on debt redemption, net of income taxes of $35	**(55)**	—	—
Cumulative effect of accounting change for income taxes..	**51**	—	—
Cumulative effect of accounting change for postretirement health care benefits, net of income taxes of $116	**—**	—	(184)
Net income	**$ 940**	$ 777	$ 80
Earnings per common share			
Primary			
Income before extraordinary charge and cumulative effect of accounting changes	**$ 3.79**	$ 3.15	$ .99
Extraordinary charge on debt redemption, net	**(.23)**	—	—
Cumulative effect of accounting change for income taxes	**.21**	—	—
Cumulative effect of accounting change for postretirement health care benefits	**—**	—	(.79)
Net income	**$ 3.77**	$ 3.15	$ .20
Fully diluted			
Income before extraordinary charge and cumulative effect of accounting changes	**$ 3.55**	$ 2.95	$ .99
Extraordinary charge on debt redemption, net	**(.21)**	—	—
Cumulative effect of accounting change for income taxes	**.19**	—	—
Cumulative effect of accounting change for postretirement health care benefits	**—**	—	(.79)
Net income	**$ 3.53**	$ 2.95	$ .20

See Notes to Consolidated Financial Statements on pages 18 through 29.

CONSOLIDATED

STATEMENTS

OF INCOME

(In millions except
per share data)
J.C. Penney Company,
Inc. and Subsidiaries

CONSOLIDATED

BALANCE

SHEETS

(In millions except share data)
J.C. Penney Company,
Inc. and Subsidiaries

Assets	1993	1992	1991
Current assets			
Cash and short term investments of $156, $405, and $126	$ 173	$ 426	$ 137
Receivables, net	4,679	3,750	4,131
Merchandise inventories	3,545	3,258	2,897
Prepaid expenses	168	157	163
Total current assets	8,565	7,591	7,328
Properties, net	3,818	3,755	3,633
Investments	1,182	991	442
Deferred insurance policy acquisition costs	426	372	313
Other assets	797	758	728
	$ 14,788	$ 13,467	$ 12,444

Liabilities and Stockholders' Equity	1993	1992	1991
Current liabilities			
Accounts payable and accrued expenses	$ 2,139	$ 2,038	$ 1,565
Short term debt	1,284	907	471
Current maturities of long term debt	348	—	237
Deferred taxes	112	64	60
Total current liabilities	3,883	3,009	2,333
Long term debt	2,929	3,171	3,354
Deferred taxes	1,013	1,012	968
Bank deposits	581	538	530
Insurance policy and claims reserves	540	462	353
Other liabilities	477	570	718
Stockholders' equity			
Preferred stock, without par value: Authorized, 25 million shares — issued, 1 million shares of Series B LESOP convertible preferred	648	666	684
Guaranteed LESOP obligation	(379)	(447)	(509)
Common stock, par value 50¢: Authorized, 500 million shares — issued, 236, 235, and 233 million shares	1,003	955	857
Reinvested earnings	4,093	3,531	3,156
Total stockholders' equity	5,365	4,705	4,188
	$ 14,788	$ 13,467	$ 12,444

See Notes to Consolidated Financial Statements on pages 18 through 29.

	1993	1992	1991
Reinvested earnings at beginning of year	$ 3,531	$ 3,156	$ 3,413
Net income	940	777	80
Unrealized change in equity securities	1	(1)	5
Two-for-one stock split	—	(59)	—
Common stock dividends declared	(339)	(309)	(308)
Preferred stock dividends declared, net of taxes	(40)	(33)	(34)
Reinvested earnings at end of year	$ 4,093	$ 3,531	$ 3,156

See Notes to Consolidated Financial Statements on pages 18 through 29.

For the Year	1993	1992	1991
Operating activities			
Net income	$ 940	$ 777	$ 80
Extraordinary charge, net of income taxes	55	—	—
Cumulative effect of accounting change for income taxes	(51)	—	—
Nonrecurring items and cumulative effect of accounting change	—	—	695
Deferred tax effects	—	—	(268)
Depreciation and amortization	316	310	316
Amortization of original issue discount	48	58	53
Deferred taxes	100	48	109
Change in cash from:			
Customer receivables	(352)	411	413
Securitized customer receivables amortized	(425)	(36)	(214)
Inventories, net of trade payables	(196)	(27)	(293)
Other assets and liabilities, net	(149)	33	20
	286	1,574	911
Investing activities			
Capital expenditures	(480)	(454)	(516)
Investment in asset-backed certificates	(12)	(419)	—
Purchases of investment securities	(351)	(325)	(169)
Proceeds from sales of investment securities	215	195	149
	(628)	(1,003)	(536)
Financing activities			
Increase (decrease) in short term debt	377	436	(433)
Issuance of long term debt	1,015	280	500
Payments of long term debt	(875)	(677)	(104)
Premium on debt retirement	(76)	—	—
Common stock issued, net	37	39	7
Preferred stock retired	(18)	(18)	(13)
Dividends paid, preferred and common	(371)	(342)	(342)
	89	(282)	(385)
Net increase (decrease) in cash and short term investments	(253)	289	(10)
Cash and short term investments at beginning of year	426	137	147
Cash and short term investments at end of year	$ 173	$ 426	$ 137
Supplemental cash flow information			
Interest paid	$ 253	$ 265	$ 267
Interest received	$ 51	$ 71	$ 22
Income taxes paid	$ 486	$ 322	$ 259

See Notes to Consolidated Financial Statements on pages 18 through 29.

CONSOLIDATED STATEMENTS OF CASH FLOWS

(In millions)
J.C. Penney Company, Inc. and Subsidiaries

SUMMARY OF

ACCOUNTING

POLICIES

Reclassifications. Certain amounts for prior years have been reclassified in the Consolidated Statements of Income to conform with the classifications used in 1993. Previously, these amounts were included in "Selling, general, and administrative expenses," "Interest expense, net," "Finance charge revenue," and "Costs and expenses of other businesses." The "Net interest expense and credit costs" caption in the Consolidated Statements of Income includes net interest expense, finance charge revenue, and credit operating costs, including bad debt expense. These reclassifications had no effect on net income. In the Consolidated Balance Sheets, the assets and liabilities of JCPenney Insurance, JCPenney National Bank, and JCP Realty, Inc., which were included in "Other assets" and "Other liabilities," respectively, in prior years, have been fully consolidated. All prior year data throughout this report has been restated to conform with the classifications used in 1993.

Basis of consolidation. The consolidated financial statements present the results of J.C. Penney Company, Inc. and all of its wholly-owned and majority-owned subsidiaries. All significant intercompany transactions and balances have been eliminated in consolidation.

Definition of fiscal year. The Company's fiscal year ends on the last Saturday in January. Fiscal year 1993 ended January 29, 1994, 1992 ended January 30, 1993, and 1991 ended January 25, 1992. They comprised 52 weeks, 53 weeks, and 52 weeks, respectively. The accounts of JCPenney Insurance and JCPenney National Bank are on a calendar year basis.

Retail sales. Retail sales include merchandise and services, net of returns, and exclude sales taxes.

Earnings per common share. Primary earnings per share are computed by dividing net income less dividend requirements on the Series B LESOP convertible preferred stock, net of tax, by the weighted average common stock and common stock equivalents outstanding. Fully diluted earnings per share also assume conversion of the Series B LESOP convertible preferred stock into the Company's common stock. Additionally, it assumes adjustment of net income for the additional cash requirements, net of tax, needed to fund the LESOP debt service resulting from the assumed replacement of the preferred dividends with common stock dividends. The number of shares used in the computation of fully diluted earnings per share was 261 million in 1993, 258 million in 1992, and 234 million in 1991.

Cash and short term investments. Cash invested in instruments with remaining maturities of three months or less from time of investment is reflected as short term investments. The carrying value of these instruments approximates market value due to their short maturities.

Merchandise inventories. Substantially all merchandise inventories are valued at the lower of cost (last-in, first-out) or market, determined by the retail method.

Depreciation. The cost of buildings and equipment is depreciated on a straight line basis over the estimated useful lives of the assets. The principal annual rates of depreciation are 2 per cent for buildings, 5 per cent for warehouse fixtures and equipment, 10 per cent for selling fixtures and equipment, and 20 per cent for data center equipment. Improvements to leased premises are amortized on a straight line basis over the expected term of the lease or their estimated useful lives, whichever is shorter.

Deferred charges. Expenses associated with the opening of new stores are written off in the year of the store opening, except those of stores opened in January, which are written off in the following fiscal year. Deferred policy acquisition costs, principally marketing costs and commissions incurred by JCPenney Insurance to secure new insurance policies, are amortized over the expected premium-paying period of the related policies.

Investments. Fixed income investments (principally bonds), held by JCPenney Insurance, are carried at amortized cost. Marketable equity securities are carried at market value. Investments also include JCP Receivables, Inc. asset-backed certificates held by the Company, which are carried at amortized cost.

Insurance policy and claims reserves. Liabilities established by JCPenney Insurance for future policy benefits are computed using a net level premium method including assumptions as to investment yields, mortality, morbidity, and persistency based on the Company's experience. Liabilities for unpaid claims are charged to expense in the period that the claims are incurred.

Advertising. Costs for newspaper, television, radio, and other media are expensed as incurred, and were $523 million in 1993, $503 million in 1992, and $398 million in 1991. Direct response advertising consists primarily of catalog preparation and printing costs, which are charged to expense over the period during which the benefits of the catalogs are expected, not to exceed six months. Catalog advertising reported in prepaid expense on the balance sheet was $88 million at the end of 1993, as compared with $79 million and $81 million at the end of 1992 and 1991, respectively.

Finance charge revenue and bad debt expense, on customer accounts receivable owned by the Company, are included in the "Net interest expense and credit costs" line of the Consolidated Statements of Income. Finance charge revenue was $523 million in 1993, $509 million in 1992, and $567 million in 1991. Bad debt expense was $95 million in 1993, $122 million in 1992, and $175 million in 1991.

Nonrecurring items amounted to $395 million in 1991, and included recognition of the costs to dispose of certain real estate properties, the write-off of investments in several experimental businesses, and costs associated with consolidating and streamlining various Company activities. There were no nonrecurring items in 1993 or 1992.

Income taxes. The Financial Accounting Standards Board issued Statement No. 109, Accounting for Income Taxes, in February 1992. This statement requires an asset and liability approach to accounting for differences between the tax basis of an asset or liability and its reported amount in the financial statements. Previously, the Company accounted for income taxes under APB Opinion No. 11. The Company adopted Statement No. 109 effective January 31, 1993, and recorded a $51 million cumulative adjustment, reducing deferred taxes on the balance sheet, and increasing net income by the same amount.

Postemployment benefits. The Financial Accounting Standards Board issued Statement No. 112, Employers' Accounting for Postemployment Benefits, in November 1992. This statement, which is required to be adopted in 1994, requires employers to recognize the obligation to provide postemployment benefits on an accrual basis if certain conditions are met. The impact on the Company of adopting this standard is expected to be immaterial.

Debt and equity securities. The Financial Accounting Standards Board issued Statement No. 115, *Accounting for Certain Investments in Debt and Equity Securities,* in May 1993. This statement, which is required to be adopted in 1994 and reflected prospectively, requires that, except for debt securities classified as "held to maturity," investments in debt and equity securities be reported at fair value. Changes in unrealized gains and losses for securities classified as "available for sale" are recorded directly to stockholders' equity, net of applicable income taxes. Had this statement been adopted at year end 1993, assets and deferred taxes on the balance sheet would be increased $119 million and $45 million, respectively, and stockholders' equity would be increased $74 million, with no change in net income.

Advertising. The American Institute of Certified Public Accountants issued Statement of Position No. 93-7, *Reporting on Advertising Costs,* in December 1993. This SOP, which is effective in 1994, requires that all advertising costs be expensed as incurred or the first time the advertising takes place, except for direct response advertising, which can be capitalized and written off over the period during which the benefits are expected. The Company's reporting of advertising costs is in conformance with the provisions of this statement.

Receivables (In millions)	1993	1992	1991
Customer receivables serviced	$ 4,410	$ 4,068	$ 4,489
Customer receivables sold	725	1,150	1,186
Customer receivables owned	3,685	2,918	3,303
Less allowance for doubtful accounts	59	69	79
Customer receivables, net	3,626	2,849	3,224
JCPenney National Bank receivables	587	538	539
Other receivables	466	363	368
Receivables, net	$ 4,679	$ 3,750	$ 4,131

The Company believes that the carrying value of existing customer and bank receivables is the best estimate of fair value because of their short average maturity and bad debt losses can be reasonably estimated and have been reserved.

The Company's policy is to write off accounts when the scheduled minimum payment has not been received for six consecutive months, if any portion of the balance is more than 12 months past due, or if it is otherwise determined that the customer is unable to pay. Collection efforts continue subsequent to write off, and recoveries are applied as a reduction of bad debt losses. Concentrations of credit risk with respect to customer receivables are limited due to the large number of customers comprising the Company's credit card base and their dispersion across the country.

During the period 1988 to 1990, the Company transferred portions of its customer receivables to a trust which, in turn, sold certificates representing undivided interests in the trust in public offerings. Certificates sold during this period totaled $1,400 million. No gain or loss was recognized at the date of sale. The $250 million of certificates sold in 1988 were completely amortized by the end of 1992. Of the $800 million certificates sold in 1990, $425 million were amortized in 1993. As of January 29, 1994, $725 million of the certificates were outstanding and the balance of the receivables in the trust was $1,642 million. The Company owns the remaining undivided interest in the trust not represented by the certificates and will continue to service all receivables for the trust.

In 1993 and 1992, the Company purchased $12 million and $419 million, respectively, of its asset-backed certificates in the open market. The fair value of this total investment of $431 million at the end of 1993 was $510 million based upon quoted market value. The fair value of the $419 million investment at the end of 1992 was $465 million.

Cash flows generated from receivables in the trust are dedicated to payment of interest on the certificates (fixed rates ranging from 8.70% to 9.625%), absorption of defaulted accounts in the trust, and payment of servicing fees to the Company. The reserve funds are fully funded ($112 million at January 29, 1994. Reserves are available if cash flows from the receivables become insufficient to make such payments. None of the reserve funds has been utilized as of January 29, 1994. Additionally, the Company has made available to the trust irrevocable letters of credit of $138 million that may be drawn upon should the reserve funds be exhausted. None of the letters of credit was in use as of January 29, 1994.

In connection with the sale of $375 million of certificates in 1990, the Company entered into two offsetting interest rate swap agreements with a commercial bank, each having a notional principal amount of $375 million. Because these interest rate swap agreements are offsetting, their net fair value at the end of 1993 and 1992 was zero. Currently, the Company has no interest rate exposure from these offsetting interest rate swap agreements which terminate when all certificates have been settled in the year 2000. Under one swap the Company receives a fixed rate and pays a floating rate while under the second swap, the Company pays a fixed rate and receives a floating rate. Because of the offsetting nature of these swaps, there is no financial statement impact. The credit risk has been minimized by the selection of a high credit quality commercial bank as counter party. As long as the Company holds both swap positions, there is effectively no credit risk since there is no net exchange of cash flows.

Merchandise inventories (In millions)	**1993**	1992	1991
Merchandise inventories, at lower of cost (FIFO)			
or market	**$ 3,791**	$ 3,540	$ 3,211
LIFO reserve	**(246)**	(282)	(314)
Merchandise inventories, at LIFO cost	**$ 3,545**	$ 3,258	$ 2,897

Substantially all of the Company's inventories are measured using the last-in, first-out (LIFO) method of inventory valuation. Since 1991, the Company has applied internally developed indices that more accurately measure increases and decreases in its own retail prices. From 1974 through 1990, the Company used the Bureau of Labor Statistics price indices applied against inventory selling values to arrive at an inventory valuation. The cumulative effect of this change on reinvested earnings at the beginning of 1991 was not determinable. However, the effect of using the internal indices instead of the Bureau of Labor Statistics price indices at the end of 1991 was to increase net income by approximately $100 million, or 39 cents per share.

Properties (In millions)	**1993**	1992	1991
Land	**$ 213**	$ 212	$ 205
Buildings			
Owned	**2,119**	2,016	1,838
Capital leases	**219**	237	244
Fixtures and equipment	**2,693**	2,703	2,649
Leasehold improvements	**575**	544	569
	5,819	5,712	5,505
Less accumulated depreciation and amortization	**2,001**	1,957	1,872
Properties, net	**$ 3,818**	$ 3,755	$ 3,633

At January 29,1994, the Company owned 245 retail stores, four catalog distribution centers, one store distribution center, its home office facility, and the insurance company corporate office building.

Capital expenditures (In millions)	**1993**	1992	1991
Land	**$ 1**	$ 8	$ 7
Buildings	**119**	189	209
Fixtures and equipment	**276**	270	238
Leasehold improvements	**63**	27	52
Total capital expenditures	**$ 459**	$ 494	$ 506

Expenditures for existing stores, primarily modernizations and updates, were $130 million in 1993, as compared with $76 million in 1992 and $134 million in 1991. Expenditures for new stores opened in 1993, 1992, and 1991 were $162 million, $130 million, and $172 million, respectively.

Investments at year end 1993 totalled $1,182 million, and consisted of fixed income securities and asset-backed certificates carried at amortized cost (shown in the table below) and equity securities carried at market value. The market value of investments is based on quoted market prices.

Equity securities were $80 million (cost, $71 million) at year end 1993, $29 million (cost, $22 million) at the end of 1992, and $27 million (cost, $18 million) at the end of 1991. Gross unrealized gains and losses at year end 1993 were $10 million and $1 million, respectively. Net unrealized investment gains on equity securities included in stockholders' equity were $6 million, net of deferred income taxes of $3 million.

The market values of investments carried at amortized cost were as follows:

Investments (In millions)	1993		1992		1991	
	Amortized Cost	Market Value	Amortized Cost	Market Value	Amortized Cost	Market Value
U.S. Government obligations	$ 139	$ 153	$ 138	$ 142	$ 48	$ 52
Corporate securities	280	302	210	224	193	210
Mortgage-backed securities	158	164	148	159	140	154
Asset-backed certificates	431	510	419	465	—	—
Other..	94	92	47	45	34	35
Total..	$ 1,102	$ 1,221	$ 962	$1,035	$ 415	$ 451

Gross unrealized gains and losses were $125 million and $6 million, respectively, at year end 1993.

Investments carried at amortized cost had scheduled maturities at year end 1993, as follows:

(In millions)	Amortized Cost	Market Value
Due in one year or less	$ 12	$ 12
Due after one year through five years	147	153
Due after five years through ten years	567	657
Due after ten years	201	218
	$ 927	$1,040
Mortgage-backed securities..	158	164
Other	17	17
Total	$1,102	$1,221

Net realized investment gains are included in "Other revenue" on the Consolidated Statements of Income. These gains were $14 million in 1993, $12 million in 1992, and $5 million in 1991.

The Company limits the credit risk by diversifying its investments by industry and geographic region.

Accounts payable and accrued expenses (In millions)	1993	1992	1991
Trade payables	$ 1,034	$ 944	$ 610
Accrued salaries, vacations, profit-sharing, and bonuses	311	308	256
Taxes, including income taxes	234	238	209
Workers' compensation and public liability insurance	126	116	112
Common dividend payable	85	77	77
Other..	349	355	301
Total..	$ 2,139	$ 2,038	$ 1,565

Short term debt (In millions)	1993	1992	1991
Commercial paper	$ 1,284	$ 887	$ 414
Master notes and other...	—	20	57
Short term debt	$ 1,284	$ 907	$ 471
Average short term debt outstanding	$ 1,350	$ 1,154	$ 754
Peak outstanding	$ 2,327	$ 1,675	$ 1,489
Average interest rates	3.2%	3.7%	5.6%

Long term debt (In millions)	1993	1992	1991
Original issue discount			
Zero coupon notes and 6% debentures, due 1992 to 1994 and 2006, $700 at maturity, yields 13.5% to 15.1%, effective rates 12.5% to 13.2%	$ 101	$ 401	$ 359
Debentures and notes			
5.375% to 7.125%, due 1998 to 2023	1,000	—	—
8.25% to 8.875%, due 1992 to 2022	250	366	269
9% to 10%, due 1992 to 2021	1,000	1,750	2,007
Guaranteed LESOP notes, 8.17%, due 1998*	379	447	509
Present value of commitments under capital leases	127	141	160
Other	72	66	50
Long term debt	$ 2,929	$ 3,171	$ 3,354
Average long term debt outstanding	$ 2,471	$ 2,683	$ 2,827
Average interest rates	9.9%	10.5%	10.2%

For further discussion, see LESOP on page 26.

The fair value for long term debt at the end of 1993 and 1992, excluding capital leases, exceeded the recorded amount by $219 million and $265 million, respectively. The fair value of these instruments was determined based on the interest rate environment and the Company's credit rating.

The Company has in place interest rate swap contracts that were entered into shortly after the issuance of $250 million aggregate principal amount of 8.25 per cent sinking fund debentures in August 1992. These are four year agreements with a notional principal amount totalling $250 million. Under the swap agreements, the Company receives a fixed rate payment and disburses a floating rate payment. The counter parties to these contracts are high credit quality commercial banks. Consequently, credit risk, which is inherent in all swaps, has been minimized to a large extent. The accounting treatment for these contracts, which serve to hedge the 8.25 per cent debentures, is to record the net interest received or paid as an adjustment to interest expense on a current basis. Gains or losses resulting from market movements are not recognized. The fair value of these interest rate swaps at the end of 1993 and 1992 was $13 million and $4 million, respectively.

Changes in long term debt (In millions)	1993	1992	1991
Increases			
5.375% to 9.75% notes, due 1997 to 2023	$ 1,000	$ 250	$ 500
Amortization of original issue discount	48	43	53
Other	16	30	5
	1,064	323	558
Decreases			
Transfers to current maturities of long term debt	348	—	237
8.375% to 12.75% debentures, bonds, and notes, due 1995 to 2021, retired in 1992 and 1993.	872	423	—
Other, including LESOP amortization	86	83	102
	1,306	506	339
Net increase (decrease) in long term debt	$ (242)	$ (183)	$ 219

Maturities of long term debt (In millions)	Long term debt	Capital leases
1994	$ 352	$ 24
1995	2	18
1996	6	19
1997	257	15
1998	587	16
1999 to 2003	821	53
Thereafter	845	19
Total	$ 2,870	164
Less future interest and executory expenses		37
Present value		$ 127

Committed bank credit facilities available to the Company as of January 29, 1994, amounted to $1.25 billion. In 1993, the Company entered into two syndicated revolving credit facility agreements. These facilities include a $450 million, one-year revolver and an $800 million, five-year revolver with a group of 39 domestic and international banks. These facilities, which replaced the $500 million confirmed lines of credit and the $750 million International Revolving Credit Facility, support commercial paper borrowing arrangements. Neither of the borrowing facilities was in use as of January 29, 1994.

Preferred stock. In 1988, a leveraged employee stock ownership plan (LESOP) was adopted (see page 26 for further discussion). The LESOP purchased approximately 1.2 million shares of a new issue of Series B convertible preferred stock from the Company. These shares are convertible into shares of the Company's common stock at a conversion rate equivalent to 20 shares of common stock for each share of preferred stock. The conversion price is $30.00 per common share. The convertible preferred stock may be redeemed at the option of the Company or the LESOP, under certain limited circumstances. The redemption price may be satisfied in cash or common stock or a combination of both at the Company's sole discretion. The dividends are cumulative, are payable semi-annually on January 1 and July 1, and yield 7.9 per cent. The convertible preferred stock issued to the LESOP has been recorded in the stockholders' equity section of the consolidated balance sheet, and the "Guaranteed LESOP obligation," representing borrowings by the LESOP, has been recorded as a reduction of stockholders' equity.

The preferred dividend is payable semi-annually at an annual rate of $2.37 per common equivalent share. Preferred dividends declared were $52 million in 1993, $53 million in 1992, and $54 million in 1991; on an after tax basis, the dividends amounted to $31 million in 1993, $33 million in 1992, and $34 million in 1991.

In 1990, the Board of Directors declared a dividend distribution of one new preferred stock purchase right on each outstanding share of common stock and authorized the redemption of the old preferred stock purchase rights for five cents per share totaling $12 million. The preferred stock purchase rights, in accordance with the rights agreement, entitle the purchase, for each right held, of 1/400 of a share of Series A junior participating preferred stock at a price of $140. The rights are exercisable upon the occurrence of certain events and are redeemable by the Company under certain circumstances, all as described in the rights agreement.

Common stock. On March 9, 1994, the Board of Directors increased the quarterly common dividend to 42 cents per share, or an indicated annual rate of $1.68 per share. The regular quarterly dividend on the Company's outstanding common stock was payable on May 1, 1994, to stockholders of record on April 8, 1994. The Board of Directors also approved on March 9, 1994, the purchase of up to 10 million shares of the Company's common stock to offset dilution caused by the issuance of common shares under the Company's equity compensation and benefit plans. The shares will be purchased from time to time on the open market or through privately negotiated transactions.

The quarterly common dividend was 36 cents per share in 1993, and 33 cents per share in 1992 and 1991, or an indicated annual rate of $1.44 per share in 1993, and $1.32 per share in 1992 and 1991. Common dividends declared were $339 million in 1993, $309 million in 1992, and $308 million in 1991.

On March 10, 1993, the Board of Directors declared a two-for-one stock split in the form of a stock dividend, which was payable May 1, 1993, to stockholders of record on April 12, 1993.

The Company will request stockholder approval at its May 20, 1994 Annual Meeting of Stockholders to increase the authorized number of shares of common stock from 500 million to 1.25 billion shares.

Changes in outstanding common stock	Shares (In thousands)			Amounts (In millions)		
	1993	1992	1991	**1993**	1992	1991
Balance at beginning of year	**234,778**	233,302	233,122	**$ 955**	$ 857	$ 850
Two-for-one stock split	—	—	—	—	59	—
Common stock issued	**1,308**	1,476	180	**48**	39	7
Balance at end of year	**236,086**	234,778	233,302	**$1,003**	$ 955	$ 857

There were approximately 53,000 stockholders of record at year end 1993. In addition, the Company's savings plans, including the LESOP, had 111,000 participants and held 36.1 million shares of the Company's common stock. The savings plans also held 1.1 million shares of preferred stock, convertible into 21.6 million shares of common stock. On a combined basis, these plans held approximately 22 per cent of the Company's common shares after giving effect to the conversion of the preferred stock at the end of fiscal year 1993.

1993 Equity Compensation Plan and 1993 Non-Associate Directors' Equity Plan. In May 1993, stockholders approved the 1993 Equity Compensation Plan (1993 Plan), which replaced the expiring 1989 Equity Compensation Plan. Under the 1993 Plan, 11.6 million shares of common stock were reserved for issuance upon the exercise of options and stock appreciation rights and for the payment of stock awards over the five-year term of the 1993 Plan. No discount options nor tax benefit rights may be issued under the 1993 Plan. Participants in the 1993 Plan are generally to be selected management associates of the Company and its subsidiaries and affiliates as determined by the committee administering the 1993 Plan. It is anticipated that approximately 2,000 associates will be eligible to participate. No awards may be made under the 1993 Plan after May 31, 1998. In May 1993, stockholders also approved the 1993 Non-Associate Directors' Equity Plan (Directors' Plan). Under the Directors' Plan, 90,000 shares of common stock were reserved for issuance upon the exercise of stock options and the payment of stock awards over the five-year term of the Directors' Plan. Each director who is presently not an active employee of the Company will automatically be granted annually an option to purchase 800 shares, in tandem with an award of 200 restricted shares of common stock. An initial grant/award in this same amount will also automatically be granted to each new Non-Associate Director upon his or her first being elected as a director. Such stock options will become exercisable six months from the date of grant, but shares acquired upon such exercise will not be transferable until a director terminates service.

	1993		1992		1991	
Stock options	Shares (In thousands)	Weighted average option price	Shares (In thousands)	Weighted average option price	Shares (In thousands)	Weighted average option price
Balance at beginning of year	8,844	$ 27.42	9,490	$ 26.31	3,820	$ 24.11
Granted	159	41.24	574	35.10	6,048	27.29
Exercised	(752)	24.49	(974)	21.02	(206)	12.85
Expired and cancelled	(16)	26.89	(246)	27.66	(172)	28.20
Balance at end of year	8,235	$ 27.96	8,844	$ 27.42	9,490	$ 26.31

At year end 1993, options covering 2.2 million shares were exercisable and 11.6 million shares were reserved for future grants.

Interest expense (In millions)	1993	1992	1991
Short term debt	$ 43	$ 43	$ 42
Long term debt	246	281	288
Income on short term investments	(14)	(48)	(19)
Interest capitalized	(4)	(14)	(12)
Other, net*	(30)	(4)	9
Interest expense, net	$ 241	$ 258	$ 308

*1993 and 1992 include $34 million and $28 million, respectively, of interest income from the Company's investment in asset-backed certificates.

Rent expense (In millions)	1993	1992	1991
Minimum rent on noncancelable operating leases	$ 236	$ 244	$ 251
Rent based on sales	37	35	33
Minimum rent on cancelable personal property leases	92	107	91
Real estate taxes and common area costs	145	134	120
Total	$ 510	$ 520	$ 495

The Company conducts the major part of its operations from leased premises which include retail stores, distribution centers, warehouses, offices, and other facilities. Almost all leases will expire during the next 20 years; however, most leases will be renewed or replaced by leases on other premises.

Minimum annual rents under noncancelable operating leases and subleases (In millions)	Gross rents	Net rents*
1994	$ 247	$ 173
1995	232	163
1996	217	152
1997	197	141
1998	184	125
Thereafter	973	718
Total	$ 2,050	$ 1,472
Present value		$ 900
Weighted average interest rate		10%

*Rents are shown net of their estimated executory costs, which are principally real estate taxes, maintenance, and insurance.

Retirement plans (In millions)	1993	1992	1991
Pension			
Service cost	$ 50	$ 46	$ 37
Interest cost	123	122	114
Actual (return) loss on assets	(236)	(90)	(332)
Net amortization and deferral	59	(90)	180
Pension credit	(4)	(12)	(1)
Postretirement health care			
Service cost	3	6	5
Interest cost	24	27	26
Total	27	33	31
LESOP expense	50	49	48
Total retirement plans	$ 73	$ 70	$ 78

Pension plan. JCPenney's principal pension plan, which is noncontributory, covers substantially all United States employees who have completed 1,000 or more hours of service within a period of 12 consecutive months and have attained 21 years of age. In addition, the Company has an unfunded, noncontributory, supplemental retirement program for certain management employees. In general, benefits payable under the principal pension plan are determined by reference to a participant's final average earnings and years of credited service up to 35 years.

In 1993, the Company lowered its discount rate to 7.25 per cent due to the continuation of a lower interest rate environment. The discount rate was also lowered in 1992 to 8 per cent from 9 per cent in 1991. In 1992, the salary progression rate was reduced from 6 per cent to 4 per cent because of lower inflation. The impact of these changes increased the Company's obligation at year end 1993 and 1992. Accordingly, the Company made a cash contribution of $65 million to the plan in 1993 and expects to make a cash contribution to the plan in 1994. The 1993 contribution was the first since 1983.

Postretirement health care benefits. The Company's retiree health care plan (Retiree Plan) covers medical and dental services and eligibility for benefits is based on age and years of service. The Retiree Plan is contributory and the amounts paid by retired employees have increased in recent years and are expected to continue to do so. For certain groups of employees, Company contributions toward the cost of retiree coverage will be based on a fixed dollar amount which will vary with years of service, age, and dependent coverage. The Retiree Plan is funded on a pay-as-you-go basis by the Company and retiree contributions. The Company adopted the Financial Accounting Standards Board Statement No. 106, Employers' Accounting for Postretirement Benefits Other Than Pensions, for its Retiree Plan in 1991.

In 1993 and 1992, the Company modified several postretirement health care assumptions. The discount rate was lowered from 8 per cent to 7.25 per cent in 1993 and from 9 per cent to 8 per cent in 1992. The health care trend rate was lowered from 12 per cent to 10 per cent for 1994 with gradual reductions to 6 per cent by 2003 and beyond. In 1992, the health care trend rate was lowered from 13 per cent to 12 per cent. The health care trend rate change represents a modification from previous assumptions because of favorable experience and a lower inflation environment. The changes in plan assumptions had no significant impact on the Company's obligation at year end 1993. A one per cent increase in the health care trend rate would increase the amount reported for the accumulated obligation by $28 million and would result in $2 million additional expense for 1993.

LESOP. The Company's LESOP, adopted in 1988, is a defined contribution plan which covers substantially all United States employees who have completed at least 1,000 hours of service within a period of 12 consecutive months, and if hired on or after January 1, 1988, have attained 21 years of age.

The LESOP borrowed $700 million at an interest rate of 8.17 per cent through a 10 year loan guaranteed by the Company. The LESOP used the proceeds of the loan to purchase a new issue of convertible preferred stock from the Company. The Company used the proceeds from the issuance of preferred stock to the LESOP to purchase 28 million common shares of the Company in the open market.

The Company has reflected the guaranteed LESOP borrowing as long term debt on the Consolidated Balance Sheet. A like amount of "Guaranteed LESOP obligation" was recorded as a reduction of stockholders' equity. The convertible preferred stock issued to the LESOP for cash was recorded in the stockholders' equity section. As the Company makes contributions to the LESOP, these contributions, plus the dividends paid on the Company's preferred stock held by the LESOP, will be used to repay the loan. As the principal amount of the loan is repaid, the "Guaranteed LESOP obligation" is reduced accordingly.

The amount of compensation cost recorded by the Company represents its cash contribution to the LESOP.

The following table sets forth the status of the Company's retirement plans:

		December 31	
Retirement plans (In millions)	**1993**	1992	1991
Pension			
Present value of accumulated benefits			
Vested	$ 1,367	$ 1,227	$ 976
Non-vested	80	73	67
	$ 1,447	$ 1,300	$ 1,043
Present value of actuarial benefit obligation	$(1,781)	$(1,694)	$(1,373)
Net assets at fair market value	1,800	1,585	1,561
Unrecognized transition asset, net of unrecognized losses	216	259	(64)
Net prepaid pension cost	$ 235	$ 150	$ 124
Postretirement health care benefits			
Accumulated benefit obligation			
Retirees	$ 246	$ 205	$ 191
Fully eligible active participants	51	82	77
Other active participants	41	43	42
	338	330	310
Unrecognized net loss	(10)	(7)	—
Net liability	$ 328	$ 323	$ 310
Key assumptions			
Rate of return on pension plan assets	9.5%	9.5%	9.5%
Discount rate	7.25%	8.0%	9.0%
Salary progression rate	4.0%	4.0%	6.0%

26

Total assets and equity (In millions)	Savings plans December 31			Pension December 31		
	1993	1992	1991	**1993**	1992	1991
JCPenney preferred and common stock	**$3,030**	$2,200	$1,720	**$ —**	$ —	$ —
Equity securities	**117**	103	79	**1,424**	1,232	1,188
Fixed income investments	**1,091**	1,061	902	**302**	275	279
LESOP loan obligation, including accrued interest of $17, $20, and $21	**(431)**	(498)	(560)	**—**	—	—
Other assets, net	**47**	37	32	**74**	78	94
Net assets	**$3,854**	$2,903	$2,173	**$1,800**	$1,585	$1,561

Changes in fair value of net assets (In millions)	Savings plans December 31			Pension December 31		
	1993	1992	1991	**1993**	1992	1991
Net assets at beginning of year	**$2,903**	$2,173	$1,823	**$1,585**	$1,561	$1,284
Company contribution	**50**	49	48	**65**	—	—
Participants' contributions	**184**	169	156	**—**	—	—
Gains	**984**	794	400	**236**	93	332
LESOP interest expense	**(35)**	(40)	(45)	**—**	—	—
Benefits paid	**(232)**	(242)	(209)	**(86)**	(69)	(55)
Net assets at end of year.........................	**$3,854**	$2,903	$2,173	**$1,800**	$1,585	$1,561

Taxes. Taxes other than income taxes, over half of which were payroll taxes, totalled $416 million in 1993, as compared with $386 million in 1992 and $372 million in 1991.

The Financial Accounting Standards Board issued Statement No. 109, Accounting for Income Taxes, in February 1992. This statement requires an asset and liability approach to accounting for differences between the tax basis of an asset or liability and its reported amount in the financial statements (temporary differences). Deferred taxes are determined by applying the provisions of enacted tax laws, and adjustments are required for changes in tax laws and rates. The Company adopted Statement No. 109 effective January 31, 1993. Deferred taxes reflected on the balance sheet were reduced by $51 million, and a cumulative adjustment was recorded to increase net income by the same amount, using current tax rates in effect at the beginning of fiscal 1993.

The Omnibus Budget Reconciliation Act of 1993, which was signed into law on August 10, 1993, included an increase in the statutory Federal income tax rate from 34 per cent to 35 per cent, retroactive to January 1, 1993. This change in the tax rate resulted in higher taxes on operating income in 1993 as well as a one-time, non-cash tax expense totalling $14 million for the revaluation of deferred taxes on the balance sheet as required by Statement No. 109.

Deferred tax assets and liabilities reflected on the Company's consolidated balance sheet at January 29, 1994, were measured using enacted tax rates expected to apply to taxable income in the years in which those temporary differences are expected to be recovered or settled. The major components of deferred tax liabilities (assets) at January 29, 1994, were as follows:

Temporary differences (In millions)	Deferred (Asset)	Deferred Liability	Net (Asset) Liability
Retirement plans..	$ (191)	$ 154	$ (37)
Restructuring reserve	(49)	—	(49)
Worker's compensation/public liability	(78)	—	(78)
Leases	(36)	388	352
Accounts receivable	(22)	—	(22)
Inventories	(23)	125	102
Depreciation	—	704	704
Deferred policy acquisition costs.............................	—	147	147
Other	(153)	159	6
Total	$ (552)	$1,677	$1,125

No valuation allowances were considered necessary as of January 31, 1993 or January 29, 1994. The Company believes that the existing deductible temporary differences will be offset by future reversals of differences generating taxable income.

Deferred taxes, under APB Opinion No. 11 in 1992 and 1991, consisted principally of accumulated depreciation and accounting for leases.

Income tax expense (In millions)	1993	1992	1991
Current			
Federal	$ 443	$ 372	$ 196
State and local	67	62	62
	510	434	258
Deferred			
Federal	80	29	(29)
State and local	20	19	(25)
	100	48	(54)
Total	$ 610	$ 482	$ 204
Effective tax rate	39.3%	38.3%	43.5%

Reconciliation of tax rates	Amounts (In millions)			Per cent of pre-tax income		
	1993	1992	1991	1993	1992	1991
Federal income tax at statutory rate	$ 544	$ 428	$ 159	35.0	34.0	34.0
State and local income taxes, less federal income tax benefit	58	53	25	3.7	4.2	5.1
Revaluation of deferred taxes	14	—	—	.9	—	—
Tax effect of dividends on allocated LESOP shares	(9)	—	—	(.5)	—	—
Interest, net of tax, on prior years' audit adjustments	—	—	21	—	—	4.6
Tax credits and other	3	1	(1)	.2	.1	(.2)
Total	$ 610	$ 482	$ 204	39.3	38.3	43.5

Segment reporting. The Company operates predominantly in one industry segment consisting of selling merchandise and services to consumers through retail department stores that include catalog departments. Total assets for that industry segment at the end of the last three years were $12,888 million, $11,820 million, and $10,987 million, respectively.

QUARTERLY DATA
(Unaudited)

(In millions except per share data)	First 1993	1992	1991	Second 1993	1992	1991	Third 1993	1992	1991	Fourth 1993	1992	1991
Retail sales	$ 3,964	3,793	3,433	3,963	3,789	3,456	4,735	4,342	3,937	6,321	6,085	5,375
Per cent increase (decrease)	4.5	10.5	(2.7)	4.6	9.6	(3.5)	9.1	10.3	(1.4)	3.9	13.2	2.2
Total revenue	$ 4,106	3,918	3,538	4,106	3,912	3,567	4,888	4,472	4,050	6,478	6,213	5,493
Per cent increase (decrease)	4.8	10.7	(2.2)	5.0	9.7	(2.8)	9.3	10.4	(1.0)	4.3	13.1	2.5
LIFO gross margin	$ 1,280	1,233	1,107	1,191	1,164	1,036	1,530	1,395	1,250	1,985	1,920	1,709
LIFO gross margin, per cent of retail sales	32.3	32.5	32.2	30.1	30.7	30.0	32.3	32.1	31.8	31.4	31.6	31.8
Selling, general, and administrative expenses, per cent of retail sales	25.9	26.7	28.4	25.8	27.1	27.8	24.2	25.0	26.3	20.8	21.7	22.0
Income before extraordinary charge and cumulative effect of accounting changes	$ 172	136	80	112	80	31	221	186	116	439	375	37
Net income (loss)	$ 206	136	(104)	112	80	31	185	186	116	437	375	37
Income per share before extraordinary charge and cumulative effect of accounting changes												
Primary	$ .68	.54	.31	.43	.31	.10	.88	.75	.46	1.80	1.55	.12
Fully diluted	$ .65	.52	.31	.42	.31	.10	.83	.70	.46	1.65	1.42	.12
Net income (loss) per common share												
Primary	$ .82	.54	(.48)	.43	.31	.10	.73	.75	.46	1.79	1.55	.12
Fully diluted	$ .78	.52	(.48)	.42	.31	.10	.69	.70	.46	1.64	1.42	.12
Dividends per common share	$ .36	.33	.33	.36	.33	.33	.36	.33	.33	.36	.33	.33
Common stock price range												
High	$ 45	34	28	49	36	29	52	38	27	56	40	29
Low	$ 36	27	24	41	32	24	39	33	24	49	36	24

SUPPLEMENTAL

INFORMATION

(Unaudited)

Credit Operations. The following table presents the results of the Company's proprietary credit card operation, measuring on an all-inclusive basis the costs of granting, operating, and financing credit, net of finance charge revenue. Revenue, costs, and expenses contained in the table below relate to all customer accounts receivable generated and serviced by the Company, including those recorded as sold under asset securitization transactions. This presentation is designed to measure on an "economic basis" the total pre-tax cost of providing the JCPenney credit card to customers.

Pre-tax cost of JCPenney credit card (In millions)	1993	1992	1991
Finance charge revenue			
On receivables owned	$ (523)	$ (509)	$ (567)
On receivables sold	(129)	(166)	(197)
Total	(652)	(675)	(764)
Bad debt expense	128	171	240
Operating expenses (including in-store costs)	265	270	275
Cost of capital	399	417	496
Total	792	858	1,011
Pre-tax cost of JCPenney credit	$ 140	$ 183	$ 247
Per cent of JCPenney credit sales	1.6%	2.2%	3.1%

The cost of capital shown above represents the cost of financing both Company-owned accounts receivable and securitized accounts receivable. The cost of the sold receivables is the actual interest paid to certificate holders. The owned accounts receivable are financed with both debt and equity capital. The debt component uses the total Company weighted average interest rate, while the equity component uses the Company's minimum return on equity objective of 16 per cent. On a combined basis, for both owned and sold receivables, the debt and equity components of the total capital requirements were 88 per cent debt and 12 per cent equity, which approximates the finance industry standard debt to equity ratio.

	1993		1992		1991	
Credit sales	Amounts (In billions)	Per cent of eligible sales	Amounts (In billions)	Per cent of eligible sales	Amounts (In billions)	Per cent of eligible sales
JCPenney credit card	$ 8.8	46.4	$ 8.4	46.6	$ 7.9	49.3
American Express, Discover, MasterCard, and Visa	2.9	15.4	2.4	13.2	2.0	12.3
Total	$11.7	61.8	$10.8	59.8	$ 9.9	61.6

Key JCPenney credit card information (In millions)	1993	1992	1991
Number of accounts serviced with balances	17.2	17.5	18.3
Total customer receivables serviced	$ 4,410	$ 4,068	$ 4,489
Average customer receivables financed	$ 3,767	$ 3,901	$ 4,288
Average account balances (in dollars)	$ 256	$ 231	$ 244
Average account maturity (months)	4.0	4.1	4.7

30

Financing costs incurred by the Company to finance its operations, including those costs related to off-balance-sheet liabilities were as follows:

(In millions)	1993	1992	1991
Interest expense, net	$ 241	$ 258	$ 308
Interest portion of LESOP debt payment	35	40	45
Off-balance-sheet financing costs			
Interest imputed on operating leases	97	96	95
Asset-backed certificates interest	87	105	117
Total	$ 460	$ 499	$ 565

Debt to capital ratio shown in the table below includes both debt recorded on the Company's Consolidated Balance Sheet as well as off-balance-sheet debt related to operating leases and the securitization of a portion of the Company's customer accounts receivable.

(In millions)	1993	1992	1991
Short term debt, net of short term investments	$ 1,128	$ 502	$ 345
Long term debt, including current maturities	3,277	3,171	3,591
	4,405	3,673	3,936
Off-balance-sheet debt			
Present value of operating leases	900	950	900
Securitization of accounts receivable, net	294	731	1,186
Total debt	$ 5,599	$ 5,354	$ 6,022
Consolidated equity	$ 5,365	$ 4,705	$ 4,188
Total capital	$10,964	$10,059	$10,210
Per cent of total debt to capital	51.1%	53.2%	59.0%

31

	1993[1]	1992	1991[2]	1990	1989[3]
Results for the year					
Total revenue	$ 19,578	18,515	16,648	16,736	16,405
Retail sales	$ 18,983	18,009	16,201	16,365	16,103
Per cent increase (decrease)	5.4	11.2	(1.0)	1.6	8.6
LIFO gross margin, per cent of retail sales	31.5	31.7	31.5	31.4	33.4
FIFO gross margin, per cent of retail sales	31.3	31.5	30.9	31.7	33.2
Selling, general, and administrative expenses, per cent of retail sales	23.7	24.7	25.6	26.2	25.8
Depreciation and amortization	$ 316	310	316	299	275
Income taxes	$ 610	482	204	255	368
Income before extraordinary charge and cumulative effect of accounting changes	$ 944	777	264	577	802
Net income	$ 940	777	80	577	802
Earnings per common share					
Primary					
Before extraordinary charge and cumulative effect of accounting changes	$ 3.79	3.15	.99	2.30	3.16
Net income	$ 3.77	3.15	.20	2.30	3.16
Fully diluted					
Before extraordinary charge and cumulative effect of accounting changes	$ 3.55	2.95	.99	2.16	2.93
Net income	$ 3.53	2.95	.20	2.16	2.93
Per common share					
Dividends	$ 1.44	1.32	1.32	1.32	1.12
Stockholders' equity	$ 21.53	19.17	17.33	18.38	17.81
Return on stockholders' equity	20.1	18.6	12.0	13.3	20.8
Financial position					
Receivables, net	$ 4,679	3,750	4,131	4,303	4,872
Merchandise inventories	$ 3,545	3,258	2,897	2,657	2,613
Properties, net	$ 3,818	3,755	3,633	3,532	3,268
Capital expenditures	$ 459	494	506	601	520
Total assets	$ 14,788	13,467	12,444	12,256	12,635
Total debt	$ 4,561	4,078	4,062	4,114	4,207
Stockholders' equity	$ 5,365	4,705	4,188	4,394	4,353
Number of common shares outstanding at year end	236	235	233	234	240
Weighted average common shares					
Primary	239	236	234	236	244
Fully diluted	261	258	234	260	268
Number of employees at year end (In thousands)	193	192	185	196	198

[1] Excluding the impact of the tax rate increase on deferred taxes, after tax income was $958 million, or $3.60 per share, on a fully diluted basis.

[2] Excluding the effect of nonrecurring items and the cumulative effect of an accounting change, after tax income was $528 million, or $2.00 per share, on a fully diluted basis.

[3] Excluding the effect of nonrecurring items, after tax income was $822 million, or $3.00 per share, on a fully diluted basis.

	1993	1992	1991	1990	1989
JCPenney stores					
Number of stores					
Beginning of year	1,266	1,283	1,312	1,328	1,355
Openings	24	33	38	46	38
Closings	(44)	(50)	(67)	(62)	(65)
End of year	1,246	1,266	1,283	1,312	1,328
Gross selling space (In million sq. ft.)	113.9	114.4	114.5	114.4	112.8
Sales including catalog desks (In millions)	$ 16,846	15,698	14,277	14,616	14,469
Comparative store sales per cent increase (decrease)[1]	6.4	9.7	(1.5)	0.0	6.8
Sales per gross square foot[1]	$ 146	137	125	127	127
Catalog					
Number of catalog units					
JCPenney stores	1,246	1,266	1,283	1,312	1,328
Freestanding sales centers and merchants	543	640	697	626	501
Drug stores	101	128	134	136	126
Other, principally outlet stores	14	14	16	16	16
Total	1,904	2,048	2,130	2,090	1,971
Number of distribution centers	6	6	6	6	6
Distribution space (In million sq. ft.)	11.4	11.4	11.4	11.4	11.4
Sales (In millions)	$ 3,514	3,166	3,002	3,220	3,205
Drug stores					
Number of stores					
Beginning of year	548	530	487	471	434
Openings	35	30	46	22	39
Closings	(77)	(12)	(3)	(6)	(2)
End of year	506	548	530	487	471
Gross selling space (In million sq. ft.)	4.6	5.2	5.0	4.8	4.7
Sales (In millions)	$ 1,413	1,383	1,192	1,097	987
Sales per gross square foot[1]	$ 235	211	201	198	189
JCPenney Insurance (In millions)					
Premium income	$ 416	333	286	221	165
Policies and certificates in force	5.8	4.6	4.3	4.1	3.5
Amount of life insurance in force	$ 7,627	6,552	5,419	5,268	3,797
Total assets	$ 1,246	1,033	857	764	739

[1] 1992 is presented on a 52 week basis.

FIVE YEAR

OPERATIONS

SUMMARY

J.C. Penney Company,
Inc. and Subsidiaries

PUBLIC

AFFAIRS

Through several established programs, the Company continued its commitment to enhance the general environment of the communities in which it does business. Charitable contributions, community service, environmental affairs, and minority/women supplier development are major efforts reflecting this commitment.

Community relations. During 1993, the Company's charitable contributions totalled $23 million nationwide. Of our total contributions, over one-third were given in the area of health and welfare, including the Company's support to nearly 1,000 United Way organizations. The 1993 United Way campaign raised a record $13.8 million in JCPenney associate and unit pledges for local United Ways.

The Company's community relations programs continue to focus on kindergarten through grade twelve education and the support of volunteerism. 15 per cent of contributions were invested in education, including the replication of the JCPenney High Performance Schools Project, a project on school-based management, to two school districts in San Antonio, Texas. $650 thousand was donated to 640 colleges and universities through the Matching Gift Program, and 200 children of JCPenney associates received college scholarships through the JCPenney Super Scholars program.

Major commitments in our focal area of supporting volunteerism include the expansion of our Golden Rule Award Program to 174 markets. These awards publicly honor community volunteers and support their work with contributions. The James Cash Penney Awards for Community Service provide similar recognition to JCPenney associates for outstanding volunteer activities. The two programs contributed approximately $1.7 million to local charitable organizations.

Minority and women-owned businesses. JCPenney's Minority Supplier Development Program has been active since 1972. During 1993, purchases from minority and women-owned businesses were $406 million and $102 million, respectively. In addition to the purchasing of products and services, the Company had relationships with 36 minority-owned banks. The Company recognized, through its Minority Supplier Development Awards Program, eight minority owned-businesses and ten JCPenney associates for their contributions to the Minority Supplier Development Program.

In order to explore ethnic markets more closely, the Fashion Influences catalog was introduced and aimed at a multicultural audience. The catalog's circulation has grown from 400,000 to over 800,000 in just two years. At the same time, a special segment manager was appointed for each of the four merchandise divisions to help find appropriate merchandise for the Fashion Influences catalog as well as those stores that have large ethnic populations within their consumer base.

Environmental affairs. JCPenney is committed to doing business in an environmentally responsible manner. At the center of this commitment stands a determination to make environmental considerations a part of corporate decision making and policy.

Leadership for this effort comes from an Environmental Affairs Committee composed of senior officers. Under their direction, the Company continuously seeks to assure that its operations, to the fullest extent feasible, preserve and improve the environment and protect the health and safety of associates, customers, and communities where JCPenney does business. The Committee has set forth a Statement of Principles on the Environment reflecting the Company's commitment to these goals.

The Company also has an Environmental Issues Task Force consisting of various subcommittees that are studying specific matters such as merchandise packaging, recycling, and trash disposal.

Significant progress has been made towards the Company's environmental goals, especially in recycling. For example, JCPenney is using recycled-content paperboard for all apparel, jewelry, and gift boxes. An environmental packaging recognition award for JCPenney associates has been introduced to encourage the reduction of unnecessary merchandise packaging. In addition, stores are recycling most of the corrugated cardboard boxes in which merchandise shipments are received. The Company also continues to explore sources of high-quality, reasonably priced recycled-content paper for its advertising supplements, catalogs, and other printed matter, and to utilize them where feasible.

An office paper and plastic recycling program is in place in the Company's home office in Plano, Texas, and in a number of other facilities around the country, and a test has been launched in retail stores. State and local officials have recognized one such program, developed by associates at the Manchester, Connecticut, Catalog Distribution Center, as a model for other businesses.

Also, the Company has formal guidelines for evaluating and substantiating environmental themes and claims proposed for merchandise, packaging, labeling, and promotions.

Copies of A Special Report Update on the Company's Environmental Responsibility, including the Company's Statement of Environmental Principles, may be obtained as indicated on page 37 of this Annual Report.

Equal employment opportunity. The Company adheres to a policy of equal employment opportunity. The following employment information summary represents associates of J.C. Penney Company, Inc. and wholly-owned subsidiaries, excluding facilities in Puerto Rico and Canada. The information provided delineates minority and female representation in major job categories.

Employment information	Total employed		Per cent female		Per cent minority	
	1993	1989	**1993**	1989	**1993**	1989
Officials, managers, and professionals	**19,205**	18,959	**47.7**	40.6	**12.0**	10.1
Management trainees	**628**	1,359	**62.7**	62.3	**34.2**	18.1
Sales workers	**99,506**	107,799	**87.7**	87.9	**19.1**	16.4
Office and clerical workers	**33,847**	26,207	**89.2**	90.2	**18.3**	16.0
Technicians, craft workers, operatives, laborers and service workers	**38,911**	42,129	**68.4**	70.9	**24.3**	20.9
Total..	**192,097**	196,453	**80.0**	79.8	**19.3**	16.7

The Company is aware that many of its stockholders are interested in matters of corporate governance. JCPenney shares this interest and is, and for many years has been, committed to assuring that the Company is managed in a way that is fair to all its stockholders, and which allows its stockholders to maximize the value of their investment by participating in the present and future growth of JCPenney.

Independent Board of Directors. In keeping with its long-standing practice, the Company's Board continues to be an independent board under any reasonable definition. All but one director have principal occupations or employment outside of the Company. Nominees for directors are selected by a committee composed entirely of directors who are not Company employees. The wide diversity of expertise, experience, and achievements that the directors possess in business, investments, large organizations, and public affairs allows the Board to most effectively represent the interests of all the Company's stockholders.

Independent committees. The principal standing committees of the Board of Directors are composed entirely of directors who are not employees of the Company. These committees include the Audit Committee, Benefit Plans Review Committee, Committee on Directors, Personnel and Compensation Committee, and the Public Affairs Committee. These committees, as well as the entire Board, consult with and are advised by outside consultants and experts in connection with their deliberations as needed.

Executive compensation. A significant portion of the cash compensation received by the Company's executive officers consists of performance incentive compensation payments derived from compensation plan "values." The amounts of these plan values are directly related to the annual and long-term sales and earnings of the Company and, consequently, vary from year to year based upon Company performance. The total compensation package for the Company's executive officers is set by the Personnel and Compensation Committee, which is composed entirely of directors who are not employees of JCPenney and which receives the advice of independent outside consultants. Please refer to the Company's 1994 Proxy Statement for a report from the Company's Personnel and Compensation Committee describing how compensation determinations are made.

Confidential voting. The Company has previously adopted a confidential voting policy statement. Under this policy, all proxy (voting instruction) cards, ballots, and vote tabulations which identify the particular vote of a stockholder are kept secret from the Company, its directors, officers, and employees. Proxy cards are returned in envelopes directly to the tabulator, who receives and tabulates the proxies. The final tabulation is inspected by inspectors of election who are independent of the Company, its directors, officers, or employees. The identity and vote of a stockholder is not disclosed to the Company, its directors, officers, or employees, or any third party except (i) to allow the independent election inspectors to certify the results of the vote; (ii) as necessary to meet applicable legal requirements and to assert or defend claims for or against the Company; (iii) in the event of a proxy solicitation based on an opposition proxy statement filed, or required to be filed, with the Securities and Exchange Commission; or (iv) in the event a stockholder has made a written comment on such material.

CORPORATE

GOVERNANCE

TABLE C-1 Present Value of $1 Per Period

	1.00%	1.25%	1.50%	1.75%	2.00%	3.00%	4.00%	5.00%	6.00%	7.00%	8.00%	9.00%	10.00%	12.00%	14.00%	15.00%
1	0.9901	0.9877	0.9852	0.9828	0.9804	0.9709	0.9615	0.9524	0.9434	0.9346	0.9259	0.9174	0.9091	0.8929	0.8772	0.8696
2	0.9803	0.9755	0.9707	0.9659	0.9612	0.9426	0.9246	0.9070	0.8900	0.8734	0.8573	0.8417	0.8264	0.7972	0.7695	0.7561
3	0.9706	0.9634	0.9563	0.9493	0.9423	0.9151	0.8890	0.8638	0.8396	0.8163	0.7938	0.7722	0.7513	0.7118	0.6750	0.6575
4	0.9610	0.9515	0.9422	0.9330	0.9238	0.8885	0.8548	0.8227	0.7921	0.7629	0.7350	0.7084	0.6830	0.6355	0.5921	0.5718
5	0.9515	0.9398	0.9283	0.9169	0.9057	0.8626	0.8219	0.7835	0.7473	0.7130	0.6806	0.6499	0.6209	0.5674	0.5194	0.4972
6	0.9420	0.9282	0.9145	0.9011	0.8880	0.8375	0.7903	0.7462	0.7050	0.6663	0.6302	0.5963	0.5645	0.5066	0.4556	0.4323
7	0.9327	0.9167	0.9010	0.8856	0.8706	0.8131	0.7599	0.7107	0.6651	0.6227	0.5835	0.5470	0.5132	0.4523	0.3996	0.3759
8	0.9235	0.9054	0.8877	0.8704	0.8535	0.7894	0.7307	0.6768	0.6274	0.5820	0.5403	0.5019	0.4665	0.4039	0.3506	0.3269
9	0.9143	0.8942	0.8746	0.8554	0.8368	0.7664	0.7026	0.6446	0.5919	0.5439	0.5002	0.4604	0.4241	0.3606	0.3075	0.2843
10	0.9053	0.8832	0.8617	0.8407	0.8203	0.7441	0.6756	0.6139	0.5584	0.5083	0.4632	0.4224	0.3855	0.3220	0.2697	0.2472
11	0.8963	0.8723	0.8489	0.8263	0.8043	0.7224	0.6496	0.5847	0.5268	0.4751	0.4289	0.3875	0.3505	0.2875	0.2366	0.2149
12	0.8874	0.8615	0.8364	0.8121	0.7885	0.7014	0.6246	0.5568	0.4970	0.4440	0.3971	0.3555	0.3186	0.2567	0.2076	0.1869
13	0.8787	0.8509	0.8240	0.7981	0.7730	0.6810	0.6006	0.5303	0.4688	0.4150	0.3677	0.3262	0.2897	0.2292	0.1821	0.1625
14	0.8700	0.8404	0.8118	0.7844	0.7579	0.6611	0.5775	0.5051	0.4423	0.3878	0.3405	0.2992	0.2633	0.2046	0.1597	0.1413
15	0.8613	0.8300	0.7999	0.7709	0.7430	0.6419	0.5553	0.4810	0.4173	0.3624	0.3152	0.2745	0.2394	0.1827	0.1401	0.1229
16	0.8528	0.8197	0.7880	0.7576	0.7284	0.6232	0.5339	0.4581	0.3936	0.3387	0.2919	0.2519	0.2176	0.1631	0.1229	0.1069
17	0.8444	0.8096	0.7764	0.7446	0.7142	0.6050	0.5134	0.4363	0.3714	0.3166	0.2703	0.2311	0.1978	0.1456	0.1078	0.0929
18	0.8360	0.7996	0.7649	0.7318	0.7002	0.5874	0.4936	0.4155	0.3503	0.2959	0.2502	0.2120	0.1799	0.1300	0.0946	0.0808
19	0.8277	0.7898	0.7536	0.7192	0.6864	0.5703	0.4746	0.3957	0.3305	0.2765	0.2317	0.1945	0.1635	0.1161	0.0829	0.0703
20	0.8195	0.7800	0.7425	0.7068	0.6730	0.5537	0.4564	0.3769	0.3118	0.2584	0.2145	0.1784	0.1486	0.1037	0.0728	0.0611
21	0.8114	0.7704	0.7315	0.6947	0.6598	0.5375	0.4388	0.3589	0.2942	0.2415	0.1987	0.1637	0.1351	0.0926	0.0638	0.0531
22	0.8034	0.7609	0.7207	0.6827	0.6468	0.5219	0.4220	0.3418	0.2775	0.2257	0.1839	0.1502	0.1228	0.0826	0.0560	0.0462
23	0.7954	0.7515	0.7100	0.6710	0.6342	0.5067	0.4057	0.3256	0.2618	0.2109	0.1703	0.1378	0.1117	0.0738	0.0491	0.0402
24	0.7876	0.7422	0.6995	0.6594	0.6217	0.4919	0.3901	0.3101	0.2470	0.1971	0.1577	0.1264	0.1015	0.0659	0.0431	0.0349
25	0.7798	0.7330	0.6892	0.6481	0.6095	0.4776	0.3751	0.2953	0.2330	0.1842	0.1460	0.1160	0.0923	0.0588	0.0378	0.0304
26	0.7720	0.7240	0.6790	0.6369	0.5976	0.4637	0.3607	0.2812	0.2198	0.1722	0.1352	0.1064	0.0839	0.0525	0.0331	0.0264
27	0.7644	0.7150	0.6690	0.6260	0.5859	0.4502	0.3468	0.2678	0.2074	0.1609	0.1252	0.0976	0.0763	0.0469	0.0291	0.0230
28	0.7568	0.7062	0.6591	0.6152	0.5744	0.4371	0.3335	0.2551	0.1956	0.1504	0.1159	0.0895	0.0693	0.0419	0.0255	0.0200
29	0.7493	0.6975	0.6494	0.6046	0.5631	0.4243	0.3207	0.2429	0.1846	0.1406	0.1073	0.0822	0.0630	0.0374	0.0224	0.0174
30	0.7419	0.6889	0.6398	0.5942	0.5521	0.4120	0.3083	0.2314	0.1741	0.1314	0.0994	0.0754	0.0573	0.0334	0.0196	0.0151

Present and Future Value Tables

TABLE C-2 Present Value of an Ordinary Annuity of $1 Per Period

	1.00%	1.25%	1.50%	1.75%	2.00%	3.00%	4.00%	5.00%	6.00%	7.00%	8.00%	9.00%	10.00%	12.00%	14.00%	15.00%
1	0.9901	0.9877	0.9852	0.9828	0.9804	0.9709	0.9615	0.9524	0.9434	0.9346	0.9259	0.9174	0.9091	0.8929	0.8772	0.8696
2	1.9704	1.9631	1.9559	1.9487	1.9416	1.9135	1.8861	1.8594	1.8334	1.8080	1.7833	1.7591	1.7355	1.6901	1.6467	1.6257
3	2.9410	2.9265	2.9122	2.8980	2.8839	2.8286	2.7751	2.7232	2.6730	2.6243	2.5771	2.5313	2.4869	2.4018	2.3216	2.2832
4	3.9020	3.8781	3.8544	3.8309	3.8077	3.7171	3.6299	3.5460	3.4651	3.3872	3.3121	3.2397	3.1699	3.0373	2.9137	2.8850
5	4.8534	4.8178	4.7826	4.7479	4.7135	4.5797	4.4518	4.3295	4.2124	4.1002	3.9927	3.8897	3.7908	3.6048	3.4331	3.3522
6	5.7955	5.7460	5.6972	5.6490	5.6014	5.4172	5.2421	5.0757	4.9173	4.7665	4.6229	4.4859	4.3553	4.1114	3.8887	3.7845
7	6.7282	6.6627	6.5982	6.5346	6.4720	6.2303	6.0021	5.7864	5.5824	5.3893	5.2064	5.0330	4.8684	4.5638	4.2883	4.1604
8	7.6517	7.5681	7.4859	7.4051	7.3255	7.0197	6.7327	6.4632	6.2098	5.9713	5.7466	5.5348	5.3349	4.9676	4.6389	4.4873
9	8.5660	8.4623	8.3605	8.2605	8.1622	7.7861	7.4353	7.1078	6.8017	6.5152	6.2469	5.9952	5.7590	5.3282	4.9464	4.7716
10	9.4713	9.3455	9.2222	9.1012	8.9826	8.5302	8.1109	7.7217	7.3601	7.0236	6.7101	6.4177	6.1446	5.6502	5.2161	5.0188
11	10.3676	10.2178	10.0711	9.9275	9.7868	9.2526	8.7605	8.3064	7.8869	7.4987	7.1390	6.8052	6.4951	5.9377	5.4527	5.2337
12	11.2551	11.0793	10.9075	10.7395	10.5753	9.9540	9.3851	8.8633	8.3838	7.9427	7.5361	7.1607	6.8137	6.1944	5.6603	5.4206
13	12.1337	11.9302	11.7315	11.5376	11.3484	10.6350	9.9856	9.3936	8.8527	8.3577	7.9038	7.4869	7.1034	6.4235	5.8424	5.5831
14	13.0037	12.7706	12.5434	12.3220	12.1062	11.2961	10.5631	9.8986	9.2950	8.7455	8.2442	7.7862	7.3667	6.6282	6.0021	5.7245
15	13.8651	13.6005	13.3432	13.0929	12.8493	11.9379	11.1184	10.3797	9.7122	9.1079	8.5595	8.0607	7.6061	6.8109	6.1422	5.8474
16	14.7179	14.4203	14.1313	13.8505	13.5777	12.5611	11.6523	10.8378	10.1059	9.4466	8.8514	8.3126	7.8237	6.9740	6.2651	5.9542
17	15.5623	15.2299	14.9076	14.5951	14.2919	13.1661	12.1657	11.2741	10.4773	9.7632	9.1216	8.5436	8.0216	7.1196	6.3729	6.0472
18	16.3983	16.0295	15.6726	15.3269	14.9920	13.7535	12.6593	11.6896	10.8276	10.0591	9.3719	8.7556	8.2014	7.2497	6.4674	6.1280
19	17.2260	16.8193	16.4262	16.0461	15.6785	14.3238	13.1339	12.0853	11.1581	10.3356	9.6036	8.9501	8.3649	7.3658	6.5504	6.1982
20	18.0456	17.5993	17.1686	16.7529	16.3514	14.8775	13.5903	12.4622	11.4699	10.5940	9.8181	9.1285	8.5136	7.4694	6.6231	6.2593
21	18.8570	18.3697	17.9001	17.4475	17.0112	15.4150	14.0292	12.8212	11.7641	10.8355	10.0168	9.2922	8.6487	7.5620	6.6870	6.3125
22	19.6604	19.1306	18.6208	18.1303	17.6580	15.9369	14.4511	13.1630	12.0416	11.0612	10.2007	9.4424	8.7715	7.6446	6.7429	6.3587
23	20.4558	19.8820	19.3309	18.8012	18.2922	16.4436	14.8568	13.4886	12.3034	11.2722	10.3711	9.5802	8.8832	7.7184	6.7921	6.3988
24	21.2434	20.6242	20.0304	19.4607	18.9139	16.9355	15.2470	13.7986	12.5504	11.4693	10.5288	9.7066	8.9847	7.7843	6.8351	6.4338
25	22.0232	21.3573	20.7196	20.1088	19.5235	17.4131	15.6221	14.0939	12.7834	11.6536	10.6748	9.8226	9.0770	7.8431	6.8729	6.4641
26	22.7952	22.0813	21.3986	20.7457	20.1210	17.8768	15.9828	14.3752	13.0032	11.8258	10.8100	9.9290	9.1609	7.8957	6.9061	6.4906
27	23.5596	22.7963	22.0676	21.3717	20.7069	18.3270	16.3296	14.6430	13.2105	11.9867	10.9352	10.0266	9.2372	7.9426	6.9352	6.5135
28	24.3164	23.5025	22.7267	21.9870	21.2813	18.7641	16.6631	14.8981	13.4062	12.1371	11.0511	10.1161	9.3066	7.9844	6.9607	6.5335
29	25.0658	24.2000	23.3761	22.5916	21.8444	19.1885	16.9837	15.1411	13.5907	12.2777	11.1584	10.1983	9.3696	8.0218	6.9830	6.5509
30	25.8077	24.8889	24.0158	23.1858	22.3965	19.6004	17.2920	15.3725	13.7648	12.4090	11.2578	10.2737	9.4269	8.0552	7.0027	6.5660

TABLE C-3 Future Value of $1 Per Period

	1.00%	1.25%	1.50%	1.75%	2.00%	3.00%	4.00%	5.00%	6.00%	7.00%	8.00%	9.00%	10.00%	12.00%	14.00%	15.00%
1	1.0100	1.0125	1.0150	1.0175	1.0200	1.0300	1.0400	1.0500	1.0600	1.0700	1.0800	1.0900	1.1000	1.1200	1.1400	1.1500
2	1.0201	1.0252	1.0302	1.0353	1.0404	1.0609	1.0816	1.1025	1.1236	1.1449	1.1664	1.1881	1.2100	1.2544	1.2996	1.3225
3	1.0303	1.0380	1.0457	1.0534	1.0612	1.0927	1.1249	1.1576	1.1910	1.2250	1.2597	1.2950	1.3310	1.4049	1.4815	1.5209
4	1.0406	1.0509	1.0614	1.0719	1.0824	1.1255	1.1699	1.2155	1.2625	1.3108	1.3605	1.4116	1.4641	1.5735	1.6890	1.7490
5	1.0510	1.0641	1.0773	1.0906	1.1041	1.1593	1.2167	1.2763	1.3382	1.4026	1.4693	1.5386	1.6105	1.7623	1.9254	2.0114
6	1.0615	1.0774	1.0934	1.1097	1.1262	1.1941	1.2653	1.3401	1.4185	1.5007	1.5869	1.6771	1.7716	1.9738	2.1950	2.3131
7	1.0721	1.0909	1.1098	1.1291	1.1487	1.2299	1.3159	1.4071	1.5036	1.6058	1.7138	1.8280	1.9487	2.2107	2.5023	2.6600
8	1.0829	1.1045	1.1265	1.1489	1.1717	1.2668	1.3686	1.4775	1.5938	1.7182	1.8509	1.9926	2.1436	2.4760	2.8526	3.0590
9	1.0937	1.1183	1.1434	1.1690	1.1951	1.3048	1.4233	1.5513	1.6895	1.8385	1.9990	2.1719	2.3579	2.7731	3.2519	3.5179
10	1.1046	1.1323	1.1605	1.1894	1.2190	1.3439	1.4802	1.6289	1.7908	1.9672	2.1589	2.3674	2.5937	3.1058	3.7072	4.0456
11	1.1157	1.1464	1.1779	1.2103	1.2434	1.3842	1.5395	1.7103	1.8983	2.1049	2.3316	2.5804	2.8531	3.4785	4.2262	4.6524
12	1.1268	1.1608	1.1956	1.2314	1.2682	1.4258	1.6010	1.7959	2.0122	2.2522	2.5182	2.8127	3.1384	3.8960	4.8179	5.3503
13	1.1381	1.1753	1.2136	1.2530	1.2936	1.4685	1.6651	1.8856	2.1329	2.4098	2.7196	3.0658	3.4523	4.3635	5.4924	6.1528
14	1.1495	1.1900	1.2318	1.2749	1.3195	1.5126	1.7317	1.9799	2.2609	2.5785	2.9372	3.3417	3.7975	4.8871	6.2613	7.0757
15	1.1610	1.2048	1.2502	1.2972	1.3459	1.5580	1.8009	2.0789	2.3966	2.7590	3.1722	3.6425	4.1772	5.4736	7.1379	8.1371
16	1.1726	1.2199	1.2690	1.3199	1.3728	1.6047	1.8730	2.1829	2.5404	2.9522	3.4259	3.9703	4.5950	6.1304	8.1372	9.3576
17	1.1843	1.2351	1.2880	1.3430	1.4002	1.6528	1.9479	2.2920	2.6928	3.1588	3.7000	4.3276	5.0545	6.8660	9.2765	10.7613
18	1.1961	1.2506	1.3073	1.3665	1.4282	1.7024	2.0258	2.4066	2.8543	3.3799	3.9960	4.7171	5.5599	7.6900	10.5752	12.3755
19	1.2081	1.2662	1.3270	1.3904	1.4568	1.7535	2.1068	2.5270	3.0256	3.6165	4.3157	5.1417	6.1159	8.6128	12.0557	14.2318
20	1.2202	1.2820	1.3469	1.4148	1.4859	1.8061	2.1911	2.6533	3.2071	3.8697	4.6610	5.6044	6.7275	9.6463	13.7435	16.3665
21	1.2324	1.2981	1.3671	1.4395	1.5157	1.8603	2.2788	2.7860	3.3996	4.1406	5.0338	6.1088	7.4002	10.8038	15.6676	18.8215
22	1.2447	1.3143	1.3876	1.4647	1.5460	1.9161	2.3699	2.9253	3.6035	4.4304	5.4365	6.6586	8.1403	12.1003	17.8610	21.6447
23	1.2572	1.3307	1.4084	1.4904	1.5769	1.9736	2.4647	3.0715	3.8197	4.7405	5.8715	7.2579	8.9543	13.5523	20.3616	24.8915
24	1.2697	1.3474	1.4295	1.5164	1.6084	2.0328	2.5633	3.2251	4.0489	5.0724	6.3412	7.9111	9.8497	15.1786	23.2122	28.6252
25	1.2824	1.3642	1.4509	1.5430	1.6406	2.0938	2.6658	3.3864	4.2919	5.4274	6.8485	8.6231	10.8347	17.0001	26.4619	32.9190
26	1.2953	1.3812	1.4727	1.5700	1.6734	2.1566	2.7725	3.5557	4.5494	5.8074	7.3964	9.3992	11.9182	19.0401	30.1666	37.8568
27	1.3082	1.3985	1.4948	1.5975	1.7069	2.2213	2.8834	3.7335	4.8223	6.2139	7.9881	10.2451	13.1100	21.3249	34.3899	43.5353
28	1.3213	1.4160	1.5172	1.6254	1.7410	2.2879	2.9987	3.9201	5.1117	6.6488	8.6271	11.1671	14.4210	23.8839	39.2045	50.0656
29	1.3345	1.4337	1.5400	1.6539	1.7758	2.3566	3.1187	4.1161	5.4184	7.1143	9.3173	12.1722	15.8631	26.7499	44.6931	57.5755
30	1.3478	1.4516	1.5631	1.6828	1.8114	2.4273	3.2434	4.3219	5.7435	7.6123	10.0627	13.2677	17.4494	29.9599	50.9502	66.2118

TABLE C-4 Future Value of an Ordinary Annuity of $1 Per Period

	1.00%	1.25%	1.50%	1.75%	2.00%	3.00%	4.00%	5.00%	6.00%	7.00%	8.00%	9.00%	10.00%	12.00%	14.00%	15.00%
1	1.0000	1.0000	1.0000	1.0000	1.0000	1.0000	1.0000	1.0000	1.0000	1.0000	1.0000	1.0000	1.0000	1.0000	1.0000	1.0000
2	2.0100	2.0125	2.0150	2.0175	2.0200	2.0300	2.0400	2.0500	2.0600	2.0700	2.0800	2.0900	2.1000	2.1200	2.1400	2.1500
3	3.0301	3.0377	3.0452	3.0528	3.0604	3.0909	3.1216	3.1525	3.1836	3.2149	3.2464	3.2781	3.3100	3.3744	3.4396	3.4725
4	4.0604	4.0756	4.0909	4.1062	4.1216	4.1836	4.2465	4.3101	4.3746	4.4399	4.5061	4.5731	4.6410	4.7793	4.9211	4.9934
5	5.1010	5.1266	5.1523	5.1781	5.2040	5.3091	5.4163	5.5256	5.6371	5.7507	5.8666	5.9847	6.1051	6.3528	6.6101	6.7424
6	6.1520	6.1907	6.2296	6.2687	6.3081	6.4684	6.6330	6.8019	6.9753	7.1533	7.3359	7.5233	7.7156	8.1152	8.5355	8.7537
7	7.2135	7.2680	7.3230	7.3784	7.4343	7.6625	7.8983	8.1420	8.3938	8.6540	8.9228	9.2004	9.4872	10.0890	10.7305	11.0668
8	8.2857	8.3589	8.4328	8.5075	8.5830	8.8923	9.2142	9.5491	9.8975	10.2598	10.6366	11.0285	11.4359	12.2997	13.2328	13.7268
9	9.3685	9.4634	9.5593	9.6564	9.7546	10.1591	10.5828	11.0266	11.4913	11.9780	12.4876	13.0210	13.5795	14.7757	16.0853	16.7858
10	10.4622	10.5817	10.7027	10.8254	10.9497	11.4639	12.0061	12.5779	13.1808	13.8164	14.4866	15.1929	15.9374	17.5487	19.3373	20.3037
11	11.5668	11.7139	11.8633	12.0148	12.1687	12.8078	13.4864	14.2068	14.9716	15.7836	16.6455	17.5603	18.5312	20.6546	23.0445	24.3493
12	12.6825	12.8604	13.0412	13.2251	13.4121	14.1920	15.0258	15.9171	16.8699	17.8885	18.9771	20.1407	21.3843	24.1331	27.2707	29.0017
13	13.8093	14.0211	14.2368	14.4565	14.6803	15.6178	16.6268	17.7130	18.8821	20.1406	21.4953	22.9534	24.5227	28.0291	32.0887	34.3519
14	14.9474	15.1964	15.4504	15.7095	15.9739	17.0863	18.2919	19.5986	21.0151	22.5505	24.2149	26.0192	27.9750	32.3926	37.5811	40.5047
15	16.0969	16.3863	16.6821	16.9844	17.2934	18.5989	20.0236	21.5786	23.2760	25.1290	27.1521	29.3609	31.7725	37.2797	43.8424	47.5804
16	17.2579	17.5912	17.9324	18.2817	18.6393	20.1569	21.8245	23.6575	25.6725	27.8881	30.3243	33.0034	35.9497	42.7533	50.9804	55.7175
17	18.4304	18.8111	19.2014	19.6016	20.0121	21.7616	23.6975	25.8404	28.2129	30.8402	33.7502	36.9737	40.5447	48.8837	59.1176	65.0751
18	19.6147	20.0462	20.4894	20.9446	21.4123	23.4144	25.6454	28.1324	30.9057	33.9990	37.4502	41.3013	45.5992	55.7497	68.3941	75.8364
19	20.8109	21.2968	21.7967	22.3112	22.8406	25.1169	27.6712	30.5390	33.7600	37.3790	41.4463	46.0185	51.1591	63.4397	78.9692	88.2118
20	22.0190	22.5630	23.1237	23.7016	24.2974	26.8704	29.7781	33.0660	36.7856	40.9955	45.7620	51.1601	57.2750	72.0524	91.0249	102.4436
21	23.2392	23.8450	24.4705	25.1164	25.7833	28.6765	31.9692	35.7193	39.9927	44.8652	50.4229	56.7645	64.0025	81.6987	104.7684	118.8101
22	24.4716	25.1431	25.8376	26.5559	27.2990	30.5368	34.2480	38.5052	43.3923	49.0057	55.4568	62.8733	71.4027	92.5026	120.4360	137.6316
23	25.7163	26.4574	27.2251	28.0207	28.8450	32.4529	36.6179	41.4305	46.9958	53.4361	60.8933	69.5319	79.5430	104.6029	138.2970	159.2764
24	26.9735	27.7881	28.6335	29.5110	30.4219	34.4265	39.0826	44.5020	50.8156	58.1767	66.7648	76.7898	88.4973	118.1552	158.6586	184.1678
25	28.2432	29.1354	30.0630	31.0275	32.0303	36.4593	41.6459	47.7271	54.8645	63.2490	73.1059	84.7009	98.3471	133.3339	181.8708	212.7930
26	29.5256	30.4996	31.5140	32.5704	33.6709	38.5530	44.3117	51.1135	59.1564	68.6765	79.9544	93.3240	109.1818	150.3339	208.3327	245.7120
27	30.8209	31.8809	32.9867	34.1404	35.3443	40.7096	47.0842	54.6691	63.7058	74.4838	87.3508	102.7231	121.0999	169.3740	238.4993	283.5688
28	32.1291	33.2794	34.4815	35.7379	37.0512	42.9309	49.9676	58.4026	68.5281	80.6977	95.3388	112.9682	134.2099	190.6989	272.8892	327.1041
29	33.4504	34.6954	35.9987	37.3633	38.7922	45.2189	52.9663	62.3227	73.6398	87.3465	103.9659	124.1354	148.6309	214.5828	312.0937	377.1697
30	34.7849	36.1291	37.5387	39.0172	40.5681	47.5754	56.0849	66.4388	79.0582	94.4608	113.2832	136.3075	164.4940	241.1327	356.7868	434.7451

GLOSSARY

The chapter in which the word first appears or is uniquely defined is indicated in parentheses.

A

Ability to bear costs (24): The notion in cost allocation that the allocation base should result in more costs being allocated to products, services, or departments that are more profitable.

Accelerated Cost Recovery System (ACRS) (10): The rules for depreciation for income tax purposes.

Accelerated depreciation methods (10): A group of depreciation methods that result in depreciation expense that is higher in the earlier years but is lower during the later years of a plant asset's estimated useful life.

Account (2): A subclassification of the accounting equation used for storing and summarizing information about transactions that affect a particular element of the business's financial position.

Accountability (1): The process by which individuals and groups demonstrate to others that they have properly or effectively discharged their responsibilities.

Account analysis (23): An analysis in which the accountant uses his or her professional judgment to classify costs as either fixed or variable.

Account balance (2): The balance at the end of the period consisting of the beginning balance plus increases during the period minus decreases during the period.

Accounting (1): The process of systematically and selectively capturing financial data, recording these data, summarizing them, and preparing statements that communicate to decision makers relevant information about economic entities, transactions, and events.

Accounting controls (6): Controls implemented by management to ensure that accounting reports are reliable.

Accounting cycle (2): The sequence of procedures accountants follow to complete the financial accounting process, consisting of analyzing transactions, recording transactions to journals, posting journal entries to ledger accounts, recording adjusting entries, preparing the financial statements, and closing all temporary accounts.

Accounting entity concept (1): The concept that the accounting process focuses on specific, separate economic entities.

Accounting equation (1): The equation that governs the relationship among the three accounting elements expressed as assets equal liabilities plus owner's equity.

Accounting period (3): The period of time for which a business determines net income.

Accounting period concept (1): The concept that financial statements or other reports should be prepared at regular intervals such as every month, quarter, or year.

Accounting rate of return (28): The average after-tax income from a project divided by the average investment in the project.

Accounting system (6): An organization of physical facilities, personnel, equipment, documents, records, and procedures designed to provide relevant information and to accomplish accounting control objectives.

Accounts payable (1): Amounts owed to suppliers for goods and services purchased on credit.

Accounts receivable (1): Payments due from customers for products or services previously provided on a credit basis.

Accounts receivable subsidiary ledger (6): The ledger containing an individual account for each credit customer.

Accrual basis of accounting (3): Revenues are recorded in the period that they are earned, and expenses are recorded in the period that they are incurred.

Accrued expenses (3): Incurred but unpaid expenses.

Accrued revenue (3): Revenue earned by a business but not yet received.

Accumulated depreciation (3, 10): The cumulative depreciation of the assets since they were acquired; a valuation (contra-asset) account.

Acid-test ratio (7): Liquid current assets divided by current liabilities.

Activity-based costing (ABC) (21): A method of assigning overhead costs to products using a number of different allocation bases.

Adjusted trial balance (3): A trial balance prepared after posting the adjusting entries.

Adjusting entries (3): Those entries needed to adjust the accounts to their proper balances to conform with GAAP for purposes of preparing appropriate financial statements.

Administrative controls (6): All controls implemented by management that are not accounting controls.

Allocation base (21): The measure of activity used to calculate an overhead rate.

Allowance for uncollectible accounts (8): A valuation account representing the cumulative amount of past sales that a business estimates to be uncollectible but has not written off.

Allowance method (8): A method of accounting for accounts receivable in which the business anticipates and estimates uncollectible accounts to be recognized as uncollectible accounts expense in the period of sale.

Amortization (11): The process of allocating the cost of intangible assets to the periods benefited by the asset.

Annuity (17): Any series of equal payments to be paid or received at the ends of a series of fixed periods.

Annuity due (17): Any series of equal payments to be paid or received at the beginnings of a series of fixed periods.

Annuity value (17): The present value of an annuity of $1 equal to the sum of the present values of each of the individual $1 amounts received at the end of each of a specified number of periods in a $1 annuity.

Application controls (6): Controls over the inputs, outputs, and processing logic of a particular accounting computer application.

Application programs (6): Sets of computer instructions to accomplish specific tasks such as word processing, databases, and spreadsheets.

Appropriation of retained earnings (16): A restriction on the amount of retained earnings available for dividends.

Articles of incorporation (15): A contract between the corporation and the state which incorporators submit to states to obtain a charter.

Assets (1, 13): Probable future economic benefits owned or controlled by a business as a result of past transactions or events.

Asset utilization ratios (19): A group of ratios that assess a business's ability to efficiently use assets to generate long-run profitability.

Attainable standard (26): Standards that take into account the possibility that a variety of circumstances may lead to costs that are greater than ideal.î

Authorized shares (15): The number of shares of stock a corporation can issue.

Automated clearing house (7): A electronic system for the transfer of funds between banks.

Available-for-sale securities (16): Long-term investments in stocks and bonds that are not held to maturity or held for short-term trading. Such securities generally are accounted for by the market method.

Avoidable costs (27): Costs that can be avoided if a company takes a particular action.

B

Balance sheet (1): The financial statement that communicates a business's financial position at a specific point in time.

Balance sheet approach (8): A method for estimating uncollectible accounts expense in which a business accrues estimated uncollectible accounts expense based on its past experience with the percentage of accounts receivable that are estimated to be uncollectible.

Bank card (8): Card that permit a customer to purchase goods on credit, while the merchant receives immediate cash payment.

Bank charges (7): Various charges made by the bank reducing the amount in a customer's bank account for such things as check printing, service fees, and NSF items.

Bank reconciliation (7): A schedule that adjusts the company's cash balance and the balance on the bank statement until they each equal the correct amount of cash as of a given date.

Bank statement (7): A statement prepared by the bank showing the activity in the depositor's bank account for a month.

Bearer or coupon bonds (17): Bonds that have detachable coupons that are redeemed for interest payments with the issuer or the issuer's agent. The bearer (owner) of the bonds surrenders them when they mature in exchange for payment of the principal amount.

Bondholders (17): The creditors or lenders who purchase bonds.

Bond indenture (17): A document containing all the debt's terms and conditions.

Bonds (17): Debt securities.

Bonds held to maturity (17): In accounting for long-term investments, a classification of bonds in which no gains or losses are recorded until the bonds are sold. To qualify, the business must have a positive intent and ability to hold the bonds to maturity.

Bookkeeping (I): The mechanical and clerical aspects of the accounting process.

Book value (15): The common stockholders' equity in the corporation's net assets determined by dividing the stockholders' equity by the sum of the number of shares outstanding and the number of shares subscribed.

Break-even point (23): The number of units a company must sell to earn a zero profit.

Budget committee (25): The group responsible for preparing budgets.

Budgeted balance sheet (25): A planned (or pro forma) balance sheet prepared from the amounts in the master budget.

Budgeted income statement (25): An income statement for a future period prepared from the amounts in the master budget.

Budgets (20, 25): Formal documents that quantify a company's plans for achieving its financial goals.î

Budget variances (25): Differences between budgeted and actual amounts.

Businesses (I): Private organizations operated to earn profits for their owners.

Business risk (19): The risk associated with the nature of the business and the markets in which it operates.

Business segments (29): Identifiable collections of related resources and activities.

Bylaws (15): Specific rules adopted by the board of directors to govern the corporation's conduct.

C

Canceled checks (7): Paid checks that have been stamped or perforated by the bank at the time of payment.

Capital acquisitions budget (25): The budget for capital assets.

Capital assets (10): Tangible productive assets owned by a business that are useful for more than one year and are acquired to be used in the business's operations, not to be resold.

Capital budget (28): The final list of approved capital expenditures developed after the potential projects have been analyzed.

Capital budgeting decisions (28): Investment decisions involving the acquisition of long-lived assets.

Capital expenditure decisions (28): Investment decisions involving the acquisition of long-lived assets.

Capital expenditures (10): Those expenditures subsequent to the acquisition that extend the plant asset's useful life beyond its original useful life or those expenditures that enhance the asset's efficiency or effectiveness.

Capitalizing retained earnings (16): The process of transferring an amount from retained earnings to contributed capital resulting from such events as a stock dividend.

Capital leases (17): Long-term leases that involve the lessee's acquisition of at least some significant ownership rights and obligations, in addition to the use of the assets over the term of the lease.

Carrying amount (10): An amount representing the undepreciated cost of a plant asset as of the balance sheet date.

Cash basis of accounting (3): Revenues are recorded only in the period that cash payments are received from customers; and expenses are recorded only in the period that cash payments are made.

Cash control systems (7): Systems designed to provide adequate control of both cash receipts and cash disbursements.

Cash disbursements journal (6): The special journal used to record payments to suppliers and service providers and other cash outflows.

Cash equivalents (18): Temporary investments of excess cash in short-term, highly liquid securities.

Cash receipts journal (6): The special journal used to record cash received from customers and other cash inflows.

Cause and effect (24): A relationship in which the allocation base used results in costs being allocated to cost objectives that caused the costs to be incurred.

Charities (I): Private organizations that are operated not for profit but for humanitarian purposes.

Charter (15): A document required by state governments to establish a corporation.

Chart of accounts (2): A list of all account names and account numbers used by a business.

Check register (7): The special journal used to record all checks written.

Classified balance sheet (4): A balance sheet that presents the assets and liabilities arranged in certain customary groupings, such as current assets; long-term investments; property, plant, and equipment; and intangible assets.

Closing temporary accounts (4): The process of transferring temporary account balances to owners' capital.

Common costs (27): Costs incurred for the common benefit of all product lines.

Common-size financial statements (19): Financial statements whose numerical amounts are re-expressed as percent of an important summary figure.

Common stock (15): The residual ownership interest of the common stockholders in the corporation's net assets.

Comparability (13): The quality of financial statement information that enables users to identify similarities in and differences between two businesses or within a single business between two or more periods.

Complete set of financial statements (18): Consists of income statement, balance sheet, retained earnings statement, and statement of cash flows.

Compound interest (17): Interest earned or paid on principal and previous interest amounts.

Comprehensive income (13): The change in equity of a business during a period from transactions and other events and circumstances from nonowner sources.

Computer-controlled manufacturing systems (21): Highly automated manufacturing systems that use computers to control equipment and generally increase the flexibility and accuracy of the production process.

Computer hardware (6): All of the computer system's mechanical and electronic components.

Computer software (6): Sets of instructions that control the computer hardware's operations and direct it to perform computational and other logical tasks.

Conceptual Framework (13): A coherent system of interrelated objectives and fundamentals that can lead to consistent standards and that prescribes the nature, function, and limits of financial accounting and financial statements developed by the FASB.

Conservatism (13): A modifying convention that deals with uncertainty by requiring accountants to use the least optimistic estimate in presenting financial statements.

Consistency (13): The quality of financial statement information that means using the same accounting methods for a business from period to period.

Consolidated financial statements (16): Financial statements prepared as though the parent and subsidiary were one corporation.

Contingent liabilities (8, 12): Potential obligations that depend on the outcome of future events to determine whether the business must pay.

Contributed capital (15): The stockholders' claim to the corporation's net assets due to the purchase of the corporation's capital stock.

Contribution approach (27): An approach to pricing that basically suggests that a company should accept any order as long as it has a positive contribution margin.

Contribution margin (23): The difference between the selling price and variable costs per unit.

Contribution margin ratio (23): The contribution margin per unit divided by the selling price.

Control (6, 16): Steps taken by management to ensure that goals are achieved, only necessary costs are incurred, activities are conducted in accordance with management's policies, assets of the business are safeguarded, and financial reports are reliable. Also, when one corporation owns a majority of another corporation's voting stock.

Control account (6): The general ledger account that relates in total to the details contained in a particular subsidiary ledger.

Controllable cost (20, 24): A cost that a manager can influence by the decisions he or she makes.

Controllable overhead variance (26): The difference between the amount of overhead that would be included in a flexible budget for the actual level of production and the actual amount of overhead.

Conversion costs (22): The total costs of labor and overhead.

Co-ownership of partnership property (14): Property invested by partners in a partnership becomes the partnership's property and is owned jointly by all of the partners.

Copyrights (11): Exclusive right granted by the federal government to creative works for the lifetime of the creator plus 50 years.

Corporation (1, 15): A legal entity separate from its owners created when a state government grants a charter.

Cost allocation (24): The process of assigning indirect costs.

Cost basis (11): In exchanges of assets, the carrying amount of the old asset plus the cash payment.

Cost/benefits convention (13): A modifying convention that requires that information presented in financial statements should provide benefits to the users that exceed the costs of preparing and using the information.

Cost center (29): A business segment responsible for controlling costs, not for generating revenues.

Cost driver (21): The activity that corresponds to a particular cost pool.

Cost-effective (6): A requirement of efficient accounting systems in which the benefits must outweigh the costs.

Cost method (16): A method used to account for investments in stocks where the investor is unable to exert significant influence on the investee company's decisions and where market prices for the stock are not available. Under this method, the investment is initially recorded at cost and is carried at cost until the securities are sold.

Cost objective (24): The object of cost allocation.

Cost of capital (28): The weighted average of the costs of debt and equity financing used to generate capital for investments.

Cost of goods available for sale (9, 20): The cost of the beginning inventory plus the cost of purchases during the year, including transportation costs. Also, the sum of the beginning balance in finished goods plus the cost of goods manufactured.

Cost of goods manufactured (20): The cost of items that have been completed in the current accounting period.

Cost of goods purchased (5): Net purchases plus transportation-in.

Cost of goods sold (5): The total purchase costs of the goods the business provides to customers for the period.

Cost of goods sold ratio (5): Cost of goods sold divided by net sales.

Cost per equivalent unit (22): The sum of the cost in beginning work in process and the cost incurred in the current period divided by the sum of the units completed and the equivalent units in ending work in process.

Cost pool (21, 24): A group of overhead costs based on the major activity that create them. Also, a grouping of individual costs whose total is allocated using one allocation base.

Cost principle (1, 19): Requires that the amounts of assets and liabilities recorded in the accounting records should be the amounts paid (or promised to be paid) for the assets when acquired or the amounts received for the liabilities when incurred.

Cost-volume-profit (C-V-P) analysis (23): An analysis of how profits change when a company's volume changes.

Credit (2): The right side of a T-account.

Credit balance (2): An account balance which occurs when the sum of credits exceeds the sum of debits.

Credited (2): Recording an amount on the right side of a T-account.

Credit memorandum (7): A document reporting an increase in the bank account.

Cumulative preferred stock (15): A type of preferred stock that allows preferred stockholders an annual stated amount of dividends before the common stockholders can receive any dividends. The right to receive the dividend does not expire if the board of directors fails to declare dividends in a given year. Instead, the right to receive the preferred dividends carries over to future years.

Current assets (4): Cash and assets that the business reasonably expects to sell, consume, or convert into cash within one year or within one operating cycle, whichever is longer.

Current liabilities (4, 12): Those obligations due within one year or within one operating cycle, whichever is longer, and that must be satisfied by paying cash, providing other current assets, or incurring other current liabilities.

Current ratio (4): Current assets divided by current liabilities.

Current value (10): The amount that the asset could be sold for at its current age and in its current condition.

D

Days-purchases-in-payables (12): Accounts payable divided by purchases times the days in the period.

Days-sales-in-receivables (8): Accounts receivable divided by credit sales times days in the period.

Debit (2): The left side of a T-account.

Debit balance (2): An account balance which occurs when the sum of debits exceeds the sum or credits.

Debited (2): Recording an amount on the left side of a T-account.

Debit memorandum (7): A document reporting a decrease in the bank account.

Debt-equity ratio (17): Total liabilities divided by total stockholders' equity.

Decentralized organizations (29): Firms that grant substantial decision-making authority to the managers of segments.

Decision usefulness (13): The primary qualitative characteristic of financial statement information that requires the information to be useful in making investment, credit, and other decisions.

Declaration date (15): The date that the board of directors declares the dividend and is legally bound to pay the dividend on a stated payment date.

Defined-benefit pension plan (12): A plan that promises employees specific retirement benefits based on their lengths of service and their level of earnings.

Defined-contribution pension plan (12): A plan in which the employer sets aside a specific amount each pay period for each employee, based on the employee's level of earnings.

Deflation (19): General decreases in prices.

Demand notes (8): Promissory notes that are due at any time the payee or holder in due course presents them for payment.

Denominations of bonds (17): The amounts that appear on the face of the bonds, also referred to as par values, face values, principal amounts and maturity values.

Depletion (11): The process of allocating the cost of natural resources to the periods benefited by the assets.

Deposits-in-transit (7): Deposits made and recorded by the business but not received by the bank in time to appear on the current bank statement.

Depreciable cost (10): The cost of the plant asset minus the estimated residual value.

Depreciation (10): The process of allocating the cost of the assets to the periods benefited from the services they provide.

Depreciation expense (3): The expense that recognizes the expiration of portions of the total lifetime usefulness of plant assets.

Depreciation income tax shield (28): The tax savings resulting from depreciation.

Depreciation schedule (10): A schedule showing the allocation of depreciation expense over the plant asset's useful life.

Differential costs and revenues (27): Cost of revenue items that differ among alternatives.

Direct cost (20): A cost that is directly traceable to a product, activity, or department.

Direct costing (23): An alternative to full costing in which only variable production costs are included in inventory. All fixed production costs are treated as period costs.

Direct labor (20): All labor that is directly traced to items produced.

Direct material (20): All materials and parts that are directly traced to items produced.

Direct method (18): A method of presenting cash flows from operating activities showing major classes of cash receipts and cash payments and their sum.

Direct method of allocating costs (24): The allocation of service department costs to production departments but not to other service departments.

Direct write-off method (8): A method of accounting for uncollectible accounts in which accounts receivable and customers' accounts are credited and Uncollectible Accounts Expense is debited when amounts owed are deemed to be uncollectible. The method is not acceptable under GAAP, but is acceptable under the Internal Revenue Code.

Discount (8, 17): When notes or bonds are sold for less than face or maturity value, the discount is the difference between the selling price and the face or maturity value.

Discounting a note (8): The process of selling or assigning a note.

Dissimilar assets (11): In accounting for exchanges of plant assets, assets that serve different functions.

Distributions to owners (1, 13): Decreases in the equity of a business resulting from transferring assets, rendering services, or incurring liabilities by the business to owners.

Dividend payout (16): Dividends per share divided by earnings per share.

Dividends (1, 15): Distributions by corporations to its stockholders.

Dividends in arrears (15): The undeclared dividends on cumulative preferred stock from previous years.

Dividend yield (16): Dividends per share divided by the market price per share.

Double-declining-balance method (10): A method of depreciation that allocates depreciation expense by multiplying the asset's carrying amount by 200% of the straight-line rate.

Double-entry rule (1): Each change in an element of the accounting equation must be matched by at least one change that has an equal, but opposite, effect.

Double taxation of corporations (15): The fact that corporations pay tax on their pre-tax earnings and stockholders must include dividends (distributions of a corporation's after-tax earnings) in taxable income.

E

Earnings per share (EPS) (15): The ratio of net income available to the common stockholders to the number of shares of common stock outstanding.

Economic entities (I): Any entity that carries on economic activities such as buying or selling products or providing or consuming services.

Effective interest rate (17): The interest rate at which the present value of all the payments due on a bond equal the proceeds of issuing the bond.

Electronic funds transfers (7): A system that manages the transfer of cash electronically, rather than by coins, currency, or checks.

Elements of financial statements (13): Classes of items included in financial statements as defined by the FASB.

Employee benefits (12): Benefits such as insurance and pension plans provided to employees as part of their compensation.

Employee earnings record (12): A record of the individual employee's earnings, withholdings, and deductions for each payroll period and often cumulatively from the beginning of the year.

Employer payroll expense register (12): A special journal used to record all the payroll expenses, other than the employees' gross wages and salaries expense.

Equity (13, 24): The residual interest in the assets of an entity that remains after deducting its liabilities. In a business, the equity is the ownership interest. Also, the notion in cost allocation that suggests that the allocation base should result in allocations that are perceived to be fair.

Equity method (16): A method used to account for long-term investments in another company's stock that is large enough that the investor is able to exert significant influence on the investee company's operating and financial policies. Under this method, the investment is initially recorded at cost, and the investor recognizes in its net income the earning of income by the investee.

Equivalent units (22): Partially completed units expressed as a comparable number of whole units.

Estimated liabilities (12): Liabilities whose exact amounts will not be known until future events occur.

Estimated net realizable value (9): Estimated selling price less the estimated costs of disposing of the merchandise.

Estimated residual value (estimated salvage value) (10): Either the estimated net proceeds if the plant asset is sold or the trade-in value if the plant asset is traded in on a replacement asset.

Estimated useful life (10): The estimated period of time that the business can use the plant asset in the business.

Exchange rate (16): The value of one currency expressed in terms of another currency.

Expenses (1, 13): Decreases in net assets caused by the revenue-producing activities during a specific period. Outflows or other using up of assets or incurrences of liabilities from delivering or producing goods, rendering services, or carrying out other activities that constitute the entity's ongoing major or central operations.

Extraordinary items (19): Items that create gains or losses but are not normal parts of doing business and are not expected to repeat themselves in the foreseeable future.

F

Face amount (8): The amount stated on a bond or promissory note as the principal amount due at maturity.

Feedback value (13): A characteristic of relevance that information should be able to improve decision makers' capabilities to predict by providing feedback about earlier expectations.

Financial accounting (I): An area of accounting that specializes in the processes and principles used to prepare financial statements.

Financial auditing (I): An independent investigative activity through which public accountants lend credibility to the financial statements or other representations of economic entities.

Financial position (1): The relationship among assets, liabilities, and owner's equity.

Financial ratios (19): Numerical statistics that represent important relationships between financial statement amounts.

Financial risk (19): The risk incurred when a business uses debt financing.

Financial statement analysis (19): The art of systematically utilizing (1) financial statement data, (2) ratios and other statistics calculated from financial statement data, and (3) information related to the financial statements to answer questions about a business and to make predictions about its future.

Financial statements (I): Standardized reports prepared by organizations for use by outsiders such as owners and prospective owners of a business, lenders, customers, and creditors.

Finished goods inventory (20): The cost of goods that are completed and ready to sell.

First-in, first-out (FIFO) (9): A method of assigning cost to the ending inventory assuming that the cost of the units in ending inventory consists of the costs of the most recent units purchased.

Fiscal year (3): The specific twelve-month accounting period a business adopts.

Fixed assets (10): Tangible productive assets owned by a business that are useful for more than one year and are acquired to be used in the business's operations, not to be resold.

Fixed costs (20, 23): Those costs that do not change when there are changes in business activity.

Flexibility (6): An accounting system objective that requires the system to support new decisions without needing major modifications.

Flexible budget (25): A budget that is adjusted for the actual level of activity.

Flexible manufacturing systems (21): Manufacturing systems configured so that machines easily can be adjusted to produce a number of different products or variations of standard products.

Foreign currency transaction (16): A transaction that calls for settlement in a currency other than the U.S. dollar.

Franchise (11): A legal agreement in which one party grants the exclusive right to another party to market a product or provide a service within a designated geographical area.

Full cost (21): Product cost information that reflects the total cost of manufacturing a product.

Full cost pricing (27): A cost-based approach to pricing in which the cost marked up is the full cost of an item, including fixed and variable costs.

Full term (17): The total time between the date the bond can first be issued and the date it matures.

G

Gains (13): Increases in equity from peripheral or incidental transactions of an entity and from all other transactions and other events and circumstances affecting the entity except those that result from revenues or investments by owners.

General and administrative expenses (5): Expenses that do not relate directly to the selling function.

General controls (6): Controls oriented toward organizing the data processing function and protecting computer equipment and related documents, files, etc.

General journal (2): A chronological listing of transactions.

General ledger (2): A collection of all the business's accounts.

Generally Accepted Accounting Principles (1): Professional standards to which the financial statements published and distributed by U.S. businesses must conform.

General price changes (19): The general trend in prices in the economy as a whole, in a major sector of the economy, or in a region of the country.

Going-concern assumption (3, 13): In the absence of evidence to the contrary, the assumption that the business will continue to operate indefinitely.

Goods in transit (9): Items of merchandise in the possession of a carrier, such as a trucking, railroad, or airline company.

Goodwill (11, 16): The business's ability to generate earnings at a higher rate than is normal for the industry in which the business operates. Goodwill is only recorded when an entire business or a major portion of a business is purchased. Also, the excess of cost over the fair value of the net assets.

Government accounting (I): A category of accounting consisting of the same activities as private accounting—but performed in cities, counties, and state and federal agencies.

Governments (I): Public organizations formed to supply essential public services to the citizenry and to the state.

Gross pay (12): Total salary or wages of an employee for a period.

Gross profit (5): The difference between net sales and the cost of goods sold.

Gross profit method (9): A method of estimating inventories for interim financial statements using a cost of goods sold to sales ratio.

Gross profit ratio (5): Gross profit divided by net sales.

Gross sales (5): The sum of the prices of all goods a business sells in a period.

H

High-low method (23): A method of estimating fixed and variable cost components in which a straight line is fitted to the data points representing the highest and lowest levels of activity.

Holder in due course (8): The buyer of a negotiable promissory note having equal or greater rights than the original payee.

Horizontal analysis (19): Analysis of the rates of change across periods in the components of a particular financial statement.

I

Ideal standard (26): Standards developed under the assumption that no obstacles to the production process will be encountered.

Implicit principal payment (17): The amount by which an installment payment reduces the principal amount owed on a note, determined by subtracting the interest component from the total payment.

Improvements (10): A subsequent expenditure that makes a plant asset more efficient or effective, but does not necessarily extend the asset's useful life.

Income persistence (19): The tendency for a component of income to continue in future periods under steady-state (no change) assumptions.

Income quality (19): The degree to which management does not exercise or does not have the opportunity to manipulate the firm's income to paint an optimistic picture of ongoing income.

Income statement (1): The financial statement that communicates the revenues, expenses, and net income of a business for a period of time.

Income statement approach (8): A method in which a business accrues and estimates uncollectible accounts expense based on its past experience with average collections per dollar of credit sales.

Income Summary (4): A temporary account to which all revenue and expense accounts are closed.

Independent auditor's report (19): A report prepared by an independent auditor for the purpose of issuing an opinion whether financial statements fairly present what they are supposed to present in all material respects in conformance with GAAP.

Indirect costs (20): A cost that either is not directly traceable to a product, activity, or department or is not worth tracing.

Indirect labor costs (20): All labor costs that are not directly traced to items produced.

Indirect materials (20): All materials and parts that are not directly traced to items produced.

Indirect method (18): A method of presenting cash flows from operating activities the begins with net income and shows the adjustments necessary to determine cash flows from operating activities.

Indirect (net) method (8): A method of reporting the effect of uncollectible accounts on the balance sheet in which accounts receivable are reported net of the allowance for uncollectible accounts.

Inflation (19): General increases in prices.

Installment loan (17): A loan that is repaid with a series of equally spaced payments of a constant amount.

Installment method (13): A method of recognizing revenue from an installment sale where each receipt of cash is considered to consist of a recovery of part of the cost of the goods sold and part of the gross profit from the sale used when there is significant uncertainty about whether the cash will be collected.

Intangible assets (4, 11): Noncurrent assets that have no physical substance such as patents, copyrights, franchises, and trademarks.

Interest (8): The expense a borrower incurs and the revenue or income a lender earns for the use of the money owed in fixed-amount agreements such as promissory notes.

Interest-bearing note(8): A debt instrument that expressly states an interest rate to be applied to the face amount of the note.

Interest method of amortization (17): A method of amortization in which interest expense is determined by applying the implicit interest rate to the bond's carrying value and amortization of premium or discount is the difference between interest expense and interest paid.

Interest rate (8): The percentage rate that applies to the face amount of the note.

Interim financial reports (3): Financial statements for a period less than a year.

Internal audit (I): An investigation by accountants of an economic entity designed to determine whether: employees and departments conform to management (or government) policies; functions in the organization are performed at reasonable cost; and a department or division is fully meeting its goals and objectives.

Internal rate of return (28): The rate of return that equates the present value of future cash flows to the investment outlay.

Inventory turnover (9): The rate at which inventory passes through a business.

Inventory turnover ratio (9): Cost of goods sold divided by average inventory.

Investment center (29): A business segment responsible for generating revenue, controlling costs, and investing in assets.

Investments by owners (1, 13): Increases in equity of a business resulting from transfers to it other entities of cash or other assets from entities that wish to obtain or increase their ownership interests.

Issuer of bonds (17): An entity that borrows by issuing debt securities called bonds.

J

Job (21): An individual product or batch of which a company needs cost information.

Job cost sheet (21): A form used to accumulate the cost of producing the item or items ordered.

Joint costs (24): The costs of the common inputs to be allocated to two or more products.

Joint products (24): Two or more products that always arise from common inputs.

Journal entry (2): The recording of one event or transaction in the general journal.

Journalizing (2): The process of recording a transaction.

Just-in-time (JIT) system (21): A manufacturing system designed to minimize inventories of raw materials and work in process.

L

Labor efficiency variance (26): The difference between the standard labor hours allowed for the number of units produced and the actual number of labor hours worked times the standard labor wage rate.

Labor rate variance (26): The difference between the standard and actual wage rates times the actual number of labor hours worked.

Large stock dividend (16): A stock dividend that is greater than 20-25% of the outstanding shares.

Last-in, first-out (LIFO) (9): A method of assigning cost to the ending inventory assuming that the cost of the units in ending inventory consists of the costs of the earliest units purchased.

Legal capital (15): The minimum amount of contributed capital for the number of shares issued.

Leverage (19): The effect of using debt financing to complement owner's capital to provide the necessary funds to operate a business.

Liabilities (1, 12, 13): Probable future sacrifices or economic benefits arising from present obligations of a business to transfer assets or provide services to other entities in the future as a result of past transactions or events.

Like-kind exchanges (11): Exchanges of similar plant assets for which no taxable gain or loss may be recognized.

Limited life (14): The characteristic of a partnership that any event or act that terminates the partnership agreement terminates the partnership.

Limited partnership (14): A form of partnership in which the general partner has unlimited liability, but the limited partners are liable only for the amount of their investment in the partnership.

Liquidity (4): The expected length of time needed to convert an asset into cash.

Liquidity ratios (19): A group of ratios that assess a business's ability to meet its current obligations as they come due.

Long-term investments (4): Assets a business does not expect to sell or collect within one year or within the operating cycle, whichever is longer.

Losses (13): Decreases in equity from peripheral or incidental transactions of an entity and from all other transactions and other events and circumstances affecting the entity except those that result from expenses or distributions to owners.

Lower-of-cost-or-market rule (9): Reporting inventories at market value when the market value has fallen below cost.

Lump-sum allocation (24): Allocations of fixed costs in which predetermined amounts are allocated regardless of changes in the level of activity.

M

Majority interest (16): When a company owns more than 50% of another company's voting stock.

Maker of a note (8): The party who makes a written promise to pay.

Management by exception (20, 25): Managers investigate departures (or variances) from the plan that appear to be exceptional; they do not investigate minor departures (or variances) from the plan.

Managerial accounting (I, 20): An area of accounting that specializes in preparing information for use by managers in making decisions about the current and future activities of economic entities.

Market value (15): The price at which investors can sell and purchase assets, such as shares of stock.

Manufacturing costs (20): All costs associated with the production of goods.

Manufacturing overhead (20): The costs of all manufacturing activities other than direct material and direct labor.

Margin of safety (23): The difference between the expected level of sales and break-even sales.

Master budget (25): A comprehensive planning document that incorporates a number of individual budgets.

Matching principle (2, 13): The accounting principle that states that expenses incurred to produce products and services should be recognized in the same period that revenues from those products and services are recognized.

Material difference (17): Amount of an error or omission in financial statements that could alter the decision of a qualified and informed individual who takes the care to analyze the financial statements.

Materiality (8, 13): The amount of error or incorrectness in a set of financial statements that could change a decision of a knowledgeable user of financial statements. A modifying convention that involves judgments about whether errors and omissions in financial statements are of sufficient size to cause the financial statements to be misleading.

Material price variance (26): The difference between the standard and actual prices per unit of material times the actual quantity of material used.

Material quantity variance (26): The difference between the standard quantity of material allowed for the number of units produced and the actual quantity of material used times the standard price of the material.

Maturity value of a note or bond (8): The amount to be paid when the note or bond is due.

Measurement (13): To assign a numerical amount to the information that is recognized in the accounts.

Merchandise inventory (5): A merchandising business's stock of goods available for sale as of a particular point in time.

Merchandise inventory card (9): A record in both quantities and costs of the beginning inventory of each item, purchases of the item, and sales of the item.

Minority interest (16): Other stockholders when one investor owns more than 50% of the voting stock in a subsidiary.

Mixed costs (23): Costs that contain both variable and fixed cost elements.

Modified Accelerated Cost Recovery System (MACRS): The most current rules for depreciation for income tax purposes.

Modifying conventions (13): Constraints on the application of accounting principles adopted by the accounting profession.

Monetary measurement concept (1): The concept that the focus of accounting is on business events, resources, and obligations that can be expressed in money terms.

Mutual agency (14): The characteristic of a partnership that makes each partner an agent of the partnership, and is therefore able to enter into binding agreements on behalf of the partnership.

N

Natural resources (11): Wasting assets such as oil, gas, mineral deposits, and stands of timber.

Negotiable promissory note (8): An debt instrument that the original payee can sell readily to collect cash earlier than the due date of the note.

Net book value (10): An amount representing the undepreciated cost of a plant asset as of the balance sheet date.

Net income (1, 3): The excess of revenues over expenses for a period.

Net loss (3): The excess of expenses over revenues for a period.

Net pay (12): Gross pay minus withholdings and deductions.

Net present value (28): The sum of the present values of all cash flows.

Net purchases (5): Purchases less purchases returns and allowances and purchases discounts.

Net sales (5): The total amounts a business receives or expects to be collected for the period's sales of merchandise to customers expressed as gross sales less sales returns and allowances and sales discounts.

Neutrality (13): A characteristic of reliability that means that in choosing an accounting method, there is freedom from bias towards a pre-determined result.

Noncontrollable costs (20): A cost that a manager cannot influence.

Noncumulative preferred stock (15): A type of preferred stock that allows preferred stockholders a stated amount of dividends before the common stockholders can receive any dividends. However, if no dividend is declared for a year, the preferred stockholders right to receive dividends for that year lapses.

Noncurrent liabilities (long-term liabilities or long-term debts) (4, 12): Those obligations due in more than one year or more than one operating cycle, whichever is longer, from the balance sheet date.

Noninterest-bearing note (8): A debt instrument that does not state an interest rate to be applied to the face amount of the note.

Non-like-kind exchanges (11): Exchanges of dissimilar plant assets for which a taxable gain or loss is recognized.

Nonmanufacturing costs (20): All costs that are not associated with the production of goods.

Non-negotiable promissory note (8): A debt instrument that does not satisfy the legal conditions for negotiability.

Nonparticipating preferred stock (15): A type of preferred stock in which the stock certificate limits the dividends on preferred stock to the stated amount.

No-par value stock (15): Stock issued without a par value.

Not-for-profit (15): An entity organized to conduct business with some other purpose than earning a profit, such as charities, educational institutions, and certain medical organizations.

NSF checks (7): Checks that the banks that they are drawn on refuse to pay for lack of funds in the maker's accounts.

O

Objectives of financial statements (13): Objectives developed by the FASB to provide broad guidelines for financial statements prepared by businesses.

Off-balance-sheet financing (17): Any scheme or system through which a business effectively acquires or retains property rights in assets for future payments without showing the assets or the related liabilities on its balance sheet.

Operating cycle (4, 12): The average period of time between committing resources to providing goods or services and collecting cash from customers.

Operating expenses (5): All the expenses of running the business for a period other than the cost of goods sold.

Operating income (29): Income from continuing operations before interest and taxes.

Operating leases (17): Short-term or long-term leases that involve strictly renting assets for use in the lessee's business. No special rights or privileges are acquired, and the lessor bears all of the risks of ownership.

Operating systems (6): Fundamental programs that tell the computer how to coordinate the parts of the system.

Opportunity costs (27): The values of benefits foregone by selecting one decision alternative over another.

Organization costs (15): Costs incurred in forming a corporation.

Outstanding checks (7): Checks that a business has issued and recorded but which have not be presented to the bank for payment.

Overapplied overhead (21): The difference between the debits and credits to Manufacturing Overhead if actual overhead is less than the amount of overhead applied.

Overhead allocation (21): The process of assigning manufacturing overhead to specific jobs and recording overhead in various accounts.

Overhead allocation rate (21): Estimated overhead costs divided by the estimated quantity of the allocation base.

Overhead applied (21): The amount of overhead assigned to jobs.

Overhead volume variance (26): The difference between the amount of overhead applied to production at the standard and the amount of overhead included in the flexible budget.

Owner's equity (1): The residual interest owners have in the business's assets after deducting the liabilities.

P

Paid-In Capital in Excess of Par (15): The account used to record the difference between the par value of the stock and the selling price when the selling price is greater than the par value.

Parent corporation (16): The investor company who is able to control the investee.

Participating preferred stock (15): A type of preferred stock in which the stockholder has the right to participate in dividends in excess of the stated amount in certain circumstances.

Partnership (1, 14): An association of two or more persons to carry on a business as co-owners.

Partnership agreement (14): The agreement between two or more persons that governs their association as partners and constitutes a contract that creates that partnership.

Par value (15): The amount printed on the stock certificate and established by the corporation's charter. The par value of the stock issued determines the corporation's legal capital.

Patents (11): The exclusive right granted by the federal government to use the product or process for a period of 17 years.

Payback period (28): The length of time it takes to recover the initial cost of an investment.

Payee (8): The party to whom money is owed.

Payment date (15): The date that the corporation actually pays the dividends that have been previously declared by the board of directors.

Payroll register (12): A special journal used to record employees' gross wages, withholdings, deductions, and net pay.

Percentage-of-completion method (13): A method that recognizes revenue for long-term construction contracts by dividing the total estimated cost by the cost incurred in the current period and multiplying the resulting percentage by the total revenue on the project.

Percent-change financial statements (19): Conventional financial statements with changes and percents of changes added.

Percent utilization of a line of credit (12): Loan balance divided by the maximum available loan.

Performance reports (20, 25): Reports comparing the budget with the actual results that shows budget variances.

Period (term, duration) of a note (8): The length of time for which the promissory note is in effect.

Period costs (20): Costs identified with accounting periods rather than with goods produced.

Periodic inventory method (5): A method of accounting for inventory in which the balance in Merchandise Inventory is updated at the end of the accounting period as a result of taking a physical inventory.

Perpetual inventory method (5): A method of accounting for inventory in which the costs of purchases and the cost of goods sold are recorded on a daily, or even a continuous, basis.

Petty cash fund (7): A fund used to make small cash payments.

Petty cash receipts (7): Documents providing evidence of disbursements made from the petty cash fund stating the purpose of the payments, the amounts, the dates, and other pertinent information.

Physical inventory (5): A process of physically counting all goods of each kind in the merchandise inventory as of a particular date, assigning costs to them and calculating an inventory balance.

Plant assets (plant and equipment, or property, plant, and equipment) (10): Tangible productive assets owned by a business that are useful for more than one year and are acquired to be used in the business's operations, not to be resold.

Point-of-sale systems (7): Computer-based cash receipts systems that allow customers to transfer funds immediately from their bank accounts to the merchant's bank account at the time of a sale.

Pooling-of-interests method (16): A method of accounting for business combinations in which the acquired company's net assets are reported in the consolidated financial statements at their book values immediately preceding the combination. This method is used for combinations that involve the exchange of common stock.

Post-closing trial balance (4): A trial balance prepared immediately after closing.

Posting (2): The process of recording transactions in the general ledger accounts.

Predetermined overhead rate (21): The estimated level of allocation base divided by the estimated total overhead cost.

Predictive value (13): A characteristic of relevance that the information should help users form predictions about the outcomes of events.

Preemptive right (15): The right of common stockholders to purchase additional shares before the shares are offered for sale to others.

Preferred stock (15): Generally nonvoting stock, entitling the stockholder to certain preferences relative to those of common stockholders.

Premium (17): When bonds are sold for more than face value, the premium is the difference between the face value and the selling price.

Present value (17): The amount that a rational person would accept now in exchange for the right to receive an amount in the future.

Present value analysis (28): The method developed to equate future dollars to current dollars.

Private accounting (I): A broad category of accounting consisting of all accounting activities required to meet the information needs of private-sector managers and of outside users such as prospective owners and lenders.

Privately-owned corporation (15): Corporations whose shares are held by a relatively few number of owners. The shares are not traded on stock exchanges.

Product costing systems (21): An integrated set of documents, ledgers, accounts, and accounting procedures used to a measure and record the cost of manufactured products.

Production cost report (22): An end-of-the-month report for a process costing system that provides reconciliations of units and costs as well as the details of the cost per equivalent unit calculations.

Product costs (20): Costs assigned to goods produced.

Profitability ratios (19): A group of ratios that assess a business's ability to earn a profit in the future.

Profit center (29): A business segment responsible for generating revenue as well as for controlling costs.

Profit margin (3): The amount of net income as a percent of revenues, stated as net income divided by revenues.

Promissory note (4, 8): A written promise by one party to pay a specified amount of money, usually with interest, to another party on a specified date at a specified place.

Property, plant, and equipment (4): The long-lived assets that the business uses to sell and/or manufacture a product or to provide a service.

Proprietorship (1): A business owned by an individual.

Proxy (15): A legal document giving an agent power to cast a stockholder's votes at stockholders' meetings.

Public accounting (I): A category of accounting in which accountants provide professional accounting services to individuals, businesses, government units, and other entities for fees.

Publicly-owned corporation (15): Corporations whose shares are publicly traded on stock exchanges.

Purchase allowances (5): Adjustments to the amount owed for goods resulting from minor deficiencies in the goods.

Purchase discounts (5): Reductions in amounts owed to encourage early payments.

Purchase method (16): A method of accounting for business combinations in which the acquired company's assets and liabilities are reported at their fair values on the date of the business combination, with any excess of the cost over the fair value of the net assets reported as goodwill.

Purchase order (7): A formal offer to buy goods sent to the supplier after it has been properly authorized.

Purchase requisition (7): A request to purchase needed goods prepared by the person responsible for maintaining the stock on hand.

Purchase returns (5): A reduction in the amount owed because flawed or unacceptable goods are returned to the supplier.

Purchases journal (6): The special journal used to record purchases of merchandise and supplies.

Q

Qualitative characteristics (13): Characteristics of decision-useful financial statement information consisting of primary and secondary qualities.

Quick ratio (7): Liquid current assets divided by current liabilities.

R

Rate of return on owner's equity (1): Net income divided by average owners' equity.

Raw materials inventory (20): The cost of materials on hand that are used to produce a company's products.

Realization principle (2): The accounting principle that revenues should be recognized in the period they are earned if they either are collected in cash or they will be collected from customers in the future.

Receiving report (7): A document containing evidence of the quantities and condition of goods actually received from suppliers completed by employees who physically receive goods on the business's behalf.

Recognition (13): The recording of effects of events and transactions formally in the accounts as assets, liabilities, revenues, expenses, etc.

Recognize (2): To record in an account.

Reconciling the bank statement (7): The process of verifying the balance in the cash account against the bank balance of cash by taking into account appropriate adjustments to both balances.

Record date (15): The date the board of directors designates for determining who owns what number of shares of stock and, therefore, who is entitled to receive the dividend.

Redemption (call) price (15): The amount specified on some preferred stock at which the corporation may redeem the shares.

Registered bonds (17): Bonds issued in the buyer's name and recorded by the issuer in a bond register.

Registrar (15): The person or business who is responsible for transferring the corporation's stock.

Regression analysis (23): A statistical technique that uses all available data points to estimate the intercept and the slope of a cost equation.

Relative benefits (24): The notion in cost allocation that the allocation base should result in more costs being allocated to the cost objectives that benefit most from incurring the cost.

Relative performance evaluation (29): The evaluation of profitability of profit centers relative to the profitability of other, similar profit centers within the company.

Relative sales value method (24): A method of allocating joint costs in which the allocation is based on the relative sales values of the products at the split-off point.

Relevance (13): A primary qualitative characteristic of financial statement information that requires the information to be capable of making a difference in a decision.

Relevant costs (27): The only cost items managers need to consider when analyzing decision alternatives because they differ among alternatives.

Relevant range (23): The range of activity for which estimates and predictions are likely to be accurate.

Reliability (13): A primary qualitative characteristic of financial statement information that assures that the information is reasonably free from error or bias and faithfully represents what it intends to represent.

Remittance advice (7): A document attached to a check that notifies the payee of the purpose of the payment. Also, a duplicate invoice sent by the payee that may be returned with payment and serves the same purpose.

Repairs (10): Ordinary and routine revenue expenditures to maintain the plant asset in good working condition.

Replacements (10): Nonroutine, capital expenditures that extend a plant asset's useful life beyond its original estimated useful life.

Representational faithfulness (13): A characteristic of reliability that requires a high degree of correspondence between financial statement numbers and the assets, liabilities, transactions, and events those numbers intend to represent.

Required rate of return (29): The rate of return that a company believes should be earned on investments.

Research and development (11): The search for and the application of knowledge to new products or processes.

Reserve funds (19): Consist of dispensable assets, arranged but unused sources of credit, and untapped sources of new credit and equity capital. Reserve funds represent the margin of protection a business has against sudden financial distress.

Residual income (29): The investment center's operating income in excess of that required for the level of its assets.

Responsibility accounting system (24): A system of accounting that traces revenues and costs to organizational units and individuals with related responsibility for generating revenue and controlling costs.

Responsibility centers (29): Organizational units responsible for the generation of revenue or for the incurrence of costs.

Retail method (9): A method of estimating inventories for interim financial statements using a cost to retail ratio for the goods available for sale.

Retained earnings (15): The cumulative net income of a corporation less the cumulative dividends paid to stockholders from the beginning of the corporation's life.

Return on investment (29): Operating income divided by total assets.

Return on total assets (10): The sum of net income and interest expense divided by total assets.

Revenue expenditures (10): Those expenditures that merely maintain the plant asset's usefulness and keep it functioning at its original capacity.

Revenues (1, 13): Increases in net assets that result directly from providing products or services to customers during a specific period. Inflows or other enhancements of assets of a business or settlement of its liabilities from delivering or producing goods, rendering services, or other activities that constitute the entity's ongoing major or central operations.

Reversing entry (4): An entry that is exactly the opposite of an adjusting entry made at the end of the preceding accounting period.

S

Sales allowance (5): A reduction in the price given because merchandise is partially flawed.

Sales discounts (5): Reductions in payments to induce early payments.

Sales journal (6): The special journal used to record credit sales transactions.

Sales return (5): A refund given to the customer when merchandise previously purchased is returned.

Scattergraph (23): A graph of costs at various activity levels.

Selling expenses (5): Expenses directly related to storing, handling, displaying, selling, and shipping or delivering products to customers.

Separation of incompatible duties (7): An accounting control which divides the responsibility for various duties among employees to reduce the opportunity for dishonesty.

Sequential method of allocating costs (24): The allocation of service department costs that considers the fact that service departments make use of each other's services.

Serial bonds (17): Bonds issued under indentures that specify that certain subsets of the total issue of bonds are due at different maturity dates.

Short-term, revolving lines of credit (12): A bank's commitment to advance funds on demand to a borrower up to a limit and for a specific period.

Similar assets (11): In accounting for exchanges of plant assets, assets that serve the same function.

Slack (25): Amounts managers may add into budgets to assure that budgeted costs can be easily achieved.

Slide (2): An error that results from adding or dropping one or more zeros from a number.

Solvency ratios (19): A group of ratios that assess a business's ability to generate sufficient cash to meets its obligations.

Special journals (6): Substitutes for the general journal used to record particular classes of transactions.

Specific identification method (9): A method of assigning costs to the ending inventory by tracking the actual physical flow of units during the period.

Specific price changes (19): Changes in the prices of particular goods or services, irrespective of general trends.

Split-off point (24): The stage of production when individual products are identified.

Stable-dollar assumption (13, 19): The assumption that the U.S. dollar is a reasonably constant unit of measure and that, even though prices change, assets, liabilities, revenues, and expenses are still recorded and reported in the financial statements according to the cost principle.

Standard cost (26): The cost that management believes should be incurred to produce a good or service under anticipated conditions.

Standard cost variance (26): The difference between the standard cost and the actual cost.

Stated, nominal, or coupon rate (17): The interest rate stated in the bond indenture.

Stated value (15): A corporation's legal capital if the corporation assigns a value to no-par value stock.

Statement of cash flows (1, 18): A financial statement that displays a business's cash receipts and cash disbursements for a period according to categories of business activities—operating activities, financing activities, and investing activities.

Statement of owner's equity (1): The financial statement that reflects the effect of owners' equity of net income, owner's investments, and owner's withdrawals for a period of time.

Statement of partners' capital (14): The statement of owner's equity for a partnership.

Static budget (25): A budget that is not adjusted for the actual level of activity.

Straight-line method (10): A method of depreciation that allocates an equal amount of depreciation expense to each period in the asset's estimated useful life.

Straight-line rate (10): 100% divided by the estimated useful life.

Stock certificate (15): A document providing evidence of ownership of shares in a corporation.

Stock dividend (16): When a company issues common stock to its own common stockholders without receiving any assets in return.

Stockholders (15): The owners of the corporation.

Stockholders' ledger (15): A subsidiary ledger containing the information about stock ownership.

Stock split (16): A method of reducing the market price per share accomplished by replacing the outstanding shares with a multiple number of the shares previously outstanding.

Stock subscription (15): A sale of shares of stock in which the purchaser agrees to pay a specified price for the shares at some future date(s).

Subsidiary corporation (16): The investee controlled by the parent corporation.

Subsidiary ledgers (6): Sets of ledger accounts that contain the details of balances in individual general ledger asset, liability, and owner's equity accounts.

Sum-of-the-years'-digits method (10): A method of depreciation that allocates depreciation expense by multiplying the asset's depreciable cost by a fraction for each year.

Sunk costs (27): Costs incurred in the past and are irrelevant to present and future decisions.

Supplier's invoice (7): The supplier's billing document containing descriptions, quantities shipped, prices of goods, the total amount owed, and the terms of credit.

System flowcharts (6): Symbolic representations of systems.

T

T-account (2): The simplest representation of an account resembling the letter T and consisting of the account title, the left (debit) side and the right (credit) side.

Temporary accounts (4): Accounts that are closed at the end of the accounting period.

Term bonds (17): Bonds issued under indentures that specify that all the bonds are due at the same date.

Term to maturity (12, 17): The period of time until a liability must be paid. The time remaining before a bond matures.

Timeliness (6,13): An objective of accounting systems that requires that information be supplied with sufficient lead time to permit management to assimilate and use it in the decision at hand. A characteristic of relevance that requires information to be available to the user before it loses its capacity to influence decisions.

Time periods assumption (13): The assumption that the life of a business can be divided into a series of equal time periods.

Time tickets (21): Forms completed by workers to keep track of the amount of time spent on each job.

Total quality management (TQM) (21): Programs designed to insure high-quality products that involve listening to customers' needs, making products right the first time, reducing defective products, and encouraging workers to improve their production processes continuously.

Trademarks (trade names) (11): Words, symbols, or other devices that identify or distinguish a product or a business. If registered with the federal government, exclusive right may be granted to use the trademark or trade name for a period of 20 years.

Trading securities (17): Bonds and equity securities that are purchased and held for resale in the near future.

Transaction (I): A voluntary exchange between economic entities, typically involving a sale/purchase of products or services that changes an economic entities' financial position.

Transfer agent (15): The person or business who is responsible for transferring the corporation's stock.

Transfer price (29): The price used to value internal transfers of goods.

Transferred-in costs (22): The cost a prior processing department incurs and transfers to the next processing department.

Transposition error (2): The reversal of two digits during the process of recording the number.

Treasury stock (16): Reacquired shares of previously issued stock.

Trial balance (2): A list of debits and credits from the general ledger accounts used to test the equality of debits and credits.

U

Unadjusted trial balance (3): A trial balance prepared before posting the adjusting entries.

Uncollectible accounts expense (8): The estimated portion of a period's credit sales that a business ultimately will not collect from customers.

Uncollectible-accounts-as-a-percent-of-credit sales (8): Uncollectible accounts expense divided by credit sales.

Underapplied overhead (21): The difference between the debits and credits to Manufacturing Overhead if actual overhead is greater than the amount of overhead applied.

Unearned revenue (3): Payment received in advance of delivering the goods or performing the services.

Unitized fixed cost (24): Fixed costs stated on a per unit basis.

Units-of-production method (10): A method of depreciation that allocates depreciation expense to the time periods based on the plant asset's output.

Unlimited liability (14): The characteristic of a partnership that holds each partner personally liable for all partnership liabilities.

Useful life of an asset (3): The period of time the business estimates it can use the asset in its operations.

V

Valuation account (contra-asset account) (3, 10): An account that reduces another account to its correct balance for presentation in the financial statements. For example, Accumulated Depreciation is the valuation account for the related plant asset account.

Variable costing (23): An alternative to full costing in which only variable production costs are included in inventory. All fixed production costs are treated as period costs.

Variable costs (20, 23): Those costs that increase or decrease in response to increases or decreases in business activity.

Verifiability (13): A characteristic of reliability that results from a high degree of agreement among independent measurers.

Vertical analysis (19): Analysis of the percentage composition of the components of a particular financial statement for a particular year.

Voucher (7): The document on which relevant data about an obligation to pay are summarized for approval, recording, and payment under a voucher system.

Voucher system (7): An integrated control system in which adequate support documents (vouchers) are prepared for all acquisitions and expenditures.

W

Weighted-average cost method (9): A method of assigning costs to the ending inventory based on the average cost per unit, which consists of the combined cost of the beginning inventory and the purchases made during the year.

"What-if" analysis (23): An examination of the results of various courses of action.

Withdrawals (1): Distributions by proprietorships or partnerships.

Work in process inventory (20): The cost of goods that are only partially complete.

Z

Zero base budgeting (25): A method of budget preparation that requires each department to justify budgeted amounts at the start of each budget period, even if the amounts were supported in prior budget periods.

INDEX

Index of Real Companies